An Introduction to Policing

THIRD EDITION

D1036745

★ ★ ★

JOHN S. DEMPSEY

Captain, New York City Police Department (Retired)
State University of New York–Empire State College

LINDA S. FORST

Captain, Boca Raton Police Department (Retired)
Shoreline Community College

THOMSON

WADSWORTH

Australia • Canada • Mexico • Singapore • Spain • United Kingdom • United States

THOMSON
WADSWORTH

Senior Acquisitions Editor, Criminal Justice: Jay Whitney
Assistant Editor: Jana Davis
Editorial Assistant: Jennifer Walsh
Technology Project Manager: Susan DeVanna
Marketing Manager: Terra Schultz
Marketing Assistant: Annabelle Yang
Advertising Project Manager: Stacey Purviance
Project Manager, Editorial Production: Jennie Redwitz
Print/Media Buyer: Doreen Suruki
Permissions Editor: Kiely Sexton

Production Service: Margaret Pinette, Heckman & Pinette
Text Designer: Harry Voigt/Adriane Bosworth
Photo Researcher: Roberta Spieckerman
Copy Editor: Margaret Pinette
Cover Designer: Qin-Zhong Yu
Cover Image: Flashing police car lights: © Corbis. Collage images, clockwise from top: © Corbis; Spencer Platt/Getty Images; © Rich Meyer/Corbis; Tim Matsui/Getty Images; Danny La/Getty Images
Compositor: ATLIS Graphics
Text and Cover Printer: Edwards Brothers, Incorporated

Thomson Wadsworth
10 Davis Drive
Belmont, CA 94002-3098
USA

Asia
Thomson Learning
5 Shenton Way #01-01
UIC Building
Singapore 068808

Australia/New Zealand
Thomson Learning
102 Dodds Street
Southbank, Victoria 3006
Australia

Canada
Nelson
1120 Birchmount Road
Toronto, Ontario M1K 5G4
Canada

Europe/Middle East/Africa
Thomson Learning
High Holborn House
50/51 Bedford Row
London WC1R 4LR
United Kingdom

Latin America
Thomson Learning
Seneca, 53
Colonia Polanco
11560 Mexico D.F.
Mexico

Spain/Portugal
Paraninfo
Calle Magallanes, 25
28015 Madrid, Spain

> For more information about our products, contact us at:
> **Thomson Learning Academic Resource Center**
> **1-800-423-0563**
> For permission to use material from this text or product, submit a request online at **http://www.thomsonrights.com**. Any additional questions about permissions can be submitted by email to **thomsonrights@thomson.com**.

Library of Congress Control Number: 2004103067

ISBN 0-534-64290-X

*To my family: Marianne, John, Donna,
Cathy, Diane, John, Daniel, Nikki, and
Erin Anne Marie, and in memory of
Anne Marie (1970–2002) – J. S. D.*

**This book is dedicated to my late husband,
Captain James E. Duke, Jr., and our beautiful
daughters, Brynn and Juleigh – L. S. F.**

About the Authors

John S. Dempsey was a member of the New York City Police Department (NYPD) from 1964 to 1988. He served in the ranks of police officer, detective, sergeant, lieutenant, and captain. His primary assignments were patrol and investigations. He received seven citations from the department for meritorious and excellent police duty. After retiring from the NYPD, Mr. Dempsey served until 2003 as professor of criminal justice at the State University of New York–Suffolk County Community College on Eastern Long Island. Currently, Mr. Dempsey teaches criminal justice and public administration courses and mentors ranking members of law enforcement and criminal justice agencies at the State University of New York–Empire State College.

He is the author of *Introduction to Public and Private Investigations* (West, 1996); *Introduction to Investigations,* 2nd ed. (Wadsworth/Thomson Learning, 2003); and *An Introduction to Policing,* 3rd ed. (Wadsworth/Thomson Learning, 2005). He has earned numerous awards for his teaching, work with students, and scholarship.

Mr. Dempsey holds AA and BA degrees in behavioral science from the City University of New York, John Jay College of Criminal Justice; a master's degree in criminal justice from Long Island University; and a master's of public administration degree from Harvard University, the John F. Kennedy School of Government.

He lectures widely around the country on policing and criminal justice issues and is a member of the Academy of Criminal Justice Sciences, International Association of Chiefs of Police, ASIS International, Northeastern Association of Criminal Justice Sciences, and Criminal Justice Educators Association of New York State.

Mr. Dempsey is married and has four children and four grandchildren.

Linda S. Forst is a retired police captain from the Boca Raton (Florida) Police Services Department. She joined the department in 1977 and served as a patrol officer, investigator, sergeant, lieutenant, and captain. She spent the majority of her career in patrol but also worked in investigations, professional standards, training, hiring, and support services. She was the first female field training officer, sergeant, lieutenant, and captain in the department. She has extensive training in accident investigation, domestic violence, sexual violence, community policing, and police management, and served on the board of directors of the local battered women's shelter for many years. She received numerous commendations during her career and brought home many gold medals from the state and International Police Olympics while representing Boca Raton.

Ms. Forst earned her BA in criminal justice, MEd in community college education, and EdD in adult education from Florida Atlantic University. Her dissertation was on acquaintance rape prevention programs. She is a graduate of University of Louisville's Sex Crime Investigation School and Northwestern University's School of Police Staff and Command. She is the author of numerous publications in magazines, journals, and newspapers and presents regularly at conferences and to community groups. She is the author of *The Aging of America: A Handbook for Police Officers.* Ms. Forst has instructed for Northwestern's School of Police Staff and Command as well as Palm Beach Community College and Florida Atlantic University. She is currently a professor of criminal justice at Shoreline Community College in Seattle, Washington, and serves as a member of the Board on Law Enforcement Training Standards and Education for the State of Washington.

Ms. Forst is the mother of two daughters.

Brief Contents

Contents

Preface

TO THE STUDENT

An Introduction to Policing, Third Edition, is a basic introductory text for college students who are interested in learning who the police are, what they do, and how they do it. The policing profession is a noble one. We sincerely hope this text teaches you how to continue the great tradition of policing.

This book is designed to give you a general overview of policing in our society so that you can understand why and how policing is performed. It will show you the jobs available in policing and how you can go about getting them, what skills you will need, and what you will do if and when you get these jobs. In addition, we try to give you an idea, a sense, and a flavor of policing. We want you to get a clear look at policing, not only for your academic interest, but more importantly to help you determine if policing is what you want to do with the rest of your life. After all, shouldn't much of college be about making an intelligent, well-informed career choice, as well as learning about life?

An Introduction to Policing explores these issues from the perspectives of two practitioners, students, and teachers of policing. We wrote this new edition, in part, out of a desire to combine the practical experience gained from a collective 44 years of police work with the equally valuable insights gained from our years of formal education and teaching. It is designed to make you aware of who the police are, what they do, and how they do it, while also sensitizing you to the complexities and ambiguities of modern policing.

TO THE INSTRUCTOR

In this third edition our overall philosophy, which focuses on the needs of students who wish to learn about policing in our society, still permeates the text. This is, above all, a text for students. The book has undergone extensive revision since its first publication. In response to student and reviewer feedback, this edition provides the latest in academic and practitioner research as well as the latest statistics, court cases, Web links, information on careers, and criminalistic and technological advances.

CHANGES TO THE THIRD EDITION

Coauthor Linda Forst brings additional geographic and gender perspectives to the text. Even more attention has been given to actual examples from specific police departments—small and large—throughout the nation and world. Each chapter has been thoroughly updated to include new research and applications.

A new chapter has been added to reflect the increasing emphasis on policing and homeland security. There is also increased coverage of such important topics as diversity in policing, police ethics, and state-of-the-art police technology and criminalistics.

We have also included essays from five well-respected veterans of law enforcement and higher education to provide additional insight into several important law enforcement issues as "Guest Lectures" in the part openers and Epilogue.

A text-specific Web site is available with tutorial quizzing, online glossary, flashcards, games, Web links, InfoTrac® College Edition activities, Internet activities, and course resources and updates. Go to http://cj.wadsworth.com/dempsey_intro3e/.

PEDAGOGICAL FEATURES

Within each chapter, we have included the following pedagogical elements:

- *Chapter Goals* serve as chapter "road maps" to orient students to the main learning objectives of each chapter.

- A *Chapter Introduction* previews the material to be covered in the chapter.

- The *Chapter Summary* reinforces the major topics discussed in the chapter and helps students check their learning.

- *Learning Checks* are questions that test the student's knowledge of the material presented in the chapter.

- *Application Exercises* are projects that require students to apply their knowledge to hypothetical situations much like those they might encounter in actual police work. These exercises can be assigned as final written or oral exercises or serve as the basis for lively class debates.

- *Web Exercises* ask the student to research police topics on the Web.

- A *Glossary* defines the key terms presented in the book.

Boxed Features

In an effort to increase student interest, we have included several types of boxed features in each chapter to supplement the main text:

- *You Are There!* These boxes take the student back to the past to review the fact pattern in a particular court case or to learn the details about a significant event or series of events in history. They are intended to give the students a sense of actually being at the scene of a police event.

- *Dempsey's Law* and *Forst's Law* These features recount personal experiences from our own police careers or dialogues between students and ourselves in class. They are intended to provide a reality-based perspective on policing, including the human side of policing.

- *Patrolling the Web* These boxes provide general and specific information for students regarding the use of the Web for academic and professional growth, as well as their own interest.

Appendices

Three appendices are included on the Book Companion Web Site, http://cj.wadsworth.com/dempsey_intro3e/:

- *Sources of Employment Information in Law Enforcement* This appendix gives students ideas on where and how to find jobs in policing and is a valuable resource for class assignments or personal job hunting.

- *The Law Enforcement Code of Ethics* and the *Police Code of Conduct* These two documents provide a framework for the ethical foundations of the police profession—essential knowledge for any student of law enforcement. They can serve as background reading for dynamic and stimulating class discussions in police ethics.

- *National Law Enforcement Officers Memorial: Washington, D.C.* This section pays tribute to the memory of the heroic men and women who have paid the ultimate sacrifice to the police profession and their fellow citizens.

ANCILLARIES

The following ancillaries are available to qualified adopters to accompany this text. Please consult your local sales representative for details.

- *Instructor's Manual* Written by Rhonda K. DeLong of Ferris State University, this instructor's supplement provides a wealth of resources that will help you to bring the course material to life for your students. Included are chapter goals, key terms, chapter outlines and summaries, and a test bank, which contains multiple choice, fill-in-the-blank, true-or-false, essay, and review exercises.

- *ExamView®* This computerized testing tool allows you to create, deliver, and customize tests for use in your courses. Its built-in tutorial system makes it easy to use, and your tests can be delivered to students in both print and online formats. You can enter your own new questions or edit any question provided in the electronic test bank.

- *WebTutor™ ToolBox* Available free with this text, WebTutor ToolBox is preloaded with content that is specific to this text. It pairs the content of the text's Book Companion Web Site with the course management functionality of either WebCT or Blackboard. ToolBox includes a gradebook, online quizzing functionality, and the ability to upload your own course documents for student access.

- *Book Companion Web Site* The Web site, http://cj.wadworth.com/dempsey_intro3e/, includes chapter-based Summaries and Outlines, plus glossary reinforcement games such as Concentration, FlashCards, and Crossword Puzzle Tutorial Quizzing to provide feedback rejoinders that can be e-mailed to instructors. Internet Activities expand the chapter content.

ACKNOWLEDGMENTS

So many people have helped us make the successful transition from the world of being street cops to the world of academia and so many more helped in the publication of this book. We hope we do not forget anyone.

Both authors would like to thank editors Jay Whitney and Sabra Horne for their faith, patience, and constant assistance in this project. For the intelligent and excellent copyediting of Margaret Pinette and the super production efforts of Jennie Redwitz and photo editor Roberta Spieckerman—our sincere admiration and thanks.

To the many students who came to our offices or classes wanting to know about the material we have put into this text, you were the inspiration for this work. This book is for you. To all the great men and women we worked with in our police departments, the heart of this book comes from you.

The authors would also like to thank all the professors across the country, particularly those former women and men in blue who have made that transition from the streets to the classrooms, for their adoption of the first two editions and their kind words and sage advice. They inspired us to prepare this third edition. We would especially like to thank the reviewers of this edition: Dan Baker, University of South Carolina; Joseph Hanrahan, Westfield State University; Anthony Markert, Western Connecticut University; David Streater, Catawba Valley Community College; and Arvind Verma, Indiana University.

John Dempsey would like to thank Professors Pat Ungarino, Al Cofone, and Bob Arrigon at Suffolk County Community College for giving this kid from the Bronx his first start in the classroom and to the administrators, faculty, and staff at SUNY–Empire State College for all their inspiration and assistance over the years. Also, I have to thank the following administrative assistants for all their help and loyalty over the years: at SCCC, Fran Brasile, Annette Guerrera, and Kathy Stasky, and at ESC, Lisa Braglia, Kim Jordan, and Stacy Karlis. A special thank you to the following friends who continually serve as my academic and intellectual stimulation: to my former NYPD partners, the scholars Jim Fyfe, Bill Walsh, Pat Ryan, and Vinny Henry—you inspired me to follow in your path; to Dave Owens—thanks for your great friendship and your leadership in our professional associations; to the members of the Great Uncaught, my speaking partners around the country—Lorenzo Boyd, Jim Burnett, Pat Faiella, Jim Ruiz, Donna Stuccio, and Ed Thibault; to all my wonderful colleagues who hang with me and trade war stories with me whenever we meet throughout the country: Professors

Howard Abadinsky, Elaine Bartgis, Jack Claffey, Lynton Clark, Katie and George Eichenberg, Eugene Evans, Bob Fernandez, Irene Fiala, Denise Gosselin, Rich Hegney, Rob Hoff, Matrice (Marty) Hurrah, Dave Kramer, Ed LeClair, Tom Lenahan, Sharon RedHawk Love, John Linn, Dale McCleary, Jeff Magers, Tony and Pat Markert, Denise Owens, Kathy Pierno, Bob Riedl, Rick Steinmann, Dave Streater, Ralph Rojas, Bernie Walsh, Liz Wiinamake, Gay Young—anything I have achieved in scholarship I owe to you all. It is always an honor and privilege to be in your gracious company. Finally, to Linda, for her gracious acceptance of my offer to assist in the preparation of this third edition. I believe her input and fresh approach have caused this text to progress from a good one to a great one.

Again, as always, to my family—Marianne, my love and best friend; my children, John, Donna, and Cathy; my daughter-in-law Diane and my son-in-law John; and in memory of Anne Marie, my special hero: Your love and patience have sustained me over the years. Finally, to Daniel, Nicolette, and Erin Anne Marie, my grandchildren: Who loves you more than the Grand Dude?

Linda Forst would like to thank many people who led her down her path to a challenging and fulfilling career in law enforcement. My dad, Calvin Forst, taught me to have a great respect for the police and made sure the officers in our town of Ardsley, New York, never left hungry when they stopped by our chicken take-out restaurant. I thank my mom, Betty Forst, who supported my decision despite her reservations and fears. I also owe a lot to my first criminal justice professor, Dr. Bill Bopp (a former police officer), who, when I showed up in his class at FAU on a whim, opened up a whole new world to me and ultimately changed my life. He served as a role model and mentor for many years, and I hope that I may have the impact on students that he had on me.

Thanks to former Palm Beach County Sheriff and Boca Raton Police Chief, Charles McCutcheon, for giving this new college graduate a chance to work at the only police department she applied to because of its outstanding reputation. I thank the late Deputy Chief Charles Hobson who taught me the importance of street officers having compassion and got my husband and me together despite my determination not to get involved with a cop. And of course I am eternally grateful to my late husband, Jim Duke, who supported and encouraged females in law enforcement long before it was politically correct and who was always there for me as I confronted various challenges while rising up through the ranks. I also owe a debt of gratitude to Lori Perkins, my administrative assistant, who showed me how critical support staff can be. Lastly, I thank attorney

Michael Salnick, the best criminal defense attorney in Palm Beach County, for his part in making me a better investigator, as well as for his friendship and support.

I am forever indebted to former Washington State Patrol Captains Steve Seibert and Tom Robbins (Chief of Wenatchee PD) for their endless support and help. When we were classmates at Northwestern University in 1989, I don't think any of us knew the roles we would play in each others' lives. They epitomize the brotherhood that exists among police officers and have always been there for me personally and professionally.

In making the transition from police officer to professor, I am grateful to many people. Professor Lee Libby, my colleague at Shoreline Community College, has been generous with his time and expertise. Jack Dempsey and the friends he mentions above welcomed me into their group when I showed up unexpectedly from the West Coast at their meeting in Vermont. They have been a source of friendship and support, and I eagerly await our yearly meetings at the ACJS national conference. I also thank Professors Jeff Magers, Dave Swim, Alex del Carmen, and Joycelyn Pollock for their support and encouragement. I am espe-

cially thankful to Jack Dempsey for his belief in me in asking me to coauthor this new edition with him. I am truly honored to be part of this production and to work with such a talented and giving man.

In conclusion, I am blessed with loving and supportive daughters, Brynn and Juleigh; siblings, Janice, Barrie, Kim, and Scott; and friends, Sue and Doug Sluis, Ray and Karen Price, Mark and Elaine Gerspacher, Cindi Whalen, Pam Wachob, Nancy Lue, Mary Fleetwood, Deb Long, and Deb Ziebart, as well as Keith and Karen Neeley, who share the brotherhood and always lend support. They have all had a great impact on my life and my ability to accept this challenge. They taught me that "we're all in this together."

We owe a special tribute to all the heroes of September 11, 2001, who rushed in so that others could get out: You are truly symbols of the great public servants who work in emergency services in our nation.

Jack Dempsey

Linda Forst

Police History and Organization

GUEST LECTURE

County Sheriff's Departments: Working in Relative Anonymity

LORENZO BOYD

Lorenzo Boyd is a former Deputy Sheriff in Suffolk County, Massachusetts. He has taught at Old Dominion University and the College of William and Mary in Virginia and is currently Senior Researcher at the Juvenile Justice Institute at North Carolina Central University in Durham, North Carolina.

Although Sir Robert Peel is credited with establishing the precursor to the modern municipal police department, the office of the sheriff has origins that date back to the ninth century and England's King Alfred the Great. The office of sheriff is the oldest law enforcement office known within the common-law system and it has always been accorded great dignity and high trust.

The role of the sheriff has changed and evolved over time. Today, as in the past, the sheriff is the lead law enforcer in the county, entrusted with the maintenance of law and order and the preservation of "domestic tranquility." Sheriffs are also responsible for a host of other criminal justice functions and related activities, including law enforcement, jail administration, inmate transportation, court services, and civil process. The responsibilities of the sheriff cover a wide range of public safety functions that vary based on jurisdiction.

Sheriffs are the only elected law enforcement officials in most states. Today, for instance, sheriffs in Massachusetts are elected in each of the 14 counties, and sheriffs in Virginia are elected in each of its 95 counties and 28 major cities. The sheriff in the county that contains the state capital is called the "high sheriff" and is the ranking sheriff in the state.

In Massachusetts the primary function of the sheriff's department is administration of the county jail and house of correction (in Massachusetts, jail is pretrial only, and the house of correction is short-term postconviction). The law enforcement function, though important, is secondary to the jail function. Because "care, custody, and control" of inmates is paramount, many sheriff's deputies function more as corrections officers than as police officers. In spite of the rich, long law enforcement history of the sheriff's department, often deputies acquiesce to a support role in dealing with municipal police departments. Long before sheriff's deputies can hone their skill on the streets of Boston, they must first serve a significant amount of time working in the county jail.

In most cities, the city police handle day-to-day police work, and the sheriff's department patrols county and rural areas that do not have a municipal police force. Sheriff's deputies also handle many prisoner transport functions to and from court and jails, police raids, and "sting" operations. Sheriff's departments also employ a tactical emergency response team, similar to that of police SWAT teams. These tactical teams in the sheriff's department are referred to as SERT (Sheriff's Emergency Response Team). Inside the jail and house of correction, the SERT team is responsible for quelling cellblock riots, hostage situations, gang rivalries, and forced cell moves.

When I was first deputized in 1988, I was under the impression that I was poised to help save the world. "Fighting crime and saving lives" was the motto that I thought I would adopt. Little did I know that I had a lot to learn about the criminal justice system in general and the sheriff's department in particular. I quickly learned that being proficient at the behind-the-scenes, less glorious duties makes the sheriff's department so important.

Training for sheriff's deputies includes both tactical police training and training for correctional settings. Deputies have to be able to react to situations both in the jail and on the streets at a moment's notice. In the academy, I endured 80 hours of firearms training, 60 hours of criminal law, 40 hours of constitutional law, 20 hours of patrol procedures, 10 hours of self-defense, and a host of other seemingly peripheral topics. My time in the training academy, although critical, did little to prepare me mentally for my first assignment.

Once the academy was over, I donned a pressed uniform and a freshly polished pair of military-style boots and was ready to assume my position in the criminal justice system. I then reported for duty at the Suffolk County Jail in downtown Boston and awaited my new assignment. One thing that I will never forget happened on my first day of work. When I walked into the jail for the first time, the large steel door slammed behind me with a sound that was unnerving. That sound separated freedom from incarceration.

When I reported for duty on that first day, I was given handcuffs, a set of keys, and a radio, and I was assigned to run an inmate housing unit in the county jail. The jail is divided into different inmate housing units, which are treated as separate self-contained jails. I was assigned, on my first day, to what is often called the worst unit in the jail: the homicide unit. In this unit, over 40 men were housed, each facing a trial for murder. It is in situations like these that you find out what you are really made of, mentally. It was a bit intimidating standing face-to-face with the people that I had read about in the newspapers or seen on the evening news accused of having committed the most heinous of crimes. These are the people that I had to interact with for 8 hours per day, every day, in the jail. This is where I was sent to hone my skills, in relative anonymity. If I were good at my job, no one would ever talk about it. Only when things get out of control does the media shine a spotlight on the sheriff's department.

Every problem that occurs in municipal police departments also is present in the sheriff's department. There are power struggles, codes of silence, corruption, and intradepartmental strife. These problems are exacerbated due to the close quarters of the jail. Most of the deputies are struggling to get out of jail duty and move on to patrol, transportation, warrant-management teams, SERT teams, or other glorious assignments. Getting out of the jail onto the streets is something that both deputies and inmates strive for, sometimes with equal fervor.

Often it is the city or state police who make the big arrests in sting operations or on the streets, usually with back up from, or transportation provided by, the sheriff's department. Sheriff's deputies still tend to do the dirty work of transportation, classification, and custody when the city or state police are conducting press conferences. It is the sheriff's deputies who have to deal with the housing, classification, control, and transportation of offenders long after the city or state police have closed their cases. Much of the work of the sheriff's department goes on behind the scenes, with little or no public accolades, but nevertheless the work of the sheriff's department continues in its professional manner often unnoticed by the public.

In retrospect, I have asked myself time and time again if my time in the sheriff's department was a positive one. Overall I am happy with my experiences, both good and bad, because those experiences helped to mold a view of the criminal justice system. The sheriff's department operates in the best (or worst) of both worlds. Deputies get to patrol the streets as well as learn the inner workings of corrections. I think the sheriff's department is the backbone of criminal justice, even though the deputies tend to work in relative anonymity.

Police History

CHAPTER GOALS

- To acquaint you with the rich, colorful history of policing
- To show you how the U.S. police and, indeed, the entire U.S. criminal justice system evolved from the English law enforcement experience
- To acquaint you with early American policing—both the urban and the frontier experiences
- To introduce you to the history of policing in the early 20th century
- To acquaint you with the history and development of recent policing, from the 1960s through the present time

The word *police* comes from the Latin word *politia,* which means "civil administration." The word *politia* goes back to the Greek word *polis,* or "city." Etymologically, therefore, the police can be seen as those involved in the administration of a city. *Politia* became the French word *police.* The English took it over and at first continued to use it to mean "civil administration." The specific application of police to the administration of public order emerged in France in the early 18th century. The first body of public-order officers to be named police in England was the Marine Police, a force established in 1798 to protect merchandise in the port of London.[1]

The reference to the police as a "civil authority" is very important. The police represent the civil power of government, as opposed to the military power of government. We use the military in times of war. The members of the military, of necessity, are trained to kill and destroy. That is appropriate in war. However, do we want to use military forces to govern or patrol our cities and towns? I do not think so. Imagine that you and some of your classmates are having a party. The party gets a bit loud, and your neighbors call 911. Instead of a police car, an armored personnel carrier and tanks arrive at the party, and 20 soldiers come out pointing AK-47 assault rifles at you. Obviously, this is a silly example, but think about it. Surely we need a civil police, not the military, in our neighborhoods.[2]

This chapter will discuss early forms of policing and the direct predecessor of the American police, the English police. Then the discussion will turn to the United States, beginning with the colonial experience with policing. A summary of the 18th- and 19th-century experience will focus on urban and frontier police. The chapter will then turn to modern times—20th-century policing—and discuss the American police from 1900 to 1960, the turbulent decades of the 1960s and 1970s, and our generation, the 1980s and 1990s. It will end with a discussion of policing since the onset of the new millennium, emphasizing the dramatic, unprecedented changes in police organization and operations brought about by the terrorist attacks of September 11, 2001.

★ ★ ★

EARLY POLICING

We do not know much about the very early history of the police. Policing—maintaining order and dealing with lawbreakers—had always been a private matter. Citizens were responsible for protecting themselves and maintaining an orderly society. Uniformed, organized police departments as we think of them today were rare. In fact, as we'll see in this chapter, modern-style police departments didn't appear until the 14th century in France and the 19th century in England.

Around the fifth century B.C., Rome created the first specialized investigative unit, called questors, or "trackers of murder."[3] Around the sixth century B.C. in Athens and the third century B.C. in Rome, unpaid magistrates (judges), appointed by the citizens, were the only people we would consider law enforcement professionals. The magistrates adjudicated cases, but private citizens arrested offenders and punished them. In most societies, people in towns would group together and form a watch, particularly at night, at the town borders or gates to ensure that outsiders did not attack the town.[4]

At about the time of Christ, the Roman emperor Augustus picked out special, highly qualified members of the military to form the **Praetorian Guard.** The Praetorian Guard could be considered the first police officers. Their job was to protect the palace and the emperor. At about the same time, Augustus also established the Praefectus Urbi (Urban Cohort) to protect the city. The Urban Cohort had both executive and judicial power. Augustus also established the Vigiles of Rome. The **Vigiles** began as firefighters. They were eventually also given law enforcement responsibilities, and they patrolled Rome's streets day and night. The Vigiles could be considered the first civil police force designed to protect citizens. They were considered quite brutal, and it is from them that our words *vigilance* and *vigilante* come.[5]

Also in Rome in the first century A.D., public officials called lictors were appointed to serve as bodyguards for the magistrates. The lictors would bring criminals before the magistrates upon their orders and carry out the magistrates' determined punishments, including the death penalty. Their symbol of authority was the fasces, a bundle of rods tied by a red thong around an ax, which represented their absolute authority over life and limb.

During the 12th and 13th centuries, kings on the European continent began to assume responsibility for the administration of the law. They began to appoint officials for that purpose to replace the watch and other private forms of self-defense. In the 13th century in Paris, Louis IX created a provost, who was assigned to enforce the law and supervise the night watch. The provost was assisted by investigating commissioners and sergeants. In 1356, France created a mounted military patrol, the Maréchausée, to maintain peace on the highways. The Maréchausée evolved into the Gendarmerie Nationale, which today polices the areas outside France's major cities.

The city of Paris had an armed, professional police in the 18th century that was credited with keeping Paris a safe and orderly city. The city of Munich also had an effective police department.

★ ★ ★

ENGLISH POLICING: OUR ENGLISH HERITAGE

The American system of law and police was borrowed from the English. Therefore, we will now concentrate on the English police experience, which is colorful and related to the development of English society.

Early History

Sir Robert Peel is generally credited with establishing the first English police department, the London Metropolitan Police, in 1829.[6] However, the first references to an English criminal justice or law enforcement system appeared some 1,000 years earlier, in the latter part of the ninth century, when England's King Alfred the Great was preparing against an impending Danish invasion. Part of King Alfred's strategy against the Danes was the maintenance of stability in his own country and the provision of a method for people living in villages to protect one another. To achieve this stability, King Alfred established a system of **mutual pledge** (a form of "society control" where citizens grouped together to protect each other), which organized the responsibility for the security of the country into several levels. At the lowest level were tithings, ten families, who grouped together to protect one another and to assume responsibility for the acts of the group's members. At the next level, ten tithings, or 100 families, were grouped together into a hundred; the hundred was under the charge of a constable. People were supposed to police their own communities. If trouble occurred, a citizen was expected to raise the **hue and cry** (yell for assistance), and other citizens were expected to come to that citizen's assistance. The **constable,** who might be considered the first form of English police officer, was responsible for dealing with more serious breaches of the law.

Groups of hundreds within a specific geographic area were combined to form shires (the equivalent of today's county). The shires were put under the control of the king and were governed by a **shire-reeve,** or sheriff.

Over the centuries, as formal governments were established, early, primitive forms of a formal criminal justice system evolved in England. In 1285 A.D., the Statute of Winchester was enacted in England. It established a rudimentary criminal justice system in which most of the responsibility for law enforcement remained with the people themselves. The statute formally established (1) the watch and ward, (2) the hue and cry, (3) the parish constable, and (4) the requirement that all males keep weapons in their homes for use in maintaining the public peace.

The **watch and ward** required all men in a given town to serve on the night watch. The watch, therefore, can be seen as the most rudimentary form of metropolitan policing. The watch was designed to protect against crime, disturbances, and fire. The watchmen had three major duties:

1. Patrolling the streets from dusk until dawn to ensure that all local people were indoors and quiet and that no strangers were roaming about.
2. Performing duties such as lighting street lamps, clearing garbage from streets, and putting out fires.
3. Enforcing the criminal law.

Persons serving on the watch, if necessary, would pronounce the hue and cry, and all citizens would then be required to leave their homes and assist the watchmen. The Statute of Winchester made it a crime not to assist the watch. The statute also established the office of parish constable, who was responsible for organizing and supervising the watch. The parish constable was, in effect, the primary urban law enforcement agent in England.

In the early 14th century, we see the beginnings of a more formal system of criminal justice, with a separation of powers and a hierarchical system of authority. The office of the justice of the peace was created to assist the shire-reeve, or sheriff, in nonurban areas and the parish constable in urban areas. Eventually, the justices of the peace developed judicial functions and a status equal to that of the sheriff. Parish constables became subordinate to the justices of the peace and became their operational assistants. While retaining the duty of supervising the night watchmen, the parish constables also had the obligation to investigate offenses, serve summonses, execute warrants issued by the justices of the peace, and secure prisoners. The shire-reeve was busy with his other county duties, especially collecting taxes, and left most of the law enforcement duties to the justices of the peace and the constables.

The Seventeenth Century and Thief-Takers

In 17th-century England, as before, law enforcement was seen as the duty of all the people, even though more and more officials were being charged with enforcing the law and keeping the peace. Already we see the beginnings of a tremendously fragmented and inept criminal justice system. The next criminal justice positions to be created were magistrates and beadles. Magistrates assisted the justices of the peace by presiding in courts, ordering arrests, calling witnesses, and examining prisoners. Beadles were assistants to the constables and walked the streets removing vagrants. The impact of the magistrates, constables, and beadles was minimal, and they were mostly corrupt.

The 17th-century English policing system also used a form of individual, private police. Called **thief-takers,** these private citizens, with no official status, were paid by the king for every criminal they arrested—similar to the bounty hunter of the American West. The major role of the thief-takers was to combat highway robbery committed by highwaymen, whose heroes were the likes of such legendary outlaws as Robin Hood and Little John. By the 17th century, highwaymen such as Jack Sheppard and Dick Turpin made traveling through the English countryside so dangerous that no coach or traveler was safe. In 1693, an act of Parliament established a monetary reward for the capture of any road agent, or armed robber. A thief-taker was paid upon the conviction of the highwayman and also received the highwayman's horse, arms, money, and property.

The thief-taker system was later extended to cover offenses other than highway robbery, and soon a sliding scale of rewards was established. Arresting a burglar or footpad (street robber), for example, was worth the same as catching a highwayman, but catching a sheep stealer or a deserter from the army brought a much smaller reward. In some areas, homeowners joined together and offered supplementary rewards for the apprehension of a highwayman or footpad in their area. In addition, whenever there was a serious crime wave, Parliament awarded special rewards for thief-takers to arrest particular felons.

Often a criminal would agree to become a thief-taker and catch another criminal to receive a pardon from the king for his or her own crime. Thus, many thief-takers were themselves criminals. Thief-taking was not always rewarding, because the thief-taker was not paid if the highwayman was not convicted. The job also could be dangerous, because the thief-taker had to fear the revenge of the highwayman and his relatives and associates. Many thief-takers would seduce young people into committing crimes and then have other thief-takers arrest the youths during the offenses. The two thief-takers would then split the fee. Others framed innocent parties by planting stolen goods on their persons or in their homes. Although some real criminals were apprehended by the professional thief-takers, the system generally created more crime than it suppressed.

Henry Fielding

Henry Fielding, the 18th-century novelist best known for writing *Tom Jones,* may also be credited with laying the foundation for the first modern police force. In 1748, during the heyday of English highwaymen, Fielding was appointed magistrate in Westminster, a city near central London. He moved into a house on Bow Street, which also became his office. Fielding, in an attempt to decrease the high number of burglaries, street and highway robberies, and other thefts, established relationships with local pawnbrokers. He provided them with lists and descriptions of recently stolen property and asked them to notify him should such property be brought into their pawnshops. He then placed the following ad in the London and Westminster newspapers: "All persons who shall for the future suffer by robber, burglars, etc., are desired immediately to bring or send the best description they can of such robbers, etc., with the time and place and circumstances of the fact, to Henry Fielding Esq., at his house in Bow Street."[7]

Fielding's actions brought about what we can call the first official crime reports. Fielding was able to gain the cooperation of the high constable of Holborn and several other public-spirited constables. Together they formed a small investigative unit, which they called the Bow Street Runners. These were private citizens who were not paid by

---

YOU ARE THERE! »

England's Early Experience with a Civil Police Department

1763	Fielding creates civilian horse patrol in London.
1770	Foot patrol is established in London.
1798	River or marine police to patrol the Thames is established by Patrick Colquhoun. (Some consider this to be England's first civil police department.)
1804	Horse patrol is established in London (England's first uniformed patrol).
1829	Peel's Police are established in London (England's first large-scale, organized, uniformed, paid, civil police department).

PATROLLING THE WEB

Introduction to "Patrolling the Web"

"Patrolling the Web" is a special feature of this textbook that will be found throughout the book. Most people refer to surfing the Web, but, for obvious reasons, we'll call it "Patrolling the Web." The purpose of this feature is to show you how the Internet can be useful to students, police officers, and the public.

The Internet is fun, easy to use, and very useful in doing research and in finding jobs in policing and the criminal justice system. "Patrolling the Web" will discuss computers, the Internet, the World Wide Web, and all related topics without using computer terms, as much as possible.

As Professor Dempsey says, *I am not a computer person or an expert in anything about computers. As a matter of fact, just a few years ago I was computer phobic. I was even afraid to turn one on. Eventually, I learned how to use a word-processing program on the computers at my school. I learned enough to type up my course outlines, my examinations, and even some speeches and personal letters.*

Eventually, I wrote two textbooks on the computer, yet whenever anyone mentioned the Internet, I froze. I came from the precomputer generation—we didn't even know what a computer was. In fact, when I went to grade school, we actually used fountain pens; we filled them up from an ink bottle on our desk. Then, the ballpoint pen came into fashion. We still had never heard of a computer.

How did I learn to use the Internet? One evening I approached my secretary, Colleen, and asked her to teach me. She smiled, turned on her computer, pressed some buttons, played with the mouse, and then started walking away. I yelled, "Hey, Colleen, where are you going? I don't know what I'm doing." She said, "Hey,

you're a professor; you can figure it out!" I didn't see her again for three hours. By the time she came back, I knew the basics of the Internet. It's that easy, even for a professor, and it's a heck of a lot of fun. Hopefully, if you don't know how to use the Internet yet, or don't know how much it can help you with research, finding a job, or having fun, you'll start here. I really can't teach you how to do it. You have to just sit down and get started.

You will need a computer, a modem, Internet software, a mouse, and that's about all. What if you do not have a computer? A modem? Internet software? A mouse? Can't afford one? The majority of schools in our nation today have everything you need to get started and allow students to use them for free. Your local library probably will give you free access to the Internet. Mine does. If all else fails, talk to your classmates; plenty of them have all you need to get started. Maybe you can wash their car for them or buy them lunch. It's that easy.

Now you have to sit down and get started. One of your friends at school must have access to the Internet and the patience to let you start working on it. If not, get new friends. If you do not want to do that, take a course at school that covers the Internet. There are many of them in colleges, school district evening programs, libraries, and the like. Some of these courses are free, and some charge. Just get started and have fun. Once you get familiar with the Internet beat, you might want to look at a really good little book published by the company that published this textbook. It's only 70 pages and covers the basics of the Internet and some of the ways to use it to its fullest. Your professor probably has one. See Internet Guide for Criminal Justice *by Daniel J. Kurland and Christina Polsenberg (Wadsworth Publishing Company, 1997).*

public funds but who were permitted to accept thief-taker rewards.

Eventually, Fielding's efforts were rewarded by the government, and his Bow Street Runners were publicly financed. In 1763, Fielding was asked to establish with public funds a civilian horse patrol of eight men to combat robbers and footpads on the London streets. The patrol proved successful but was disbanded after only nine months due to a lack of government support.

Londoners debated whether to have a professional police department. Although certainly enough crime occurred to justify forming a civil police force, most people did not

want a formal, professional police department for two major reasons. Many felt that a police force would threaten their tradition of freedom. Additionally, the English had considerable faith in the merits of private enterprise, and they disliked spending public money.

Despite the widespread public fear of establishing a civil police force, a small, permanent foot patrol financed by public funds was established in London in 1770. In 1789, a London magistrate, Patrick Colquhoun, lobbied for the creation of a large, organized police force for greater London, but his ideas were rejected after much government and public debate.

In 1798, Colquhoun was able to establish a small, publicly financed special river or marine police, patterned after Fielding's Bow Street Runners, to patrol the Thames. Some consider Colquhoun's force the first civil police department in England.

In 1804, a new horse patrol was established for central London. It included two inspectors and 52 men who wore uniforms consisting of red vests and blue jackets and trousers, making them England's first uniformed civil police department. As the problems of London in the late 18th and early 19th centuries increased (the Industrial Revolution, poverty, public disorder, and crime), the people and Parliament finally surrendered to the idea that London needed a large, organized, civil police department.

Peel's Police—The Metropolitan Police for London

In 1828, Sir Robert Peel, England's home secretary, basing his ideas on those of Patrick Colquhoun, drafted the first police bill, the Act for Improving the Police in and near the Metropolis (the Metropolitan Police Act). Parliament passed it in 1829. This act established the first large-scale, uniformed, organized, paid, civil police force in London. Over 1,000 men were hired. Although a civil, as opposed to a military, force, it was structured along military lines, with officers wearing distinctive uniforms. The first London Metropolitan Police wore three-quarter-length royal blue coats, white trousers, and top hats. They were armed with truncheons, yesterday's equivalent of today's police baton. The police were commanded by two magistrates, later called commissioners. The control of the new police (called Bobbies in honor of their founder, Sir Robert Peel) was delegated to the home secretary, a member of the democratically elected government. Thus, the police as we know them today were, from their very beginning, ultimately responsible to the public.

Sir Robert Peel has become known as the Founder of Modern Policing. Peel's early police were guided by his nine principles (**Peel's Nine Principles**):

1. The basic mission for which the police exist is to prevent crime and disorder.
2. The ability of the police to perform their duties is dependent upon public approval of police actions.

YOU ARE THERE! »

Sir Robert Peel—The Founder of Modern Policing

Sir Robert Peel was one of the most important persons in 19th-century British history. He dominated parliament throughout the period 1830 to 1850. He became a Member of Parliament (MP) in 1809 at the age of 21 after his father bought him a seat in Parliament and became undersecretary of war and the colonies in 1810.

In 1812, Peel was appointed Chief Secretary for Ireland. In that post he attempted to bring an end to corruption in Irish government by trying to stop the practice of selling public offices and the dismissal of civil servants for their political views. Eventually he became seen as one of the leading opponents to Catholic Emancipation. In 1814, he established a military-type "peace preservation" force in Ireland which eventually evolved into the Royal Irish Constabulary (RIC). In 1818, he resigned his post in Dublin and returned to London.

He became Home Secretary from 1822 to 1827. Distressed over the problems of law and order in London, he persuaded the House of Commons to pass the Metropolitan Police Act in 1829. The first Metropolitan Police patrols went onto the streets on September 29, 1829.

He was prime minister twice, from 1834 to 1835 and from 1841 to 1846. Peel died in 1850 as the result of injuries he sustained in a fall from his horse while riding up Constitution Hill in London. Many have called him among the most important statesmen in the history of England

Because of Peel's connection with the creation of both the modern Irish and English police, the Irish police were known as "peelers" and the English police as "bobbies," thus magnifying Peel's role in the development of modern policing.

Source: Thomas A. Reppetto, *The Blue Parade* (New York: The Free Press, 1978), pp. 16, 22; A Web of English History, retrieved on July 14, 2003, from http://www.adw03.dial.pipex.com/pms/peelbio.htm; Peel Web home page, retrieved on July 14, 2003, from http://dspace.dial.pipex.com/town/terrace/adw03/peel/peelhome.htm; Metropolitan Police Service Historical Archives, retrieved on July 14, 2003, from http://www.met.police.uk/history/archives.htm; Robert Peel, retrieved on July 14, 2003, from http://www.partacus.schoolnet.co.uk/PRpeel.htm

An English "bobbie" on foot patrol.

3. Police must secure the willing co-operation of the public in voluntary observance of the law to be able to secure and maintain the respect of the public.

4. The degree of co-operation of the public that can be secured diminishes proportionately to the necessity of the use of physical force.

5. Police seek and preserve public favour not by catering to public opinion but by constantly demonstrating absolute impartial service to the law.

6. Police use physical force to the extent necessary to secure observance of the law or to restore order only when the exercise of persuasion, advice and warning is found to be insufficient.

7. Police, at all times, should maintain a relationship with the public that gives reality to the historic tradition that the police are the public and the public are the police, the police being only members of the public who are paid to give full-time attention to duties which are incumbent on every citizen in the interests of community welfare and existence.

8. Police should always direction their action strictly towards their functions and never appear to usurp the powers of the judiciary.

9. The test of police efficiency is the absence of crime and disorder, not the visible evidence of police action in dealing with it.[8]

As a result of the formation of the new police force, the patchwork of private law enforcement systems in use at the time was abolished. The English model of policing eventually became the model for the United States.

London's first two police commissioners were Colonel Charles Rowan, a career military officer, and Richard Mayne, a lawyer. Rowan believed that mutual respect between the police and citizens would be crucial to the success of the new force. As a result, the early Bobbies were chosen for their ability to reflect and inspire the highest personal ideals among young men in early 19th-century England.

The Metropolitan Police was organized around the **"beat system,"** in which officers were assigned to relatively small permanent posts and were expected to become familiar with them and the people residing there, thereby making the officer a part of neighborhood life. This system differed from the patrols of the Paris police, which consisted of periodic roving surveillance of areas. Paris police patrols were never assigned to the same area on successive nights, thus discouraging a close familiarity between the police and the public.

The main jobs of the new police were the suppressing of mob disorder, the winning of support from the public, and the development of a disciplined force. The development of a professional and disciplined force was difficult, as Thomas Reppetto tells us:

On September 29, 1829, the force held a muster of its first 1,000 recruits. It was a rainy day, and some of the men broke out very un-military umbrellas, while others, carrying on the quite military habit of hard drinking, showed up intoxicated. The umbrella problem was eliminated by an order issued that day, but drinking was not so easily handled. In the first eight years, 5,000 members of the force had to be dismissed and 6,000 resigned. After four years only 15 percent of the 3,400 original recruits were left.[9]

Unfortunately, the new police were not immediately well received. Some elements of the population saw the police as an occupying army, and open battles between the police and citizens occurred. The tide of sentiment turned in favor of the police, however, when an officer was viciously killed in the Cold Bath Fields riot of 1833. At the murder trial, the jury returned a not-guilty verdict, inspiring a groundswell of public support for the much-maligned police. Eventually, Peel's system became so popular that all English cities adopted his idea of a civil police department.

★ ★ ★

AMERICAN POLICING: THE COLONIAL EXPERIENCE

The American colonists did not have an easy life.[10] They were constantly at risk from foreign enemies, their brother and sister colonists, and Native Americans. Their only protection was their own selves and, at times, the military or militia. By the 17th century, the colonies started to institute a civil law enforcement system that closely replicated the English model. The county sheriff was the most important law enforcement official. However, in addition to law enforcement, he collected taxes, supervised elections, and had much to do with the legal process. Sheriffs were not paid a salary but, much like the English thief-taker, were paid fees for each arrest they made. Sheriffs did not patrol but stayed in their offices.

In cities, the town marshal was the chief law enforcement official, aided by constables (called *schouts* in the Dutch settlements) and night watchmen. Night watch was sometimes performed by the military. The city of Boston created the first colonial night watch in 1631 and three years later created the position of constable. In 1658, eight paid watchmen replaced a patrol of citizen volunteers in the Dutch city of Nieuw Amsterdam. This police system was inherited by the British in 1664 when they took over the city and renamed it New York. By the mid-1700s, the New York night watch was described as follows: "a parcel of idle, drinking, vigilant snorers, who never quell'd any nocturnal tumult in their lives; but would perhaps, be as ready to joining in a burglary as any thief in Christendom."[11]

When serious breaches of the peace occurred, including riots or slave revolts, the governors called on the colonial militia or the British army. Many cities, including Fort Pontchartrain (Detroit), New Orleans, and Fort Washington (Cincinnati), were under martial law for much of their early existence.

Despite the presence of law enforcement officials in the colonies, law enforcement was still mainly the responsibility of the individual citizen, as it had been in early England. There was little law and order on the colonial frontier. When immediate action was needed, the frontier people took matters into their own hands, which led to an American tradition of vigilantism.

★ ★ ★

AMERICAN POLICING: EIGHTEENTH AND NINETEENTH CENTURIES

Historically, American policing attempted to control crime and disorder in an urban and frontier environment. Although the urban and frontier experience differed in many ways, both could be classified as brutal and corrupt.

The Urban Experience

During the 18th century, the most common form of American law enforcement was the system of constables in the daytime and the watch at night. Crime, street riots, and drunkenness were very common, and law enforcement personnel were totally incompetent.

From 1790 to 1845, New York City's population rose from 33,000 to 370,000 people, and most were new immigrants. The increased population and poverty dramatically increased crime. An 1840 New York newspaper reported:

> Destructive rascality stalks at large in our streets and public places, at all times of day and night, with none to make it afraid; mobs assemble deliberately. . . . In a word, lawless violence and fury have full dominion over us.[12]

In 1842, a special citizens' committee of New Yorkers wrote:

> The property of the citizen is pilfered, almost before his eyes. Dwellings and warehouses are entered with an ease and apparent coolness and carelessness of detection which shows that none are safe. Thronged as our city is, men are robbed in the street. Thousands that are arrested go unpunished, and the defenseless and the beautiful are ravished and murdered in the daytime, and no trace of the criminals is found.[13]

EARLY POLICE DEPARTMENTS   The first organized American police department was created in Boston in 1838. In addition to police duties, until 1853 the Boston police were charged with maintaining public health. The first Boston Police Department consisted of only eight members and worked only in the daytime. By 1851, the night watch was assumed by the new Boston Police Department. In 1853, the office of police chief was created, and in 1854, police stations were constructed. The Boston police force was not fully uniformed until 1859, when members were required to wear blue jackets and white hats.

In 1844, the New York State legislature authorized communities to organize police forces and gave special funds to cities to provide 24-hour police protection. In New York City, under the leadership of Mayor William F. Havermeyer, a London-style police department was created on May 23, 1845. The first New York City police officers were issued copper stars to wear on their hats and jackets but were not allowed to wear full uniforms until 1853. In fact, the first New York cops did not even want to wear their copper stars, because doing so made them targets for the city's ruffians. The New York City police were also in charge of street sweeping until 1881.

Philadelphia started its police department in 1854. By the outbreak of the Civil War, Chicago, New Orleans, Cincinnati, Baltimore, Newark, and a number of other large cities had their own police departments. The new police departments replaced the night watch system. As a result, constables and sheriffs were relieved of much of their patrol and investigative duties. However, they performed other duties in the fledgling criminal justice system, such as serving court orders and managing jails.

POLITICS IN AMERICAN POLICING   Policing in 19th-century America was dominated by local politicians and was notorious for brutality, corruption, and ineptness:

PATROLLING THE WEB

New York City Police Department
 http://www.nyc.gov/html/nypd/home.html
New York City Police Museum
 http://www.nycpolicemuseum.org

YOU ARE THERE! >>

New York City Police Museum

The NYPD has protected the city for over 150 years. Its period of development to its modern-day structure dates back to the 17th century. The New York City Police Museum is located at 100 Old Slip in Manhattan's financial district within view of the Brooklyn Bridge and the Fulton Fish Market. The building was built in 1909 as the new home for the First Precinct. It was considered a model police facility when built, and chiefs of police from throughout the country visited the new station house looking to copy some of its features in their own buildings.

The museum captures the history of the NYPD as well as a present-day look at the world of law enforcement through the eyes of its officers. Its exhibits include an array of weapons, police shields, fingerprinting and forensic art stations, a drug awareness display, and a tactics simulator.

The museum collects, preserves, and interprets objects related to the history of the NYPD and provides information about its history through exhibitions, lectures, the Internet, publications, school events, and other educational programs. It houses one of the largest collections of police memorabilia in the United States, as well as an extensive photo collection and some police records dating back to the inception of the NYPD in 1845.

Source: New York City Police Department at http://www.nycpolicemuseum.org

In addition to the pervasive brutality and corruption, the police did little to effectively prevent crime or provide public services. . . . Officers were primarily tools of local politicians; they were not impartial and professional public servants.[14]

In his 1991 book, *Low Life: Lures and Snares of Old New York,* Luc Sante says,

The history of the New York police is not a particularly illustrious one, at least in the nineteenth and early twentieth centuries, as throughout the period the law enforcement agents of the city continually and recurrently demonstrated corruption, complacency, confusion, sloth and brutality.[15]

In 1857, political differences between the Democrats, who controlled New York City, and the Republicans, who controlled New York State, caused a full-scale police war. The corrupt New York City police, the Municipal Police, under the control of New York's mayor Fernando Wood,

What a Police Officer's Uniform Means

The police badge—known in some departments as the shield, chest piece, or tin—is the outward symbol of a police officer's legal status and entitlement. It is symbolic of the authority vested in that individual by the public. The badge and other parts of the police officer's uniform are vestiges of the armor worn by government warriors centuries ago.

The badge's history can be traced back to two pieces of armor: the handheld shield used to deflect blows and the chest plating intended to protect the warrior's chest from penetration. The shield often displayed the heraldry and symbols of the warrior's lord or head of state, just as today's badges reflect symbols of the officer's municipality, county, or state.

Shoulder epaulets or shoulder patches represent the shoulder plating worn to protect the warrior from the heavy, flat swords of the time. The officer's hat is reminiscent of helmets worn by warriors in battle. The hat badge or shield is a vestige of the plumage or insignia on the helmets.

Source: Adapted from *Police Chief* (Sept. 1988), p. 66.

was replaced by the Metropolitan Police, created and controlled by Governor John A. King. Wood, however, refused to disband the Municipals. Thus, the city had two separate police departments, each under the control of one of the two enemies.

On June 16, 1857, the two police departments clashed at New York's City Hall. Fifty Metropolitan police arrived at City Hall with a warrant to arrest Wood. Almost 900 members of the Municipal Police attacked the Metropolitans, causing them to retreat. As the Metropolitans were retreating, the state called in the Seventh Regiment of the National Guard under the command of General Sandford. The members of the National Guard marched on City Hall and raised their weapons as if to fire at the Municipals and City Hall. Eventually Wood surrendered to arrest, and no shots were fired. In court, the mayor was released and the judge decided that the Metropolitan Police would be the official New York City police.

The primary job of 19th-century police was to serve as the enforcement arm of the political party in power, pro-

tect private property, and control the rapidly arriving foreign immigrants. In the late 1800s, police work was highly desirable, because it paid more than most other blue-collar jobs. The average factory worker earned $450 a year, whereas a police officer was paid, on average, $900.

Politics dominated police departments, and politicians determined who would be appointed a police officer and who would be promoted to higher ranks. Chicago, New Orleans, Cincinnati, Baltimore, Newark, and a number of other large cities created police departments around the time of the start of the Civil War. Security was nonexistent, because when a new political party gained control of city government, it would generally fire all police officers and hire new ones.

Regarding the influence of politics on the hiring of police officers, Samuel Walker wrote:

> Ignorance, poor health, or old age was no barrier to employment. An individual with the right connections could be hired despite the most obvious lack of qualifications. Recruits received no formal training. A new officer would be handed a copy of the police manual (if one could be found) containing the local ordinances and state laws, and sent out on patrol. There he could receive on-the-job training from experienced officers who, of course, also taught the ways of graft and evasion of duty.[16]

You Decide: How Did the Term "Cops" Come About?

Did "cops" refer to the copper stars worn by the first New York City police officers?

When the first members of the NYPD began to patrol in the summer of 1845, they had no standard uniforms; they only wore badges on their civilian clothing. The badges were eight-pointed stars (representing the first eight paid members of the old Watch during Dutch times) with the seal of the City at the center and were made of stamped copper. The newspapers of the time referred to the new force as the "Star Police," but people, seeing the shiny copper shields, began to call them "coppers," which was later shortened to "cops."

Or, was "cops" a shortened way of saying Constables on Patrol (COPs)? There is also a British police term, Constable on Patrol, which may account for the use of the term "cops" in England as well.

Robert M. Fogelson wrote about the political impact of politicians on the police:

> Most patrolmen who survived for any length of time quickly . . . learned that a patrolman placed his career in jeopardy more by alienating his captain than by disobeying his chief and more by defying his wardman, who regulated vice in the precinct, than by ignoring [his sergeant].[17]

According to one researcher,

> They [the police] knew who put them in office and whose support they needed to stay there. Their job was to manage their beat; often they became completely enmeshed in the crime they were expected to suppress. Corruption, brutality, and racial discrimination, although not universal, were characteristic of most big city departments.[18]

ARMING OF THE POLICE

THE EARLY POLICE OFFICER'S JOB   Police work was primitive. The role of the American urban police in the 18th and 19th centuries was varied and often not limited to law enforcement. The early police performed many duties they do not have today, including cleaning streets, inspecting boilers, caring for the poor and homeless, operating emergency ambulances, and performing other social services.

American police, in the English tradition, were not issued firearms. However, this changed quickly. In 1858, a New York City police officer shot a fleeing felon with a personal weapon. The case was presented to a grand jury, which did not indict the officer. Police officers in New York then began to arm themselves. A similar incident in

---

YOU ARE THERE! »

First Urban U.S. Police Departments

Boston

1838	Boston Police Department is created with eight officers who only worked in the daytime.
1851	Boston Police Department assumes the night watch.
1853	First Boston police chief is appointed.
1854	First Boston police stations are built.
1859	Boston police officers receive first uniforms.

New York

1845	New York City Police Department is created—with officers on the job twenty-four hours a day, seven days a week.
1853	New York City police are required to wear uniforms.
1857	Police "civil war" erupts at New York City Hall.

Philadelphia

1854	Philadelphia Police Department is created.

Boston led to the arming of that police force. By the early 1900s, cities commonly issued revolvers to their police officers. Officers patrolled on foot with no radios, backup, or supervision. They relied on brute force and brutality to avoid being beaten up or challenged by local toughs. (See the description of the turn of-the-last-century New York City police captain Alexander "Clubber" Williams in Chapter 12.)

Citizens had a tremendous hatred for 19th-century police officers and saw them as political hacks. The police were subjected to frequent abuse by street gangs, and suspects often had to be physically subdued prior to arrest. Commenting on this lack of respect by citizens, Walker notes, "A tradition of police brutality developed out of this reciprocal disrespect. Officers sought to gain with their billy clubs the deference to their authority that was not freely given."[19] Regarding this brutality, the social reformer Lincoln Steffens wrote: "He saw the police bring in and kick out their bandaged, bloody prisoners, not only strikers and foreigners, but thieves too, and others of the miserable, friendless, troublesome poor."[20]

YOU ARE THERE! »

Saved by the Badge

A Kansas prosecutor literally owes his life to his badge. Eric Stonecipher, a special narcotics prosecutor for the Geary County, Kansas, attorney's office, was ambushed August 11, 1992, while driving on a Kansas highway. At least five bullets struck his car. Stonecipher's special prosecutor's badge, carried in his breast pocket, deflected a bullet that would have struck him in the heart. Three bullets struck his car headrest, one passed through his upper left arm, and the fifth bounced off his badge.

Source: Adapted from "Saved by the Badge," *Law Enforcement News* (Sept. 30, 1992), p. 4.

Corruption, mismanagement, and brutality were rampant. Consequently, between 1860 and 1866, the police forces of Baltimore, St. Louis, Chicago, Kansas City, Detroit, and Cleveland were placed under state control.

Boston was the first city to form a detective division to investigate past crimes. However, early detectives were as corrupt as their uniformed counterparts, private thief-takers, or bounty hunters.

In the latter part of the 19th century, we begin to see some practical and technological advances in policing. The public health and social welfare responsibilities that formerly were the province of the police, including sweeping sidewalks and housing the homeless, were transferred to newly created municipal agencies. In the 1850s, precincts began to be linked to central headquarters by telegraph machines. In the 1860s, telegraph signal stations were installed, first in Chicago and then in Cincinnati. These enabled officers, using Morse code, to check with their precincts for instructions or to call for assistance. In 1881, the Morse code signal system was replaced by telephone call boxes in Cincinnati. A police officer could now call from his beat for a patrol wagon to transport prisoners. A red light on the top of a call box could summons officers for messages from their precinct headquarters.

As primitive as the 18th and 19th century urban policing was, policing America's frontier was even more primitive, as we shall see in the next section.

The Frontier Experience

Life on the American frontier was not easy.[21] Early settlers faced tremendous problems from the weather, the terrain, Native Americans, and the criminals within their own ranks. Formal law enforcement on the frontier was rare. What little law enforcement existed in the Old West consisted mainly of the locally elected county sheriff and the appointed town marshal, and sometimes the U.S. marshal, the U.S. Army, or the state militia.

SHERIFFS AND TOWN MARSHALS   The locally elected county sheriffs and the appointed town marshals (appointed by the mayor or city council) were usually the only law enforcement officers available on the frontier. Most of the sheriff's time was spent collecting taxes and performing duties for the courts.

If a crime spree occurred or a dangerous criminal was in an area, the sheriff would call upon the **posse comitatus,** a common-law descendent of the old hue and cry. (The term *posse comitatus,* in Latin, means "the power of

the county.") No man above the age of 15 could refuse to serve as a member of a legally constituted posse. The posse was often little more than a legalized form of vigilantism. Vigilantism and lynch mobs were common in the Old West because of the lack of professional law enforcement. Many famous town marshals, such as James Butler (Wild Bill) Hickok of Hays City, Kansas, and later, Abilene, Kansas, and Wyatt Earp of Dodge City, Kansas, were really semireformed outlaws. There was little to distinguish between the good guys and bad guys in the American frontier's criminal justice system.

FEDERAL MARSHALS   Federal marshals played a role in frontier law enforcement. The Federal Judiciary Act of 1789, which created the office of the U.S. marshal, also gave the marshals the power to call upon the militia for assistance, a power formalized under federal posse comitatus legislation in 1792. The militia were technically members of the federal marshal's posse and aided him in performing his civil duties. In 1861, Congress passed a law empowering the president to call upon the militia or regular army to enforce the law when ordinary means were insufficient.

THE MILITARY   After the Civil War, from 1867 to 1877, law enforcement duties were provided by the military in the military districts created from the Confederacy. U.S. marshals in occupied southern states often called upon federal troops to form a posse to enforce local laws. Once southern states regained representation in Congress, they tried to prevent such practices. In both the North and the South, the military was also used by civilian authorities. In the South, the army guarded polling places and curbed the actions of the Ku Klux Klan; in the North, the army was used to suppress labor disturbances.

Excesses by the military in enforcing the law resulted in Congress passing the Posse Comitatus Act of 1879, forbidding the use of the military to enforce civilian law except where expressly authorized by law. Some of these exceptions applied in the Old West to prevent trespassing on Native American reservations or to enforce unpopular federal decisions regarding territories such as Arizona and New Mexico. The use of the military in the Old West ended around the last quarter of the 19th century.

STATE POLICE AGENCIES   Some states and territories created their own police organizations. In 1823, Stephen Austin hired a dozen bodyguards to protect fellow

YOU ARE THERE! >>

The Drug Enforcement Administration (DEA) Museum

The Drug Enforcement Administration (DEA) Museum is open to the public with regular hours, but admission is by appointment only. Located in Arlington, Virginia, the museum is operated by the DEA's Office of Public Affairs. It also conducts programs and tours for schools and other community groups.

Inside the museum a variety of exhibits outline the DEA's mission, history, and some of its more notable feats in enforcing U.S. controlled-substance laws. One featured exhibit is "Illegal Drugs in America: A Modern History." This exhibit traces drug use in America from the opium dens of the 1800s to the international crime organizations that run the "narcobusiness" today. The exhibit traces the impact drugs have had on American society and the counternarcotics efforts used to combat the problem. It also traces the DEA's evolution from part of the Treasury Department to the force it is today.

Sources: Sheila Burnette, "Police Museums Worldwide," *Law and Order* (August 2001), pp. 71–74; Drug Enforcement Administration, http://www.usdoj.gov/dea/museum

"Texicans" from Native Americans and bandits. Austin's hired guns were officially named the Texas Rangers upon Texas's independence in 1835. The Texas Rangers served as a border patrol for the Republic of Texas, guarding against marauding Native Americans and Mexicans. When Texas was admitted to the Union in 1845, the Texas Rangers became the first U.S. state police agency.

Unlike present-day state police, the Texas Rangers and their counterparts, the Arizona Rangers (1901) and the New Mexico Mounted Patrol (1905), were primarily border patrols designed to combat cattle thievery and control outlaw activities along the Rio Grande. By the 1850s, they had received general police powers. The Rangers were disbanded during the post–Civil War reconstruction period but reemerged in 1874.

With Pennsylvania leading the way in 1905, states outside the Southwest began to create their own state police agencies. The twentieth century saw the creation of state police agencies in each state, with the exception of Hawaii.

PRIVATE POLICE   Private police were much more effective than public law enforcement agencies on the frontier. The private police acted in the same manner as the English thief-takers; however, the American private police were more professional and honest than the English version.

Allan Pinkerton, a native of Scotland, was a former police detective who established a detective agency in Chicago in 1850. The Pinkerton Agency first gained notoriety just before the Civil War, when it thwarted the alleged "Baltimore Plot" to assassinate president-elect Abraham Lincoln. By the 1880s, Pinkerton's National Detective Agency had offices in nearly two dozen cities. In the West, Pinkerton's customers included the U.S. Department of Justice, various railroad companies, and major land speculators. The agents arrested train robbers and notorious gangsters, including the James Gang in the 1880s and Robert Leroy Parker (Butch Cassidy) and Harry Longbaugh (the Sundance Kid) in the early 1900s. The agents also arrested John and Simeon Reno, who organized the nation's first band of professional bank robbers. They were also hired in the East by mining and manufacturing companies to suppress labor organizations, such as the Molly Maguires in 1874 to 1875, as well as to suppress the Homestead Riots in Pittsburgh in 1892. The Pinkertons employed informants throughout the United States and its territories and offered cash rewards for information. The Pinkertons mainly protected the interests of the railroads, wealthy eastern bankers, and land speculators.

In competition with the Pinkerton Agency during the latter part of the 19th century was the Rocky Mountain Detective Association, which pursued and apprehended bank and train robbers, cattle thieves, murderers, and the road agents who plundered highways and mining communities throughout the Southwest and Rocky Mountain area.

Also in competition with the Pinkertons was Wells, Fargo and Company, started in 1852 by Henry Wells and William G. Fargo as a banking and stock association designed to capitalize on the emerging shipping and banking opportunities in California. It operated as a mail-carrying service and stagecoach line out of more than a hundred offices in the western mining districts. Because the company carried millions of dollars in gold and other valuable cargo, it created a guard company to protect its shipments. The Wells Fargo private security employees were effective in preventing robberies and thefts; moreover, criminals who were able to hold up its banks and carriers were relentlessly hunted down by specially trained and equipped agents.

★ ★ ★

AMERICAN POLICING: TWENTIETH CENTURY

The first half of the 20th century saw such dramatic negative events as the Boston Police Strike, National Prohibition, and the issuance of the Wickersham Commission Report. However, innovation and an increase in professionalism grew to characterize the American police in part through the efforts of such early police professionals as August Vollmer, O. W. Wilson, and J. Edgar Hoover.

Policing from 1900 to 1960

As we have seen, American policing has historically been characterized by ineptness, corruption, and brutality.[22] At the start of the 20th century, serious attempts were made to reform the police.

Even earlier, Theodore Roosevelt attempted reform as one of the New York City Board of Police Commissioners between 1895 and 1897. Roosevelt raised police recruitment standards and disciplined corrupt and brutal officers. However, despite much publicity and some superficial changes, Roosevelt's efforts failed when the corrupt Tammany Hall political machine was returned to power in 1897.

During the progressive era of American government, 1900 to 1914, attempts at reforming the police were originated outside police departments by middle-class, civic-minded reformers. For the most part, however, these attempts failed.

TECHNOLOGY   In the 20th century, the use of technology grew phenomenally in American police departments. By 1913, the police motorcycle was being used by departments in the Northeast. The first police car was used in Akron, Ohio, in 1910, and the police wagon was first used in Cincinnati in 1912. By the 1920s, the patrol car was in widespread use. The patrol car began to change police work by allowing the police to respond quickly to crimes and other problems, as well as by enabling each officer to cover much more territory.

The widespread use of the one-way radio in the 1930s and the two-way radio in the 1940s, combined with the growing use of the patrol car, began to revolutionize police work. A person could call police headquarters or a precinct, and a police car could be dispatched almost immediately, providing rapid response to calls for service and emergencies. Although this innovation was greeted with

great joy by police administrators, motorized patrol eventually forced a separation of the police from the community and played a part in the serious problems in policing that arose in the 1960s.

THE BOSTON POLICE STRIKE   The Boston police strike of 1919 was one of the most significant events in the history of policing, and it increased interest in police reform. While other professions were unionizing and improving their standards of living, police salaries lagged behind, and the police were becoming upset with their diminished status in society. The fraternal association of Boston police officers, the Boston Social Club, voted to become a union affiliated with the American Federation of Labor (AFL). On September 9, 1919, 70 percent of Boston's police officers—1,117 men—went on strike. Rioting and looting immediately broke out, and Governor Calvin Coolidge mobilized the state militia. Public support went against the police, and the strike was broken. All the striking officers were fired and replaced by new recruits. The strike ended police unionism for decades. Calvin Coolidge became a national hero and went on to become president of the United States. Many say that his action in firing the Boston police propelled him to the presidency.

NATIONAL PROHIBITION   Another significant event in 20th-century policing, and one that stirred up another police reform movement, was the experiment with the prohibition of alcohol in the United States. The **Volstead Act** (National Prohibition) was passed in 1919 and became law in 1920 with the adoption of the **Eighteenth Amendment** to the Constitution. It forbade the sale and manufacture of alcohol, attempting to make America a dry nation. Traditional organized crime (TOC) families received their impetus during this period as gangsters banded together to meet the tremendous demand of ordinary Americans for alcohol. When the Eighteenth Amendment was repealed in 1933 with the adoption of the Twenty-first Amendment, the organized crime families funneled the tremendous amount of capital that they had received in the alcohol trade into other vice crimes, such as illegal gambling, prostitution, loan sharking, labor racketeering, and later, drug dealing.

Local law enforcement was unable to stop the alcohol and vice operations of organized crime and became even more corrupt as many law enforcement officers cooperated with organized crime. As a result, between 1919 and 1930, 24 states formed crime commissions to study the crime problem and the ability of the police to deal with crime.

After 70 percent of Boston's police officers went on strike on September 9, 1919, rioting and looting broke out, resulting in the mobilization of the Massachusetts state militia by then-governor Calvin Coolidge. Here the militia round up a crowd of "cop shooters" who had tried to harm volunteers filling in for the striking officers. All the striking officers were fired and replaced by new recruits, and the incident ended unionism within law enforcement for decades.

THE WICKERSHAM COMMISSION   In 1929, President Herbert Hoover created the National Commission on Law Observance and Enforcement with George W. Wickersham as its chair. The commission was popularly known as the **Wickersham Commission** and conducted the first national study of the U.S. criminal justice system. The commission issued a report in 1931, popularly known as the Wickersham Report. The report criticized the Volstead Act, which created Prohibition, saying it was not enforced because it was unenforceable. The following year National Prohibition was repealed.

The commission found that the average police commander's term of office was too short and that his responsibility to politicians made his position insecure. It said there was a lack of effective, efficient, and honest patrol officers, as well as no effort to educate, train, or discipline officers or to fire incompetent ones. The commission found further that police forces, even in the biggest cities, did not have adequate communication systems or equipment.

Two volumes of the Wickersham Report, *Lawlessness in Law Enforcement* (volume 2) and *The Police* (volume 14), concerned themselves solely with the police. *Lawlessness in Law Enforcement* portrayed the police as inept, inefficient, racist, and brutal, and accused them of committing illegal acts. The volume concluded that "the third degree—the inflicting of pain, physical or mental, to extract confessions or statements—is extensively practiced."[23]

The Wickersham Report blamed the shortcomings of the police on a lack of police professionalism. *The Police*, written primarily by August Vollmer, discussed methods that could be used to create a professional police force in the United States. The methods the commission advocated included increased selectivity in the recruitment of officers, better pay and benefits, and more education for police officers.

The Wickersham Report angered citizens and started another groundswell for police reform. With the onset of the Great Depression, however, police reform became less important than economic revival, and another attempt at police reform failed.

PROFESSIONALISM   An early attempt at police reform was the creation in 1893 of a professional society, the International Association of Chiefs of Police (IACP). Its first president was the Washington, D.C., chief of police, Richard Sylvester. The IACP became the leading voice of police reform during the first two decades of the 20th century by consistently calling for the creation of a civil service police and for the removal of political influence and control over the police. The IACP remains a significant force in policing today.

Eventually a federal law, the **Pendleton Act,** was passed in 1883 to establish a civil service system that tested, appointed, and promoted officers on a merit system. The civil service system was later adopted by local governments, and political influence slowly evaporated from police departments. However, today not all U.S. police agencies are governed by civil service rules. Furthermore, despite civil service systems, politics continued to play some part in American law enforcement.

Several people were pioneers in modern policing, and two men, August Vollmer and O. W. Wilson, stand out in the 20th century as the founders of police professionalism.

AUGUST VOLLMER   The chief of police in Berkeley, California, from 1905 to 1932 was August Vollmer. Vollmer instituted many practices that started to professionalize the U.S. police. Among those practices was incorporating university training as a part of police training. Also, Vollmer introduced the use of intelligence, psychiatric, and neurological tests to aid in the selection of police recruits and initiated scientific crime detection and crime-solving techniques. In addition, Vollmer helped develop the School of Criminology at the University of California at Berkeley, which became the model for programs related to law and criminal justice throughout the United States. Vollmer, as stated earlier, was also the author of the Wickersham Report's volume entitled *The Police.* Additionally, he trained numerous students who went on to become reform-oriented and progressive police chiefs. August Vollmer can certainly be considered the father of modern American policing.

O. W. WILSON   A disciple of Vollmer's, O. W. Wilson pioneered the use of advanced training for police officers when he took over and reformed the Wichita, Kansas, police department in 1928. While there, Wilson conducted the first systematic study of the effectiveness of one-officer squad cars. Despite officers' complaints about risks to their safety, his study showed that one-officer cars were more efficient, effective, and economical than two-person cars. Wilson developed modern management and administrative techniques for policing. He was the author of the first two textbooks on police management: the International City Management Association's *Municipal Police Administration* and his own text, *Police Administration,* which became the Bible of policing for decades.

Wilson was dean of the School of Criminology at the University of California at Berkeley from 1950 to 1960 and the superintendent of the Chicago police from 1960 to 1967. The core of Wilson's approach to police administration was managerial efficiency. He believed that police departments should maximize patrol coverage by replacing foot patrols with one-person auto patrols. He advocated rapid response to calls for service as a key criterion by which to judge the effectiveness of police departments.

Almost every U.S. police department since the 1950s has been organized around the principles espoused in Wilson's books. He developed workload formulas based on reported crimes and calls for service on each beat. Wilson's 1941 workload formula remained unchanged for decades.

RAYMOND BLAINE FOSDICK AND BRUCE SMITH
Other early pioneers in the movement toward police professionalism were Raymond Blaine Fosdick and Bruce Smith. Neither was a police officer. Fosdick is noted for the first scholarly research regarding the police. In 1915, he published *European Police Systems,* which examined the police structures and practices of Europe. In 1920, he published *American Police Systems* after studying the police of 72 U.S. cities.

Bruce Smith, a researcher and later manager of the Institute of Public Administration, also contributed to our early knowledge of the police. His efforts in surveying and researching police departments in approximately 50 leading American cities in 18 states led to his noteworthy 1940 book *Police Systems in the United States;* a second edition was published in 1949.

JOHN EDGAR HOOVER   One cannot discuss law enforcement in the 20th-century United States without mentioning John Edgar Hoover, usually known as J. Edgar Hoover. In 1921, President Warren G. Harding appointed Hoover, an attorney working for the U.S. Department of Justice, to the position of assistant director of the Bureau of Investigation, the forerunner of the Federal Bureau of Investigation (FBI). In 1924, President Calvin Coolidge, upon the retirement of the bureau's director, appointed

Hoover as the director. Over the next 48 years, Hoover was reappointed as director of the FBI by every U.S. president; he remained director until his death in 1972.

Under Hoover's leadership, the FBI changed from an inefficient organization into what many consider to be the world's primary law enforcement agency. Among his major contributions were the hiring of accountants and lawyers as special agents; the introduction of the FBI *Uniform Crime Reports,* which since 1930 have been the leading source of crime and arrest statistics in the United States; the development of the National Crime Information Center (NCIC); the development of the FBI's Ten Most Wanted Criminals Program, otherwise known as Public Enemies; the development of the FBI Academy at Quantico, Virginia; and the popularizing of the FBI through the media as incorruptible, crime-fighting G-men.

During the past few decades, Hoover's reputation has diminished. Revelations have surfaced about his use of the media to build a myth about the FBI, his single-mindedness about Communism, and his domestic surveillance operations over prominent Americans.

KEFAUVER COMMITTEE   In 1950, in response to fear about crime and the corruption of law enforcement officers, the U.S. Senate's Crime Committee, chaired by Senator Estes Kefauver, was created. The Kefauver Committee held televised public hearings that led to the discovery of a nationwide network of organized crime, a syndicate that has commonly been called the Mafia or Cosa Nostra. The hearings also revealed that many law enforcement officers nationwide were on the syndicate's payroll. The public was shocked over these tales of corruption, and another attempt at police reform began. David R. Johnson wrote about this decade:

> The 1950s marked a turning point in the history of professionalism. Following major scandals, reformers came to power across the nation. Politicians had real choices between the traditional and new models of policing because a number of professional police reformers were available for the first time. With an enraged middle class threatening their livelihoods, the politicians opted for reform.[24]

Policing in the 1960s and 1970s

The 1960s and 1970s, times of great tension and change, were probably the most turbulent era ever for policing in U.S. history. Numerous social problems permeated these decades, and the police were right in the middle of each one of the problems. In this era the struggle for racial equality reached its height, accompanied by marches, demonstra-

tions, and riots. These riots burned down whole neighborhoods in U.S. urban centers. In this era the Vietnam War was reaching its height, soldiers were dying, and students across the United States were protesting the war and governmental policies. The Supreme Court decided in case after case to protect arrested persons from oppressive police practices. During this time, the police seemed to be more the targets of radical groups than the respected protectors of the people. In short, in this time of dramatic social change in the United States, the police were not only right in the middle of it all, but were often the focus of it all.

The police, because of their role, were always in the middle—between those fighting for their civil rights and the government officials (the employers of the police) who wanted to maintain the status quo, between demonstrating students and college and city administrators. The police received much criticism during these years. Some of it was deserved, but much of it was beyond their control.

James Q. Wilson perhaps described the decade of the 1960s best when he wrote, "It all began about 1963, that was the year, to overdramatize a bit, that a decade began to fall apart."[25]

This section briefly describes some of the problems experienced by the police during this period and some of the encounters between the police and what were seen at the time as rival groups. It should be noted that one of the authors of this text served as a uniformed police officer in New York City during this time. During the day, he policed antiwar marches, civil rights demonstrations, and urban riots, and at night he attended college, sitting next to fellow students, many of whom he had encountered as adversaries on the street.

SUPREME COURT DECISIONS   The 1960s saw the Warren Court at its height, a U.S. Supreme Court that focused dramatically on individual rights. Police actions, ranging from arrests to search and seizure and custodial interrogation, were being declared unconstitutional. (Chapter 11 will focus on these decisions.) The Court made dramatic use of the exclusionary rule, a Supreme Court ruling in 1914 that declared that evidence seized by the police in violation of the Constitution could not be used against a defendant in federal court, thus leading to the possibility that a guilty defendant could go free because of procedural errors by the police.

Many important police-related cases were decided in this era. *Mapp* v. *Ohio* (1961) finally, after much warning, applied the exclusionary rule to all states in the nation.[26] *Escobedo* v. *Illinois* (1964) defined the constitutional right to counsel at police interrogations.[27] *Miranda* v. *Arizona*

(1966) required the police to notify a person who is in police custody and who is going to be interrogated of his or her constitutional rights.[28]

THE CIVIL RIGHTS MOVEMENT   Legal segregation of the races finally ended with the landmark Supreme Court case of *Brown v. Board of Education of Topeka* (1954), which desegregated schools all over the nation. However, equal treatment of the races did not occur overnight. Numerous marches and demonstrations were to come before the Civil Rights Act of 1964 was passed.

In the 1960s African Americans and other civil rights demonstrators participated in freedom marches throughout the United States, particularly in the South. Because the police are the enforcement arm of government, they were used to enforce existing laws, which in many cases meant arresting and inhibiting the freedom of those marching for equality.

In 1960, the Freedom Riders left Washington, D.C., by bus to confront segregation throughout the South. The buses and protesters were harassed and were temporarily halted and attacked by violent white mobs in Anniston and Birmingham, Alabama. The police were again used to inhibit these marches for equality.

During the 1960s, the Reverend Martin Luther King, Jr., was at the forefront of the civil rights marches. In 1962, there were mass arrests of civil rights demonstrators in Albany, Georgia. Also in 1962, James Meredith became the first African American to enroll at the University of Mississippi. President John F. Kennedy was forced to send U.S. marshals and the armed forces into Mississippi to protect Meredith against attacks by segregationists, because the local police were unable or unwilling to protect him.

In 1963, Dr. King led 25,000 demonstrators on a historic march on Washington that culminated in his "I have a dream" speech. During this speech, a defining moment of the movement, a white uniformed police officer stood behind King in a highly visible position, perhaps as a symbolic representation of the new role of the police in America's social history. Officers were to act as defenders rather than oppressors.

Also in 1963, in Birmingham, Alabama, four African American girls were killed when a bomb exploded during a church service at the 16th Street Baptist Church. In the same year, King led a peaceful march against segregation in Birmingham, Alabama, while Birmingham's sheriff Bull Connor unleashed fire hoses and police dogs against the demonstrators. The actions of police personnel like Bull Connor caused the police much negative press and has affected police–minority group relationships ever since.

In 1964, the Student Non-Violent Coordinating Committee (SNCC) launched the Mississippi Freedom Summer Project as thousands of students from northern campuses flocked to Mississippi for the summer voter registration drive, attempting to get African Americans to register to vote. During that summer, three civil rights volunteers were brutally murdered in Philadelphia, Mississippi.

In 1965, African Americans and other civil rights demonstrators attempted a peaceful march to Selma, Alabama. During the march, Alabama state police stopped the marchers at the Edmund Petus Bridge in Selma, where a Boston minister was murdered and many others were beaten by white toughs. A massive civil rights march then proceeded from Selma to Montgomery, Alabama, under the protection of the National Guard.

In 1966, activist Stokely Carmichael was elected chair of the SNCC and coined the term "black power." In the same year, James Meredith, the first African American student at the University of Mississippi, began a solitary March against Fear through Mississippi and was wounded by a sniper. African American leaders continued Meredith's march using the slogan "black power," which began to symbolize the movement toward equality for some African Americans. Also in 1966, King led an antidiscrimination march in Chicago and was stoned by a hostile crowd.

The civil rights movement continued and succeeded in part by enrolling more minorities as voters, outlawing forms of government-sanctioned segregation, and ensuring that more minorities participated in government. Today, many of our large-city mayors and politicians are members of minority groups.

Although the civil rights movement was necessary in the evolution of our nation, the use of the police by government officials to thwart the movement left a wound in police–community relations that has still not healed. The 1991 beating of Rodney King in Los Angeles and the 1992 jury verdict acquitting the four Los Angeles police officers who were charged in King's beating (described later) angered people across the United States. The resultant riots in Los Angeles and other cities seemed to bring the United States back to the same strained racial conditions that existed in the 1960s.

ASSASSINATIONS   In the 1960s three of the most respected leaders in the United States were assassinated: President John F. Kennedy in 1963 in Dallas; his brother Robert Kennedy in 1968 in Los Angeles; and the Reverend Martin Luther King, Jr., also in 1968 in Memphis. These assassinations clearly reflected the turbulence of the decade.

Many say that the person who assassinated President Kennedy as he rode in a Dallas motorcade is still unknown. Lee Harvey Oswald was captured and charged with Kennedy's murder after shooting and killing a Dallas police officer, J. D. Tippett, an hour after the president was killed. Several days later, Oswald himself was shot and killed by Jack Ruby as Oswald was being led out of a Dallas police station. The debate over these incidents in Dallas continues today.

ANTI–VIETNAM WAR DEMONSTRATIONS   The Vietnam War was another turbulent, heartrending experience in American history, and again the police were used in a manner that tarnished their image. There were numerous and violent confrontations between opponents of the Vietnam War and the government's representatives—the police—on college campuses and city streets.

In 1967, hundreds of thousands of people using civil disobedience tactics marched in antiwar demonstrations in New York City, Washington, D.C., San Francisco, and numerous other cities around the nation, often clashing with the police, whose job it was to enforce the law and maintain order.

At the Democratic Party presidential convention in Chicago in 1968, police–citizen violence occurred that shocked the nation and the world. With information that 10,000 protesters organized by antiwar groups, including the Youth International Party (Yippies), were coming to Chicago for the 1968 Democratic National Convention, Chicago's mayor, Richard J. Daley, mobilized the National Guard and the Chicago police. On August 28, the protesters attempted to force their way into the convention. Police and the National Guard chased the crowd through downtown Chicago. Many report that the police command structure broke down and that the police became a mob that ran through the streets and assaulted protesters, reporters, and bystanders. A study subsequent to the convention, the Walker Report, called the actions of the police a police riot.

There are many different viewpoints of the chaotic disturbances that occurred on the U.S. streets during this period. What some perceived as a police riot others perceived as the police doing their job. Many stress that the Yippies and other protesters were attempting to break up a lawfully gathered assembly by illegal means.

Eight members of the Yippies were charged with conspiracy for starting the disturbances in Chicago and were dubbed the "Chicago Eight." In 1969, the Chicago Eight trial began (it was later called the Chicago Seven trial due to the severance from the trial of Bobby Seales, the co-

founder of the Black Panther Party). A Students for a Democratic Society (SDS) splinter group, the Weathermen, organized the Days of Rage in Chicago, which resulted in violent rampaging in the streets and more confrontation with the police. In 1970, all of the Chicago Eight were acquitted of conspiracy charges; convictions on lesser charges were later overturned as well.

CAMPUS DISORDERS   In addition to the civil rights movement of the 1960s, demonstrations, marches, and civil disobedience also took place on college campuses across the nation. These events protested a perceived lack of academic freedom, the Vietnam War, the presence of Reserve Officers' Training Corps (ROTC) units on campuses, and many other issues. Again, the police were used to enforce the law.

In 1960, the SNCC was organized to coordinate student civil rights protests. In 1961, the SDS held its first national convention in Port Huron, Michigan. These two groups had a tremendous impact on the 1960s. Teach-ins, rallies, student strikes, takeovers of campus buildings, and the burning of draft cards were some of the tactics used on the campuses.

The protests on the campuses caused college administrators to call in local police departments to maintain order. That, in turn, caused students to complain about the actions of the police. Again, the police became the focus of anger and attention.

In 1968, a state of civil disorder was declared in Berkeley, California, following recurring police–student confrontations. Protests, riots, and violent clashes between students and the police replaced education on many college campuses in the United States.

Probably the most widely publicized campus protest of the 1960s was the student takeover at Columbia University, in New York City, in the spring of 1968. Students employed every tactic that had been used in earlier campus protests, including teach-ins, rallies, picketing, sit-ins, a student strike, and the takeover of university buildings. As negotiations between the college administration and the student rebels broke down, the administration decided to call in the police.

In the early morning of April 30, 1968, after students had taken over many college buildings, 2,000 police officers moved onto the campus and methodically cleared five occupied buildings. The effort to clear the remaining buildings became violent. Finally, the police were able to secure all buildings by arresting 692 students. In late May, the students again took over two buildings on Columbia's campus. The administration again called the police. The

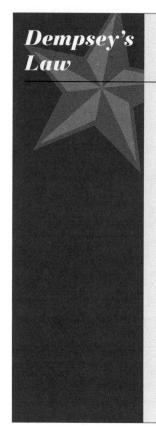

Dempsey's Law

What a Difference Eighteen Years Make

In 1968, I was at Columbia University in Morningside Heights, New York City. I was not a student. I was a cop. My job: evict protesting students from the college buildings. I was doing my job, earning a paycheck. For several nights, I was spit at and called a pig. I listened to chants calling my mother, and other cops' mothers, obscenities, and I had bags of human waste thrown at me.

In 1986, 18 years later, I was at Harvard University, as a student. One day, in a large auditorium at the Kennedy School of Government, a woman started a conversation with me.

Hi, my name is Ardyth, I'm from Boise, Idaho.

Hi, I'm Jack, I'm from New York.

I never would have known that, with that accent! I went to school in New York, for a year.

Oh, where?

Barnard College.

Barnard College? That was the women's

school at Columbia, right? [Would you believe that in those years, Columbia had different colleges for men and women?]

Yes.

What year did you go there?

1968.

1968! I was there, then, too.

What was your major?

No, I wasn't a student, I was a cop.

Were you the _____ _____ cop who threw me into the rose bushes and made my arm bleed?

Were you the girl who threw the bag of _____ at me?

During the year at Harvard, Ardyth and I became friends and discussed the 60s often. It was interesting. Now she seemed to understand the role of the cops back then, and now I seemed to understand why the kids were protesting. Isn't it interesting how smart we can get in 18 years?

Cox Commission, formed to investigate the violence at Columbia University, reported on the police action that followed:

> Hell broke loose. One hundred students locked arms behind the barricades at Amsterdam Avenue. Hundreds more crowded close to the gate. The police swiftly dismantled the obstruction. The hundred broke and ran. But 2,000 students live in dormitories facing South Field. Many of them and hundreds of other people were crowded on the campus. For most, the character of the police action was a profound shock; neither they nor others in the Columbia community appreciated the extent of the violence which is the probable concomitant of massive police action against hundreds, if not thousands, of angry students. As police advanced, most students fled. . . . Some police first warned the students; others chased and clubbed them indiscriminately. But not all students went to their dormitories and some who fled came back out to attack the police. Bottles and bricks were hurled by students. A number of police were injured. The action grew fierce. . . . By 5:30 A.M. the campus was secured.[29]

The campus antiwar riots reached their height in 1970. The firebombing of a University of Wisconsin ROTC

building began a wave of some 500 bombings or arsons on college campuses. Students rampaged through Cambridge's Harvard Yard; two students were killed and nine wounded by police gunfire at Jackson State College in Mississippi; and four students were killed by the National Guard at a protest at Kent State University, causing many U.S. colleges and universities to close for the year. Again, clashes between the police and students caused wounds that were hard to heal.

URBAN RIOTS   Major riots erupted in the ghettos of many U.S. cities during the 1960s. Most started directly following a police action. This is not to say that the riots were the result of the police; rather, a police action brought to the surface numerous underlying problems, which many say were the actual causes of the riots.

In the summer of 1964, an off-duty white New York City police lieutenant shot an African American youth who was threatening a building superintendent with a knife. This shooting precipitated the 1964 Harlem riot. Riots also occurred that summer in Rochester, Jersey City, and Philadelphia. In 1965, riots occurred in Los Angeles (the

Watts district), San Diego, and Chicago. In 1966, riots again occurred in Watts, as well as in Cleveland, Brooklyn, and Chicago. In 1967, major riots occurred in Boston's Roxbury section, in Newark, and in Detroit.

The riot in Detroit was responsible for 43 deaths, 2,000 injuries, and property damage estimated at over $200 million; 7,000 persons were arrested. The Watts riot was responsible for the deaths of 34 people, over 1,000 injuries, and the arrests of nearly 4,000 people. The Newark riot was responsible for 26 deaths and 1,500 injuries.

In 1968, riots occurred in cities all over the United States—including Baltimore, Boston, Chicago, Detroit, Kansas City, Newark, New York City, Washington, D.C., and scores of other cities—in the wake of the murder of the Reverend Martin Luther King, Jr. The worst riot occurred in Washington, D.C., with 12 people killed, 1,200 injured, and 7,600 people arrested, and nearly $25 million in property damage. Nationwide, 55,000 federal troops and National Guard members were called out. Forty-six deaths resulted from the riots, and 21,270 people were arrested.

Again, the efforts of the police to maintain order during these massive shows of civil disobedience and violence caused wounds in police–community relations that have yet to heal. Problems between the minority communities and the police continued, as did the riots. Several radical groups, including the Black Panther party and the Black Liberation Army, waged urban warfare against the police, resulting in many deaths among their members and the police.

YOU ARE THERE! »

The Urban Riots of the Sixties

1964	Harlem (New York City), Rochester, Jersey City, Philadelphia
1965	Watts (Los Angeles), San Diego, Chicago
1966	Watts (Los Angeles); Cleveland; Brooklyn, the Bronx, and the Barrio (New York City); Chicago
1967	Roxbury (Boston), Newark, Detroit
1968	Washington, D.C., and much of the urban United States

CREATION OF NATIONAL COMMISSIONS   In the wake of the problems of the 1960s, particularly the problems between the police and citizens, three national commissions were created. The first was the **President's Commission on Law Enforcement and Administration of Justice**, which issued a report in 1967, *The Challenge of Crime in a Free Society*, and a collection of Task Force Reports covering all aspects of the criminal justice system.

The second national commission was the **National Advisory Commission on Civil Disorders (Kerner Commission)**, which released a report in 1968 that decried white racism and a rapidly polarizing society. The report stated, "Our nation is moving toward two societies,

---

Dempsey's Law

It Was a Tough Time to Be a Cop; It Was a Tough Time to Be a Cop's Spouse

I was married in 1967. My wife, Marianne, was expecting our first child in either March, April, or May of 1968. On April 4, 1968, my day off, we went to see the obstetrician, on the Grand Concourse in the Bronx. It was about 4:45 P.M., and we heard on the radio in the doctor's waiting room that the Reverend Martin Luther King, Jr., had been assassinated in Memphis. I said to Marianne, "I want to be around to help you when the baby comes. Have the baby right now, or you have to wait a couple of weeks, because America is going to burn, and I won't have much time off."

I was called in for riot duty that night and worked 12-hour tours without a day off for two weeks. Marianne, the tough spouse that all cops need, held on until the riots were over. Our first child, a 10-pound boy, John Daniel, was born on April 19, 1968. John Daniel's first child, a 10-pound, 2-ounce boy, Daniel Joseph, was born on October 24, 1992. John Daniel did see the 1992 Los Angeles riot. It is my hope that Daniel Joseph never has to see a riot.

Dempsey's Law

Thank You, LEEP

I started college in 1963 as a full-time student. However, finances forced me to leave school and work full-time. In 1964, having been fortunate enough to obtain a position as a New York City police trainee, I applied for admission to the City University of New York and was accepted. My college was called the College of Police Science (now the John Jay College of Criminal Justice). My entire four-year college degree, which took me ten years to complete, was paid for by the Law Enforcement Education Program (LEEP). My first graduate degree, from Long Island University, was also paid for by LEEP. My second master's degree, from Harvard, was supported in part by New York City and the New York City Police Foundation.

---

one black, one white, separate and unequal." The commission concluded that "abrasive relationships between police and Negroes and other minority groups, have been a major source of grievance, tension, and, ultimately, disorder."[30]

The third was the President's Commission on Campus Unrest. Its report, issued in 1970, called the gap between youth culture and mainstream society a threat to U.S. stability. These commissions are mentioned often in this text.

CORRUPTION   The corruption that has historically permeated American policing in the past has continued into the present. Approximately every 20 years, the nation's largest and most visible police department, the New York City Police Department (NYPD), has been the subject of a major scandal involving police corruption: the Seabury Hearings in the 1930s, the Gross Hearings in the 1950s, and the Knapp Commission in 1970.

The Knapp Commission resulted from allegations made by New York City plainclothes police officer Frank Serpico and New York City police sergeant David Durk. Serpico was a Bronx plainclothes police officer (assigned to enforce antigambling laws) who was aware of widespread graft and bribe receiving in his unit. He took his tales of corruption to major police department officials, including the second-highest-ranking officer in the department; to the city's Department of Investigation; and eventually even to the mayor's office. When Serpico finally realized that no one was taking his claims seriously, he and Durk went to a *New York Times* reporter, who wrote a series of stories about corruption in the department that shocked the public. The *Times* articles forced the mayor, John Lindsey, to appoint a commission to investigate police corruption, which became known as the Knapp Commission. Chapter 12 will focus on the Knapp Commission and police corruption

and misconduct. The revelations of the Knapp Commission regarding widespread, systemic, organized corruption in the NYPD led to sweeping changes in the department's organization, philosophy, operations, and procedures.

POLICE RESEARCH   The decades of the 1960s and 1970s saw tremendous research into policing, which brought about sweeping changes in thinking about how police work is done in the United States. One of the most significant developments in modernizing and professionalizing the police was the creation of the Law Enforcement Assistance Administration (LEAA) within the U.S. Department of Justice through Title 1 of the Omnibus Crime Control and Safe Streets Act of 1968. The LEAA spent over $60 million in its first year alone, and between 1969 and 1980 it spent over $8 billion to support criminal justice research, education, and training.

LEAA required each state to create its own criminal justice planning agency, which in turn was required to establish an annual, comprehensive, statewide criminal justice plan to distribute LEAA funds throughout the state. One of LEAA's primary benefits to police officers was its Law Enforcement Education Program (LEEP), which provided funds for the college education of police officers.

An independent organization, the Police Foundation, joined LEAA as a funding source for research on innovative police projects. The most significant of these projects were the Kansas City Preventive Patrol Experiment, the Rand Corporation's study of the criminal investigation process, the Police Foundation's study of team policing, and the Newark Foot Patrol Experiment. These innovative studies began to change the way we thought about policing in the United States.

As we will see later, traditional policing involved three major strategies: (1) routine random patrol, (2) rapid response to calls by citizens to 911, and (3) retroactive investigation of past crimes by detectives. Academic research, starting in the 1960s and 1970s and continuing to this day, has indicated that these three strategies have not worked. This research has led police administrators to implement the innovative approaches to policing that will be discussed in this text.

Policing in the 1980s and 1990s

The tremendous turmoil that permeated society and policing during the decades of the 1960s and 1970s gave way to somewhat more peaceful times in the 1980s and 1990s. The police, as always, were confronted by a myriad of issues and events that severely tested their professionalism and ability. Prominent among those events were terrorist bombings of New York City's World Trade Center and the Federal Building in Oklahoma City. In these

Forst's Law

History Is All Relative

I remember when I started at the police department in 1977. I finished the police academy and went on to eight weeks of field training with a more senior officer. The department didn't have a formalized program at the time, they simply put rookie officers with more experienced officers who they felt could teach them how our department did things.

Besides my training officer, I met lots of other officers eager to share their knowledge with me on how to "really do the job." I had some "old timers" tell me about how different it was when they started with the department. "They handed me a badge and a gun and told me to go out and enforce the laws . . . we didn't have any of this training stuff" one told me. This was hard for me to imagine as I thought of all the information I had learned in the academy and was learning during training—not to mention the liability involved. "We never had air-conditioned cars," another told me as I cringed at the thought of driving around in the south Florida heat and humidity without the benefit of air conditioning. "There was no such thing as backup," another said, "we just broke up the fights in the projects and threw 'em in the drunk tank to sober up for a few hours." Again the thought of detaining people for drunkenness with no real reason to deprive them of their liberty made me nervous. I chalked it up to "the old days" and smiled smugly at how far we'd come and how advanced we were now.

Now I teach my classes, and as we talk about the "history" of law enforcement and

how police officers actually relied on car radios and worked without the luxury of portable radios, and how we used .38 revolvers and were ecstatic when speed loaders became part of our equipment, they are shocked to realize I worked that way. They are shocked to learn we used pay phones as a means of communication when we didn't want to use the radio. They can't imagine life without everyone having cell phones. Their jaws really hit the desks when I talk about our early use of "cell phones." I was a lieutenant in charge of the midnight shift when we got our first portable phone. The shift commanders carried the phone in their cars for use in emergency situations where we did not want the press or others to hear our radio transmissions or we had to call "the brass" at home to brief them on situations. This "portable" phone (and I use the term loosely) was mounted in a briefcase and weighed over 15 pounds. If a situation occurred where we were setting up at a scene, I would take the briefcase out of the car, lay it on the trunk, and screw antennas into the phone assembly. Then I hoped the bad guys couldn't hear me pushing the numbers (it sounded loud at 3 A.M. in the quiet streets) or see all the lights associated with the phone, and most of all I hoped it worked. Sometimes, I just felt it wasn't worth all the trouble to use it. If nothing else, these stories make students appreciate the ease of communications that law enforcement enjoys today.

cases, police agencies from all over the nation performed numerous heroic and successful actions that saved lives and resulted in the eventual criminal prosecution of the offenders.

Some of the many positive developments of the 1980s and 1990s included the development of a computer revolution in policing involving communications, record keeping, fingerprinting, and criminal investigations; a drastic reduction in violent crime; and the birth of two major new concepts of police work: community policing and problem-solving policing. Community policing and problem-solving policing can be seen either as new approaches to policing or as a return to the policing of the past—the cop on the beat. Chapter 10 of this text covers these concepts. The computer and technology revolution in policing is covered in Chapter 14.

Some believe that the highlight of recent developments in policing is the significant crime reductions that occurred throughout the nation in the late 20th century. In 1997, the FBI reported that serious crime for 1996 had declined 3 percent, the fifth annual decrease in a row since 1992. Violent crime, including homicide, robbery, rape, and aggravated assault, dropped 7 percent from the previous year. This decrease in violent crime was the largest in 36 years. The homicide rate was the lowest it had been nationwide since 1969.[31] These crime decreases continued throughout the decade and into the next century.

Some criminologists attributed this decline to a series of factors, including community policing, problem solving policing, and aggressive zero-tolerance policing. Other factors mentioned were increased jail and prison populations; demographic changes in the numbers of crime-prone young people; and community efforts against crime.

The explanation, however, that has gained the most popularity among some law enforcement officials, politicians, and criminologists is that the reduced crime rates are the result of aggressive police tactics like those introduced in New York City by its former commissioner William J. Bratton. Bratton completely reengineered the NYPD to make reducing crime its primary objective.[32] The keynote behind Bratton's reengineering was a process known as **Compstat.**[33]

Compstat was originally a document, referred to as the "Compstat book," which included current year-to-date statistics for criminal complaints and arrests developed from a computer file called Compare Stats—hence Compstat. Central to Compstat are the semiweekly crime-strategy sessions conducted at police headquarters. At each Compstat meeting, sophisticated computer-generated maps addressing a seemingly unlimited variety of the latest crime details

confront and challenge the precinct commanders. The commanders are held responsible for any increases in crime and must present innovative solutions to address their precincts' crime problems. In these sessions, crime-fighting techniques are developed and expected to be implemented. The four-step process that is the essence of Compstat is

1. Timely and accurate intelligence.
2. Use of effective tactics in response to that intelligence.
3. Rapid deployment of personnel and resources.
4. Relentless follow-up and assessment.

One writer summed up the essence of NYPD's new policing strategy:

> The multifaceted Compstat process is perhaps best known to law enforcement insiders for its high-stress, semiweekly debriefing and brain-storming sessions at police headquarters, but it is far more. . . . Compstat is enabling the NYPD to pinpoint and analyze crime patterns almost instantly, respond in the most appropriate manner, quickly shift personnel and other resources as needed, assess the impact and viability of anti-crime strategies, identify bright, up-and-coming individuals from deep within the ranks, and transform the organization more fluidly and more effectively than one would ever expect of such a huge police agency.[34]

Only history will tell if the crime reductions of the mid-1990s can continue, and no one can attribute them solely to the police, but Bratton seems convinced: "We've changed course, and the course will be changed for all time."[35]

Despite all the successes of the police in the 1980s and 1990s, many of the problems of earlier decades carried over into this time. Some of the negative issues and problems confronting the police in our generation were the continuing debate over misconduct by the police and the continuing occurrence of riots in our communities.

The endemic corruption that has always characterized U.S. policing seemed to have subsided somewhat during the 1980s and 1990s, although there were sporadic corruption scandals. The most noticeable of these included the Miami River Cops scandal of the 1980s, involving murders, extortions, and drug violations, and New York City's 77th and 32nd Precincts and "Cocaine Cops" scandals, involving drug corruption. Many other police departments throughout the nation also suffered embarrassing corruption and misconduct scandals. Chapter 12 of this text covers this area in detail.

In 1991, the Rodney King incident in Los Angeles shocked the public and may have set the police back 30 years in the progress they had made in improving relationships with the community. A video camera captured on tape the police beating of Rodney King, an African American. King had taken the police on a 115-mile-per-hour chase throughout Los Angeles and, when finally stopped by the police, allegedly lunged at one of the officers. The videotape shows four Los Angeles police officers beating King with 56 blows from batons while a dozen other officers stood by and watched. King seemed to be in a defenseless, prone position on the ground. Four of the officers were arrested and charged with the assault of King. They were originally acquitted in a criminal trial but were subsequently convicted in a federal trial.

The Rodney King incident was followed in 1997 with allegations that at least two police officers from New York City's 70th Precinct assaulted a Haitian American prisoner, Abner Louima, by placing a wooden stick into his rectum and then shoving the blood- and feces-covered stick into his mouth. This incident shocked the world as the King incident did.[36] One officer was eventually convicted and imprisoned for the assault on Louima.

In 1994, a criminal trial also brought negative attention to the police. Former football star Orenthal James (O. J.) Simpson was charged by the Los Angeles police with the brutal murder of his former wife, Nicole Brown, and her friend Ronald Goldman. The trial was covered on national television and captured the attention of the world. Two hundred and fifty days and 126 witnesses later, the jury, despite overwhelming scientific evidence to the contrary, voted to acquit Simpson of all charges. Many said the verdict was jury nullification; others said it was an indictment of the Los Angeles Police Department. The LAPD was accused of gross incompetence in its handling of the crime scene and forensic evidence, and one of its main witnesses, Detective Mark Fuhrman, later pled guilty to charges that he had lied while testifying in the trial.

In 1997, the Justice Department's inspector general reported that the FBI's renowned crime laboratory was riddled with flawed scientific practices that had potentially tainted dozens of criminal cases, including the bombings of the Federal Building in Oklahoma City and the World Trade Center in New York. The inspector general's findings resulted from an 18-month investigation that uncovered extremely serious and significant problems at the laboratory that had been a symbol of the FBI's cutting-edge scientific sleuthing.[37] The dramatic series of problems associated with the FBI and its alleged bungling of scientific evidence and criminal investigations led the national magazine *Time* to produce a cover article entitled, "What's Wrong at the FBI: The Fiasco at the Crime Lab."[38]

Riots again scarred our sense of domestic tranquility. The city of Miami experienced two major riots in its Overtown district in the 1980s. New York City experienced riots in the 1990s in Crown Heights and Washington Heights. Many other cities witnessed racial and civil unrest and skirmishes between the police and citizens.

Perhaps the worst riot in our nation's history occurred in 1992 in the wake of the not-guilty verdicts against the officers in the Rodney King case. The riot began in Los Angeles and spread to other parts of the country.

By the second day of the riot, at least 23 people had been killed, 900 injured, and 500 arrested. Hundreds of buildings burned as the violence spread from south-central Los Angeles to other areas. Entire inner-city blocks lay in ruin. The riot quickly spread to Atlanta, San Francisco, Madison, and other cities. Fighting between African Americans and whites was reported at high schools in Maryland, Tennessee, Texas, and New York. By the end of the second day, over 4,000 National Guard troops had entered Los Angeles, as well as over 500 U.S. Marines. Less than a week after the riot started, calm began to appear. The final toll of the Los Angeles riot revealed that 54 people were killed; 2,383 people were injured; 5,200 buildings, mostly businesses, were destroyed by arson; and over $1 billion in property damage occurred. The riot resulted in the loss of approximately 40,000 jobs. Almost 17,000 arrests were made.

The following is a vivid newspaper description of the events of the first days of the riot:

> The violence in Los Angeles jumped a boundary from the South-Central area today, bringing racial conflict for the first time into the insulated, mostly white areas of West Los Angeles and Beverly Hills. Shops were looted and burned in Hollywood and nearby Santa Monica. A gunfight broke out this afternoon between Korean merchants and a group of black men in the Korea-town section, a sharp escalation in the tensions that have divided the groups in recent months. Tall plumes of smoke rose from burning shops in the neighborhood, just north of South-Central.
>
> As fires, police sirens and pockets of violence spread, most of the city shut down, with offices and shops closing and public transport scaling back its operations early. As the guard members were taking up positions in the badly battered South-Central area, convoys of cars carrying young men headed out into affluent West Los Angeles and Beverly Hills, shouting, brandishing hatchets, crowbars and bottles, beating passersby and looting shops.
>
> As night fell, what had been scattered pillars of smoke broadened to become a huge black cloud reminiscent of the burning oil wells of Kuwait during the Persian Gulf War.[39]

A special commission under the direction of William H. Webster (the former director of both the Federal Bureau of Investigation and the Central Intelligence Agency), created to study the causes of the Los Angeles riots, issued a report highly critical of the Los Angeles Police Department.[40]

YOU ARE THERE! >>

The Nicole Brown Simpson and Ronald Goldman Murder Case

On Sunday, June 12, 1994, somewhere between the hours of 10:00 P.M. and 11:00 P.M., Nicole Brown Simpson (the ex-wife of former football star Orenthal James [O. J.] Simpson) and a male acquaintance, Ronald Goldman, were brutally murdered in front of Nicole's expensive town house in Brentwood, California.

Investigation by the Los Angeles Police Department revealed that Nicole and O. J. had attended a dance recital that day in West L.A., which they left at approximately 6:00 P.M. At approximately 6:30 P.M. Nicole, her two children, and other family members and friends dined at the trendy Mezzaluna Trattoria restaurant in Brentwood. O. J. was not invited to the dinner. At approximately 8:30 P.M. Nicole and her party left the restaurant, and Nicole returned home with her children. Later, she received a call from her mother stating that she might have left her eyeglasses at the restaurant. Nicole called the restaurant and was told the eyeglasses were located. Ronald Goldman, a waiter at the restaurant, offered to bring the glasses to Nicole's home after he was off duty. At approximately 9:45 P.M. Goldman left the restaurant. At approximately midnight on June 12 the dead bodies of Nicole Simpson and Ronald Goldman were found by neighbors.

Detectives investigating the murder left the murder scene and responded to O. J. Simpson's $5-million mansion several miles away, also in Brentwood. While attempting to notify Simpson regarding the murder of his former wife, the detectives received no answer at his gate and then observed blood on the left door of Simpson's white Ford Bronco, which was parked outside the house. The detectives, fearing that there could be further injuries inside the Simpson property, entered the property without a search warrant and began to interview people residing there. While inside the property the detectives found evidence, including bloodstains and a bloody glove that matched a bloody glove found at the murder scene.

At approximately 10:45 P.M. on the night of the murder, O. J. Simpson traveled from his residence to Los Angeles International Airport, where he boarded a flight to Chicago. At approximately 5:34 A.M., June 13, 1994, he arrived in Chicago

and checked into a room at the O'Hare Plaza Hotel, where he had made reservations days earlier. That morning the police telephoned Simpson at his hotel room and notified him of his ex-wife's murder. He then flew back to Los Angeles. At approximately noon on Monday, Simpson was taken to L.A. police headquarters for several hours of questioning and then released.

During the week that followed there was intense media attention to the case, including reports of spousal abuse by Simpson against his ex-wife. These reports covered a 1988 arrest of Simpson for spousal abuse and a 1993 911 tape recording of a frantic call to the police by Nicole Brown Simpson with the angry voice of Simpson in the background.

On Friday, June 17, 1994, at 8:30 A.M., the LAPD called Simpson's attorney Robert Shapiro, saying they were ready to arrest Simpson for the murder of his ex-wife and Mr. Goldman. Shapiro reported that he would bring Simpson to police headquarters. At approximately 2:00 P.M., police reported that Simpson had not surrendered and was being considered a fugitive. At approximately 5:00 P.M., the police, responding to a citizen's tip, pinpointed Simpson as a passenger in his friend Al (A. C.) Cowlings's Ford Bronco, which was being driven on southern California freeways. The police then proceeded on a nearly 50-mile "low-speed pursuit" of Cowlings's car. During the pursuit, Simpson called 911 from the car cellular phone, stated he was armed, threatened to kill himself, and asked to talk to his mother. At approximately 8:00 P.M., Cowlings's car entered Simpson's property. After about 45 minutes of hostage negotiations, police persuaded Simpson to leave the car and enter his house. After being searched, Simpson was allowed to call his mother, use the bathroom, and drink a glass of orange juice. The low-speed pursuit and negotiations were watched by approximately 90 million Americans on live television.

A six-day preliminary hearing held in late June and early July resulted in O. J. Simpson being bound over for a murder trial.

Policing in the 2000s

As the world welcomed in a new millennium, some of the same myriad of issues that influenced policing since the creation of the first organized police forces in the early 19th century continued to dominate the police landscape. Among these issues were police misconduct,

corruption, and brutality. There were also many positives for the police as the crime rate decline that started to occur in the 1990s continued into the 2000s, and local, state, and federal law enforcement agencies reorganized and reengineered themselves to address the concerns of the new millennium. The Compstat program that developed in New York City was adopted by numerous departments throughout the nation. Crime in New York City, in particular, dropped to levels not seen since the 1960s.

Despite their tremendous successes in reducing crime, the NYPD again hit the headlines with a major controversial police shooting. An African immigrant, 22-year-old Amadou Diallo, was shot and killed by four members of the NYPD, who fired 41 shots at him. Investigation revealed that plainclothes police were on patrol in an area of the Bronx looking for a suspect in a series of rapes. They encountered Diallo standing on the steps of his apartment building, called out to him, and began to approach him. Diallo, who had difficulty understanding English, reached into his pocket. The police shot him because they believed he was reaching for a gun. It turned out that he was reaching for his wallet. There were numerous protests on the streets of New York. The four officers were arrested for second degree murder; but, in February 2000, a state jury found the officers innocent of any criminal wrongdoing.

The LAPD also was involved in a major corruption scandal involving their antigang unit operating out of the department's Rampart division. Many of the unit's members were accused of framing hundreds of people, planting evidence, committing perjury, brutalizing people, and forcing confessions through beatings. Officers were also accused of several illegal shootings. One officer, Rafael Perez, caught stealing $1 million worth of cocaine from the police property room, turned informant and cooperated with the prosecutors. After this scandal came to light, hundreds of falsely obtained convictions were thrown out of court and numerous civil lawsuits ensued against the department. Perez was eventually convicted and sentenced to five years in prison. Other officers were convicted and also went to prison.

The periods of civil unrest which dominated earlier times did not end with the new millennium. In 2001, a four-day riot occurred in Cincinnati after a white police officer was charged with shooting and killing an unarmed man.

Paramount to the new issues facing the police were the tragic **terrorist attacks against the United States of America on September 11, 2001.** Chapter 16, "Policing and Homeland Defense," will cover these attacks in detail.

As the twin towers of New York City's World Trade Center's Buildings 1 and 2 were struck by planes within minutes of each other, went on fire, and then imploded into the ground, a massive emergency response including the New York City Police Department, the New York City Fire Department, the police and rescue operations of the

©Richard Levine

Police mobilize on September 11, 2001, to help victims of the World Trade Center collapse. Many officers lost their lives in their efforts to rescue others. In the wake of the tragic events of that day, many large police departments throughout the nation started specialized antiterrorism units and trained their members in disaster control and antiterrorism duties.

Port Authority of New York–New Jersey, and the city's emergency medical service was immediate. These people entered the buildings in an attempt to rescue those within them. Many of these brave rescuers were lost forever, including much of the high command of the fire and Port Authority departments. Medical, law enforcement, and emergency response personnel from around the world responded. Triage centers went into operation, and ordinary residents passed out bottled water to the responding emergency personnel. By the evening of September 11, Buildings 5 and 7 of the World Trade Center had also collapsed, and many buildings began to tremble and show signs of imminent collapse. The fires, smoke, and eerie ash continued blowing through the streets. Almost 3,000 innocent persons were murdered that day in New York City.

Twenty-three New York City Police Officers, 37 Port Authority of New York–New Jersey officers, three New York City Court Officers, and over 300 New York City firefighters paid the ultimate price to their professions that day.

Within minutes of the attacks on the World Trade Center, another plane slammed into one of the five-sided, five-story concrete-walled structures of the U.S. Pentagon in northern Virginia—the headquarters and command center of the military forces of the United States of America.

The swiftness, scale, and sophisticated coordinated operations of the terrorists, coupled with the extraordinary planning required, made most people realize that terrorism and mass murder had hit New York City, the United States, and indeed, the world. These attacks shocked the world. Many law enforcement officers, emergency response personnel, and ordinary citizens will never be the same after September 11, 2001; 9/11 had indeed changed the world.

In the wake of the tragic events of 9/11, many large police departments throughout the nation started specialized antiterrorism units and trained their members in disaster control and antiterrorism duties. As one example, the New York City Police Department started a counterterrorism bureau under the command of a deputy commissioner who is a retired general with the U.S. Marine Corps. The counterterrorism bureau, consisting of over 1,000 officers, is under the command of a three-star chief and consists of a counterterrorism section and investigating units.

Additionally, there was a major reorganization of the federal government creating the massive Department of Homeland Security. Chapter 2, "Organizing Public and Private Security in the United States," and Chapter 16, "Policing and Homeland Defense," will address the enormous organization and operational changes in federal and state law enforcement as a result of the terrorist attacks.

The new focus of U.S. law enforcement was seen clearly as the U.S. began war against Iraq in March 2003. The counterterrorism units of law enforcement agencies in the United States matched the dramatic preparations of the military forces abroad:

> As the United States wages war on Iraq, New Yorkers and others across the region are witnessing an extraordinary state of heightened security. Police officers are armed like assault troops outside prominent buildings, police boats are combing the waterfronts and trucks are being inspected at bridges and tunnels.[41]

The NYPD's war contingency plan, Operation Atlas, described as the most comprehensive terrorism-prevention effort the city had ever conducted, cost at least $5 million a week in police overtime alone, including expanded patrols on the streets, focusing on government buildings, tourist attractions, financial institutions, hotels and houses of worship, and in the subways, on the waterways, and in the harbor. It also strengthened checkpoints at bridges and tunnels and on the streets. There were extra patrols in Jewish neighborhoods deemed to be terrorist targets, 24-hour police coverage of Wall Street, harbor patrols to protect commuter ferries, and bomb-sniffing dogs on the Staten Island Ferry. Officers were also posted outside television news outlets to prevent possible takeovers by terrorists who were feared to want to broadcast anti-American messages. The NYPD also opened its command center at Police Headquarters in Lower Manhattan as well as a backup command center.[42]

These precautionary measures were not limited to New York City as random car searches were reinstated at many airports throughout the nation. In Ohio, weigh stations on highways stayed open around the clock for inspections; in South Dakota, six satellite parking lots at Mount Rushmore were shut down, and park rangers, brandishing shotguns, screened each vehicle. In San Francisco, California Highway Patrol officers, some on bikes, joined National Guard troops stationed at the Golden Gate Bridge.[43] Also, Washington State Troopers rode on ferries and questioned passengers, while the boats themselves were shadowed by Coast Guard cutters with .50-caliber machine guns mounted on the sterns and bows.[44]

The war efforts of 2003 also brought back memories of the massive social protests of earlier decades. Reminiscent of the antiwar protests of the 1960s, protesters again took to the streets in March 2003 in response to the U.S. invasion of Iraq. There were massive street marches and skirmishes and attacks on the police in New York City, San Francisco, Washington, D.C., and Madison, Wisconsin, on March 20, 2003.

San Francisco was the epicenter of the antiwar movement's efforts, and more than 1,000 protesters were arrested in the financial district on March 20. Demonstrators blocked the Bay Bridge and about 40 intersections during the morning rush hour. They set fire to bales of hay near the Transamerica Building, opened fire hydrants, and smashed police car windows. They vomited on the pavement outside a federal building and linked themselves with metal chains, forcing firefighters to use circular saws to separate them.[45]

Similarly, in Washington, D.C., protesters forced the police to close Potomac River crossings during the morning commute. In Chicago, protesters shut down Lake Shore Drive during the evening rush hour. Protesters in Atlanta and Boston also shut down major streets. About 100 protesters were arrested in Philadelphia, 8 in Los Angeles, and in New York City 21 people were charged with disorderly conduct after a crowd of several thousand lay down in Times Square. In Madison, Wisconsin, protesters smashed the windows of the state Republican Party headquarters, splattering red paint that they said symbolized blood.[46] In Chicago, police arrested 543 antiwar protesters for civil disobedience that closed downtown streets for hours. A

top-ranking police official denounced the demonstrators as anarchists.[47]

In New York City, on March 22, 2003, during a protest by almost 200,000 marchers, 89 persons were arrested. Someone in the crowd had released a canister of pepper spray, injuring 14 officers, including several who were taken to the hospital.[48]

Clearly, the 21st century promises to be another turbulent and challenging time for the police.

CHAPTER SUMMARY

This chapter covered over 2,000 years of recorded history in its discussion of the history of policing, and it concentrated on the past three centuries in England and the United States. The concept of preserving the peace and enforcing the law has moved from primitive forms like the watch and ward to highly organized, professional police departments. The history of policing has included brutality, corruption, incompetence, innovation, research, heroism, and professionalism.

Academic interest in policing began in earnest in the 1960s with programs in police science, which later were expanded to include the entire criminal justice system and renamed criminal justice programs. Courses similar to the one for which you are using this text were offered. Much of the impetus for these programs came from recommendations made by commissions investigating criminal justice agencies and violence in the United States. Many of the recommendations of these commissions have been implemented by governments and police agencies. Billions of dollars have been spent in an attempt to ameliorate the inequalities that were seen as the underlying problems that caused the violence and disorder of the 1960s. Police departments have been totally revamped since those days. Human relations training has been implemented. Better recruitment efforts and hiring practices have made police departments more reflective of the communities they serve. Community relations units and numerous programs have been in effect for four decades, attempting to improve relationships between the police and the community. Community policing and problem-oriented policing are being implemented throughout the United States to build relationships and partnerships between the police and the communities they serve, as well as to maintain order and fight crime.

Policing has changed dramatically since we first put on police uniforms. Great progress has been made in policing over the years, and the profession is much better today than it was—more technically sophisticated and professional. Certainly, the Rodney King and Abner Louima incidents have hurt the image of policing. Much will be said of these incidents in the rest of this text. Those of us who police our nation, or aspire to police it, cannot erase these incidents and the image they presented of our police to the world. What we can do, what we must do, and what we will do is accept that they happened while still regretting them and continue with the progress we have just read about. We must hope that by our study and by our example, incidents like these will not occur again.

The September 11, 2001, terrorist attacks on the United States have also changed policing to a degree that we cannot yet imagine. The demands on the police to confront the serious crime and disorder problems they face on the streets, as well as to attempt to ameliorate all the social problems they confront there, have been increased with the new duties to protect citizens from terrorist attacks.

Learning Check

1. Discuss the primary means of ensuring personal safety prior to the establishment of formal, organized police departments.
2. Talk about the influence of the English police experience on American policing.
3. Compare and contrast the urban and frontier experiences in 18th- and 19th-century U.S. policing.
4. Identify at least four people instrumental in the development of 20th-century U.S. policing and list some of their accomplishments.
5. Explain how the turbulent times of the 1960s and the early 1970s affected U.S. policing.

Application Exercise

As part of an honors program at your college, the chair of the so-cial science division has nominated you to represent the criminal justice department in a 21st-century time-capsule project. She is asking all departments to contribute material to be placed in a sealed, weatherproof container that will be buried on the campus grounds. The capsule will be opened on January 1, 2105.

The chair asks you to include at least ten simulated, represen-tative documents or artifacts that reflect your study of the U.S. criminal justice system for the years 1900 to the present. What would you include?

Web Exercise

As part of your school's "Dawning of the New Millennium" conference, you have been asked by your depart-ment chair to represent the criminal justice department and pre-sent a brief history of your local police department. He asks that you gather your information from the World Wide Web and be prepared to give a 20-minute oral presentation on it. If your local department is not on the Web, find one close by, possibly your state police.

Key Concepts

Beat system
Compstat
Constable
Eighteenth Amendment
Hue and cry
Metropolitan Police (London)
Mutual pledge
National Advisory Commission on Civil Disorders (Kerner Commission)
Peel's Nine Principles
Pendleton Act
Posse comitatus
Praetorian Guard
President's Commission on Law Enforcement and Administration of Justice
Shire-reeve
Terrorist attacks against the United States of America on September 11, 2001
Thief-takers
Vigiles
Volstead Act (National Prohibition)
Watch and ward
Wickersham Commission

Organizing Public and Private Security in the United States

CHAPTER GOALS

- To acquaint you with the many and diverse local and state public agencies that attempt to enforce the law and ensure public safety in the United States
- To introduce the numerous federal law enforcement agencies that enforce federal laws and regulations and assist local and state police departments
- To describe the size, scope, and functions of law enforcement agencies in the private sector
- To explain methods that private communities can use to ensure their safety
- To acquaint you with the number and type of jobs available to you in public and private policing
- To alert you to the many changes made in U.S. public and private law enforcement in the aftermath of the September 11, 2001 terrorist attacks against the United States

The tragic events of September 11, 2001, the terrorist attacks against New York City's World Trade Center and the U.S. Pentagon, brought the issues of safety and security to the forefront of the minds of most people in the United States and, indeed, the world.

The public and private security industry—those institutions and people who attempt to maintain law and order and enforce the law in the United States—is enormous. We can almost say that it is a growth industry, expanding every year. In the wake of September 11, this industry is expanding even more.

The U.S. security industry spends an immense amount of money and provides jobs for millions of people. The industry operates on all governmental levels: the local level (villages, towns, counties, and cities), the state level, and the federal level. The public agencies are funded by income taxes, sales taxes, real estate taxes, and other taxes. Additionally, the security industry is served by the private sector, which hires more people and spends more money than all the public agencies put together. Students interested in seeking a career in policing will find a vast number and many different types of law enforcement jobs from which to choose.

This chapter will discuss the U.S. public security industry including local, state, and federal law enforcement, as well as international police, Interpol. It will also discuss private security, private investigations, private employment of public police, and community self-protection.

★ ★ ★

THE U.S. PUBLIC AND PRIVATE SECURITY INDUSTRY

Ensuring the safety of U.S. citizens by providing law enforcement services is an extremely complex and expensive undertaking. The U.S. approach to law enforcement is unique when compared with the rest of the world. Japan and some western European countries, including Denmark, Finland, Greece, and Sweden, have single national police forces.[1] The U.S. does not have a national police force, although many people think of the Federal Bureau of Investigation (FBI) as one. We will see later in this chapter that the FBI is an investigative agency, not a police agency.

U.S. law enforcement has developed over the years based on a philosophy of **local control**, the formal and informal use of local neighborhood forms of control to deter abhorrent behaviors. To understand why, remember that the U.S. was built on the fear of a large central government,

The private security industry has grown tremendously in recent years and is one of the nation's expanding industries. Here a private security guard stands watch at a commercial shipping dock on the Miami River in Miami, Florida. What do you think is fueling the growth of private security?

as had existed in England when the colonists came here. The primary responsibility for police protection still falls to local governments (cities, towns, and counties). Although we have state and federal law enforcement agencies, they are minuscule in size and importance when compared with the law enforcement agencies of local government.

Because of the tremendous number of law enforcement agencies and their employees in the United States and the lack of a unified system for the reporting of police personnel, it is very difficult to get a perfect picture of the U.S. law enforcement industry. Every few years the Bureau of Justice Statistics (BJS) of the U.S. Department of Justice attempts to do this as part of its **Law Enforcement Management and Administrative Statistics (LEMAS)** program. For the latest reporting period, LEMAS reports that state and local governments in the United States operated almost 18,000 full-time law enforcement agencies. These included approximately 12,666 general purpose local police departments (mostly municipal and county departments), almost 3,070 sheriff's offices, 49 state police departments, and approximately 1,400 special district police departments, including park police, transit police, constable offices, and other specialized state and local departments.[2]

Dempsey's Law

There Is More to Law Enforcement than Policing

Professor Dempsey, I want a job in law enforcement, but I don't want to be a police officer. That's not the job for me—carrying a gun and working all those strange hours. Are there any jobs in law enforcement other than police officer?

The criminal justice field consists of more than the police. There are jobs in courts and corrections as well. Also, in law enforcement plenty of jobs do not require what we normally call "police work." Let me give you examples of jobs that some of our criminal justice students have obtained.

Most of our graduates have become police officers, deputy sheriffs, state troopers, or investigators in many of the federal agencies. However, many have gone on to four-year colleges, and many have gotten jobs in nonpolice agencies.

Some I remember, such as Diana, have gotten jobs in legal services. Diana worked for the County Victim's Services Agency, and others have become investigators for the county legal aid society.

Some students have obtained police jobs that do not involve enforcement duties. For example, Paul is now a dispatcher with the county police department, and Marianne is a forensic technician with the city police department.

Some have gone on to law school after getting their baccalaureate. One I remember is Tony, who went on to open his own legal firm. Another who comes to mind right away is Rick Steinmann, who graduated in 1971. Rick went on to get a four-year degree and then graduated from law school. Besides doing legal work, Rick has been a criminal justice professor at colleges and universities in Ohio, Kentucky, Florida, and Missouri. In addition to his formal education, Rick also worked as a police officer and a prison counselor, which really gives him great credentials for teaching criminal justice courses.

Another successful graduate is Joe Terry. Joe graduated from our college and then went on to St. John's University, where he received his four-year degree in criminal justice. He started his career as a salesperson for West Publishers, which published the first edition of this textbook. He then became a developmental editor and then an acquisitions editor for West. Joe was one of the people instrumental in the publication of this book's first edition. Now Joe is an executive editor for one of the major publishing companies in the United States.

The report indicates that these state and local law enforcement agencies employed approximately 1,019,500 persons on a full-time basis. This total included 708,000 full-time sworn personnel (69 percent) and 311,500 nonsworn or civilian personnel (31 percent). See Chapter 3 for a discussion of sworn and nonsworn or civilian personnel. These agencies also had about 99,000 part-time employees, including nearly 43,000 part-time sworn personnel.[3] See Table 2.1.

The latest operating expenditures for law enforcement agencies in the United States amounted to approximately $65 billion, which was almost half of all the operating expenditures for the entire U.S. criminal justice system. The police represent the largest segment of the criminal justice system in terms of people employed and money spent.[4]

In addition to state and local law enforcement agencies and personnel, federal law enforcement agencies employed more than 93,000 full-time federal law enforcement personnel authorized to make arrests and carry firearms.[5]

Of the almost 18,000 state and local law enforcement agencies, only 6 percent employed 100 or more full-time officers (77 agencies had 1,000 or more officers); 52 percent employed fewer than 10; and nearly 31 percent employed fewer than 5. Eleven percent had only one full-time officer. Although state and local agencies with 100 or more full-time sworn officers accounted for just 6 percent of all agencies, they employed 63 percent of all state and local full-time sworn personnel. The 77 agencies with 1,000 or more officers accounted for about 31 percent of all full-time sworn personnel.[6]

Table 2.1	Employment by State and Local Law Enforcement Agencies in the United States, 2000						
		Number of employees					
		Full-time			Part-time		
Type of agency	Number of agencies	Total	Sworn	Civilian	Total	Sworn	Civilian
Total	17,784	1,019,496	708,022	311,474	99,731	42,803	56,928
Local police	12,666	565,915	440,920	124,995	62,110	27,323	34,787
Sheriff	3,070	293,823	164,711	129,112	22,737	10,300	12,437
Primary state	49	87,028	56,348	30,680	817	95	722
Special jurisdiction	1,376	69,650	43,413	26,237	13,583	4,667	8,916
Texas constable	623	3,080	2,630	450	484	418	66

Source: Brian A. Reaves and Matthew J. Hickman, *Census of State and Local Law Enforcement Agencies: 2000* (Washington, D.C.: Bureau of Justice Statistics, 2002), Table 1, p. 2.

California had the most full-time state and local law enforcement employees, followed by New York, Texas, Florida, and Illinois. The states with the lowest number of state and local law enforcement agencies were Vermont and North Dakota.

Nationwide, there were 362 full-time state and local law enforcement employees for every 100,000 residents for a nationwide **Law Enforcement Employee Average** of 3.62 (law enforcement employees per 1,000 citizens). The states with the highest law enforcement averages were the District of Columbia, 8.59; Louisiana, 5.27; and New York, 5.0. The states with the lowest were West Virginia, 2.29; Kentucky, 2.37; and Vermont, 2.4. The nationwide **Sworn Law Enforcement Employee Average** was 2.52 (sworn law enforcement officers per 1,000 citizens), with the District of Columbia, with 6.93, as the highest; next were Louisiana, 4.15; New York, 3.84; New Jersey, 3.45; and Illinois, 3.21. The states with the lowest sworn law enforcement averages were Vermont, with 1.70, and West Virginia, with 1.74.

In addition to the publicly funded federal, state, and local law enforcement agencies, it has been estimated that the enormous **private security industry** in the United States employs 1.5 million people and spends over $100 billion yearly. Private policing is growing at a much faster rate than public policing.[7]

Statistics can sometimes be cumbersome and confusing. When we translate them into words, however, we can make some generalizations about the U.S. law enforcement industry:

1. The size and scope of the U.S. law enforcement industry is enormous.

2. The U.S. law enforcement industry is tremendously diverse and fragmented.

3. The U.S. law enforcement industry is predominantly local.

4. There are many employment opportunities in U.S. law enforcement at the federal, state, local, and private levels.

PATROLLING THE WEB

Some Law Enforcement Sites and Law Enforcement Associations

Law Enforcement Jobs on the Net
   http://www.lawenforcementjobs.com
Officer.com (Note: This site is the author's favorite site for accessing a tremendous amount of police information. For example, from officer.com, one can access any law enforcement agency in the world's Web site—just click onto Agencies, then country, state, and so on.)
   http://www.officer.com
International Association of Chiefs of Police (IACP)
   http://www.iacp.org
National Sheriff's Association
   http://sheriffs.org

★ ★ ★

LOCAL LAW ENFORCEMENT

When we use the term *local police,* we are talking about the vast majority of all the law enforcement employees in the United States, including metropolitan police and sheriff's offices. Jobs in these agencies increase yearly.

The United States Department of Labor's Bureau of Labor Statistics reported that the employment of police and detectives is expected to increase faster than the average for all occupations through the year 2010. A more security-conscious society and concern about drug-related crimes contribute to the increasing demand for police services. Police and sheriff's patrol officers had median annual earnings of $39,790 in 2000. Police supervisors had median annual earnings of $57,210, and the median annual earnings of detectives and criminal investigators were $48,870.[8]

Local law enforcement agencies include metropolitan law enforcement, county law enforcement, and rural and small town enforcement.

Metropolitan Law Enforcement

Municipal governments operate the vast majority of the nearly 12,666 general purpose local police departments in the United States. The remainder are operated by county, tribal, or regional (multijurisdictional) jurisdictions.[9]

About 65 percent of full-time local officers primarily perform patrol duties, while 16 percent primarily perform criminal investigations. Other primary duty areas include administrative, training, and technical support.

The largest local department is the New York City Police Department (NYPD) with nearly 53,000 full-time employees, including over 40,400 sworn officers. (Twenty-three sworn members of NYPD were killed in the September 11, 2001, terrorist attack on New York City's World Trade Center.) The next-largest local police department is Chicago, with nearly 13,500 total employees, followed by Los Angeles, with 9,340; Philadelphia, with 7,000; and Houston, with 5,300. About 1 out of every 6 full-time local police officers in the United States works for one of these five largest forces. The largest county police departments (not sheriff's offices) in the United States are the Nassau County, New York, Police Department with 3,000 full-time officers; the Miami–Dade, Florida, Police Department with 3,000 officers; and the Suffolk County, New York, Police Department with 2,600 officers.

The majority of police today work for these metropolitan police departments. These departments can be extremely large. Metropolitan police departments generally provide the duties and services we typically associate with the police. These include arresting law violators, performing routine patrol, investigating crimes, enforcing traffic laws (including parking violations), providing crowd and traffic control at parades and other public events, and issuing special licenses and permits.

Many larger metropolitan areas have overlapping police jurisdictions. For example, in New York City, the NYPD is assisted by other federal, state, and local police and law enforcement agencies that police the city's public schools, colleges, hospitals, buildings, social service centers, parks, bridges, tunnels, airports, and the like. (Formerly, the city's many public housing developments and the city's mass transit system were policed by the New York City Housing Authority Police and the New York City Transit Authority Police, but these were merged into the NYPD in the mid-1990s. It should be noted that before the merger the separate transit and housing authority police departments were bigger than the police departments in the vast majority of the largest cities in the United States.) As another example, in Washington, D.C., there are many separate local and federal departments that have concurrent jurisdiction throughout the city.

Most academic and professional studies of policing focus on municipal departments, because this is where "the action" is in the law enforcement world. This action includes problems with crime, budgeting and funding, politics, and population changes, as well as social problems, including homelessness, unemployment, drug addiction, alcoholism, and child abuse. Additionally, after the terrorist bombings of September 11, 2001, these metropolitan departments have also had to deal increasingly with the problems of terrorism facing their cities. Also, large

---

PATROLLING THE WEB

Some Local Law Enforcement Agencies' Web Sites

Las Vegas Metropolitan Police Department
  http://www.lvmpd.com
Pinellas County (Florida) Sheriff's Office
  http://www.pinellas.fl.us/sheriff
Metropolitan Police Department, Washington, D.C.
  http://www.mpdc.gov

Large municipal police departments face their own unique challenges in keeping residents, business people, and tourists safe. They often respond to the challenge with specialized units that can be utilized as various demands arise.

municipal departments are highly visible because of their size, complexity, budgets, and innovative programs. In addition to attempting to control crime, municipal police have significant problems maintaining public order and solving quality-of-life problems that bother neighborhood residents. The police handle social problems that other public and private agencies either cannot or will not handle. In a big city, when there is a problem, citizens generally do not call the mayor's office; they call 911.

In many geographic areas metropolitan police are supplemented by special jurisdiction police agencies. In the latest reporting period, nearly 1,400 state and local law enforcement agencies with special geographic jurisdictions or special enforcement responsibilities were operating in the United States with over 43,400 full-time sworn personnel. About 68 percent of the full-time sworn personnel handled patrol duties, while 17 percent were criminal investigators. Approximately one percent were responsible for court-related duties. These agencies performed such duties as guarding government buildings and facilities; enforcing conservation, agricultural, and parks and recreation laws; performing special criminal investigations; patrolling transportation systems and facilities; and engaging in special enforcement duties relating to various functions such as alcohol enforcement, gaming or racing law enforcement, business relations enforcement, or drug enforcement.[10]

The largest special jurisdiction agency in the United States, with over 1,200 sworn full-time personnel, is the Port Authority of New York–New Jersey Police Department (PAPD) which polices the facilities owned and operated by the bistate Port Authority of New York–New Jersey, which includes the area's major airports, tunnels, bridges, and transportation systems, as well as New York City's former World Trade Center. (Thirty-seven PAPD police officers were killed in the September 11, 2001, terrorist attacks against the World Trade Center.) The next-largest special jurisdiction agencies are the Florida Game and Fresh Water Fish Commission, with over 670 full-time sworn officers; the California Department of Parks and Recreation, with about 560 sworn officers; and the Texas Parks and Wildlife Department, with about 485 sworn employees.

County Law Enforcement

Most counties in the United States are patrolled by a sheriff's department under the leadership of an elected sheriff (as mentioned in the previous section, several very large counties in New York and Florida have county police departments).

The role of sheriff has evolved in several stages since the early English sheriff (shire-reeve), whose main duty was to assist the royal judges in trying prisoners and enforcing sentences. During the development of the West in the Untied States and until the development of municipal departments, the sheriff often served as the sole legal authority over vast geographical areas.

Today the duties of a county sheriff's office vary according to the size and urbanization of the county. The sheriff's office may perform the duties of coroners, tax assessors, tax collectors, keepers of county jails, court attendants, and executors of criminal and civil processes, as well as law enforcement officers.

There are several different types of sheriff's departments. Some are oriented exclusively toward law enforcement; some carry out only court-related duties; some deal exclusively with correctional and court matters and have no law enforcement duties; others are full-service programs that perform court, correctional, and law enforcement activities.[11]

In the latest reporting year, there were approximately 3,070 full-time sheriff's offices operating nationwide with a total of over 294,000 full-time employees (165,000 sworn and 129,000 civilian or nonsworn). Nearly all sheriff's offices are responsible for responding to citizen calls for service. In addition to handling calls for service, about 80 percent of the offices operate one or more jails, and nearly all have court-related responsibilities such as the serving of process and court security. Forty-one percent of sheriffs' deputies were regularly assigned to patrol duty, 12 percent to investigative duties, and 24 percent to jail-related duties, while 17 percent primarily performed court-related duties, mostly court security.[12]

The largest sheriff's office in the nation is the Los Angeles County, California, Sheriff's Department, which employs over 8,400 full-time sworn personnel, followed by the Cook County, Illinois, Sheriff's Office, which employs 5,300 full-time sworn personnel.

Rural and Small Town Law Enforcement

Sometimes, rural and small town police face different problems than large metropolitan and county police. The state of Wyoming, for example, has the lowest population in the United States and has vast open areas where one can drive over 100 miles between small towns. The law enforcement officers in this state must routinely face the problem of not having immediate backup in most situations. As Mike Roy, the lead instructor at the Wyoming Law Enforcement Academy, says,

> We deal with great distances out here and there is a different mentality. Every other pickup truck you stop out here has a rifle in a gun rack or a pistol in the glove box. Most of the problems we have in law enforcement center around people— where you have people you will have problems.[13]

Regarding the lack of readily available backup, Roy says, "Everyone completing our academy is instructed not to get stupid by acting alone in known volatile situations. Officers are instructed to get used to waiting for the closest help to arrive even if it's 60 miles away."[14]

Although everyone seems aware of the drug problems and dangers to police in our large urban communities, many are not aware of the large-scale problems in the many small towns throughout America's heartland. Police officers searching a modest home on the outskirts of Kansas City, Missouri, encountered a perverse vision of middle-American domesticity:

In the living room sat the computer where Dad had just been forging driver's licenses, while in another room Mom kept their towheaded children, 8 and 4 years old, away from the family's sawed-off shotgun and a crude laboratory that turned out methamphetamine from ingredients bought in local stores. Toxic waste from the illegal drugmaking had been dumped down the drain. When officers looked in the kitchen, . . . a police detective [said], "we found several jars of meth in the freezer next to the children's Popsicles."[15]

Authorities say that locally made methamphetamine, long popular on the West Coast, has become the small town Midwest's drug of choice, similar to the scourge that crack or rock cocaine has been to the inner city. Methamphetamine is a stimulant variously called meth, crank, ice, and speed. For years it was made and distributed by outlaw motorcycle gangs, but today in the Midwest it is a "Mom-and-Pop" operation. Medical experts and some users say meth delivers a stronger, cheaper psychoactive kick than crack cocaine, unleashing aggression and leading to long binges that end with physical collapse.

In the first half of 1997, more than 60 clandestine methamphetamine laboratories were seized by the Jackson County drug task force, whose officers are drawn from seven towns from western Missouri. In 1996, over 300 labs were seized in the Drug Enforcement Administration (DEA) field office covering small towns in Missouri, Kansas, Iowa, Nebraska, South Dakota, and southern Illinois. (In contrast, no labs were seized in New York and only one in New Jersey for the same period.)

In addition to the violence associated with meth users, their labs also prove dangerous to the police. A Missouri detective told of finding an overhead lightbulb in a dark basement laboratory in Independence that was filled with tiny lead pellets and gunpowder, rigged to explode when the switch was turned on. He has also found a couple of pipe bombs and rattlesnakes, as well as toxic gases, in his raids on the labs.[16]

Rural and small town law enforcement agencies engage in mutual assistance programs with neighboring agencies and come to one another's aid when necessary.

Attention to the needs of rural law enforcement agencies gave birth to the National Center for Rural Law Enforcement (NCRLE), a part of the Criminal Justice Institute, located in Little Rock, Arkansas. To assist law enforcement officials throughout the United States, the NCRLE provides management education and training courses ranging from principles of supervision to detailed courses on the legal aspects of domestic violence. NCRLE also provides research and Internet assistance. The NCRLE brings sheriffs, police chiefs, citizens, and social service agency representatives together to discuss the needs of

PATROLLING THE WEB

National Center for Rural Law Enforcement
http://www.ncrle.net

Rural and small town law enforcement agencies are facing the overwhelming challenge of controlling the proliferation of methamphetamine labs like the one shown here from a bust in Arkansas. These labs present very real dangers to rural officers, who engage in mutual assistance programs and task forces in order to come to one another's aid when necessary. What are some other strategies these departments could employ to minimize the danger to their officers?

rural communities and explore the process of creating a community coalition. [17]

★ ★ ★

STATE LAW ENFORCEMENT

Forty-nine of the fifty U.S. states have a state law enforcement agency. The only state without a state police agency is Hawaii. (This may surprise those who are familiar with the television series *Hawaii 5-0,* which was based on a fictional Hawaiian State Police.) In the latest reporting year, the 49 primary state law enforcement agencies had 87,000 full-time employees. There were over 56,000 full-time sworn personal. Of the full-time sworn personnel about 69 percent were patrol officers, 11 percent were investigators, and the rest were ranking officers.[18]

The largest state law enforcement agency is the California Highway Patrol, which has about 9,700 employees; the next two largest are the Texas Department of Public Safety with 7,000 employees and the Pennsylvania State Police with over 5,600 employees. The smallest state police agencies are the North Dakota Highway Patrol, with 126 sworn employees; the Wyoming Highway Patrol, with 148 sworn personnel; and the South Dakota Highway Patrol, with 153 sworn employees.

Historically, state police departments were developed to deal with growing crime in nonurban areas of the country, which was attributable to the increasing mobility of Americans, the proliferation of cars, and the ease of travel. The state police agencies were formed by governors and legislators to lessen reliance on metropolitan and county police departments, which were seen to be more closely linked with politics and urban and county corruption.

PATROLLING THE WEB

Some State Law Enforcement Agencies' Web Sites

Ohio State Highway Patrol
    http://www.dw.ohio.gov/ohiostatepatrol
State of Nevada Department of Public Safety
    http://www.dps.nv.gov
North Carolina State Highway Patrol
    http://www.ncshp.org
South Carolina Highway Patrol
    http://www.schp.org

Generally, state police patrol small towns and state highways, regulate traffic, and have the primary responsibility to enforce some state laws. The state police also carry out many duties for local police agencies, such as the managing of state training academies, criminal identification systems, and crime laboratories.

At the state level, there are two distinct models of law enforcement agencies. The **centralized model of state law enforcement** combines the duties of major criminal investigations with the patrol of state highways. The centralized state police agencies generally assist local police departments in criminal investigations when requested and provide the identification, laboratory, and training functions for local departments.

The second state model, the **decentralized model of state law enforcement**, has a clear distinction between traffic enforcement on state highways and other state-level law enforcement functions. The states that use this model—many southern and midwestern, and some western, states—generally have two separate agencies, one a highway patrol and the other a state bureau of investigation. California, for example, has the California Highway Patrol and the California Division of Law Enforcement.

Although the duties of the various state-level police departments may vary considerably, the most common duties include highway patrol, traffic law enforcement, and the patrol of small towns.

★ ★ ★

FEDERAL LAW ENFORCEMENT

Although the U.S. Constitution created three branches of government—executive, legislative, and judicial—it did not create a national police force. However, it did give the national government power over a limited number of crimes.

Traditionally in the United States, the creation of laws and the power to enforce them have been matters for the states. The states have given much of their enforcement powers to local police agencies. Policing has largely been local. However, in recent years, the number of crimes included in the U.S. Criminal Code has multiplied greatly, as has the number of people assigned to enforce these crimes. As of the latest reporting year, there were almost 93,000 full-time federal law enforcement employees within 67 federal agencies authorized to make arrests and carry firearms. These numbers do not include officers in the U.S. Armed Forces (Army, Navy, Air Force, Marines, and Coast Guard) and also do not include federal air marshals and CIA security protective service officers, because of classified information restrictions.[19] With the increased attention to border security and homeland defense in the aftermath of the terrorist attacks of September 11, 2001, the number of federal law enforcement officers increases daily.

PATROLLING THE WEB

Some Federal Law Enforcement Agencies' Web Sites

U.S. Department of Justice
  http://www.usdoj.gov
U.S. Department of the Treasury
  http://www.ustreas.gov
U.S. Department of Homeland Security
  http://www.dhs.gov
U.S. Department of the Interior
  http://www.doi.gov
Federal Bureau of Investigation
  http://www.fbi.gov
Drug Enforcement Administration
  http://www.usdoj.gov/dea
U.S. Marshals Service
  http://www.usdoj.gov/marshals

Internal Revenue Service—Criminal Investigation
  http://www.ustreas.gov/irs/ci
Bureau of Alcohol, Tobacco, Firearms and Explosives
  http://www.atf.gov
National Park Service
  http://www.nps.gov
U.S. Capitol Police
  http://www.uscapitolpolice.gov
U.S. Postal Inspection Service
  http://www.usps.com/postalinspectors
U.S. Department of State Bureau of Diplomatic Security
  http://www.state.gov/m/ds/

Exhibit 2.1   Major Federal Law Enforcement Agencies

- **Department of Justice**
  - Federal Bureau of Investigation
  - Drug Enforcement Administration
  - U.S. Marshals Service
  - Bureau of Alcohol, Tobacco, Firearms and Explosives
  - Bureau of Prisons

- **Department of the Treasury**
  - Internal Revenue Service—Criminal Investigation Division
  - Treasury Executive Office for Asset Forfeiture
  - Executive Office for Terrorist Financing and Financial Crime
  - Office of Foreign Assets Control
  - Financial Crimes Enforcement Network

- **Department of Homeland Security**
  - U.S. Immigration and Customs Enforcement
  - U.S. Citizenship and Immigration Services
  - U.S. Customs and Border Protection
  - U.S. Secret Service
  - U.S. Coast Guard
  - Federal Protective Service
  - Federal Law Enforcement Training Center

- **Department of the Interior**
  - National Park Service
  - Fish and Wildlife Service
  - U.S. Park Police
  - Bureau of Indian Affairs
  - Bureau of Land Management

- **Department of Defense**
  - Defense Criminal Investigative Service
  - Army Criminal Investigation Division
  - Naval Criminal Investigative Service
  - Air Force Office of Special Investigations

- **U.S. Postal Service**
  - Postal Inspection Service

- **Department of State**
  - Bureau of Diplomatic Security

- **Department of Agriculture**
  - U.S. Forest Service

- **Department of Commerce**
  - Bureau of Export Enforcement
  - National Marine Fisheries Administration

- **Department of Labor**
  - Office of Labor Racketeering

- **Other Federal Law Enforcement Agencies**
  - AMTRAK Police
  - U.S. Mint Police
  - Bureau of Engraving and Printing Police
  - U.S. Capitol Police
  - U.S. Supreme Court Police
  - Library of Congress Police
  - National Gallery of Art Police

YOU ARE THERE! »

Internships at the FBI

Many federal agencies offer intern programs for students. The following is one of the programs offered by the FBI.

Each summer, a special group of outstanding undergraduate and graduate students are selected to participate in the FBI Honors Internship Program in Washington, D.C. The program offers students an exciting insider's view of FBI operations and provides an opportunity to explore the many career opportunities within the Bureau. At the same time, the program is designed to enhance the FBI's visibility and recruitment efforts at colleges and universities throughout the United States.

Due to the very selective and highly competitive nature of the Honors Internship Program, a limited number of internships are awarded each summer. Only individuals possessing strong academic credentials, outstanding character, a high degree of motivation, and the willingness to represent the FBI upon returning to their respective campus will be selected. In order to be considered, individuals must meet the following qualifications:

- Undergraduate students should be enrolled in their junior year at the time they apply to the program.

- Graduate-level students must be enrolled in a college or university and attending full-time.

- Students must have a cumulative grade point average of 3.0 or above.

- All candidates must be U.S. citizens.

- The applicant must supply a copy of one of his or her college term papers.

- The applicant must prepare a completed SF-86, *Questionnaire for National Security Position*.

Applicants must travel at their own expense for an interview at the FBI Academy. Final selection will be contingent upon background investigation by the FBI, who will coordinate all internships with appropriate school officials.

Sources: Federal Bureau of Investigation, *Honors Internship Program,* retrieved on July 7, 2001, from http://www.fbi.gov/employment /honors.htm

Four major U.S. cabinet departments administer the majority of federal law enforcement agencies and personnel: the Department of Justice, the Department of the Treasury, the Department of Homeland Security, and the Department of the Interior. Numerous other federal agencies have law enforcement functions. Each of the agencies discussed in this section have a presence on the Web, and students are urged to access these sites to obtain information regarding these agencies, their duties, and the many jobs they have available.

This text pays special attention to federal law enforcement agencies because many of these agencies require a four-year college degree for appointment. See Exhibit 2.1 on page 42 for a list of the major federal law enforcement agencies.

The Department of Justice

The U.S. Department of Justice is the primary legal and prosecutorial arm of the U.S. government. The Department of Justice is under the control of the U.S. Attorney General and is responsible for: (1) enforcing all federal laws; (2) representing the government when it is involved in a court action; and (3) conducting independent investigations through its law enforcement services. The Department's Civil Rights Division prosecutes violators of federal civil rights laws, which are designed to protect citizens from discrimination on the basis of their race, creed, ethnic background, or gender. These laws apply to discrimination in education, housing, and job opportunity. The Justice Department's Tax Division prosecutes violators of the tax laws. Its Criminal Division prosecutes violators of the Federal Criminal Code for such criminal acts as bank robbery, kidnapping, mail fraud, interstate transportation of stolen vehicles, and narcotics and drug trafficking.

The Justice Department also operates the **National Institute of Justice (NIJ)** as its research arm. The National Institute of Justice maintains the **National Criminal Justice Reference Service (NCJRS)** as a national clearinghouse of criminal justice information.

The NCJRS is one of the most extensive sources of information on criminal justice in the world. Created by the NIJ in 1972, it contains specialized information centers to provide publications and other information services to the constituencies of each of the U.S. Department of Justice, Office of Justice Programs (OJP), bureaus, and to the Office of National Drug Control Policy. Each OJP agency has established specialized information centers, and each has its own 800 number and staff to answer questions about the agency's mission and initiatives.

On the NCJRS Web site you can:

- Search the abstracts database, with summaries of more than 160,000 criminal justice publications, including federal, state, and local government reports; books; research reports; journal articles; and unpublished research.
- Search the collection of 1,500 full-text publications.
- Obtain information on criminal justice grants and funding.
- Obtain the calendar of events for significant criminal justice meetings.
- Order all print publications of the Department of Justice.
- Subscribe to the *Justice Information* electronic newsletter.
- Join the NCJRS mailing list.

The NCJRS maintains a monthly catalogue that provides timely and important information for students and practitioners in the criminal justice system. The catalogue also gives abstracts of the most recent research. You can subscribe to the catalogue at no cost and get on the NCJRS mailing list by writing to NCJRS, P.O. Box 6000, Rockville, Maryland, 20849-6000 or through the Web site at http://www.ncjrs.org.

The National Institute of Justice also conducts the National Crime Victimization Survey (NCVS), a twice-yearly survey of a random sample of the American public that polls citizens about their criminal victimization. Finally, the Justice Department also maintains administrative control over the Federal Bureau of Investigation (FBI), the Drug Enforcement Administration (DEA), the U.S. Marshals, and the Bureau of Alcohol, Tobacco, Firearms and Explosives (ATF).

THE FEDERAL BUREAU OF INVESTIGATION   The Federal Bureau of Investigation (FBI) is the best known of the federal law enforcement agencies. The FBI has over 11,000 special agents and is the primary agency charged with the enforcement of all federal laws not falling under

PATROLLING THE WEB

National Criminal Justice Reference Service (NCJRS)
http://www.ncjrs.org

the purview of other federal agencies. The main headquarters of the FBI is in Washington, D.C. It also has field offices in major American cities and abroad. The head of the FBI is known as the Director and is appointed by the President of the United States, subject to confirmation by the Senate.

In addition to the 11,000 special agents, the FBI employs over 13,000 nonenforcement personnel who perform such duties as fingerprint examinations, computer programming, forensic or crime laboratory analysis, and administrative and clerical duties.

All special agents must attend the FBI Academy, located in Quantico, Virginia. In addition to the special agents, other law enforcement officers and officers from some foreign governments attend the Academy.

Contrary to popular opinion, the FBI is not a national police force. It is an investigative agency that may investigate acts that are in violation of federal law. The FBI may also assist state and local law enforcement agencies and investigate state and local crimes when asked to do so by those agencies.

The FBI was created in 1908, when President Theodore Roosevelt directed the attorney general to develop an investigative unit within the Justice Department. It was first named the Bureau of Investigation; in 1935, it was renamed the Federal Bureau of Investigation. Its most prominent figure and longtime director from 1924 to 1972 was J. Edgar Hoover.

The FBI has had a colorful history. It captured the attention of the media during the Great Depression with nationwide searches and the capture of such notorious criminals as George "Machine Gun" Kelly in 1933, John Dillinger in 1934, and Charles "Pretty Boy" Floyd in 1934.

Critics, however, allege that the FBI under Hoover's regime ignored white-collar crime, organized crime, and violations of the civil rights of minority groups. After Hoover's death in 1972, it was discovered that under his direction the FBI had committed many violations of citizens' constitutional rights, including spying, conducting illegal wiretaps, and burglarizing premises. These violations were mostly aimed at individuals and groups because of their political beliefs.[20]

Hoover's successors reoriented the mission of the bureau and put more emphasis on the investigation of white-collar crime, organized crime, and political corruption.[21]

In addition to its investigative capacity, the FBI today provides many important services.

Identification Division   The FBI's Identification Division, created in 1924, collects and maintains a vast fingerprint file. This file is used for identification pur-

poses by the FBI, as well as state and local police agencies.

National Crime Information Center   The National Crime Information Center (NCIC) is a tremendous computerized database of criminal information. It stores information on stolen property that has identifying information, such as serial numbers or distinctive markings. The NCIC also contains information on outstanding warrants and criminal histories.

FBI Crime Laboratory   The FBI Crime Laboratory, created in 1932, provides investigative and analysis services for other law enforcement agencies. It is the world's largest forensic or criminalistic (scientifically crime related) laboratory and provides microscopic, chemical, and DNA analyses, as well as spectrography and cryptography. Skilled FBI technicians examine such evidence as hairs, fibers, blood, tire tracks, and drugs.

Uniform Crime Reports   The Uniform Crime Reports (UCR) is an annual compilation that includes information on crimes reported to local police agencies, arrests, and police killed or wounded in the line of duty, along with other data. The Uniform Crime Reporting Program is the result of a nationwide, cooperative statistical effort by the majority of the nation's city, county, and state law enforcement agencies voluntarily reporting data on crimes brought to their attention by the public and is published once a year as *Crime in the United States*. Since 1930, the FBI has administered the program and issued periodic assessments of the nature and type of crime in the nation. Although the program's primary objective is to provide a reliable set of criminal statistics for use in law enforcement administration, operation, and management, over the years its data have become one of the leading social indicators for the United States. The American public looks to the UCR for information on fluctuations in the level of crime. Criminologists, sociologists, legislators, municipal planners, the press, and students of criminal

PATROLLING THE WEB

FBI Crime Laboratory
  http://www.fbi.gov
FBI Uniform Crime Reports
  http://www.fbi.gov

justice use the statistics for varied research and planning purposes.

The specific crimes measured by the UCR are called Part I—Index crimes. They are murder and nonnegligent manslaughter, forcible rape, robbery, aggravated assault, burglary, larceny/theft, motor vehicle theft, and arson. One of the latest additions to the UCR is the collection of hate-crime statistics, mandated by the Hate Crime Statistics Act passed by the U.S. Congress and signed by President Bush in April 1990. This collection of data is being used to study crimes motivated by religious, ethnic, racial, or sexual orientation prejudice.

Investigatory Activities   The FBI investigates more than 200 categories of federal crimes and also has concurrent jurisdiction with the Drug Enforcement Administration (DEA) over drug offenses under the Controlled Substances Act.

Traditionally the FBI focused its investigations on organized crime activities, including racketeering, corruption, and pornography; bank robbery; and white-collar crime, including embezzlement and stock and other business fraud. The FBI is also at the forefront of our government's efforts against domestic terrorist activity and trains special antiterrorist teams to prevent and respond to terrorist attacks. It also maintains surveillance on foreign intelligence agents and investigates their activities within this country.

Realizing that both international and domestic terrorism were serious national concerns, the federal government took several law enforcement measures to deal with terrorism even before September 11, 2001. However, in May 2002, in the wake of massive criticism that the FBI had failed to properly handle information that could have led to the prevention of the September 11 attacks, Director Robert S. Mueller issued a press release outlining its complete reorganization and creating a new strategic focus for the agency. The FBI's new focus placed the following as its three priorities: (1) protecting the United States from terrorist attack, (2) protecting the United States against foreign intelligence operations and espionage, and (3) protecting the Untied States against cyber-based attacks and high-technology crimes. The main organizational improvements Mueller enacted were a complete restructuring of the counterterrorism activities of the Bureau and a shift from a reactive to a proactive orientation; the development of special squads to coordinate national and international investigations; a reemphasis on the Joint Terrorism Task Forces; enhanced analytical capabilities with personnel and technological improvements; a permanent shift of additional resources to counterterrorism; the creation of a more mobile, agile, and flexible national terrorism response; and targeted recruitment to acquire agents, analysts, translators, and others with specialized skills and backgrounds.[22]

See Chapter 16, "Policing and Homeland Defense," for further discussion of the FBI's new role in counterterrorism and homeland security.

THE DRUG ENFORCEMENT ADMINISTRATION   The Drug Enforcement Administration (DEA) was previously part of the Treasury Department and was called the Bureau of Narcotics. It was renamed and shifted to the Justice Department in 1973. The DEA is at the vanguard of the nation's "war on drugs" by engaging in drug interdiction, conducting surveillance operations, and infiltrating drug rings and arresting major narcotics violators. The agency also tracks illicit drug traffic; registers manufacturers, distributors, and dispensers of pharmaceutical drugs and controlled substances; tracks the movement of chemicals used in the manufacture of illegal drugs; and leads the nation's marijuana eradication program.[23]

THE U.S. MARSHALS SERVICE   The U.S. Marshals Service performs many functions. Its primary functions are the transportation of federal prisoners between prisons and courts and the security of federal court facilities. The marshals also protect witnesses at federal trials, apprehend federal fugitives, execute federal warrants, operate the Federal Witness Security Program, and are in charge of the federal government's asset seizure and forfeiture programs, handling the seizure and disposal of property resulting from criminal activity.

The Federal Witness Security program, or Federal Witness Protection Program, is responsible not only for the protection of federal witnesses but also for the relocation and creation of new identities for witnesses who "turn" or "flip" against former associates and testify against them in court. (To turn or flip means to cooperate with authorities and obtain or give evidence regarding former partners in crime.) Two notable criminals who have participated in the Federal Witness Protection Program are Henry Hill (the protagonist in Nicholas Pillegi's *Wiseguy: Life in a Mafia Family*, which served as the source of the 1991 movie hit *Goodfellas*) and Salvatore "Sammy the Bull" Gravano (the underboss of the Gambino crime family and the self-admitted participant in 19 murders, whose testimony led to the conviction in 1992 of his boss, John Gotti).

It is interesting to note that Gravano, while living under the protection of the Federal Witness Protection Program in Arizona, was arrested in 2001 for being the kingpin of one of the largest wholesale ecstasy rings in the United States. After his arrest, he was removed from the program and, since conviction, is currently back in prison.

THE BUREAU OF ALCOHOL, TOBACCO, FIREARMS AND EXPLOSIVES   The Bureau of Alcohol, Tobacco, Firearms and Explosives (ATF), formerly part of the Department of the Treasury, was transferred to the Justice Department in 2002. It is the nation's primary agency for enforcing federal laws relating to alcohol, tobacco, and firearms violations. It enforces laws pertaining to the manufacture, sale, and possession of firearms and explosives; attempts to suppress illegal traffic in tobacco and alcohol products; collects taxes; and regulates industry trade practices regarding these items.

The ATF assists other domestic and international law enforcement agencies as the nation's primary agency for tracing of weapons and explosives. The ATF traces these weapons through its records of manufacturers and dealers in firearms. The ATF also investigates cases of arson and bombing at federal buildings or other institutions that receive federal funds, as well as investigating arson-for-profit schemes. The ATF received much criticism for its 1993 raid on the compound of religious cult leader David Koresch in Waco, Texas, but also suffered the ultimate in agency sacrifice, the murder of four agents in that incident.

The Department of the Treasury

The Department of the Treasury has administrative control over the Internal Revenue Service–Criminal Investigation Division and several very important offices related to the financial aspects of crime, drug trafficking, and terrorism, including the Treasury Executive Office for Asset Forfeiture (TEOAF), the Executive Office for Terrorist Financing and Financial Crime (EOTF/FC), the Office of Foreign Assets Control (OFAC), and the Financial Crimes Enforcement Network (FinCEN).

THE INTERNAL REVENUE SERVICE   The Internal Revenue Service (IRS), the nation's primary revenue-collection agency, is charged with the enforcement of laws regulating federal income tax and its collection. The investigative arm of the IRS is its Criminal Investigation Division (CID). CID agents investigate tax fraud, unreported income, and hidden assets.

In its efforts against organized crime figures and major drug dealers, the federal government often uses the CID to target these individuals with the goal of prosecuting them for tax evasion. Also, many other law enforcement agencies solicit the help of the CID in an attempt to prosecute major drug dealers and other criminals who are in possession of large amounts of undeclared income.

THE TREASURY EXECUTIVE OFFICE FOR ASSET FORFEITURE (TEOAF)   The Treasury Executive Office for Asset Forfeiture (TEOAF) administers programs involving applying the forfeiture laws to the infrastructure of criminal enterprises, limiting the ability of these organizations to continue their illegal activities. It primarily directs its efforts against drug cartels, criminal syndicates, and terrorist organizations by removing their assets and minimizing their profits.

THE EXECUTIVE OFFICE FOR TERRORIST FINANCING AND FINANCIAL CRIME (EOTF/FC)   The Executive Office for Terrorist Financing and Financial Crime (EOTF/FC) develops and implements U.S. government strategies to combat terrorist financing domestically and internationally. It also develops and implements the National Money Laundering Strategy.

THE OFFICE OF FOREIGN ASSETS CONTROL (OFAC)   The Office of Foreign Assets Control (OFAC) administers and enforces economic and trade sanctions based on U.S. foreign policy and national security goals against targeted foreign countries, terrorists, international narcotics traffickers, and those engaged in activities related to the proliferation of weapons of mass destruction.

THE FINANCIAL CRIMES ENFORCEMENT NETWORK (FinCEN)   The Financial Crimes Enforcement Network (FinCEN) coordinates information sharing among law enforcement agencies to deal with the complex problem of money laundering.

The Department of Homeland Security (DHS)

After much study since the terrorist attacks of September 11, 2001, the cabinet-level U.S. Department of Homeland Security (DHS) was established in March 2003. Much study and input was put into this reorganization.[24] See Chapter

16, "Policing and Homeland Defense," for a complete description of the DHS and other government and private efforts to prevent terrorism and ensure homeland defense.

The new agency merged 22 previously disparate domestic agencies into one department to protect the nation against threats to the homeland. The new agency consists of more than 170,000 employees; its creation was the most significant transformation of the U.S. government since 1947, when President Harry S. Truman merged the various branches of the U.S. Armed Forces into the Department of Defense to better coordinate the nation's defense against military threats.

The DHS represents a similar consolidation, both in style and substance. The DHS assumed the former duties

Forst's Law

Communication Is Crucial

Communication among various law enforcement agencies has always been a challenge. The tragedies of September 11, 2001, taught us just how critical communication and the sharing of information can be in our global community.

During my career in South Florida, drug smuggling and arms smuggling were major concerns of law enforcement. Federal agencies, state agencies, and county sheriff's departments, as well as local law enforcement, all had units and divisions in place to combat these crimes. The problem was attacked through covert as well as overt investigations. Sometimes agencies spent months infiltrating organizations and setting up drug deals with "bad guys" to buy or sell large amounts of drugs or weapons. Law enforcement wanted to keep these investigations quiet in order to avoid information getting back to the "bad guys." The problem arose (and it did happen) when two different law enforcement agencies were buying from and selling to each other or working the same group without knowing about it. The potential for someone getting hurt was significant. After a couple of close calls, it became apparent that policies and procedures needed to be implemented to minimize the chance of that occurring. Information sharing was encouraged in the safest way possible with the fewest people knowing about it.

Communication is also important to minimize duplication of effort. Why waste time doing steps of an investigation that have already been done? By coordinating investigative efforts, time and money could be saved. Additionally, we realized that by pooling resources we could be more effective. This is especially appropriate when we recognize the fact that bad guys know no boundaries. They are not concerned about crossing city and county jurisdictions and perhaps favored it, banking on our traditional lack of communication.

During the 1980s the use of task forces became a popular tool in the south Florida area to address the growing crime problem. One large and powerful task force was established when then-vice-president George Bush established a task force to combat the extensive drug and crime problem in south Florida. Federal agents and attorneys from other parts of the country were temporarily assigned to the task force in south Florida, typically for a year or 18 months. For several months, I served as part of this task force, which involved federal agents from ATF, DEA, and Customs, as well as officers and deputies from Palm Beach, Broward, and Dade Counties. It was a great experience and an opportunity to learn from the other officers/agents how things were done in their agencies. We worked together surveilling the major players in a large crime organization and communicated via numerous portable radios incorporating various radio frequencies and varying signals and codes. In the end, this efficient use of personnel and equipment resulted in many arrests, the recovery of property, the seizure of drugs and money, and the dismantling of major crime organizations. It was a clear example to me of how teamwork can work to the advantage of all involved in accomplishing a mission and also in fostering positive relationships among the organizations.

of the U.S. Coast Guard, the U.S. Customs Service, the Secret Service, the Immigration and Naturalization Service, and the Transportation Security Administration, along with numerous other federal communications, science, and technology agencies. The DHS does not include the FBI, CIA, or National Security Agency, but these agencies have to share their data with DHS's new intelligence center.[25]

The department's major priority is the protection of the nation against further terrorist attacks. The department's units analyze threats and intelligence, guard our borders and airports, protect our critical infrastructure, and coordinate our nation's responses to future emergencies.

The DHS's major law enforcement division is its Border and Transportation Security (BTS) directorate, which is responsible for maintaining the security of our nation's borders. It assumed the former professional workforce, programs, and infrastructure of the Coast Guard; the Customs Service; the Immigration and Naturalization Service, including the Border Patrol; and the Transportation Security Administration. Through these agencies, the DHS enforces the nation's immigration laws. Its first priority is to prevent the entry of terrorists and the instruments of terrorism while simultaneously ensuring the efficient flow of lawful traffic and commerce.

It is the nation's primary border interdiction agency and maintains an extensive air, land, and marine interdiction force and investigative component. It has investigative responsibilities covering more than 400 laws related to customs, drugs, export control, and revenue fraud.

It conducts inspections and collects import duties and import taxes at more than 300 ports of entry into the United States. It also detects and intercepts illegal drugs, counterfeit consumer goods, and other contraband entering the country. It also plays a major role in the war on drugs. The agency seizes and holds for **civil forfeiture** boats, planes, and other vehicles used to transport illegal drugs into the country. Civil forfeiture results in the owner's loss of legal ownership of his or her confiscated property, and the individual must sue the government for its return.

It also polices the thousands of miles of land and sea borders of the United States, trying to prevent the entrance of illegal aliens. It also conducts investigations of smuggling rings that bring thousands of illegal immigrants into the country each year. It is in charge of admitting foreigners who qualify for United States citizenship.

The U.S. Coast Guard, which falls under the administrative control of the DHS's Border and Transportation Security directorate, is responsible for routine patrol and law enforcement, as well as lifesaving and rescue operations in U.S. waters. Additionally, the Coast Guard enforces boating safety, pollution, and fishery regulations. The Coast Guard makes major efforts in the U.S. war on drugs as it searches for and boards ships suspected of smuggling drugs into the country. Using the civil forfeiture laws, it seizes numerous ships for violation of drug laws.

DHS's Emergency Preparedness and Response (EPR) subdirectorate is responsible for ensuring that our nation is prepared to deal with and recover from terrorist attacks and natural disasters and assumed the personnel and duties of the Federal Emergency Management Administration (FEMA). The Federal Protective Service, which guards all government buildings and installations, and the Federal Law Enforcement Training Center, which trains most federal investigators, are also under the control of the DHS. The U.S. Secret

©Reuters/Corbis

Armed U.S. Marshals patrol a security checkpoint at Logan Airport in Boston, Massachusetts, on September 17, 2001. How has the role of federal law enforcement changed since 9/11?

Service was also placed under the administration of the DHS in 2003.

THE U.S. SECRET SERVICE   The U.S. Secret Service has as its primary mission the protection of the President and his or her family, and other government leaders and foreign dignitaries, as well as the security of designated national events. The Secret Service is also the primary agency responsible for protecting U.S. currency from counterfeiters and safeguarding Americans from credit card fraud, financial crimes, and computer fraud. It provides security for designated national events and preserves the integrity of the nation's financial and critical infrastructures. It uses prevention-based training and methods to combat the cybercriminals and terrorists who attempt to use identity theft, telecommunications fraud, and other technology-based crimes to defraud and undermine American consumers and industry.

In their role of protecting the president, vice president, and other government officials and their families, along with former presidents and presidential and vice presidential candidates, the Secret Service coordinates all security arrangements for official presidential visits, motorcades, and ceremonies with other federal government agencies and state and local law enforcement agencies. The Secret Service has uniformed and nonuniformed divisions. The uniformed division provides protection for the White House complex and other presidential offices, the Main Treasury Building and Annex, and foreign diplomatic missions.

The Secret Service was created by Congress in 1865 as a bureau of the Department of the Treasury to deal with the counterfeiting and forgery of products of the government's monetary system. Because the Secret Service was the federal government's only general law enforcement agency at the time, its responsibilities were expanded to include smuggling, piracy, mail robbery, and land fraud. The Secret Service also conducted post–Civil War investigations of the Ku Klux Klan and served as intelligence and antiespionage agents during the Spanish-American War and World War I. In 1901, after the assassination of President William McKinley, the Secret Service was given the responsibility of protecting the president.

The Department of the Interior

The Department of the Interior's myriad law enforcement agencies provide law enforcement services for the property under its purview, utilizing the National Park Service, the United States Park Police, the Bureau of Indian Affairs, the Fish and Wildlife Service, the Bureau of Land Management, and the Bureau of Reclamation. They are responsible for protecting most of the nation's historic icons, like Mount Rushmore, the Washington Monument, the Hoover and Grand Coulee Dams and 350 other dams, and millions of acres of uninhabited wilderness in national parks, preserves, and other lands controlled by the federal government.

Enforcement agents for the National Park Service are known as commissioned park rangers. They are responsible for law enforcement, traffic control, fire control, and search and rescue operations in the 30 million acres of the National Park Service. Additional rangers serve seasonally as part-time commissioned rangers. In addition to park rangers, the Park Service also uses park police officers, mainly in the Washington, D.C., area.

Enforcement agents for the Department of the Interior's Fish and Wildlife Service are called Wildlife Law Enforcement Agents. They investigate people who are illegally trafficking in government-protected animals and birds, such as falcons. The Interior Department's Bureau of Indian Affairs provides law enforcement services on Indian reservations. In addition, many tribal governments operate their own police departments.

For decades and especially since the terrorist attacks of September 11, 2001, and the subsequent fear of more attacks directed at our nation's landmarks, the Department of the Interior has been under continuing criticism and scrutiny for having no intelligence, terrorism, or domestic security officers; having no capability to gather crime and enforcement statistics; and being permeated with organizational dysfunction. In 2002, a former senior FBI official was appointed to be the director of law enforcement and security in the Interior Department with a broad mandate to professionalize the agencies.[26]

The Department of Defense

Each branch of the U.S. military has its own law enforcement agency. The military police agencies are organized in a manner similar to the civil police, using uniformed officers for patrol duties on military bases and investigators to investigate crimes. The Army's investigative arm is the Criminal Investigation Division (CID); the investigative arm of the Navy and Marines is the Naval Criminal Investigative Service (NCIS); and the Air Force's is the Air Force Office of Special Investigations (OSI).

The U.S. Postal Service

The Postal Inspection Division of the U.S. Postal Service is one of the oldest of the federal law enforcement agencies, having been created in 1836. Postal inspectors investigate illegal acts committed against the Postal Service and its property and personnel, such as cases of fraud involving the use of the mails; use of the mails to transport drugs, bombs, and firearms; and assaults upon postal employees while exercising their official duties. Postal Inspectors are responsible for criminal investigations covering more than 200 Federal statutes related to the postal system. Postal Police Officers provide security for postal facilities, employees, and assets; escort high-value mail shipments; and perform other protective functions.

Other Federal Law Enforcement Agencies

Many other federal agencies have law enforcement responsibilities. The Department of Agriculture has enforcement officers in its U.S. Forest Service, and its Office of Investigation investigates fraud in the areas of food stamps and subsidies to farmers and rural home buyers. The Department of Commerce has enforcement divisions in its Bureau of Export Enforcement and the National Maritime Fisheries Administration. The Department of Labor has the Office of Labor Racketeering as an enforcement division.[27]

The Food and Drug Administration (FDA) oversees the enforcement of the laws regulating the sale and distribution of pure food and drugs. Criminal law enforcement divisions are also found in the Securities and Exchange Commission (SEC), the Interstate Commerce Commission (ICC), the Federal Trade Commission (FTC), the Department of Health and Human Services, the Tennessee Valley Authority, the Environmental Protection Agency, the Library of Congress, and the National Oceanic and Atmospheric Administration.

The Department of State has the Bureau of Diplomatic Security to investigate matters involving passport and visa fraud. The U.S. Supreme Court has its own police department. Even the National Gallery of Art has its own law enforcement unit.

The U.S. Capitol Police employs over 1,200 officers to provide police services for the U.S. Capitol grounds, buildings, and area immediately surrounding the Capitol complex. The U.S. Mint has a police department that provides police and patrol services for U.S. Mint facilities, including safeguarding the nation's coinage and gold bullion reserves. The Bureau of Engraving and Printing has a police department providing police services for their facilities, including those where currency, stamps, securities, and other official U.S. documents are made. The National Railroad Passenger Corporation, better known as AMTRAK, has officers who provide police response, patrol, and investigative services for the railroad.

Joint Federal/Local Task Force Approach to Law Enforcement

In the 1970s, federal enforcement agencies implemented an innovative approach to law enforcement by using **joint federal/local task forces** involving local, state, and federal law enforcement officers acting as a team. In these task forces, investigators from local police departments and state police agencies are temporarily assigned to a federal law enforcement agency to work with federal agents in combating particular crimes. The local and state officers provide knowledge of the area, local contacts, informants, and street smarts, and federal agents provide investigative experience and resources. The Drug Enforcement Administration has been using joint drug enforcement task forces in many areas of the country since the early 1970s. The joint task force approach has also been used successfully in ongoing programs to investigate bank robbery, arson, kidnapping, and terrorism. See Chapter 16, "Policing and Homeland Defense," for a complete description of the Joint Terrorism Task Forces.

★ ★ ★

INTERNATIONAL POLICE

INTERPOL (the International Criminal Police Organization) is a worldwide organization established for the development of cooperation among nations regarding common police problems. INTERPOL was founded in 1923, and the United States became a member in 1938. The mission of INTERPOL is to track and provide information that may help other law enforcement agencies apprehend criminal fugitives, thwart criminal schemes,

PATROLLING THE WEB

INTERPOL
http://www.interpol.int

exchange experience and technology, and analyze major trends of international criminal activity. It attempts to achieve its mission by serving as a clearinghouse and depository of intelligence information on wanted criminals.

INTERPOL's main function is informational; it is neither an investigative nor an enforcement agency. Police officials of any member country may initiate a request for assistance on a case that extends beyond their country's jurisdiction. INTERPOL is headquartered in France, and its U.S. representative is the U.S. Department of the Treasury.

★ ★ ★

PRIVATE SECURITY

The preceding sections of this chapter showed the tremendous size and scope of the public law enforcement industry on the local, state, federal, and international levels.

However, that was only the tip of the iceberg. Another cast of players is associated with providing safety and security in the United States. The vast industry that provides security to much of corporate America and, increasingly, to much of public America is generally known as the private security industry.

In 1980, the National Institute of Justice commissioned Hallcrest Systems, Inc., to conduct a comprehensive study of the private security industry in the United States. The **Hallcrest Reports** are the most in-depth study of the private security industry in the United States. Hallcrest's *The Hallcrest Report I: Private Security and Police in America*, released in 1985, estimated that 1.1 million people were employed in private security and that almost $22 billion was spent for private security.[28]

Commissioned to do a follow-up report for the government, Hallcrest produced *The Hallcrest Report II: Private Security Trends: 1970–2000*, released in 1990. This report

YOU ARE THERE!»

Private Security at Macy's, 2003

As an example of private security in 2003, the department store Macy's detained and processed for shoplifting more than 12,000 persons in 105 Macy's stores nationwide, including more than 1,900 at their Manhattan store alone. Only 56 percent of these people were processed through the police, although 95 percent of the persons detained confessed to shoplifting and quite a few paid an in-store penalty before leaving. The Manhattan store alone lost $15 million to theft in 2002.

The Macy's Manhattan store's security includes 100 security officers, four German shepherds, hundreds of cameras, and a sophisticated closed-circuit television center. Plainclothes store detectives roam the 10 selling floors, keeping in contact with uniformed guards by radio. The movement and activities of shoppers is tracked by over 300 cameras, some controlled by joysticks, as security workers watch images on dozens of closed-circuit television monitors. Macy's spent approximately $28 million on security in 2002—$4 million at their Manhattan store alone.

Macy's policy is to call the police if anyone requests legal representation or asks to be set free immediately, but most people prefer to settle the matter privately. Private security is not legally required to provide the same safeguards as are the police. Retailers are held to a standard known as the "merchant's privilege," which allow stores to detain people on suspicion of shoplifting without police involvement. These

laws also provide "civil recovery statutes," allowing retailers to hold shoplifters liable for the cost of catching them and for the losses they cause, charging penalties even if an item is recovered in perfect condition. In New York State, retailers are allowed to demand five times the value of the item stolen as civil recovery.

Critics of private security procedures such as Macy's say, whether guilty or not, accused shoplifters are often deprived of some of the basic assurances usually provided in public law enforcement proceedings, including the right to legal representation before questioning and rigorous safeguards against coercion.

Wal-Mart's policy, in contrast, is to always contact the police when they detain a suspected shoplifter, according to a company spokesman. According to Donna Lieberman, executive director of the New York City Civil Liberties Union, "The issue of private security guards is a difficult one. On the one hand, stores have an interest in protecting their business. But on the other hand, security guards have neither the training nor the same legal obligations as police officers and the danger of interfering with individual rights is huge."

Source: Andrea Elliott, "In stores, private handcuffs for sticky fingers," *New York Times* (June 17, 2003), pp. A1, C14.

revealed that spending for private security had risen to $52 billion in 1990. Additionally, 1.5 million people were employed annually by private security agencies. They estimated that private security expenditures would rise to $104 billion by the year 2000.[29]

As of 1997, it was estimated that the private security industry had a three-to-one employment ratio to public security, with approximately 1.8 million private security personnel and specialists in the United States. It was also estimated that private security responds to 50 percent of all crimes committed on private property.[30] Most recent estimates report that private security services cost American industries yearly almost $65 billion, while money spent on public policing only totals $40 billion.[31]

As one example of the increasing use of private security, during the 2002 Olympic winter games in Salt Lake City, Utah, almost $213 million was spent for security arrangements, and more than 40,000 private security personnel were employed.[32]

Many of the major private security firms, as well as many small ones, have a presence on the Web. Students are urged to access these sites to find the many jobs and career opportunities in this area. Also, there are several professional organizations in this industry that have a presence on the Web.

In 2003, the United States Department of Labor's Bureau of Labor Statistics reported in its *Occupational Outlook Handbook* that security guards and gaming surveillance officers held more than 1.1 million jobs in 2000 and that opportunities for most jobs as security guards and gaming surveillance officers should be very favorable through the year 2010. Employment of security guards and gambling surveillance officers is expected to grow faster than the average for all occupations through 2010 as concern about crime, vandalism, and terrorism continue to increase the need for security. The median annual earnings of security guards were $17,570 in 2000. Industrial security firms and guard agencies **(contract security)** employed 60 percent of all wage and salary guards. These organizations provide security services on a contract basis, assigning their guards to buildings and other sites as needed. Most other security guards were employed by the organizations they are responsible for guarding **(proprietary security),** such as banks, building management companies, hotels, hospitals, retail stores, restaurants, bars, schools, and government agencies.[33]

The Department of Labor identifies the duty of guards, who are also called security officers, as patrolling and in-

specting property to protect against fire, theft, vandalism, and illegal activity. These workers protect their employer's investment, enforce laws on the property, and deter criminal activity or other problems. The Department of Labor subdivides security guards into "static security positions" and "mobile patrol." Guards assigned to static security positions usually stay at one fixed location for a specific length of time. In contrast, guards assigned to mobile patrol duty drive or walk from location to location and conduct security checks within an assigned geographical zone. Guards work in department stores, shopping centers, theatres, office buildings, banks, hospitals, public buildings, factories, laboratories, government buildings, data processing centers, military bases, universities, parks, sports stadiums, and air, sea, and rail terminals, and they also serve as armored car guards. They protect people, records, merchandise, money, and equipment.

David H. Bayley and Clifford D. Shearing, in their 2001 study, *The New Structure of Policing: Description, Conceptualization and Research Agenda*, reported that policing is being restructured and transformed in the modern world by the development of private protective services as important adjuncts to public law enforcement. They report that a host of nongovernmental agencies have begun to provide security services. They report that, in most countries, private police outnumber public police.[34]

The Economist reported that there are three times as many private police as public, and Americans are spending $90 billion a year on private security compared to $40 billion in taxes for public police.[35] It has been estimated that there are 60,000 private security firms in the U.S.[36]

The issues of private security versus public policing do not affect only the United States. A 2002 report by the Law Commission of Canada discusses the movement in Canada to rely more and more on private security firms to provide for economic and physical security.[37]

Researchers have identified nine categories in the private security industry:

1. Proprietary (in-house) security. (Proprietary security means that a particular company has its own security department.)

2. Contract guard and patrol services. (Contract services are services that are leased or rented to another company.)

3. Alarm services.

4. Private investigations.

5. Armored car services.

6. Manufacturers of security equipment.

7. Locksmiths.

8. Security consultants and engineers.

9. Other, including such categories as guard dogs, drug testing, forensic analysis, and honesty testing.[38]

William C. Cunningham and Todd H. Taylor divide the private security industry into three distinct components: physical, information, and personnel security.[39]

The physical security component of the private security industry involves protecting people and property. Typical activities of physical security include guarding building entrances, preventing shoplifting, patrolling premises, and maintaining order. Information security involves protecting information. Typical activities of information security are protecting against the unauthorized use of computer programs and preventing the theft of corporate research and development plans. Personnel security means protecting people. Activities of personnel security include being bodyguards for company executives or celebrities and conducting background investigations of prospective employees.

Most major corporations in the United States have private security forces performing overt and covert functions. Overtly, they perform visible patrol designed to provide protection and loss prevention. Covertly, private security forces engage in surveillance or countersurveillance regarding trade secrets. The covert functions of private security are increasing. According to the Society of Competitor Intelligence Professions, over 80 percent of the Fortune 1000 companies have regular in-house "snoops" on the payroll. Corporate spying has reached the point where companies everywhere are now concerned with finding and eliminating spies and securing their files and corporate secrets.[40]

Private security officers are not restricted by the provisions of the U.S. Constitution in their duties, as the public police are. Private security officers do not have to give suspects Miranda warnings before questioning, and the exclusionary rule does not apply to the evidence they seize. (Constitutional limitations on the police will be discussed in Chapter 11, "Police and the Law.") However, private security officers must be very careful in their operations, as they can be sued and suffer monetary losses.

Traditionally, there has been a lack of personnel standards and training for private security employees. A study by the Rand Corporation in the 1970s found that fewer than half of the private security guards in the United States were high school graduates, their average age was 52, and most were untrained and poorly paid. Rand provided the following stereotype of the "typical security guard": "an aging white male who is poorly educated and poorly paid—between 40 and 55; he has little education beyond the ninth grade; he has had a few years of experience in private security; he earns a marginal wage— some have retired from a low-level civil service or military career."[41]

Although the professionalization of private security has improved somewhat since the 1970s, a 2002 report advises that security services need to devote extensive time and resources to hiring the right people, developing them, and striving to ensure they are the right people for the clients' needs.[42]

In the wake of September 11, 2001, security is now a rising star in the corporate structure. The people responsible for security have become much more visible to the top of the business and much more important to the business itself. The shift in business attitudes is also evident in a recent market report on the security industry by Lehman Brothers in which the analyst writes that global security industry "has moved from a peripheral activity to center stage."[43]

Because of the proliferation of private security employees in the United States and their clouded history, a number of states have required a licensing process for them. Some states require training if the security guard is to be armed. Some states, however, require only an application and a minor fee.[44]

In 1955, a number of private security professionals developed a professional association to improve the image of private security—the American Society for Industrial Security (ASIS). Over the years membership has increased greatly, and the society has indeed improved the image of private security.

Today, ASIS is known as **ASIS International** and has more than 33,000 members and is the preeminent international organization for professionals responsible for security, including managers and directors of security. In addition, corporate executives, other management personnel, consultants, architects, attorneys, and federal, state and local law enforcement become involved with ASIS International to better understand the constant changes in security issues and solutions. ASIS International provides educational programs and certifications that address broad security concerns.[45]

PATROLLING THE WEB

Security Management magazine
  http://www.securitymanagement.com

It offers three certification programs:

- *Certified Protection Professional (CPP).* This certification designates individuals who have demonstrated competency in all areas constituting security management. Nearly 10,000 individuals have received the CPP certification since its inception in 1977.[46] (See Exhibit 2.2.)

- *Professional Certified Investigator (PCI).* Holders of the PCI certification have demonstrated education and/or experience in the fields of case management, evidence collection, and case presentation.

- *Physical Security Professional (PSP).* The PSP designation is the certification for those whose primary responsibility is to conduct threat surveys; design integrated security systems that include equipment, procedures, and people; or install, operate, and maintain those systems.

ASIS International offers numerous Professional Development Programs throughout the country each year (see Exhibit 2.3) and also offers a variety of online courses

at http://wwww.asisonline.org/onlinecourses.html. It also operates an Annual Seminar and Exhibits in a major city each year which is attended by security directors and managers, security consultants, law enforcement professionals, homeland security officials, high-level executives of critical infrastructure businesses, government and military personnel with security responsibilities, and other professionals responsible for security operations. The 2002 meeting was in Chicago; the 2003 meeting was in New Orleans.

ASIS International is seeking to professionalize the ranks of private security by appealing to college students. In 1997, ASIS had eight separate panels dealing with jobs in security at a career exposition at the John Jay College of Criminal Justice in New York City. It has distributed more than 30,000 "Careers in Security" booklets to universities, colleges, and career centers.[47]

In 1976, only five colleges in the United States offered a bachelor's degree in private security, and no master's programs were available. By 1990, 46 colleges offered a bachelor's degree, and 14 offered a master's degree.[48] Today, college education is becoming more important in private security.

Ph.D. programs in security are still rare, but academic and professional certifications are more prevalent and more attainable, particularly using online options. The American Military University (AMU) has partnered with ASIS International to deliver an abundance of online degree programs. AMU offers certificates and degrees at the undergraduate and graduate levels focusing on such topics as

Exhibit 2.2	The Certified Protection Professional (CPP) Examination

The CPP examination is a one-day, multiple-choice test consisting of two parts, a mandatory test administered in the morning and specialty subjects administered in the afternoon.

- Mandatory Subjects
    Emergency Planning
    Investigations
    Legal Aspects
    Personnel Security
    Physical Security
    Protection of Sensitive Information
    Security Management
    Substance Abuse
    Loss Prevention
    Liaison
- Specialty Subjects
    Banking and Financial Institutions
    Computer Security

Credit Card Security
Department of Defense Industrial Security Program
    Requirements
Educational Institutions Security
Fire Resources Management
Health Care Institutions Security
Manufacturing Security
Nuclear Power Security
Public Utility Security
Restaurant and Lodging Security
Retail Security
Transportation and Cargo Security
Oil and Gas Industrial Security
Telephone and Telecommunications Security

The CPP certification is valid for three years and must be renewed thereafter.

Source: ASIS International.

Exhibit 2.3	ASIS International Professional Development Programs

The following is a sample of ASIS International Training Programs currently available:

Managing Your Physical Security Program
Security Force Management
Executive Protection
Facility Security Design
Professional Certified Investigator (PCI) Review
Physical Security Professional (PSP) Review
Certified Protection Professional (CPP) Review
Gaming Security and Surveillance
Investigating Corruption and Fraud Within Your Company
Interview and Interrogation Techniques

Source: Adapted from *Security Management,* May 2003.

homeland security, intelligence, information technology, and counterterrorism.[49]

Enrollment in academic security programs and internships is on the rise, both at the undergraduate and graduate level, says Doctor Robert McCrie, professor of security management at John Jay College of Criminal Justice: "Those going into security see a correlation between the private sector and serving the country as a whole. They see private security as a part of homeland security."[50]

Security executives responding to the 2002 ASIS International Employment Survey reported that they earned on average 26 percent more if they held a four-year degree, and those with a master's degree even 15 percent more.[51]

The increased demand for quality security education since the terrorist attacks of September 11, 2001, has altered course content and caused many new degree programs, including:

- Johns Hopkins University is introducing an undergraduate concentration in security management as part of its Bachelor of Science degree in business and management.
- Georgetown University is offering a Master of Arts in Security Studies through its School of Foreign Service.
- The University of Houston is offering a Master of Science degree in Security Management.
- Drexel University, in conjunction with area community colleges, will offer degrees in emergency management and planning.

- George Washington University offers a security management concentration in its Master of Forensic Sciences degree program with an emphasis on the integration and communication between corporations and government services. It features courses on emergency preparedness, disaster planning, crisis management, and crisis prevention.
- Webster University offers a master's degree program in security management.
- The University of Denver is designing a security concentration in its Master of Professional Studies degree program as well as graduate- and undergraduate-level certificate programs in homeland security. Courses offered will include managing violence, conflict management systems, crisis public relations, risk assessment and management, and information systems security.

ASIS International has sponsored Academic Practitioners Symposiums where academicians and practitioners have engaged in discussions to develop courses to introduce business students to the subject of security. These symposiums provide a forum for academicians and security practitioners to meet, share ideas, and discuss potential improvements in security education. They have been held at the University of Nevada, the University of Cincinnati, the University of Oklahoma, and the University of Maryland.[52]

New professional certifications have also been developed, some centered around a homeland security theme, such as the one offered by the American College of Forensic Examiners, and others focusing on specific technical subjects, such as the PCI and PSP certifications offered by ASIS International. According to Professor McCrie, "The statistics paint a bright future for private security and those students looking to enter the market. It also looks bright for those looking to make a career change."[53]

★ ★ ★

PRIVATE INVESTIGATIONS

A major area of private security is private investigations. The Bureau of Labor Statistics of the U.S. Department of Labor reported that private detectives and investigators held about 39,000 jobs in 2000 and reports that employment of private detectives and investigators is expected to grow faster than the average for all occupations through 2010. Median annual earnings were $26,750 in 2000.[54]

PATROLLING THE WEB

Private Investigations Agencies' Web Sites

Pinkerton Security and Investigation Services
    http://www.pinkertons.com
Wackenhut Corporation
    http://www.wackenhut.com
Equifax Employment Services
    http://www.equifax.com
Kroll's Associates
    http://www.krollworldwide.com

In the wake of the academic studies of detective operations (see Chapter 7, "Police Operations: The Traditional Approach") that revealed that much of what detectives do is unproductive work and does not lead to solving crimes, many police departments drastically cut the number of persons they assigned to detective units. Today, generally only 10 percent of a department's personnel are assigned to detective duties. If you are the victim of a crime that does not merit an investigation, your only recourse may be to hire a private investigator if you want the crime solved.

Also, we need private investigators because police power and resources are limited. There are areas of criminal and noncriminal activity where conventional law enforcement is either ill equipped or otherwise prohibited from getting involved. In cases of suspected insurance fraud, for example, most public police agencies have neither the personnel nor the financial resources to undertake intensive investigations. The search for runaway children is also far too large a problem for public agencies, and the surveillance of unfaithful spouses is beyond the authority and jurisdiction of any public service agency.

A review of popular magazines and newspapers reveals that private investigators are involved in the following broad areas: investigating art thefts,[55] investigating terrorism cases,[56] investigating kidnapping cases,[57] following lovers and spouses,[58] helping Hollywood stars clear their names of damaging gossip,[59] conducting financial investigations for corporations and foreign governments,[60] checking prospective mates (with the threat of AIDS this could be very important),[61] attempting to free wrongly convicted convicts,[62] exposing defense fraud,[63] investigating business fraud,[64] working for corporate clients, investigating corporate drug rings, tracing stolen goods, tracking lost assets,[65]

Dempsey's Law   Jobs for College Students in Private Security

Professor Dempsey, are there jobs for college students in the private investigations business?

Sure, there are many jobs for college students in the private investigations business— both part-time jobs while you are in college and full-time jobs when you finish college. Let me give you a few examples. Eric, Vanessa, Nancy, and Nick all worked for local private investigators while attending our college. They served subpoenas, made observations, and did surveillances. Many local private investigators call me at my office and ask me to recommend students for them to interview.

What about full-time jobs after graduation, Professor?

I'll give you some examples here also. Rich became a police officer with the county five years ago. He had such an outstanding record that he was recently promoted to detective/investigator and is now working in a robbery squad. Cindy was hired as an investigator with U.S. Customs. She had a 4.0 grade point average here and at her four-year school. I have had other students hired by large national companies as investigators in their proprietary security departments and other students hired by the largest private investigating firms, such as Pinkerton and Wackenhut.

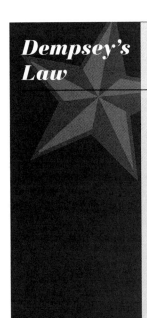

Dempsey's Law

More Jobs for Students in Private Security: Integrity Shoppers

Professor Dempsey, a friend of mine was just arrested and lost her job as a cashier at the Feel-Well drugstore in town. She said that she was the victim of integrity shoppers. What's that?

Many retail businesses employ integrity shoppers to test employee's honesty and adherence to the rules and regulations established by the business. Let me give you the following scenario. It describes the actual operation of a team of integrity shoppers who were students of mine in a night class here at the college.

Mary, age 40, rushing through the busy aisles of a large pharmacy downtown, hurriedly selects an item of cosmetics costing $4.50. Clutching the item and a five-dollar bill, she passes other customers waiting on the checkout line and addresses the cashier in an excited manner: "I have to get back to work, or I'll be fired. Look, take the five. That'll cover the tax." She then quickly places the five-dollar bill on the counter in front of the cashier. Without waiting for a reply, she turns and rushes out of the store.

At the same time, Mary's daughter Linda, age 21, who is also Mary's partner, waits by the hair dye in the front of the store looking as if she cannot make up her mind which product to buy. Linda, in actuality, is carefully watching the cashier to determine what the cashier will do with the five-dollar bill.

If the cashier puts the money into his or her pocket instead of ringing it up on the cash register, Linda signals her mother, who is waiting outside. The two women then approach the store manager, identify themselves as company security, and report the transaction. The cashier is removed from her or his station and brought to the manager's office.

Mary and Linda generally try to get the employee to prepare a written statement regarding her or his actions and any other previous illegal acts he or she has engaged in at the store. Because Mary and Linda are not police officers or government officials, they do not have to read the subject his or her Miranda Rights prior to questioning. Often the employee will give the names of other employees who steal from the store.

After obtaining the written statement, Mary and Linda notify the police, who respond and arrest the employee on the written complaint of the store manager.

Professor Dempsey, isn't that entrapment?

No! Providing someone an opportunity to commit a crime is not entrapment. The cashier did not have to pocket the five. He or she should have followed proper company procedures, which, no doubt, involved ringing up the sale or notifying the store manager to account for any cash overage or shortage.

---

finding lost pets,[66] investigating insurance fraud, and serving subpoenas.[67]

The following is a comprehensive list of duties that can be performed by the private investigator:[68]

- Assist attorneys in case preparation.
- Perform accident reconstruction for insurance companies and attorneys.
- Review police reports for attorneys (many private investigators are former members of police departments and thus are able to interpret police terminology and jargon).
- Conduct surveillance and observations for insurance companies and attorneys.
- Do background investigations of possible spouses.
- Do background investigations of possible employees.
- Investigate criminal cases that police do not investigate due to lack of resources or lack of solvability.
- Run credit checks.
- Run financial resources checks.
- Investigate missing persons cases that the police cannot investigate due to a lack of resources.

YOU ARE THERE! »»

Jobs in Private Security and Private Investigating: Pinkerton and Wackenhut

Pinkerton and Wackenhut, two of the largest employers of private security employees and private investigators in the United States, like most modern corporations today, advertise and recruit on the Internet. They have special sections on their Web sites for this purpose.

For Pinkerton, go to http://pinkertons.com

For Wackenhut, go to http://www.wackenhut.com

- Investigate missing persons cases that are not police cases because no crime was involved.
- Check into conduct of spouses or lovers.
- Conduct suicide investigations.
- Provide personal protection.
- Provide executive protection.
- Provide premises or meeting protection.
- Prepare travel itineraries for business executives and others to ensure they will have safe traveling connections.
- Conduct honesty or "shopper" testing.
- Investigate insurance or workers' compensation frauds.
- Perform auto accident reconstruction.
- Work undercover for private firms to uncover criminal activity, drug use, or work rule violations.
- Investigate product liability claims.
- Serve subpoenas.

The fundamental difference between the private investigator and public investigator is the investigative objective. While police and public investigators are primarily concerned with the interests of society, the private detective serves organizational and individual interests.

Many private investigators are former police detectives or federal agents. As with the public investigation, the private investigation may overlap into a criminal area. However, the private investigator has no authority by state law to investigate a legally proscribed crime and should in

all cases involving criminal violations inform the appropriate law enforcement agency.

★ ★ ★

PRIVATE EMPLOYMENT OF PUBLIC POLICE

Many public police officers **moonlight** (work on their off-duty hours) as private security guards.[69] Almost all police departments require an officer to obtain the department's permission before obtaining private security employment. In some departments, the officers must find their own private employer; in others, the police union serves as a broker in assigning off-duty officers to private employers. In some areas (for example, Boston, Colorado Springs, New Haven, and St. Petersburg), the police department itself actually serves as the broker between the private employers and the off-duty officers.[70]

The Seattle Police Department reported that 47 percent of its police officers had security work permits (department permission to work as private security officers while off duty). The Colorado Springs Police Department reported that 53 percent of its officers had work permits and worked a total of 20,000 off-duty hours in uniform, earning an average of $1,333 per officer. The Metro-Dade, Florida, police department reported that its uniformed off-duty officers made approximately $4 million in a year while working as private security guards.[71]

Three-quarters of the police departments that permit officers to perform private security on their off-duty hours allow the officers to wear their uniforms. Also, many departments permit the off-duty use of other department equipment, including radios and vehicles.[72]

The use of public police as private security guards can lead to obvious problems. To whom is the officer responsible—the primary employer (the police department) or the private company? Who is responsible for the officer's liability in the event he or she makes a mistake? Should a police department continue to pay an officer who is out on sick report due to injuries sustained while working for a private firm? If an officer is guarding a local business and he or she observes a crime on the street, which obligation comes first—the obligation to the private business for security or the obligation to his or her oath of duty?[73]

COMMUNITY SELF-PROTECTION

Chapter 10, "Community Policing: The Debate Continues," will discuss the two most current philosophies affecting police departments today, community policing and problem-solving policing. These two philosophies acknowledge that the police, by themselves, cannot eliminate or control crime; the community has to get involved. There must be a working relationship between the police and the community. Chapter 9, "Police and the Community," will discuss numerous police–community partnerships. Two of the most effective strategies in community crime prevention are target hardening and neighborhood watch programs.

One way citizens can protect themselves from crime is through **target hardening**—making a home or business as crime-proof as possible by installing locks, bars, alarms, and other protective devices. One survey of 11,000 households across the United States found that one-third of the households reported taking one or more crime prevention measures, including installing a burglar alarm (7 percent), participating in a neighborhood watch program (7 percent), or engraving valuables with an identification number (25 percent). Other commonly used crime prevention techniques included window bars, watchdogs, warning signs, fences or entrance barricades, guards or door attendants, and intercoms or surveillance cameras in building entrances.[74]

Another program is **neighborhood watch.** A National Institute of Justice report discussed the various neighborhood patrol and block watch programs created by communities and the police. These programs are designed so that people in communities watch for suspicious people, lobby for improvements like increased lighting, report crime to the police, conduct home security surveys, and generally work with the police to make neighborhoods safer. Chapter 9, "Police and the Community," will discuss this report and these programs in greater detail.[75]

CHAPTER SUMMARY

The tragic events of September 11, 2001, the terrorist attacks against New York City's World Trade Center and the U.S. Pentagon, brought the issues of safety and security to the forefront of the minds of most people in the United States and, indeed, the world. As a result of these attacks and the need to protect the nation from terrorism and provide homeland defense, there were numerous changes in the public and private law enforcement industry.

The federal government, in particular, responded to September 11 by creating the huge cabinet-level Department of Homeland Security, which merged and improved the many disparate federal agencies concerned with terrorism, homeland defense, and response to catastrophic emergencies. The FBI completely changed its mission, orientation, and practices to address the terrorist threat against our homeland. Other federal agencies did the same. Local, state, and private agencies also reengineered themselves to address the need for homeland defense.

This chapter discussed the changes indicated above, as well as the entire U.S. public security industry including local, state, and federal law enforcement, as well as international police, INTERPOL. It also discussed private security, private investigations, private employment of public police, and community self-protection.

Learning Check

1. In terms of personnel and money spent, talk about how extensive the safety industry is in the United States.
2. Most U.S. police are local, as opposed to state and federal. Discuss why this is so.
3. Discuss how state police differ from local police.
4. Explain how federal law enforcement agencies differ from local and state police.
5. Discuss the scope of the private security industry in the United States.

Application Exercise

You have been given the opportunity to create a new town or city based on your specifications. To do this, you must also create the institutions that will govern this locality. What type of police agency would you create to ensure a safe and orderly environment? You must assume that crime and disorder are possible, even in your new city. Consider the qualifications you want these officers to possess, what power you would give them, and whether you would design them as private or public.

Web Exercise

Patrol the Web to the National Institute of Justice's home page and obtain the Bureau of Justice Statistics' latest update regarding the number of law enforcement agencies in the United States, including local departments, sheriff's offices, state police agencies, and federal law enforcement agencies.

Also obtain the latest statistics on the number of sworn officers in local, state, and federal law enforcement agencies.

Key Concepts

ASIS International
Centralized model of state law enforcement
Civil forfeiture
Contract security
Decentralized model of state law enforcement
Hallcrest Reports
Joint Federal/Local Task Force
Law Enforcement Employee Average
Law Enforcement Management and Administrative Statistics (LEMAS)
Local control
Moonlighting
National Criminal Justice Reference Service (NCJRS)
National Institute of Justice (NIJ)
Neighborhood watch
Private security industry
Proprietary security
Sworn Law Enforcement Employee Average
Target hardening

Organizing the Police Department

CHAPTER GOALS

- To acquaint you with the organizational and managerial concepts necessary to organize and operate a police department
- To acquaint you with the complexities of modern police organizations
- To show you how police departments are organized on the basis of personnel, area, time and function
- To introduce you to the major ranks in a police department and to the responsibilities connected with those ranks
- To introduce you to the major units of a police department and the functions they perform

Some of you reading this text want to become members of a police department, while some of you are just interested in what the police do and how they do it. Reading this chapter will give you a good insight into how a police department actually works. Did you ever wonder how a police officer gets promoted to the detective rank or to a supervisory position or gets assigned to a particular area of your city or town?

This chapter deals with organizing a police department. Although this chapter uses the term *police department,* it is used as a generic term and includes other law enforcement agencies, such as federal, state, and county law enforcement agencies, including sheriffs' offices. In any organization, someone must do the work the organization is charged with doing; someone must supervise those doing the work; and someone must command the operation. Certain commonly accepted rules of man-

agement must be followed to accomplish the goals of the organization. This chapter will include the organization of the police department by personnel (rank), area, time, and function or purpose. It will look at the various ranks in a police department and examine the responsibilities of the people holding those ranks. Then it will discuss how a police department allocates or assigns its personnel by area, time, and function or purpose. This chapter is designed to give you an awareness of the complexities involved in policing 7 days a week, 24 hours a day.

Not all police organizations are as complex as those described here. In fact, most police departments in the United States are small. The intent of this chapter, however, is to cover as many complexities of the police organization as possible to give you the broadest possible view of policing in the United States.

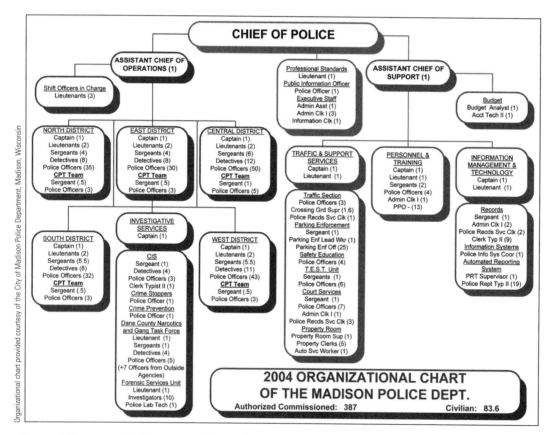

By providing a graphic illustration of how a department is organized, organization charts like this one for the Madison, Wisconsin, police department help officers understand their chain of command and the division of labor. Increasingly, departments are placing their organizational charts on the Web to help educate and inform the public as well.

ORGANIZING THE DEPARTMENT: MANAGERIAL CONCEPTS

Before discussing the organization of a police department, some managerial concepts common to most organizations should be understood. These concepts include division of labor; chain of command (hierarchy of authority); span of control; delegation of responsibility and authority; unity of command; and rules, regulations, and discipline.

Division of Labor

Obviously, all the varied tasks and duties that must be performed by an organization cannot be performed by one, a few, or even all of the members of the organization. The different tasks and duties an organization performs must be divided among its members in accordance with some logical plan.

In police departments, the tasks of the organization are divided according to personnel, area, time, and function or purpose. Work assignments must be designed so that similar (homogeneous) tasks, functions, and activities are given to a particular group for accomplishment. In a police department, patrol functions are separate from detective functions, which are separate from internal investigative functions. Geographic and time distinctions are also established, with certain officers working certain times and areas. The best way to think of the division of labor in an organization is to ask the question, "Who is going to do what, when, and where?"

The division of labor should be reflected in an organization chart, a pictorial representation of reporting relationships in an organization (Figure 3.1). A good organizational chart is a snapshot of the organization. Workers can see exactly where they stand in the organization (what functions they perform, whom they report to, and who reports to them).

Chain of Command (Hierarchy of Authority)

The managerial concept of **chain of command** (also called hierarchy of authority) involves the superior–subordinate or supervisor–worker relationships throughout the department, wherein each individual is supervised by one immediate supervisor or boss. Thus, the chain of command as pictured in the organizational chart shows workers which supervisor they report to; the chain of command also shows supervisors to whom they are accountable and for whom they are responsible. All members of the organization should follow the chain of command. For example, a patrol officer should report to his or her immediate sergeant, not to the captain. A captain should send his or her orders through the chain of command to the lieutenant, who disseminates the directions to the sergeants, who disseminate the information to the patrol officers (see Figure 3.2). Chain of command may be violated, however, when an emergency exists or speed is necessary.

Span of Control

The number of officers or subordinates that a superior can supervise effectively is called the **span of control.** Although no one can say exactly how many officers a sergeant can supervise or how many sergeants a lieutenant can supervise, most police management experts

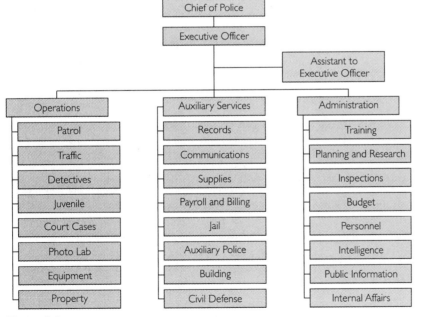

Figure 3.1
Organization of a Police Department by Function

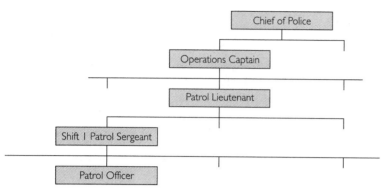

Figure 3.2
Chain of Command from Chief to Patrol Officer

Source: Used with permission from *Introduction to Police Administration,* 2d ed., p. 33. Copyright 1998 Matthew Bender & Company, Inc., a member of the LexisNexis Group. All rights reserved.

say the chain of command should be one supervisor to every six to ten officers of a lower rank. Nevertheless, it is best to keep the span of control as limited as possible so that the supervisor can more effectively supervise and control. The number of workers a supervisor can effectively supervise is affected by many factors, including distance, time, knowledge, personality, and the complexity of the work to be performed.

Delegation of Responsibility and Authority

Another important managerial concept in police organizations is delegation of responsibility and authority. Tasks, duties, and responsibilities are assigned to subordinates, along with the power or authority to control, command, make decisions, or otherwise act in order to complete the tasks that have been delegated or assigned to them.

Unity of Command

The concept of **unity of command** means that each individual in an organization is directly accountable to only one supervisor. The concept is important, because no one person can effectively serve two supervisors at one time. Unity of command may be violated in emergency situations.

Rules, Regulations, and Discipline

Most police organizations have a complex system of rules and regulations designed to control and direct the actions of officers. Most departments have operations manuals or rules and procedures designed to show officers what they must do in most situations they encounter. Rule books are

often complex and detailed. In some major police departments, the police rule book can be a foot thick.

Police departments have disciplinary standards that are similar to, but less stringent than, the military's. Violation of department standards in terms of dress, appearance, and conduct can lead to sanctions against officers in terms of reprimands, fines, or even dismissal from the department.

★ ★ ★

ORGANIZING BY PERSONNEL

A police department faces the same organizational challenges as any organization, and a major challenge is personnel. The civil service system plays a large role in police hiring. This section will describe that role, along with the quasi-military model of police, sworn versus nonsworn personnel, rank structure, and other personnel issues.

The Civil Service System

The **civil service system** is a method of hiring and managing government employees that is designed to eliminate political influence, favoritism, nepotism, and bias. Civil service rules govern the hiring, promoting, and terminating of most government employees. The Pendleton Act created a civil service system for federal employees in 1883, in the wake of the assassination of President James Garfield, who was killed in 1881 by a person who had been rejected for appointment to a federal office. Eventually, many state and local governments adopted their own civil service systems.

Today over 95 percent of all government employees at the federal, state, and local levels are covered by the civil service system. Civil service has reduced political interference and paved the way for merit employment, a system in which personal ability is stressed above all other considerations. However, some civil service systems seem to guarantee life tenure in the organization and provide an atmosphere of absolute employee protection instead of stressing the merit that the system was initially designed to emphasize.

Most police departments, particularly larger departments, are governed by civil service regulations. Some complain that the civil service system creates many problems for police administrations, because a chief or commissioner cannot appoint or promote at will but must follow the civil service rules and appoint and promote according to civil service lists. Additionally, it is often difficult to demote or terminate employees under the civil service system.[1] Although many criticize civil service rules, it must be remembered that they help eliminate the autocratic power of a supervisor to hire, fire, or transfer employees on a whim.

Quasi-Military Model of Police

As Chapter 1 indicated, the U.S. police are a civil, as opposed to a military, organization. Despite this, our police departments are **quasi-military organizations** (organizations similar to the military). Like the military, the police are organized along structures of authority and reporting relationships; they wear military-style, highly recognizable uniforms; they use military-style rank designations; they carry weapons; and they are authorized by law to use force. Like the military, police officers are trained to respond to orders immediately.

Despite similarities, however, the police are far different from the military. They are not trained as warriors to fight foreign enemies but instead are trained to maintain order, serve and protect the public, and enforce the criminal law. Most important, the power of the police is limited by state laws and by the Bill of Rights.

However, despite the dissimilarity of the police and the military, in the aftermath of the terrorist attacks of September 11, 2001, many departments have assumed a more military stance and equipped their officers with more tactical weapons to deal with the possibility of future terrorist attacks. See Chapter 16, "Policing and Homeland Defense," for examples of this.

Sworn and Nonsworn (Civilian) Personnel

People who work for police departments fall under two major classifications: sworn members of the department, or police officers, and nonsworn members of the department, or civilians.

SWORN MEMBERS   **Sworn members** are those people in the police organization we usually think of as police officers, troopers, or deputy sheriffs. They are given traditional police powers by state and local laws, including penal or criminal laws and criminal procedure laws. Additionally, upon appointment, sworn members take an oath to abide by the U.S. Constitution and those sections of state and local law applicable to the exercise of police power.

The best example of police power is the power to arrest. Regular citizens also have the power to arrest (citizen's arrest). However, these powers differ.

As an example, the *Criminal Procedure Law* of New York State grants arrest powers to both police officers and ordinary citizens:

> Section 140.10 . . . a police officer may arrest a person for:
> (a) Any offense when he has reasonable cause to believe that such person has committed such offense in his presence; and
> (b) A crime when he has reasonable cause to believe that such person has committed such crime, whether in his presence or otherwise. . . .
> Section 140.30 . . . any person (citizen) may arrest another person:
> (a) For a felony when the latter has in fact committed such felony; and
> (b) For any offense when the latter has in fact committed such offense in his presence.[2]

The law is quite specific. Police officers need only to have probable cause (not definite proof) to make arrests for any crimes committed in their presence or not. They can make arrests for any offenses (including minor infractions) committed in their presence.

Probable cause is a series of facts that would indicate to a "reasonable person" that a crime is being committed or was committed and that a certain person is committing or did commit it. A good example of facts leading to probable cause:

1. At 3 A.M., screams from a female are heard in an alley.

2. An officer sees a man running from the alley.

3. Upon the officer's command, the man refuses to halt and rushes past the officer.

This gives the officer probable cause to stop the man, even though there is no "proof" yet of a crime. If it later turns out that no crime was committed, the officer has done nothing wrong, because he or she acted under probable cause.

Citizens, in contrast, cannot use probable cause, and the crime must have actually happened. (In fact, this leaves citizens open for false-arrest lawsuits). Additionally, citizens can only arrest for offenses actually committed in their presence, unless that offense was a felony.

In addition to the power of arrest, the police officer has the power to stop temporarily and question people in public places, to stop vehicles and conduct inspections, and to search for weapons and other contraband. Additionally, the police officer has significantly more power to use physical force, including deadly physical force, than does the citizen.

NONSWORN (CIVILIAN) MEMBERS   **Nonsworn (civilian) members** of police departments are not given traditional police powers and can exercise only the very limited arrest power given to ordinary citizens. Thus, they are assigned to nonenforcement duties in the department. They serve in many different areas of a police organization and in many roles. When we think of nonsworn members, we usually think of typists, 911 operators, and police radio dispatchers. However, nonsworn members serve in many other capacities as well, including clerical, technical, administrative, and managerial jobs. Their rank structure is generally not as vertical as that of sworn officers.

Rank Structure

Sworn members generally have a highly organized rank structure (chain of command). The lowest sworn rank in the police organization is usually the police officer, although many organizations have lower-ranked sworn officers, such as cadets or trainees, who generally perform duties similar to nonsworn members or assist sworn members in performing nonenforcement duties. Many cadets or trainees aspire to an eventual sworn position or are in training for one. In most organizations, those in training at the police academy are known as recruits or cadets and generally have the same legal authority as regular officers, except that they are generally not assigned to enforcement duties while still in training.

To say the police officer is the lowest rank in a police department may sound demeaning to the rank. However, it only refers to the relative rank in the organizational chart, not to the police officer's power or to the quality and importance of the service performed.

Officers of all ranks and from different departments come together for a memorial service. Sworn members of law enforcement generally have a highly organized rank structure (chain of command). The lowest sworn rank in the police organization is usually the police officer.

The following sections describe the various ranks in the police organization using generic terms. Most departments use the titles police officer, detective or investigator, sergeant, lieutenant, and captain. However, some organizations, such as state police departments and county sheriff's offices, use different terms to describe their members. In a state police force, the rank of trooper is almost identical to the rank of police officer. In a sheriff's office, the rank of deputy sheriff is synonymous with the rank of police officer.

The police officer/trooper/deputy sheriff is the most important person in the police organization. He or she is the person who is actually working on the streets, attempting to maintain order and enforce the law. A police agency is only as good as the quality of the men and women it employs.

POLICE OFFICER   Police officers serve as the workers in the police organization. The average police officer is assigned to patrol duties. (See Chapters 7 and 8 for a complete discussion of the activities of patrol officers.) Police officers perform the basic duties for which the organization exists. They are under the control of supervisors, generally known as ranking officers or superior officers. Ranking officers are generally known as sergeants, lieutenants, and captains. At the highest level in most police organizations are inspectors and chiefs. In some state police organizations, military ranks such as major and colonel are used instead of inspector and chief. In federal law enforcement organizations, nonmilitary terms are used to reflect rank structure, such as agent, supervisor, manager, administrator, and director.

CORPORAL OR MASTER PATROL OFFICER   Many police departments have established the corporal or master patrol officer rank as an intermediate rank between the police officers and the first-line supervisor, the sergeant. Often this rank is given to an officer as a reward for exemplary service or for additional services performed, such as training or technical functions.

DETECTIVE/INVESTIGATOR   Some police officers in a department are designated as detectives, investigators, or inspectors. (The various names for ranks may be confusing because investigators in the San Francisco Police Department are called inspectors, whereas in the New York City Police Department, and many others, the rank of inspector is that of a senior manager.) Their role is to investigate past crimes. (See Chapter 7 for a complete discussion of the role and activities of the detective.) Detectives exercise no supervisory role over police officers except at a crime scene (the location where a serious crime occurred

Dempsey's Law

Making Rank

Professor Dempsey, how do you make rank in a police department? How do you get promoted?

All police departments are different, Erin. Would you like me to tell you how I made rank in the NYPD?

Sure, that would be great.

I was appointed to the rank of police trainee in 1964, based upon my successful passing of the police officer civil service examination and the psychological, medical, physical aptitude, and background investigation that we will discuss in Chapter 4. I was appointed to the rank of police officer in 1966. At that time, the entry-level rank in the NYPD was called patrolman instead of police officer. It was changed to police officer for reasons we will discuss when we get to Chapter 13. I worked in the Forty-first (41) Precinct in the South Bronx, until 1973, when I was transferred to the police academy as a recruit instructor. I was promoted to detective in 1973. There is no examination for the rank of detective in the NYPD; generally, officers make detective based on merit and performance.

I was promoted to sergeant in 1974 and transferred to the Sixtieth (60) Precinct in Coney Island, Brooklyn. Promotion to sergeant was based on a civil service examination and an assessment center. I spent my years as a sergeant in the 60 and the Organized Crime Control Bureau (OCCB). OCCB concentrated on organized crime vice activities, including controlled substances and drugs, gambling, loan sharking and extortion, and prostitution.

I was promoted to lieutenant in 1983 and assigned to the 60 once again. Promotion to lieutenant involved a three-stage civil service examination, including administrative, operational, and oral exercises and an assessment center.

I was promoted to captain in 1985 and transferred to Patrol Borough Brooklyn North. Promotion to captain was also based on a three-stage civil service examination. I spent my years as a captain in Patrol Borough Brooklyn North, the Seventy-ninth (79) Precinct in Bedford Stuyvesant, Brooklyn; the Civilian Complaint Review Board; and the Personnel Bureau.

I retired in 1988 after 24 years of service.

Professor, you must have worked very hard to get all those promotions.

I sure did.

Was it worth it?

I would say so. My pension today and for the rest of my life is over $50,000 a year, and I had a great time.

---

and where possible evidence may be present), where they are in charge and make most major decisions.

The role of the detective is generally considered more prestigious than that of police officer. Detectives generally receive a higher salary and do not wear uniforms. They are usually designated detectives not through the typical civil service promotional examination but rather by appointment, generally for meritorious work. Often detectives do not possess civil service tenure and can be demoted back to the police officer rank without the strict civil service restrictions applicable to the other ranks in a police organization.

SERGEANT   The first supervisor in the police chain of command is the sergeant. The sergeant is the first-line supervisor and, as many will say, the most important figure in the police supervisory and command hierarchy. The sergeant has two main responsibilities in police operations. First, the sergeant is the immediate superior of a number of officers assigned to his or her supervision. This group of officers is generally known as a **squad.** (Generally, six to ten officers make up a squad, and several squads may work on a particular tour of duty.) The sergeant is responsible for the activities and conduct of members of his or her squad. Second, the sergeant is responsible for decisions made at the scene of a police action until he or she is relieved by a higher-ranking officer.

The sergeant is responsible for getting the job done through the actions of people. Thus, he or she must possess numerous important personal qualities, such as intelligence, integrity, and dedication. The sergeant also draws on numerous organizational, motivational, and communication skills.

LIEUTENANT   Just above sergeant in the chain of command is the lieutenant. Whereas the sergeant is generally in charge of a squad of officers, the lieutenant is in charge of the entire platoon. The **platoon** consists of all of the people working on a particular tour (shift). Not only is the lieutenant in charge of employees; he or she also is in charge of all police operations occurring on a particular tour.

CAPTAIN   Next in the chain of command above the lieutenant is the captain. The captain is ultimately responsible for all personnel and all activities in a particular area, or for a particular unit, on a 24-hours-a-day basis. The captain must depend on the lieutenant and sergeants under his or her command to communicate his or her orders to the officers and to exercise discipline and control over the officers.

RANKS ABOVE CAPTAIN   Many larger municipal agencies have a hierarchy of ranks above the rank of captain. Inspectors generally have administrative control over several precincts or geographic areas, whereas assistant chiefs or chiefs have administrative control of major units, such as personnel, patrol, or detectives.

CHIEF OF POLICE/POLICE COMMISSIONER   The head of the police agency is usually termed the chief of police or the police commissioner. Chiefs of police and police commissioners are generally appointed by the top official of a government (mayor, county executive, or governor) for a definite term of office. Generally commissioners and chiefs do not have civil service tenure and may be replaced at any time.

One of the major exceptions to this lack of civil service tenure is the chief of the Los Angeles Police Department (LAPD). The LAPD chief of police is not subject to the direction of the Los Angeles mayor but rather to a board of officials called the Police Commission, who may remove the chief from duty, but only for cause. In effect, the chief has a permanent appointment. This proved to be a complicating factor in the 1991 Rodney King case in that the Police Commission fired Chief Daryl Gates, who was then returned to his post by the Los Angeles City Council. Gates maintained his post, despite much pressure, during the 1992 Los Angeles riots.

Gates resigned after the riots and was replaced by former Philadelphia top cop Willie Williams, who was granted a five-year contract. Williams was instrumental in planning the city's strategy to deal with possible problems in the wake of the 1993 retrial of the officers involved in the Rodney King case and was generally credited with maintaining order on Los Angeles streets during that time.

Other Personnel

Police departments are increasingly using nonsworn employees and civilians to perform tasks in the police department. This effort can increase efficiency in the use of human resources and cut costs. Community service officers and police auxiliaries also help some departments operate more efficiently.

CIVILIANIZATION   The process of removing sworn officers from noncritical or nonenforcement tasks and replacing them with civilians or nonsworn employees is **civilianization.** Civilians with special training and qualifications have been hired to replace the officers who formerly did highly skilled nonenforcement jobs (traffic control, issuing parking tickets, taking past-crime reports, and so on). Additionally, civilians with clerical skills have been hired to replace officers who were formerly assigned to desk jobs. Approximately one quarter of all local police department employees are civilians.

The replacement of sworn officers by civilians in nonenforcement jobs is highly cost effective for police departments, because civilian employees generally earn much less than sworn officers. This strategy also enables a department to have more sworn personnel available for patrol and other enforcement duties.

A study of civilianization programs found that managers and officers were favorably impressed with the use of civilians for nonenforcement duties. Many officers observed that civilians performed some tasks better than the sworn officers they replaced. Perhaps, because the civilians were not subject to rotation and emergency assignment, they

©Lester Lefkowitz/Corbis

Many departments employ civilians or community service officers in the demanding position of emergency service operator.

could concentrate better on their specific duties. Additionally, many officers tended to consider some of the noncivilianized jobs as confining, sedentary, a form of punishment, and not proper police work. Others in the study felt that civilians want careers in police work, and a sizable number of officers recommended that more be hired.[3]

COMMUNITY SERVICE OFFICERS   The President's Commission on Law Enforcement and Administration of Justice recommended that three distinct entry-level police personnel categories be established in large and medium-size police departments: (1) police agents, (2) police officers, and (3) **community service officers**.[4] Police agents would be the most knowledgeable and responsible entry-level position. They would be given the most difficult assignments and be allowed to exercise the greatest discretion. The commission suggested a requirement of at least two years of college and preferably a bachelor's degree in the liberal arts or social sciences. Some departments have adopted this recommendation and give these officers the title of corporal or master patrol officer.

Police officers would be the equivalent of the traditional and contemporary police officer. They would perform regular police duties, such as routine preventive patrol and providing emergency services. The commission recommended that a high school degree be required for this position.

Community service officers (CSOs) would be police apprentices, youths 17 to 21 years of age, preferably from minority groups. They would have no general law enforcement powers and no weapons. The commission reasoned that because of their social background and greater understanding of inner-city problems, community service officers would be good police–community relations representa-tives. The commission suggested that the CSOs work with youths, investigate minor thefts, help the disabled, and provide community assistance. The commission also recommended that the lack of a high school diploma and the existence of a minor arrest record not bar the CSOs from employment. It also recommended that the CSOs be allowed to work their way up to become regular police officers.

POLICE RESERVES/AUXILIARIES   Personnel shortcomings in police departments may be perennial or seasonal, depending on the jurisdiction. Some resort communities face an influx of vacationers and tourists during a particular season that can more than double the normal size of the population. In response to this annual influx, some communities employ "summertime cops."

The use of the term **reserve officer** has been very confusing. In many jurisdictions reserve officers are part-time employees who serve when needed and are compensated. In other jurisdictions, reserves are not compensated. The key element regarding the reserve officer is that he or she is a nonregular but sworn member of the department who has regular police powers. Other volunteer officers, sometimes referred to as auxiliaries, do not have full police power. Perhaps the best definition of a reserve officer has been provided by the International Association of Chiefs of Police (IACP):

> The term "reserve police officer" usually is applied to a nonregular, sworn member of a police department who has regular police powers while functioning as a department's representative, and who is required to participate in a department's activities on a regular basis. A reserve officer may or may not be compensated for his or her services, depending on each department's policy.[5]

Police agencies in some communities employ part-time officers throughout the year. These men and women, sometimes referred to as reserve or auxiliary officers, are either unpaid volunteers or paid less than full-time officers. In Illinois and North Carolina, for example, they are sworn officers who carry firearms. In Arizona, the highway patrol has used unpaid reserve officers for more than 30 years. These troopers are fully certified state law enforcement officers. Regarding the Arizona Highway Patrol reserve troopers, two researchers have written, "The only distinguishing element of their uniform is the word 'Reserve' written on the badge. The public sees reserve officers as Highway Patrol officers, which, by statute and training, they are. Reserves issue traffic citations, effect felony or misdemeanor arrests, investigate accidents and perform all the functions of a full-time officer."[6]

PATROLLING THE WEB

Some Reserve Police Officer Organizations

National Reserve Law Officers Association (NRLO)
   http://www.nrlo.net
California Reserve Peace Officers Association (CRPOA)
   http://www.crpoa.org
Baltimore County Auxiliary Police Team
   http://www.auxpolice.org

Reserve officers augment the regular force in police departments throughout the nation. Whether paid or not, they have full police powers. Many augment the traditional police force by providing law enforcement services, including patrol, traffic control, assistance at natural and civil disasters, crime prevention, dispatch operations, and numerous other functions.[7]

Each state varies in its requirements to become a reserve officer. South Carolina, for example, requires a minimum of 60 hours of police instruction and a firearms qualification conducted by a certified firearms instructor. The reserve candidate must then pass a rigid examination conducted by the South Carolina Criminal Justice Academy. The reserve officer in South Carolina cannot be paid.

In North Carolina, however, a reserve candidate must receive the same training as a full-time officer. He or she must attend the Basic Law Enforcement Training Course, which consists of 488 hours of instruction at a host of community colleges or at the central North Carolina Justice Academy at Salemburg, North Carolina. Upon completion of the basic training, the student must pass a state board examination. Reserve officers in North Carolina can receive a salary from their employer.

The following are some examples of successful reserve programs:

- Belding, Michigan, with a population of 5,800 and nine full-time officers, organized a ten-member reserve unit, which contributes over 6,000 hours of volunteer service a year. Under Michigan state law, reserve officers do not require any special or mandatory training. Consequently, the Belding Police Department trains all reserve officers at the department using the full-time officers as trainers.[8]

- Selma, North Carolina, a community 22 miles southeast of Raleigh, the state capital, has a permanent population of 6,000, with 15 sworn police officers and 5 civilians. In 1990 it added six reservists. The reserves are required to perform a minimum of twelve hours of service per month, mostly on Friday and Saturday evenings and during holidays. The department's normal three-car shift is boosted by up to five vehicles because of the reserves. Recently when the department added three full-time officers, they were selected from the reserve force. Because all reservists eventually desire full-time appointment, the program is important in allowing the command staff to evaluate each reserve officer's performance under normal and emergency operating conditions.[9]

In some cities, auxiliary officers are unpaid volunteers. Although they wear police-type uniforms and carry batons, these auxiliaries are citizens with no police powers, and they do not carry firearms. They usually patrol their own communities, acting as a deterrent force and providing the police with extra eyes and ears. New York City has more than 8,000 of these unpaid volunteer auxiliary officers. Chapter 9 of this text, "Police and the Community," provides coverage of police volunteer programs.

Some Personnel Issues

Like all organizations with employees, police departments have a distinct set of personnel issues. Some important issues are lateral transfers, police unions, and other police affiliations (for example, fraternal organizations and professional organizations).

LATERAL TRANSFERS   **Lateral transfers,** or lateral movement, in police departments can be defined as the ability and opportunity to transfer from one police department to another. Some states allow lateral transfers from one department in the state to another department and also allow lateral transfers from out-of-state departments. Some states allow only in-state lateral transfers, and some states do not allow lateral transfers at all. Table 3.1 lists some police departments that allow lateral transfers.

The major problem with lateral transfers is that many police pension systems are tied into the local government, and funds put into one fund cannot be transferred into other funds. Thus, lateral transfers in those departments can cause officers to lose all or some of their investments.

The President's Commission on Law Enforcement and Administration of Justice recommended developing a national police retirement system that would permit the transfer of personnel without the loss of benefits. A few experiments with portable police pensions have been tried.[10]

POLICE UNIONS   Police unionism has a long and colorful history. Police employee organizations first arose as fraternal associations to provide fellowship for officers, as well as welfare benefits (death benefits and insurance policies) to protect police families. In some cities, labor unions began to organize the police for the purpose of collective bargaining, and by 1919, 37 locals had been chartered by the American Federation of Labor (AFL). The Boston Police Strike of 1919, as we saw in Chapter 1, was triggered by the refusal of the city of Boston to recognize the AFL-affiliated union. In response to the strike, Calvin Coolidge, then the governor of Massachusetts, fired all of the striking officers—almost the entire police department. Because of the Boston strike, the police union movement stalled until the 1960s, when it reemerged.[11]

Table 3.1	Sample of Police Departments Allowing Lateral Transfers		
Police Department		In-State Lateral	Out-of-State Lateral
Mesa (Arizona) Police Department		✓	
Alachua County (Florida) Sheriff's Office		✓	✓
Prince Georges County (Maryland) Police Department		✓	✓
Bethlehem (Pennsylvania) Police Department		✓	
Florence (South Carolina) Police Department		✓	

Today, nearly 75 percent of all U.S. police officers are members of labor unions. About two-thirds of all states have collective bargaining laws for public employees. In those states, the police union bargains with the locality over wages and other conditions of employment. In the states that do not have collective bargaining agreements, the police union serves a more informal role.[12]

Police unions are predominantly local organizations that bargain and communicate with the local police department and the mayor's or chief executive's office. Local unions often join into federations on a state or federal level to lobby state and federal legislative bodies. Some of the major national federations of local police unions are the International Union of Police Associations (IUPA), the Fraternal Order of Police (FOP), the International Conference of Police Associations (ICPA), and the International Brotherhood of Police Officers (IBFO). Some officers are also members of national federations of civil service workers, such as the American Federation of State, County, and Municipal Employees (AFSCME).

Unions exist in order to harness the individual power of each worker into one group, the union, which can then speak with one voice for all the members. The ultimate bargaining tool of the union has traditionally been the strike. Members of many organizations, such as the telephone company, the department store, the factory, and so on, strike to win labor concessions from their employers.

Should police officers be allowed to strike? Many feel that police officers are special employees and should not have the right to strike. In fact, most states have laws that specifically prohibit strikes by public employees. New York State has one of the toughest laws against strikes by public employees in the nation, the Taylor Law.

Despite the presence of the Taylor Law and similar laws, there have been strikes by police employees. In 1970, members of the New York City Police Department staged a wildcat strike, for which all officers were fined two days' pay for each day they participated in the strike. Police strikes have also been staged in Baltimore, San Francisco, and New Orleans.

To avoid the penalties involved in a formal police strike, police union members occasionally engage in informal job actions to protest working conditions or other grievances felt by the officers. These job actions include the **blue flu** (where officers call in on sick report) and a refusal to perform certain job functions, such as writing traffic summonses.

OTHER POLICE AFFILIATIONS   Police officers affiliate on levels other than unions. The two major types of affiliations are fraternal and professional.

Fraternal organizations generally focus on national origin, ethnic, or gender identification. In the New York City Police Department, some examples include the Emerald Society (Irish American officers), the Columbian Society

PATROLLING THE WEB

Some Police Unions and Federations

Fraternal Order of Police (FOP)
http://www.grandlodgefop.org
Fraternal Order of Police Associates (FOPA)
http://www.grandlodgefop.org/associates
National Association of Police Organizations (NAPO)
http://www.napo.org
St. Louis Police Officers' Association (SLPOA)
http://www.slpoa.org

PATROLLING THE WEB

Some Police Professional Organizations

International Association of Chiefs of Police (IACP)
   http://www.theiacp.org
Police Executive Research Forum (PERF)
   http://www.policeforum.mn-8.net

(Italian American officers), the Guardian Association (African American officers), the Schomrin Society (Jewish officers), the Policewoman's Endowment Society (female officers), and the Gay Officers Action League (gay and lesbian officers).

The two major professional organizations for police officers, designed as a forum to exchange professional information and provide training, are the International Association of Chiefs of Police (IACP) and the Police Executive Research Forum (PERF), a research-oriented organization.

★ ★ ★

ORGANIZING BY AREA

Police departments must be organized not only with regard to personnel but also with regard to the geographic area they serve. Each officer and group of officers must be responsible for a particular well-defined area. Geographic areas may be beats or posts, sectors or zones, and precincts. In very large police departments that have numerous precincts, the precincts may be grouped together to form divisions. Figure 3.3 shows a map of a precinct divided into sectors.

Beats/Posts

The **beat** or post is the smallest geographic area that a single patrol unit—one or two people in a car or on foot—can patrol effectively. A beat may be a foot beat, patrol car beat, mounted beat, motorcycle or scooter beat, or even bicycle beat. Obviously, patrol car beats can be much larger than foot beats.

The beat officer ideally should know everyone living or doing business on his or her beat, as well as conditions

and problems on the beat that require police assistance or concern. For this reason, a beat should be as geographically limited as possible, without being so small that it is nonproductive or boring to the officer.

Sectors/Zones

A sector or zone is a number of individual beats grouped together. A patrol car sector may patrol several foot beats. A supervisor's zone may include numerous foot beats and several auto sectors.

Precincts

A **precinct** is generally the entire collection of beats and sectors in a given geographic area. In a small department, generally only one precinct serves as the administrative headquarters for the entire department. The Long Beach Police Department, in Nassau County, New York, which patrols a city of 35,000 people with 70 police officers, has one precinct. The Corning (Iowa) Police Department, which serves 2,100 people, has one precinct. The Suffolk County (New York) Police Department, which serves over 1.5 million people with about 2,000 officers, has seven precincts geographically placed throughout the county. The city of Imperial Beach, California, policed by the San Diego County Sheriff's Office, has one precinct. The New York City Police Department, which serves over 8 million people with almost 40,000 officers, has 76 police precincts spread throughout the five boroughs of the city.

The building that serves as the administrative headquarters of a precinct is generally called a precinct house or station house. The station house usually contains detention cells for the temporary detention of prisoners awaiting a court appearance after an arrest, locker rooms in which officers can dress and store their equipment, administrative offices, meeting rooms, and clerical officers.

The focus of the precinct or station house in many large police departments is the desk. The desk is usually an elevated platform, near the entrance of the station house, where all major police business is carried on. Prisoners are booked at the desk, and officers are assigned to duty from it. A ranking officer, generally a sergeant or lieutenant, is assigned as the desk officer and supervises all activities in the station house. The desk officer is usually in charge of the police blotter, a record in chronological order of all police activities occurring in a precinct each day. The blotter traditionally has been a large bound book in which all entries are handwritten by

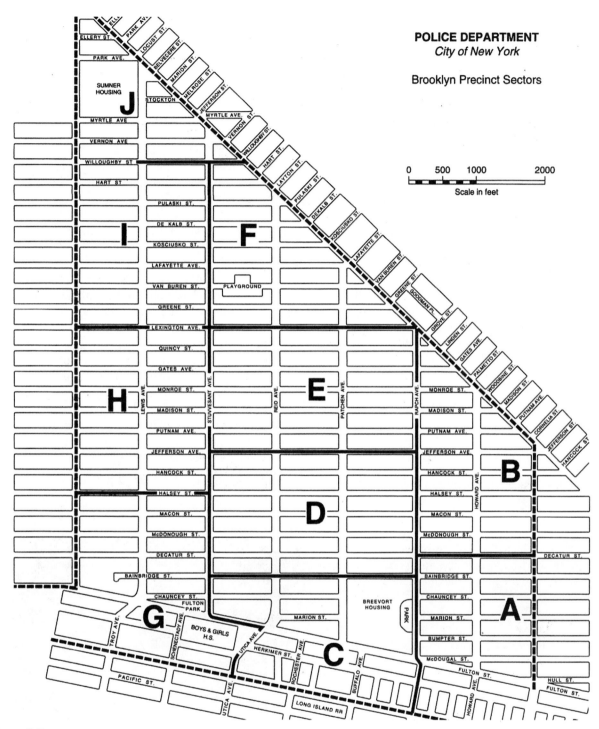

Figure 3.3
Map Dividing Precinct into Sectors

Source: Courtesy of New York City Police Department.

the desk officer. Although some departments still maintain the classic handwritten blotter, that term is now used more generically as the written record of all activity in a precinct. The blotter can include typed and computerized reports.

★ ★ ★

ORGANIZING BY TIME

In addition to being organized by personnel and by area, a police department must organize its use of time. The following discussion will describe the tour system, including the common three-tour system, tour conditions, and steady (fixed) tours.

The Three-Tour System

Common sense dictates that police officers, like other workers, can work only a certain number of hours and days before fatigue sets in and they lose their effectiveness. Tradition and civil service rules have established the police officer's working tour (also called the shift or platoon) as eight hours. The traditional police organization separates each day or 24-hour period into three tours (also called shifts, platoons, or watches): a midnight or night tour (shift, platoon, or watch) which generally falls between the hours of 12 midnight and 8 A.M.; a day tour (shift, platoon, watch) which generally falls between the hours of 8 A.M. and 4 P.M.; and an evening tour (shift, platoon, watch) which generally falls between the hours of 4 P.M. and 12 midnight. Shifts or tours do not necessarily have to fall between these exact hours; they can be between any hours, as long as all 24 hours of the day are covered. Some departments have shifts that last longer than eight hours, and they use the overlapping time as training time. Also, some departments use variations of the three-tour system, including two 12-hour tours a day or four 10-hour tours a week. An example of a department using 12-hour tours is the Nassau County (New York) Police Department, which uses a 7 A.M. to 7 P.M. and a 7 P.M. to 7 A.M. tour system. This department and others like it that use 12-hour tours thus have only two platoons as opposed to the traditional three-platoon system.

Table 3.2 shows a duty chart, a schedule of assigned working tours for one year for all members of the New York City Police Department who work steady midnight-to-8 A.M. tours (the first shift, platoon, or watch). The chart is divided into the three squads that work that tour, Squads, 1, 2, and 3. There are other duty charts for the other platoons.

By a quick glance, officers working the first platoon can tell if they are working or off for any day of the year. For example, an officer from Squad 1 or 2 knows he or she is working on January 13 and January 28 (the first box after the word January), whereas an officer from Squad 3 knows he or she is off duty. The number 1 in the box indicates the first platoon. An administrator who wants to know who is working January 1 can immediately tell that Squads 1 and 3 are working and Squad 2 is off.

Officers take these charts very seriously, because they also affect their private lives. For example, Squad 3 has Christmas Day (December 25) off but must be back on duty at midnight after Christmas Day, at 0001 hours, December 26. Squad 3 members will consider themselves very fortunate in that they have the dreaded New Year's Eve off.

Using the traditional three-tour system, it takes three officers to cover each day, one on the night tour, one on the day tour, and one on the evening tour. When days off, vacation time, and sick time are factored into the three-tour system, approximately five officers are required to cover each beat 24 hours a day, 7 days a week, 365 days a year. (Formulas to allocate personnel are available in police organization and management texts.)

Historically, police officers have been allocated evenly during the three tours of duty each day, with equal numbers of officers assigned to each of the tours. However, the academic studies of the police beginning in the 1960s discovered that crime and other police problems do not fit neatly into the three-tour system. Studies indicated that the majority of crime and police problems in the United States

Roll call or briefing is a crucial function in a police agency. Briefings occur at shift change and provide the officers coming on duty with information about what has occurred since their last tour of duty.

Table 3.2	Patrol Duty Chart

	First Platoon Duty Schedule 243 Appearances														
	1	2	3	4	5	6	7	8	9	10	11	12	13	14	15
Squad No. 1	1	1	1	1	1			1	1	1	1	1			
Squad No. 2	1	1				1	1	1	1	1			1	1	1
Squad No. 3															
January	13–28	14–29	15–30	1–16–31	2–17	3–18	4–19	5–20	6–21	7–22	8–23	9–24	10–25	11–26	12–27
February	12–27	13–28	14	15	1–16	2–17	3–18	4–19	5–20	6–21	7–22	8–23	9–24	10–25	11–26
March	14–29	15–30	1–16–31	2–17	3–18	4–19	5–20	6–21	7–22	8–23	9–24	10–25	11–26	12–27	13–28
April	13–28	14–29	15–30	1–16	2–17	3–18	4–19	5–20	6–21	7–22	8–23	9–24	10–25	11–26	12–27
May	13–28	14–29	15–30	1–16–31	2–17	3–18	4–19	5–20	6–21	7–22	8–23	9–24	10–25	11–26	12–27
June	12–27	13–28	14–29	15–30	1–16	2–17	3–18	4–19	5–20	6–21	7–22	8–23	9–24	10–25	11–26
July	12–27	13–28	14–29	15–30	1–16–31	2–17	3–18	4–19	5–20	6–21	7–22	8–23	9–24	10–25	11–26
August	11–26	12–27	13–28	14–29	15–30	1–16–31	2–17	3–18	4–19	5–20	6–21	7–22	8–23	9–24	10–25
September	10–25	11–26	12–27	13–28	14–29	15–30	1–16	2–17	3–18	4–19	5–20	6–21	7–22	8–23	9–24
October	10–25	11–26	12–27	13–28	14–29	15–30	1–16–31	2–17	3–18	4–19	5–20	6–21	7–22	8–23	9–24
November	9–24	10–25	11–26	12–27	13–28	14–29	15–30	1–16	2–17	3–18	4–19	5–20	6–21	7–22	8–23
December	9–24	10–25	11–26	12–27	13–28	14–29	15–30	1–16–31	2–17	3–18	4–19	5–20	6–21	7–22	8–23

Note: 1 = 0001 to 0800 hours. Each tour consists of 8 hours and 35 minutes, as described in Operations Order 105S78.

Source: Courtesy of New York City Police Department.

occurred during the late evening and early morning hours. Many police departments began to change their methods of allocating police personnel. Most now assign their personnel according to the demand for police services, putting more officers on the street during those hours when crime and calls for police officers are highest.

Many departments now distribute patrol officers according to a workload formula based on reported crimes and calls for service. The Dallas Police Department, for example, assigns 43 percent of its officers to the tour from 4 P.M. to midnight, 25 percent to the tour from midnight to 8 A.M., and 32 percent to the tour from 8 A.M. to 4 P.M.[13]

Tour Conditions

Each of the three shifts in the three-tour system has its own characteristics, as any police officer will tell you.

The midnight tour is sometimes called the overnight or the graveyard shift. Most people are sleeping during this time, although in some large cities a good deal of commerce and business occurs. The most common problems for police officers during this tour are disorderly and intox-

icated people at home and on the street, disorderly tavern patrons, commercial burglaries, prostitution, and drug sales. In addition to handling these specific problems, the police provide their normal duties, such as routine patrol, response to emergency calls, aiding the sick and injured, and solving disputes. Generally, the least amount of police activity occurs on this tour, and the lowest number of officers are on duty.

The day tour occurs during the normal business hours in the United States. Stores and offices are open, highway and construction crews are working, and children are in school and at play. The most common activities for police officers during this tour are facilitating the traffic flow and ensuring the safety of those traveling to and from work by enforcing parking and moving violations, ensuring the safety of children walking to and from school and entering and leaving school buses, preventing robberies and other property thefts in commercial areas, and providing other normal police services. Generally, the second-highest amount of police activity occurs on this tour, and the second-largest number of police officers are on duty.

The evening tour is generally the busiest for the police. The work day and school day are over, the sun goes down, and the hours of darkness arrive. During the evening hours, normal adherence to acceptable ways of behavior often gives way to alcohol and drug abuse, fights, and disputes. The most common activities of the evening tour are facilitating traffic for the homeward-bound commuter; dealing with bar fights, violence at home, and violence on the streets; preventing and dealing with street and commercial robberies; and providing normal routine police services. The largest amount of police activity occurs on this tour, and the majority of officers are assigned to it.

Steady (Fixed) Tours

Traditionally, most police departments have assigned their officers to rotating tours of duty: one week of night tours, one week of day tours, and one week of evening tours. Officers' days off rotate to accommodate the three-tour system. This practice has caused tremendous problems for police officers in both their on-duty and off-duty lives. The strain of working a new shift every other week has a negative effect on eating, living, sleeping, and socializing. It creates tremendous levels of stress.

There has been a move in recent years, therefore, to place officers on steady, or fixed, tours of duty, much like most other workers in the United States. Today, officers in many jurisdictions are assigned to steady night tours, day tours, or evening tours based on seniority or the officer's own choice. Police administrators hope that these steady tours will make officers' on-duty and off-duty lives more normal, thus eliminating the many problems created by shift work.

Forst's Law

We're All Working Together

In many police departments a disparity arises between the sworn and nonsworn personnel. Our department was no different. Smart police officers realize how important the support personnel are to their mission. The help you get when you need it from these essential areas of the department can make an officer's life much easier or harder.

Think of the difference it can make when you're running late for a court appearance and need to pick up some crucial evidence or paperwork and the individual who supplies that evidence or paperwork is very busy with lots of people before you. You didn't plan ahead and allow the time for the request that the department requires. If you're on good working terms with that employee, he or she might go out of the way and make the extra effort to help you out so you don't get in trouble. But if, on the other hand, you have treated that employee as a second-class citizen, that will be remembered, and you will wait your turn; no special effort will be made.

During my career I had a few officers who didn't see the relationship between the jobs we were all doing and treated some of the support personnel in a less than equal manner. If I ever saw this behavior, I would sit the officer down, and we'd have a chat about human relations and how we all work together and how these coworkers can make officers look good or bad. Officers usually heeded this advice, but some had to learn the hard way.

I know when I became a patrol captain and went from five years of the midnight shift to working days with 100 people in my division and the politics and events involved with day shift, I relied very heavily on my secretary, Lori. She had been working as the uniform division secretary for many years and had a great depth of knowledge and command of the history of the department. Perhaps she spoiled me, but for any question I asked, she was able to go to the files and pull out a file with all the backup documentation I needed to understand and plan. She was a crucial part of the working of the department, and luckily I had realized her expertise early in my career when I was a sergeant and appreciated all she did. She greatly eased my transition to uniform division captain and contributed to my success in that role.

★ ★ ★

ORGANIZING BY FUNCTION OR PURPOSE

The best way to organize a police department in this way is to place similar functions performed by the police into similar units. Thus, all members of the department performing general patrol duties are placed into a patrol division, whereas all officers performing detective duties are placed into a detective division.

Line and Staff (Support) Functions

Police departments, like all organizations, must be organized by function or purpose. The first and simplest grouping of units or divisions of a department differentiates between line functions and staff (support) functions. Line functions are those tasks that directly facilitate the accomplishment of organizational goals, whereas staff (support) functions are those tasks that supplement the line units in their task performance.

YOU ARE THERE! »

What Cops Do, as Told by Cops

The police department is a service organization, open for business 24 hours a day, 7 days a week. Dial their number, and somebody has to answer, no matter what it is you want. As one officer put it, "People'll [sic] call us for everything. If their toilet runs over, they call the police before they call the plumber." A police officer deals with the desperate, the disturbed, and all those people out there who are just plain lonely in the middle of the night. Their duties put them on intimate terms with the bizarre things people are doing to each other and to themselves behind all the closed doors and drawn shades in the community. While the rest of us look the other way, they cart away the societal offal we don't want to deal with—suicides, drunks, drug addicts, and derelicts. We call it keeping the peace, but the police officer often thinks of him- or herself as society's garbage collector. All smart cops carry a pair of rubber gloves in the car for handling dirt, disease, and death. They use their gloves much more than they use their guns.

Here are some stories cops tell.

The woman who opened the door for me was just a medium-sized female. The thing unique about her was that I could not see either one of her eyes. Her nose no longer existed. And she had a cavernous opening where there would have been a mouth and teeth. Her cheekbones were broken. In my entire career, I had never seen anybody who was so thoroughly battered. I asked her what the problem was and she said, "My husband beat me up." . . . I'm holding him by his left arm, escorting him down in handcuffs. As we stepped through the front door of the building, she tried to bury a twelve-inch butcher knife right between my shoulder blades. Kachunk! She hit me right in the old bulletproof vest. . . . It's human

nature. When I walked in there she was upset because he beat her up so bad. When she saw her true love going out the door with the big bad police hauling him off, then no longer is he the villain. The police is the villain. It just tears your mind up. In spite of all that damage he did to her, she still loved him so much that she wanted me dead as opposed to taking him away.

So it goes, each shift ticked off by one stomach-curdling cup of coffee after another, enlivened only by the knowledge that something hairy just might happen. In those dead hours on the underbelly of the night when the orange glare of streetlights slowly gives way to the dawn, when the worst bar brawler is home in bed or sleeping it off in a cell and the ugliest hooker has made her quota, the hardest part of the job is staying awake until quitting time. By then the cop is running on residual adrenaline alone, struggling to remember that the next wife beater might have a deer rifle, that the next empty warehouse might not be empty after all, that the next underaged driver he stops for speeding might just be crazy enough to poke a pistol in a policeman's face and pull the trigger.

Police work is basically 99 percent pure bull___t, because there is just not that much going on. But it is punctuated by one percent of just sheer terror. And it happens just that quick. That's the reason a lot of policemen keel over from heart attacks, because of all that adrenaline pumping all of a sudden all of the time. Ulcers, too. You ride around for five or six shifts in utter boredom, worried to death about when the next time is going to happen.

Source: From Mark Baker, *Cops: Their Lives in Their Own Words* (New York: Simon & Schuster, 1985), pp. 41–44.

One of the organizational goals of a police department is order maintenance. Thus, the patrol officers who actually patrol the streets to preserve order would be grouped under a patrol unit or patrol division. Another organizational goal of a department is to investigate past crime. Thus, the detectives charged with investigating past crimes would be grouped together under a detective unit or detective division. Patrol and detective units directly facilitate the accomplishment of the organizational goals of a police department; thus, they perform line functions.

Staff (support) functions are those functions of the police department that are not directly related to the organizational goals of the department but nevertheless are necessary to ensure the smooth running of the department. Investigating candidates for police officers, performing clerical work, and handing out paychecks are examples of staff (support) functions.

Police Department Units

Scholars Robert Sheehan and Gary W. Cordner provided an excellent and comprehensive description of the basic tasks of a police department.[14] They describe 30 tasks or duties the police must perform to have an effective police department. They state that in very large police departments, separate units may be established to perform each task. In smaller departments, the tasks may be grouped together in various ways to be performed by certain units or people. Sheehan and Cordner divided the 30 tasks into three subsystems, which are similar to the previously mentioned division of line and staff functions. Their three task subsystems are operations, administration, and auxiliary services. Table 3.3 summarizes the Sheehan and Cordner system of organizing a police department by function or purpose.

OPERATIONAL UNITS   Operations are activities performed in direct assistance to the public. These are the duties most of us think about when we think of police departments, including crime fighting, crime detection, and providing service. Operational units include patrol, traffic, criminal investigations, vice, organized crime, juvenile services, community services, crime prevention, and community relations.

The patrol unit performs the basic mission of the police department: maintaining order, enforcing the law, responding to calls for assistance, and providing services to citizens. Patrol officers, who are usually on auto or foot patrol, are the backbone of the police service. They are the most important people in police service. Police patrol will be the subject of Chapters 7 and 8.

The traffic unit performs traffic control at key intersections and in other heavily traveled areas, enforces the traffic laws, and investigates traffic accidents. The police traffic function will be covered in Chapter 7.

The criminal investigations unit investigates past crimes reported to the police in an effort to identify and apprehend the perpetrators of those crimes. Criminal investigations will be covered in Chapter 7 of this text.

Table 3.3	Organizing a Police Department by Function or Purpose	
Operations	Administration	Auxiliary Services
Patrol	Personnel	Records
Traffic	Training	Communications
Criminal investigations	Planning and analysis	Property
Vice	Budget and finance	Laboratory
Organized crime	Legal assistance	Detention
Juvenile services	Public information	Identification
Community services	Clerical/secretarial	Alcohol testing
Crime prevention	Inspections	Facilities
Community relations	Internal affairs	Equipment
	Intelligence	Supply
		Maintenance

Source: Used with permission from *Introduction to Police Administration*, 2d ed., pp. 114–115. Copyright 1998 Matthew Bender & Company, Inc., a member of the LexisNexis Group. All rights reserved.

The vice unit enforces laws related to illegal gambling, prostitution, controlled substances and other illegal drugs, pornography, and illegal liquor sales.

The organized crime unit investigates and apprehends members of criminal syndicates who profit from continuing criminal enterprises, such as the vice crimes just mentioned, extortion, loan sharking, and numerous other crimes.

The juvenile services unit provides a multitude of services to juveniles, including advice and referral to appropriate social agencies designed to assist youth, particularly youthful offenders. This function also investigates cases of child abuse and neglect.

The community services unit provides a multitude of services to the community, including dispute resolution, crime victim assistance, counseling, and other routine and emergency services. Relationships between the police and the community, including numerous partnership programs between the police and the community, will be covered in Chapters 9 and 10 of this text.

The police crime prevention unit attempts to organize and educate the public on measures people can take alone and with the police to make themselves less vulnerable to crime. Some techniques include target hardening, neighborhood watch programs, and operation identification programs. Crime prevention will be covered in Chapter 9.

The community relations unit attempts to improve relationships between the police and the public so that positive police–community partnerships can develop to decrease crime and improve the quality of life in U.S. neighborhoods. Community relations will be covered in Chapter 9.

ADMINISTRATIVE UNITS   Administration in a police department is defined as those activities performed not in direct assistance to the public but for the benefit of the or-ganization as a whole, usually from 9 A.M. to 5 P.M. five days a week. Administrative units include personnel, training, planning and analysis, budget and finance, legal assistance, public information, clerical/secretarial, inspections, internal affairs, and intelligence.

The personnel unit performs the duties generally associated with corporate personnel departments, including recruiting and selecting candidates for police positions and assigning, transferring, promoting, and terminating police personnel. The training unit provides entry-level training to newly hired recruits and in-service training for veteran officers. Police training is covered in Chapter 4 of this text.

The planning and analysis unit conducts crime analyses to determine when and where crimes occur in order to prevent them. This unit also conducts operational and administrative analysis to improve police operations and the delivery of police services.

The budget and finance unit of the police department is involved in the administration of department finances and budgetary matters, including payroll, purchasing, budgeting, billing, accounting, and auditing. The legal assistance unit provides legal advice to members of the department, including patrol officers.

The public information unit informs the public, through the news media, about police activities, including crime and arrests. This unit also informs the public about methods they can take to reduce their chances of becoming crime victims. The clerical/secretarial unit prepares the necessary reports and documents required to maintain police record keeping.

The inspections unit conducts internal quality control inspections to ensure that the department's policies, procedures, and rules and regulations are being followed. The internal affairs unit investigates corruption and misconduct by officers. Corruption, misconduct, and internal affairs

Dempsey's Law

Becoming a Police Detective/Investigator

Professor Dempsey, I want to become a detective with the city police, but I want to skip the uniform stuff. I want to just become a detective right away.

It doesn't work that way, Frank. Most police departments do not put new people in their detective units. Becoming a detective is a pro-motion from the uniformed patrol police officer, trooper, or deputy sheriff rank. It takes many years of experience and an outstanding record of achievement to be considered for promotion to detective or investigator.

Table 3.4	Staffing of a Police Department by Function and Time								
	Chief	Captain	Lieutenant	Sergeant	Police Officer	Civilian	Coordinators	Crossing Guards	Total
Office of the Chief	1					1			2
Operations Division		1				½			1½
Patrol Bureau									
8–4			1	3	21				25
4–Midnight			1	3	23				27
Midnight–8			1	3	15				19
Detective Bureau									
8–4			1		4				5
4–Midnight					1				1
6–2					1				1
Juvenile Bureau									
8–4			1		2				3
6–2					1				1
Traffic Bureau									
8–4				1	3		2	57	63
4–Midnight					3				3
Midnight–8					2				2
Prosecutions Unit					2				2
Fingerprint and Photography Unit					None full-time				
Administration and Services Division		1	1			½			2½
Planning and Records Bureau					1	2			3
Payroll, Billing and Budget Unit					1				1
Community Services and Training Unit					2				2
Custodial Services						1			1
Total	1	2	6	10	82	5	2	57	165

will be covered in Chapter 12. Finally, the intelligence unit conducts analyses of radical, terrorist, and organized crime groups operating in a police department's jurisdiction.

AUXILIARY SERVICES UNITS   Auxiliary services are defined as activities that benefit other units within the police department, but on a more regular and frequent basis than do administrative activities. Auxiliary services functions are usually available to assist the police officer 24 hours a day. Auxiliary services units include records, communications, property, laboratory, detention, identification, alcohol testing, facilities, equipment, supply, and maintenance.

The records unit of a police department maintains department records, including records of crimes and arrests, statistics and patterns regarding criminal activity, and records of traffic accidents. The communications unit answers incoming calls to the department's 911 telephone lines and assigns police units to respond to emergencies and other requests for police services. Communications will be discussed in Chapter 14 of this book.

The property unit inventories and stores all property coming into the custody of the police, including evidence, recovered property, and towed and recovered vehicles. The laboratory unit examines and classifies seized evidence, including drugs, weapons, and evidence found at crime scenes (for example, fingerprints, fibers, and stains). The police laboratory will be discussed in Chapter 14.

The detention unit provides temporary detention for prisoners awaiting their appearance in court. The identification unit fingerprints and photographs criminals, classifies prints, and maintains identification files. The alcohol testing unit administers driving-while-intoxicated tests for court prosecution.

The facilities unit of a police department maintains buildings designed for police use, such as station houses, offices, and detention facilities. The equipment unit maintains the numerous types of equipment necessary for the department's effective operation. The numerous supplies necessary for the proper operation of the department are purchased by the supply unit. Finally, the maintenance unit keeps all facilities and equipment serviceable.

Table 3.4 shows the breakdown, by rank and assignment, of a police department. By reading the top line of the chart and following it down to the bottom line ("Total"), one can easily see that there are a total of 165 employees in this department, with 82 police officers, 19 ranking officers (1 chief, 2 captains, 6 lieutenants, and 10 sergeants), 5 civilians, 2 coordinators, and 57 crossing guards.

By reading the details under "Police Officers" from the top line down, one can see that 59 of the officers are assigned to the Patrol Bureau (21 to 8 A.M. to 4 P.M. tours, 23 to 4 P.M. to midnight tours, and 15 to midnight to 8 A.M. tours); 6 to the Detective Bureau; 2 to the Juvenile Bureau; 8 to the Traffic Bureau; 2 to the Prosecutions Unit; 1 to the Planning and Records Bureau; 1 to the Payroll, Billing, and Budget Unit; and 2 to the Community Services and Training Unit.

CHAPTER SUMMARY

This chapter described the tremendous complexity involved in a police organization. The discussion covered managerial concepts relating to a police department, such as division of labor, chain of command, span of control, and delegation of responsibility and authority. The chapter described the civil service system, the quasi-military nature of the police, the police rank structure, civilization, police auxiliaries, and police unions and other police affiliations.

The size of the geographic area many police agencies cover forces them to subdivide the area into beats (posts), sectors (zones), precincts, and sometimes divisions. Because of the responsibility of being available 24 hours a day, 7 days a week, the police must employ a three-tour system.

The functions the police are charged with performing are complex and diverse. The primary responsibility of the police is to maintain order, enforce the law, and provide services to citizens. These functions are generally charged to a department's operational units—primarily patrol, criminal investigations, traffic, and community services units. The police also perform administrative duties and auxiliary services.

Learning Check

1. Identify the major managerial concepts that must be considered when organizing a police department.

2. Discuss how police departments exercise their quasi-military nature.

3. Name some ways in which civilianization can benefit a police department.

4. Discuss the special problems that must be dealt with in organizing a police department that operates 7 days a week, 24 hours a day.

5. Identify the backbone of the police department and tell why this is the most important person in police service.

Application Exercise

You have been appointed the new commissioner of the Anycity Police Department. Anycity is a suburban city 60 miles from a major U.S. city; it has a population of 30,000 people and a police department of 100 officers. The major police problems in Anycity are disorderly teens making unnecessary noise at night, parking and traffic problems in Anycity's commercial district during business hours, and daytime residential burglaries.

The former commissioner's assistant informs you that the department has no organizational chart, no written rules and procedures, and "has always done a great job in the past."

Anycity's city manager, however, tells you that the former commissioner was incompetent and that the department is totally disorganized and ineffective. You review the department's personnel records and find that of the 100 officers in the department, 30 percent are patrol officers, 30 percent are detectives, and 40 percent are supervisors. Additionally, the entire department is divided evenly into the three tours of duty.

In view of what you learned in this chapter, would you reorganize the department? Why or why not? If you would reorganize, how would you do it?

Web Exercise

Patrol the Internet and find information on civilian or nonsworn employment opportunities in several police departments of your choice. Select one department and one advertised employment opportunity and prepare a resume and cover letter applying for that position.

Key Concepts

Beat
Blue flu
Chain of command
Civil service system
Civilianization
Community service officers (CSOs)
Lateral transfers
Nonsworn (civilian) members
Platoon
Precinct
Quasi-military organizations
Reserve officer
Span of control
Squad
Sworn members
Unity of command

The Personal Side of Policing

GUEST LECTURE

The Learning Process Continues

MICHELLE BENNETT

Michelle Bennett has worked for the King County Sheriff's Office in Washington State since 1990. She is currently a sergeant supervising school programs, community police centers, and day shift patrol officers. She has a master's degree in psychology and is currently working on her doctorate in education.

March 25, 1991, was my first day on patrol, and as a brand new deputy I was really excited. I'd spent three months in the basic academy, then a month in a postacademy class learning about our department, and finally a week sitting on my hands riding with a seasoned veteran officer, observing what I could. Now, after months of training, I was ready to get into a patrol car and inflict my newfound knowledge of the law on unsuspecting citizens. Little did I know I would be the one learning most of the lessons on that day.

I walked into the precinct roll-call room and was greeted by my first field-training officer, another female deputy. "Hi, I'm Diana," she said and suddenly paused, "How old are you anyway?"

"Twenty-one," I replied excitedly.

She groaned, "Great," then said, "C'mon let's go; it's getting busy out there." I got into the passenger seat of her patrol car. As a first-month deputy, I was told I was not allowed to drive yet. We were immediately dispatched to help an apparently disoriented senior citizen who was wandering around a residential neighborhood. We arrived, and Diana explained that I was to handle this; she would jump in if I needed any help. I put on my best professional face and proceeded to try out my best problem-solving skills as I began to ask this elderly gentleman a series of questions in order to determine where he lived. He ignored me and continued rambling on, not listening to a word I said. He finally turned to look me in the eye. Raising a craggy, wrinkled finger, he pointed to my face and said, "I think you're a little too young to be troubleshooting, Missy!" Diana began laughing behind me as my facade of composure began to fade. Diana finished the questioning, and she was able to locate the man's family.

Okay, so it was my first call. Overall it could have been worse. I could not help my youth; I would just show them all that it was not the age, but the seasoning that mattered. Our second call was an area check for criminal activity in a local park. We walked through a construction site to get into the park and were greeted by the construction workers, "Hey Cagney, Lacey, come arrest me!" "No, come arrest me, will you handcuff me?" "No, come over here and search me!" I was embarrassed and shocked that any person would address a police officer in such a way. We arrived on the scene to find nothing but were greeted on our way back out by another construction worker. "Would you like to share my cupcakes with me, cupcake?" he said as he pulled some Hostess cupcakes out of his lunch box. Diana ignored him and continued walking. "No, thank you," I said politely and ran to catch up with my trainer. "You had better get used to this," she said. "It will get worse."

Next, we took a tour of the precinct area. We drove down the main highway, a street laced with seedy motels, strip bars, and taverns. We came upon a group of juveniles jaywalking across the highway. They turned away quickly when they saw us. "Let's go talk to them," Diana said. "You start, and I'll jump in if you need help." No problem, I thought—two years of college and four months of training, I can handle a group of misguided kids. I began speaking to the youth I felt was the ringleader. He largely ignored what I was saying and began mouthing off to me in an apparent attempt to impress his peers. "Don't you be flippant with me, young man," I said, pointing my finger in his face. Diana interrupted me at that point and finished the questioning, satisfied that we could find nothing on them. We got back into the car, and she turned to me with an incredulous look on her face and said, "'Don't be flippant with me, young man?' Look, I don't even know what 'flippant' means, how in the hell is that kid going to know what it means? You've really got to dumb down, or this isn't going to work! I need a break. Let's get lunch."

We drove to the nearest cozy diner, and I sat immersed in thought about my first day. It was nothing like I thought it was going to be. Respect had to be earned. I had no idea how to talk to people. All of my logical, pragmatic thought processes and problem-solving abilities seemed lost upon the public. To make matters worse, my new bulletproof vest was so tight and uncomfortable that it was hard to breath. I voiced this last concern to Diana. "Well," she said, "you need to get one with boobs built into it." After some clarification, I realized that I had received a male fitted vest from our property management unit, and the female vests actually had a curved chest allowing the female wearer to breathe.

"I'll take care of this first thing tomorrow," I thought to myself. We sat down to eat, and I noticed that it seemed as though everyone in the restaurant was staring at us. Then people started coming up to us, asking questions while we were trying to enjoy the meal. "This is why I usually get food to go and sit behind a building somewhere," Diana said. I thought about that for a minute . . . wow, here we were public servants, yet we were hiding from the people we were supposed to be serving? It would take me years to understand that concept.

Our next call was a three-car accident blocking the roadway. Upon our arrival, I learned the importance of multitasking at a scene. Who needs aid? Who will block the roadway? Who will call the tow trucks? When do we get the driver's

information, and how do we write the report? As all of these things were running through my mind, things got even worse when I realized the driver who caused the accident was intoxicated. I performed field sobriety tests and decided to take the driver into custody. I told her she was under arrest. I soon realized it was a big mistake (and was duly chastised) not to handcuff her first. Suddenly, the fight was on. I could not believe someone would actually fight with a police officer. Weren't we there to protect the public? Were we not there to help and serve? Did we not command the respect of all those we dealt with? After all, we had guns! I utilized my newly learned defensive tactics and techniques to put the woman into custody as we struggled. Diana yelled for me to call for backup, and I did as I was instructed. A few days later I was given a private speech from a male officer warning me about how it sounds when female officers call for backup. He told me to not do it too often, as the men will think I can't handle myself (another lesson it took me years to unlearn). However, before backup arrived, Diana and I were able to subdue the extremely drunk and agitated woman. The woman hurled every nasty name in the book at me . . . another huge shock. "Get used to it," Diana said. "Drunk women always want to fight female officers." Over the course of my career, I realized how true her statement was. In my 13 years of police work, approximately 85 percent of all of my physical confrontations have been with women; and, of those, approximately 84 percent of those women were under the influence of an intoxicating substance.

We drove back to the precinct and finished the case report and booking information on our arrested female. It was then I learned another important fact about police work. For every two minutes of excitement on the job, there are at least two hours of paperwork. We spent the rest of our shift completing all of the paperwork from our DUI accident, and I ended up staying late trying to get things done. "I'm going home," Diana said. "See you tomorrow, and we'll start all over again."

I could barely sleep that night, just thinking about the day's events. I wrote everything down in a journal just to get my thoughts out on paper. I was excited about the job, but it was so different from what my perceptions had been. It was so real and exciting, yet at times so tedious, difficult, embarrassing, and dangerous. To me, as a woman, it seemed like there was a whole set of unwritten rules and lessons that I had yet to learn. I have learned and will continue to discover many of those lessons for years to come. I started my first day thinking about all the things I had to teach people and all the knowledge I could impart about the law. In the end, I discovered little of the job had to do with the law; it had to do with people, emotion, respect, and wisdom. The learning process continues . . .

Becoming a Police Officer

CHAPTER

4

CHAPTER OUTLINE

Finding Information on Jobs in Policing
The Recruitment Process
The Job Analysis
The Selection Process
    Characteristics of Good Police Officers
    Guidelines for the Selection Process
    Written Entrance Examination
    Oral Interview
    Psychological Appraisal
    Polygraph Examination
    Medical Examination
    Physical Agility Test
    Smoking
    Background Investigation
Standards in Police Selection
    Physical Requirements
    Age Requirements
    Education Requirements
    Prior Drug Use
    Criminal Record Restrictions
    Residency Requirements
    Sexual Orientation
The Police Training Process
    Recruit Training
    Firearms Training
    In-Service, Management, and Specialized Training
    Training for the Police Corps
    Community Policing Training
    Probationary Period

CHAPTER GOALS

- To show you where you can find information on jobs in law enforcement
- To make you aware of the police selection process
- To acquaint you with the standards that must be met to be accepted for employment as a police officer
- To give you a sense of the type of individuals police departments are interested in employing
- To acquaint you with the police academy training, field training, community policing training, and probationary periods required in many police departments

Becoming a police officer is very different from obtaining most other jobs in the United States. The men and women applying for police jobs in the United States must be carefully screened to determine if they have the necessary attributes for this challenging position. Why? Because we trust these individuals with our liberty and safety. We give them guns and enormous discretion.

Many reading this textbook are interested in becoming police officers. Some want to become officers because it is a secure job with a good salary and good benefits. Some are attracted to police work because they find the work exciting or because of the opportunity to help others. When police officer candidates are asked why they are looking for a police officer position, they often cite these reasons. Additionally, it has been found that the new generation of police recruits' work values have shifted. These new candidates value their active participation in the workplace. They are less compelled by loyalty to a company or organization and do not want to be limited to taking orders and adhering to strict job duties. They want to actively participate in their work role and want work that is meaningful and in which they feel valued. They want to be actively involved in the decision-making processes at the workplace.[1] Many are realizing that the police role can fill these requirements.

This chapter is designed to show how the average person begins a police career. It will discuss the recruitment process, the job analysis, the selection process, standards (necessary qualifications to become a police officer), the police training process, and the probationary period. The chapter contains several highlighted boxes giving the latest possible examples of standards, testing procedures, and requirements for selected police departments.

Today's officer is better educated, better trained, and more representative of the entire community than ever before. Educational levels have risen; training programs have improved; and there are more African American, Hispanic, other minority, and female police officers than in the past.[2]

For many years, stereotypes have existed about police officers. The dominant stereotypes have fallen into two basic categories, both essentially undesirable. The negative stereotype views officers as uneducated, poorly trained, biased and prejudiced, violence prone, and corrupt. The positive stereotype views them as heroic saints who risk their lives in the face of hostility from the public, the media, and the courts.[3] Some police officers probably fall into these two stereotypes, but most do not. Most police officers are like people everywhere: some good, some bad, but all human.

★ ★ ★
FINDING INFORMATION ON JOBS IN POLICING

Where do you find information about available jobs in policing or criminal justice in general? There are many sources. One possible source is media advertising. Many police departments today are recruiting through radio, television, and newspaper advertising. Civil service publications are another source. Many large cities have weekly or monthly civil service newspapers on sale in local stores. These newspapers carry information regarding openings in civil service jobs, and some even carry advertisements for courses to help you prepare for civil service exams.

Many cities have an office in their city hall or other government buildings that contains up-to-date job information on civil service jobs. You can also easily obtain information regarding the next police entrance examination or other information regarding the police by visiting or calling the local police station or headquarters. Many police departments, in an effort to recruit college-educated men and women, participate in college job fairs. Additionally, many high school career days include representatives from local police departments or other criminal justice agencies.

Another source of information on jobs in policing is national publications. Appendix A of this text, on our Web site at http://cj.wadsworth.com/dempsey_intro3e/, contains subscriber information for numerous publications that list police jobs and other criminal justice jobs in the United States. Searching the Internet for "law enforcement job opportunities" results in numerous Web sites with links to job listings. The U.S. Department of Labor Web site at www.bls.gov/oco/ocos160.htm also provides job descriptions and responsibilities for various law enforcement positions.

Word-of-mouth advertising by family members and friends is a common way people receive information about jobs in policing and criminal justice.

Many police departments view their current officers as effective recruiters. Through their daily interactions with citizens they come into contact with individuals they may view as good officer candidates. They can informally provide valuable information to these individuals and perhaps start them on their way to a law enforcement career. Some departments even provide financial incentives to officers who recruit successful candidates.

Today, one of the best and easiest ways to obtain information on jobs in law enforcement is the Internet. Most police departments have their own sites on the Web that include employment information among other information provided to the public. Most departments provide information on their requirements and the hiring process. Many address frequently asked questions, give advice on training for the physical agility portion of the test, and provide contact information for further clarification. The Internet provides a time-saving and nonthreatening way of obtaining information about a law enforcement career. There are also Web sites for private enterprises that have assumed the testing role for many smaller law enforcement agencies in various regions of the country. They also provide current information regarding their process and requirements. Finally, many colleges and universities have intern programs, in which students work for a local government agency for a semester while earning college credit. These programs are valuable for two reasons: (1) Students see firsthand what working in a particular agency is like and thus are better equipped to make well-informed decisions regarding future career plans; and (2) students may obtain inside information regarding job opportunities that may not be available to the general public.

★ ★ ★

THE RECRUITMENT PROCESS

According to Robert Sheehan and Gary W. Cordner, police departments seem to discourage applicants from applying. Sheehan and Cordner also point to the low esteem in

which police are held in some communities and the fictitious television image of the police as other factors that discourage qualified applicants from applying for police jobs.[4]

Some potential candidates may have negative images of police, while others may perceive the physical attributes as being beyond their reach. Since 9/11, the law enforcement occupation has been more favorably viewed; and, as the media focused on the heroes who served on 9/11, many realized they were everyday people with a desire to help and contribute to society. With dedication and hard work these individuals had attained their goals.

To attract more qualified candidates, particularly among minority groups, the Commission on Accreditation for Law Enforcement Agencies has recommended a number of standards that departments should adhere to regarding recruiting candidates for selection as police officers. Among these standards are

1. Individuals assigned to recruitment activities for a law enforcement agency should be knowledgeable in personnel matters, especially **equal opportunity employment regulations** and **affirmative action regulations** that affect the management and operations of the agency. Equal employment opportunity regulations are designed to ensure that members of minority groups are treated equally with members of dominant groups. These regulations should ensure that race, gender, ethnicity, and religion will not affect a person's chances of being hired or promoted. Affirmative action regulations are designed to achieve a ratio of minority group employees in approximate proportion to their makeup in the population of a locality, as well as to remedy past discriminatory employment and promotional practices. These concepts will be discussed at length in Chapter 13.

2. The law enforcement agency should seek recruitment assistance, referrals, and advice from community organizations and leaders.

3. The agency should have an equal employment opportunity plan.

4. The agency should advertise as an equal opportunity employer on all employment applications and recruitment advertisements.

5. The agency's recruitment literature, if any, should depict women and minorities in law enforcement roles.[5]

©PhotoEdit

Police cadets engage in a physical training drill at the academy. Why is this training important? Should it continue once officers are hired and working the streets?

Successful police recruiters recruit in high schools and colleges, among other places. In an effort to attract minorities, many departments recruit at predominantly minority colleges in their region. Recruiters also often attend church gatherings and women's shows to reach others who may not have considered a law enforcement career. Also, numerous departments throughout the United States use the local media (especially television and radio) to recruit for their examinations.

Rapid changes in U.S. demographics have made the recruiting of minorities for police careers more essential than ever before. The U.S. Census Bureau predicts that by 2050 minority populations will be 49.9 percent of the population. Hispanics will comprise approximately 25 percent, African Americans 15 percent, and Asians 8 percent of the population.[6]

Police departments in the United States, however, have had problems hiring qualified minority group members in a way that properly represents the racial, ethnic, and gender makeup of the community. Chapter 13 of this text shows how women, African Americans, Hispanic Americans, and other minorities have used the federal courts and affirmative action programs to enter law enforcement positions and move up through the ranks.

In addition to the racial and ethnic changes occurring in the United States, the age of the population is changing, and the percentage of the population between the ages of 16 and 24 (the ages traditionally recruited from for police jobs) is declining. According to the U.S. Census Bureau, by 2050 the percentage of Americans age 65 and over will increase from 12 to 21 percent. Ralph S. Osborn, in a 1992 *FBI Law Enforcement Bulletin,* wrote that because of the changing demographics just discussed, "Recruitment strategies of the past will not be sufficient to provide agencies with quality applicants."[7] Osborn makes a number of recommendations that departments may implement to improve recruitment efforts:

1. Try to understand the values of the current entry-level applicants and make changes in the department that will encourage these people to take pride in the department and have a sense of belonging in it.

2. Improve the retention of current officers by understanding the wants, needs, and desires of employees, thus decreasing the need to do so much recruiting.

3. Examine the department's employee benefits package to determine whether it addresses issues that are important to women. During the next ten years, two of every three employees in all occupations will be women, and the police will need to obtain their fair share of them.

4. Increase recruitment in high schools, colleges, and the military.

5. Increase programs for young people, including police cadet and explorer programs. Allow youths to take the police entrance exam; the knowledge of a good career ahead may help young people stay out of trouble.

6. Develop programs aimed at changing traditional ethnic community attitudes toward law enforcement careers by showing newly arrived minority group members that the U.S. police are interested in providing services to them rather than in oppressing them, which may have occurred in their home countries.[8]

In recent years, a number of factors have resulted in better and more efficient police recruitment. The depressed job market in some areas has made the security of a police career particularly inviting; the growing numbers of criminal justice programs in colleges and universities have attracted a pool of educated young people seeking careers in law enforcement. The media attention to the heroes of 9/11 has also increased interest among young people for a law enforcement career. Additionally, the development of a competitive salary structure, as well as the addition of educational pay incentives, has provided new officers annual starting salaries in the range of $35,000 to $40,000 a year.

In recent years, law enforcement agencies around the country have found themselves in the unusual position of having to compete among themselves as well as with the private sector to fill vacancies. This has led to departments reexamining their employment requirements as well as employing new and smarter recruitment techniques. These techniques included signing bonuses to obtain new recruits and increased salaries to keep officers and reduce turnover. Agencies are conducting more targeted advertising as well as recruiting trips across the country, targeting lateral transfers and emphasizing the benefits as well as the quality of life in their jurisdiction. In Boca Raton, Florida, the "Guess Who's Coming to Dinner?" campaign received national attention and response after announcing that Chief Andrew Scott or another high-ranking police official would bring dinner and a pitch for the job to the candidate's home. The campaign was paid for by donations from a business in town. Boynton Beach, Florida, advertised heavily in the northeast United States in ads that included pictures of the "Boynton Beach Snowman," which was a puddle of water on the beach.[9] Duane L. West, of the Tallahassee, Florida, Police Department writes of the new procedures used by his department in aggressively recruiting a diverse group of officers who meet the highest standards both personally and educationally and who are also

Increased competition among law enforcement agencies for qualified candidates has inspired innovative recruiting techniques. The Boca Raton, Florida, police department has initiated the "Guess Who's Coming to Dinner?" campaign, in which Chief Andrew Scott or another high-ranking police official brings dinner and a job pitch to a candidate's home.

representative of the community they may serve. He reports that hiring benchmarks have been established based on both race and gender to ensure that the department mirrors the community's ethnic and gender demographics.[10]

★ ★ ★

THE JOB ANALYSIS

Before the selection process for new members can actually begin, a police department must know what type of person it is interested in hiring. To determine this, the department must first decide what type of work is done by officers and then determine the type of person who would be most qualified to do that type of work. This **job analysis** identifies the important tasks that must be performed by police officers and then identifies the knowledge, skills, and abilities necessary to perform those tasks.

In the past, women and members of minority groups were rejected from police departments because they didn't meet certain standards, such as height, weight, and strength requirements. A good job analysis can avoid that situation by measuring what current police officers in a department actually do. From this study, the department then

can establish the standards and qualifications necessary for its officers to perform the needed duties.

If a competent job analysis is performed, the knowledge, skills, and abilities necessary for performance in that department are judged to be **job related**. If a certain qualification is deemed to be job related, that requirement can withstand review by the courts, and the specific test measuring for that knowledge or those skills or abilities is nondiscriminatory.

The case of ***Guardians Association of New York City Police Department* v. *Civil Service Commission of New York*** (1980) is a landmark appellate court decision regarding the job analysis.[11] In this case, the federal courts accepted the job analysis of the New York City Department of Personnel and the New York City Police Department. Two researchers have outlined these departments' procedures in preparing the job analysis, which were considered to be nondiscriminatory.

First, the Department of Personnel identified 71 tasks that police officers generally perform; the department based the choice of tasks on interviews with 49 officers and 49 supervisors. Second, a panel of seven officers and supervisors reviewed the list of tasks in order to add any tasks that might have been omitted and to eliminate duplicate tasks and tasks not performed by entry-level officers. Certain tasks were combined, and some were added or deleted. This process resulted in a final list of 42 tasks commonly performed by entry-level police officers. Third, a questionnaire was sent to 5,600 officers requesting them to rate each of the 42 tasks on the basis of frequency of occurrence, importance, and the amount of time normally spent on performing the task. The 2,600 responses received were analyzed by computer to yield a ranking of the 42 tasks. The ranking was confirmed by observations made by professors from the John Jay College of Criminal Justice in New York City. Next, the Department of Personnel divided the list of 42 ranked tasks into clusters of related activities. Each one of the clusters was then analyzed by a separate panel of police officers to identify the **knowledge, skills, and abilities (KSAs)** for the cluster as a whole.[12] KSAs are a shortened way to indicate the knowledge, skills, and abilities needed to do police work. Candidates are not expected to know how to do police work, but they must have the KSAs to learn how to perform the duties of the profession. Some KSAs are the ability to read, write, reason, memorize facts, and communicate with others. Additional KSAs include physical ability, such as physical agility and endurance. The fact that this job analysis and the entrance examination based on it successfully passed the court's examination of job relatedness shows that a police department must carefully construct its entrance examinations based on the duties actually performed by police officers.

★ ★ ★

THE SELECTION PROCESS

Becoming a police officer is much more difficult than getting a job as a security officer in a retail store. The **police selection process** is lengthy, difficult, and competitive. The police selection process is a series of examinations, interviews, and investigative steps designed to select the best candidate to appoint to a police department from the many who apply. Many practitioners relate that in many agencies only 1 out of 100 applicants makes it into the employment ranks.

According to the Bureau of Justice Statistics, municipal police agencies utilized the following screening procedures:[13]

- Written aptitude testing (43 percent)
- Personal interview (96 percent)
- Physical agility (44 percent)
- Polygraph exam ((21 percent)
- Voice stress analyzer (2 percent)
- Psychological evaluation (61 percent)
- Drug testing (67 percent)
- Medical exam (81 percent)
- Background investigation (96 percent)

The report also indicated that the percentage of departments utilizing the screening methods increased significantly as the size of the department increased.

According to their Web site, the Madison, Wisconsin, Police Department has numerous recruiting and hiring goals. They seek men and women who reflect the diversity of their community. They want to recruit applicants who can communicate effectively both verbally and in writing. They also seek individuals who are committed to improving the quality of life and who can enforce the law while protecting the constitutional rights of all (www.ci.madison .wi.us). Though positions are open to individuals over 18 by state law, Madison finds that the most successful applicants tend to have an average age of 27 or 28 and have previous work experience in various professions.

Applicants fill out an extensive application form, and after it is reviewed they are invited to take a written exam testing reading comprehension, vocabulary, and the ability to organize thoughts and communicate them on paper.

After the successful completion of the written test, an internal review panel will determine which applicants will proceed further in the process. These candidates will continue on to the physical agility exam, and the internal panel will then reconvene and determine which applicants will proceed to the oral interview in front of a panel.

The remaining steps include a thorough background investigation, an interview with the Chief of Police, a ride along with a Field Training Officer, a personality assessment, and other interviews with departmental personnel. Eventually a conditional job offer will be made to the selected candidates, which will be followed by a thorough medical exam conducted at city expense. For out-of-town applicants, Madison tries to condense some of these steps to minimize the cost and time to the applicant.

Timothy N. Oettmeier, of the Houston, Texas, Police Department, recently discussed the selection process in view of the increasing adoption of the community policing philosophy throughout the United States. He warned that departments must not radically change existing approaches to selecting the right personnel to adapt to this innovative policing philosophy; a commitment to community policing does not necessarily mean a department must make radical changes to its selection procedures. In fact, before implementing any changes, department members should reach consensus about an officer's role and responsibilities in a community-based department.[14] He recommends departments take the following four general steps before restructuring the selection process for community policing:

1. Redefine the role of the officer.
2. Reevaluate knowledge, skills, and abilities.
3. Place a new emphasis on marketing police positions.
4. Proceed with caution.

The Community Policing Consortium addresses this issue on their Web site (www.communitypolicing.org). They believe there are efforts that can be undertaken by agencies that will facilitate hiring individuals with talents geared toward community polcing and that these efforts will benefit overall police hiring as well. The organization believes that education and experience should be stressed. This would include having educational requirements in place, providing tuition reimbursement, recruiting more mature applicants, and removing artificial boundaries such as residency requirements. They emphasize the use of psychological exams coupled with thorough background investigations and the use of good job analysis and assessment centers to screen applicants. The more an applicant can be evaluated based on performance in realistic situations, the better the

YOU ARE THERE! >>

Fort Lauderdale, Florida, Police Officer Examination Process

The city of Fort Lauderdale receives a large number of police officer applications, both local and out-of-state. Written and physical agility tests are conducted on a weekly basis through the Criminal Justice Testing Center at Broward Community College. The following list represents the testing process and order of testing:

1. Written test; 40 percent of final score
2. Oral interview; 60 percent of final score (minimum score of 70 required)
3. Polygraph examination; pass/fail
4. Basic motor skills test (administered by the Criminal Justice Testing Center); pass/fail
5. Psychological examination; pass/fail
6. Background investigation; pass/fail
7. Medical examination, including drug screen; pass/fail
8. Swim test (administered by the Criminal Justice Testing Center); pass/fail

WRITTEN TEST

Noncertified candidates are responsible for taking the Criminal Justice Basic Aptitude Test (CJBAT) for Law Enforcement Officer prior to their application being submitted. The written test covers topics such as written comprehension and expression, inductive and deductive reasoning, information ordering, and visualization.

PRELIMINARY BACKGROUND INVESTIGATION

This may be conducted for applicants who pass the written exam. The focus of the investigation will include, but not be limited to, verification of education and training, previous employment and work history, driving history, arrest and conviction record, and past or present use of drugs. Discrepancies found in the background investigation from information given at any other point in the selection process will be grounds for disqualification from the process.

PHYSICAL AGILITY TEST

Noncertified applicants are responsible for taking the Basic Motor Skills Test (agility) prior to their application being submitted. The agility test includes: trigger pull, long jump, vehicle push, half-mile run, and a job-task course, which includes high wall, ladder/platform/ramp, fixed railing, chain link fence, window, door, fixed railing, maze, tunnel, overhead ladder, rope grid, log, parallel bars, low wall, and pole run. Further description can be obtained at their Web site: http://ci.ftlaud.fl.us/police. Additionally, while in the academy each trainee must demonstrate proficiency in pull-ups, push-ups, sit-ups, treadmill, bend and twist, squat thrust, half-mile run, and obstacle course. Levels are detailed on their Web site.

ORAL INTERVIEW

Once a candidate's application has been approved, he or she will be mailed official notification to schedule an oral board examination. The applicant must bring required, completed paperwork to the interview. A three-member panel consisting of two ranking officers from the police department and one human resources representative will rate applicants in a formally structured interview. The applicant will be rated on characteristics important to the police officer position, including command presence, integrity, initiative/interest, communication skills, tolerance for stress, judgment, and decisiveness.

MEDICAL EXAMINATION

Prior to being hired, applicants must successfully complete a medical examination by the city of Fort Lauderdale's licensed physician. Candidates will be required to meet specified body-fat standards along with height/weight requirements. A drug screen is part of this examination.

VISION REQUIREMENTS

Applicants must be free from color blindness and have no permanent abnormality of either eye; they must have at least 20/100 vision in each eye without correction (glasses or contacts) and must have 20/30 vision in each separately with correction.

SWIM TEST

Applicants must swim 50 yards (any recognized stroke).

Source: Fort Lauderdale, Florida, Police Department, 2003; http://ci.ftlaud.fl.us/police/

chance of hiring individuals with the desired flexibility and interpersonal skills. This would be good for law enforcement in general and community policing specifically.

Characteristics of Good Police Officers

What are the "right characteristics" police administrators should look for when selecting future police officers? There have been a number of efforts to determine the specific criteria that predict future police performance, including a comprehensive analysis by Allan and Norma Roe.[15]

The Roes' data were reanalyzed and simplified in a subsequent study by researchers Bernard Cohen and Jan Chaiken.[16] Cohen and Chaiken found that performance on written civil service entrance tests was the best predictor of subsequent police performance. They identified this police performance as arrest activity, investigative skills, evidence gathering, and crime scene management. They also found that performance on written civil service exams was associated with future supervisory ratings and career advancement. Thus, the Cohen and Chaiken study indicates that police candidates who score best on written entrance exams become better police officers in terms of arrest and investigative activity, are seen as better officers by their supervisors, and have more successful careers. Cohen and Chaiken found that other factors, such as oral interviews, prior work experience, numerical ability, intelligence quotient (IQ), age, and education, also may predict above average performance as a police officer. They also found that unsatisfactory police performance was observed in officers with low educational levels, prior work problems, and poor probationary periods.[17]

It is interesting to note that Cohen and Chaiken had conducted an earlier study, in 1973, examining the background characteristics of 1,608 New York City police officers in an attempt to correlate these background characteristics with the officers' subsequent performance. These background characteristics included race, age, IQ, father's occupation, previous job history, exam score, recruit training score, military record, marital status, education, criminal record, and others, for a total of 39 factors. None appeared to predict subsequent performance except for the individual's recruit training score, which Cohen and Chaiken found was one of the most powerful and consistent predictors of later police performance.[18]

The inconsistencies among the two Cohen and Chaiken studies and numerous other studies indicate the difficulty of predicting the future job performance of police officers and, thus, the difficulty in finding suitable measurement or selection tests.

YOU ARE THERE! >>

Florida Highway Patrol Qualifications

ENTRANCE-LEVEL REQUIREMENTS

- U.S. citizenship
- At least 19 years of age at the time of employment
- High school diploma or GED and one of the following:
  - One year of sworn or nonsworn law enforcement experience
  - Two years of active and continuous military service
  - Two years of public contact experience
  - Successful completion of 30 semester hours or 45 quarter hours at an accredited college or university
- Minimum corrected vision of 20/30 in each eye, minimum field of vision of 140 degrees
- Weight in proportion to height

SELECTION PROCESS

- Application
- Written examination
- Physical abilities test
- Polygraph examination
- Eye and medical examination
- Psychological screening
- Drug screening
- Background investigation

Candidates who are eliminated from the selection process may be able to reapply after 12 months, depending on the reason(s) for rejection.

Source: Florida Highway Patrol, 2003; www.fhp.state.fl.us

Another researcher, Hrand Saxenian, a former professor at the Harvard Business School and a management consultant, also attempted to find which personal qualities eventually make a successful police officer. Saxenian determined that maturity is the single most important criterion in the selection process. He has attempted, with some success, to measure maturity by determining "the extent to which a man expresses his own feeling and convictions, with consideration for the thoughts and feelings of others."

In an experiment conducted with a state police agency, Saxenian, using his own unique system for determining maturity, interviewed the 50 recruits in the 12-week police academy. Each recruit was interviewed for a half hour. The recruits were then ranked from 1 to 50 based on Saxenian's system of measurement. At the end of the recruit training, the staff of the academy ranked the recruits from 1 to 50 based on overall performance. The two sets of rankings were remarkably similar and statistically showed a high rate of correlation. Several years later, follow-up studies verified the statistical validity of Saxenian's findings. Those recruits identified by Saxenian as being the most mature were overwhelmingly the best officers.[19]

Despite these studies and probably many more studies in the future, the major difficulty in attempting to determine what characteristics make the best officer is the definition of the term *best officer*. Who is the best officer? The one who makes the most arrests, or the one with the best record in promoting goodwill in the community by doing such things as organizing local youths and forming after-school recreational programs?

With the expansion of the community policing philosophy, the emphasis continues to be on the importance of attracting and hiring ethical individuals who are capable of making good decisions, keeping a cool head, acting independently, and communicating with all types of people in a positive and effective manner. Police organizations and private companies are exploring ways to best test for these skills before actually hiring an individual. One company used by law enforcement around the country and with a presence on the Internet is the Behavioral Personnel Assessment Device (B-PAD) Group (www.bpad.com). The company states that their product assesses judgment and human relations skills and results in no "adverse impact" in the hiring process Candidates for a position watch a series of video simulations and respond verbally as if they were at the scene. Their responses are videotaped and scored using validated criteria. This results in a court-defensible test, according to the company. This type of process, like assessment centers, allows agencies to see how a candidate performs in realistic situations.

Guidelines for the Selection Process

According to the Bureau of Justice Statistics (2003) and the U.S. Department of Labor, and as can be observed by perusing law enforcement Web sites, despite the difficulties in predicting which characteristics produce the best police

---

YOU ARE THERE! »

Indiana State Police Qualifications

BASIC ELIGIBILITY REQUIREMENTS

1. Must be a United States citizen

2. Must be at least 21 and a maximum of 34 years old when appointed as a police employee

3. Eye requirement: correctable to 20/50

4. Must possess a valid driver's license

5. Must be willing, if appointed, to reside and serve anyplace within the state of Indiana

6. Applicants must have completed at least 60 semester or 90 quarter hours of credit from an accredited college or university and have at least a 2.0 grade point average based on a 4.0 grading scale and evidenced by a certified transcript, or possess a high school diploma or GED, plus one of the following: at least three years' full-time accredited successful (sworn) law enforcement experience having graduated from a state accredited police academy, or at least two years'

successful, active, military duty, honorably discharged or currently serving at the rank or E-4 (or its equivalent) or above in a U.S. military service

SELECTION PROCESS

1. Submission of completed application form

2. Written test

3. Oral interview

4. Polygraph/psychological tests

5. Physical ability test

6. Background investigation

7. Fitness examination/psychological examination

8. Superintendent's review

Source: Indiana State Police Web site, 2003; www.ai.org/isp/career

officers, most police departments in the United States use a combination of some of the following selection techniques in their selection process: written entrance examinations, oral interviews, psychological appraisals, polygraph examinations, medical examinations, physical agility tests, and background investigations. A candidate must pass each and every stage of the testing process before being appointed as a police officer. The multiple testing process, which will be described in detail later, is designed to weed out all but the best possible candidates for police work and has proven to be very competitive in most agencies. Once a candidate fails to qualify on the medical, psychological, or background investigation, he or she is dropped from the list and is no longer considered.[20]

A crucial element of the police selection process is that each step is court defensible and has validity to the job performance of a police officer. Under EEOC guidelines, "adverse impact" or a different rate of selection occurs when the selection rate for any gender, race, or ethnic group is less than 80 percent of the selection rate for the group with the highest selection rate. If "adverse impact" is noted and the test or selection criteria can not be shown to be valid, the EEOC would classify the test as impermissible discrimination.[21] This could result in legal problems for a police agency.

In addition to uniformed or sworn members of law enforcement agencies, nonsworn or civilian members of many departments—for example, 911 operators and dispatchers—often receive preemployment screening similar to that of police officers.

Written Entrance Examination

A police department's written entrance examination is usually a pen-and-pencil test administered in schools or police facilities near prospective candidates' homes. Some departments test at regular intervals, such as once a year or once every four years; other departments test continually as candidates appear.

Larry K. Gaines and his fellow researchers have stated that the written examination is the hurdle that screens out the most applicants and that has been the subject of most court litigation.[22] Many minority groups have claimed that most written entrance exams are discriminatory and biased. To reduce claims of discrimination, many innovative tests have been designed to eliminate bias. Some testing professionals argue that most written police tests used to screen large numbers of entry-level candidates are incapable of bringing in the right types of applicants and culling from the field those who are ill-suited to perform

the duties of today's police officer, because these exams primarily test for cognitive abilities, rather than common sense. Stephen A. Lazer argues for better testing. Finding the perfect testing instrument may be a futile search, but seeking to improve existing tools is a worthy endeavor. Testing for common sense and public service orientation will go a long way toward identifying candidates who can cope with the demands placed on those ultimately selected to serve and protect. While no one test can do everything, entry-level law enforcement tests aimed at measuring more than just cognitive abilities are much needed and are likely to be well received in the future.[23]

Some new tests incorporate features to eliminate bias and screen for common sense. Some have culturally equivalent language—language that does not discriminate against people on the basis of their cultural background. This change allows African Americans to perform better than they did on the standard tests. Some measure candidates' ability to take quick and reasonable action in stressful situations, with correct answers determined by analyzing responses given by experienced, qualified police officers. Some tests provide candidates with job-related materials—memos, reports, and procedural guides—and ask them to make decisions on the basis of these materials.[24] Additionally, some of the new exams use nonwritten group exercises that have candidates interact with one another in problem-solving situations. Candidates are asked to participate in role plays that involve the need for leadership, problem-solving, and conflict-resolution skills.

Many departments use tests specifically developed for the police selection process. Most of these new tests are administered through the use of computer simulations or assessment centers. Law enforcement agencies either purchase these systems, contract with private providers, or turn the testing or certain aspects of the testing over to a private enterprise with the cost to be absorbed by the applicant. Many departments have found the testing process to be costly, time consuming, and legally challenging. They have also found that applicants are willing to absorb the cost of testing, especially when it results in less inconvenience to the applicant. Consequently, private enterprises have arisen to fill this niche and provide legally defensible consolidated testing for many agencies (typically smaller agencies) within a region. One such company, Public Safety Testing (www.publicsafetytesting.com), provides written and physical agility testing for many agencies throughout Washington and Idaho. Their Web site stresses the convenience for applicants, including convenient testing venues with one application, one written test, and one physical agility test, which may be accepted by more than one agency. The company will then send the applicant's scores to all the agencies they want to pursue.

Oral Interview

The oral interview in the police selection process can be conducted by a board of ranking officers, a psychologist, the police chief, or an investigator. There often are multiple oral boards or interviews conducted by numerous representatives of the department. The goal is to solicit input from many stakeholders in the organization and to minimize the chance of a personality conflict that might result in an applicant being kept out of the selection pool. The oral interview may merely discuss the candidate's application and background or may be used to test the candidate's ability to deal with stressful situations. The oral board is a more structured and court defensible process than an unstructured one-on-one oral interview. Generally, the oral board will consist of at least three members of the department who develop specific, standardized questions. All candidates are asked the same questions and rated on their responses.

Psychological Appraisal

Psychological testing has become very important in the police selection process. Job-related stress is a major health problem, especially in law enforcement. There is a need for a thorough background investigation, along with a comprehensive psychological-psychiatric evaluation, in order to eliminate candidates with psychiatric problems, personality disorders, problems with impulse control, substance abuse, or questionable character. The Minnesota Multiphasic Personality Inventory (MMPI) and the California Personality Inventory (CPI) are administered to prospective police recruits in California and other states, as well as in some foreign countries, including Canada. These instruments measure personality dimensions, such as anxiety, sociability, personal adjustment, and social adjustment.[25] Police departments use these tests to screen out applicants who have maladjusted or problem personalities.[26]

Larger police departments often use sophisticated screening devices, such as the Wechsler Adult Intelligence Scale–Revised (WISC–R), to measure intelligence. They use the Inwald Personality Inventory (IPI), as well as the CPI and the MMPI, to evaluate personality structure and determine whether recruits have any disorders that would adversely affect their functioning.[27] Some research has indicated that these tests, taken independently or used together with clinical interviews, can often be valid predictors of future police performance.[28] However, there is a continuing debate on the effectiveness of psychological testing. Some researchers report a growing consensus that psychological testing can determine the emotional and psychological fitness of recruits. Unfortunately, psychologists and psychiatrists often do not agree on what makes a good

Jacksonville, Illinois, police academy students role play a domestic violence call. Why is role play being used increasingly in preservice training?

police officer. Therefore, they do not agree on what they are looking for in the prospective police officer, or how to test for it.[29] Additionally, a number of researchers indicate that although psychological tests are valid, their predictive value tends to diminish over time.[30] A review of the literature by Elizabeth Burbeck and Adrian Furnham found not only significant methodological problems in the administration of psychological tests but also little success by most tests in distinguishing between good and bad police officers.[31] In a review of police selection procedures, J. Douglas and Joan Grant found that methods used to screen out recruits who will not become good police officers have generally not been successful. They argue that the psychological tests currently employed may screen out serious mental health problems but fail to predict future behavior as a law enforcement officer.[32]

In recent years, the trend has been away from using general psychologists and psychiatrists and utilizing those in the field who are specializing in law enforcement hiring and fitness-for-duty exams. Due to their expertise, as well as open communication with the agencies hiring them, these specialists understand the unique requirements of law enforcement personnel and the major issues involved in fitness for duty as well as the constraints of conforming to the requirements of the Americans with Disabilities Act (ADA). These psychologists will typically make one of three recommendations to a law enforcement agency regarding an applicant: "recommended," "recommended with reservations," and "not recommended." The agency will then choose whether to follow this recommendation. There could be legal problems in the future if an agency hires an individual against the psychologist's recommendation and that officer becomes involved in a questionable situation.

Polygraph Examination

The polygraph, often called the lie detector, is a mechanical device designed to ascertain whether a person is telling the truth. It was first used by the Berkeley, California, Police Department in 1921. The polygraph records any changes in such body measurements as pulse, blood pressure, breathing rate, and galvanic skin response. The effectiveness of the polygraph is based on the belief that a person is under stress when telling a lie. Therefore, if a person lies, the machine will record that stress in the body measurements. The use of the polygraph is an attempt to determine the truth through scientific instruments. The name *polygraph* means "many writings." During a polygraph test, several measurements of the body's activity are recorded on

YOU ARE THERE! »

Sample Areas Covered in a Polygraph Examination

1. Questions regarding the applicant's failure to disclose pertinent information on the application that would have an impact on the selection decision

2. Questions regarding undetected felony acts of murder, rape, robbery, burglary, arson, and the like

3. Questions in regard to the current usage of drugs or narcotics (without prescription). Attention will be directed to the type of illegal usage, the number of times used, and time frame of usage

4. Questions regarding thefts: when, volume, how much (dollar amount); also to include deception-type theft, such as check fraud

5. Questions regarding the omission of information from the application or deception in furnishing information during the background investigation or oral interview

6. Questions regarding the sale and delivery, or participating in the sale or delivery, of illegal drugs, narcotics, and marijuana

7. Questions regarding current alcohol abuse

8. Questions regarding *illegal* sexual conduct

Source: Indiana State Police, 1997

a visible graph. The three major sections of the polygraph are the pneumograph, which measures respiration and depth of breathing; the galvanograph, which measures changes in the skin's electrical resistance; and the cardiograph, which measures blood pressure and pulse rate. It is interesting to note that the subject does not actually have to verbally answer a question for the machine to measure the mental and emotional response of the person to the question. Some state that the polygraph, although not infallible, can detect physiological changes indicating deception anywhere from 75 to 96 percent of the time. Its accuracy depends on the subject, the equipment, and the operator's training and experience. In some cases, the polygraph may fail to detect lies because the subject is on drugs, is a psychopathic personality, or makes deliberate muscular contractions.[33] Formerly, the polygraph was used extensively within private industry for screening job appli-

Dempsey's Law

Some Advice on Becoming a Cop

Professor Dempsey, I'm taking the police test Saturday. Do you have any advice?

Professor Dempsey, I'm meeting my investigator for the first time next week. Do you have any advice?

These are questions I receive every day from my students. I do have advice for them.

Make a test run. A few days before your appointment, go to the location where you are scheduled to appear. Know how long it will take you to get there. Learn where you can park, where to get coffee or a bite to eat, where you can find a public bathroom. If you are late, you may not be allowed to take the test. If you are late meeting your investigator, it will give him or her a very bad impression of you.

Whenever you are scheduled to meet your investigator, wear proper business attire. For a man, that is a conservative suit and tie. For a

woman it is a simple dress or business suit. Select conservative colors—gray, blue, or black. Polish your shoes. Be neat. Take off the earring. You can always put it back after the interview. Accessories that are appropriate for the club scene are not appropriate for an interview. Men and women should eliminate jewelry of any type except for a functioning watch.

If it moves, call it sir or ma'am. A friend of mine told me that when he was in the army, he was so afraid of getting in trouble for not saluting ranking officers that he would salute every person he saw. By doing that, he knew he could never make a mistake. You do not have to salute your investigator. However, whenever answering or asking a question, call your investigator sir or ma'am. In fact, while at your investigator's office, take my friend's advice: If it moves, call him sir and her ma'am.

cants and preventing employee theft. The use of the polygraph in preemployment screening was severely limited in the Employee Polygraph Protection Act (EPPA) signed into law in June 1988. The EPPA prohibited random polygraph testing by private sector employers and the use of the polygraph for preemployment screening. However, the law exempts the U.S. government or any state or local government from its provisions and restrictions. The EPPA allows the use of the polygraph for preemployment screening for police departments and other employers whose primary business is the provision of certain types of security services, companies that manufacture or dispense controlled substances, and for businesses doing sensitive work under contract to the federal government.[34] Although the results of polygraph tests may not be admissible in court, they are still used in the police selection process.

Some departments have switched from the polygraph to the voice stress analyzer, as they find it to be easier to administer and less intrusive to the candidate. According to the Bureau of Justice Statistics' 2003 report on local police departments, 21 percent of all local police departments use the polygraph in the screening process, and an additional 2 percent use the voice stress analyzer.

Medical Examination

Police departments generally want candidates who are in excellent health, without medical problems that could affect their ability to perform the police job. There are long-range and short-range reasons for using medical examinations in the police selection process. The short-range purpose is to ensure that candidates can do the police job. The long-range purpose is to ensure that candidates are not prone to injuries that may lead to early retirement and an economic loss to the department. Gaines and his associates state that every applicant should be given a complete and thorough medical examination to detect any disqualifying diseases (such as diabetes, epilepsy, or heart disease) or any physical abnormalities or medical conditions (such as back problems or high blood pressure) that might later render the applicant physically unqualified for duty or allow the candidate to be able to retire early on a service disability. They also warn departments about carefully monitoring the medical examination. They cite examples where applicants took drugs to control hypertension (high blood pressure), used insoles to increase height, and obtained urine specimens from friends to conceal drug use or other medical ailments.[35] The Americans with Disabilities Act

(ADA), signed into law in 1990, extended the basic protection of the Rehabilitation Act of 1973 to government and private industry. This law took effect in 1992 and mandated that discrimination on the basis of disability is prohibited by all governmental entities and all but the smallest private employers. The ADA prohibits discrimination against disabled persons who can perform the essential functions of the job in spite of their disability. If a police agency rejects a disabled person for employment, it must show that the disabled person cannot adequately perform the job. The law provides an affirmative duty for employers to reasonably accommodate qualified disabled persons unless doing so would create an undue hardship. Areas covered by ADA include physical agility tests, psychological tests, and drug testing.[36]

Physical Agility Test

It is common knowledge that police departments are interested in police candidates who are physically fit. In the past 20 years, physical agility testing has been criticized for discriminating against some candidates, particularly women and physically small members of certain minority groups. Some argue that the tests relate to aspects of the police job that are rarely performed. Others argue that, while these aspects of the police job are not routinely and frequently performed, they are critically important.[37] Not possessing the strength, endurance, or flexibility needed for the job could result in injury or death to the officer or a citizen. It also may increase the likelihood of an officer having to resort to deadly force.

The question that law enforcement needs to answer is how fit officers must be; and then law enforcement has to prove job relatedness to the standards, or the courts will find against them. A recent study, conducted over 15 years and collecting data from 34 physical fitness standards validation studies performed on more than 5,500 officers from federal, state, and local law enforcement, enables law enforcement to document that fitness areas underlie specific task performance. Through the use of several police officer job scenarios, the authors were able to tie in the need for aerobic power (1.5-mile run), anaerobic power (300-meter run), upper body absolute strength (bench press), upper body muscular endurance (push-ups), abdominal muscular endurance (sit-ups), explosive leg power (vertical jump), and agility (agility run) to the police job.[38]

A related issue that is often raised by officers, applicants, unions, and scholars is the issue of maintaining fitness once someone is employed as a police officer. How

can an agency justify having rigorous agility tests to get hired if there is nothing done to follow through on this stated job qualification once the officer is hired? Traditionally, police officers have had no standards to adhere to once they were hired. With the inherent physical demands that can be placed on an officer in a moment's notice, this is a recipe for disaster. This is slowly changing but it is a complicated issue involving standards, discipline, incentives, compensation for time, and liability regarding injuries.

Most officers keep themselves in top shape, motivated by personal pride and a desire to be healthy, minimize their chance for injury, and better serve the community. This effort is facilitated by departments providing on-site workout facilities, on-duty time to work out, and various incentives for maintaining certain levels of fitness. Many provide "fitness coordinators" to guide employees in their efforts.

YOU ARE THERE! »

Sample Agility Tests

ARLINGTON, TEXAS, POLICE DEPARTMENT

1. Rapid-acceleration agility course (includes hurdles, walls, and actions simulating low hedges, fences, storm drains, bridges, and running through crowds)
2. Trigger squeeze
3. Dummy drag
4. Ladder climb with shotgun
5. Endurance run

Arlington also provides tips and guidelines on their Web site about preparing for the test.

PORTLAND, OREGON, POLICE BUREAU

1. 440-yard mobility (agility) run
2. 165-lb dummy drag
3. Modified squat thrust and stand using rail vault
4. 80-lb torso bag carry

Sources: Arlington, Texas, http://www.arlingtonpd.org/; Portland, Oregon, http://www.portlandonline.com/police/

Smoking

Though over the years many police departments have prohibited smoking in public due to concerns for a professional appearance, health and monetary considerations have now become issues for law enforcement agencies. In an effort to respond to rising medical costs for personnel and to keep officers healthy and productive for a longer time, many departments have instigated no-smoking policies. Generally, current officers are grandfathered in, but new hires must sign affidavits stating they have not smoked tobacco for a year and will not smoke tobacco once employed by the agency. This prohibition applies on or off duty, and it is a condition of employment. Some departments are afraid of civil rights implications in these types of rules but prohibit smoking in police facilities and vehicles in an effort to reduce smoking and to minimize exposure for other employees to secondhand smoke. Some departments have had no-smoking policies in place for over ten years, and so far they have withstood court challenges. Courts have traditionally upheld that public safety employers have a legitimate interest in the health and fitness of their employees.[39]

Background Investigation

In an effective background investigation, a candidate's past life, past employment, school records, medical records, relationships with neighbors and others, and military record are placed under a microscope. The investigator looks for evidence of incidents that might point to unfavorable traits or habits that in turn might affect the individual's ability to be a good police officer. Such factors are poor work habits, dishonesty, use of alcohol or drugs, or a tendency to violence. Thomas H. Wright offers the following basics for a thorough background investigation:

1. *Preliminary interview.* In a preliminary interview, the investigating officer should advise the applicant of the details of the background investigation process and the facts about employment in the department, including salary, benefits, and responsibilities.

2. *Background investigation booklet.* Applicants should receive a booklet that contains questions for them to answer regarding all important aspects of their past, including residences, schools, jobs, military service, arrests or summonses, and any other information the department wishes to investigate. This booklet becomes the basic document for the background investigation.

3. *Photographs and fingerprints.* Photographs should be taken and used to show to neighbors and former employers in case they do not recognize the applicant by name. Fingerprints should be sent to the FBI and the local state criminal identification agency to determine any previous police record.

4. *Education.* The applicant's school experience should be investigated to determine attendance and disciplinary history.

5. *Employment.* The applicant's employment experience should be investigated to determine honesty, self-initiative, attitudes, job performance, absenteeism, tardiness, and use of sick leave.

6. *Credit check.* The applicant's credit history should be examined to ensure a previous history of fulfilling obligations.

7. *Criminal history.* Every police agency that covers areas where the applicant might have lived or attended school should be contacted to gather any available information regarding his or her conduct while living or attending school there.

8. *Driving record.* The applicant's record of traffic accidents and traffic summonses/citations should be investigated.

9. *Military history.* The applicant's military record should be investigated to determine any disciplinary actions or medical problems that may affect his or her police employment.[40]

★ ★ ★

STANDARDS IN POLICE SELECTION

Each police department sets standards, or necessary qualifications, that it requires in selecting its prospective police officers. In recent years these standards have changed to allow a greater number of females and minorities to become police officers, but they are still more stringent than standards in most other professions. The police standards cover physical, age, and education requirements, criminal record restrictions, and residency requirements.

Physical Requirements

At one time, the main requirement for becoming a police officer was the size of a young man's body and his physical strength and courage. Over the years, we have come to realize that brains are more important than brawn in police

Forst's Law

The Oral Interview

When I am asked for advice by students, I give them advice similar to that Professor Dempsey gives them. I will add a couple of examples and pieces of advice gathered over my many years of participating in oral boards and conducting background investigations.

1. The number one piece of advice is, *"Don't lie,"* and that includes exaggerating facts and leaving information out. You will be found out. Investigating is law enforcement's strong point. I was constantly amazed by applicants who would lie in interviews or about their backgrounds, sometimes about trivial things that would not have affected their chances and sometimes about big things that were very easy to verify. Once a candidate lies, he or she is out of the game. No second chances.

2. As Professor Dempsey stated, dress appropriately. I remember participating on oral boards (as a lieutenant) with a male captain who frequently was heard to exclaim to a candidate—"Look how I'm dressed, and I have a job!" The common perception (and in my experience, accurate perception) among law enforcement executives is that the candidate's demeanor, appearance, and attitude are likely to be the best they will ever be during the hiring process. If it is not top notch at that time, the future is bleak. How will the applicant dress for court appearances?

3. To add to Professor Dempsey's comments, showing respect for the position of the inter-

viewers is an excellent idea. I have been called both "sir" and "ma'am." In the case of the former, the applicant either had a vision problem, was extremely nervous, or, in the worst-case scenario, was a sexist trying to make a point. Personally, I never liked to be referred to as "ma'am" as it made me feel old. I've heard other female executives make the same comment. I believe if it is at all possible, the preferred method is making note of the interviewer's rank or title and using that. It shows respect for the time and effort required to attain the rank and shows a basic understanding of police organizations and the rank structure.

4. I also recommend you prepare. Know the organization. Research the jurisdiction and the agency on the Internet. Be aware of the vision of the agency as well as specific goals and initiatives the department is involved in. This preparation will allow you to ask good questions of the interviewers (most oral boards will allow you to ask them questions at the end of the interview) as well as illustrate your understanding of the agency and its challenges and philosophies and to show your initiative. This will be viewed positively by the board.

5. Lastly, "be yourself." Trying to project an image or persona that you think they want to see, but is not you, will result in a less than positive interview process. Better to let your true personality come through and thereby determine if it is a fit or not with the agency.

work. Also, the former physical requirements discriminated against women and minorities. Today, physical requirements are still stringent.

HEIGHT AND WEIGHT REQUIREMENTS   Height and weight requirements for police department applicants have changed dramatically in recent years. Only a few decades ago, nearly all police departments required officers to be at

least 5 feet 8 inches tall.[41] Because this is no longer so, women and minorities can enter the police ranks more easily.

In 1977, in *Dothard* v. *Rawlinson,* the Supreme Court threw out a 5-foot 2-inch, 120-pound minimum height and weight hiring qualification for a correctional officer, stating that the employer failed to demonstrate this requirement as necessary for performance of the job.[42]

Courts typically do not support minimum height and weight requirements but do support the need for maximum weight standards or the weight and height relationship.

VISION REQUIREMENTS   Many police departments require an applicant to have very good uncorrected vision that must be correctable to 20/20 vision with eyeglasses, as well as to be free from color blindness. These requirements have created a roadblock for many qualified candidates. Some contest this requirement, because many police officers wear glasses, and police work does not require perfect uncorrected vision. One researcher noted that a person with 20/200 uncorrected vision may be able to function adequately as a police officer, depending on the type of vision problem he or she has.[43] Other researchers noted that an applicant's specific vision problem should be considered before rejecting a candidate because of poor vision.[44] In recent years, the majority of agencies require vision that is correctable to 20/20, as illustrated by Madison, Wisconsin's vision requirement of "binocular vision correctable to 20/20; normal peripheral vision & no significant eye disease."

Gaines and his associates explain that many police departments' vision requirements are based on tradition rather than need. It was long thought that a police officer should have relatively good vision because of the potential for officers to lose their glasses during an altercation with a suspect, which would render the officer helpless.[45] They tell us, however, that two researchers, Good and Augsburger, found that 50 percent of the police officers in a survey had experienced "spectacle dislodgement" (their glasses fell off), with an average of 4.09 occurrences during their career.[46] That rate does not appear to be a significant problem. Furthermore, the popularity of contact lenses makes this even less of a problem. With the increased utilization and success of vision correction surgery, vision is less of a concern for applicants today than it was even five years ago.

Age Requirements

Until recently, most police departments required that an officer be between the ages of 21 and 29 at the time of appointment. Anyone over the age of 29 was considered too old for employment. Sometimes, exceptions were made for those with previous military or police experience. The number of years a candidate served in the military or in previous police employment were added to the maximum age limit. The percentage of departments with maximum age limits has dropped significantly in recent years, largely due to age discrimination issues. Many police departments, however, still do not want to accept candidates past a certain age.

A few years ago, several applicants who took a NYPD police officer examination when they were under the age limit weren't called until much later but still expected to be hired. However, on May 31, 1997, a Manhattan Supreme Court justice upheld the NYPD's policy of limiting new officers to applicants under age 35. The judge said that age limits on public-safety jobs are acceptable exceptions to laws against age discrimination. The applicants had passed the necessary physical, psychological, and educational tests but were denied appointment at the last minute before they were to be appointed. A city law setting a maximum age of 34 for new recruits expired in 1993 and was not renewed, but the city argued that police work is stressful and physically demanding and therefore better left to people under 35. Eighty passing applicants were denied appointment.[47]

Despite this court ruling, most departments do not have an official upper age limit. Their concerns in hiring revolve around pensions and health issues and the related medical costs. Some departments will hire officers retiring after 20 years with another department, and it is not necessarily unusual to see officers enjoy two lengthy police careers in two different departments.

Education Requirements

Among local law enforcement agencies, as reported by the Bureau of Justice Statistics (2003), 83 percent of departments required a high school diploma, 15 percent had some type of college requirement, and only 1 percent required a four-year college degree. However, the same report indicated that the percentage of officers employed by a department with some type of college requirement was 32 percent in 2000, which was three times as many as in 1990. It should be noted that the minimum high school diploma requirement may not necessarily reflect actual selection practices, because many departments favor applicants who meet more than the minimum standards.

In reviewing requirements nationally, it appears that most departments with college requirements have major universities nearby, perhaps giving them a larger pool of candidates to draw from as well as providing access to higher education for in-service personnel. As we saw in Chapter 2, most federal law enforcement agencies require a four-year college degree for employment. The more sought-after departments, with better pay and benefits, are more likely to require college degrees.

The development of college programs for the police was first stimulated by the recommendations of the National Commission on Law Observance and Enforcement (Wickersham Report) in 1931, which discussed, among other police problems, the poor state of police training in the United States. However, the real impetus behind the relatively high levels of police education in recent decades was the Law Enforcement Education Program (LEEP), a federal scholarship and loan program operated by the U.S. Department of Justice between 1968 and 1976. LEEP spent more than $200 million in grants and loans to students in "law enforcement–related" college programs. LEEP funds supported more than 500,000 "student years" of college education. About 90 percent of the students in the program were in-service sworn officers.[48]

Considerable debate has arisen over the desirability of college education for police officers. Many experts believe that all police officers should have a college degree. As early as 1967, the President's Commission on Law Enforcement and Administration of Justice recommended, "The ultimate aim of all police departments should be that all personnel with general enforcement powers have baccalaureate degrees."[49] Some studies have shown that college-educated officers receive fewer citizen complaints and have better behavioral and performance characteristics than those without college.[50] Higher levels of education have also been associated with fewer on-the-job injuries, fewer injuries by assault, fewer disciplinary actions from accidents, fewer sick days per year, and fewer physical force allegations.[51] Other research has shown that higher education results in higher aspirations; decreased dogmatism, authoritarianism, rigidity, and conservatism; fewer disciplinary problems; fewer citizen complaints; increased promotions; greater acceptance of minorities; decreased use of discretionary arrests; increased perception of danger; and a better ability to tolerate job-related excitement.[52]

In a 1992 article, Mitchell Tyre and Susan Braunstein reported on two studies they conducted regarding higher education and ethics in policing. In one study, the authors found that educational levels had a direct positive effect upon all individuals in the survey and that the correlation between a college degree and ethical decisions was 12 times greater for police officers than for the control group. In another study, the authors found that officers who had not attained a two-year college degree were approximately four times more likely to be brought before the Florida Department of Law Enforcement for decertification proceedings.[53]

However, the report of the National Advisory Commission on Higher Education for Police Officers, often called the Sherman Report, stated that there is some evidence that officers with more education become dissatisfied with policing as a career more often than officers with less education. Additionally, the report said that the lack of career opportunities for the educated and ambitious officer is a serious problem in law enforcement agencies, and that new officers with college degrees are often resented by veteran officers with no college experience. Additionally, the report concludes that there is evidence that some departments punished officers with more education by denying them career opportunities.[54] The Sherman Report criticized current police higher education programs for "servicing the status quo." It suggested that higher-education programs for the police should offer them a "broadening" experience, which would enable them to expand their ability to deal with their professional problems. The Sherman Report also recommended recruiting college-educated young people rather than sending recruits to college. It also argued that police departments should recruit students from liberal arts programs rather than law enforcement programs.[55]

The issue of whether those who are college educated make better police officers has not been decided. The thought that officers with college educations might be better decision makers and more effective officers contributed to the creation of the Police Corps program.[56]

While some research has indicated that education has little impact on police performance, other studies indicate that college-educated officers have fewer disciplinary problems and citizens' complaints and write better reports.[57] Education alone cannot determine an officer's success; other strong influences include academy training, department training, supervision, and the organizational climate. There is a belief that college-educated officers will be better able to relate to the various types of people they will encounter than will officers who have not attended college.

One of the most common objections to requiring some college education for police officers is that this practice limits the pool of applicants and has a negative impact on racial minorities who may have been the victims of inferior schooling. Also, some argue that there is no conclusive evidence that officers with college degrees perform more effectively than those without degrees.[58] Regarding their objections to the college requirement for police officers, Robert Sheehan and Gary W. Cordner write:

> Education is very often seen as a vehicle for professionalization. . . . Yet a demand that all police applicants be college graduates necessarily narrows the field from which the applicants may be drawn. By establishing the college degree as an entrance-level requirement the police administrator precludes thousands of capable prospective applicants from applying for entrance-level positions.[59]

Some departments have instituted college education requirements for promotion to higher ranks. Some departments provide tuition reimbursement to encourage officers to continue their education, and some departments or states provide officers educational incentive money, which varies by the amount of education they have. In the state of Florida, the state pays police officers a set amount of money per month depending on the amount of college they have. This is over and above their salary and continues for the duration of their career. It can add up to quite a bit of money over 20 years.

Prior Drug Use

Departments have continually faced the problem of a candidate's prior drug use. Should a candidate be disqualified because of prior drug use? Is experimentation with marijuana enough to dismiss a candidate? What about cocaine? How many prior uses of drugs are acceptable? In 1997, the Maryland Legislature passed a bill that established minimum standards on prior drug use by those seeking certification as law enforcement officers. The bill was proposed to replace a patchwork of policies throughout the state.[60]

Recently, many departments around the country have liberalized their policies regarding drug use due to a smaller applicant pool as well as societal changes. According to John Firman, the research director for the International Association of Chiefs of Police (IACP), the most common restriction is 10 years for hard drugs and 5 for marijuana.[61] A recent study found a lot of flexibility in department policies on police applicants and marijuana use. The most important issues to departments were the number of times and when it was used. Thirty-five percent of the departments surveyed did not reject outright candidates who had used marijuana. They may have guidelines in writing, but there is a considerable amount of flexibility in the policies, and the word used is often "may" as to whether or not marijuana use will disqualify an applicant. Applicants are usually given an opportunity to explain their drug use, and the circumstances as well as how many times and when are examined by the hiring agency.[62] Drug restrictions can and do vary widely from agency to agency and will require research by interested applicants for whom this is an issue. A policy or action that is too liberal can raise issues of liability for agencies. Most departments also have random drug testing, and officers can be fired and stripped of their state certificate if found to be using drugs.

Criminal Record Restrictions

Obviously, people wishing to become police officers must respect the rules of our society and must adhere to these rules. The lack of a significant criminal record is a requirement to become a police officer. However, many police departments recognize that people may make mistakes, especially when young, that might result in an arrest. Also, police departments distinguish between arrests and convictions. A Justice Department survey discovered that 95 percent of all police departments reject applicants with an adult felony conviction, and 75 percent reject those with a juvenile felony conviction. Only 30 percent, however, reject applicants with either an adult or a juvenile misdemeanor conviction. Twenty percent of departments reject those with an adult felony arrest but no conviction, and 25 percent reject those with a juvenile arrest but no conviction.[63] Remember that in the U.S. criminal justice system, a person is not considered guilty until convicted in court.

Along with the issue of criminal records is undetected criminal activity. This will be explored during the background investigation, polygraph exams, and interviews.

Residency Requirements

The majority of larger departments have dropped their residency requirements and recruit nationwide, whereas many of the smallest departments recruit only within their own local community—possibly a reflection on local politics. Some experts believe that a department should recruit from the largest possible area to maximize the potential of the qualified applicant pool.[64] Other groups, such as the ACLU, believe police officers should be part of the community they serve, or at least not appear to be an "outside force" hired to police the community.[65] The theory is that the more an officer knows about the community he or she serves and the more that officer has vested in the community, the better the job of serving the community he or she will be able to do. The opposing view is that residency requirements restrict the officers' freedom of choice, narrow the selection pool, and in fact have shown no definite correlation to better police service.

Sexual Orientation

One of the more controversial police personnel issues is the recruitment of gay and lesbian officers. Some police administrators have decided not to make an issue of sexual orientation on background investigations; others are vigorously recruiting openly gay officers. These decisions are most likely influenced by the overall change in society's social and sexual mores. They are also supported by the views of equal rights for all groups within our society. This issue is particularly challenging in the area of law enforcement, where the image has traditionally been one of tough, macho male officers responding to citizens' cries for help.

Police departments must face the problems of discrimination against gay officers in their own ranks. Over the years, some gay officers have been forced to resign because of pressures placed on them, and gays in police departments have formed organizations to protect themselves. In the 1970s, gay officers in California started the Golden State Peace Officers Association (GSPOA). Another of the nation's first gay officers' associations was the New York City Police Department's Gay Officers Action League (GOAL), which was established in 1981 and, as explained on their Web site (www.goalny.org), holds yearly conferences and provides links with ten U.S. and eight international gay and lesbian police organizations. Law Enforcement Gays and Lesbians (LEGAL) and similar support groups around the country also offer support to gay, lesbian, bisexual, and transgender workers in the criminal justice system. They hope to improve the environment within law enforcement agencies for gays and ultimately improve the relationship between the police and the gay community. The issue of discrimination against gay officers and the recruitment of gay officers is further discussed in Chapter 13, "Women and Minorities in Policing."

★ ★ ★

THE POLICE TRAINING PROCESS

Once an individual has been chosen to be a member of a police department, he or she begins months of intensive training. Recruit training and in-service training programs vary from department to department, and, in reality, police training never ends. Veteran police officers continue their education and training in many areas to keep up with the latest trends in fighting crime as well as keeping up with changing laws and procedures. They also receive specialized training in preparation for serving in specialized units or managerial positions.

Recruit Training

Recruit training is the initial training a police officer receives. It teaches officers the state laws and state procedures and educates them in the goals, objectives, and procedures of the department. It provides them with the knowledge, skills, and abilities to do the job. In most po-

lice departments, new officers must attend a formal training course at an academy operated by, or associated with, the department. The first police training school in the United States was developed in 1908 by the Berkeley, California, chief of police, August Vollmer.[66]

VARIATIONS IN TRAINING REQUIREMENTS   The majority of big cities in the United States have their own police academies. About 85 percent of cities with a population of 250,000 or more and approximately half of cities with a population between 100,000 and 250,000 operate their own police academies.[67] Localities without their own academy use a nearby state or county academy. Regional academies are increasingly serving the training needs of several departments in an area. Also, many academies are now operated by community colleges on a contract basis or using police personnel as staff.

A history of the Northern Virginia Criminal Justice Academy (formerly called the Northern Virginia Police Academy) illustrates the evolution in police training of many police academies over the last quarter of a century. The Northern Virginia Police Academy was established in 1965 to train police from Arlington County, the city of Alexandria, and Fairfax County. In the academy's early years, the training consisted of 11 weeks divided into academic, firearms, physical, and driver training.[68] The academic training consisted of an introduction to police science (police methods and techniques), government and law, police and community life, and laboratory techniques. The firearms and physical training curricula consisted of learning to fire a service revolver and shotgun, as well as calisthenics, judo, and close-order drill (military-type marching and calisthenics). The driver training consisted of driving around traffic cones on a simplified course. In 1970, the state of Virginia formed its first training commission to promulgate mandatory requirements governing both basic and in-service training. The commission insisted that all sworn officers receive 160 hours of training during the first year of employment and that each veteran officer attend 40 hours of in-service training every two years. As a result of the new regulations, the academy added blocks of instruction on community relations, crisis intervention, tactical decisions, judgmental shooting, officer survival, crisis management, advanced driver training, and sensitivity training.

A study of police training revealed that, in the 1950s, training was considered a minor position in the department, whereas in the 1980s, most big city academies had been elevated to a higher level within the organization.[69] In the last three decades, there has been a dramatic increase in the quality and quantity of police training and departments are paying more attention to curriculum, training methods, and the development of training facilities. Perhaps the improvement in police training can be traced to the 1967 recommendation by the President's Commission on Law Enforcement and Administration of Justice that police departments provide "an absolute minimum of 400 hours of classroom work spread over a 4- to 6-month period so that it can be combined with carefully selected and supervised field training." The commission also recommend in-service training at least once a year, along with incentives for officers to continue their education.[70] The number of hours devoted to recruit training since then has increased dramatically.

In 2000, new police officers in cities with over 100,000 in population completed an average of 853 hours of academy training, whereas in jurisdictions serving a population of less than 2500, the average was 532 hours.[71]

The basic law enforcement academy in the state of Washington provides recruits with 720 hours of instruction, including criminal law and procedures, traffic enforcement, cultural awareness, communication skills, emergency vehicle operator's course, firearms, crisis intervention, patrol procedures, criminal investigation, and defensive tactics.

The Madison, Wisconsin, Police Department's academy is 1,120 hours long and provides extensive training in law, crisis intervention, firearms, and use of community resources.

Field training is on-the-job training of recently graduated recruits from the police academy. The training is provided by specially selected patrol officers and is designed to supplement the theory taught at the police academy with the reality of the street. The San Jose (California) Police Department created a field training program as early as 1972 that has been adopted by many police departments across the country. The San Jose program consists of two phases of training: (1) 16 weeks of regular police academy classroom training and (2) 14 weeks of field training. During the field training phase, a recruit is assigned to three different **field training officers (FTOs).** Each FTO works with the recruit on patrol for four weeks. The recruit then returns to the first FTO for the last two weeks. Each recruit receives a daily evaluation report by his or her FTO and a weekly evaluation report by the FTO's supervisor.[72] A survey found that nearly two-thirds (64 percent) of departments had a field training program. More than half indicated that their program was directly modeled after the innovative San Jose program.[73] Today, many departments continue to use the San Jose program or a variation of it. The Mesa, Arizona, Police Department explains on their Web site (www.ci.mesa.az.us/police/fto/) that they model their program after the San Jose program but have

©Stephen D. Cannerelli/Syracuse

Officers face "Shoot, Don't Shoot" firearms training simulators throughout their careers. Here, Syracuse, New York, police officer Maureen Buckland tests her ability to react to dangerous situations on a simulator. Is this type of training more or less valuable than traditional target shooting practice?

modified it to be a four-phase, 18-week program that exposes the recruit to at least three FTOs. In fact, so widespread is field training that in 1992, the National Association of Field Training Officers (NAFTO) held its first annual conference in Monterey, California. The organization was chartered for the purpose of furthering and representing the interests of law enforcement, corrections, and communications field training officers. The association expects to establish chapters in all 50 states.[74] According to their Web site (www.nafto.org/about.htm), there were 16 state chapters at the time of this writing.

Firearms Training

In the 1960s, most **police firearms training** in the United States consisted of firing at bull's-eye targets. Later, training became more sophisticated, using more realistic silhouette targets shaped like armed adversaries. The FBI's Practical Pistol Course began to modernize firearms training; the course required qualification not only from different distances but also from different positions, such as standing, kneeling, and prone positions. As firearms training progressed, shoot/don't shoot training was introduced using **Hogan's Alley** courses. Targets depicting "good guys" and "bad guys" would pop up, requiring officers to make split-second decisions. Today, many agencies have replaced Hogan's Alley programs with computer-controlled visual simulations.[75]

Departments nationwide are reviewing actual shooting incidents and, in an attempt to increase officer safety and minimize litigation, are attempting to make their training as realistic as possible and incorporate stressors that occur in street situations. Administrators have realized that shootings rarely occur with warnings in sterile and controlled situations involving stationary targets. They've incorporated inclement weather, realistic dress, flashing lights, blaring sirens, and other distractions, as well as multiple individuals or targets involved in the scenarios. They've found that training in this manner together with stressing the decision to shoot or not shoot is better equipping officers when confronted with situations on the street.

In-Service, Management, and Specialized Training

Police training generally does not end at the recruit level. In many departments, in-service training is used to regularly update the skills and knowledge base of veteran officers. Because laws and developments in policing are constantly changing, officers need to be kept up-to-date. Many states have chosen to mandate a required number of in-service training hours for officers to maintain their state certification. Primarily, this was done as a way to ensure departments were keeping their officers updated on the latest laws and procedures and ensure some degree of uniformity from jurisdiction to jurisdiction. The average annual number of hours required for in-service officers was 69 hours in 2000, which included an average of 26 annual state-mandated hours.[76] Some popular topics for in-service training around the country include ethics, use of force, cultural awareness, stress, domestic violence, workplace harassment, critical incidents, hate crimes, victim assistance, hostage situations, pursuits, interviews and interrogations, fraud, identity theft, and computer crime.

PATROLLING THE WEB

Law Enforcement Training at FLETC

According to their Web site, www.fletc.gov, the Federal Law Enforcement Training Center (FLETC) was established by Congress in 1970 and is located near Brunswick, Georgia. The Center's parent agency is the Department of Homeland Security. This center provides training for officers from federal agencies, with the exception of the FBI and DEA, which have their own training academies. Since 1983, the FLETC also has provided the opportunity for advanced or specialized training for state and local police. Together with its 75 partner organizations for which it provides training, the curriculum and policies are developed and reviewed. The average training curriculum consists of legal studies, enforcement techniques, behavioral science, enforcement operations, computer/economic crime, firearms, and physical techniques. One of the major benefits of the FLETC concept is that each agency does not have to operate its own training unit and thus can save significant funds through consolidated training.

In addition to in-service training, many departments use management training programs to teach supervisory and management skills to newly promoted supervisors and managers. Some of them send supervisors and managers to regional or state sites for this training in supervision or management. There are several well-known law enforcement administrative officers' courses around the country that departments may use to improve the managerial skills of their mid- and upper-level managers. These include the FBI Academy in Quantico; the Southern Police Institute at the University of Louisville; the Center for Public Safety at Northwestern University; the Senior Management Institute for Police in Boston; the Management Institute at the Federal Law Enforcement Training Center in Glynco, Georgia; the Institute of Police Technology and Management at the University of North Florida in Jacksonville; and the Southwestern Law Enforcement Institute in Texas. Typically administrators attend these schools for anywhere from 8 to 13 weeks and are paid a salary while they attend. The managers obtain the latest information concerning law enforcement practices and network with other managers from around the country. This is a valuable source of information and subsequent resources for mid- and upper-level managers who often spend their entire career in one department.

Many departments also offer specialized training programs for officers assigned to new duties. These may be conducted on site or at other locations.

In Florida, community colleges are the site of many regional training opportunities. They routinely host in-service training for officers who need to learn new skills to specialize in new assignments. These include drug investigations, traffic homicide investigations, radar, surveillance, investigation, DARE, School Resource Officer, Firearms Instructor, Crowd Control, Instructor Certification, Crime Scene Investigation, Child Abuse, Sex Crimes, Robbery Investigations, Interview and Interrogation and other classes that chiefs request.

Training for the Police Corps

The Police Corps, which has been proposed for over 30 years by Adam Walinsky, since he was an aide to former New York Senator Robert F. Kennedy, finally came to fruition in March 1997. This program models training after the military's successful Reserve Officer Training Corps (ROTC). As part of the 1994 federal anticrime law, $10 million was appropriated for six states to develop these programs. The programs reimburse as much as $30,000 in educational costs to college graduates who agree to serve four years in a participating police agency. Currently, there are programs in Alaska, Arizona, Arkansas, Colorado,

Connecticut, Florida, Georgia, Illinois, Indiana, Kentucky, Maryland, Massachusetts, Minnesota, Mississippi, Missouri, Nevada, North Carolina, Ohio, Oklahoma, Oregon, South Carolina, Texas, Utah, Virginia, Washington, and Wisconsin. The Police Corps reduces costs to agencies by providing funds to the states to provide 16 to 24 weeks of rigorous residential Police Corps training for each participant. Proponents of the Police Corps say it will transform policing, not just by attracting college graduates, but by having these older, better-educated recruits trained in a different way. They will have a new curriculum focusing on the community and emphasizing leadership, sensitivity, and social skills as tools to break down the friction and distrust that officers often encounter. To deal with these problems, recruits will learn not only regular police procedures but also the demographics of neighborhoods and communication and note-taking skills. Role play will also be a major part of training. For further information on the Police Corps program visit their Web site at www.ojp.usdoj.gov/opclee/.

Community Policing Training

Numerous departments throughout the United States have begun to develop low-cost and effective local and regional community policing training to inculcate community awareness into their recruits and in-service personnel.[75] In fact, in 2000, 59 percent of local departments provided at least eight hours of training in community policing. This ranged from 87 percent of departments serving populations over 1 million to 42 percent of departments serving populations under 2500.[76] The U.S. Department of Justice, Office of Community Oriented Policing Services (COPS), funds training provided by the Community Policing Consortium, a group of five of the leading policing organizations in the United States: the International Association of Chiefs of Police (IACP), the National Organization of Black Law Enforcement Executives (NOBLE), the National Sheriffs' Association (NSA), the Police Executive Research Forum (PERF), and the Police Foundation. This consortium delivers free community policing training to all recipients of COPS grants under the 1994 Crime Bill in the form of regional training. Sessions include community policing orientation, sheriff-specific training, cultural diversity/building community partnerships, problem solving, personnel needs and managing calls for service, and train-the-trainer courses.[77]

Probationary Period

A **probationary period** is the period of time that a department has to evaluate a new officer's ability to perform his or her job effectively. Generally, a probationary officer can be dismissed at will without proof of specific violations of law or department regulations. Once officers are off probation, civil service rules often make it very difficult to dismiss them. Probationary periods can last anywhere from six months to three years. Today, the average probationary period nationwide is twelve months. The probationary period in policing has been called the "first true job related test . . . in the selection procedure."[78]

CHAPTER SUMMARY

Numerous jobs are available in policing on the federal, state, local, and private levels. The police selection process can be complicated and time consuming. Before selection actually begins, a department must conduct a job analysis to determine the type of candidate the department wants to hire. Next comes the actual selection process. This process can include a written entrance examination, an oral review, a psychological appraisal, a polygraph examination, a medical examination, a physical agility test, and a background investigation.

The standards required to become a police officer have changed significantly in recent years to allow more females and minorities entry into policing. The current standards to be a police officer are high and rigorous in most agencies. Newly hired police officers generally receive academy training and field training. A probationary period must then be served. In addition, officers continue their educations throughout their careers through in-service, management, and specialized training programs.

Learning Check

1. Discuss why the job analysis is such a vital phase in the police hiring practice.

2. Explain the typical selection process most police departments use to identify and select qualified police officers.

3. Explain the standards most police departments use to select qualified police officers.

4. Discuss why field training programs and probationary periods are vital phases in the police training practice.

5. In your own words, describe the average newly hired U.S. police officer, in view of the police recruitment and selection process.

Application Exercise

Based on your reading of this chapter, prepare a resume and cover letter designed to apply for employment in a police department. If you have never prepared a resume and cover letter, this may be the time to go to the library or Internet sites and obtain information on the process.

Web Exercise

Visit the sites of three law enforcement agencies, list the hiring requirements, and describe the hiring process for someone who wants to become a sworn police officer.

Key Concepts

Affirmative action regulations
Equal opportunity employment regulations
Field training
Field training officers (FTOs)
Guardians Association of New York City Police Department v. *Civil Service Commission of New York*
Hogan's Alley
Job analysis
Job related
Knowledge, skills, and abilities (KSAs)
Police firearms training
Police selection process
Probationary period

The Police Role and Police Discretion

CHAPTER GOALS

- To explore the police role and its many interpretations
- To introduce you to the goals and objectives of policing
- To explore various operational styles of the police
- To introduce you to the concept of police discretion
- To explore the concept of police discretion, seeking to understand how and why discretion is exercised and the methods that have been used to control it

The role of the police and the exercise of police discretion are among the most important issues in policing. Who are the police? What do they do? How do they do what they do? What should they do instead?

This chapter will look at the role of the police in society, including the crime-fighting role, the order-maintenance role, the ambiguity of the police role, and the effects of the terrorist attacks on the United States on September 11, 2001. It will discuss the goals and objectives of the police, as well as various police operational styles discovered by researchers who study the police. Additionally, the chapter will discuss police discretion. It will examine what discretion is, how and why discretion is exercised, what factors influence discretion, and how discretion can be controlled by police administrators.

★ ★ ★
THE POLICE ROLE

What is the **police role?** Who are the police in the United States? What do they do? What should they do? These are very difficult questions to answer. The scholar Herman Goldstein warns, "Anyone attempting to construct a workable definition of the police role will typically come away with old images shattered and a newfound appreciation for the intricacies of police work."[1]

Two major views of the role of the police exist (Exhibit 5.1):

1. The police are crime fighters concerned with law enforcement (**crime fighting**).

2. The police are order maintainers concerned with keeping the peace and providing social services to the community (**order maintenance**).

Crime-Fighting Role

Movies and television shows about the police emphasize the police crime-fighting role. If we believe these stories, the police engage in numerous daily gunfights, car chases, and acts of violence, and they arrest numerous people

Exhibit 5.1	The Police Role

Crime fighting (law enforcement)
 or
Order maintenance (peacekeeping)?

every day. Fictional books about police work also emphasize the crime-fighting role. Even the news media emphasize this role; television news shows and newspaper headlines dramatize exciting arrests and action by the police.

The police themselves also emphasize their role as crime fighters and play down their job as peacekeepers and social service providers. As a former professor turned police officer, George L. Kirkham, states:

> The police have historically overemphasized their role as crime fighters and played down their more common work as keepers of the peace and providers of social services, simply because our society proffers rewards for the former (crime fighting) but cares little for the latter (peace-keeping and providing services). The public accords considerable recognition and esteem to the patrol officer who becomes involved in a shoot-out with an armed robber or who chases and apprehends a rapist, and therefore so do the officer's peers and superiors.[2]

At first glance, there appears to be some truth to the belief that police are primarily crime fighters. Statistics for the latest reporting year reveal that the U.S. police made almost 14 million arrests for all criminal infractions, not including traffic violations.[3]

An analysis of the arrests, however, shows a different perspective. About 2.23 million of the arrests were for the FBI's Index or Part I crimes. Of these arrests, about 620,000 were for violent crimes (murder, forcible rape, robbery, and aggravated assault) and about 1.6 million of the arrests were for property crimes (burglary, larceny/theft, motor vehicle theft, and arson). However, the following accounted for the other 11.75 million arrests:

1. Driving under the influence (DUI) or driving while intoxicated (DWI)—1,462,000 arrests

2. Drug abuse violations—1,539,000 arrests

3. Misdemeanor assaults—1,289,000 arrests

4. Liquor law violations, drunkenness, disorderly conduct, vagrancy, and loitering—1,924,000 arrests

5. A large variety of lesser offenses excluding traffic offenses

From the analyses of the arrests made by police, we can see that the vast majority of the arrests are not serious Index crimes but rather what we might call crimes of disorder or actions that annoy citizens and negatively affect their quality of life (for example, offenses involving drugs and alcohol). Even the vast majority of crime fighting the police do is related to order maintenance rather than serious crime.

Though officers do not spend the majority of their time as crime fighters, it is an important role for them. Procedures and safety are important considerations even when officers have K-9 backup.

Dorothy Littell Greco/The Image Works

Table 5.1	Arrests, United States, 2002		
Total[1]	**13,741,438**	Embezzlement	18,552
		Stolen property; buying, receiving, possessing	126,422
Murder and nonnegligent manslaughter	14,158	Vandalism	276,697
Forcible rape	28,288	Weapons; carrying, possessing, etc.	164,446
Robbery	105,774	Prostitution and commercialized vice	79,733
Aggravated assault	472,290	Sex offenses (except forcible rape and prostitution)	95,066
Burglary	288,291	Drug abuse violations	1,538,813
Larceny/theft	1,160,085	Gambling	10,506
Motor vehicle theft	148,943	Offenses against the family and children	140,286
Arson	16,635	Driving under the influence	1,461,746
		Liquor laws	653,819
Violent crime[2]	620,510	Drunkenness	572,735
Property crime[3]	1,613,954	Disorderly conduct	669,938
Crime index[4]	2,234,464	Vagrancy	27,295
		All other offenses	3,662,159
Other assaults	1,288,682	Suspicion	8,899
Forgery and counterfeiting	115,735	Curfew and loitering law violations	141,252
Fraud	337,404	Runaways	125,688

[1]Does not include suspicion.
[2]Violent crimes are offenses of murder, forcible rape, robbery, and aggravated assault.
[3]Property crimes are offenses of burglary, larceny/theft, motor vehicle theft, and arson.
[4]Includes arson.

Source: Federal Bureau of Investigation, *Uniform Crime Reports,* 2002. Retrieved on March 19, 2004, from http://www.fbi.com

PATROLLING THE WEB

Police Forums / Ask a Cop
http://www.officer.com
Officer.com has an interesting group of public forums that enable you to discuss police issues and converse with police officers. Go to officer.com and click on "forums." You may want to just read the entries, or you may post your own questions or comments and get replies.

A 2001 report regarding a national survey of the U.S. public revealed that approximately 44 million citizens have contacts with the police each year. The majority involve motor vehicle or traffic-related issues. Only about .9 of 1 percent involved the use of force by the police.[4]

Order-Maintenance Role

If police are not primarily crime fighters, then what are they? In an effort to determine the proper role of the police, researchers have conducted numerous studies to determine what it is that police do and why people call on their services. A summary of the key studies follows.

In a study of patrol activities in a city of 400,000, John Webster found that providing social service functions and performing administrative tasks accounted for 55 percent of police officers' time and 57 percent of their calls. Activities involving crime fighting took up only 17 percent of patrol time and amounted to about 16 percent of the calls to the police.[5]

A study by Robert Lilly found that of 18,000 calls to a Kentucky police department made during a four-month period, 60 percent were for information, and 13 percent concerned traffic problems. Fewer than 3 percent were about violent crime, and about 2 percent were about theft.[6]

In the Police Services Study (PSS), a survey of 26,000 calls to police in 24 different police departments in 60 neighborhoods, researchers found that only 19 percent of calls involved the report of a criminal activity.[7] Table 5.2 shows a breakdown of all citizens' calls for service in this

PATROLLING THE WEB

Officer Personal Pages
http://www.officer.com
Officer.com has an interesting group of officer personal pages that allow you to get an inside look at officers' and retired officers' professional and personal lives and interests. Go to officer.com and click on "personal pages." The personal page index is arranged according to U.S. states and countries all over the world.

YOU ARE THERE! »

Police TV Series

Since the original *Dragnet* television series, which first ran in 1952, police shows have been very popular on television.

The following is a list of very popular long-running shows and the years they were on. Did you watch any of them? Many of them are still on in reruns. Ask Dad or Mom; they probably remember some of these shows, and it will bring back some memories for them.

Dragnet	1952–59; 1967–70;
	2003–present
Naked City	1958–63
Adam 12	1968–75
Hawaii Five-O	1968–80
Mod Squad	1968–73
McMillan and Wife	1971–76
Columbo	1971–77
Kojak	1973–78
Police Woman	1974–78
Starsky and Hutch	1975–79
Baretta	1975–78
Barney Miller	1975–82
CHiPS	1977–83
Hill Street Blues	1981–87
Cagney and Lacey	1982–88
Miami Vice	1984–89
21 Jump Street	1987–91
In the Heat of the Night	1988–94
Law and Order	1990–present
The Commish	1991–95
Homicide: Life on the Street	1993–99
N.Y.P.D. Blue	1993–present
CSI	2001–present
CSI – Miami	2002–present

Table 5.2	Analysis of Citizens' Calls for Police Service by Percentage
Nonviolent crime	17%
Interpersonal conflict	7
Medical assistance	3
Traffic problem	9
Dependent person	3
Public nuisances	11
Suspicious circumstances	5
Assistance	12
Citizen wants information	21
Citizen wants to give information	8

Source: Adapted from Eric J. Scott, *Calls for Service: Citizen Demand and Initial Police Response* (Washington, DC: U.S. Government Printing Office, 1981), pp. 28–30.

study by general problem types. Similar studies were conducted by Michael Brown in California, Norman Weiner in Kansas City, and Albert J. Reiss in Chicago, with similar results.[8] Additionally, Steven Meagher analyzed the job functions (duties) of 531 police officers in 249 municipal departments and found that, regardless of their size, most police agencies and police officers have similar functions and do pretty much the same thing.[9]

The academic studies clearly indicate that what the police do is maintain order and provide services. People call the police to obtain services or to get help in maintaining order.

Ambiguity of the Police Role

The police role is extremely diverse, **ambiguous**, and dynamic. We must remember that England's Sir Robert Peel, who arranged for the organization of the first paid, full-time, uniformed police department, conceived of the police role as a conspicuous community-oriented patrol designed more for prevention and deterrence than for enforcement. Peel designed the police to be an alternative to the repression of crime and disorder that could have been achieved through military might and severe legal sanctions. (See Chapter 1, "Police History.")

The early American settlers brought Peel's ideas on the role of the police to our shores. As Alan Coffey tells us, however, as the United States began to pass more and more statutory laws, the police role expanded from maintaining order to enforcing the law. Coffey states, "It is this combination of role expectations that generates controversy, particularly with those who emphasize the peacekeeping segment of police work as opposed to actual enforcement."[10]

One way of defining the police role may be to say that it is whatever the community expects the police to be. However, we must remember that most communities consist of many diverse groups with different goals and interests. One group in the community may expect police to do something entirely different from what another group expects. For example, older people in a community or store owners may want the police to hassle teenagers hanging on the street, yet the teenagers, for their part, may feel that if the police do hassle them, the officers are abusing them. Parents in a community may want the police to search and arrest drug dealers and drug users yet not want the police to search their own children. In these and many other ways, the police are often in a no-win situation.

One researcher, George Pugh, writing on the expansive and varied role of the police, states that a good police officer must have the qualities of common sense and mature judgment and must react quickly and effectively to problem situations. A good police officer, Pugh says, must be able to adopt the appropriate role of policing to the situation he or she encounters. Common roles include law enforcer, maintainer of social order, and public servant. Finally, a good police officer must have the appropriate concepts of policing that guide and prioritize the role the officer should employ in particular situations. These concepts governing police work, Pugh says, are (1) an effort to improve the welfare of the community and (2) a respect for the individual's rights, worth, and dignity.[11]

Robert Sheehan and Gary W. Cordner, using the work of previous scholars, offer the following synopsis of the police role:

1. The core of the police role involves law enforcement and the use of coercive force.

2. The primary skill of policing involves effectively handling problem situations while avoiding the use of force.

3. Skillful police officers avoid the use of force primarily through effective, creative communication.[12]

In summing up the police role, we might agree with Joseph J. Senna and Larry J. Siegel. They say that the police role has become that of a social handywoman or handyman called to handle social problems that citizens wish would simply go away.[13]

YOU ARE THERE! ≫

Policing Mardi Gras in New Orleans: Jim Ruiz says, "It happens; guide it, then get out of its way."

The two major views of the role of the police are crime fighting and order maintenance or keeping the peace. While policing parades, officers generally play both roles. As a New York City police officer I was assigned to police a myriad of parades and major events each year. These parades and events included various festive and exciting ethnic parades such as those celebrating St. Patrick's Day, West Indian Day, Columbus Day, Steuben Day, Puerto Rican Day, and the like, as well as New Year's Eve, when millions of partygoers flocked into a very small area of midtown Manhattan. To get a different perspective on policing parades, I have turned to my good friend Professor Jim Ruiz of Pennsylvania State University–Harrisburg, who was formerly a sergeant in the New Orleans, Louisiana, Police Department and a veteran of 18 Mardi Gras seasons as an officer. I've asked him to tell us all about policing what is perhaps the granddaddy of all parades, the 11-day Mardi Gras celebration in New Orleans.

Mardi Gras has been described as "11 days of planned madness." In New Orleans, it is an 11-day parade season. Most parades on the weekdays are scheduled to begin between 6 and 7 P.M. and are not over until 10 P.M., and on weekends they end much after midnight. Officers doing parade duty on weekends often have to work 16- to 18-hour shifts. Often officers who are assigned to the parade formation area or an early portion of the route are collected by police buses after the parade has passed their location and are spirited to another location ahead of the parade (second and third assignments) for crowd control.

Policing Mardi Gras is somewhat of a misnomer. For the police, Mardi Gras is something that happens. Police attempt to guide it and then get out of its way. Most officers attempt to place themselves strategically so they can see what is going on around them. Should they see something amiss, they will usually go in and handle whatever is required and then move out to the fringes once more.

Unlike the traditional Christmas, Thanksgiving, or football bowl parades where those gathered to watch are passive, either sitting on the curb or in lawn chairs, Mardi Gras parade goers are dynamic. Often, the crowd can be compared to rolling surf on the seashore. Because the maskers on the floats are throwing beads, cups, doubloons, Frisbees, and other trinkets, the crowd surges toward the base of a float as it nears and passes. It is important for police officers to stand with their backs to the float, facing the crowd. To do otherwise would be to put

them in a position to be jammed against the float or have someone jumping for throws fall or hit them.

Most parades stop to have various groups perform; this doesn't happen in a Mardi Gras parade. Bands and groups are not to stop to perform. If they do, they are warned once. A second offense results in cutting the unit out of the parade. The parade stops only for the king of each crew to toast the mayor and the queen.

On Mardi Gras day, there is what sometimes seems to be an endless procession of over 350 flatbed 18-wheelers creeping along the parade route. The main duty of the officers assigned to parade route coverage is to try to prevent injury or death to parade goers. In the madness and excitement of the moment people, especially small children, are scampering on the ground for the throws. It is not uncommon for throws to land in front of or roll under a float. Children and even adults will dive for the throws totally oblivious to the danger of the wheels of the float or the tractor pulling it. It is not uncommon to have 30 to 50 maskers on each truck throwing trinkets. Also, it is not uncommon to have someone die because of such an accident.

Danger also lurks behind the crowd, often unknown to those attending the parade, from what is called "The Second Line." This line often forms on the outer edges of the crowd where certain high school bands are marching; it follows the band on both sides of the crowd. The line can consist of upwards of 100 or more youths dancing to the music and passing directly through and sometimes assaulting those standing on the parade route. When I was assigned to the Mounted Division, we would take up positions to the rear of the crowd at a major intersection along with a contingent of motorcycle officers. With Mounted in front and motorcycles as backup, the line was shepherded down a street away from the parade. However, this was rarely successful because the line would run around the block and eventually catch up with the band again. These maneuvers would be performed numerous times along the route. Also, because of the density of the crowd in many places, pickpockets are a problem. Visitors as well as rookie police officers are cautioned not to carry wallets in their rear pockets.

Officers are discouraged from making arrests because most are headed to second and third assignments. To make an arrest would mean that the officer would have to take the person to the rear and require that one or two more officers accompany

YOU ARE THERE! >>

Policing Mardi Gras in New Orleans (*continued*)

him. There they would have to wait for transportation, which is next to impossible because it is common for many areas to be boxed in by the parade.

There are several main issues for officers during the Mardi Gras season. Perhaps first and foremost is the weather. Because Mardi Gras can start as early as the end of January and end as late as the end of February, it has a tendency to occur when low temperatures are common in New Orleans. Add in the high humidity and even a moderate wind, and it can be most uncomfortable for officers standing parade duty. Second is the lack of availability of restroom facilities. It is not uncommon for officers to be stationed in residential neighborhoods, be-

cause most parades begin in the various neighborhoods across the city. The same can be said for officers stationed in the central business district, which is usually closed during parade times. Third are provisions for food and drink. The department makes no provisions for this, and officers are left to find what they can, when they can. Last is fatigue. Long hours, weather, and constant demands of the crowd take their toll on officers in the latter part of the parade season.

Despite the apparent chaos and challenges visitors see at the parades, most New Orleans police officers approach each season as just another one, as we grew up attending Mardi Gras.

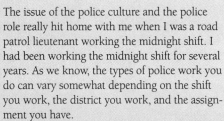

Forst's Law

The Changing View

The issue of the police culture and the police role really hit home with me when I was a road patrol lieutenant working the midnight shift. I had been working the midnight shift for several years. As we know, the types of police work you do can vary somewhat depending on the shift you work, the district you work, and the assignment you have.

On the midnight shift you spend a lot of time working with "bad guys," as most average citizens are home in bed. Obviously, there are exceptions to this; but, overall, officers on midnights are dealing with people on the street who are up to no good. This observation or feeling starts to ingrain itself in an officer's head, and he or she becomes suspicious of everyone encountered. What are they *really* doing? Are they lying? Why? The officer develops a protective attitude physically and mentally when approaching and talking to people during the shift. He or she will assume the worst. This is not necessarily a negative trait when looking at

it in terms of officer safety and survival, but it can have an impact on the officer's interactions with people he or she encounters.

I remember one night seeing a car driving in an area of warehouses where we had numerous burglary problems during the midnight shift hours. I watched the vehicle for a few minutes and then pulled it over. I approached the young male driver and asked him what he was doing out here at this time of day—in other words, what was he really up to? He looked at me quizzically and replied that he was just going to work. He was able to produce paperwork that documented this (which of course doesn't necessarily mean he wasn't doing burglaries in the area). I allowed him to go on his way and thought about the encounter. Though it was still dark, it was just after 6 A.M. and good, hardworking people were in fact getting up and going to work; but I was still thinking of "bad guys" being out and about and up to no good.

Dempsey's Law

Should I Search Her Book Bag, or Should We Take the Chance That She'll Shoot Us? The Inherent Conflict

Diane: *Professor, you always talk about a police officer's responsibility to protect people's individual rights under the U.S. Constitution, but my mom says that an officer's job is to protect society's rights, and the heck with criminals' rights.*

Diane, your mother and I are both discussing the biggest problem in the criminal justice system: the inherent conflict between the rights of the individual, including the criminal, and the rights of society. Let's try an experiment. I hear that Dawn here has a gun in her book bag. If I'm an officer, I should search it, right? [Dempsey takes Dawn's book bag from the floor in front of her desk and acts as if he is going to open it and look in it.] What do you think about that, Dawn?

Dawn: *I don't think that's right, Professor Dempsey. An officer can't just look into anyone's property. I don't think you should look into my bag.*

What's your problem, Dawn? You have a gun in here?

Dawn: *No!*

You have drugs in here?

Dawn: *No!*

But what about Diane's mother's feelings? What about the rights of the students in this society—in this classroom? Do you people want Dawn to pull a gun out of this bag and shoot you?

Dawn: *Yeah, Professor, but what about my rights? What about the Fourth Amendment?*

That's the whole issue. There is an inherent conflict between the rights of the individual as expressed in our Bill of Rights and the rights of society to be free of crime. There is the conflict between Dawn's right that I not search her property unreasonably, based on a hunch, and the rights of the students here not to be shot by Dawn, if she does have a gun. Does anyone know the source of this inconsistency?

Mike: *Yes, our founding fathers created the Bill of Rights, or the first ten amendments to the Constitution, to ensure that government would not violate their rights. They were afraid that the government oppression they faced in England could appear here, too.*

Exactly right, but our founding fathers placed us in a dilemma. There is an inherent conflict between the rights of the individual and the rights of society. Crime is the price we pay for this conflict. The police must balance that conflict. Police officers have a very special obligation to protect society and also to protect everyone's individual rights. I remember one afternoon when I was assigned to the Plaza Hotel in midtown Manhattan. President Reagan was in town, and he always stayed at the Plaza. I was in charge of about a hundred officers who were assigned to the demonstration area in front of the hotel. Our job was to ensure that the demonstration was orderly and that there was no conflict between the demonstrators protesting President Reagan's foreign policy and onlookers. It was raining tremendously, and there was only one demonstrator. He obviously had a mental problem. It was 1985, and this man was holding up signs and screaming, "U.S. get out of Vietnam! Stop the Vietnam War! Reagan is a war criminal!" The man obviously had a problem. Then I saw one of my officers engaged in a rather loud argument with this sole demonstrator. I pulled the officer aside and asked him what the problem was between him and the man. He said to me, "Lieutenant, this man is a nut. Do you hear what he is saying about the president? I told him to stop or I would arrest him, and he started to argue with me about his First Amendment rights." Seeing that the officer had his priorities a little mixed up, I asked if he knew what his role in the demonstration was. He replied, "I'm here to protect the president from this nut." I replied, "Officer, you are here to protect everyone, including this nut."

Diane: *Yeah, professor, I understand all that, but who is right? You or my mom? I respect you both, but who is right?*

John: *Diane, they are both right. The job of the police is to strike a balance between the rights of society and the rights of the individual. Right, Professor?*

You got it, John. And it's not an easy job!

Egon Bittner has stated that from its earliest origins, police work has been a "tainted occupation":

> The taint that attaches to police work refers to the fact that policemen are viewed as the fire it takes to fight fire, that in the natural course of their duties they inflict harm, albeit deserved, and that their very existence attests that the nobler aspirations of mankind do not contain the means necessary to insure survival.[14]

The Police Role in the Aftermath of September 11, 2001

The role of the police and its ambiguity have been further complicated by the terrorist attacks against the United States on September 11, 2001. Since 9/11 the police have been seen by many as the front line of homeland defense against terrorists. Police departments, themselves, have responded to this by forming specialized, military-like antiterrorist units that appear in public as a strong deterrent force against would-be terrorists. This has concentrated attention on the law enforcement role of the police.

The order-maintenance and social service roles of the police have also been reemphasized, as the police are the first responders to all emergencies and unusual occurrences in the nation and are tasked with the many duties that this entails, including crowd control, emergency medical response and treatment, and maintenance of public order in often catastrophic conditions.

See Chapter 16, "Policing and Homeland Defense," which discusses the new duties placed on the police for homeland defense.

★ ★ ★

GOALS AND OBJECTIVES OF POLICING

Much study and research has gone into determining the proper **goals and objectives** of a police department. This topic can be discussed more easily by thinking in terms of primary goals and objectives and secondary goals and objectives.

Primary Goals and Objectives

The two primary goals and objectives of police departments, according to Sheehan and Cordner, are maintaining order and protecting life and property.[15] These are among the most basic roles of government, and government hires the police to perform these services. To achieve these goals, the police perform a myriad of duties. As Senna and Siegel say,

Police are expected to perform many civic duties that in earlier times were the responsibility of every citizen: keeping the peace, performing emergency medical care, and dealing with civil emergencies. Today, we leave those tasks to the police. Although most of us agree that a neighborhood brawl must be broken up, that the homeless family must be found shelter, or the drunk taken safely home, few of us want to jump personally into the fray; we'd rather "call the cops."[16]

Secondary Goals and Objectives

Sheehan and Cordner also list six secondary goals and objectives toward which police resources and activities are used to meet the primary two objectives:

1. Preventing crime
2. Arresting and prosecuting offenders
3. Recovering stolen and missing property
4. Assisting the sick and injured
5. Enforcing noncriminal regulations
6. Delivering services not available elsewhere in the community[17]

The police attempt to prevent crime by trying to create a sense of omnipresence (the police are always there)

Richard Lord

Police officers spend a good part of their days interacting with the residents of their communities. This interaction includes keeping the peace and assisting citizens in various ways.

through routine patrol; responding to calls by citizens to deal with problems that may cause crime; and establishing and participating in police–citizen partnerships designed to prevent crime.

Arresting offenders and assisting prosecutors in bringing charges against defendants is one of the primary methods used by the police to maintain order and protect life and property.

When people find property on the street, they generally bring it to a police officer or to a police station. The police then attempt to find the owner. If that is not possible, they store the property in the hopes that the rightful owner will come in to claim it. When people lose property, they generally go to the police station in the hopes that someone has turned it in. Besides all of their other duties, then, the police serve as society's foremost lost-and-found department.

Because they are available 7 days a week and 24 hours a day and because they are highly mobile, the police generally are the closest government agency to any problem. In many jurisdictions, the police are called to emergency cases of sickness and injury to assess the situation before an ambulance is dispatched, or they are called to assist ambulance, paramedical, or other emergency response personnel.

In the absence of other regulatory personnel or during the times they are not available, the police enforce numerous noncriminal regulations, including traffic and parking regulations, liquor law regulations, and many others.

The police are generally the only government officials available every day, round the clock. When government offices close, the police become roving representatives of the government who assist people with problems no one else is available to handle. When the lights go off in an apartment building, people call the police. When the water main breaks, people call the police. When your neighbor's dog barks all night and keeps you awake, whom do you generally call? You call the police. After all, who else can you call at 3:00 in the morning? The police respond and take whatever action they can to ameliorate problems and deal with emergencies. They direct traffic, evacuate residents, and decide whom to call for assistance.

★ ★ ★

POLICE OPERATIONAL STYLES

People who research the police write about **police operational styles**—styles adopted by police officers as a way of thinking about the role of the police and law in society and how they should perform their jobs. The findings of two

leading researchers, John J. Broderick and James Q. Wilson, will be discussed here. The concept of operational styles is useful in analyzing the police role and police behavior. However, it must be remembered that no officer conforms solely to one of these styles to the exclusion of the others. Many officers show characteristics of several of these styles.

Broderick's Police Operational Styles

John J. Broderick, in his *Police in a Time of Change,* presents four distinct police operational styles: enforcers, idealists, realists, and optimists.[18]

ENFORCERS   Many officers believe that their major role is maintaining order on their beat, keeping society safe, and protecting society by arresting criminals. These "enforcers" place less value on the rights of the individual and on the due process of law granted under the U.S. Constitution than they do on their perceived role, which is maintaining social order and keeping society safe. Enforcers are critical of police administrators, politicians, and the court decisions that favor the rights of the individual over the rights of society.

Enforcers do not like their jobs. They spend much of their time arresting people and then watching these people win court cases based on what the enforcers see as legal technicalities. Furthermore, they often see offenders receiving probation or being released from prison. Enforcers are resentful, cynical, and distrustful, and they tend to stereotype individuals. They seek to return to the "good old days" when, they believe, there was more respect for law and order and the cop on the beat.[19]

IDEALISTS   The officers Broderick calls idealists are similar to enforcers, yet they place a higher value on individual rights and the adherence to due process as required by the U.S. Constitution. Idealists believe that it is their responsibility to keep the peace, to protect citizens from criminals, and to preserve the social order. Idealists tend to be cynical, because they see a system of justice with significant problems. They would like understanding and respect for their contributions to society, but they find that they do not receive it and feel that the public is against them. Idealists would like to be in a position to have some impact on the problems they constantly encounter. Seeing no chance of that, however, they tend to feel powerless.[20]

REALISTS   Broderick's realists suffer many of the same resentments and dissatisfactions with the criminal justice system as enforcers and idealists, but they are more secure

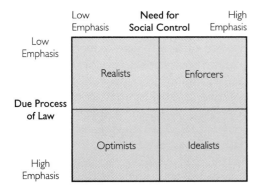

**Figure 5.1
Differences among Broderick's Police
Operational Styles**

Source: Based on John J. Broderick, *Police in a Time of Change,* 2d ed.
(Prospect Heights, IL: Waveland Press, 1987), pp. 21–116.

in themselves and less frustrated with their role in life.
They place a relatively low emphasis on both social order
and individual rights. Realists see due process of law as being an obstacle to criminal justice. They believe that the
goals and objectives of the police (maintaining order and
protecting life and property) are impossible, so they concentrate their efforts on the concept of police loyalty and
the mutual support of their fellow officers. They are complete cynics and do not make attempts to change or affect
the system.[21] As Broderick says, "Realists do not try to
change the world, the offenders, or even the police department. They learn that if you cannot succeed at the job, because of politicians, offenders, and ordinary citizens who
do not understand, then the hell with it—just don't let it
get to you."[22]

OPTIMISTS   Finally, Broderick describes the optimists—
officers who place a relatively high value on individual
rights and see their job as people oriented, as opposed
to crime oriented. Optimists concentrate their efforts on
helping people in trouble rather than on keeping society
safe. They tend to like their jobs and are not cynical.[23]
Figure 5.1 summarizes Broderick's four police operational
styles.

Wilson's Police Operational Styles

In his seminal work *Varieties of Police Behavior: The
Management of Law and Order in Eight Communities,* James
Q. Wilson described three distinct styles of policing that
a police department can deploy in maintaining order and
responding to less serious violations of law. (Within
each style, the police treat serious felonies similarly.)

Wilson discussed the watchman style, the legalistic style,
and the service style.[24] He found that the political culture
of a city, which reflects the socioeconomic characteristics
of the city and its organization of government, exerts a
major influence on the style of policing exercised by the
police.

WATCHMAN STYLE   Departments that operate using
the watchman style are primarily concerned with order
maintenance—maintaining order and controlling illegal
and disruptive behavior. Officers in a watchman-style department exercise a great deal of discretion (see the section
entitled "Police Discretion") and ignore many minor violations, especially those involving juveniles and traffic.
These departments tolerate a certain amount of vice and
gambling.

Watchman-style departments maintain order, when
necessary, through informal police intervention. Officers
use persuasion and threats, or even "hassle" or "rough up"
disruptive people, instead of making formal arrests. This
style, Wilson says, is generally found in working-class
communities with partisan mayor–city council forms of
government.

LEGALISTIC STYLE   Legalistic departments, according
to Wilson, enforce the letter of the law. They issue many
summonses and make many misdemeanor arrests. They
proceed vigorously against illegal enterprises. The legalistic
style of enforcement envisions a single standard of conduct
in a community and ensures that all members of the community live up to this standard. This style does not make
allowances for juveniles, minorities, or intoxicated people.
The legalistic style of enforcement, Wilson says, occurs in
reform administrations' government styles. Furthermore,
this style often occurs in the aftermath of a scandal in a
watchman type of department that results in the hiring of a
"reform" police chief.

SERVICE STYLE   Wilson's service departments stress servicing the needs of the community. The officers see themselves more as helpers than as soldiers in a war against
crime. Service-oriented departments work hand in hand
with social service agencies to provide counseling for minor offenders and to assist community groups in preventing crimes and solving problems. Service departments take
all requests for service, law enforcement, or order maintenance seriously. They have a high rate of police intervention, but without the arrests and summonses found in legalistic departments. The service style, Wilson says, is
generally found in more affluent suburban areas.

★ ★ ★

POLICE DISCRETION

The use of discretion is one of the major challenges facing U.S. police today. The following sections will discuss the meaning of police discretion, how and why it is exercised, what factors influence discretion, and how it can be controlled.

What Is Discretion?

Discretion means the availability of a choice of options or actions one can take in a situation. We all exercise discretion many times every day in our lives. At a restaurant, we have discretion in selecting a steak dinner or a fish dinner. At the video store, we have discretion in picking a mystery or a comedy to view. Discretion involves making a judgment and a decision. It involves selecting one from a group of options.

The criminal justice system involves a tremendous amount of discretion. A judge exercises discretion in sentencing. He or she can sentence a defendant to a prison term or to probation. A judge can release a defendant on bail or order the defendant incarcerated until trial. Prosecutors exercise discretion: They can reduce charges against a defendant or drop the charges entirely. Parole boards exercise discretion: They can parole a person from prison or order him or her to serve the complete sentence. The entire criminal justice system is based on the concept of discretion.

Why is there so much discretion in the U.S. system of criminal justice? In our system, we tend to treat people as individuals. One person who commits a robbery is not the same as another person who commits a robbery. Our system takes into account why the person committed the crime and how he or she committed it. Were there any mitigating or aggravating circumstances? The U.S. system is interested in the spirit of the law, in addition to the letter of the law.

When a judge, a prosecutor, or a parole board member exercises discretion, each generally has sufficient time and data necessary to make a careful, reasoned decision. The judge can read the presentence report prepared by the probation department or consult with the probation department staff member preparing the report. The judge can also consult with the district attorney or the defense attorney. The prosecutor and parole board member also have sufficient data and time in which to decide what action to take in a case.

However, the majority of the most crucial decisions made in the criminal justice system do not take place as described in the previous paragraph. The most important decisions do not take place within an ornately decorated courtroom or a wood-paneled conference room. They take place on the streets. They take place any time of the day or night and generally without the opportunity for the decision makers to consult with others or to carefully consider all the facts. These split-second decisions are often based on little information. They take place at the very lowest level in the criminal justice system. The police officer is generally the first decision maker in the U.S. criminal justice system and is often the most important.

James Q. Wilson described the police officer's role in exercising discretion as being "unlike that of any other occupation . . . one in which sub-professionals, working alone, exercise wide discretion in matters of utmost importance (life and death, honor and dishonor) in an environment that is apprehensive and perhaps hostile."[25]

Two researchers state, "The police really suffer the worst of all worlds: they must exercise broad discretion behind a facade of performing in ministerial fashion; and they are expected to realize a high level of equality and justice in their discretionary determinations though they have not been provided with the means most commonly relied upon in government to achieve these ends."[26] Kenneth Culp Davis, an expert on police discretion, says, "The police make policy about what law to enforce, how much to enforce it, against whom, and on what occasions."[27]

Not much happens in the U.S. criminal justice system without the use of discretion by the police. How does a police officer exercise discretion on the street?

How Is Discretion Exercised?

The police exercise discretion to perform the following crucial actions:

- To arrest
- To stop, question, or frisk
- To use physical force
- To use deadly force
- To write traffic summonses
- To use certain enforcement tactics (harassment, moving loiterers, warning, and so on)
- To take a report on a crime
- To investigate a crime

The extent of police discretion is indicated by the following research findings. Donald Black found that only 58 percent of adults suspected of felonies were arrested.[28] John A. Gardiner found that Dallas police officers wrote traffic tickets at a rate 20 times higher than that of Boston police.[29] The Police Foundation noted that the police in Birmingham, Alabama, shot and killed citizens at a rate of 25 per 1,000 officers, compared with 4.2 per 1,000 in Portland, Oregon.[30]

Why Is Discretion Exercised?

Discretion is an extremely necessary part of police work. Sheehan and Cordner tell us that there are seven reasons why the police exercise discretion:

1. If the police attempted to enforce all the laws all the time, they would be in the station house or court all the time and would not be on the street maintaining order and protecting life and property.

2. Because of political realities, legislators pass some laws that they do not intend to have strictly enforced all the time.

3. Lawmakers pass some laws that are vague and ill-defined, making it necessary for the police to interpret these laws and decide when to apply them.

4. Most violations of the law are minor (for example, traffic violations) and do not require full enforcement.

5. The complete enforcement of all the laws all the time would alienate the public from the police and the entire criminal justice system.

6. The full enforcement of all the laws would overwhelm the courts, jails, and prisons.

7. The police have so many duties to perform and such limited resources that good judgment must be exercised in when, where, and how they enforce the law.[31]

YOU ARE THERE! >>

You Decide

Think about what you would do as a police officer under the following circumstances. This is a perfect example of a case calling for the exercise of police discretion.

FACTS

You receive a call to respond to a boy who is bleeding on the street. You arrive at the location, and you find a 14-year-old Asian boy, naked and with blood on his buttocks; a male in his late 20s or early 30s; and two women. The two women tell you that the man must be trying to kill the boy. The boy is too dazed to respond and remains mute. The man tells you that he and the boy are homosexual lovers and were having an argument.

WHAT WOULD YOU DO?

If you were the police officer at the scene, which of the following actions would you take?

- Further question all parties at the scene.
- Bring all parties to the station house for further investigation.
- Request that your supervisor or the detectives meet you at the scene.

- Arrest the man for assault and sexual relations with a minor.
- Ignore the situation and let these people solve their own problems.

THE ACTUAL CASE

The previous facts are from an actual case you probably recognize. Shortly after midnight on May 27, 1990, two women saw a man chasing a 14-year-old Asian boy, naked and with blood on his buttocks, down an alley behind the Oxford Apartments in a low-income area of Milwaukee, Wisconsin. The women called the police. Two police officers arrived in a patrol car. The man told the police officers that he and the boy were gay lovers having a spat. The officers told all parties to go home and resumed patrol.

The boy was later identified as Konerak Sinthasomphone after his remains were found amid the carnage at Apartment 213 of the Oxford Apartments in 1991. The man was later identified as Jeffrey Dahmer. When the police searched Dahmer's apartment, they found parts of at least 11 bodies. These included three severed heads in the refrigerator; decomposed hands and a genital organ in a lobster pot; five full skeletons; and the remains of six other bodies, three of which were in a chemical-filled, 57-gallon plastic drum in the basement. Dahmer later confessed to the murder of 17 males.

What Factors Influence Discretion?

We know that officers practice discretion, and we know that discretion is necessary. Are there factors, however, that cause the police to exercise discretion in a certain way? Scholars have been studying this issue for quite a while.

Herbert Jacob says that four major factors influence police officers in determining the exercise of discretion:

1. *Characteristics of the crime.* A serious crime leaves the police less freedom or ability to ignore it or exercise discretion regarding it.

2. *Relationship between the alleged criminal and the victim.* Generally, the police tend to avoid making arrests when a perpetrator and a victim have a close relationship. In recent years, however, many departments have limited discretion in family-related assault cases and have adopted proarrest policies. Family-related assault cases will be discussed in Chapter 15.

3. *Relationship between police and the criminal or victim.* Generally, a respectful, mannerly complainant is taken more seriously and treated better by the police than an antagonistic one. In the same way, a violator who acts respectfully to the police is also less likely to be arrested than an antagonistic one.

4. *Department policies.* The preferences of the police chief and city administration, as expressed in department policy, generally influence the actions of the officer.[32]

In *Varieties of Police Behavior,* Wilson found that an officer's discretion varied depending on the type of situation he or she encountered. Wilson found that police have wide latitude in self-initiated situations, such as the enforcement of traffic or drug violations, because there is usually no complainant or victim demanding police action. However, in citizen-initiated situations, an officer has less discretion, and the preferences of the citizen will often influence the officer's decision whether to arrest or not to arrest.[33]

Research has identified five other specific factors that may influence police discretion to arrest: the subject's offense, attitude, race, socioeconomic status, and gender. Studies of police discretion have shown that the most significant factor in the decision to arrest is the seriousness of the offense committed. This factor is supplemented by other information, such as the offender's current mental state, the offender's past criminal record (when known to the arresting officer), whether weapons were involved, the availability of the complainant, and the relative danger to the officer involved.[34]

Irving Pilavin and Scott Briar found that the subject's attitude greatly influenced an officer's discretion to arrest. With the exception of offenders who had committed serious crimes or who were wanted by the police, the disposition of juvenile cases depended largely on how a youth's character was evaluated by the officer. This evaluation and the decisions that followed from it were limited to information gathered by police during their encounter with the juveniles.[35]

Numerous studies have looked at discretion to arrest as it relates to the race of the offender and the race of the victim. A study by Dennis Powell found that a community's racial makeup may influence police discretion. Powell studied five adjacent police jurisdictions and found that the police in predominantly African American, urban communities demonstrated a higher use of discretion and were more punitive toward whites than toward African Americans, whereas police in predominantly white areas were significantly more punitive toward African American offenders than toward white offenders.[36] Dale Dannefer and Russel Schutt found that racial bias was often present in the patrol officer's decision to arrest juveniles and bring them to juvenile court.[37]

Some studies have indicated that the victim's race rather than the criminal's race was the key to racial bias in the use of discretion. It was discovered that the police are more likely to take formal action when the victim of a crime is white than they are when the victim is a minority group member.[38] Cecil Willis and Richard Wells found that police were more likely to report child abuse involving white families than African American families.[39]

There is also evidence that the influence of race on police discretion varies from jurisdiction to jurisdiction and may be a function of the professionalism of the individual department.[40] However, a number of studies have produced data indicating that racial bias does not influence the decision to arrest and process a suspect.[41]

Douglas Smith and Jody Klein found that the socioeconomic status of a neighborhood had a great deal of influence on police discretion in domestic violence cases. The researchers found that the police were much more likely to arrest spouse abusers in lower-class neighborhoods than in middle- and upper-class neighborhoods. They also found that a person's income level influenced whether the police took a complaint seriously.[42]

As for a subject's gender, Douglas Smith and Christy Visher found that males and females were equally likely to be arrested and formally processed for law violations

Police officers arrest Iraq war protestors blocking the entrance to Lockheed Martin in Pennsylvania, January 20, 2003. Although officers usually have a good deal of discretion, some incidents restrict this discretion and may require officers to make arrests regardless of their political or social beliefs.

when encountered by the police.[43] Other researchers have found that gender bias has decreased from earlier years.[44]

Some studies have found that more than one of the factors just discussed affect police decision making. For example, Christy Visher found that police were more likely to arrest women whose attitude and actions deviated from the stereotype of "proper" female behavior. Visher also found that older white female suspects were less likely to be arrested than younger African American women.[45]

Studies on factors influencing police discretion and police decision making continue. A review of recent literature points to the tremendous complexity of the issue and the concern we all should have regarding it.[46]

How Can Discretion Be Controlled?

In recent years, much attention has been given to the need to prepare police for the appropriate use of discretion.[47] Most experts believe that discretion itself is not bad, but that the real problem is uncontrolled or unregulated discretion. The experts feel that discretion cannot and should not be abolished but believe that police departments should attempt to control or regulate it.[48]

Most researchers believe that discretion should be narrowed to the point where all officers in the same agency are dealing with similar issues in similar ways. They feel there should be limits on discretion that reflect the objectives, priorities, and operating philosophy of the department. The limits on discretion should be sufficiently specific to enable an officer to make judgments in a wide variety of unpredictable circumstances in a proper, unbiased manner that will achieve a reasonable degree of uniformity in handling similar incidents in the community.[49]

One approach to managing police behavior involves requiring obedience to a formal set of policies or guidelines that can ensure the just administration of the law. The New York City Police Department established written policies regarding the use of deadly force as far back as the early 1970s. These policies dramatically reduced the number of shootings of civilians by the police, as well as reduced the number of officers shot by civilians. In the 1980s, the NYPD and many other departments established formal procedures for dealing with emotionally disturbed persons and other issues.

Wilson tells us that controlling discretion involves more than just establishing policies and ensuring that they are obeyed. Managing discretion involves an effort by management to instill a proper value system in officers. According to Wilson, controlling discretion "depends only partly on sanctions and inducements; it also requires instilling in them a shared outlook or ethos that provides for them a common definition of the situations they are likely to encounter and that to the outsider gives to the organization its distinctive character or 'feel.'"[50]

PATROLLING THE WEB

Police Discretion at NCJRS
  http://www.ncjrs.org
NCJRS has an online library of numerous important issues in policing and criminal justice. Go to ncjrs.org, click on "abstracts," and enter "police discretion" in the subject area. You will get numerous studies on police discretion.

CHAPTER SUMMARY

This chapter has concerned the role of the police in the United States. It discussed two major ways of looking at the police role—the crime-fighting role (law enforcement) and the order-maintenance role (peacekeeping and providing social services)—as well as the ambiguity of the police role and the changing role of the police in the aftermath of the terrorist attacks of September 11, 2001.

Two primary goals and objectives of police departments are maintaining order and protecting life and property. Secondary goals may include preventing crime, arresting and prosecuting offenders, recovering stolen and missing property, assisting sick and injured people, enforcing non-criminal regulations, and delivering services not available elsewhere in the community.

Police officers adopt a police operational style in thinking about the role of police and law in society and how they should do their jobs. John J. Broderick identifies these styles as enforcers, idealists, realists, and optimists. James Q. Wilson describes three styles police departments adopt: the watchman, legalistic, and service styles.

An important aspect of a police officer's job is the exercise of discretion. The chapter examined what discretion means, how and why it is exercised, what factors influence the use of discretion by the police, and how police departments can attempt to control discretion.

Learning Check

1. Explain the basic difference between the crime-fighting role and the order-maintenance role of the police.
2. List the major goals and objectives of the police.
3. Compare and contrast each of James Q. Wilson's police department operational styles.
4. Discuss some of the major ways police exercise discretion.
5. Identify some of the major factors that influence police discretion.

Application Exercise

Interview or ride with officers from your local police or sheriff's department. Determine the following:

1. To which role—crime fighting or order maintenance—do the officers seem to subscribe?
2. Which of Broderick's police operational styles do the officers' styles most resemble?
3. Which of James Q. Wilson's styles does the department seem to resemble?
4. What factors influence the decisions the officers make regarding stopping, summonsing, and arresting people?

Web Exercise

Patrol the Internet and click onto a police department's home page of your choice. Review and analyze the content of their Web site and determine which role this department seems to reflect: the crime-fighting role or the order-maintenance role.

Key Concepts

Ambiguous role
Crime-fighting role
Discretion
Order maintenance
Police operational styles
Police role

The Police Culture and Personality and Police Stress

CHAPTER GOALS

- To acquaint you with the research indicating the existence of a distinct police culture or subculture
- To familiarize you with studies of the police personality, including attempts made to define the police personality and to determine whether it comes from officers' own personalities or from the occupation
- To present studies of police cynicism and to familiarize you with the Dirty Harry problem. Do good endings justify the use of bad means to achieve those endings?
- To discuss one of the most serious police problems, police stress, and to see why it occurs, how it is exhibited, and what means can be taken to deal with it
- To discuss the serious and sad problems of police officer suicide and "suicide by cop"

On September 11, 2001, police officers throughout New York City, many responding while off duty, raced through the streets to respond to a 911 call reporting that a plane had crashed into New York City's World Trade Center. The rest is history. Many rushed into the building to help citizens get out. They rushed in while regular citizens rushed out. Thirty-seven Port Authority of New York/New Jersey police officers, 23 New York City police officers, and 3 New York court officers lost their lives in their valiant effort to protect and serve. Were these brave officers displaying the traits of the police culture?

Many experts and researchers studying the police write about such concepts as a distinct police culture or subculture and a distinct police personality. Are the police different from most other people? Much research indicates that they are. If they are different, were they born that way, or did police work make them like that?

This chapter will discuss such concepts as the police culture or subculture, the police personality, police cynicism, the Dirty Harry problem, police stress, police suicide, and "suicide by cop." Police stress is a serious issue facing the police. Therefore, this chapter will attempt to define it and to show why it occurs, how it exhibits itself, and how police agencies can deal with it. The problems of stress and the need for departments to address it was emphasized in the aftermath of the terrorist attacks of September 11, 2001, when the NYPD ordered all 55,000 of its employees to attend mental health counseling to deal with the stress brought about due to this event.[1]

This chapter will also discuss police suicide and "suicide by cop" and how these problems can be dealt with.

★ ★ ★

THE POLICE CULTURE OR SUBCULTURE

Numerous academic studies have indicated that the nature of policing and the experiences officers go through on the job cause them to band together into their own subculture, which many researchers call the police culture or police subculture.[2] For example, if someone who was not a police officer walked into a bar at 1:00 A.M. and overheard a group of men and women engaged in animated conversation using such words as collars, mopes, skells, perps, EDPs, and shooflies, he or she would have great difficulty understanding. However, to the off-duty police officers having a few drinks and talking about their previous tour of duty, each word has a precise meaning.

Exhibit 6.1	Traits of the Police Culture / Subculture

- Clannishness
- Isolation from the public
- Secrecy
- Honor
- Loyalty
- Individuality

A subculture may be defined as the culture of a particular group that is smaller than, and essentially different from, the dominant culture in a society. The **police culture** or **police subculture**, then, is a combination of shared norms, values, goals, career patterns, lifestyles, and occupational structures that is substantially different from the combination held by the rest of society. The police subculture, like most subcultures, is characterized by clannishness, secrecy, and isolation from those not in the group. Police officers work with other police officers during their

Courtesy of Linda Forst

Due to challenging work schedules, police officers often socialize more frequently with other officers than with the average citizen. Though this might increase isolation, in some cases it can be beneficial for stress reduction by providing a healthy opportunity to ventilate and exercise.

tours of duty. Many socialize together after work and on days off, often to the exclusion of others—even old friends and family. When socializing, off-duty officers tend to talk about their jobs.

Working strange shifts of duty—especially 4 to 12s (4:00 P.M. to 12:00 midnight) and midnights (12:00 midnight to 8:00 A.M.) and working weekends and holidays—make it difficult for the police officer to socialize with the average person, who works a 9-to-5 job Monday through Friday. Many police officers find it difficult to sleep after a tense, busy evening tour. If officers want to socialize or relax after work instead of going home to a house whose inhabitants have to get up at 6:00 A.M. to go to regular jobs, they tend to socialize with their comrades from the precinct. When officers work weekends, their days off fall during the average person's workweek, so again, many tend to socialize with other officers. Police spouses tend to socialize with other police spouses, and police families tend to associate with other police families. After a while, the police world (the Job) is the only world for many officers.

Michael K. Brown, in *Working the Street*, tells us that police officers create their own culture to deal with the recurring anxiety and emotional stress that is endemic to policing. Brown believes that the police subculture is based on three major principles: honor, loyalty, and individuality.[3]

Honor is given to officers for engaging in risk-taking behavior. (An example of risk-taking behavior is being the first one in the door to challenge an armed adversary when taking cover and waiting for backup would have been the more prudent course of action.)

Loyalty is a major part of the police subculture, and police loyalty is extremely intense. The word *backup* occurs often in police officer conversations. Backup involves not only assisting other officers in emergency situations but also coming to their aid when they are challenged, criticized, or even charged with wrongdoing. Brown explains the importance of backup by pointing out that the violence that police must deal with and the strong bonding that occurs among police officers "places the highest value upon the obligation to back up and support a fellow officer."[4]

The ideal officer, then, according to the police subculture, takes risks (honor), is first on the scene to aid a fellow police officer (loyalty), and is able to handle any situation by doing it her or his own way (individuality).

The idea of danger permeates the police subculture. George L. Kirkham, a college professor who became a police officer to better understand his police students, discusses the police mistrust of civilians and police reliance upon their own peer group support to survive on the streets: "As someone who had always regarded policemen

as a 'paranoid lot,' I discovered in the daily round of violence which became part of my life that chronic suspiciousness is something that a good cop cultivates in the interest of going home to his family each evening."[5]

Bittner also has said that an esprit de corps develops in police work as a function of the dangerous and unpleasant tasks police officers are required to do. Police solidarity, a "one for all, and all for one" attitude, Bittner says, is one of the most cherished aspects of the police occupation.[6]

A student interested in studying the police culture might be interested in seeing some police officer homepages or personal pages on the Internet, where active and retired police officers from all over the nation and abroad have created their own personal pages. Often, retired officers will contact former colleagues through the Internet. A good Web site to search for these officer personal pages is officer.com.

★ ★ ★

THE BLUE WALL OF SILENCE

Studies of the police culture indicate that police officers protect one another from outsiders, often even refusing to aid police superiors or other law enforcement officials in investigating wrongdoing of other officers. Many believe that this part of the police culture or the police subculture produces a protective barrier known as the **"blue wall of silence."**[7]

Writing about the police subculture and the "blue wall of silence," Egon Bittner says, "Policing is a dangerous occupation and the availability of unquestioned support and loyalty is not something officers could readily do without."[8]

Robert Sheehan and Gary W. Cordner write about how this aspect of the police subculture can destroy the reputation and integrity of a police department: "The influence of dominant police subcultural role expectations can have a devastating effect on a police department. In fact the existence of such unofficially established, negative, institutionalized role expectations is the primary reason that so many police departments are held in such low esteem by the public."[9]

High-ranking San Francisco law enforcement officials pled innocent after being indicted in March 2003 for allegedly covering up a street fight that involved off-duty officers. What message does this type of incident send to the public?

©Frederic Larson/San Francisco Chronicle/Corbis

Sheehan and Cordner give two examples of how the police subculture can create a "blue wall of silence" and adversely affect a police department in two fictional cities, Cod Bay and Tulane City.[10] In Cod Bay, a police sergeant is dealing with an irate motorist whose car was towed because it was parked illegally. As the sergeant talks to the officer who wrote the summons that caused the car to be towed, the sergeant realizes that the motorist's car was indeed parked legally, and the towing was in error. The sergeant, however, following the dominant police subcultural expectation that he must back the officer whether he was right or wrong, tells the motorist that in order to get his car back, he must pay the towing charge.

In Sheehan and Cordner's other fictional city, Tulane City, politics rules the police department. A police chief who is appointed by local politicians accepts corruption, incompetence, and brutality by his officers because he realizes that when another mayor takes office, that mayor will select his own police chief, and he himself will return to the department in a lower rank. If he had tried to reform the police department while chief he would be ostracized by officers when he returned to a lower status. Failing to adhere to the existing police subculture would have been dangerous to the chief in the future.

Another example of the police subcultural "blue wall of silence" is William Westley's classic study of the Gary (Indiana) Police Department, in which he found a police culture that had its own customs, law, and morality. Westley says these values produce the **"blue curtain"**—a situation in which police officers trust only other police officers and do not aid in the investigation of wrongdoing by other officers. Westley calls the "blue curtain" a barrier that isolates police officers from the rest of society.[11]

★ ★ ★

THE POLICE PERSONALITY

The police subculture leads to what scholars call the **police personality**, or traits common to most police officers. Scholars have reported that this personality is thought to include such traits as authoritarianism, suspicion, hostility, insecurity, conservatism, and cynicism.[12]

This section will attempt to describe the characteristics of the police personality, what shapes the police personality, and the causes and effects of police cynicism.

What Is the Police Personality?

The scholar Jerome Skolnick coined the phrase "working personality of police officers."[13] Skolnick stated that the police officer's "working personality" is shaped by constant exposure to danger and the need to use force and authority to reduce and control threatening situations.[14] Skolnick wrote

> The policeman's role contains two principal variables, danger and authority, which should be interpreted in the light of a "constant" pressure to appear efficient. The element of danger seems to make the policeman especially attentive to signs indicating a potential for violence and lawbreaking. As a result the policeman is generally a "suspicious person." Furthermore, the character of the policeman's work makes him less desirable as a friend since norms of friendship implicate others in his work. Accordingly the element of danger isolates the policeman socially from that segment of the citizenry whom he regards as symbolically dangerous and also from the conventional citizenry with whom he identifies.[15]

Elizabeth Burbeck and Adrian Furnham have identified three important features of an officer's working personality: danger, authority, and isolation from the public.[16] Additionally, Burbeck and Furnham reviewed the literature comparing the attitudes of police officers with those of the general population and found that police officers place a higher emphasis on terminal values (such as family security, mature love, and a sense of accomplishment) than on social values (such as equality).

One example of the studies Burbeck and Furnham looked at was the Rokeach study. Social psychologist Milton Rokeach and his colleagues studied police officers in Lansing, Michigan. He compared their personality traits with a national sample of private citizens and concluded that police officers seemed more oriented toward self-control and obedience than the average citizen. Also, police were more interested in personal goals, such as "an exciting life," and less interested in social goals, such as "a world of peace." Rokeach also compared values of veteran officers with those of recruits and discovered no significant differences. Rokeach believed police officers have a particular value orientation and personality before they start their police career.[17]

Exhibit 6.2   Traits of the Police Personality

- Authoritarianism
- Suspicion
- Hostility
- Insecurity
- Conservatism
- Cynicism

Many social scientists have attempted to duplicate the Rokeach study to see if the recruit police officer has values that differ from those of the ordinary citizen. The results have been mixed and inconclusive. Some researches have found that police officers are actually psychologically healthier, less depressed and anxious, and more social and assertive than the general population.[18]

Are They Born Like That, or Is It the Job?

Two opposing viewpoints on the development of the police personality exist. One says that police departments recruit people who by nature possess those traits that we see in the police personality. The second point of view holds that officers develop those traits through their socialization and experiences in the police department.[19]

Edward Thibault, Lawrence M. Lynch, and R. Bruce McBride tell us that the majority of studies have found that the police working personality derives from the socialization process in the police academy, field training, and patrol experience.[20] John Van Maanen also asserts that the police personality is developed through the process of learning and doing police work. In a study of one urban police department, he found that the typical police recruit is a sincere individual who becomes a police officer for the job security, salary, belief that the job will be interesting, and the desire to enter an occupation than can benefit society.[21] Van Maanen found that, at the academy, highly idealistic recruits are taught to have a strong sense of camaraderie with follow rookies. The recruits begin to admire the exploits of the veteran officers who are their teachers. From their instructors, the recruits learn when to do police work by the book and when to ignore department rules and rely on personal discretion.[22]

Van Maanen says that the learning process continues when the recruits are assigned to street duty and trained by field training officers. The recruits listen to the folklore, myths, and legends about veteran officers and start to understand police work in the way that older officers desire them to. By adopting the sentiments and behavior of the older officers, the new recruits avoid ostracism and censure by their supervisors and colleagues.[23]

Richard J. Lundman says that the formal training at the police academy—courses in law and criminal procedure—do not teach the recruits what they really want to know. Recruits, according to Lundman, want to know the following: "What is it really like out there on the streets? How do I arrest someone who doesn't want to be arrested? Exactly when do I use my nightstick, and how do I do it? What do the other patrol officers think of me?"

Dempsey's Law

Do Any of You Have Parents Who Are Police Officers?

We have just discussed the police personality. Does anyone in the class have a parent who is a police officer, who might have displayed aspects of the police personality?

Neill: *Professor, my father was an officer for 20 years. He's retired now, and he's slowed down a lot. But when he was a cop, he was really wired up. If a car he didn't recognize drove down the block, he would really stare down the driver. And once, when I was 16, I got a speeding ticket. You know how sometimes parents will ground a kid—take away driving privileges—for a while over something like that. Well, he told me I was grounded until I was 21.*

Sounds reasonable to me. Cathy, how about you? I know your mom is a deputy sheriff with the county. Is she different from other moms?

Cathy: *Well, she's very suspicious. Whenever I'm going out, she wants to know where I'm going, whom I'm going with, and what I'm doing. She's always warning me about bad things that can happen to me when I go out. And her hours are terrible. Every week she has to work different tours, and also weekends and holidays. Even though she tried, she could never go to my high school plays or my band recitals. Most of the other kids had their parents there. I know she loves her job, but in a way, she's kind of sad she can't be like most moms.*

Kim: *Professor, my father's a cop in the city, and because of him I couldn't even get a date to my senior prom. Every time a guy would come to the house, my dad would interrogate him—ask him questions like "Where do you work? Where do you go to school? Why is your car so noisy?" He always had something to say about their clothes. When the boys would leave, he would interrogate me, like "Who was that kid? How come his hair was so long?" Guys don't want to hang out with a girl who has a father like that.*

Well, Kim, I find that quite reasonable conduct for a father. Let me tell you about my daughter Anne Marie's first date. This young man asked her to go to a dance with him in Great Neck, which is quite a distance from our home. She was about 16, and it was her first formal date. Knowing my police personality, I guess, she told me he was coming over Saturday afternoon to meet me before their date the following Friday night. Saturday afternoon he shows up in a suit, and it was a hot summer day. I can just imagine what Anne Marie told him about me.

When I interrogated him—I mean talked to him—I asked him how they were going to get to Great Neck. He said that he didn't have a car, so they would take the railroad. I said to him, "Instead of taking the railroad and paying all that money, I'll drive you to the dance." He didn't object. On the following Friday, he showed up to pick up my daughter, and I drove them to the dance. I sat in my car outside drinking coffee until it was over, and I drove the young man back to his house and then took my daughter home. He never called her again. I wonder . . .

Daniel: *Now that you are retired, Professor Dempsey, has anything about your personality or conduct changed?*

That's a good question, Daniel. I think I'm much less suspicious than I was. I remember my wife used to get very annoyed whenever we went out to a restaurant for dinner. I always had to sit in a chair with my back to a wall and in a position where I could see whoever was coming into the restaurant. Whenever people came in the door, I would check them out. My wife thought I was ignoring her. The other night we went out to eat, and I sat with my back to the door. She noticed it and remarked about it to me. But it took a long time to change. I've been retired about 16 years now.

To answer these questions, Lundman says, instructors tell war stories. Most of the war stories stress police defensiveness (the distrust police officers have of outsiders, or non–police officers) and police depersonalization (the tendency of police officers to treat violence, victims, and other unpleasant experiences in a matter-of-fact way in an attempt not to get emotionally affected by all the human misery they see).[24] By stressing the danger of police work and the need for officers to group together and defend themselves from civilians, the instructors reinforce the police subculture and help to create the police personality.

A recently completed longitudinal study of attitudes of police over time as they were exposed to police work certainly showed an effect. The study tested police recruits during the first week of the academy and then at several follow-up periods up to almost four years after the academy. The testing included the MMPI, standard demographic questions, questions concerning the respondent's physical exercise program and tobacco use, an alcohol consumption assessment, and Niederhoffer's cynicism scale. There was clear evidence that the personality characteristics of the officers started to change shortly after their induction into the policing environment. With rare exceptions, officers tended to become more cynical, more paranoid, more depressed, angrier, more dominant, and more hostile, the longer they were in the policing environment. White females were the least affected group, and black females were the most affected group. Black males were more affected by their exposure to policing than white males.[25]

Conversely, a number of researchers have found little evidence that a "typical" police personality actually exists. Studies by sociologists Larry Tifft, David Bayley and Harold Mendelsohn, and Robert Balch indicate that even experienced police officers are quite similar to the average citizen.[26] Nevertheless, the weight of existing evidence generally points to the existence of a unique police personality that develops from the police socialization process.

★ ★ ★

POLICE CYNICISM

Police cynicism is an attitude that there is no hope for the world and a view of humanity at its worst. This is produced by the police officer's constant contact with offenders and what he or she perceives as miscarriages of justice, such as lenient court decisions and plea bargaining.

Arthur Niederhoffer described police cynicism:

Cynicism is an emotional plank deeply entrenched in the ethos of the police world and it serves equally well for attack or defense. For many reasons police are particularly vulnerable to cynicism. When they succumb, they lose faith in people, society, and eventually in themselves. In their Hobbesian view, the world becomes a jungle in which crime, corruption and brutality are normal features of terrain.[27]

Niederhoffer, a former New York City Police Department lieutenant and then professor at John Jay College of Criminal Justice, wrote what is one the best known studies of the police personality, *Behind the Shield: The Police in Urban Society*. Niederhoffer examined the thesis that most police officers develop into cynics as a function of their experience

as police officers.[28] Niederhoffer tested Westley's assumption that police officers learn to mistrust the citizens they are paid to protect as a result of being constantly faced with keeping people in line and believing that most people are out to break the law or injure a police officer.[29] Niederhoffer distributed a survey measuring attitudes and values to 220 New York City police officers. Among his most important findings were that police cynicism increased with length of service in the police department, that police officers with a college education became quite cynical if they were denied promotion, and that quasi-military police academy training caused new recruits to become cynical about themselves quickly. For example, Niederhoffer found that nearly 80 percent of first-day recruits believed that the police department was an "efficient, smoothly operating organization." Two months later, fewer than a third held that belief. Also, half the new recruits believed that a police superior was "very interested in the welfare of his subordinates." Two months later, that number declined to 13 percent.[30]

Robert Regoli and Eric Poole found evidence that police officers' feelings of cynicism intensify their need to obtain the respect of citizens and increase their desire to exert authority other others. Regoli and Poole note, however, that as police escalate the use of authority to obtain respect, citizens learn to mistrust and fear them. In turn, the citizens' feelings of hostility and anger create feelings of potential danger among police officers, resulting in "police paranoia."[31] Regoli and Poole also found that negative attitudes of the police contribute to their tendency to be very conservative and resistant to change—factors that interfere with the efficiency of police work.[32]

Cynicism may hurt the relationship between the police and the public, but it may help advance an officer in his or her career within the department. In a longitudinal study of police officers in Georgia, Richard Anson, J. Dale Mann, and Dale Sherman found that the officers with the most cynical attitudes were the ones most likely to get high supervisory ratings. The researchers concluded, "Cynicism is a valued quality of the personality of the police officer and is positively evaluated by important individuals in police organizations."[33]

★ ★ ★

THE DIRTY HARRY PROBLEM

Police officers are often confronted with situations in which they feel forced to take certain illegal actions to achieve a greater good. Indeed, one of the greatest and oldest ethical questions people have ever faced is, "Do the good ends ever justify the bad means?"[34]

Carl B. Klockars has dubbed this moral dilemma of police officers as the **Dirty Harry Problem,** from the 1971 film *Dirty Harry*, starring Clint Eastwood as Detective Harry Callahan. In the film, a young girl has been kidnapped by a psychopathic killer named Scorpio, who demands $200,000 in ransom. Scorpio has buried the girl with just enough oxygen to survive a few hours. Harry eventually finds Scorpio, shoots him, and tortures him to find out where the girl is. Finally, Scorpio tells Harry where the girl is. Harry finds her, but she has already died from lack of oxygen.

Let's change the plot of the movie and say that Harry's action resulted in his finding the girl and saving her life. This would be a great Hollywood ending, but think about it. Harry had a good end in mind (finding the girl before she dies), but what about the means (torturing Scorpio and not giving him his constitutional rights prior to interrogation)?

Harry was wrong, right? He violated police procedure. He violated the precepts of the Fifth Amendment to the U.S. Constitution, which he swore an oath to obey. He has committed crimes, the most obvious of which is assault.

Harry was wrong, right? If Harry had used proper police procedure, had not violated the law, had not violated the Constitution of the United States, and had advised Scorpio of his right to an attorney, and if Scorpio had availed himself of one, there is no doubt the attorney would have told him to remain silent, and the little girl would have died.

Which is more wrong morally? Is it more wrong to (1) torture Scorpio, thereby violating the police oath of office and legal obligations but therefore finding the girl and saving her life, or (2) act in accordance with the rules of the system and not make every effort, illegal or not, to force Scorpio to talk and thus permit the girl to die?

Sure, this is only Hollywood. You would never be faced with this dilemma as a police officer, would you? As Klockars writes:

> In real, everyday policing, situations in which innocent victims are buried with just enough oxygen to keep them alive are, thankfully, very rare. But the core scene in *Dirty Harry* should only be understood as an especially dramatic example of a far more common problem: real, everyday, routine situations in which police officers know they can only achieve good ends by employing dirty means. Each time a police officer considers deceiving a suspect into confessing by telling him that his fingerprints were found at the scene or that a conspirator has already confessed, each time a police officer considers adding some untrue details to his account of probable cause to legitimate a crucial stop or search . . . that police officer faces a Dirty Harry Problem.[35]

We can sympathize with Harry Callahan, and surely we can sympathize with the plight of the little girl about to die. However, despite Hollywood portrayals, police officers must operate within the boundaries of the law, because the law is what the people, through their representatives, want to be governed by. The police cannot make their own laws. Harry Callahan, although he attempted to save the life of the child, was wrong. In our system of law, we cannot use unlawful means to achieve worthy goals. Police work is a tough business. Tough choices must be made. As Klockars says,

> Dirty Harry Problems are an inevitable part of policing. They will not go away. The reason they won't is that policing is a moral occupation which constantly places its practitioners in situations in which unquestionable good ends can only be achieved by employing morally, legally, or politically dirty means to their achievements.
>
> The effects of Dirty Harry Problems on real police officers are often devastating. They can lead officers to lose their sense of moral proportion, fail to care, turn cynical, or allow their too passionate caring to lead them to employ dirty means too readily or too crudely. They make policing the most morally corrosive occupation.[36]

Is the Dirty Harry Problem a serious ethical problem facing our police? It certainly is. Police officers must be always alert to the fact that bad means never justify good ends. The police swear allegiance to their oath of office, the U.S. Constitution, and their state constitution. Although it may be tempting, police cannot solve all the problems of this world, and they certainly cannot solve them by violating their oath of office and their dedication to the Constitution of our land. Much more will be discussed regarding ethics in Chapter 12.

★ ★ ★

POLICE STRESS

Police officers are faced with stressful situations often during a routine tour of duty. The dispatcher assigns them to respond to a "gun run." (A gun run is a dispatcher's order to patrol units to respond to a certain location because of a report over 911 that a person has a gun in his or her possession. These calls receive immediate police response.) Citizens stop them to report a crime or dangerous condition. Officers find an open door to a factory and search for a possible burglar. They wait in a stakeout for an armed felon to appear. Police officers are always ready to react. Their bodies' response to these stressful situations is good in that it prepares them for any emergency, but the stress response takes its toll on officers' physical and mental states.

What Is Stress?

Stress is the body's reaction to internal or external stimuli that upset the body's normal state. A stimulus that causes stress (stressor) can be physical, mental, or emotional. The term *stress* is used to refer to both the body's reaction and the stimuli that caused it.

The body's reaction to highly stressful situations is known as the **flight-or-fight response.** Under stressful cir-

Researchers have identified four general categories of stress with which police officers are confronted: external stress (stress produced by real threats and dangers); organizational stress (stress produced by elements inherent in the quasi-military character of the police service); personal stress (stress produced by the interpersonal characteristics of belonging to the police organization); and operational stress (stress produced by the daily need to confront the tragedies of urban life).

cumstances, quantities of adrenaline, a hormone produced by the adrenal glands, are released into the bloodstream. This stimulates the liver to provide the body with stored carbohydrates for extra energy. It also results in quickened heartbeat and respiration, as well as increased blood pressure and muscle tension. The body is getting prepared for extraordinary physical exertion; this is good. However, if the need for this extraordinary exertion does not materialize, the frustrated readiness may cause headache, upset stomach, irritability, and a host of other symptoms.[37]

Some experts say that stress alone probably does not cause illness, but it contributes to circumstances in which diseases may take hold and flourish. Stress weakens and disturbs the body's defense mechanisms and may play a role in the development of hypertension, ulcers, cardiovascular disease, and as research indicates, probably cancer.[38] Exhibit 6.3 lists some of the mental and physical problems associated with stress.

The Nature of Stress in Policing

Although most people have stress in their careers or lives, studies have found evidence of particularly high rates of stress in certain professions. Some have called policing the most stressful of all professions. The American Institute of Stress ranked police work among the top ten stress-producing jobs in the United States.[39]

Exhibit 6.3	Mental and Physical Problems Associated with Stress

- Psychiatric problems
  Posttraumatic stress syndrome
  Neuroses
  Transient situational disturbances
- Immunology problems
  Reduced resistance to infection
  Tumors
- Cardiovascular problems
  Heart attacks
  Coronary artery disease
  Hypertension
  Stroke
- Genitourinary problems
  Failure to menstruate
  Impotence
  Incontinence
- Gastrointestinal problems
  Ulcers

Source: Adapted from Edwin S. Geffner, ed., *The Internist's Compendium of Patient Information* (New York: McGraw-Hill, 1987), sec. 30.

A reporter riding with the police addressed the stress that officers experience:

> The world inside the patrol car is a world of its own, two officers who are slave to the dispatcher on the crackling radio who can send them speeding into adrenaline overdrive racing to catch a suspect with a gun and then can order "slow it down" after enough cars are already at a crime scene. The result is an emotional up and down in just six blocks.[40]

Some studies indicate that police have higher rates of divorce, suicide, and other manifestations of stress than other professions.[41] One writer said, "It would be difficult to find an occupation that is subject to more consistent and persistent tension, strain, confrontations and nerve wracking than that of the uniformed patrolman."[42]

Researchers have identified four general categories of stress with which police officers are confronted:

1. *External stress.* Stress produced by real threats and dangers, such as responding to gun runs and other dangerous assignments and taking part in auto pursuits.

2. *Organizational stress.* Stress produced by elements inherent in the quasi-military character of the police service, such as constant adjustment to changing tours of duty, odd working hours, working holidays, and the strict discipline imposed on officers.

3. *Personal stress.* Stress produced by the interpersonal characteristics of belonging to the police organization, such as difficulties in getting along with other officers.

4. *Operational stress.* Stress produced by the daily need to confront the tragedies of urban life: the need to deal with derelicts, criminals, the mentally disturbed, and the drug addicted; the need to engage in dangerous activity to protect a public that appears to be unappreciative of the police; and the constant awareness of the possibility of being legally liable for actions performed while on duty.[43]

A recent study of police stress in Canada involving full-shift ride-alongs with randomly selected officers from 12 municipal departments in British Columbia found significant levels of physical stress among police officers. Using heart rate, coupled with observed physical-activity data, researchers found the highest physical stress to occur during officers' physical enforcement activities; marked psychosocial stress when responding to critical incidents, particularly during the interaction with a suspect both during the critical incident and then during each subsequent interaction with suspects for the remainder of the shift. The average heart rate of those involved in a critical incident remained elevated for the remainder of the shift for all tasks, including report writing in the last hour of the shift. The evidence also suggests that officers anticipate stress as they conduct their work, experiencing anticipatory stress at the start of each shift.[44]

Factors Causing Stress in Policing

According to researchers, factors leading to stress in police work include poor training, substandard equipment, poor pay, lack of opportunity, role conflict, exposure to brutality, fears about job competence and safety, and lack of job satisfaction. Researchers also say that the pressure of being on duty 24 hours a day leads to stress and that the police learn to cope with that stress by becoming emotionally detached from their work and the people they are paid to serve.[45] Fatigue can also affect officers' stress. Working long hours and overtime produces fatigue and consequently stress in officers.[46]

One researcher attributes stress problems to a lack of emphasis on physical fitness once an officer leaves the police academy: "Without police fitness standards, a police

---

Exhibit 6.4   Sources of Law Enforcement Stress

- External stressors
  Lack of consideration by courts in scheduling officers for court appearances
  Public's lack of support
  Negative or distorted media coverage

- Internal stressors
  Policies and procedures that are offensive
  Poor or inadequate training and inadequate career development opportunities
  Lack of identity and recognition
  Poor economic benefits and working conditions
  Excessive paperwork
  Inconsistent discipline
  Perceived favoritism

- Stressors in law enforcement work itself
  Rigors of shift work
  Role conflict
  Frequent exposures to life's miseries
  Boredom
  Fear
  Responsibility for protecting other people
  Fragmented nature of the job
  Work overload

- Stressors confronting the individual officer
  Necessity to conform
  Necessity to take a second job
  Altered social status in the community

Source: Adapted from Richard M. Ayres and George S. Flanagan, *Preventing Law Enforcement Stress: The Organization's Role* (National Sheriff's Association, Bureau of Justice Assistance, 1990).

department has too many 'loose wires' to account for. It is unfair to place the burden of quality effectiveness on each individual without presenting a plan that will achieve these goals."[47]

Critical incidents and **critical incident responses,** particularly police shootings, are extremely stressful. Two recent studies revealed the prevalence of acute traumatic dissociative responses in officers who have been involved in these critical incidents.[48]

Exhibit 6.4 presents an extensive list of sources of stress for those in law enforcement. These include both external and internal stressors, stressors in law enforcement work itself, and stressors confronting the individual officer.

Effects of Stress on Police Officers

Too much stress affects health, as Exhibit 6.3 showed. Police officers face the stress created by always being ready for danger day in and day out. In addition, the working hours of police officers and the resultant living conditions have a further negative effect on their health. One writer reports that police officers may be among those with the most unhealthy diets in the United States, due to a very high rate of consumption of fast food and junk food.[49] In fact, a study by Dorothy Bracey found that due to a poor diet and lack of exercise, a significant sample of U.S. police possessed a body composition, blood chemistry, and general level of physical fitness greatly inferior to that of a similarly sized sample of prison convicts.[50]

A recent National Institute of Justice report has listed the following as consequences of job-related stress commonly reported by police officers:

- Cynicism and suspiciousness
- Emotional detachment from various aspects of daily life
- Reduced efficiency
- Absenteeism and early retirement
- Excessive aggressiveness (which may trigger an increase in citizen complaints)
- Alcoholism and other substance abuse problems
- Marital or other family problems (for example, extramarital affairs, divorce, or domestic violence)
- Posttraumatic stress disorder.
- Heart attacks, ulcers, weight gain, and other health problems
- Suicide[51]

One study of 2,300 police officers in 20 U.S. police departments revealed that 37 percent had serious marital problems; 36 percent, health problems; 23 percent, problems with alcohol; 20 percent, problems with their children; and 10 percent, drug problems.[52] Other researchers estimate that between 20 and 30 percent of all police officers have alcohol problems. The typical drinker is single, over 40 years of age, with 15 to 20 years of police experience.[53]

Other studies indicate that police officers are 300 percent more likely to suffer from alcoholism than the average citizen;[54] the average life expectancy of a police officer is 57 years, compared to 71 for the general public; and officers rank at the top among professions in rates of heart disease, hypertension, and diabetes.[55]

Professors at Michigan State University have found that officers who have had to kill someone in the line of duty suffer postshooting trauma that may lead to severe problems, including the ruin of their careers. Studies indicate that 70 percent of these officers leave the police force within seven years after the shooting.[56]

A recent study on officer gender and stress revealed that female officers had higher levels of depression compared to male officers but that male and female police officers did not differ statistically in clinically developed measures of anxiety.[57]

Stress and Police Families

Police work not only affects officers; it also affects their families, loved ones, and friends: "Police work . . . affects, shapes, and at times, scars the individuals and families involved."[58] Studies of stress in the immediate families of male police officers reveal that between 10 and 20 percent of all police wives are dissatisfied with their husbands' jobs and would like to see their husbands leave the police department.[59] In addition, rotation shift work interferes with planning and celebrating holidays and important family events, such as birthdays and anniversaries. Rotating shifts also make it difficult for a spouse to pursue another career.[60]

Ellen Scrivner, the director of the Psychological Services Division of the Prince George's County (Maryland) Police Department and president of the Psychologists in Public Service Division of the American Psychological Association, identified a number of job-related issues that contribute to family dysfunction in police families:

1. *Family disruption due to rotating shifts.* Problems caused by rotating shifts include providing child care, unavailability on holidays and at other family events, and

physical problems caused by overtime and shift work, which cause irritability and increased tension.

2. *Unpredictable work environment.* The constantly changing work setting of the police officer leads to crisis and emergency responses, as well as fear of death or injury and of being the target of internal investigations.

3. *Job-related personal change and family relationships.* An officer is forced to see much human tragedy and is always personally affected. Changes in the officer's personality and attitudes, in turn, affect the family.

4. *Community expectations and demands.* The public seems to hold police officers to a higher standard of behavior in comparison with other workers. Neighbors often expect their police officer neighbors to take care of neighborhood problems and be available for emergencies.

5. *Intrusion into family life.* The police officer may have to carry parts of his or her job home. For example, police officers generally carry weapons, which they must secure in a safe place at home. Officers also must be available 24 hours a day.[61]

A recent National Institute of Justice report has reported the following as sources of stress commonly cited by officers' spouses:

- Shift work and overtime

- Concern over the spouse's cynicism, need to feel in control in the home, or inability or unwillingness to express feelings

- Fear that the spouse will be hurt or killed in the line of duty

- Officers' and others' excessively high expectations of their children

- Avoidance, teasing, or harassment of the officer's children by other children because of the parent's job

- Presence of a gun in the home

- The officer's 24-hour role as a law enforcer

- Perception that the officer prefers to spend time with coworkers rather than with his or her family

- Too much or too little discussion of the job

- Family members' perception of the officer as paranoid or excessively vigilant and overprotective of them

- Problems in helping the officer cope with work-related problems

- "Critical incidents," or the officer's injury or death on the job[62]

Police Departments Dealing with Stress

A report by the U.S. Commission on Civil Rights emphasized the need to provide stress management programs and services for police. The commission noted that most police departments lack such programs, despite the recent emphasis on stress as "an important underlying factor in police misconduct incidents." The commission recommended the following: "Police officials should institute comprehensive stress management programs that include identification of officers with stress problems, counseling, periodic screening and training on stress management."[63]

For example, the New York City Police Department has responded to the problem of police suicides by training 100 officers as peer counselors. The NYPD also established telephone hotlines in four precincts; officers needing help in stressful situations could call for help 24 hours a day, 7 days a week.[64] A recent summary report on this program revealed a reduction in the number of police suicides, numerous telephone calls on the help line, referrals to mental health clinicians, and families participating in family support seminars.[65]

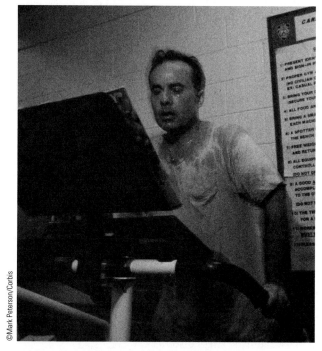

©Mark Peterson/Corbis

Many police departments have fitness facilities and programs to support cardiovascular health. By encouraging physical fitness, departments hope to keep their officers healthy and help them combat stress.

Scrivner describes the Prince George's County Police Department's Psychological Services Division, which was initiated by a grant from the Maryland Governor's Commission on Law Enforcement. According to Scrivner, the program provides a wide range of psychological services to the department, including research, training, and management consultation services. The keystone of the program is the confidential counseling services provided to sworn and civilian police personnel and their families. The counseling services are free and offered at a nonpolice facility. An employee or family member can contact the service, receive an initial assessment of the problem, and receive follow-up therapeutic intervention. The program also offers a 24-hour crisis intervention service and a critical incident response (an immediate response to an emergency situation) for personal or job-related problems for officers and their families.[66]

Officers who perform as hostage negotiators experience a great deal of stress. In the California counties of Riverside and San Bernardino, hostage negotiators receive four hours of training from a psychologist. The topics of instruction include sources and symptoms of stress and techniques officers can use to reduce stress both during and after negotiations.[67]

Stress management has a physical as well as a psychological component. The FBI's Training Division Research and Development Unit mailed a training needs survey packet to 2,497 police agencies across the nation. The survey results indicated that handling personal stress and maintaining an appropriate level of physical fitness ranked first and second in programs most requested by police officers. In another survey, 90 percent of the nearly 2,000 officers questioned reported that they were in favor of a department-sponsored physical fitness program.[68]

Some departments have instituted health and fitness programs to ensure their officers' physical and emotional well-being. For example, the Ohio State Patrol has implemented a mandatory health and fitness program for all its officers. The Ohio program is designed to ensure a "high quality of life during the troopers' active career period and into retirement."[69]

Speaking of the need for physical fitness, James J. Ness and John Light state

> The adverse effects of the lack of fitness are overwhelming, while the positive benefits of fitness are often overlooked. Being physically fit diminishes stress, promotes self-esteem, improves firearms accuracy, increases an officer's confidence in confrontations, makes him more effective with impact weapons and defense tactics, and generally improves his quality of life.[70]

Police officers themselves use many coping strategies to deal with stress, including humor and keeping an emotional distance from themselves and stressful events.[71]

In the aftermath of the terrorist attacks of September 11, 2001, the NYPD ordered all 55,000 of its employees to attend mental health counseling to deal with the stress brought about due to this event.[72] A similar program of mental health counseling was implemented to help Oklahoma City rescue workers in 1995 in the wake of the terrorist attack in that city.[73]

The Worcester, Massachusetts, Police Department has used peer counselors as "stress responders" to assist other officers in dealing with stressful incidents for over 20 years. A recent book describes the work of police peer counselors and presents their history, describes their strategies and tactics, and identifies the obstacles they face in their work.[74] High among the counselors' recommendations is immediate response to critical incident stress events by counselors and the necessity to conduct immediate critical incident stress debriefings (CISDs) for officers who have been exposed to potentially traumatic circumstances. The counselors report that this can help minimize or eliminate the secondary trauma that often occurs and that the counselor can be an understanding listening ear and often a strong bond may be forged between the officer and the counselor that can foster follow-up care.[75]

PATROLLING THE WEB

Some Support Groups for Police and Their Families Concerning Police Stress and Police Suicide

International Critical Stress Foundation, Inc.
   http://www.icisf.org
Concerns of Police Survivors, Inc.
   http://www.nationalcops.org
Central Florida Police Stress Unit, Inc.
   http://www.policestress.org
Police Suicide Prevention Center
   http://www.policesuicide.com
National Police Suicide Foundation
   http://www.psf.org
Policefamilies.com
   http://www.policefamilies.com

The National Institute of Justice has created the Corrections and Law Enforcement Family Support program (CLEFS) to deal with some of the problems of police stress. It has sponsored research and program development in some 30 agencies and related organizations (labor unions and employee professional organizations, for example). These projects include the development of innovative treatment and training programs as well as research into the nature and causes of stress.[76]

There are numerous training programs and support groups for police officers and their families. Many of them have a presence on the Web. See the listing of some sample groups in the nearby "Patrolling the Web" box.

Testing for Ability to Handle Stress

Law enforcement agencies in at least 42 states administer psychological tests to police applicants to avoid the appointment of officers who may overreact to law enforcement stress.[77] Some departments also routinely test current officers for their ability to handle stress.

The Officer at Risk Examination (ORE) is a paper-and-pencil test developed to detect individual police officers who may tend to get into trouble on the job by being overaggressive or underagggressive. Based on test results, officers can receive individual counseling, reassignment, or department sanctions. The examination consists of 143 multiple-choice questions and takes 20 minutes to administer. It contains a built-in reliability index and consists entirely of law-enforcement-specific questions designed to minimize falsification. The test has been administered to law enforcement officers in Alabama, California, Florida, Michigan, and Wisconsin. According to its developers, William Nagler and David Carlington, the examination is so specific to police officers that most officers actually enjoy taking the examination: "Many laugh with self-recognition while taking the test and discuss the ORE and its results for days after."[78]

The New York City Police Department has established a policy requiring all police officers applying for a specialized assignment to undergo additional psychological testing. Prior to the implementation of this policy, the NYPD conducted psychological testing only as a part of the pre-employment screening process. The psychological testing consists of a battery of written tests and an oral interview. Qualities measured or identified include reaction time, psychosomatic disorders, ability to concentrate without distraction, decision-making ability, impulsivity, manual dexterity, perceptual abilities, distortion of reality, organic brain damage, and possible violent or psychotic personalities. In short, the testing provides an up-to-date assessment of a police officer's mental well-being.

★ ★ ★

POLICE SUICIDE

Closely associated with the problem of stress in policing is the problem of **police suicide,** which seems to worsen over the years. Despite all the programs existing to deal with officer problems that may cause suicide, the toll continues to mount. Studies indicate that the suicide rate among police officers is anywhere from two to three times higher than that of the general population, and the rate of police suicides doubled in the 1990s:[79]

- In September 2002, a distraught Nebraska state trooper committed suicide because he believed that a clerical error he had made the previous week contributed to the murders of five people during a deadly bank robbery. A week before the robbery, the trooper had stopped one of the eventual perpetrators of the crime and given him a ticket for carrying a concealed weapon. However, in filing his report he had inadvertently transposed two of the gun's serial numbers, and thus did not learn that the defendant's firearm was stolen—an offense that would have put him in jail instead of back on the street.[80]

- On January 1996, a New York City police officer shot herself at the City Island home she shared with her boyfriend, another New York police officer.[81]

- In September 1996, authorities in Texas found the body of a former deputy in the reserve unit of the county sheriff's department. A handgun was found beside the body, which had what looked like a bullet wound to the head.

- An Oklahoma City police sergeant was found dead in May 1997, an apparent suicide. He had been up for a medal of valor the previous year for rescuing people from the bombing of the Federal Building.

Dr. John M. Violanti, a professor in the Criminal Justice Department of the Rochester Institute of Technology in Rochester, New York, and a member of the Department of Social and Preventive Medicine, University of New York at Buffalo, works on the problem of police suicide under a National Institute of Mental Health grant.[82] Dr. Violanti, who also served 23 years with the New York State Police, notes that the police culture and the reluctance of police officers to ask for help complicates the problem of police suicide. His study revealed that police are at higher risk for committing suicide for a variety of reasons, including access to firearms, continuous exposure to human misery, shift work, social strain and marital difficulties, drinking problems, physical illness, impending retirement, and lack of control over their jobs and personal lives. Violanti's work indicates that police commit suicide at a rate up to 53 percent higher than other city workers.[83]

Leonard Territo and Harold J. Vetter have attempted to explain the high rates of suicide among police officers. The stressors they identify shed a light on the particularly stressful nature of police work:

1. Police work is a male-dominated profession, and men have higher suicide rates than women.

2. The use, availability, and familiarity with firearms by police in their work make it fairly certain that suicide attempts will be successful.

3. There are psychological repercussions to being exposed to potential death on a constant basis.

4. Long and irregular working hours do not promote strong friendships and strain family ties.

5. There is constant exposure to public criticism and dislike toward the police.

6. Judicial contradictions, irregularities, and inconsistent decisions tend to negate the value of police work in officers' lives.[84]

Traditionally, no matter what their problems, police officers refrain from asking for help. There are various reasons for this reluctance. The primary reason, however, is that officers do not wish to appear weak or vulnerable in front of their peers. Individuals who perceive themselves as problem solvers often have great difficulty admitting that they have problems of their own. As a result, some officers who feel that they can no longer tolerate psychological pain choose to solve the problem themselves through suicide rather than by asking others for help.[85]

Stressing the role of police management in developing programs for dealing with police suicides, Thomas E. Baker and Jane P. Baker write

> A suicide prevention program can work only if members of the department feel free to take advantage of it. Police administrators and supervisors must play a nonpunitive role. They must communicate to officers four clear messages: (1) seek-

ing help will not result in job termination or punitive action; (2) all information will be respected and kept confidential; (3) other ways exist for dealing with a situation, no matter how hopeless it seems at the time; and (4) someone is available to help them deal with their problems. Police training and departmental policy, as well as the everyday examples set by police leaders, must communicate these four messages consistently.[86]

Violanti, who feels that a stress-management program needs to be a key part of any effort to prevent police suicides, also believes that police management must address the problem. He echoes the Bakers' feelings:

> [Denial of the problem] runs right through an entire organization. Middle management is probably a perfect place to train sergeants, lieutenants and captains about how to recognize this problem.[87]

A recent conference on suicide and law enforcement was held at the FBI Academy in Quantico, Virginia, in which 61 papers were presented describing causes of police suicide and how various law enforcement agencies in the United States and Canada have sought to prevent and respond to these events.[88]

★ ★ ★

SUICIDE BY COP

Compounding the stress problems of police officers is the phenomenon known as **suicide by cop,** in which a person wishing to die deliberately places an officer in a life-threatening situation, causing the officer to use deadly force against that person. Such a case occurred on a Long Island, New York, expressway in November 1997, when a 19-year-old man, despondent over a gambling debt, forced police to pull him over for driving erratically and then pulled a "very real-looking gun" (actually a $1.79 toy revolver) on them. Police shot and killed the youth. Inside the youth's auto were good-bye cards for his friends and a chilling suicide note addressed "To The Officer Who Shot Me" in which he apologized for getting the police involved.[89]

The "suicide by cop" phenomenon became widely reported in 1996 by a Canadian police officer, Richard Parent, in a landmark report, "The Phenomenon of Victim-Precipitated Homicide." Parent, who interviewed cops after they were involved in such incidents, said many quit the police department, got divorced, and abused drugs or alcohol after the killings.[90]

Dempsey's Law

Why Did He/She Do It? Is There Any Hope?

Professor Dempsey, I have been reading the academic research on police suicides. It disturbs me, because I want to be a police officer. Am I going to be subjecting myself to this potential problem? Do you have any firsthand experience with the problem? Do you have any advice for me?

Yes, Emily, unfortunately I certainly do. During my career in policing I have lost some friends and numerous acquaintances through suicide. All the stressors and problems discussed in the academic studies were present in each case. The biggest factors, as I saw them, were the tremendous stress that goes with policing, the sense of frustration and helplessness in experiencing and watching what human beings do to each other, the sense of isolation from the public and sometimes the officer's own family, and the reluctance of police officers to admit they have personal problems in dealing with the experience of policing. Certainly, when you combine these stressors with other conditions police officers regularly face—problems with relationships, alcohol, and the ready, immediate access to firearms—the problem is compounded.

The problem, however, Emily, can be dealt with. For all the personal tragedies I have encountered in this area, there have also been successes. It all depends on the officers' peers and supervisors. They must attend to fellow officers' problems and warning signs. As a police manager, I felt compelled numerous times to recommend officers for psychological counseling. On a couple of occasions I even removed an officer's firearms. Sure, the immediate reaction was that I had damaged the officer's career; however, in the long run, those officers and others understood and thanked me for caring enough to intercede and get them the help they needed.

I can never forget one particular guy, a terrific cop who worked for me in a Brooklyn precinct. He was a great cop, but his productivity had recently declined, and he had become the subject of much station house gossip about what many considered his bizarre behavior. When I confronted him, he admitted to me that he was having tremendous marital problems. He said that his wife was pregnant, but he believed he was not the father. He said that he was drinking heavily but didn't feel he needed any help. I removed his firearms and drove him myself downtown to the department's psychological unit for counseling. At first, he hated me for this, but eventually I think he understood. When I retired, I received a call from him. He thanked me for caring about him and told me, "You know, Captain, if you hadn't removed my gun that night, I would have blown my brains out when I got home." There is always hope, Emily, but people have to pay attention and they have to care.

In a Los Angeles study of 437 officer-involved shootings during the years 1987 through 1997, "suicide by cop" accounted for 11 percent of the shootings and 13 percent of all officer-involved justifiable homicides. The victims in these cases enacted elaborate schemes, including doing something to draw officers to the scene, disobeying commands to put down the weapon, continuing to threaten officers and other individuals, and escalating the encounter to the point where police had to use deadly force to protect themselves, their partners, and civilians.

The study indicated that the majority of the subjects in these cases were male and had a past history of domestic violence, suicide attempts, and alcohol and drug abuse. Police officers involved in these incidents experienced emotions ranging from shock and remorse to shame, anger, and powerlessness.[91]

A study of the psychological effects of suicide by cop on involved officers revealed that the short-term effects seemed to involve the same psychological impacts experienced by officers involved in most critical incidents, in-

Forst's Law

Losing a Good Friend

Suicide is something that happens to other people. You never think it is going to happen to someone you know and never anticipate experiencing suicidal thoughts. Over my police career and through my interactions with the families of suicide victims as well as people experiencing thoughts of suicide or who attempt suicide, I sadly found this was not true.

One of the saddest times of my career was when a friend and coworker committed suicide. Bernie was in his mid-40s when I joined the department. He was a detective and highly respected within the agency and throughout our local criminal justice system. He was known as a great investigator and interviewer and worked relentlessly to get to the truth and then pursue the case to its conclusion. He had the highest ethical standards and never took shortcuts.

I was very fortunate, as Bernie took me under his wing and became my mentor when I joined the department. He said he saw a lot of potential and wanted to help me in any way he could. He worked "crimes against persons" and had become our resident expert in sex crimes. He called me out whenever he was called in for a sex crime. We worked together regularly, and I learned a tremendous amount from Bernie. The strongest impact he made on me was how to interact with people. He had an unassuming and compassionate style that made people feel comfortable and encouraged them to talk. This resulted in many confessions to sex crimes that other officers were surprised were obtained.

I can only guess that though Bernie was able to encourage others to talk, he was not as able to open up to others. We spent some off-duty time together, and I knew that he was divorced and his children were up north. But he was dating someone and seemed well adjusted to his lifestyle.

After I had been in the department five years, Bernie took some leave time for minor surgery and a friend took care of taking him to and from the hospital. I talked to the friend; Bernie didn't want any visitors while he was home recuperating and would see us when he got back to work. A week later, that friend (a detective bureau supervisor) came to my door in the evening. I could tell by the look on his face that something was wrong, but I assumed it was an official visit. We sat down and he told me that Bernie was dead. Sometime that day Bernie had shot himself with his service weapon.

I had the feelings of guilt that survivors often experience. I should have seen something, I should have visited him even though he didn't want visitors, I should have spent more time with him, I should have encouraged him to talk more . . . all the things you wish you'd done.

Bernie had a lasting impact not only with all the victims and families he worked with but with all the many officers he trained and the officers they went on to train. I have taught many investigators Bernie's techniques and philosophies, so he lives on in the efforts of many.

cluding replaying the event repeatedly, disruption of sleep, feelings of irritability, detachment, being hypercritical, sensory disturbance, and hypervigilance. The most dominant emotion experienced by the officers was anger toward the subject for controlling the situation and forcing the officer to use deadly force. Some long-term effects were feelings of vulnerability, being more protective of family, and being less trusting of the general public. Over half of the officers interviewed seriously considered retiring or quitting the department. Often these thoughts were reinforced by family members, who experienced intensified fears of their loved one being killed in the line of duty. Officers reported that psychological debriefing was particularly important in helping them through the impact of the incident.[92]

CHAPTER SUMMARY

This chapter addressed the police culture, or subculture, the police personality, police cynicism, the Dirty Harry Problem, and police stress. Most researchers believe that there is a distinct police subculture and police personality. Most believe that this subculture and this personality arise from the type of socialization specific to police work rather than from police departments recruiting only people who already have the attributes of the police subculture and personality. Police cynicism is very common and seems to get more intense the longer a person stays in policing.

The Dirty Harry Problem is the conflict over whether to use illegal means to accomplish good ends. It is a problem that seems to permeate many aspects of policing.

Finally, the chapter looked at the issues of police stress. It discussed what stress is, what factors produce it, the results of stress, the effects of stress on police families, and efforts on the part of departments to deal with stress among their ranks. Many police departments test candidates and in-service members on their ability to handle stress. The problems of police suicide and "suicide by cop" and their causes and effects were also discussed.

Learning Check

1. Explain what the police subculture is and how it expresses itself.

2. Define the police personality and discuss how it expresses itself.

3. List some reasons for the existence of a police subculture and a police personality.

4. Give some reasons why police officers experience high levels of stress.

5. Discuss what police departments can do to deal with the high levels of stress present in their officers.

Application Exercise

You are confronted with the following Dirty Harry Problem.

Your friend Bill became a police officer in your hometown, the city of Bigproblems. During Bill's academy training and field training he was very happy about the job and constantly conveyed this to you. However, after several months on patrol as a community beat officer in a high-crime public housing development, Bill's personality seems to be changing. You begin to worry about him, and one night when you are out to dinner together, you ask him if anything has happened.

Bill confides in you that he had arrested a 20-year-old resident, Bigman Doper, for dealing drugs on his beat several weeks ago and had been disappointed that the court had only sentenced Bigman Doper to probation, even though it was his second drug arrest.

You tell Bill that you understand his disappointment. However, you caution him to remember that the actions of courts are beyond his control and that he should just continue to do his job.

Bill then tells you that the court's decision is not his major concern. He relates that he had been complaining in the locker room about the court decision and had been approached by Hotshot Cassidy, a 20-year veteran of the department, who said, "Hey kid, don't worry about it. I'll fix Bigman for you." Bills says that a week later, he observed Bigman walking through the streets of the development and noticed that he appeared to have been the victim of a serious recent beating. Later, at the station house, Cassidy approached Bill and said, "You see what I did to Bigman, kid?"

Bill asks your advice.

Web Exercise

Use the Internet to get into some police officer personal pages at www.officer.com and try to get a sense of the content and flavor of a few of the officer personal pages. Do their stories and comments remind you of anything you have read about in this chapter? Do the officers show the features of the police culture and the police personality?

Key Concepts

Blue curtain
Blue wall of silence
Critical incident response
Dirty Harry Problem
Flight-or-fight response
Police culture or police subculture
Police cynicism
Police personality
Police suicide
Suicide by cop

Police Operations

GUEST LECTURE

Community Policing with the Aging Population

ANDREW SCOTT

Andrew J. Scott III began his career in law enforcement in 1978 at the North Miami Police Department in Miami/Dade County. After several years, Chief Scott moved to the North Miami Beach Police Department. He remained there until 1998 and ascended to the rank of Assistant Chief of Police. He was appointed as the Chief of Police of the city of Boca Raton in 1998 and currently holds that position. Chief Scott earned a master of science degree in management from St. Thomas University in Miami in 1993 and a bachelor of arts degree in psychology from Florida International University in 1977. He is a graduate of the FBI National Academy (183rd Session, 1995) and the FBI Leeds Session (#42, 2001). He is currently a commissioner on the Commission for Florida Law Enforcement Accreditation, Inc. Chief Scott is also an assessor for the Commission on Accreditation for Law Enforcement Agencies, Inc. (CALEA), as well as an assessor for the Commission for Florida Law Enforcement Accreditation, Inc. He has been nationally recognized for promoting equality for women in law enforcement.

The city of Boca Raton has an interesting demographic makeup—over 30 percent of our population is over the age of 60. As in the United States as a whole (according to the 2000 U.S. Census), our 85 and older citizenry is currently the fastest growing segment of the population. Moreover, this population is comprised overwhelmingly of women, many of whom have outlived their spouses, their financial resources, and, in some cases, their children and other relatives.

As calls for service increased among the elder population, officers looked for resources to assist residents but often did not know how to help. Concerned neighbors and family living out of state also contacted our agency. Though in most cases no actual crime occurred, quality of life issues such as failing health, isolation, depression, and competency arose repeatedly. Social service agencies, both public and nonprofit, also alerted our attention to the aging population phenomenon as they sought assistance in aiding these citizens.

An Alzheimer's or dementia diagnosis further complicates domestic situations, as officers are increasingly responding to victims who are abused by their caregivers or to caregivers who are incapable of taking care of their loved ones and are battered by the patient. We soon discovered that there is a tremendous gap in services for frail and vulnerable adults, unless they are in extreme poverty and qualify for services through the Department of Children and Families.

As a result, it became apparent that our city's increased elder population were vulnerable adults, at an increased risk to become victims of crime. In response, the Boca Raton Police Services Department wanted to augment the current social services provided and implement proactive measures to this underserved population. Although bridging the gap between state legal protection and social service providers is difficult, the Boca Raton Police Services Department endeavored to establish an in-house position to assist elders who fall through the cracks.

The Elder Crime Specialist position is a relatively new addition to the Boca Raton Police Services Department, initiated in February 2002. Most notably, it is a position that did not exist within any other Palm Beach County law enforcement agency. This civilian position was added to address the increased victimization of the elder population in Boca Raton. In recent years, we have seen an increase in elder crime, especially consumer fraud and financial exploitation. In 2001, 10 percent of crimes committed in the city were against the elderly. In 2002, the percentage jumped to almost 13 percent.

The primary objective in designating an Elder Crime Specialist was to reach out to the senior community and provide a police department liaison to the elders in our city. In this way, law enforcement becomes proactive in identifying and targeting particular issues that affect city residents. Another goal was to educate elders, focusing on crime awareness and prevention. Telemarketing fraud is the most prevalent crime committed against elders, with other types of white-collar crimes following a close second. Making elders aware of their own vulnerabilities and the types of crimes that most affect them is the first step in reducing their risk level.

In the summer of 2002, Boca Raton Police initiated the first-ever Elder Education Seminar. The program educates seniors on county and state agencies providing free services to people over the age of 60. Over 25 state agencies and nonprofit organizations covered topics such as Medicare fraud; consumer fraud; Alzheimer's and dementia diagnosis and care; elder abuse, neglect, and exploitation; health care facility and health care professional licensing requirements; transportation; fixed incomes; assisted living facilities and nursing home standards; and volunteer opportunities. Two seminars have been completed, with over 50 attendees at each eight-week session. Education is a crucial piece in crime prevention, and the Elder Education Seminars seek to provide elders with the information they need to protect themselves and each other.

In the winter of 2002, Boca Raton Police initiated a free cellular telephone program for city seniors to ensure constant access to 911. Area businesses and high schools have been an integral part of this program by collecting and donating used phones. The Boca Raton Police Explorers (a high school student group) clean and program the phones, preparing them for distribution to the elder community. The Elder Crime Specialist meets with each phone recipient to instruct and educate the elder about the phone. To date, we have distributed over 300 phones to Boca Raton residents.

The state-operated Long Term Care (LTC) Ombudsman Council has partnered with our agency to train staff members and residents at assisted living facilities and nursing homes. The state of Florida is currently experiencing a significant nursing shortage, affecting staffing ratios at many long-term care facilities. Unfortunately, crimes such as elder abuse and neglect are on the rise in these facilities, as staffing shortages continue and traditional nursing positions are filled with unlicensed certified nursing assistants. Educating the staff about resident rights is imperative, as many caregivers in these facilities are unaware of the special rights that protect residents. Further, staff often is uneducated about behaviors that not only violate these special rights but also can be prosecuted by state law under the elder abuse, neglect, and exploitation chapter. The Elder Crime Specialist and LTC Ombudsman representative conduct both staff and resident training at 12 facilities in the city.

Home visits to frail and vulnerable elders by our Elder Crime Specialist provide intervention and situation assessment. As law enforcement becomes aware of these individuals, either through calls for service or a phone call made to our agency by a concerned friend or neighbor, we can mitigate potentially dangerous circumstances. Identifying elders at risk gives us an opportunity to protect an elder and possibly prevent a future crime from occurring. Further, we can actively participate in making certain that quality of life measures are upheld. Sometimes that means a simple phone call to an out-of-state relative. Many times it is as easy as making sure the elder has meals delivered to his or her home. More complicated cases involve elders with no family or means of supporting themselves.

Participation in committees such as the State Attorney's Crimes Against the Elderly Task Force enables our department to interface with other law enforcement agencies and various state and county agencies to share information, discuss prevention and intervention techniques, and troubleshoot difficult cases. BRPSD in-service training is held in conjunction with agencies such as Adult Protective Services, the Legal Aid Society, and the state attorney's office to educate road patrol officers about crimes against the elderly and the importance of detailed incident reports.

The Elder Crime Specialist regularly speaks about crimes against the elderly to homeowner association meetings, civic organizations, and assisted and independent living facilities. Educating and warning elders about recent telemarketing scams and other fraud schemes empowers them to be aware of common ploys to exploit them or their friends.

Our community partners include state, county, and nonprofit agencies charged with providing services to vulnerable adults in Palm Beach County and the city of Boca Raton. They include the Department of Children and Families division of Adult Protective Service, the Area Agency on Aging, the Long Term Care Ombudsman Council, the Department of Elder Affairs, Alzheimer's Community Care, the Mae Volen Senior Center, and the Center for Information and Crisis Services, to name a few. These agencies engage in collaborative efforts with local law enforcement to share information and provide resources for elder residents of our city.

Partnerships with agencies such as Alzheimer's Community Care and the Legal Aid Society division greatly assisted our agency in mitigating the magnitude of elder abuse, neglect, and exploitation occurring in our city. These agencies have aggressively fought to assist vulnerable adults by responding in unconventional ways, including making home visits to victims.

Local businesses have responded with tremendous generosity, both financially and by donating their valuable time. Key contributors include Publix Supermarkets and Florida Power and Light, who combined to make the holiday food and gift basket drive an overwhelming success. Additionally, several local merchants donated cell phones that ultimately were distributed to city elders.

Community input also comes from Boca Raton Police Department volunteers, most over the age of 65. Their role serves two primary purposes: to identify and prioritize concerns of the elderly and, more importantly, to retain their independence by giving back to the city.

7 Police Operations: The Traditional Approach

★ ★ ★

CHAPTER GOALS

- To acquaint you with the three traditional methods of doing police work and examine their effectiveness
- To introduce you to the academic studies of police patrol and detective operations
- To introduce you to police patrol—what the police do on patrol and how they do it
- To supply you with basic information regarding police detective operations
- To acquaint you with police traffic operations and special operations

This chapter is about police operations: what the police do and how they do it. It covers police patrol operations, detective operations, traffic operations, and special operations.

The chapter will discuss the academic studies of the 1960s and 1970s, particularly the Kansas City Study, which has changed our understanding of the effectiveness of the traditional methods of doing police work. The Kansas City Study, as well as other studies, forced academics and progressive police administrators to look closely at their operations to see if there were better, more effective ways to do police work. The following chapter, Chapter 8, "Police Operations: A New Approach," will discuss these better and more effective ways of policing.

Most of this chapter will be related to police patrol operations, the "backbone" of policing. Patrol operations involve the activities and role of the patrol officer and the various methods of doing patrol work, including motorized and foot patrol. Additionally, the chapter will discuss detective operations, traffic operations, and special operations, including SWAT teams and emergency service units.

★ ★ ★
TRADITIONAL METHODS OF POLICE WORK

Robert Sheehan and Gary W. Cordner identify the following three traditional methods of doing police work: (1) random routine patrol, (2) rapid response to calls by citizens to 911, and (3) retroactive investigation of past crimes by detectives.[1]

The average U.S. police officer arrives at work at the beginning of his or her shift and receives the keys and the patrol car from the officer who used it on the previous tour. The officer then drives around a designated geographic area (**random routine patrol**). When the officer receives a call from the police dispatcher, he or she responds to the call and performs whatever police work is required—an arrest, first aid, breaking up a fight, taking a crime report, and so on (**rapid response to citizens' calls to 911**). If the call involves a crime, the officer conducts a preliminary investigation and often refers the case to a detective, who conducts a follow-up investigation of the crime (**retroactive investigation of past crimes by detectives**). As soon as the officer is finished handling the call, he or she resumes patrol and is ready to respond to another call.

These are the methods of traditional police work. However, are random routine patrol, rapid response to citizens' calls to 911, and retroactive investigation of past crimes by detectives the proper ways for the police to safeguard our communities? Are these methods effective? Is this combination of methods the only way to do police work? This chapter will attempt to answer these questions.

★ ★ ★
EVALUATING THE EFFECTIVENESS OF POLICE WORK

Evaluating the effectiveness of police work is very difficult. If a city has a high crime rate, does it follow that its police department is not effective? If a city has a low crime rate, does it follow that its police department is an effective one? When we talk about crime, we are talking about many different and complex variables. The police cannot control all the variables that might produce crime, such as social disorganization; anger; poverty; hostility; revenge; psychological, social, or biological problems; and the desire to commit crime as an alternative to the world of work.

Despite the difficulties and problems associated with conducting academic and scientific research in policing, the research has been influential in the development of policing strategies over the last two decades. As Joan Petersilia, one of the early researchers, has written,

> Although systematic research on policing began less than 15 years ago, it has already influenced major changes in the way police departments operate and in public perceptions of policing. Changes in policy and practice around the country suggest that research has had particularly important conceptual and operational effects in patrol operations, criminal investigation, and specialized offense and offender operations.[2]

One of the problems in conducting scientific studies of policing involves attempting to set up controlled experiments. When scientists conduct academic studies of the effects of a variable on something—for example, to see if a particular drug cures a particular illness—they conduct a controlled experiment. In a **controlled experiment,** two categories of groups are used. One group is the **experimental group,** and the other is the **control group.** The experimental group, in the drug example, is given the drug, whereas the control group is not given the drug. If the drug is effective, the experimental group will recover from the illness, and the control group will not.

Another example of a controlled experiment could be changing the packaging of a particular product sold in a store to see if putting a product in a red package results in more people buying the product than when the same product is offered in a blue box. The new red packages would be the experimental group, and the old blue packages would be the control group. If we leave all other variables the same (the price, where the packages are located in the store, and so on) and the red boxes sell at a better rate than the blue boxes, it can be said that the red boxes make a difference.

Can we have controlled experiments to see if a police department is effective? Can we eliminate police patrols from one neighborhood and compare the crime rate in that neighborhood with the crime rate in the neighborhood where there are police patrols? Obviously, a myriad of problems accompany controlled experiments with crime. Is such experimentation ethical? Is it legal? This chapter will look at several controlled experiments with crime and see how they have affected our traditional concepts of doing police work.

★ ★ ★

RANDOM ROUTINE PATROL: THE KANSAS CITY STUDY

Random routine patrol, otherwise known as preventive patrol, involves a police officer's driving around and within a community when he or she is not on an assignment from the radio dispatcher or a supervisor. Tradition has held that random routine patrol creates a sense of omnipresence and deters crime, because a criminal will not chance committing a crime if a police officer might be just around the corner. It was also felt that random routine patrol enabled police officers to catch criminals in the act of committing their crimes. Just how effective is random routine patrol? The **Kansas City Study** was the first attempt to actually test the effectiveness of random routine patrol.

The Kansas City Study in Brief

During 1972 and 1973, the Kansas City Police Department, under the leadership of Police Chief Clarence Kelly (who later became the director of the FBI) and with the support of the Police Foundation, conducted an experiment to test the effects of routine preventive patrol. This year-long experiment has been both influential and controversial.

Fifteen patrol beats in Kansas City's South Patrol Division were used for the study (see Figure 7.1). Five of these beats were assigned to a control group with no changes in normal patrol staffing or tactics. Five other beats were chosen as reactive beats, and all preventive patrolling was eliminated. Outside patrol units handled calls

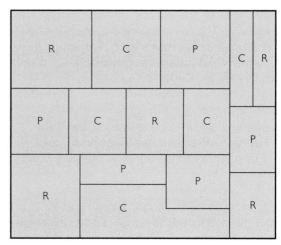

P = Proactive   C = Control   R = Reactive

Figure 7.1
A schematic representation of the Kansas City Patrol Experiment. In the proactive areas, routine random police patrol was increased; in the control areas, it remained the same; and in the reactive areas, it was eliminated.

Source: Adapted from George L. Kelling et al., *The Kansas City Preventive Patrol Experiment: A Summary Report* (Washington, DC: Police Foundation, 1974), p. 9.

in the reactive beats, and units left the beats once they had handled the calls. The final five beats in the experiment were proactive beats, in which two to three times the usual level of preventive patrolling was provided. Thus, the reactive beats (with all routine patrol eliminated) and the proactive beats (with routine patrol increased) were the experimental groups. If random routine patrol is an effective way of policing our communities, we should expect to see changes in the reactive and proactive beats.

Prior to the outset of the experiment, researchers collected data on reported crime, arrests, traffic accidents, response times, citizen attitudes, and citizen and business victimization for each of the 15 beats. The researchers collected similar data after the conclusion of the year-long experiment. During the experiment, the activities of the police officers assigned to the beats were observed and monitored. No one in the community was advised of the experiment.[3]

Results of the Kansas City Study

When the Kansas City Study was finished, the researchers concluded, "Decreasing or increasing routine preventive patrol within the range tested in [the] experiment had no effect on crime, citizen fear of crime, community attitudes

Exhibit 7.1	Results of the Kansas City Study

- No change in crime
- No change in citizen fear of crime
- No change in community attitudes toward the police
- No change in police response time
- No change in traffic accidents

Source: Adapted from George L. Kelling et al., *The Kansas City Preventive Patrol Experiment: A Summary Report* (Washington, DC: Police Foundation, 1974), p. 16.

toward the police on the delivery of police service, police response time or traffic accidents."[4] In effect, the study failed to demonstrate that adding or taking away police patrols from an area made any difference within the community (see Exhibit 7.1). At the end of the experiment, no one in the community had any idea that an experiment regarding policing had been conducted in their community.

The conclusions of the Kansas City Study shocked many people and differed from all the assumptions we had always made regarding police patrol. It had been commonly believed that putting more officers on patrol would cause a decrease in crime, and taking away police would cause an increase in crime. The Kansas City Study told us that this basic assumption about police work was wrong. Or did it?

Critiques of the Kansas City Study

In an evaluation of the Kansas City Study, James Q. Wilson cautions that the results should not be misinterpreted: "The experiment does not show that the police make no difference and it does not show that adding more police is useless in controlling crime. All it shows is that changes in the amount of random preventive patrol in marked cars does not, by itself, seem to affect over one year's time in Kansas City, how much crime occurs or how safe citizens feel." Wilson says that very different results might have occurred if changes had been made in how the police were used and not merely in the number of marked patrol cars placed in one area.[5]

Joseph D. McNamara, who succeeded Kelly as chief of the Kansas City Police Department in 1974 and later served as chief of the San Jose (California) Police Department, warned that "a great deal of caution must be used to avoid the error that the experiment proved more than it actually did. One thing the experiment did not show is that a visible police presence can have no impact on crime in selected circumstances." McNamara stressed the fact that the experiment seemed to show that police officers' uncommitted time (time they are not responding to calls to 911 or doing self-initiated police work)—approximately 50 percent of their time—could be used more effectively. Uncommitted time probably should be devoted to activities with more specific objectives than routine patrol.[6]

George Kelling, director of the Kansas City Study, said that it would be a mistake to conclude that patrol was completely unnecessary or that police departments could manage with far fewer resources. He argued that "the experiment has demonstrated that the time and staff resources do exist within police departments to test solutions to the many complex and interrelated problems of police service."[7] Thus, it seems to Kelling that the police can actually experiment with ways to do better work.

Richard C. Larson, in contrast, reported that he found serious flaws in the research design of the experiment. He noted that when police cars in the reactive beats entered the area in response to calls, they made a visible police presence. In the eyes of citizens and potential criminals, this was the same as routine patrol. Larson also pointed out that police vehicles from other specialized units (who were not part of the experiment) operated in the reactive beats, thereby creating a visible police presence. Larson found other differences in the reactive beats. Officers undertook a higher rate of self-initiated activities (such as vehicle stops), and they used sirens and lights more often in responding to calls. Furthermore, there was a higher incidence of two or more cars responding to a call for service.[8]

The major proponent of the effectiveness of patrol, O. W. Wilson, and his associate Roy Clinton McLaren, argued that despite the conclusions of the researchers, the value of police patrol cannot be measured by a statistical study like the Kansas City one and must be evaluated based on historical experience. Wilson and McLaren stated, "The fact remains that in the few situations in recent history in which police response was obviously not immediately available . . . wholesale looting and lawlessness have been the result."[9]

Wilson made that statement in 1977. In 1992, the absence of police patrols by the Los Angeles Police Department was blamed for the rioting and looting in the area near the intersection of Florence and Normandy after the not-guilty verdict in the Rodney King trial. Was Wilson prophetic? It must be remembered, however, that a myriad of reasons led to the riots in addition to the paucity of police patrols.

To date, only one attempt has been made to replicate the Kansas City experiment. A similar study in Albuquerque, New Mexico, reached essentially similar conclusions.[10]

Another analysis revealed that the relationship between crime and the time police spend on patrol may be more complex than previously recognized. For example, in some instances, the rates of robbery have actually increased when police patrol has increased. This may be because citizens are more likely to report robberies when they know that police are concentrating more time and effort on detecting that crime.[11]

Value of the Kansas City Study

Sheehan and Cordner describe the value of the Kansas City Study by saying that the study did not result in the elimination of preventive or random routine patrol but rather set the stage for further experimentation with alternative patrol strategies and tactics. Because of the study, police executives realized that they could try alternative patrol tactics without fearing that reduced random routine patrol would result in calamity.[12] In that regard, Samuel Walker says, "It seems to indicate that possibilities exist for more flexible and creative approaches to the use of patrol officers."[13]

In summary, the Kansas City Study indicated that our traditional three cornerstones of policing might not be the most effective way to do police work. The Kansas City Study definitely set the stage for the academic study of policing, which in turn has caused tremendous changes in our thinking about policing. A later section of this chapter will further explore police patrol—what patrol officers do and how they do it. Chapter 8 will look at new approaches to police work that resulted from the Kansas City Study.

★ ★ ★

RAPID RESPONSE TO CITIZENS' 911 CALLS

Rapid response to citizens' calls to 911 has traditionally been thought of as a way in which the police could catch criminals while they were in the act of committing their crimes or as they were escaping from their crimes. The ideal scenario is this: A citizen observes a person committing a crime and immediately calls 911. The police respond in seconds and arrest the perpetrator. This sounds great, but it rarely works that way.

Another scenario follows: A citizen is mugged and, just after the mugging, immediately calls 911 and reports the crime. The police respond in seconds and catch the perpetrator as he or she is at the crime scene or in immediate flight from it. This also sounds great, but again, it rarely works that way. The traditional approach of rapid response

to 911 calls was based on unexamined assumptions about police patrol. Research over the past 20 years has pointed out that we cannot depend on this television portrayal of police work.

Early Studies of Rapid Response

In 1967, the President's Commission on Law Enforcement and Administration of Justice, in its *Task Force Report: Science and Technology*, found that quick response to a citizen's report of a crime to 911 made an arrest more likely. However, the commission emphasized that only extremely quick response times were likely to result in arrest. The commission discovered that when police response time was one or two minutes, an arrest was likely, and improvements in the response time of even 15 to 30 seconds greatly improved the likelihood of an arrest. In contrast, when response time exceeded three or four minutes, the probability of an arrest dropped sharply.[14]

The U.S. National Advisory Commission on Criminal Justice Standards and Goals in 1973 recommended that "urban area response time . . . under normal conditions should not exceed 3 minutes for emergency calls and 20 minutes for non-emergency calls." The commission stated that "when the time is cut to 2 minutes, it can have a dramatic effect on crime."[15]

Later Studies of Rapid Response

In time, further studies of rapid response to citizens' calls to 911 were carried out. These studies took into account the complexity of response time, which the earlier research by the two commissions had failed to do. Total response time (from the moment of the crime to the arrival of the first police officer) consists of three basic components:

1. The time between the crime and the moment the victim or a witness calls the police

2. The time required for the police to process the call (answer the phone, obtain details from the citizen, and dispatch a patrol car)

3. Travel time from the moment the patrol car receives the call from the dispatcher until it arrives at the scene[16]

Two later studies looked even more carefully at response time and at the different types of situations that spur calls to 911 for police assistance. These studies found that victims often delay calling the police after a crime or other incident occurs. Sometimes no phone is available; sometimes the victims are physically prevented from calling by the perpetrator. Often, victims of crime are temporarily disori-

Rapid response to 911 calls has traditionally been looked at as a pillar of police operations. Studies conducted over the last three decades have caused law enforcement to reexamine that belief. Response to calls for service is now prioritized, but rapid response to emergency calls will always be an essential element of law enforcement.

© Lester Lefkowitz/Corbis

ented, frightened, ashamed, or even apathetic. Some people in one study reported that they first called parents, insurance companies, or their doctors. The later studies reported that the average citizen delay in calling the police for serious crimes was between five and ten minutes. The discovery that citizens often wait several minutes before calling the police puts response time in a different light and suggests that rapid response may not be as significant as was once thought.[17]

The later studies also made an important distinction between involvement crimes and discovery crimes. In involvement crimes, the victim is actually present when the crime occurs. Rapid response might be productive if the citizen has not delayed too long before calling 911. In discovery crimes, a citizen comes home (from work or vacation, for example) and discovers that a burglary has occurred. In this case, rapid police response is unlikely to matter, because the crime probably occurred a long time before the call to the police. Frequently, then, the actual time of occurrence may be hours or days earlier, making even instantaneous police arrival irrelevant.[18]

The emphasis on rapid response time (one or two minutes) makes no sense for several reasons. First, citizens generally cannot or do not report crimes immediately. Second, it is unlikely that a police car can get to a given location in one or two minutes. Consider the delay in calling the po-

lice, the time involved in processing the call by the 911 operator, and the distance the available police car has to travel and the traffic with which the car's driver has to contend.

Obviously, we will always need some type of rapid police response to citizens' calls to 911, even though we have to realize that a one- or two-minute response is highly unrealistic. We will always need rapid response to take people injured in traffic accidents to hospitals, to respond to violent arguments and fights, to deliver babies when their mothers cannot get to the hospital, and to respond to those crimes where rapid response may be effective (the victim or witness calls immediately, and the perpetrator is still on the scene or is in immediate flight from it). Also, quick response improves the chances for finding and interviewing possible witnesses and securing and retrieving physical evidence for analysis. However, as the academic studies have indicated, alternative strategies to rapid response to citizens' calls to 911 are needed to make better use of police officers.

Chapter 8 will discuss an alternative to rapid response, differential response to calls for service in which the police carefully screen all calls to 911 and only provide immediate response to serious crimes, crimes in progress, or other emergencies. In other types of calls, the police may provide a delayed response, take the report on the telephone, or advise the reporter to come into the station house to report the crime.

Dempsey's Law

Does It Help When the Police Get There Really Fast?

For the past 15 years, I have performed an experiment in my Introduction to Policing class to determine the validity of studies that indicate that police response time is not critical in apprehending perpetrators of past crimes. I generally pose the following scenario to a female student:

It's 1:00 A.M. You have just left the Noisy Barn (a local nightclub known for a rowdy, drunken, college-age crowd; in my generation we called these places buckets of blood). As you are walking to your car, you get pushed to the ground, and a person you never see takes your purse. You get back on your feet. What do you do?

The students in my classes give a variety of answers:

"I'd chase him."

"I'd scream. Maybe someone would come and help me."

"I don't know."

"I'd call my boyfriend."

"I'd call my insurance company."

"I'd call my dad."

"I'd call 911."

"I'd call 911" is rarely the answer. When a student gives that answer, I generally ask a follow-up question: "Where do you find a phone, and if you do, do you think the 911 operator can hear you?" Think about your last evening at your local Noisy Barn! Also, think about the description you would give the police of your attacker!

Is rapid response to citizens' calls to 911 really an effective way for the police to apprehend criminals?

★ ★ ★

RETROACTIVE INVESTIGATION OF PAST CRIMES BY DETECTIVES

Prior to the **Rand Study of the Criminal Investigation Process**, the investigation of almost all felonies and some misdemeanors was the sole responsibility of the detective division of a police department.[19] The patrol officer merely obtained information for a complaint or incident report and referred the case to the detectives for follow-up investigation. Theoretically, detectives would interview each complainant and witnesses again, respond to the scene of the crime, and search for clues and leads that could solve the crime.

In 1975, the Rand Corporation think tank found that much of a detective's time was spent in nonproductive work—93 percent of their time was spent on activities that did not lead directly to solving previously reported crimes—and that investigative expertise did little to solve cases. The Rand report said that half of all detectives could be replaced without negatively influencing crime clearance rates:[20]

The single most important determinant of whether or not a case will be solved is the information the victim supplies to the immediately responding patrol officer. If information that uniquely identifies the perpetrator is not present at the time the crime is reported, the perpetrator, by and large, will not be subsequently identified. Of those cases that are ultimately cleared but in which the perpetrator is not identifiable at the time of the initial police incident report, almost all are cleared as a result of routine police procedures. . . .

Our data consistently reveal that an investigator's time is largely consumed in reviewing reports, documenting files and attempting to locate and interview victims on cases that experience shows will not be solved. For cases that are solved (i.e., a suspect is identified), an investigator spends more time in post-clearance processing than he does in identifying the perpetrator.[21]

The effectiveness of detectives was also questioned by a study conducted by the Police Executive Research Forum (PERF) in 1981. Data from the study disclosed that if a crime is reported while it is in progress, police have about a 33 percent chance of making an arrest. However, the probability of arrest declines to about 10 percent if the crime is reported one minute later and to 5 percent if more than 15 minutes elapse before the crime is reported. In addition, as time elapses between the crime and the arrest, the chances of a conviction

Forst's Law

Rushing to the Scene

When I entered policing, responding to calls with lights and siren was not that uncommon. We did it a lot more frequently than officers do today. I can remember responding to bar fights with lights and siren, as was the procedure at the time. After responding to many of these calls in this manner, I began to question the rationale of running red lights and driving over the speed limit with cars pulling over in every direction to get out of my way. I began to wonder why I was risking my life and the lives of other motorists as very rarely was there still a fight going on when I got there. Most of the time friends had separated the individuals involved, and it was usually a situation of mutual (drunk) combatants. It didn't seem to be a call worth risking lives over. Over the years police departments looked at this situation and came to a similar conclusion. Our department started to strictly limit which calls we could respond to in an emergency mode due to the potential for injuries and death and the liability involved.

But early in my career we were very cognizant of police response times, and a bar fight was a call with potential injuries; we wanted to have a good response time. We were not considering the fact that often the fight had been going on for a while or might even be over before someone—usually management—decided to call the police. It was often a threat made by management when the subjects wouldn't leave the lounge. When the subjects didn't leave, the management picked up the phone and called police, the subjects saw they were serious and left, and consequently they were often gone or leaving when we got there.

When police departments started examining the philosophy of immediate response and response time, it became apparent there were other factors that determined whether our response was in fact immediate. Often there was a delay before the call was even made so our "immediate" response lost a lot of its value. When departments weighed the issues of danger to the public and officers, departments severely restricted the types of calls that required an emergency response.

It took a long time, and still today officers like to respond as an emergency vehicle and would like to do it more often. They may argue it's better to get to most situations earlier rather than later, but with streets increasingly more crowded at all hours of the day, it just isn't safe.

---

are reduced, probably because the ability to recover evidence is lost. Once a crime has been completed and the investigation is put into the hands of detectives, the chances of identifying and arresting the perpetrator diminish rapidly.[22]

The Rand and PERF findings were duplicated in a study of detective work by Mark Willman and John Snortum in 1984. The researchers analyzed 5,336 cases reported to a suburban police department. They found that the majority of cases that were solved were solved when the perpetrator was identified at the scene of the crime; scientific detective work was rarely necessary.[23]

These early studies of detective operations indicate that detectives are not very successful in the criminal investigation process. Chapter 8 will explore better techniques police departments have developed to investigate past crimes.

POLICE PATROL OPERATIONS

When we think of the police, our first image is that of the man or woman in uniform driving a police car, at rapid speeds with lights and siren, to the scene of a crime or an accident. We also may think of the uniformed officer on foot patrol ("walking a beat") in a downtown business area, moving a drunk and disorderly citizen away from a group of ordinary shoppers. (**Foot patrol** is a method of deploying police officers that gives them responsibility for all policing activity by requiring them to walk around a defined geographic area.) We may think of a police officer on horseback or one on a motorcycle. All these officers have one thing in common: They are patrol officers.

Since the time of Robert Peel (the promoter of the first organized, paid, uniformed police force in London in

1829), patrol has been the most important and visible part of police work to the public. Peel's major innovation and contribution to society was the idea of a continuous police presence throughout a community that is organized and delivered by means of regular patrol over a fixed beat by uniformed officers. Patrol is the backbone of policing.

Activities of the Patrol Officer

Former Minneapolis police chief Anthony Bouza described the patrol division of a police department as follows: "The patrol forces are the backbone of the agency. They are the uniformed troops, the infantry. They do the bulk of what is known as 'police work': responding to calls, handling emergencies, policing events or demonstrations and just simply being available."[24]

According to Samuel Walker, the basic purpose of patrol has not changed since 1829. Patrol has the following purposes:

1. The deterrence of crime
2. The maintenance of a feeling of public security
3. Twenty-four-hour availability for service to the public[25]

The American Bar Association offers the following as the major purposes of police patrol:

1. To deter crime by maintaining a visible police presence
2. To maintain public order
3. To enable the police department to respond quickly to law violations or other emergencies
4. To identify and apprehend law violators
5. To aid individuals and care for those who cannot help themselves

6. To facilitate the movement of traffic and people
7. To create a sense of security in the community[26]

The patrol officer is the police department's generalist and foremost representative to the public. He or she performs numerous and varied duties in and for the community. Patrol officers face numerous complex problems on a daily basis and see things that most human beings never see. As W. Clinton Terry III wrote

> Patrol officers respond to calls about overflowing sewers, reports of attempted suicides, domestic disputes, fights between neighbors, barking dogs and quarrelsome cats, reports of people banging their heads against brick walls until they are bloody, requests to check people out who have seemingly passed out in public parks, requests for more police protection from elderly ladies afraid of someone entering their residence, and requests for information and general assistance of every sort.[27]

The word *patrol* may be derived from the French word *patrouiller,* which originally meant "to tramp about through the mud of a military camp."[28] This translation reflects the feelings of one authority, who has called patrol a function that is "arduous, tiring, difficult, and performed in conditions other than ideal."[29]

The majority of police patrol today is performed by uniformed officers in radio-equipped patrol cars or on foot. Police also patrol on motorcycles, scooters, boats, planes, helicopters, horses, and bicycles. Officers also patrol in golf carts, in all-terrain vehicles, and on roller skates. In 1997, the city of Philadelphia actually started a patrol unit using officers on in-line skates.[30] As of 2001, there were more than 2,000 active police bicycle units in the United States.[31] In 2003, many police departments began experimenting with patrols using the battery-operated self-balancing vehicle, the Segway.

A 2003 article explains the versatility of certain specialized patrol vehicles for patrol:

- The police motorcycle's maneuverability and acceleration make it ideal for traffic enforcement, escort details, and crowd control.

- Bicycles are quiet and efficient and provide a bridge between motorized vehicles and foot patrol. They provide efficient transportation to areas that are normally available only by walking, such as parks, public housing developments with limited street access, tourist areas, college campuses, business plazas, and sports arenas.

- Electric bikes provide all of the advantages of the pedal bicycle but require less physical effort by the rider.

- Scooters are more maneuverable than cars, yet offer many of the features of a car in a compact space. They also provide shelter from the weather and enable officers to carry more equipment than bicycles. They are especially suited for parking enforcement and specialized patrol on college campuses and business premises.

- Multiterrain vehicles are useful when officers are required to travel into remote areas such as mountains and beaches. Their low-pressure, high-flotation tires and motorcycle-type engines and handlebar steering provide maneuverability in traversing rough terrain. They can often be used for search and rescue missions.

- Mobile substations or precincts can be driven to a specific area to provide a base of operations for beat officers and to facilitate community interaction. They can function as self-contained community policing headquarters and be used in daily community policing programs. They can also be used as a command center at the scene of a crime or disaster.[32]

Some police patrol wearing civilian clothes; they try to blend into the community in an effort to catch criminals in the process of committing crimes. Chapter 8 will discuss civilian-clothes patrol in detail.

The Legacy of O. W. Wilson

Until the 1970s, most of what we knew about patrol was written by O. W. Wilson, former dean of the School of Criminology at the University of California at Berkeley and a former police chief in Wichita (Kansas) and Chicago, and his associate Roy C. McLaren, in the classic *Police Administration*.[33] Wilson called patrol "the backbone of policing" and stated that patrol is designed to create "an impression of omnipresence," which will eliminate "the actual opportunity (or the belief that the opportunity exists) for successful misconduct."[34] The word **omnipresence** can be defined as "the quality of always being there." Thus, if the police are "always there" or seem to be always there, criminals cannot operate. Wilson's patrol ideas were designed to make the police appear to be as omnipresent as possible.

Wilson defined the distribution of patrol officers as the "assignment of a given number of personnel according to area, workload, time or function."[35] Under Wilson's theory some police officers work the day shift; others, the evening shift; and others, the night shift. They are assigned to certain areas based on the work load (number of crimes, arrests, and calls for service) in a particular area. Patrol officers are also assigned according to the type of work they

YOU ARE THERE! »

O. W. Wilson

Orlando Winfield Wilson (1900–1972) has been considered as one of the foremost thinkers and reformers in policing in the 20th century. Wilson was a student and protégé of August Vollmer, having enrolled at the University of California at Berkeley in 1920, attracted by a campus newspaper ad placed by Vollmer. He studied under Vollmer at Berkeley and worked for him as a Berkeley police officer. He held numerous posts during his long career in policing, including Military Police Governor in post–World War II Berlin, Germany; Chief of Police in Fullerton, California (1925); Chief of Police in Wichita, Kansas (1928–1939); and Superintendent of Police in Chicago (1960–1971). He also served as Dean of the School of Criminology at the University of California at Berkeley.

As chief of police in Wichita, Wilson popularized many of the innovations he had observed at Berkeley, including the use of the polygraph, marked police cars, and a crime laboratory. In addition to his seminal landmark textbook, *Police*

Administration (1950), he also wrote the International City Management Association's *Municipal Police Administration*, *Police Records,* and *Police Planning*. In his second edition of *Police Administration* (1963) he coined a term we often use today—"crime analysis."

By the 1960s, Wilson had become a giant in the field of policing, and his recommendations were taken as gospel. His *Police Administration* was the first textbook for police executives and continues to be used today. Wilson firmly believed in honest law enforcement. He believed that corruption was the by-product of poor organization, lack of planning, and tangled lines of command. He developed the concept of preventive patrol and believed that an aggressive omnipresent patrol force could thwart criminal behavior by reducing the opportunity for crime.

Source: O. W. Wilson, Central Missouri State University, Criminal Justice homepage. Retrieved on September 25, 2003, from http://www.cmsu.edu.

perform—foot, radio car, traffic, canine, or some other type of patrol function. Professional police management has consistently followed Wilson's ideas emphasizing the rational distribution of patrol officers according to a work load formula.

Implicit within Wilson's concept of random routine patrol by marked police vehicles was his insistence that the cars should contain one officer, not the two officers that were commonly used earlier. This was quite controversial at the time and remains so. Wilson believed that one-officer patrols could observe more than two-officer patrols could; they would respond more quickly to calls for service; and officers patrolling by themselves were actually safer than officers patrolling in pairs. In a 2003 study of police officer attitudes toward one-officer versus two-officer patrol, officers generally agreed that they would perform the same regardless of whether they were in a one- or two-officer patrol car; however, they believed that two-officer units should be used during the evening or midnight shift as well as in areas of the city where people mistrust the police and that they were generally more effective.[36]

Academic Studies of the Police Patrol Function

Prior to the 1960s, there was little study of the police patrol function—what patrol officers do and how they do it. For years, O. W. Wilson's writings were the bible of policing.[37] It took many years of study to realize that much of what Wilson had taught us about police patrol was wrong and was based on faulty assumptions. Despite the fact that many of Wilson's ideas were replaced by new ideas and concepts based on the subsequent research revolution in policing, we still owe a tremendous thanks to him as the first researcher to really study and write on police operations. As three of the leading police researchers of the 1980s, 1990s, and today, James J. Fyfe, Jack R. Greene, and William F. Walsh, said in their 1997 revised edition of Wilson's classic *Police Administration:*

> Other materials in this edition also are new and, in some cases, actually in conflict with information included in past editions. These conflicts, however, do not indicate that Fyfe, Greene, and Walsh are in disagreement with the Wilson/McLaren tradition. The Wilson/McLaren tradition is to present readers with the state of the art of police administration, rather than to perpetuate information that may be time-locked in earlier years. The fact is that the state of the art has changed since 1976: It is our honor to continue in the tradition of O.W. Wilson and Roy C. McLaren by attempting to present the state of the art as it exists at this writing.[38]

George L. Kelling and Mary A. Wycoff, in their 2001 *Evolving Strategy of Policing: Case Studies of Strategic Change,* write that during the era dominated by O. W. Wilson and his colleagues, roughly the 1920s through the 1970s, police strategy and management emphasized bureaucratic autonomy, efficiency, and internal accountability through command and control systems that focused on countering serious crime by criminal investigation, random preventive patrol by automobile, and rapid response to calls for service.[39] During the 1970s, however, research into police practices called into question the core competencies of police preventive patrol and rapid response to calls for service.

What do the police hope to accomplish through the use of patrol? William Gay, Theodore H. Schell, and Stephen Schack define the goals of patrol as follows: "crime prevention and deterrence, the apprehension of criminals, the provision of non-crime related service, the provision of a sense of community security and satisfaction with the police and the recovery of stolen property."[40] They then divide routine patrol activity into four basic functional categories:

1. *Calls for services.* Responding to citizens' calls to 911 relative to emergencies or other problems accounts for 25 percent of patrol time.

2. *Preventive patrol.* Driving through a community in an attempt to provide what O. W. Wilson described as omnipresence accounts for 40 percent of patrol time.

3. *Officer-initiated activities.* Stopping motorists or pedestrians and questioning them as to their activities account for 15 percent of patrol time.

4. *Administrative tasks.* Paperwork accounts for 20 percent of patrol time.[41]

James Q. Wilson's pioneering work, *Varieties of Police Behavior: The Management of Law and Order in Eight Communities,* attempted to study what police officers do. Wilson concluded that the major role of the police was "handling the situation." Wilson believed that the police encounter many troubling incidents that need some sort of "fixing up." He says that enforcing the law might be one tool a patrol officer uses; threats, coercion, sympathy, understanding, and apathy might be others. Most important to the police officer, Wilson says, "is keeping things under control so that there are no complaints that he is doing nothing or that he is doing too much."[42]

For many years, the major role of police patrol was considered to be law enforcement. However, research conducted in the 1960s and 1970s by academics showed that very little of a patrol officer's time was spent on crime-fighting duties.

PATROL ACTIVITY STUDIES   To determine what police actually do, researchers have conducted patrol activity studies. This research involved studying four major sets of data: data on incoming calls to police departments (calls to 911), calls radioed to patrol officers, actual activity by patrol officers, and police–citizen encounters.

The nature of incoming calls to police departments reveals the kinds of problems or conditions for which citizens call 911. Data from these calls can usually be retrieved from telephone logs or from recordings of conversations between callers and 911 operators. The nature of the calls radioed to patrol officers, or assignments given to police patrol units by 911 dispatchers, reveals not only the types of problems for which people call the police but also the types of problems the police feel deserve a response by patrol units.

The collection of data regarding the actual activity of patrol officers during each hour of their tour is probably the best answer to the question, "What do police officers do?" This information includes activities the police are directed to perform from the 911 dispatcher, as well as the officers' self-initiated activities. These data can usually be retrieved from officers' activity reports and observations by researchers riding with police patrol officers.

Data on what occurs when an officer encounters a citizen—either when the officer is on assignment from the dispatcher or is on self-initiated activities—can best be retrieved from observations by researchers riding with police patrol officers.[43]

The following sections summarize findings by researchers in each of the categories just described.

Studies of Calls to 911   Robert Lilly found that of 18,000 calls to the Newport (Kentucky) Police Department made over a four-month period, 60 percent were requests for information and 13 percent concerned traffic problems. Only 2.7 percent of the calls were about violent crime; 1.8 percent of the calls concerned theft.[44] In a survey of 26,000 calls to the police in 21 different jurisdictions, George Antunes and Eric Scott found that only 20 percent of the calls involved the report of criminal activity.[45] James Q. Wilson conducted a study of all calls to the Syracuse (New York) Police Department during a six-day period. He discovered that only one-tenth of the calls involved incidents in which the police would have to perform a law enforcement function.[46]

Albert Reiss monitored all calls to the Chicago Police Department over a 28-day period. Of all the calls, 58 percent were in regard to criminal or potentially criminal matters. Of these calls, 26 percent involved breaches of the peace; 16 percent, offenses against property; 6 percent, offenses against persons; 5 percent, violations regarding automobiles; and 3 percent, suspicious persons. Reiss noted that the Chicago police themselves categorized as noncriminal some 83 percent of the incidents reported to them.[47]

Summarizing these studies of calls to 911, Cordner reports that most of the calls to police departments are requests for information, requests for services, and reports of disputes and disturbances.[48]

Studies of Calls Radioed to Patrol Officers   Bercal analyzed a sample of over 200,000 calls dispatched to patrol officers in Detroit and St. Louis. He discovered that in Detroit, 39 percent of the calls involved predatory crimes; 35 percent, public disorder; 12 percent, accidents; and 15 percent, service-related requests. In St. Louis, 51 percent of the calls involved predatory crimes; 27 percent, public disorder; 10 percent, accidents; and 12 percent, service-related requests.[49]

Tien, Simon, and Larson discovered that 57 percent of dispatched calls in Wilmington, Delaware, dealt with crime; 14 percent, with traffic; 8 percent, with alarms; 3 percent, with medical problems; and 18 percent, with miscellaneous matters.[50] Lawrence Sherman analyzed over 300,000 dispatches in Minneapolis and discovered that 32 percent involved conflict management; 28 percent, property crime; 19 percent, traffic problems; 13 percent, service; 5 percent, miscellaneous; and 2 percent, stranger-to-stranger crime.[51]

Cordner states that these studies show that a much greater portion of calls handled by patrol officers are crime related than earlier studies regarding only calls to 911 had suggested. He also points out that sizable portions of patrol workload are calls regarding order maintenance, traffic, and service responsibilities.[52]

Studies of Actual Activity by Patrol Officers   Reiss found that the average police officer's typical tour of duty does not involve a single arrest.[53] Egon Bittner found that patrol officers average about one arrest per month and only three Index crime arrests per year.[54] O'Neill and Bloom found that patrolling and nonduty activities accounted for 45 to 50 percent of patrol time in 18 California cities.[55] Finally, Kelling and his associates in the Kansas City Study found that 60 percent of patrol time in Kansas City was uncommitted.[56]

Cordner, commenting on these studies, writes that the majority of patrol work involves not doing anything very specific, but rather taking breaks, meeting with other officers, and engaging in preventive patrolling. He states that administrative duties are the most common in police patrol, and the remaining time is divided among police-initiated activities (33 percent) and calls from the police dispatcher (67 percent). Cordner says the police-initiated activities are mostly related to law enforcement (particularly traffic enforcement). The calls from the dispatcher involve a blend of crimes, disputes, traffic problems, and service requests, with crimes and disputes being the most common.[57]

Studies of Police–Citizen Encounters   The Police Services Study examined patrol work in 60 different neighborhoods. Observers accompanied patrol officers on all shifts in 24 different police departments. The observers collected information on each encounter between a police officer and a citizen, detailing nearly 6,000 encounters. The study found that only 38 percent of all police–citizen encounters dealt primarily with crime-related problems. Most of these were nonviolent crimes or incidents involving suspicious circumstances. The next most common kinds of encounters were disorder problems and traffic-related matters, each accounting for 22 percent of the total. Finally, 18 percent of the police–citizen encounters were primarily of a service nature.

The Police Services Study data also indicated that the police invoked the law relatively rarely, making arrests in only 5 percent of the encounters and issuing tickets in less than 10 percent of the encounters. Additionally, officers used force or the threat of force in only 14 percent of the encounters, with force actually used in only 5 percent of the encounters. Most of this force involved only handcuffing or taking a suspect by the arm.[58]

In 2001, the National Institute of Justice reported the results of a national survey of contacts between the police and citizens, the **Police–Public Contact Survey (PPCS).** The report revealed that about 21 percent of the total population, age 16 or older, have face-to-face contacts with the police each year. About half of these contacts involve some form of motor vehicle- or traffic-related issue, about 20 percent contact the police to report a crime, and about 3 percent of the contacts occur because the police suspected them of involvement in a crime.[59]

THE GREENE AND KLOCKARS STUDY   Jack R. Greene and Carl B. Klockars have described a survey of a full year's worth of computer-aided dispatch (CAD) data for the Wilmington (Delaware) Police Department. Their survey has given us a new look at police activity.[60] Greene and Klockars also describe many of the previous studies regarding police activity and note that most of these studies, as we have seen, reveal that much of police work deals with problems that are not related to crime.

Table 7.1	Distribution of Police Patrol Time
Activity	**Percentage of Time**
Criminal matters	26
Order maintenance matters	9
Service-related matters	4
Traffic matters	11
Medical assistance	2
Administrative matters	12
Unavailable for patrol	5
Random routine patrol	30

Source: Adapted from Jack R. Greene and Carl B. Klockars, "What Police Do," in *Thinking about Police: Contemporary Readings,* 2d ed., Carl B. Klockars and Stephen D. Mastrofski, eds. (New York: McGraw-Hill, 1991), pp. 273–284.

The study revealed that the police spent 26 percent of their time on criminal matters, 9 percent on order maintenance assignments, 4 percent on service-related functions, 11 percent on traffic matters, 2 percent on medical assistance, and 12 percent on administrative matters. Five percent of their time, they were unavailable for service, and almost 30 percent of the time was clear or unassigned, when the officers performed random routine patrol (see Tables 7.1 and 7.2).

Two of the significant findings of this study follow. First, when the percentage of time involved in unavailable, administrative, and clear time is excluded from the data, the data indicate that the police spent almost 50 percent of their time on criminal matters, 16 percent on order maintenance, 8 percent on service, 21 percent on traffic, and 4 percent on medical assistance. Second, 47 percent of the officers' time was spent on activities other than actual assignments.

Table 7.2	Why Police Are Not on Assignment	
Activity	**Percentage of Time**
Administrative time: traveling to and from headquarters, hospitals, or courts	12
Unavailable time: meals, personal time	5
Clear time: random routine patrol	30

Source: Adapted from Jack R. Greene and Carl B. Klockars, "What Police Do," in *Thinking about Police: Contemporary Readings,* 2d ed., Carl B. Klockars and Stephen D. Mastrofski, eds. (New York: McGraw-Hill, 1991), pp. 273–284.

Dempsey's Law

College Intern Programs Are Great

Has anyone in this class participated in the college's intern program with the county police?

I have, Professor Dempsey.

OK, Troy, tell us about it.

Well, we have to work 100 hours with the police, attend a weekly seminar with the other students where we talk about what we are doing on our jobs, and write a 15-page paper on our experiences. We get 4 credits for it.

Troy, what do you do with the police?

We get to work in many different units. I spent one tour on patrol in the patrol car and went to all the calls the officer went on. One day I worked with the precinct detectives and another day with the precinct crime control team, where we busted some prostitutes and raided a crack house. That was cool!

Another day I worked with speed enforcement on the expressway. Man, I'll never speed again. I worked another tour at the Equipment Bureau, but that was just administrative work.

Just administrative work? They don't let you do police work, do they?

Sure, but we have to sign a waiver that we won't sue the department and the county if we get hurt. When we were at the crack house, the perps thought I was a cop. One called me officer; another called me sir.

Troy, we have had a lot of students who have worked the intern program with the police. Some have decided that police work wasn't for them after their experiences. How about you?

Mr. Dempsey, I want it more than ever, now!

OBSERVATIONS ON THE STUDIES   We have seen that the police spend their time performing numerous types of duties. They spend significant time on criminal matters, but the measurement of this time varies depending on the study.

Looking at all the police activity studies, it is obvious why most experts today agree that the great bulk of police patrol work is devoted to what has been described as random routine patrol, administrative matters, order maintenance, and service-related functions. Sheehan and Cordner state that, although the studies performed a valuable function by challenging the crime-fighting image of police work, by the late 1970s many police chiefs and scholars carried them too far and began to downplay and de-emphasize the crime-related and law enforcement aspects of police work.[61] James Q. Wilson noted that he would "prefer the police to act and talk as if they were able to control crime."[62]

Sheehan and Cordner sum up all the studies on "what do cops do" as follows:

Taking all of these studies into consideration, we think a middle of the road position is advisable. It is obvious now that police work is not so completely dominated by crime fighting as its public image and media misrepresentations would suggest. However, it is equally clear that crime-related matters occupy an appreciable portion of the police work load. The available research conclusively demonstrates that those who have been arguing that police work has little or nothing to do with crime know little or nothing about police work.[63]

A former police chief gives a vivid description of police patrol work that may point more to the truth of the matter than can academic studies:

Cops on the street hurry from call to call, bound to their crackling radios, which offer no relief—especially on summer weekend nights. That is the time when the ghetto throbs with noise, booze, violence, drugs, illness, blaring TVs, and human misery. The cops jump from crisis to crisis, rarely having time to do more than tamp one down sufficiently and leave for the next. Gaps of boredom and inactivity fill the interims, although there aren't many of these in the hot months. Periods of boredom get increasingly longer as the night wears on and the weather gets colder.[64]

From the Foot Beat to the Patrol Car

Patrol allocation models give the police answers as to where and when to assign officers. However, over the years, different methods of deploying police officers have been used. The two major deployments are motorized patrol and foot patrol.

Police patrol, as we saw in Chapter 1, is a historical outgrowth of the early watch system. The first formal police

YOU ARE THERE! »

What Do Cops Do? A Reporter Finds Out!

Reporter Alison Mitchell tells some tales of her days riding with police officers:

They hurtled up three steep flights of stairs, six police officers racing to answer a 911 call about a deranged man with a knife. What they found in the small Brooklyn apartment was a skinny man sitting quietly, surrounded by frantic family members.

"We don't want him to get hurt—he's real passive," a nephew said. But when the officers suggested that the relatives should bring the man to a hospital themselves, the story changed. "He's dangerous—he's walking around with this," said a stepson, grabbing a large steak knife to demonstrate how the man had been threatening to kill Fidel Castro.

After several minutes of argument, the officers—two women and four men—cuffed the man's hands behind his back and led him downstairs to await an ambulance. There, as neighbors watched from nearby stoops, the bewildered man began struggling and officers forced him to lie on his stomach on the sidewalk.

"They're kicking him," a spectator holding a bagged beer cried, though, in fact, the officers had done nothing more than stand in a protective circle since putting the man on the ground.

It was a typical call on a typical night on patrol. . . .

On busy nights, the 911 calls are as likely to involve domestic disputes as crime. Police Officer Hanna Tonuzi, 27, and her partner, Officer Nicole Medico, 23, were on the 4-to-midnight tour on a recent balmy Saturday evening when they received the call about the man with the knife. But they had scarcely any time to dwell on the case, which was sandwiched somewhere between the brother who beat his sister so savagely that her blood was splattered on the floor outside their apartment and a 911 report of a woman with a gun.

The gun call was the one that left them talking. Seven officers responded, only to find that it was in reality a woman with an infant. The long-haired redhead in a black tights outfit had shown up to confront her child's father at his home, where he and his wife also had a newborn. A screaming fracas was under way between the women. The police quickly separated everyone. The girlfriend was pulled into the yard. The man and his wife were quizzed in their home.

Officer Tonuzi, her blond hair in a ponytail, calmed the girlfriend with down-home feminist advice: Forget him. "I'm sure you still love him," she said to the intruder, who was in tears and would get a desk-appearance ticket for harassment. "To come here is not good. She's going to fight you because she's here too." . . .

He [Police Officer Louis Marino] was speeding toward a burglary when a new call of officer needing assistance sent him into reverse. His patrol car pulled up where two plainclothes officers, Eddie Mattera and Carlos Pacheco, had just arrested a 19-year-old carrying a .25 caliber semiautomatic pistol. The young man was handcuffed. The only problem was his dog.

The uniformed officers pulled the animal into their car, to return it to the man's mother. She wasn't home, but a young neighbor was. They told him his friend was under arrest. "His dog's under arrest too," Officer Marino deadpanned. They handed over the dog with instructions that it be returned to his owner's mother, along with the news that her son could be found at the precinct station house.

"I don't know the dog's name," the teenager called back to the officers.

"Call him Pistol," Officer Tomasi answered.

Source: Reprinted with permission from Alison Mitchell, "A Night on Patrol: What's behind Police Tensions and Discontent," *New York Times* (Oct. 19, 1992), pp. B1, B2. Copyright © 1992 by The New York Times Company.

---

patrols were on foot, and the cop on the beat became the symbol and very essence of policing in the United States. Furthermore, the cop on the beat became the embodiment of American government to most citizens. However, as early as the 1930s—even before the automobile had become an integral part of American life—foot patrols were beginning to vanish in favor of the more efficient and faster patrol car.[65]

By the late 1930s and 1940s, police management experts stressed the importance of motorized patrol as a means of increasing efficiency. The International City Management Association (ICMA) reported that the number of cities using motorized patrols increased from 840 in 1946 to 1,000 in 1954 and to 1,334 in 1964.[66]

By the 1960s, the efficiency of the remaining foot patrols was being challenged. Foot patrols were considered geographically restrictive and wasteful of personnel. Foot officers, who at the time had no portable radios (these did not become available until the 1970s), were not efficient in terms of covering large areas or being available to be

Police are expanding their methods of patrol to best address the needs and challenges of their communities. These patrol strategies can include marine patrol and patrol on all-terrain vehicles.

signaled and sent on assignments. Thus, to management experts, foot patrols were not as efficient as the readily available radio cars.

In 1968, the District of Columbia Crime Commission, criticizing the District of Columbia's continued use of foot patrol, stated: "The department's continued reliance on foot patrol is an inefficient and outdated utilization of manpower resources. . . . As long as the Department uses foot patrol as the primary method of patrol, however, available economics will not be realized and the city will not be provided the best possible police service."[67]

At about this time, many cities—including Kansas City, Missouri; Dallas; Phoenix; Omaha; Oklahoma City; Birmingham, Alabama; and other large cities—had shifted

almost totally away from foot patrols, replacing them with more deployable two-person car patrols. However, as a report of the Kansas City (Missouri) Police Department pointed out, in 1966, the number of foot patrol beats per shift in Boston, Baltimore, Pittsburgh, and other major urban centers still remained in the hundreds.[68]

At almost the same time these reports from Kansas City and the District of Columbia were prepared, the International Association of Chiefs of Police (IACP) went one step further, strongly advocating the idea of a conspicuous patrol that conveyed a sense of police omnipresence. The association felt that this could be best achieved using a highly mobile force of one-person cars:

> The more men and more cars that are visible on the streets, the greater is the potential for preventing a crime. A heavy blanket of conspicuous patrol at all times and in all parts of the city tends to suppress violations of the law. The most economical manner of providing this heavy blanket of patrol is by using one-man cars when and where they are feasible.[69]

The change from foot to motor patrol revolutionized U.S. policing. It fulfilled the expectations of the management experts by enabling police departments to provide more efficient patrol coverage—that is, covering more areas more frequently and responding more quickly to calls for service.[70] However, one major unforeseen consequence of the shift to motorized patrol continues to haunt us to this very day. As William A. Westley pointed out in 1970, "In contrast to the man on the beat, the man in the car is isolated from the community."[71]

Motor patrol was very efficient in terms of coverage, but it involved a trade-off in terms of the relationship between the police and the community. Now police officers had few contacts with ordinary citizens in normal situations; most calls involved problems, either crime or order maintenance problems. A growing rift began to develop between the police and the public. Few people noticed this change in policing until the riots of the 1960s dramatized the problem of police–community relations.[72]

As early as 1968, experts began to realize the problems created by the emphasis on the efficiency of the patrol car. They realized the absence of the foot officer's closeness to the community. The *Task Force Report* of the President's Commission on Law Enforcement and Administration of Justice noted, "The most significant weakness in American motor patrol operations today is the general lack of contact with citizens except when an officer has responded to a call. Forced to stay near the car's radio, awaiting an assignment, most patrol officers have few opportunities to develop closer relationships with persons living in the district."[73]

Despite the drawbacks, by 1978, the *Police Practices Survey* found that more than 90 percent of all beats were handled by motor patrol. Foot patrol accounted for less than 10 percent.[74]

Return to Foot Patrol

Obviously, police officers on motorized patrols are more efficient than foot officers. Cars get to locations much more quickly; they can cover much larger areas; and they provide the officers more comfort in inclement weather. However, as we have seen, some police managers and other experts feel that automobile patrolling had led to a police alienation from neighborhoods and a loss of the feelings of safety by citizens that is generated by foot patrol.[75]

In the mid-1980s, in an attempt to get the police closer to the public and to avoid the problems caused by the alienation of radio car officers from the community, an emphasis on foot patrol began to return to many cities. By 1985, foot patrol had returned to Newark, Oakland, Los Angeles, Detroit, Flint (Michigan), Houston, Boston, New York City, Atlanta, Tampa, Minneapolis, Cincinnati, and many other cities. A 1984 survey revealed that approximately two-thirds of medium-sized and large police departments utilized foot patrol in some form.[76]

Researchers arrived at the following conclusions about the reinstitution of foot patrol in Newark and Flint:

1. When foot patrol is added in neighborhoods, levels of fear decrease significantly.
2. When foot patrol is withdrawn from neighborhoods, levels of fear increase significantly.
3. Citizen satisfaction with police increases when foot patrol is added in neighborhoods.
4. Police who patrol on foot have a greater appreciation for the values of the neighborhood residents than do police who patrol the same area in automobiles.
5. Police who patrol on foot have greater job satisfaction, less fear, and higher morale than do officers who patrol in automobiles.[77]

A thorough study conducted in Newark regarding foot patrols was unable to demonstrate that either adding or removing foot patrol affected crime in any way. However, Newark citizens involved in this study were less fearful of crime and more satisfied with services provided by officers on foot patrol than services by officers on motorized patrol. Also, Newark citizens in this study were aware of additions and deletions of foot patrol from their neighborhoods, in contrast to the Kansas City Study, where citizens did not perceive changes in the level of motorized patrol.[78] Thus, the **Newark foot patrol studies** do not prove that foot patrols reduce crime but that foot patrols actually make citizens feel safer. Experience indicates that citizens clearly want to see a return to the old "cop on the beat."

The best evidence that citizens want foot patrols may have been shown in Flint. Despite the highest unemployment rate in the nation, citizens there voted in 1982 and 1985 to increase their taxes to extend foot patrol to the entire city.[79]

Interviews over a four-year period disclosed that the Neighborhood Foot Patrol program in Flint improved relationships between the police and the community. Residents of the community indicated their belief that the police on foot patrol were more responsive to their needs than had been the case before the experimental program.[80]

Research has indicated that more active citizen involvement in policing has occurred where foot patrol programs have been implemented. In Boston, for example, citizens actively participate with police officers on neighborhood crime and street patrol committees.[81] In Atlanta, a Bureau of Police Services Partnership against Crime program has actively involved citizens with police in devising ways of attacking crime through more aggressive prevention and control.[82]

A Tampa, Florida, patrol experiment, the Permanent Patrol Assignment system, was supplemented with golf cart patrols. Like foot patrols, golf cart patrols can get closer to the people, but they are more mobile than foot patrol. The golf car patrols responded more rapidly to citizen calls and increased dispatcher efficiency in dealing with citizen complaints.[83]

Why Walking Works Better Than Driving

Citizens want and like foot patrol officers. Why does this more expensive form of policing seem more effective than traditional radio car patrol?

Researchers have found that foot patrol officers pay more attention to disorderly behavior and minor offenses than do motor patrol officers. Foot patrol officers are in a better position to manage their beats—to see, understand, and deal with threatening or inappropriate behavior. They are more likely to pay attention to derelicts, petty thieves, disorderly persons, vagrants, panhandlers, noisy juveniles, and street people—people who are not committing serious crimes but are causing concern and fear among many citizens.[84]

The existence of the foot patrols themselves does not seem to be the critical factor that makes them effective.

Rather, it is the actions of the officer on the foot beat. As Robert C. Trojanowicz, evaluator of the Flint experiment, points out, "If an officer's walking along in the traditional way, he won't affect the crime rate. Patrolmen who operate that way are just motorized officers without a car. Basically, they're doorshakers. But when the officers become actively involved in the community, that's when crime problems begin to be solved."[85]

James Q. Wilson and George L. Kelling, in "'Broken Windows': The Police and Neighborhood Safety," talk about a Newark street cop they call "Kelly," with whom Kelling spent many hours walking a beat:

> As he saw his job, he was to keep an eye on strangers; and make certain that the disreputable regulars observed some informal but widely understood rules. Drunks and addicts could sit on the stoops, but could not lie down. People could drink on side streets, but not at the main intersection. Bottles had to be in paper bags. Talking to, bothering, or begging from people waiting at the bus stop was strictly forbidden. . . . Persons who broke the informal rules, especially those who bothered people waiting at bus stops, were arrested for vagrancy. Noisy teenagers were told to keep quiet.[86]

Kelly obviously separated the people on his beat into strangers versus regular people and reputable versus disreputable people, and he created rules to enforce a distance between them. By walking around and enforcing the rules, Kelly maintained peace and a sense of equilibrium on his beat.

As we saw in Chapter 1, there have been drastic crime reductions in U.S. cities from the mid-1990s up to today. Much of this crime reduction, not surprisingly, can be attributed to aggressive zero-tolerance policing by individual foot patrol officers in our major cities. The lessons taught by Wilson and Kelling through "Kelly" surely have made our urban streets safer for residents and visitors.

★ ★ ★

DETECTIVE OPERATIONS

Most of the activities of a police department involve police patrol operations. However, as we saw in Chapter 3, the police engage in numerous other activities. Detective operations are an important part of police work.

What Do Detectives Do?

The detective division of a police department is charged with solving, or clearing, reported crimes. In traditional detective operations, detectives conduct a follow-up investigation of a past crime after a member of the patrol force takes the initial report of the crime and conducts some sort of preliminary investigation.

According to police tradition, a detective or investigator reinterviews the victim of the crime and any witnesses, collects evidence, and processes the crime scene (searches the scene of a crime for physical evidence, collects the evidence, and forwards it to the police laboratory for analysis). The detective or investigator also conducts canvasses (searches of areas for witnesses); interrogates possible suspects; arrests the alleged perpetrator; and prepares the case, with the assistance of the district attorney's or prosecutor's office, for presentation in court.

The detective generally begins an investigation upon receipt of an incident report (complaint report) prepared by the officer who conducted the initial interview with the victim. The incident report contains identifying information regarding the victim, details of the crime, identifying information regarding the perpetrator (or perpetrators) or a description; and identifying information regarding any property taken.

As the detective begins the investigation, he or she maintains a file on the case, using follow-up reports for each stage of the investigation. The incident report and the follow-up reports are generally placed in a case folder and serve as the official history of the crime and its investigation. The case folder is then used by the prosecutor to prosecute the case in court. (To prosecute means to conduct criminal procedures in a court of law against a person accused of committing criminal offenses. The people performing this duty are generally called prosecutors. They are also called, in various jurisdictions, district attorneys, state attorneys, or U.S. attorneys.) The incident report and the follow-up reports may also be subpoenaed by a defendant's defense attorney under the legal process known as discovery, which allows a defendant, prior to a trial, to have access to the information the police and prosecutor will use at the trial.

Detective units may be organized on a decentralized or centralized basis. In a decentralized system, each precinct in a city has its own local detective squad, which investigates all crimes occurring in the precinct. Detectives or investigators in a decentralized squad are considered generalists.

In a centralized system, in contrast, all detectives operate out of one central office or headquarters and are each responsible for certain particular types of crime in the entire city. These detectives are considered specialists. Some departments separate centralized or specialty squads into crimes against persons squads and crimes against property squads. Some departments operate specialized squads for most serious crimes—for example, they may have a homicide squad, sex crime squad, robbery squad, burglary squad, forgery squad, pickpocket squad, and bias crimes squad (which investigates crimes that are motivated by bigotry or hatred of a person's race, ethnic origin, gender, or sexual orientation).

Some cities use both decentralized and centralized investigatory units. The decentralized squads operate out of a local precinct and refer some of their cases to the specialized centralized squads, such as sex crime, homicide, or arson squads. The decentralized squads then investigate less serious cases themselves.

The Detective Mystique

Detectives work out of uniform, perform no patrol duties, and are generally paid at a higher rate than regular uniformed officers. The assignment to detective duties is generally considered a promotion. Detectives generally enjoy much greater status and prestige than patrol officers. They have historically been seen as the heroes of police work in novels, television, and the movies—consider Sherlock Holmes, Cagney and Lacey, Andy Sipowicz, Crockett and Tubbs, Dirty Harry Callahan, and other fictional detectives. Are real life detectives as heroic, smart, individualistic, tough, hardworking, and mysterious as their fictional counterparts? Or is there a mystique attached to the detective position?

The **detective mystique** is the idea that detective work is glamorous, exciting, and dangerous, as it is depicted in the movies and on television. In reality, however, detectives spend most of their time filling out reports and reinterviewing victims on the telephone. Commenting on the detective mystique, Herman Goldstein has written

> Part of the mystique of detective operations is the impression that a detective has difficult-to-come-by qualifications and skills, that investigating crime is a real science, that a detective does much more important work than other police officers, that all detective work is exciting and that a good detective can solve any crime. . . . [In] the context of the totality of police operations, the cases detectives solve account for a much smaller part of police business than is commonly realized. This is so because in case after case, there is literally nothing to go on: no physical evidence, no description of the offender, no witness and often no cooperation, even from the victim.[87]

Prior to the Rand Study of the Criminal Investigation Process, which will be discussed in Chapter 8, the detective mystique was considered to be an accurate representation of reality. It was believed that each crime was completely investigated, that all leads and tips were followed to their logical conclusion, and that each case was successfully solved. This was not true, as we will see when we discuss the Rand study. The reality of detective work usually has little in common with its media representations.

Because of the Rand study and other studies, police administrators can now make some generalizations about detective operations. First, the single most important determinant of whether or not a crime is solved is not the quality of the work performed by the detectives but the information the victim supplies to the first patrol officer who reports to the scene of the crime.[88] Next, detectives are not very effective in solving crimes. Nationally, police are only able to clear (solve) about 21 percent of all serious crime reported to them.[89] (It must be remembered however, that this 21 percent clearance figure refers to all crimes and that the police have much higher clearance rates in the most serious crimes, such as murder, sexual assault, and aggravated assault). Furthermore, because only about one-third of all crimes are ever reported to the police at all, the real clearance rate of crime is much lower than 21 percent. (Police cannot clear crimes not reported to them.)[90] Finally, patrol officers, not detectives, are responsible for the vast majority of all arrests. In fact, in one study, patrol officers made 87 percent of all arrests.[91]

★ ★ ★

POLICE TRAFFIC OPERATIONS

Controlling the movement of vehicular traffic and enforcing the traffic laws is another one of the important activities the police engage in. The proliferation of automobiles, motorcycles, and trucks in the United States has been accompanied by a tremendous amount of traffic fatalities, injuries, and property damage. For the latest reporting year, 2002, a total of 42,815 persons died, 2.92 million persons were injured, and $230.6 billion dollars in economic loss occurred due to traffic accidents.[92] Alcohol-related fatalities made up 41 percent of the total, and 59 percent of those who died were not wearing safety belts.

The states have enacted numerous laws dealing with vehicle use, and it falls upon the police to enforce those laws. Thibault, Lynch, and McBride define the traffic role of the police as follows:

1. The elimination of accident causes and congestion

2. The identification of potential traffic problems and hazards

3. The regulation of parking on streets and municipal facilities

4. The investigation of property damage and personal injury automobile accidents

5. Directing public awareness toward the proper use of automobiles, bicycles, and motorcycles

6. The arrest of offenders[93]

The vast majority of local and state law enforcement agencies have the responsibility of enforcing state and local traffic laws and ordinances. Some states have a state highway patrol, whose primary duties are the enforcement of traffic laws. Many police departments create a special unit, such as a traffic division, to pay special attention to traffic problems. However, the enforcement of traffic regulations is generally the duty of all officers in a department. In some municipalities, nonsworn officers or civilians are hired for traffic control and the enforcement of local parking regulations.

★ ★ ★

POLICE SPECIAL OPERATIONS

One type of police work that has increased greatly in recent years includes special weapons and tactical teams (SWAT) and emergency service units (ESUs). SWAT teams and ESUs address specific emergency and lifesaving situations that regular officers on routine patrol do not have the time or expertise to handle.

SWAT Teams

SWAT teams were created in many cities during the 1960s, generally in response to riots and similar disturbances. The first SWAT team was the Philadelphia Police Department's 100-officer Special Weapons and Tactics (SWAT) squad, which was organized in 1964 in response to the growing number of bank robberies throughout the city.[94]

Members of SWAT teams are carefully chosen and trained in the use of weapons and strategic invasion tactics. SWAT teams are used in situations involving hostages, serious crimes, airplane hijackings, and prison riots,

© AP Photo/Mary Altaffer

The tragedy at the World Trade Center has had an impact on the day-to-day operations of all police organizations. Here the New York Police Department Emergency Service Unit patrols Wall Street with a drug-sniffing dog and machine guns in 2003 during an extended level-orange terror alert.

as well as in other situations requiring specialized skills and training.

A recent study by Professors Peter B. Kraska and Victor E. Kappeler, of Eastern Kentucky University, said that paramilitary police units are becoming a standard feature of

American policing, even in small- and medium-sized departments. Their study found that from 1982 to 1995, the proportion of police agencies with SWAT teams in departments servicing populations of 50,000 residents had risen from 59 percent to 89 percent.[95]

Emergency Service Units

Police departments provide numerous emergency services, including emergency first aid to sick and injured citizens, rescues of people trapped in automobiles at accident scenes, rescues of those trapped in burning or collapsed buildings, and often rescues of people attempting to commit suicide by jumping from buildings and bridges. These duties involve specialized training and, often, sophisticated rescue equipment. The first aid and rescue services are often provided by patrol officers as part of their routine services. Many larger cities or counties, however, provide special patrol units whose primary responsibility is to respond to these emergencies. Often these emergency duties are merged into a department's SWAT operations or are pro-

vided by specialized emergency service units with sophisticated rescue and lifesaving equipment.

The New York City Police Department has had its Emergency Service Unit (ESU) since 1930. This unit spends most of its time on rescue missions, as well as on performing traditional hostage and SWAT operations. An emergency service volunteer recruit described his training:

> [The ESU recruit] is schooled in a staggering syllabus of skills. He is trained as a marksman so he can play a key role when an armed perpetrator takes cover or a terrorist takes hostages. Then he is taught the psychology of barricaded criminals so he can avoid using his marksmanship talents. He is certified as an emergency medical technician and can administer cardiopulmonary resuscitation and oxygen to victims of coronaries, respiratory ailments, smoke inhalation and asphyxiation. He is versed in the art of extrication and rescues people trapped in not only elevators but also vehicles, heavy machinery and cave-ins. He knows how to secure dangerous cornices and scaffolds, repair downed electrical wires and poles . . . and navigate an armored personnel carrier for rescuing people pinned down by gunfire.[96]

CHAPTER SUMMARY

This chapter has discussed the traditional methods of doing police work: random routine patrol, rapid response to citizens' 911 calls, and retroactive investigation of past crimes by detectives. Prior to the academic studies of the 1960s and 1970s—particularly the Kansas City Study—most of what we knew about police work, and most of the way police work was done in the United States, relied on untested assumptions. We assumed that adding more police to a community reduced crime. Routine random patrol by officers driving in and around a neighborhood in marked police cars, rapid response to citizens' calls to 911 for assistance, and retroactive investigations of past crimes by detectives were the only ways we did police work, and we assumed they were effective. The Kansas City Study forced academics and progressive police administrators to look closely at police operations to see if there were better, more effective ways to do them. This chapter looked at some of the academic studies regarding policing.

Most of the chapter involved police patrol operations—the "backbone" of policing. The chapter discussed the activities and role of the patrol officer and the various methods of doing patrol work, including motorized and foot patrol. Additionally, the chapter discussed detective opera-

tions, traffic operations, and special operations, including SWAT teams and emergency service units.

Chapter 8 will look at new ways of policing based on the academic studies and experiences of police administrators discussed in this chapter.

Learning Check

1. Name the three basic methods used by the police to fulfill their mission.
2. Discuss whether the three basic methods used by the police to fulfill their mission are effective. If they are effective, why? If they are not effective, why not?
3. Identify the major value of the Kansas City Study.
4. Explain what the academic studies regarding police patrol revealed about what the police do while on patrol.
5. Discuss what the academic studies regarding police detective operations revealed about what detectives do.

Application Exercise

Your professor in this course is attending the annual national convention of the Academy of Criminal Justice Sciences (ACJS) in March and has invited you and your fellow students to accompany her. She has indicated that students may present student papers at the convention on any issue in policing.

The paper must be 10 pages long, double spaced. In addition to preparing the paper, the student will be required to present it to an assembled panel of other students from all over the United States in a 10- to 15-minute oral report.

Your professor has recommended that you select one of the following topics and write a report on it:

1. Traditional methods of policing—What are they? How effective are they?

2. Police patrol operations—What do patrol cops do?

3. Police detective operations—What do detectives do?

Web Exercise

Patrol the Internet, find several examples of police departments using foot patrols, and describe what these departments say about their benefits.

Key Concepts

Control group
Controlled experiment
Detective mystique
Experimental group
Foot patrol
Kansas City Study
Newark foot patrol studies
Omnipresence
Police–Public Contact Survey (PPCS)
Rand Study of the Criminal Investigation Process
Random routine patrol
Rapid response to citizens' calls to 911
Retroactive investigation of past crimes by detectives

8 Police Operations: A New Approach

CHAPTER GOALS

- To acquaint you with alternatives to the traditional methods of random routine patrol and rapid response to citizens' 911 calls, as discussed in Chapter 7
- To introduce you to alternatives to retroactive investigation of past crimes by detectives, as discussed in Chapter 7
- To acquaint you with the most recent proactive tactics being used by the police to fight crime, including tactical operations, decoy operations, sting operations, civil liability and code enforcement teams, and new efforts against drunk drivers
- To acquaint you with undercover operations, including police, federal, and private security operations, and undercover drug operations
- To define entrapment and show how it relates to police tactical and undercover operations

Despite the unprecedented crime decreases of the mid-1990s, as discussed in Chapter 1, public and media attention to crime has intensified. In fact, in August 1997, a study by the Washington, D.C.–based Center for Media and Public Affairs showed that the amount of network news devoted to stories regarding murder cases in the United States soared 721 percent from 1993 to 1996.[1] In 1999, despite the fact that the murder rate had been steadily declining for several years, network news coverage continued to climb, reaching the highest rate in 10 years if the O. J. Simpson case coverage is excluded.[2] Police operations and efforts against crime, therefore, remain a critical component of policing. Chapter 7 discussed the three traditional methods of police work—random routine patrol, rapid response to citizens' calls to 911, and retroactive investigation of past crimes by detectives—and why they are not very effective.

Police departments throughout the nation have learned that they must be more specific and focused in addressing crime and disorder problems. They have created new policies, procedures, and units to address these concerns. This chapter will discuss and examine some of these innovations. Despite all of the criticism of traditional police patrol methods by academic researchers, no one is calling for the elimination of police patrol. Rather, researchers and police administrators are exploring various innovative alternatives to supplement traditional methods of patrol. These alternatives involve organizational and procedural changes in the makeup and use of the patrol force. The first three alternatives—directed patrol, split force patrol, and differential response to requests for service—are modifications of normal routine preventive patrol and rapid response to calls for service. Traditional detective operations have also been modified in response to academic studies that have indicated that new methods can be used in the investigation of past crimes and the apprehension of career criminals. Improved investigations of past crimes include changes made in detective operations in response to research conducted by the Rand Corporation and other think tanks, as well as the use of cold case squads. Increased attention to career criminals has led to a proliferation of repeat offender programs (ROPS) throughout the United States. Additionally, new tactics and operations have been developed over the past two decades in an attempt to provide more effective policing. The tactics discussed in this chapter include uniformed tactical operations, such as aggressive and saturation patrol; decoy operations; stakeout operations; sting operations; code enforcement teams; and efforts against drunk and aggressive drivers.

The chapter also discusses the major types of undercover operations, including police, federal, and private security undercover operations. The chapter concludes with a discussion of the legal aspects of entrapment and how it relates to undercover work and other law enforcement tactics.

★ ★ ★

ALTERNATIVES TO RANDOM ROUTINE PATROL AND RAPID RESPONSE TO CITIZENS' 911 CALLS

The current popular alternatives to random routine patrol and rapid response to citizens' 911 calls are directed patrol, split force patrol, and differential response to calls for service. These innovative approaches to policing are designed to make better use of officers' patrol time, as well as to make better use of a department's resources.

Directed Patrol

An alternative to random routine patrol is **directed patrol,** in which officers are given specific directions to follow when they are not responding to calls. The directed patrol assignments are given to officers before they begin their tour and are meant to replace uncommitted random patrol time with specific duties that police commanders believe will be effective. Directed patrol assignments can be based on crime analysis, specific problems, or complaints received from the community. In departments utilizing the community policing philosophy, patrol officers are often given the freedom of determining where and when their directed patrol efforts should be directed based on crime analysis and their experiences.

Several studies present some evidence that target crimes were reduced by directed patrol. By basing directed patrol assignments on statistical studies, many of the inadequacies of random, unstructured patrol may be overcome. The data suggest that citizen satisfaction and crime control efforts increase when patrol is based on a systematic analysis of crime.[3] A significant recent example of a directed patrol program that achieved positive results was the "Kansas City Gun Experiment." Working with the University of Maryland, the Kansas City, Missouri, Police Department focused extra directed patrol attention to gun crimes in a "hot spot" area that was determined by computer analysis. Two two-officer patrol cars focused exclusively on gun detection from 7 P.M. to 1 A.M., seven days a week. They focused on the directed patrol assignment and did not respond to any radio calls or service assignments.[4] During the course of the 29-week experiment, the officers worked a total of 200 nights involving over 4,500 officer hours and over 2,200 patrol car hours (70 percent of their time was spent processing arrests and performing other necessary duties). During the 29-week experiment, the gun patrol officers made thousands of car and pedestrian checks, traffic stops, and over 600 arrests. They confiscated 29 guns; an additional 47 weapons were seized by other officers in the experimental area. The gun seizures represented a 65 percent increase over the number of guns seized in the target area during the previous six months. The gun patrol efforts also affected crime rates. There were 169 gun crimes in the target beat in the 29 weeks prior to the experiment, but only 86 during the experimental period, a decrease of 49 percent. Drive-by shootings and homicides decreased significantly. Interestingly, none of the seven contiguous beats showed a significant increase in gun crime, indicating that there was little crime displacement effect.

Community surveys conducted before and after the program was initiated indicated that citizens in the target area were less fearful of crime and more satisfied with their neighborhood than residents in companion areas. After the extra directed patrols were ended, crime rates went back to their normal levels.

Senna and Siegel indicated that the Kansas City gun patrol experiment suggests that a modest police patrol effort targeting a specific crime problem can produce dramatic effects on the crime rate.[5] Whether such efforts should be made part of general police policy remains to be seen. They could produce risks to officer safety, provoke hostile reactions from citizens, and make people subject to police searches hostile and angry. These risks may be acceptable if aggressive police action could significantly reduce the threat of gun violence.

Split Force Patrol

As we have just seen, directed patrol is designed so officers can pay particular attention to specific crimes and disorder while they are not on assignment from the police dispatcher. One of the problems with directed patrol, however, is that calls for service often interrupt the performance of directed patrol assignments. **Split force patrol**

Dempsey's Law

A Typical Directed Patrol Assignment

Professor Dempsey, what does "directed patrol" mean? Who directs what? Can you give me an example?

Directed patrol is designed to address specific problems when police are not involved in any other police work. It is an alternative to routine random patrol. Based on a review of a precinct's crime statistics, complaints from the community, and other data, the precinct commander prepares a list of directed patrol assignments that officers can concentrate on when they are not on assignment from the radio dispatcher. The assignments are then given to the officers who patrol that particular area at that particular time when they report for duty.

Consider the following example of a typical police problem. Outside a local rock club, the Sundance Heavy Metal Trash Club, numerous fights have broken out in the parking lot during the hours when the club is open (Friday and Saturday nights between 9 P.M. and 4 A.M.). Generally, police respond, bring the victims to

the hospital for first aid, and sometimes arrest the perpetrator. But the problem does not go away. The precinct does not have the personnel to assign directly to the lot due to the need to answer emergency calls.

A directed patrol assignment might be used to correct this condition. The following instructions could be given to two or three patrol cars on the Friday and Saturday evening and night tours: "Between 9 P.M. and 4 A.M., while not on assignment, sit in the parking lot of the Sundance Heavy Metal Trash Club, located at 711 Sunrise Highway, to prevent fights between youths." Possible combatants might feel the police presence and realize the police were serious about this problem. At the same time, the police would still be available for rapid response to emergencies. Think about it. If you had a dispute at a club and decided to go outside and settle it, would the presence of several police cars make you think more rationally? Think about some problems in your own community that could benefit from directed patrol.

offers a solution to this problem. One portion of the patrol force is designated to handle all calls dispatched to patrol units. The remaining portion of the officers working that tour are given directed patrol assignments with the assurance that except for serious emergencies, they will not be interrupted. The most extensive test of the split force strategy was conducted in Wilmington, Delaware. The evaluation of the experiment found that this patrol improved both call-handling productivity and patrol productivity, while also enhancing patrol professionalism and accountability.[6]

The Houston Police Department, faced with a spiraling crime rate, implemented a form of split force patrol called the high-intensity patrol (HIP). HIPs are an effort to put more officers on the streets in different parts of the city during peak crime hours. The Houston patrols, funded from a $2 million overtime account, are staffed by as many as 35 officers working on their days off or outside their regular duty hours. The HIP officers perform highly visible patrol in specific areas to emphasize the police presence. They are directed not to answer 911 calls but to remain patrolling in their assigned areas.[7] Some critics of the Houston program state that it is mismanaged and a waste of time and money. They say that calls for service are put on hold and accumulated because there are not enough regular patrol officers to respond to them. Some officers have jokingly referred to the HIPs as "the drive-by-and-wave program." One officer stated, "Meanwhile, the calls for service just continued to pile up. It was unbelievable. The regular officers were really upset because they are running from one call to another while the other guys weren't doing anything. The guys in the HIP weren't to blame. They were ordered not to answer calls."[8]

As of 2004, the Houston Police Department continued to emphasize directed patrol as a strategy in addressing crime issues as well as nuisance calls. While the department could not credit a slight reduction in crime to this strategy, they do believe these patrols have led to a decrease in fear of crime and an increase in citizen satisfaction with the police. They meet regularly with citizens' groups to discuss issues of importance and develop plans to address these issues. Approximately 30 percent of the patrol force is devoted to specialty units working directed patrols; and, though there is still some resistance among officers, it has declined dramatically. This decline can be attributed in part to the fact that commanders are now allowing these specialty units to handle calls for service at peak times, in particular at shift changes. This has minimized the problem of calls stacking up at busy times for the patrol units handling calls for service.

Differential Response to Calls for Service

Differential response to calls for service is a policy that abandons the traditional practice of responding to all calls for service. In differential response, responses to citizens' calls to 911 for service are matched to the importance or severity of the calls. Reports of injuries, crimes, or emergencies in progress, as well as reports of serious past crimes, continue to receive an immediate response by sworn police. However, less serious calls are handled by alternative methods. Conditions for which delayed or alternative responses are appropriate include the following: delayed burglaries, thefts, vandalisms, lost property, and insurance reports.

Differential response alternatives can replace sending a patrol unit to investigate a past crime. A patrol unit can be sent later, when there are fewer calls for service. The caller can be asked to come into the precinct headquarters to report the crime. The call can be transferred to a nonsworn member, who then takes the report over the phone. In some departments the report can be made online. Finally, the dispatcher can make an appointment for a nonsworn member to respond to the caller's home to take a report. Differential response to calls for service is designed to reduce and better manage the workload of patrol officers. It gives patrol officers more time to devote to directed patrol, investigations, or crime prevention programs.[9]

Differential response is based on the research described in Chapter 7 on the effectiveness of rapid response to citizens' calls to 911. The policy arises from an evaluation of questions such as these: Is there any value in sending a patrol unit immediately to a past burglary, particularly when the owner has just returned from a weeklong vacation? Must a patrol unit be sent right away when the likelihood of the arrest of the perpetrator or the obtaining of leads to solving the crime is extremely low, even with an extremely rapid response of one to two minutes? Perhaps rapid response is good for police public relations—"See how fast we respond when you call!"—but the allocation of scarce patrol resources should depend on police effectiveness rather than public relations. Research has shown that most citizens will accept explanations of alternative police responses if the explanations are politely and logically presented. However, researchers have suggested that providing such explanations goes beyond the traditional role of police communications personnel and requires additional training and supervision.[10] Departments have different ways of presenting this information and educating the public about their policies, and the Internet can increase the available options. The Arlington, Texas, Police Department explains on their Web page about their policy regarding response to 911 calls and how and why they prioritize calls.[11]

Departments suffering from financial difficulties that prevent them from hiring additional officers may benefit most from differential response. They can spread out the workload while still ensuring that all emergency calls are responded to and all reports to past crimes and incidents are recorded and investigated. They also make use of less expensive nonsworn personnel and perhaps even volunteers in some of this report taking by stacking nonpriority calls until the zone car is available and not sending an adjacent zone car immediately. This saves department resources and identifies a need to realign the zones if a disparity in workload becomes apparent. Studies also indicate that, in addition to the benefits to the departments, citizens are not unhappy with delayed response from police departments even when they must wait an hour or more for a police response.[12] This is especially true when the citizen is aware there will be a delay, and the rationale is explained. Many citizens find the new options, including online reporting, phone reporting, and referrals, more convenient for their busy schedules.

★ ★ ★

ALTERNATIVES TO RETROACTIVE INVESTIGATION OF PAST CRIMES BY DETECTIVES

Current popular alternatives to retroactive investigation of past crimes by detectives are improved investigation of past crimes and repeat offender programs. These innovative techniques are designed to concentrate investigative resources on crimes that have a high chance of being solved.

Improved Investigation of Past Crimes

The National Advisory Commission on Criminal Justice Standards and Goals has recommended the increased use of patrol officers in the criminal investigation process. The commission recommended that every police agency direct patrol officers to conduct thorough preliminary investigations and recommended that agencies establish written priorities to ensure that investigative efforts are spent in a manner that best achieves organizational goals. The commission further recommended that investigative specialists (detectives) only be assigned to very serious or complex preliminary investigations.[13] As a consequence of the Rand

Study of the Investigative Process and other studies discussed in Chapter 7, the Law Enforcement Assistance Administrative (LEAA) funded research that led to the publication and wide dissemination of a new proposal regarding methods that should be used to investigate past crimes.[14] The proposal, **Managing Criminal Investigations (MCI)**, offers a series of guidelines that recommend (1) expanding the role of patrol officers to include investigative responsibilities and (2) designing a new method to manage criminal investigations by including solvability factors, case screening, case enhancement, and police and prosecutor coordination.[15] Solvability factors and case screening will be covered in this part of the chapter, and case enhancement and police and prosecutor coordination will be discussed in the next section, "Repeat Offender Programs." Under an MCI program, the responding patrol officer is responsible for a great deal of the follow-up activity that used to be assigned to detectives. These duties include locating and interviewing the victim and witnesses, detecting physical evidence, and preparing an initial investigative report that will serve as a guide for investigators. This report must contain proper documentation to indicate whether the case should be assigned for continued investigation or immediately suspended for lack of evidence.[16] The other major innovation under MCI involves the use of a managerial system that grades cases according to their solvability; detectives then work only on cases that have a chance of being solved. Some solvability factors include:

1. Is there a witness?

2. Is a suspect named or known?

3. Can a suspect be identified?

4. Will the complainant cooperate in the investigation?

Each solvability factor is given a numerical weight. In the next process, case screening, the total weight of all solvability factors—the total score—determines whether the case will be investigated or not.[17] The MCI method of managing investigations is designed to put most of an investigator's time and effort into only very important cases and cases that actually can be solved. Research conducted by numerous police departments has demonstrated that scoring systems using checklists and point scores successfully screen out cases with a low probability of being solved and identify promising cases.[18]

There are times that the solvability factors may be disregarded and a case investigated that does not meet the numerical criteria, due to officers' concern, political rea-

As recommended by the Rand Study and proposed by the Law Enforcement Assistance Administration in *Managing Criminal Investigations,* patrol officers are assuming more responsibility in crime investigations. Here officers in Austin, Texas, separate and interview witnesses at a robbery scene.

sons, or public safety. It gives investigators a more manageable caseload and an opportunity to be more organized and methodical in their efforts. Even with all the changes recommended by the Rand and other studies, and even though police departments have implemented many changes in the investigatory process, the police are still not very successful in clearing by arrest (also just referred to as *clearing,* a police term for solving) crimes reported to them. Only 21 percent of the serious crimes called to police attention are cleared.[19] (It must be remembered again, as was stated in Chapter 7, that the 21 percent clearance rate refers to all crime and that the police have much higher clearance rates in the very serious crimes of murder, rape, and felonious assault.) The improved methods of investigation, however, have resulted in less waste and more efficiency in police detective operations and have allowed departments to use personnel in more proactive policing.

Cold Case Squads

The advances of DNA technology have led to the increase in the use of cold case squads to solve crimes. Cold case squads reexamine old cases that have remained unsolved. They use the passage of time coupled with a fresh set of eyes to help solve cases that had been stagnant for years and often decades.

Over time, relationships change. People may no longer be married, may no longer be friends, or may no longer be intimidated or afraid of the same people. Someone who was reluctant to talk due to fear or loyalty may decide to tell the truth years later. Individuals may have found religion or changed their lifestyle and years later realize that what they did or witnessed or knew about was bad and they need to set the record straight. Cold case detectives reinterview all individuals involved and hope someone has had a change of heart over the years or forgotten what was said initially, allowing them to uncover new information.

Cold case detectives also use the passage of time in another way. They take advantage of the tremendous advances in forensic science, especially DNA testing. Much smaller samples are necessary now to get a more definitive match through DNA than even a couple of years ago. Cold case detectives are able to solve many cases solely by reexamining the evidence. In 1977, a 6-year-old girl was reported missing in Reno, and 23 years later the detectives had her clothes retested, finding previously undetected DNA evidence, tying the crime to a convicted felon.[20] In 2003, an individual was arrested in Miami for a 10-year-old, previously unsolved murder in Seattle after he was arrested for another crime and his DNA was obtained and compared to DNA from the victim's body resubmitted by investigators. This had been a random sexual assault and murder by an individual with no known connection to the victim. The investigation revealed that the suspect had in fact lived in Seattle for a brief period of time, during which the murder occurred.

Investigators who make up the cold case squad must think outside the box and also not be afraid to use whatever means may help their case, including the media. Some use shows such as "America's Most Wanted" to help bring a suspect or a crime back into the mind of the public. They use innovative ideas to obtain evidence they may need for comparison purposes. A man from New Jersey was recently arrested for a decades-old murder of a teenage girl in Seattle, when he too was a teen. He had been a prime suspect but investigators had no evidence linking him to the crime. In 2003, they sent him a form to fill out to participate in a suit regarding parking fines in Seattle. He filled out the form, put it in the envelope, licked the envelope, and mailed it back to Seattle. Detectives were able to match the DNA from his saliva to that found on evidence, and he was arrested.

Cold case squads are providing great hope and comfort to families of victims of old unsolved crimes and a sense of justice to the community when they are able to solve these long-unsolved cases and bring defendants to justice.

Repeat Offender Programs (ROPS)

U.S. criminologist Marvin Wolfgang discovered that only a few criminals are responsible for most of the predatory street crime in the United States. Most Americans do not commit street robberies; only a relatively small group of people do, but they commit a tremendous amount of crime each year. Borrowing from Wolfgang's research, police started to address their investigative resources to the career criminal using **repeat offender programs (ROPS)**. These programs can be conducted in two major ways.

First, police can identify certain people to be the target of investigation. Once a career criminal is identified, the police can use surveillance techniques, follow the criminal, and wait to either catch the person in the act of committing a crime or catch him or her immediately after a crime occurs. These target offender programs are labor intensive.

The second way police can operate a repeat offender program is through case enhancement. Specialized career criminal detectives can be notified of the arrest of a robbery suspect by other officers and then determine from the suspect's conviction or arrest rate whether or not the arrest merits enhancement. If the case is enhanced, an experienced detective assists the arresting officer in preparing the case for presentation in court and debriefs the suspect to obtain further information. A major tactic behind case enhancement is liaison with the district attorney's office to alert the prosecuting attorney to the importance of the case and to the suspect's past record. Such information helps ensure zealous efforts by the prosecutor. Houston Police Department's Targeted Offender program uses a prearrest targeting and postarrest case enhancement to get violent career criminals off the street.[21] The Maricopa County, Arizona, attorney's office targets repeat offenders for special prosecution with the belief that 10 percent of known offenders are responsible for 90 percent of crime.[22]

A study in Washington, D.C., found that a proactive repeat offender unit was successful in arresting targeted offenders. In addition, those offenders who were apprehended had much more extensive and serious prior records than other arrested offenders. The tactics of this unit included conducting surveillances of active offenders, locating wanted serious offenders, acting on tips from informants, and employing decoy and sting methods.[23]

Marcia Chaiken and Jan Chaiken, in their report *Priority Prosecutors of High-Rate Dangerous Offenders,* distinguished among persistent offenders (those who commit crimes over a long period of time), high-rate offenders (those who commit numerous crimes per year), and dangerous offenders (those who commit crimes of violence).[24]

Chaiken and Chaiken suggest that the most accurate way to identify high-rate dangerous offenders is through the use of a two-stage screening process. The first stage, they say, should look for evidence of a serious previous felony conviction, failure to complete a previous sentence, arrests while in pretrial release, or a known drug problem. The authors state that defendants falling into three of these categories have a 90 percent chance of being high-rate dangerous offenders and should be further screened. The second screening involves looking for evidence of the following: use of a weapon in the current crime, one or more juvenile convictions for robbery, or status of wanted for failure to complete a previous sentence.[25] The presence of any of these aggravating factors would cause the defendant to be considered a high-rate dangerous offender. The authors suggest that any defendant considered a high-rate dangerous offender should receive special attention by investigators and prosecutors.

The Chicago Police Department is implementing a new program targeting repeat offenders in Englewood, a 4-square-mile section of the city in which over 700 people have been murdered in the last decade, including 61 in 2002.[26] The Repeat Offender Geographic Urban Enforcement Strategies (ROGUES) project will assign a Cook County prosecutor to the police districts that have a lot of narcotics trafficking taking place around schools and churches. When law enforcement identifies an individual as a problem due to gang membership, violent history, or being a repeat offender, the ROGUES team will be notified, and the assigned prosecutor will follow the case through its entirety.

★ ★ ★

NEW PROACTIVE TACTICS

In addition to alternatives to random routine patrol, rapid response to citizens' 911 calls, and retroactive investigation of past crimes by detectives, police departments are using new, proactive tactics to supplement traditional patrol techniques. These innovations include uniformed tactical operations, decoy operations, stakeout and sting operations, code enforcement teams, and efforts against drunk drivers.

Uniformed Tactical Operations

Uniformed tactical operations involve the use of traditional patrol operations in a more aggressive manner. The two basic kinds of uniformed tactical operations are aggressive patrol tactics and saturation patrol. Uniformed tactical units are officers who are relieved of routine patrol responsibilities, such as random routine patrol and handling calls for service, in order to concentrate on proactive crime control. Uniformed tactical units often saturate an area that is experiencing a serious crime problem. The tactical units are aggressive and make numerous pedestrian and vehicle stops to increase the likelihood of encountering offenders. These specially assigned officers make numerous field interrogations (FIs). An FI is a contact with a citizen initiated by a patrol officer who stops, questions, and sometimes searches a citizen because the officer has reasonable suspicion that the subject may have committed, may be committing, or may be about to commit a crime. One researcher says that field interrogations "serve to generate information about the activities of probable suspects and, more importantly for deterrence, they make the suspects aware that the police know of their presence in a given area, regard them as suspicious and are watching them closely."[27]

Among the most controversial, and perhaps the forerunner, of these tactical groups was New York City's Tactical Patrol Force (TPF), a unit of rapidly moving officers trained in mob control. They were selected from the very best of police academy recruits. During the 1960s and early 1970s, the 1,000-member TPF viewed itself as the elite of incorruptible law enforcement. In addition to mob and riot control, TPFs swept into high-crime areas to hunt down muggers and robbers, often using a variety of decoy units that readily blended into life on the street.[28]

Although New York City's Tactical Patrol Force was successful in reducing crime, it was frowned on by many citizens, especially in minority communities. Eventually the unit's name was changed to Tactical Patrol Unit to avoid the connotations of the word *force*. In the 1980s, the Tactical Patrol Unit was discontinued altogether.

One can only wonder whether highly mobile, aggressive units like the TPF could have reduced the numerous civilian and police injuries that resulted from civil disorders in the early 1990s—for example, the disturbances on the streets of Chicago in 1992 and 1993 in the wake of the Chicago Bulls National Basketball Association championships; the disturbances in Montreal after the Canadians won hockey's 1993 Stanley Cup; the 1992 street riots in south central Los Angeles in the wake of the not-guilty verdicts in the Rodney King case; or the disturbances on the streets of Crown Heights, Brooklyn, in 1991 and Washington Heights, Manhattan, in 1992.

Many departments have much smaller tactical units. Typically these units work flexible schedules and employ varying techniques depending on what particular problem they're addressing. Santa Barbara Police Department has a tactical patrol force made up of one sergeant and four officers.[29] Their primary responsibility is street crime in the central and beachfront business districts. These officers do not handle calls; working closely with community policing units and crime analysis, they proactively address street crime and quality-of-life issues. Their goal is to reduce crime and the perception of crime. They often use bicycle patrol and foot patrol in their efforts.

Bicycles are a tool employed by many departments in addition to Santa Barbara in their tactical policing efforts. They can be used in covert surveillance by plainclothes officers who will have a better ability to blend in with their surroundings on bicycles. They can also prove valuable for officers in uniform, allowing them to maneuver in crowded conditions and to quietly and quickly approach individuals they suspect are involved in suspicious activity.

AGGRESSIVE PATROL TACTICS   Uniformed tactical operations make use of aggressive patrol tactics: stopping numerous people and vehicles in an attempt to find evidence that they may have committed a crime or may be committing a crime. Aggressive patrol tactics using field interrogations can be very effective in reducing crime. However, they often cause problems with the community due to their potential for abusing citizens' rights.

A study in San Diego tested the effects of field interrogations. In this study, field interrogation activity was suspended for nine months in one experimental area but maintained at normal levels in two control areas. Crime in the area where field interrogations were suspended increased by a substantial amount while it remained about the same in the control areas where field interrogations continued to be used. With the resumption of FI activity in the experimental area, crime decreased to about the same level it had been before the experiment.[30]

Another study used the number of traffic citations issued by police as a measure of patrol aggressiveness and developed a sophisticated mathematical model to determine the relationship between aggressive patrol and the robbery crime rate. The analysis suggested that aggressive patrol contributes to a higher robbery arrest rate, which in turn leads to a lower robbery crime rate.[31]

For quite some time it was believed that police action had little deterrent effect or, if it did, that the effect was short-lived.[32] However, some academic studies have proved otherwise. Researchers James Q. Wilson and Barbara Boland found that proactive, aggressive law enforcement styles may help reduce crime rates. They found that jurisdictions that encourage patrol officers to stop motor vehicles to issue citations and to aggressively arrest and detain suspicious persons experience lower crime rates than jurisdictions that do not follow such proactive policies.[33] Robert Sampson and Jacqueline Cohen found that departments that more actively enforced disorderly conduct and traffic laws also experienced lower robbery rates.[34]

In a study using data acquired in Scandinavia, Perry Shapiro and Harold Votey found that an arrest for drunk driving can actually reduce the probability of offender recidivism. Arrests apparently increase people's beliefs that they will be rearrested if they drink and drive and also heighten their perceptions of the unpleasantness associated with an arrest.[35] Similarly, Douglas Smith and Patrick Gartin's research shows that getting arrested reduces the likelihood that a novice offender will repeat criminal activity. Their study also shows that experienced offenders have reduced future offending rates after an arrest.[36]

Lawrence W. Sherman's review of 18 case studies of varying types of police crackdowns revealed that the effects of these crackdowns "began to decay after a short period, sometimes despite continued dosage of police presence or even increased dosage of police sanctions."[37] Jay S. Albanese and Robert D. Pursley report that law enforcement "sweeps" are essentially mass arrests of gang members on minor charges, and that they are similar to an enforced curfew in that they take young people off the streets at night and release them by the next day.[38]

Some of the innovative aggressive tactics regarding crime are based on research that indicates that a great deal of urban crime is concentrated in a few "hot spots." Lawrence Sherman, Patrick Gartin, and Michael Buerger have found that a significant portion of all police calls in Minneapolis came from a relatively few locations: bars, malls, the bus depot, hotels, and certain apartment buildings. They believed that concentrating police resources on these hot spots of crime could appreciably reduce crime.[39]

Many claim that the drastic drop in crime rates in the mid-1990s, particularly in cities like New York, were the results of aggressive, zero-tolerance anticrime policies. During this period, New York City's crime rates dropped to 30-year lows under the administration of then Police Commissioner William Bratton. As part of his crime-fighting strategy, he ordered his officers to crack down on such minor offenses as public urination, loitering, loud radios, and unlicensed street vending to improve the city's quality of life. He told his uniformed street officers to resume making low-level drug arrests and not leave them to specialized units, which the NYPD had done for many years for fear of corruption scandals. Under his policies, all minor offenders were frisked for guns and checked for outstanding warrants. Computer-plotted maps were made daily to track crime on each and every block in the city. Bratton said, "I want to challenge the old idea that policing can't make a substantial impact on social change. American policing has been swatting at mosquitoes for 20 years. In New York we've learned how to drain the swamp."[40]

Fugitive and warrant programs have been added to the aggressive patrol actions of police departments. In Houston, in 1996, warrant enforcement generated 8,860 arrests and cleared over 38,000 cases. In New York City, the NYPD, with help from the U.S. Marshals Service and the FBI, began going after as many as 87,000 fugitive felons and 403,000 misdemeanor offenders.[41]

Regarding aggressive policing techniques, Marie Simonetti Rosen wrote

> Clearly, 1996 was the year of the crackdown, but perhaps the most common approach was a crackdown on quality-of-life crime. In city after city, quality-of-life enforcement became a priority, in part because such a focus was desired by the community, but as important, because evidence increasingly points to the fact that going after minor violators contributes directly to reductions in major crime. . . .
>
> In growing numbers, police executives are convinced that effective policing can decrease crime, and even a growing cohort of criminologists is conceding that police work is responsible for the recent notable decline in crime. Nationwide, there are clear signs of departments reorganizing, refocussing and implementing anti-crime strategies, targeting problems and attacking them with verve. And from all indications it appears that their efforts are paying off, as 1996, like the years immediately preceding it, witnessed significant drops in the crime rate.[42]

The evidence seems to suggest that proactive, aggressive police strategies are effective in reducing crime, at least in target areas. However, many believe that aggressive patrol tactics breed resentment in minority areas; citizens there often believe they are the target of police suspicion and reaction. There is evidence that such aggressive police tactics as stop-and-frisk and rousting teenagers who congregate on street corners are the seeds from which police–citizen racial conflict grows.[43] This leads to a serious conflict for police administrators. Do they reduce crime rates by using effective yet aggressive police techniques and therefore risk poor relationships with lawful members of the community? It must be stated, however, that, despite the credit paid to the police in reducing crime, many criminologists and other students of crime and criminal justice point to other possible reasons for crime reduction, including the aging of the criminal-age-prone population, the increased prison and jail populations, the increased commitment of community groups in addressing crime conditions, and other such issues.

SATURATION PATROL   Another kind of uniformed tactical operation is saturation patrol. A larger number of uniformed officers than normal is assigned to a particular area to deal with a particular crime problem. The results of this type of strategy are mixed, according to several studies involving saturation patrol. In a study of a New York City precinct, researchers concluded that a 40 percent increase in patrol personnel resulted in 30 to 50 percent decreases in street crime.[44] A study that analyzed New York subway robberies in relation to increased patrol over an eight-year period also found that saturation patrol reduced crime. In this instance, the deployment of substantially more subway patrol officers in the evening hours resulted in a decrease in subway robberies during the hours of the patrols. After a brief decrease, however, daytime robberies increased steadily.[45]

In a study of saturation patrol in Nashville, Tennessee, three patrol areas experiencing high burglary incidences during daylight hours were given increased patrols between 8:00 A.M. and 4:00 P.M. The level of saturation raised the number of patrol cars per area from one to between four and eight. During the five weeks of the study, the number of burglary arrests increased, but there were no changes in the incidence of burglary.[46] A year later, in Nashville, four high-crime areas were given increased patrol, two during daytime hours and two during evening hours. Patrol in all areas during the saturation times was increased from one to five cars. The results indicated that daytime saturation patrols had no effect on crime, but that evening saturation patrols did decrease crime.[47]

One of the most effective tactical operations employed by the New York City Police Department during the 1980s was Operation Pressure Point. Located in the city's Lower East Side, Operation Pressure Point involved using numerous young rookie officers on foot patrol. The officers were encouraged to use aggressive field interrogation techniques and undercover operations to combat the sale and possession of drugs, which had ravaged the neighborhood for

years.[48] Operation Pressure Point was so successful that real estate prices began to skyrocket, turning the Lower East Side into a gentrified, high-rent section of the city. Although crime was reduced in the target area, it actually was merely displaced to adjoining neighborhoods.

Other initiatives have had mixed results. Programs evaluated by M. Kleiman in 1988 that were similar to Operation Pressure Point had little effect on street drug sales in Harlem; slightly improved crime statistics in Lynn, Massachusetts; and did improve crime statistics in Lawrence, Massachusetts. A program in Jersey City examined by Weisburg and Green in 1995 found a reduction in drug trafficking, and not merely displacement, with a neighborhood crackdown coupled with police surveillance in high-crime and drug-trafficking locations.[49]

Decoy Operations

One of the primary purposes of police patrol is to prevent crime through the creation of a sense of omnipresence; potential criminals are deterred from crime by the presence or potential presence of the police. Obviously, omnipresence does not work well. We have crime both on our streets and in areas where ordinary police patrols cannot see crime developing, such as the inside of a store or the hallway of a housing project. Additionally, we have seen that retroactive investigations of crimes, with the intent to identify and arrest perpetrators, are not very effective.

© Frances M. Roberts/Levine-Roberts Photography

Whether conducting decoy operations or surveillance, it is essential that officers blend in with the people in the community. Who among this group might be a police officer?

Forst's Law

Jogging on the Job

Decoy work varies tremendously in challenge and desirability. In large departments it can be an officer's regular assignment, but in most midsized and smaller departments it will be utilized as necessary depending on crime issues that arise. In these cases it will usually be a break from an officer's regular assignment. Over my police career, I had many occasions to work decoy assignments in which females were targeted victims. I found these assignments to be a challenge and a welcome break to my routine, whether I was assigned to patrol or the detective bureau at the time.

One June we had a couple of incidents of indecent exposure at a popular but somewhat isolated jogging trail. We then had an incident where a female was grabbed at 8:00 A.M. and pulled into the bushes along this jogging trail. She fought her attacker off and managed to get away but it was clearly an attempted rape. We decided that for two weeks we would put a female out jogging this same trail in the early morning hours. Since I was known to be a runner, I was chosen for the assignment. It

sounds pretty cool, get paid to run and work out on duty, but the conditions were less than ideal.

June in South Florida is *very* hot and humid, and this trail was in a scrub area with lots of bushes but not many trees; consequently, there was little shade. I put on a wire so that I had voice communication when I was out of sight of the two backup officers along the three-mile course. I had to be covered up enough to hide the wire, which meant I would be even warmer. I ran and walked for about two hours a day around this course; and, as I sweated profusely, jumped over and avoided snakes, and was bitten by the biggest horseflies I had ever seen, I started singing Helen Reddy's song "Ain't No Way to Treat a Lady" for the entertainment of my backup officers (and perhaps to make a point). We saw nothing of interest during the two weeks, and there were never any more attacks there, so the offender must have moved on or been arrested for something else. Or maybe he heard me singing and got scared off?

During the past three decades, an innovative proactive approach to apprehending criminals in the course of committing a crime has developed—**decoy operations**. Decoy operations take several forms, among them blending and decoy. In **blending,** officers dressed in civilian clothes try to blend into an area and patrol it on foot or in unmarked police cars in an attempt to catch a criminal in the act of committing a crime. Officers may target areas where a significant amount of crime occurs, or they may follow particular people who appear to be potential victims or potential offenders. In order to blend, officers assume the roles and dress of ordinary citizens—construction workers, shoppers, joggers, bicyclists, physically disabled persons, and so on—so that the officers, without being observed as officers, can be close enough to observe and intervene should a crime occur.

In decoy, officers dress as, and play the role of, potential victims—drunks, nurses, businesspeople, tourists, prostitutes, blind people, isolated subway riders, or defenseless

elderly people. The officers wait to be the subject of a crime while a team of backup officers is ready to apprehend the violator in the act of committing the crime. Decoy operations are most effective in combating the crimes of robbery, purse snatching, and other larcenies from the person; burglaries; and thefts of and from automobiles.

Descriptions of decoy operations in major cities contain numerous successful applications.[50] A successful decoy operation was begun by the Miami Police Department in 1991 with the establishment of an undercover decoy operation targeting tourist robberies, known as STAR (Safeguarding Tourists Against Robberies). Members of this 12-officer unit pose as tourists sitting in parked rental cars near busy areas. When robbers strike, a backup team moves in to assist in the arrest. STAR has resulted in a 33 percent decrease in tourist robberies.[51]

The NYPD's Street Crime Unit (SCU) has been extremely successful and has served as a model for numerous other police agencies. The SCU consists of experienced volunteer officers who are aggressive and street smart. The SCU members, who receive extensive training in decoy techniques, are assigned to high-crime areas.[52] Each of New York City's 76 patrol precincts has its own decoy unit, called an anticrime unit, composed of volunteer officers with high arrest records.

Among the more effective decoy and blending operations was another NYPD unit, the Taxi-Truck Surveillance Unit, which was organized to combat the growing number of nighttime assaults on truck and cab drivers. For a period of five years, specially equipped officers from both patrol and detective units were selected to play the roles of cabbies and truckers. This undercover approach ultimately reduced assaults and robberies of cabbies and truckers by almost 50 percent.[53] An interesting recent decoy program in New York City to combat a rash of robberies at McDonald's and other fast-food restaurants involved officers donning McDonald's uniforms and posing as employees. In one case, a robber was apprehended by the store's "cleaners" when he passed a holdup note to a cashier.[54] Another recent use of disguises involved a police officer in Paulsboro, New Jersey, who was facing a growing list of persons wanted on arrest warrants. On Halloween evening, 1995, he donned a clown's outfit over his bulletproof vest and went trick-or-treating. As his subjects opened their doors, they had a real treat—they were arrested. The officer cleared 12 warrants by arrest that evening.[55]

Anticrime and decoy strategies focus on reducing serious and violent street crimes, apprehending criminals in the act, making quality arrests, and maintaining a high conviction record. In achieving successful prosecutions in their cases, decoy operations overcome the problem police encounter when witnesses and victims are reluctant to cooperate with police and prosecutors because of fear, apathy, or interminable court delays.[56]

A San Francisco police sergeant successfully defined the goals and operations of a decoy program: "The underlying theory . . . is that the type of criminal that is responsible for the most violent street crime is an opportunist. The criminal walks the streets looking for a victim that is weaker than himself, looking for an opportunity to make a 'score' without any danger to himself, or any danger of apprehension. The decoy program is intended to respond to this type of criminal."[57] There has been some criticism of decoy operations. As one former police commander says, "Decoy operations are often seen as entrapment, even though they rarely come close to it."[58] Also, decoy programs, in which officers dress and assume the roles of victims, can be very dangerous to the officers involved.

Decoy Vehicles

There is another type of decoy operation that has been used with great success. It involves no danger to officers, but its primary goal is not catching criminals but rather preventing crime violations. This decoy operation involves using unoccupied marked police vehicles in strategic locations to give the perception of omnipresence. This tactic has been used successfully to address less serious yet demanding crime problems and traffic violations. It is a way of addressing issues that are a problem in the least resource-intensive way.

It is not uncommon for police agencies to park a marked vehicle on a roadside where there is a problem with speeding. Drivers see the unit in the distance and slow down. Even if they see that the vehicle is unoccupied, it serves as a reminder that it could have been occupied and they could have gotten a ticket. It helps drivers become more aware of their driving habits and slows them down. Some agencies have taken this a step further and placed inflatable dummies in the driver's seat. This serves as a technique to increase awareness and educate drivers, much like the portable radar devices that post the speed limit and measure and show drivers their speed. This technique allows police agencies to address traffic problems without tying up an officer for extended periods of time.

This idea can be and has been expanded upon. When faced with numerous and persistent "smash and grabs" at exclusive women's clothing stores, the Boca Raton, Florida, Police Department had a problem. There was no discernable pattern to these burglaries, which were occurring throughout Dade, Broward, and Palm Beach Counties, yet store owners were outraged by repeat victimization that occurred over many months. With a limited number of midnight shift officers, many square miles of territory, and a high number of women's clothing stores, the police department had to come up with a method to address this problem and reassure the community that they considered this problem a priority. They started parking unoccupied marked vehicles in front of some of the more vulnerable targets. The hope was that the offender driving on the main roadways looking for a target would bypass these stores thinking either that there was an officer in the car, in the store, or in the area.

While this strategy alone would not solve the crime, if a surveillance effort was put into effect at the remaining stores, the criminals might be displaced to those establishments, and an arrest could result. At the least, it was a preventative technique for the businesses and led to displacement of the crime to another area or town. Unfortunately, as with "target hardening" prevention techniques, this can be all we hope to do.

Stakeout Operations

Many crimes occur indoors, where passing patrol officers cannot see their occurrence. A stakeout consists of a group of heavily armed officers who hide in an area of a store or building waiting for an impending holdup. If an armed robber enters the store and attempts a robbery, the officers yell "Police!" from their hidden areas. If the perpetrators fail to drop their weapons, the officers open fire. Stakeouts are effective in cases in which the police receive a tip that a crime is going to occur in a commercial establishment or in which the police discover or come upon a pattern. A typical pattern would be a group of liquor stores in a certain downtown commercial area that have been robbed at gunpoint in a consistent way that indicates it might happen again. Stakeouts are extremely expensive in terms of police personnel. They are also controversial, because they invariably involve death or serious injury to the perpetrator. Detroit, which once had a stakeout unit called STRESS (Stop the Robberies, Enjoy Safe Streets), disbanded it because of the many deaths of perpetrators and the public furor that attended a series of highly publicized killings of robbers.[59]

Sting Operations

Sting operations, which have become a major law enforcement technique in recent years, involve using various undercover methods to apprehend thieves and recover stolen property. For example, the police rent a storefront and put the word out on the street that they will buy any stolen property—no questions asked. The police set up hidden video and audio recorders that can be used to identify "customers," who are then located and placed under arrest several months later. The audio and video recorders make excellent evidence in court. There are numerous examples of successful stings.

An FBI-run high-tech electronics store in Miami was used by drug traffickers to purchase beepers, cellular phones, and computers. The 17-month operation resulted in 93 arrests.[60] Another FBI sting in New Jersey, in which agents posed as fences who bought 170 stolen trucks and luxury cars worth $9 million over a two-year period, netted 35 arrests.[61] Another type of sting operation is directed against people wanted on warrants. These wanted persons are mailed a letter telling them that they have won an award (such as tickets to an important ball game) and that

they should report to a certain location (usually a hotel) at a certain time to pick up the prize. When the person appears, he or she is arrested.

Studies of sting operations have found that they account for a large number of arrests and the recovery of a significant amount of stolen property. However, the studies have failed to demonstrate that the tactic leads to reductions in crime.[62] A major drawback to sting operations is that they can serve as inducements to burglary and theft, because they create a market for stolen goods. Additionally, sting operations can lead to questions regarding ethics. Consider the congressional Abscam operations. Abscam was a 1978–1980 sting conducted by FBI agents against members of Congress. The agents, posing as Arab sheikhs, offered bribes to members of Congress in order to receive favors. The sting resulted in the conviction of seven members of Congress and other officials, as well as harsh criticism (by some) of the FBI for its undercover methods.

Civil Liability and Code Enforcement Teams

Many cities have turned to civil liability enforcement to attempt to deal with local problems that have a negative effect on the quality of life in their communities. These cities use civil, as well as criminal, laws to force landlords and others in control of premises to correct illegal conditions. These cities have established code enforcement teams, which consist of a number of agents from different municipal agencies working together using local ordinances and codes, as well as the criminal law, in an attempt to solve particular problems.

Fort Lauderdale, Florida, has established a code enforcement team with members representing the police, fire, building, and zoning departments. In a three-year period, Fort Lauderdale's code enforcement team demolished 124 crack cocaine houses and boarded up another 587. They collected $600,000 in fines from 300 landlords and property managers of substandard housing. Additionally, they pressured landlords into spending $5.7 million on repairs to deteriorating properties. Drug activity in the code enforcement team's targeted area dropped 57 percent.[63] As of 2003, the team was up to six members and the command issue that arose had been addressed by forming a steering committee. Executives from the affected departments as well as the assistant city manager serve on the steering committee to handle policy issues. The code team works closely with the community policing unit and has an extensive range of enforcement options to deal with quality-of-life issues, which has led to success).[64] Milwaukee formed an interagency team to combat crack houses in the city. Representatives from the city's police department, building inspection department, city attorney's office, and Community Outreach joined forces to attack drug houses in the community. In its first year, the team closed 264 drug houses. A key to the success of the programs, says Milwaukee's police chief, was the information provided by citizens calling a community hotline.[65]

In 1997, a zero-tolerance program targeting drug houses in Worcester, Massachusetts, was so successful that it had rid neighborhoods of locations where drug activity flourished. At least 60 drug houses were driven out of business, and police made hundreds of arrests in the interagency effort. The city put pressure on landlords to clean and make repairs to their properties. The owners were also put on notice that they could lose their properties under the city's nuisance laws if criminal activity reoccurs.[66] Worcester uses very aggressive methods to conduct their zero-tolerance program. Uniformed and undercover police officers flood the streets of the target areas, making arrests and maintaining a high-profile presence that keeps potential drug buyers away from the area. The following is a very graphic example of the squalid and dangerous conditions code enforcement teams are designed to combat. Vacant apartments have become a maze of traps, meant to block out drug dealers' rivals and the police. Electrified wires have been stretched across window frames. Holes have been smashed in the walls and floors to provide easy escape routes. And hallway floors have been smeared with Vaseline to trip unwary intruders. The hallways are spray-painted with directions to where the drugs are sold, and with a warning that informers will be killed.[67]

Efforts against Drunk Drivers

During the 1990s, much attention has been paid to the tremendous damage done on our highways by drunk drivers. Efforts by such groups as Mothers Against Drunk Driving (MADD) and Students Against Drunk Driving (SADD) have caused the police to pay particular attention to the problem. The worst-ever year for alcohol-related fatalities was 1986, when 24,045 deaths occurred.[68] According to the National Highway Traffic Safety Administration (NHTSA), in 2000 the United States experienced the largest percentage of increase in alcohol-related traffic deaths when 17,380 people were killed in alcohol-related crashes—one every 30 minutes. The number continues to go up, with 17,400 people killed in 2001 and 17,419 killed in 2002. In 2002, this accounted for 41 percent of people killed in traffic crashes nationally, according to

©Nancy Pierce/The New York Times

In an effort to keep the motoring public safe, many police agencies conduct DWI roadblocks or field sobriety checkpoints. Drivers are systematically stopped and paperwork examined. The driver may then be asked to perform a field sobriety test or take a Breathalyzer test.

MADD's Web site.[69] Patrol officers cannot be expected to deal effectively with the problem of drunk drivers, because so much of the officers' time is occupied by other duties but there are things they can do. To enforce the laws against driving while intoxicated (DWI) or driving under the influence (DUI), the police have resorted to sobriety checkpoints. The following describes the typical DWI checkpoint or roadblock: Officers conducting a roadblock may stop all traffic or some numerically objective number, such as every fifth vehicle. After a vehicle is directed to the side of the road, an officer may request to see an operator's license and vehicle registration and may ask several questions to observe the driver's demeanor. If the officer detects the signs of inebriation, the motorist may be directed to move the vehicle to a secondary area, step out, and submit to a roadside sobriety coordination or Breathalyzer test. The failure to pass either test constitutes sufficient probable cause for arrest.[70]

Sobriety Checkpoints

In an effort to control driving under the influence of alcohol and drugs, the director of the Michigan Department of State Police appointed state and local police officials, prosecutors, and the University of Michigan's transportation researchers to a Sobriety Checkpoint Advisory Committee. This committee created guidelines governing the following issues regarding sobriety checkpoints: site selection, publicity, and police procedures while conducting the sobriety checks. Under Michigan's program, checkpoints were set up at selected sites, and all drivers passing through the checkpoints were stopped and briefly examined for signs of intoxication. Drivers who showed evidence of being under the influence were directed out of the traffic flow for a license and registration check and further sobriety tests. If the tests showed intoxication, arrests were made. One court case that arose from Michigan's policy was *Michigan Department of State Police* v. *Sitz*. The checkpoint at issue in the case conformed to the guidelines just described and operated for one hour and fifteen minutes, during which the state police stopped 126 individuals for an average delay of 25 seconds each. Officers detained two drivers for field sobriety testing, one of whom they arrested for driving under the influence (DUI). A third motorist, who drove through the checkpoint without stopping, was pulled over by an officer in an observation vehicle and arrested for DUI. To determine the constitutionality of the sobriety checkpoint in this case, the court focused on (1) the gravity of the public concerns addressed by the checkpoint, (2) the effectiveness of the checkpoint, and (3) the severity of the checkpoint's interference with individual liberty. The court found that Michigan's procedures were constitutional.

Source: *Michigan Department of State Police* v. *Sitz* 110 S.Ct. 2481 (1990); and Louis DiPietro, "Sobriety Checkpoints: Constitutional Considerations," *FBI Law Enforcement Bulletin* (Oct. 1992), pp. 27–32.

Police are also using saturation patrol to combat the drunk driving problem. Officers will saturate a predesignated area with roving police officers to monitor traffic for signs of impaired driving. They also emphasize speeding and seat belt violations. The Chicago Police Department has had success with their program, which is funded by a grant from the NHTSA. To expedite the processing of violators, the Breath Alcohol Testing (BAT) Mobile Unit is deployed. According to their Web site, Chicago's saturation patrols typically are from 7:00 P.M. to 3 A.M. and have averaged between 230 and 300 total violations in their efforts.[71]

Studies indicate that laws establishing administrative license revocation (ALR) have reduced alcohol related crashes by almost 40 percent.[72] Police can continue to work with legislative bodies to implement these types of drivers' license sanctions.

NHTSA supports all these efforts targeting impaired drivers. In an effort to assist departments in running saturation patrols and sobriety checkpoints, they provide guidelines on their Web sites and issues that need to be addressed to successfully run checkpoints.[73]

Fighting Aggressive Driving

In recent years, road rage and aggressive driving have become a problem. People have been assaulted and even murdered in road rage incidents. Sometimes this road rage takes the form of aggressive driving, and innocent people have ended up dead due to the reckless driving of aggressive drivers. Aggressive driving is not necessarily defined as a specific offense but rather is a combination of several violations including speeding, tailgating, driving on the shoulder, and not signaling when changing lanes. NHTSA defines aggressive driving as "the commission of two or more moving violations that is likely to endanger other persons or property, or any single intentional violation that requires a defensive reaction of another driver." According to the Washington State Patrol Web site, the state of Washington defines road rage as "an assault with a motor vehicle or other dangerous weapon by the operator or passenger(s) of one motor vehicle on the operator or passenger(s) of another motor vehicle caused by an incident that occurred on a roadway."[74]

The frustration caused by heavy traffic, traffic jams, and drivers who make errors due to inattention results in some individuals resorting to driving behavior to "get back" at the other driver. These actions may include passing a vehicle and then stopping suddenly or tailgating a vehicle the driver perceives as moving too slowly. If the other driver buys into this behavior, it can result in a verbal or physical confrontation at a traffic light. The Washington State Patrol describes symptoms of road rage and aggressive driving and allows individuals to evaluate themselves via an instrument on their Web site.[75]

Sometimes drivers are just frustrated with slow-moving traffic or traffic jams and will do whatever they feel will help them move faster, such as passing cars, quickly changing lanes, or tailgating to intimidate other drivers into changing lanes. When this behavior includes inappropriately passing vehicles, it has resulted in fatal head-on crashes. Many states are targeting this aggressive driving in an effort to reduce crashes and make the roads safer.

The Colorado State Patrol has an aggressive driving program known as Aggressive Drivers Are Public Threats (ADAPT), which uses unmarked vehicles, motorcycles, and aircraft for enforcement coupled with an extensive media campaign. There is a designated cell phone number to call and report aggressive driving. If the reported incident requires police response, a unit will be sent; if not, the incident will be logged in the computer database and the complainant allowed to vent his or her frustration. The system can track the vehicles with repeated aggressive behavior; with three logged offenses, the owner of the car is notified. Additionally, in their media campaign to educate the public, the Colorado State Patrol advocates that motorists use the two-finger "peace" or "victory" sign to mean "thank you," "sorry," or "excuse me."[76]

The Washington State Patrol has formed the "Aggressive Driver Apprehension Team," which utilizes unmarked vehicles armed with cameras in the windshield to record traffic stops. In 2002, they pulled over approximately 29,000 drivers for aggressive driving, more than twice the number stopped in 2001, and are viewed as having a successful program.[77]

★ ★ ★

UNDERCOVER OPERATIONS

An **undercover investigation** may be defined as one in which an investigator assumes a different identity in order to obtain information or achieve another investigatory purpose. The undercover investigator generally plays the role of another person. In an undercover investigation there are many things the investigator can be doing, including merely observing or performing certain actions that are designed to get other people to do something or to react to or interact with the investigator in a certain way. The primary function of the investigator in these cases is to play a role without anyone realizing that he or she is playing a role. In policing, the primary purpose of the undercover operation most often is the collection of evidence of crimes.

Gary T. Marx has identified several general types of undercover investigations, including police undercover investigations, federal undercover investigations, and private security undercover investigations.[78] This section will discuss these types of investigations and operations and will pay particular attention to the drug undercover investigation.

Other types of investigations and police proactive tactics that could be described as undercover investigations, sting operations, decoy operations, and stakeouts were previously discussed in depth in this chapter.

Police Undercover Investigations

These investigations generally include drug undercover investigations; stings, including warrant stings and fencing stings that involve the buying and selling of stolen goods and other contraband; decoy operations targeted against the crimes of robbery, burglary, and assault; antiprostitution operations; and operations involving the infiltration and arrest of people involved in organized crime, white-collar crime, and corruption. Police undercover officers have a dangerous yet often rewarding job. In a 1994 news article, some of the 200 undercover officers of the New York City Transit Authority Police Department talked about their jobs. "Undercovers are a better breed—more gutsy," said Officer William Diaz, a 34-year-old transit officer in an elite anticrime unit in downtown Brooklyn. To conceal his identity from the criminals who work the stations he patrols, he continually grows a beard, cuts it off, and grows it again. Officer Diaz's 33-year-old partner, Denise James, said her commitment to undercover work arose from seeing crime's toll on her own neighborhood. She said, "I got tired of people taking crack and robbing people in hallways. I wanted to make a small dent on crime in my neighborhood. What I like is surprising people. You get the perpetrator. The victim is thankful. When you make the collar, the criminal says, 'You're a cop?' That's what I call satisfying."[79]

Federal Undercover Investigations

These investigations generally include efforts at detecting and arresting people involved in political corruption, insurance fraud, labor racketeering, and other types of organized conspiracy-type crimes. Perhaps the classic case of a successful undercover investigation was the work of FBI Special Agent Joseph D. Pistone, who assumed the cover identity of Donnie Brasco. Pistone began his infiltration of La Cosa Nostra (the American Mafia) in 1976 and continued it for six years. Pistone was so completely accepted by the Mafia that he was able to move freely among all the Mafia families and learn their secrets. He was so effective that he had to terminate his undercover operations because he was about to be inducted into the Mafia as a "made man" and was expected to kill another Mafioso. As a result of Pistone's work more than 100 federal criminal convictions were obtained, dealing a severe blow to Mafia operations throughout the United States.

Dempsey's Law

But She Was 6 Feet Tall and Looked Like She Was 23!

Professor, you're talking about proactive and covert investigations—are they, like, stings?

Yes, Daniel. Stings are generally proactive and covert investigations, meaning that they are police initiated and secret or undercover.

My father was the victim of a sting last night. He owns a deli, and this young woman came in about 6 P.M. She took a six-pack of Bud from the box, paid my father for it, and immediately left the deli. Five minutes later the police came in, told my father that he had just sold beer to a minor, and issued him a summons.

Dan, business owners have to be very careful selling beer, alcohol, or cigarettes to youthful-looking people. The police in your father's area are very aggressive in enforcing the laws regarding beer, alcohol, and cigarette sales. Many of the students in our criminal justice program volunteer to work with the police participating in these sting operations.

Yeah, Professor, but my father said she looked like she was about 23 years old, not 19, like the police told him. He said she was about 6 feet tall, real foxy, and dressed to the nines. Doesn't the fact that my father thought she looked older relieve him of criminal responsibility?

Not in this state, Dan. We have a legal concept called strict liability regarding certain laws. Sale of alcohol is one of those laws. Strict liability means that the prosecutor does not have to prove criminal intent on the part of the person committing a crime. Just the mere fact that he

sold her the alcohol and the fact that she was less than 21 is enough to charge him with the crime.

Professor Dempsey, I probably shouldn't admit it, but I think I'm the one Dan is talking about. Sorry about that, Dan. I didn't know that was your father's store.

Kimberly, you were volunteering with the 6th Precinct again yesterday evening?

Yeah, we hit eight delis and two liquor stores on Route 25. I was only carded in one place, and I couldn't make a buy because I didn't have proof and the guy refused to sell me the beer. The police gave summonses in the other nine places because they sold to me without carding me.

[Note: Kimberly is actually Kimberly Dean of East Setauket, New York. Kimberly, who does stand 6 feet tall, was actually 19 years old when this event occurred. Kimberly volunteered many hours working with the Suffolk County Police Department doing proactive, covert sting operations regarding the illegal sale of alcohol. Regarding her work with police, Kimberly says, "It definitely makes store owners aware of who they are selling alcohol to. Fifteen-year-olds can go in and get beer sometimes—it's pathetic." Kimberly's parents, Marie and Sandy, are proud of their daughter's involvement with the police and say, "Kimberly is certainly aware of the important issues in our community, and we couldn't be more proud of her." Kimberly is pursuing her college career and is considering law enforcement as a career choice.]

An FBI undercover investigation shows the success of the undercover investigation concept. For two years, FBI agents conducted Operation Road Spill, in which they established a bogus company, Southern Leasing Systems of South Kearny, New Jersey. The agents posed as shady business people who were willing to pay cash for stolen BMWs, Acura Legends, and other luxury cars. During the investigation they bought 120 stolen cars for a fraction of their value.[80]

The federal agencies, including DEA, Customs, and ATF, often form joint task force investigations with local, county, and state law enforcement agencies. This allows them to

pool resources and expertise. This approach has been particularly successful in South Florida. Many major drug smuggling operations were broken up, arrests made, and millions of dollars worth of property confiscated.

Private Security Undercover Investigations

According to Marx, these investigations generally involve inventory losses, pilferage, willful neglect of machinery, unreported absenteeism, "general employee attitudes," and

YOU ARE THERE! »

The Legality of Police Undercover Drug Investigations: *Gordon* v. *Warren Consolidated Board of Education*

High-school officials had placed an undercover officer into regular classes to investigate student drug use. After the investigation, several students were arrested and convicted of participating in the drug trade. They appealed their convictions claiming that the actions of the school officials violated their rights under the First Amendment of the United States Constitution. Their appeal was dismissed by appellate court ruling that the presence of the police officer working undercover did not constitute any more than a "chilling" effect on the students' First Amendment rights, because it did not disrupt classroom activities or education and it did not have any tangible effect on inhibiting expression of particular views in the classroom.

Source: Based on Gordon v. Warren Consolidated Board of Education, 706 F.2d 778 6th Cir. (1983).

"delicate investigations."[81] In addition to Marx's categories, many other categories can be added to private security undercover investigations, including criminal, marital, civil, and child custody cases, to name only a few. This section will cover four important private security undercover investigations: shopping services, silent witness programs, internal intelligence programs, and the store detective.

SHOPPING SERVICES   Wackenhut Investigations offers prospective business clients its "Integrity Testing" and other "Shopping Services." Wackenhut calls its integrity analysis the single most important element of a shopping service. This test of employees' honesty is performed by "shoppers" (undercover agents) posing as customers and is designed to act as a deterrent to inventory shrinkage, detect dishonest employees, and provide evidence for prosecuting employees caught stealing.[82]

SILENT WITNESS PROGRAMS   Wackenhut also offers prospective corporate clients its Silent Witness Program. The function of the program is to provide a method for honest, dedicated employees who are concerned about wrongdoing in the workplace to volunteer helpful informa-

tion without compromising themselves. Wackenhut reports that it created the program because of its conviction that the vast majority of employees are honest, that they are disturbed by the threat of illegal activities to their employer, their own morale, and their jobs but are reluctant to speak out because they fear being revealed as informers.[83] The Wackenhut program uses some techniques familiar to the Neighborhood Crime Watch and media TIPS programs. Silent Witness utilizes a telephone number readily available to employees throughout the facility or company. Materials explain the program and guarantee anonymity, and all calls are monitored by trained Wackenhut personnel in its Communications Center. Wackenhut simply acts as a third-party conduit, accepting the volunteered information and passing it on to the client employer. The employee is never asked for his or her name or for other information that would lead to the caller's identity, is invited to call again, and is given a way to claim any reward offered.

INTERNAL INTELLIGENCE PROGRAM   Private investigative firms offer corporations undercover internal intelligence programs in which they plant undercover agents into a corporation's business operations to make observations and report back to the company. Wackenhut reports that its internal intelligence program has been used successfully in combating theft of funds and merchandise, use of alcohol or drugs on the job, gambling, sabotage, and planned disruption by antimanagement activists. Pinkerton Inc. reports that one of the most effective ways to combat avoidable losses is through undercover investigations. It describes its undercover operations in the following way: Specially selected and trained individuals are temporarily hired as members of the workforce. They mix into the company in ordinary capacities, then observe and report activities to their supervisor. The net result of an effective investigation should be an objective and unbiased assessment of employee behavior, morale, and supervisory competence. In the best undercover work, both good and bad information is reported by individuals with the experience and objectivity to find the truth under difficult circumstances.[84]

THE STORE DETECTIVE   One of the most common types of undercover private investigations is the store detective (also known as a loss prevention specialist). Shoplifting is one of the most common crimes in the United States. Statistics available through the U.S. Department of Justice reveal that shoplifting is the fastest-growing crime in the larceny-theft category, with more than one million arrests reported each year since 1989. However, these figures may be only the tip of the iceberg; some experts speculate that for every shoplifter caught, as many as 10 to 20 others go undetected.[85]

Shrinkage is a major problem for retailers. The term *shrinkage* is used by retailers to describe the difference between inventory on hand at the beginning of the year and inventory on hand at year's end, taking into account the year's sales. In a national retail security survey, the average shrinkage for surveyed department stores was 2.09 percent. Using this rate, a department store chain with merchandise sales of $1 billion would have shrinkage of almost $21 million. In the judgment of the survey's respondents, 38.4 percent of all shrinkage was caused by shoplifting.[86] Another major cause of shrinkage is employee theft.

The goal of the store detective is to apprehend persons stealing property from the store. After apprehending the shoplifter, the store detective retrieves the stolen property. In many cases, the police are called to arrest the violator and process him or her through the criminal justice system. Some stores use sophisticated camera equipment to scan the store for people stealing merchandise, whereas other stores rely on a store detective "roaming" the store, appearing to look like an ordinary shopper. Many college students work their way through college by working as store detectives or loss prevention specialists. Store detective is also a good entry-level job in private security from which employees can work their way up to security management.

Drug Undercover Investigations

At least three general methods can be used in conducting drug undercover investigations. The first involves infiltrating criminal organizations that sell large amounts of drugs. The method of that kind of undercover operation is to buy larger and larger amounts of drugs to reach as high as possible into the particular organizational hierarchy. Lower members of the criminal hierarchy have access only to a fixed quantity of drugs. To obtain larger amounts, they have to introduce the investigator to their source or connection, who is generally someone in the upper echelon of the organization or a member of a more sophisticated organization. These operations generally require sophisticated electronic surveillance measures and large sums of money. Also, they can be very lengthy and dangerous to undercover investigators. The next method that can be used to attack drug syndicates or drug locations is the process of "staking out" (a fixed surveillance) a particular location and making detailed observations of the conditions that are indicative of drug sales, such as the arrival and brief visit of numerous autos and people. These observations are best if recorded on video to establish probable cause for obtaining a search warrant. If a judge agrees with the probable cause, he or she can issue a search warrant, which can then be executed against a particular person, automobile, or premises. These investigations can be very lengthy and involve extensive sophisticated electronic surveillance. The third method is the undercover "buy-and-bust."

Proper preparation for serving a search warrant or arrest warrant is essential for officer and citizen safety as well as to prevent flight or destruction of evidence. Here, backup officers get in position outside a second-floor apartment.

The undercover drug buy-and-bust is an operation in which an undercover police officer purchases a quantity of drugs from a subject, then leaves the scene, contacts the backup team, and identifies the seller. The backup team, in or out of uniform, responds to the location of the sale and arrests the seller, based on the description given by the undercover officer. The legal basis of the arrest is probable cause to believe that a crime was committed and that the subject is the perpetrator of the crime. Based upon the legal arrest, the backup team can search the subject and seize any illegal drugs. If the arrest occurs inside a premises, the backup team can seize any illegal substances that are in plain view. The undercover officer then goes to the police facility the subject was brought to and makes a positive identification of the subject from a hidden location, generally through a one-way mirror or window. By viewing the suspect through the one-way mirror or window, the undercover officer cannot be seen and can be used again in the same role. The buy-and-bust is generally utilized in low-level drug operations that receive numerous complaints from the community. The purpose is to take the person into custody as quickly as possible to relieve the quality-of-life problem in the neighborhood. A sufficient number of officers is extremely important in undercover "buy-and-bust" operations. The basic players in the game are

1. *The undercover officer (U/C).*
2. *The ghost officer.* This officer closely shadows or follows the U/C as she or he travels within an area and approaches the dealer.
3. *The backup team.* This should consist of at least five officers, if possible, who can watch from a discreet location to ensure the safety of the U/C and ghost and who can move in when ready to arrest the dealer.
4. *The supervisor.* He or she is the critical member of the team who plans and directs the operation and makes all key decisions.

The arrest in the buy-and-bust operation can also be delayed until the officers obtain an arrest warrant.

★ ★ ★

ENTRAPMENT

Often people believe that undercover operations by the police are entrapment. What is entrapment? **Entrapment** is defined as inducing an individual to commit a crime he or she did not contemplate, for the sole purpose of instituting a criminal prosecution against the offender.[87] Entrapment is a defense to criminal responsibility that arises from improper acts committed against an accused by another, usually an undercover agent. *Inducement* is the key word; when police encouragement plays upon the weaknesses of innocent persons and beguiles them into committing crimes they normally would not attempt, it can be deemed improper as entrapment and the evidence barred under the exclusionary rule.

The police, by giving a person the opportunity to commit a crime, are not guilty of entrapment. For example, an undercover officer sitting on the sidewalk, apparently drunk, with a 10-dollar bill sticking out of his or her pocket, is not forcing a person to take the money but giving a person the opportunity to take the money. A person who takes advantage of the apparent drunk and takes the money is committing a larceny. The entrapment defense is not applicable to this situation. However, when the police action is outrageous and forces an otherwise innocent person to commit a crime, the entrapment defense may apply.

The U.S. Supreme Court in *Jacobson v. U.S.* (1992) ruled that the government's action of repeatedly, for two and a half years, sending a man advertisements of material of a sexual nature, causing the man to order an illegal sexually oriented magazine, constituted entrapment. It ruled that law enforcement officers "may not originate a criminal design, implant in an innocent person's mind the disposition to commit a criminal act, and then induce commission of the crime so that the government may prosecute."[88] Regarding this case, Thomas V. Kukura's article in the *FBI Law Enforcement Bulletin* made the following recommendations: To ensure that undercover investigations do not give rise to successful claims of entrapment or related defenses, all law enforcement offices should consider the following three points before conducting undercover investigations. First, while reasonable suspicion is not legally necessary to initiate an undercover investigation, officers should nonetheless be prepared to articulate a legitimate law enforcement purpose for beginning such an investigation. Second, law enforcement officers should, to the extent possible, avoid using persistent or coercive techniques, and instead, merely create an opportunity or provide the facilities for the target to commit a crime. Third, officers should document and be prepared to articulate the factors demonstrating a defendant was disposed to commit the criminal act prior to government contact.[89]

YOU ARE THERE! »

Jacobson v. United States, 1992

In February 1984, a 56-year-old Nebraska farmer (hereinafter the defendant), with no record or reputation for violating any law, lawfully ordered and received from an adult bookstore two magazines that contained photographs of nude teenage boys. Subsequent to this, Congress passed the Child Protection Act of 1984, which made it illegal to receive such material through the mail. Later that year, the U.S. Postal Service obtained the defendant's name from a mailing list seized at the adult bookstore, and, in January 1985, began an undercover operation targeting him.

Over the next two and a half years, government investigators, through five fictitious organizations and a bogus pen pal, repeatedly contacted the defendant by mail, exploring his attitudes toward child pornography. The communications also contained disparaging remarks about the legitimacy and constitutionality of efforts to restrict the availability of sexually explicit material, and finally, offered the defendant the opportunity to order illegal child pornography. Twenty-six months after the mailings to the defendant commenced, government investigators sent him a brochure advertising photographs of young boys engaging in sex. At this time, the defendant placed an order that was never filled. Meanwhile, the investigators attempted to further pique the defendant's interest through a fictitious letter decrying censorship and suggesting a method

of getting material to him without the "prying eyes of U.S. Customs." A catalogue was then sent to him, and he ordered a magazine containing child pornography. After a controlled delivery of a photocopy of the magazine, the defendant was arrested. A search of his home revealed only the material he received from the government and the two sexually oriented magazines he lawfully acquired in 1984. The defendant was charged with receiving child pornography through the mail in violation of 18 U.S.C. 2252(a)(2)(A). He defended himself by claiming that the government's conduct was outrageous, that the government needed reasonable suspicion before it could legally begin an investigation of him, and that he had been entrapped by the government's investigative techniques. The lower federal courts rejected these defenses; but, in a 5–4 decision, the Supreme Court reversed his conviction based solely on the entrapment claim. In *Jacobson*, the Supreme Court held that law enforcement officers "may not originate a criminal design, implant in an innocent person's mind the disposition to commit a criminal act, and then induce commission of the crime so that the government may prosecute."

Source: Based on *Jacobson v. United States,* 112 S.Ct. 1535 (1992); and Thomas V. Kukura, J.D., "Undercover Investigations and the Entrapment Defense: Recent Court Cases," *FBI Law Enforcement Bulletin* (April 1993), pp. 27–32.

CHAPTER SUMMARY

This chapter discussed new approaches to traditionl police operations. Alternatives to random routine patrol and rapid response to citizen's calls to 911 for service include directed patrol, split force patrol, and differential response to calls for service. Alternatives to retroactive investigation of past crimes by detectives include improved detective operations, career criminal or repeat offender programs, and cold case squads. New proactive tactics in police operations include uniformed tactical operations (aggressive patrol and saturation patrol), decoy operations, stakeout operations, sting operations, code enforcement teams, and efforts against drunk and aggressive drivers.

The chapter also discussed undercover operations, including police, federal, and private security undercover operations, as well as the legal concept of entrapment

and how it affects undercover operations and proactive tactics.

Learning Check

1. Name and describe three alternatives to random routine patrol and rapid response to citizens' calls to 911.

2. Discuss the innovations to police detective operations motivated by the Rand study and other studies.

3. Name some of the new proactive tactics employed by the police to deal with crime problems and criminals.

4. Discuss the rationale behind repeat offender programs (ROPS) and give some examples.

5. Describe the three major types of undercover drug operations.

6. Define entrapment and give some examples.

Application Exercise

After you receive your degree in criminal justice, you are hired by the Averagetown Police Department as an assistant and consultant to the police commissioner. Averagetown has several crime problems, including robberies at its fast-food restaurants, thefts from autos in public parking lots, burglaries, and some low-level drug dealing in the town's commercial area and at the local high school. Of the department's 100 officers, 10 are assigned to the detective unit to investigate past crimes, 5 are assigned to traffic duties, 5 are assigned to administrative duties, and the rest are assigned to the uniformed patrol force. Based on your reading of this chapter, what would you advise the police commissioner to do?

Web Exercise

Go to the National Highway Traffic Safety Administration Web site and look at the material on saturation patrols and safety checkpoints. List at least five of the tips the Web site gives officers or agencies wishing to conduct an operation. Go to the Washington State Patrol Web site and do the self-evaluation for aggressive driving.

Key Concepts

Blending
Decoy operations
Differential response to calls for service
Directed patrol
Entrapment
Managing Criminal Investigations (MCI)
Repeat offender programs (ROPS)
Split force patrol
Sting operations
Undercover investigations

CHAPTER

9 Police and the Community

CHAPTER GOALS

- To illustrate the meaning of police–community relations and their importance to the safety and quality of life in a community
- To explore public attitudes regarding the police and efforts undertaken around the nation to improve public perceptions
- To describe various minority populations and some of their issues regarding police interactions
- To explore the challenges various populations, including the aging population, youth, the homeless, crime victims, and the physically challenged, face when interacting with the police
- To identify efforts being made to better serve these populations
- To describe some innovative community crime prevention programs that focus on crime reduction and improving the quality of life in communities

This chapter deals with relationships between the police and the citizens they are paid to protect: the community. This chapter, along with Chapter 10, forms the focus of the police and community section of this text. While Chapter 10 will deal with the philosophies of community policing and problem-solving policing, this chapter will discuss the relationships between the police and the public. It will describe numerous programs being implemented by police agencies to better serve these populations.

The chapter emphasizes the need for proper relationships between the police and the community and presents definitions of police human relations, police public relations, and police–community relations. It also explores public opinion of the police as well as the challenges presented by an increasingly diverse population. It will also explore the relationships between the police and minority communities (including African American, Hispanic American, Asian American, Native American, Muslim, and Jewish communities; women; the gay community; and new immigrants). It will also look at relationships between the police and some special populations, including senior citizens, young people, the homeless, crime victims, and physically and mentally challenged individuals.

Additionally, the chapter will discuss community crime prevention programs, including Neighborhood Watch programs, Crime Stoppers, citizen patrols, citizen volunteer programs, home security surveys, Operation Identification, National Night Out, police storefront stations or ministations, citizen police academies, mass media campaigns, and other police-sponsored crime prevention programs and police and citizen initiatives.

★ ★ ★

THE NEED FOR PROPER POLICE–COMMUNITY RELATIONSHIPS

The police are needed to handle emergencies, maintain order, regulate traffic, and promote a sense of security within the community. To accomplish this, the police must be part of the community. They cannot be viewed as mercenaries or as an army of occupation. When the police see themselves as an occupying army or are seen as one by the community, urban unrest results. The police can best serve the community when they are regarded as part of the community both by the residents and themselves.

The police and community need each other to help communities to be as vibrant and safe as possible. Police–community relationships must be two-way partnerships. Additionally, in a democratic society, the legitimacy of the police depends on broad and active public acceptance and support. Police chiefs or police commissioners have the responsibility and obligation to educate the public about the many causes of crime and the inability of the police, acting alone and on their own, to control crime. Former New York City police commissioner Lee P. Brown (also former police chief of Houston and Atlanta) has said that the police chief must "take the lead in addressing broadened local social service needs that could, if neglected, produce greater crime problems."[1] The more educated a community is concerning the role of the police and the challenges the police face in meeting multiple demands, the more supportive and helpful they can be.

The leadership of the chief in reaching out to the community is essential. As R. C. Davis says, "Initiating positive interaction with the community generally results in increased citizen support, higher morale in the work force, protection against or insulation from many hostile external forces, and increased resources."[2] Although it is very important for a chief to seek the support and cooperation of the public to improve efforts to police the community, the most important person in the police department, in terms of improving police community relations, is the individual police officer. Patrol officers, traffic officers, and detectives are the individuals within the department who come into contact with the public on a regular basis. Most people receive their impression of a particular police department through the actions of the police officers they encounter. A person who has a bad experience with a particular officer may believe that the entire department mirrors that officer. Additionally, due to the high visibility of uniformed officers, many citizens will form opinions based on behavior they may observe in restaurants, stores, on car stops, or at scenes, or even by police driving their marked police vehicles. The officer most likely won't even be aware he or she is being scrutinized in these situations. Officers are constantly serving as ambassadors for their departments. The Police Foundation has stated that "it is imperative that every . . . officer see a great deal of community relations as part of his daily patrol or investigative assignment."[3]

★ ★ ★

HUMAN RELATIONS, PUBLIC RELATIONS, COMMUNITY RELATIONS

A tremendous emphasis on police community relations has arisen since the civil disorders of the 1960s. Numerous textbooks and courses exist on police community relations and police human relations. What do these terms mean?

Are they interchangeable? Are community relations and human relations the same as police public relations? Steven M. Cox and Jack D. Fitzgerald perhaps best define these terms. They define **police human relations** as follows: "In the most general sense, the concept of human relations refers to everything we do with, for, and to each other as citizens and as human beings."[4] Human relations thus connotes treating others with respect and dignity and following the Golden Rule—acting toward others as you would want others to act toward you. Cox and Fitzgerald define **police public relations** as "a variety of activities with the express intent of creating a favorable image of themselves . . . sponsored and paid for by the organization."[5] Then, using these two definitions, they define **police community relations** as follows:

> Community relations are comprised of the combined effects of human and public relations. Police community relations then encompass the sum total of human and public relations, whether initiated by the police or other members of the community. . . . Police community relations may be either positive or negative, depending upon the quality of police interactions with other citizens (human relations) and the collective images each holds of the other (which are derived from public as well as human relations).[6]

The President's Commission on Law Enforcement and Administration of Justice, in 1967, reported that "police relations with minority groups had sunk to explosively low levels."[7] The commission defined police community relations in its summary report, *The Challenge of Crime in a Free Society:*

> A community relations program is not a public relations program "to sell the police image" to the people. . . . It is a long-range, full-scale effort to acquaint the police and the community with each other's problems and to stimulate action aimed at solving these problems.[8]

Louis A. Radelet, a pioneer in studying the role of the police in the community, traced the development of the **police community relations (PCR) movement** to an annual conference begun in 1955.[9] However, some believe that the PCR movement grew out of the riots and civil disorders of the 1960s. The PCR movement should not be confused with today's community policing. The PCR movement involved assigning a few officers in a department as community affairs or community relations specialists. These officers attended community meetings and tried to reduce tensions between members of the department and the public. Some of the programs were shams or merely public relations attempts. The PCR movement had no real effect on the philosophy or culture of most police departments. Egon Bittner has said that for PCR programs to be effective, they need to reach to "the grassroots of discontent," where citizen dissatisfaction with the police exists.[10] In short, police human relations skills are needed.

Since the urban disorders of the 1960s, training in human relations has become part of the police academy and in-service training in many departments. Sensitivity training—sometimes referred to as T-groups, or encounter groups—is designed to provide participants an opportunity to learn more about themselves and their impact on others, as well as to learn to function more effectively in face-to-face situations. In a typical encounter group, officers may engage in a role play face to face with a group of minority citizens, teenagers, or others who have had problem relationships with the police. The police officers play the role of the other group, and the members of the other

In order to strengthen their relationships with people they serve, police departments are striving to make themselves more diverse and representative of their communities. Their commitment to communication may be paying off: The approval rating of police by younger people has risen in the past few years.

group play the role of the police. The goal of this training is to facilitate the ability of police officers to understand the perceptions and behaviors of the citizen group.

The International Association of Chiefs of Police (IACP) understands the importance of public relations and the interactions between the police and the community. In recent years they have issued training keys on managing anger, police–citizen contacts, dealing with the mentally ill, elderly victimization, and hate crimes. There is also an understanding that crucial to police–community relations is the community's faith in the police department to police itself. It must be understood by all that allegations of police misconduct will be thoroughly and fairly investigated. In 2001, the IACP issued three training keys pertaining to the investigation of public complaints to assist departments in this process.

Cox and Fitzgerald tell us that human relations training in police departments has focused on the police and youth, women, and the elderly, in addition to racial and ethnic minorities. This training uses films, lectures, discussion sessions, and the analysis of written case studies.[11]

★ ★ ★

PUBLIC OPINION AND THE POLICE

While it's well known the police have a difficult job, the role of the police has always been somewhat ambiguous. The perception of the police mission by police leaders as

well as the community leaders has varied over the last few decades. With the adoption of the community policing philosophy (discussed in the next chapter), many law enforcement agencies have seen their roles expand to include activities that previously were not viewed as police functions. Additionally, in the fiscally challenged times of post-9/11, agencies have found it necessary to turn some previous police duties over to other entities. These methods include privatization, the use of volunteers, and civilianization within the department. Despite this reassessment, the police role continues to be viewed in three primary areas—crime fighters, order maintainers, and service providers. Though views differ, it is a common refrain from police and citizens alike that there are not enough police officers on the streets.

Given the difficult job the police have, it is easier for them to perform their duties if they have the support of the public. The media often portray a police force that is not liked by the public. However, this is a false perception.

In a nationwide poll asking people how much respect they have for the police, 61 percent answered "a great deal," 29 percent answered "some," and 9 percent answered "very little." (See Table 9.1.) With regard to police in their area, the numbers were similar, with 60 percent of respondents having "a great deal" of respect for police in their area.[12]

The public's opinion of the police has remained relatively constant over time, with the vast majority of the public giving favorable ratings to the police. Whites and older citizens generally give the police better ratings than do African Americans and younger people.

Interestingly, the approval ratings of police by younger people has risen. In a 1991 national poll, 49 percent of people aged 18 to 29 had a "great deal" of respect for police, whereas in 2002, 56 percent of the same age group felt that way.[13] Perhaps this is a reflection of the efforts police agencies have made regarding the youth in their communities.

In a nationwide poll conducted by the Gallup organization in 2003,[14] citizens were questioned regarding how much confidence they had in some

Table 9.1	Reported Confidence in the Police, 2003			
	A Great Deal	Some	Very Little	None
Nationwide	61%	29%	9%	1%
By gender				
Male	60%	28%	11%	1%
Female	61%	31%	7%	1%
By race				
White	65%	27%	7%	1%
Nonwhite	43%	37%	18%	2%
Black	43%	30%	24%	3%
By age				
18–29	61%	25%	12%	2%
30–49	59%	31%	10%	
50+	64%	28%	8%	

Source: Adapted from *Sourcebook of Criminal Justice Statistics, 2003.* http://www.albany.edu/sourcebook/1995/wkl/t213.wkl, retrieved 03/28/2004.

American institutions. The percentage reporting they had a "great deal" or "quite a lot" of confidence in the police was 61 percent, slightly outscoring the presidency (55 percent). It was less than the military (82 percent), but more than organized religion (50 percent), Congress (29 percent), the medical system (44 percent), TV news (35 percent), and the U.S. Supreme Court (47 percent). (See Table 9.2.)

James Q. Wilson has said, "The single most striking fact about the attitudes of citizens, black and white, toward the police is that in general these attitudes are positive, not negative."[15] The polls mentioned here clearly indicate that Wilson was right. The police, however, feel that the public does not like them or support them. William A. Westley found that 73 percent of officers questioned thought that the public was against the police or hated the police. Only 12 percent of the officers felt that the public liked the police.[16] Wilson, acknowledging the fact that most police officers feel that the public does not like or appreciate them, concluded that the police "probably exaggerate the extent of citizen hostility."[17]

Perhaps one reason many officers believe the public does not like them is that officers, particularly in high-crime areas, spend a significant proportion of their time dealing with criminals and unsavory-type people. Further confusing perceptions, any conflicts or negative issues that arise are played out repeatedly in the media and the community.

★ ★ ★

POLICE AND MINORITY COMMUNITIES

One of the most significant problems facing the police over the past three decades has been the tension, and often outright hostility, between the police and minority group citizens. Most of this tension has focused on relationships between African Americans and the police. However, tension has existed between police and Hispanic Americans, Native Americans, Asian Americans, and other minority groups, including women and the gay community. One of the best ways to improve relationships between the police and minority groups is to ensure that minority groups are adequately represented in a jurisdiction's police department. Recently, minority representation has increased significantly in U.S. police departments. This should improve relationships between the police and minority communities. However, as Chapter 13 will discuss, African Americans, Hispanic Americans, and other minorities (including women) are still seriously underrepresented in U.S. police departments.

While increasing diversity within the law enforcement workforce will facilitate cultural awareness and understanding with various minority populations, there are other efforts law enforcement can make. Having and conveying respect for these cultures is critical. Opening up the lines of communication with the informal leaders of these communities in order to discuss their issues and their needs will result in greater cooperation.

Officers should be trained in the background and cultures of the various communities to aid in understanding. If language is a barrier, the identification of reliable, honest translators within the community will be helpful. In turn, education of the community in police goals and operations will increase residents' understanding and lessen their fear. The Community Relations Service (CRS) of the Department of Justice has published a guide, "Avoiding Racial Conflict," that may be helpful in improving and maintaining good

Table 9.2	Reported Confidence in Selected U.S. Institutions 2003

Question: "I'm going to read you a list of institutions in American society. Please tell me how much confidence you, yourself, have in each one—a great deal, quite a lot, some, or very little?"

Institution	Percent Answering "A Great Deal" or "Quite a Lot"
Banks	50%
Big business	22%
Church/organized religion	50%
Congress	29%
Criminal justice system	29%
Medical system	44%
Military	82%
Newspapers	33%
Organized labor	28%
Police	61%
Presidency	55%
Public schools	40%
TV news	35%
U.S. Supreme Court	47%

Source: The Gallup Organization, Inc., The Gallup Poll (online). Available at http://www.gallup.com/poll/releases/pr 030619.asp (June 24, 2003).

relations between the police and the various minority groups.

Multiculturalism

The 2000 U.S. Census reports that 11.5 percent of the total U.S. population is foreign born, accounting for 32.5 million people. Of these, 52 percent were born in Latin America, 26 percent in Asia, and 14 percent in Europe, with the remainder coming from other areas of the world, including Africa. Significantly, more than 20 percent of these foreign-born residents have less than a ninth-grade education. Additionally, almost 18 percent of American households now report that they speak a language other than English at home.[18] These factors have implications for police officers responding to calls involving these residents. Not only is there likely to be a communication problem, but there may be a lack of trust and understanding of police, possibly resulting in fear.

In 1994, the Police Executive Research Forum (PERF) conducted a cultural diversity conference. Sherman Block, Sheriff of Los Angeles County, California, serving as the keynote speaker, stated that, in regard to cultural diversity in his community,

> The merging of cultures and ethnic backgrounds produced both a richness of diversity and a myriad of problems. The richness of diversity is evident in the new communities that have evolved from people relocating here in hopes of establishing a better life for their families. . . . The myriad of problems are as diverse as the mix of individuals who now comprise Los Angeles. Each ethnic community strives and struggles to overcome life's challenges to acquire part of the American Dream—the dream to be free to live, work, worship and pray as it sees fit. However, the cultural mix itself can cause problems. . . . When internal cultures conflict, it can be as destructive as a collision between an iceberg and an ocean liner. Misunder-

standing between two cultural groups can lead to conflict and, taken to the extreme, physical confrontations.[19]

To improve relations between his department and their multicultural clientele, Block instituted a 36-hour block of multicultural training in his academy. He also established a "Host a Deputy Program" in which families within the community voluntarily host a deputy in their homes for an evening.[20]

A study of how police departments in four California cities responded to demographic changes that took place in their communities between 1980 and 1994 revealed that the four departments, San Jose, Long Beach, Stockton, and Garden Grove, have embraced the diverse communities they serve by innovative new strategies in recruitment and hiring, citizen participation, training programs both for employees and community members, community outreach initiatives, and community policing. African Americans, Asians, and Hispanics represented almost 50 percent of the population of these cities in 1994, an increase of 17 percent over 1980.[21]

Numerous training programs have been developed to address the issues of cultural diversity. Two recent examples include the following. The International Association of Chiefs of Police (IACP) offers two two-day training courses in this area to departments throughout the nation, "Cultural Diversity Training for Law Enforcement Personnel," and "Development of Cultural Diversity Training: Train the Trainer."[22] The Long Beach, California, Police Department, collaborating with the National Conference of Christians and Jews, has developed a 40-hour cultural awareness training course for all department employees.[23]

The African American Community

The face of the U.S. population is changing as it has continued to become more diverse year after year. Whereas in 1950 caucasians represented approximately 87 percent of the U.S. population, it is predicted that by 2030 they will make up only 59 percent of the American population.[24] African Americans currently are 13 percent of the population, as compared to 10 percent in 1950. Their percentage of the population is expected to remain relatively constant with projections of 13 percent in 2030.[25]

African Americans have historically faced discrimination in U.S. society. Not until 1954, with the landmark Supreme Court case of *Brown* v. *Board of Education of Topeka,* was legal segregation of the races officially declared unconstitutional.[26] This case overturned the old "separate but equal" doctrine regarding race and public schools. A

PATROLLING THE WEB

The Community Relations Service (CRS) of the Department of Justice

The publication "Avoiding Racial Conflict" is available and more information can be found at the CRS Web site: http://www.usdoj.gov/crfs/pubs/avoidracial.htm

decade later, the Civil Rights Act of 1964 was passed by Congress, strengthening the rights of all citizens regardless of race, religion, or national origin.

Access to equal rights did not come easily. The 1950s and 1960s saw demonstrations, marches, and protests by minority groups to win these rights. Often the police, being the official agents of government bodies seeking to block equality for all people, were forced to enforce laws against minority groups, sometimes by arresting them and breaking up their gatherings. Additionally, the police were also forced to confront protests by people opposing equality for all. The police were constantly in the middle between those striving for equality and those expressing "white backlash."

Although some might disagree, police contacts with African Americans were not the only—and perhaps not even the major—cause of the urban riots in the 1960s. However, police actions generally were the immediate precipitators or the precipitating events of these riots. The riots in Harlem, Watts, Newark, and Detroit were all precipitated by arrests of African Americans by white police officers.[27]

In the wake of the 1960s riots, police departments throughout the United States established community relations programs designed to improve relationships with minority members of the community. Police departments increased their recruitment and hiring of African American officers. The 1980s, 1990s, and early 21st century saw the election of African American mayors and other officials in many large cities, as well as the appointment of African American police commissioners in many of the largest U.S. police departments.

Despite the elimination of legal racism and the increased acceptance of minorities into mainstream society, however, the problems of African Americans did not disappear. Racism and hatred still exist in our society. Many African Americans in the inner cities remain unemployed or underemployed. Many live below the poverty level and remain in a state of chronic anger or rage. It is this rage that many say led to the 1992 Los Angeles riots.

Cox and Fitzgerald, writing in 1992 (before the Los Angeles riots), seem to have been prophetic. After discussing the urban riots of the sixties, they state

> We have the distinct impression that the horrors of the 1960s have receded into the backs of the minds of many police administrators; the same appears to be true of the general public. There is little doubt in our minds, however, that the same tensions that found temporary release on the streets of

the urban centers of our country still exist. The growing "underclass" of minority-group members presents a real and present problem which we cannot afford to ignore. Well-thought-out, well-planned police minority relations programs are essential if the mistakes of the 1960s are not to be repeated.[28]

If police administrators had heeded the advice of Cox and Fitzgerald, they might have been more prepared for the 1992 Los Angeles incident. Serious problems still remain between the police and the African American community. In a 1996 survey by the Joint Center for Political and Economic Studies, about 43 percent of the African Americans polled said police brutality and harassment were serious problems where they live, whereas only 13 percent of the general population responded similarly. A 1995 report by the Sentencing Project, a public-interest group that advocates sentencing reform, reported that one in every three young black males in the United States is imprisoned, on probation, or on parole. A similar study in 1991 had found that one out of every four young black men was under some type of criminal justice supervision. The new figure represents an increase of 31 percent.[29]

There continues to be a concern among individuals in the African American community of unfair treatment by law enforcement and the criminal justice system. The terms *racial profiling* and *driving while black* have become commonplace. Racial profiling is a "form of discrimination and singles out people of racial or ethnic groups because of a belief that these groups are more likely than others to commit certain types of crimes. Race-based enforcement is illegal."[30] This issue will be discussed later in this text.

The controversy over racial profiling has resulted in many states passing legislation requiring officers to document the race and ethnicity of individuals being stopped by police as well as requiring sensitivity training for police officers.[31] One of the goals of this legislation is to ensure that individuals are not stopped based on their race or ethnicity and also to document to the public that this is not occurring or what steps have been taken if statistics indicated it was perhaps being done. These statistics, documentation, and efforts will go a long way to smoothing relations between minority community members, in particular African Americans, and the police, but there are other areas that also need to be addressed.

When examining perceptions of police brutality in respondents' area, the Gallup Organization found that while

28 percent of whites believed there was a problem with police brutality in their area, a much higher 53 percent of blacks felt there was a problem.[32] Furthermore, high school seniors in 2001 were asked the question "How good or bad a job is being done for the country as a whole by . . . the police and other law enforcement agencies?" The responses differed by race. Just over 37 percent of white seniors felt law enforcement was doing a "good" or "very good" job whereas only 20 percent of black high school seniors felt that way.[33] Clearly, the relationship between police and African Americans remains an area that needs to be addressed.

Special Agent Ronnie A. Carter of the U.S. Bureau of Alcohol, Tobacco, Firearms and Explosives wrote in a 1995 article regarding police relations with minorities:

> Officers must attempt to understand the attitudes of all community members, including those of minority residents. By joining with the many citizens who want fair and equitable law enforcement, police officers will find that the real minority is not defined by race or class. The real minorities are comprised of the few criminals who victimize society with little fear of being brought to justice.[34]

The Hispanic American Community

The Hispanic community is composed of many different cultures. Officers must understand and acknowledge this diversity. In 1950, Hispanics comprised approximately 3 percent of the U.S. population. By 2030, this proportion is projected to be approximately 20 percent.[35] The 2000 U.S. Census reports that 11.1 percent of the U.S. population was born outside of the United States. Of these, almost 52 percent were born in Latin America (including South America, Central America, Mexico, and the Caribbean).[36] Officers can't assume that all of the Hispanic groups share the same culture and beliefs. Though there are similarities, each is unique. If police officers group all Hispanics together due to a lack of understanding or knowledge, this can lead to resentment within the community.

Hispanic Americans have suffered discrimination, and many are also handicapped by language and cultural barriers. Their relationships with the police have often been as tense as the relationships between the police and the African American community.

Considerable attention has been given to recruiting and hiring Hispanic Americans as police officers. In addition, affirmative action programs have been used to appoint and promote Hispanic Americans to higher ranks, and many

police departments offer courses to teach their employees how to speak Spanish. Two examples of departments offering Spanish-language training are Los Angeles and Phoenix.

In 1996, the Los Angeles Police Department sent 19 officers to Guadalajara, Mexico, for a 10-day crash course in Spanish language and culture. According to LAPD Deputy Chief Mark Kroeker, "Officers learn enough Spanish in the Academy to give basic commands to suspects. We also need to be able to say, 'How's your family? or How's work?'"[37] In 1995, the Phoenix, Arizona, police department provided Spanish-language training courses for all its officers. It also had a program enabling Spanish-speaking translators to ride on patrol with Phoenix police officers. Five of the first ten translators were Arizona State University students.[38]

The Asian American Community

According to the 2000 U.S. Census, of the 11 percent of the population who were born outside the United States, 26.4 percent were born in Asia.[39] These Asian Americans include many distinct and separate cultures with people from China, Japan, Korea, Vietnam, Laos, Cambodia, Thailand, and other countries of the Far East. Chinese Americans are among the most visible of the Asian American community, with Chinatowns in many large U.S. cities. The Chinese community has traditionally been viewed as relatively crime free. However, as Delbert Joe and Norman Robinson stated as far back as 1980, "Over the past decade and a half Chinatowns in the major urban centers of North America have ceased to be lands of law and order and have instead become places in which crime is increasingly prevalent."[40] As crime and social problems increase in Asian American communities, some departments are making special efforts to recruit and hire Asian Americans. For example, in California, the San Jose, Long Beach, Garden Grove, and Stockton police departments have taken affirmative steps to recruit and hire more Asian American personnel.[41]

Many departments are also strengthening their relationships with the Asian population by reaching out to the community and educating them about the role of police in the United States. There are often misperceptions and misunderstandings about what the police do and why they do it, especially given what the various cultures have experienced in their homelands.

Opening the lines of communication with the various groups and understanding their history, beliefs, and culture go a long way toward facilitating an open relationship. Of particular importance for officers to understand would be the political culture of their native country, including the police role, both formal and informal. This will help officers understand reactions they are encountering on the street and minimize the opportunity for misunderstandings.[42]

Establishing a liaison program between the police department and community leaders with the goal of educating both the residents and police officers will have a positive affect on the relationship. The Minneapolis Police Department has established an initiative to reach out to their Asian communities, the Southeast Asian Community Leaders Forum. They have found this forum to have positive effects, including increased communication and information sharing and enhanced recruiting efforts. The schools have also noticed benefits from this increased community investment in the Asian students.[43]

Native Americans

In the 2000 Census, Native Americans numbered almost 2.4 million, or a little under one percent of the U.S. population.[44] Native American nations, reservations, colonies, and communities with criminal jurisdiction have traditionally been policed in two ways: by use of federal officers from the Bureau of Indian Affairs (BIA) or by use of their own police departments, like any other governmental entity. In a few cases, tribes contract police services with a local or state agency or the U.S. Bureau of Land Management. The trend in recent years is for tribes to assume their own police responsibilities and phase out reliance on BIA police and investigators.[45] As indicated in recent investigations by the U.S. Congress, police have traditionally had problems with Indian communities and much more needs to be done regarding police–Native American relationships.[46]

Despite the obstacles, progress is being made. Throughout the United States, there are over 100 different tribal groups, all with different beliefs. In an interview with *Building Bridges* in 1994, Nancy Bill, the Injury Prevention Specialist for the Navajo Area, stressed the importance of taking cultural beliefs into consideration when developing safety programs with Native Americans. The various cultural beliefs will filter the residents' perceptions of information they receive from governmental personnel or law enforcement. These beliefs also influence how Native Americans interact with others, including law enforcement, and may result in misunderstandings if officers aren't aware of these cultural differences. For the Navajo, a direct statement that sounds like a warning, such as "you better wear

The trend in recent years is for tribes to assume their own police responsibilities. Officer Carlis G. Yazzie, a Native American officer in the Navajo Tribal Police, is on patrol in Chinle, Arizona.

your seatbelt or you could get killed," is likely to be interpreted as the speaker wishing that event on them.[47]

Law enforcement in tribal areas is typically very complex. There are overlaps as well as gaps in law enforcement, depending on whether the officer is a Native American or Anglo and/or whether the individual involved is a tribal member or an Anglo. This, coupled with the alarming statistics regarding an increased crime rate involving American Indians, spurred the International Association of Chiefs of Police (IACP) to address this issue with tribal communities through the summit "Improving Safety in Indian Country."[48]

Two recent Bureau of Justice Statistics studies had indicated a high victimization rate and offender rate for Native American in the 90s at a time when the crime rate in the rest of the U.S. population was declining. Problems that are being addressed outside Indian country are not being adequately addressed inside.[49] The summit was held to come up with some ideas on how to reverse this trend. Recommendations include cross-jurisdictional cooperation, elimination of jurisdictional authority issues that impede

PATROLLING THE WEB

The U.S. Department of Justice Community Relations Service is also involved in the issue of conflict resolution in Indian country, and they also recommend cross-deputization of law enforcement between tribal and non-tribal law enforcement agencies. Additional recommendations can be seen at

http://www.usdoj.gov/crs/pubs/
pubflyernativeamerican52002update.htm

law enforcement, improved crime prevention programs and funding, training for law enforcement working in or near tribal country regarding Native American culture, improved data collection and information sharing, and improving victims' services in order to minimize revictimization.

Many reservations employ both Native Americans and non-Native Americans as police officers. Some have a preference for Native American officers due to the cultural issues, but many agencies have found that with training and communication on both sides, ethnic background shouldn't be a factor. Many are also involved in community relations programs in an outreach effort to residents of the tribal lands.

The Menominee Tribal Police Department in Wisconsin has found a way to reach out to the residents and open up the lines of communications. They did it with softball. They sponsored a series of co-ed softball games and found that this program allowed members of the community to interact with police officers in a nonthreatening arena. The officers and community have both benefited from the improved communications.[50] Law enforcement is continuing to examine issues involving Native Americans and what efforts can be undertaken to address those issues.

Arab Americans, Muslims, and Sikhs

Since 9/11, there has been an increased awareness of the needs and issues with the Middle Eastern community. After it was revealed that the 9/11 terrorists had lived and worked and gone to school in many South Florida communities without arousing any suspicion, many residents became alarmed at any individual of Middle Eastern descent living in their neighborhood. The Muslim community has raised concerns for their civil rights and the suspicion that seems to have been generated within their communities.

Many Muslims have asked law enforcement for extra protection as they are in fear of hate crimes being perpetrated because of their ethnicity. The Community Relations Service of the Department of Justice has written a guide to help law enforcement respond to this issue.[51] They recommend conducting a community assessment to determine the vulnerable targets. Increasing high-visibility patrol in those areas would be one strategy, as well as opening the lines of communication with the Muslim community to determine their fears, concerns, and tensions. It is also felt a proactive approach by the police department, speaking out against hate crimes and promising vigorous investigation and prosecution, will set the tone for the community. They also recommend initiating dialogues via task forces or committees among representatives of the various ethnic and/or religious groups within the community. This will help to break down barriers and destroy stereotypes among residents. Training for police officers and education for community residents in the Muslim beliefs and traditions is also advocated for spreading the truth and minimizing misunderstandings. Having access to community leaders and good translators will help the communication process. (AT&T has a service if there are no local individuals available; 1-800-628-8486).

For the long term, increasing recruiting efforts within these ethnic minorities will facilitate understanding. All of these efforts should help members of the community of Middle Eastern descent feel less threatened and less ostracized.

The Jewish Community

In these increasingly tense post–9/11 times, there is a fear among the Jewish population of being a "soft" terrorism target. In cities with large Jewish populations this is particularly dramatic. These fears and concerns for the safety of the Jewish residents, synagogues, temples, schools, and group homes can cause a surge in demand for police protection.

There are some innovative programs being put in place in areas with large Jewish populations to make the community feel safer and make police officers and other non-Jewish residents of the community more sensitive to the needs of the Jewish population. The Metropolitan Police Department in Washington, D.C., has implemented a police training program for police recruits. Through a partnership with the Anti-Defamation League (ADL) and the United States Holocaust Memorial Museum (USHMM), Chief Charles Ramsey has mandated that all police recruits attend a tour of the museum as part of their "hate crimes" component of their training.[52] Following the tour, the recruits engage in educational sessions emphasizing case studies from the Holocaust. This program was a 2001 IACP award-winner in the education and training section.

The Boca Raton, Florida, Police Department has teamed up with the American Jewish Committee to create a program called Safe Community Initiative.[53] The program, which is viewed as a model for the nation, will instruct leaders of the local Jewish community on how to respond to terrorism threats and other emergencies. It will take "crime prevention" a step farther due to the "times" and the "current war" and the possibility of Jewish facilities being considered "soft" targets. The attendees will learn how to react to a gun threat, to deal with suspicious packages and threatening phone calls, and to respond to catastrophic events. They will learn how to respond in the time before police and/or rescue workers arrive to assume control. The program is modeled after one in England in which Jewish leaders work with Scotland Yard.

Women

Women have often been critical of police methods of handling domestic violence cases. They also have often complained of insensitivity by the police in rape and other sexual assault cases. As Chapter 15 will explain, the police have heeded complaints regarding the handling of domestic violence cases by the increasing adoption of proarrest policies in these cases. During the past three decades, the police have also been much more sensitive to women in rape and sexual assault cases. Numerous police departments have formed special investigating units to handle sex crimes (often using female investigators). Many departments conduct sensitivity sessions to help officers understand the concerns of women. Also, today, much of the prior discrimination against women in terms of hiring and promotions in police departments has been officially eliminated, and women are active members of law enforcement agencies throughout much of the nation. However, as Chapter 13 will show, women still face problems in law enforcement agencies.

With the increased numbers of women in law enforcement and the slowly increasing number in the upper administration of police organizations, the policies and procedures in place are more reflective of the female perspective than ever before. As the female officers become more visible in the community, the perception of the police as being more supportive of women should increase.

This extends to the support of victim/witness services that exist in many departments around the country. These individuals or units receive specialized training in crime victimization, including domestic and sexual violence. Police departments are utilizing these units within their own agencies to better serve the victims and witnesses of crime, many of whom are women. This effort also represents an effort to be more receptive to women's needs within the criminal justice system.

The Gay Community

In cities with large gay populations, such as San Francisco and New York, there are numerous verbal and physical attacks on members of the gay community (sometimes called "gay bashing"). Police departments across the United States have created bias units to investigate crimes that are the result of racial, religious, ethnic, or sexual orientation hatred. In addition, as we saw in Chapter 4, the International Association of Chiefs of Police has rescinded its policy of opposing the employment of gay and lesbian officers. Many police departments have not discriminated against homosexuals in recruiting and hiring officers, and some cities have made special efforts to recruit future officers from the gay community. These efforts have certainly improved relationships between the police and this minority population. One author has even indicated that the special efforts of the San Francisco Police Department to recruit homosexuals have reduced fears of reporting crimes among many members of that city's gay community, who for years had been victims of organized assaults by bikers and street gangs.[54] Despite efforts by the police, however, crimes against homosexuals are increasing in some communities and are still a sad reflection on our society.[55]

The murder of Matthew Shepard made it clear that hate-motivated violence is still a problem for the gay community. The Lambda Legal Defense and Education Fund—a legal organization dedicated to the civil rights of lesbians, gay men, people with HIV and AIDS, and the transgendered community—proposes increased prevention efforts to target antigay attitudes and violent tendencies that start at a young age.[56] While hate crime legislation seeks to appropriately punish individuals perpetrating such crimes, it is felt that if attitudes and socialization issues can be changed we could reduce the number of these types of crimes and allow these minority populations to live free of fear.

As mentioned in Chapter 4, Law Enforcement Gays and Lesbians (LEGAL) and other similar support groups around the country also offer support for gay, lesbian, bisexual, and transgendered workers in the criminal justice system. They hope to improve the environment within law enforcement agencies for gays and ultimately improve the relationship between the police and the gay community.

New Immigrants

A great proportion of new immigrants, particularly in South Florida and New York City, are Haitians and Cubans. The numbers of people arriving on Florida shores seeking political asylum and improved economic conditions have proven challenging for the local governments and schools. These immigrants often bring strong religious and cultural beliefs with them that law enforcement is unfamiliar with. These beliefs and rituals can have an impact on police services and has presented a challenge to police, resulting in the desire to learn as much as possible about these cultures to minimize misunderstandings and danger to officers or to the immigrants.

Law enforcement procedures have evolved over the years as more and more immigrants have arrived in larger numbers. Police strive to better serve the new arrivals as well as minimize the impact to police services.

There are currently over 250,000 Haitian Americans living in New York City. Though the largest population of Haitian immigrants in the United States, they have not attained the political voice that their compatriots in South Florida have acquired. Relations between these residents and police have been strained since August 1997 when Haitian immigrant Abner Louima was beaten and sodomized by a New York City police officer. There has been a fear and suspicion associated with the Haitians' view of police officers in New York. The New York Police Department has striven to change this and implemented the "Streetwise" program to teach recent police academy graduates about the culture and language of the Haitians. (They have developed programs for other immigrant populations also.) So far, they have trained 5,000 new officers and plan to begin training veteran officers.[57]

South Florida police agencies and police academies have developed similar programs and have experienced success with improved understanding and communication between the groups. Qualified Haitian Americans are also eagerly recruited as police officers. Non–Haitian American officers are also assigned to these communities with the goal of being highly visible and getting to know the residents. All of these officers are able to assist in bridging the gap between the community and the police. In 1998, some Haitian NYPD officers founded the Haitian American Law Enforcement Fraternal Organization (HALEFO) to foster understanding between the police and the Haitian immigrants.[58] There have been improvements in relations in both areas of the country due to these efforts.

The Cuban immigrants arriving on the Florida shores tend to stay in South Florida where there is a large support group of Cuban Americans ready to render any kind of assistance that is needed. Cuban Americans in South Florida are a powerful group and a strong political force. The Cuban immigrants have used anything available to escape Cuba and travel the 90 miles to Florida, from inner tubes and rickety fishing ships even to Cuban-owned vessels. They then scramble to the shore and have been seen kissing the sand and smiling widely, knowing they had "made it" and would be allowed to stay. The Cuban community in residence in South Florida has served greatly to help integrate the newcomers into the community, and relations with the police do not seem to be an issue.

As new immigrants move to the United States every year to create a new life for themselves, they also have an impact upon the police. Almost 30 years ago, the New York City Police Department created a New Immigrants Unit to establish a working liaison with representatives of new immigrant groups in the city. This action was prompted by census surveys showing that approximately 25 percent of the city's population was foreign born. Many of these immigrants come from countries where the role of the police is much different from ours. Part of the mission of the New Immigrants Unit is to inform these newcomers to the United States that our police operate differently than the police in their former lands and to make sure that they understand that here the police serve the people. The unit is staffed by a group of ethnically and culturally diverse uniformed officers, who participate in hundreds of community meetings annually.[59]

★ ★ ★

POLICE AND SPECIAL POPULATIONS

As we have seen, the community the police serve is extremely diverse. Special populations offer unique challenges for police departments. Some of the groups with special needs are senior citizens, young people, the homeless, crime victims, and the disabled.

Forst's Law

Risking All for the American Dream

I was a police officer in Boca Raton, Florida, when Haitians started to arrive on our shores. I was a sergeant on the road when the issue first presented itself in the mid-80s. It was something we had never dealt with before, and we had no idea how to address this new challenge. The first time it happened was around 4 or 5 in the morning; we got a call from a citizen that there was a group of blacks who were soaking wet, walking up to State Road A1A from the beach.

Previously we had been confronted with drug dealers using boats to smuggle marijuana and cocaine to the beaches. At times their boats broke up, and people and drugs scattered; other times, the drugs were dumped offshore as the occupants of the vessel were scared by the possibility of law enforcement being in the area, either on the water or in the air. If and when word got out of drugs washing up, there was often a response by locals trying to gather up some of the drugs.

Because this had been my previous experience, that was my assumption regarding the call as I responded to back up the zone officer. When we arrived we found about eight black men and women walking in two different directions on A1A. We stopped them and attempted to communicate with them. None

of us knew Creole, and the Haitians did not speak English. One Haitian knew a little English, and we were able to ascertain that they had come from Haiti on a small boat that had broken up a few hundred yards offshore, and that they had swum and then walked to shore. These people were wet, cold, tired, hungry, and scared. We tried to talk to them as best we could; but, in addition to the language barrier, they would not look us in the eye, which made us suspicious that they were perhaps lying to us.

We ended up using several police vehicles to transport them to the police station. Once at the station we searched all of them (there were those drug smuggling fears again) and ultimately ended up transporting them to Miami where INS would take custody of them.

This began to happen with increased regularity, and the numbers got larger and larger. Tragedy also resulted on several occasions with people drowning on their way to shore. We also saw pregnant women and children arriving with these groups. We learned some things about these new arrivals with each group that came, and we also sat down as a police organization and with other groups such as Immigration to decide how these situations should be handled.

Programs for the Aging Population

Senior citizens experience particular problems that necessitate special attention from the police. Although seniors have the lowest criminal victimization rates of all age groups, they experience a tremendous fear of crime, often refusing to leave their homes because of the fear of being a victim. Additionally, many senior citizens are infirm and require emergency services. Often police provide special programs and services for senior citizens. The population of the United States is aging rapidly. It is projected that by the year 2030, there will be 66 million older people in our society. The increasing number of older persons, coupled with their fear of victimization, yields new problems for law enforcement. Fear of victimization and percep-

tions of rising crime rates rank high among the concerns of the elderly.[60]

Also of concern to older Americans is the desire to retain their independence. An AARP (formerly American Association of Retired Persons) study found that 85 percent of people over the age of 60 want to remain living independently as they age. Only one in eight lives with other relatives.[61]

While there are many innovative programs to assist the aging population, law enforcement has realized that education and training of their officers must occur for the line officer to foster a good relationship with this segment of the population. As has been mentioned earlier, the line officer is the ambassador for the department. The way these

Forst's Law

Risking All for the American Dream (*continued*)

We found that economic conditions in Haiti were deplorable, and people were fleeing to the United States for an opportunity to work. Others were persecuted by the dictatorship in Haiti and in fear of their lives. The police were different in Haiti and they often shot citizens for no reason. Knowing this, I was surprised these people were so docile and cooperative when we stopped them. I can only attribute it to fear. In fact, their reluctance to look us in the eye was a cultural sign of respect.

For the most part, reports of them sailing the ocean in the rickety boats they were getting off of were false. Most were transported most of the way by smugglers and then placed on the old boats to go the rest of the way, or they were simply forced to jump off the smugglers' boats, often resulting in death.

When I searched the females early on in this process, I found that they were wearing several layers of clothing in an effort to bring as many clothes with them as possible. They carried nothing. They literally came to this country with just the clothes on their backs.

Our procedures changed as this became a more regular occurrence and with larger groups. We stopped bringing them to the station and searching them and began calling INS to respond directly to the beach. We often had groups of over 100 Haitians, and we would have officers stay with them in a designated area on or near the beach and await buses that INS sent. Most of these arrivals spent months in the Krome Detention Center in Miami waiting for their cases to be heard and decided by Immigration.

South Florida has a large population of Haitians, and as a police officer I frequently interacted with them. They quickly went to work at any job they could find. Overall, I found them a very hardworking, peaceful group of people. They were happy to be able to work and send money home to Haiti to their families and often spent their nonworking time studying English. They also brought some unique cultural beliefs, in particular concerning voodoo, which were new to me as well as other officers. It was something we learned about and had to be aware of when we were investigating crimes. The department did provide us with training regarding the Haitian culture as well as some basic Creole to facilitate communication. It was an eye-opening experience for me to witness these people risking everything, including their lives, for an opportunity to work at (usually) very menial positions. The situation reminded me how lucky we are here in the United States.

officers treat older people will set the stage for what the seniors think of the department.

It is important for officers to understand the physical, emotional, and social challenges that people face as they age. They can then adapt some of their procedures to minimize the affect of some of the physical challenges (changes in vision, hearing, and mobility) on their interactions with older people.[62] An officer who understands the psychological and social issues will be able to understand an unexpectedly emotional reaction to what he or she perceives as a routine event. An example would be an overreaction by an older person to being involved in an automobile crash. To the person involved, this accident could be seen as a threat to his or her independence. A citation could affect a senior's ability to keep his or her license and consequently to remain independent. The social issues confronting older Americans include adjusting to retirement, loosing family and friends to death, coping with illness and impairments, and perhaps facing a terminal illness. To have these things happen in close proximity to each other enhances the effects.[63]

Line officers also need to be aware of special issues facing the older person, including driving, fraud, self-neglect, and elder abuse. Increased awareness will help the officer to take action or make the proper referrals as well as helping the department to develop appropriate programs to address these issues.

Many departments are realizing what a valuable resource their retired citizens can be. According to the U.S.

YOU ARE THERE! »

Elder Abuse—What a Shame

Officers of the Austin, Texas, Police Department discovered the partially clothed body of a 68-year-old woman in an apartment she shared with her son. The woman wore a diaper fashioned from a vacuum cleaner bag and was found on the kitchen floor in a fetal position. Police later learned that the victim did not die of any aggressive action—she died of starvation.

An 81-year-old woman received treatment in a hospital emergency room twice in one month for serious wounds and abrasions. The woman admitted that her two sisters beat her. Although hospital officials counseled her on filing criminal charges, she refused. The woman died a month later. The coroner's inquest found that the victim had died from unnatural causes due to the intentional and unlawful conduct of her sisters.

A deputy found an elderly man abandoned by his children with no heat or hot water in his home. The bed was saturated with urine, and the man was covered with his own excrement. His body was a mass of lesions and sores that were infested with maggots. A foot had to be amputated.

Officials closed down the Riverside Nursing Home in Tampa and removed 19 residents on stretchers after the administrators ignored repeated citations and scores of deficiencies. One resident restricted to soft foods died from choking on a hot dog. Another was treated for dehydration and malnutrition after not being fed for five days.

A home health aide—previously convicted of dealing in stolen property and grand theft—was assigned by a hospital in Sun City, Florida, to care for an 86-year-old man after open-heart surgery. The woman and her husband systematically drained his assets to buy cars and gamble. They took out a $22,000 mortgage on his home and attempted to divert his direct-deposit checks to their own use before they were finally caught. The bank threatened foreclosure, but—after public pressure—announced that "no further actions will be taken for 30 days."

These are only a few stories from the myriad of sad tales of elder abuse by relatives and loved ones. Incidents of elder abuse in domestic settings are estimated at 1.5 million cases per year, yet only one out of eight cases comes to the attention of state elder abuse reporting systems. Because many older persons wish to maintain their privacy, they either do not report the abuse and neglect or they tell practitioners they do not wish to take any action against the abuser. Mel E. Weith of the St. Clair County Sheriff's Department, Belleville, Illinois, argues for more attention by police to education regarding this dramatic problem.

Proper training regarding basic gerontology and the problems that face our elders on a daily basis is greatly needed. If it is not provided, we are failing to address the issues that concern a large segment of our at-risk population. Through education of law enforcement personnel, we have the potential to eliminate this fear and guarantee that the elder population does more than just survive.

Sources: Adapted from Mel E. Weith, "Elder Abuse: A National Tragedy," *FBI Law Enforcement Bulletin* (Feb. 1994), pp. 24–26; Ronald J. Getz, "Protecting Our Seniors: Elder Abuse and Neglect Is Coming Out of the Closet as Police Network with Social Agencies to Improve the Quality of Life for Senior Citizens," *Police* (Sept. 1995), pp. 40–41; Douglas A. Campbell, "Elder Abuse: The Needless Death of Cassandra," *50 Plus* (1988), pp. 18–19; D. Quirk, "Agenda for the Nineties and Beyond," *Generations, 15* (1991), p. 25.

Census in 2000, there were 25 million men and 31 million women aged 55 and older. These individuals make up a major consumer market as well as a strong political force. If these people are knowledgeable about police resources and programs, they can be a valuable political ally at budget time. Today's older citizen is wealthier, healthier, and better educated than ever before. Many of these residents strongly believe in contributing to the community and "giving back" and have a strong desire to stay active. What they need are ways to contribute in a meaningful way. Smart police departments assess their needs and determine areas in which these residents can make a contribution. The use of volunteers will be discussed in a later section. Currently, many special programs that are offered by police

departments can be found on their Web sites. If older people have access to computers and are computer literate, this information (as well as crime statistics) is at their fingertips. It is a good avenue of outreach for police departments.

Today, numerous special programs have been created by police departments to deal with the problems of seniors. One such program is Triad, a joint partnership between the police and senior citizens to address specific problems seniors encounter with safety and quality-of-life issues. Triad was started by the International Association of Chiefs of Police (IACP) in cooperation with the American Association of Retired Persons (AARP) and the National Sheriff's Association (NSA). The three associations have designated members to serve as a national Triad policy

Courtesy of the Boca Raton Police Department

Police departments are realizing what a valuable resource and ally the older residents can be. Many are expanding their outreach efforts with their older citizens and developing ways that they can contribute to the community. Sgt. Eric Lawrence shares a laugh with a resident in Boca Raton, Florida.

board, which is responsible for providing guidance and technical support to local Triads.[64] One example of a Triad program involves the plight of some seniors in personal care homes in Columbus, Georgia. The local Triad council devised a strategy to investigate elder abuse with the assistance of the sheriff's office and the police and health departments. They obtained a search warrant for the homes, arranged for proper lodging and care for those seniors living in unhealthy and unsafe conditions, and planned for more careful monitoring of such homes.[65] Triads are also involved in training police officers to deal with seniors. In Illinois, "elder service officers" from local police agencies are given 40 hours of training in issues related to the elderly. Similar programs exist in Rhode Island, Florida, and Georgia.[66]

Some examples of programs that offer assistance to older residents include the following.

The St. Martin Parish, Louisiana, Sheriff's Department has created an Adopt a Senior program. Deputies are made "adoptive grandchildren" for isolated seniors and are assigned two or three elderly people to visit once or twice each week.[67]

Another valuable program is the Wanderer's Program, developed by the Alzheimer's Association in cooperation with law enforcement. This program identifies people afflicted with the disease and returns them to safety if they become lost, as well as providing a registry for patients who suffer from memory disorders and have a tendency to wander. An engraved ID bracelet or necklace lists the patient's name, a code number, and the words "memory impaired" with a central telephone number for the county. See Exhibit 9.1 for guidelines developed for police officers who encounter Alzheimer's victims.

In Bridgeport, Connecticut, seniors participate in a weekly Senior Safe Walk Program, where they get exercise and hear crime prevention presentations. The seniors learn about safe ways to carry money and valuables, home

PATROLLING THE WEB

Senior Programs

The Glendale, California, Police Department Web page
   http://police.ci.glendale.ca.us/volunteers
gives information about their volunteer activities, including the Retired Senior Volunteer Patrol (RSVP).
The Richmond, Virginia, Police Department site
   http://www.rpdonline.net/main/citizensacademy.htm
invites residents of the community to participate in the Citizen Police Academy. They add a special invitation to seniors to apply, offering to arrange transportation for those in need and thus addressing seniors' common reluctance to drive at night.

Exhibit 9.1	How to Deal with an Alzheimer's Victim

When confronting an apparent Alzheimer's victim, a police officer should:

- Identify him- or herself as a police officer.
- State why he or she is there, even if it appears obvious.
- Speak slowly and use a low-pitched voice.
- Use short, familiar words.
- Use "yes or no" questions.
- Ask one question at a time, allowing sufficient response time.
- If necessary, repeat questions using the same words. A victim may have only comprehended part of the question.
- Maintain eye contact.
- Use nonverbal communication if necessary.
- Avoid the use of restraints unless necessary; they may trigger an increase in the victim's symptoms. Restraints should be used only as a last resort to ensure the safety of the victim, officers, and others.

security, or carjacking prevention. Often, the appeal of companionship and exercise draws seniors who might otherwise not hear these presentations.[68]

The Colorado Springs, Colorado, Police Department has the Senior Victim Assistance Team (SVAT). SVAT members have assisted at car accident scenes, listened to the fears and frustrations of robbery victims, transported domestic violence victims to a safehouse, and referred seniors to other appropriate agencies.[69]

The Waltham, Massachusetts, Police Department has a comprehensive Triad program that stresses crime prevention and quality of life for the senior residents. Like all Triad programs, the Waltham program stresses cooperation and coordination with many other government and community organizations and protective services. One of the components of their program is the "file of life," a magnetized card placed on the resident's refrigerator with his or her medical information. They also have a Postal Carrier Alert program in which residents fill out an information card with emergency contacts that can be utilized when postal employees notice mail accumulating.[70]

Miami–Dade and Broward Counties, Florida, operate referral programs for their older residents. Paramedics and law enforcement personnel who respond to calls involving senior citizens may ask whether the resident needs assistance with various living tasks. Together with visual assessments made while at the residence, they determine whether a referral to social service organizations is warranted. In Miami–Dade County, this program is called Elder-Links; Broward calls it Senior Connection. They work closely with the Area Agency on Aging. These referrals have been found to aid thousands of older residents who didn't know how to ask for help.[71]

Seattle, Washington, has a coordinated program called Protecting Our Elderly Together (POET) that involves the domestic violence unit of Seattle Police Department, the city attorney's office, and victims' advocates and case workers from Family Protective Services, Geriatric Mental Health Services, and Aging and Disability Services. A lawyer representing a legal assistance organization also participates in the meetings. They have monthly meetings where they review cases and look for solutions to difficult

YOU ARE THERE! »

Alzheimer's Disease Victims

Many of our seniors face the dreaded Alzheimer's disease. This disease was first described by Dr. Alois Alzheimer in 1906. There are about 4 million Alzheimer's victims in the United States, with 19 million Americans having a family member afflicted and 37 million saying they know someone with the disease. Most victims are older than 65, but this disease can strike people in their 40s and 50s. It is found in 10 percent of persons over 65 years old and in nearly half of those over age 85. A patient can live from 3 to 20 years after the onset of symptoms, but the average is 8 years. It is the fourth leading cause of death among adults. As our population ages, it has been estimated that the number of people affected will reach 14 million by the middle of this century unless a cure or treatment is found.

Symptoms of Alzheimer's include gradual memory loss, decline in the ability to perform routine tasks, disorientation, difficulty in learning, loss of language skills, impairment of judgment, and personality changes. Patients have been known to wander aimlessly.

Now there is help for law enforcement agencies in dealing with Alzheimer's. In 1994, the Alzheimer's Association developed the Safe Return program, which provides a national registry for people with Alzheimer's or who suffer memory impairment for other reasons. Since its inception, more than 400 patients who were lost have been returned safely. About 15,000 people are currently registered in the program. Through Safe Return, caregivers register their loved ones or patients through the Alzheimer's Association, providing the name, address, phone number, characteristics, distinguishing features, and other information, as well as names and phone numbers of contact persons. The registrant receives an identity bracelet or necklace, wallet cards, and clothing labels with his or her Safe Return ID number and Safe Return's 24-hour toll-free number. If a registrant is found, Safe Return is contacted and, through the ID number, his or her information is provided. Also, if a registrant is reported missing, Safe Return notifies the National Crime Information Center (NCIC) so law enforcement agencies are alerted to the missing person and his or her medical condition.

Source: Adapted from Sheila Schmitt, "'Safe Return' Program Assists Alzheimer's Disease Victims and Police," *Law and Order* (June 1996), pp. 60–64.

cases, making sure all necessary services are utilized and coordinated.[72]

AARP has cooperated with law enforcement by publishing several brochures on crime prevention for the elderly. The brochures contain practical advice on how to reduce criminal opportunity.[73]

Programs for Young People

Young children are a special target of police community relations programs because they are impressionable, and it is believed that if children learn something early enough in life, it will stay with them forever. The problem of crime and young people is very serious. Over a recent 10-year period, the number of juveniles arrested for violent crimes increased by 68 percent, whereas the change in the number of adults arrested for violent crime was 46 percent. More shockingly, the number of juveniles arrested for murder for this 10-year period increased by nearly 168 percent, whereas the number of adults arrested for murder increased by only 13 percent.[74] Youths are also victims of serious crimes. Approximately three million official reports of child abuse and neglect are filed in the United States yearly.[75]

In a 1996 nationwide poll of police chiefs, 92 percent said that government must invest in programs that help children and youth if it is really serious about reducing crime.[76] Regarding this poll, former Chicago Police Superintendent Matt Rodriquez said

> Every day, police officers in Chicago and across the country see gangs and drug dealers competing with parents and law-abiding citizens for the allegiance of America's youth—bidding to recruit our children for their army, investing in our kids to lead them down a path to disaster. If we are going to win the fight for the souls of America's children, if we are going to make America safe for our families, then we are going to have to invest in the services that help kids get the right start they need in life.[77]

Former New York City Police Commissioner Patrick Murphy said

> When I hear someone say we can't afford investments in programs that help kids get the right start, I see more bright yellow crime-scene tape, more prisons, hundreds of police officers and thousands of good men and women and boys and girls lying in pools of blood, more families crying. I've seen too much of that.[78]

There are numerous special police programs for young people. The most important, perhaps, are antidrug programs.

ANTIDRUG PROGRAMS FOR YOUNG PEOPLE   Currently, the most popular antidrug program aimed at children is **Drug Abuse Resistance Education (DARE).** In DARE programs, police officers teach students in their own classrooms about the dangers of drug abuse. The program is designed to help youths (1) build self-esteem, (2) build self-confidence, (3) manage youthful stress, (4) redirect behavior to viable alternatives, and (5) see police officers as positive role models.

The DARE curriculum is organized into 17 classroom sessions conducted by a police officer, coupled with suggested activities taught by the regular classroom teacher. The course includes classroom lectures, group discussions, role plays, workbook exercises, and questions and answers.[79]

DARE is the single largest and most widely used substance abuse prevention program in the world. It is being used in all 50 states and 54 countries around the world; it benefits more than 36 million school children each year.[80] It operates in 80 percent of all school districts around the country and reaches 36 million students per year.[81]

A 1994 study confirmed the popularity of DARE and revealed that its appeal cuts across racial, ethnic, and socioeconomic lines. It indicated considerable support for expansion of the program, yet reported that DARE had little, if any, statistical impact on drug use by young people.[82]

A 1999 study of 3,150 high school juniors in Ohio found that students who completed two or more semesters of DARE in elementary school were 50 percent less likely to become high-risk abusers of drugs and alcohol than were students not exposed to DARE. The program also strengthened peer resistance skills regarding drugs and alcohol.[83]

A study conducted in Houston, Texas, in 2000, reported increased awareness of drug, alcohol, tobacco, weapons, and theft problems on their campus among middle and high school students who took the program; parents strongly supported its continuance.[84] There is generally great support for the program as a community relations tool.

Although DARE has been popular, some believe that it is not an effective use of resources in combating drug use among young people and point to other programs that are more effective.[85] For example, in 1996, police officials in Seattle and Spokane, Washington, decided to shelve their DARE programs in favor of less costly, homegrown, antidrug programs aimed at their schoolchildren.[86] However, the executive director of DARE America, a national information and resource clearinghouse for local DARE programs, downplayed the Seattle and Spokane decisions, saying that their scrapped programs represent only a very small percentage of all of the DARE officers in Washington State. The executive director further emphasized that 300 to 400 police departments add DARE programs each year. He praised the New York City Police Department, which in 1996 budgeted $8.8 million for the program, in which 101 officers teach the 17-week curriculum to 600,000 students in 1,100 schools.[87]

The national research strongly supports the short-term efforts of DARE, but the long-term success in terms of drug avoidance is mixed. Researchers believe DARE's effects can be strengthened when it is part of a more comprehensive effort by communities. Recently, a study indicated that DARE students were five times less likely to start smoking.[88]

In a continuing effort to improve its program as well as address concerns regarding benefits, DARE has developed some new curricula and joined forces with the University of Akron to conduct research. Nationwide, a total of 80 high schools and 176 feeder middle schools will participate, and evaluations will be conducted over a five-year period. The results obtained from this national study should help clarify the issue.[89]

OTHER PROGRAMS FOR YOUNG PEOPLE   Police programs for young people exist to address concerns other than drugs. The following section discusses some of the most popular programs.

Gang Resistance Education and Training (GREAT) is a program modeled after DARE but specifically addressing the issues of gangs. It is a confidence-building class with the emphasis on resisting peer pressure regarding gangs and what they offer.

Youth Crime Watch of America is a youth-led movement to create a crime-free, drug-free, and violence-free environment in the schools and neighborhoods.[90] They offer a variety of components based on the "watch out, help out" philosophy which can be tailored to fit different communities. These include crime reporting, youth patrols, drug, crime and violence education, bus safety, mentoring, conflict resolution, mediation, peer and cross-age teaching and action projects. They also provide a monthly newsletter and on-line chats.

Antibullying programs are becoming more prevalent. In the wake of recent school violence, many schools and communities are addressing the area of bullying in their schools with various education and prevention programs. State legislatures are also addressing this issue. Bullying and being bullied have been correlated with violence and also with lack of student success. It's been found that the more invested a student is in the school, the better he or she performs academically.

The Oak Harbor High School in Washington state implemented an antibullying program in 1999. It was a joint effort involving the police, a youth advocate from Citizens Against Domestic and Sexual Abuse, and school personnel. Their goal and slogan emphasized catching verbal assaults and intervening in order to prevent physical assaults. Data indicate that bullying, harassment, and intimidation have decreased.[91]

Youth Hate Crime Prevention Programs have grown as many schools have also recognized that hate crimes are a problem in the community and that a significant proportion involve young people. It is believed that these crimes are caused by attitudes that are learned and that, by providing educational materials to prevent or change these prejudiced attitudes and tendencies toward violence, the problem can be greatly reduced. These programs also hope to enable young people to resist recruiting efforts by hate groups.[92]

Community Emergency Response Team (CERT) training has been made available to high school students in many schools throughout the country. After 9/11 there was increased awareness of the importance of civilians being trained in basic emergency response, first aid, and search and rescue. It was also realized that students would be a great asset to improving safety in their schools in the event of a disaster. Students view this as an opportunity to learn valuable skills that could enhance their chances of obtaining employment in police and fire departments.

PATROLLING THE WEB

Youth Programs

You can visit the Youth Crime Watch of America on the Internet at
    www.ycwa.org/
The Community Policing Consortium has information on Oak Harbor High School at
    www.communitypolicing.org/publications/
"Preventing Youth Hate Crime," a manual published by the Department of Justice, is available on their Web site:
    www.usdoj.gov/

Successful programs have been launched in many schools, including Los Altos High School in California, Northport High School in Sarasota, Florida, Glencoe High School in Hillsboro, Oregon, and Grants Pass High School in Grants Pass, Oregon.[93]

Officer Friendly and other programs designed to help children see and talk to police officers are popular with schools and police administrators alike. The intent of the Officer Friendly programs is to encourage young children to view police officers as friends by getting to know some.[94] Some officers may dress up as clowns or old-time police officers and perform clown-type tricks with balloons. This has proven to be popular with young children.

Musical programs attract young people. One is the Fayetteville, North Carolina, Police Department's Roll'rz Band, which performs for elementary schools, public housing projects, civic events, and community meetings in an effort to prevent drug use and violence.[95]

Police Explorer programs are very popular. (See the nearby "Dempsey's Law" feature.) The Fontana, California, Police Department has an Explorer post whose primary function is emergency preparedness. These Explorers have been used during actual emergency responses, including hazardous material spills, earthquakes, floods, major accidents, and a plane crash.[96] Being an Explorer is a great way to determine if a law enforcement career is right for a young person. Most Police Explorer units have Web pages attached to their police department's site with information regarding their post.

Police trading cards are another popular youth program. For example, the Waterloo, Iowa, Police Department produces trading cards that feature the photographs and personal information of officers in the department. Young people often go to the police station in order to find officers from whom they want a card or autograph.[97] Other departments that have had success in using their police officer trading cards are the Campbell and Santa Fe, California, police departments. The Campbell department has printed and distributed 250,000 cards. Chief Jim Cost reports, "We even use them as business cards. I haven't given out a real business card in four years. . . . When an angry citizen comes in, I say, 'Here, let me give you my card,' and it starts the conversation with a smile."[98]

Some police departments feature a "card of the week" or "card of the month," which will be printed in the local paper and available at the front desk for pick-up. Police administrators are often surprised at the number of youth responding to add to their collection.

A big hit with kids are robots that teach crime prevention and safety programs. The robots are lifelike and come in all sizes, shapes, and colors. Some police robotic programs are P.C. the Patrol Car, Safety Sam, and a 9-foot-tall Officer Friendly.[99]

The school resource officer, a position designed to combat the increase of juvenile crime and improve relationships between school children and the police, has proven to be effective. This program assigns uniformed police officers to schools, generally junior and senior high schools, to provide a wide variety of services.[100] The Phoenix, Arizona, Police Department has such a program. A three-year study revealed that the truancy rate at schools with resource officers dropped by 73 percent, and crimes committed at the schools and in the surrounding neighborhoods decreased significantly.[101]

Anti–child abduction programs are also very popular. The U.S. Department of Justice estimates that more than a million children run away or are reported missing every year. Many law enforcement agencies provide parents with free photo ID documents and crucial information on safety for their children.[102] Recently, some departments have begun to facilitate the collection of DNA from children via a swabbing kit. The specimen is then retained by the parents. In 2003, President Bush signed the Protect Act of 2003. Although many states have had Amber Alert systems in place since this program originated in Texas in 1996, the Protect Act formally established the federal government's role in the Amber Alert system. The goal is to get entire communities involved in the search for missing children by joining the efforts of law enforcement and the media. Using the media to quickly alert the public to the descriptions of individuals endangering children has already had a number of successes.[103]

In conjunction with these efforts, many departments offer Internet safety brochures and programs to guide parents in keeping their children safe on the computer.

Police athletic programs or police athletic leagues (PALs) have long been one of the most popular programs involving the police and youth. These programs include boxing, baseball, football, and basketball leagues (including midnight basketball) and summer camps. Some prominent former members of PALs around the nation include boxers Mohammed Ali and Evander Holyfield and entertainer Bill Cosby. PAL is the largest organization of law enforcement agencies using athletics, recreation, and education to instill positive life principles and character-building tools to deter crime and violence. As of 2004, there were over 350 chapters serving over two million youths nationwide.[104]

Police department/college intern programs are also common throughout the nation. A good example of a police/college intern program is that of the Spring Lake Park,

Dempsey's Law

Check It Out! Police Exploring

Professor Dempsey, I think I want to be a police officer, but I'm not sure. How can I tell if it's for me?

I get this question every day. I tell students that there are several ways they can find out firsthand what police work is all about. If your school has an intern program with the local government, try to get into it and request to work with the police department. If your police department has an auxiliary program that allows you to contribute your time to the department, try that out. If your police department has a "ride-along" program, take advantage of it. I tell the students about these programs and also about one of my former students, Cindy Grob, who was a Police Explorer. Grob, of Port Jefferson Station, New York, had been a member of the Sixth Precinct Explorers in Suffolk County, New York, since the age of 14. She said, "Being a Police Explorer has made me more aware of the needs and problems of my community. The program has strengthened my direction in wanting to become a police officer." Grob, who rose to the rank of captain in the Explorers, hoped to use the experience she gained as an Explorer in a law enforcement career. Grob's parents, Jack and Judy Grob, also had positive feelings about the Explorer program. They said, "Cindy's involvement with the Police Explorers has enhanced her direction toward choosing the occupation she wants to pursue. We are very proud to have a daughter who has set her standards high and has chosen the field of law enforcement."

The Law Enforcement Exploring program involves young men and women, ages 14 through 20 years, in a hands-on look at law enforcement as a potential career. Youths interested in Law Enforcement Exploring join posts sponsored by a law enforcement agency. The law enforcement agency provides a sworn officer as the post leader. There are approximately 2,100 posts, with more than 23,000 members nationwide. More than half the posts are sponsored by local police and sheriff's de-

partments; the rest are sponsored by state police agencies, federal law enforcement agencies, and schools and civic organizations. Liability insurance is provided by the Boy Scouts of America (BSA), which offers Law Enforcement Exploring as a program for older youths. The BSA also operates regional and national events for Explorers. In a typical post, Explorers are required to work approximately 20 hours a month to maintain their eligibility, but they may work more hours if they wish. Some of the ways in which Explorers work with the police include assisting the police in crowd, traffic, and parking control at parades and festivals; staging crime prevention programs for neighborhood associations and assisting with Operation Identification by marking citizens' valuables; assisting the police in performing clerical functions; and serving as role models for younger children and assistants for officers teaching DARE. Explorers can attend regional events in which they compete in pistol shooting, crime scene searches, hostage negotiations, report writing, traffic accident investigations, and other events based on aspects of law enforcement. Every other year, a national conference with interpost competition is held. According to the BSA, approximately 40 percent of Explorers become either law enforcement officers or lawyers.

Note: In 1996, Cindy Grob was hired by the U.S. Customs Service, under the federal government's Outstanding Scholars Program. Cindy had achieved 4.0 grade point averages in our school and her four-year school. In 1997, Cindy, after extensive training, became a Customs Service canine operator, monitoring people and cargo at New York City's Kennedy Airport. In 2003, was promoted to supervisor of canine enforcement.

Source: Used with permission from personal communication with Cindy Grob, Jack Grob, and Judy Grob, 1993, 1997; and Ordway Burden, "Law Enforcement Exploring: An Effective Intro to Policing," *CJ The Americas* (August/September 1992), pp. 9–10.

Minnesota, Police Department. The program spans 10 weeks; interns participate for 200 to 400 hours and prepare a research project or paper on a topic approved by the college and the department. Interns work on routine and proactive patrol. On their own, they handle calls for motorist assists, complaints about animals, and vehicle lockouts. They also work with investigators, tour jails and crime labs, spend a shift at the communications center, and observe district and municipal court proceedings.[105]

Assistance for the Homeless

Police departments are generally the only agency available 24 hours a day, 7 days a week. Therefore, the police are frequently called to deal with alcoholics, the mentally ill, and the homeless (street people). Tremendous numbers of people live on the streets today. Many of these people are often in drug or alcoholic stupors or frenzies, or they exhibit wild and chaotic behavior. The roots of the homeless problem include the policy in the 1960s and 1970s of releasing the institutionalized mentally ill, today's jail overcrowding, the decriminalization of public intoxication, and the lack of affordable housing.

Community residents often call the police and insist they remove homeless people from their streets. Residents do not realize, do not understand, and perhaps do not care

Police officers frequently handle calls involving the homeless. These calls can be challenging and emotionally draining. A New York City Police Department officer holds a woman's kitten while assisting in the eviction of a homeless encampment in a vacant lot.

that the police have very few options for dealing with these unfortunate members of the community.

One group of researchers has reported that "Handling the mentally ill is, perhaps, the single most difficult type of call for law enforcement officers. . . . Police officers usually found themselves saddled with sole responsibility for suspected mentally ill persons whose public behavior warranted some form of social intervention."[106]

A 1990 U.S. Supreme Court case, *Zinermon* v. *Burch,* added another barrier to those already impeding the treatment of the mentally ill.[107] In this ruling, the Court held that all patients must be "competent" to sign themselves voluntarily into a mental hospital. Because of this ruling, patients who are marginally competent may have to be admitted involuntarily and have their treatment validated by the courts.

Today's homeless population, as compared to the homeless prior to the 90s, have special problems, as pointed out by Allan Coffey. Coffey writes, "The homeless are no longer the group of vagrants that police have traditionally encountered. Although hobos are still among the homeless in America, many urban areas are witnessing the inclusion of women and children, even whole families, in this group."[108]

The following gives a sense of the problems encountered by the homeless in the dangerous environs of the New York City subway system: "An indeterminate number of the homeless . . . have sought refuge underground in the city's hundreds of miles of subway tunnels. There, they face other dangers beyond the routine perils of homelessness—the possibility of being electrocuted by rails crackling with 600 volts of electricity, and the risk of being crushed by several tons of fast-moving subway trains."[109]

Who are the homeless? The National Institute of Justice reported that 25 to 45 percent of the people living on the streets are alcoholics, and that about 30 percent of all homeless people suffer from severe mental disorders. Many more homeless suffer from less severe psychological disorders that may prevent them from holding stable jobs. It also reports that a surprising number of homeless people are military veterans. Runaways also account for many of the homeless. Others are neither alcoholic nor suffering from mental illness, but they have instead experienced economic hard times or cannot afford housing.[110]

Nationally, 49 percent of homeless people are homeless for the first time, 28 percent of the homeless have been homeless for 3 months or less, but 30 percent have been homeless for more than 2 years.[111] The homeless are no longer living just in subways, along railroad tracks, or in urban downtown areas. They are in suburban and rural towns, living along rivers, in wooded areas, and in business districts. They live almost anywhere in cars, trucks, tents, and tarps. It is difficult to locate these individuals to even offer various available services.

Many of the homeless who come to the attention of the police do so as a result of committing a crime or being the victim of a crime. Typically, these incidents include drinking in public, disturbing the peace, fighting, thefts, and more serious offenses including sex crimes, robberies, and murders.

Businesses frequently call the police to remove these members of the population as they believe they are keeping customers away from their businesses because of begging, harassment, odors, urine or excrement in the area, noise, litter, and narcotics usage. They feel that this population poses a health and public safety concern to themselves and the community.

The homeless issue today is a multifaceted one and requires many organizations working together to attempt to solve the underlying problems. Many police departments have realized this and have taken a proactive approach.

The Fort Lauderdale, Florida, Police Department has a homeless outreach program that has proven to be successful. Instead of making arrests, the officers are trained to provide aid and referrals to the homeless population. After taking a three-hour training session on homeless issues, they are more sensitive to the needs and rights of these people. They are in partnership with a homeless assistance center that provides help with social services and educational and employment programs, as well as a place to sleep and eat. Staff of both organizations meet monthly to discuss issues regarding their efforts.[112] The Los Angeles and Baltimore police departments also have active homeless outreach programs that include officer training, communication, and referrals.

A proactive approach to these problems has been taken in Reno, Nevada, which has instituted a Homeless Evaluation Liaison Program (HELP), with the goal of uniting the police with various social service agencies in order to find alternatives to jailing the homeless.[113]

Working with Crime Victims

"Victim issues and concerns are becoming an integral part of policing in the 21st century. We have to prioritize this in our law enforcement mission," according to Chief Frank Winters, Chairman of the IACP Victim Services Committee.[114]

It is estimated there are as many as 31 million victims of violent or property crime in the U.S. annually.[115] Many efforts have been undertaken to assist victims of crime, including victims' rights laws, victim assistance programs,

and crime compensation funds. Recently, law enforcement has realized that by working more closely with these victims, not only can they better serve the victims and enhance community support, but they can also help to advance the law enforcement mission and goal of reducing and solving crime and reducing fear of crime.

Victims have traditionally been considered law enforcement clients, as they receive law enforcement services. Recently, the criminal justice system has recognized that victims are powerful and resourceful stakeholders in the system; by working more closely with them and incorporating their assistance, police can have a greaer impact on crime and perception of community safety.[116] There has also been increased demand on law enforcement to be responsive to the needs of victims, especially in the arena of domestic violence.[117]

Many departments around the country have established victim's services units within their agency and have found this to be a very positive undertaking. Victim's services staff can have a more rapid response and consequently obtain more and better information regarding the crime and the victim's needs than they would by reading the report the next day or even later. Crisis counseling can be initiated earlier, and police time can be devoted to investigation. This supportive atmosphere may also encourage citizens to report more crime, cooperate more fully, and consequently increase conviction rates.

The city of Austin, Texas, has initiated a comprehensive program. The Victim Services Division within the Austin Police Department provides crisis and trauma counseling to victims, families, witnesses, and others and provides assistance to street officers and investigators on cases. Austin is a large department with a large Victim Services Division. In the 20 years since its implementation, this division has grown to 35 full- and part-time staff and 300 volunteers. They see 14,000 victims a year.[118] Smaller departments can implement similar programs on a smaller scale. One victim/witness coordinator or victim advocate may be enough to serve a smaller community but still make a valuable contribution to the community.

Police also have instituted special investigative units over the past decades and use special tools to make the investigative process less threatening to victims of crime.

Many police departments have created special investigatory units to deal specifically with victims of sexual abuse. Many of these units use female investigators to ease the interview process with both adult and juvenile victims. Many police departments use **anatomically correct dolls** made to resemble actual people and their body parts, including sexual organs, in an effort to facilitate interviews of child victims of sexual abuse. These dolls can be useful in reducing stress, establishing rapport, determining competency, and learning the child's sexual vocabulary. Great care is needed, however, in the use of anatomically correct dolls; experts warn that the improper use of dolls can block communication and cause severe case problems for prosecutors.[119]

One successful police assistance program for crime victims is the Police Crisis Intervention Unit in Scottsdale, Arizona. The program provides 24-hour crisis intervention, interviews with victims to offer support and assistance, referrals to appropriate agencies, orientation to court procedures, and transportation of victims to court. The staff also provides emotional support to many victims during municipal court proceedings, and city judges often call the unit when victims become upset in court. Police refer victims for assistance, even after regular business hours, by telephoning the specialists at home or by paging them on beepers.[120]

Marion County, Indiana, has established the Child Advocacy Center, where children can be questioned in cases of possible child abuse and molestation. The center maintains child-friendly, toy-filled, cheerful playrooms where investigators can question and assist children. Since the child-friendly atmosphere was created, the number of

cases handled by the center's detectives has risen almost 50 percent, and the clearance rate has risen to over 97 percent. Most of the detectives agree that it is the center's atmosphere, which makes children feel comfortable and at ease, that has led to this extraordinarily high clearance rate. The detectives claim that when children feel at ease, they are much more willing to talk about their abuse.[121]

Working with the Physically Challenged

Depending on the definition of physically challenged, there are between 40 million and 70 million physically challenged people in the United States. According to the Census Bureau, among the 53 million adults with disabilities in the United States in 1997, 33 million had a severe disability and 10 million needed assistance in their daily lives. In 1997, almost 1 in 5 adults had some type of disability and the likelihood of a disability increased with age.[122] They include the deaf and hard of hearing; those who use wheelchairs, walkers, canes, and other mobility aids; the blind and visually impaired; those with communication problems; the mentally ill; and the retarded.

The Deaf Community can present a difficult challenge to law enforcement, particularly when they are involved in a

©AP Photo/Richard Sheinwald

The inability of many law enforcement officers to communicate with people of the Deaf Community can be potentially dangerous. Officers mistakenly thought that Franklin Ash, right, who is deaf, was acting suspiciously at the scene of a shooting. In fact, he was trying to communicate with them using American Sign Language, which he eventually explained to these officers, who could sign with him.

How a Hearing-Impaired Person May Communicate His or Her Disability

How does a police officer determine if someone is hearing impaired? The most likely indications are the following: The subject might say, "I am deaf." Many hearing impaired people can speak, but it should not be assumed that because they can speak that they can also hear. Their speaking ability may range from normal to unintelligible. A manual sign may be given to indicate deafness. This may be a movement of the hand pointing first to the ear and then to the mouth, or by pointing to the heart and putting their two hands together in front of them. The hearing impaired person may have a printed card that states that he or she is deaf and how a person can best communicate with him or her.

Source: Adapted from Suzanne M. Youngblood and Thomas W. Lynch, "Officer, I Can't Hear You!," *Law and Order* (Feb. 1995), pp. 51–53.

crisis situation. As communication is always a vital part of police response, being unable to communicate with a member of the Deaf Community can be a significant hurdle.

The Washington, D.C., police encountered such a hurdle after a Gallaudet freshman was found bludgeoned to death in his dorm room in September of 2000. The crime resulted in panic at the famous college for the deaf and hard of hearing. The police missed some clues and arrested a student who admitted fighting with the victim, as they interpreted this to be a confession to murder. The student was released, and ultimately another suspect was arrested.

District Police have installed TTY telephones for the deaf in their seven stations, given cultural training to the officers, and provided training in sign language to interested officers. Officer Myra Jordan has proposed establishing a liaison unit for the Deaf Community, as has been provided for other minority communities, and has offered to lead the unit. She learned sign language at a young age and attends Gallaudet.[123]

Officer Randy Melton with the Houston police has served as the deaf and hard of hearing liaison for 15 years and has developed a training session for law enforcement that he presents all over the country, "Bridging the Gap between Law Enforcement and the Deaf and Hard of Hearing." Departments host the class in an effort to reach out to the Deaf Community.[124] He also presents an educational session to the Deaf Community on "Understanding the Law Enforcement Culture." There is a big demand for his seminars as agencies around the country realize the importance of this issue.

The Houston Police Department has issued a visor card that identifies members of the Deaf Community and also gives them instructions on how to respond if stopped by a police officer.

Police Officer Elizabeth Cook has a talent only a few other officers have—the ability to use sign language. In 1996, as a deaf and mute man climbed to a ledge of a 32-story building and threatened to jump, the call went out for Officer Cook. "I'm here to help you," Cook signed, "Tell me what happened." The man indicated to Cook that he was despondent over the death of his girlfriend in a car accident the previous week. Cook counseled the man and reminded him of the friends and relatives who loved him and how he had the power to change his life. Within half an hour, the man surrendered to the police. Previously, Cook had used sign language to deal with crime victims, but this was the first time she had used it to save a life.[125]

Diabetics also have significant problems of which the police should be aware. Because of the prevalence of drug abuse in our society, officers frequently confront people who are in possession of hypodermic syringes and needles or are actually using a hypodermic needle. Some, however, may be people suffering from diabetes, treating themselves by injecting insulin. Diabetics often wear easily recognizable identification alerting first responders and police that they have insulin-treated diabetes. Officers might also encounter diabetics who appear to be suffering from drug- or alcohol-related impairment, are unconscious, or are suffering from seizures.[126]

★ ★ ★

COMMUNITY CRIME PREVENTION PROGRAMS

Police expert George L. Kelling has written that citizens have "armed themselves, restricted their activities, rejected cities, built fortress houses and housing complexes both inside and outside the cities, and panicked about particular groups and classes of citizens."[127] Surely, citizens are worried about crimes and have taken measures to isolate or protect themselves against it. However, the police have an obligation to help citizens protect themselves against crime. It is obvious that the police cannot solve the crime and disorder problems of the United States by themselves, and they cannot let citizens take the law into their own hands. To address these problems, the police must turn to the public for its support and active participation in programs to make the streets safer and improve the quality of life. As Wesley G. Skogan has written, "Voluntary local efforts must support official action if order is to be preserved within realistic budgetary limits and without sacrificing our civil liberties."[128]

Community crime prevention programs include Neighborhood Watch, Crime Stoppers, citizen patrols, citizen volunteer programs, home security surveys, Operation Identification, National Night Out, police storefront stations or ministations, mass media campaigns, and other police-sponsored programs.

Neighborhood Watch Programs

Citizen involvement in crime prevention programs has increased greatly in the past decade. The National Institute of Justice has reported that one family in five lives in a neighborhood with a crime prevention program. In those neighborhoods, 38 percent of the citizens participate in the program.[129] Another report indicates that more than 6 million U.S. residents are members of citizens' crime watch groups. In Detroit, Neighborhood Watch is organized on 4,000 of the city's 12,000 blocks. In New York City, 70,000 homes are involved in Blockwatcher programs, and in Dade County, Florida, 175,000 members belong to the Citizen Crime Watch.[130]

Crime prevention programs in which community members participate have different names in various parts of the country. Examples are Crime Watch, Block Watch, Community Alert, and, most commonly, **Neighborhood Watch**.[131] Neighborhood Watch groups engage in a wide range of specific crime prevention activities, as well as community-oriented activities. Citizens watch over activities on their block and alert the police to any suspicious or disorderly behavior. Neighborhood Watch blocks have clear signs alerting people that the block is protected by a Neighborhood Watch group.

In some jurisdictions, regular service providers have gotten involved in various crime watch programs. Providers such as postal employees, power company employees, and delivery personnel who are routinely out in residential areas are trained in identification of suspicious activity. They radio or call in this activity to their dispatchers, who in turn notify the police.

It has been reported that Neighborhood Watch programs can produce at least short-term reductions in certain crimes—particularly house burglaries—and are more likely to be effective when they are part of general purpose or multi-issue community groups rather than when they only address crime problems.[132]

Voluntary community organizations are often more successful in middle-class or high-income neighborhoods. Community watch programs are less likely to be found in poor neighborhoods, areas in which disorder is generally high. Skogan has found that in lower-income areas, "residents typically are deeply suspicious of one another, report only a weak sense of community, perceive they have low levels of personal influence on neighborhood events, and feel that it is their neighbors not 'outsiders' whom they must watch with care."[133]

One of the keys is the transient nature of the community. The more rooted the residents feel, the more they have invested in the community. Their tendency would be to get involved to maintain the highest level of quality of life. If the residents envision living there for only a few months, they don't care about the long-term future of the area. Therefore, the more stable the residents, the more successful a program will be.

Crime Stoppers

Crime Stoppers originated in 1975 in Albuquerque, New Mexico, and quickly spread across the country. In the typical Crime Stoppers program, the police ask television and radio stations to publicize an "unsolved crime of the week." Cash rewards are given for information that results in the conviction of the offender.[134] As of 2004, there were an estimated 911 Crime Stoppers programs in the United States. Based on information from 433 of the 911 known programs, Crime Stoppers U.S.A. has resulted in 316,724 arrests, recovered over $3 billion in property and narcotics, and paid out over $47 million in rewards.[135] Virginia Beach, Virginia's, successful program recovered over $603,000 in property and narcotics in 2003 and paid out over $29,000 in rewards. Since its inception in 1982, this program has received more than 22,500 calls, resulting in over 6,000 arrests and the recovery of over $24 million in property and narcotics.[136]

Similar to Crime Stopper programs are programs that provide citizens the opportunity to leave anonymous tips regarding crimes and criminals for the police. Along the same lines, there have been some television shows that focus on locating wanted persons. One show that has enjoyed great success is *America's Most Wanted*, hosted by John Walsh. The show precipitated one of its highest-profile captures on March 12, 2003. Information aired by the show led to citizens calling the police when they spotted

Elizabeth Smart and her kidnappers. That call, together with good police work by the officers who responded, led to a happy conclusion. Elizabeth was a 14-year-old girl kidnapped from her bedroom as she slept at home in Salt Lake City, Utah. She had been missing for many months, and her captors had many contacts with people who didn't recognize them. The show put the information back in peoples' minds, and the country rejoiced when she was safely reunited with her family. This capture was the 747th influenced by the show. This is an example of the public and private sector working together for the good of the community.

Citizen Patrols

Citizen patrols are very popular around the nation. They involve citizens patrolling on foot or in private cars and alerting the police to possible crimes or criminals in the area, thus being the eyes and ears of the police. The best-known citizen patrol is the Guardian Angels. The group, begun by Curtis Sliwa in 1977 to patrol New York City subway cars and stations, now has chapters in many other parts of the United States. The Angels are young people in distinctive red berets and T-shirts who patrol on buses, subways, and streets. Their main function is to act as an intimidating force against possible criminals or potentially disruptive people. Many people report that the mere presence of the Guardian Angels reassures them. Despite their popularity with citizens, however, the Guardian Angels have not been welcomed by police executives, who argue that only well-trained officers can maintain order.[137] In 1996, however, the Guardian Angels finally received official acceptance by the NYPD when it was announced the department would train 12 Guardian Angels in civilian crime-fighting techniques and make them part of a police-sponsored rollerblade patrol to improve safety in New York City's famed Central Park.[138]

Researcher Susan Pennell evaluated the Guardian Angels' impact on crime in San Diego and 20 other localities in the United States. The impact of the Angels on crime was inconclusive. However, the study revealed that a majority of citizens knew that the Guardian Angels were patrolling their neighborhood, and most of those who knew about the Angels felt safer as a result of their presence.[139] Recently, the Guardian Angels have developed an academy, which is licensed in New York and is working in conjunction with the U.S. Department of Homeland Security to make the nation more secure.[140]

Another noted citizen patrol group is the Nation of Islam Security Agency, affiliated with the Reverend Louis Farrakhan's Nation of Islam. In 1992, the Los Angeles Police awarded the group a permit to patrol 15 drug-ridden apartment buildings. Some African American residents praise the idea, saying, "The Nation carries respect because they give it, they are courteous and we know they won't just look the other way," and "People out here, even the drug dealers, respect the Nation. More than the police."[141] In Washington, D.C., the Nation of Islam Security Agency is credited by tenants with improving conditions at two housing projects that the agency has been patrolling for about four years.[142] The Nation of Islam caused some controversy in late 2003 by providing security for Michael Jackson as he was fighting child molestation charges.

Many police departments are now utilizing citizens as observers in more formal ways. Volunteers with training (often graduates of the Citizens' Police Academy) are uniformed and drive in department vehicles. These vehicles are marked but carefully painted differently than police cars.

These citizens patrol in teams and are another set of eyes and ears for the police guided by strict policies on noninvolvement and instructions how to report suspicious activity.

The Nashville Police Department has an active BOLO ("Be on the Lookout") patrol. Citizens are trained to make observations in their neighborhoods and report suspicious activity to patrol officers. When they are out patrolling, they wear special insignias designating they are with the BOLO program. They address quality-of-life issues including things such as graffiti or lights out. In a business–community partnership, GTE Wireless donated 100 phones and service to the BOLO program.[143]

Citizen Volunteer Programs

Citizen volunteer programs—in which citizens volunteer to do police jobs, thus freeing police officers to return to patrol duties—have become numerous and popular, involving about 600,000 citizens in numerous U.S. police departments. Citizens perform such jobs as crime analysis, clerical work, victim assistance, and crime prevention. Ordway P. Burden reports that although police unions are often critical of volunteers, the volunteers typically are accepted by the police officers with whom they work once their ability to do the job has been demonstrated.[144]

The use of volunteers in police departments has increased tremendously in the last five years. Departments have realized the value of utilizing the talents of their residents from many perspectives. A police department that doesn't actively seek to recruit volunteers in fact is not practicing good management.

The volunteers feel a vested interest in their police department and can often be counted on for support when departments are trying to expand, start new programs, or hire additional personnel. The police officers have increased involvement with the citizens at times other than crisis situations. Administrators can redirect sworn employees to more hazardous duties when volunteers assume nonhazardous jobs. The department may be able to try new programs they wouldn't have ordinarily been able to attempt due to a lack of personnel. The city or county government benefits from reduced or flat expenditures and the ability to not raise taxes in these budget-strapped times. The community benefits with a more educated citizenry and an increased feeling of safety. It is a win–win situation for all involved.

How to utilize volunteers is limited only by police managers and/or volunteer imagination. Nationwide, departments use volunteers for parking enforcement, help at special events, as crime prevention specialists, for telephone follow-ups and pawnshop investigations, and as receptionists and in clerical positions, as well as tour guides of the facility. They may volunteer with PAL, at community-wide safety fairs conducting fingerprinting, and even for role play situations in police training.

Some retirees have special talents that prove extremely valuable to police departments such as computer expertise, printing know-how, writing abilities (for brochures or notices), photographic or video expertise, or even cooking or catering skills to supply refreshments for special occasions.

Departments are actively recruiting volunteers and have Web pages devoted to the volunteer effort, including application forms. The Nashville, Tennessee, Police Department site has a page entitled "Get Involved: Get involved, help

make a difference in your community." It then lists the various ways community members can get involved in their department.[145]

The Glendale, California, Police Department has a page devoted to volunteers, asking for people to help at the substations, serve as docents for police facility tours, or join the Retired Senior Volunteer Patrol (RSVP). The page directs them to the Volunteer Coordinator for questions.[146]

The San Antonio, Texas, Police Department site has a page entitled "Volunteers in Policing VIP" that presents various opportunities for citizens of San Antonio to get involved and assist their police department. The VIP program began in 1997 with 12 volunteers; by 2001 there were over 300 VIPs working in various capacities within the department. They have links to an overview of the program, job descriptions, application and training, and a calendar of activities.[147]

Home Security Surveys and Operation Identification

Target-hardening programs have become very popular in the last few decades. Target hardening involves installing burglar alarms, installing protective gates, and using other devices and techniques to make it more difficult for criminals to enter premises to commit crime. To facilitate target hardening, numerous police departments offer home security surveys and business security surveys free of charge.

Operation Identification programs involve engraving identifying numbers (usually Social Security numbers) onto such property as bicycles, televisions, and other personal electronic items with the goal of returning the property to owners if it is stolen and then recovered by the police. The program also involves displaying decals on windows announcing that a house is equipped with an alarm or has participated in an Operation Identification program.

National Night Out

Every year citizens are encouraged to turn on all outside lighting and step outside their homes between 8:00 P.M. and 9:00 P.M. on a well-publicized, designated night, called National Night Out. In addition, a growing number of residents are expanding their participation by staging parades and concerts and securing corporate sponsors for the annual event. One of the program's primary objectives is to enable neighbors to get to know one another so suspicious people and activities can be detected and reported as soon as possible. Other objectives include the generation of community support for, and participation in, local anti-crime efforts, the strengthening of community spirit, and the placing of criminals on notice that neighborhood residents are watching them.[148]

Police Storefront Stations or Ministations

In an effort to get closer to the public, many police departments operate **police storefront stations** or **ministations.** In these programs, a small group of police officers is assigned to patrol in the immediate area of a ministation or storefront station and to engage in crime prevention programs with members of the community. The city of Elizabeth, New Jersey, operates a ministation precinct program that doubles as an antidrug education program. Each ward in the city has a ministation staffed by patrol officers and civilian volunteers. Under this program, the officers and volunteers visit each school within their ministation precincts and present an antidrug program.[149] In East Dallas, Texas, four sworn Dallas police officers and three civilian employees operate the East Dallas Police Storefront, which has forged a lasting bond with the community for nearly 20 years. The East Dallas Storefront is one of five in the Central Patrol Division.[150]

Although they would not be considered ministations, many businesses, such as 7-11, McDonald's, and the pharmacy chain CVS, are opening up their stores to the local police to use as temporary community police stations by reserving workstations for them at a table near the front of the store.

Some police departments, including that in Baltimore, Maryland, have borrowed an idea that has worked for the Japanese police for years—the "koban" or kiosk-style police ministation. In 1995, the Baltimore version of the koban opened up in the city's popular Market Center shopping district. The 8-by-12-foot steel-and-bulletproof-glass structure is equipped with telephones, a fax machine, a computer, closed-circuit television monitors, and a bathroom. It is staffed by a police officer for 12 to 16 hours a day.[151] The major difference between the Baltimore koban and the Japanese model is that Japanese officers live in their kobans, which are usually two stories tall and staffed around the clock.

Many jurisdictions have consolidated services in their police storefronts or ministations. Their goal is to get more efficient use of their tax dollars and make city services as accessible as possible for their taxpayers. They may be able to conduct minor water department or zoning business or ob-

tain various city forms at the station. Paramedics often host "wellness fairs" at these facilities, where health information is distributed along with blood pressure tests and the like.

Mass Media Campaigns

Mass media campaigns, such as the "Take a Bite Out of Crime" advertisements in newspapers, magazines, and on television, provide crime prevention suggestions for citizens. The "Take a Bite Out of Crime" national media campaign features the crime dog McGruff, a trench-coated cartoon figure. McGruff advises readers or viewers of actions they should take when they witness criminal activity.

Chaplain Programs

Departments around the country have discovered the benefits of having an active, involved chaplains program. These volunteers serve as liaisons with various religious institutions in the community. They are indispensable in the event of a tragedy. They can provide counseling and referral services to victims and families and police officers as needed. When they show up to assist at a suicide or homicide scene, they can help to free up officers from the emotional demands of the scene to concentrate on their investigation.

A well-rounded chaplains program will attempt to have representatives from all religious groups in the community. In the event of disharmony in the community, they can also provide a calming voice to their constituents and serve to help solve problems within the community. It is believed that the faith community concept is an essential ingredient in making law enforcement more sensitive to the needs of the community.[152]

In Oklahoma, they have taken the role even further. They have implemented a 36-hour academy for police chaplains. It is felt that this academy better prepares chaplains for the role they find themselves frequently filling in the community. That role is as an advocate for issues facing law enforcement personnel; chaplains find themselves increasingly in the role of mediator between law enforcement personnel and the community. The academy also reassures the public that they are being served by a well-trained, qualified, and motivated individual.[153]

Citizen Police Academies

Many police departments have established citizen police academies. Through these academies, police agencies seek to educate community members about the roles and responsibilities of police officers and to familiarize the public with the departments and how they work within the community.[154] The goal of most citizen police academies is not to provide civilians trained in law enforcement but to create a nucleus of citizens who are well informed about a department's practices and services.

Many departments use their citizen police academy as a form of training and preparation for their volunteer pool. It gives the volunteer an excellent overview of the police department. At times, departments may tailor their citizen academy to meet the needs of a specific group, such as older residents or high school students. It also may be held off-site to facilitate attendance by groups with transportation problems. Web sites often describe the course and provide application forms online.

The Boca Raton, Florida, Police Department has run a successful citizen police academy three times a year since 1992. This has helped to provide a resource of informed citizens in the community.

The Farmington, Connecticut, Police Department has had a 10-week citizen police academy since 1993 with the goal of improving communication with the community and serving as a valuable problem-solving resource.[155] The Lakewood, Colorado, Police Department offers a nine-week citizen police academy that educates community members about various aspects of policing, such as basic law, patrol procedures, drugs, vice investigations, SWAT, K-9, officer survival, firearms, arrest control, and building searches.[156]

Other Police-Sponsored Crime Prevention Programs

To allow citizens to get an inside look at how the police perform their jobs and to help them understand the police better, many police departments offer such programs as ride-alongs and tours of precincts and other police facilities. In the ride-along programs, citizens actually ride in patrol cars with police officers and respond to calls for police services with the officers. Citizens get a firsthand look at the activities the police perform and the special problems they encounter. Police departments providing ride-along programs require participants to sign a waiver freeing the jurisdiction from civil liability if a participant gets injured. Many departments also provide tours of police stations, police headquarters buildings, shooting ranges, and other facilities to allow citizens to see how their tax dollars are spent.

Always a popular activity with the community are the K-9 exhibitions and mounted unit exhibitions for the

---

PATROLLING THE WEB

Emergency Preparedness

The Long Beach, California, Police Department
www.longbeachpd.org

---

agencies that have them. These are great ways to bridge the gap between the police and the community.

In recent years, police agencies have facilitated the forming of Community Emergency Response Teams (CERT). The team members undergo training to help them act in the event of an emergency or disaster. The training enables them to respond before emergency services arrive on the scene and to assist the emergency service personnel when they do arrive. Many larger departments address this role on their Web sites and have links to the organization conducting the training. This training provides communities with a pool of trained civilians able to respond in disaster situations. It also encourages a feeling of teamwork in the community.

Terrorism and homeland security advisories can also be found on many department's Web sites, along with guidance in how to be prepared for emergency situations.

The Long Beach, California, Police Department has a page devoted to "Emergency Preparedness for Terrorism Activity," which displays the threat level in effect. It also gives advice for reporting suspicious activity and how to prepare for terrorism. The terrorism information reporting phone number is also published, as are links to emergency preparedness information from the federal government, terrorism's most wanted, and the American Red Cross. The belief is that a more informed and prepared public can be of valuable assistance in an emergency and less likely to panic in the event of an incident.[157]

★ ★ ★

POLICE AND BUSINESS COOPERATION

Businesses throughout the United States have recently begun to take a proactive role in assisting their local police departments:

- The Crown Point, Indiana, Police Department was able to refurbish 19 of its patrol vehicles in 1995 with help from local business sponsors.[158]

- In East St. Louis, Missouri, advertising on patrol cars pays for the local drug awareness programs.[159]

- In 1995, the Alliance for a Safer L.A. donated 30 computers to the Los Angeles Police Department.[160]

- In South Florida, weekly newspapers print trading cards for law enforcement officers to distribute to children.[161]

- In Norfolk, Virginia, local businesses fund the police department's twenty-one-officer bicycle patrol.[162]

- The five-person Hesston, Kansas, Police Department, in an effort to alert citizens to the need to wear seat belts, cooperates with a local printing company and local restaurants in obtaining place mats bearing the slogan, "We care, Buckle up." The police also lecture in classrooms about the importance of seat belt safety and provide free T-shirts and McDonald's Happy Meal certificates donated by local businesses. The Hesston police also provide free year-round meals to needy citizens by picking up food from merchants and restaurants and discreetly dropping it off with needy families.[163]

AMERICORPS AND POLICING

AmeriCorps is a program that uses the services of thousands of Americans of all ages and backgrounds to perform vital functions in communities across the nation. In exchange for either one or two years of service, AmeriCorps members earn a small living allowance and an education award to help finance a college education or vocational training or to pay back student loans. Many departments throughout the nation are using AmeriCorps members in programs designed to prevent and control crime and violence and prevent fear. In 1996, AmeriCorps members were walking the beat with police officers in New York City; supporting neighborhood policing centers in Wilmington, North Carolina; targeting crack houses for closure in Kansas City, Missouri; conducting safety escorts for seniors in St. Louis, Missouri; hardening targets in high-crime areas of Bridgeport, Connecticut; augmenting community policing in Clearwater and St. Petersburg, Florida; assisting victims of domestic violence in New Hampshire; and expanding safe havens in five Weed and Seed sites across the nation.[164]

The Police Corps is a Federal program designed to address violent crime by increasing the numbers of officers with advanced education and training who serve on community patrol. "The mission of the office of Police Corps and Law Enforcement Education is to increase the professional capabilities and stature of law enforcement officers through training and education. By engaging these officers with distinct communities, we will increase trust and respect between law enforcement and all of our citizens, thereby creating safer communities while protecting individual liberties."[165]

CHAPTER SUMMARY

This chapter discussed the importance of positive relationships between the police and the public and the concepts of police human relations, police public relations, and police community relations. Public opinion and the police and the relationships between the police and minority communities and special groups were covered. Police programs involving young people appear to have the greatest potential for success in creating positive relationships with the police and causing youths to develop positive ways of behaving that will lead to future success.

The chapter also discussed community crime prevention programs, including Neighborhood Watch, Crime Stoppers, citizen patrols, citizen volunteer programs, home security surveys, and other programs designed to fight crime and improve the quality of life in U.S. communities.

As we move on to Chapter 10 and cover the philosophies of community policing and problem-solving policing and their importance in dealing with the entire community, let us not forget the lessons learned in this chapter, specifically that particular groups of people, such as minorities, young people, seniors, the homeless, and the physically challenged, have special needs and require special attention from the police.

Learning Check

1. Explain why it is essential that the police maintain positive relationships with the community.

2. Discuss why there has been a tradition of negative relationships between the police and the African American community.

3. Explain the rationale behind DARE programs.

4. Discuss how effective community crime prevention programs are.

5. Identify some special populations and how the police help them with their problems.

Application Exercise

You are the president of Smalltown's police community council, a group of citizens who work with the police to improve the quality of life and the quality of police–citizen relationships in Smalltown. Two days ago, a Smalltown police officer was captured on a video camera while brutally beating a Smalltown resident, who remained motionless on the ground. The tape was turned over to a local cable station, which has played it numerous times each day, causing many residents to complain openly of police brutality and harassment. Smalltown police officers have reported that numerous teenagers are screaming insults at them as they pass in their police cars. One officer reported that a teenager openly challenged him to a fight. The police chief has called the police community council into session and asks for advice in correcting the rapidly deteriorating relationship between the police and the community. What measures would you recommend to the chief?

Web Exercise

Patrol the Web, find some examples of police programs that help citizens help themselves in preventing crime in their neighborhoods, and explore the opportunities available to individuals from the community who wish to volunteer within the police agency.

Key Concepts

Anatomically correct doll
Crime Stoppers
Drug Abuse Resistance Education (DARE)
Neighborhood Watch
Operation Identification
Police community relations
Police community relations (PCR) movement
Police human relations
Police public relations
Police storefront station or ministation

10 Community Policing: The Debate Continues

CHAPTER OUTLINE

CHAPTER GOALS

- To acquaint you with the most current thinking about corporate strategies for policing, including strategic policing, community policing, and problem-solving policing
- To explore the philosophy and genesis of the current corporate strategies of community policing and problem-solving policing
- To discuss the effect of community policing and problem-solving policing on current policing
- To discuss the implementation of community policing strategies, including the most recent methods, the role of the federal government, and some recent community policing successes
- To explain why some scholars and practitioners do not agree with the implementation of community policing strategies
- To discuss how community policing strategies can be useful in the fight against terror

Chapter 9 discussed police and the community. Specifically, it explored the concepts of police community relations, public relations, and human relations; public opinion and the police; and problems and relationships between the police and many specific populations, including minority groups and such special populations as senior citizens, young people, the homeless, the disabled, and crime victims. It also discussed numerous forms of crime-prevention services the police offer the community and numerous partnerships between the police and the community to deter crime and improve the quality of life in our communities.

This chapter continues discussing relationships between the police and the community but deals with more philosophical and strategic issues about reducing crime and improving our quality of life. It addresses the concepts of community policing and problem-solving policing, concepts that many consider new strategies of policing. Others feel these concepts are not new strategies, but rather a return to the policing of the past. In 1988, the scholar George Kelling stated

> A quiet revolution is reshaping American policing. Police in dozens of communities are returning to foot patrol. In many communities, police are surveying citizens to learn what they believed to be their most serious neighborhood problems. Many police departments are finding alternatives to rapidly responding to the majority of calls for service. Many departments are targeting resources on citizen fear of crime by concentrating on disorder. Organizing citizens' groups has become a priority in many departments. Increasingly, police departments are looking for means to evaluate themselves on their contribution to the quality of neighborhood life, not just crime statistics. Are such activities the business of policing? In a crescendo, police are answering yes.[1]

By 1998, many said the face of policing had changed dramatically. Community policing and problem-solving policing had been practiced for over a decade and had proven to be tremendously popular with some citizens, academics, politicians, and police chiefs. Many believe that community policing and problem-solving policing could be the best strategies to use in policing our nation. These two ideas emphasize community involvement and the building of partnerships between the police and the community. In many areas where community policing and problem-solving policing have been implemented, crime rates have gone down, quality of life has been improved, and people have felt safer.

By 1999, state and local law enforcement agencies had almost 113,000 full-time sworn personnel who served as community policing officers or were involved in community policing activities. Additionally, 64 percent of departments representing 86 percent of the U.S. population served by local police had full-time officers engaged in community policing activities.[2] Many, however, are not enthusiastic about this new philosophy and argue over its definition and implementation.

This chapter is intended to present the facts, explore the issues, and continue the debate. The chapter will discuss three corporate strategies for modern policing: strategic policing, community policing, and problem-solving policing. It will discuss the underlying philosophy and the genesis of the thinking about community policing and problem-solving policing and then discuss some examples of how these concepts can be translated into action.

We will also discuss the federal government and its influence over community policing, including the 1994 Crime Bill, the Office of Community Oriented Policing Services, and the Community Policing Consortium. We will present some empirical and anecdotal evidence of the accomplishments of community policing but will also show how some scholars and practitioners do not agree with these policing strategies.

It is hoped that, by presenting the issues and exploring them, we may continue the process begun by Sir Robert Peel in 1829 of making the police an essential part of life in the community.

★ ★ ★

CORPORATE STRATEGIES FOR POLICING

Police chiefs and academics throughout the United States are discussing changes in the traditional methods of policing that were discussed in Chapter 7—random routine patrol, rapid response to citizens' calls to 911, and retroactive investigation of past crimes by detectives. Since the mid-1980s, Harvard University's prestigious John F. Kennedy School of Government has held periodic meetings to discuss the current state of policing in the United States. These Executive Sessions on Policing were developed and administered by the Kennedy School's Program in Criminal Justice Policy and Management. Under the leadership of Professor Mark H. Moore, the chair of Harvard's program, leading police administrators and academics gathered at Harvard to focus and debate on the use and price of such strategies as strategic policing, community policing, and problem-solving policing.

Beginning in 1988, the National Institute of Justice and Harvard produced a series of monographs that have shaped the current state of police thinking. These monographs discussed community policing, problem-oriented policing, police values, corporate strategies of policing, crime and policing, policing and the fear of crime, the history of policing, police accountability, and drugs and the police.[3]

Harvard's Executive Sessions on Policing identified three **corporate strategies for policing** that are presently guiding U.S. policing: (1) strategic policing, (2) community policing, and (3) problem-solving policing.[4] Strategic policing involves a continued reliance on traditional police operations, but with an increased emphasis on crimes that are not generally well controlled by traditional policing (for example, serial offenders, gangs, organized crime, drug distribution networks, and white-collar and computer criminals).

Strategic policing represents an advanced stage of traditional policing using innovative enforcement techniques, including intelligence operations, electronic surveillance, and sophisticated forensic techniques. Much of this textbook, particularly the chapters on police operations and technology, deals with strategic policing issues.

Community policing is an attempt to involve the community as an active partner with the police in addressing crime problems in the community.

Problem-solving policing emphasizes the fact that many crimes are caused by underlying social problems. It attempts to deal with those underlying problems instead of just responding to each criminal incident.

Community policing and problem-solving policing are very similar approaches to the crime and disorder problems in our communities. Most departments adopting a community policing program also follow many of the tenets of problem-solving policing. These two philosophies or strategies tend to go hand in hand.

★ ★ ★
THE PHILOSOPHY OF COMMUNITY POLICING AND PROBLEM-SOLVING POLICING

In the 1960s, increases in crime, technological advances, and changes in police management thinking led to the abandonment of police foot patrols and their resultant ties to the community. They were replaced by a highly mobile police department able to drive from one incident to another in minutes.

At about the same time, many urban communities were experiencing drastic demographic changes. Longtime community residents were moving from the inner city to newly opened suburbs and being replaced by newly arrived people from rural areas and Caribbean and Latin American countries. These people were not used to urban life and the culture, norms, and mores of their adopted neighborhoods. Often there was a language barrier between the immigrants and older members of the community. These changes brought severe social problems to our cities and, of course, problems to our police. In addition, the heroin epidemic hit the United States in the 1960s, causing crime, social disorganization, and fear and mistrust. Recall the descriptions of the urban riots of the late 1960s described in Chapter 1 of this text.

Many problems developed between the police and the newly arrived residents as rapidly moving police mobile units, with flashing lights and roaring sirens, arrived in a community to answer someone's request for assistance or report of a crime. Often a lack of communication and mistrust ensued because of the police's need to take quick action and get violent people off the street as soon as possible and then to return to more serious emergencies. The police were no longer seen as members of the community, as the old beat cop had been; they were more and more seen as an invading army or an army of occupation. As a result, many police departments began to establish community relations units to address problems between themselves and the community. The units were part of what was called the Police Community Relations movement (PCR).

The police community relations units were supposed to address this communication gap. These units were not effective, however, because they usually appeared only after an ugly incident. Although the community relations units were well intentioned, in reality they could not work. The real responsibility for proper police–community relations, as any professional, experienced police officer knows, rests with each and every police officer, not a select, small group of community relations officers. Today's community policing is completely different from the earlier community relations movement and should not be confused with it.

Modern community policing, as compared to the PCR movement, entails a substantial change in police thinking. As Albert J. Reiss, Jr., says, the change must be "one where police strategy and tactics are adapted to fit the needs and requirements of the different communities the department serves . . . and where there is considerable involvement of the community with police in reaching their objectives."[5]

Many believe that the modern stage of community policing began with the seminal 1982 article in the *Atlantic Monthly* by James Q. Wilson and George Kelling, "'Broken Windows': The Police and Neighborhood Safety." Theirs has come to be known as the **broken windows**

model of policing.[6] The Wilson and Kelling article made several very critical points.

First, disorder in neighborhoods creates fear. Urban streets that are often occupied by homeless people, prostitutes, drug addicts, youth gangs, and the mentally disturbed, as well as regular citizens, are more likely than other areas to have high crime rates. Second, certain neighborhoods send out "signals" that encourage crime. A community in which housing has deteriorated, broken windows are left unrepaired, and disorderly behavior is ignored may actually promote crime. Honest and good citizens live in fear in these areas, and predatory criminals are attracted. Third, community policing is essential. If police are to reduce fear and combat crime in these areas, they must rely on the cooperation of citizens for support and assistance. Wilson and Kelling argued that community preservation, public safety, and order maintenance—not crime fighting—should become the primary focus of police patrol.[7] From this concept, many believe, the modern concept of community policing began.

Expanding on the work of Wilson and Kelling, Wesley G. Skogan surveyed numerous neighborhoods and identified two major categories of disorder that affect the quality of life in the community: human and physical disorder. The human behaviors found to be extremely disruptive to the community were public drinking, corner gangs, street harassment, drugs, noisy neighbors, and commercial sex. The physical disorders that Skogan found extremely destructive to the community were vandalism, dilapidation and abandonment, and rubbish.[8]

Using the Wilson and Kelling and Skogan ideas as a philosophical and practical framework, many scholars and progressive police chiefs jumped onto the community policing bandwagon.

★ ★ ★

COMMUNITY POLICING

Robert C. Trojanowicz, director of the National Center for Community Policing in East Lansing, Michigan, said that community policing can play a vital role in reducing three important kinds of violence in the community: (1) individual violence, ranging from street crime to domestic abuse to drug-related violence; (2) civil unrest, which can often include gang violence and open confrontations among various segments of society, specifically the police; and (3) police brutality.[9]

Scholars Jerome Skolnick and David Bayley have pointed out the following in regard to community policing:

"Among the world's industrial democracies, community-oriented policing represents what is progressive and forward-looking in policing. In Western Europe, North America, Australia, New Zealand, and the Far East, community policing is being talked about as the solution to the problems of policing. Papers exploring it have become a cottage industry."[10]

In 1997, Jeremy Travis, Director of the National Institute of Justice, speaking about community policing strategies in response to the dramatic decreases in crime during the mid- to late 1990s, noted

> The dramatic decline in crime occurring in many of our nation's cities has generated an intense public debate over the cause or causes. . . . It is interesting to note that many authorities—among them a number of eminent criminologists—have credited much of the drop in crime to better and smarter policing. In fact, after a long period of reluctance to say the police can prevent crime, a consensus is emerging that gives at least partial credit for lower crime to the transformation in policing.[11]

Community policing mandates that the police work with the community, not against it, to be effective. The foot patrol experiments described in Chapter 7 in Newark, New Jersey, and Flint, Michigan, are examples of the community policing model suggested by Wilson and Kelling in their "broken windows" approach to policing.

The scholar Herman Goldstein offers the following list of the most important benefits of community policing:

1. A more realistic acknowledgment of police functions

2. A recognition of the interrelationships among police functions

3. An acknowledgment of the limited capacity of the police to accomplish their jobs on their own and of the importance of an alliance between the police and the public

4. Less dependence on the criminal justice system and more emphasis on new problem-solving methods

5. Greatly increased use of the knowledge gained by the police of their assigned areas

6. More effective use of personnel

7. An increased awareness of community problems as a basis for designing more effective police response[12]

Community policing seeks to replace our traditional methods of police patrol with joint community and police efforts to find proactive, innovative solutions to crime and disorder on our streets. In *Beyond 911: A New Era for Policing,* Malcolm K. Sparrow, Mark H. Moore, and David M. Kennedy offer the following observation on community

YOU ARE THERE! »

Academic Research Resulting in Today's Emphasis on Community Policing

The academic research regarding policing, discussed in Chapters 1, 7, and 8 of this text, revealed many facts about policing that have led to the current emphasis on community policing. According to Professor David L. Carter, the research indicates:

- Random, marked patrol does not prevent crime.

- Patrol officers have a notable amount of "uncommitted" time.

- Quick response to citizen calls does not increase the probability of apprehending criminals.

- Fulfillment of citizen expectations of response time—not the actual speed of response—shapes citizen satisfaction with the police.

- Call management plans, such as Differential Response to Calls for Service, can increase the efficiency and effectiveness of policing without sacrificing citizen safety.

- Assigning patrol officers to geographic locations based on population ratios does not meet the variability of demands for police service.

- Meaningful deployment of patrol officers requires careful analysis of environmental factors, thus calling for service that can fluctuate according to season, time of day, and geographic location.

- Because most citizen calls can be handled effectively by one officer, single-officer patrol cars are significantly more efficient than two-officer units.

- One-officer patrol cars do not pose undue threats to officer safety.

- Teams of police officers working in a cooperative effort toward commonly defined goals can provide more comprehensive police service than nonteam efforts.

- Unique patrol deployment schemes, or specialized patrols, can be useful in handling special circumstances and problems.

- Patrol officer job enlargement and job enrichment helps increase job satisfaction, thus fostering an environment in which officers become more productive.

- Citizen demands for police assistance and problem solving related to noncriminal matters must be addressed.

Source: Adapted from David L. Carter, *Community Policing and DARE: A Practitioner's Perspective* (Washington, DC: National Institute of Justice, 1995), p. 2.

policing: "Community policing, with its emphasis on openness and partnerships . . . has broadened police awareness and extended police capabilities. The police have been willing to accept community help in both setting priorities and carrying out operations."[13]

Some examples of very early attempts at community policing involved the experiences of Detroit, New York City, and Houston.

In Detroit, one innovative approach developed by community policing advocates was the development of decentralized neighborhood-based precincts that serve as "storefront" police stations. One well-known program is the Detroit Mini-Station Program, which established over 36 such stations around the city. At first, the community did not accept the program because the officers assigned to the ministations seemed to lack commitment. Later, however, officers were chosen for ministation duty on the basis of their community relations skills and crime prevention ability; since then the program has met with much greater community acceptance.[14]

A study in Houston that involved patrol officers visiting households to solicit viewpoints and information on community problems reported both crime and fear decreases in the study area.[15]

The New York City Police Department began a Community Patrol Officer Program (CPOP) in 1984. CPOP officers did not respond to calls from 911 but instead were directed to identify neighborhood problems and develop short- and long-term strategies for solving them. Each officer kept a beat book in which he or she was expected to identify major problems on his or her beat and list strategies to deal with them. Officers thus were encouraged to think about problems and their solutions.[16]

David L. Carter, of Michigan State University, explains that community policing did not suddenly materialize as a new idea; rather, it evolved from research conducted by a wide range of scholars and police research organizations. Beginning primarily in the early 1970s, a great deal of research was conducted on police patrol.[17]

(text continues on p. 232)

PATROLLING THE WEB

The Web and Community Policing—How Can It Help?

The philosophy of community policing has hit the Internet. Community policing focuses on solving problems at the neighborhood level by involving government organizations, citizens, and community groups in an effort to help to improve the quality of life in a neighborhood. The Internet provides a great opportunity to establish an information resource for the community and to solicit citizens' comments and questions.

For example, statistical information related to criminal offenses, arrests, and calls for police service are of considerable interest to individual community members, as well as community and business groups. Linking statistics to maps provides a graphical connection to this data.

Crime prevention material and information about agency programs also can be provided efficiently via the Web. Photographs can be published with textual information that duplicates—or even surpasses—the quality of printed material. Some police departments publish an electronic list of most-wanted fugitives with digitized photographs, physical descriptions, and details of the crimes for which they are wanted.

Many departments, to support the goal of improving access and communication between the agency and the community, publish a directory of all their units. Such a directory can be updated in a few minutes at any time and could include unit addresses, telephone numbers, the names of commanders or contact persons, and the like.

E-mail links from this directory can make it even easier for citizens to send messages to the right people or places to deal with most particular problems.

YOU ARE THERE! »

What Is Community Policing? What Is a CPO?

Robert Trojanowicz and Bonnie Bucqueroux, in *Community Policing: A Contemporary Perspective,* define community policing as follows:

> Community Policing is a new philosophy of policing, based on the concept that police officers and private citizens working together in creative ways can help solve contemporary community problems related to crime, fear of crime, social and physical disorder, and neighborhood decay. The philosophy is predicated on the belief that achieving these goals requires that police departments develop a new relationship with the law-abiding people in the community, allowing them a greater voice in setting local police priorities and involving them in efforts to improve the overall quality of life in their neighborhoods. It shifts the focus of police work from handling random calls to solving community problems. . . .
>
> The community policing philosophy is expressed in a new organizational strategy that allows police departments to put theory into practice. This requires freeing some patrol officers from the isolation of the patrol car and the incessant demands of the police radio, so that these officers can maintain direct, face-to-face contact with people in the same defined geographic (beat) area every day. This new Community Policing Officer (CPO) serves as a generalist, an officer whose mission includes developing imaginative, new ways to address the broad spectrum of community concerns. . . . The goal is to allow CPOs to own their beat areas, so that they can develop the rapport and trust that is vital in encouraging people to become involved in efforts to address the problems in the neighborhoods. . . . The CPO not only enforces the law, but supports and supervises community-based efforts aimed at local concerns. The CPO allows people direct input in setting day-to-day local police priorities, in exchange for the cooperation and participation in efforts to police themselves.

Source: Adapted from Robert Trojanowicz and Bonnie Bucqueroux, *Community Policing: A Contemporary Perspective* (Cincinnati, OH: Anderson, 1990), p. 5.

YOU ARE THERE! >>

Critical Attitudes Associated with Community Policing: What the Community Police Officer Needs

1. A sense of personal responsibility for an area and its people. A feeling of ownership for what happens.

2. Belief in the importance of attempting to improve conditions within an area. A desire to assess what you have control over and act responsibly as it relates to crime and disorder.

3. Belief that the concerns of neighborhood residents matter. Recognizing that police do not always know what citizens want and are not afraid to ask.

4. Belief that citizens possess information necessary for police to do their jobs well. An understanding that police are heavily dependent on assistance from citizens to be successful.

5. Commitment to educating and empowering citizens to act. A desire to teach citizens how to help themselves.

6. Belief in working with citizens to solve problems. Recognizing limitations and a willingness to pursue alternative courses of action.

7. Belief in working with other government or community agencies to solve problems. Understanding the importance and being capable of working in teams to accomplish results.

8. Willing to make "extra efforts." Is willing to go above and beyond what is normally expected.

Source: Mary Ann Wycoff and Thomas Oettmeier, *Evaluating Patrol Officer Performance Under Community Policing: The Houston Experience* (Houston, TX: Houston Police Department, 1993).

Dempsey's Law

Professor: What Is Community Policing? Did You Ever Do That Stuff?

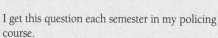

I get this question each semester in my policing course.

When I first started as a police officer in the 41st Precinct in the Bronx, in 1966, I was a foot patrol cop, as were most of us. During my first two years there, there were only four RMP (Radio Motor Patrol) sector cars in the entire precinct, plus the sergeant's car. Our foot patrol beats generally covered five or six blocks. Early in my career there, the precinct earned the nickname Fort Apache because of the wild conditions and crime that permeated the precinct. It was considered the busiest and most dangerous precinct in the City of New York, and probably the world, in the 1960s and 1970s. Later, a movie was made, starring Paul Newman, called *Fort Apache—the Bronx,* detailing life as a police officer in the days I was there. You can still see the movie on TV or get it from your video store. Believe me, the movie made the place seem too tame. It was much crazier than that.

My foot patrol post, Post 28, covered all of Westchester Avenue from Southern Boulevard to Kelly Street, both sides of the streets and all of the side streets including Simpson Street, Fox Street, Tiffany Street, and Kelly Street. Westchester Avenue, under the el, was the commercial hub of the area, and all of the side blocks were covered by wall-to-wall five-story tenements. It was the height of the heroin crisis in New York City, and crime and disorder were rampant. I patrolled this post alone without the portable radio you see officers carry today. I loved it. I made hundreds of collars [arrests], mostly gun collars and junk [drug] arrests. I also broke up fights, delivered babies, brought kids home to their parents, directed traffic, gave comfort and advice, and helped as many people as I could. Whatever the time, day or night, whenever I was working, people knew they could talk to me. Whenever they had a problem, they could come to me. The good people on my post loved me—they called me their

Dempsey's Law

Professor: What Is Community Policing? Did You Ever Do That Stuff? (*continued*)

amigo. The people who wanted to annoy the good people on my post learned to avoid me—they went someplace else. The criminals . . . well, they didn't like me too much. I put them in jail. In summary, I was the *cop*.

Everyone knew me. I was part of the life of that community, part of the life of that little spot of the world—Patrol Post 28 of the 41st Precinct. We didn't have a concept known as community policing then. We were all just cops, doing our job. As the years went by, the number of patrol car sectors assigned to the precinct increased and increased until by 1970 we had over 14 sectors, almost four times the number we had when I started. I guess this was due to new management thinking in the department: A radio motor patrol unit can cover so much more territory than a foot cop, thus officers in a car are more economical, cost effective, and efficient. Also, 911 had taken over the NYPD by then. We would race from one 911 call to another—handle one incident after another—do what we had to do and then do it all over again, time after time. No longer did we deal with prob-

lems. We just dealt with incidents. Although this change from foot patrol to the more cost-effective motorized patrol may have been necessary because of 911, I think it was a big mistake. Most of us were assigned to regular seats in the radio cars and never walked our foot beats again. What we gained in efficiency, we lost in closeness to the community. Many of the people on my beat felt they had lost their amigo—I was always busy running around the entire precinct handling 911 jobs.

Today's community police officer, I believe and hope, is a return to the past, a return to the cop on the beat who knows, and is known by, everyone. The major difference between today's community officer and the beat cop of my day is structure. Today, the officers receive training and support from the department and other city agencies. They have offices and answering machines and fill out paperwork. Hopefully, they also become what I was on Post 28 in the 41st Precinct—part of life in that little part of the world—the good people's amigo.

Forst's Law

My Experience with Community Policing

My experience with community policing began when we got a new chief of police from outside the agency in the early 1980s. He used the term *team policing,* but the philosophy was similar to community policing.

I was a road sergeant at the time and was given supervisory responsibility for everything that happened in a particular sector of the city. The chief had divided the city into three sectors, and the supervisory staff was responsible for everything occurring in all the zones within that sector; the lieutenants and captain were accountable for everything that occurred in that sector whether they were on duty or not.

Personnel were assigned to sectors and this assignment never changed. Staffing was the responsibility of the sector supervisors, and they did not get help from the other sectors. The lieutenants were most affected by this change in philosophy, and some did not like it, but they seemed to accept it well. The new chief also implemented changes in the detective bureau that appeared to diminish some of their authority and autonomy. Patrol officers were following up minor crimes, and some detectives were reporting to sector supervisors. That chief didn't last too long, due to other issues, but some of his philosophies and changes remained.

(continued)

Forst's Law

My Experience with Community Policing (*continued*)

BOCA RATON POLICE

CAPTAIN
LINDA S. FORST

Courtesy of Boca Raton Police Department

Captain Linda Forst joined the Boca Raton Police Services Department in 1977. She has spent time in Investigative Services, Training, The Professional Standards Unit, and Support Services. The majority of her career has been spent in Road Patrol which she also commanded for three years.

Captain Forst has represented the Department in state and international Police Olympic swimming competitions bringing more than 25 gold medals home to Boca Raton. She is also a graduate of "Outward Bound", a wilderness survival course.

Linda is married and she and her husband have two daughters. Her hobbies include reading, running, swimming, camping, cooking, and studying Chinese culture.

"Challenge yourself physically and mentally to be the best you can be."

ID ➡ O

"Buckle Up For Safety"

PHOTO BY: Claudia Reilly

BOCA RATON POLICE SERVICES DEPT.
Chief Peter Petracco   **99**

Printing trading cards of police officers is one of the strategies departments use to promote their philosophy of community policing. The cards assist members of the community in seeing police officers as individuals. They also encourage interaction and communication when community members—particularly youth—contact officers to obtain their cards.

When a new chief was appointed who had risen through the ranks, he continued with many of these ideas but also expanded further and implemented various strategies to address problems within our community. He put together various task forces to address certain problems and instructed them to work with the community to attempt to come up with solutions. He recognized the need for training when implementing these changes and PERF came to the department to provide training in problem-oriented policing. The training started with the supervisors and then progressed to the officers. We used real problems in our community to practice the steps in problem solving. Later we would actually implement some of these ideas. Most importantly, this training got us thinking

"outside the box" in addressing some of our persistent problems.

My experience as well as that of a lot of other officers and supervisors was that a lot of the strategies that community policing stressed were in fact things we were already doing and enjoyed doing. Getting out of my police vehicle and talking with business owners, residents, and tourists was something I loved to do. I had found it was also a great way to develop relationships and obtain information. I preferred to work the same zone so that I could get to know the comings and goings of the people living and working in the zone. Most supervisors also believed in this and assigned people to the same zone for extended periods of time whenever they were able to. The response of some officers

Forst's Law

My Experience with Community Policing (*continued*)

and supervisors to this training was, "What else is new? We already know this and already do this . . . they're just giving it a new name." Most went along with the change and encouraged their coworkers to try new things.

We had a particular section of town called Pearl City, a lower socioeconomic area that was experiencing crime and drug problems. The neighborhood was centrally located along main highways and railroad tracks and had been splintered by road expansion as the city grew. A minority police officer was assigned to foot patrol in this predominantly minority-populated section of town. He spent all his time in the neighborhood and established relationships with the community. He became a friend to older and younger residents, someone they knew and could come to with problems. He worked with them in addressing the problems the community was facing. In 1987, he established the CATS (Children and Teens Service) Program in the community. He worked with other resources in the community to provide positive role models, mentors, after-school and summer activities, and educational opportunities. He worked with other city agencies to clean up the neighborhood. He was a charismatic officer and was good at marketing his program and getting community leaders to donate effort, time, and money. This program grew and became successful in many ways and ultimately was used as a model in other neighborhoods in the city. These programs became known as the Neighborhood Improvement Programs and encompassed various programs under that heading. Educational funding for college was guaranteed for students maintaining certain standards in school, computer labs were built and staffed by high school and college students, tutoring and recreational programs were available in an effort to provide wholesome activities and even the playing field in school for some of these children from less affluent homes. These programs were successful and gained national recognition. There were TV documentaries, magazine articles, and national awards.

This was of course great news for the organization, right? Yes, but the fame and attention that this one officer received caused some resentment in other officers. Some officers felt that their efforts at aggressive law enforcement, conducted in addition to these "softer" methods to clean up the area, were ignored. They felt they had risked injury and worked hard to clean up the area, and only one officer was getting the credit. They believed these were good programs but also felt the one officer couldn't have accomplished what he did without other officers backing him up and covering the calls for service that he would have been handling had he not had this special assignment. Luckily, this resentment was small-scale and didn't grow, as most officers realized that the ultimate goal was to improve the quality of life for the residents of that community as well as everyone else in the city and to minimize our repeat responses to problems. Those goals were being accomplished, and most knowledgeable people would realize that it took a coordinated effort throughout the department.

One of the most significant changes within the department occurred when supervisors allowed officers to take risks in addressing problems in unconventional ways. When supervisors truly allowed officers to "fail" without marking them down on their evaluations, this encouraged officers to try new things. One of the most difficult issues to deal with in our department and probably any department was the fact that some officers and some supervisors just don't want to do the thinking or work involved in problem solving. They would rather just continue to do law enforcement the traditional way and then just throw their hands up and blame other conditions or factors when they can't solve a problem.

The other philosophy that I have carried with me since leaving law enforcement, and look for in other law enforcement agencies and personnel, is the realization that the police department belongs to the community and is an extension of the community. Police organizations need to be

(continued)

Forst's Law

My Experience with Community Policing (*continued*)

responsive to the residents and realize the residents are in fact their "bosses." The effort to improve the quality of life for all residents, not just lower socioeconomic populations, should be ongoing. Making it easier for residents to file reports, obtain reports, understand the department, obtain information, and speak with employees should always be a concern. Whether through the various strategies we have mentioned, such as on-line reporting, telephone reporting, Web pages, ministations throughout the community, citizen academies, or public forums, or just the philosophy of always giving the citizens the best service possible, we must be willing to go the extra mile to build the partnership between the police and community.

Regarding community policing, Joseph E. Braun, of the U.S. Department of Justice, wrote in 1997 that

> The traditional role of law enforcement is changing. . . . Community policing allows law enforcement practitioners to bring government resources closer to the community. Hence, participation and cooperation are key. . . . we cannot expect law enforcement to solve crime and social disorder problems alone. Community involvement is imperative. . . . With the implementation of community policing practices, officers and deputies still retain their enforcement duties and powers. Community policing does not mean that authority is relinquished; rather, its proactive nature is intended to reduce the need for enforcement in the long term as problems are addressed up front and much earlier. This can only occur with the cooperation and participation of the community.[18]

In *"Broken Windows" and Police Discretion,* George Kelling notes that the community policing model expands and encourages the use of discretion among officers at all levels of the organization. The traditional method of telling officers what they can and can't do, as is commonly found in police manuals, will not greatly improve the quality of policing. He advocates teaching officers how to think about what they should do, do it, and then review their actions with coworkers. With time, this should lead to improved practices and the sharing of values, knowledge, and skills that will prove valuable in the performance of their job.[19] Kelling supports "guideline development" in police agencies to facilitate the discretionary behavior of police officers and enable them to better work with the public in enhancing the quality of life.

It must be noted here that community policing is not a totally new concept. As we saw in Chapter 1 of this text, policing, from its early English roots, has always been community oriented. As one officer reminded us in 1997,

> The concept of community policing goes as far back as London's Sir Robert Peel, when he began building his public police in 1829. In his original principles, he said, "The police are the public and the public are the police; the police being only members of the public who are paid to give full-time attention to duties which are incumbent on every citizen in the interests of community welfare and existence."[20]

Though not a new phenomenon, the community policing philosophy has grown tremendously in the last few years. Departments are expanding their efforts to work with their communities, including incorporating new technology, and the public seems to like this trend.

In 1999, the Department of Justice conducted a study of residents in 12 cities across the country. The percentage of residents who were "very satisfied" or "satisfied" with the police ranged from 97 percent in Madison, Wisconsin, to 78 percent in Washington, D.C.[21] Over 50 percent of these residents knew what community policing was, and 54 percent said their departments practice community policing in their neighborhood.

According to Deputy Attorney General Eric Holder,

> The high degree of citizen support for America's neighborhood police officers is a testament to the dedicated men and women who work day in and day out to establish relationships with the residents in their communities. These relationships help citizens and police work together to promote community safety.[22]

From 1997 to 1999, the percentage of police officers designated as community policing officers increased from 4 percent to 21 percent. State and local law enforcement agencies had almost 113,000 community policing officers during 1999. Sixty-four percent of departments had full-time community policing officers, and 63 percent of agencies used foot and/or bicycle patrols. It could be argued that these practices have been in place with a different name for quite some time or are perhaps a type of window dressing. Consequently, more interesting is the indication of departments' interest in providing training in the area of community policing and incorporating problem solving into how they do business. Eighty-seven percent of law enforcement officers were employed by departments that provided community policing training to new recruits, and 85 percent are employed by departments that provided such training to in-service officers. Another encouraging sign is that 90 percent of police agencies serving a population of over 50,000 gave officers responsibility for specific geographic beats, which is a major tenet of the community policing philosophy. Also noteworthy, 50 percent of police officers are working in agencies that encouraged them to engage in problem-solving projects in their beats.[23]

Community policing is also more easily facilitated with todays' technology. Departments are taking advantage of that, using computers and the Internet to their greatest ability, trying to maximize their outreach to the community. In 1999, 62 percent of residents were served by a police agency that had an Internet home page, compared with 48 percent in 1997. A presence on the Internet with a high-quality interactive Web page can be a highly successful way of sharing the department's philosophy, beliefs, and practices with the community, as well as sharing information about the law enforcement personnel, aiding in familiarity with employees, facilitating a relationship, and encouraging a partnership. Sharing procedures, resources, and crime statistics with the community in an open way can show the community the department's commitment to a partnership and to providing them with as much information as possible in an effort to meet their needs. Communication is further enhanced with links and e-mail.

★ ★ ★
PROBLEM-SOLVING POLICING

The idea of problem-solving policing can be attributed to Herman Goldstein, a law professor at the University of Wisconsin, who spent a great deal of time in the trenches with different police departments. The problem-solving approach to policing was first mentioned by Goldstein in a 1979 article calling for a new kind of policing, which he termed problem-oriented policing.[24]

In traditional policing, most of what the police do is incident driven—they drive to incident after incident, dealing with each one and then responding to the next. Problem-solving policing, or problem-oriented policing, however, forces the police to focus on the problems that cause the incidents.

Commenting on incident-driven policing, John E. Eck and William Spelman stated

> Often officers tend to respond to similar incidents at the same location numerous times—burglaries in a certain housing project—car thefts in a certain parking lot. Because the police have traditionally focused on incidents, rarely have they sought to determine the underlying causes of these incidents. Problem-oriented policing tries to find out what is causing citizen calls for help.[25]

Sparrow, Moore, and Kennedy explain the need for problem-solving policing:

> By relying on patrol to prevent crime and rapid response to catch criminals police had backed themselves into an isolated, reactive corner. The beat officers of old had naturally seen crime on their beats in terms of patterns: they were responsible for all incidents on their turf, and a rash of burglaries or overdoses signaled a burglar or a dealer who needed to be dealt with. Modern officers, tied to their radios, saw crime as an endless string of isolated incidents. Fourteen burglaries in the same neighborhood might draw fourteen different cars.[26]

The Newport News, Virginia, and Baltimore County, Maryland, Police Departments have gained national recognition for their implementation of problem-solving policing. Their programs involved officers and the community working together to find solutions that would reduce crime, disorder, and fear.

The problem-oriented policing strategy consists of four distinct parts: scanning, analysis, response, and assessment (see Figure 10.1). Problem-oriented policing practitioners

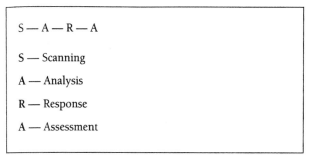

Figure 10.1
Problem-Solving Technique—SARA

YOU ARE THERE! >>

Problem-Solving Policing Solves Problems

Newport News, Virginia, is a Navy town with a population of 155,000 that has many of the same crime problems as other major cities. It was the location of one of the first studies of problem-solving policing. The following selection shows how Newport News used the problem-solving approach, dealing with its robbery problem as a general problem rather than as a series of incidents:

> At 1:32 A.M., a man identified as Fred Snyder dials 911 from a downtown corner phone booth. The dispatcher notes his location and calls the nearest patrol unit. Police Officer Knox arrives four minutes later.

> Snyder says he was beaten and robbed 20 minutes earlier but did not see the robber. Under persistent questioning, Snyder admits he was with a prostitute he picked up in a bar. Later, in a hotel room, he discovered the prostitute was actually a man, who then beat Snyder and took his wallet.

> Snyder wants to let the whole matter drop. He refuses medical treatment for his injuries. Knox finishes his report and lets Snyder go home. Later that day, Knox's report reaches Detective Alexander's desk. She knows from experience that the case will go nowhere, but she calls Snyder at work. Snyder confirms the report but refuses to cooperate further. Knox and Alexander go on to other cases.

> Months later, reviewing the crime statistics, the city council deplores the difficulty of attracting business or people downtown. Midnight-watch patrol officers are tired of taking calls like Snyder's. They and their sergeant, James Hogan, decide to reduce prostitution-related robberies, and Officer James Boswell volunteers to lead the effort.

> First, Boswell interviews the 28 prostitutes who work the downtown area to learn how they solicit, what happens when they get caught, and why they are not deterred. They work downtown bars, they tell him, because customers are easy to find, and police patrols do not spot them soliciting. Arrests, the prostitutes tell Boswell, are just an inconvenience; judges routinely sentence them to probation, and probation conditions are not enforced.

> Based on what he has learned from the interviews and his previous experience, Boswell devises a response. He works with the Alcohol Beverage Control Board and local bar owners to move the prostitutes into the street. At police request, the commonwealth's attorney agrees to ask the judges to put stiffer conditions on probation: Convicted prostitutes would be given a map of the city and told to stay out of the downtown area or go to jail for three months.

> Boswell then works with the vice unit to make sure that downtown prostitutes are arrested and convicted and that patrol officers know which prostitutes are on probation. Probation violators are sent to jail, and within weeks all but a few of the prostitutes have left the downtown area.

> Then Boswell talks to the prostitutes' customers, most of whom do not know that almost half the prostitutes working the street are actually men posing as women. He intervenes in street transactions, formally introducing the customers to their male dates. The U.S. Navy sets up talks for him with incoming sailors to tell them about the male prostitutes and the associated safety and health risks.

> In three months, the number of prostitutes working downtown drops from 28 to 6, and robbery rates are cut in half. After 18 months, neither robbery nor prostitution show signs of returning to their earlier levels.

Source: Adapted from John E. Eck et al., *Problem Solving: Problem-Oriented Policing in Newport News* (Washington, DC: Police Executive Research Forum, 1987), pp. 100–101.

call this scanning, analysis, response, and assessment process by the acronym SARA. In the scanning process, groups of officers discus incidents as "problems" instead of as specific incidents and criminal law concepts, such as "robberies" or "larcenies." A robbery, which used to be thought of as a single incident, in the scanning process is thought of as being part of a pattern of robberies, which in turn might be related to another problem, such as prostitution-related robberies in a particular area of the city.

After defining the problem, officers begin analysis. They collect information from a variety of sources, including nonpolice sources, such as members of the business community, other city agencies, or local citizens. The officers then use the information to discover the underlying nature of the problem, its causes, and options for solutions.

After scanning and analysis, the police begin response. They work with citizens, business owners, and public and private agencies to prepare a program of action suitable to the specifics of the particular problem. Solutions may include arrest but also may involve action by other community agencies and organizations. In the assessment process—after the police make their response to the problem—they evaluate the effectiveness of the response. They may use the results to revise the response, collect more data, or even to redefine the problem.[27]

Problem-oriented policing involves officers' thinking, not just responding to yet another call for duty. It involves officers dealing with the underlying causes of incidents to prevent those incidents from happening again, and it involves officers' using all sources, not only police department sources, to deal with problems. Sparrow, Moore, and Kennedy offer the following commentary on problem-oriented policing:

> Problem-solving policing, with its emphasis on thoughtful police work . . . has challenged police to pay renewed attention to the causes and patterns of crime. It has also added to their arsenal new techniques of analysis, dispute resolution, and crime prevention, and an increased willingness to engage in productive cooperative relationships with other municipal agencies.[28]

There are many new tools available to law enforcement today to assist with this problem analysis. Herman Goldstein defined problem analysis as "an approach/method/process conducted within the police agency in which formal criminal justice theory, research methods, and comprehensive data collection and analysis procedures are used in a systematic way to conduct in-depth examination of, develop informed responses to, and evaluate crime and disorder problems."[29]

It is hoped that this problem analysis occurs within the department, using the latest research to develop appropriate procedures to successfully address problems in the community. Developing partnerships with local universities may prove to be a win–win solution for police organizations. By understanding the underlying factors leading to the problems, the most realistic solutions can be developed.[30]

New technology enhances law enforcement's ability to analyze crime and geography and consider factors such as repeat victimization, repeat offending, and *modus operandi* (M.O.'s) and therefore obtain the data that will facilitate their successfully addressing the crime problem. With improved technology this can be accomplished, despite recent budgetary constraints; and, together with criminological theories and up-to-date research, the new technologies may lead to innovative ways to reduce crime.[31]

★ ★ ★

CURRENT WAYS OF DOING COMMUNITY POLICING

The concepts of community policing and problem-solving policing have merged in the past decade and can generally be looked at as one philosophy. There have been several names that have been given to this philosophy in addition to community policing and problem-solving policing, including community-oriented policing. Whatever the name given to this philosophy, the concept is the same—the involvement of the community as a partner in the policing process and an emphasis on proactive, problem-oriented policing as opposed to incident-driven policing. This section will address several of the methods, techniques, or ways of implementing community-oriented policing.

The police have implemented the philosophy of community policing with numerous methods. Primary among these is the refocusing of a department's overall philosophy and operations in order to view the community not only as a partner but as a consumer of the department's products.

Accordingly, Harvey Rachlin, a freelance writer who reports prolifically on police programs, wrote in 1997:

> Community policing has grown to be more than just a philosophy calling for police to cooperate with the public in addressing crime problems. Today, police agencies are beginning to mirror financial, telecommunications, and other industries and institutions by offering various "products" other than their core service to satisfy the ever-changing public.[32]

Rachlin then presents a staggering list of creative community policing "products" offered by a number of police departments in the state of Kansas. This list includes over 30 specific programs that focus on the consumers of the police product, including young people and other members of the community. Many of his products were referred to and discussed in Chapter 9.

Elgin, Illinois, a community of 77,000 located 35 miles northwest of Chicago, has refocused its department on numerous products that have supported a comprehensive, innovative community policing philosophy. This philosophy emphasizes that policing is done by everyone in the community and that police officers are the paid professionals who facilitate it. Its refocusing includes many of the programs discussed in Chapter 9 and the philosophies discussed in this chapter. Among their programs are

■ A Gang Unit that tracks gang activity and saturates areas manifesting an increase in gang crime

- A Neighborhood Officer Program (NOPE) through which officers are assigned to particular neighborhoods within the city

- Housing Authority officers who work in the public housing areas

- A Community Restitution Division in which sworn officers supervise offenders' probation and restitution

- A liaison officer who works with senior services and the local crisis center to enhance services through better criminal investigation, information, and education

- School liaison officers who provide support for the schools, teach gang resistance education and awareness training programs, and attend students' social and sporting activities

- A social services coordinator who offers immediate assistance to victims of crime and domestic violence

- Community outreach workers who offer special services to the city's Laotian and Hispanic population

- A phone line for reporting crime anonymously

- Crime prevention/community relations programs, including Neighborhood Watch, Citizens Patrol, and other volunteer activities

- Police officer involvement on numerous community boards and committees that are working to prevent crime, drug use, and gang activity

- Use of an AT&T language line that provides translation for more than 200 foreign languages[33]

The keystone, perhaps, of the Elgin program is their Resident Officer Program (ROPE), in which an officer is assigned to live and work in a neighborhood that has been identified as needing direct police attention due to criminal and social issues. Elgin's was the first such program in the United States. Resident officer programs are becoming very popular throughout the nation, as we will see later in this chapter.

Elgin's former police chief, Charles A. Gruber, emphasized the role of the police and citizens together in improving the quality of life of members of the community. Speaking of conditions that cause neighborhood deterioration, Gruber said

> Neighborhoods do not decay overnight. They decay one apartment or one home at a time, and the only way to recover that is to take them back one at a time, and bring about a stabilization to where people can believe that the government is going to meet its public-safety requirements.[34]

YOU ARE THERE! >>

What Some Community Policing Cops Do in Dallas

In 1997, Dallas police officers, along with employees from animal control, code enforcement, the fire department, the Dallas County Sheriff's Department, and the FBI, worked with residents living in the River Bottoms section of the city to remove junked motor vehicles and demolish more than 30 dilapidated buildings (many of which were used for drug trafficking). Officers carried employment applications from neighborhood businesses and were able to find work for 60 residents. The police officers also made friends with youths and senior citizens at neighborhood recreation centers in the area. Eight months later, Part I criminal offenses had decreased 47 percent in the River Bottoms neighborhood.

Dallas officers coordinated a graffiti paintout in the southwest section of the city. Dozens of citizen volunteers painted a concrete quarter-mile-long retaining wall. The effort was possible because of those volunteers and the 84 gallons of paint that a neighborhood store donated.

In the northeast part of Dallas, officers coordinated a Juneteenth Celebration that was attended by more than 500 citizens and included cultural dancing, storytelling, African art, an exhibit about black inventors, a parade, and ethnic food. The day of fun went a long way to blend cultures and tear down barriers.

Source: Adapted from Ben Click, "Changed Perceptions, Expectations Spell Success," *Community Policing Exchange* (July/August 1997), p. 1.

Regarding the successes of his community policing programs and residents' attitudes toward police, Gruber says

> It's changed dramatically. On occasion, you'd go out and have to fight with people to make an arrest. Now we go out, bust a drug house or a drug dealer on the corner, and people come out and clap. They're working with us to get that done.[35]

Chicago's Alternative Policing Strategy (CAPS), one of the nation's most ambitious community policing initiatives, also embodies the philosophies discussed earlier in this chapter. In an average month, some 6,000 Chicagoans connect with their beat officers through the 230 community meetings held throughout the city. The purpose of the beat officer is to identify and resolve problems of crime and disorder in Chicago's neighborhoods. Both the police and community members have been trained in problem solving and partnership building, resulting in the formation of meaningful partnerships. Other city agencies have been brought into the process to address quality-of-life issues. Beat officers work the same neighborhood and watch for one year to ensure they become a familiar presence in the community.[36]

According to a 1999 CAPS press release provided on the Northwestern University Web site, Chicago's program has made strides in involving the public in securing neighborhood safety. The majority of the city's population (79 percent) knows about the program, largely due to the TV campaign, and participation has been maintained in the communities that need it most. Though participation in community meetings appears low, those who do attend feel positive about the process. One criticism is that it appears to be the police who propose solutions to the problems rather than the community. Community policing training in the police department is ongoing, and progress has been made, but the department is looking to address the concerns and weaknesses in their program.[37]

Although most of the academic and professional writing about policing centers on our nation's big cities, many crime and disorder problems occur in small towns. Community-oriented policing strategies have also been directed toward these small towns. Consider the example of Sagamore Hills, Ohio, a small rural community with a population of 10,000 and a police department of 8 full-time and 11 part-time officers, who cover a jurisdiction of 16 square miles. The department transitioned to community policing in 1995.

The benefits of its community policing focus can be seen in the following results of a 1996 citizen perception survey:

- In 1995, 18 percent of the population surveyed stated they always felt safe, whereas in 1996, 53 percent stated the same.

- In 1995, 29 percent of the citizens reported that crime had increased. In 1996, only 9 percent reported that crime increased.

- In 1995, 26 percent of citizens reported knowing someone in Sagamore Hills who had been a victim of crime. In 1996, this dropped to 4 percent.[38]

According to a Sagamore Hills officer,

Before 1995, the department did little to squash rumors, inform citizens of arrests, or arrange meetings to discuss neighborhood problems. As the department transitioned to community policing, however, management recognized that giving citizens ownership in the process would instill a sense of stability and security.[39]

The Irvine, California, Police Department has built itself around the community policing philosophy since its inception in 1975. In 2002, the International Association of Chiefs of Police (IACP) recognized Irvine's efforts to promote safety in the community in response to some blatant gang-related violence it was experiencing. They initially found that the stakeholders in the youth violence issue in the city were more concerned with protecting themselves from blame than in working together to come up with solutions. In response they formed a Safe Community Task Force comprised of many community partners. They were charged with researching the issue of community safety and making recommendations for solutions.

The primary goals were to reduce the use of alcohol, tobacco, and drugs and the level of violence among youth; increase attendance in school; and ensure that all students feel connected to their school and their home. Many innovative programs were eventually developed. These included the IPD Youth Services Unit, a discrete youth crimes investigation unit to consistently be present around the schools; Operation Safe Campus, an interagency organization that regularly meets to discuss emerging trends and issues around school safety; Alternative to Suspension; a School Attendance Review Board; a High-Risk Youth Interagency Intervention Team; an interagency team to manage high-risk students; FOR Families, providing free information and short-term support to needy residents; Families Forward, serving families with a food bank program and transitional housing; Human Options, serving victims of domestic violence; Pennies for Prevention, collecting pennies in the schools to support prevention efforts; Pizza Night, designed to promote block parties throughout the community; Community Education, providing cross-training opportunities; and Youth Development, hosting teen forums.

Though prevention is difficult to measure, Irvine experienced a 39.8 percent decrease in violent crime in 2000–2001 and is a leader in developing partnerships to prevent problems.[40]

The Louisville, Kentucky, Division of Police was also recognized by the International Association of Chiefs of Police in 2002 for a community policing initiative they de-

PATROLLING THE WEB

International Association of Chiefs of Police award-winning programs
  www.theiacp.org

veloped to improve their success on calls involving mental illness. In consulting with mental health professionals in the community they developed a 24-hour proactive city-wide crisis intervention team based on a program in place in Memphis, Tennessee, composed of specially trained CIT officers. The primary objective of the program included increased training for all officers in the area of mental health issues and a reduction in the use of force as well as an increase in options involving less than lethal force in the handling of these calls.

The program seems to be successful; in the first quarter of 2002, CIT officers responded to 503 calls. Of those, 401 of these individuals were hospitalized for evaluation or treatment; 11 were charged with offenses; and force was used in only 3 cases, and that was "empty-hand control" only. The program continues to be closely monitored and evaluated by the CIT committee formed to implement a plan initially.[41]

The University of Vermont Department of Public Safety was also given recognition by IACP in 2002 for its community policing initiative, designed to address poor relations with students resulting in tension, lack of reporting of crime, and lack of trust. Their primary goal was to improve communications and work together with the students to solve the problems of the campus community. They appointed liaison officers for various groups and solicited input from the students, faculty, and staff via surveys regarding issues on the campus. Police Services also became more involved in university-wide staff development and training regarding safety issues. Evaluation continues, but initial survey results found that 57.4 percent of the campus community was either very satisfied or satisfied with Police Services.[42]

In Michigan City, Indiana, the police department has opened a substation in a poorer section of town in an attempt to improve their relationship with the community. The primary goal is education; the substation is equipped with computers, printers, a reading library, and Internet access. The secondary goals of providing a safe place for neighborhood children to study after school as well as improving police–community relations have also been met.[43] Youth from the neighborhood are routinely hanging out at the center and using the computers, and they have even brought their parents to the computer classes offered at the center.

Resident Officer Programs— The Ultimate in Community Policing?

Numerous initiatives generally known as **resident officer programs** have sprung up around the nation since the early 1990s. Key proponents of the programs, such as Elgin's Chief Gruber, believe resident officer programs capture the essence of community policing: improved relationships between police and their neighbors, who team together to fight crime and address quality-of-life conditions that contribute to crime.

Another strategy involved in community policing, as well as in strengthening police–community relations as discussed in Chapter 9, is outreach to the community. This police kiosk in San Francisco's Japan Center helps bring police services to the community as well as make officers more approachable.

YOU ARE THERE! >>

A Sample of Community Policing Programs in Kansas

- Handicapped parking enforcement
- Youth summer camps
- Ride-alongs
- Trading cards
- Police chief for a day
- Open house
- Rewarding good behavior
- Adopt-a-house
- Safety town
- Radio broadcasting
- Children's I.D.
- Print publications for youth
- Newsletters
- McGruff House
- Junior police academy
- Block watch

- Community surveys
- Police play day
- Solidarity marches
- Student youth forum
- Crime prevention unit
- Citizens police academy
- Sports competitions
- Crime line
- Training videos
- Bubblegum handouts
- Bicycle safety rodeos
- Bicycle patrols
- Safety incentive giveaways
- Leadership programs

Source: Adapted from Harvey Rachlin, "Creative Community Policing Programs," *Law and Order* (April 1997), pp. 24-34.

Elgin's ROPE program, which started in 1991 with three officers, grew to six officers by 1995. The ROPE officers, living in donated or subsidized homes or apartments, normally work an eight-hour day; but, for all practical purposes, they are on 24-hour-a-day call, because residents call them at all hours for assistance. In addition to a residence, the city provides the officers with utilities, a bicycle and squad car for patrol, an answering machine, and whatever expenses are necessary for special needs in the neighborhood. The officers decide on their own how to improve the quality of life in their neighborhood so residents can live without fear of drugs, gangs, prostitution, and crime, as long as their methods are legal, moral, and ethical.[44]

Generally, the stated term of an officer in the program is two years; however, most end up staying longer because of the bond that forms between the officers and residents. One officer reports, "When I first started, I'd go out in the morning and there'd be anonymous notes under my car's wipers, tipping me to crimes in the area. Now, people come up to me and tell me in person."[45]

The program's effectiveness can be seen by the change in answers to a survey distributed to one area's residents. When ROPE first started in the neighborhood, a question-

naire asked what problems concerned the residents. "Drugs and gangs" were the major problem then; two years later the same residents answered that loud stereos and speeding cars were now their biggest concerns.

Elgin's former chief Gruber reported that ROPE has made a tremendous difference for the better in targeted neighborhoods, helping to reduce violent crime by as much as 60 percent since its inception. He says of the officers,

> They're expected to work with the neighborhood to come up with solutions to problems, whether it's gangs, drugs or kids littering, working with public works to get new sidewalks, visiting schools or working with kids—whatever it takes. . . . They work whenever they need to work; they work for the neighborhood.[46]

The current Elgin chief of police, William Miller, continues to support this innovative program.

The Macon, Georgia, Police Department also implemented a resident officer program in 1995 in which officers agree to live in rent-free, city-owned housing in exchange for working with at-risk youths for 24 hours a month.[47]

© AP Photo/Alan Diaz

Bicycle patrol is a strategy that enhances community policing while at the same time effectively fights crime. It allows officers to get out in the community without the barrier of a car. It also allows officers to patrol in situations that might be difficult for motor vehicles.

According to their Web site, Macon's Youth Enrichment Service is a cooperative effort with the Economic and Community Development Department to place resident police officers in inner-city neighborhoods to serve as role models and mentors for at-risk youth between the ages of 10 and 14.

Columbia, South Carolina, has created resident officer programs by establishing the Police Homeowners Loan Program, which offers officers low-interest, no-money-down mortgages to buy houses in neighborhoods that have high crime rates or deterioration. The mortgages include renovation costs, so officers and their families can live in newly rehabilitated homes they otherwise might not have been able to afford. At the same time, the officers are a physical presence to deter crime. By 1992, seven police officers owned homes in high-crime and deteriorating neighborhoods as a result of the program, and in 1995 the number grew to 11.[48] By 2004, the Community Development Division reported that 26 officers wre involved in the program as its success continued to grow. Since the program's inception, Columbia has added take-home patrol cars for participating officers, and feedback from residents showed that the vehicles were definitely noticed. Former police chief and now city manager Charles Austin

reported in 1995 that there had been a decline in both major and minor crimes and that the program had helped bridge the communications gap between the police and the community.[49]

The city of Phoenix, Arizona, has initiated a Police Officer Placement Solutions (POPS) program. According to the police department Web site, the purpose of the POPS program is to enable the city to assist neighborhoods in recruiting police officers to become residents in their community. City leaders feel it will enhance the quality of life for all residents in the neighborhoods. The officers become familiar with the neighborhood and function as an avenue of communication as well as a deterrent to crime. The officers benefit with financial incentives regarding rent and utilities and the opportunity to drive a marked take-home police vehicle. The officers are expected to be good neighbors and act as resources for the community, with police service and 911 calls being handled by on-duty personnel. This program was started in 1993; in 2003 it was still going strong with guidelines for participation and application procedures available on the department's Web site.[50]

In 1997, New York City adopted a resident officer program. A limited number of two-bedroom apartments in New York City's public housing developments have been provided for up to 63 police officers and their families at an unbelievably low (for New York City) rents. In exchange for the reduced rent, the officers reside in the apartments and provide five hours a month of community service in addition to their normal police work. The new program leapfrogs police officers over an estimated 200,000 families now on the waiting list for public housing.[51]

In 1997, President Clinton came onto the resident officer bandwagon when he announced a plan to give 50 percent discounts to 2,000 police officers to buy federally foreclosed homes in 500 low-income neighborhoods nationwide. Participants must agree to live in the homes for at least three years. This program, called Officer Next Door, is part of a wide-ranging Urban Homestead Initiative designed to reduce crime and make low-income neighborhoods more attractive to homeowners.[52] In 2000, the Teacher Next Door program was added to this initiative; and, since both programs' inceptions, over 6,000 police officers and teachers in 41 states and the District of Columbia have purchased the homes. The programs were suspended for several months in 2001 after fraud and criminal convictions involving some of the participants. According to their Web site, the U.S. Department of Housing and Urban Development (HUD) has reopened their Officer Next Door and Teacher Next Door Programs after implementing corrective actions to eliminate abuse and allow these winning programs to continue to benefit and strengthen the communities involved.[53]

Other communities adopting resident officer programs include Alexandria, Virginia; Bloomington and Springfield, Illinois; Jackson, Michigan; and Waterloo, Iowa. Officials in these cities say that resident officers provide a high-profile presence that helps to prevent crime.[54]

Unfortunately, a resident officer program did not get off to such a good start in Denver, Colorado. The home of the first Denver police officer to move into a high-crime area under the program was burglarized. Thieves took the officer's computer, compact disks, and ski parka.[55]

★★★

THE FEDERAL GOVERNMENT AND COMMUNITY POLICING

In the 1992 presidential race, Bill Clinton championed the concept of community-oriented policing and promised to add 100,000 more police officers to the nation's streets. After the election, the federal government made tremendous contributions to the state of community policing strategies throughout the nation. This section will discuss the 1994 Crime Bill, the Department of Justice's Office of Community Oriented Policing Services, and the Community Policing Consortium.

The Crime Bill

After much political debate, the Violent Crime Control and Law Enforcement Act (the **Crime Bill**) was signed into law by President Clinton in 1994. The provisions of this bill authorized the expenditure of nearly $8 billion over six years for grants to law enforcement agencies to reduce crime.

Office of Community Oriented Policing Services (COPS)

As the research and evaluation arm of the Department of Justice, the National Institute of Justice (NIJ) has mounted a broad agenda to study changes in policing. In the wake of the passage of the Crime Bill, Attorney General Reno established the **Office of Community Oriented Policing Services (COPS)**.[56] The COPS office was established to

President Bill Clinton signing the 1994 Crime Bill. This bill provided federal grant money to police organizations seeking to expand their community policing efforts.

administer the grant money provided by the Crime Bill and to promote community-oriented policing.

The mission statement reflecting the values and goals of the COPS office reads

> We . . . dedicate ourselves, through partnerships with communities, policing agencies and other public and private organizations, to significantly improve the quality of life in neighborhoods and communities . . . by putting into practice the concepts of community policing in order to reduce levels of disorder, violence, and crime through the application of proven, effective programs and strategies.[57]

All indications are that progress is being made in the COPS mission. On the COPS home page, current U.S. Attorney General John Ashcroft states, "Since law enforcement agencies began partnering with citizens through community policing, we've seen significant drops in crime rates."

There are four primary goals of the program. These include increasing the numbers of officers on the street, encouraging partnerships between police and the community, promoting innovation in policing, and developing new technologies to help reduce crime and its consequences.[58]

COPS allocated the funds in three ways. The first was for three-year grants to hire police officers to work in community policing initiatives. The second method was to award grants for improved productivity through acquiring technology or hiring civilians to free up sworn-officer time, which could then be devoted to community policing activities. The third approach was to award grants to agencies for special programs attacking specific crime issues.[59] To maximize participation by the agencies that needed the resources and to facilitate the most equitable distribution of funds throughout the nation, the act establishing COPS required simplified application procedures and equal distribution of funds between jurisdictions with more and less than 150,000 population.

The COPS program appears to be a success. Though falling short of its original goal to put "100,000 new cops on the beat," it did greatly increase the numbers of police officers out in the field. In examining the data, it's estimated that in 2003 the level of policing on the street will increase by the equivalent of 62,700 to 83,900 full-time officers. (This includes the numbers of police officer hires and the full-time equivalents gained through increased productivity).[60] Additionally, though it is difficult to document, it is believed that the effort facilitated the growth of community policing in the country. Due to the fact that non–grant recipients also initiated community policing initiatives, it's difficult to conclusively link the two. It was

noted, however, that most departments were pleased with the simplified application process and the technical support available from the COPS office.

The COPS office has continued to expand its services over the years. Between 1994 and 2002, COPS awarded more than $9.4 billion in total to local, state, and tribal agencies, including over 31,000 grants to over 12,000 state and local law enforcement agencies.[61] COPS has supported other law enforcement community policing initiatives, including $10.9 million in antigang initiatives, $21.7 million in training since 1999 for "COPS in Schools," and $69.6 million for community policing initiatives to combat domestic violence. In March 2004, the COPS Web site announced that $20.7 million in grants had been awarded to hire 194 new police officers in schools across the nation.[62]

COPS is examining the character of police officers, including exploring changes in how law enforcement officers are recruited and hired through their program Hiring in the Spirit of Service, started in 2000. They've also allocated $35 million since 1997 through their Police Integrity Training Initiative.

In responding to issues deemed to be community problems, COPS has allocated financial backing to law enforcement agencies developing innovative community policing responses to problems created by methamphetamine, through grants that have reached $223 million since 1998. They believe that a strong relationship between law enforcement and the community can help to combat the methamphetamine problem.[63]

COPS also supports the Regional Community Policing Institutes (RCPIs), which consist of partnerships across a variety of police agencies, community groups, and organizations to create a delivery system for training police officers in community-oriented policing. By early 2003, over $93 million had been spent for training through COPS Regional Community Policing Institutes. This represents the training of over 209,000 officers and citizens across the country in community policing. There are over 30 RCPIs. Each RCPI develops innovative, region-specific curricula for community policing training as well as providing technical assistance opportunities for policing agencies and community members. The RCPI network is facilitating the growth of community policing throughout the United States.

Another program financed by COPS is the Police Corps. This program, which was allocated $20 million for fiscal year 1997, allows participants to receive a college education by providing up to $7,500 per academic year, with a per-student maximum of $30,000. Upon graduation with the baccalaureate degree, the student is obligated to serve four years with a police agency. Yet another program sponsored by COPS is Troops to Cops, in which former military personnel separating from active service, with some training and background in law enforcement, are trained as community-oriented policing officers. As of early 2003, $7.8 million had been spent in the Troops to Cops initiative.[64]

Showing its commitment to community policing and partnerships with the community, NIJ officials wrote in 1997:

> Policing is undergoing a broad and dramatic transformation. The strategic shift toward community-oriented policing and problem-solving strategies has changed the ways in which police departments organize themselves, the strategies that departments employ to combat crime and disorder, and the types of partnerships formed in order to enhance effectiveness.[65]

At the opening of the 2002 COPS National Conference, Attorney General John Ashcroft stated, "The responsibility to protect our community does not reside solely with law enforcement. It rests, as I have said before, in the hands of every American citizen . . . . (it) makes a difference when the citizens join in."[66]

COPS funding is helping to continue to encourage police–community partnerships. One successful program was developed in Phoenix, Arizona, to facilitate the collaborative partnership between the police and the citizens. The Phoenix Neighborhood Patrol (PNP) empowers neighborhood residents to be the eyes and ears of the Phoenix PD. The PNP participants receive eight hours of training in patrol procedures, observation skills, the 911 system, reporting techniques, confrontation avoidance, and safety practices. They also have the opportunity to ride along with a patrol officer. After this training, they are issued an identification card and an official shirt so they are easily identifiable in their community. They patrol their own community with which they're very familiar and report any suspicious activity to the police. Some have also been trained to patrol schools and shopping centers, as well as assist in finding missing persons and Alzheimer's patients. This program, in addition to others Phoenix has employed, has allowed officers and the residents to keep the lines of communication strong.

Utilizing a COPS methamphetamine grant, Salt Lake City established a task force involving over 30 government agencies working together to prevent the use and production of methamphetamine. One result of the initiative, the Drug Endangered Children Program (DEC), succeeded in changing the child endangerment statutes to better protect drug-exposed children.[67]

The COPS office continues to respond to the changing needs of law enforcement and the American community. After 9/11, they reassessed some of law enforcement's processes and decided to address the information-sharing aspect of law enforcement. They funded a project by the International Association of Chiefs of Police (IACP) to determine ways to improve information sharing between federal, state, local, and tribal law enforcement agencies. The result was a report entitled "Criminal Intelligence Sharing: A National Plan for Intelligence-Led Policing at the Local, State and Federal Levels." Among other things, the report recommends the creation of a Criminal Intelligence Coordinating Council (CICC) to help the Department of Homeland Security share criminal intelligence.[68] As COPS views community policing as a strong weapon in the fight against terror, they will continue to address the issue.

In viewing the success of the COPS program, the weak area appears to be the problem-solving and relationship-building initiatives.[69] Relationship building is somewhat dependent on the community and their willingness to participate in the process. In some communities, the residents have been reluctant or unable to participate. Problem solving as a methodology spans a wide continuum. Some departments are truly practicing problem solving as Goldstein defined it. In other agencies, problem solving may occur in name only as things are done in the same traditional law enforcement manner with some additional steps added.[70]

Community Mapping Planning and Analysis for Safety Strategies (COMPASS)

Community Mapping Planning and Analysis for Safety Strategies is a program initiated by the National Institute of Justice (NIJ) in partnership with other agencies in 1999. The other partners are the Bureau of Justice Assistance, Bureau of Justice Statistics, Executive Office for Weed and Seed, and the Office of Juvenile Justice and Delinquency Prevention and Community Oriented Policing Services. An additional key component of the COMPASS program is a research partner. COMPASS is a strategic approach to improving community safety. It is a data-driven approach for enhancing community safety through collaborative, proactive problem solving. There are four components to COMPASS:[71]

1. A collaborative policy group spanning various community interests to guide the initiative

2. A comprehensive wide-ranging data infrastructure consisting of data from many sources

3. Strategic analysis of the data to identify and target specific public safety problems

4. A research paper to analyze the information and provide feedback and documentation of the impacts and outcomes of the interventions

Community Policing Consortium

The **Community Policing Consortium** comprises five of the leading policing associations in the United States: the International Association of Chiefs of Police (IACP), the National Organization of Black Law Enforcement Executives (NOBLE), the National Sheriffs' Association (NSA), the

---

PATROLLING THE WEB

How to Really Learn about Community Policing

The Community Policing Consortium (Office of Community Oriented Policing Services, or COPS) has established its own Web site, loaded with community policing success stories, contact information, and upcoming events. Anyone interested can visit their Web site at:

   http://www.communitypolicing.org

You can also visit the Web site of COPS at
   http://www.cops.usdoj.gov
and obtain the latest information regarding community policing initiatives and programs. There you can link to issues of homeland security, training, funding, and resources, as well as grants announcements and applications to obtain federal funding. This is a valuable site to any organization wanting to research community policing ideas or obtain funding to implement their programs.

The Compass site,
   www.ojp.usdoj.gov/nij/compass
will provide information on their program as well as quarterly reports on the pilot projects currently underway in Seattle, Washington, and Milwaukee, Wisconsin.

Bonnie Bucqueroux, who spent almost a decade as associate director of the National Center for Community Policing, working closely with the late Dr. Robert Trojanowicz, created a Web site devoted to community policing that has a discussion forum and articles of interest as well as links to other sites:

   http://policing.com

Police Executive Research Forum (PERF), and the Police Foundation. The consortium, funded by COPS, issues a bimonthly publication, *Community Policing Exchange,* dedicated to reporting the newest developments in community policing partnerships.

Its statement of purpose reads, "*Community Policing Exchange* strives to assist law enforcement practitioners in bridging the distance between communities, facilitating the exchange of information, and giving voice to all involved in the implementation of community policing."[72]

The Community Policing Consortium maintains a Web site providing information and links regarding community policing. Its primary mission is to deliver community policing training and technical assistance to police departments and sheriff's offices that are designated COPS grantees. The Web site provides information, resources, tools, publications, and a chat room regarding community policing.

The Community Policing Consortium also publishes *Sheriff Times* and the *Community Policing Information Access Guide,* as well as *Community Policing Exchange* and *Community Links.* These publications highlight various programs around the nation, promoting an exchange of information and sharing of ideas. A recent issue of *Community Links* described a successful program being implemented in California. The Santa Ana Police Department is assisting the University of California–Irvine in teaching medical students and family medicine physicians about domestic violence. This supplements a family violence emergency response team, in place for 10 years, in which victim advocates respond with police officers to domestic violence calls. Since 1999, medical students are required to ride with the Family Violence Emergency Response Team. It's been found that this program provides insight for the medical personnel into the cycle of violence, increased awareness when they go into practice for medical personnel, and improved screening for victims seeking medical treatment.[73]

★ ★ ★

SOME ACCOMPLISHMENTS OF COMMUNITY POLICING

As reports of overall crime rate decreases hit the presses in the mid- and late 1990s, some police officials associated this decrease to closer relationships with their communities through community policing, as well as the addition of new community policing officers.[74] Some examples:

- Fort Worth, Texas, police attribute a 7 percent decrease in overall crime and a 50 percent drop in homicides to a closer relationship between the department and the community: "There's an unended line of communication between the police department and the citizens. . . . [They are] more aware about crime prevention efforts—what they can do to harden targets, get involved and keep an eye out for their neighbors."[75] Fort Worth police say that constituents are treated as equal players in the fight against crime and cite the city's successful Citizens on Patrol program, a recent auxiliary police innovation. Program participants are issued police radios and patrol neighborhoods in specially designated vehicles. Police report that this program has had a major impact on property crimes, such as larceny and burglary. Also, residents have approved a special sales tax that will provide the police department with an additional $25 million a year, earmarked for equipment and personnel.

- Wichita, Kansas, police also attribute an 11 percent decease in crime to community policing. "It's a whole different mindset toward problem-solving and that in itself can have a dramatic impact on how we serve the community."[76]

- Los Angeles police attribute a 4 percent crime decline to police–community participation. "There truly is a significant partnership with the community, with a lot more emphasis on problem-solving than there has been in the past. We'd like to believe that's at the root of these reductions."[77]

- Responding to the third decrease in crime in as many years, police officials in Baton Rouge, Louisiana, gave much of the credit to the community. "Community organizations and civic groups have come out of the woodwork in the last few years. All of that has made a difference."[78]

- Denver, Colorado, police officials, noting a 13 percent decrease in crime, said, "When the neighborhood takes stock in their community and they're serious they don't want crime, then you start to see crime go down."[79]

- Police officials in Austin, Texas, also credit increased citizen involvement with the community for a 23 percent drop in crime. Residents and police also reclaimed a city park that had become a haven for drug deals. The police chief reported that she had many people coming up to her and shaking her hand to thank her for giving them back their park.

- New Orleans police reported that a community policing plan had helped cut the murder rate by 18 percent. In three public housing developments, where police deployed community oriented police teams, homicide dropped by 83 percent.[80]

Although many attribute crime reduction to community policing strategies, many do not. Some believe that these new philosophies are merely rhetoric. Many others attribute the drastic decrease in crime rates in the mid- and late 1990s to more aggressive, strategic, and legalistic law enforcement, similar to that practiced in New York City and other metropolitan areas, as discussed in Chapter 1.

★ ★ ★

NOT ALL AGREE WITH COMMUNITY POLICING

Not all community policing efforts have been successful. A study of community constables in England found that the constables actually spent very little of their time in direct contact with citizens, despite role expectations that emphasized community contact.[81] Research on the effectiveness of community-oriented policing has yielded mixed results. Foot patrol seems to make citizens feel safer, but it may not have much of an effect on the actual amount of crime.[82]

Many experts are not overly enthusiastic over the idea of community policing. Jack Greene and Steve Mastrofski are among those who argue that the most significant problem in community policing is to define what is meant by *community*. They found that in most community policing projects, the concept of community is defined in terms of "administrative areas" traditionally used by police departments to allocate patrols, instead of in terms of "ecological areas" defined by common norms, shared values, and interpersonal bonds. Greene and Mastrofski find this to be a very significant problem, because a major goal of community policing is to activate a community's norms and other methods of social control. If the police are using administrative areas instead of ecological areas, the authors say, they lose what they should be trying to get.[83]

Robert Sheehan and Gary W. Cordner tell us how some police may define community differently: "For the working police officer, the community generates police activity (law violations and calls for service) and provides the setting within which police work must be performed. For the police executive, the community represents a source of both support and complaints and most importantly, is the final arbiter of the quality of police services and the effectiveness of the police department."[84]

Additionally, many feel that community policing can actually have a negative effect on certain people. An analysis of a victim callback program established by the Houston Police Department found that the program, which was originally designed to help victims, had a generally negative effect on some minority groups (Asian Americans and Hispanic Americans), whose members may have been suspicious of the department's intentions.[85]

Also, an audit of the Houston Police Department by a consulting firm criticized the department's neighborhood-oriented policing (NOP) approach. It concluded that although "well-conceived," NOP faced a number of difficulties and had not produced any comprehensive improvements in police services. The report acknowledged that NOP has the potential to enhance the quality of police services without adding costs but claimed that the Houston program did not have tangible effects on citizens' security and quality of life. The report said that the program, which had been implemented at the expense of more proactive law enforcement functions, such as arresting criminals, had resulted in mediocre performance in response time to emergency calls for service.[86]

According to Schobel, Evans, and Daly, the empirical evidence for community policing's effectiveness in solving the crime problem is both limited and contradictory.[87] Other researchers admit there are a number of documented successes of community policing programs, but there is also an indication that community policing may serve to displace crime. Indeed, several studies indicate there has been an increase in crime in the areas surrounding the community policing impact area.[88]

The debate continues to rage regarding community policing, even among officials of the same agency. Take, for example, the following statements by current and former members of the Baltimore County Police Department.

Kevin Novak, department spokesperson, comments

> You put 10 people in a room you'll get 20 different definitions. Each one is torn between at least two. . . . There are some areas where it's really not completely applicable. . . . Some things, like the widespread armed-robbery problem we had earlier this year, are best handled through traditional enforcement—using informants, conducting aggressive patrol and enforcement strategies—and that's what we did.[89]

Captain James Johnson, patrol commander of a high-crime Baltimore precinct, has said

> [The effectiveness of community policing] really depends on how you define community policing. That's part of the problem. Academics and practitioners can't agree, and there's no

agreement among police leaders in America today over what it really is. . . . Part of the problem for the line officer is that there's this nebulous terminology . . . and this makes it very clouded and obscure.[90]

Neil Behan, former police chief who led the department when it adopted the community-based policing philosophy in 1982, disagrees with the others and says community policing has had a concrete definition from the beginning:

> Community policing is a partnership with the community to improve the quality of life. What the Captain does not understand is that community policing never rejected traditional policing. It is an enhancement of traditional policing—sometimes in a different direction—but it never abandoned traditional policing.[91]

Present Baltimore Chief Terrence B. Sheridan, who has questioned the wisdom of some current practices involving community policing, has abandoned some of its policies in favor of more "enforcement-directed" policing. However, as of 2004, he continued to express the department's commitment to community-oriented policing on the department's Web page.[92]

Researchers traveled to St. Petersburg, Florida to observe changes occurring in police roles and police–community relations after the implementation of community policing. They found that the citizens seemed satisfied with community policing, as well as finding high levels of cooperation in everyday police–citizen contact; they found that 85 percent of those interviewed were "very" or "somewhat" satisfied with neighborhood policing services.[93] The department seems to be attaining their goal of high visibility as approximately one-third of those surveyed said they had seen the police in the previous 24 hours. Of more interest, they found that the perception of police officers toward community policing had improved, although they noted distinctions between community policing officers and road officers. Generally, community policing officers were more supportive of the importance of assisting citizens and enforcing minor laws than were the officers handling calls for service. An interesting finding was that, among all the police officers, a still rather high 25 percent said they have reason to distrust most citizens.[94]

An initial concern in the early stages of the COPS grants was whether departments would permanently retain the police officers hired through the grants and absorb the costs locally. In September 1997 it was reported that the first cycle of U.S. Justice Department grants, begun in 1994 and mentioned earlier in this chapter, were coming to a close. This would require agencies throughout the nation to fund all of the new officers added since the 1994 Crime Bill without the help of the federal government, which had been funding 75 percent of the cost. It was reported that local officials might be tempted to scrap community policing programs or shift officers around in order to avoid retaining COPS hires.[95]

This fear seems to be unfounded. At the time of this writing, 98 percent of respondents indicated they had kept the COPS-funded officers or quickly filled any vacancies that arose. Additionally, 95 percent reported that the officers were or would be part of the department's budget by time grant funding ended.[96] But some departments are experiencing hurdles in this area. As an example of problems now being faced by departments, consider the example of Toledo, Ohio. The city was originally awarded $10 million to add 125 new officers to its police department but refused some of the money and hired fewer officers. According to its police chief,

> All of a sudden, they [the federal government] gave us 75 officers in one crack, for a total award of $5.6 million. The cost for one officer in Toledo, with benefits, is $150,000. The city has to match $75,000, and that $5.5 million bill has come out of the general fund. There's no way we can fund that.[97]

Toledo is not alone. According to the chief of the South Pasadena, California, Police Department, "Every police chief I've talked to is worried about how to keep the officers hired with Federal money once the grant runs out."[98]

The debate continues.

★ ★ ★

THE FUTURE, TERRORISM, AND COMMUNITY POLICING

Though the debate continues, research continues to add to the literature, and police administrators are looking to using the community policing philosophy to address new issues that arise. Though more time may be needed to examine the initiatives more closely and over longer periods of time, some preliminary research has indicated success. The State of California has conducted statewide research in an effort to answer the big question, "Does community policing work at reducing the crime rate?" Their results indicate that "broken windows" law enforcement strategies can be effective in reducing more serious crime and agencies that are exploring the issue can be reassured that these strategies are likely to work.[99]

As issues are recognized as community concerns, law enforcement agencies are looking to the community polic-

---

PATROLLING THE WEB

There are many sites on the Internet with information on community policing. In addition to the previously mentioned sites, community policing information can also be obtained at:

"Community Policing Pages" dedicated to continuing the work of Robert C. Trojanowicz
   www.concentric.net/~dwoods/

Police Executive Research Forum
   www.policeforum.org

International Association of Crime Analysts
   www.iaca.net

Michigan State University School of Criminal Justice
   www.cj.msu.edu

National Institute of Justice "COMPASS" Community Mapping Planning and Analysis for Safety Strategies
   www.ojp.usdoj.gov/nij/compass

Center for Court Innovation—section on problem-solving courts
   www.courtinnovation.org/

West Chicago Police Department problem-oriented policing
   www.westchicago.org

SUNY Albany School of Criminal Justice
   www.albany.edu/scj

John Jay College of Criminal Justice
   www.jjay.cuny.edu

---

ing philosophy to devise ways to successfully address these issues. Domestic violence is one such issue. The Santa Ana, California, police department has developed an initiative in this area, working closely with medical students to increase the awareness of the problem. In addition, better police–community relationships and more familiarity between residents and their neighborhood police officer might bring the problem out in the open.[100] Victims of domestic violence might be more likely to report incidents if they feel they can trust their police department. Those who believe they will be treated with sensitivity and respect will be more likely to come forward with their problems. According to an article in *Community Policing and Domestic Violence,* sharing information with the community may involve going to laundromats or country clubs to reach people. A community policing officer would know his or her neighborhood and how to best reach the people that need the information. An officer trained in the philosophy of community policing will work with other agencies to best solve the underlying issues in the domestic violence calls handled and consequently build a strategy toward addressing the problem and breaking the cycle of violence.[101]

The philosophy of community policing has been viewed in such favorable light that communities are expanding the idea to the area of city or government services and to the entire criminal justice system.

The community policing Web site, www.policing.com (see the "Patrolling the Web" box on page 244), encourages an integrated criminal justice system working as a whole to benefit the community. It is compared to the medical model, where the citizen shares the responsibility for quality of life in the community as the patient bears some responsibility for his or her good health. The criminal justice system working together with the community, as doctors work together with their patients in the holistic approach, emphasizes prevention and early response to minimize the escalation of problems.

Many municipal and county governments are also using the philosophy of community policing to encourage citizen participation in governmental services and in solving problems in the community. Many have expanded their "mini-police stations" in the community into mini–city halls to bring services to the citizens and open up the lines of communication. Citizens seem to be receptive to and appreciative of this concept.

As mentioned earlier, many police departments and governments are posting their values and mission statements on their Web pages. The community policing philosophy is explained to the residents, and participation is encouraged. The Web site for the Grand Rapids, Michigan, Police Department includes the department's *Five-Year Strategic Plan to Implement Community Policing as Part of Community-Oriented Government*. Included in this plan are a brief history, definitions, mission statement, core values, vision, and goals of the plan. Given access to this information, residents can truly be partners in this strategic plan.

Since 9/11, there has been an increased effort by some to get back to essential police services. Budget dollars are at a premium and "extra" programs may be viewed as nonessential. Some feel that by going back to more traditional law enforcement with more militaristic tactics is the only way to fight the war on terror.

In examining the events leading up to 9/11 and in an effort to prevent these types of informational gaps from happening in the future, community policing could fill a vital role. In an article posted on the COPS Web site, "Community Policing: Now More Than Ever," Rob Chapman and Matthew Scheider illustrate the strengths of community policing and how they would prove beneficial in the war on terror.

One of the primary goals would be the prevention of terrorist acts. Through partnerships with other agencies and the community, "hard" and "soft" targets can be identified, vulnerability assessed, and responses planned. Additionally, with established, positive, trusting relationships, members of the community will be more likely to come forward with good intelligence information allowing law enforcement to "connect the dots" before it is too late.[102]

If such an incident were to occur again, knowing the community and neighborhood would prove beneficial. Community leaders—possibly already CERT trained (discussed in Chapter 9)—could be called upon to assist with response. Previous relationships and knowledge of the neighborhood would facilitate response. Additionally, police officers used to making decisions and not having to rely on superiors to make decisions would be an advantage in a crisis situation where events are unfolding, communication challenged, and innovative responses needed.[103]

CHAPTER SUMMARY

The face of policing has changed dramatically. Community policing and problem-solving policing have been practiced for over one decade, and some say it has been tremendously popular and successful. Others have disagreed. The debate continues, and that is good for policing.

This chapter discussed three corporate strategies for modern policing, including strategic policing, community policing, and problem-solving policing. It discussed the underlying philosophy and genesis of community policing and problem-solving policing and then discussed how these strategies are designed to work.

The chapter then focused on numerous ways of implementing community-oriented policing and focused on one particular strategy, the resident officer program.

The chapter also discussed the federal government and its current role in community policing, including the 1994 Crime Bill, the Office of Community Oriented Policing Services, and the Community Policing Consortium. It discussed some empirical and anecdotal evidence of the benefits of COPS but also showed how some scholars and practitioners do not agree with community policing strategies.

Despite many recent innovations in police departments throughout the United States, many problems still remain. There is much evidence that not all police officers are ready to accept new images of police work. Some researchers have warned that the police subculture is so committed to the traditional ways of policing that efforts to change it can demoralize an entire department, making the department ineffective in doing its basic tasks.[104] Some researchers of the police subculture warn that police departments will not become effective until the values of the average police officer match the formal values espoused by today's innovative police administrators.[105] It is hoped that our exploration of these issues will continue to add to the debate.

Learning Check

1. Define community policing and problem-solving policing and give three actual examples of each.

2. Discuss the importance of the research of scholars James Q. Wilson and George Kelling to the concept of community policing.

3. Discuss the contributions of Herman Goldstein to the concept of problem-solving policing.

4. Define a resident officer program and give three actual examples.

5. Name three of the programs administered and supported by the Office of Community Oriented Policing Services (COPS) of the U.S. Department of Justice and discuss them.

Application Exercise

After you receive your degree in criminal justice, you are hired by the Littletown Police Department as an assistant and consultant to the police chief. Littletown has no major crime problem, but residents of the town's only public housing development are constantly complaining about youths who loiter in and around their buildings, causing noise and disorder problems, such as littering and fighting.

The chief tells you that she is thinking about ways to improve her department. She says she read an article once about broken windows, but does not remember it. Based on your reading of this chapter, what would you tell the police chief?

Web Exercise

Visit the COPS Web site and find out what the Regional Community Policing Institute (RCPI) that your state belongs to is planning. Is their any specific training going on related to community problems in your state? Then visit a police department and note what programs they are using to further their community policing efforts.

Key Concepts

"Broken windows" model
Community policing
Community Policing Consortium
Corporate strategies for policing
Crime Bill of 1994
Office of Community Oriented Policing Services (COPS)
Problem-solving policing
Resident officer programs

CHAPTER

11   Police and the Law

CHAPTER OUTLINE

Crime in the United States
  How Do We Measure Crime?
  How Much Crime Occurs in the United States?
  Arrests in the United States
The Police and the U.S. Constitution
  The Bill of Rights and the Fourteenth Amendment
  The Role of the Supreme Court in Regulating the
    Police
  The Exclusionary Rule
  Impact of the Exclusionary Rule on the Police
The Police and Arrest
  Probable Cause
  Reasonable and Deadly Force in Making Arrests
  Stopping Vehicles
The Police and Search and Seizure
  The Warrant Requirement and the Search Warrant
  Exceptions to the Warrant Requirement
The Police and Custodial Interrogation
  The Path to *Miranda*
  The *Miranda* Ruling
  The Erosion of *Miranda*
  The *Dickerson* Ruling and Beyond
  Surreptitious Recording of Suspects' Conversations
The Police and Identification Procedures
  Lineups, Showups, and Photo Arrays
  Other Identification Procedures

CHAPTER GOALS

- To acquaint you with the amount and type of crime in the United States, as well as the number and type of arrests made by the police
- To apprise you of the role of the Bill of Rights and the U.S. Supreme Court in regulating the actions of the police
- To explain the role of the police in making arrests, searching people and places, and stopping automobiles
- To make you aware, through the exploration of case law, of the changing philosophy of the U.S. Supreme Court in areas regarding search and seizure, custodial interrogation, and identification procedures
- To make you aware, through the exploration of case law, of current standard police procedures in search and seizure, custodial interrogation, and identification procedures

When people think about the police, they generally think about the power of the police to arrest someone, about the power of the police to issue a citation for driving violations, or about some other enforcement activity. People think of the police in terms of the law. As this text has shown, the police do much more than enforce the law. But, although the police role is not limited to law enforcement, that is definitely a major part of the police role.

This chapter will discuss the amount and types of crime in the United States, along with the amount and types of arrests made by the police. It will also discuss the U.S. Constitution and its first ten amendments, the Bill of Rights, focusing on the relationship between the police and the Bill of Rights as interpreted by the U.S. Supreme Court over the years. It will explore significant areas of police power, including the power to arrest people, to stop people and inquire as to their conduct, to search people and places and seize property, and to question people about their participation in a crime. Landmark Supreme Court cases will be used to show how the police have altered their procedures to comply with the provisions of the U.S. Constitution. The chapter provides the fact pattern behind some of the cases. A fact pattern is the events in a criminal case that led to the arrest, as well as the facts of the investigation and arrest. The fact pattern is considered by the courts in adjudicating a case. Reading these fact patterns will help you see that law is not abstract principles but rather the result of personal and dynamic events.

This chapter is perhaps the most important one in this text. The role of the police is a very special one in our society. The police enforce the law. When enforcing the law, they sometimes have to arrest people. By arresting people, the police take away what Americans value most highly— their freedom and their liberty. The police must know the law and must apply it correctly.

★ ★ ★

CRIME IN THE UNITED STATES

Crime is part of life in the United States. We read about crime in our newspapers, and often details of the crimes are the lead stories on our television news broadcasts. The following sections will discuss how we measure crime in the United States, how much crime occurs, and how many arrests are made.

How Do We Measure Crime?

Two major methods are used to measure crime in the United States. They are (1) the Uniform Crime Reports and (2) the National Crime Victimization Survey.

UNIFORM CRIME REPORTS   The **Uniform Crime Reports (UCR)** are collected and published by the FBI based on reports of crimes made to the police across the United States. The FBI publishes a yearly report, *Crime in the United States,* based on all reports made to the police for the year and forwarded to the FBI. The Uniform Crime Reports have four major sections, the Crime Index, Crime Index Offenses Cleared, Persons Arrested, and Law Enforcement Personnel.

The FBI's Crime Index consists of data regarding the major Index crimes (murder and nonnegligent manslaughter, forcible rape, robbery, aggravated assault, burglary, larceny-theft, motor vehicle theft, and arson). The Crime Index section of the yearly Uniform Crime Reports generally comprises several hundred pages of tables and graphs regarding the Index crimes. Included on these pages are five-year analyses of each of the crimes, using numerous variables, such as the relationship between perpetrator and victim; weapons used; age, race, and gender; crime trends; and crime rates for all offenses reported to the police for the previous year for each of the reporting cities, towns, universities/colleges, and suburban and rural counties.

The Crime Index Offenses Cleared section lists the clearance rates (rates of crimes solved by arrest) for the Index crimes according to certain variables, such as population group and geographic region of the country.

The section on Persons Arrested lists all arrests in the United States for the Index crimes and other crimes according to certain variables. These include geographic area, age, race, and gender.

The Law Enforcement Personnel section lists the number of all uniformed and civilian law enforcement employees for each reporting town, city, and county.

Prior to 1972, the Uniform Crime Reports were the only nationwide measure of crime in the United States. Scholars, however, became skeptical of the crime report data in the Uniform Crime Reports because they

PATROLLING THE WEB

Uniform Crime Reports
   http://www.fbi.gov/ucr/ucr.htm
National Crime Victimization Survey
   http://www.ojp.usdoj.gov.bjs

were based solely on reports made to the police and did not recognize the fact that many crimes are not reported to the police. To get a truer account of crime, the National Crime Victimization Survey was started.

NATIONAL CRIME VICTIM-IZATION SURVEY   The **National Crime Victimization Survey (NCVS)** is prepared by the National Institute of Justice (NIJ), the research arm of the U.S. Department of Justice. The National Crime Victimization Survey, as the name implies, is a survey of a random sample of U.S. households, asking them if a crime was committed against anyone in the household during the prior six months. It also asks certain questions about the incident. Data from the NCVS is published by the NIJ yearly as *Criminal Victimization in the United States*. The NIJ also issues periodic reports regarding trends in particular crimes.

How Much Crime Occurs in the United States?

Crime information for the latest year available for each of the Index crimes is shown in Table 11.1. The data in the Uniform Crime Reports are easy to read. For example, when we look at the figures for murder and nonnegligent manslaughter, we see that there were 16,204 murders, which amounts to 5.6 murders for every 100,000 Americans.

The other crime measure, the National Crime Victimization Survey, reports the crime data shown in Table 11.2. Notice that the number of incidents for each crime is quite different in the two reports. The UCR data only include incidents actually reported to the police, whereas the NCVS data are based on results of interviews with people, many of whom did not report their criminal victimization to the police. Note that the figures for motor vehicle theft (auto larceny) are closest in both reports. This is because most people in the United States are covered by automobile insurance and thus report an

Table 11.1	Uniform Crime Reports Data, 2002	
Index Crime	Number of Crimes	Per 100,000 Inhabitants
Murder and nonnegligent manslaughter	16,204	5.6
Forcible rape	95,136	33.0
Robbery	420,637	145.9
Aggravated assault	894,348	310.1
Burglary	2,151,875	746.2
Larceny	7,052,922	2,445.8
Motor vehicle theft	1,246,096	432.1

Source: Federal Bureau of Investigation, *Uniform Crime Reports, 2002,* at http://www.fbi.com, 4/1/2004

automobile theft to the police in order to make a claim with their insurance company.

Arrests in the United States

For the latest reporting year, the U.S. police made about 14 million arrests a year for all criminal infractions except traffic violations. About 2.2 million of these arrests were for the FBI's Index or Part 1 crimes. Of these crimes about 621,000 were for violent crimes (murder, forcible rape, robbery, and aggravated assault) and about 1.6 million were for property crimes (burglary, larceny/theft, motor vehicle theft, and arson. (See Exhibit 11.1.)

The remaining 11.77 million arrests were for various other offenses. The major categories of these arrests and their approximate totals were misdemeanor assaults, 1.3 million; drug abuse violations, 1.5 million; driving under the influence, 1.5 million; and liquor-related disorderly conduct, vagrancy, and loitering, 1.9 million.[1]

Table 11.2	National Crime Victimization Survey Data	
Crime	Number of Victimizations	Victimization Rate per 1,000 Households
Violent crimes	5,341,410	23.1
Rape/sexual assault	247,730	1.1
Robbery	512,490	2.2
Aggravated assault	999,110	4.3
Simple assault	3,591,090	15.5
Property crimes	17,539,220	159.0
Household burglary	3,055,720	27.7
Motor vehicle theft	988,760	9.0
Theft	13,494,750	122.3

Source: Adapted from Callie Marie Rennison and Michael R. Rand, *Criminal Victimization, 2002* (Washington, DC: Bureau of Justice Statistics, 2003), p. 2.

Exhibit 11.1	Crime Clock, 2002

Every 2.7 seconds, one Crime Index offense

Every 22.1 seconds, one violent crime
    Every 35.3 seconds, one aggravated assault
    Every 1.2 minutes, one robbery
    Every 5.5 minutes, one forcible rape
    Every 32.4 minutes, one murder

Every 3.0 seconds, one property crime
    Every 4.5 seconds, one larceny-theft
    Every 14.7 seconds, one burglary
    Every 25.3 seconds, one motor vehicle theft

Note: The crime clock is designed to convey the annual reported crime experience by showing the relative frequency of the index offences. This mode of display should not be taken to imply a regularity in the commission of the Part I offenses; rather, it represents the annual ratio of Part I offenses to fixed time intervals.

THE POLICE AND THE THE U.S. CONSTITUTION

The United States is a nation governed by law. The primary law regulating life in the United States is the U.S. Constitution, including its many amendments. The following sections will discuss the first ten amendments to the Constitution (the Bill of Rights), the Fourteenth Amendment, the role of the U.S. Supreme Court in regulating the police, and the exclusionary rule and its impact on the police.

It must be remembered that the U.S. Constitution is a continuing, dynamic document constantly being reviewed by the United States Supreme Court. This chapter discusses hundreds of Supreme Court decisions, "landmark cases," which have affected the police and the entire criminal justice system, as well as our society. As this judicial review process of the Court is constantly reinterpreting the Constitution and constantly changing the rules that govern police behavior, all officers must constantly review their own organization's rules and directives with the realization that the law is always changing.

The Bill of Rights and the Fourteenth Amendment

The U.S. criminal justice system is based on the Bill of Rights, the first ten amendments to the U.S. Constitution. Five of the first ten amendments specifically address freedoms or rights that people possess when involved with the criminal justice system. See Exhibit 11.2 for the amendments that specifically affect the U.S. criminal justice system.

To understand the U.S. system of criminal justice, we must go back to the birth of the United States. The early colonists came to escape persecution by the English king and to seek freedom. The colonists, however, continued to be persecuted and to be denied freedom. They rebelled, wrote the Declaration of Independence, fought for independence from England, and were able to defeat the British troops. As newly freed people, the former colonists wrote the U.S. Constitution to govern themselves. They then wrote the first ten amendments to the Constitution, which form the basis of our criminal justice system—the rights and freedoms we possess that can be used against government tyranny.

The Fourteenth Amendment also has an effect on the U.S. criminal justice system. The Supreme Court, over the years, has extended the Bill of Rights to the states through the due process clause of the Fourteenth Amendment. The due process clause is that section of the Fourteenth Amendment that protects all citizens of the United States against any state depriving them of life, liberty, or property except through the proper legal processes guaranteed by the U.S. Constitution. The section has been the vehicle through which much of the Bill of Rights has been interpreted to apply to state courts as well as federal courts.

PATROLLING THE WEB

The Constitution of the United States
    http://www.law.cornell.edu/constitution/
    constitution.overview.html
Supreme Court of the United States
    http://www.supremecourtus.gov
Supreme Court Cases
    http://supct.law.cornell.edu/supct/
American Bar Association
    http://www.abanet.org
Cornell Law School—Legal Information Institute
    http://www.law.cornell.edu/lii.html
Law.Com
    http://www.law.com
RefDesk.com—Legal Resources
    http://www.refdesk.com/factlaw.html

Exhibit 11.2　U.S. Constitution: Amendments Governing the U.S. Criminal Justice System

First Amendment
Congress shall make no law respecting an establishment of religion, or prohibiting the free exercise thereof; or abridging the freedom of speech, or of the press; or the right of the people peaceably to assemble, and to petition the government for a redress of grievances.

Fourth Amendment
The right of the people to be secure in their persons, houses, papers, and effects against unreasonable searches and seizures, shall not be violated, and no warrants shall issue, but upon probable cause, supported by oath or affirmation, and particularly describing the place to be searched, and the persons or things to be seized.

Fifth Amendment
No person shall be held to answer for a capital, or otherwise infamous crime, unless on a presentment or indictment of a grand jury, except in cases arising in the land or naval forces, or in the militia, when in actual service in time of war or public danger; nor shall any person be subject for the same offense to be twice put in jeopardy of life or limb; nor shall be compelled in any criminal case to be a witness, against himself, nor be deprived of life, liberty, or property, without due process of law; nor shall private property be taken for public use, without just compensation.

Sixth Amendment
In all criminal prosecutions, the accused shall enjoy the right to a speedy and public trial, by an impartial jury of the State and district wherein the crime shall have been committed, which district shall have been previously ascertained by law, and to be informed of the nature and cause of the accusation; to be confronted with the witnesses against him; to have compulsory process for obtaining witnesses in his favor, and to have the assistance of counsel for his defense.

Eighth Amendment
Excessive bail shall not be required, nor excessive fines imposed, nor cruel and unusual punishments inflicted.

Fourteenth Amendment (Section 1)
All persons born or naturalized in the United States and subject to the jurisdiction thereof, are citizens of the United States and of the State wherein they reside. No State shall make or enforce any law which shall abridge the privileges or immunities of citizens of the United States; nor shall any State deprive any person of life, liberty, or property, without due process of law; nor deny to any person within its jurisdiction the equal protection of the laws.

The Role of the Supreme Court in Regulating the Police

The U.S. Supreme Court, through its policy of **judicial review,** has made a significant impact on the way the police do their job. As early as 1914, in *Weeks* v. *United States,* the Court influenced the police by regulating how they should conduct their searches and seizures.[2] In 1936, in *Brown* v. *Mississippi,* the Court began to affect the police by ruling certain methods of police interrogation unconstitutional.[3]

Most Supreme Court cases regarding criminal justice try to strike a balance between the rights of the individual and the rights of society. But what do we mean by the rights of the individual and the rights of society? A simple example, which could have occurred today in your classroom, might explain it. You and your fellow students want a safe classroom. You do not want a student walking into class with an illegal gun that could be used to shoot you (rights of society). However, which of you would like the police to be at the classroom door each morning searching you for illegal guns without just cause (rights of the individual)?

The Supreme Court has the difficult task of bringing balance between these two often-conflicting goals. There is an inherent inconsistency between protecting the rights of the in-

dividual and the rights of society. To have unlimited individual rights risks the chance of limiting the rights of society to be safe from crime. To have unlimited rights of society to be safe from crime risks giving up individual rights. It falls upon the Supreme Court to balance these two precious rights.

In police matters, the Supreme Court hears cases, on appeal, from people who have been the subject of police actions, including arrest, search and seizure, and custodial interrogation. The justices then decide whether or not the police action violated the person's constitutional rights. In most cases, they do this by interpreting one of the amendments to the Constitution. Supreme Court decisions can bring about changes in police procedures. Certain significant cases, such as *Mapp* v. *Ohio* and *Miranda* v. *Arizona,* are known as landmark cases.[4] The major method used by the Supreme Court to ensure that

Table 11.3	Landmark Supreme Court Decisions: Exclusionary Rule in Police Search and Seizure Cases
Case	Decision
Weeks v. *United States*	Exclusionary rule applies to federal law enforcement agents
Rochin v. *California*	Exclusionary rule applies in shocking cases
Mapp v. *Ohio*	Exclusionary rule applies to all law enforcement agents

Dempsey's Law

Law Is History—Know Your Facts

Professor Dempsey, I know we have to know the law, but I don't understand why we have to know the specific cases. Like Mapp v. Ohio—*that was in 1961; that's ancient history! Why don't you just tell us that the police can't make an unreasonable search of a dude's house? And* Terry v. Ohio—*that was 1969. Why do we have to know the fact pattern, as you call it? Can't we just know that cops can make stops and frisks under certain circumstances?*

Those are good questions, John. There are several reasons why I insist that you know the fact patterns of cases, not just specific principles of law, to which you seem to be referring.

First, I want you to know that the law is not mere theory or the application of reason to problems. U.S. law is as much history as it is reason and logic. As you know, I frequently paraphrase Justice Oliver Wendell Holmes in class by saying that there is more law in a page of history than in a volume of logic. This means that the law is dynamic. It changes over time, and it changes because it is responsive to the thoughts, feelings, and needs of society.

Second, I want you to know that the law—specifically, case law—is based on real experiences of real people. (Case law is the body of law that results from court interpretations of statutory law—law written by the legislative or executive branch of the government—or from court decisions, where rules have not been fully codified or have been found to be vague or in error). In this class, you often hear the names Dollree Mapp, Danny Escobedo, Ernesto Miranda and even Donald or Don King, Mike Tyson's former boxing promoter. Sure, they were people who were often on the "other side of the law," but as Justice Felix Frankfurter once observed, "the safeguards of liberty have frequently been forged in controversies involving not very nice people."* Sure, Dollree Mapp was a small-time gambler and was hiding a man wanted by the police, Danny Escobedo was a murderer, and Ernesto Miranda was a rapist. But they influenced legal history, and they did it by exercising their rights under the U.S. Constitution—those very rights that also apply to all of us in this room.

Also, as you further your studies in criminal law, or if you enter law school, a text or a professor might refer to a "*Terry* stop" or say "as the Court ruled in *Chimel*" and assume that you know these concepts. And you should know these concepts.

*Fred W. Friendly and Martha J. H. Elliot, *The Constitution: That Delicate Balance: Landmark Cases That Shaped the Constitution* (New York: McGraw-Hill, 1984), p. vii.

the police do not violate people's constitutional rights is the use of the exclusionary rule.

The Exclusionary Rule

The **exclusionary rule** is not a part of the U.S. Constitution. It is an interpretation of the Fourteenth Amendment by the Supreme Court that holds that evidence seized in violation of the U.S. Constitution cannot be used in court against a defendant. Such evidence is suppressed (not allowed to be used in court).

The exclusionary rule evolved in U.S. law through a series of Supreme Court cases. Since at least 1914, the Supreme Court has been concerned with police use of illegal means to seize evidence in violation of the

Constitution and then using that evidence to convict a defendant in court. Because the Bill of Rights, when written, applied only to agents of the federal government—not to those of local governments—the Court first applied the exclusionary rule only to federal courts and federal law enforcement officers. The Court continually warned state courts and law enforcement agencies that they must amend their procedures in order to comply with the U.S. Constitution or risk the exclusionary rule's being imposed on them as well. By 1961, the Supreme Court, noting that states had not amended their procedures to conform to the Constitution, applied the exclusionary rule to state courts and law enforcement agencies, as well as federal ones. The following four landmark

YOU ARE THERE! »

The Exclusionary Rule: Judge Kennedy-Powell's Ruling on the Admissibility of Evidence in the O.J. Simpson Case

This decision concerns the court's determination as to whether the warrantless entry into the property of O. J. Simpson and the recovery of certain important items of physical evidence (bloodstains and a bloody glove, which matched a bloody glove found at the murder scene) on the morning of Monday, June 13, 1994, was justified in the light of exigent circumstances.

Judge Kathleen Kennedy-Powell:

The detectives testified that they were concerned about those children [the Simpson children had been taken to a Los Angeles police station after their mother's dead body was found] and wanted to make arrangements with regard to those children. They get to the gate and here, again, it seems to me they really do extraordinary things to try to make contact with the persons inside. I mean the testimony was that they rang the bell for some fifteen minutes to try to rouse somebody from within the house. They could hear that phone ringing from out at the gate. There's no response. But what do they see? And this, apparently, also is uncontroverted in light of the testimony that was presented. There's a light on upstairs; there's a light on downstairs. There's several vehicles in the driveway, a suggestion that there are persons inside.

They see what they believe to be blood on the door handle or near the door handle of this white Bronco. A white Bronco that is parked on a public street where the officers have a right to be, and the court sees no problem with the observing or recovery of the blood samples from the door of the Bronco.

So, seeing what they believe to be blood and having seen droplets of blood leading away from the location, the officers even now are doing more to get in touch with the people inside by calling the Westec Security, who apparently dispatches at least one, if not two, vehicles to the location and eventually gives the police the telephone number. What they get at that point is an answering machine.

Defense lawyers in this case did an excellent job on cross-examination. But, when one looks at the result of that cross-examination, basically there were really no holes put in any of those detectives' testimonies that they felt that they were acting in an emergency situation at the time. This would be a very easy decision for me if, in fact, these officers went in there like storm troopers, fanning out over the property, examining every leaf, every car,

every closet, every nook and cranny of this location, but the testimony as elicited by the officers and as supported by the witnesses that testified on behalf of the defense, show that this was not what happened.

What the testimony was, is that the officers went in search of persons on the property. They went into the guest quarters of Mr. Kaelin, woke him up.

We have to judge the officers' conduct and the exigency if there was one, not based upon what all of us know today, but based upon what the officers knew at the time. And the information that they had been provided by Westec Security was that there was a live-in maid at the location. Additionally, Westec Security advised them that they had not been informed that there was going to be a vacation and absence of the residents from that location.

We know now, obviously, that there was no dying person or injured person on the property at the Simpson estate at that time. We know that all the persons who were supposed to be there were accounted for. Mr. Simpson was in Chicago, Mr. Kaelin was in his quarters, Ms. Arnelle Simpson had been out and returned about one o'clock in the morning. And GiGi, the maid, was on her night off. But the officers didn't know that at the time.

And we know from Mr. Kaelin's testimony that there was a loud, jarring, banging on the wall of his guest quarters, one that scared him, that he didn't know the origin of, that he had mentioned to several other persons but had never really investigated himself. So the officers have that information from Mr. Kaelin and Detective Fuhrman walks down that path.

He doesn't go anywhere else on the property. Officers make no attempt to go upstairs; they don't start opening cupboards, lifting up carpets, opening vehicles. He goes down that path to the area approximately adjacent to the air-conditioner where that noise was seen and the picture jarred from the wall and finds a glove. A glove that appears to be the apparent mate to the glove found at the crime scene.

Contrary to the suggestions in the defense argument that a ruling allowing the officers' conduct—finding that it was reasonable and that there were exigent circumstances—would mean the end of the Fourth Amendment and the Constitution and anarchy, I disagree.

YOU ARE THERE! »

The Exclusionary Rule: Judge Kennedy-Powell's Ruling on the Admissibility of Evidence in the O.J. Simpson Case (*continued*)

The court finds that they [the detectives] were, in fact, acting for a benevolent purpose in light of the brutal attack and that they reasonably believed that a further delay could have resulted in the unnecessary loss of life. And, therefore, the court denies the defense motion to suppress and will allow the introduction into evidence of the glove that was

recovered and of the spattered blood spots that were located on the driveway once the sun came up, as well as the bloodstains from the Bronco, which was in plain view on the public street.

Source: Preliminary hearing in *People v. Orenthal James Simpson,* July 8, 1994.

---

cases show how the exclusionary rule developed in this country.

WEEKS V. UNITED STATES   *Weeks* v. *United States* (1914) was the first case in which the exclusionary rule was used.[5] It involved federal law enforcement personnel entering an arrested person's home and seizing evidence without a warrant. The evidence was used against him in court, and he was convicted based on it.

On appeal, the Supreme Court overturned the man's conviction and established the exclusionary rule. Expressing the opinion of the Court, Justice William R. Day wrote

YOU ARE THERE! »

Weeks v. United States

Freemont Weeks was arrested at his place of business and charged with using the U.S. mail to conduct an illegal lottery. The police then searched Weeks's house and turned over articles and papers to a U.S. marshal. The marshal, then, together with the police, searched Weeks's room and confiscated other documents and letters. All the searches were conducted without a warrant.

Weeks was convicted based on the evidence seized from his home. On appeal to the U.S. Supreme Court, his conviction was overturned, and the exclusionary rule was established.

Source: Based on *Weeks* v. *United States,* 232 U.S. 383 (1914).

If letters and private documents can thus be seized and held and used in evidence against a citizen accused of an offense, the protection of the Fourth Amendment, declaring his right to be secure against such searches and seizures, is of no value, and so far as those thus placed are concerned, might as well be stricken from the Constitution. The efforts of the courts and their officials to bring the guilty to punishment, praiseworthy as they are, are not to be aided by the sacrifice of these great principles established by years of endeavor and suffering which have resulted in their embodiment in the fundamental law of the land.

The exclusionary rule provided that any evidence seized in violation of the Fourth Amendment could not be used against a defendant in a criminal case. The exclusionary rule, as enunciated in the *Weeks* case, applied only to evidence seized in an unconstitutional search and seizure by a federal agent and used in a federal court. It did not apply to state courts.

The exclusionary rule gave rise to another form of police misconduct that has been called the **silver platter doctrine.** Under the silver platter doctrine, federal prosecutors were allowed to use "tainted" evidence obtained by state police officers seized through unreasonable searches and seizures, provided that the evidence was obtained without federal participation and was turned over to federal officers. In *Silverthorne Lumber Co.* v. *U.S.* (1920), the Court ruled that this tainted evidence is essentially the "fruit of the poisoned tree" and cannot be used in court.[6]

WOLF V. COLORADO   Another case that involved the exclusionary rule was *Wolf* v. *Colorado* in 1949.[7] Mr. Wolf was suspected of being an illegal abortionist. A deputy sheriff seized his appointment book without a warrant and interrogated people whose names appeared in the book. Based on the evidence from these patients, Wolf was arrested, charged with committing illegal abortions, and convicted in court.

On appeal, the Supreme Court issued what could be seen as a rather strange decision. It ruled that although the Fourth Amendment did bar the admissibility of illegally seized evidence, it would not impose federal standards (the exclusionary rule) on state courts. The Court directed that the states create stronger state rules that would prevent illegally obtained evidence from being admitted into state courts. At the time of the *Wolf* decision, 31 states had rejected the exclusionary rule, and the Court had accepted this, respecting states' rights. By 1961, when *Mapp* v. *Ohio* reached the Supreme Court, many states had accepted the exclusionary rule.

Justice Felix Frankfurter, speaking for the Court, wrote, "We hold, therefore, that in a prosecution in a State Court for a State crime the Fourteenth Amendment does not forbid the admission of evidence obtained by an unreasonable search and seizure."

ROCHIN V. CALIFORNIA   In *Rochin* v. *California* (1952), another landmark case in the development of the exclusionary rule, the police entered Mr. Rochin's home without a warrant and, upon seeing him place what they believed to be narcotics into his mouth, forcefully attempted to extract the narcotics from him.[8] Failing this, they brought Rochin to a hospital, where his stomach was pumped. The stomach pumping produced two capsules as evidence of illegal drugs. Rochin was convicted in court and sentenced to 60 days' imprisonment. The chief evidence against him was the two capsules.

The Supreme Court overturned Rochin's conviction, considering the forcible seizure of evidence as a violation of the Fourteenth Amendment's due process clause. Speaking for the Court, Justice Felix Frankfurter wrote

> This is conduct that shocks the conscience. Illegally breaking into the privacy of Rochin, the struggle to open his mouth and remove what was there, the forcible extraction of his stomach's contents—this course of proceedings by agents of government to obtain evidence is bound to offend even hardened sensibilities. They are methods too close to the rack and screw to permit of constitutional differentiation.

In the *Rochin* case, the Court did not make the exclusionary rule applicable in all state cases, but only in those

YOU ARE THERE! »

Rochin v. California

On July 1, 1949, based on information received that Mr. Rochin was selling narcotics, three Los Angeles County deputy sheriffs entered Rochin's house without a warrant and forced open the door to his apartment within the house. When the police entered Rochin's bedroom, they saw two capsules on his bedside table and asked him what they were. Rochin picked up the capsules and swallowed them. A struggle ensued between Rochin and the police, and the police attempted to open Rochin's mouth to get to the capsules. Failing to do this, they handcuffed him and forcibly took him to a hospital. At the hospital, under the direction of one of the police officers, a doctor forced an emetic solution through a tube into Rochin's stomach against his will. The stomach pumping caused Rochin to vomit. In the vomited matter were found two capsules, which proved to be morphine.

Source: Based on *Rochin v. California,* 342 U.S. 165 (1952).

cases of extremely serious police misconduct—misconduct that, in Justice Frankfurter's words, "shocks the conscience." The Court again urged the states to enact laws prohibiting the use of illegally seized evidence in state courts and threatened that if the states did not enact those laws, the Court might impose the exclusionary rule upon the states.

MAPP V. OHIO   *Mapp* v. *Ohio* (1961) was the vehicle the Supreme Court used for applying the exclusionary rule to state courts.[9] The case involved the warrantless entry of police into a woman's home to search for a man in connection with a bombing. While in her home, the police searched it and found "obscene materials," for which she was arrested and ultimately convicted in court.

Speaking for the Supreme Court, Justice Tom C. Clark wrote

> The ignoble shortcut to conviction left open to the State tends to destroy the entire system of constitutional restraints on which the liberties of the people rest. Having once recognized that the right to privacy embodied in the Fourth Amendment is enforceable against the States, and that the right to be secure against rude invasions of privacy by state officers is, therefore, constitutional in origin, we can no longer permit that right to

YOU ARE THERE! »

Mapp v. *Ohio*

On May 23, 1957, three Cleveland police officers went to the home of Dollree ("Dolly") Mapp to search for a man named Virgil Ogletree, who was wanted in connection with a bombing at the home of Donald King. (Donald King was the well-known boxing promoter who promoted former heavyweight champion Mike Tyson, among other fighters.) The police knocked at the door and demanded entry. Mapp telephoned her lawyer and, on his advice, refused to allow the police to enter without a warrant.

Three hours later, the police again arrived with additional officers. The police then forced their way into the house. At this point, Mapp's lawyer arrived but was not allowed to see his client or to enter the house. As the police were rushing up the stairs to Mapp's second-floor apartment, Mapp was halfway down the stairs, rushing the police and demanding to see the warrant. In response to Mapp's demand, one of the officers held up a piece of paper purported to be a warrant. Mapp grabbed the piece of paper and stuffed it down the front of her clothing. A struggle ensued, during which the officers retrieved the piece of paper and then handcuffed Mapp because she was acting "belligerent." The officers then forcibly took her to her bedroom, where they searched a dresser, a chest of drawers, a closet, and some suitcases. They also looked through a photo album and some of Mapp's personal papers. The police also searched the living room, dining area, kitchen, and Mapp's daughter's bedroom. They then went to the basement and searched it and a trunk located there. During the search, the police found an unspecified amount of pornographic literature.

Mapp was charged with possession of "lewd and lascivious books, pictures and photographs" and subsequently convicted in court for possessing obscene materials. The warrant was never produced in court.

On appeal, the Supreme Court reversed Mapp's conviction based on the police's violation of the Fourth Amendment. It then extended the exclusionary rule to all state courts and law enforcement personnel.

Note: Do you know what happened to Dollree Mapp after this case?

In 1970, Dollree Mapp was arrested by New York City police for the possession of drugs. Suspecting that Mapp was dealing in stolen property, the police obtained a search warrant. While executing it, they found 50,000 envelopes of heroin and stolen property valued at over $100,000. Mapp was convicted and sentenced to a term of 20 years to life. On New Year's Eve in 1980, the governor of New York commuted her sentence.

Sources: Description of case based on *Mapp* v. *Ohio*, 367 U.S. 643 (1961); description of Mapp's subsequent career adapted from James A. Inciardi, *Criminal Justice*, 3rd ed. (Orlando, FL: Harcourt Brace Jovanovich, 1990), p. 280.

---

remain an empty promise. Because it is enforceable in the same manner and to like effect as other basic rights secured by the Due Process Clause, we can no longer permit it to be revocable at the whim of the police officer who, in the name of law enforcement itself, chooses to suspend its enjoyment. Our decision, founded on reason and truth, gives to the individual no more than that which the Constitution guarantees him, to the police officer no less than that to which honest law enforcement is entitled, and to the courts, the judicial integrity so necessary in the true administration of justice.

Impact of the Exclusionary Rule on the Police

Many police officers and citizens feel that the exclusionary rule is unfair—that it is procriminal and antipolice. They feel that the rule allows hardened criminals the chance to escape justice and be released "on a technicality." Since the *Mapp* and *Miranda* decisions, many have claimed that the Supreme Court has "handcuffed" the police and that the police no longer have the tools to fight crime. (The *Miranda* case will be discussed later in this chapter.) Academic studies of the effect of the exclusionary rule have not confirmed these fears. One study revealed that the exclusionary rule is overwhelmingly used with drug offenses, not violent crimes, and that the rule was responsible for evidence being suppressed in less than 1 percent of all criminal cases in the study.[10] Another study—a review of 7,500 felony cases in nine counties in three states—found that only .6 percent were dismissed because of the exclusionary rule.[11]

The remainder of this chapter will deal with constitutional limitations on the police in the areas of arrest, search and seizure, custodial interrogation, and identification procedures.

★ ★ ★
THE POLICE AND ARREST

The police authority to arrest is restricted by the Fifth Amendment, which forbids depriving citizens of life, liberty, or property without due processes of law. An arrest is also controlled by the Fourth Amendment's restrictions on searches and seizures, because an arrest is the ultimate seizure—the seizure of one's body. A state's criminal procedure law defines an arrest and directs who can make an arrest, for what offenses, and when. Most states define an arrest as "the taking of a person into custody, in the manner authorized by law for the purpose of presenting that person before a magistrate to answer for the commission of a crime." (See Exhibit 11.3.)

In 2001, in *Atwater* v. *City of Lago Vista*, the Supreme Court ruled that custodial arrests are reasonable seizures under the Fourth Amendment regardless of the possible punishment for the crime that resulted in the arrest.[12] In this case, police in Lago Vista, Texas, arrested Gail Atwater for driving her vehicle with her two children, ages 3 and 5, in the front seat, without seat belts, which is a misdemeanor in Texas punishable by a maximum fine of $50. (Neither Atwater or the two children were wearing seat belts.) Texas law permits police to make warrantless arrests for misdemeanors. Atwater was handcuffed, transported to the police station for booking, and placed in a cell for an hour before being seen by a magistrate. Atwater, after pleading no contest to the seat belt violation and paying a $50 fine, sued the police and the city of Lago Vista for being subjected to an unreasonable Fourth Amendment seizure. She argued that her offense carried no jail time and there was no need for her immediate detention. In this case the Supreme Court ruled that Atwater's arrest satisfied constitutional requirements because it was based on probable cause to believe that Atwater had committed a crime in the arresting officer's presence.

Arrests can be made with or without a warrant (a writ, or formal written order, issued by a judicial officer that directs a law enforcement officer to perform a specified act and affords the officer protection from damages if he or she acts according to the order). In general, police officers can arrest a person (1) for any crime committed in the officers' presence, (2) for a felony not committed in the officers' presence if they have probable cause to believe that a felony has occurred and that the person they have arrested committed the felony, or (3) under the authority of an arrest warrant. As an example of the first circumstance, officers can arrest a man they observe committing a robbery with a gun. An arrest can also be made in the following scenario: An officer is called to a scene where there is a dead body and is told by witnesses that a woman in a black leather jacket was engaged in an altercation with the deceased and took out a gun and shot him. The officer searches the area around the crime scene and finds a woman in a black jacket; she is hiding under a staircase. Upon searching the woman, the officer finds a gun. In the event the officer does not find the woman after the crime, but witnesses positively identify her, the officer can go to court and obtain an arrest warrant for the woman and a search warrant to search her house for the gun.

However, if a routine arrest is to be made in a suspect's home, an arrest warrant is necessary unless the suspect gives consent or an emergency exists. In *Payton* v. *New York* (1980), New York City police were attempting to arrest Payton based on probable cause for a murder. They attempted to gain entrance to Payton's apartment, but there was no response to their knocks. They then went into the apartment by breaking down the door. Upon entering the apartment they observed in plain view a .30 caliber shell casing that was used as evidence of the murder. The Supreme Court ruled that this was a routine arrest and the police had ample time to gain a warrant prior to entry.[13]

Probable Cause

Most of the arrests made by the average police officer do not involve a warrant, because most crimes an officer becomes aware of on the street necessitate immediate ac-

---

Exhibit 11.3	**A Police Officer's Power to Arrest**

The Tennessee Code, Section 40.803, reads

Grounds for arrest by officer without warrant—An officer may, without a warrant, arrest a person:

1. For a public offense committed or a breach of the peace threatened in his presence.
2. When the person has committed a felony, though not in his presence.
3. When a felony has in fact been committed, and he has reasonable cause for believing the person arrested to have committed it.
4. On a charge made, upon reasonable cause, of the commission of a felony by the person arrested.

tion and do not allow the officer the time necessary to go to court to obtain a warrant. Most of the arrests made by the police are based on the probable cause standard.

Probable cause can be defined as evidence that may lead a reasonable person to believe that a crime has been committed and that a certain person committed it. Probable cause is less than beyond a reasonable doubt, which is the standard used by a court to convict a person of a crime. Probable cause is more than reasonable suspicion. **Reasonable suspicion** is a standard of proof that would lead a reasonable person (a police officer) to believe a certain condition or fact (that a crime is or will be occurring, or has occurred) exists. This is the standard necessary for police officers to conduct stop-and-frisks.

The evidence needed to establish probable cause must be established prior to arrest. For example, if an officer sees a man, walking down a block, adjust his jacket to the extent that a gun can be seen protruding from his waistband, the officer has reasonable suspicion to stop and question the man. If the possession of the gun is illegal, the officer has probable cause to make an arrest. Because the arrest is legal, the search that produced the gun is legal; therefore, the gun can be entered into evidence. In contrast, if an officer stops all people walking down the street and searches them without sufficient justification, any arrest for possession of a gun would be illegal, and the gun would be suppressed in court.

In 1959, *Henry v. United States* set the precedent than an arrest must be made on firmer grounds than mere suspicion and that the Fourth Amendment applies to searches and arrests.[14] The Supreme Court, in *Brinegar v. United States* (1949), ruled that relaxations of the fundamental requirements of probable cause, as it relates to the power of arrest, would leave law-abiding citizens at the mercy of police officers' whims.[15] *Draper v. United States* (1959) held that the identification of a suspect by a reliable informant may constitute probable cause for an arrest, where the information given is sufficiently accurate to lead the officers directly to the suspect.[16]

In 1991, in *County of Riverside v. McLoughlin*, the Court ruled that a person arrested without a warrant must generally be provided with a judicial determination of probable cause within 48 hours after arrest, including intervening weekends and holidays, meaning that weekends and holidays could not be excluded from the 48-hour rule.[17] (See Table 11.4.)

Reasonable and Deadly Force in Making Arrests

When making an arrest, an officer can use **reasonable force**. Reasonable force is that amount of force necessary to overcome resistance by the person being arrested by the police. For example, if a person is punching the officer in an effort to avoid the arrest, the officer may use similar force in an attempt to subdue the person and control him or her. As an attacker's force escalates, an officer may escalate his or her use of force.

The best way to define reasonable force may be to define unreasonable force. Punching, kicking, or otherwise using force against a person who is not resisting and who is willingly submitting to an arrest would be the unreasonable use of force. Continuing to strike at a person after he or she is subdued, handcuffed, and under the officer's physical control would be an unreasonable use of force. The videotape of the Rodney King incident (1991) discussed in Chapter 12, "Police Ethics and Police Deviance," would appear to be an excellent example of unreasonable force, even though the jury apparently saw it differently in the first trial. King does not appear to be resisting, yet the officers continue to hit him with their batons.

The use of deadly force (force sufficient to cause a person's death) has long been a controversial topic in policing. Chapter 15, "Specific Police Problems and Issues," covers it in depth. However, for the purposes of this chapter, it should be stated that the use of deadly force by the police is generally permitted (1) when an officer's life or another's life is at peril from the person against whom deadly physical force is directed, (2) where the officer has probable cause to believe the suspect has committed a crime involving serious physical harm to another, or (3) in other serious felony cases.

Stopping Vehicles

"It was a routine traffic stop," many officers used to testify in court regarding summonses and arrests for drivers of automobiles. The routine traffic stop came to an end,

Table 11.4	Landmark Supreme Court Decisions: Arrests by Police
Issue	**Cases**
Probable cause	*Henry v. United States* (1959), *Brinegar v. United States* (1949), *Draper v. United States* (1959), *Atwater v. City of Lago Vista* (2001)
48-hour rule	*County of Riverside v. McLoughlin* (1991)

however, in 1979, with the case of *Delaware* v. *Prouse*.[18] In this case, the Supreme Court ruled that the police cannot make capricious car stops and that "random spot checks" of motorists are a violation of a citizen's Fourth Amendment rights.

The Court, however, stated that police may still stop automobiles based on reasonable suspicion that (1) a crime was being committed or (2) a traffic violation occurred. The Court also said that the police can establish roadblocks as long as (1) all citizens are subject to the stop or (2) a pattern is set, such as stopping every third car.

Can a police officer legally order a driver or a passenger out of the vehicle after he or she has stopped it? Yes, ruled the Supreme Court in two cases. In *Pennsylvania* v. *Mimms* (1977), the Court ruled that the Fourth Amendment allows a law enforcement officer who has made a lawful routine stop of a vehicle for a traffic offense to order the driver to exit the vehicle without requiring any additional factual justification.[19] In this case, the defendant was stopped for driving with an expired license plate. The officer then ordered the defendant to exit the vehicle. The officer later testified that he routinely ordered all drivers to exit vehicles following routine traffic stops out of a concern for his safety. When Mimms stepped out of the vehicle, the officer noticed a bulge in his jacket, prompting the officer to conduct a limited search for weapons and leading to the discovery of a handgun.

In *Maryland* v. *Wilson* (1997), a Maryland state trooper pulled over a vehicle for speeding.[20] The trooper, out of concern for his safety, directed the defendant, Wilson, a

YOU ARE THERE! »

Delaware v. Prouse

On November 30, 1976, at about 7:30 P.M., a New Castle County, Delaware, police officer stopped an automobile owned by William Prouse. Another man was driving Prouse's car, and Prouse was an occupant. As the officer approached the vehicle, he smelled the odor of marijuana. He then observed marijuana on the floor of the automobile. Prouse was arrested and later went on trial. At the trial, the officer testified that his stop of Prouse's car was "routine." He stated that he saw the car, and, because he was not answering any other calls, he decided to stop the car. He further testified that he saw no traffic violations or vehicle equipment violations.

The trial court ruled that the stop and detention had been capricious and was a violation of Prouse's Fourth Amendment rights. The state of Delaware appealed the case to the Supreme Court, which affirmed the opinion of the trial court. The Supreme Court ruled that random spot checks of automobiles are a violation of citizens' Fourth Amendment rights.

Source: Based on *Delaware* v. *Prouse,* 440 U.S. 648 (1979).

Table 11.5	Landmark Supreme Court Decisions: Police Traffic Stops
Issue	**Case**
Routine traffic stops	*Delaware* v. *Prouse* (1979)
Ordering driver out of vehicle	*Pennsylvania* v. *Mimms* (1977)
Ordering passenger out of vehicle	*Maryland* v. *Wilson* (1997)
DWI checkpoints	*Michigan Department of State Police* v. *Sitz* (1990)
Drug checkpoints	*City of Indianapolis* v. *Edmond* (2000)
Pretext stops	*Whren* v. *United States* (1996)

passenger in the vehicle, to step out of the vehicle. As the man exited the car, the trooper observed a bag of cocaine fall to the ground.

In both cases, the Court recognized the inherently dangerous nature of the traffic stop. In fact, in *Maryland* v. *Wilson*, the Court cited statistics showing that in the year in which the Mimms stop occurred, almost 6,000 officers were assaulted and 11 killed during traffic pursuits and stops.[21]

In 1990, the Supreme Court, in *Michigan Department of State Police* v. *Sitz*, ruled that brief, suspicionless seizures at highway checkpoints for the purpose of combating drunk driving were legal.[22] However, in 2000, in *City of Indianapolis* v. *Edmond*, the Court ruled that when the checkpoint is to locate illegal drugs, the seizure involved is unconstitutional.[23] Thus, highway checkpoints for DWI enforcement are constitutional, but for drug enforcement they are not legal. In this case the Court reasoned that the drunk driving checkpoint was clearly aimed at reducing the immediate hazard posed by drunk drivers on the

Forst's Law

Crime and the Community

The law and enforcing the law are not always cut and dried. Politics and community values and priorities will influence what police officers do in their jurisdiction. They are two of the factors that influence officer discretion.

I remember that, when I was a detective, we had a robbery go down in our business district. It was a time of very high crime rates; the public was fed up with "bad guys," and they wanted them arrested and punished. They wanted to feel safe in their community and be able to walk the streets without fear of being robbed or of going home and finding their house broken into.

This robbery, in fact, was similar to many we'd been having throughout the city. There was no weapon involved—just physical force. Two young men walked into a jewelry store in a crowded strip mall. It was around 1 P.M. on a beautiful day in the middle of December, the height of both the tourist season and the busy holiday shopping season. These two young men asked to look at some gold chains and were shown several by the employees. Leery because they had been victimized on several prior occasions by "snatchers," the employees showed only a couple at a time and didn't stray far from the counter.

After a few minutes of looking at chains and discussing pros and cons the two "customers" grabbed several and ran out the door. The owner pulled a gun and told them to stop. They did not. They ran out the door, and the owner followed. He let off some rounds and hit one of the subjects in the butt as he exited the store. The owner continued running after the other subject and fired off two more rounds but missed him. Shoppers were diving for cover,

and the two rounds lodged in the wall of an adjacent store (the strip mall was L-shaped, with several stores perpendicular to the jewelry store).

When I got to the scene, the injured offender was still there. Though he wasn't seriously injured, he was transported to the hospital where the bullet was removed, and he was released. The second subject was apprehended not far from the scene. It turned out these two subjects were juveniles—big juveniles (about 6′) but only 16 years old. They were charged with their crime and sent to the detention center. I wanted to charge the store owner with firing his weapon, as it was not a case of self-defense and there was a significant potential for harming innocent bystanders. I consulted with the state attorney's office, and the ultimate decision was that we would present the case to a grand jury. The state attorney recognized the political nature of this case (as did I) in this time of soaring crime rates and citizens' anger and impatience with "bad guys." He didn't think it would be a good move politically to charge the owner outright but rather to let a grand jury of 21 citizens make the decision.

We took the case to the grand jury; after listening to the testimony, they decided not to charge the owner. With many of the jurors having been crime victims or knowing crime victims, they could relate to the frustration of the business owner. They felt he was justified in doing what he did because he had been victimized so many times and was just trying to protect his business and livelihood. I'm just glad no one got hurt in this reckless action.

---

highways, while general crime control (such as drug enforcement) stops needed some quantum of individualized suspicion.

In *Whren v. United States*, in 1996, the Supreme Court ruled that pretextual traffic stops, also known as pretext

stops (the temporary detention of a motorist upon probable cause to believe that he has violated the traffic laws even if another reasonable officer may not have stopped the motorist absent some additional law enforcement objective) do not violate the Fourth Amendment. In this

Police officers may stop vehicles based on reasonable suspicion that a crime was/is being committed or that a traffic violation occurred.

case, plainclothes vice officers were patrolling a high drug activity area in an unmarked car when they noticed a vehicle with temporary license plates and youthful occupants waiting at a stop sign. The truck remained stopped at the intersection for what appeared to be an unusually long time while the driver stared into the lap of the passenger. When the officers made a U-turn and headed toward the vehicle, it made a sudden right turn without signaling and sped off at an "unreasonable" speed. The officers overtook the vehicle when it stopped at a red light. When one of the officers approached the vehicle, he observed two large plastic bags of what appeared to be crack cocaine in Whren's hands. He was arrested. At trial, Whren sought to suppress the evidence, saying that the plainclothes officer would not normally stop traffic violators and that there was no probable cause to make a stop on drug charges; therefore, the stop on the traffic violation was merely a pretext to determine whether Whren had drugs.[24]

★ ★ ★

THE POLICE AND SEARCH AND SEIZURE

Search and seizure is the search for and taking of persons and property as evidence of crime by law enforcement officers. Searches and seizures are the means used by the police to obtain evidence that can be used by the courts to prove a defendant's guilt. Police searches are governed by

the Fourth Amendment, which prohibits all unreasonable searches and seizures and requires that all warrants be based on probable cause and that they particularly describe the place to be searched and the persons or things to be seized. For the legal definitions of terms pertinent to searches and seizures, see Exhibit 11.4 on page 266.

The sanctity of one's home is very important in U.S. legal tradition and it is commonly assumed that "a person's home is his or her castle." The U.S. Supreme Court has consistently ruled that the police must use due process to enter a home. In *Payton* v. *New York* (1980), discussed earlier in this chapter, the Court ruled that the police need a warrant to enter a person's home to make a routine arrest absent consent or emergency situations.[25] In *Minnesota* v. *Olson* (1990), the Supreme Court held than an overnight guest had a sufficient expectation of privacy in a host's dwelling and is entitled to the Fourth Amendment protection against unreasonable searches and seizures.[26] In *Minnesota* v. *Carter* (1998), the Court refused to extend Fourth Amendment protections to a person who is merely present with the consent of the householder.[27]

In 2002, in *Kirk* v. *Louisiana*, the Court reaffirmed their previous ruling in *Payton* that the police many not enter a person's home without a warrant, unless emergency or exigent circumstances are present. In this case, police had entered Kirk's apartment after observing what they believed to be drug purchases therein and then stopping one of the apparent buyers on the street to verify the drug sales. Officers testified that "because the stop took place within a block of the apartment [they] feared that evidence would be destroyed and ordered the apartment be entered." They immediately knocked on the door of the apartment, arrested Kirk, searched him, found a drug vial in his underwear, and then observed contraband in plain view in the apartment. The Court ruled that police officers need either a warrant or probable cause plus exigent circumstances in order to make a lawful entry into a home.[28]

A good example to explain the meaning of a legal Fourth Amendment search is the 2000 U.S. Supreme Court landmark case *Bond* v. *United States*. In this case, Dewayne Bond was a passenger with carry-on luggage on a bus. When the bus stopped at a Border Patrol checkpoint, a Border Patrol agent boarded the bus to check the passengers' immigration status. In an effort to locate illegal drugs, the agent began to squeeze the soft luggage, which some passengers had placed in the overhead storage space above their seats. The agent squeezed the canvas bag above Bond's seat and noticed that it contained a "bricklike" object. Bond admitted that the bag was his and consented to its search. When the agent looked inside the bag, he discovered a "brick" of methamphetamine. Bond was arrested and then indicted and convicted for federal drug charges. Upon appeal, the Supreme Court reversed the conviction and ruled that the agent's manipulation of the bag was an unreasonable search and that it violated the Fourth Amendment.

In *Bond,* the Court ruled that the agent did in fact conduct a search and that that search was unreasonable because he conducted it without a warrant and the search did not fall under any of the recognized exceptions to the warrant requirement. Although Bond consented to a search of his bag, his consent was not an issue. The agent's squeezing of Bond's bag was at issue—Bond argued, and the Court agreed, that the agent's squeezing of his bag was an illegal search and occurred before any consent given by Bond.[29]

In explaining the legality of a search and seizure, the Court's reasoning in this case was that the search was in violation of the Fourth Amendment, in that, according to *Katz v. United States* (1967), a search is a government infringement of a person's reasonable expectation of privacy and that a search must be reasonable to comply with the Fourth Amendment. The Court has ruled that any government search conducted without a warrant is *per se* unreasonable, unless the search falls under a few recognized exceptions to the warrant requirement (for example, consent searches, emergency searches, motor vehicle searches, inventory searches, searches incident to arrest, and the like).[30]

The Warrant Requirement and the Search Warrant

In the United States, the general rule regarding search and seizure is that law enforcement officers obtain a search warrant prior to any search and seizure. (However, there are many exceptions.) A **search warrant** is an order from a court, issued by a judge, authorizing and directing the police to search a particular place for certain property described in the warrant and directing the police to bring that property to court. Generally, to get a search warrant, a police officer prepares a typed affidavit applying for the warrant and then personally appears before a judge. The judge reads the application; questions the officer, if necessary; and signs the warrant if in agreement with the officer that there is probable cause that certain property that may be evidence of a crime, proceeds from a crime, or contra-

YOU ARE THERE! »

Katz v. United States

Mr. Justice Stewart delivered the opinion of the Court:

The petitioner was convicted in the District Court of the Southern District of California under an eight-count indictment charging him with transmitting wagering information by telephone from Los Angeles to Miami and Boston, in violation of a federal statute. At trial the Government was permitted, over the petitioner's objection, to introduce evidence of the petitioner's end of telephone conversations, overheard by FBI agents who had attached an electronic listening and recording device to the outside of the public telephone booth from which he had placed his calls. In affirming his conviction, the Court of Appeals rejected the contention that the recordings had been obtained in violation of the Fourth Amendment, because "there was no physical entrance into the area occupied by the petitioner." We granted certiorari in order to consider the constitutional questions. . . . Wherever a man may be, he is entitled to know that he will remain free from unreasonable searches and seizures. The government agents here ignored "the procedure of antecedent justification" . . . that is central to the Fourth Amendment, a procedure that we hold to be a constitutional precondition of the kind of electronic surveillance involved in this case. Because the surveillance here failed to meet that condition, and because it led to the petitioner's conviction, the judgment must be reversed.

It is so ordered.

Source: Based on: *Katz v. United Sates,* 389 U.S. 347 (1967).

band (material that is illegal to possess, such as illegal drugs or illegal weapons) is present at a certain place.

Generally, a warrant can be executed only during daylight hours and within a certain time period. However, there are many exceptions. Officers executing a warrant generally must announce their presence before entering. At times, judges may add a "no knock" provision to the warrant, which allows the officers to enter without announcing their presence.[31]

Most searches by police officers are not made with warrants, because they are made on the street, where there is no time for an officer to proceed to court to obtain a warrant. Most searches are made in accordance with one of the exceptions to the search warrant requirement—situations involving **exigent circumstances** (emergency situations). Exceptions to the warrant requirement will be discussed at length in the next section.

Often, the cases in which search warrants are generally used are lengthy investigations in which immediate action is not required. Also, warrants are often used in organized crime and other conspiracy-type investigations.

One of the major uses of warrants is after an informant provides information to the police that certain people are engaged in continuous illegal acts, such as drug dealing. For example, a man tells the police that a certain person is a drug dealer and sells the drugs from her house. The police get as much information as they can from the informant and then dispatch a team of plainclothes officers to make undercover observations of the house. The officers do not see actual drug dealing, because it is going on inside the house, but they see certain actions that go along with the drug trade, such as cars stopping at the house and people entering the house for a short time and then leaving and driving away. Based on these observations, the police

Table 11.6	Landmark Supreme Court Decisions: Search Warrants
Decision	Cases
Two-pronged test	*Aguilar v. Texas* (1964), *Spinelli v. United States* (1969)
Totality of circumstances test	*Illinois v. Gates* (1983)

can then go to court and request that a judge issue a search warrant. If a search warrant is issued, the police can enter and search the house.

The Supreme Court has had several standards by which to determine what evidence would constitute probable cause for a judge to issue a warrant. (See Table 11.6.) The first standard was a two-part (two-pronged) test that mandated that the police show (1) why they believed the informant and (2) the circumstances that showed that the informant had personal knowledge of the crime. This standard was articulated in two major Supreme Court cases, *Aguilar*

Exhibit 11.4   Legal Definitions Relating to Arrest and Search and Seizure

Affidavit   A statement in writing subscribed by a signature of a person that was affixed under oath before a notary public, a magistrate, or a commissioner of deeds.

Arrest   The initial taking into custody of a person by law enforcement authorities to answer for a criminal offense or violation of a code or ordinance.

Crime   Any act that the government has declared to be contrary to the public good, that is declared by statute to be a crime, and that is prosecuted in a criminal proceeding. In some jurisdictions, crimes include only felonies and/or misdemeanors.

Evidence   All matter of proof offered in a trial to prove or disprove an issue of fact.

Exclusionary Rule   A judicially contrived procedure that prevents evidence unconstitutionally obtained by law enforcement officers from being introduced into evidence at a criminal trial and that is not to be considered by the triers of the facts of the case in arriving at a verdict.

Felony   A crime for which a person may be imprisoned for at least a year and a day.

Frisk   The patting down of the outer clothing of a person who is suspected of carrying a concealed weapon.

Informant   A person who supplies information to a law enforcement officer referring to the commission of a crime or to some set of facts requiring the attention of the law enforcement agency.

Misdemeanor   A class of criminal deviance that is usually punished by a maximum of $1,000 fine and/or up to one year in a county or

city jail. A misdemeanor is less serious than a felony. Different jurisdictions classify misdemeanors and sanctions for violation thereof differently.

Plain view   A phrase that is applied to items of evidence that a law enforcement officer sees without having violated a person's constitutional rights and that the officer came upon inadvertently while performing normal duties.

Probable cause   The reasoning process that a reasonable person uses to conclude that (1) there is a good reason to make an arrest and (2) there is good reason to suspect that a person has contraband or evidence of crime in his or her possession.

Search warrant   A court order directing a law enforment officer to search for, and return to the court, particular items of personal property to be used for the prosecution of a person for violation of a statute.

Stop and frisk   The act of an officer stopping a suspected person and patting that person's outer clothing to search for a concealed weapon. The officer must have reason to believe that the suspect is armed and dangerous.

Suppression of evidence   What occurs when evidence is unconstitutionally obtained by law enforcement authorities and the defendant makes a motion to suppress this evidence. After a hearing before a judge, the judge will indicate that the motion is granted. This means that the prosecutor is not permitted to use the unconstitutionally obtained evidence in the trial of the defendant. Often, the prosecutor is unable to proceed with the case without this evidence.

YOU ARE THERE! »

Illinois v. Gates

The Bloomingdale (Illinois) Police Department received by mail the following anonymous handwritten letter:

> This letter is to inform you that you have a couple in your town who strictly make their living on selling drugs. They are Sue and Lance Gates, they live on Greenway, off Bloomingdale Rd. in the condominiums. Most of their buys are done in Florida. Sue his wife drives their car to Florida, where she leaves it to be loaded up with drugs, then Lance flys down and drives it back. Sue flys [sic] back after she drops the car off in Florida. May 3 she is driving down there again and Lance will be flying down in a few days to drive it back. At the time Lance drives the car back he has the trunk loaded with over $100,000.00 in drugs. Presently they have over $100,000.00 worth of drugs in their basement.
>
> They brag about the fact they never have to work, and make their living on pushers. I guarantee if you watch them carefully you will make a big catch. They are friends with some big drug dealers who visit their house often.

Obviously, the *Aguilar–Spinelli* two-pronged test could not apply to this case. The writer was anonymous; the police could not produce the writer and prove his or her reliability.

Based on this letter, however, the police performed the following investigatory actions:

1. They verified the Gates's address.
2. They obtained information from a confidential informant about Lance Gates.
3. They obtained information from an O'Hare Airport police officer that "L. Gates" had made a reservation on Eastern Airlines to West Palm Beach, Florida, departing Chicago on May 5 at 4:15 P.M.
4. They arranged for the Drug Enforcement Administration to conduct a surveillance of the May 5 Eastern Airlines flight.

The surveillance resulted in the information that Lance Gates arrived in West Palm Beach and went to a Holiday Inn room registered to one Susan Gates, as well as other information verifying the information in the letter. A judge issued a search warrant for the Gates's apartment and automobile. Using the warrant, the police seized approximately 350 pounds of marijuana, weapons, and other contraband.

The Gateses were arrested and indicted for violation of state drug laws. The evidence, however, was suppressed in a pretrial motion, as the judge ruled that the affidavit submitted in support of the application for the warrant was inadequate under the *Aguilar–Spinelli* standard. Upon appeal, the U.S. Supreme Court replaced the *Aguilar–Spinelli* standard with the totality of circumstances standard.

Source: Based on *Illinois v. Gates*, 462 U.S. 213 (1983).

v. *Texas* (1964) and *Spinelli v. United States* (1969).[32] Obviously, there were problems with this standard. To show why the police believed the informant and how the informant obtained the information, the police would have to identity the informant or show how the informant was trustworthy in the past, or both. The identifying of the informant and the description of past tips could put the informant in danger.

In *Illinois v. Gates*, the Supreme Court in 1983 reversed the *Aguilar–Spinelli* two-pronged test.[33] The Court replaced it with the totality of circumstances test, which holds that an informant could be considered reliable if he or she gives the police sufficient facts to indicate that a crime is being committed and if the police verify these facts.[34]

Exceptions to the Warrant Requirement

Many exigent circumstances arise in which the police cannot be expected to travel to court to obtain a search warrant. The evidence might be destroyed by a suspect, the suspect might get away, or the officer might be injured. The following are the major exceptions to the search warrant requirement and the rules established by the Supreme Court that govern these exceptions. (See Table 11.7.)

INCIDENT TO LAWFUL ARREST   In *Chimel v. California* (1969), the U.S. Supreme Court established guidelines regarding searches at the time of arrest.[35] In this case, the Court ruled that incident to (at the time of) an arrest, the police may search the defendant and only that area immediately surrounding the defendant for the purpose of preventing injury to the officer and the destruction of evidence. This has become known as the "arm's reach doctrine."

On September 13, 1965, three police officers from the Santa Ana, California, Police Department arrived at Ted Chimel's house with a warrant to arrest him for the burglary of a coin shop. The police showed Chimel the arrest warrant and asked him if they could "look around." Chimel objected, but the officers told him they could search the house on the basis of the lawful arrest. The officers then searched the entire three-bedroom house for 45 minutes. They seized numerous items, including some coins. The coins were admitted into evidence, and Chimel was convicted at trial of burglary.

Upon appeal, the U.S. Supreme Court ruled that the warrantless search of Chimel's home was a violation of his constitutional rights. The Court thus established the "arm's reach doctrine."

In 1973, in *United States* v. *Robinson*, the Court ruled that because a probable cause arrest is a reasonable Fourth Amendment intrusion, a search incident to that arrest requires no additional justification.[36]

In 1990, in *Maryland* v. *Buie*, the Court, considering officers' safety extended the authority of the police to search locations in a house where a potentially dangerous person could hide while an arrest warrant is being served.[37] In a similar vein, in 2001, in *Illinois* v. *McArthur*, the Court held that a police officer's refusal to allow residents to enter their homes without a police officer until a search warrant was obtained did not violate the Fourth Amendment.[38]

In *Knowles* v. *Iowa* (1998) the Supreme Court considered the right of the warrantless search incident to arrest to the search of a motor vehicle stopped by the police incident to a traffic citation. In *Knowles*, Patrick Knowles was stopped for speeding by a police officer in Newton, Iowa. The officer issued Knowles a citation and then conducted a thorough search of Knowles's car without his consent, found a bag of marijuana and a pot pipe, and arrested and

Table 11.7	Landmark U.S. Supreme Court Decisions: Exceptions to the Warrant Requirement in Police Search and Seizure Cases
Issue	**Cases**
Abandoned property	*Abel* v. *United States* (1960), *California* v. *Greenwood* (1988), *California* v. *Hodari, D.* (1991).
Automobile exception	*Carroll* v. *United States* (1925), *United States* v. *Belton* (1981), *United States* v. *Ross* (1982), *California* v. *Acevedo* (1991), *Florida* v. *Jimeno* (1991), *Pennsylvania* v. *Labron* (1996), *Maryland* v. *Dyson* (1998), *Florida* v. *White* (1998), *Wyoming* v. *Houghton* (1998)
Border searches	*United States* v. *Martinez-Fuerte* (1976)
Buses	*Florida* v. *Bostick* (1991)
Canine searches	*United States* v. *Place* (1983)
Computer error	*Arizona* v. *Evans* (1995)
Consent	*Schneckloth* v. *Bustamonte* (1973), *United States* v. *Matlock* (1974), *Bumper* v. *North Carolina* (1968), *Illinois* v. *Rodriquez* (1990)
Exigent circumstances	*Warden* v. *Hayden* (1967), *Mincey* v. *Arizona* (1978), *Wilson* v. *Arkansas* (1995), *Bond* v. *United States* (2000), *Illinois* v. *McArthur* (2001), *Kirk* v. *Louisiana* (2002)
Good faith	*United States* v. *Leon* (1984), *Massachusetts* v. *Sheppard* (1984), *Illinois* v. *Krull* (1987), *Maryland* v. *Garrison* (1987)
Incident to arrest	*Chimel* v. *California* (1969), *United States* v. *Robinson* (1973), *Knowles* v. *Iowa* (1998)
Inventory	*Colorado* v. *Bertine* (1987).
Open fields	*Hester* v. *United States* (1924), *Oliver* v. *United States* (1984), *California* v. *Ciraola* (1986), *Florida* v. *Riley* (1989).
Motor homes	*California* v. *Carney* (1985)
Plain view	*Harris* v. *New York* (1968).
Protective sweep	*Maryland* v. *Buie* (1990)
Private persons	*Burdeau* v. *McDowell* (1921)
Stop and frisk, field interrogations	*Terry* v. *Ohio* (1968), *Minnesota* v. *Dickerson* (1993), *Illinois* v. *Wardlow* (2000), *Florida* v. *J.L.* (2000)
Watercraft	*United States* v. *Villamonte-Marquez* (1983)

charged him with violation of the controlled substances statutes. The Court ruled that when the police officer stopped Knowles, he had probable cause to believe Knowles had violated traffic laws. He could have arrested Knowles for that violation but chose instead to issue a citation. It ruled that the search incident to an arrest exception does not apply to a traffic citation.[39]

FIELD INTERROGATIONS (STOP AND FRISK)   In 1968, the Supreme Court established the standard for allowing police officers to perform a **stop and frisk** (pat down) of a suspect in *Terry v. Ohio*.[40] A stop and frisk is the detaining of a person by a law enforcement officer for the purpose of investigation, accompanied by a superficial examination by the officer of the person's body surface or clothing to discover weapons, contraband, or other objects relating to criminal activity. In *Terry v. Ohio*, the Court

© AP Photo/The Progress-Index, Jeff Mankeie

Pursuant to the *Terry v. Ohio* case (1968), an officer who has reasonable suspicion to believe an individual has committed or is committing a crime may conduct an investigatory stop. An officer who has reasonable suspicion to believe the subject is armed may frisk for weapons.

YOU ARE THERE! »

Terry v. Ohio

Detective Martin McFadden, a veteran of the Cleveland Police Department's robbery squad, was on routine stakeout duty in a Cleveland downtown shopping district when he observed two men acting suspiciously on the street in the vicinity of Huron Road and Euclid Avenue. One of the suspects looked furtively into a store, walked on, returned to look at the same store, and then joined a companion. The companion, another male, then went to the store, looked in it, and then rejoined his companion. The two men continually repeated these actions and looked into the store numerous times. The two men then met with a third man.

McFadden suspected that the males were casing the store for a stickup and believed that they were armed. He approached the three men, identified himself as a police officer, and asked the men their names. The men mumbled something, whereupon McFadden patted them down (frisked them, or ran his hands over their outer clothing). His frisk and subsequent search revealed that one of the men, Terry, was in possession of a gun. Another frisk and subsequent search revealed that one of his companions, Richard Chilton, also had a gun.

Terry and Chilton were arrested for possession of a gun and were convicted. Upon appeal, the Supreme Court ruled that McFadden's actions were constitutional.

Source: Based on *Terry v. Ohio*, 392 U.S. 1 (1968).

ruled that a police officer could stop a person in a public place to make reasonable inquiries as to the person's conduct. It ruled that when the following five conditions exist, a police officer is justified in patting down, or frisking, a suspect:

1. Where a police officer observes unusual conduct which leads him reasonably to conclude in light of his experience that criminal activity may be afoot . . .

2. . . . and that the person with whom he is dealing may be armed and dangerous . . .

3. . . . where in the course of investigating this behavior he identifies himself as a policeman . . .

4. . . . and makes reasonable inquiry . . .

5. . . . and where nothing in the initial stages of the encounter serves to dispel his reasonable fear for his own or others' safety . . . he is entitled to conduct a carefully limited search of the outer clothing of such persons in an attempt to discover weapons which might be used to assault him. Such search is a reasonable search under the Fourth Amendment and any weapons seized may properly be introduced in evidence against the person from whom they were taken.[41]

In 1993, in *Minnesota* v. *Dickerson*, the Court placed new limits on an officer's ability to seize evidence discovered during a pat-down search conducted for protective reasons when the search itself is based merely upon suspicion and fails to immediately reveal the presence of a weapon.[42] In this case, Timothy Dickerson was stopped by Minneapolis police after they noticed him acting suspiciously while leaving a building known for cocaine trafficking. The officers decided to investigate and ordered Dickerson to submit to a pat-down search. The officer testified that he felt no weapon but did feel a small lump in Dickerson's jacket pocket, which he believed to be a lump of cocaine upon examining it with his fingers. Dickerson was arrested and convicted of drug possession. Upon appeal, the U.S. Supreme Court ruled that the search was illegal, saying, "While *Terry* entitled [the officer] to place his hands on respondent's jacket and to feel the lump in his pocket, his continued exploration of the pocket after he concluded that it contained no weapons was unrelated to the sole justification for the search under *Terry*."

In *Illinois* v. *Wardlow* (2000), the Court held that a police officer's initial stop of a suspect was supported by reasonable suspicion if the suspect was both present in an area of expected criminal activity and fled upon seeing the police.[43] In this case, two police officers were investigating drug transactions while driving in an area known for heavy drug trafficking. They noticed Mr. Wardlow holding a bag. When Wardlow saw the officers, he fled. The officers pursued and stopped him. One of the officers conducted a protective pat-down search for weapons because, in his experience, it was common for weapons to be in the vicinity of drug transactions. During the pat down, the officers squeezed Wardlow's bag and felt a heavy, hard object in the shape of a gun. When the officer opened the bag, he did in fact discover a handgun with ammunition. Wardlow was arrested. Upon appeal that the arrest was illegal because the officers did not perform a lawful stop and frisk, the Court held that the initial stop was reasonable and supported by reasonable suspicion and cited *Terry* v. *Ohio*, "Under *Terry*, an officer may, consistent with the Fourth Amendment, conduct a brief, investigatory stop when the officer has a reasonable, articulable suspicion that criminal activity is afoot."[44] Thus, in *Wardlow*, the Court ruled that several factors can be used to determine whether an officer has reasonable suspicion to make a *Terry* stop, including: (1) whether the stop occurred in a high-crime area; (2) a suspect's nervous, evasive behavior; and (3) a suspect's unprovoked flight upon noticing the police.[45]

Regarding anonymous tips to the police, the Supreme Court has ruled that if an officer is relying on an anonymous tip to make a *Terry* stop, then the tip must be sufficiently reliable to provide the officer with reasonable suspicion to make the stop. Generally, an anonymous tip alone is not sufficiently reliable. The Court explained that an anonymous tip that is suitably corroborated may be sufficiently reliable to provide the officer with reasonable suspicion to make a *Terry* stop, considering two factors: (1) what the officers knew—either by their own observations, their experience, or prior knowledge of the suspect or area—before they conducted their stop; and (2) whether the anonymous tip showed that the informant had predicted accurately the suspect's movements or had knowledge of concealed criminal activity. A tip that merely identifies a specific person is not reliable enough to show knowledge of concealed criminal activity.

In *Florida* v. *J. L.* (2000), the Court held than an anonymous tip that a person is carrying a gun, without more information, does not justify a police officer's stop and frisk of that person. In this case, an anonymous caller reported to the police that a young black man standing at a particular bus stop and wearing a plaid shirt was carrying a gun. There was no audio recording of the tip and nothing was known about the informant. Officers went to the bus stop and saw three black men. One of the men, J. L., was wearing a plaid shirt. Aside from the tip, the officers had no reason to suspect the three of illegal conduct. The officers did not see a firearm or observe any unusual movements. One of the officers frisked J. L. and seized a gun from his pocket.[46]

EXIGENT CIRCUMSTANCES   Although the general rule on searches within a home without a warrant is that they are presumptively unreasonable,[47] the Supreme Court has established a few narrowly crafted exceptions to the warrant requirement. These exceptions allow the police to act when "the public interest requires some flexibility in the application of the general rule that a valid warrant is a prerequisite for a search."[48] The Court has recognized the following "exigent" or emergency circumstances as ones in which there are insufficient time to obtain a search warrant:

1. To prevent escape
2. To prevent harm to the officers or others
3. To prevent the destruction of evidence
4. While in hot pursuit of a criminal suspect
5. To render immediate aid to a person in need of assistance[49]

As some examples, in *Warden* v. *Hayden*, 1967, the Court approved the warrantless search of a residence after reports that an armed robber had fled into a building;[50] in *Mincey* v. *Arizona* (1978) the Court held that the Fourth Amendment does not require police officers to delay an investigation if to do so would gravely endanger their lives or others;[51] in 1990 in *Maryland* v. *Buie*, mentioned earlier, the Court extended the warrantless authority of police to search locations in a house (protective sweep) where a potentially dangerous person could hide while an arrest warrant is being served;[52] and in *Wilson* v. *Arkansas* (1995) it ruled that officers need not announce themselves while executing a warrant if evidence may be destroyed, officers are pursuing a recently escaped arrestee, or officers' lives may be endangered.[53] Also, in 2001, in *Illinois* v. *McArthur*, the Court ruled that officers with probable cause to believe that a home contains contraband or evidence of criminal activity may reasonably prevent a suspect found outside the home from reentering it while they apply for a search warrant.[54]

A call to 911, even an anonymous one, obviously, is an example of a possible exigent circumstance. In these situations, however, to make a lawful warrantless, nonconsensual entry and search to render aid, the police must reasonably believe that an emergency situation exists requiring immediate police intervention, the search must not be motivated primarily by intent to arrest and seize evidence, and there must be some reasonable basis, approximating probable cause, to associate the emergency with the area or place to be searched. Although it may be best for police to verify and corroborate an anonymous call to 911, the Court acknowledged in 2003, in *United States* v. *Holloway*, "when an emergency is reported by an anonymous caller, the need for immediate action may outweigh the need to verify the reliability of the caller."[55]

Michael L. Ciminelli, in a 2003 *FBI Law Enforcement Bulletin*, while acknowledging that officers should not hesitate to act reasonably to preserve life and protect others in potentially dangerous situations, says officers can follow the following guidelines to help support the legal justification to enter a home when answering an anonymous 911 call:

- Take reasonable steps to identify the caller before making the entry if circumstances permit; however, in certain cases—for example, screams for help, sounds of a struggle, or shots fired—this may not always be possible.
- Where safe and feasible, take reasonable steps to investigate and corroborate the anonymous call before acting by speaking to neighbors and other persons in the vicinity.
- Where safe and feasible, attempt to obtain a valid consent to enter.
- Accurately document the information given by the anonymous caller.
- Accurately document conditions found at the scene that may corroborate the anonymous call.[56]

CONSENT SEARCHES   A police officer can also search without a warrant if consent is given by a person having authority to give such consent. Consent searches have some limitations. The request cannot be phrased as a command or a threat; it must be a genuine request for permission. An oral reply must be received by the police; a nod of the head is not consent. Also, the search must be limited to the area for which consent is given.[57] Following is a discussion of some of the most important consent search decisions made by the Supreme Court.

In *Schneckloth* v. *Bustamonte* (1973), the Supreme Court ruled that a search conducted pursuant to lawfully given consent is an exception to the warrant and probable cause requirements of the Fourth Amendment; however, because a consensual search is still a search, the Fourth Amendment reasonableness requirement still applies. The court ruled that to determine whether an individual voluntarily consented to a search, the reviewing court should consider the totality of the circumstances surrounding the consent.[58] In *United States* v. *Matlock* (1974), the Court ruled that for a consent search to be constitutionally valid, the consent must be voluntarily given by a person with proper authority. In this case, the Court ruled that a person sharing a room with another person had the authority to allow the police to search the room.[59]

An example of a search that was considered unconstitutional occurred in *Bumper* v. *North Carolina* (1968) in which the police searched a defendant's house by getting the permission of the defendant's grandmother, who also occupied the house.[60] To get the grandmother's permission, the police told her they had a lawful search warrant, which they actually did not have. The Court ruled that the government has the burden of proving that an individual voluntarily consented to the search; and, in this case, they did not.

In 1990, in *Illinois* v. *Rodriguez*, the Court declared constitutional the actions of the police in entering the defendant's Chicago apartment with his former girlfriend's consent and key after she claimed he had seriously assaulted her.[61] Upon entry, the police found the defendant, Rodriguez, and a quantity of cocaine and drug paraphernalia. Rodriguez's claim that his former girlfriend had no control over the apartment because she had moved out at least a month earlier did not sway the Court.

In 1991, in *Florida* v. *Bostick*, the Supreme Court reinterpreted consent searches by ruling that police requests to look into a person's luggage do not require that the officer have reasonable suspicion that he or she is violating the law.[62]

The Supreme Court has also established a "consent once removed" exception to the search warrant requirement. Under that exception, officers are permitted to make a warrantless entry to arrest a suspect based on the consent to enter given earlier to an undercover officer or informant.[63] An example is the 2000 case of *United States* v. *Pollard* in which an informant and an undercover officer entered a residence to purchase four kilograms of cocaine. Upon seeing the cocaine in the apartment, the informant gave the arrest signal. In response to the arrest signal, approximately six officers, without knocking or announcing, immediately broke down the front door and arrested the defendants. The U.S. Court of Appeals for the Sixth Circuit ruled that the entry by the backup officers to arrest the defendants was lawful under the consent once removed doctrine. The Court found that once the defendants gave the undercover officer and the informant permission to enter, the entry by the arrest team did not create any further invasion of privacy.[64]

PLAIN VIEW   **Plain view evidence** is unconcealed evidence inadvertently seen by an officer engaged in a lawful activity. If an officer is at a location legally doing police work and observes contraband or other plain view evidence, its seizure without a warrant is legal, according to the U.S. Supreme Court in *Harris* v. *United States* (1968).[65] In *Arizona* v. *Hicks* (1987), the Court ruled that the evidence must indeed be in plain view without the police moving or dislodging objects to view the evidence.[66]

Many people think that there is a **crime scene** exception to the search warrant. This is not so. In *Mincey* v. *Arizona* (1978), the Court refused to recognize a crime scene search as one of the well-delineated exceptions to the search warrant requirement. As a result, crime scenes are given no special consideration under the Fourth Amendment. If a crime occurs in an area where there is a reasonable expectation of privacy, law enforcement officers are compelled to obtain a search warrant before the crime scene search.[67] To obtain a valid search warrant, officer must meet two critical requirements of the Fourth Amendment. First, they must establish probable cause to believe that the location contains evidence of a crime; and, second, they must particularly describe that evidence. It is very simple to justify the granting of a search warrant for a crime scene, because by its very nature a crime scene establishes the probable cause for obtaining the warrant. Descriptions of the evidence believed to be present at the scene is generally relatively generic; for example, blood, a weapon, and the like.[68]

Yet, despite the general requirement to obtain a search warrant, it is very common that most crime scenes do not permit the police sufficient time to obtain a search warrant before making initial entries onto the scene. Consequently, they are forced to rely on exceptions to the warrant requirement to justify these searches. The most common justifications in these cases are consent, emergencies (exigent circumstances), public place, and plain view.

The consent exception can apply to many crime scenes because often the person who has summoned the police to the scene is someone who can consent to the search. However, in order for the crime scene search to be constitutional, consent must be given voluntarily by a person reasonably believed by law enforcement officers to have lawful access and control over the premises.[69]

The emergency exception also applies to many crime scenes. Traditionally, courts have recognized three different types of emergencies: threats to life or safety, destruction or removal of evidence, and escape. It is indeed difficult to imagine a crime scene that would not automatically present officers with the necessary belief that at least one of these exigent circumstances exists. However, once they are inside the premises and have done whatever is necessary to resolve the emergency, the emergency is over. The officers must have a warrant or one of the other exceptions to the warrant requirement either to remain on the premises or to continue their search.

Although officers cannot conduct a full-scale search of a crime scene under the emergency exception, there are certain investigative steps that may lead to the discovery of evidence that fall well within its scope. For instance, officers arriving on the scene of a violent crime unquestionably can sweep the premises in an effort to locate other victims or the suspect if they reasonably suspect that either is present. If a body is found at the scene, taking the medical examiner to view and collect the body is deemed a reasonable step. If officers have probable cause to believe a crime scene contains evidence that will be destroyed if not quickly recovered, that evidence may be retrieved as part of the emergency. Officers may also secure doors and control people on the premises, to guarantee that the scene is not contaminated. Finally, if the crime scene is in a public place or evidence is in plain view, a warrant is not required.[70]

ABANDONED PROPERTY   In *Abel* v. *United States*, the U.S. Supreme Court in 1960 established a standard regarding police searches of abandoned property.[71] A hotel manager gave an FBI agent permission to search a hotel room that had been previously occupied by Abel. The agent found incriminating evidence in a wastepaper basket. Abel was arrested and convicted based on this evidence. On appeal to the U.S. Supreme Court, the Court ruled that once Abel vacated the room, the hotel had the right to allow law enforcement agents to search it.

In *California* v. *Greenwood* (1988), the Supreme Court extended the abandoned property rule to include garbage left at the curb.[72] In this case, the police in Laguna Beach, California, received information from an informant that Billy Greenwood was engaged in drug dealing from his house. They made observations of the house and found numerous cars stopping there at night. The drivers would leave their cars and enter the house for a short time and then leave. The police made arrangements with the local garbage collector to pick up Greenwood's trash, which he left in brown plastic bags in front of his house, and to take it to the station house. The police searched the garbage and found evidence indicating a drug business, including razor blades and straws with cocaine residue and discarded telephone bills with numerous calls to people who had police records for drug possession. Using this evidence, the police obtained a search warrant. When they executed the warrant, they found hashish and cocaine, and they arrested Greenwood.

The U.S. Supreme Court ruled that searches of a person's discarded garbage were not violations of the Fourth Amendment. Speaking for the Court, Justice Byron White stated, "It is common knowledge that garbage bags left on or at the side of a public street are readily accessible to animals, children, scavengers, snoops and other members of the public. Requiring police to seek warrants before searching such refuse would therefore be inappropriate."

In 1991, in *California* v. *Hodari, D.*, the Court ruled the police were proper in arresting a defendant who fled from the police and threw away evidence as he retreated.[73] In this case, a group of youths in Oakland, California, fled when they saw the approach of two police officers. The officers retrieved a rock of crack cocaine thrown away by one of the youths.

INVENTORY   In *Colorado* v. *Bertine*, the Supreme Court ruled in 1987 that the police may enter a defendant's automobile, which they impounded for safekeeping and were going to return to the defendant after initial police and court processing, and inventory its contents without a warrant to ensure that all contents were accounted for.[74] In this case, Bertine had been arrested for driving while intoxicated. Upon making an inventory of his van's contents, the police found canisters of drugs. Bertine was additionally charged with violation of the drug laws. The Supreme Court ruled that the police action did not violate Bertine's constitutional rights.

OPEN FIELDS   In *Hester* v. *United States* (1924), the Supreme Court established an "open fields exception" to the warrant requirement.[75] The Court said that fields not immediately surrounding a home did not have the protection of the Fourth Amendment and that no warrant was required to enter them and search. Justice Oliver Wendell Holmes, speaking for the Court, wrote

> The special protection accorded by the Fourth Amendment to the people in their "persons, houses, papers, and effects," is not extended to the open fields. The distinction between the latter and the house is as old as the common law.

In *Oliver* v. *United States*, the Supreme Court was asked in 1984 to reexamine its open fields exception under the following circumstances:

> Acting on reports that marijuana was being raised on the farm of petitioner Oliver, two narcotics agents of the Kentucky State Police went to the farm to investigate. Arriving at the farm they drove past petitioner's house to a locked gate with a "No Trespassing" sign. . . . The officers found a field of marihuana over a mile from petitioner's house.[76]

Speaking for the Court, and reaffirming the open fields exception, Justice Lewis F. Powell, Jr., wrote, "We conclude that the open fields doctrine, as enunciated in *Hester,* is consistent with the plain language of the Fourth Amendment and its historical purpose."

Two additional cases in the 1980s expanded the power of the police to watch over citizens without a warrant. In 1986, in *California* v. *Ciraola*, the Court ruled on the actions of the police who had received a tip that marijuana was growing in the defendant Ciraola's backyard.[77] The backyard was surrounded by fences, one of which was 10 feet high. Police flew over the yard in a private plane at an altitude of 1,000 feet in an effort to verify the tip. On the basis of their observations, the police were able to secure and execute a search warrant, which resulted in the seizure of marijuana. Ciraola was convicted on the drug charges, and on appeal the Court ruled that the police actions were not unconstitutional.

In 1989, in *Florida* v. *Riley*, the police flew a helicopter 400 feet over a greenhouse in which Riley and his associates were growing marijuana plants.[78] Based on their observations, the police arrested Riley on drug charges. On appeal, the Court ruled that the police did not need a search warrant to conduct such a low-altitude helicopter search of private property because the flight was within airspace legally available to helicopters under federal regulations.

THE AUTOMOBILE EXCEPTION   Many students complain about the actions of police officers who search their automobiles. "Don't we have Fourth Amendment rights when we are in our cars?" they ask. "Yes," the professor answers, "but less than in your house."

The automobile exception to the search warrant requirement goes all the way back to 1925, in *Carroll* v. *United States*.[79] In this case, the Supreme Court ruled that distinctions should be made between searches of automobiles, persons, and homes, and that a warrantless search of a vehicle, which can be readily moved, is valid if the police have probable cause to believe that the car contains evidence they are seeking. This decision has become known as the **Carroll doctrine.**

In 1981, in *New York* v. *Belton*, the Supreme Court ruled that a search incident to a lawful arrest of the occupant of an automobile can extend to the entire passenger compartment of the automobile, including the glove compartment and luggage boxes or clothing found in them.[80] This ex-

YOU ARE THERE! »

Carroll v. United States

On September 29, 1921, during Prohibition, two federal agents were in an apartment in Grand Rapids when George Carroll and John Kiro entered. The agents arranged to buy a case of whiskey from them. Arrangements were made for the two men to deliver the whiskey the next day, but they never returned. A few days later, on October 6, 1921, the agents observed Carroll and Kiro driving an automobile on a highway. They pursued them but lost them. Two months later, on December 15, 1921, the agents again observed them on the same highway and were able to overtake them and stop them. The agents searched the car and found 68 bottles of whiskey behind the seats. Carroll and Kiro were arrested for violation of the Prohibition laws. Upon appeal, the Supreme Court established the automobile exception to the Fourth Amendment.

Source: Based on *Carroll* v. *United States*, 267 U.S. 132 (1925).

tended the Chimel "arm's reach doctrine," but only in the case of automobiles.

In *United States* v. *Ross* (1982), the Supreme Court held that if probable cause exists to believe than an automobile contains criminal evidence the police may make a warrantless search of the automobile.[81] In 1983 in *United States* v. *Villamonte-Marquez,* the Court extended the Carroll doctrine to include watercraft; and, in 1985, in *California* v. *Carney,* it extended it to include motor homes.[82]

In 1991, the Supreme Court further extended police rights in vehicle searches. In *California* v. *Acevedo* and a similar case, *Florida* v. *Jimeno*, the Court ruled that the automobile exception not only covers vehicles but also permits warrantless searches of immobile packages that have been placed in cars.[83] In the *Acevedo* case, the police had observed the defendant leaving his house and carrying a brown paper bag the size of marijuana packages they had seen earlier. The defendant placed the bag in the car's trunk. As he drove away, the police stopped the car, opened the trunk, and seized and opened the bag.

In 1996, the Court in *Pennsylvania* v. *Labron* reaffirmed the Carroll doctrine by ruling that, in probable cause cases, there is no need for a warrant in vehicle searches if the vehicle is readily mobile, even if there is time to obtain a warrant.[84]

In its 1998–1999 term, the Supreme Court provided further clarification of the constitutionality of searching a motor vehicle without a warrant in three separate cases. In *Maryland* v. *Dyson*, the Court remained consistent with its prior rulings by ruling that a warrantless search of a vehicle is permitted when officers have probable cause to believe that a motor vehicle contains evidence or contraband, even in the absence of exigent circumstances.[85] In *Florida* v. *White*, a forfeiture case, the Court ruled that the police do not have to obtain a warrant prior to seizing a vehicle while it is parked in a public place. In *Wyoming* v. *Houghton*, the Court held that when an officer has probable cause to search a vehicle, the officer may search objects belonging to a passenger in the vehicle provided the item(s) the officer is looking for could reasonably be in the passenger's belongings.[86]

BORDER SEARCHES   In *United States* v. *Martinez-Fuerte* (1976), the Supreme Court ruled that border patrol officers do not have to have probable cause or a warrant to stop cars for brief questioning at fixed checkpoints.[87]

GOOD FAITH   The Supreme Court established a "good faith" exception to the exclusionary rule in *United States* v. *Leon* (1984). It waived the exclusionary rule in cases in

YOU ARE THERE! ≫

United States v. Leon

In August 1981, Officer Cyril Rombach, an experienced and well-trained narcotics investigator, prepared an application for a search warrant to search the homes and automobiles of several suspects in a drug investigation. In September 1981, a search warrant was issued by a state superior judge. The officer executed the search warrant and found large quantities of drugs at three residences and in two automobiles listed on the warrant. Rombach arrested several people, including Alberto Leon, for drug violations.

The defendants were indicted by a grand jury and charged with conspiracy to possess and distribute cocaine. The defendants filed motions to suppress the evidence, and the district court granted the motions to suppress in part. It concluded that the affidavit was insufficient to establish probable cause. The court recognized that Rombach had acted in good faith, but it rejected the government's suggestion that the Fourth Amendment exclusionary rule should not apply where evidence is seized in reasonable good faith reliance on a search warrant.

Upon appeal, the Supreme Court overruled the district court and established the "good faith doctrine." It ruled that evidence obtained in good faith, where the officers reasonably believed they had sufficient probable cause to get a warrant, is admissible in court. The Court said that the exclusionary rule should be applied only in cases in which the police purposely, recklessly, or negligently violate the law.

Source: Based on *United States v. Leon*, 468 U.S. 897 (1984).

In 1995, in *Arizona v. Evans*, the Court extended the "good faith" exception by creating a "computer errors exception." In this case the police arrested Evans for a traffic violation. A routine computer check reported an outstanding arrest warrant for Evans, and he was arrested; a search of his vehicle revealed possession of a controlled substance. Later, it was determined that the arrest warrant should have been removed from the computer a few weeks earlier. However, the Court reasoned that officers could not be held responsible for a clerical error made by a court worker and did, in fact, act in good faith.[90]

SEARCHES BY PRIVATE PERSONS   In *Burdeau v. McDowell* (1921), the Supreme Court ruled that the Bill of Rights applies only to the actions of government agents; it does not apply to private security employees or private citizens not acting on behalf of, or with, official law enforcement agencies.[91] The fact that private security personnel are not bound by the tenets of the Constitution and cannot obtain warrants, however, does not mean that they can indiscriminately violate the rights of offenders. If they do, they can be sued at civil law and suffer severe financial damages.

CANINE SEARCHES   In *United States v. Place* (1983), the U.S. Supreme Court ruled that exposure of luggage in a public place to a trained drug canine did not constitute a search within the meaning of the Fourth Amendment.[92] The Court explained that the dog's alert to the presence of drugs created probable cause for the issuance of a search warrant for drugs. It explained that the dog's sniff is nonintrusive and reveals only the presence of contraband. Many cases have ruled that a dog's positive alert alone generally constitutes probable cause to search a vehicle under the motor vehicle exception to the search warrant requirement.[93]

Special Agent Michael J. Bulzomi, a legal instructor at the FBI Academy, writes that drug detection dogs remain extremely important in drug interdiction. They represent a highly efficient and cost-effective way to establish quickly whether probable cause exists to execute a search for contraband. The use of drug detection dogs has met with few real legal challenges in the courts. The only notable area that has been challenged is a dog's reliability. Drug detection dog handlers should be prepared to establish a dog's reliability by providing prosecutors with a complete record of the dog's training, success rate, and certification in drug detection.[94] Jayme S. Walker, in an excellent 2001 article in the *FBI Law Enforcement Bulletin*, shows many examples of court decisions declaring dog sniffs not searches under

which the police act in reasonable reliance and good faith on a search warrant that is later ruled faulty or found to be unsupported by probable cause.[88]

Speaking for the Court, Justice Byron R. White stated

In the absence of an allegation that the magistrate abandoned his detached and neutral role, suppression is appropriate only if the officers were dishonest or reckless in preparing their affidavit or could not have harbored an objectively reasonable belief in the existence of probable cause. . . .

During the 1980s the Court continued its emphasis on "good faith" exceptions to the Fourth Amendment in *Massachusetts v. Sheppard* (1984), *Illinois v. Krull* (1987), and *Maryland v. Garrison* (1987).[89]

the Fourth Amendment in cases involving luggage, packages, warehouses or garages, buses, trains, motel rooms, apartments, and homes.[95]

★ ★ ★

THE POLICE AND CUSTODIAL INTERROGATION

Kimberly A. Crawford has written that the U.S. Supreme Court has recognized two constitutional sources of the right to counsel during interrogation. One source is the Court's interpretation, in *Miranda* v. *Arizona*,[96] of the Fifth Amendment right against self-incrimination; the other is contained within the language of the Sixth Amendment. The impetus for the creation of the *Miranda* rights was the Supreme Court's concern that **custodial interrogations** are intrinsically coercive; therefore, the right to counsel contained within *Miranda* applies only when the subject of interrogation is in custody.[97]

In English common law, the lack of a confession was often viewed as a serious deficiency in the government's case, enough to cause a judge or jury to acquit an accused person. Although not required to prove guilt, the emphasis on securing a confession from a suspect remains today.[98]

Louis DiPietro, a special agent and legal instructor at the FBI Academy, states that a confession is probably the most substantiating and damaging evidence that can be admitted against a defendant. To be admissible, due process mandates that a confession be made voluntarily. In addition, it mandates the investigator's scrupulous compliance with the U.S. Supreme Court's requirements emanating from the landmark *Miranda* case and other constitutional rights of an accused. DiPietro warns that a nonvoluntary confession will be excludable on the grounds of denial of due process of law.[99]

This section will pay particular attention to cases leading to the *Miranda* ruling; the *Miranda* case and its ruling; cases that seem to have led to the erosion of the *Miranda* rule; the *Dickerson* ruling; and surreptitious recording of suspects' conversations.

The Path to *Miranda*

The police have many crimes to investigate and often not enough resources to accomplish their mission. Also, in many cases there is not enough physical evidence or there are no eyewitnesses to assist the police in their investigation. Thus, police must seek to gain a confession from a defendant, particularly in murder cases, in order to gain a

Exhibit 11.5	The Path to *Miranda*

Brown v. Mississippi (1936)
McNabb–Mallory rule (1957)
Escobedo v. Illinois (1964)
Miranda v. Arizona (1966)
The *Miranda* rules (1966)

conviction. The history of methods used by the police to obtain confessions from suspects has been sordid, including beatings and torture by the police that came to be known as "the third degree." From 1936 until 1966, the Supreme Court issued a number of rulings to preclude this misconduct and ensure compliance with due process as guaranteed by the Bill of Rights. The following landmark cases show the development of rules regarding custodial interrogation during those three decades. (See Exhibit 11.5.)

THE END OF THE THIRD DEGREE   In *Brown* v. *Mississippi* (1936), the Supreme Court put an end to the almost "official" practice of brutality and violence used by the police to obtain confessions from suspects. The case involved the coerced confessions, through beatings, of three men. The Supreme Court suppressed the confessions and emphasized that the use of confessions obtained through barbaric tactics deprived the defendants of their right to due process under the Fourteenth Amendment. The Court, in effect, said that coerced confessions were untrustworthy, unreliable, and unconstitutional.[100] (See Exhibit 11.6.)

Exhibit 11.6	Legal Definitions Relating to Interrogation

Admission   A voluntary statement, contrary to a person's position on trial, that falls short of a confession.

Confession   A direct acknowledgment of guilt.

Custodial interrogation   The confinement of a person by law enforcement agents-officers. The person is not free to leave and is questioned about a crime.

Exculpatory   Statements or evidence that tends to prove that a person was not the perpetrator of a criminal offense.

Incriminate   To involve either oneself or another as responsible for criminal conduct.

Interrogation   Questioning of a person to ascertain facts.

Sources: Irving J. Klein, *Constitutional Law for Criminal Justice Professionals*, 3d ed. (Miami, FL: Coral Gables Publishing, 1992), pp. 691–699; and Irving J. Klein, *The Law of Arrest, Search, Seizure, and Liability Issues: Principles, Cases, and Comments* (Miami, FL: Coral Gables Publishing, 1994).

Brown v. Mississippi

On March 30, 1934, Raymond Steward was murdered. On that night Deputy Sheriff Dial went to the home of Ellington, one of the defendants, and requested him to accompany him to the house of the deceased. There a number of white men were gathered, who began to accuse the defendant of the crime. Upon his denial they seized him and hanged him by a rope to the limb of a tree, twice. When they took him down the second time they tied him to a tree and whipped him. The trial record showed that the signs of the rope on his neck were plainly visible during the trial. He was again picked up a day or two later and again severely beaten until he confessed. The other two defendants, Ed Brown and Henry Shields, were also arrested and taken to jail. In order to obtain the confession the defendants were "made to strip and they were laid over chairs and their backs were cut to pieces with a leather strap with buckles on it and they were likewise made by the said deputy definitely to understand that the whipping would be continued unless and until they confessed, and not only confessed, but confessed to every matter of detail as demanded by those present."

The defendants made their confession on April 1, 1934, were indicted on April 4, went on trial on April 5, and were convicted and sentenced to death on April 6, 1934. The deputy sheriff who administered over the beatings, Deputy Sheriff Dial, testifying in court, responded to an inquiry as to how severely a defendant was whipped by stating "Not too much for a negro; not as much as I would have done if it were left to me."

On appeal, the Supreme Court ruled that the actions against the three men were violations of their due process rights.

Source: Based on *Brown v. Mississippi*, 297 U.S. 278 (1936).

Speaking for the court, Chief Justice Charles E. Hughes wrote

Because a State may dispense with a jury trial, it does not follow that it may substitute trial by ordeal. The rack and torture chamber may not be substituted for the witness stand. The State may not permit an accused to be hurried to conviction under mob domination—where the whole proceeding is but a mask—without supplying corrective process. . . . The due process clause requires "that state action, whether through one agency or another, shall be consistent with the fundamental principles of liberty and justice which lie at the base of all

our civil and political institutions." . . . It would be difficult to conceive of methods more revolting to the sense of justice than those taken to procure the confessions of these petitioners, and the use of confessions thus obtained as the basis for conviction and sentence was a clear denial of due process.

THE PROMPT ARRAIGNMENT RULE   *McNabb* v. *United States* (1943) and *Mallory* v. *United States* (1957) were cases that involved confessions obtained as a result of delays in the "prompt arraignment" of the defendants before a federal judge.[101] The Court did not address whether or not the confessions were voluntary, the previous standard for admitting them into evidence. Instead, it consid-

McNabb v. United States and Mallory v. United States

The McNabb family consisted of five Tennessee mountain people who operated an illegal moonshine business near Chattanooga. During a raid on their business by federal agents, a police officer was killed. The five were arrested and subjected to continuous interrogation for two days. Two of the McNabbs were convicted based on their confessions, and each was sentenced to 45 years in prison for murder. In *McNabb v. United States,* the Supreme Court ruled that these confessions were in violation of the Constitution because they violated the Federal Rules of Criminal Procedure, which required that defendants must be taken before a magistrate without unnecessary delay.

In *Mallory v. United States,* the defendant was a 19-year-old male of limited intelligence who was arrested for rape in Washington, D.C. He was arrested the day after the crime and taken to the police station and questioned over a 10-hour period. He confessed under interrogation by the police officer administering the polygraph examination. The Supreme Court again ruled that the delay in bringing the defendant before a magistrate was a violation of the Federal Rules of Criminal Procedure.

In both of these cases, the court did not even consider the question of voluntariness. The new standard that the Court adopted was called the *McNabb–Mallory* rule and considered only the time element between the arrest and the first appearance before a judge. This rule applied only to actions of federal law enforcement officers.

Source: Based on *McNabb v. United States,* 318 U.S. 332 (1943) and *Mallory v. United States,* 354 U.S. 449 (1957).

ered how long it took for law enforcement agents to bring the suspects before a judge and whether the confessions should be admissible because of this delay.

THE ENTRY OF LAWYERS INTO THE STATION HOUSE   In 1964, the Supreme Court ruled in *Escobedo v. Illinois* that the refusal by the police to honor a suspect's request to consult with his lawyer during the course of an interrogation constituted a denial of his Sixth Amendment right to counsel and his Fifth Amendment right to be free from self-incrimination—rights made obligatory upon the states by the Fourteenth Amendment.[102] The decision rendered any incriminating statement elicited by the police during such an interrogation inadmissible in court. The Court ruled that once a suspect becomes the focus of a police interrogation and is taken into custody and requests the advice of a lawyer, the police must permit access to the lawyer.

The *Miranda* Ruling

The well-known case of *Miranda v. Arizona* (1966) was the culmination of many Supreme Court decisions focusing on the rights of individuals during police interrogations.[103] The *Miranda* decision was, in fact, a combination of cases involving four persons: Ernesto Miranda; Michael Vignera, arrested in New York City for robbery; Carl Westover, arrested in Kansas City for robbery; and Roy Stewart, arrested in Los Angeles for robbery. What we now call the *Miranda* rules could have been called the Vignera, or Westover, or Stewart rules; however, the Court decided to issue their ruling under Ernesto Miranda's case.[104]

In *Miranda*, the Supreme Court ruled that confessions are by their very nature inherently coercive and that custodial interrogation makes any statements obtained from defendants compelled and thus not voluntary. The Court felt that interrogations violate the Fifth Amendment, which guarantees that no one shall be compelled to be a witness against him- or herself in a criminal case, and that this guarantee is violated anytime a person is taken into custody and interrogated.

The Court then established the now well-known **Miranda rules** or **Miranda warnings**, which state that prior to any interrogation of a person in custody the police must

- Advise the suspect that he or she has the right to remain silent
- Advise the suspect that anything he or she says can and will be used in court against him or her
- Advise the suspect that he or she has the right to consult a lawyer and to have the lawyer present during questioning
- Advise the suspect that if he or she cannot afford an attorney, an attorney will be provided, free of charge

The Court further ruled that if, prior to the interrogation or during the interrogation, the suspect, in any way, indicates a wish to remain silent or to have an attorney, the interrogation may no longer proceed.

YOU ARE THERE! »

Escobedo v. Illinois

On the evening of January 19, 1960, Danny Escobedo's brother-in-law, Manuel, was shot to death. The next morning the Chicago police arrested Escobedo and attempted to interrogate him. However, his attorney obtained a writ of habeas corpus, requiring the police to free him.

On January 30, Benedict DiGerlando, who was then in police custody, told the police that Escobedo had fired the fatal shots at his brother-in-law. The police then rearrested Escobedo and brought him to police headquarters. Escobedo told the police he wanted to consult his lawyer. Shortly after the arrest, Escobedo's attorney arrived at headquarters and attempted to see him, but he was denied access to him. During their stay at headquarters the police caused an encounter between Escobedo and DiGerlando during which Escobedo made admissions to the crime. Later a statement was taken from Escobedo. He was never advised of his rights. He was convicted of the murder of Manuel based on his statements.

The Supreme Court reversed Escobedo's conviction based on the fact that the police violated Escobedo's Sixth Amendment rights, rights made obligatory on the states through the Fourteenth Amendment.

Note: Do you know what happened to Danny Escobedo after this case? Subsequent to his landmark Supreme Court case, Escobedo was arrested for burglary and selling drugs. He was sentenced to prison and paroled in 1975. In 1984 he was again sentenced to prison on sex crime charges involving a 13-year-old girl. While free on bond pending an appeal on that conviction he was arrested in Chicago for attempted murder. He pled guilty.

Source: Based on *Escobedo v. Illinois* 378 U.S. 478 (1964); and James A. Inciardi, *Criminal Justice*, 3rd ed. (Orlando, FL: Harcourt Brace Jovanovich, 1990), pp. 280–281.

© UPI/Corbis-Bettman

Ernesto Miranda (right) with his attorney in Phoenix, Arizona, in 1967. The successful appeal of his case to the U.S. Supreme Court established the well-known *Miranda* warnings.

the suspect is *both* in custody and subject to interrogation.[105] Even interrogations taking place at the police station may not fall within the meaning of custodial interrogation. For example, in *Oregon v. Mathiason* the Court held that a suspect who was invited to come to the police station, voluntarily arrived unaccompanied by the police, and was told before the interrogation that he was not under arrest was not in custody for the purpose of *Miranda*.[106] The court has also found routine traffic stops and questioning at the suspect's home to be noncustodial situations.[107]

When giving the *Miranda* warnings, officers must ensure that a suspect makes a knowing, intelligent, and voluntary waiver of his rights as a prerequisite to questioning. Also, if a suspect clearly indicates unwillingness to answer questions and invokes the right to silence, police must scrupulously honor that request. Where a suspect makes a clear request to consult with an attorney, police must immediately cease any further questioning and may not contact the suspect about any crime unless a lawyer is present or

It must be remembered that the *Miranda* rule applies to all custodial interrogations; however, this does not mean every police interview requires the warnings. The Supreme Court has made it clear that *Miranda* applies only when

YOU ARE THERE! >>

Miranda v. *Arizona*

On March 2, 1963, in Phoenix, Arizona, an 18-year-old woman walking to a bus stop after work was accosted by a man who shoved her into his car and tied her hands and ankles. He then took her to the edge of the city where he raped her. The rapist drove the victim to a street near her home and let her out of the car. On March 13, the Phoenix police arrested a 23-year-old, eighth-grade dropout named Ernesto Miranda and charged him with the crime. Miranda had a police record dating back to when he was 14 years old, had been given an undesirable discharge by the army for being a Peeping Tom, and had served time in federal prison for driving a stolen car across a state line.

Miranda was placed in a lineup at the station house and positively identified by the victim. He was then taken to an interrogation room where he was questioned by the police without being informed that he had a right to have an attorney present. Two hours later, police emerged from the interrogation room with a written confession signed by Miranda. At the top of the statement was a typed paragraph stating that the

confession was made voluntarily, without threats or promises of immunity and "with full knowledge of my legal rights, understanding any statement I make may be used against me."

At trial Miranda was found guilty of kidnapping and rape and sentenced to 20 to 30 years in prison. Upon appeal, the Supreme Court ruled that Miranda's confession was inadmissible.

Note: Do you know what happened to Ernesto Miranda after this decision? Ernesto Miranda was subsequently given a new trial. He was convicted of rape and kidnapping after his common-law wife, Twila Hoffman, testified that he had admitted kidnapping and raping the victim. He was sentenced to a 20- to 30-year prison term and was paroled in 1972. In 1974 he was arrested for the illegal possession of a gun and drugs. In 1976, at age 34, Miranda was murdered in a Phoenix skid row bar during a quarrel over a card game.

Source: Based on *Miranda v. Arizona,* 384 U.S. 436 (1966); and James A. Inciardi, *Criminal Justice,* 3rd ed., (Orlando, FL: Harcourt Brace Jovanovich, 1990), pp. 280–281.

unless the suspect initiates the contact with the police.[108] Also, the Court has ruled that persons who cannot understand the *Miranda* warnings because of their age, mental handicaps, or language problems cannot be legally questioned without an attorney being present.[109] In *Arizona v. Roberson*, the Court held that the police may not avoid a suspect's request for a lawyer by beginning a new line of questioning, even if it is about an unrelated offense.[110]

The Erosion of *Miranda*

In the aftermath of the *Miranda* decision, there was tremendous confusion in the legal community over its exact meaning. Consequently, a large number of cases were brought to the Court challenging and questioning it. Eventually the Supreme Court of the 1970s and 1980s under Chief Justice Burger began to impose a series of exceptions to the *Miranda* decision. These decisions led noted civil liberties lawyer and Harvard law professor Alan Dershowitz to write an article in 1984 entitled "A Requiem for the Exclusionary Rule," in which he said, "The Burger Court has chipped away at the exclusionary rule—carving out so many exceptions that it is falling of its own weight."[111] Dershowitz added

> Our twenty-five year experiment with the exclusionary rule may well be coming to an end. We have learned precious little from it, because the exclusionary rule was never really given a chance. The public, spurred by politicians' rhetoric, closed its eyes and ears to facts like the following: that only a tiny fraction of defendants (less than half of one percent, according to a federal study) are freed because of the exclusionary rule; and that there has been a marked improvement both in police efficiency and in compliance with the Constitution since the exclusionary rule was established.[112]

Despite Dershowitz's thoughts, the *Miranda* rule still stands, and defendants in custody must still be advised of their constitutional rights prior to any interrogation. However, the Court does recognize certain exceptions to *Miranda*. Several of the post-*Miranda* cases that have led to its weakening follow.

HARRIS V. *NEW YORK*   In *Harris v. New York* (1971), the Court ruled that statements that are trustworthy, even though they were obtained without giving a defendant *Miranda* warnings, may be used to attack the credibility of a defendant who takes the witness stand.[113] The prosecutor accused Harris of lying on the stand and used statements obtained by the police, without *Miranda* warnings, before the trial to prove it.

Justice Burger, speaking for the Court relative to the *Miranda* rule, wrote, "The shield provided by *Miranda* cannot be perverted into a license to use perjury by way of a defense, free from the risk of confrontation with prior inconsistent utterances. We hold, therefore, that petitioner's credibility was appropriately impeached by use of his earlier conflicting statements."

MICHIGAN V. *MOSLEY*   In *Michigan v. Mosley* (1975), the Court ruled that a second interrogation, held after the suspect had initially refused to make a statement, was not a violation of the *Miranda* decision. In the second interrogation, which was for a different crime, the suspect had been read the *Miranda* warnings.[114]

BREWER V. *WILLIAMS*   In *Brewer v. Williams* (1977), the Supreme Court seemed to extend the meaning of the word *interrogation* by interpreting comments made by a police detective as "subtle coercion."[115] This case affirmed *Miranda* but is presented here because of a second decision in the case of *Nix v. Williams* (1984).[116] In this case, the state of Iowa continued to appeal the decision reached in *Brewer v. Williams*. In 1984, the Supreme Court, in *Nix v. Williams*, promulgated the "inevitability of discovery rule." Victim Pamela Powers's body would have been discovered inevitably, so it should be allowed to be used as evidence in the trial.

RHODE ISLAND V. *INNIS*   In *Rhode Island v. Innis* (1980), the Supreme Court clarified its definition of interrogation by ruling that the "definition of interrogation can extend only to words or actions on the part of police officers that *they should have known* [Court's emphasis] were reasonably likely to elicit an incriminating response."[117] In this case, a man told the police where he had left a shotgun he had used in a shooting after the police had made remarks about the possibility of a disabled child finding it. (There was a home for disabled children nearby.)

NEW YORK V. *QUARLES*   In *New York v. Quarles* (1984), the Supreme Court created a "public safety" exception to the *Miranda* rule.[118] In this case, a police officer, after arresting and handcuffing a man wanted in connection with a crime, and after feeling an empty shoulder holster on the man's body, asked him where the gun was without giving the man the *Miranda* warnings. The gun was suppressed as evidence because the officer's question was not preceded by the warnings. The Supreme Court, however, overruled the state court and said the officer's failure to read the *Miranda* warnings was justified in the interest of public safety.

YOU ARE THERE! »

Brewer v. *Williams* and *Nix* v. *Williams*

On Christmas Eve, 1968, 10-year-old Pamela Powers was at a Des Moines, Iowa, YMCA with her parents to watch her brother participate in a wrestling match. Pamela told her parents that she was going to use the bathroom. She was never seen alive again. At about the time of Pamela's disappearance, a young boy saw a man, later identified as Robert Williams, walking out of the YMCA carrying a bundle wrapped in a blanket to his car. The boy told police that he thought he saw two legs under the blanket. Robert Williams was a resident of the YMCA, a religious fanatic, and an escaped mental patient. On Christmas Day Williams's car was found abandoned near the city of Davenport, Iowa, 160 miles from Des Moines. On the day after Christmas Williams walked into the Davenport police station house and surrendered to the police. The Davenport police notified the Des Moines police, who arranged to pick up Williams.

When Detective Leaming arrived at the Davenport police station to pick up Williams, he was advised by Williams's lawyer, Henry McKnight, that he did not want Williams to be the subject of any interrogation during the trip from Davenport to Des Moines. Leaming agreed to the lawyer's request.

In the car on the way back to Des Moines, Detective Leaming, knowing that Williams was a religious fanatic, addressed him as "Reverend" and made what has become known as the "Christian Burial Speech":

> I want to give you something to think about while we're traveling down the road. . . . Number one, I want you to observe the weather conditions. It's raining, it's sleeting, it's

freezing, driving is very treacherous, visibility is poor, it's going to be dark early this evening. They are predicting several inches of snow for tonight, and I feel that you yourself are the only person that knows where this little girl's body is, that you yourself have only been there once, and if you get a snow on top of it you yourself may be unable to find it. And, since we will be going right past the area on the way into Des Moines, I feel that we could stop and locate the body, that the parents of this little girl should be entitled to a Christian burial for the little girl who was snatched away from them on Christmas Eve and murdered. And I feel we should stop and locate it on the way in rather than waiting until morning and trying to come back out after a snowstorm and possibly not being able to find it at all.

After this speech, Williams directed the police to the young girl's dead body. Williams was convicted of her murder.

On appeal to the Supreme Court, the Court voted 5–4 that Leaming's "Christian Burial Speech" constituted custodial interrogation and that the evidence, the body, was illegally obtained and therefore not admissible in court.

But the state of Iowa continued to appeal the Brewer decision, and in 1984 the Supreme Court in *Nix* v. *Williams* promulgated the "inevitability of discovery rule" saying in effect that Pamela Powers's body would have been discovered inevitably, thus it should be allowed to be used as evidence in a trial.

Source: Based on *Brewer* v. *Williams*, 430 U.S. 222 (1977) and *Nix* v. *Williams*, 467 U.S. 431 (1984).

The Court wrote

We conclude that the need for answers to questions in a situation posing a threat to the public safety outweighs the need for the prophylactic rule protecting the Fifth Amendment's privilege against self incrimination. We decline to place officers such as Officer Kraft in the untenable position of having to consider, often in a matter of seconds, whether it best serves society for them to ask the necessary questions without the *Miranda* warnings and render whatever probative evidence they uncover inadmissible, or for them to give the warnings in order to preserve the admissibility of evidence they might uncover but possibly damage or destroy their ability to obtain that evidence and neutralize the volatile situation confronting them.

MORAN V. *BURBINE*   In *Moran* v. *Burbine* (1986), a murder case, the Supreme Court ruled that the police failure to inform a suspect undergoing custodial interrogation of his attorney's attempts to reach him does not constitute a violation of the *Miranda* rule.[119] The Court reasoned that events that are not known by a defendant have no bearing on his capacity to knowingly waive his or her rights.

Speaking for the Court, Justice O'Connor, commenting on the actions of the police in lying to the lawyer, Munson, wrote

> Focusing primarily on the impropriety of conveying false information to an attorney, he [Burbine] invites us to declare that such behavior should be condemned as violative of

YOU ARE THERE! >>

Rhode Island v. Innis

On the night of January 12, 1975, John Mulvaney, a Providence, Rhode Island, cabdriver, disappeared after being dispatched to pick up a fare. His body was discovered four days later buried in a shallow grave in Coventry, Rhode Island. He had died from a shotgun blast to the back of his head.

Five days later, shortly after midnight, the Providence police received a phone call from a cabdriver who reported that he had just been robbed by a man with a sawed-off shotgun. While at the police station, the robbery victim noticed a picture of his assailant on a bulletin board and informed a detective. The detective prepared a photo array, and the complainant identified the suspect again. The police began a search of the area where the cabdriver had brought the suspect. At about 4:30 A.M., an officer spotted the suspect standing in the street. Upon apprehending the suspect, the officer, Patrolman Lovel, advised him of his *Miranda* rights. A sergeant responded and advised the suspect of his *Miranda* rights. A captain responded and also advised the suspect of his constitutional rights. The suspect stated that he understood his rights and wanted to speak with an attorney. The captain directed three officers in a caged wagon, a four-door police car with a wire screen mesh between the front and rear seats, to bring the suspect to the police station. While en route to the police station two of the officers engaged in conversation. One, Patrolman Gleckman, testified at the trial:

> At this point, I was talking back and forth with Patrolman McKenna stating that I frequent this area while on patrol and that (because a school for handicapped children is located nearby) there's a lot of handicapped children running around in this area, and God forbid one of them

might find a weapon with shells and they might hurt themselves.

Patrolman McKenna testified:

> I more or less concurred with him that it was a safety factor and that we should, you know, continue to search for the weapon and try to find it.

The third officer, Patrolman Williams, didn't participate in the conversation but testified as to the conversation between the two officers:

> He (Gleckman) said it would be too bad if the little—I believe he said a girl—would pick up the gun, maybe kill herself.

According to police testimony, the suspect then interrupted the conversation, stating that the officers should turn the car around so he could show them where the gun was located. When they reached the crime scene the suspect was again advised of his *Miranda* rights and the suspect said he understood his rights but that he "wanted to get the gun out of the way because of the kids in the area in the school." The suspect then led the police to the area where the shotgun was located.

The defendant Innis was convicted; but, upon appeal, the evidence of the gun was suppressed. However, in 1980, the United States Supreme Court heard the case and reversed the Rhode Island appeals court, ruling that the officers' statements were not interrogation and the gun was allowed to remain in evidence.

Source: Based on *Rhode Island v. Innis*, 446 U.S. 291 (1980).

---

canons fundamental to the "traditions and conscience of our people." . . . We do not question that on facts more egregious than those presented here police deception might rise to a level of a due process violation. . . . We hold only that, on these facts, the challenged conduct falls short of the kind of misbehavior that so shocks the sensibilities of civilized society as to warrant a federal intrusion into the criminal processes of the States.

ILLINOIS V. PERKINS   In *Illinois v. Perkins* (1990), the Supreme Court further clarified its *Miranda* decision.[120] In the *Perkins* case, police placed an informant and an undercover officer in a cellblock with Lloyd Perkins, a suspected

murderer incarcerated on an unrelated charge of aggravated assault. While planning a prison break, the undercover officer asked Perkins whether he had ever "done" anyone. In response, Perkins described at length the details of a murder-for-hire he had committed.

When Perkins was subsequently charged with the murder, he argued successfully to have the statements he made in prison suppressed because no *Miranda* warnings had been given before his conversation with the informant and undercover officer. On review, however, the Supreme Court reversed the order of suppression.

Rejecting Perkins's argument, the Supreme Court recognized that there are limitations to the rules announced in

YOU ARE THERE! »

New York v. Quarles

At 12:30 A.M., police officers Frank Kraft and Sal Scarring were on routine patrol in Queens, New York, when a young woman approached them and told them that she had been raped by a black male, approximately 6 feet tall, who was wearing a black jacket with the name "Big Ben" printed in yellow letters on the back. She then told the officers that the man had just entered an A&P supermarket located nearby and that the man had a gun. The officers put the woman into the police car and drove to the A&P, where Officer Kraft entered the store while his partner radioed for backup. Kraft observed the suspect, Mr. Quarles, approaching a checkout counter. On seeing the officer, Quarles turned and ran toward the rear of the store. Kraft took out his revolver and chased Quarles. When Quarles turned the corner at the end of an aisle, Kraft lost sight of him for several seconds. On regaining sight of Quarles, Kraft apprehended him and ordered him to stop and put his hands over his head. Kraft then frisked Quarles and discovered that he was wearing an empty shoulder holster. After handcuffing him, Kraft asked him where the gun was. Quarles nodded in the direction of some empty cartons and said, "The gun is over there." Kraft retrieved a loaded .38 caliber revolver from one of the cartons and then formally arrested Quarles and read him his *Miranda* warnings. At trial the judge suppressed Quarles's statement, "The gun is over there," and suppressed the evidence of the gun because Kraft had not given Quarles his *Miranda* warnings before asking "Where's the gun?"

On appeal from the prosecutor to the United States Supreme Court, the Court reversed the New York ruling and created a "public safety" exception to the requirement that police give a suspect his *Miranda* warnings before interrogation.

Source: Based on *New York v. Quarles*, 104 S.Ct. 2626 (1984).

Miranda. The Court expressly declined to accept the notion that the *Miranda* warnings are required whenever a suspect is in custody in a technical sense and converses with someone who happens to be a government agent. Rather, the Court concluded that not every custodial interrogation creates the psychologically compelling atmosphere that *Miranda* was designed to protect against. When the compulsion is lacking, the court found, so is the need for *Miranda* warnings.

The Court in *Perkins* found the facts at issue to be a clear example of a custodial interrogation that created no compulsion. Pointing out that compulsion is determined from the perspective of the suspect, the Court noted that Perkins had no reason to believe that either the informant or the undercover officer had any official power over him, and therefore, he had no reason to feel any compulsion to make self-incriminating statements. On the contrary, Perkins bragged about his role in the murder in an effort to impress those he believed to be his fellow inmates. *Miranda* was not designed to protect individuals from themselves.

PENNSYLVANIA V. MUNIZ   In *Pennsylvania v. Muniz* (1990), the Court ruled that the police use of the defendant's slurred and drunken responses to booking questions (he was arrested for driving under the influence of alcohol) as evidence in his trial was not a violation of *Miranda* rights even thought he was never given his *Miranda* warnings.[121]

ARIZONA V. FULMINANTE   In 1991, in *Arizona v. Fulminante,* the Supreme Court further weakened *Miranda* by ruling that a coerced confession might be a harmless trial error.[122] In this case the Court overruled years of precedent to hold that if other evidence introduced at trial is strong enough, the use of a coerced confession could be considered harmless and a conviction upheld. In other words, a coerced confession, by itself, is not sufficient to have a conviction overruled if there is other compelling evidence of guilt.

MINNICK V. MISSISSIPPI   In *Minnick v. Mississippi* (1991), the Court clarified the mechanics of *Miranda* by ruling that once a suspect in custody requests counsel in response to *Miranda* warnings, law enforcement officers may no longer attempt to reinterrogate that suspect unless the suspect's attorney is present or the suspect initiates the contact with the law enforcement agents.[123]

McNEIL V. WISCONSIN   In *McNeil v. Wisconsin* (1991), the Court ruled that an in-custody suspect who requests counsel at a judicial proceeding, such as an arraignment or initial appearance, is only invoking the Sixth Amendment right to counsel as to the charged offense and is not invoking the Fifth Amendment right to have an attorney present during the custodial interrogation.[124]

WITHROW V. WILLIAMS   In *Withrow v. Williams* (1993), the Supreme Court distinguished *Miranda* violations from Fourth Amendment violations with respect to habeas corpus proceedings.[125] The Court held that criminal

Moran v. Burbine

On March 3, 1977, Mary Jo Hickey was found unconscious in a factory parking lot in Providence, Rhode Island. Suffering from injuries to her skull apparently inflicted by a metal pipe found at the scene, she was rushed to a nearby hospital. Three weeks later she died from her wounds.

Several months after her death, the Cranston, Rhode Island, police arrested Brian Burbine and two others for burglary. Shortly before the arrest, Detective Ferranti of the Cranston police had learned from a confidential informant that the man responsible for Ms. Hickey's death lived at a certain address and was also known by the nickname "Butch." On learning from the arresting officer that Burbine went by the nickname Butch and that he gave his address as the same one previously given by the informant, Ferranti advised Burbine of his constitutional rights. Burbine refused to speak to the detective. Ferranti spoke to Burbine's two associates and obtained more incriminating information. Ferranti then called the Providence police, who sent three detectives to Cranston to interrogate Burbine.

That evening Burbine's sister called the Providence Public Defender's Office to obtain legal assistance for her brother. A lawyer from the office, Allegra Munson, called the Cranston detective division. The conversation went as follows:

A male voice responded with the word "Detectives." Ms. Munson identified herself and asked if Brian Burbine was

being held; the person responded affirmatively. Ms. Munson explained to the person that Burbine was represented by attorney and she would act as Burbine's legal counsel in the event that the police intended to place him in a lineup or question him. The unidentified person told Ms. Munson that the police would not be questioning Burbine or putting him in a lineup and that they were through with him for the night. Ms. Munson was not informed that the Providence Police were at the Cranston police station or that Burbine was a suspect in Mary's murder.

Less than an hour after Munson's call, Burbine was brought to an interrogation room and questioned about Mary Jo Hickey's murder. He was informed of his *Miranda* rights on three separate occasions, and he signed three written forms acknowledging that he understood his right to the presence of an attorney and indicating that he did not want an attorney called or appointed for him. Burbine signed three written statements fully admitting to the murder. Based on his written statements Burbine was convicted of murder. Upon appeal the Rhode Island Court of Appeals reversed the conviction.

The United States Supreme Court reversed the court of appeals ruling and ruled that Burbine's constitutional rights were not violated.

Source: Based on *Moran v. Burbine*, 475 U.S. 412 (1986).

---

defendants can continue to raise *Miranda* violations in habeas corpus proceedings, even though it had previously restricted habeas corpus petitions that raised Fourth Amendment issues.

DAVIS V. UNITED STATES   In *Davis v. United States* (1994), the Court ruled that, after law enforcement officers obtain a valid *Miranda* waiver from an in-custody suspect, they may continue questioning him when he makes an ambiguous or equivocal request for counsel during the questioning.[126] The Court stated that although it may be a good law enforcement practice to attempt to clarify an equivocal request for counsel, that practice is not constitutionally required.

In *Davis*, Naval Criminal Investigative Service (NCIS) agents investigating a murder obtained both oral and written *Miranda* waivers from the defendant. After being inter-

viewed for approximately 90 minutes, the defendant said: "Maybe I should talk to a lawyer." After asking some clarifying questions, the NCIS agents continued to interrogate him. The Court ruled that the defendant's statement was not sufficiently unequivocal to constitute an assertion of his *Miranda* right to counsel.

STANSBURY V. CALIFORNIA   In *Stansbury v. California* (1994), the Court reaffirmed the principle that an officer's uncommunicated suspicions about a suspect's guilt are irrelevant to the question of whether that suspect is in custody for purposes of *Miranda*.[127] Thus, a custody for *Miranda* purposes is a completely objective determination based on facts and circumstances known to the subject.

The Court reiterated its earlier holding in *Oregon v. Mathiason* (1977) that *Miranda* warnings are required only when a person is in custody, which can be defined as either a formal arrest or a restraint on freedom of movement to the degree associated with a formal arrest. The Court then stated that this determination of custody depends on objective factors and not on the subjective views of the officers or the subject. (See Table 11.8.)

The *Dickerson* Ruling and Beyond

In *Dickerson* v. *United States* (2000), the Supreme Court ruled that *Miranda* was a constitutional decision that cannot be overruled by an act of Congress.[128]

Charles Thomas Dickerson was charged with conspiracy to commit bank robbery and other offenses. Before trial, he moved to suppress a statement he had made to the FBI on grounds that he had not received *Miranda* warnings before being interrogated. The District Court suppressed the statement. The government appealed saying that two years after *Miranda*, Congress enacted 18 USC 3501, providing that a confession shall be admissible in federal court if it is voluntarily given. The government felt that Congress intended to overrule *Miranda* because the new law required merely voluntariness—not the four warnings as per *Miranda*—as the determining factor as to whether a statement will be admissible.

After several appellate decisions the Supreme Court held that *Miranda* was a constitutional decision—that is, a decision that interprets and polices the Constitution—that cannot be overruled by an act of Congress, such as 18 USC 3501. While conceding that Congress may modify or set aside the Court's rules of evidence and procedure that are not required by the Constitution, the Court emphasized that Congress may not overrule the Court's decisions that interpret and apply the Constitution.

The Court cited various other reasons for reaching its conclusion that *Miranda* is a constitutionally based rule. Among them, the Court noted that *Miranda* had become part of our national culture because the warnings were embedded in routine police practice. By holding *Miranda* to be a constitutional decision, the Court reaffirmed that *Miranda* governs the admissibility of statements made during custodial interrogation in both state and federal courts. In light of the *Dickerson* decision, a violation of *Miranda* is now clearly a violation of the Constitution, which can result in suppression of statements in both federal and state courts.[129]

Prior to *Dickerson*, some constitutional scholars expected that the Court might find a way to use the many cases mentioned in the "Erosion of *Miranda*" section to overrule *Miranda*. The Court expressly declined to do so in *Dickerson*. The Court's decision in this case did not attempt to find and defend an underlying rationale that would reconcile *Miranda* with those previous relevant cases that threatened to undermine or erode *Miranda*.[130]

After *Dickerson* came *Texas* v. *Cobb* (2001) in which the U.S. Supreme Court ruled that the Sixth Amendment right to counsel only applies to the case for which that right was invoked by the suspect and not other cases affecting the suspect.[131]

Raymond Cobb, 17, was accused of burglarizing the home of Lindsey Owings. When Owings returned from work he found his house burglarized and his wife and daughter missing. The police conducted an investigation and eventually questioned Cobb about the incident. At the time of the questioning, Cobb was incarcerated on an unrelated offense. After being advised of and waiving his *Miranda* rights, Cobb admitted to the burglary but denied any knowledge of the whereabouts of the woman and child. He was indicted on the burglary and invoked his Sixth Amendment right to counsel. After being freed on bond, Cobb confessed to his father that he had killed the woman and the child. The father reported his son's confession to the police and a warrant was obtained for the boy's arrest on charges of murder.

After the arrest, Cobb was advised of his *Miranda* rights and waived them. He then admitted to the police that he stabbed the wife to death with a knife he had brought with him and then took her body into a wooded area behind the house to bury her. He then returned to the house and found the 16-month-old child sleeping on its bed. He took the baby into the woods and laid it near the mother. He

Table 11.8	Landmark Supreme Court Decisions: Custodial Interrogation
Issue	**Cases**
Physical torture	*Brown* v. *Mississippi* (1936)
Prompt arraignment	*McNabb* v. *United States* (1943), *Mallory* v. *United States* (1957)
Refusal to allow counsel	*Escobedo* v. *Illinois* (1964)
Must advise of constitutional rights	*Miranda* v. *Arizona* (1966)
Inevitability of discovery	*Brewer* v. *Williams* (1977), *Nix* v. *Williams* (1984)
Public safety	*New York* v. *Quarles* (1984)
Lying to lawyers	*Moran* v. *Burbine* (1986)
Placing informer in prison cell	*Illinois* v. *Perkins* (1990)
Harmless trial error	*Arizona* v. *Fulminante* (1991)
Equivocal request for counsel	*Davis* v. *United States* (1994)

then obtained a shovel and dug a grave. Before Cobb had put the mother's body in the grave, the child awoke and began stumbling around, looking for her mother. When the baby fell into the grave, Cobb put the mother's body on top of her and buried them both. Cobb subsequently led police to the grave.

Cobb was convicted of capital murder and sentenced to death. He appealed his conviction on the grounds that the interrogation following his arrest on the murder charges violated his Sixth Amendment right to counsel that had attached and been invoked with respect to the burglary charge. An appellate court agreed, and Cobb's conviction was reversed.

But the Supreme Court reversed the appellate court, ruling that the interrogation did not violate Cobb's Sixth Amendment right to counsel and the confession was admissible. The Court argued that the Sixth Amendment right to counsel is "offense specific," and applied to the burglary charge only and not the murder charge.

Surreptitious Recording of Suspects' Conversations

Kimberly Crawford reports that the surreptitious recording of suspects' conversations is an effective investigative technique that, if done properly, can withstand both constitutional and statutory challenges.[132] She cites several cases in which the courts have ruled that the surreptitious recording of suspects' conversations did not violate the custodial interrogation rules decided in *Miranda*.

In *Stanley v. Wainwright* (1979), two robbery suspects were arrested and placed in the backseat of a police car. They were unaware that one of the arresting officers had turned on a tape recorder on the front seat of the car before leaving the suspects unattended for a short period of time. During that time, the suspects engaged in a conversation that later proved to be incriminating. On appeal, the defense argued that the recording violated the ruling in *Miranda* because the suspects were in custody at the time the recording was made and placing of the suspects alone in the vehicle with the activated recorder was interrogation for purposes of *Miranda*. The appeals court summarily dismissed this argument and found that the statements were spontaneously made and not the product of interrogation.[133]

In a similar vein, in 1994, in *United States v. McKinnon*, the Eighth Circuit Court of Appeals held that individuals have no reasonable expectation of privacy in police vehicles, stating that a police car is "essentially the officer's office and is frequently used as a temporary jail for housing and transporting arrestees and suspects. The general public

has no reason to believe that it is a sanctuary for private discussions."[134]

In *Kuhlmann v. Wilson* (1986), the Supreme Court held that placing an informant in a cell with a formally charged suspect in an effort to gain incriminating statements did not amount to a violation of the defendant's constitutional rights, stating

> Since the Sixth Amendment is not violated whenever—by luck or happenstance—the State obtains incriminating statements from the accused after the right to counsel was attached, a defendant does not make out a violation of that right simply by showing that an informant, either through prior arrangement or voluntarily, reported his incriminating statements to the police. Rather, the defendant must demonstrate that the police and their informant took some action, beyond merely listening, that was designed deliberately to elicit incriminating remarks.[135]

In a 1989 case, *Ahmad A. v. Superior Court*, the California Court of Appeals confronted a Fourth Amendment challenge to the admissibility of a surreptitiously recorded conversation between the defendant and his mother. The defendant, a juvenile arrested for murder, asked to speak with his mother when advised of his constitutional rights. The two were thereafter permitted to converse in an interrogation room with the door closed. During the surreptitiously recorded conversation that ensued, the defendant admitted his part in the murder. Reviewing the defendant's subsequent Fourth Amendment challenge, the California court noted that at the time the mother and her son were permitted to meet in the interrogation room, no representations or inquiries were made as to privacy or confidentiality. Finding the age-old truism "walls have ears" to be applicable, the court held that any subjective expectation that the defendant had regarding the privacy of his conversation was not objectively reasonable.[136]

In 2001, in *Belmar v. Commonwealth*, the Virginia Appellate Court ruling on a case similar to *Ahmad A. v. Superior Court* wrote that police interrogation rooms are "designed for disclosure, not the hiding, of information."[137]

These cases and others show that the mere placing of a recorder in a prison cell, interrogation room, or police vehicle does not constitute a violation of a suspect's rights. Instead, in order to raise a successful Sixth Amendment challenge, the defense has to show that someone acting on behalf of the government went beyond the role of a mere passive listener (often referred to by the courts as a "listening post") and actively pursued incriminating statements from the suspect.

Crawford suggests that law enforcement officers contemplating the use of this technique comply with the following guidelines:

- To avoid a Sixth Amendment problem, this technique should not be used after formal charges have been filed or the initial appearance in court, unless the conversation does not involve a government actor, the conversation involves a government actor who has assumed the role of a "listening post," or the conversation pertains to a crime other than the one with which the suspect has been charged.

- To avoid conflicts with both the Fourth Amendment and Title III of the Omnibus Crime Control and Safe Streets Act, suspects should not be given any specific assurances that their conversations are private.[138]

★ ★ ★

POLICE EYEWITNESS IDENTIFICATION PROCEDURES

Often law enforcement officers apprehend suspects based on descriptions given by victims of violent crimes. To ensure that the apprehended person is actually the perpetrator, the police must obtain assistance from the victim or employ other identification procedures. The following sections discuss procedures to identify suspects properly as the actual perpetrators of crimes.

Lineups, Showups, and Photo Arrays

Lineups, showups, and photo arrays are important parts of the police investigation process, as are procedures requiring suspects to give samples of their voice, blood, and handwriting to be used in identification comparison procedures.

A **lineup** is the placing of a suspect with a group of other people of similar physical characteristics (such as race, age, hair color, hair type, height, and weight) so that a witness or victim of a crime has the opportunity to identify the perpetrator of the crime. Lineups are usually used after an arrest.

A **showup** involves bringing a suspect back to the scene of the crime or another place (for example, a hospital where an injured victim is) where the suspect can be seen and possibly identified by a victim or witness. The showup must be conducted as soon as possible after the crime, and with no suggestion that the person is a suspect. A showup is usually used after an arrest.

A **photo array** is similar to a lineup, except that photos of the suspect (who is not in custody) and others are shown to a witness. Photo arrays are used prior to arrest.

Could these procedures be construed as violating a defendant's freedom against self-incrimination as provided by the Fifth Amendment to the U.S. Constitution? The following sections detail the key landmark decisions of the Supreme Court in lineup, showup, and photo array cases.

UNITED STATES V. WADE   In *United States v. Wade* (1967), the Supreme Court made two very important decisions about lineups.[139] It ruled that a person can be made to stand in a lineup and perform certain actions that were performed by the suspect during the crime, such as saying certain words or walking in a certain fashion. The Court also ruled that once a person is indicted, that person has a right to have an attorney present at the lineup.

KIRBY V. ILLINOIS   In 1972, in *Kirby v. Illinois*, the Supreme Court ruled that the right to counsel at lineups applies only after the initiation of formal judicial criminal proceedings, such as an indictment, information, or

---

YOU ARE THERE! »

United States v. Wade

On September 21, 1964, a man with a piece of tape on each side of his face forced a cashier and a bank official to put money into a pillow case. The robber then left the bank and drove away with an accomplice, who was waiting outside in a car.

In March 1965, six months after the robbery, an indictment was returned against Wade and an accomplice for the robbery. Wade was arrested on April 2, 1965. Two weeks later, an FBI agent put Wade into a lineup to be observed by two bank employees. Wade had a lawyer, but the lawyer was not notified of the lineup. Each person in the lineup had strips of tape on his face, similar to those worn by the robber, and each was told to say words that had been spoken at the robbery. Both bank employees identified Wade as the robber. Wade was convicted based on the identification by the witnesses.

On appeal, the Supreme Court ruled that placing someone in a lineup and forcing that person to speak or perform other acts at the lineup did not violate the Fifth Amendment privilege against self-incrimination. The Court held, however, that because Wade had been indicted and was represented by counsel, the lawyer should have been allowed to be there.

Source: Based on United States v. Wade, 388 U.S. 218 (1967).

arraignment—that is, when a person formally enters the court system.[140] An information is a formal charging document drafted by a prosecutor and presented to a judge. An indictment is a formal charging document returned by a grand jury based on evidence presented to it by a prosecutor. The indictment is then presented to a judge. Indictments generally cover felonies. An arraignment is a hearing before a court having jurisdiction in a criminal case, in which the identity of the defendant is established, the defendant is informed of the charge or charges and his or her rights, and the defendant is required to enter a plea. In *Kirby*, the Court reasoned that because a lineup may free an innocent person, and the required presence of an attorney might delay the lineup, it is preferable to have the lineup as soon as possible, even without an attorney.

Thus in a postarrest, preindictment lineup, there is no right to have an attorney present. Many police departments, however, will permit an attorney to be present at a lineup and make reasonable suggestions, as long as there is no significant delay of the lineup.

STOVAL V. *DENNO*   In *Stoval* v. *Denno* (1967), the Supreme Court ruled that showups are constitutional and do not require the presence of an attorney.[141] The Court addressed the issue:

> The practice of showing suspects singly to persons for purpose of identification, and not a part of a lineup, has been unduly condemned. . . . However, a claimed violation of due process of law in the conduct of a confrontation depends on the totality of the circumstances surrounding it and the record in the present case reveals that the showing of Stoval to Mrs. Behrendt in an immediate hospital confrontation was imperative.

Subsequent to *Stoval* v. *Denno*, a federal appellate court established a set of guidelines phrased in the form of questions that could decide the constitutionality of a showup. A careful review of the questions reveals that the court clearly prefers lineups to showups but will permit showups if certain conditions are met:

- Was the defendant the only individual who could possibly be identified as the guilty party by the complaining witness, or were there others near him or her at the time of the showup so as to negate the assertion that he or she was shown alone to the witness?
- Where did the showup take place?
- Were there any compelling reasons for a prompt showup so as to deprive the police of the opportunity of securing other similar individuals for the purpose of holding a lineup?

- Was the witness aware of any observation by another or any other evidence indicating the guilt of the suspect at the time of the showup?
- Were any tangible objects related to the offense placed before the witness that would encourage identification?
- Was the witness identification based on only part of the suspect's total personality?
- Was the identification a product of mutual reinforcement of opinion among witnesses simultaneously viewing the defendant?
- Was the emotional state of the witness such as to preclude identification.[142]

UNITED STATES V. *ASH*   In *United States* v. *Ash* (1973), the Supreme Court ruled that the police could show victims or witnesses photographic displays containing a suspect's photograph (photo arrays) without the requirement that the suspect's lawyer be present.[143]

Other Identification Procedures

We know that any type of testimony is governed by the Fifth Amendment. However, in most cases coming before it, the Supreme Court declared that procedures that are not testimonial are not under the purview of the Fifth Amendment. (*Testimonial* refers to oral or written communication by a suspect, as opposed to the taking of blood or exemplars as indicated in this section.) Samples of such cases follow. (See also Table 11.9.)

SCHMERBER V. *CALIFORNIA*   In 1966, in *Schmerber* v. *California*, the Supreme Court ruled that the forced extraction of blood by a doctor from a man who was arrested for driving while intoxicated was not a violation of that man's constitutional rights.[144]

WINSTON V. *LEE*   In *Winston* v. *Lee* (1985), the Supreme Court clarified its position on medical provisions regarding prisoners.[145] When the Court decided the Schmerber case, it warned, "That we today hold that the Constitution does not forbid the States' minor intrusions into an individual's body under stringently limited conditions in no way indicates that it permits more substantial intrusions, or intrusions under other conditions."[146] The Rudolph Lee case provided the test of how far the police can go in attempting to retrieve evidence from a suspect's body.

Lee, a suspect in a robbery, was shot by the victim. The police endeavored to have a bullet removed from Lee's body in order to use it for a ballistics examination.

YOU ARE THERE! »

Winston v. Lee

On July 18, 1982, Ralph E. Warkinson was shot during a robbery attempt at his place of business. Warkinson fired at the shooter and believed he hit him in the side. The police brought Warkinson to a local hospital emergency room. Twenty minutes later, the police responded to a reported shooting and found Rudolph Lee suffering from a gunshot wound to the left chest area. Lee said he had been shot during a robbery attempt by two men. When Lee was taken to the hospital (the same one to which Warkinson had been taken), Warkinson identified Lee as the man who had shot him. After a police interrogation, Lee was arrested for the shooting.

In an effort to obtain ballistics evidence, the police attempted to have Lee undergo a surgical procedure under a general anesthetic for the removal of the bullet lodged in his chest. Lee appealed to the courts, which ruled in his favor and against the operation. The Commonwealth of Virginia appealed the case to the U.S. Supreme Court. The Court ruled that such surgical procedure, without Lee's permission, would be a violation of his Fourth Amendment rights.

Source: Based on *Winston v. Lee*, 470 U.S. 753 (1985).

Table 11.9	Landmark Supreme Court Decisions: Police Identification Procedures
Issue	Cases
Lineups	*United States v. Wade* (1967), *Kirby v. Illinois* (1972)
Showups	*Stoval v. Denno* (1967)
Photo arrays	*United States v. Ash* (1973)
Medical procedures	*Schmerber v. California* (1966), *Winston v. Lee* (1985)

Justice William J. Brennan, speaking for the Court, wrote, "We conclude that the procedure sought here is an example of the 'more substantial intrusion' cautioned against in *Schmerber*, and hold that to permit the procedure would violate respondent's right to be secure in his person guaranteed by the Fourth Amendment."[147]

UNITED STATES V. DIONISIO   In *United States v. Dionisio* (1973), the Supreme Court ruled that a suspect must provide voice exemplars (samples of his or her voice) that can be compared with the voice spoken at the time of the crime.[148]

UNITED STATES V. MARA   In 1973, in *United States v. Mara*, the Supreme Court ruled that it was not a violation of constitutional rights for the police to require a suspect to provide a handwriting exemplar (a sample of his or her handwriting) for comparison with handwriting involved in the crime.[149]

EYEWITNESS IDENTIFICATION   Concerning eyewitness identification, in 2001, the National Institute of Justice produced a guide for law enforcement for the collection and preservation of eyewitness evidence that represented a combination of the best current, workable police practices and psychological research. It describes practices and procedures that, if consistently applied, will tend to increase the overall accuracy and reliability of eyewitness evidence. Although not intended to state legal criteria for the admissibility of evidence, this guide sets out rigorous criteria for handling eyewitness evidence that are as demanding as those governing the handling of physical trace evidence. It outlines basic procedures that officers can use to obtain the most reliable and accurate information from eyewitnesses.[150]

CHAPTER SUMMARY

This chapter discussed crime in the United States, including how we measure it, how much crime occurs, and how many arrests are effected; the police and the United States Constitution, including the Bill of Rights and the Fourteenth Amendment; and the role of the Supreme Court in regulating the police and the exclusionary rule and its impact on the police. It also covered the police and arrest, including probable cause, reasonable and deadly force in making arrests, and stopping vehicles.

Also, the chapter discussed the police and search and seizure, including the warrant requirement, the search warrant, and exceptions to the warrant requirement; the police and custodial interrogation, including the path to *Miranda*, the *Miranda* ruling, the erosion of *Miranda*, the *Dickerson* ruling and beyond; and the police and identification procedures, including lineups, showups, photo arrays, and other identification procedures.

Learning Check

1. Explain how crime is measured in the United States. Determine how much crime occurs in the United States. Tell how many arrests are made in the United States and what the majority of the arrests are for.

2. Explain how the Bill of Rights and the actions of the U.S. Supreme Court regulate the police.

3. List several of the exceptions to the warrant requirement in search and seizure cases and cite and discuss several U.S. Supreme Court cases to illustrate the exceptions.

4. Describe the development of the requirement to be advised of one's constitutional rights prior to police interrogation when in police custody. Cite and discuss several U.S. Supreme Court cases to show the changes in police interrogation procedures over time.

5. Explain the differences between lineups, showups, and photo arrays. Give an example of how each one can be legally used.

Application Exercise

Your younger brother, a high school sophomore, brags to his Future Government Leaders Club that you know everything there is to know about the U.S. Supreme Court. The club's faculty advisor calls you and asks you to participate in a debate at a future club meeting. The subject to be debated is "The Supreme Court of the 1980s and 1990s has swung too far to the right by overemphasizing the rights of society and underemphasizing individual rights." The advisor gives you a choice as to which side you wish to take and tells you to be prepared to quote as many cases as possible in the areas of search and seizure and custodial interrogation in order to defend your stand. Prepare yourself for the debate.

Web Exercise

Patrol over to the FBI homepage and obtain the latest (as current as possible to the date you are using this textbook) statistics on the Index crimes and arrests in the United States. Then patrol over to the NIJ homepage and obtain latest statistics for the NCVS.

Key Concepts

Carroll doctrine
Crime scene
Custodial interrogations
Exclusionary rule
Exigent circumstances
Judicial review
Lineup
Miranda rules (*Miranda* warnings)
National Crime Victimization Survey (NCVS)
Photo array
Plain view evidence
Probable cause
Reasonable force
Reasonable suspicion
Search and seizure
Search warrant
Showup
Silver platter doctrine
Stop and frisk
Uniform Crime Reports (UCR)

Police Ethics and Police Deviance 12

CHAPTER GOALS

- To acquaint you with the various definitions, the types, and the extent of police corruption
- To explore various reasons for police corruption
- To acquaint you with forms of police misconduct other than police corruption, including misuse of alcohol and illegal drugs, cooping, and police deception
- To discuss the definition, types, and extent of police brutality
- To explore various responses to police brutality, including citizen complaint review boards

One of the authors recalls being asked by a student why there are so many studies of deviance by police officers, when other occupational groups rarely study deviance in their ranks. His answer was simple: "We give loaded guns and almost unlimited power to the men and women we appoint as police officers. We don't do that for most other occupations."

Police officers in the United States are given tremendous authority and wide latitude in using that authority. In addition, to the average citizen, the police are the most visible symbol of not only the U.S. criminal justice system, but also the U.S. government.

Many police officers complain that the press overdoes coverage of corrupt or brutal police officers. The 1991 Rodney King tape (the home videotape of the beating of African American motorist Rodney King by four white Los Angeles police officers) was broadcast over every television network in the United States for weeks. The 1997 Abner Louima case (in which a New York City police officer allegedly inserted a stick into the rectum of a prisoner and then put the feces- and blood-covered stick into the prisoner's mouth) was worldwide news and will probably continue to be so for years. Police officers always ask, "Why do they [the media] try to make us all look bad? It was only a few cops, not all cops." Officers also complain about the media attention given to the allegations of racism, brutality, and abuse of authority of Detective Mark Fuhrman in the worldwide television coverage and commentary in the O. J. Simpson murder trial. "Hey, he's only one cop; we're not like that."

We must remember that the media operate under the following philosophy: If a dog bites a person, that is not news. Dogs bite people every day of the week. But if a person bites a dog, that's news. The news is that which is different and not normal. Police officers across the United States do hundreds of thousands of good acts a day. They arrest lawbreakers, find lost children and people suffering from Alzheimer's, walk the elderly across the street, bring the sick and injured to the hospital, deliver babies, stop fights and arguments, and counsel the confused. That is their job, and they do it well, but that is not news. But when the very people we trust to uphold our law—to serve as the model of what our law is and what it stands for—violate that law, that is news. That is the person biting the dog. It is healthy that police misconduct is news. Imagine if this misconduct were so common that it did not qualify as news.

It must be remembered, before reading this chapter, that the vast majority of the over 800,000 men and women in our nation's law enforcement agencies are extremely ethical.

Unfortunately, a few are not. Therefore, this chapter must exist. However, it is, indeed, about the person biting the dog, not the dog biting the person. This chapter will discuss ethics; police deviance, including police corruption and other misconduct such as drug and alcohol abuse, cooping, police sexual violence, domestic violence in police families, police deception and abuse of authority; and police brutality.

★ ★ ★

ETHICS AND THE POLICE

What is ethics? James N. Gilbert, in his article "Investigative Ethics," tells us that ethics can be defined as the practical, normative study of the rightness and wrongness of human conduct. He says that all human conduct can be viewed in the context of basic and applied ethical considerations. Basic ethics are the rather broad moral principles that govern all conduct, while applied ethics focuses these broad principles upon specific applications. For example, a basic ethical tenet assumes that lying is wrong. Applied ethics would examine and govern under what conditions such a wrong would indeed take place.[1] Gilbert concludes

> The ethical dilemmas which face our police will not disappear as the world becomes more sophisticated and technological. On the contrary, such developments only widen the gap between professional behavior and possible unethical actions. As judicial guidelines become more complex, criminal operation more skilled, the temptation towards unethical conduct increases. Accordingly, education and training which addresses the poignant issue of ethical decision making will truly aid the investigator [and police officer].[2]

There has been a growing interest in ethics in the academic and law enforcement literature over the past few decades, including textbooks, studies, journal articles, and media articles.[3] Many departments and law enforcement organizations are promoting in-service training in the area of ethics. The International Association of Chiefs of Police (IACP) offers courses in ethics including "Ethical Standards in Police Service, Force Management, and Integrity Issues" and "Value-Centered Leadership: A Workshop on Ethics and Quality Leadership." Some departments, such as the Santa Monica Police Department, have facilitated ethics training as part of their commitment to community policing. The department recognized that trust is a vital element of community policing and that ethical people inspire trust while unethical people do not. They realized that ethics training would help the department recognize its full potential.[4]

The Greek philosopher Aristotle in his classic *Nicomachean Ethics* stated that "every art and every inquiry and similarly every action and choice is thought to aim at some good."[5] Is Aristotle's "good" what we mean as ethics? This author thinks so. Could Aristotle's definition of good or ethics be the same as our modern saying "do the right thing?" Yes! If one is ethical, he or she does the right thing. If one does the right thing, he or she is ethical. Remember, the vast majority of the over 800,000 men and women in our police departments and other law enforcement agencies are ethical. They do the right thing hundreds of times a day. Unfortunately, some are not ethical. Some do the wrong thing. How do we measure police ethical standards? What standards have been established to determine how police officers should act? Joycelyn Pollock, in her excellent book, *Ethics in Crime and Justice: Dilemmas and Decisions,* identified some of these standards:

- Organizational value systems or codes of ethics designed to educate and guide the behavior of those who work within the organization

- An oath of office, which can be considered a short-hand version of the value system or code of ethics

- The Law Enforcement Code of Ethics as promulgated by the International Association of Chiefs of Police (IACP) (See Appendix B of this text for the Law Enforcement Code of Ethics and the Police Code of Conduct.)[6]

Other standards governing police ethics are the U.S. Constitution and the Bill of Rights, case law as determined by appellate courts and the U.S. Supreme Court, and federal and state criminal laws and codes of criminal procedure.

Although these standards appear on the surface to set a perfect example for police officers and mandate exemplary performance by them, how widely accepted and followed are they by individual officers and departments? As Pollack explains, the police subculture, as discussed in Chapter 6 of this text, often works against these official ethical precepts:

> It is apparent that the formal code of ethics or the organizational value system is quite different from subculture values. Violations of formal ethical standards such as the use of force, acceptance of preferential or discriminatory treatment, use of illegal investigation tactics, and differential enforcement of laws are all supported by the subculture. The police subculture has an ethical code of its own.[7]

Perhaps it is the police subculture, or perhaps it is just the individual actions of officers or groups of officers that create police deviance. Whatever the reason, deviance certainly occurs in policing. However, remember, as most officers know and apparently the public knows, most of our nation's police officers are highly ethical. Albert Cantara, a psychologist for the Austin, Texas, Police Department, addresses some of these issues in his article entitled "An Open Letter from a Police Psychologist to all officers." He states that training and education in ethics can be very beneficial and helpful to the officer in putting the "code of honor" before the "code of silence." He also emphasizes the role of the organization and supervisors in protecting their personnel—especially those in "high-risk" specialties. He stresses proper selection techniques, mandatory periodic counseling, and proactive supervisors who are quick to take action if they observe any potential problems arising.[8]

Evidence exists that the U.S. public believes to a great extent that our police are good, and ethical, and do the right thing. In a 2001 Gallup poll asking respondents to rate the honesty and ethical standards of various occupations, the police came in with an 94 percent positive rating, with 23 percent of the public rating them very high, 45 percent rating them high, and 26 percent rating them average. Only 6 percent of respondents gave them a low or very low rating. Ranking lower than police officers in honesty and ethical standards were bankers, journalists, business executives, stockbrokers, lawyers, labor union leaders, insurance salespeople, advertising practitioners, members of Congress, and even doctors, dentists, and college teachers. Only a few occupations rated higher than police, including firefighters, military, nurses, and clergy.[9]

In fact, in a report prepared by the Administration of Justice Program at George Mason University for the IACP in October of 2001, the authors found that not only do the police consistently rank among the institutions and occupations in which the public expresses the highest confidence and trust, but most citizens are satisfied with police service in their own neighborhood. Interestingly, the majority of citizens have not had face-to-face contact with police and therefore their opinions are primarily based on secondhand information and media accounts.[10]

★ ★ ★

THE DILEMMA OF LAW VERSUS ORDER

Police corruption and police brutality have always been part of policing. The names, places, and times change, but corruption and brutality remain. There has always been an inherent conflict in the role of the police in maintaining law and order in U.S. society. Jerome Skolnick calls this conflict the "dilemma of law versus order," referring to police efforts at maintaining law and order but doing so under the restraints of the law.[11] It would be very easy to maintain law and order by ensuring that our cops were bigger, meaner, and tougher than our criminals, and by letting the cops just beat up all the criminals to ensure a safe society. Of course, we cannot do that. We must have our police comply with the same law they are paid to enforce. As Howard Abadinsky says, "Whatever goals and objectives we assign the police, we insist that they be achieved in conformity to law, and this is no small task."[12]

Elmer Johnson points out that "police observance of individual rights is essential to making democracy a reality in a mass society but achievement of this ideal is made particularly difficult by demands that the police also be efficient in protecting the community against criminals and the disorder attending social unrest."[13]

Police officers face ethical dilemmas everyday. They make difficult decisions on a daily basis utilizing discretion. Every situation is different, and circumstances surrounding an incident may determine whether or not an arrest is made. Officers have to weigh many variables and sometimes contemplate accomplishing the most good for the greatest number of people. Whenever they do this, they are open to questioning and criticism. If they considered the wrong factors (race, ability to gain influence, payoffs) in making these decisions, they could be on the slippery slope to corruption.

Frank Serpico testifying at the Knapp Commission hearings on police corruption in 1970.

In addition to the national commissions, numerous state and local commissions, panels, and hearings have looked into the behavior and operations of the police. The most notable was the Knapp Commission to Investigate Allegations of Police Corruption in New York City (known as the **Knapp Commission**).[15] The Knapp Commission was created in 1970 by New York City mayor John V. Lindsay in response to a series of articles in the *New York Times* detailing organized, widespread police corruption in New York City. It held public

★ ★ ★

REVIEW OF THE POLICE

Possibly because of the dilemma of law versus order, the police are constantly under review by government agencies, including federal, state, and local agencies; the courts; academics; the media; and the general public. Numerous national commissions have looked into the operations of the police. Among the most noteworthy were the National Commission on Law Observance and Enforcement, more popularly known as the Wickersham Commission (1931); the President's Commission on Law Enforcement and Administration of Justice (1967); the National Advisory Commission on Civil Disorders (1968); the National Advisory Commission on Criminal Justice Standards and Goals (1973); and the Commission on Accreditation for Law Enforcement Agencies (1982).[14]

YOU ARE THERE! »

National Commissions Overseeing the Police

1931	National Commission on Law Observance and Enforcement
1967	President's Commission on Law Enforcement and Administration of Justice
1968	National Advisory Commission on Civil Disorders
1973	National Advisory Commission on Criminal Justice Standards and Goals
1982	Commission on Accreditation for Law Enforcement Agencies

The Knapp Commission Discovers Corruption

The Knapp Commission was created in 1970 by New York City mayor John V. Lindsay in response to allegations brought by New York City police officers Frank Serpico and David Dirk of widespread corruption in the New York City Police Department. These allegations were detailed in several articles in the *New York Times* and received national attention. The hearings conducted by the commission also received national attention in the media. The committee's final report was issued in 1972, and its findings were responsible for widespread changes in the policies and operations of the NYPD. The types of corruption in the NYPD discovered by the Knapp Commission through its hearings, investigations, and informants were so many and so varied that they could fill volumes. The Knapp Commission discovered corruption in the following areas:

1. *Gambling.* Officers assigned to plainclothes (antigambling) units received regular monthly payments from the operators of illegal bookmaking, policy, and other gambling operations. The regular monthly payments were called "the pad." Other payments that involved one-time-only payments were called "scores."

2. *Narcotics.* Officers assigned to narcotics units extorted money and other bribes, including drugs, from drug addicts and dealers. The officers also conducted illegal wiretaps and used other unlawful investigatory techniques. Officers engaged in flaking people (claiming someone was in possession of narcotics when he or she was not—the drugs used for evidence were from the officer's own supply) and padding arrests (similar to flaking, but involving adding enough extra narcotics, or felony weight, to the defendant's total to raise the charge to a felony).

3. *Prostitution.* Officers involved in plainclothes units had maintained pads and received scores from houses of prostitution, prostitute bars, and prostitutes.

4. *Construction.* Uniformed officers received payoffs from contractors who violated city regulations or who did not possess proper licenses and permits.

5. *Bars.* Officers received payoffs from licensed and unlicensed bars to overlook crimes and violations.

6. *Sabbath law.* Officers received payoffs from food store owners to allow the owners to violate the Sabbath law,

a former New York City law that required certain food stores—such as delicatessens, groceries, and bodegas—to close down on Sundays.

7. *Parking and traffic.* Officers received payoffs from motorists who wanted to avoid traffic summonses, as well as from business establishments to discourage officers from issuing summonses for illegal parking in front of their businesses.

8. *Retrieving seized automobiles from the police.* Officers at city automobile storage yards received payments from owners to retrieve their automobiles.

9. *Intradepartmental payments.* Certain officers received payments for doing paperwork for other officers and for temporary assignments, permanent assignments, and medical discharges.

10. *Sale of information.* Officers received payments for the sale of confidential police information to criminals and private investigation firms.

11. *Gratuities.* Officers received free meals, drinks, hotel rooms, merchandise, Christmas payments, and other gifts and tips for services rendered.

12. *Miscellaneous.* Officers received payments from fortune-tellers, loan sharks, automobile theft rings, hijackers, and peddlers. Officers stole money and property from dead bodies (DOAs) and their apartments. They burglarized stores and other premises.

The Knapp Commission's report distinguished between two types of corrupt officers: grass eaters and meat eaters. Grass eating, the most common form of police deviance, was described as illegitimate activity that occurs from time to time in the normal course of police work, such as taking small bribes or relatively minor services offered by citizens seeking to avoid arrest or to get special police services. Meat eating, in contrast, was a much more serious form of corruption involving the active seeking of illicit moneymaking opportunities. Meat eaters solicited bribes through threat or intimidation, whereas grass eaters made the simpler mistake of not refusing those that were offered.

Source: Adapted from Knapp Commission, *Report on Police Corruption* (New York: Braziller, 1973), pp. 1–5.

hearings, and its findings caused widespread changes in the policies and operations of the New York City Police Department.

The police are also under constant review by the U.S. judicial system through the process of judicial review, as was discussed in Chapter 11. **Judicial review** is the process by which the actions of the police in such areas as arrests, search and seizure, and custodial interrogation are reviewed by the U.S. court system at various levels to ensure the constitutionality of those actions. Judicial review has resulted in such landmark Supreme Court cases as *Mapp v. Ohio* and *Miranda v. Arizona,* which were discussed in Chapter 11. In addition, the police are reviewed daily by the media: newspapers, magazines, radio, and television. Finally, they are under constant review by citizens, many of whom do not hesitate to report what they consider to be deviant conduct to the media, to the police themselves, or to other legal authorities. Officers' high visibility often puts them under the microscope.

The police today act in many types of situations, and it is difficult for courts or police administrators to predict every possible situation that could arise. This, coupled with the fact that the legal authority of the police is constantly changing as is the interpretation of the constitutional limitations of the police by the courts, leads to a dynamic and challenging situation.[16]

★ ★ ★

POLICE CORRUPTION

Police corruption has many definitions. Herman Goldstein defines it as "acts involving the misuse of authority by a police officer in a manner designed to produce personal gain for himself or others."[17]

Frederick A. Elliston and Michael Feldberg define corruption as "the acceptance of money or the equivalent of money by a public official for doing something he or she is under a duty to do anyway, that he or she is under a duty not to do, or to exercise legitimate discretion for improper reasons."[18] Richard J. Lundman defines police corruption as "when officers accept money, goods, or services for actions they are sworn to do anyway. It also exists when police officers accept money, goods, or services for ignoring actions they are sworn to invoke legal procedures against."[19]

Although these definitions differ, we can find enough commonalities to define corruption for our purposes as follows: A police officer is corrupt when he or she is acting under his or her official capacity and receives a benefit or something of value (other than his or her paycheck) for doing something or for refraining from doing something.

It is often difficult to distinguish among bribes, gratuities, and gifts. Is giving an officer a free cup of coffee or a sandwich an act of corruption? Michael Feldberg writes, "Sometimes, it is difficult to distinguish between genuine gifts (such as Christmas gifts), gratuities, bribes and corruption. At times, however, accepting any kind of gift is the beginning of the slippery slope syndrome where the path is paved for accepting other, larger gratuities in the future and eventually bribes.[20]

In the wake of the allegations of tremendous corruption in the New York City Police Department that led to the establishment of the Knapp Commission, reform police commissioner Patrick V. Murphy told his officers, "Except for your pay check there is no such thing as a clean buck.[21] Although some would dispute this, there is no question that Commissioner Murphy knew what he considered to be corruption and that he was holding his officers accountable for it.

Corruption Makes Good Books and Films

Police corruption is a popular topic in literature and film. Does life imitate art, or does art imitate life? This eternal question is easily answered when we discuss police corruption: Art imitates life.

As an example, the novel *Serpico,* by Peter Maas, and the movie starring Al Pacino were great successes.[22] *Serpico* tells the true tale of an honest NYPD plainclothes officer, Frank Serpico, who roams the police department and city government for a seemingly endless time in an attempt to report that there is corruption in his plainclothes division in the Bronx. Serpico tells his supervisors, his commanders, the chief of personnel, an assistant to the mayor, and the city's Department of Investigation his tale, and nothing is done; corruption remains rampant. Finally, frustrated in his efforts, Serpico and a friend, Sergeant David Dirk, report their allegations to a reporter for the *New York Times.* This leads to the formation of the Knapp Commission and widespread changes in the NYPD's policies and procedures initiated by Commissioner Murphy, who was appointed soon after the allegations were made.

The novel *Prince of the City: The Story of a Cop Who Knew Too Much,* by Robert Daley, and the movie of the same name starring Treat Williams also were great successes.[23] *Prince of the City* tells the true story of a corrupt, experienced narcotics detective, Robert Leuci, assigned to the elite Special Investigations Unit of the New York City Police Department's Narcotics Division. Leuci was a corrupt cop who, to save his own skin, worked as a federal informer to obtain evidence to put his partners behind bars.

The book *Buddy Boys: When Good Cops Turn Bad,* by Mike McAlary, was a best seller.[24] *Buddy Boys* is also a true tale of 13 corrupt police officers in Brooklyn's 77th Precinct who stole drugs from drug dealers, sold drugs and guns, and committed other nefarious crimes.

The movie *L.A. Confidential,* which was released in 1997, portarys life in the 1940s in Hollywood. Police corruption together with other types of corruption is portrayed throughout the story. Some of the factors that contribute to or facilitate police corruption can be seen throughout the movie, including power, financial gain, and job advancement.

Examples of Police Corruption

Despite all the attention police corruption has received in history and the efforts by police administrators to detect and eradicate it, there are still numerous recent examples of large-scale police corruption.

During the 1980s, 75 Miami police officers were arrested for serious acts of police corruption. Seven of these officers, who were dubbed the "Miami River Cops," were charged with high-level drug dealing. Three of them have also been charged with murder.[25]

In 1992, six New York City police officers, including Police Officer Michael Dowd, were arrested and charged with buying drugs in their inner-city precincts and selling them in the suburban communities in which they lived. This arrest led to allegations of murders committed by some of the officers, as well as charges that NYPD internal affairs investigators had known about the corrupt acts by these officers for years prior to the arrests and had taken no action. This resulted in the formation, by Mayor David Dinkins, of another Knapp-style commission to investigate corruption in the New York City Police Department.[26] This case supports the theory that a major corruption scandal surfaces every 20 years in the NYPD. The theory holds that after the scandal and the resultant investigatory commission, the department vigorously fights corruption and prevents large-scale, organized corruption from resurfacing. However, approximately 20 years later, it will resurface anyway.

In 1996, three Detroit police officers and one former officer were named in a federal indictment that accused them of being key players in a Texas-to-Michigan cocaine-smuggling ring. Also, six current and former police officers from Ford Heights, Illinois, 30 miles south of Chicago,

> ### YOU ARE THERE! >>
>
> ## The Twenty-Year Theory of Corruption in the NYPD
>
> History has proved the theory that a major corruption scandal occurs in the New York City Police Department approximately every 20 years. These scandals have resulted in major investigations and public hearings. This theory was again proved with the Mollen Commission, which in September and October 1993 investigated charges of corruption in several NYPD precincts. This commission was brought about by the arrest of corrupt officer Michael Dowd and his associates, who stole drugs in their inner-city precincts and sold them in their suburban communities. The following time line lists the scandals:
>
> | | |
> |---|---|
> | 1890s | The Lexow Commission and the Mazet Commission |
> | 1910s | The Curran Committee and the Becker/ Rosenthal Scandals |
> | 1930s | The Seabury Hearings |
> | 1950s | The Harry Gross Investigation |
> | 1970s | The Knapp Commission |
> | 1990s | The Mollen Commission |

were indicted for taking bribes to look the other way as more than 20 drug dealers conducted a brisk, brazen business in the small, impoverished town.[27]

Also in 1996, former New Orleans police officer Len Davis was sentenced to death for arranging the murder of a woman who had filed a brutality complaint against him. Davis was only one of several New Orleans officers charged in a 1994 FBI sting for transporting and guarding shipments of cocaine. Davis is not the only New Orleans officer on death row. Another officer, charged with the murder of a fellow officer during a robbery, has also been sentenced to death.[28]

In 2003, a Federal Jury convicted three Miami officers of conspiracy for covering up questionable shootings that occurred from 1995 to 1997. Eleven officers had been indicted, two had previously pled guilty and testified at the trial, three were found not guilty, and mistrials were declared regarding the remaining three officers. The officers received sentences ranging from 13 months to 37 months in prison coupled with 3 years of supervised release.[29]

Corruption is not limited to rank-and-file police officers. In 1992, Chief William L. Hart, Detroit's police chief since 1976, retired after a federal jury convicted him of stealing $2.6 million from police department funds.[30] In 1996, Newark, New Jersey, Police Director William Celester was forced out of office after being named in a wide-ranging indictment. He was charged with numerous counts of malfeasance, including mail and wire fraud, tax fraud, accepting illegal gratuities, making a false statement, and forging documents. In a plea bargain in July 1996, Celester pleaded guilty to using nearly $30,000 from a police account to pay for vacations, airline tickets, gifts for his girlfriends, and other personal expenses.[31]

In 2001, a city manager in Miami who had previously been the police chief was charged with taking almost $70,000 from a youth anticrime group while he was police chief during the 1990s. He was on the charity's board of directors for nine years. He served a year in prison, was ordered to repay the money, and lost his police pension.[32]

In 2003, a Hackensack, New Jersey, police officer who was also the union treasurer pled guilty to stealing $180,000 from the union to support his gambling habit. Most of the money came from the union's death benefits fund, meant to help deceased officers' families.[33]

Corruption and misconduct are by no means restricted to local police. Federal law enforcement agents have also succumbed to this temptation. In 1997, former FBI agent Earl Edwin Pitts was sentenced to 27 years in prison for spying first for the Soviet Union and, after that government fell, Russia. Pitts sold U.S. intelligence secrets for almost one-quarter million dollars from 1987 to 1992. Pitts is not the only FBI agent charged with selling out his country. Richard W. Miller was imprisoned for 20 years for similar acts in 1984.[34]

Also in 1997, Jerome R. Sullivan, a 25-year veteran of the FBI, was indicted on charges of stealing more than $400,000, including at least $104,000 that the FBI said was mob money he had helped seize. Sullivan was the lead FBI agent in the arrest of Nicholas Corozzo, a leader in an organized crime family in South Florida, who was poised to take the place of imprisoned John Gotti as the family leader. Sullivan's lawyer reported that his client had alcohol and gambling problems that the FBI had been aware of but had not done enough to help him with.[35]

In a case that caused a lot of controversy in South Florida and led to procedural changes in the Florida Highway Patrol (FHP), an FBI agent was convicted on misdemeanor charges in the 1999 traffic deaths of two young men and also agreed to a financial settlement stemming from a civil suit. The deaths occurred in an early morning collision on I-95 in which one of the vehicles was traveling the wrong way. The FHP had initially stated the two young men were driving the wrong way but a month later reversed itself saying the FBI agent had been the wrong-way driver after a night of drinking with a supervisor at a sports bar. Questions arose as to whether the agent was treated differently during the initial investigation due to his status as an FBI agent. The jury was unable to determine whether the agent was driving the wrong way, and he was acquitted of felony charges but convicted of the lesser charges, including driving under the influence and reckless driving. The agent was also sued by the victims' family for $50 million and settled out of court for an undisclosed amount.[36]

Several recent books have focused specifically on the issues of police deviance. For example, see Victor Kappeler, Richard Sluder, and Geoffrey Alpert's *Forces of Deviance, Understanding the Dark Side of Policing;* Jerome H. Skolnick and James J. Fyfe's *Above the Law: Police and the Excessive Use of Force;* and Michael J. Palmiotto's *Police Misconduct: A Reader for the 21st Century.*[37]

Types and Forms of Corruption

Corruption is not limited to the present day. Lawrence W. Sherman reports, "For as long as there have been police, there has been police corruption."[38] Herman Goldstein says, "Corruption is endemic to policing. The very nature of the police function is bound to subject officers to tempting offers."[39] Frank Schmalleger says, "Police deviance has been a problem in American society since the early days of policing. It is probably an ancient and natural tendency of human beings to attempt to placate or 'win over' those in positions of authority over them."[40]

Samuel Walker describes four general types of police corruption: taking gratuities, taking bribes, theft or burglary, and internal corruption.[41] Gratuities are small tips or discounts on goods purchased. In many communities, taking gratuities is not considered corruption but merely the showing of good will to the police (with, of course, the hope that the police might perform their duties a little better for the person who shows them goodwill).

Police corruption also may involve taking bribes—the payment of money or other consideration to police officers with the intent to subvert the aims of the criminal justice system. According to Walker, bribes may take two forms: (1) the pad (formal, regular, periodic payments to the police to overlook continuing criminal enterprises) and (2) the score (a one-time payment to avoid arrest for illegal conduct).

Dempsey's Law

Do Police Officers Have to Pay for Their Lunch?

Professor Dempsey, don't police officers have to pay for their lunches? The other day I saw an officer get a sandwich and a soda at the convenience store. He said thank you and left, but I never saw him give the cashier any money.

I get this question often. I generally respond that different departments around the country may have different standards regarding free or discounted meals for police officers. However, Dempsey's Law says that officers should pay for their meals, just as any other citizen should.

*Yeah, Professor Dempsey, but once I saw an officer try to pay for a cup of coffee at the local diner, and the cashier wouldn't take the money. The officer looked really embarrassed. If that's corrup-*tion, should the officer have arrested the cashier for bribery?

No, the officer should not have arrested the cashier for bribery. That would be pretty stupid. However, there are ways to get around embarrassing situations like that. I used to always have several $1 bills in my wallet and have them ready in my hand at the register. If such a situation occurred, I would merely smile and say, "Thank you very much." Then I would leave the approximate cost of the meal on the counter. If the cashier continued to protest, I would return by my table and leave the money as a tip for the waiter. Hey, I made good money as an officer. I could afford the price of a meal.

Theft or burglary, the taking of money or property by the police while performing their duties, is another form of police corruption, according to Walker. The police have access to numerous premises, including warehouses and stores, while investigating burglaries. They also have access to homes while on official business. A corrupt police officer has plenty of opportunity to take property from others.

Walker's final type of police corruption is internal corruption. Officers pay members of their departments for special assignments or promotions.

Thomas Barker and Julian Roebuck identified the following types of police corruption:

1. Acceptance of free or discounted meals and services
2. Acceptance of kickbacks for referrals for services
3. Opportunistic theft from helpless citizens or unsecured premises
4. Shakedowns
5. Protection of illegal activities
6. Acceptance of money to fix cases
7. Planned theft[42]

Sherman discusses three general levels of police corruption.[43] The first is the "rotten apples and rotten pockets" theory of police corruption, which holds that only one officer or a very small group of officers in a department or precinct is corrupt. At first thought, this may not seem very serious. If only one officer or a handful of officers is corrupt, a department needs only to arrest the officer or group and use the arrest as an example to other officers of what might happen to them also, if they were to become corrupt. The dangerous part of this theory is that if police commanders believe that only a few officers are bad, they will not take the tough, proactive policies necessary to uncover and eradicate corruption in the entire precinct or department. New York City's Commissioner Patrick V. Murphy, in the wake of the Serpico allegations, faced a dilemma. He could accept the rotten apple theory, or he could admit that the entire barrel might be rotten. To his credit, and for the betterment of the NYPD, Murphy chose the latter and took the steps necessary to correct the situation.[44]

The second level of corruption that Sherman found might exist in a police department was pervasive, unorganized corruption, where a majority of the officers are corrupt but are not actively working with one another on an organized or planned basis.

Sherman's third level of corruption was pervasive, organized corruption, where almost all members of a department or precinct are working together in systematic and organized corruption. This type is essentially what the Knapp Commission discovered, particularly in the NYPD plainclothes units.[45]

Several stages of the moral decline of police officers have been identified. Sherman tells us about certain stages in an officer's moral career. The first stage involves the acceptance of minor gratuities, such as free meals. Peer pressure from other officers is extremely important at this stage. The second and third stages involve accepting gratuities to overlook regulatory offenses, such as accepting money to allow bars to remain open past regular closing hours or accepting money from a motorist instead of giving him or her a summons. Peer pressure from other officers is also very important at this stage. The final stage involves changing from passively accepting gratuities to actively seeking bribes. As the corruption continues, it becomes more systematic. It involves larger amounts of money and includes numerous types of crimes, ranging from gambling violations and prostitution to dealing in narcotics.[46]

Noble Cause Corruption

"Noble cause" corruption refers to situations where a police officer may bend the rules in order to attain the "right" result. This is also often referred to as the "Dirty Harry" syndrome. In the extreme situation an officer might justify violating a suspect's rights in order to save someone's life. More commonly, the rights violation would be justified in the officer's mind by the ultimate good of putting the bad guy in jail where he belongs. These behaviors involve police officers misusing their legal authority but they are not doing it for personal gain. They rationalize the behavior to get the bad guys behind bars and consider it a noble cause type of corruption.[47] Delattre, in his 1996 book, *Characters and Cops,* presents ethical dilemmas that illustrate the noble cause corruption issue:

> A police officer in plainclothes approaches an individual to question on the street and momentarily loses sight of the individual as he goes around a corner and drops narcotics on the ground. The officer finds the contraband and arrests the individual. What should the officers do? Writing an accurate report might lead to the case being dismissed and the bad guy going free—but there is no choice. Fabricating reports compounds and leads to a department without integrity and fosters a philosophy of vigilantism and a we–they view of life, society and right and wrong.[48]

Effects of Police Corruption

"Nothing undermines public confidence in the police and in the process of criminal justice more than the illegal acts of [police] officers," said the President's Commission on Law Enforcement and Administration of Justice.[49] David Burnham, a *New York Times* writer, offered an interesting analysis of the social costs of police corruption. Burnham identified what he calls four hidden social costs of police corruption:

- It represents a secret tax on businesses that have to pay off the police to avoid harassment.

- It undermines the enforcement of the law, allowing widespread illegal activity to flourish.

- It destroys the department itself, robbing the police officer of self-respect and respect for superior officers and the department as a whole. Effective discipline becomes impossible when corruption is systematic.

- Knowledge of the existence of corruption undermines the public's faith in the police and the entire criminal justice system.[50]

Law enforcement has come to the realization that it can be far more effective in its mission with the help of the community. It's also been shown that citizens won't help the police if they don't trust the police. Citizens must feel that they will be treated fairly and treated with respect.

Morale within the department will suffer as the officers may feel they are "painted with the same wide brush." This happens even with incidents that happen in other jurisdictions and even other states. Many officers will tell you they were questioned by citizens for months after the Rodney King incident regardless of what state or what type agency they worked for.

An incident that occurs within an officers' organization is often complicated by rumors and lack of official information. During an investigation, it is quickly common knowledge that an investigation is occurring, and rumors fly. Departments typically do not release any information or discuss the investigation prior to the conclusion of the investigation. Officers are left with rumors as their source of information, and everyone is nervous as to what is going on, what will happen next, who else is involved, and whether or not they will be questioned. Officers don't know whom to trust, and morale plummets. There is an air of suspicion that can last for months while the investigation is conducted. This type of atmosphere is emotionally draining for officers and will greatly contribute to the stress they experience.

An incident of corruption can result in an organization writing a policy or implementing training that might have prevented this particular incident from occurring but is not a realistic policy or training session nor needed for the majority of the personnel. Officers may find their work lives or personal lives made more difficult or complicated in an inappropriate manner for an incident involving someone else.

Just one or two incidents of corruption can ruin a department's reputation and destroy the trust the community has in the department. It can take years to overcome this bad publicity. It will affect the department in many ways. There will be a lack of trust, resulting in a lack of cooperation and information from the community. The department will be less attractive to highly qualified police officer candidates as well as police administrators. Consequently the department will stagnate for years under this perception unless drastic and highly visible changes are made.

Reasons for Police Corruption

Numerous theories attempt to explain corruption in law enforcement agencies. Frank Schmalleger offers an interesting theory about the reason some police officers become corrupt by tying Edwin H. Sutherland's theory of differential association to police corruption.[51] Sutherland's theory of differential association holds that crime is basically "imitative"; we learn crime the same way we learn other behavior. We tend to imitate the behavior that surrounds us. Schmalleger asks us to consider a police officer's typical day—associating with and arresting petty thieves, issuing traffic citations and other summonses to citizens who try to talk their way out of the tickets, dealing with prostitutes who feel hassled by the cops, and arresting drug users who think what they are doing is not wrong. Schmalleger asks us to combine these everyday experiences with the relatively low pay officers receive and the sense that police work is not really valued to understand how officers might develop a jaded attitude toward the double standards of the civilization they are sworn to protect. Such a jaded attitude, Schmalleger says, may entice officers into corruption.[52]

When we consider the enormous authority given to our police officers, the tremendous discretion they are allowed to exercise, and the existence of the police personality and police cynicism (discussed in Chapter 6), it is easy to see that police work is fertile ground for the growth of corruption. Add to this environment the constant contact police have with criminals and unsavory people, the moral dilemma they face when given the responsibility of enforcing unenforceable laws regarding services people actually want (illegal drugs, gambling, alcohol, and prostitution), and the enormous amount of money that can be made by corrupt officers. Based on all these factors, it is little wonder that corruption is pervasive in police departments.

The current drug problem in the United States, including the desirability of drugs and the tremendous profits available from their sale, seems to increase the risks of police corruption. The Wickersham Commission in 1931 warned that the presence of laws against alcohol (National Prohibition) had the potential for corruption by police and other officials.[53] Is today's illegal drug business as tempting to corruption-prone law enforcement officers as the alcohol trade was to officers during National Prohibition?

The style of policing employed by a department may be somewhat responsible for the degree of corruption in that department. James Q. Wilson analyzed corruption according to the different styles of policing he described in *Varieties of Police Behavior: The Management of Law and Order in Eight Communities.*[54] He says that the greatest degree of police corruption is found in departments characterized by the "watchman style," in which police are expected merely to maintain order, not to deal with the causes of crime or to make attempts to improve conditions that may lead to crime. Wilson says that low salaries and the expectation that police will have other jobs increase the probabilities that the police will be involved in corruption in watchman-style departments.

Corruption is found to a lesser degree, Wilson says, in departments characterized by the "legalistic style." These departments emphasize formal police training, recruiting from the middle class, offering greater promotional opportunities, and viewing law as a means to an end rather than an end in itself. In this departmental style, formal sanctions are used more frequently than informal ones; police give less attention to community service and order maintenance than to law enforcement.

Wilson says that corruption is not a serious problem in the third type of police department style, the "service style." In this management style, law enforcement and order maintenance functions are combined with an emphasis on good relationships between the police and the community. The command of the department is decentralized; police on patrol work out of specialized units. Higher education and promotional opportunities are emphasized, and police are expected to lead exemplary private lives.

Responses to Police Corruption

The most important step in eliminating or reducing police corruption is to admit that corruption exists. The need for candor, Herman Goldstein argues, is paramount. Police officials have traditionally attempted to ignore the problem and deny that it exists.[55] Many police departments have established **internal affairs divisions (IADs or IAs)** as their major department resource to combat corruption. Internal affairs divisions or units are the police who police the police department. Internal affairs investigators are not very popular with other members of the department, because many officers see them as spies who only want to get them in trouble. Internal affairs units are also used to investigate allegations of police brutality by most departments.

In understanding both the negative connotations of the "Internal Affairs" title and the need for systematic preventive initiatives regarding corruption, many departments have implemented "Professional Standards" units, "Compliance" units or "Integrity" units. These divisions within the police department will investigate allegations of wrongdoing but will also be actively involved in developing and implementing policies and procedures that will minimize the chances of corruption occurring. This unit will conduct audits and inspections to insure these safeguards are in place and procedures are being adhered to. Good record keeping is essential in preventing corruption, and then, if it occurs, it is helpful in the investigative process.

Internal affairs divisions can attack corruption in two ways, reactively and proactively. In a reactive investigation, the investigator waits for a complaint of corruption from the public and then investigates that specific complaint using traditional investigative techniques. In a **proactive investigation** into police corruption, investigators provide opportunities for officers to commit illegal acts, such as leaving valuable property at a scene to see if officers follow normal procedures regarding found property. Proactive investigations are often called **integrity tests.**

An excellent example of an integrity test or a proactive investigation that nabbed a corrupt officer occurred in the 33rd Precinct in New York City's Washington Heights in June 1997. Acting on tips that a precinct officer was corrupt, internal affairs investigators set up a sting for the officer. Reporting that they had just raided an apartment in a drug case, investigators had the suspect officer assigned to guard the apartment. The raid, however, was bogus, a ruse to allow the investigators to set up video surveillance equipment in the apartment and leave behind $20,000 and fake drugs. Upon the officer's return to the station house at the end of his shift, he was caught carrying $6,000 in cash. The officer was arrested on charges of grand larceny and official misconduct.[56]

Police corruption can also be investigated by local district attorneys, state and federal prosecutors, and special investigative bodies, such as the Knapp Commission (New York City police corruption, 1970s), the Mollen Commission (New York City police corruption, 1990s), and the Christopher Commission (Los Angeles police brutality, 1991). In addition, the FBI has jurisdiction to investigate police corruption, and their investigations have had a major effect on several police departments, including the Philadelphia and the New Orleans departments.

As recently as 1998, a three-year investigation by the FBI and the Internal Revenue Service resulted in a 74-page indictment and the arrest of nine current and former members of the West New York, New Jersey, Police Department and numerous others for widespread police corruption.[57]

As a result of the New Orleans Police Department's deep rooted problems, many reforms were instituted by the new chief hired from the outside in 1994, Superintendent Richard Pennington. He formed a Public Integrity Division in 1995 to eradicate police corruption and raise the department's ethical standards. This is a partnership between the FBI and Louisiana law enforcement officers.[58] New Orleans is the first department to have FBI agents assigned to it full-time and working closely with them on the PID initiatives, and they have been able to regain citizens' confidence. They instituted an off-site location for the PID, implemented a toll-free hotline to report misconduct or provide feedback, utilized undercover personel to detect wrongdoing, staged integrity checks, employed a computerized "early warning system," and expanded relevant training programs. The superintendent wants the department and the citizens to know they're checking to make sure everyone is doing their job as it should be done. They believe the community confidence in the police department has steadily risen.

The recent gun and conspiracy scandal in Miami was the biggest corruption scandal since the famous Miami River Cops scandal of the 1980s. The convictions came in the third month of the new chief, John Timoney, brought in to clean up the department. "He cleaned house at the police department and moved the Internal Affairs office out of headquarters to strengthen its ability to operate independently and began an extensive review of the department's policies."[59]

San Francisco suffered negative publicity as allegations were made of widespread corruption in the department regarding cover-ups. It started over a police brawl involving off-duty officers in November 2002. The three junior officers involved were indicted on assault and battery charges, and seven command officers, including the chief of police and an assistant chief whose son was one of the junior officers involved, were indicted on charges of conspiracy to obstruct justice. The chief went on medical leave after he was indicted and announced his retirement several days after he was cleared of conspiracy in August 2003.[60] Although charges against the top brass were dropped, the case has brought attention to the "code of silence" that exists in police organizations.

★ ★ ★

OTHER POLICE MISCONDUCT

Police corruption and police brutality are the most serious forms of police deviance. Police brutality will be discussed later in the chapter. Other types of police deviance also exist. Chief among them are illegal drug use and trafficking by officers, drinking and alcohol abuse, cooping, police deception, and abuse of authority, sexual violence, and domestic violence.

Drug Abuse and Trafficking

The abuse of drugs has been a serious problem in U.S. society for many years. In the 1960s and 1970s, we saw the terror of the heroin epidemic, as well as the problems caused by psychedelic drugs and other drugs, especially in cities. The 1980s and 1990s brought the rock cocaine, or crack, crisis, as well as the reemergence of the heroin crisis.

The police are not immune to the problems that face the rest of society. They are also participants in, or victims of, the drug crisis. Given that illegal drug use is a problem among police officers, should police departments conduct drug testing? The use of drug testing, particularly random drug testing without cause, has become a major issue in the U.S. criminal justice system. Some argue that drug testing is a violation of one's constitutional rights. Many agree that an employer can insist that an employee not use drugs when he or she is working, but that because drugs remain in one's system many days after use, drug tests do not differentiate between on-duty and off-duty use.

In an article in the *FBI Law Enforcement Bulletin,* Jeffrey Higginbotham cited numerous reasons supporting urinalysis drug testing programs for law enforcement officers: (1) to maintain public safety, (2) to maintain public trust in the police, (3) to reduce the potential for the corruption of the police, (4) to allow the presentation of credible testimony by the police, (5) to boost morale in the workplace, (6) to avoid loss of productivity, and (7) to avoid civil liability.[61]

The U.S. Supreme Court, in **National Treasury Employees Union** v. **Von Raab** (1989), ruled that the random testing of U.S. Customs personnel involved in drug interdiction and/or carrying firearms was constitutional.[62] Prior to this case, police departments had tremendous problems trying to get drug testing—primarily random drug testing—accepted by police unions. In many cases, the unions fought the departments to prohibit the drug testing of officers. This case made it much easier for local government agencies to engage in drug testing of their employees.

In one year, the New York City Police Department gave drug tests to 5,174 probationary officers. (These tests are capable of discovering controlled substances, including marijuana, in a person's system.) Only 18 tested positive for drug use—an extremely low positive rate of 0.003 percent. The New Jersey State Police also tested 2,300 of its members, and only five showed evidence of drug use—again an amazingly low positive rate of 0.002 percent.[63]

The National Institute of Justice conducted a telephone survey of 33 large police departments regarding measures being taken to identify officers and civilian employees using drugs. The survey found that almost all departments had written procedures to test those employees reasonably suspected of drug abuse. Of the departments surveyed, 73 percent tested applicants, and 21 percent reported that they were actively considering testing all officers. Also, 21 percent said they might offer treatment to identified violators rather than dismiss them, depending upon their personal circumstances.[64]

The International Association of Chiefs of Police (IACP) has made available to police departments a model drug testing policy that suggests:

1. Testing all applicants and recruits for drug or narcotics use

2. Testing current employees when performance difficulties or documentation indicates they may have a potential drug problem

3. Testing current employees when they are involved in the use of excessive force or when they suffer or cause on-duty injury

4. Routine testing of all employees assigned to special high-risk areas, such as narcotics and vice[65]

Despite these efforts, there are still officers who use and get addicted to drugs. In 2002, an 18-year veteran lieutenant in Delray Beach, Florida, was arrested in Miami after driving there in his city-owned vehicle, buying $20 worth of cocaine from an undercover officer, and then trying to flee from officers.[66]

Drug-Related Corruption

Drug-related corruption is also a concern to modern law enforcement agencies. In a report by the General Accounting Office to the U.S. House of Representatives, it was found that there was no central data source from which to gather this information, but through research and interviews the report was able to provide some valuable insight.[67]

While finding that the vast majority of police officers are honest, it was found that in cities where drug dealing was a concern there is a potential for drug-related police corruption. Typically, it involved small groups of officers who assisted and protected each other in criminal activities, including protecting criminals or ignoring their activities, stealing drugs and/or money from drug dealers, selling drugs, and lying about illegal searches. Profit was the most frequent motive.[68]

The report also cited four management-related factors associated with drug-related corruption, including a culture characterized by a code of silence and cynicism, officers with less education and maturity, ineffective supervision, and a lack of emphasis on integrity and internal oversight within the department. Strategies to combat drug-related corruption were discussed in the report; these will be addressed later in the chapter.

Without the proper procedures in place, close supervision, and oversight, it will be easier for officers to fall victim to the lure of the quick buck around the drug trade or to use their power and opportunities to steal from those they feel will never report it. In 2002, a West Palm Beach, Florida, officer was indicted on money-laundering charges after being paid by a cocaine distributor to use his cash to pay the construction costs of three houses; and two officers in Hiahleah, Florida, were sentenced to over 20 years in connection with federal robbery, narcotics, and firearms charges. Some of these incidents occurred while officers were on duty, using their marked police vehicles as escape vehicles after robberies.[69]

Drinking and Alcohol Abuse

As Chapter 6 discussed, police stress and police suicide are special problems in police departments. Alcohol is generally involved in both problems.

Numerous academic studies have confirmed that alcohol abuse is a major problem in policing. Jerome Skolnick, in "A Sketch of the Policeman's Working Personality," concluded that officers drink heavily and usually drink together to avoid public criticism.[70] Danielle Hitz found that mortality rates for alcohol-related cirrhosis of the liver among the police officers studied were significantly higher than the rates for the general population.[71] W. Kroes estimated that 25 percent of all police officers have a serious alcohol dependence, and R. C. Van Raalte reported that 67 percent of a sample of police officers admitted to drinking on duty.[72] Obviously, drinking and guns do not mix well. Drinking and driving also do not mix well. Alcohol problems correlate with DUI violations both on and off duty.

These incidents are further complicated when officers on duty in the same or other jurisdictions then have to make discretionary decisions regarding DUI violations. These discretionary decisions take place routinely involving citizens, but when the driver is a police officer they will be very closely scrutinized. These types of cases are some of the most frequently occurring; perusing newspapers will show the publicity they generate. Therefore, it is crucial that police departments be vigilant in preventing alcohol abuse by officers.

Cooping

Police officers refer to the practice of sleeping, resting, or avoiding work while on duty as "cooping." The coop is where the cooping occurs. Former officer Gene Radano, in *Walking the Beat,* gives a very good description of cooping: "A coop is a shelter where cops go to sit down, grab a smoke, escape the weather or to lie down. . . . Cops move in like the proverbial camel nosing his way into the tent, and soon squatter's rights prevail."[73]

If a police officer is so inclined, it is very easy to coop. Supervisors generally must cover a very large area and are not likely to observe a police radio car at rest in the back of a school yard, by a closed factory, or in another desolate location. This behavior, while not good for the community, also has the potential for being very dangerous for the officer and his or her coworkers.

Police Deception

Another form of police misconduct is police deception, which includes perjury while testifying in court and attempts to circumvent rules regarding searches and seizures of evidence.

Anyone familiar with the works of the novelist and former Los Angeles Police Department sergeant Joseph Wambaugh, particularly his classic *The Blue Knight,* is aware of the possibility that police may perjure themselves on the witness stand to secure a conviction against a defendant. In *The Blue Knight,* Wambaugh's protagonist, Police Officer Bumper Morgan, illegally entered a man's hotel room to arrest him on a warrant and then fabricated probable cause well after the event to cover his actions. In a dramatic scene in the book, after Morgan falsely testifies in court, evidence is presented to show clearly that Morgan perjured himself on the stand. The judge severely rebukes him in her chambers.[74]

Skolnick states that police deception, if it occurs, usually occurs at three stages of the police detection process: investigation, interrogation, and testimony in court.

"Particularly objectionable," says Skolnick, "is the idea that a police officer would not be truthful when testifying under oath in court. However, much evidence suggests that there are 'tolerable' levels of perjury among police officers when testifying in court."[75]

Columbia University law students analyzed the effect of the landmark U.S. Supreme Court case *Mapp* v. *Ohio* on police practices in the seizure of narcotics.[76] This case, which was covered in depth in Chapter 11, severely restricted the power of the police to make certain searches of persons or premises. The students found that before *Mapp* v. *Ohio,* police officers typically testified that they found narcotics hidden on the defendants' persons. After the *Mapp* case, police officers testified that the narcotics they found were dropped on the ground by the defendants. This became known as dropsy (from "drop-see testimony"). Prior to the *Mapp* case, narcotics evidence obtained from suspects by police, even when illegally seized, was admissible in court. After *Mapp,* this was no longer so. Hence, the researchers said, police officers began to commit perjury to circumvent the illegal seizure of evidence rule and to ensure that their testimony and the evidence would be admissible against defendants charged with narcotics possession.[77]

The FBI was involved in numerous deceptive practices during the time J. Edgar Hoover was at its head. Tony G. Poveda, in *Lawlessness and Reform: The FBI in Transition,* details the illegal conduct engaged in by the FBI. This conduct included disrupting political groups, performing illegal burglaries, maintaining secret files, and attempting to deceive the public.[78]

Police corruption continues to be a concern. Here, FBI agents escort five handcuffed Miami police officers to a van outside FBI headquarters in Miami in September 2001, after they were indicted regarding cover-ups in shooting incidents.

There have also been cases of police officers fabricating stories for more unusual reasons, believing their status as officers will lead them to be believed. An officer in Toledo, Ohio, was found guilty of tampering with evidence after producing false documents and staging incidents in an attempt to make it appear she was being stalked. She was trying to gain sympathy from fellow officers.[79] In 2003, in San Jose, California, an eight-year veteran officer concocted a story about a robbery to cover up an alleged drunken driving accident. While off duty and calling the emergency dispatcher, he identified himself as an officer and stated he'd been robbed by two black males. Though his story quickly unraveled, the description of the offenders as black caused concern and hurt in the community.[80]

Abuse of Authority

The tremendous power and discretion given to the police provide them with numerous opportunities to abuse their power or authority. In describing police deviance, Thomas Barker and David L. Carter distinguish between occupational deviance and abuse of authority. Occupational deviance, they say, is motivated by the desire for personal benefit. Abuse of authority, in contrast, occurs most often to further the organizational goals of law enforcement, including arrest, issuing tickets, and the successful conviction of suspects.[81] This is the most common type of noble cause corruption, as discussed earlier.

Alan N. Kornblum gives us a definition of corruption of authority: "that corruption that comes from the broad discretion police have in much of their work and the tension between efficiency standards versus the activities that must ensure due process."[82] Robert D. Pursley defines corruption of authority by saying it means that the police either employ, or might be tempted to employ, certain corrupt practices, such as the violation of a person's civil rights, in an effort to be more efficient.[83]

Many people were shocked at the alleged reports of abuse of power by Los Angeles police detective Mark Fuhrman in the widely covered O. J. Simpson murder case. In addition to his self-reported acts of brutality and racism, he seemed proud to admit to numerous acts of abuse of his police authority and the violation of citizens' human and constitutional rights. Many say that the verdict of not guilty in the Simpson case, in spite of overwhelming forensic evidence to the contrary, was in reality an act of jury nullification brought about by Fuhrman's alleged actions.

Police Sexual Violence

Police sexual violence incorporates many behaviors and involves "those situations in which a citizen experiences a sexually degrading, humiliating, violating, damaging or threatening act committed by a police officer, through the use of force or police authority."[84] These are very serious offenses against the public trust. The vast majority of police officers detest this behavior by the few bad apples who perpetrate it. It shocks the conscience of the community to think an officer would use his position of trust to violate some of the most vulnerable citizens. The average officer has a hard time believing this type of abuse occurs, but a perusal of newspapers across the country indicates that it does in fact occur.

It is imperative that police administrators be aware of this type of violation and be vigilant in looking for warning signs. Often there is behavior that could signal a potential problem; if that behavior is handled quickly and effectively, administrators could avert a bigger problem or give the organization documented behavior for a discipline case.

Examples of warning signs might include an officer who pulls over female drivers, spends a lot of time outside bars at closing time, spends an inordinate amount of time at any place women tend to congregate, or conducts inappropriate follow-ups that he wouldn't conduct for the average citizen. Most of these activities can be explained away in the context of performing good police service, but together they could be a pattern of behavior worth watching.

Police officers using their position of authority to sexually abuse females occurs more often than one would expect given the serious nature of this offense. In El Paso, Texas, two deputies were arrested; one was sentenced to 10 years and another was wanted for failure to appear for depriving a woman of her civil rights after raping her when she was stranded with a flat tire.[85] In Margate, Florida, an officer had sex with a 16-year-old girl in the backseat of his patrol car after arresting her for DUI after an accident.[86] In Lakewood, Ohio, a seven-year police veteran pled guilty to sexual battery for having sex with a woman in the backseat of his patrol car. He took the woman into custody on Christmas Eve 2002, though he never charged her. He didn't use physical force, but his position of authority, not to mention his gun, made the sex illegal.[87] In Los Angeles, an officer referred to by the prosecutor as a "Wolf in LAPD clothing" was sentenced in April 2003 to three consecutive

25-years-to-life terms for three rapes he committed while on duty. He was armed with a gun each time, and two of his victims were bound or tied. He was convicted of 14 felony counts, including forcible rape, sexual penetration by a foreign object, sodomy by use of force, and sodomy under color of authority.[88]

Domestic Violence in Police Families

Some studies indicate that domestic violence may be more prevalent in police families than in the general population.[89] It has traditionally been a hidden problem with victims hesitant to report it. Domestic violence is an issue only beginning to be addressed, and it is an uphill battle. If the victim is a spouse of a police officer, then the offender has friends and supporters in the department who may not believe the allegations, the offender has a gun, and the offender knows the system and knows where the shelters are. A victim who is a police officer must deal with all sorts of psychological issues as to why he or she can't handle this problem alone. The victims fear for their safety and also for the economic future of their family, as an act of domestic violence could cost the officer his or her job.

If departments get a report, many choose to handle it informally in an effort to protect the officer. This has resulted in tragedy. How departments handle domestic violence has been found to be inconsistent between departments and even within departments. A 1994 survey of 123 police departments documented that 45 percent had no specific policy for handling officers involved in domestic violence, and the most common form of discipline for sustained allegations was counseling.[90] The International Association of Chiefs of Police has developed a model policy on police-involved domestic violence, and some departments are building on that policy and becoming proactive. The 1996 Federal Law (18 U.S.C. 925) that prohibits anyone convicted of a misdemeanor from owning or using a firearm further complicates the law enforcement issue.

In 1997, a task force studying LAPD found that out of 227 cases of alleged domestic violence cases investigated between 1990 and 1997, 91 were sustained. In over 75 percent of these, the sustained allegations were not mentioned in the officer's yearly evaluations; and, in fact, 26 of these officers were promoted.

Tragically, a case that exemplifies this type of response happened in Tacoma, Washington. On April 26, 2003, David Brame, the Chief of Police in Tacoma, Washington, fatally shot his wife and then himself in front of his children

Forst's Law

Deviance and the Job

Police departments strive to hire the most ethical individuals that they can. In my opinion, they do an outstanding job. When you realize the vast opportunities officers have to do the "wrong thing" and look at the fact that very few choose to follow that path, that says something about the quality of the individual working the street. Officers are confronted on a daily basis with ethical issues.

I remember as a police officer working the street being constantly challenged by citizens and business owners who wanted to show their appreciation for the job we were doing. The crime rate was very high, and citizens were grateful when we gave them the service they deserved even in matters they may have perceived as minor.

Half-price meals or free coffee were fairly common offerings. The arguments that ensued over payment were embarrassing and usually resulted in my leaving the full price of the meal on the table or counter; they could use it as a tip if nothing else. Unfortunately, it sometimes resulted in my avoiding that restaurant and going elsewhere, which of course was the exact opposite of what the business owner wanted.

The text of this chapter mentions studies that found that often the biggest complaint citizens had about officers' behavior toward them was abusive or derogatory language rather than excessive force. While I feel that everyone should be treated with respect, I was also concerned with the safety of the community and my own safety as well as that of other officers. There were times when people I encountered on the street did not respond to my requests. There were times when I resorted to crazy language, bad language, or harsh orders in order to avoid the need for a physical confrontation. One time I spotted a unarmed robbery suspect while I was patrolling the edge of town. I confronted him, and the chase was on. Because I was out in the woods on the edge of town, I knew there would be no backup anywhere close. I yelled all sorts of things at this guy, because I wanted him to think I was crazy and might not "play by the rules." It worked. He stopped and put his hands up, and I was able to cuff him and take him in.

I also feel that public education can help in these complaint situations and aid in smoothing misunderstandings between the police and the community. I remember as a road patrol captain I used to get calls from angry citizens complaining about the harsh treatment they received from an officer. I explained the officer's point of view and police procedure, including the officer's need to control the situation. I also explained that the officer encounters all types of people during the day and that many officers get killed or injured during car stops. I found that after being made aware of these factors, the citizen usually no longer wanted to make a complaint.

Lastly, I think it is critical that departments make it as difficult as possible for officers to be tempted to deviate from their good ethical conduct. They need to have good, solid policies and procedures in place to protect the officers from temptation and to protect the officers from any possible allegations of wrongdoing. I went to many scenes as a road supervisor where the narcotics unit had made some arrests. There were often bags of money and/or drugs all around with no one sure exactly how much was there. Once there was half a million dollars in duffle bags. How tempting it might be for an officer having trouble paying the mortgage to take some cash from bad guys that no one would even miss—or . . . how easy for someone to make that accusation. There must be policies in place to provide checks and balances and protections for the officers on the scene. Police departments owe it to their organization and their officers.

in a parking lot in a neighboring community. This came several days after allegations of abuse and the divorce paperwork became public, despite his wife's efforts to minimize his anger and embarrassment by filing the divorce papers in a neighboring county. His wife, Crystal, had filed for divorce and moved out of the home with the children in February, alleging that her husband was abusive and possessive. Brame was assistant chief and a 20-year veteran of the department when he was named chief in December 2001. There are allegations that the city manager knew of rumors of abuse and an acquaintance rape issue in his past but did not investigate them thoroughly before appointing him chief. The state of Washington concluded an investigation of the incident in November 2003 and found no grounds for criminal charges but significant evidence of mismanagement within the city of Tacoma. Both noncriminal and federal investigations are ongoing. Relatives of Crystal Brame have filed a $75 million wrongful-death civil suit, with the belief that the city's inaction or inappropriate actions ultimately led to Crystal's death.[91]

★ ★ ★

POLICE BRUTALITY

Police brutality has been defined as "the excessive or unreasonable use of force in dealing with citizens, suspects, and offenders."[92] Police violence in this country and charges of police brutality are not new; however, neither is brutality or excessive force very common, despite what the media may lead us to believe. A National Institute of Justice Study found that most police officers in the U.S. disapprove of the use of excessive force, and the overwhelming majority do not believe that officers regularly engaged in the excessive use of force. Almost all surveyed officers (97.1 percent) agreed that serious cases of misconduct—like the Rodney King or Abner Louima cases—were "extremely rare" in their departments.[93]

Tradition of Police Brutality

In a classic and frequently cited article on police brutality, Albert J. Reiss, Jr., began his discussion with a 1903 quotation by a former police commissioner of New York City:

> For 3 years, there has been through the courts and the streets a dreary procession of citizens with broken heads and bruised bodies against a few of whom was violence needed to effect an arrest. Many of them had done nothing to deserve an arrest. In a majority of such cases, no complaint was made. If the victim complains, his charge is generally dismissed. The police are practically above the law.[94]

Police Captain "Clubber" Williams coined the phrase "There is more law in the end of a policeman's nightstick than in a decision of the Supreme Court."[95] Another 19-century police officer recalls being told by his sergeant, "There's more religion in the end of a nightstick, than in any sermon preached to the likes of them."[96]

In the 1920s, the Wickersham Commission detailed numerous instances of police brutality, including the use of the third degree to obtain confessions.[97] The general acceptance of police brutality in the past can be seen in the landmark 1936 U.S. Supreme Court case *Brown* v. *Mississippi*. In this case, the deputy sheriff who administered beatings to three defendants to force them to confess to a murder actually answered the judge's inquiry at trial as to how severely a defendant had been beaten by saying, "Not too much for a negro."[98]

Police violence became a major topic for public discussion in the 1940s, when rioting by citizens provoked serious police backlash and brutality against citizens. Former Supreme Court associate justice Thurgood Marshall, then a lawyer for the National Association for the Advancement of Colored People (NAACP), referred to the Detroit police as a "Gestapo" after a 1943 race riot left 34 people dead.[99]

Examples of Police Brutality

Charges of police brutality have not disappeared. They were common during the civil disorders of the 1960s and 1970s. As recently as the 1990s, people in the United States were stunned by the use of excessive force by police officers in the Abner Louima and Rodney King cases.[100]

Recent history shows us the current public reaction to the use of force by the police against minority citizens. The shootings of African American men by police officers were the sparks that set off three riots in Miami between 1980 and 1989. The last disturbance, which occurred from January 16 to January 18, 1989, was set off by the shooting of an unarmed African American motorcyclist by a Hispanic American police officer; 11 citizens were wounded and 13 buildings burned to the ground.[101] The 1992 Los Angeles riots, perhaps the most severe civil disturbance in U.S. history, came on the heels of not-guilty verdicts in the trials of the four LAPD officers accused of assaulting Rodney King.

Brutality seems as intractable in policing as corruption is. Consider just a few examples. In 1979, the U.S. Department of Justice filed an unprecedented civil rights suit charging Philadelphia's Mayor Frank Rizzo and the Philadelphia Police Department with pervasive and systematic police brutality, as well as violations of the 1964 Civil

Dempsey's Law

When It's Over, It's Over

Professor Dempsey, did you see that tape from Los Angeles [the 1991 Rodney King incident]?

Tony, I had no chance to avoid it. It must have been shown every hour on television.

Well, what did you think?

It was disgusting! I think it set police work and relationships with the community back decades, if not centuries!

Yeah, but my friend said that the guy might have been resisting, and the police should have continued to hit him until he stopped moving. When is police physical force considered excessive force?

Look, Tony, sometimes police work is a contact sport. Sometimes you have to roll around in the mud. But like any contact sport, when it's over, it's over. You don't hit your opponent after the bell or after the ref blows the play dead. Do you know what I mean?

Yeah.

Was it over?

Yeah, it was.

That was excessive force, Tony.

Rights Act, federal laws, and the U.S. Constitution. This was the first time the federal government had charged an entire police department with indiscriminate brutality rather than proceeding against specific officers. The government reported, "The conditions we're addressing seem institutionalized, and putting away individual officers doesn't solve the problem."[102] The suit also said that the Philadelphia Police Department followed "procedures which resulted in widespread, arbitrary, and unreasonable physical abuse or abuse which shocks the conscience."[103] The suit also accused the department of "inflicting disproportionate abuse on black persons and persons of Hispanic origin."[104]

In 1986, a ranking officer and officers from the 106th Precinct in New York City were convicted of torturing an accused drug dealer with an electronic stun gun. This caused an enormous shake-up in the command structure of the NYPD, including transfer of each supervisor assigned to the precinct.

Recently, a mistrial was declared due to a hung jury in the case of an Inglewood, California, officer caught on videotape "manhandling" a 16-year-old in July 2002. The amateur video showed the officer slamming the youth on the trunk of the patrol car and hitting him in the face while he was handcuffed.[105] Shortly after the incident occurred, the *Los Angeles Times* identified more than a dozen complaints of excessive force against Inglewood officers in recent years, including physical abuse resulting in broken noses and missing teeth.[106]

In 1989, Don Jackson, an African American police officer from a neighboring town, began a ride through the streets of Long Beach, California, secretly accompanied by an NBC camera crew. In less than three minutes, Jackson's car was pulled over. He was verbally abused by a Long Beach police officer, his head was pushed through a plate glass window, and then his head was pounded on the trunk of a police car.[107]

Why do cases of police brutality dominate the headlines for weeks at a time? Is police violence against citizens that pervasive? Or does police brutality receive so much attention because it is so repugnant to our concept of "order under law"?

Is Brutality Really the Problem?

Despite the high incidence of headlines about police brutality, evidence suggests that the verbal abuse of citizens by officers is a more serious problem. The President's Commission on Law Enforcement and Administration of Justice reported

> The commission believes that physical abuse is not as serious a problem as it was in the past. . . . Most persons, including civil rights leaders, believe that verbal abuse and harassment, not excessive use of force is the major police community relations problem today.[108]

Albert J. Reiss, Jr., of Yale University, conducted a classic study of police abuse. For several weeks, 36 observers (college students with backgrounds in law, police administration, and social science) rode in patrol cars in high-crime areas of Boston, Chicago, and Washington, D.C. The observers recorded and reported the outcomes of 5,360 interactions between the police and citizens.[109] Of the 5,360 encounters between police and citizens, Reiss found only 27 cases in which the police were observed using force improperly. He found that police verbal abuse toward citizens was far more common than the use of excessive force. Police behavior was observed to be uncivil toward 13 percent of all citizens with whom the police interacted. The study found that the most common complaints of citizens against police, in order of frequency, were

1. Use of profane and abusive language
2. Use of commands to move on or get home
3. Stopping and questioning people on the street or searching them and their cars
4. Use of threats to use force if not obeyed
5. Prodding with a nightstick or approaching with a pistol
6. Actual use of physical force or violence itself

Reiss found that in cases in which offenders were taken into custody, the factors leading to the unnecessary use of force by police were the citizens' social class and behavior (deferring to versus defying the authority of the police). About half of the cases of unnecessary force involved people's openly defying police authority. Reiss found that the police were more likely to use excessive force against suspects and citizens when the police considered it necessary to clarify who was in charge and when the police were harassing drunks, members of the gay community, and narcotics users.

Although three-fourths of the white police officers in the Reiss study were observed making prejudicial statements about African American citizens, they did not actually treat African Americans any more uncivilly than they treated whites. Furthermore, there was no evidence of racial discrimination against African Americans in cases where the police unnecessarily assaulted citizens.

In more than half of the instances of excessive force, officers who were present but not party to the violence did not restrain or report their fellow officers. Reiss emphasizes that what the citizens he studied found especially disturbing was the status degradation aspect of police behavior. They felt they had not been treated with the full rights and dignity due to citizens in a democratic society.

Paul Chevigny notes that police abuses often stem from the traditions of police work and from the expectations of the police when confronting citizens. The police expect deference to, or at least acceptance of, their authority. Behavior that is inconsistent with the officers' expectations—ranging from a show of disrespect to outright resistance—usually brings a strong physical reaction by officers.[110]

To make citizens aware of the police reaction to conduct challenging their authority (as discovered by Reiss and Chevigny), Peter Scharf and Arnold Binder suggested "a community education program informing citizens about police expectations and about typical police responses to citizen threats. . . . [so] that citizens might communicate with police officers to avoid violent confrontations."[111] Also, as communication is a two-way street, police need to consider the appropriateness of their expectations of deference from citizens.

In a research study, David Bayley and James Garofalo observed 350 eight-hour tours in three precincts in New York City. They discovered that incidents of violence between police officers and citizens are relatively rare, even in a large urban area such as New York City. Of 467 potentially violent incidents they encountered, only 78 resulted in some type of actual conflict. Of these, in only 42 encounters was force used by the police against citizens or by citizens against the police. The force used by police consisted almost exclusively of grabbing and restraining; firearms were never used.[112]

Findings similar to these emerged from the questioning of citizens in 15 cities about police misconduct for the National Commission on Civil Disorders. Gerald D. Robin and Richard H. Anson say, "Police incivility (verbal disrespect) rather than police brutality (physical abuse) is the salient issue in the public's criticism of the police."[113]

Also, the 1997 National Criminal Victimization Survey conducted by the Bureau of Justice Statistics revealed that less than 1 percent of the persons who reported a contact with the police during the prior reporting period said the police had used or threatened to use physical force on them. If force was used, respondents said it was usually because they provoked the officers.[114]

Police Department Responses to Police Brutality

Police departments respond to the problem of excessive force by the police with a variety of solutions. Carl B. Klockars tells us that the leading proposed solutions to police brutality are improved training, better screening of applicants, citizen review, more aggressive internal affairs investigations, increased discipline, closer press scrutiny, community policing, clearer policy, tighter rules, and stronger leadership.[115]

Police departments have several responses to documented cases of police brutality. Sometimes they arrest, suspend, or terminate the officer. In the 1991 Rodney King incident and the 1997 Abner Louima case, the officers were arrested and immediately suspended. The officers in the 106th Precinct stun gun case were all arrested, suspended from duty without pay, and eventually convicted. After conviction, they were terminated from the department.

Most states allow for another avenue of discipline. Officers must be licensed or certified in the state in order to be a police officer. When an officer participates in conduct that falls outside state guidelines, the state must be notified. The charges may warrant a decertification hearing. This process adds to the checks and balances in police discipline. A problem that arose in the '80s and '90s was when departments would allow an officer to resign after misconduct to avoid the costly termination process and potential legal fight. Officers were often hired to be officers on other departments that did not conduct as thorough a background investigation as they should have. An exposé by the press in Florida revealed there were some officers moving around the state from department to department after resigning due to misconduct that had never been reported to the state.

Samuel Walker reports that some police departments take more proactive action to prevent officer–citizen violence, such as instituting specialized training programs to reduce brutality and amending and adding detailed rules of engagement limiting force in police and citizen encounters. Walker points out, however, that these rules usually are a reaction to a crisis situation in the department rather than a systematic effort to improve police–citizen interactions.[116]

A good example of rules made in response to a crisis situation is the response to the 1984 Bumpers case in New York City. An emotionally disturbed person, Eleanor Bumpers, while being evicted from a city housing project, attempted to stab one of the officers and was subsequently killed by an Emergency Services officer using a shotgun. The shooting caused serious disturbances in the minority community in the Bronx. The officer who fired the weapon was subsequently arrested by the Bronx district attorney for criminally negligent homicide but was later found not guilty at trial. In the wake of the shooting and the demonstrations, Police Commissioner Benjamin Ward changed department procedures regarding the police response to calls involving emotionally disturbed persons. The new rules called for the elimination of shotguns being carried in these cases by members of the Emergency Services Division and also mandated that a captain must respond to all such cases as the primary decision maker.

Some say that improved hiring practices can cause a reduction of police brutality. The U.S. Commission on Civil Rights, after field investigations and public hearings in Philadelphia and Houston, emphasized the importance of hiring more members of racial minority groups and upgrading their positions in police departments. The commission cited the study of the National Minority Advisory Council on Criminal Justice: "Central to the problem of brutality is the underrepresentation of minorities as police officers. . . . It has been shown that the presence of minority police officers has a positive effect on police–community relations."[117]

Many police administrators hope that personality or psychological tests can be instituted that may help to identify individuals prone to corruption or abuse of power before they are hired. This would save departments money, time, and aggravation as well as protect or preserve the police–community relationship. The National Institute of Justice is currently examining this issue and has identified some personality traits that seem to correlate with officers involved in corruption. Included in these traits were difficulty in getting along with others and immaturity. An initial recommendation NIJ makes to police departments is to carefully conduct and review background investigations. They provide further information at their Web site.

Citizen Oversight

Another important innovation suggested to reduce police brutality is **citizen oversight**, the process by which citizens (nonpolice) appointed by government executives review allegations of brutality or abuse by police officers. Generally, these boards have no power to discipline offending officers but can make recommendations to police officials. Many local governments have created citizen complaint review boards (CCRBs) to investigate alleged cases of police brutality. Citizen complaint review boards existed in the 1950s and early 1960s but became most popular after the civil disturbances of the 1960s and 1970s, primarily in areas where minorities believed that police were discriminating against them. CCRBs were bitterly opposed by some members of the police, and most either lasted only a short time or were not very powerful.[118]

Wayne Kerstetter has identified three different types of citizen complaint review boards based on the extent of citizen involvement. First, the citizen review model agency is outside of and independent from the police department and has the authority to receive and investigate complaints and to recommend discipline. Second, the citizen input model agency employs nonsworn police personnel to receive and investigate complaints, but the power to recommend discipline remains with sworn police officials. Finally, the citizen monitor model agency is part of the police department, and the agency receives, investigates, and adjudicates complaints. However, an independent citizen board serves as a check or safeguard over the process.[119]

In the 1980s, 30 cities established new citizen oversight agencies. Staff members from these agencies formed their own professional organization, the International Association for Citizen Oversight of Law Enforcement (IACOLE). By 1995, the National Association for Civilian Oversight of Law Enforcement (NACOLE) began operations in the United States. Of the nation's 100 largest cities, 71 have citizen review mechanisms; and, since 1996, NACOLE has assisted more than 20 cities in their establishment of systems. Citizen review boards created to hear complaints against police have not always been successful. The Civil Rights Commission found the following about CCRBs: "Their basic flaws were that they were advisory only, having no power to decide cases or impose punishment, and that they lacked sufficient staffs and resources." The commission recommended that although disciplinary action must remain with the police department, there must be some outside review to assist the complaining citizen who is unsatisfied with the police department's finding.[120] Despite calls for citizen complaint review boards to investigate allegations of police misconduct, some communities are not entirely comfortable with these boards.

In 1991, the residents of Miami, Florida, defeated a resolution that would have given subpoena powers to citizen review boards. One proponent of this resolution—an attorney for the currently inactive Overtown Independent Review Panel, which was established in the wake of the 1989 Miami riots—complained, "If we can't even get an officer to come in and say what happened, then you don't have a real investigation." The president of the Miami Fraternal Order of Police, however, stated that the granting of subpoena powers to citizen boards would have given rise to "perceptions that someone had to be the fall-guy, and needless to say, it was going to end up being a policeman."[121]

PATROLLING THE WEB

National Association for Civilian Oversight of Law Enforcement

NACOLE has annual conferences and provides newsletters and training to interested parties:
www.nacole.org

Terry Hensley, chief of staff inspections for the St. Petersburg, Florida, Police Department, reports that law enforcement is generally opposed to the idea of citizen review, whereas community and civil liberty organizations are generally in support of it. In his review of the current literature regarding citizen review, Hensley lists the pros and cons of the process. In favor of citizen review, Hensley cites the following:

- There is a lack of communication and trust between the law enforcement and minority group communities.
- The lack of trust between law enforcement and minorities is accentuated by the belief that law enforcement agencies fail to discipline their own employees who are guilty of misconduct.
- Citizen review would theoretically provide an independent evaluation of citizen complaints.
- Citizen review would ensure that justice is done and actual misconduct is punished.
- Citizen review would improve public trust in law enforcement.[122]

Against citizen review, Hensley writes that:

- Citizen complaint review boards ignore other legal resources that citizens have for registering complaints (for example, states' attorneys' offices, the federal EOC, civil suits, FBI civil rights investigations, and so forth).
- Citizens cannot understand the operations of law enforcement agencies and the laws, ordinances, and procedures that law enforcement officers must enforce.
- Citizen review boards have a destructive effect upon internal morale.
- Citizen review boards invite abdication of authority by supervisors and management.
- Citizen review boards weaken the ability of upper-level management to achieve conformity through discipline.
- Creating citizen review boards is tantamount to admitting that the police cannot police themselves.[123]

Despite their problems, however, many still favor CCRBs. As Albert J. Reiss, Jr., wrote, "Greater citizen involvement in police administration is one community response to police corruption and citizen review boards may have merit, despite the negative sentiments of some police chiefs."[124]

In a 1997 report, Samuel Walker and Eileen Luna were highly critical of police oversight in Albuquerque, New Mexico. They stated that the oversight mechanisms were ineffective and in some cases, actually served to aggravate tension between residents and the Albuquerque police department.[125]

In 1997, in Tucson, Arizona, officials approved a plan that provided a double layer of oversight for their police department, with the establishment of a 10-member Citizen Police Advisory Review Board, as well as an independent auditor to monitor the investigation of complaints against officers.[126]

Despite the valid arguments on both sides of the issue of citizen oversights, processes involving citizens are widely used. Seventy-five percent of the largest U.S. cities have established some form of review in which citizens participate. Therefore, the issue may have been settled from the public's point of view as to the value of these reviews. The only decision to be made is what type of review system to incorporate. The issue, as viewed from the police perspective, is that these types of boards are most often implemented after a highly publicized and emotionally charged incident has occurred. Consequently, they are sometimes hastily put together and may not be the system best designed to serve the particular police department. To have more time and input in choosing the system that best complements the police organization, many departments are taking a proactive approach and putting a system in place before a crisis erupts. Ultimately, this may contribute to the success of the system for all concerned.[127]

The Emotional Toll

The emotional toll that internal affairs investigations can cause is a subject often ignored by academics. While it is agreed that it is important to receive, document, and track complaints against the police for many reasons, it does need to be noted that people have all sorts of reasons for complaining about police officers. Many mistakenly hope to get out of whatever charges they face from traffic tickets to arrests. Oftentimes the person charged is not even the one to make the complaint. He or she tells someone about it, and that third party may decide to make an issue of it. These complaints can generate a lot of media attention. The media love to report on "bad cops," sometimes even without the facts all being in.

The public reads about it in the paper or hears about it in the news, and the statement is often made that "Officer Smith would not comment," which the public may view negatively. The press does not usually mention that most of the time department policy and sometimes state law may prevent an officer from discussing an ongoing investiga-

tion. This results in the citizen complainant getting to tell his or her story, often over and over, with that account not being disputed by the police until the conclusion of the investigation. Unfortunately, this procedure can take weeks or months, depending on how involved the investigation is.

This has a drastic impact on the psychological well-being of the officers involved, as well as their families, as they see their names trashed in the papers and on the news. Sometimes fellow officers may unintentionally distance themselves from an accused officer, wanting to avoid any negative publicity or association. Command staff and supervisors may also avoid contact with the officer in hopes of not contaminating the investigation, and the involved officer is often placed on administrative leave. This leads to the officer feeling abandoned and alone, with no one to talk to about the incident. Departments often don't take this into consideration, as their most pressing concern becomes distancing the department and their policies from the officer's behavior if necessary. Police administrators and officers need to remind themselves that police officers go into law enforcement to serve the public and do the right thing. If by being wrongly accused or by making a mistake they are now vilified, the effects can be devastating. The worst-case scenario is the officer who commits suicide as his or her world crumbles; and lesser problems include turning to alcohol, marital problems, or extreme cynicism for the remainder of his or her career. Police administrators need to be cognizant of the emotional toll of internal investigations and have some procedures in place to help minimize those effects.

Promoting Integrity

The ideal way for police agencies to handle the deviance and corruption issue is through prevention. If a department takes a proactive stance toward promoting integrity throughout the department, the environment will not be conducive toward the development of corruption or deviance. First, departments need to promote integrity throughout the organization, starting with the top executive. If the chief uses department resources or personnel to work on his or her home, what is the message the officers get? Chiefs need to examine their behavior and make sure everything is above board with nothing that could be misinterpreted. Rank and file who see the command staff taking shortcuts will assume it is tolerated. Training and education should also be provided for the officers to encourage them to role play potential ethical dilemmas, understand what is acceptable behavior and what is not, and know what to do when a situation arises that needs to be addressed. Officers need to be aware of the department policies as well as state laws regarding critical areas such as use of deadly force, use of less than lethal force, pursuits, workplace harassment, and racial profiling.

Departments need to make sure their policies and procedures are clear and provide guidelines to the officers in their behavior. They need to be realistic, relevant, and regularly reviewed and updated. Policies and procedures should not be used or be viewed by officers as being used as a way to hang the officer.

Citizens should be informed of the procedure of making a complaint against a department employee. They should be allowed to make the complaint via phone, by mail, or in person. The department should have a procedure in place to govern taking these complaints to make sure they all get investigated and a determination is made regarding the validity of the complaint. Cases should be able to be tracked. It can cause problems and bad press when citizens bring up former complaints that were made and claim that nothing was done; if a complaint was not properly documented or recorded the department/officer can't properly defend themselves when in fact the officer was cleared or the behavior was justified. Proper documentation and tracking shows the community that the department is not afraid to examine allegations and then take disciplinary action when an officer is wrong. This will promote a feeling of trust between the police and the community.

It is also helpful if the department takes a proactive approach to misconduct. This is often done through various "early warning" systems.[128] It has been understood that it is usually a small percentage of police officers that cause departments most of their problems. Bigger departments may need help in trying to determine who these people are before a problem reaches the critical stage. The department will decide what factors or criteria they want to look at to aid them in recognizing if an officer has a tendency toward violence or excessive force before it becomes a serious problem. In a small department, most supervisors will know all the officers working the street and their personalities and reliability. Bigger departments with their changing shifts, zones, and supervisors may not be immediately aware of potential problem officers. These systems must be coupled with the common sense of supervisors and management. Officers with more aggressive assignments and generally working the nighttime shifts will generate the most complaints because their assignment is to be proactive and prevent crime. Also, sometimes more senior officers have learned that the best way to stay out of trouble and avoid controversy is to avoid contacting people on the street if they don't have to. Consequently, these officers will generate very few citizens' complaints. If a flag is raised regarding an officer who seems to have a tendency toward rudeness or excessive force, the department can use counseling or training to help correct the problem.

Most departments have standard procedures to investigate any police-involved shootings, as well as use of the stun gun or chemical spray. Again, the routine documentation and, when necessary, investigation will let both the officers and the community know these are important issues and help the department to identify at-risk officers.

Lastly, open communication with the public will help promote integrity. The public should have access to policies and procedures, and they (as well as the officers) should know what the expected behavior is for officers and the department. Soliciting input and actually considering it or using it will also provide valuable relationships with the public.

The 1998 Government Accounting Office report mentioned earlier also recommended changing the police culture, spreading accountability throughout the department, raising the age and education requirements for police officers, improving/implementing integrity training for recruits and in-service officers, and establishing an independent monitor to oversee the department and internal affairs investigations as well as the implementation of community policing. These efforts, together with integrity testing, early warning systems, and proactive investigations of officers and/or units with corruption complaints, will aid in the detection and cessation of corruption and deviance.

Additionally, the Department of Justice (DOJ) advocates having good, solid policies and procedures in place so that everyone—rank and file, supervisors, administrators, and the public—knows what is expected. These policies recognize and respect the value and dignity of all people, encourage courtesy in all contacts, and discourage the use of force unless absolutely necessary.[129]

PATROLLING THE WEB

The Department of Justice

The Department of Justice provides examples of model police practices and policies, including high-liability areas and complaint investigations, on their Web site:
   http://www.ojp.usdoj.gov

When a department promotes integrity and consequently works together with the community to solve problems and reduce crime, this will lead to an improved quality of life for all. Former Attorney General Janet Reno called attention to the inscription on the side of the Justice Department Building in Washington, D.C., that reads "The common law is derived from the will of mankind, issuing from the life of the people, framed by mutual confidence and sanctioned by the light of reason." She followed this, in concluding her introduction to the DOJ report on integrity, with the comment, "Policing at its best can do more than anything to frame that confidence and bring together all of the people, in the knowledge that the law speaks fairly to them."[130]

CHAPTER SUMMARY

Police deviance, which has a long tradition in U.S. police departments, appears to be intractable. This chapter discussed the many forms of police deviance, including corruption, drug and alcohol abuse, cooping, police deception, abuse of authority, verbal abuse of citizens, sexual violence, domestic violence, and police brutality.

The chapter detailed examples of police corruption, types and forms of corruption, reasons for police corruption, and responses to police corruption. It also discussed the tradition of police brutality, gave some recent examples of police brutality and police abuse, and talked about responses to police brutality (including citizen oversight).

The extremely serious problems that this chapter discussed tarnish the image of police departments and all police officers. Stories of police deviance sell newspapers. A police officer or a group of officers who commit deviant acts occupy the front pages of newspapers for weeks.

The temptations leading to corrupt and brutal acts by police officers are tremendous. However, not all police officers commit deviant acts. In fact, a very small percentage of police officers are brutal or corrupt. It would be nice if we could eliminate all police deviance. Unfortunately, however, we recruit our police from the human race, so we will always have some bad police officers along with the many excellent ones. Police departments must do all that is necessary to prevent police deviance. Also, honest police officers must bring to light the actions of the few deviant police officers in their midst to keep the profession as honest as possible. Policing can then become a better and easier profession.

Learning Check

1. Define police corruption. Identify some of the forms it takes.
2. Explain why some police officers become corrupt.
3. Discuss whether something about police work makes police corruption and other police deviance intractable.
4. Define police brutality. Identify some of the forms it takes.
5. Identify and discuss forms of police deviance other than corruption and brutality.

Application Exercise

Because of your experience in taking this course, you have been appointed assistant to the police commissioner of Anyburgh, USA. Anyburgh has had a 10-year tradition of numerous brutality and corruption complaints against its officers. The commissioner requests your advice regarding the effects of these allegations on the integrity and effectiveness of the department, as well as methods he can take to reduce them.

Web Exercise

Go to the IACP Web site (www.theiacp.org) and examine their "code of ethics" as well as the "oath of honor" and determine what the difference is between these two items. What kind of training does IACP offer on the topic of ethics? Also visit a state, county, and municipal law enforcement agency site on the Internet. What procedures are in place for someone to make a complaint against a police officer? Will these procedures encourage or discourage complaints?

Key Concepts

Citizen oversight
Integrity test
Internal affairs division (IAD or IA)
Judicial review
Knapp Commission
National Treasury Employees Union v. *Von Raab* (1989)
Proactive investigation

GUEST LECTURE

The Message

JEFF MAGERS

Dr. Jeffrey S. Magers is an assistant professor in the Department of Justice Administration and Southern Police Institute at the University of Louisville. He retired as a captain with the Jefferson County Police Department in Louisville, Kentucky (now called the Louisville Metro Police Department). Dr. Magers is a Lieutenant Colonel in the U.S. Army Reserve (retired). He attended the Southern Police Institute Administrative Officers Course and the FBI National Academy.

The criminal justice system relies upon the credibility, integrity, and professional conduct of police officers under the supervision of ethical police leaders. Police leaders often underestimate the influence they have on the ethical climate of an organization and the ethical conduct of individual police officers under their command. This essay will present a true story illustrating how much influence a single, determined, ethical police leader can have when he or she takes the opportunity and demonstrates the conviction of strong moral character and ethical leadership.

Early in my police career I was a detective in the violent crime unit of a 450-officer county police department. At that time, I worked the evening shift with four other detectives and a sergeant. One evening, early in the shift, I was sitting at my desk writing reports. The other detectives with whom I worked were doing the same. I looked up from my report for a moment and saw our lieutenant walking in the squad room with a determined look on his face. Visits from the lieutenant were not unusual; he worked the day shift and often visited us in the squad room before departing for the day. This evening, with no greeting, he walked directly to the chair in front of my desk. Without prelude, the lieutenant immediately began a speech that I will never forget. He said, "I hate liars, I will not tolerate liars under my command, and anyone under my command whom I catch lying, I will personally do everything I can to see to it that they are terminated." Good evening LT, how are you today! Needless to say the lieutenant had my attention, because he was sitting directly across from my desk. I immediately wondered, "Is he talking to me?" I quickly discerned that he had not focused on me alone. His gaze was scanning the room. I realized he was making a blanket statement to all who could hear, and without a doubt he had our undivided attention. He continued to elaborate by saying he would not tolerate lying to him, the sergeant, the captain, to other officers, to the media, to prosecutors, and I expected him to say and to our parents, spouses, and children, but he left them out of this speech. He continued speaking on this theme for several more minutes. He was not happy about something, and it was apparent he felt that someone in his command had lied. He was angry and disappointed.

To this day I think he suspected that someone had lied about some aspect of a politically sensitive case we had been working on. I suspect he did not know who the culprit was, because no one lost their job that day. The lieutenant finished his tirade, lifted himself from the chair, and left the room abruptly. I remember the general comments in the room after he left focused on what had the LT bent out of shape. That was not what I was thinking. I had just heard the most definitive, firm stance on police ethics that I had ever heard in my relatively short police career. He left no doubt in my mind as to his expectations of ethical conduct for his detectives and for all police officers in general. As impressive a speech as it had been, at that moment I did not fully realize how much it would influence my career.

Months later, I was assigned a particularly difficult investigation. It was an unusual case because it was one that to my knowledge no one in our unit had ever tried to investigate and prosecute. Because this was an extraordinary case for which no one had any experience in how to proceed, I was investigating the case without much help or guidance. During the course of the investigation I made a serious mistake. The mistake was one I should not have made, but I had not intentionally done so. I came to work one day as the investigation of this case was nearly complete, and we were beginning the prosecution phase. I was confronted with my error by the lieutenant. He informed me of my mistake in no uncertain terms and asked me to explain. I could have lied that day and told the LT a story that maybe would have shifted the blame, but I was looking into the eyes of the man who just a few months earlier had given the "speech." My parents had taught me not to lie, and this was reinforced by an honor code as a commissioned officer in the U.S. Army (my first job after college), but under pressure, the temptation to lie is intense. If we are truthful with ourselves, we know this temptation all too well. Looking at the LT I realized lying was *not* an option, as well it should never have been. I told the lieutenant the truth about my error, because when presented with the facts, I realized, I had to be responsible for my actions involving this investigative mistake. I know you want to know what the mistake was, but that is irrelevant to this story. It was not criminal; it was just a procedural error

that could have jeopardized the case and certainly caused everyone working on the case more work. I still obtained a conviction in the case.

After I had confessed my error, the LT gave me a vigorous oral reprimand, as did the captain, the major, and the deputy chief of police. Thank goodness the chief was off that day and I was spared that nightmare, although I must admit I was undeserving of a break that day. When the ordeal was over I went about the task of correcting my error. It was only days later that I realized that I had faced a crucial moment in my career. Had I lied that day, I truly believe it would have been the end of my police career. Without the lieutenant's speech, I may have had the strength of character to tell the truth that day, but maybe I would not have. I will never know. I do know the words of the LT echoed in my head, setting the standard for ethical policing. The lieutenant's definitive ethical message was the support I needed at that critical moment. Later when I reflected on the situation, I realized how important the lieutenant's words were to me and to my young career. I do not know if the other detectives in the squad room heard the message in the same way I did, but the influence it had on me was profound.

After this incident I thought about the three officers in my recruit class who had been terminated for separate ethical lapses. If they had heard this same message, would they have heeded the warning and lived up to the ethical expectations so effectively expressed by my lieutenant, a police leader who took the time to clearly set the standard for ethical conduct of the police officers in his command? We will never know. Years later, as a sergeant, I was selected for an assignment by that same lieutenant, who by then was a major and the commander of a joint city–county narcotics unit. He chose me to be the asset forfeiture manager for the unit. After I was with the unit for a while, I asked him why he chose me for the job. He said I was the one sergeant he knew he could trust for this highly sensitive position, involving the handling of considerable amounts of cash.

While still working as a police officer I returned to college to earn a doctorate in leadership education. A considerable amount of my coursework concerned ethics and leadership. I began teaching basic and in-service training ethics classes for police officers and police supervisors in my department, the state, and various venues throughout the country. In every class I have told this story, repeating the lieutenant's message each time. All police leaders, police officers, police recruits, and criminal justice students in college must hear the same message. Because ethical decision-making for police officers is such an important issue, I chose to complete my doctoral dissertation on the topic of how police supervisors influence police officers to lie to cover up unethical behavior. Needless to say my research indicated what the lieutenant intuitively knew: Police supervisors have a significant effect on the ethical behavior of police officers.

The burden to create an ethical police environment rests not just with police leaders. Individual officers are responsible for their conduct. Leaders can set the tone, but each officer must make a conscious decision to accept or not accept the wise counsel of ethical police leaders. So, in this era where people often blame others for their crimes or ethical lapses, one should not shift the blame entirely to supervisors for the ethical conduct of their subordinates. Police leaders providing clear ethical messages certainly help those who would choose to make sound, ethical decisions in the course of their daily police lives. Ultimately it is an individual decision. It is your decision to hold yourself accountable and to hold other officers accountable for their actions when police leaders are not physically present.

I retired from policing; I now teach criminal justice/law enforcement at a regional state university in Texas and provide seminars for police leaders. Every time I tell this story, I hope there are those who hear the same clear, concise, ethical message I heard from the lieutenant to whom I owe so much.

13 Women and Minorities in Policing

CHAPTER GOALS

- To describe the history and problems of women and minorities in policing
- To illustrate how discrimination affected women and minorities in obtaining employment and promotions in policing
- To discuss the provisions of the U.S. legal system that enabled women and minorities to overcome job discrimination.
- To introduce the academic studies showing that women and African Americans can perform police patrol duty as effectively as white men
- To portray a sense of the problems women and minorities still face in law enforcement, even in the 21st century

Female police officers on uniformed patrol duty are common today, as are officers who are African American or members of other minority groups. In fact, all races and ethnic groups are represented in U.S. police departments. However, this was not always the case. Until quite recently, white males dominated the ranks.

African Americans were traditionally excluded from U.S. police departments. As just one example among many, before 1948, African Americans were not allowed to be members of the Atlanta Police Department.[1] A police historian notes that the underrepresentation of minorities in police departments has not been limited to southern cities. He found that every major municipal jurisdiction in the United States has a history of discriminating against minorities.[2]

Although the United States has had organized, paid police departments since the 1840s, the first female police officer was not appointed until 1905. By 1919, over 60 police departments employed female officers. However, they were given only clerical duties or duties dealing with juveniles or female prisoners. It was not until the late 1960s that women were permitted to perform the same patrol duties as men.[3]

This chapter will focus on the roles of women and minority groups in U.S. police departments. It will review their experience and the methods they used to secure the same job opportunities as white males. The chapter will also show the extent to which women and minorities have influenced today's police departments and explore the capabilities of women in performing what has traditionally been viewed as a male occupation. Finally, it will examine the status of women and minorities in U.S. law enforcement today.

★ ★ ★

DISCRIMINATION IN POLICING

The United States has a long history of job **discrimination** against women and minorities. Discrimination is the unequal treatment of persons in personnel decisions (hiring, promotion, and firing) on the basis of their race, religion, national origin, gender, or sexual orientation. Only in the past several decades have women and minorities been able to share the American dream of equal employment. Their treatment in police departments was not much different from their treatment in other jobs and in society in general. The federal government admitted this fact in 1974 in an affirmative action guidebook for employers: "American law guarantees all persons equal opportunity in employment.

However, employment discrimination has existed in police departments for a long time. The main areas of discrimination are race/ethnic background and gender."[4]

In addition to discrimination against women and ethnic and racial minorities, police departments have had a history of discrimination in employment decisions against homosexuals. As we will see later in this chapter, much of this discrimination has disappeared.

Discrimination against Women

Women have faced an enormous uphill struggle to earn the right to wear the uniform and perform the same basic police duties that men have performed for years. Why were women excluded from performing regular police work? Until the 1970s, it was presumed that women, because of their gender and typical size, were not capable of performing the same type of patrol duty as men. Additionally, other social forces discriminated against women. Gerald Carden points to several possible reasons why women were kept out of policing: Men did not want to put up with the social inhibitions placed on them by the presence of women; they did not want to be overshadowed by, or to take orders from, women; and they did not want to be supported by females in the performance of potentially dangerous work.[5] Other possible reasons for discrimination against women certainly existed, including the jealousy of male police officers' wives.

Prior to 1967, women constituted only a very small percentage of U.S. police officers. The early female officers were restricted to issuing parking tickets or performing routine clerical tasks. Additionally, in the early days of female policing, women were normally used in only three actual police-related jobs: vice, juvenile work, and guarding female prisoners.[6] Catherine Milton, writing in 1972, found that female officers were used mainly as secretaries and dispatchers, and they were rarely afforded equal status with men.[7]

In the late 1960s and early 1970s, the role of women in U.S. police departments began to change. Samuel Walker states that one of the possible causes for this change could have been the suggestion by the President's Commission on Law Enforcement and Administration of Justice that the greater use of female officers could help solve the police personnel crisis discovered by the commission. Walker also attributes the change to the woman's rights movement and to the efforts by female officers themselves to gain the right to perform patrol duty in order to achieve equality with male officers.[8] Even as late as the mid-1970s, however, Timothy Egan writes, women were often still allowed

The History of Women in the NYPD

In 1924, the Bureau of Policewomen was established in the New York City Police Department with Mary Hamilton named as its director. (Female officers were called policewomen, and male officers were patrolmen.) In 1938, the first test for appointment to the rank of policewoman was given. In 1959, policewomen were first used on foot patrol in midtown Manhattan. The real rise of women into the NYPD rank structure, and the impetus for the eventual unification of policewoman and patrolman ranks into the rank of police officer, began in 1961. An NYPD policewoman, Felicia Shpritzer, filed a lawsuit to achieve the right to take a promotional exam to the rank of sergeant. The city had always maintained that policewomen were not part of the civil service career path from patrolman to captain. In April 1964, the city gave a promotional examination to the rank of sergeant; and, because of Shpritzer's lawsuit, women were given the right to take a makeup examination for that rank on March 12, 1965. Shpritzer and another policewoman, Gertrude Schimmel, successfully passed the examination and became the first women in NYPD history to hold the rank of police sergeant. In December 1967, Shpritzer and Schimmel successfully passed the promotional examination to the rank of lieutenant. In December 1971, Schimmel became the first female police captain in New York City's history.

In June 1972, a pilot project was established in three New York City police precincts using policewomen on regular uniformed patrol, acting in the same capacity as patrolmen. In 1973, the title of all New York City policewomen was changed to police officers; the ranks of patrolman and policewoman were replaced with the unisex rank of police officer.

In 1973 and 1974, the female ranks in the NYPD began to swell. Nearly 20 percent of the incoming police academy classes were women, due to the creation of the first unisex police examination and the settlement of numerous court cases. The future for women in the NYPD was promising, and many of the women were preparing for promotional examinations. In 1975, however, the city of New York, immersed in a financial crisis, was forced to terminate nearly 5,000 police officers. Because of civil service rules, the officers were laid off in reverse seniority, and the jobs of the newest 5,000 officers were terminated. This group included a significant number of women and minorities.

Within a few years, many of the laid-off officers were rehired. Some, however, including many women, elected not to return because they had found new careers or started families. It was not until 1980 that the city again hired new police officers. In December 1976, for the first time, a New York City police precinct—the First Precinct, which covers Lower Manhattan, including the Wall Street area—was commanded by a woman, Captain Victoria Renzullo.

The gains of women have not been without their losses. On February 12, 1980, Mary Bembry became the first female officer to be shot in the line of duty. A few years later, Irma Losado, a New York City Transit Police officer, became the first female officer in New York City to be killed in the line of duty; she was attempting to subdue a robbery suspect.

to work only with juvenile offenders. In many cities (Chicago for one), female officers could not ride in patrol cars after dark.[9]

For an excellent look at the history of women in U.S. police departments and their transition and evolution from quasi-social workers to fully qualified police officers, see former police captain, and now professor, Dorothy Moses Schulz's excellent 1995 book, *From Social Worker to Crime Fighter: Women in United States Municipal Policing*[10]

Discrimination against Racial and Ethnic Minorities

Members of racial and ethnic minority groups, like women, have experienced entry-level discrimination in police jobs. This section will focus on the history of African Americans in U.S. policing and then discuss the dawning of the awareness of discrimination against all minorities in U.S. police departments.

DISCRIMINATION AGAINST AFRICAN AMERICANS
The first African American police officer was appointed to the Chicago Police Department in 1872. In 1886, another African American man was appointed to the Washington, D.C., Police Department. By 1890, there were approximately 2,000 African American police officers in the United States, mostly employed by large cities. By the turn of the last century, African Americans made up 2.7 percent of all watchmen, police officers, and firefighters. The number of African American officers then decreased over the years until the 1970s, when the number of African Americans entering police work began to rise again with

the move to abolish job discrimination. Kuykendall and Burns report that African Americans have been hired by police departments since the 1940s because of political pressure from African American communities' complaints about the behavior of white officers.[11]

Historically, African American police officers have experienced significant discrimination. Their work assignments were frequently restricted to patrolling African American neighborhoods, and their chances of promotion to higher ranks were restricted. In some areas, they had limited arrest powers and were required to call white police officers to make an arrest. Additionally, they were subjected to prejudicial attitudes by many white officers. As late as the 1950s, some white officers refused to ride in a patrol car with African American officers.[12]

In his classic study of African American police officers in the New York City Police Department, *Black in Blue: A Study of the Negro Policeman,* Nicholas Alex discovered that African Americans were excluded from the department's Detective Division. Alex also found that African American officers were usually accepted by white officers as fellow police officers but were socially excluded from the white officers' off-duty activities.[13] Alex's major finding was that African American police officers had to suffer **double marginality**—the simultaneous expectation by white officers that African American officers will give members of their own race better treatment and hostility from the African American community that they are traitors to their race. Additionally, the African American officers were subjected to racist behavior of white cops. Alex found that African American officers, to deal with this pressure, adapted behaviors ranging from denying that African American suspects should be treated differently from whites to treating African American offenders more harshly to prove their lack of bias. Thus, African American cops, Alex found, not only suffered from the racism of their fellow officers but also were seen to be rougher on African Americans in order to appease whites.[14] In a repeat of his study in 1976, *New York Cops Talk Back,* Alex claimed to have found a more aggressive, self-assured African American police officer. The officers he studied were less willing to accept any discriminatory practices by the police department.[15]

Stephen Leinen, in his book *Black Police, White Society,* found significant discrimination in the New York City Police Department until the 1960s. African American police officers were assigned only to African American neighborhoods and were not assigned to specialized, high profile units. Leinen also noted that disciplinary actions against African American officers were inequitable when compared with those against white officers.[16] He found, however, that institutional discrimination had largely disappeared in subsequent years. He attributes this to the legal, social, and political events of the civil rights era, along with the efforts of African American police officer organizations, such as the NYPD's Guardians.[17]

NATIONAL COMMISSIONS TO STUDY DISCRIMINATION   In the 1960s and early 1970s, the U.S. government recognized the problems caused by the lack of minorities in policing. Various national commissions were established to study, and make recommendations toward improving, the criminal justice system.

The National Advisory Commission on Civil Disorders stated that discriminatory police employment practices contributed to the riots of the middle and late 1960s. It found that in every city affected by the riots, the percentage of minority group officers was substantially lower than the percentage of minorities in the community. The commission noted that in Cleveland, minorities represented 34 percent of the population but only 7 percent of the sworn officers; and, in Detroit, minorities represented 39 percent of the population but only 5 percent of the sworn officers. The commission also noted that although African Americans made up at least 12 percent of the U.S. population, they represented less than 5 percent of police officers nationwide. The Commission also reported that minorities were seriously underrepresented in supervisory ranks in police departments.[18] Another commission formed at this time, the President's Commission on Law Enforcement and Administration of Justice, commented on the low percentage of minorities in police departments: "If police departments, through their hiring or promotion policies indicate they have little interest in hiring minority group officers, the minority community is not likely to be sympathetic to the police."[19] Another group, the **National Advisory Commission on Criminal Justice Standards and Goals,** realized the need to recruit more minorities into U.S. police departments. This presidential commission, which was formed to study the criminal justice system, issued standards to which police agencies should adhere in order to reduce job discrimination. Among these were standards on the employment of women and minority recruitment. On the employment of women, the commission stated

> Every police agency should immediately insure that there exists no agency policy that discourages qualified women from seeking employment as sworn or civilian personnel or prevents them from realizing their full employment.[20]

Minority recruiting was discussed:

> Every police agency immediately should insure that it presents no artificial or arbitrary barriers (cultural or institutional) to discourage qualified individuals from seeking employment or from being employed as police officers.
>
> Every police agency should engage in positive efforts to employ ethnic minority group members. When a substantial ethnic minority population resides within the jurisdiction the police agency should take affirmative action to achieve a ratio of minority group employees in approximate proportion to the makeup of the population.[21]

Discrimination against Gay Officers

In addition to discrimination against women and racial and ethnic minorities, police departments have had a history of discriminating against job applicants because of their sexual orientation. Until the beginning of the focus on equal employment opportunity, many police departments discriminated against homosexuals in employment decisions, and the International Association of Chiefs of Police (IACP) maintained a policy of opposing the employment of gay officers. In 1969, the IACP rescinded its policy of opposing the employment of gay officers. It was estimated that, by 1990, 20 percent of the sworn officers in the San Francisco County Sheriff's Department and perhaps 10 percent of officers in the Los Angeles Police Department were gay men or lesbians.[22] The percentage of gay and lesbian officers is a difficult number to determine. Many departments are not asking about sexual orientation; and, because of a fear of making their sexual orientation known to their coworkers, many police officers hide the fact that they are gay or lesbian.

As stated, many police administrators have decided not to make an issue of sexual orientation in the background investigation. Charles R. Swanson, Leonard Territo, and Robert W. Taylor believe that this decision may reflect an overall change in society's social and sexual mores, as well as a concern by police administrators that if they do not voluntarily take the lead, the federal courts may be called upon to intercede on the behalf of the gay community, as the courts have already done in the case of minorities and women.[23]

Some cities are recruiting openly gay officers in an attempt to bridge a perceived gap with their gay community. The Key West Police Department has the largest number of openly gay officers in south Florida (seven) relative to the city's population.[24] Sgt. Alan Newby, an openly gay officer with Key West and also the president of the Florida chapter of *Law Enforcement for Gays and Lesbians*, states that though officers may receive training in diversity and sexual orientation, "the important thing is that the agency support gay and lesbian police officers and let that officer know he is going to be judged on work product, not sexual orientation." Though Newby sees no need for publicizing officers' sexual orientation, he believes that gay officers are needed in any city with a significant gay population. A gay officer may be more sensitive to issues that arise in the gay community. In advising other departments that are interested in actively recruiting openly gay officers, Newby relates that more internal preparations will need to be made if a gay man rather than a lesbian joins the department. "Police work traditionally is viewed as a macho job, and departments are usually more accepting of lesbian officers than gay officers," he states.[25]

Other departments believe that providing a welcoming climate for gay officers is important but recruitment isn't necessary. Miami Beach Police Department Detective Bobby Hernandez states they've hired their openly gay officers by doing what they always do: "We hire the most qualified applicants. It's not an issue and quite frankly it's none of our business." Perhaps an openly gay citizen in Wilton Manors, Florida, a town looking to actively recruit openly gay officers, summed it up best: "It does not matter to me whether a police officer is openly gay, closeted, or straight, as long as the police department keeps my neighborhood safe."[26]

★ ★ ★

HOW DID WOMEN AND MINORITIES ACHIEVE EQUALITY?

Despite pronouncements by national commissions, women and minorities were forced to take their cases to the U.S. courts in an attempt to achieve equality with white men in U.S. police departments. The primary instrument governing employment equality, as well as all equality, in U.S. society is the **Fourteenth Amendment** to the U.S. Constitution. This amendment, passed in 1868, guarantees "equal protection of the law" to all citizens of the United States. It states

> Section 1. All persons born or naturalized in the United States, and subject to the jurisdiction thereof, are citizens of the United States and of the State wherein they reside. No State shall make or enforce any law which shall abridge the privileges or immunities of citizens of the United States; nor shall any State deprive any person of life, liberty, or property, without due process of law; nor deny to any person within its jurisdiction the equal protection of the law.

More than the Fourteenth Amendment was needed, however, to end job discrimination in policing (or any government agency). The path to equality had as milestones not only the Fourteenth Amendment but also the Civil Rights Act of 1964, Title VII of the same law, the Equal Employment Opportunity Act of 1972 (EEOA), the Civil Rights Act of 1991, federal court cases on discrimination, and government-mandated affirmative action programs.

The Civil Rights Act of 1964

Despite the existence of the Fourteenth Amendment, discrimination by U.S. government agencies continued. In an effort to ensure equality, the **Civil Rights Act of 1964** was passed by Congress and signed into law by President Lyndon B. Johnson in 1964.[27] **Title VII** of this law was designed to prohibit all job discrimination based on race, color, religion, sex, or national origin. It covered all employment practices, including hiring, promotion, compensation, dismissal, and all other terms or conditions of employment.

The Equal Employment Opportunity Act of 1972

The **Equal Employment Opportunity Act of 1972 (EEOA)** extended the 1964 Civil Rights Act and made its provisions, including Title VII, applicable to state and local governments.[28] The EEOA expanded the jurisdiction and strengthened the powers of the Federal Equal Employment Opportunity Commission (EEOC). It allowed employees of state and local governments to file employment discrimination suits with the EEOC, strengthened the commission's investigatory powers by allowing it to document allegations of discrimination better, and permitted the U.S. Department of Justice to sue state and local governments for violations of Title VII. The EEOA stated that all procedures regarding entry and promotion in agencies—including application forms, written tests, probation ratings, and physical ability tests—are subject to EEOC review, in order to determine whether there has been any unlawful act of discrimination.

The Civil Rights Act of 1991

The Civil Rights Act of 1991, also administered by the EEOC, allows for the awarding of punitive damages regarding civil rights violations under certain conditions based on the number of employees a company has. Though it does not apply to governmental agencies, it is a significant development in the civil rights movement and influences behavior throughout the community.

Federal Courts and Job Discrimination

Job discrimination may take several forms. The most obvious, of course, is where there is a clear and explicit policy of discrimination—for example, separate job titles, recruitment efforts, standards, pay, and procedures for female or minority employees. The second, and probably most prevalent, form of job discrimination is **de facto discrimination.** De facto discrimination is discrimination that is the indirect result of policies or practices that are not intended to discriminate but do, in fact, discriminate.

Under EEOC guidelines, discrimination in testing occurs when there is a substantially different rate of selection in hiring, promotion, or another employment decision that works to the disadvantage of members of a particular race, sex, or ethnic group. Let us say that a substantially different rate of passing a particular examination occurs for different racial or ethnic minority groups or members of a certain gender and that this works to the disadvantage of a particular group. For example, if a certain examination results in the vast majority of females failing that test and the vast majority of males passing it, it can be said that the particular examination had an **adverse impact** on females. Adverse impact can be seen as a form of de facto discrimination. In the 1970s and 1980s, women and minorities began to use Title VII and the courts (particularly the federal courts) to attempt to achieve equality.

JOB RELATEDNESS   The first important job discrimination case was *Griggs v. Duke Power Company* in 1971, which declared that the practices of the Duke Power Company were unconstitutional because they required that all of its employees have a high school diploma and pass a standard intelligence test before being hired.[29] The court ruled that these requirements were discriminatory unless they could be shown to measure the attributes needed to perform a specific job. The decision in *Griggs* v. *Duke Power Company* established the concept that job requirements must be job related—they must be necessary for the performance of the job a person is applying for.

De facto discrimination or adverse impact was found to be most prevalent in employment standards and entrance examinations. These standards and tests discriminated against certain candidates, particularly women and minorities. To eliminate the discriminatory effect of recruitment and testing practices, the EEOC required that all tests and examinations be job related. To prove that a test or standard is job related, an agency must provide evidence that the test, examination, or standard measures qualifications and abilities that are actually necessary to perform the specific job for which an applicant is applying or being tested. In the words of the EEOC, to be job related, a test must be "predictive or significantly correlated with important elements of work behavior which comprise or are relevant to the job or jobs for which candidates are being evaluated."[30]

How did all these regulations apply to police departments? Candidates who formerly were denied acceptance into police departments because they could not meet certain standards (height and weight) or could not pass certain tests (strength) began to argue that these standards were not job related—that is, the standards did not measure skills and qualifications needed to perform police work.

The requirement that officers not be less than a certain height (height requirement) was probably the strongest example of discrimination against female candidates. With very few exceptions, police departments lost court cases involving the height requirement. In *Mieth* v. *Dollard* (1976), a lawsuit against the Alabama Department of Public Safety, the court ruled

> Evidence failed to establish . . . that tall officers hold an advantage over smaller colleagues in effectuating arrests and administering emergency aid; furthermore, the contention that tall officers have a psychological advantage was not, as a measure of job performance, sufficient constitutional justification for blanket exclusion of all individuals under the specified height."[31]

In another court case regarding height, the court in *Vanguard Justice Society* v. *Hughes* (1979) noted that the Baltimore Police Department's height requirement of 5 feet, 7 inches was a prima facie case of sex discrimination, because it excluded 95 percent of the female population, in addition to 32 percent of the male population.[32] (*Prima facie* is from the Latin, "at first sight." It refers to a fact or evidence sufficient to establish a defense or a claim unless otherwise contradicted.)

Previous forms of physical ability testing were also challenged and found discriminatory by the courts. Newer tests, known as physical agility tests, were developed to reduce adverse impact. These newer physical agility tests required much less physical strength than the former tests and relied more on physical fitness. Some researchers who have studied these physical agility tests

have found that some still had an adverse impact on females. One study discovered that females were four times more likely than males to fail physical agility testing for deputy sheriff positions.[33] Another study concluded that these physical agility tests did not represent realistic job samples, because they related to aspects of the job that were rarely performed.[34] In cases in which the courts decided that these tests still discriminated against females, the police departments were ordered to create new ones. This issue is still being examined throughout the country.

While it is recognized that it is crucial for police officers to be fit, law enforcement administrators have struggled with exactly how to define *fit* and how fit officers should be. A recent study conducted over the past 15 years and examining validation studies from over 5,500 police officers from federal, state, and local law enforcement allowed job-related fitness areas to be documented. This study and the results were discussed in Chapter 4.

THE JOB ANALYSIS   Today, as indicated in Chapter 4, to ensure that entry and promotion examinations are job related, police departments perform a job analysis for each position. An acceptable job analysis, declared constitutional by the courts, includes identification of tasks officers generally perform. This identification is based on interviews of officers and supervisors; reviews by another panel of officers and supervisors; computer analyses of questionnaires to determine the frequency of tasks performed; and analyses of the knowledge, skills, and abilities needed to perform the task.[35]

The courts have issued numerous rulings regarding testing and the job analysis. In *Vulcan Society* v. *Civil Service*

YOU ARE THERE! >>

The Path to Equality—Court Cases

1971	*Griggs* v. *Duke Power Company*
1973	*Vulcan Society* v. *Civil Service Commission*
1976	*Mieth* v. *Dollard*
1979	*Vanguard Justice Society* v. *Hughes*
1979	*United States* v. *State of New York*
1980	*Guardians Association of New York City Police Department* v. *Civil Service Commission of New York*

Commission (1973), the court rejected personnel tests because of the lack of a job analysis.[36] In *United States* v. *State of New York* (1979), the court rejected the New York State Police Department's entrance examination because it was validated using a faulty job analysis.[37]

However, in the case of *Guardians Association of New York City Police Department* v. *Civil Service Commission of New York* (1980), which is considered a landmark ruling, the court actually accepted the job analysis of the New York City Department of Personnel and the New York City Police Department as being nondiscriminatory.[38] This ruling showed that police departments had begun to follow the mandates of the federal courts without being ordered to do so.

Affirmative Action Programs

The most controversial method of ending job discrimination is the concept of **affirmative action.** In 1965, in Executive Order 11246, President Johnson required all federal contractors and subcontractors to develop affirmative action programs. Subsequent orders have amended and expanded the original executive order. In essence, the concept of affirmative action means that employers must take active steps to ensure equal employment opportunity and to redress past discrimination.

Affirmative action must be result oriented—it must focus on the result of employment practices. It is not enough for an agency merely to stop discriminating; the agency must take steps to correct past discrimination and give jobs to those against whom it has discriminated in the past.[39] Basically, affirmative action is designed to make up for, or to undo, past discrimination. Affirmative action programs involve several major steps. First, the agency must study its personnel makeup and determine a proper level of minority and female representation. If it does not meet that level, the agency must establish goals, quotas, and timetables to correct female and minority representation. It must make every effort to

---

YOU ARE THERE! >>

The Walls Come Tumbling Down

Throughout the years, numerous lawsuits involving affirmative action were filed by and on behalf of women and minorities. The judicial findings and consent decrees (agreements between parties before, and instead of, a final decision by a judge) did much to ease the way for women and minorities into U.S. police departments. A sampling of these cases follows.

A lawsuit filed against the San Francisco Police Department resulted in a federal court order establishing an experimental quota of 60 women as patrol officers. The department also revised the height and weight requirements that had barred women from patrol jobs. In response to a lawsuit filed by the Department of Justice, Maryland agreed to recruit more female state police officers.

Similarly, the New Jersey State Police agreed to establish, within a year, hiring goals for women in both sworn and nonsworn positions.

A rejected female applicant filed suit against the California Highway Patrol, charging that its male-only standards unlawfully discriminated against women under Title VII of the Civil Rights Act. Following the results of a two-year feasibility study, a decision was made in the plaintiff's favor. As a result, the California Highway Patrol officially began accepting qualified women for state trooper positions, ending a 46-year tradition of using only men as traffic officers.

With the threat of a lawsuit in the offing, the New York City Police Department ended its height requirements, unfroze its list of female applicants, and increased its female officers on patrol to 400 in a brief period of time.

The Los Angeles Police Department signed a consent decree with the Justice Department awarding $2 million in back pay to officers who were discriminated against, agreeing that 45 percent of all new recruits would be African American or Hispanic American and that 20 percent of all new recruits would be women.

A consent decree required that one-third of all promotions in the Miami Police Department be given to women and minorities.

Sources: Adapted from The New York Times (Sept. 14, 1976), p. 8; The New York Times (Oct. 8, 1975), p. 45; Glen Craig, "California Highway Patrol Officers," Police Chief (Jan. 1977), p. 60; Anthony V. Bouza, "Women in Policing," FBI Law Enforcement Bulletin (Sept. 1975), pp. 4–7; Criminal Justice Newsletter (Dec. 1980), p. 6; and Dianne Townsey, "Black Women in American Policing: An Advancement Display," Journal of Criminal Justice, 10 (1982), pp. 455–468.

California Highway Patrol officers recruiting at the Chinese New Year celebration in San Francisco. Departments are expanding their recruitment efforts in order to attract quality minority candidates.

advertise job openings and actively seek out and encourage female and minority applicants. All tests and screening procedures must be validated as being job related, and any potentially discriminatory procedures must be eliminated.

The major concept behind affirmative action, and possibly the most disturbing concept to many, is the establishment of **quotas.** Under a quota arrangement, a certain percentage of openings are reserved for particular groups. In 1974, for example, the Detroit Police Department adopted a policy of promoting one African American officer to sergeant for each white officer promoted. Largely as a result of its policy, Detroit has one of the best records for minority employment in the United States.[40]

Robert Sheehan and Gary W. Cordner provide an excellent summation of the efforts of women and minorities to gain equal employment through the courts and affirmative action:

> Such decisions have thrown the police service into some turmoil and have angered many white male police officers, who charge reverse discrimination. . . . That police administrators have been forced to hire and promote minority group members rather than attempting to do this on their own, is, in our opinion, a sad reflection on the administrators' real commitment to justice. The personnel task has been complicated significantly by this turn of events.[41]

It should be noted that in the late 1990s and early 2000s, the concept of affirmative action was under attack on numerous fronts, ranging from U.S. Supreme Court cases to state and local laws.

★ ★ ★

WHITE MALE BACKLASH

As more police jobs and promotions began to go to women and minorities, fewer white males, obviously, received these jobs and promotions. White males were passed over on entrance and promotion examinations by females and minorities, some of whom had received lower test scores. This resulted in the turmoil and angry white males referred to by Sheehan and Cordner in the quotation cited earlier. Anger, resentment, and counter lawsuits followed.

Though the EEOC prohibits all discrimination and consequently does not use the theory of "reverse discrimination," majority individuals often label the preferential treatment received by minority groups as "reverse discrimination."[42] They argue that selecting police officers based on their race or gender actually violates the 1964 Civil Rights Act and is discriminatory. Critics also argue that selecting officers who have scored lower on civil service tests lowers the personnel standards of a police department and will result in poorer performance by the department. Sociologists James Jacobs and Jay Cohen relate that white police officers view affirmative action hiring and promotion programs as a threat to their job security.[43]

Even in law enforcement, with the loyalty that generally exists and where officers depend on each other when responding to calls, tensions can arise between various groups in the workplace. In Chicago, white officers intervened on the side of the city when an African American police officer organization filed suit to change promotion criteria.[44] In Detroit, the Detroit Police Officers Association filed suit to prevent the police department from setting up a quota plan for hiring African American police sergeants.[45]

In 1995, a sergeant with the Los Angeles County Sheriff's Department formed the Association of White Male Peace Officers to protect the rights of white male officers through zero discrimination in hiring, promotion, or assignment. The Sheriff's Department said it cannot prevent officers from joining the group but reported that it does not sanction the group or understand the reason for its formation.[46]

Also in 1995, 18 white Dallas police officers filed a $1.8 million lawsuit alleging they were passed over for promotion to senior corporal in favor of minority officers who scored lower on a promotional exam. The lawsuit called for an order barring the city from imposing quotas to implement its affirmative action plan.[47]

The continued need for affirmative action programs is under renewed challenge from critics who contend that they have achieved their original goals of ending discrimination against minorities and providing parity with white males. In April 1995, Maryland State Police agreed to provide approximately $250,000 in back pay to 99 white male troopers who claimed they were unfairly passed over for promotions in 1989 and 1990.[48]

★ ★ ★

CAN WOMEN AND MINORITIES DO THE JOB?

Much of the discrimination against women in police departments was based on a fear that they could not do police work effectively because of their gender and size. Much of the discrimination against minorities was based on a fear that they would not be accepted by nonminority citizens, if not just on outright racism. The academic studies and anecdotal evidence presented in this section show that women and minorities do indeed make effective police officers.

Academic Studies of Female Officers

In the 1970s, many police officials argued that female officers could not handle the tasks of patrol duty effectively. According to this traditional, macho perspective, policing required physical strength and a tough, masculine attitude. Two important academic studies, however—one by the Police Foundation and the other by the Law Enforcement Assistance Administration (LEAA)—found that female officers were just as effective on patrol as comparable males.[49] The latter study was performed for the Law Enforcement Assistance Administration, the precursor of the National Institute of Justice.

The study performed for the Police Foundation, *Policewomen on Patrol: Final Report,* evaluated and compared the performance of female recruits during their first year on patrol in Washington, D.C., with that of a matched group of new male officers in the same department. This was the first time a police department had integrated a substantial number of female officers into the backbone of the department. This research project was designed to determine: (1) the ability of women to perform patrol work successfully, (2) their impact on the operations of a police department, and (3) their reception by the community. The study found that female officers exhibited extremely satisfactory work performance. The female officers were found to respond to similar types of calls as male officers, and their arrests were as likely as the male officers' arrests to result in convictions. Additionally, the report found that women were more likely than their male colleagues to receive support from the community, and they were less likely to be charged with improper conduct.[50]

The study for LEAA was titled *Women on Patrol: A Pilot Study of Police Performance in New York City.* The study involved the observation of 3,625 hours of female police officer patrol in New York City, and it included 2,400 police–citizen encounters. The report concluded that female officers were perceived by citizens as being more competent, pleasant, and respectful than male officers. This study found that women performed better when serving with other female officers, as well as that women, when serving with male partners, seemed to be intimidated by their partners and were less likely to be assertive and self-sufficient.[51]

Thus, the first two large-scale studies of female patrol officers dispelled the myth that they were not able to do the job. Follow-up anecdotal evidence and empirical studies further bolstered the assertion that women make effective patrol officers. The findings of the Washington, D.C., and New York City studies were supported by anecdotal reports of experiences in the Boston, Miami, and Dayton police departments.[52]

In addition to the studies cited above, numerous other academic studies of job performance by female police officers were conducted, with similar results. James David studied the behavior of 2,293 police officers in Texas and Oklahoma and found that the arrest rates of male and female officers were almost identical, despite the stereotype that women make fewer arrests than men. David also found that women were more inclined to intervene than were their male counterparts when violations of the law occurred in their presence.[53]

Dempsey's Law

The Dirty Harriet or Jane Wayne Syndrome

Professor Dempsey, you know, if we had more female officers, we wouldn't have cases like Rodney King. Women wouldn't use excessive force like those macho males do.

Maybe you're right, but I don't think we should generalize by gender. Female officers can use excessive force, just as male officers can. As a matter of fact, Connie Fletcher, a journalism professor at Loyola University who interviewed 125 Chicago police officers for her book *What Cops Know,* says that female police officers are not immune from using excessive force. Fletcher identified a tendency by some rookie female officers to overreact as they try to live up to a

tough image. She said the cops call this the Dirty Harriet or Jane Wayne Syndrome, just as some male cops are said to have the Dirty Harry or John Wayne Syndrome. Fletcher says that most brutality cases involve rookie cops who want to impress older officers. I tend to agree with her. In my experience, the vast majority of citizen complaints regarding excessive force concerned officers with less than five years on the job.

Source: Some of the material in this box is based on Connie Fletcher, *What Cops Know: Cops Talk about What They Do, How They Do It, and What It Does to Them* (New York: Random House, 1991).

A study of police perceptions of spouse abuse, by Robert Homant and Daniel Kennedy, concluded that female officers were more understanding of, and sympathetic to, the victims of spouse abuse than were male officers, and they were more likely than male officers to refer those victims to shelters.[54]

Loretta Stanlans and Mary Finn supported this finding when their study revealed that though there was no difference between male and female officers in arrest rates on domestic violence calls, experienced female officers were more likely to recommend battered womens' shelters and less likely to recommend marriage counseling than were their male counterparts. This difference did not occur among rookie officers. Is this variation due to their experience over the years with domestic violence calls or due to the fact that they were willing to act contrary to the mens' norms?[55]

In an analysis of the existing research on female police officers, Merry Morash and Jack Greene found that the traditional male belief that female officers could not be effective on patrol was not supported by existing research. Morash and Greene concluded that evidence existed showing that women make highly successful police officers.[56]

Former New York City police detective Sean Grennan's study of patrol teams in New York City found no basic difference between the way males and females, working as a patrol team, reacted to violent confrontations. Grennan also found that female police officers, in most cases, were far more emotionally stable than their male counterparts. Female officers also lacked the need to project the macho

image, which, Grennan believes, seems to be inherent in the personality of most of the male officers he studied. He found that the female officer, with her less aggressive personality, was more likely to calm a potentially violent situation and less likely to cause physical injury. She was also less likely to use a firearm and no more likely to suffer on-the-job injuries.[57]

Similar results were found by the Christopher Commission in 1991 while conducting a review of the practices of the Los Angeles Police Department after the Rodney King incident. The commission reported that, of the 120 officers with the most allegations concerning the use of force, all were male.[58]

A councilman for the city of Los Angeles introduced five motions following the Christopher Commission report that would encourage the hiring of more female officers and substantially decrease police violence in the LAPD. These included making the police department and the police commission more gender balanced and making this an important issue in the selection of the new chief of police. He believed that true change in the philosophy of the department would result from achieving more gender balance.[59]

An article in *Time* magazine, written around the same time and related to the Commission's work, indicates that female officers have a strong ability to talk people out of violent acts and that they also generate fewer citizen complaints.[60]

This was supported by a study conducted in a large police department in the Southeast in which 527 internal

Dempsey's Law

When You Really Get to Know Someone . . .

Professor Dempsey, there are many women in this class, and some want to be police officers. But I know a lot of guys who say women can't do police work because they're not strong enough. What do you think?

I get this question often. I generally respond to it with my own experience rather than the empirical evidence that says women can be very effective officers. When women were first entering my department in large numbers, many male officers complained about female officers. However, I never heard a male officer with a steady female partner complain at all about her. Also, I never heard a female officer who had a steady male partner complain about him. I guess what that says to me is that when we get past things like gender—and even race, ethnic group, and age—we start to see the real people we are working with, and we start to respect them for themselves. I generally conclude by saying that some women make excellent police officers and some make poor officers, just as some men make excellent officers and some make poor officers.

---

affairs complaints of misconduct over a three-year period were examined. These incidents translated into 682 allegations of wrongdoing (more than one officer was involved in some incidents). The analysis revealed that male officers were overrepresented in these complaints. Female officers accounted for 12.4 percent of those employed by the agency, but they accounted for only 5.7 percent of the allegations.[61]

Recently, a study was conducted in which 40 patrol officers (20 male and 20 female) were observed over a 10-week period while working the 3-to-11 shift in Syracuse, New York. Their attitudes were also assessed by using surveys and scenarios. Results indicated there were no differences in how the officers viewed or performed their jobs.[62]

Despite these indications that females are performing no differently than males—or perhaps better, in some situations—resistance or lack of acceptance still exists, though to a lesser degree, among the public and fellow police officers. Kristen Leger found that there is a growing acceptance by the public for females in the law enforcement role. Especially noteworthy is that the unfounded skepticism concerning the females' ability to handle violent encounters, which is often raised, no longer exists among the majority of citizens. The public attitude toward women in law enforcement is changing, and police officers and administrators should take note of that.[63]

While citizens are more accepting, they do also have certain preconceived notions as to male and female officers' stong and weak areas within law enforcement. These stereotypes affect citizen expectations and consequently act on their reactions to police officers. When college students were given three scenarios (domestic violence, shoplifting, and a noisy party) and the gender of the officer was manipulated, students rated the officers differently based on what they expected the officer's strengths to be. (In this case, it was expected that females would be extremely knowledgeable and capable in the area of domestic violence.) Officers who didn't live up to these preconceived stereotypes were rated as being less effective. This phenomenon could lead to unrealistic expectations and inappropriate judging of females' performance.[64]

One of the biggest obstacles to women's entering the ranks of police officer has been the contention that women lack the necessary physical strength to do the job. In a review of the existing literature on female police officers, Michael Charles found that women can train themselves to achieve a level of strength and fitness well within the normal demands of the police profession.[65]

The IACP conducted a study of 800 police departments in 1998. They found that law enforcement administrators felt overwhelmingly that women possess exceptional skills in the area of verbal and written communications as well as outstanding interpersonal skills in relating to all types of people and being sensitive to their needs whether they are victims, witnesses, or suspects.[66]

The National Center for Women and Policing agrees that in fact, women offer unique advantages to the contemporary field of law enforcement with its emphasis on community policing and the high volume of calls involving diversity issues and violence against women and the strengths that will prevail in these situations.[67]

An examination of use of excessive force as related to officer gender found that female officers were significantly underrepresented compared to male officers in both citizen complaints and sustained allegations of excessive force. They also cost their departments significantly less than male officers in civil liability payouts involving excessive force. In the Los Angeles Police Department between 1990–1999, when the male officers outnumbered the female officers on patrol by a ratio of 4:1, the payouts for excessive force for males exceeded those for females by a larger ratio of 23:1.[68]

Clearly, although women have been assigned to patrol duties for only three decades, evidence exists that they are very effective as patrol officers. The former belief that they lacked the size, strength, and temperament to do the job has given way to a realization that being a patrol officer requires more than size, strength, and a tough attitude.

Academic Studies of African American Officers

Unlike the situation for women, there have been no studies regarding the ability of African Americans to do police work. Anecdotal evidence, however, suggests that they perform as well as any other group. For example, in a 1984 study in the aftermath of the 1980 Miami riots, Bruce Berg, Edmond True, and Marc Gertz found that African American police officers were far less detached and alienated from the local community than were white or Hispanic American police officers.[69] Considering that the 1968 National Advisory Commission on Civil Disorders reported a significant problem of alienation between the police and the community, the addition of minority officers has to be considered a plus for policing.

★ ★ ★

WOMEN AND MINORITIES IN POLICING TODAY

As this chapter has shown, during the past three decades, U.S. police departments have attempted to better reflect the communities they serve. Police administrators have intensified the recruitment of women and minorities to have more balanced police departments. They've also directed their efforts toward the retention of these officers. Many departments have links on their Web sites for the targeted population providing additional information and outreach as well as mentoring services.

They have altered their entry requirements and training curriculums—sometimes willingly, and sometimes under court mandate—to facilitate the hiring and training of women and minority officers. Today women and minorities serve in all aspects of police work and in all neighborhoods of all towns and cities across the United States.

As an example, as of 1996, minorities made up 64 percent of the San Francisco Sheriff's Department, up from 45 percent in 1985, when the agency first began tracking efforts to bring diversity to the 649-deputy force. According to Sheriff Michael Hennessey, the diversity helps increase public esteem in the agency. Members of minority groups, he said, will be more trusting knowing that others of the same race, gender, or ethnicity are represented on the force. He also said that the improved racial and gender mix can also reduce the number of gender- or race-based complaints against officers from both within and without the department.[70]

On another positive note, the International Association of Women Police, a fraternal organization, reports that the number of women in command positions and serving as chiefs of police grows slowly but steadily. Elizabeth Watson was the first woman to lead a police department in a city of over 1 million when she headed the Houston, Texas, Police Department from 1990 to 1992; upon leaving Houston, she became the first woman chief to head the Austin, Texas, Police Department.[71]

In 1996, Paula Meara became the first female chief in the history of the 500-officer Springfield, Massachusetts, Police Department. Meara is used to being first; she was the first Springfield female officer to have a college degree, the first to make sergeant, and then the first to make lieutenant.[72] In 1997, Deborah K. Ness, who was the first of three women ever hired as patrol officers by the Minot, North Dakota, Police Department, became the first woman ever to be named police chief in North Dakota when she assumed command of the Bismarck Police Department.[73]

In 1995, Annette Sandberg, a female lieutenant with the Washington State Patrol, was appointed to lead the department as chief. It was the first time a woman had been named to lead a state police agency.[74] She was followed by Anne Beers, who currently serves as Colonel of the Minnesota State Patrol.

Despite these notable accomplishments, females are still significantly underrepresented in upper management in law enforcement agencies. According to the IACP survey of 800 police agencies in 1998, only 9 percent of the agencies had any women in policy making positions and only 13 percent had women at the command level.[75] Despite this, there was great interest among the law enforcement execu-

©AP Photo/Victoria Arocho

Boston Police Commissioner Kathleen O'Toole speaks to the media on March 31, 2004, regarding a new law enforcement consortium in New England. Standing behind her is Paula Meara, the Springfield, Massachusetts, police chief. Both women are the first female chiefs in their respective agencies.

©AP Photo/Ben Margo

San Francisco Police Chief Heather Fong speaks at a press conference in January 2004. Ms. Fong, named chief in 2004, is the first female to head the department.

tives in expanding the base of women in law enforcement. The IACP conducted this survey in an effort to examine the role of women in policing and issues of concern. They made recommendations for law enforcement agencies to accomplish the goal of strengthening the position of women in policing that stressed recruiting, testing, education and training, policy development, and mentoring. More information can be found on their Web site.

Female Representation Today

A 2003 Bureau of Justice Statistics (BJS) publication reports that, in the year 2000, 10.6 percent of all full-time sworn officers in local law enforcement were females. This represented a 59 percent increase from 1990. Numbers ranged from 16.5 percent in departments serving populations of 500,000 or more to 4 percent in departments serving fewer than 2,500.[76] To put these percentages into perspective, although the presence and status of women in law enforcement have risen, the percentage of female officers falls below 44.7 percent, the percentage of the labor force that women currently occupy. Women in policing appear to be lagging behind women in other traditionally male professions.

Commenting on the increased female representation in U.S. police departments, Dean J. Champion notes that although female representation in policing is well below the proportional representation of women in the United States, "Few critics propose the creation of a 50–50 balance of males and females in law enforcement."[77] Larry K. Gaines, Mittie D. Southerland, and John E. Angell state that the use of female officers in all aspects of police work has increased in the past decade and that women are accepted as capable, competent police officers and managers by most people.[78]

More females are now attaining the length of service and breadth of experience typically associated with command positions. Consequently, recent years have seen a significant increase in the numbers of women in administrative positions and serving as chiefs and sheriffs.

In 2002, Connie Patrick became the director of the Federal Law Enforcement Training Center in Glynco, Georgia, after a long and distinguished law enforcement career. In 2003, Nannette H. Hegerty became the first female chief in the history of the Milwaukee Police Department. In 2004, Heather Fong was named chief of police in San Francisco, followed soon after by Kathleen O'Toole, who was appointed chief of the Boston Police Department. Reports are beginning to be received of mothers and daughters serving in the same police departments, as with Chrissie Coon, who joined the North Las Vegas Police Department, where her mother, Sandy Hanes, is the head detective in the fugitive squad.

A recent study found that consent decrees over the last couple of decades have been very effective in increasing the numbers of women in law enforcement. A consent decree is an agreement that in this situation binds the agency to a particular course of action in regard to hiring and promoting women in law enforcement. The study reported that the representation of female officers in agencies with a consent decree was substantially higher than in agencies without consent decrees and higher than the national average for that type of department. Municipal agencies were found to employ 17.8 percent sworn females (25 percent higher than the national average for municipal agencies), county agencies 12 percent (9 percent higher than the national average for counties), and state police agencies 7.2 percent females (23 percent higher than the national average for state police agencies). Unfortunately, the report states that once the consent decree ends, the progress for women tends to slow in the agency. The authors believe the consent decree may be a worthwhile tool to stick with until agencies progress on their own in this area.[79]

Others believe this is unnecessary. Though the percentages of women in law enforcement today are nowhere near the 50 percent that women represent in society, many argue that this is a result to some degree of self-selection and that law enforcement is simply not a career for everyone. The current numbers of females in law enforcement are a big improvement, considering they have been actively engaged in the profession for only a few decades. There is some concern, however, that the growth appears to have slowed in the last decade.

In their report, *The Status of Women in Policing: 2001,* the National Center for Women and Policing found that females accounted for only 12.7 percent of all sworn officers in large agencies (those with more than 100 sworn personnel), which is only 4 percentage points higher than the 9 percent they comprised in 1990. In small or rural agencies, women make up an even smaller percentage, at 8.1 percent of sworn personnel. When all types of agencies are factored together, females represent 11.2 percent of all sworn officers nationally. The authors attribute these low figures to bias in the hiring and selection process (in particular the physical fitness training), as well as inadequate recruitment policies and the image of police officers and agencies as macho and militaristic.[80]

It is encouraging, however, that these are all issues that law enforcement executives are currently addressing in a desire to recruit and retain more female officers. Some of these innovative strategies are discussed in the next section. The slow, steady increase in numbers already seen, coupled with new efforts to eliminate bias in the hiring process and with proactive police administrators, will help increase the numbers of women in law enforcement. This will be greatly aided by females attaining rank in agencies, as mentioned earlier, and becoming more visible as well as having increased input regarding policies and procedures.

African American and Other Minority Representation Today

In the 1970s and 1980s, African Americans were appointed as police commissioners or chiefs in some of the nation's biggest city police departments. Among them were William Hart, Detroit; Lee P. Brown, Atlanta, Houston, and New York City; and Benjamin Ward, New York City.

In the 1990s this trend continued with Willie Williams in Los Angeles in 1992. In 1997, Melvin H. Wearing was named police chief of New Haven, Connecticut, the first African American to hold that post.[81] Also in 1997, Mel Carraway became the first African American to be appointed to head the Indiana State Police.[82] However, many feel that African Americans are still discriminated against in promotional assignments.[83]

As of 2004, many police departments had African Americans in their command staff or serving as chiefs of police. These include the notable and progressive agencies of Arlington, Texas, with Dr. Theron Brown as chief of police; Madison, Wisconsin, with Chief Noble Wray; and Charleston, South Carolina, with long-term Chief Ruben Greenberg.

Another traditional minority group in policing, Asian Americans, received good news in 1996, as the San Francisco Police Department appointed Fred Lau to become the first Asian American police chief in the department's history.[84] As mentioned earlier, another Asian American, Heather Fong, was named chief in 2004.

According to a Bureau of Justice Statistics Report, in the year 2000, 22.6 percent of full-time local law enforcement officers were members of a racial or ethnic minority, a 61 percent increase since 1990. African American officers represented 11.7 percent of all law enforcement officers, which was an increase of 35 percent compared to 1990. Their representation is highest in agencies serving 500,000 to 999,999, where they compose 25.2 percent of all officers. Similarly, Hispanic or Latino officers were 8.3 percent of all local law enforcement officers, with their

Forst's Law

We've Come a Long Way!

While in college at Florida Atlantic University (FAU), I participated in a "field experience" at the Boca Raton Police Department. I was impressed with the individuals I met there and the progressive chief, Charles McCutcheon, who also taught at FAU. I knew that going into law enforcement as a female in the mid-70s would be a challenge and I would not be uniformly welcomed. But I felt that Boca with its high percentage of college-educated officers and a progressive, educated chief would be less of a hurdle than many other departments. It was the only department I applied to. After graduating from the Police Academy, I was assigned a Platoon and Field Training Officer. It was common knowledge that I would be going to C Platoon, as there were already three female officers in the department, one on every platoon except C. The consensus was that they wanted to evenly distribute the female officers. I was happy with the way this worked out as I knew a lot of the guys on C Platoon, and we'd become friends. My Field Training Officer was chosen because he was the only married officer on the platoon, and the administration didn't want two young, single officers riding around together for eight hours a day . . . who knew what might happen? The chosen officer had no training in being a training officer, didn't particularly want to be one, and in fact seemed to not be very much in favor of female officers on the road.

During my first couple of years, I was touched and propositioned by a couple of superiors, had a snake put in my patrol car and a rat in my briefcase, and was locked in the mens' restroom and the back of a patrol car. These were things I put up with to be "one of the guys."

I watched as the department grew and more females came to the job. I met personally with each one to offer support and a shoulder if they

needed it. I offered to serve as a "mentor" in any way that I could and always encouraged them to apply for new assignments and take promotional exams. When I became the Uniform Division Captain in 1991, there were many women working the road among the 100 or so personnel in the division. One of my proudest moments came one day when I was looking at the deployment of personnel and realized some squads had 50 percent females and even higher, while others had lower percentages—someone's race or gender had ceased to be an issue. Everyone was simply an officer choosing a schedule by seniority, and gender, race, or ethnicity was never brought up by anyone in the process.

We also had a "workplace harassment" policy in place that was strictly adhered to. Employees were disciplined and even fired for inappropriate comments or behavior, depending on the severity of the offense. There were department representatives designated for employees who had harassment issues, and each incident was investigated. We strived to make all employees feel safe, and we educated all employees on what constituted harassment in the workplace. Employees didn't have to quietly go through what I did in my early career.

Later in my career, when I was involved in the hiring process and did a report regarding female and minority representation, I realized we had greatly diversified our employees with our major efforts aimed simply at hiring the best employees possible. We had female FTOs, supervisors, and specialists in all areas. I was proud of the fact that someone could drive down the streets of Boca, go into a DARE classroom, walk into a community policing outreach center, or get pulled over by an officer on a motorcycle, and be likely to see a female or a person of color. We've come a long way!

highest representation (17.3 percent) coming in departments serving populations over 1 million. The biggest increase in representation has occurred among other minorities (Asians, Pacific Islanders, Native Americans) with a 150 percent increase from 1990 to 2000, when they represented 2.7 percent of all local police officers.[85]

Many states are also tracking their progress in staffing departments that are representative of the community they serve. In 2004, the Washington State Patrol reported that blacks represented 3.9 percent of state troopers, compared to 3.2 percent of the state population. Asian Americans and Pacific Islanders equaled 3.0 percent of troopers and 7.5 percent of the population in the state. Hispanic officers accounted for 2.9 percent of troopers and 7.5 percent of the population, and Native Americans were 2 percent of troopers and 1.6 percent of the state population. Females accounted for only 7.8 percent of troopers, but the State Patrol noted that they represented 15 percent of new hires.[86]

Progress is occurring in the representation of females and minorities in U.S. police departments, but progress comes slowly. It has been a slow, gradual process from the 1960s into the 21st century, and the progress has sometimes been accompanied by failures; but strides are being made, and police departments are becoming more representative of the people they serve.

★ ★ ★

PROBLEMS PERSIST FOR WOMEN AND MINORITIES IN POLICING

Despite gains in actual numbers, women and minorities still encounter difficulties in being accepted in policing.[87]

Problems for Women

Gaines, Southerland, and Angell report that, despite the gains women have made in policing during the last two decades, policing remains a male-dominated profession, and females still face discrimination. They state, however, that today's discrimination is more subtle than in the past. They said that women have not really received equal opportunity in policing; they have just overcome the traditional barriers to entry into the profession.[88]

Great progress has been made, but at times true acceptance can seem elusive. It might be hoped that criminal justice majors (and future coworkers) might be more understanding and supportive of females in law enforcement. But a study conducted involving 835 college students

---

YOU ARE THERE! »»

The Benefits of a Law Enforcement Career

- A secure job with good benefits and advancement open to all

- Varying and exciting job assignments

- Opportunities for extensive training and education and experiences

- Increased confidence and self-esteem after successfully confronting dangerous and difficult situations

- Camaraderie and close relationships with other officers; a support group

- Opportunity to serve as a role model within the community

Source: Adapted from an article by Penny Harrington, former Chief of Police in Portland, Oregon, and the Director of the National Center for Women and Policing, which appeared in *Women and Criminal Justice,* 14(1, 2002), pp. 1–13.

---

found that male students, particularly criminal justice majors, were far less likely to be supportive of females in law enforcement than are female students. The two most interesting findings were that male criminal justice students were twice as likely to disagree with the statement, "Females have the physical skills and strength to do police work," than female criminal justice majors; and, amazingly, 40 percent of male criminal justice majors and 35 percent of male nonmajors believed that female officers should be limited to working with female offenders.

The encouraging fact is that these numbers are still a significant improvement over previous studies and that over two-thirds of male criminal justice majors are supportive of female officers overall, while over 90 percent of female students feel positively about females in law enforcement.[89]

A study with some limitations (due to sample size and lack of randomness) but viewed as an exploratory analysis found that field training officers had a bias against female trainees after the FTOs rated the performance of trainees in written training scenarios in which the gender of the officer was manipulated.[90] This should be researched further, because if it truly is an issue, this could be a real career inhibitor for females.

Field training officers are extremely important individuals in the career of a police officer. They can make or break an officer's career and can certainly affect the officer's self-esteem. If there is a bias there, the female officer will feel it. In a small study, female officers surveyed believed that law enforcement has changed with the times and the discrimination that existed in the first 20 years has decreased and also changed. The discrimination is less overt, but the officers feel it exists in more subtle ways. The officers perceived discrimination from coworkers, supervisors, administrators, and the public. They were most concerned with discrimination from supervisors, because those individuals are crucial to their careers as keys to recognition, rewards, promotions, and transfers.[91]

The International Association of Chiefs of Police (IACP) believes this is an important issue for law enforcement today. They have become involved in investigating the climate in law enforcement regarding women and have actively educated departments on recruiting and retaining female officers.

Ironically, current issues challenging departments concern workplace romances and pregnancy. Many departments do not address these issues at all, resulting in some cases in lawsuits. Other departments are feverishly drafting policies in an attempt to insulate themselves from such litigation.[92]

YOU ARE THERE! »

Advice to Women Starting a Law Enforcement Career

- Seek out good advisors and mentors.
- Always tell the truth.
- Join a women's police organization.
- Stay current on police matters.
- Don't complain about your job to coworkers.
- Seek out varied work experiences and opportunities.
- Stay in good physical and emotional shape.
- Read the paper every day.
- Join community organizations.
- Know your community, community leaders, and political leaders.

Source: Adapted from an article by Penny Harrington, former Chief of Police in Portland, Oregon, and the Director of the National Center for Women and Policing , which appeared in *Women and Criminal Justice*, 14(1, 2002), pp. 1–13.

Policies on pregnancy and job assignment are issues that need to be addressed by police agencies for legal reasons as well as for the message these policies send to the female officers. Departments have to offer the same benefits to pregnant officers as to officers with other conditions, such as a temporary back injury or recovery from surgery. If officers in those situations are allowed to work limited or light-duty assignments, then pregnant officers must be allowed the same choice. Policies and benefits must be equitable. The Pregnancy Discrimination Act (PDA), which amended Title VII of the Civil Rights Act of 1964, states that discrimination on the basis of pregnancy constitutes a type of sex discrimination.

Many departments are allowing the pregnant officer to choose whether to take light or limited duty or to stay in her job assignment. This is the policy of the San Diego County Sheriff's Department (SDCSD), and the administrators make sure supervisors know and adhere to the policy. Chief Vicky Pelzer of the University of Washington Police Department and president of the National Association of Women Law Enforcement Executives (NAWLEE), agrees that the officer should make the decision and the department shouldn't dictate when or if an officer will go on limited duty.[93] Some officers elect to remain in their job assignments throughout the pregnancy, while some assume limited duty after the first trimester and others wait until the last trimester. It depends on what their job assignment is and how they feel physically. Some departments even provide maternity uniforms for officers who will be in the public eye.

In the past, some agencies have forced pregnant officers to take sick leave or to go to a limited-duty assignment despite their desires. Besides the potential liability if this differs from what is offered to an officer who gets injured in another way, this action also sends a message to the officer and her female coworkers. Administrators interested in recruiting and retaining females have noticed that many left after giving birth, not necessarily because they wanted to stay home with their babies but rather because of the atmosphere and workplace culture. They felt unwelcome and as if they were a burden to the agency.

There is a concern among chiefs and sheriffs for the safety of the unborn child. This issue is a bit murky, according to Professor Sam Marcosson of the Brandeis School of Law at the University of Louisville, who served as a litigator in the Appellate Division of the Equal Employment Opportunity Commission. He believes that in a circumstance where a department has to allow a pregnant officer to continue at her job until such time that she or her doctor requests limited duty, the courts will probably not hold the department liable for job-related injuries. However, many departments are taking a conservative approach regarding exposure to lead, which results from firearms qualifications exercises. Many departments allow pregnant females to forego firearms training until they come back from maternity leave.[94] Having a fair and equitable policy in place will aid the department in creating a supportive and welcoming atmosphere for female officers and is likely to lead to more applicants and a higher rate of retention for female officers.

Workplace dating is another murky area that some agencies are trying to address. Some sexual harassment cases have arisen from relationships that have soured, leading some departments to want to prohibit fraternization. Though this situation is not unique to the law enforcement workplace, it can be a bit more problematic because of lack of supervision and the variety of locations and situations in which law enforcement can place officers. The issue is complicated by the police culture and the need to socialize with coworkers, regardless of gender. Departments are struggling with this tough issue in an effort to forestall bad situations.

In the past two decades, state, regional, national, and international organizations have been started to lend support to female officers and to address and present a unified voice on issues that affect females in law enforcement. The International Association of Women Police (IAWP) is committed to several goals in striving to achieve their mission, including serving as a support system and source of info and referral and providing networking and training opportunities. Many states and/or regions around the country also have women police officer organizations. More recently (since 1995), the National Center for Women and Policing has been working to educate criminal justice policy makers, the media, and the public about the impacts of increasing the representation of women in policing.

PATROLLING THE WEB

The International Association of Women Police (IAWP)
    www.iawp.org
The National Center for Women and Policing
    www.womenandpolicing.org
The Los Angeles Police Department
    www.lapdonline.org

Police departments are also making additional efforts to recruit and retain females. They are exploring innovative ways of attracting applicants and encouraging them in the process. They are also researching why females leave law enforcement and trying to address those issues. An example of a proactive approach (in an organization that has been strongly encouraged to hire more women) can be seen on the Los Angeles Police Department Web page. Their site provides a link to "Women in the LAPD," which includes biographies of some high-ranking female officers and information on three support programs the department has put in place. The Candidate Assistance Program (CAP) is a program available to candidates who have passed the written test for the LAPD. It helps them to prepare for the physical portion of the police academy training. The Academy Trainee (AT) Program is offered to qualified police officer candidates who have successfully completed all steps in the application process. They receive a salary commensurate with their duties while they're trained in the curriculum in the academy that has been identified as most crucial to success. ATs usually spend five weeks in the program before entering recruit training. The Women's Coordinator is a counselor and advisor who is available to all female employees (sworn and civilian) to assist them in promotional and assignment opportunities. The coordinator also acts as a spokesperson for female officers in the resolution of problems and is involved in efforts to recruit and retain female officers. With the expansion of proactive programs such as these to departments around the country, the numbers of women turning to a career in law enforcement should increase.

Real change will occur as more women move into the policy-making positions in law enforcement and have the ability to substantively affect the working conditions women face. Addressing the issues that are retarding recruitment and retention will encourage more women to enter and remain in the profession. Increased visibility as these women are seen on the street and in the media will further the recruitment effort as women discount some of the previous myths they held and relate to the women they see in the public domain. Realistic books (even fiction), movies, and news and magazine articles will also respond to the curiosity that females may have about the profession. Books such as Marion Gold's *Top Cops: Profiles of Women in Command* portray women who have risen to the top in the law enforcement culture and provide their perspective on law enforcement as a career. A former police officer and now college professor, Donna Stuccio, turned her talent for playwriting into a way to spread the word about women in law enforcement. Her play *Blue Moon,* which has been pro-

©Frances M. Roberts/Levine-Roberts Photography

Women are represented in all areas of law enforcement, from patrol to investigations to motorcycles. Here a female member of the NYPD Emergency Services Unit works with her team to search for a suspect.

duced on stage, takes place predominantly in the womens' locker room of a police department and brings out some of the issues and challenges women face.[95]

Despite the problems women still experience in police departments, they have shown that they will do all that is necessary to attain the job, and they have shown that they can do the job. Many have given the ultimate sacrifice, their lives. There are currently 188 women's names included among the 14,000 law enforcement officers killed, listed on the National Law Enforcement Memorial in Washington, D.C. As women continue to serve and contribute to law enforcement in this country, the face of law enforcement will evolve, and their future in policing will be dynamic and interesting.

Problems for African Americans and Other Minorities

Some lawsuits in the 1990s revealed that discrimination against African Americans and other minorities still exists in policing.

In 1995, 30 African American and Hispanic police officers in Suffolk County, New York, filed a discrimination suit with the U.S. Equal Employment Opportunity Commission. The suit alleged that little had been done to integrate the 2,575-member force since a 1986 consent decree promised to remove barriers to hiring and promotion.[96]

In 1996, the Bureau of Alcohol, Tobacco, Firearms, and Explosives agreed to pay $5.9 million in damages and legal fees to African American agents who filed a lawsuit claiming they were assigned to lower-ranking jobs than whites and paid less. The ATF agreed to overhaul its hiring, recruiting, and promotion methods as part of the settlement.[97]

The 1992 shooting of an African American New York City Transit Authority police officer, Derwin Pannell, by fellow police officers is indicative of another problem faced by African American officers, particularly those working in plainclothes assignments. Pannell and his partner, Kenneth Donnelly, both in plainclothes, were arresting a woman for fare evasion. Three other plainclothes officers observed Pannell with his gun pointed at the arrested woman and mistakenly believed they had come upon a robbery in progress. They fired shots at Pannell, hitting him three times.[98] One reporter investigating the case wrote, "The subsequent wounding of Officer Pannell confirmed the worst fear of these black and Hispanic officers that as they blend in with their surroundings, especially in high crime minority neighborhoods, they become an invisible presence camouflaged even to the brother and sister officers when it matters most."[99] An African American undercover transit officer said, "Let's face it, when I'm down there, the white cops see me like I'm a mutt, I hear them. That's what they call the teenagers who wear their pants low and their caps backwards. When I'm in the hang-out pose looking for fare beaters, I dress that way. If I'm in a bad spot, if the going is bad and they don't recognize me, they'll think I'm a mutt too."[100]

Another shooting of an African American police officer in a New York City subway points to the problems minority group police officers face. In 1994, Desmond Robinson, an undercover New York City Transit Authority police officer, was mistaken for a criminal and shot four times by an off-duty New York City police officer, Peter Del-Debbio. The incident was set in motion by the freak misfiring of a shotgun dropped by a suspect trying to escape the transit police and the pandemonium that followed on a Lexington Avenue subway platform.[101]

As these stories indicate, problems still persist for police officers who are members of minority groups. The National Organization of Black Law Enforcement Executives (NOBLE) is an organization trying to address some of these problems and further the status of blacks in law enforcement. Their motto is "Justice by Action." NOBLE aggressively pursues its goals by conducting research, speaking out, and performing outreach activities. NOBLE plays a major role in shaping policy in areas of importance to minorities and the law enforcement community including the recruitment, retention, and promotion of minority officers. It is hoped that efforts of organizations such as NOBLE, individual police organizations' efforts, and the minority officers' increased visibility in uniform will help to improve the situation for minorities in law enforcement.

CHAPTER SUMMARY

This chapter discussed the history and extent of discrimination against women and racial and ethnic minorities in U.S. police departments. It explained how women and minorities used the Civil Rights Act of 1964, the Equal Employment Opportunity Act of 1972, the federal courts, and affirmative action programs to achieve job equality. The chapter also showed how this movement toward equality caused a white male backlash. The chapter also discussed relevant academic studies and anecdotal evidence that women and minorities are effective in police work. It discussed the representation of women and minorities in policing today, as well as the problems that persist for them. Women and minorities have had a difficult time gaining admission into U.S. police departments. However, through their own efforts, and with the help of new laws and the federal courts, they have accomplished in a relatively short time gains that many would have thought impossible. Women and minorities have proved that they can perform the patrol officer's job as well as anyone else. In the future, most hope, discrimination in U.S. police departments will be completely eliminated.

Learning Check

1. Describe the role the federal government played in removing equal employment opportunity barriers to women and minorities in policing.

2. Discuss how police standards and testing procedures have changed in recent years to enable more women and minorities to enter policing.

3. Describe how affirmative action policies have affected white males in hiring and promotional policies.

4. Talk about how effective women are as patrol officers, as compared with their male counterparts.

5. Identify ways in which women and minorities still face problems in policing.

Application Exercise

You have been appointed personnel director of the city of Anywhere, USA. Anywhere, with a population of 60,000, has a police department of 120 officers. The department currently has no female officers, and it is expected to lose 30 officers through retirement this year. The local chapter of the National Organization for Women (NOW) is claiming that Anywhere is discriminating against females in its police hiring process. Develop a comprehensive plan to increase female representation in the department. Consider ideas presented in this chapter and in Chapter 4.

Web Exercise

Visit the NOBLE Web site (www.noblenatl.org) and explore the various links. Describe some of their outreach efforts. Also visit the IAWP site (www.iawp.org) and click on "Women Police Organizations" to view other organizations. Does your state have a local organization for supporting female officers? Also look at the "speakers' bureau" and ascertain the types of presentations IAWP speakers are giving.

Key Concepts

Adverse impact
Affirmative action
Civil Rights Act of 1964
De facto discrimination
Discrimination
Double marginality

Equal Employment Opportunity Act of 1972 (EEOA)
Fourteenth Amendment
Griggs v. *Duke Power Company*
National Advisory Commission on Criminal Justice Standards
    and Goals
Quota
Title VII

14 Computers, Technology, and Criminalistics in Policing

CHAPTER GOALS

- To acquaint you with the latest technological advances in policing
- To show you how the computer and technology are revolutionizing policing
- To acquaint you with the latest uses of computers in police operations, criminal investigations, and police management tasks
- To introduce you to the latest criminalistic and forensic techniques, including DNA profiling
- To alert you to the threat to civil liberties caused by rapidly advancing technology

Computers, technology, and modern forensic or criminalistic techniques have revolutionized policing and have made the police more effective in crime-fighting and other duties. As one example, John Lee Malvo, the teenage sniper responsible for the 2002 shootings that shocked the Washington, D.C., metropolitan and suburban areas, was identified as a result of one of the latest fingerprinting innovations that will be described later in this chapter.

Video cameras, videocassette recorders (VCRs), microcomputers, personal computers, cash machines, cellular telephones, satellites, and the Internet are all very familiar to the students reading this text. However, many might not be aware that little was known of this technology on the day they were born. The past few decades have seen advances in technology that most of us would never have foreseen. The computer chip has revolutionized society. The criminal justice system and the police in particular have benefited greatly from this technological revolution. Also, the terrorist attacks of September 11, 2001, and other cases have heightened public awareness of the police and forensic and scientific evidence to an extent that had never existed before. As you will see in this chapter, policing is adapting to this new technology.

As U.S. Attorney General John Ashcroft stated in 2001,

> The wave of technological advancement that has changed the lives of almost every individual, business, and institution in the nation has also changed the world of criminal justice— from how we fight crime to how we manage law enforcement resources to the types of crimes we face. New technologies can help law enforcement agencies prevent crime, apprehend criminals, manage offender populations, and protect the public from the threat of terrorism.[1]

This chapter will discuss technology in policing, including computers and their application in record keeping, crime analysis, communications, personnel allocation, investigations, administration, and training. It will also discuss fingerprint technology, including basic categories of fingerprints and automated fingerprint and palmprint identification systems. Additionally it will discuss less-than-lethal weapons, including chemical irritant sprays, the Taser and other stun devices, and the safety and effectiveness of these innovative alternatives to the use of deadly force.

The chapter will cover emerging state-of-the-art surveillance technology, including surveillance vans, vehicle tracking systems, night vision devices, global positioning systems and surveillance aircraft, as well as advanced photographic techniques such as mug shot imaging, age progression photographs, and composite sketches. Also, it will cover forensics and criminalistics including the modern crime lab, crime lab accreditation, and DNA profiling including the science of DNA, the history of DNA in U.S. courts, current DNA technology, DNA databases, and other current issues.

Biometric identification, videotaping, robots in policing, and the fear of the increased police use of modern technology will be discussed.

★ ★ ★
COMPUTERS IN POLICING

In 1964, St. Louis was the only city in the United States with a computer system for its police department. By 1968, 10 states and 50 cities had computer-based criminal justice information systems. Today, every department serving a population of more than 25,000 uses computers.[2]

As Charles R. Swanson, Leonard Territo, and Robert W. Taylor tell us,

> Literally thousands of software packages are available that provide singularly or in combination a number of functions directly related to law enforcement. Records management, data analysis, graphics, telecommunications, and word processing are application programs that currently exist in the software market. Most of these software packages require little customizing or adapting for police usage.[3]

Some people may think that computerization has to be an expensive undertaking available only to a large police department, but this is far from the truth. In recent years, a small department of 20 officers, with an operating budget of less than $100,000 per year (not including salaries), could become computerized with a basic $2,500 computer system, including easily available database software management programs.[4]

Today, computers have become more geared toward law enforcement, giving agencies more choices and a better ability to tailor the technology to their specific needs. Officers are using laptops, embedded or modular systems, and handheld personal digital assistants (PDAs) for transporting computers back and forth between their police vehicle or field assignment and the police station.[5] The following sections discuss the most commonly used applications of computers in police work.

Computer-Aided Dispatch (CAD)

Prior to the computer revolution, the police communications system was slow and cumbersome. A citizen would call the police with a seven-digit telephone number. A police telephone operator would take the information, write

©AP Photo/E. B. McGovern

Captain Jeff Schneider of the Yakima, Washington, Police Department demonstrates the new digital video system that will be installed in patrol cars. Each system includes a mounted camera, microphones, and computer. These systems have proven valuable in recording evidence and documenting incidents when there are complaints against police officers.

Today **computer-aided dispatch (CAD)** allows almost immediate communication between the police dispatcher and police units in the field. Numerous CAD system software packages are available for purchase by police departments. With typical CAD systems, after a 911 operator takes a call from a citizen, the operator codes the information into the computer, and the information immediately flashes on the dispatcher's screen. The CAD system prioritizes the calls on the dispatcher's screen, putting more serious calls (such as crimes in progress and heart attacks) above less serious calls (such as past crimes and nonemergency requests for assistance). The system also verifies the caller's address and telephone number, as well as determining the most direct route to the location. It also searches a database for dangers near the location to which the officers are responding, calls to the same location within the last 24 hours, and any previous history of calls to that location. The CAD system also constantly maintains the status of each patrol unit. In this way, the dispatcher knows which units are available and where all units are located. The system also determines which patrol unit is closest to the location needing police assistance.

it on an index card, and put the card on a conveyor belt, where it would travel to the dispatcher's desk. The dispatcher would then manually search maps and records for the police car that covered the area from which the call originated and then call the car, giving the officer all the information from the index card. All records were kept manually.

The 911 emergency telephone number system was introduced by American Telephone and Telegraph (AT&T) in 1968. Today, almost all U.S. police departments in cities with a population over 250,000 operate a 911 system.[6]

Some CAD systems have automatic transponders within patrol units. These enable dispatch personnel to monitor visually all patrol vehicles via a computer monitor and to assign them in coordination with this computer-generated information.

Newer CAD systems, including **enhanced CAD** and **enhanced 911 (E-911)**, use **mobile digital terminals**

Dempsey's Law

No Computers for Me! Forget About It!

Professor Dempsey, one of the reasons I want to be a police officer is that I hate office work. I'd never want to work with computers, and computers have taken over offices. I'm going to be a cop and ride around in my police car and just deal with people, not machines.

Jason, let me read this quote to you from Rich Owens, a member of the Idaho State Police:

All of the various electronic tools that are at our disposal are finding their way into the patrol car. The toughest thing right now is finding room for the officer.

Source: Adapted from *Law Enforcement News* (Jan.15/31, 1991), p. 5.

YOU ARE THERE! »

Translators on Call

The AT&T Language Line Services offer interpreters in some 140 foreign languages. If a call comes in that a police dispatcher cannot understand, the dispatcher can roll it over to the Language Line, and an interpreter will come on. The Monterey-based Language Line Services operations center can readily identify virtually any language presented to it and have an interpreter on the line immediately. According to Major William Devine, commanding officer of the Providence (Rhode Island) Police Department Night Uniform Division, "When you have a victim whose language you don't understand, you just dial the number and you've got an operator who can get you an address, get you to the area, tell you what happened and what was taken. Then we can put the whole thing together."

Source: Adapted from Harvey Rachlin, "Meeting the Demands of Foreign Languages in Small and Medium-Sized Communities," *Law and Order* (Sept. 1992), pp. 99–102.

(MDTs) in each patrol unit. In systems using MDTs, voice communications are replaced by electronic transmissions that appear on an officer's MDT, a device put into a police vehicle that allows the electronic transmission of messages between the police dispatcher and the officer in the field. Officers receive messages via a computer screen and transmit messages via a keyboard. Enhanced CAD, or enhanced 911, systems are the latest, most sophisticated, state-of-the-art communications systems. Most involve MDT transmissions as well as the option of traditional voice transmissions, along with sophisticated databases.

MDT systems offer the following advantages over voice systems:

1. A direct interface between the patrol unit and local, county, state, and federal criminal justice information system computers, enabling an officer to query names, license plates, and driver's licenses with almost immediate response, and without interfering with radio communications or requesting the services of a dispatcher

2. The elimination of many clerical duties

3. The availability of more detailed information, including addresses displayed with the nearest cross streets and map coordinates (and in some cases, even floor plans)

4. Better coordination of all emergency agencies, because their movements can be monitored visually by both officers at the scene and dispatchers

5. Automatic processing of incident information via a preformatted incident form, eliminating the need for the officer to drop off an incident report at the station house and the need for someone to type up a report

6. A dramatic increase in response time as the entire dispatch process, from call to arrival, is fully automated

7. The capability for the accumulation of large amounts of data regarding police incidents and personnel, which can be used in crime analysis and staff allocation planning to assign personnel when and where crime is highest or calls for assistance are heaviest[7]

Jerome H. Skolnick and David H. Bayley report on the computer terminals in the Houston Police Department's patrol cars:

> The terminals increase enormously the amount of relevant information patrol officers have. For example, they can determine before they step out of their cars if the vehicle they have just signaled to a stop is stolen or if its owner, who may be the driver, is wanted in any connection. Officers cruising down the street often idly type in the license plate numbers of cars driving ahead or parked at sleazy motels . . . in the faint hope that something interesting will turn up, like hitting a jackpot in a slot machine.[8]

The Nassau County (New York) Police Department is among the many departments in the nation that have established an enhanced 911 (E-911) system. When a person calls 911 for assistance, vital information is immediately flashed on a screen in front of the operator. The screen gives the exact address of the telephone being used; the name of the telephone subscriber; whether it is a residence, business, or pay telephone; the police patrol beat it is on; the nearest ambulance; and the closest fire department.[9] This system gives the police the ability to assist people at risk even if they cannot communicate because of illness, injury, or an inability to speak English. For example, if a sick or injured person initiates a call to 911 for assistance and then passes out or can no longer continue the conversation for some other reason, the police, having the information in the computer, are still able to respond with assistance.

A good example of the use of newly available communications systems is the experience of the Union/Essex Counties Auto Task Force. The New Jersey counties of Essex and Union experience the highest number of vehicle thefts in the nation. In an effort to suppress these thefts

YOU ARE THERE! »

How the LAPD Works the Phones

The Los Angeles Police Department's 911 system, which handles over 3 million calls a year, uses the Emergency Command Control Communications System (ECCCS). The main components of the ECCCS are the central dispatch center (CDC), the mobile digital terminal (MDT), and the handheld remote out-of-vehicle emergency radio (ROVER). The CDC is the nerve center of Los Angeles's 911 system and is located in City Hall East in Los Angeles. Citizens' calls for service are received at the CDC, and when appropriate, CDC operators issue dispatch orders based on the computer-displayed recommendation for field unit assignment. The MDTs are mounted in LAPD vehicles. They receive and transmit dispatch and status information, including officer-initiated emergency messages and database inquiries. The MDT has a keyboard for entering data and a screen for displaying messages and data. The ROVERs are used by field officers for voice communications throughout the city. ROVERs are used for high-priority communications and to back up the MDT

communications. Using a ROVER, a field officer can talk to CDC operators and with other field officers. The ROVER has an emergency trigger that transmits an instant "officer needs help" message to the CDC, bypassing normal voice channels to obtain faster assistance.

The New York City Police Department's 911 system is the primary answering point for requests for police, fire, and emergency medical assistance. The system receives approximately 22,700 calls each day. The police dispatch almost 12,000 radio runs. In addition, 331 calls are forwarded to the fire department for dispatch, as are almost 1,900 calls for emergency medical service runs. New York City has implemented an E-911 system similar to the one operated by the LAPD. The project cost over $200 million.

Source: Personal correspondence with the vendor, System Development Corporation, 2500 Colorado Ave., Santa Monica, CA 90406; and personal communication with supervising communications technician Martin Stander of the NYPD Communications Division.

---

and to arrest auto thieves, 12 law enforcement agencies established the Union/Essex Counties Auto Theft Task Force. The task force officers are equipped with portable mobile data terminals (MDTs). In the first five months of the Task Force's existence, they recovered 160 vehicles worth $1.5 million and arrested 60 adult auto theft suspects and 101 juvenile suspects. Auto thefts dropped significantly. Each MDT is linked directly to the NCIC and New Jersey's State Criminal Information Center. Each MDT has an emergency "hot key" that, when pressed, summons all other vehicles with MDTs to back up an officer in distress.[10]

A report on the use of mobile data access to law enforcement databases reveals that officers with in-car data access technology make more than eight times as many inquiries on driving records, vehicle registrations, and wanted persons or property per eight-hour shift than do officers without in-car computers.

REVERSE 911   The latest in 911 technology is **reverse 911 (R-911).** R-911 is a way for the police to contact the community by telephone, by a simple digital click, in the event of an emergency or serious situation, more quickly and over a larger area than if the officers had to go door to door to notify residents. This technology was first used in

DuPage County, Illinois, in 1996 and has been utilized by many municipalities since the terrorist attacks of September 11, 2001. It was used very successfully in Arlington, Virginia, in the aftermath of the terrorist attack on the Pentagon, enabling rapid mobilization of off-duty officers.[11]

Automated Databases

As we have come into the 21st century, computer technology is doing things that were previously unthinkable in policing. A simple example of how far we have come is a new system in Mesa, Arizona. The Mesa Police Department's Cellular Digital Packet Data (CDPD) technology, an automated database, gives officers immediate access, via mobile computers, to critical information contained in the city's mainframe computer. The department's divisions using this system include homicide, pawn detail, auto theft, public information, gang control, and hostage negotiation.[12]

The availability of automated databases has revolutionized police work. An automated database is an enormous electronic filing cabinet that is capable of storing information and retrieving it in any desired format. The FBI created a major automated database, the **National Crime Information Center (NCIC),** in 1967. The NCIC collects

PATROLLING THE WEB

National Crime Information Center (NCIC 2000)
http://www.fbi.gov/hq/cjisd/ncic.htm

and retrieves data about people wanted for crimes anywhere in the United States; stolen and lost property, including stolen automobiles, license plates, identifiable property, boats, and securities; and other criminal justice information. The NCIC also contains criminal history files and the status (prison, jail, probation, or parole) of criminals. The NCIC has millions of active records, which are completely automated by computers that process over 270,000 inquiries every 24 hours. The NCIC provides virtually uninterrupted operation day or night, seven days a week. Although the NCIC is operated by the FBI, approximately 70 percent of its use is by local, state, and other federal agencies.

In 2000, the NCIC was renamed **NCIC 2000** and provided a major upgrade to the services mentioned above and extended these services down to the patrol car and the mobile officer. With this system, police are able to identify fugitives and missing persons quickly using automated fingerprint identification system (AFIS) technology, which will be discussed later in this chapter. The officer may place a subject's finger on a fingerprint reader in a patrol car, and the reader will transmit the image to the NCIC computer at FBI Headquarters. Within minutes, the computer will forward a reply to the officer. A printer installed in patrol cars will allow officers to get copies of a suspect's photograph, fingerprint image, signature, and tattoos, along with artist's conceptions and composite drawings of unknown subjects. The printer will also be able to receive images of stolen goods, including cars. The new system also provides for enhanced name searches (based on phonetically similar names); prisoner, probation, and parole records; convicted sex offender registries; and other services.[13]

Additionally, the FBI maintains the National Instant Criminal Background Check System (NICS) which provides access to millions of criminal history records from all 50 states and the District of Columbia for matching subject information for background checks on individuals attempting to purchase a firearm.[14]

The FBI also maintains the Violent Criminal Apprehension Program (ViCAP) database, which contains information on unsolved murders. ViCAP has helped local and state law enforcement agencies solve violent crimes for almost 20 years.[15]

In addition to these national databases, local law enforcement agencies maintain their own databases. For example, the Los Angeles Police Department uses a computer to maintain a database of over 60,000 gang members.[16]

Another system for storing and reading databases is the CD-ROM, which is capable of storing massive files of data. The advantages of CD-ROM technology are that it is

YOU ARE THERE! »

Where Are Computers Taking Us?

In the near future, an officer may pull his patrol vehicle in behind a violator and with a simple touch of a button instantly access all pertinent information available on that subject.

As the scanner behind the vehicle's grill reads the bar-coded license plate, the MDT (mobile digital terminal) will display complete registration information almost instantly. In addition, it will check NCIC 2000 (National Crime Information Center) and warn if there's a "want" involving the plate.

With the touch of another button, the terminal will position the patrol unit's location from the satellite locator system and send a signal to the dispatcher that the subject vehicle has been stopped at that location. Accuracy will be within a few feet.

After advising the driver that he or she is being cited for failing to stop at a stop sign and after returning to the patrol vehicle, the officer will position the driver's license on a little screen on the MDT. Bar-coded information on the license will be checked automatically and displayed with the vehicle information.

If there are no red flags, simply touching another precoded button will activate the miniprinter and produce the proper citation completely filled out. The offender is presented with hard copy and is quickly on his or her way. . . .

If there was some reason to be suspicious of the operator of the vehicle, . . . the subject could be asked to place a finger into the small box presented to him or her and touch the surface inside. When the officer plugs the box into the computer console, the fingerprint is quickly checked against the state's AFIS (automated fingerprint identification system) file to confirm the driver's identity.

Source: Adapted from Bill Clede, "Where Are Computers Taking Us?" Law and Order (Nov. 1991), p. 40.

inexpensive and has numerous law enforcement applications. Police departments and investigators can store numerous types of archived files onto CD-ROM, such as closed cases, mug shots, fingerprint cards, motor vehicle records, firearm registration information, wanted notices, court decisions, missing person photos and information, and known career criminal files, including photographs and fingerprints.[17]

Automated Crime Analysis (Crime Mapping)

Numerous software application programs aid the police in **automated crime analysis** or **crime mapping.** Crime analysis entails the collection and analysis of data regarding crime (when, where, who, what, how, and why) to discern criminal patterns and assist in the effective assignment of personnel to combat crime. The most basic use of crime analysis is to determine where and when crimes occur, in order to assign personnel to catch perpetrators in the act of committing the crime or to prevent them from committing it.

The forerunner in the use of modern sophisticated automated crime analysis was the New York City Police Department's COMPSTAT program, which was discussed in Chapter 1. COMPSTAT provides instant statistical updating of all reported crimes, arrests, and other police activities, such as traffic and other citations. This program and its movie screen-type visual displays provide the framework for the weekly crime analysis meetings at NYPD's headquarters in which precinct commanders must account for all increases in crime and must provide strategies to combat these crimes. The keynote of the NYPD re-engineering program of the mid-1990s and the envy of police departments throughout the world, COMPSTAT is a process that began to evolve in early 1994 when, after changes in the leadership of many of the NYPD's bureaus, disturbing information emerged. It appeared that the NYPD did not know most of its own current crime statistics, and there was a time lag of three to six months in its statistical reporting methods. Upon learning this, the department made a concerted effort to generate crime activity data on a weekly basis. COMPSTAT has been credited with causing crime in New York City to drop to levels not seen since the 1960s.[18] Some of the major municipalities using systems similar to New York's are Minneapolis, Los Angeles, and New Orleans.

The National Institute of Justice has reported that 36 percent of police agencies with 100 or more sworn officers are now using some form of computerized crime mapping.[19]

Computer-Aided Investigation (Computerized Case Management)

Computer-aided investigation and **computer-aided case management** are revolutionizing the criminal investigation process. For example, the New York City Police Department's Detective Division has created an automated mug shot file called CATCH (Computer-Assisted Terminal Criminal Hunt). Using CATCH, detectives feed the description and modus operandi information of an unknown robbery perpetrator into the computer and then receive a computer printout that lists, in rank order, any potential suspects. The detectives can then obtain photographs of possible suspects and show them in photo arrays to victims for possible identification. A computer database, HITMAN, has been used by the Los Angeles Police Department since 1985 and operates in a manner similar to CATCH.[20]

HOLMES (an acronym for Home Office Large Major Enquiry System and a reference to the legendary fictional detective Sherlock Holmes) is a sophisticated computer program developed for British investigators to aid them in managing complex investigations. (In Great Britain, an investigation is called an enquiry.) HOLMES is a complete case management system that can receive, process, organize, recognize, interrelate, and retrieve all aspects of information on a case. It also keeps track of ongoing progress, or the lack of it, in investigations. The system was created in response to the infamous Yorkshire Ripper case, in which 13 women were killed between 1974 and 1981. When the perpetrator was finally apprehended in 1981, it was discovered that he had been detained and questioned by at least six different police departments in connection with the attacks. Because sharing of information on related cases was so cumbersome for the neighboring forces at that time, the connection was never made.[21]

Sergeant Glenn Moore of the St. Petersburg, Florida, Police Department traveled to England to study HOLMES for the St. Petersburg department. Moore points out that every person involved in an investigation can be up to date on its status in minutes: "All they have to do is ask HOLMES."[22]

The St. Petersburg Police Department adopted HOLMES and uses 10 computer terminals tied into it. Information on criminal cases is constantly being entered, evaluated, reviewed, processed, and analyzed on the various screens. Thousands of pages of information are readily available to any investigator working on the case at any time.

Every piece of paper in a case is first evaluated by a "receiver and indexer" who decides how it is to be entered into the system so it can be retrieved quickly. Inputters then enter the material into any of the six "indexes" or data classifications in the system. A document may suggest that certain follow-up actions are required, such as interviewing a new lead mentioned. These actions will be brought up by the "statement reader" and sent to the "action allocator." Thus all potential leads are noted and immediately assigned to follow-up action. These follow-up actions are entered into the computer, and HOLMES enters them into a master progress report. Every time the case manager checks on the progress of a case, he or she knows immediately what has and has not been done by all those connected with the case. Even news releases issued are entered into the computer. Then, if a suspect is questioned later about facts on the case, the investigators know whether or not any pertinent details were leaked to the press.

Information in the system can be recalled or combined in any desired format. For example, the investigator might ask to see information on anyone whose name has come up more than two or three times during the investigation. If this program had been used in the Yorkshire Ripper case, the suspect's name would have appeared regularly early in the investigation.

HOLMES can locate multiple uses of one name in the records of any one case at the lightning speed of more than one million words a minute. It can also scan all descriptions of people connected in any way to a case and advise if any of them comes close to the description of the main suspect. This description can include such items as the make or color of the car or boat driven or owned.

The system helps investigators follow up on leads, generate new leads, and then piece together seemingly unrelated information by organizing evidence in new ways and by linking scattered leads. Access to all information is so streamlined that it is estimated that thousands of human resource hours are saved on each case.

Investigators in Washington State battle violent crime with the Homicide Investigation and Tracking System (HITS/SMART). HITS/SMART, an electronic investigation system, stores, collates, and analyzes characteristics of all murders and sexual offenses in Washington State. Investigators statewide can then retrieve information from the system on these violent crimes to help them solve related cases. The system relies on the voluntary submission of information by law enforcement agencies throughout the state. These agencies submit data on murders, attempted murders, missing persons (when foul play is suspected), unidentified dead persons believed to be murder victims, and predatory sex offenders.[23]

Based on the information provided by the detectives, HITS/SMART analysts can query the database for any combination of the victim's gender, race, lifestyle, method and cause of death, geographic location of the crime, the absence or presence of clothing on the body, concealment of the body, and/or the dates of death and body discovery. In this way, analysts can identify other murder cases with common elements. Once the database is accessed, analysts can then supply detectives with the names of similarly murdered victims (if known), investigating agencies, case numbers, and the primary investigator's name and telephone number. Designing the query usually takes only a few minutes, as does the data search.

A database connected to HITS/SMART stores information contained in records from the Washington State Department of Corrections. This file gives HITS/SMART immediate access to the identification of present and former inmates with murder and sexual assault convictions. Their physical descriptions can be checked against the physical descriptions of unidentified suspects in recent sexual assault investigations.

As one example of the success of HITS/SMART, after a brutal rape, a detective made a request to the system for information about offenders having certain physical descriptions and MOs. The system staff provided the investigator with a list of known sexual offenders released from prison during the past five years and the areas to which they had been released. Along with this information, the HITS/SMART staff provided a collection of photographs to

---

YOU ARE THERE! »

Modus Operandi

The term *modus operandi* (MO) comes from the Latin and can be translated as "method of operation." An MO includes a summary of the habits, techniques, and peculiarities of a person's behavior. The same criminal will generally use a similar MO when committing different crimes.

Some examples of MOs that can be fed into a computer to assist investigators in solving crimes follow:

- *Robbery cases:* Armed with a gun; states "Your money or your life."

- *Murder cases:* Commits sexual acts with the dead body, then dismembers it.

- *Rape cases:* Breaks into college dormitories between 3 and 5 A.M.

YOU ARE THERE! »

His Personal Computer Solved the Crime

A burglar was identified and picked up just a few hours after committing a crime. Released from prison only two weeks before, he was identified by fingerprints recovered at the scene. The Danbury, Connecticut, police officer investigating the 8 P.M. burglary was back in his lab by 9:45 P.M. and identified the perpetrator by 10 P.M. Detectives spotted the burglar strolling on the avenue just 45 minutes later.

How did the investigating officer break the case? Using a software program called Felon/Find'r on his personal computer, he entered the classification of the listed latent print, and a list of suspects appeared on the screen. The suspect that he sought was among them.

Source: Adapted from Bill Clede, "Computer Chatter," *Law and Order* (Jan. 1994), p. 45.

the detective, and the victim immediately identified one of the former offenders as her assailant.

The Institute of Police Technology and Management in Florida has developed "SHERLOCK" (again, a reference to the legendary investigator Sherlock Holmes), a major case and death investigation management system. This program is designed for the personal computer and can index and cross-reference people, places, things, and vehicles; automatically generate leads; create a "time clock" of victims or suspects; generate a status report on all phases of investigations; provide management controls of evidence and documents; and handle serial crimes.[24]

The Royal Canadian Mounted Police has created a crime analysis computer program, the Major Crime Organizational System, that enables police to compare immediately similarities in homicides and sexual assaults. It uses guidelines from the HITS/SMART, the Iowa sex crimes section, and the FBI criminal profiling system. From those sources, investigators have compiled a list of 200 questions to be answered in each murder, sexual assault, and missing persons case.[25]

Microset, a Canadian company, has developed a program whose focus is on managing the volumes of paperwork needed before a case can be brought before the crown attorney (the Canadian counterpart of the U.S. pros-

ecutor). Based on the philosophy that a police force is made up of work groups that need specific tools to do their jobs, the company created a case tracking program for the Toronto Metropolitan Police Department that was originally designed to run on a laptop computer. The program helps investigators prepare the paperwork needed for court and track the evidence and supplementary reports involved in each case.[26]

It must be emphasized that, despite the influence of the computer in the investigative process, it will never replace the investigator. The successful investigation of crimes and other police incidents will always primarily depend on the intelligence and hard work of investigators and police officers.

Computer-Assisted Instruction

Computers are valuable teaching tools in police departments. Computer-assisted instruction (CAI) is a learning process in which students interact one on one with a computer, which instructs them and quizzes them. One of the most popular CAI systems is the Firearms Training System (FATS), a computer-driven laser disk mechanism, to train police officers to make decisions in life-threatening situations. FATS assists both veteran officers and new recruits in making shoot/don't shoot decisions.

Administrative Uses of Computers

Police departments use computers to perform many administrative functions. Management information systems and automated clerical processing systems free personnel to concentrate on serving the public. Software packages can assist police departments in jail and prisoner management. Automated patrol allocation is also possible.

MANAGEMENT INFORMATION SYSTEMS   Police departments, like other U.S. businesses, use management information systems. Robert Sheehan and Gary W. Cordner define management information systems as "those systems that provide information needed for supervisory, allocation, strategic, tactical, policy and administrative decisions."[27] They list management information systems found in police departments: (1) personnel information systems, (2) warranty control information systems, (3) equipment inventory systems, (4) evidence and property control systems, (5) booking information systems, (6) detention information systems, (7) case-tracking systems, (8) financial information systems, and (9) fleet maintenance information systems.[28]

Computers are perfect vehicles for management information systems, especially in larger police departments. Their use eliminates the need to keep handwritten records and conduct manual searches. Many of the management information systems just listed are now computerized in most large, modern police departments. For example, in 1997, the Prince George's County, Maryland, Police Department joined a growing roster of law enforcement agencies nationwide that have instituted computer-aided early-warning systems to identify officers who are experiencing stress or other problems so that positive interventions can be made before the situation becomes career-threatening.[29]

AUTOMATED CLERICAL PROCESSING SYSTEMS

Policing involves a tremendous amount of paperwork, including arrest reports, incident and follow-up reports, and accident and injury reports. The computer simplifies the report-writing process. Most police departments today use automated clerical processing systems, and many officers use these systems in their patrol cars with portable or laptop computers.

JAIL AND PRISONER MANAGEMENT   Many software packages can assist in jail and prisoner management. This application of computers is useful for police departments and sheriff's offices that are responsible for the lodging of prisoners awaiting appearance in court. These packages perform booking, updating, record inquiry, daily logs and audit trails, medical accounting, classification/pretrial release, inmate cash accounting, and billing.[30]

PATROL ALLOCATION DESIGN   Patrol allocation is a very important responsibility for police administrators. Sheehan and Cordner summarize the major issues in patrol allocation:

1. Determining the number of patrol units needed in each precinct, at each time of the day, and for each day of the week
2. Designing patrol beats
3. Developing policies to dispatch and redeploy patrol units
4. Scheduling patrol personnel to match variations in the number of units on duty[31]

Several computerized models are available for automated patrol allocation. These software packages determine the number of patrol units needed by precinct,

day of the week, and shift, based on predetermined objectives.

Computer Networks / The Internet

A computer network allows users from many different areas to communicate with one another and also to access the network's database. Computer networks are becoming common in policing.

The International Association of Chiefs of Police (IACP) has formed a nationwide computer network for the exchange of semiofficial and informal communications among police departments. The IACP network updates news and provides legislative information, special topic reports, calendars of events, department profiles, electronic mail, and a "Yellow Pages" of IACP. Today, a great many police departments, large and small, have created their own Web sites and homepages on the Internet. Students using the Web exercises at the end of each of the chapters of this text know how easy, interesting, and enjoyable it is to surf or patrol police Web sites.

The Internet provides quick and easy access to literally millions of organizations and people around the world, including persons, organizations, businesses, and government and education sources. All a user needs is a computer, a modem, Internet software, and a mouse. Millions of people today use the Internet as a form of communication, entertainment, and business. Today, most students are very familiar with the Internet and use it for their personal business and research. Much of the information in this chapter can be accessed through the Internet without taking the time to travel to a library, call a corporation, or look for a book. The Internet not only has revolutionized society but has revolutionized policing by enhancing the ability of officers and investigators to access tremendous amounts of data at a moment's notice without leaving their workplace. The ability to surf the Net through search engines, business, media, educational, and government Web sites and by exploring links attached to many Web sites is becoming essential in policing. Students are urged to use the numerous Web sites throughout this text to improve their knowledge.

As an example of how the Internet can help the police interact with the public, many cities, counties, and states in all regions of the nation are putting their crime maps on the Web, enabling citizens to view them. Some examples of Web sites with excellent crime maps are Vacaville and Sacramento, California, and Cambridge, Massachusetts.[32]

YOU ARE THERE! »

How High Tech and the Internet Have Helped Police Departments

The *FBI Law Enforcement Bulletin* polled police departments all over the nation regarding their use of the Internet. All of the responding agencies reported they use their homepages to provide basic information about their departments to citizens. This information generally includes the agency's mission statement, a brief history of the department, and a message from the commanding officer. Departments also feature local fugitives (some even include a list of the FBI's Ten Most Wanted), crime prevention tips, and crime tip hotlines. Some agencies use the Internet to obtain product information or simply to contact other police agencies. The majority of responding agencies provide a list of state and local criminal statutes. Also, many of the agencies use their Internet sites to provide citizens with detailed information about criminal activity occurring in the community and to provide numerous community and law enforcement services.

Here are some specific representative responses and programs:

■ The King County, Washington, Police Department worked with a local computer firm to develop a software application that enables the department to include electronic pin maps on its homepage. These maps display information on all arrests, residential burglaries, aggravated assaults, auto thefts, and other crimes occurring throughout the county.

■ The Chicago, Illinois, Police Department developed an online form for residents to register their bicycles with the department.

■ The Beaufort City, South Carolina, Police Department issues press releases to local media via the Internet, eliminating the scheduling problems caused by officers having to meet in person with different news organizations that

need information. The department now posts all press releases on its Web site, making them instantly available to media groups and the general public alike.

■ In Davis, California, the police department's youth services division assisted in the development of an online coloring book that allows young students to color pictures via the Internet. When completed, the pictures—each of which reinforces a different safety message—can be printed or sent via e-mail to other computers.

In addition to creating homepages, several responding agencies have applied more interactive approaches to their Web sites:

■ The Wakefield, Massachusetts, Police Department established an interactive e-mail capability coupled with voice mailboxes routed to officers' work stations. This capability allows citizens—most notably crime victims and witnesses—to leave messages for individual officers.

■ The Des Moines, Washington, Police Department hosts various e-mail conferences on its Web site—including a popular "ask a cop" conference in which citizens get direct answers to law enforcement-related questions.

■ The city of Tempe, Arizona, recently established several computerized information kiosks that draw information from the Internet server. This year, the police department's homepage will be included in this system, significantly broadening its potential audience.

Source: Adapted from "FaxBack Response: Previous Question: How Has the Internet Helped Your Agency?," *FBI Law Enforcement Bulletin* (Jan. 1997), pp. 23–25.

★ ★ ★

FINGERPRINT TECHNOLOGY

Fingerprints offer an infallible means of personal identification.

Criminal identification by means of fingerprints is one of the most potent factors in apprehending fugitives who might otherwise escape arrest and continue their criminal activities indefinitely. This type of identification also makes possible an accurate determination of the number of previous arrests and convictions, which results in the imposition of more equitable sentences by the judiciary.

In addition, this system of identification enables the prosecutor to present his or her case in the light of the offender's previous record. It also provides probation officers and the parole board with definite information upon which to base their judgment in dealing with criminals in their jurisdiction.[33]

Fingerprints may be recorded on standard fingerprint cards or can be recorded digitally and transmitted electronically to the FBI for comparison. By comparing fingerprints at the scene of a crime with the fingerprint record of suspect persons, officials can establish absolute proof of the presence or identity of a person.[34]

Exhibit 14.1	Some Fingerprint Facts

Three Classifications

Three fingerprint classifications form the basis for all ten-print classification systems presently in use:

- *Loops:* Fingerprints that are characterized by ridge lines that enter from one side of the pattern and curve around to exit from the same side of the pattern. Some 60 percent of fingerprints are loops.

- *Whorls:* Fingerprints that include ridge patterns that are generally rounded or circular in shape and have two deltas. Some 30 percent of fingerprints are whorls.

- *Arches:* Fingerprints characterized by ridge lines that enter the print from one side and flow out of the other side. Some 5 percent of fingerprints are arches.

Three Types

Most people refer to any fingerprint discovered at a crime scene as a latent fingerprint. But there are really three basic types of prints:

- *Visible prints:* Made by fingers touching a surface after the ridges have been in contact with a colored material such as blood, paint, grease, or ink.

- *Plastic prints:* Ridge impressions left on a soft material such as putty, wax, soap, or dust.

- *Latent (invisible) prints:* Impressions caused when body perspiration or oils present on fingerprint ridges adhere to the surface of an object.

Source: Adapted from: Richard Saferstein, *Criminalistics: An Introduction to Forensic Science,* 7th ed. (Upper Saddle River, NJ: Prentice-Hall 2001), p. 401.

Basic Categories of Fingerprints

There are two basic categories of fingerprints: **inked prints,** or **ten-prints,** and **latent prints.**

Inked prints or ten-prints are the result of the process of rolling each finger onto a ten-print card (each finger is rolled onto a separate box on the card) using fingerprinting ink. Inked prints are kept on file at local police departments, state criminal justice information agencies, and the FBI. When a person is arrested, he or she is fingerprinted and those inked prints are compared with fingerprints on file of known criminals. Inked prints or ten-prints are also taken for numerous other types of investigations such as employment background and license applications.

Latent prints are impressions left on evidence. These prints may be "lifted" and then compared with inked prints on file in order to establish the identity of the perpetrator. Latent prints are impressions produced by the ridged skin on human fingers, palms, and soles of the feet. Latent print examiners analyze and compare latent prints

to known prints of individuals in an effort to make identifications or exclusions. The uniqueness, permanence, and arrangement of the friction ridges allow examiners to positively match two prints and to determine whether an area of a friction ridge impression originated from one source to the exclusion of others.

A variety of techniques, including use of chemicals, powders, lasers, alternate light sources, and other physical means, are employed in the detection and development of latent prints. In instances where a latent print has limited quality and quantity of detail, examiners may

Exhibit 14.2	How to Find and Develop Latent Fingerprints

- *Carbon dusting powders:* When finely ground carbon powder is applied lightly to a surface with a camel's-hair or fiberglass brush, it will adhere to perspiration residues left on the surface and can render an invisible impression visible. Generally the print technician will apply powder of a contrasting color to the color of the surface being dusted. The raised print is photographed, lifted off the surface using transparent tape, and then transferred to a card that has a contrasting color to the color of the powder used on the tape.

- *Iodine fuming:* Crystals of iodine are placed in a glass container called a fumer along with the article suspected of containing latent prints. When the crystals are heated, iodine vapors will fill the chamber and make the latent print visible. Iodine prints are not permanent and begin to fade once the fuming process is stopped. The resultant fingerprint must be immediately photographed. This method is particularly useful for obtaining prints from paper or cardboard.

- *Silver nitrate:* A solution of silver nitrate in distilled water is sprayed or saturated on paper believed to have latent prints. When the paper is exposed to light, the print becomes visible.

- *Ninhydrin:* The chemical ninhydrin is sprayed over large cardboard or paper containers and if a latent print is present it will become visible.

- *Super glue fuming:* Super glue (cyanoacrylate) treated with sodium hydroxide is placed within a chamber with an object believed to contain latent prints. The resultant fumes from the glue adhere to the latent print, making it visible.

- *Ultraviolet light:* A UV lamp (black light) can be effective in a darkened environment to expose latent prints.

- *Laser:* The laser, when directed at a surface, can cause the perspiration forming a latent fingerprint to fluoresce, thus making the print visible.

- *Alternative light sources (ALS):* An ALS operates under the same principle as a laser and can make latent fingerprints fluoresce and become visible. It is much more portable than the laser.

Source: Adapted from Larry Ragle, *Crime Scene* (New York: Avon, 1995), pp. 101–108; Richard Saferstein, *Criminalistics: An Introduction to Forensic Science,* 7th ed. (Upper Saddle River, NJ: Prentice-Hall, 2001), pp. 405–413.

Dempsey's Law

Can a Person Change Fingerprints?

Professor Dempsey, can a person change his or her fingerprints?

Many students ask this question. It is impossible to change one's fingerprints, although many criminals have tried to obscure them. Perhaps the most celebrated attempt to obliterate one's fingerprints was the efforts by the notorious 1930s gangster John Dillinger, who tried to destroy his own fingerprints by applying a corrosive acid to them. However, prints taken at the morgue after he was shot to death, compared with fingerprints taken at the time of a previous arrest, proved that his efforts had been a failure.

Richard Saferstein, the noted criminalistics expert, has indicated that efforts at intentionally scarring the skin on one's fingerprints can only be self-defeating, for it would be totally impossible to obliterate all the ridge characteristics on the hand, and the presence of permanent scars merely provides new characteristics for identification.

Source: Adapted from Richard Saferstein, *Criminalistics: An Introduction to Forensic Science,* 7th ed. (Upper Saddle River, NJ: Prentice-Hall, 2001), p. 400.

---

perform microscopic examinations in order to effect conclusive comparisons.

Sometimes, a latent fingerprint found in dust may be the only clue in an investigation in which there are no other leads. Even though this kind of print was actually caused by some of the dust being removed—because it adhered to the ridges of the skin that touched there—methods of lifting these prints are now available.[35]

Lasers can be used to lift prints from surfaces that often defy traditional powder or chemical techniques, including glass, paper, cardboard, rubber, wood, plastic, leather, and even human skin.[36] The use of lasers in fingerprint lifting allowed the FBI to detect a 40-year-old fingerprint of a Nazi war criminal on a postcard.[37] In a recent article, the special agent in charge of the Forensic Services Division of the U.S. Secret Service cited numerous cases of the suc-

cessful use of sophisticated fingerprint technology. He mentioned such high-profile cases as the original bombing of the World Trade Center and the killing of two CIA employees in Langley, Virginia.[38]

Automated Fingerprint Identification Systems

By the 1980s, **automated fingerprint identification systems (AFIS)** began to be developed. An AFIS enables a print technician to enter unidentified latent prints into the computer. The computer then automatically searches its files and presents a list of likely matches, which can then be visually examined by a fingerprint technician in order to find the perfect match. Additionally, using the AFIS technology, a person's prints can be taken and stored into memory without the use of traditional inking and rolling techniques.[39]

The first locally funded, regional automated fingerprint identification system in the United States was NOVARIS (Northern Virginia Regional Identification System). NOVARIS can look for prints having similar characteristics at the rate of 297 prints per second. It then prints out a listing of individuals whose fingerprint patterns match 75 percent or more of the fingerprint detail pattern submitted.[40] The Los Angeles Police Department estimates that fingerprint comparisons that in the past would have taken as long as 60 years can now be performed in one day.[41] Washington, D.C., police report that computerized print systems enable them to make more than 100 identifi-

PATROLLING THE WEB

Biomet.org: The Biometric Resource Center
    http://www.biomet.org
International Association for Identification
    http://www.theiai.org
FBI Latent Print Examinations
    http://www.fbi.gov/kq/lab/org/lpee.htm
Fingerprint Identification Technology in Civil Applications
    http://www.morpho.com/

YOU ARE THERE! >>

Fingerprints Are Infallible Evidence—Aren't They?

Fingerprint evidence rests on the idea that no two people have the same print. First admitted into court in 1911, fingerprint evidence has generally been accepted by the relevant scientific community and very easily passed the Frye test on acceptability of scientific evidence. Since then courts have accepted fingerprint evidence without much scrutiny. However, some legal experts say that this may be changing, based on the landmark 1993 *Daubert* v. *Merrell Dow Pharmaceutical* case

In *Daubert*, the U.S. Supreme Court asserted that "general acceptance" or the Frye standard is not an absolute prerequisite to the admissibility of scientific evidence and relegated to the trial judge the task of ensuring that an expert's testimony rests on a reliable foundation and is relevant to the subject of the trial. Thus, the Court ruled that trial judges must serve as the "gatekeeper" in judging the admissibility and reliability of scientific evidence presented in their courts. The Court suggested the following guidelines:

- The scientific technique or theory can be and has been tested;

- The technique or theory has been subject to peer review and publication;

- The technique's potential rate of error has been judged;

- Standards controlling the technique's operation exist and are maintained; and

- The scientific theory or method has attracted widespread acceptance within a relevant scientific community.

Some experts now question our confidence in the accuracy of a match between prints carefully taken in a police station and often less-than-perfect prints recovered at a crime scene. They also question whether fingerprint identification could be challenged on the grounds that it has not been adequately tested, that the error rate has not been calculated, and that there are no standards for what constitutes a match. The first recent challenge to fingerprint identification was in *United States* v. *Byron C. Mitchell*, 1999.

The admissibility of fingerprint evidence was challenged in this case in the Eastern District of Pennsylvania, involving the trial of a man accused of driving a getaway car in a robbery. The prosecution said the man's prints were on the gearshift and door of the car. The defense argued that fingerprints could not be proven to be unique. Government experts vigorously disputed this claim. After a hearing, the judge upheld the admissibility of fingerprints as scientific evidence and ruled that human friction ridges are unique and permanent and human friction ridge skin arrangements are unique and permanent.

Since Mitchell, other case challenges have been filed in courts, but none has yet kept fingerprints out of a trial. The debate continues.

Sources: Adapted from Malcolm Ritter, "Fingerprint Evidence Faces Hurdles." Retrieved on June 16, 2001, from http://www.aafs.org/leadstory1.htm; *Frye* v. *Untied States*, 293 Fed. 1013 (1923); *Daubert* v. *Merrell Dow Pharmaceutical, Inc.*, 113 S.Ct. 2786 (1993); *United States* v. *Byron C. Mitchell*; Richard Saferstein, *Criminalistics: An Introduction to Forensic Science*, 7th ed. (Upper Saddle River, NJ: Prentice-Hall, 2001), pp. 12–14, 397.

cations a month from fingerprints taken at a crime scene. Other departments reporting successful results using automated fingerprint identification systems are San Jose, California; Houston, Texas; and Minneapolis, Minnesota.[42]

Here are some more examples of the success of automated fingerprint identification systems:

- Since the Milwaukee, Wisconsin, Police Department implemented its AFIS, 232,000 ten-print cards have been entered into the system with a 37 percent identification rate on unknown latent prints. A Milwaukee police official reports that many serious crimes in the area are now solved with "no suspect information at all—just a fingerprint."[43]

- The Royal Canadian Mounted Police (RCMP) operate a national AFIS system that takes prints from all Canadian law enforcement agencies and holds 2.6 million ten-print cards. A networking system has been in place since early 1990 that allows seven remote sites with compatible equipment to access the central site's system in Ottawa. At its central AFIS site, alone, the RCMP made 1,700 latent hits in one year.[44]

- An example of the way in which AFIS technology can help in criminal investigation was its use in Nevada by the Washoe County Sheriff's Office. Nevada is one state, along with Alaska, California, Idaho, Oregon, Utah, Washington, and Wyoming, that uses the services of

Forst's Law

"What a Difference Technology Makes"

During my police career I saw some great improvements in technology. Many tasks that took hours to complete and document began to be done by computers. We handwrote reports that had five copies and were turned in to the supervisor who read them, signed off on them, and sent them to records (after perhaps having us rewrite it a few times). A data entry clerk then entered the data so that very basic information could be retrieved for future reference. When it was time to go to court, the officer went back to records and requested a copy of the report to take to court. When I left the department, officers had been using laptops for several years with state-of-the-art programs; they wrote their reports, and the supervisors retrieved and reviewed them electronically and uploaded them to the main computer system. Much more extensive data was then available for retrieval without the use of a data entry clerk. Reports were then generated on a daily basis to gather needed information for units like Crime Analysis, Press Information Office, and the Detective Bureau.

In my opinion, the most significant improvement I saw over my career was the advent of the Automated Fingerprint Identification System (AFIS). When I started with the police department we had a sworn officer, a sergeant in fact, doing fingerprint comparisons. If we arrested a suspect and thought he might have committed some specific crimes, we could request that his prints be compared to the latents lifted at the scenes. If we worked a scene and had some possible suspects, we could request that the latents be compared to the suspect's prints—if we had them. If we had no suspect, the sergeant could compare the prints to those of some local offenders known to have commited similar crimes, but other than that, we were out of luck. This man spent eight hours a day comparing prints with little productive results.

Now, when an officer works a scene, he or she turns in any latents, and they can be compared with all the latents in the database within minutes if not seconds. Clearance rates have been greatly enhanced by this technology. We are also able to put that sergeant position out on the street where it is needed. Dusting for fingerprints is no longer seen as an exercise in futility. This is just one way technology has made law enforcement much more productive and effective.

Western Identification Network, Inc. (WIN), a regional AFIS. The Washoe County Sheriff's Office arrested an unknown person on charges of using stolen credit cards to obtain money from automatic teller machines. A WIN AFIS search identified the suspect as a repeat offender with a prior criminal record in Oregon, which led in turn to an FBI record check indicating that the suspect was wanted by the U.S. Secret Service, the state of North Carolina, and the District of Columbia for fraud and weapons violations. The suspect had also been arrested in seven states, using multiple aliases.[45]

- In the late 1990s, the Providence, Rhode Island, police department purchased an AFIS system and in a short time entered more than five hundred thousand latent fingerprints into the system and solved numerous crimes that would not have been solved using previous systems.[46]

- As of 1998, the Maryland automated fingerprint system had linked 435 offenders to unsolved crimes, including 4 homicides, 65 rapes, and 59 robberies.[47]

- The Hennepin County (Minnesota) Sheriff's Department, along with the police departments of Redlands and Ontario, California, is experimenting with the latest AFIS technology, IBIS (Identification Based Information System), which captures fingerprint and photo images at a crime scene on a handheld remote data terminal (RDT). IBIS is described later in this chapter.[48]

NEWER, LESS COSTLY SYSTEMS   Until very recently, AFIS technology has been extraordinarily expensive and therefore procured only by the largest agencies. The technology provided excellent high-speed fingerprint matching once fingerprint databases became large enough. Still, a drawback was that each system has been stand-alone—that is, systems could not exchange information rapidly. But there are now software-based systems using open-system architecture. In other words, any computer based on the UNIX operating system will work with them.[49] These systems are also designed to exchange fingerprint and other data over the wire with other criminal justice information systems, using the widely accepted Henry System of fingerprint classification.

These systems, designed for use in a booking facility, can use ink-and-paper fingerprints or can employ Live-Scan, an optical fingerprint scanning system, to read the suspect's prints. The scanner uses electronic capture of the suspect's fingerprint pattern, using 500 DPI resolution, electronic quality analysis, and automatic image centering. The booking officer begins with a single-finger or dual-digit search, placing the suspect's finger on the scanner for reading. If the computer finds a possible match, the officer gets news of a "hit" within minutes. The computer selects the most likely matches, which then must be verified by a human operator. If there is no hit, the computer adds the fingerprint to its database automatically. Only one hour's training is necessary for a booking officer to operate the system.

These systems also have electronic quality checking, image enhancement, and ten-print system capability. They can scan fingerprint cards, reducing them to electronic records, and store them for future reference. They can also print fingerprint cards from electronically scanned Live-Scan fingerprints. Training for a latent fingerprint examiner takes several days because of the numerous features in this system. A latent fingerprint examiner can link separate crime scenes using single latent prints, which can point to a common perpetrator or a pattern.

LIVE-SCAN   The use of **Live-Scan** stations allows fingerprints and demographic information to be electronically captured, stored, and transmitted in minutes. Greater use of applicant fingerprints is among the many reasons why the use of ten-print Live-Scan stations is increasing nationwide. Built-in quality-control software helps reduce human errors. Because there is no ink, there is no smearing. If a mistake is made, a print can be retaken until one high-quality record is obtained. There is no need to print a person again for local, state, and federal agencies, because Live-Scan can make copies. Higher-quality fingerprints mean a higher likelihood of the AFIS finding a match in its database without human verification.[50]

Nationwide, smaller law enforcement agencies have found that they receive much faster response times from these systems when they use Live-Scan equipment that is connected to the AFIS. California uses such a system to fingerprint applicants for school employment in background checks, as is required under state law.

IAFIS   In 1999, the FBI Laboratory began using the FBI Criminal Justice Information Services (CJIS) Division's **Integrated Automated Fingerprint Identification System (IAFIS).** This system provides the capability to search latent fingerprints against the largest criminal fingerprint repository in the world, which contains the fingerprints of almost 45 million individuals. This allows the FBI

YOU ARE THERE! »

DNA Couldn't Find the Suspect, but IAFIS Did

The Georgia Bureau of Identification (GBI) and the Pleasant Prairie, Wisconsin, Police Department (PPPD) were both looking for the same rape suspect in crimes committed in their jurisdictions. The PPPD contacted the GBI because they noted common characteristics in the rapes: The victims all worked as clerks at retail strip malls near interstates. The PPPD sent fingerprint and DNA samples for examination. Through DNA testing, the GBI tied those two rapes to a rape in Florence, Kentucky, but could not identify the suspect.

After exhaustive investigation efforts with the PPPD, including a requested subject analysis by the FBI's Violent Crime Apprehension Program, had yielded no viable leads, the GBI submitted the Wisconsin print for examination by the FBI's IAFIS database. Within minutes, the search produced the name of a suspect.

The man was located in jail at Lawrenceville, Georgia, where he was being held on an unrelated crime. The GBI was granted a search warrant to obtain a blood sample. Although he denied any involvement in the crimes, his blood was matched to DNA samples from the serial rapes. A few days after the sample was taken, he used a bedsheet to hang himself in his jail cell. He implicated himself in other rapes before his death.

The lesson from this investigation is the value of the IAFIS latent search technique. In spite of exhaustive investigative efforts, none of the other organizations' efforts were able to identify a suspect for these serial crimes. IAFIS did.

Source: Adapted from: "Unsolved Case Fingerprint Matching," *FBI Law Enforcement Bulletin* (Dec. 2000), pp. 12–13.

to make identifications without benefit of a named suspect to help solve a variety of crimes.[51]

IAFIS is primarily a ten-print system for searching an individual's fingerprints to determine whether a prior arrest record exists and then maintaining a criminal arrest record history for each individual. The system also offers significant latent print capabilities. Using IAFIS, a latent print specialist can digitally capture latent print and ten-print images and perform several functions with each, including enhancing to improve image quality; comparing latent fingerprints against suspect ten-print records retrieved from the criminal fingerprint repository; searching latent fingerprints against the ten-print fingerprint repository when no suspects have been developed; doing automatic searches of new arrest ten-print records against an unsolved latent fingerprint repository; and creating special files of ten-print records to support major criminal investigations.[52]

The IAFIS Project has its roots in the 1960s and 1970s, when the FBI began investigating the feasibility of automating the fingerprint identification process. During that time, the Identification Division, predecessor to CJIS, began working with the National Institute for Standards and Technology to develop algorithms for searching and matching fingerprints using computer technology.

In the year 2000, the fingerprint databases of the FBI, the FBI's IAFIS, and the Immigration and Naturalization Service (INS) were merged. Formerly, federal, state, and local law enforcement officials did not have access to all fingerprint information captured by Border Patrol agents, and the INS did not have access to the FBI's records when its agents apprehended suspects at the border. The merging of the two systems was prompted by the inadvertent release by the INS in 1999 of Angel Maturino-Resendez, the suspected serial killer—known as the "railroad killer"—who was alleged to have stowed away on trains and murdered eight people near rail lines during a three-state killing spree. Border Patrol agents had picked up Maturino-Resendez for illegal entry into the U.S. and sent him back to Mexico. The agents were unaware that he was wanted by the Houston police and the FBI for questioning in the murders. Within days of his release, Maturino-Resendez killed four of his victims. Eventually he surrendered to Texas Rangers in July 1999.[53]

As of 2003, IAFIS had almost 45 million records and provided an international standard for providing fingerprints electronically. After a criminal ten-print search is submitted electronically, the FBI guarantees a response within two hours, and the prints are compared to those of anyone who has been arrested in the U.S. since the 1920s. One of the biggest current problems with IAFIS is that eight states still do not electronically submit standardized criminal fingerprints to the system, and 20 states do not submit latent fingerprints. IAFIS was instrumental in the capture of John Lee Malvo, one of the two suspects in the 2002 Washington, D.C., area sniper case. A latent print entered into IAFIS matched Malvo, whose prints were in the system because he had been previously arrested by the Immigration and Naturalization Service.[54]

IBIS   A new device, IBIS (Identification Based Information System) is available as a portable, handheld tool that delivers on-the-spot positive identification when a suspect has no driver's license or seems to be presenting a false identification. The IBIS captures thumbprints and mugshots and receives text and mugshots from databases with criminal histories, warrants, and images. It even has a silent assist button in the event the investigator requires help from fellow officers. The IBIS offers a high-resolution camera to make images of latent fingerprints at a crime scene, a digital voice recorder, and a geographic informa-

YOU ARE THERE! ≫

Solve This Crime

A man meets a woman in a singles bar. She invites him to her apartment. He has a drink with her in the apartment and then shoots and kills her. The detectives investigating the case can find no one who saw the man and woman together, and they have no suspects. While processing the crime scene, they find the two glasses from which the man and woman were drinking. Using forensic techniques, they dust the glasses and come up with a partial latent print (an impression caused by the contact of the man's finger against the glass).

Comparing an unknown latent print or an unknown partial latent print to a known print was once an extremely difficult undertaking. There are millions of fingerprint files in law enforcement agencies around the United States. To match the unknown print to a known print—assuming that our murderer has been fingerprinted—a latent print examiner must search through countless numbers of fingerprints, hoping to find a match. This is similar to searching for the proverbial needle in the haystack.

Fortunately, automated fingerprint identification system (AFIS) technology is available today. Using it, investigators may be able to solve this case.

YOU ARE THERE! >>

The Power of Fluorescent Print Detection: The Polly Klass Case

The power of fluorescent print detection was demonstrated in the Polly Klass kidnap/murder case in Petaluma, California. The young victim was abducted from her bedroom by an unknown intruder. Police used black powder methods to discover several prints, none of which matched the subsequently identified suspect.

In an effort to locate more evidence, the FBI's Evidence Response Team (ERT) was called upon. ERTs are trained and equipped with the latest forensic technology. Agents from the San Francisco ERT processed the scene using an Omniprint 1000. After the victim's wooden bed frame was dusted with Redwop illumination at 450nm, a clear palmprint was revealed.

A suspect was subsequently arrested, but he denied any knowledge of the crime. However, when learning of the palmprint evidence, he admitted to the crime and directed investigators to the location of the victim's body. The palmprint was the only print that matched the suspect and could not have been found by traditional fingerprint techniques.

Unfortunately, solving the crime did not prevent the death of the victim. The FBI is building a computerized fingerprint database of all convicted sex offenders. It is hoped that rapid matching of any prints found at an abduction scene will lead to the apprehension of the suspect before the victim is physically harmed. Fluorescent print detection is clearly going to be a widely used tool in these efforts.

Source: Adapted from Mary C. Nolte, "The Role of the Photon in Modern Forensics," *Law and Order* (Nov. 1994), pp. 51–54.

---

tion system. Local agencies will be able to connect with state and federal communications and information systems when the system is fully developed.[55]

INNOVATIONS IN OTHER COUNTRIES   Other countries have also made innovations in fingerprinting technology. The New Zealand police have combined several advanced techniques to put their fingerprint experts at the forefront of world technology. They combine high-intensity forensic light, video cameras, computer enhancement technology, and AFIS technology to obtain information at a crime scene. In one case, a section of clear tape had been used to tie up a victim during an armed robbery. When the tape was brought in for fingerprint processing, it was discovered that fingerprints were superimposed on both sides of the tape. Technicians used sophisticated lighting and computerized technology to uncover a workable print in 35 minutes despite problems with background detail and complexity. A search through AFIS revealed matching prints on record, and the perpetrator was arrested.[56]

The United Kingdom is using its National Automated Fingerprint Identification System (NAFIS) in most of the police forces in England and Wales. NAFIS integrates automated fingerprint technology and criminal justice records at a national level, linking a database of about five million ten-print fingerprints sets and two million crime scene marks. NAFIS is capable of making one million comparisons per second for the most urgent cases, enabling fin-

gerprints taken from the scene of a crime to be searched against local or national databases in a matter of minutes.[57]

The International Association for Identification (IAI) is a professional organization for those interested in fingerprint identification, latent prints and AFIS.

Automated Palmprint Technology

Recent advances in biometrics have made it possible for automated **palmprint** systems to complement standard AFIS technology. The technology works in the same manner as its AFIS counterpart; but, instead of fingerprints, it captures the four core areas of the palm and converts them into data for storage in a palmprint repository. On arrest, suspects have their palms scanned along with the fingerprints. After a palmprint is lifted from a crime scene, it too is scanned and entered into the database for matching. The palmprint matching processor will then return a rank-ordered notification of match candidates to the workstation. Before palmprint technology, if police didn't have a suspect to compare prints to, the only way they could make a palmprint match was to manually compare latent palmprints with hundreds of thousands of individual prints sitting in repositories. In most cases, for obvious reasons, this simply was not possible.[58]

Automated palmprint technology has been in development for some time, but it has only recently come onto the market. One reason for this is the complicated nature of the palmprint itself. The palm area contains up to 1,000 minutiae (small characteristics), compared to the approximate 100 minutiae found in the average fingerprint. This difference in size means that an automated palmprint system must actively scan and match a larger area, requiring complex refining of the technology to ensure the highest accuracy rate possible.

★ ★ ★

LESS-THAN-LETHAL WEAPONS

Police departments are using technological devices to stop and disable armed, dangerous, and violent subjects without resorting to the use of firearms. The term **less-than-lethal weapons,** or nonlethal weapons, is used to identify innovative alternatives to traditional nonfirearm weapons (such as batons and flashlights) and tactics (such as martial arts techniques and other bodily force techniques, including tackles and choke holds). Nonlethal weapons can be seen as shooting-avoidance tools, because these weapons can control unarmed but resisting suspects early in a con-

frontation, before they have the opportunity to become armed and attack an officer. Also, these weapons can be used against a subject who is armed with less than a firearm—for example, a knife, club, or other instrument that can cause injury to officers. Among the most popular nonlethal weapons being used by the police are chemical irritant sprays and the TASER and other stun devices.[59]

Chemical Irritant Sprays

Chemical irritant sprays are handheld liquid products that contain the active ingredients of cayenne pepper or CS or CN tear gas. They can be sprayed into the face of a resisting suspect from a distance of up to 15 feet in order to cause discomfort and temporary disorientation. Thus, officers gain the necessary time to subdue the subject safely.

For many years, the aerosol CN tear gas, originally introduced by Smith and Wesson under the name Chemical Mace, was regarded by law enforcement as the closest thing to a perfect nonlethal weapon. Today, however, police are experimenting with other types of aerosol sprays. Aerosol subject restraints (ASRs), for example, are different from CS or CN sprays in that they do not rely on pain. They cause a subject's eyes to close and double the subject over with uncontrollable coughing. They also cause a temporary loss of strength and coordination. ASRs cause no physical damage and require no area decontamination. Among popular ASRs are oleoresin capsicum (OC, the hot ingredient in chili peppers), Aerko (Punch), Def-Tee (Pepper Mace), Guardian Personal Security Products (Bodyguard), and Zarc (Cap-Stun).[60]

In 1997, the NYPD announced that it was switching to a more powerful form of pepper spray. Pepper spray is an aerosol-propelled mist that is composed partly of cayenne pepper and causes people to gag, cough, close their eyes, and sometimes experience shortness of breath. It has been used by the NYPD since 1993, but recently police officials said it has not been strong enough. The department is now issuing larger cans of spray that can shoot nearly twice as far, 15 feet rather than 8 feet. The new spray is mixed with citrus fibers, which give it a foamy quality and help it stick to its target, causing a stronger reaction.[61] Former Chief of Department Louis R. Anemone said, "We're encouraging the use of pepper spray. We want the cops to use this

©AP Photo/Wilfredo Lee

A Miami police officer advances toward a man on a railroad crossing light fixture in July 2003. The man threatened to kill himself by jumping off the 25-foot pole and threw rocks, small pipes, and cups of urine at police and passersby. Officers used a TASER and beanbag gun to subdue the subject, and no one was injured. Do you think less-than-lethal weapons are effective in subduing resistant suspects?

rather than a nightstick or hand-to-hand combat or the butt of a gun or radio or firing a weapon. We think this is an effective less-than-lethal tool."[62]

Shortly after pepper spray was first widely used in the early 1990s to largely replace tear gas and Chemical Mace, several people who had been exposed to it died in police custody, raising fears about its safety. But after reviewing a national sample of such deaths, the National Institute of Justice in 1997 concluded that pepper spray did not cause any of these deaths.[63]

A recent National Institute of Justice (NIJ) study of officer and arrestee injuries in three North Carolina police jurisdictions before and after pepper spray was introduced found a correlation between pepper-spray use and a decline in injuries. Also, the NIJ report covered another study of 63 cases in which deaths of in-custody suspects followed pepper spray use. The study disclosed that in only two of these cases was pepper spray found to have been a factor in the deaths, but not the cause of the deaths.[64]

The Taser and Other Stun Devices

The Taser, an acronym for Thomas A. Swift's Electric Rifle, is a handheld electronic stun gun that discharges a high-voltage, low-amperage, pulsating current via tiny wires and darts, which can be fired from up to 15 feet away. When the darts strike the subject, the electric current causes a temporary incapacitation of the muscles. This gives the officers the necessary time to subdue the subject safely. The electricity can penetrate up to two inches of clothing. The Taser discharges only a few watts of power and is not harmful to cardiac patients with implanted pacemakers, nor can it be modified to produce a lethal charge.[65]

The Taser has been used by the LAPD since 1980 and was used more than 600 times in one year alone. It has proved to be an effective tool in confrontations with violent people under the influence of phencyclidine (PCP). PCP, "angel dust," is an illegal drug that can cause users to exhibit bizarre behavior coupled with extreme violence. Such people are very hard to control, because they exhibit the phenomenon known as superhuman strength. Officers frequently refer to people under the influence of PCP as "dusters."[66]

Another increasingly popular less-than-lethal weapon is the "beanbag" gun. The one-inch-square canvas bag, filled with bird shot, has been used by SWAT teams for several years and more recently by regular patrol officers. The beanbag gun produces a velocity of 320 feet per second

within a range of a few inches to 30 feet away with nonlethal force.[67]

However, in the 2001 *Deorle* v. *Rutherford* court decision by the U.S. Court of Appeals for the Ninth Circuit, the court decided that firing beanbag rounds at an unarmed suspect without first issuing a verbal warning represented excessive force and ruled that the beanbag round represented force with a significant risk of serious injury.[68]

Safety and Effectiveness of Less-Than-Lethal Weapons

J. P. Morgan, chief of the Goldsboro (North Carolina) Police Department, points to a possible drawback of the less-than-lethal weapon: "Sometimes . . . it can give a false sense of security, as evidenced by an officer's response to the offer of a back-up. 'I don't need one, I got my OC' [oleoresin capsicum, a pepper spray]."[69]

Just how safe are less-than-lethal weapons? A study of 502 use-of-force incidents not involving the use of firearms attempted to discover the injury rate to officers and subjects from eight specific types of force used by the officers. The force was used to cause a suspect to fall to the ground so that the officers could safely subdue him or her. The types of force studied were (1) striking with a baton; (2) a karate kick; (3) a punch; (4) striking with a flashlight; (5) swarming techniques, or organized tackles by a group of officers; (6) miscellaneous bodily force, including pushing, shoving, and tackling; (7) chemical irritant sprays (CS and CN); and (8) the Taser.[70]

The most used types of force in the study were the baton, miscellaneous bodily force, and the Taser; the least used were chemical irritant sprays, flashlights, and punches. The Taser was used in 102 cases and chemical irritant sprays in 21 cases. The Taser was about as effective as the other forms of nonlethal force in subduing a subject, and it resulted in fewer injuries to officers and subjects. The researcher concluded, "Expanded use of nonlethal weapons, along with the concurrent development of the next generation of such devices, will lead to fewer and less severe injuries to suspects and officers, reduced civil liability claims and payments, reduced personnel complaints, reduced disability time out of the field, reduced disability pension payments and an improved public image for law enforcement."[71]

The use of the Taser has been upheld in court. In *Michenfelder* v. *Sumner*, a federal court found the following: "Authorities believe the Taser is the preferred method for controlling prisoners because it is the 'least confrontational' when compared to the use of physical restraint, billy clubs, mace or beanbag guns. . . . When contrasted to alternative methods for physically controlling inmates, some of which can have serious after-effects, the Taser compared favorably."[72]

However, more recent studies present a less promising picture of less-than-lethal weapons. In 2001, the Toronto, Canada, Police Service conducted a comprehensive survey of less-than-lethal weapons to assist in the reduction of the use of force and deadly force by the police. The emphasis of the study was to evaluate the practicality and effectiveness of these devices. Their conclusion was that there are presently no less-than-lethal weapons available that could replace the police firearm in certain life-and-death situations. Impact projectile launchers, capture nets, and electronic stun devices were determined to be impractical and ineffective, although they did report that batons or pepper spray were useful in less deadly situations and could sometimes prevent an officer from having to use deadly force.[73] Also, a 2001 report by the Great Britain Home Office discussing the United Kingdom's police need for less-lethal weapon technologies, after reviewing all current commercially available weapon possibilities, concluded only that further testing of all the devices will continue to assess their potential use in policing.[74] Furthermore, according to a 2002 article in *Law Enforcement Technology*, recent research has found that technological gadgetry, such as beanbag devices and rubber bullets, have caused death and serious injuries over the past years. Also, the author asserts that there is a fear that if common criminals see law enforcement using more force and more lethal trends, they will also; and he concludes that less-than-lethal technologies have not been able to coexist with lethal force because, in most street-level confrontations, they have turned out worse than using lethal force.[75]

★ ★ ★

SURVEILLANCE TECHNOLOGY

Police agencies use surveillance for a variety of reasons. Surveillance might be used to provide cover for an undercover officer and an arrest team in a buy-and-bust narcotics operation or to gather intelligence or to establish probable cause for arrest. Today's advances in technology provide us with more surveillance devices than ever before.[76]

Formerly, surveillance equipment consisted of a nearly broken down undercover van used to store the typical surveillance equipment: a camera and a pair of binoculars.

Times have changed. Today's police have high-tech state-of-the-art listening, recording, and viewing devices, high-tech surveillance vans, night vision devices, vehicle tracking systems, global positioning systems, and surveillance aircraft, among other innovations.

Scientific breakthroughs in the areas of surveillance, mobile communications, and illicit drug detection are arming law enforcement agencies with increasingly sophisticated tools in their fight against illegal drug traffickers and other criminals.[77] This section will discuss the latest in surveillance devices.

Surveillance Vans

A vehicle specialist describes today's state-of-the-art surveillance van: "When talking about surveillance vehicles today, . . . we tend to think of a van whose interior looks slightly less complex than the bridge of Star Trek's USS Enterprise." He describes the ideal surveillance van as having the following equipment: power periscopes operated by a videogame-like joystick; six cameras to cover 360 degrees of the van's exterior, plus a periscope-mounted observer's camera; videotape decks to record everything happening on the street; quick-change periscope camera mounts; portable toilets; video printers; motion detection cameras; night vision cameras; cellular telephones; AM/FM cassette entertainment systems; CB radios, police radios, and police scanners; and other personalized equipment.[78]

Vehicle Tracking Systems

Vehicle tracking systems, also sometimes referred to as transponders, bumper beepers, or homing devices, enable officers and investigators to track a vehicle during surveillance. These systems are actually transmitters that can be placed on a subject's vehicle. The tracking system consists of the transmitter on the subject's vehicle and a receiver, which picks up the signal from the transmitter. There are three basic vehicle tracking systems on the market:

- *RF (radio frequency) tracking systems* are usually short-range systems that operate on a transmitted signal from a transmitter placed on the target vehicle. The receiver receives the signal using three or four antennas and determines the direction of the target vehicle.

- *Cellular tracking systems* work similarly to RF tracking systems but make use of transmitters that link to cellular telephone towers to track the target vehicle. Often, a cellular telephone serves as the transmitter signal that the tracking system employs. Tracking range is limited to the range of towers in the area.

■ *Global positioning system (GPS) tracking* makes use of GPS satellites to pinpoint the location of a target vehicle. GPS technology can locate a target vehicle anywhere in the world. Mapping software allows the target vehicle's location to be displayed on detailed street maps. Global positioning systems will be discussed further in this chapter.

Night Vision Devices

Among the most sophisticated surveillance devices in use today are enhanced **night vision devices**, including monocular devices small enough to hold in one hand, which can be adapted to a camera, video camera, or countersniper rifle. An expert describes the potential of such devices:

> Perhaps an automobile slowly approaches you in the dark with its lights out. With a normal night vision scope you can see it clearly—but you can't see through the windshield to see who's driving the car. Switch on the infrared (IR) laser, and it illuminates a spot through the windshield so you can identify the operator. In another case, at night a man lurks on the porch of a mountain cabin. In normal mode only the cabin and porch are clearly visible. The IR laser illuminates a spot to show the person waiting in the shadows.[79]

As far back as 1800, Sir William Herschel discovered the fact that every object emits thermal energy in the infrared (IR) wavelengths. His son, Sir John Herschel, took the first IR photographs of the sun approximately 40 years later. Infrared surveillance systems appeared toward the end of World War II as a covert way to observe the enemy at night. The Germans were the first to use IR systems as impressive nighttime tank killers. The Soviets developed IR systems in the 1960s and 1970s. Since then, these systems have been used by the United States during the Korean, Vietnam, and Gulf Wars.[80]

A more sophisticated form of infrared technology is thermal imaging (TI), which does not require any light at all. Traditional night vision equipment requires minimal light, such as from the moon. Thermal imaging not only can see through the night, it can also see through fog, mist, or smoke. It is especially useful in penetrating many types of camouflaging. Thermal imaging takes advantage of the infrared emission but does it passively, so only the user knows when it is in operation, not the subject.[81]

IR and TI systems can be mounted on police vehicles and pan possible subjects in all directions. Display screens can be mounted in patrol cars or investigators' cars, and joysticks can be used to direct the panning of the cameras.[82]

Law enforcement agents from U.S. Customs and Border Protection make extensive use of thermal imagers. These heat-sensing cameras detect the presence and location of a human; then an image intensifier makes the image clearer so that identification is possible. They are used for myriad law enforcement and investigatory purposes, such as search-and-rescue missions, fugitive searches, perimeter surveillance, vehicle pursuits, flight safety, marine and ground surveillance, structure profiles, disturbed surfaces, hidden compartments, environmental hazards, and officer safety. Other emerging uses of thermal imaging are the obtaining of more accurate skid-mark measures at a crash scene and the obtaining of evidence at a crime scene that cannot be observed with the human eye.[83] U.S. Customs and Border Protection also uses many other different night vision technologies in their duties including infrared cameras, night vision goggles, handheld searchlights with a band that reaches more than a mile, seismic and infrared sensors, and fiberscopes.[84]

Global Positioning Systems

Global positioning systems (GPS) are the most recent technology available to help law enforcement and investigators. The GPS is a network of twenty-four satellites used by the U.S. Department of Defense to pinpoint targets and guide bombs. They are equipped with atomic clocks and equally accurate position measuring telemetry gear. GPS has been used for everything from helping hikers find their way through the woods to guiding law enforcement officers to stolen vehicles.[85] When GPS is combined with geographic information systems (GIS) and automatic vehicle locations (AVL), officers can tell where they are on a map, and the dispatch center can continuously monitor the officers' location. Police departments can determine the location of each patrol vehicle without any communication from the officer who is driving. In a car wreck, such a system could automatically notify the dispatcher of a possibly injured officer at a specific location. Also, if an officer engages in a high-speed chase, such a system would provide the vehicle's location automatically; or, if an officer is injured in an encounter with a suspect, it can suggest that help be sent immediately.

GPS is also used by fleet operators in the private sector to track fleets for routing purposes and for rolling emergencies. It can be used to track the route over time and to monitor the vehicle's speed. GPS is also used for crime mapping, tracking, and monitoring the location of probationers and parolees around the clock.[86]

Surveillance Aircraft

Airplanes are being added to law enforcement's arsenal of surveillance devices. These aircraft do not require extensive landing fields and have proved to be very successful in surveillance operations. Fixed-wing aircraft and rotorcraft complement ground-based vehicles in hundreds of police agencies worldwide and aid search-and-rescue operations, surveillance, and investigative missions. Advanced electronic and computer systems for aircraft now include real-time video downlinks and low-light surveillance.[87]

★ ★ ★

ADVANCED PHOTOGRAPHIC TECHNIQUES

Photography has always played a major role in policing. Innovations and advanced techniques have increased this role. This section discusses mug shot imaging systems, age-progression photography, and composite sketching.

Mug Shot Imaging

Mug shot imaging is a system of digitizing a picture and storing its image on a computer so that it can be retrieved at a later time. The picture is taken with a video camera and is then transferred to a color video monitor, where it appears as an electronic image. When the image is filed, the operator enters the identifying data such as race, gender, date of birth, and the subject's case number. Using this system, victims of crimes can quickly view possible mug shots on a computer screen. The Orange County, Florida, sheriff's office is using a mug shot imaging system with a laser printer to produce "wanted" flyers for those sought on warrants. The pictures on these flyers are very clear, with excellent resolution.[88]

Major John J. Pavlis, who commands the Court Services Bureau of this sheriff's office, writes about other ways this system could also be used:

■ Photos of missing children or other missing people, once digitized, could be sent to all locations that have imagery workstations. Quality pictures could then be sent quickly to officers in the field.

■ Photos of all department employees could be digitized and kept in files for use in internal affairs investigation.

■ Photos of wanted individuals, once digitized, could be sent to other agencies via computer.[89]

A good example of mug shot imaging is the ALERT (Advanced Law Enforcement Response Technology) System. This system allows a photo of a subject to be transmitted from one police vehicle to others with the necessary equipment, giving officers an immediate view of a wanted suspect or a missing person.[90] In the first demonstration of this system in 1997, digital photographs were transmitted between two specially equipped police vehicles—one parked in College Station, Texas, the other sitting in an Alexandria, Virginia, hotel parking lot. The Alexandria Police Department spokesperson said it took about 20 seconds.[91]

Automated systems that capture and digitize mugshots can incorporate biometric facial recognition. The Los Angeles County Sheriff's Department installed a system that can take the composite drawing of a suspect or a

YOU ARE THERE! »

In Just 20 Minutes the Carjacker Was Identified by a Computerized Composite Photo System

Los Angeles County Sheriff's Sergeant William Conley used the latest technology to apprehend a carjacker who had stolen a 1997 Honda and beaten the vehicle's owner. Using the victim's recollection of the suspect's appearance, Conley entered those features into a computerized composite photo system to form a composite mug shot that was compared to thousands on file in the county's database of digitized photos. In just 20 minutes, Conley was able to pull up a likeness of the suspect as well as his address. Deputies arrested the man at his home; he subsequently confessed to the crime and is now serving a five-year sentence.

Source: "Adapted from: "No More Pencils, No More Books," *Law Enforcement News* (Jan. 31, 1998), p. 5.

video image of someone committing a crime and search it against its database of digitized mugshots. The department also intends to search for suspects on "Megan's Law CD," a photo database of registered sex offenders.[92]

Age-Progression Photographs

One of the newest innovations in police photography is the **age-progression photo.** The ability to recognize a face may be thwarted by the changes that naturally occur to the face with age. To counter this, two medical illustrators, Scott Barrows and Lewis Sadler, developed techniques for producing age-progression drawings in the early 1980s. Today, thanks to a computer algorithm, the same process that used to take hours using calipers, ruler, and pen can be completed in seconds. Developed by a colleague of Barrows and Sadler, the age-progression program systematizes the knowledge of the anatomy of 14 major bones and more than 100 muscles and how they grow. It also shows the change in relationship, over time, of 48 facial landmarks, such as the corners of the eyes and the nose. Computers have enabled the National Center for Missing and Exploited Children to arrange to have thousands of age-progressed pictures printed onto milk cartons and flyers.[93]

The FBI uses its own age-progression program for adult faces. The system allows artists to do such things as thin hair, add jowls, or increase wrinkles while maintaining the basic facial proportions. The FBI's software for aging children's faces allows pictures of parents and older siblings to be fused into photos of missing children to obtain a more accurate image.[94]

Composite Sketches

Police have for many years sought the assistance of forensic artists in preparing **composite sketches.** The FBI began to use composite sketching in 1920; other agencies had been using it even earlier. These portrait-style drawings generally require hours of interview, drawing, and revision.

YOU ARE THERE! »

Capture of John List through Age-Progression Photo

In 1987, the FBI's Newark, New Jersey, field office forwarded a request for forensic assistance to the Special Projects Section of the FBI Laboratory for age-enhanced photos of J. E. List, who had eluded detection since murdering his entire family 17 years previously.

The FBI produced age-enhanced photographs of List and forwarded them to the field office. The office then publicized an age-enhanced photograph in various national publications. A woman recognized her neighbor as List, who lived under the assumed name Robert P. Clark. She had seen List's age-enhanced photograph in a supermarket tabloid. The neighbor dared Clark's wife to confront her husband with the photo but the wife never did.

Two years later, in 1989, the television show *America's Most Wanted* featured a plaster bust, prepared by a forensic artist, that was based on the photograph of List. By this time List had moved to Midlothian, Virginia, a suburb of Richmond. Convinced that Clark was, in fact, John List, his former neighbor asked her son-in-law to call the FBI and provide investigators with List's new address. When agents confronted the man, he denied he was List. But fingerprints from a gun permit application filed a month before the slayings revealed the truth. List was arrested and returned to New Jersey where he was convicted of murder and sentenced to life in prison.

Source: Adapted from Gene O'Donnell, "Forensic Imaging Comes of Age," *FBI Law Enforcement Bulletin* (Jan. 1994), pp. 5–10.

YOU ARE THERE! »

Finding Missing Children through Age-Enhanced Photos

An investigator from Oakland, California, reached out across the United States and Canada with age-enhanced images of two missing brothers. After exhausting every lead, the investigator turned to the television program *Unsolved Mysteries.*

On the evening of the broadcast, hundreds of calls poured in from the Albuquerque, New Mexico, area. Authorities located the children in a trailer on the outskirts of town, where they lived with their mother and her new husband—a known drug dealer. The boys were returned to their father, who had not seen them in several years. Although the aged images of the boys were very accurate, the relentless determination of the investigator and the assistance of the public ultimately solved the case.

Source: Adapted from Gene O'Donnell, "Forensic Imaging Comes of Age," *FBI Law Enforcement Bulletin* (Jan. 1994), p. 9.

Today the FBI has converted its book of photographs, used for interviewing witnesses for composites, into hand-drawn images using forensic imaging. The hand-drawn images are entered into a computer, where they form the basis of a database that will automatically generate images similar to those that are hand drawn. Once the witness selects features from the catalog, the composite image appears on the computer screen in just a few minutes.[95]

Computer software can also allow officers to produce a digitized composite photo of a suspect based on the recollections of victims and witnesses. The resulting photo can then be compared with thousands of digital mug shots stored in the growing number of databases in jurisdictions all over the nation, including those states that now issue digitized photos on driver's licenses. Included in this software is a data bank of thousands of facial features from which witnesses select the ones that best fit their description of suspects. Software users, who need no formal artistic training, can adjust the composite by using a scanner to adjust the facial features chosen by the witness.[96]

Often, an artist is not even necessary. With practice, investigators can place the features on the screen and modify the image as the witness instructs. The system can be loaded into a laptop computer to further speed up the process by taking it directly to a crime scene. It can also be accessed via a modem hookup or put online, with an artist in another city available to prepare the composite while a witness views and suggests changes.

A new CD-ROM program, called "Faces, the Ultimate Composite Picture," has been developed that provides nearly 4,000 facial features that can be selected to create billions of faces. The designers used photos taken of approximately 15,000 volunteers, ages 17 to 60, to acquire images of hair, eyes, chins, and more. Instead of a police artist trying to coax the memory of an offender's face from a frightened victim, artists and even victims themselves can create photo-quality composites in about 30 minutes.[97]

There remains a controversy over the value of forensic artistry versus the use of digital imaging composite software. Hand-drawn sketches are seen as having the ability to include subtleties that cannot compare to composite software programs and can increase the number of unique facial features possible. Digital composites, on the other hand, can be made in the field immediately following an incident and printed out and dispersed to field units almost immediately. Hand-drawn sketches once completed can then be scanned into a digital imaging program.[98]

★ ★ ★

MODERN FORENSICS OR CRIMINALISTICS

The use of scientific technology to solve crime is referred to as **forensic science,** or **criminalistics.** The terms forensic science and criminalistics are often used interchangeably. Forensic science, the more general of the two terms, is that part of science applied to answering legal questions. It is the examination, evaluation, and explanation of physical evidence related to crime.[99]

Criminalistics is actually just one of several branches of forensic science. Others include pathology, toxicology, physical anthropology, odontology, psychiatry, questioned documents, ballistics, tool work comparison, and serology. In order to simplify the information in this chapter for the nonscience student, however, the word *criminalistics* will be used interchangeably with *forensic science.*

The California Association of Criminalists defines criminalistics as "that profession and scientific discipline directed to the recognition, identification, individualization, and evaluation of physical evidence by the application of the natural sciences to law-science matters."[100] Criminalistic evidence includes such clues as fingerprints, blood and blood stains, semen stains, drugs and alcohol, hairs and fibers, and firearms and toolmarks. Forensic technicians, forensic scientists, forensic chemists, or the more generic term, criminalists, generally specialize in one or more of the following areas: analysis of trace evidence, serology, drug chemistry, firearms/toolmarks, and questioned documents.

The purpose of criminalistics is to take physical evidence from a crime or a crime scene and to use it to (1) identify the person who committed the crime and (2) exonerate others who may be under suspicion. For example, was the revolver found on a suspect the one that fired the bullet found in the body of a murder victim? If so, did the suspect fire it? Criminalistic evidence also can be used to establish an element of the crime and reconstruct how the crime was committed.

In court, criminalistic evidence is presented via laboratory analysis by an expert prepared to interpret and testify to the scientific results, thus distinguishing forensic evidence from other forms of physical or tangible evidence such as stolen goods, articles of clothing, and other personal property.

In a study of criminalistic evidence and the criminal justice system, the National Institute of Justice discovered that the police are on average about three times more likely to clear (solve) cases when scientific evidence is gathered and analyzed; prosecutors are less likely to agree to enter into plea negotiations if criminalistic evidence strongly associates the defendant with the crime; and judges issue more severe sentences when criminalistic evidence is presented at trials.

The 1990s and the beginning of the 2000s have brought significant negative attention to the problems of crimes labs and scientific evidence. In 1994, the criminal trial of former football star Orenthal James (O. J.) Simpson for the brutal murder of his former wife, Nicole Brown, and her friend Ronald Goldman, was covered on national television and captured the attention of the world. The jury, despite overwhelming scientific evidence to the contrary, voted to acquit Simpson of all charges. The LAPD was accused of gross incompetence in its handling of the crime scene and forensic evidence.

As another example, in 1997, the Justice Department's inspector general reported that the FBI's renowned crime laboratory was riddled with flawed scientific practices that had potentially tainted dozens of criminal cases, including the bombing of the Federal Building in Oklahoma City and the original bombing of the World Trade Center in New York. The inspector general's findings resulted from an 18-month investigation that uncovered extremely serious and significant problems at the laboratory that had been a symbol of the FBI's cutting-edge scientific sleuthing.[101] The dramatic series of problems associated with the FBI and their alleged bungling of scientific evidence and criminal investigations led the national magazine *Time* to produce a cover article entitled, "What's Wrong at the FBI: The Fiasco at the Crime Lab."[102]

Also, in 2001, an Oklahoma City Police Department forensic scientist was accused of a series of forensic errors involving at least five cases in which she made significant errors or overstepped the acceptable limits of forensic science. In response, the Oklahoma governor launched a review of every one of the thousands of cases the scientist had handled between 1980 and 1993. In 12 of these cases the defendants were awaiting the death penalty, and in another 11 the defendants had already been put to death.[103]

Also, in 2003, DNA evidence in 64 criminal cases from Marion County, Indiana, has been attacked because of concerns that a laboratory technician may have cut corners.[104] There have also been laboratory problems in Houston, Texas, and other departments around the nation.

A professional society for the professionals dedicated to the application of science to the law is the American

YOU ARE THERE! »

Problems with Police Chemist Cast Doubt on Suspects' Guilt

Jeffrey Pierce was convicted of rape in 1986 on the basis of forensic evidence, including scalp hairs, pubic hairs, and semen samples, collected and analyzed by an Oklahoma City Police Department forensic scientist. In 2001, under a new state law, the Oklahoma Indigent Defense System won approval to submit the forensic evidence in the case for independent DNA testing. In April 2001, the preliminary results showed that the DNA taken from the rapist's hair did not match Mr. Pierce. In addition, an FBI analysis of the hair samples contradicted the scientist's original hair testimony. As a result of the new test results, Mr. Pierce was released from prison. The chemist, Joyce Gilchrist, was placed on administrative leave from her position.

Ms. Gilchrist analyzed forensic evidence like blood, hair, semen, and fibers from 1980 until she was promoted to a supervisory position in 1994. After the Pierce case revelations, the Oklahoma governor ordered a review into every felony conviction linked to analyses done by Ms. Gilchrist to make certain that no one else had been wrongly convicted. Among those hundreds of cases were 11 in which the defendant was executed and 12 in which the defendant was on death row. Additionally, the state gave the Oklahoma Indigent Defense System $725,000 to hire two attorneys and conduct DNA testing of any evidence analyzed by Gilchrist that led to a conviction. A preliminary FBI study of eight cases found that, in at least five, she had made outright errors or overstepped the acceptable limits of forensic science. Also, there are allegations that she withheld evidence from the defense and failed to perform tests that could have cleared defendants. Over the years, Ms. Gilchrist's work began coming under criticism from her peers, defense lawyers, and judges. She was reprimanded by one professional organization and expelled from another. Despite all the criticism, the local police and prosecutors never scrutinized her work.

Academy of Forensic Sciences (AAFS), whose membership includes physicians, criminalists, toxicologists, attorneys, dentists, physical anthropologists, document examiners, engineers, psychiatrists, educators, and others who practice and perform research in the many diverse fields relating to forensic science.

The Modern Crime Lab

There are more than 300 crime laboratories in the United States today. Eighty percent of them are located within police agencies. Most large police departments operate their own police laboratories. Smaller departments may contract out the use of large county crime labs, or state police crime labs. Some departments use the services of the FBI lab.[105]

Private (that is, nongovernment) labs are taking on greater importance in the U.S. legal system. Their analyses are increasingly being introduced into criminal and civil trials, often not only as evidence but also to contradict evidence presented by a prosecutor that was analyzed in a police lab.

As indicated in Table 14.1, most crime labs have the following sections which concentrate on different criminalistics evidence: ballistics, serology, criminalistics, chemistry, and documents analysis. Table 14.2 lists the different sections of a police lab used in the O.J. Simpson case. Services provided by the F.B.I. lab are listed in Exhibit 14.3.

Table 14.2	The O.J. Simpson Case and the Police Lab
Piece of Evidence	Section of Police Lab
Bloody glove	Serology
Hair from the blue watch cap	Criminalistics
Blood droplets	Serology
Shoeprint impressions	Criminalistics
O.J.'s apology letters to Nicole	Document analysis

BALLISTICS   The **ballistics** section of the crime lab conducts scientific analysis of guns and bullets. (Ballistics is the science of the study of objects in motion and at rest.) Examination of firearms evidence involves the identification, testing, and classification of firearms submitted to the lab. Technicians microscopically examine a bullet, cartridge case, or shotgun shell in order to determine whether it was fired from a specific firearm to the exclusion of any other firearm.

The ballistics examination provides the investigator with such information related to shooting cases as comparison of a spent (that is, fired) bullet to a suspect weapon; the type and model of weapon that may have been used in a shooting; the description and operating condition of a suspect weapon; the bullet trajectory of a bullet wound (the line of fire and firing position of the shooter); the possibility of an accidental discharge of a weapon as opposed to a purposeful discharge; the trigger pull (amount of force required to fire a particular weapon); the shooting distance in possible suicide cases; and restored serial numbers from a weapon in which the original serial numbers were altered or obliterated.

In order to determine whether a suspect firearm was used in a particular shooting, ballistics experts test fire a bullet from it into a tank of water known as a ballistics recovery tank. The spent bullet is then compared to the bullet taken from a victim or the crime scene using a ballistic comparison microscope. The rationale behind this testing is that bullets fired from a gun receive a mark on them from the lands and grooves of the barrel of the gun. These small individualistic markings are called striae. Bullets fired from the same gun should have similar markings.

In 1994, a computerized ballistics identification system that stores bullet "signatures" in a database was established in order to allow ballistics examiners to quickly determine whether a spent bullet may be linked to a crime. The new technology was hailed as a revolutionary advance in the painstaking, time-consuming science of ballistics. This new

Table 14.1	Police Forensic Laboratories
Major Section	Function
Ballistics	Examination of guns and bullets
Serology	Examination of blood, semen, and other body fluids
Criminalistics	Examination of hairs, fibers, paints, clothing, glass, and other trace evidence
Chemistry	Examination of drugs and alcohol
Document analysis	Comparison of handwriting
Specialty Sections	Function
Forensic toxicology	Analysis of poisons and other toxic substances in a person's body
Forensic pathology	Examination of dead bodies
Forensic physical anthropology	Examination of skeletal remains
Forensic odontology	Study of teeth formation
Forensic entomology	Examination of insect activity at death scenes

technique, called Bulletproof (a trademarked name), was used on a pilot basis by the Bureau of Alcohol, Tobacco, Firearms, and Explosives (ATFE) and the Washington, D.C., Metropolitan Police Department. "It's an amazing system," said Jack Killorin, the ATFE's chief spokesperson. "We're literally at a point where the technology is going to allow us to do the same kinds of things for the unique marks left on expended projectiles that's now being done for fingerprints."[106]

YOU ARE THERE! »

How Luminol Solved a Murder

In a rural community, the dismembered body of a dead woman—a waitress at a local restaurant—was found on the side of a road. The woman had been sexually assaulted and her body mutilated. Neither the victim's clothing nor a murder weapon could be found. There were no witnesses. Examination of the body revealed that the woman's arms and legs had been severed with either a saw or a large knife with a serrated edge.

Investigators were able to find out that a certain man, who frequented the restaurant where the woman worked, had been unsuccessfully attempting to date the woman. Witnesses told the police that on the night she disappeared, the man appeared to be agitated when she refused to wait on his table.

Several years later, investigators were able to gain further evidence against the man that gave them the necessary facts to obtain a search warrant. While executing the warrant, they found a large table saw in a workshop behind the suspect's house. A close examination of the saw led to the discovery of several hairs that appeared to be human. There was no blood visible on the saw or in the workshop.

The area was then sprayed with Luminol, a substance that, when sprayed on an area, produces a luminescence if blood had been there. Luminol is used in cases in which the police believe an attempt was made to hide or alter bloodstains. Based on the Luminol testing, it was determined that a wall in the workshop, the saw, and other items in the workshop contained enough traces of the victim's blood for identification.

The suspect was arrested and tried for the murder. He was found not guilty by reason of insanity. He remains confined to a state hospital.

Source: Adapted from: Dusty Hesskew, *Law and Order*, November 1991, pp. 31–33.

The software-driven Bulletproof system includes a customized microscope, a video camera, a specimen manipulator, an image digitizer, and a series of computers. The video camera and microscope record the unique, telltale markings and grooves made as a soft lead bullet is fired through a gun barrel, then digitally translate the information for computer storage and future analysis. The system alerts the operator if a possible match has already been entered into the data base by providing the examiner with a list ranked numerically. The examiner can then retrieve the stored image for a side-by-side visual comparison, eliminating the need to track down the original specimen. It also allows examiners to magnify any portion of the stored images.

Ballistics experts with the Metro-Dade, Florida, Police Department tested the system with 230 fired bullets—including five "unknowns." It searched more than 1,500 comparisons before homing in on the two matches for each unknown entered into the database—"hits" the system made during its first search. The same task—a manual search and comparison that usually involves rifling through drawers containing thousands of samples collected over time by police—would have taken years.

In addition to examining guns and bullets, firearms examiners can help investigators determine if a suspect recently fired a weapon. Investigators can use the dermal nitrate or paraffin test to determine if there is any gunpowder residue on a suspect's hands or clothing.

Another new computerized ballistics system, DRUG-FIRE, has also come on line. This system, which deals with the comparison of shell casings and bullets, is a national database giving firearms examiners the capability to link firearms and projectiles used in drive-by, serial, gang, and drug-related shootings across the nation. DRUGFIRE is maintained by the FBI.[107] The ATF maintains the Integrated Ballistics Information System (IBIS). Another of the ATF's weapons against illicit gun sales is ONLINE LEAD, a computerized database of the records the AFT keeps on more than a million guns seized in crimes. The system allows investigators to tell almost instantly whether the same person or store keeps showing up repeatedly as the source of a gun used in the commission of a crime. The data can then be sorted in ways that could lead to the identification of organized gun-distribution rings. By 2000, the various national law enforcement ammunition-tracing databases created since 1993 held more than 800,000 images of bullets and shell casings. More than 8,000 matches have been made in over 16,000 cases. Law enforcement officials say that computer ballistic imaging technology is the most important forensic advancement since the development of the comparison microscope over 70 years ago.[108]

A professional organization for persons interested in firearms and ballistics examinations is the Association of Firearms and Tool Mark Examiners (AFTE).

SEROLOGY   The crime lab's **serology** section analyzes blood, semen, and other body fluids found at a crime scene—obviously, important evidence in homicide and sexual assault cases. If blood on a suspect's shirt can be matched to the victim's blood, it can place the suspect at the crime scene. If semen found in a rape victim or on her clothing can be matched to a suspect's, it can link the perpetrator to the crime. Certain tests are useful in this process. The hemin crystal test will determine if a particular stain is actually blood. The precipitin test will determine if the blood is human, animal, or a mixture of both. Other tests can determine the specific blood type of the stain. Tests can also detect the existence of semen in stains and match the semen to a particular blood type. Laboratory tests can reveal if a stain is semen, if sperm is present, if the person was a secretor and, if so, establish blood groups.

The use of the chemical Luminol can produce evidence that blood was at a scene even if the area was meticulously cleaned. When Luminol is sprayed on an area, a luminescence or glow is produced if blood has been present. The development of DNA profiling or genetic fingerprinting, which will be discussed later in this chapter, has revolutionized the serology capacity of the crime lab.

CRIMINALISTICS   The criminalistics section of the crime lab studies myriad pieces of physical evidence that may connect a suspect to a crime or a crime scene. Often this evidence is crucial to the understanding of the crime scene and the identification of perpetrators. A perpetrator may unknowingly take something from a crime scene (for example, fibers from the victim's carpet may be found on the suspect's clothing) or may leave something at the crime scene (a shoe print in the mud outside the victim's window or marks from a tool used to pry open the victim's window).

The matching of samples of evidence found at the crime scene to a particular subject can be instrumental in the identification and successful prosecution of a suspect. The following are some examples of crime scene evidence that can be of value in an investigation.

Glass   Fragments of glass found at a crime scene can give an investigator a great deal of useful information. Traces of blood, clothing, hair, or fingerprints can be found on glass fragments. When a suspect is arrested, these same fragments can conclusively establish the individual's presence at the scene if they are also found on his or her clothing.

YOU ARE THERE! »

Criminalistics and Good Old Detective Work Find Suspect in Hit-and-Run

In January 2001, Marjorie Cordero, the wife of famed jockey Angel Cordero, was struck and killed by an auto driven by a hit-and-run driver as she crossed a road near her home in Greenvale, New York. Among the evidence left at the scene was a headlight and a 2-inch by 3-inch plate of fiberglass from a header panel of the car. Eventually this evidence enabled police to make an arrest in May 2001.

Criminalists from the Nassau County Police Department's Scientific Investigation Bureau analyzed the headlight and the fiberglass and determined that these pieces of evidence came from a 1987 or 1988 black Mercury Cougar. They ran that description through the state Department of Motor Vehicles database and found there were hundreds of cars of that model in the Nassau County and eastern Queens area. During the weeks that followed, investigators looked at more than 300 Mercury Cougars—staking out driveways, glancing at header panels—before zeroing in on the suspect's car. They obtained a warrant to search it, and the piece of black fiberglass recovered at the scene fit into the header panel of the suspect's car like a missing piece of a jigsaw puzzle.

Source: Adapted from: Oscar Corral, "Hit-Run Arrest: Cops Find Suspect in Incident That Killed Marjorie Cordero," *Newsday* (May 2, 2001), p. A3.

Glass can also tell an investigator how a crime was committed. Investigators can study conchoidal fractures, radial fractures, and concentric breaks to determine how the glass was broken, the angle at which a bullet was fired, and even which bullet was fired first through a window with multiple bullet holes.

Glass offers a wealth of information because of differences in the way it is made. It varies widely in physical and chemical composition, and has numerous impurities. Through the use of refractive index analysis, dispersion analysis, densities analysis, and spectrographic analysis, a crime lab can link glass from a suspect's clothing to that collected at a crime scene, or specify the type of vehicle from fragments collected at a hit-and-run accident.

YOU ARE THERE! ››

How Criminalistics Evidence Led to a Serial Killer: The Wayne Williams Case

For 22 months in 1980 and 1981, the residents of Atlanta, Georgia, lived in growing fear and outrage as a serial killer methodically hunted their children. The body count reached 30 victims before the killer was apprehended. The victims ranged in age from 7 to 28, and most were young males. Some were shot or strangled; others were stabbed, bludgeoned, or suffocated. All were African American. The deaths of so many black young people gave rise to a variety of theories and accusations, including belief in a plot by white supremacists to systematically kill all African American children. Atlanta became a city under siege and inevitably attracted the attention of the entire country, including the resources of the federal government.

It appeared the murders would never stop until one night, as police staked out a bridge over the Chattahoochee River, they heard a car on the bridge come to a stop, followed by a distinct splash caused by something being dropped into the river. They pulled Wayne B. Williams, 23, over for questioning and finally arrested him as a suspect in the child murder cases. Williams was found to be a bright young African American man who lived with his retired parents and involved himself in photography. A media and police "groupie," Williams would often listen on his shortwave radio and respond to ambulance, fire, and police emergency calls. He would then sell his exclusive pictures to the local newspapers. At age 18, he was arrested for impersonating a police officer. He spent one year at

Georgia State University but dropped out when he felt his "rising star" was moving too slowly.

Wayne's freelance work as a cameraman was never steady, and he began to focus his energies on music. As a self-employed talent scout, he eventually lured his victims into his control. He was known to distribute leaflets offering "private and free" interviews to African Americans between the ages of 11 and 21 who sought a career in music. At his trial, Williams was depicted as a man who hated his own race and wanted to eliminate future generations. He was described as a homosexual, or a bisexual, who paid young boys to have sex with him. A boy, age 15, claimed he had been molested by Williams, and several witnesses testified they had seen him with some of the victims.

Williams denied guilt, and the prosecution had only elaborate forensic evidence on which to base their case against him. The forensic evidence suggested a distinct link between Williams and at least 10 of the homicides and indicated a pattern surrounding the murders. The judge ruled the evidence admissible, and Williams was found guilty of murdering two of his older victims, Nathaniel Cater, 27, and Ray Payne, 21. Due to the nature of the circumstantial evidence, the judge sentenced Williams to two consecutive life sentences. He was eventually named as being responsible for 24 of the Atlanta slayings.

Source: Adapted from Eric W. Hickey, Serial Murderers and Their Victims (Pacific Grove, CA: Brooks/Cole, 1991), p. 168.

Hairs and Fibers   Hairs and fibers can be vital pieces of evidence. They can be found on a victim's clothing and in objects at the crime scene, such as bed linen, carpets, and furniture. Hair can tell the perpetrator's race and gender. Investigators can tell which part of the body the hair came from. They can see whether it was pulled out forcibly or fell out naturally, or if it was smashed with a blunt object or sheared with a sharp instrument.

Fibers are also very specific in the information they reveal. Because they vary dramatically in color, source, shape, and composition, they actually have more identifying characteristics than hair. A major case involving fibers as criminalistics evidence was the Atlanta child murders case in 1981 and 1982 in which approximately 30 young African American boys were murdered.

Fingernail Scrapings   Two types of evidence can be taken from fingernail scrapings and fingernails at a crime scene.

First, when fingernails are trimmed and collected from a victim, scrapings of hairs, fibers, skin, or blood from under the nail can reveal a variety of information about the crime and the perpetrator, especially in cases in which the victim struggled with the perpetrator. Second, when a broken fingernail is left at the scene and later compared to the nails of a suspect, it can include or exclude that person from the list of suspects. Much like fingerprints, nails are unique to each individual and rarely change through a person's life. Fingernails can be examined in much the same way as tool marks, bullets, and casings. Because the striae on nails are on the same scale as those found on fired bullets, the same type of comparison microscope is used.

Impressions and Casts   Impressions and casts taken of footprints at a crime scene can be very important to the investigator because no two people will wear shoes in precisely the same pattern or show damage in the same places.

Footprints can include or exclude a suspect, as well as tell investigators whether he or she was walking or running, was carrying a heavy object, or seemed unfamiliar with the area or unsure of the terrain.

CHEMISTRY   The chemistry section studies alcohol and possible drugs or controlled substances gathered in investigations and arrests. This section analyzes most of the cases handled by the crime lab.

The most commonly used standard for the degree of intoxication in criminal cases such as driving while intoxicated (DWI) or driving under the influence (DUI) is the measure of alcohol concentration in the suspect's blood. The alcohol concentration level determined by the lab is instrumental in the eventual prosecution of these alcohol-related crimes.

The chemistry section also tests substances believed to be in violation of the drug laws. Using chemical and other tests, chemists can identify the type of drug in a substance, as well as the percentage of a drug in a particular mixture.

Testing employees for the use of drugs and controlled substances is very common in private industries today. An expert in corporate drug testing has provided businesses that wish to test their employees for drug use with the following advice:

> It is critical that the company selects a laboratory carefully. It should pick the highest quality lab and make sure it is certified by the National Institute of Drug Awareness (NIDA). NIDA only certifies labs that are specialists in forensic drug testing. Personnel of a non-NIDA lab may not be trained in, or consistently follow procedures that will stand up in court. The lab should test a sample twice, first with a screening test, usually enzyme multiplied immunoassay testing (EMIT) and second, if the first test is positive, a confirmation test using gas chromatography/mass spectrometry (GC/MS) testing. The lab should be required to keep all positive samples for one year. Employees will appreciate knowing that if they ever test positive for substance abuse, the sample will be available for them to test independently at another lab.[109]

DOCUMENT ANALYSIS   The document analysis section studies handwriting, printing, typewriting, and the paper and ink used in the preparation of a document in order to provide investigators with leads on the identity of the writer. The document technician can compare requested handwriting exemplars (samples of the suspect's handwriting requested by the police) with the questioned document. This is a very important type of analysis in investigating ransom notes, anonymous letters, and possible forgeries.

Document analysis can also determine if there were any additions, changes, or deletions made. The paper on which a document is written can provide a number of clues to the investigator, such as the manufacturer, date of production, the pH and fiber composition, trace elements, and chemical elements including fibers, waxes, dyes, fluorescent brighteners, and fillers.

A private lab specializing in document analysis describes its services this way: "Scientific examination of anonymous letters; printed, written and typewritten documents to determine authenticity, alterations, and indented writing. Court qualified, expert witness and lecturer."[110]

The U.S. Secret Service has developed a new computer tool, the Forensic Information System for Handwriting (FISH). The innovative automated handwriting technology allows examiners to treat writing data with special mathematical programs and search them against previously entered writings. According to Richard A. Dusak, a document analyst for the U.S. Secret Service in Washington, D.C., "The Secret Service has been able to effect case solutions, consolidate investigative information and identify previously unknown individuals with the aid of the Forensic Information System for Handwriting."[111]

Exhibit 14.3	Services Provided by the FBI Laboratory

- Chemistry
- Computer analysis and response
- DNA analysis
- Evidence response
- Explosives
- Firearms and tool marks
- Forensic audio, video, and image analysis
- Forensic science research
- Forensic science training
- Hazardous materials response
- Investigative and prosecutive graphics
- Latent prints
- Materials analysis
- Questioned documents
- Racketeering records
- Special photographic analysis
- Structural design
- Trace evidence

Source: Adapted from: FBI Laboratory Services. Retrieved on May 15, 2001, from www.fbi.gov/hq/lab/org/labchart.htm.

The American Society of Questioned Document Examiners (ASQDE) is a professional organization for forensic document examiners.

Crime Lab Accreditation

Crime lab accreditation is designed to ameliorate some of the problems raised earlier in this chapter: mistakes made by our nation's crime labs.

The American Society of Crime Laboratory Directors (ASCLD) is a nonprofit professional society of crime laboratory directors, devoted to the improvement of crime laboratory operations through sound management practices. Its purpose is to foster the common professional interests of its members, to promote and foster the development of laboratory management principles and techniques. Its Crime Laboratory Accreditation Program is a voluntary program in which any crime laboratory may participate to demonstrate that its management, operations, personnel, procedures, equipment, physical plant, security, and personnel safety procedures meet established standards. The accreditation process is part of a laboratory's quality assurance program, which should also include proficiency testing, continuing education and other programs to help the laboratory give better overall service to the criminal justice system. The ASCLD maintains that the process of self-evaluation is in itself a valuable management tool for the crime laboratory director.[112]

The American Board of Criminalists (ABC) certifies lab employees. Because it ensures that lab personnel are all held to the same standard, certification helps analysts fend off courtroom salvos about their experience, background, and training.

Accreditation and certification is certainly needed in the nation's labs. According to Ron Urbanovsky, director of the Texas Department of Public Safety's statewide system of crime labs, "Part of the Simpson case fallout was that we've seen much longer and stiffer cross-examinations in court. Testimony that used to take two to three hours now takes eight to 12 hours, and it's grueling. We are asked to be perfect in a non-perfect world."[113]

★ ★ ★

DNA PROFILING/GENETIC FINGERPRINTING

DNA profiling, also called **genetic fingerprinting** or **DNA typing,** has shown much promise in helping investigators solve crimes and ensuring that those guilty of crimes are convicted in court. This section will cover the science of DNA, the history of DNA in U.S. courts, current DNA technology, DNA databases, and current DNA issues.

The Science of DNA

Deoxyribonucleic acid (DNA) is the basic building code for all of the human body's chromosomes and is the same for each cell of an individual's body, including skin, organs, and all body fluids. Because the characteristics of certain segments of DNA vary from person to person, it is possible to analyze certain substances such as blood, hair, semen, or body tissue and compare them to a sample from a suspect.

Forensic science consultant Richard Saferstein, former chief forensic scientist of the New Jersey State Police Laboratory and author of the text *Criminalistics: An Introduction to Forensic Science*, tells us that portions of the DNA structure are as unique to each individual as fingerprints. He writes that inside each of the 60 trillion cells in the human body are strands of genetic material called chromosomes. Arranged along the chromosomes, like beads on a thread, are nearly 100,000 genes. Genes are the fundamental unit of heredity. They instruct the body cells to make proteins that determine everything from hair color to susceptibility to diseases. Each gene is actually composed of DNA specifically designed to carry out a single body function. Scientists have determined that DNA is the substance by which genetic instructions are passed from one generation to the next.[114]

DNA profiling, also called genetic fingerprinting or DNA typing, has shown much promise in helping investigators

---

PATROLLING THE WEB

American Society of Crime Laboratory Directors
   http://www.ascld.org
American Board of Criminalistic**s**
   http://www.criminalistics.com
American Academy of Forensic Sciences
   http://www.aafs.org
FBI Crime Lab
   www.fbi.gov/hq/lab/labhome.htm
Association of Firearms and Tool Mark Examiners
   http://www.afte.org
FirearmsID.com
   http://www.firearmsID.com
American Society of Questioned Document Examiners
   http://www.asqde.org

YOU ARE THERE! >>

The Blooding—The First Use of DNA Typing in a Criminal Case

DNA profiling was the subject of *The Blooding,* by Joseph Wambaugh. This book describes the brutal beating and murder of two young girls in the English county of Leicestershire. Although the police had no clues to the identity of the killer, eventually, a young man, whom Wambaugh called only the "Kitchen Porter," confessed to the murder of the first girl and was also charged by the police with the second murder. Hoping to get physical evidence to corroborate this confession, the police asked Alec Jeffreys, a young geneticist at nearby Leicestershire University and the man who discovered genetic fingerprinting, to compare DNA samples from the victims with the DNA of the defendant.

After performing his testing, Jeffreys told the police that their suspect definitely did not commit the murders. He also told them that the same one man—not their suspect, however—was responsible for the murders of both girls.

The police decided to embark on a campaign of "blooding" to find the killer. They "requested" that all men within a cer-

tain age group who lived, worked, or had business in the area appear at the police station and submit to a venipuncture (the drawing of a vial of blood). The blood was then analyzed using Jeffrey's technique. But even after more than 4,500 men gave samples of their blood, the police had no suspects. Eventually it was discovered, over a few beers in a local pub, that a young man, Colin Pitchfork, had paid another young man, Ian Kelly, to appear and be "blooded" for him. When the police approached Pitchfork, he willingly confessed to both murders. His blood samples were then tested, and the DNA tests revealed that he was, indeed, the murderer of both girls.

It must be emphasized that the DNA analysis did not solve the case, although it did eliminate a suspect, and it did confirm guilt. Even if DNA profiling is fully accepted by the scientific community, it will never replace regular detective work.

Source: Based on Joseph Wambaugh, *The Blooding* (New York: William Morrow, 1989).

---

solve crimes and ensuring that those guilty of crimes are convicted in court. It is the examination of DNA samples from a body fluid to determine whether they came from a particular subject. For example, semen on a rape victim's jeans can be positively or negatively compared with a suspect's semen.

DNA is powerful evidence. Howard Safir, former police commissioner of New York City, described DNA typing as the primary tool for law enforcement in reducing crime in the 21st century. Elizabeth Devine, former supervising criminalist in the Scientific Services Bureau of the Los Angeles County Sheriff's Department says, "The power of what we can look for and analyze now is incredible. It's like magic. Every day we discover evidence where we never thought it would be. You almost can't do anything without leaving some DNA around. DNA takes longer than fingerprints to analyze but you get a really big bang for your buck."[115]

DNA profiling has been used in criminal investigations since 1987.[116] The FBI has made great progress in improving the technology since opening its first DNA typing laboratory in October 1988.

To show the further utility of DNA profiling, the U.S. Defense Department has established a repository of genetic information for the more than two million members of the U.S. armed forces as a way of identifying future casualties

of war. DNA is collected and stored by the Armed Forces Institute of Pathology. Formerly, unidentified dead were identified, if possible, by fingerprints and medical records. However, DNA can now be used to identify people from body parts, like a single leg.[117]

DNA technology in law enforcement has changed rapidly. The latest procedure—**PCR-STR** (polymerase chain reaction–short tandem repeat)—has several distinct advantages for law enforcement over **RFLP** (restricted fragment length polymorphism), an earlier DNA procedure. The newer PCR-STR requires only pin-size samples, rather than the dime-size samples needed for RFLP. Also with this process samples degraded or broken down by exposure to heat, light, or humidity can be analyzed; only two days are needed for laboratory analysis, compared to eight weeks for RFLP; and the entire DNA process can be automated, greatly reducing the possibility of human error.[118]

The DNA Analysis Unit of the FBI Laboratory analyzes body fluids and body fluid stains recovered as evidence in violent crimes. Examinations include the identification and characterization of blood, semen, saliva, and other body fluids using traditional serological techniques and related biochemical analysis. Once the stain is identified, it is characterized by DNA analysis using RFLP or PCR-STR techniques. The results of the analyses are compared to results obtained from known blood or saliva samples submitted from the victims or suspects.[119]

The unit also uses **mitochondrial DNA (MtDNA)** analysis, which is applied to evidence containing very small or degraded quantities of DNA from hair, bones, teeth, and body fluids. The results of MtDNA analysis are then also compared to blood or saliva submitted from victims and suspects.

Another current DNA innovation is **CODIS (Combined DNA Index System)**. CODIS contains DNA profiles obtained from subjects convicted of homicide, sexual assault, and other serious felonies. Investigators are able to search evidence from their individual cases against the system's extensive national file of DNA genetic markers.[120]

CODIS provides software and support services so that state and local laboratories can establish databases of convicted offenders, unsolved crime scenes, and missing persons. It allows these forensic laboratories to exchange and compare DNA profiles electronically, thereby linking serial violent crimes, especially sexual assaults, to each other, and to identify suspects by matching DNA from crime scenes to convicted offenders. As of 2001, CODIS was installed in 104 laboratories in 43 states and the District of Columbia. (All 50 states have enacted DNA database laws requiring the collection of a DNA sample from specified categories of convicted offenders. Most currently take samples from convicted felons, but they vary on which types of felons. Some states are trying to pass legislation to take samples from all persons charged with a felony; some are even considering collecting them from people convicted of misdemeanors.) More than 500 federal, state, and local DNA analysts have received CODIS training. The FBI laboratory has even provided CODIS software and training to criminal justice agencies in other countries. The **National DNA Index System (NDIS)** is the final level of CODIS and supports the sharing of DNA profiles from convicted offenders and crime scene evidence submitted by state and local forensic laboratories across the United States.[121]

The current version of CODIS contains two indexes: a Convicted Offender Index and a Forensic Index. The former contains DNA profiles from those convicted of violent crimes, and the latter contains DNA profiles acquired from crime scene evidence. The CODIS system is also separated into different segments, from the local to the national level. The system stores the information necessary for determining a match (a specimen identifier, the sponsoring laboratory's identifier, the names of laboratory personnel who produced the profile, and the DNA profile). To ensure privacy, it does not include such things as social security numbers, criminal history, or case-related information.[122]

The FBI maintains a national database, whereas each state has one designated database location, and each participating locality maintains its own local database. Thus, it is possible for each locality to cross-reference a DNA profile against other DNA profiles across the country. Furthermore, it is likely that an international DNA database may be implemented, allowing law enforcement officials to identify suspects both nationally and internationally.

In March 2000, the FBI reported that the CODIS program has assisted in more than 1,100 investigations in 24 states. As of 2001, CODIS contained DNA profiles from approximately three hundred thousand convicted offenders. DNA evidence has been used to clear suspects. By 1999, more than 61 people had been exonerated as a result of DNA typing.[123]

New technologies regarding DNA evidence emerge constantly. The latest is Low Copy Number (LCN) DNA, which attempts to provide unprecedented levels of detection by obtaining DNA profiles from objects that were simply touched by a suspect. LCN DNA can be obtained from as little as a fingerprint or residue from the lip of a drinking glass. However there are still some complications and limitations of this technology. The DNA could be transferred from one person to another (for example, through a handshake) and then to an object. This calls into question the reliability of placing a person at a crime scene through this type of analysis. More research is being conducted of this promising technology to reduce the dangers of contamination.[124]

The History of DNA in U.S. Courts

The use of DNA in U.S. courts has an interesting history. (See Table 14.3.) The process has gained popularity at an exponential rate since its introduction in the United States in 1987. It was initially hailed as "foolproof" and 99 percent positive. Most of the positive claims about DNA profiling were based on the testimony of interested parties, such as prosecutors and scientists from companies involved in DNA testing. Defense attorneys were often unable to combat DNA evidence in court or to find experts to testify against it. Generally, defendants, when confronted with a DNA match, pleaded guilty in a plea bargain—until the Castro case.

On February 5, 1987, 23-year-old Vilma Ponce and her 2-year-old daughter were stabbed to death in their apartment in the Bronx, New York. There were few leads until police arrested the building's superintendent, Joseph Castro, and found some dried blood in the grooves of his watch. When questioned, he said the blood was his own.

Prosecutors sent the blood from the watch, samples of the victims' blood, and a sample of Castro's blood to a firm called Lifecodes for testing.

Lifecodes declared a match between the DNA from the blood on the watch and the DNA from Vilma Ponce's blood. Defense attorneys Barry Scheck and Peter Neufeld located experts who agreed to testify against the admission of the DNA typing evidence. For 12 weeks the evidence was argued before New York Supreme Court Acting Justice Gerald Sheindlin, who listened to experts from both sides. The experts for the defense were able to uncover such serious blunders committed by Lifecodes in its performance of the tests that the prosecution's expert witnesses recanted their position. In an unprecedented move, two expert witnesses for the defense and two for the prosecution issued a joint statement:

> The DNA data in this case are not scientifically reliable enough to support the assertion that the samples . . . do or do not match. If these data were submitted to a peer-reviewed journal in support of a conclusion, they would not be accepted. Further experimentation would be required.[125]

Ultimately, Justice Sheindlin ruled the evidence of the match inadmissible, and the case against Castro was dismissed. (You may remember the names of the two attorneys in this case: Scheck and Neufeld. They later played a pivotal role in the acquittal of O. J. Simpson.)

The main problem with DNA profiling at the Castro stage was that it could not pass the **Frye test**. The Frye Test was based on the court case *Frye* v. *United States*, in which the court ruled that novel scientific evidence will not be accepted into evidence until it has gained general acceptance in the particular scientific discipline in which it belongs.[126] Although DNA was accepted by some courts and rejected by others, its reliability had to be held in question until it gained general acceptance by the scientific community.[127]

A 1992, a unanimous decision by the U.S. Court of Appeals for the Second Circuit, one of the most influential federal appeals courts, began to change court rulings nationwide on DNA evidence. The court approved the use of DNA evidence and affirmed the kidnapping conviction of Randolph Jakobetz for kidnapping and rape. The evidence on which he was convicted involved an FBI analysis of the DNA from semen recovered from the woman and matched to Jakobetz from a blood test.

Legal experts have said that this decision was the first clear-cut guidance from the federal appellate bench on the use of DNA fingerprinting. Previously, many courts would not allow DNA evidence to be used at a trial unless it was presented first at a pretrial hearing. Under the new ruling, courts could allow DNA evidence without such hearings and let the jury determine the worth of the evidence. In this case, the court seems to have overruled the Frye test by ruling that "scientific evidence was like any other and that it could be admitted if its 'probativeness, materiality and reliability' outweighed any tendency to mislead, prejudice and confuse the jury."[128]

The Jakobetz case was followed by two other important U.S. Supreme Court cases, *Daubert* v. *Merrell Dow Pharmaceuticals, Inc.* (1993) and *General Electric Co.* v. *Joiner* (1997), which further undermined the restrictive Frye test by ruling that federal courts should generally allow admission of all relevant evidence. This ruling applied to all evidence in civil and criminal cases, including DNA evidence and other forensic science issues.[129]

In 1992, after a two-year study, a 12-member panel consisting of forensic, legal, and molecular biology experts endorsed DNA profiling in the identification of suspects in criminal cases. Conducted under the auspices of the National Academy of Sciences, the study concluded that DNA fingerprinting is a reliable method of identification for use as evidence in criminal trials, but it found problems with current methods of sampling, labeling, and general quality assurance. The panel of experts recommended that accreditation be required of forensic laboratories performing this work.[130]

The panel also advised the courts to consider the reliability of new DNA typing techniques on a case-by-case basis when determining the admissibility of DNA evidence. The panel's report, *DNA Technology in Forensic Science*, called for the creation of a national DNA profile data bank that would contain DNA samples and document information on the genetic makeup of felons convicted of violent crimes. This report led to the creation of CODIS, described earlier.

The National Commission on the Future of DNA Evidence was created in 1998 at the request of the U.S. Attorney General. Its mission is to examine the future of DNA evidence and how the Justice Department could encourage its most effective use. One of the duties of the commission is to submit recommendations to the Attorney General that will ensure more effective use of DNA as a crime-fighting tool and foster its use through the entire criminal justice system. Other focal areas for the Commission's consideration include crime scene investigation and evidence collection, laboratory funding, legal issues, and research and development.[131]

Current Technology

In 2000, the National Commission on the Future of DNA Evidence reported:

> The great variability of DNA polymorphisms has made it possible to offer strong support for concluding that DNA from a suspect and from the crime scene are from the same person. Prior to this . . . it was possible to exclude a suspect, but evidence for inclusion was weaker than it is now because the probability of a coincidental match was larger. DNA polymorphisms brought an enormous change. Evidence that two DNA samples are from the same person is still probabilistic rather than certain. But with today's battery of genetic markers, the likelihood that two matching profiles came from the same person approaches certainty.[132]

Although the evidence that two samples came from the same person is statistical, the conclusion that they came from different persons is certain (assuming no human or technical errors). As a result of DNA testing, more than 70 persons previously convicted of capital crimes and frequently having served long prison terms have been exonerated. And there are everyday

Table 14.3	Milestones in the Development of DNA Testing
Date	**Development**
1900	A, B, O blood groups discovered
1923	*Frye v. United States*
1983	PCR first conceived by Kerry Mullis
1984	First DNA profiling test developed by Alec Jeffreys
1986	First use of DNA to solve a crime and exonerate an innocent subject (Colin Pitchfork case)
1986	First acceptance of DNA testing in a U.S. civil court
1987	First use of DNA profiling in a U.S. criminal court
1987	Castro case
1992	Publication of *DNA Technology in Forensic Science*
1992	Jakobetz case
1993	*Daubert v. Merrell Dow Pharmaceuticals, Inc.*
1997	*General Electric Co. v. Joiner*
1998	Creation of the National Commission on the Future of DNA Evidence
2000	Publication of *The Future of Forensic DNA Testing*

Source: Adapted from National Institute of Justice, *The Future of Forensic DNA Testing: Predictions of the Research and Development Working Group* (Washington, DC: National Institute of Justice, 2000); Norah Rudin, "Forensic Science Timeline." Retrieved on May 12, 2001, from http://www.forensicdna.com/Timeline.htm.

YOU ARE THERE! »

New State DNA Data Bank Leads to Arrest in Three-Year-Old Rape

In the early morning hours of December 21, 1999, a female television producer was attacked by a man who forced her down a stairwell in a building on a busy street in midtown Manhattan. He then raped her and tried to force her to withdraw money from a nearby automated teller machine before fleeing with her watch and umbrella.

In May 2001, a suspect Lashange LeGrand, 34, a convicted robber who had been released from prison three years earlier, was arrested by the NYPD and arraigned on rape, robbery and sodomy charges. The arrest resulted from information provided to the police from the state police laboratory, which matched DNA from a semen sample on the victim's blouse to a DNA sample taken from LeGrand the previous year under a state law that requires certain felons, particularly violent ones, to submit DNA samples even after their release.

The state law took effect in December 1999, and in less than two years the state collected 82,000 samples from convicted offenders and registered 53 matches for previously unsolved crimes.

At the time of the attack LeGrand, who has eight aliases and an arrest record stretching back more than a decade on charges including grand larceny, burglary, and drug possession, was still on parole from a 1991 robbery conviction for which he had served seven years. Apparently aware of the increasing collection of DNA evidence, the suspect used tissues in an effort to wipe up after the attack, but the police were still able to retrieve the semen sample.

exculpations, since about a quarter of analyses lead to exclusions.

The Commission made the following conclusions and projections for the near future:[133]

- We emphasize that current state-of-the-art DNA typing is such that the technology and statistical methods are accurate and reproducible. . . .

- Methods of automation, increasing the speed and output and reliability of STR methods, will continue. In particular we expect that portable, miniature chips will make possible the analysis of DNA directly at the crime scene. This can be telemetered to databases, offering the possibility of immediate identification. . . .

- By 2005, the CODIS database should be well established, with more than 1 million convicted felon profiles on file. Interstate comparisons will be commonplace and international comparisons increasingly feasible. . . . Greater automation and higher throughput approaches will help reduce the backlog. . . . We also expect integration of computers and Internet with analytical techniques to permit direct transmission of test data between laboratories. . . .

- By 2010, we expect portable, miniaturized instrumentation that will provide analysis at the crime scene with computer-linked remote analysis. This should permit rapid identification and, in particular, quick elimination of innocent suspects.

- In the future, it is likely that an increasing number of suspects will be identified by data-based searches.

YOU ARE THERE! »

CODIS Case Highlights

Using CODIS, the Illinois State Police Laboratory linked a 1999 solved sexual assault case to three other sexual assaults in which the suspect was previously unknown. The 1999 case involved a sexual assault on two female college students who were unable to identify the offender. Police, however, were able to develop a suspect from witnesses' descriptions and circumstantial evidence. CODIS matched this suspect's DNA profile to three other cases that occurred in 1994 and 1995.

In another case, a DNA profile developed by the Virginia Division of Forensic Science in Richmond resulted in the resolution of an unknown subject rape case. In March 1997, a man raped and sodomized a woman after breaking into her home. The police had no suspects in the case but were able to retrieve biological evidence from the crime scene. This evidence was sent to the Richmond laboratory, where a DNA profile was developed and searched in CODIS. In March 1999, CODIS linked the crime to a profile in Virginia's Offender Index. At the time of the identification, the offender was serving time in a New York prison for robbery, with a prior conviction in Virginia for grand larceny.

Source: Adapted from Federal Bureau of Investigation, *CODIS Case Highlights,* pp. 1–2. Retrieved on June 2, 2001, from http://www.fbi.gov/hq/lab/org/systems.htm.

DNA Databases and Current Issues

Initially, DNA fingerprinting or profiling was used to confirm the identity of an individual already suspected of committing a specific crime, but now the use of offender DNA databases has altered the way a criminal investigation can proceed. Very small amounts of DNA recovered from a crime scene can be used to link an otherwise unknown suspect to the crime. The existing offender DNA databases have been upheld over Fourth Amendment challenges, because of the minimal privacy expectations offenders have due to their status as offenders.

Some believe that the growing practice of using voluntary DNA samples to link the donor to other unsolved crimes should be curbed. However, police and prosecutors defend the strategy, claiming that it allows them to take full advantage of the technology to solve crimes. Darrell Sanders, chief of police in Frankfort, Illinois, says, "If we get someone's DNA legally, how can we justify giving him a free pass on something else he once did?" Defense attorneys, such as Barry Scheck, foresee the potential for abuse: "As it is, there's nothing to stop police from setting up a DNA data base of 'the usual suspects'."[134]

Another issue is the implementation of a universal DNA database containing DNA fingerprints from every member of society. Some believe this would not withstand constitutional scrutiny because free persons have no diminished expectations of privacy, as prisoners do. In addition, some feel that allowing a universal DNA database would allow the government to intrude without suspicion on an individual's privacy.[135]

A 2003 report by the Executive Office of the President of the United States praised DNA technology for becoming increasingly vital to identifying criminals, clearing suspects, and identifying missing persons. However, it acknowledged that the current federal and state DNA collection and analysis needs improvement because crime labs are overwhelmed and ill equipped to deal with the influx of DNA samples and evidence. President Bush has proposed federal funding for the improvement of the use of DNA in these labs.[136]

The Executive Office of the President's report indicating that crime labs are overwhelmed and ill equipped to deal with the influx of DNA samples and evidence was followed by the *National Forensic DNA Study Report,* commissioned by the National Institute of Justice, which concluded that there is a staggering backlog of either nonsubmitted or nonanalyzed biological evidence that could aid in the solving of crimes, sitting untested in police departments and crime labs.[137] Specifically, the report stated that:

- The number of rape and homicide cases with possible biological evidence that local law enforcement agencies *have not submitted to a laboratory for analysis* is over 221,000 (52,000 homicide cases and 169,000 rape cases).

- The number of property crime cases with possible biological evidence that local law enforcement agencies *have not submitted to a laboratory for analysis* is over 264,000.

- The number of *unanalyzed* DNA cases sitting in state and local crime laboratories is more than 57,000.

- Total crime cases with possible biological evidence either still in the possession of local law enforcement or backlogged at forensic laboratories is over one-half million.

The report indicated that the reason so many cases have not been submitted to laboratories for analysis is that the law enforcement agencies did not realize that DNA was a tool for crime investigation or that they were poorly funded. It also found that the crime labs with unanalyzed cases indicated that they were overworked, understaffed, and insufficiently funded.

Other countries are making effective use of DNA technology in crime fighting. The National DNA Data Bank of Canada (NDDB) became operational in June 2000. Since then, the NDDB has helped to revolutionize the way crimes are investigated in Canada. The NDDB maintains DNA profiles in two indexes, the Crime Scene Index (CSI) and the Convicted Offender Index (COI). As of January 2003, the Canadian system has made over 452 matches between crime scenes and convicted offender samples and 29 crime scene to crime scene matches.[138] Australia, also, has been very successful using DNA to investigate their serious crimes by using its National Crime Investigation DNA Database.[139]

DNA TRAINING   The National Commission on the Future of DNA Evidence has produced a CD-ROM, *What Every Law Enforcement Officer Should Know about DNA Evidence*. It is designed to teach law enforcement officers about the best practices for the identification, preservation, and collection of DNA evidence at various types of crime scenes. The training CD-ROM details collection and packaging procedures for DNA evidence and offers an overview of the history of the use of DNA evidence in criminal trials. Lessons teach how a crime scene is processed for DNA evi-

YOU ARE THERE! »

Royal Canadian Mounted Police Extends DNA Technology to Trees

The Royal Canadian Mounted Police (RCMP) Forest Crime Investigation Unit is working with researchers in British Columbia to develop DNA identification systems that would allow them to source stolen trees back to the stumps left in the ground.

The British Columbia government estimates that lost taxes from foresters' stolen downed trees are in excess of $20 million a year; the value of the stolen timber is much higher. The forest sector and its related activity is the leading industry in British Columbia and many towns and cities rely directly on the sector. But here is the problem: if the RCMP gets a call that somebody's cutting, they can do surveillance and try to get the person in the act. But if they don't actually observe the cutting, they have to physically match the wood to the site—that is, unload a truck and try to fit the tree back together. If they can't determine where the wood came from, they can't charge anyone with theft.

Using DNA to identify lumber could make life much tougher for lumber thieves, but the technology is in its infancy. DNA evidence pertaining to wood has not yet been entered into a court of law in Canada.

Source: Adapted from Alan Harman, "RCMP Extends Technology to Trees," *Law and Order* (Nov. 2000), pp. 58–61.

dence; how to collect, package, and transport DNA evidence; identifying the sources, locations, and the limitations of DNA evidence; the importance of elimination and reference samples; and learning how to use the CODIS to solve crimes. The training also covers applications of DNA evidence at specific types of crime scenes, including a homicide, a sexual assault, a burglary, and a violent crime. Students enter each crime scene as an evidence technician and are given choices about how to handle DNA evidence. After completing the CD, students take a test.[140]

In 2001, the National Institute of Justice released a bulletin, *Understanding DNA Evidence: A Guide for Victim Service Providers*. This discusses the important role forensic DNA evidence plays in solving criminal cases, particularly brutal sexual assaults and homicides, and advises victim service providers that they need to know the significance of DNA evidence in the cases they are dealing with. The bulletin explained how to identify DNA evidence and counsel victims on its value in apprehending and convicting offenders. The bulletin included three case studies that reflect the power of a DNA match and reveal the complexities involved in the criminal justice system.[141]

DNA WARRANTS   In October 1999, the Milwaukee, Wisconsin, county prosecutor made an innovative legal move regarding DNA in an effort to prevent the statute of limitations from expiring in a case against an unknown person suspected in a series of kidnappings and rapes. The prosecutor filed a "John Doe" warrant, not uncommon in cases where a suspect's identity is unknown. What made this case different was the means used to identify the suspect. The warrant identifies the assailant as "John Doe, unknown male with matching deoxyribonucleic acid (DNA) at five locations."[142] Since this happened, DNA warrants have been used a great deal.

In 2003, New York City criminal justice officials announced a sweeping, innovative plan, termed the "John Doe Indictment Project," in which prosecutors, investigators, and scientists will seek to match the DNA profiles of unknown sexual offenders in the most serious unsolved sex attacks to specific DNA profiles in the state DNA known-offender data bank, then file John Doe warrants before they have linked a name to the DNA or arrested a suspect. The first 600 cases for which evidence will be reviewed concern attacks in 1994. If the indictments are completed before the statute of limitations clock (10 years) runs out they can arrest and prosecute the offender anytime in the future.[143]

★ ★ ★

BIOMETRIC IDENTIFICATION

Fingerprints and palmprints are only two of the forms of **biometric identification.** Biometric systems use a physical characteristic to distinguish one person from another. Other systems involve the face, the eyes, the hands, and the voice. A 1998 study of the accuracy, applications, costs, legal issues, and privacy issues associated with potential uses concluded that biometric systems have enormous potential for public and private organizations alike.

Biometric systems serve two purposes: identification and authentication. They can help identify criminals, prevent welfare fraud, aid security in corrections, support border control, conduct criminal background checks, and establish identities on driver's licenses.[144]

Biometric systems already on the market can identify and authenticate people with a high degree of accuracy. Fingerprints remain the best choice for applications involving large numbers of users. Iris-based systems (which scan the human eye) may equal or exceed fingerprints in accuracy, but the limited number of vendors and lack of precedent for iris recognition make them less attractive. Hand-geometry systems have proven themselves in physical control, particularly in prisons, which require high levels of accuracy and security. Voice recognition proves least accurate but might be the best alternative to verify someone's identity over the phone. Facial-recognition systems create opportunities to identify people unobtrusively and without their cooperation, as in video surveillance, and they can be added to digital photo systems used for mug shots or driver's licenses.

Facial identification technology and its potential impact on crime control were examined in a futures study that focused on the history of identification systems, the nature and status of the technology, and privacy issues. The study noted that facial recognition technology compares a real-time picture from a video camera to digital pictures in a computerized database to identify a person. It has the potential for both access security and the identification and apprehension of criminals.[145]

A project funded by the National Institute of Justice developed a surveillance system using real-time face recognition technology to increase the usefulness of currently existing CCTV-compatible surveillance software. The system is a state-of-the-art, automated facial recognition surveillance system that could be extremely useful to law enforcement, intelligence personnel, and CCTV control room officers.[146]

British police plan to automatically monitor closed-circuit surveillance video cameras with facial-recognition software. In Britain, more than 200,000 video cameras are used for surveillance, many watching streets and shopping areas. In Newham, a borough of London, the local police use a system that includes 140 street cameras and 11 mobile units. A computer will monitor video cameras set to watch for known criminals. When the system recognizes someone, it will alert the police.[147]

In July 2001, Tampa police started using security cameras to scan the city's streets for people wanted for crimes. The computer software program used, *FaceIt*, was linked to 36 cameras scanning crowds in Tampa's nightlife district, matching results against a database of mug shots of people with outstanding arrest warrants. Tampa is the first city in the country to use this technology on such a wide basis. A city spokesperson said, "It's a public safety tool, no different than having a cop walking around with a mug shot." He added that on a local street of restaurants, nightclubs, and stores crowded with 20,000 people, "Your expectation of privacy is somewhat diminished, anyway." But the legal director for the American Civil Liberties Union of Florida disagreed, saying it amounted to subjecting the public to a digital lineup. "This is yet another example of technology outpacing the protection of people's civil liberties. It has a very Big Brother feel to it."[148]

Using the *FaceIt* software, police officers in a nondescript command center in a neighborhood building monitor a bank of television screens filled with faces in the crowd, zooming in on individuals and programming the equipment to scan them. The computer breaks down each facial image into something similar to a map, checking 80 reference points. If the system matches more than a dozen of those points against an image in its database, it indicates a match. The system operator then determines if the images are similar enough to radio a uniformed officer who investigates and makes an arrest if appropriate. The system doesn't catalogue anything; if a face is not in the database, the system does not store it.

A similar system was used at the Super Bowl in January 2001 at Raymond James Stadium in Tampa. During the game, the computer spotted 19 people in the crowded stadium who had outstanding warrants. In the intense security efforts following the September 11, 2001, terrorist at-

tacks, *FaceIt* technology has been used extensively to screen visitors to federal facilities. A recent example was its use to screen visitors to Liberty Island in New York, the site of the Statue of Liberty. The technology attempted to match the faces of visitors waiting to board the ferry to the island with its terrorist database.

★ ★ ★

VIDEOTAPING

The use of handheld compact videotaping equipment is an example of the growing use of technology as a policing tool. For many years, the police have also been using videotape in investigations, undercover operations, and recording the confessions of suspects.

Two examples show the potential of the use of videotaping in police work. The Franklin County, Ohio, Sheriff's Office and the Columbus, Ohio, Police Department were the recipients of several video cameras donated by insurance companies and Mothers Against Drunk Drivers (MADD). The cameras are mounted to the dashboards of police cars. When an officer sees a vehicle that appears to be operated by an alcohol-impaired driver, the officer begins to record the suspect's driving and notes on tape the location and the circumstances raising suspicions of drunk driving. When the vehicle is stopped, the officer approaching the car wears an activated wireless microphone that is able to record conversations up to 500 feet from the camera. The videotape provides corroborating evidence to the officer's testimony.[149]

The other example of a promising application of videotaping involves departments equipping its patrol vehicles with video recorders. These cameras automatically record everything said or done within their range. The system was originally intended to aid in drug interdiction cases, in prosecuting alcohol-impaired drivers, and in accident investigations. However, the police discovered that the video cameras provided reliable, unbiased evidence in citizen complaint cases. In one case, a trooper was accused of being rude and using profanity during a traffic stop. The videotape proved that the charges were unfounded. In another case, a trooper was accused of shooting an unarmed motorist. The videotape revealed that the trooper had issued

©AP Photo/Visionics

FaceIt® surveillance software works with security cameras to quickly scan thousands of faces at places like town centers, airports, and border crossings. The software examines 80 facial characteristics to compare a person's unique "faceprint" to a database of suspected criminals. If 12 of the features match up, an alarm is sounded. What benefits or drawbacks do you see in this system?

at least 26 warnings for the person to drop his gun before the officer fired. The videotape can also confirm wrongdoing by an officer. In one case in which a trooper was accused of raping a motorist he had stopped for a traffic violation, the videotape was admitted into evidence against him.[150]

There have been numerous cases of officers catching their own assault, and several, their own felonious death, on the patrol vehicle's video recorder. One, on January 3, 1997, involved Deputy Sheriff Henry Huff, a member of the Walton County, Georgia, Sheriff's Office, who was shot at point-blank range during a traffic stop by a 9mm-wielding 16-year-old. Since Huff's squad car was equipped with an automatic surveillance camera, the entire incident was recorded on videotape. Fortunately, despite being shot twice in the chest, Huff was spared serious injury by his bullet-resistant vest and has since returned to duty.[151]

★ ★ ★

ROBOTS

Robots have been available to law enforcement since the early 1970s. However, because of their high cost, they were seldom purchased for law enforcement use. Since the mid-1980s, robots have become very popular in police departments for bomb disposal.

The bomb robots can be operated by an electric cable or by radio control. They can take X-rays and photographs of packages, search suspect locations, and place explosive devices into a transport vessel, thus keeping bomb personnel safely away from the immediate area. Robots can have closed-circuit video systems, audio systems, and spotlights. Some of the more sophisticated robots can climb stairs, cross ditches, and knock down doors.[152]

FEAR OF TECHNOLOGY BY CIVIL LIBERTARIANS

Civil libertarians fear that technological developments, such as improved computer-based files and long-range electronic surveillance devices, will give the police more power to intrude into the private lives of citizens. A Congressional report found reason to believe that DNA fingerprinting may work against a suspect's reasonable expectation of privacy.[153]

Even the magazine *Popular Mechanics* worries about the civil liberties issues of enhanced police technology:

> Along with the advantages, however, has come new potential for abuse. For example, the same computer databases that make AFIS possible could also be used for random searches that might focus suspicion on people because they have stayed in a homeless shelter, or because they fall into certain categories based on age, race or other discriminatory criteria.[154]

The noted civil liberties lawyer Alan M. Dershowitz, of Harvard University Law School, in *Taking Liberties: A Decade of Hard Cases, Bad Laws, and Bum Raps*, comments on the 1986 U.S. Supreme Court case *California* v. *Ciraolo*.[155] In this case, the Court ruled that evidence obtained by the police's flying over and photographing a person's property was not a violation of the person's Fourth Amendment rights. Dershowitz says, "You can be sure that our Constitution's Founding Fathers would have been appalled at this breach of privacy. A person's home—whether it be a walled estate, a plantation, or small cottage—was regarded as his castle, free from the intruding eye of government, without a warrant based on probable cause."[156]

CHAPTER SUMMARY

Tremendous improvements have been made in the police use of technology in the past few decades in the fields of computers, communications, criminal investigation, surveillance, and criminalistics. Computers have enabled the police to dispatch officers immediately to any calls for service. They have also aided the police in the investigation process by enabling officers to feed descriptions and MOs into the computer and to receive almost instantaneous printouts on possible suspects. Computers have enabled

police to maintain better records more easily. The computer has also caused a revolution in the processing of fingerprints through automated fingerprint identification system (AFIS) terminals.

In recent years, the police have also used science to develop less-than-lethal weapons, such as Tasers and chemical irritant sprays, as an alternative to using deadly force. Other technology, including improved surveillance devices and improved forensic techniques (such as DNA profiling) is enhancing the ability of the police to solve crime.

As technology continues to improve, and if the police remain receptive to testing and accepting new technology, unheard-of methods of investigating crimes and processing evidence will seem commonplace tomorrow. It must be remembered, however, that despite the advances that science brings to police work, the key to police work will always be people—the men and women we hire to serve and protect us.

Learning Check

1. Discuss the advantages of computer-aided dispatch (CAD) systems, including enhanced CAD.

2. List and discuss some of the major uses of the computer in police departments today.

3. Explain the latest advances in fingerprint processing.

4. Define DNA and talk about the accuracy of the results of genetic fingerprinting (DNA profiling).

5. Discuss some of the threats to civil liberties posed by the use of recent technology.

Application Exercises

1. You have been hired by the Typical City Police Department as a consultant to implement computerization in the department. The department now has no computerized systems at all. The commissioner tells you that he has a large but limited budget for the computerization of the department. He wants the following department functions to receive priority this year: (1) the 911 system, (2) crime analysis, and (3) the police laboratory.

    Based on your reading of this chapter, prepare a report to the commissioner specifying the equipment he or she should purchase using the budgeted funds.

2. Arrange to tour a public or private crime laboratory and prepare a report on what you observed.

3. Conduct research on a recent criminal case and show how forensic evidence resulted in a conviction or acquittal in court.

4. As a private investigator, you have been hired to investigate the following case. John and Diane Wilson, the son and daughter of Doctors Marianne and Jack Wilson, two prominent surgeons in your town, were kidnapped as they played on their front lawn nearly 20 years ago. The twins were 3 years old when they were abducted. The police conducted a massive nationwide investigation, with negative results. The case received extensive media attention for several years.

    Last week the Wilsons received a telephone call from a woman, Donna Anne, who told the following story:

I am a 23-year-old woman whose parents have just died. Our parents told my twin brother and me that we were adopted by them when we were very young, but they were always secretive about who our real parents were. Last week, while researching a report for my criminal investigations course, I came upon the story of the kidnapping of the Wilson twins, your children. I talked to my Aunt Cathy about the case and she became agitated and refused to discuss it with me any further. My brother and I believe that we could be your children.

The Wilsons ask you to investigate the possibility of this story being true before they agree to meet with the twins. They report that they are very distraught over the phone call and could not tolerate meeting them if there wasn't a chance that they could be their long-lost children. They also tell you they are afraid that this call could be a scam. They provide you with family photographs of the children taken before they were kidnapped. They tell you that their children were never officially fingerprinted by the police before their disappearance. However, they give you several toys that were handled by the twins when they were young. They tell you that the police reported to them, at the time of the disappearance, that the toys and photographs could not help in this case.

Based on your reading of this chapter, list the primary steps you can take to investigate this case.

Web Exercises

1. You are working as an intern with a small local police department that does not have a crime lab and sends their evidence to the state lab. The chief, knowing of your interest in forensic science and computers, asks you to help her understand DNA. She says she uses the Internet and would like to look at a few sites that will help her to understand DNA as a layperson. Select at least three sites that may help the chief and provide her with the name and Internet address of each site and a few sample pages of each site's coverage of DNA.

2. The Honors Program of your school is sponsoring a symposium, "The Challenge to Privacy Faced by Increased Law Enforcement Technology." You have been selected by your professor to research this subject and present some background information to your class prior to the symposium. She asks you to search the Web, find several Web sites regarding this issue, and prepare a brief report regarding some major issues that might arise in the symposium.

3. Patrol over to the National Institute of Justice's Web site and find the latest reports on its grants and assistance to local police departments in the fields of computerization and technology.

Key Concepts

Age-progression photos
Automated crime analysis (crime mapping)
Automated fingerprint identification systems (AFIS)
Ballistics
Biometric identification
Combined DNA Index System (CODIS)
Composite sketches
Computer aided dispatch (CAD)
Computer-aided investigations (computer-aided case management)
Criminalistics
DNA profiling (genetic fingerprinting, or DNA typing)
Enhanced CAD (enhanced 911) (E-911)
Fingerprints
Forensic science
Frye test
Global positioning systems (GPS)

Inked prints (ten-prints)
Integrated automated fingerprint identification system (IAFIS)
Latent prints
Less-than-lethal weapons
Live-Scan
Mitochondrial DNA (MtDNA)
Mobile digital terminal (MDT)
Mug shot imaging
National Crime Information Center (NCIC) (NCIC 2000)
National DNA Index System (NDIS)
Night vision devices
Palmprints
PCR-STR
Reverse 911 (R-911)
RFLP
Serology
Vehicle tracking systems

Specific Police Problems and Issues

15

CHAPTER GOALS

- To increase awareness of dangers facing the police, including being killed and injured in the line of duty and dealing with contagious diseases, such as AIDS
- To introduce the academic studies involving police shooting incidents, the "fleeing felon" rule, the landmark Supreme Court case *Tennessee* v. *Garner,* and current police policies regarding the use of deadly force
- To discuss the problem of police high-speed auto-mobile pursuits and current policies being utilized around the country
- To discuss the unique role of police officers in the domestic violence issue
- To introduce some of the radical and hate groups operating in our nation today and the problems they present to the police and society
- To discuss the issue of bias-based policing
- To explore the issue of police civil and criminal liability

This chapter focuses on some specific issues that face police departments and the people who serve in them. This book has discussed numerous problems that are endemic to police work, such as corruption, brutality, cynicism, and racism. The police issues and problems discussed in this chapter are as serious as the ones discussed earlier.

One problem is danger. How often are police officers killed or injured in the line of duty? What are the specific threats to the police regarding personal safety? Closely connected to police officer safety is the issue of police shootings—the use of deadly force by the police. One question to be investigated is, when can a police officer legally shoot a criminal? The issue of using less-than-lethal force will also be discussed. Another action by police that may lead to death and serious injuries to both officers themselves and the public is high-speed police pursuits. How fast officers drive, how long they continue to pursue motorists, and what policies are currently being used to guide this behavior will be examined.

The chapter will also discuss the special problems presented to the police by domestic violence, along with evolving procedures police are using in these cases. Radical and hate groups and the threats they pose to our society and the police are considered. Bias-based policing is examined. The chapter concludes with a discussion of what can happen if the police make mistakes in using force or in pursuing fleeing motorists, or even if the police do not make mistakes but an innocent citizen is killed or injured. The concept of civil liability and its ramifications for communities, police departments, and individual officers will be examined.

★ ★ ★

POLICE AND DANGER

No one would disagree with the statement that police work is dangerous. Unfortunately, its dangers are increasing, too. Each year many officers are injured or killed in the line of duty. Also, the chances of contracting life-threatening diseases, such as AIDS, are increasing as more of the general population is affected. This section, and the entire chapter, puts these dangers into perspective.

Officers Killed in the Line of Duty

The tragic assassination of 22-year-old rookie New York City police officer Edward Byrne by vicious drug dealers in 1988 shocked the United States. This murder was particularly shocking because the drug dealers were attempting to send a message that they, not ordinary citizens, controlled our streets. Officer Byrne was assigned to guard a man, Arjune, who was helping the police identify drug dealers in his Jamaican neighborhood. Three men shot Byrne to death as he was sitting alone in his police car at 3:25 A.M., guarding Arjune's house. The killers were acting under the orders of a drug kingpin who ordered the police assassination from his prison cell to teach law enforcement officers a lesson—to stop harassing his drug dealers. Officer Byrne was murdered not because he was Eddie Byrne but because he represented us—decent, law-abiding U.S. citizens.

Deputy Sheriff Patrick Behan, who had just started working for the Broward Sheriff's Office in Florida in 1990 after several years as a Boca Raton police officer, was murdered outside a convenience store during his midnight-shift tour. He had just taken a routine report and was sitting in his marked unit writing the report when he was approached by an assailant. Apparently, Pat did not perceive a threat and rolled down his window to talk to the assailant; he was shot in the head. It took months to solve the case, but two juveniles were charged and served time. In 2003, the case was appealed based on additional information that came to light in 2001 indicating a former jail detention officer may have committed the murder. The detention officer allegedly thought he was killing another deputy whom he held responsible for his losing his corrections job. The defense attorney for the individual in prison alleged the defendants were coerced into confessing to a crime they did not commit. Though the detectives and prosecutor did not feel this was valid information, the verdict was overturned by a federal judge, and the individual still in prison was freed. Currently the state is weighing its options.

How dangerous is police work? Are murders similar to that of Officer Byrne and Deputy Behan and the murders and deaths of other officers common in the United States?

WHY IS POLICE WORK DANGEROUS?   According to the Department of Justice, law enforcement officers are most at risk for workplace violence, followed by corrections officers and taxicab drivers.[1] Police officers perform necessary and often dangerous tasks. They deal constantly with what may be the most dangerous species on this planet—the human being—often in the most stressful and dangerous situations. They regularly respond to people shooting at each other, stabbing each other, and beating each other. In a typical tour of duty, officers can deal with the full range of human emotions. They also respond to calls where they may meet armed adversaries such as robberies in progress and hostage situations. Most frequently officers respond to "unknown problems" or "unknown distur-

Dempsey's Law

Where Is the Real Danger in Police Work?

Professor Dempsey, isn't police work dangerous? Isn't it easy to get killed or hurt as a police officer?

Empirical data suggest that police work is not the physically dangerous occupation that many say it is. However, the real danger in police work is not death and physical injury. It is the toll that police work takes on your personal and family life. John, suppose you're an officer right now. You have just come off a busy 4 to 12; your nerve endings are electrified. Do you think you can go right home and go to sleep?

No.

You're newly married. You have a small apartment. Your wife is a schoolteacher, and she has to be up at 6:00 A.M. Can you go home and wake her up to talk to you while you relax?

No.

Can you go home and play music or watch television or a tape in your little apartment?

No, that would wake her up.

Can you expect her to meet you at a local restaurant or bar to have something to eat and drink with you?

No.

So, John, what do you do to relax to come down after the highs of the tour?

Probably go out to the bar with my friends from work.

Yeah, John, and guess who else is at the bar? Yeah, Cathy, over there. And she's there because she had a tough tour, too, and her husband has to be up at 5 A.M. to go to his highway job. If you're not careful, John and Cathy, more than just friendship can occur at these meetings. Police work is dangerous. If you're not careful, it can be dangerous to your family life.

---

bances" types of calls, where someone is calling for help, but the officers are unable to gather further information and really don't know what they're walking into. The dangerous conditions facing U.S. police officers are compounded by the irrationality produced by alcohol and drugs. The urban drug business since the 1980s has been characterized by an emphasis on tremendous inflows of cash and instant gratification. The proliferation of young, urban, uneducated, and unemployable males, armed with a plethora of weapons (including military-like automatic assault weapons), makes officers more and more fearful for their safety. As Barbara Raffel Price of the John Jay College of Criminal Justice says, "It would be foolish not to recognize that the violence associated with the drug business puts the police and citizens in greater jeopardy and that it makes the job of policing almost impossible."[2]

FBI STATISTICS ON POLICE MURDERS   Despite the dangers the police face, the FBI (which maintains records of all law enforcement officers murdered in the line of duty each year) reported that 142 law enforcement officers were feloniously slain in the line of duty during 2001. This figure included 72 from the terrorist attacks of 9/11. Excluding that number, the figure represents an increase of 37

percent over the year 2000, but it is still slightly below the number in 1996.

Accidents claimed 78 law enforcement officers in 2001, with 50 dying in automobile, motorcycle, or plane crashes and 19 struck by vehicles. Additionally, 5 were accidentally shot.

In analyzing the murder of police officers from 1976 through 1998, the FBI looked at numbers, demographics, and circumstances. This information is gathered by the deceased officer's agency, which voluntarily sends the information to the FBI.

The analysis reveals that 1,820 law enforcement officers were murdered between 1976 and 1998, with an average of 79 per year. The number is actually dropping with 93 officers murdered in 1978, 78 murdered in 1988, and 61 murdered in 1998.[3]

One possible explanation for this decrease is the increased use of body armor. Unfortunately, there are no statistics regarding the percentage of officers wearing body armor; however, whether an officer is wearing body armor at the time of the attack is recorded. If these percentages are similar, we can draw some conclusions, as the percentage of murdered officers wearing body armor has risen. In 1988, 26 percent of officers murdered were

Police Officer Steven McDonald marches proudly up Fifth Avenue during the annual St. Patrick's Day Parade in New York City. McDonald was paralyzed in the line of duty on July 12, 1986, at the age of 28. While the decline in the numbers of police officers killed in the line of duty is encouraging, dealing with the effects of on-the-job injuries on officers whose lives have been changed forever is often overlooked.

wearing body armor; in 1993, 56 percent were wearing body armor; and, in 1998, 57 percent were wearing it.[4]

Additionally, recent reports indicate that 77 percent of all local departments provide body armor to their officers, and 64 percent of the departments required at least some officers to wear it.[5] This, coupled with better training, communications, and police practices are likely to have contributed to the decline.

Firearms claimed the lives of 92 percent of the officers murdered from 1976 to 1998; 12 percent were killed with their own guns. On average, 39 percent of officers lost their lives during arrest situations, 16 percent while answering disturbance calls, 14 percent enforcing traffic laws, and 11 percent in ambush situations.

Regarding officer characteristics, it was found that of the officers murdered from 1976 to 1998:

- 98 percent were male
- 65 percent were over 30 years of age
- 86 percent were white
- 72 percent were wearing their uniforms
- the officers had an average of 9 years' law enforcement service

Regarding the offenders, it was found that 54 percent of those who murdered officers were between the ages of 18

and 30, 97 percent were male, and 54 percent were white. African Americans make up 12 percent of the population but were 43 percent of the murderers; whites were 83 percent of the population and 54 percent of the murderers of police officers.[6]

The most recent statistics for law enforcement officers killed and assaulted are from 2002. The FBI reports that, in 2002, 56 law enforcement officers were feloniously killed in the line of duty. This is a decline of 25 percent from the 70 who were killed (without including the 9/11 deaths) in 2001. Twenty-five of these deaths occurred in the South, 12 in the Midwest, 9 in the West, and 5 in the Northeast. Five officers were killed in Puerto Rico. Analysis shows that 15 of the officers were killed in ambush situations, 10 in traffic stops or pursuits, 10 during arrest situations, 9 handling disturbance calls, and 8 while investigating suspicious incidents. The additional 4 officers were murdered by mentally deranged individuals. Firearms were used in most cases; 4 of the officers were shot with their service weapons. Of the offenders, 3 were killed by the victim officers, 8 were justifiably killed by someone other than the officer, 4 committed suicide, and 1 is at large. The remainder were arrested. In addiiton to the 56 officers feloniously killed, 77 officers were accidentally killed in the line of duty in 2002.[7]

The FBI reports that 142 officers were killed in 2001, with 72 of them dying on 9/11. Of those officers, 105 worked for city police departments, 24 for county agencies, and 3 for state agencies. Four of the officers were with federal agencies, and 6 were from Puerto Rico. Eighty of the officers (including the 72 from 9/11) were investigating suspicious incidents, 24 were making arrests, 14 were answering disturbance calls, 10 were ambushed, 9 were enforcing traffic laws, 3 were slain by mentally deranged individuals, and 2 were transporting prisoners.[8]

Further examination of the 70 officers killed (without including the 9/11 deaths) reveals that the average age of the officers was 37, 67 of the officers were male, 61 were white, 8 were African American, and 1 was American Indian/Alaskan Native. Twenty-nine officers were killed in the South, 18 in the West, 14 in the Midwest, and 3 in the Northeast. Six were in Puerto Rico. Sixty-one of the murders involved firearms (46 handguns, 11 rifles, and 4 shotguns). Three officers were killed with their own guns, and 38 of the officers were wearing body armor at the time of their death. Seventy-three suspects were identified in connection with 70 of the deaths, 52 were arrested, 10 were justifiably killed, 5 committed suicide, and 4 died under other circumstances.[9]

ACCIDENTAL POLICE DEATHS   In addition to the 801 officers feloniously slain during the 1980s and the total of 1,217 slain feloniously from 1980 to 1995, 1,076 officers lost their lives in accidents while performing official duties from 1980 to 1995. Automobile accidents were the leading cause of accidental deaths (496). Other automobile-related accidental deaths of officers included officers' being struck by vehicles while engaging in traffic stops, performing road blocks, directing traffic, and assisting motorists. Other accidental deaths were the result of aircraft accidents, accidental shootings, motorcycle accidents, falls, and drowning.[9] The most recent figures are for the year 2001 in which 78 officers were accidentally killed. Fifty officers were victims of automobile, motorcycle, and aircraft accidents. Nineteen officers were struck by vehicles, 5 were accidentally shot, and 4 died in other types of accidents.[10]

OTHER STUDIES OF POLICE MURDERS   Other studies over the years give us information regarding the murder of police officers. William Geller and Michael S. Scott's study revealed that in 1971 police were feloniously killed at a rate of 38 per 100,000 officers, but this rate decreased steadily until it reached 12 per 100,000 officers in the 1990s.[11]

David Lester's study of the characteristics of cities that have high rates of police officer fatalities indicated that these cities were mainly located in the South. The cities had low population densities, high murder rates, and a high proportion of gun ownership.[12]

Research by William Geller has shown that off-duty police officers and plainclothes officers have high rates of shooting fatalities.[13] His explanation for these high rates was that off-duty officers, who are usually armed, are expected to take appropriate action when they encounter criminal situations. However, they suffer from the lack of normal tactical advantages, such as communication, cover, and backup. Additionally, Geller indicated that plainclothes officers may often be mistaken for perpetrators in criminal situations.

Police officers themselves comprehend the dangers in policing better than does the average citizen. In a study involving police officers and perceptions of danger, Frances T. Cullen found that police officers were aware of the difference between the possibility of danger and its actual occurrence in police work. When officers were asked whether they felt that "a lot of people" were hurt in the line of duty, 87 percent of the officers disagreed. At the same time, however, nearly 75 percent of the officers interviewed stated that they worked in a dangerous occupation.[14]

The Web site of the National Law Enforcement Officers Memorial Fund illustrates that the organization has accomplished many of its goals. The Law Enforcement Officers Memorial is visited by over 150,000 people each year and enhances public knowledge of and appreciation for law enforcement officers and the dangers they face. They also collect and catalog information on law enforcement fatalities in an effort to educate the public about officer safety and with the goal that no officer slain in the line of duty will ever be forgotten.

The National Law Enforcement Officers Memorial Fund site reports some interesting facts:[15]

- As of June, 2003, there were approximately 850,000 sworn law enforcement officers in the United States.

- Since 1792, over 16,000 police officers have been killed in the line of duty.

- More than 56,000 law enforcement officers are assaulted each year, resulting in approximately 16,000 injuries.

- The deadliest decade for police officers was the 1970s, with 2,240 officers losing their lives.

- The deadliest day in law enforcement history was September 11, 2001, when 72 officers were killed.

- The NYPD has lost more officers in the line of duty (576) than any other department, and California has lost more (1,334) than any other state.

- During the last 10 years, more officers were killed on Friday and fewer on Sunday than any other days; the most deadly hours are between 8 P.M. and 10 P.M.

PATROLLING THE WEB

The National Law Enforcement Officers Memorial Fund

The Web site of the National Law Enforcement Officers Memorial Fund provides facts and figures about law enforcement officers killed, the reported causes, and a historical overview:

www.nleomf.com

Concerns of Police Survivors Inc. (COPS) is an organization started in 1984 to provide resources to survivors of law enforcement officers killed in the line of duty. Their Web site provides information to survivors and police agencies. They also provide training and assistance to departments in how to respond to a law enforcement death in their department in the hopes of reducing the trauma suffered by coworkers. As COPS states on their Web site, "In 2001, a law enforcement officer was killed in the line of duty every 39 hours. Every 39 hours on average another family joined the COPS organization. There is no membership fee to join COPS, for the price paid is already too high."[16]

EXPLANATIONS FOR LOW POLICE MURDER RATE
What accounts for the relatively low murder rates of police officers despite the constant possibility of violence with which they are faced? There are several explanations.

People who would not think twice about shooting a fellow citizen might hesitate in shooting a police officer, knowing that society places a special value on the lives of those they depend on for maintaining law and order on the streets. They also know that the criminal justice system reacts in a harsher way to a "cop killer" than to an ordinary killer.

Also contributing to the relatively low level of officer killings is the fact that professional criminals, including organized crime members and drug dealers, know that killing a police officer is "very bad for business." Such a killing will result in tremendous disruption of their business while the police hunt for, and prosecute, the killer.

Another reason for the relatively low number of killings of police officers is their awareness of the dangers they face every day and the resultant physical and mental precautions they take to deal with such dangers. The discussion of the police personality in Chapter 6 characterized it as suspicious, loyal, and cynical. Most experts believe that the police personality is caused by the dangers of police work. It's possible that the negative aspects of the police personality keep officers relatively safe.

Lastly, as stated earlier, improved training and equipment have helped to keep officers safe. Officers are now trained not to blindly rush into situations but to obtain as much information as possible (aided by improved records systems) while enroute and upon arrival. Obtaining cover and waiting for backup are also stressed. Officers being trained in more less-than-lethal weapons and agreeing to wear their body armor has also helped keep officers alive.

Officers Assaulted in the Line of Duty

Police officers have relatively low murder rates, but how often are officers injured by criminal assaults in the line of duty? In 2001, there were 56,666 assaults committed against police officers. These assaults most commonly involved personal weapons such as hands, feet, and fists. These attacks accounted for just over 80 percent of attacks on police officers in 2001 and resulted in 30 percent of the injuries to officers. Firearms were used against officers in 3.2 percent of assaults, knives or cutting instruments in 2.1 percent of the assaults, and other weapons in 14.5 percent of assaults against officers.[17] This number increased in 2002 with 58,066 law enforcement officers assaulted in the line of duty. As in 2001, personal weapons were used in just over 80 percent of assaults.[18]

Police and AIDS

Since the 1980s, human immunodeficiency virus (HIV), acquired immune deficiency syndrome (AIDS), and hepatitis B and C have become sources of great concern to U.S. police officers, as well as to everyone else. AIDS, a deadly disease, is transmitted mainly through sexual contact and the exchange of body fluids. Although AIDS was formerly associated mainly with male homosexuals, intravenous drug users, and prostitutes, it is now known that anyone could be subject to infection by this disease.

The impact of HIV/AIDS is readily apparent. According to the Centers for Disease Control (CDC), the estimated number of AIDS diagnoses in the United Stated through 2002 is 886,575, with 9,300 of those being children under 13. The estimated deaths from AIDS are 501,669, including 5,315 children under 15. Worldwide, the statistics are even more frightening, with over 40 million people believed to be living with HIV/AIDS as of 2003. During 2003 alone, the disease was acquired by 5 million people and caused the deaths of 3 million people worldwide.[19]

These figures do not include individuals infected with HIV who may carry the disease for years before any symptoms of AIDS appear. These individuals are still contagious. Though there is no cure for AIDS, advances have been made in the treatment of the disease, allowing infected individuals to live longer lives.[20]

Police officers frequently come into contact with all types of people—including those having infectious diseases—and officers often have contact with blood and other body fluids. Therefore, officers are at special risk for catching communicable diseases. They must take precau-

San Francisco police officers finish up at a shooting scene. Officers respond to many calls involving contact with body fluids—while rendering first aid, subduing and arresting a suspect, or processing a crime scene. It is imperative that officers receive training regarding communicable diseases and be provided with proper equipment in order to minimize their chances for exposure.

tionary measures during searches and other contacts with possible carriers of infectious diseases, as well as at crime scenes, where blood and other body fluids may be present.[21]

The International Association of Chiefs of Police (IACP) model policy stresses education and the use of "universal precautions" or generic precautionary rules. This is the practice of treating all body fluids as potentially hazardous, including the routine use of gloves, plastic mouthpieces for CPR, and the adoption of policies and behaviors that minimize the chance of being exposed to HIV/AIDS, such as changing the way searches are conducted.[22] Universal precautions mitigate the fact that, due to confidentiality issues in most states, officers will not know who is or is not infected with a communicable disease. With appropriate training and the use of universal precautions, the police mission can be carried out with a near zero chance of being infected with HIV/AIDS.

The IACP's policy on HIV/AIDS prevention was published in May 2000. The policy defines an exposure as "any contact with body fluids including, but not limited to, direct contact with skin, eyes, nose and mouth, and through needle sticks." The policy stresses prevention of HIV/AIDS exposure and recommends behaviors and procedures to minimize the chance of becoming exposed. It also addresses the supplies that departments should have on hand and procedures to be utilized for clean-up in the event of a body fluid spill or deposit in a patrol vehicle or booking area. The policy also discusses the importance of documenting and following through on an exposure for educational purposes and to ensure the officers are covered if the disease has been contracted.

The FBI has published 16 recommendations on how to collect and handle evidence that might be infected with the viruses, bacteria, and germs of infectious diseases.[23] The National Institute of Justice has also published recommendations on dealing with possibly infected evidence.[24] Despite serious medical risks, police officers may not refuse to handle incidents involving persons infected with the AIDS virus or with other infectious diseases. Failing to perform certain duties—such as rendering first aid, assisting, or even arresting a person—would be a dereliction of duty, as well as discrimination against a class of people.[25] Police officers assume the risks associated with law enforcement when they accept their commission, and the low risk of contracting HIV/AIDS when utilizing proper training and equipment supports any kind of legal claim against an officer refusing to perform a duty.[26] This risk is a part of the job but certainly more able to be controlled than many risks that officers face.

★ ★ ★

POLICE SHOOTINGS: USE OF DEADLY FORCE

Historically, the shooting of a citizen by the police has been a major problem facing the police. Police shootings have had a serious negative impact on police–community relations. Numerous incidents of civil unrest have followed police shootings of civilians. James Q. Wilson has stated, "No aspect of policing elicits more passionate concern or more divided opinions than the use of deadly force."[27]

Police shootings receive tremendous media attention. However, James J. Fyfe, a former New York City police lieutenant and one of the leading experts on the police use of deadly force in the United States, reported that the systematic examination of the use of deadly force was largely neglected until a series of police shootings and other police problems precipitated the urban violence of the 1960s.[28]

Number of Citizens Shot by the Police

The FBI has been collecting information on justifiable homicides by police since 1968. When a police officer deliberately kills someone, a determination is made as to whether the killing occurred in the line of duty and whether it was justified. In other words, was it necessary in order to prevent imminent death or serious bodily injury to the officer or someone else? If this determination is made, the information is voluntarily sent by the police agency to the FBI. An unjustified killing would then be reported to the FBI as a murder; and there is currently nothing to distinguish murder by a police officer from murders by others.[29]

According to this report, an average of 373 people per year are killed justifiably by police officers, with 1987 having the smallest number (296) and 1994 the most (459). In 99 percent of these homicides, police used a firearm. Ninety-eight percent of persons justifiably killed by police were males, and 98 percent of the officers involved in justifiable homicides were male. The average age of the officers was 33 years.

From 1976 to 1998, the officers involved in 84 percent of justifiable homicides were white, while 15 percent were African American. This percentage is in keeping with their average percentage in the police ranks across the nation (approximately 87 percent of police officers are white). In 65 percent of justifiable homicides by police, the officer's race and the offender's race were the same.[30]

According to the FBI, there were 8,578 felons justifiably killed by police officers from 1976 to 1998. The largest number were killed in 1994 (459) and the smallest number in 1987 (296). This is an average of 373 a year. Though the U.S. population age 13 and over had increased by 47 million people in this time, and the number of police officers had increased by approximately 200,000, the number of felons justifiably killed by police did not significantly increase.[31]

It would appear perhaps the police are becoming more judicious with their use of deadly force. This may be the result of better training, better procedures, or the expansion of less-than-lethal alternatives.

Numerous studies have been conducted to determine if there is, in fact, racial discrimination in the police use of deadly force. If one considers only total numbers, the overwhelming difference in the percentage of African Americans shot over the percentage of whites shot could lead to the conclusion that discrimination does indeed exist.

The FBI report mentioned earlier indicates that there is a disproportionate number of African Americans justifiably killed by police officers. From 1976 to 1998, they made up 12 percent of the population aged 13 and up but were 35 percent of felons killed by police. However, this percentage is similar to that of African Americans (40 percent) arrested by police for violent crime. It was also reported, however, that the rate at which African Americans are killed by police declined from 1976 to 1998, while the rate at which whites are killed has remained steady.[32]

It is also shown that a growing percentage of people killed by police officers are white, with 50 percent being white in 1978, 59 percent in 1988, and 62 percent in 1998. While the rate at which blacks were killed by police in 1998 was four times that of whites, this is much lower than the eight-times rate in 1978.[33]

In one of the first studies of police shootings, Robin found that Chicago police, over a ten-year period, shot and killed African Americans at a rate of 16.1 per 100,000 citizens, compared with 2.1 whites per 100,000 citizens. Other cities had even greater disparities. In Boston, the police shot and killed African Americans 25 times more often than they did whites.[34]

Fyfe's analysis in the late 1970s of citizens shot and killed by the Memphis police over a five-year period found a pattern of extreme racial disparity, particularly with respect to unarmed citizens. Overall, 26 of the 34 people shot and killed in that period (85.7 percent) were African American. In the category of nonassaultive and unarmed people, the Memphis police shot and killed 13 African Americans and only one white. Half of all the African Americans shot and killed were nonassaultive and unarmed. The data suggest that the Memphis police were much more likely to shoot unarmed African Americans than unarmed whites. Fyfe states that "blacks and Hispanics are everywhere overrepresented among those on the other side of police guns."[35]

There is another side, however, to the analysis of race and police shootings. Two studies indicate that people who engage in violent crime or who engage the police in violent confrontations are much more likely to be the victims of police shootings. In one study, participation in violent crime was used as a relevant variable in police shootings, because generally, participation in crime places a person at risk of being confronted by the police and being shot by the police. The Chicago Law Enforcement Study Group examined shootings by Chicago police over a five-year period. The group first analyzed the rate at which whites, African Americans, and Hispanic Americans were shot and killed according to their number in the population and then the rate at which the same groups were shot and killed while participating in violent crimes. The data indicated that African Americans were shot and killed six times as often as whites in terms of the total population, but the disparity disappeared when participation in violent crimes was a factor. Whites were shot and killed at a rate of 5.6 per 1,000 arrests for forcible felonies, compared with 4.5 African Americans shot and killed per 1,000 arrests for the same category of crime.[36]

In the other study—Fyfe's pioneering Ph.D. dissertation, "Shots Fired," a study of New York City police shootings over a five-year period in the 1970s—Fyfe found that police officers are most likely to shoot suspects who are armed and with whom they become involved in violent confrontations. Fyfe found that if factors such as being armed with a weapon, being involved in a violent crime, and attacking an officer are considered, the racial differences in the police use of deadly force became nonsignificant.[37]

In a 1993 study, David Lester, pointing to the jurisdictional variation of police use of deadly force, reported that police officers kill more people in communities with high violence rates and during years in which the homicide rates were highest.[38]

Researchers acknowledge that many factors are involved in the quick decision-making process involved in a police shooting, including the victim's actions, the officer's actions, the type of assault against the officer, and the type of weapon involved, as well as other options available to the officer in addition to deadly violence. These are in addition to the environmental factors such as community characteristics and organizational factors such as the department's policies and organizational climate. We need to continue to analyze all these factors.[39]

An interesting study involving ordinary citizens was conducted by some researchers at the University of Washington. A psychology professor showed 208 shooting scenarios to 106 undergraduate psychology students on computers. They had one second to "shoot," send a "safety signal" that they saw a police officer, or do nothing. The students were told before the scenario that the criminal, who was always armed, was either African American or white. In the scenarios, African Americans were found to be mistaken more often for the criminal than were whites. African Americans were wrongly shot 35 percent of the time and whites 26 percent of the time. A sergeant with the State of Washington Criminal Justice

Training Commission does not believe this translates to police recruits due to their training. In training over 2,000 recruits on simulators, he found they were likely to err on the side of not shooting and in fact are more focused on the weapon and often aren't aware of the race of someone they had just "shot."[40] The FBI statistics mentioned earlier would tend to back up this sergeant's observation.

Departure from the "Fleeing Felon" Rule

Before the great amount of attention given to police shootings in the wake of the civil disorders of the 1960s, most U.S. police departments operated under the common-law **"fleeing felon" doctrine,** which held that law enforcement officers could, if necessary, use deadly force to apprehend any fleeing felony suspect. This doctrine evolved in the common law tradition of medieval England, when all felonies were capital offenses. Because there was very little official law enforcement in those days, and very few escaping felons were able to be apprehended, the law allowed a person who had committed a felony to be killed while fleeing the scene.

The fleeing felon rule, like most of England's common law, came to the United States. Today, however, there is little need for the fleeing felon rule in the United States, because we have sufficient armed police and modern communications systems to aid in the apprehension of fleeing felons. Also, the legality and morality of the fleeing felon rule comes into question because of the U.S. legal concept of presumption of innocence. Most U.S. states, however, maintained the fleeing felon rule well into the 1960s and 1970s. In 1984, the fleeing felon rule was declared unconstitutional by the U.S. Supreme Court in the landmark case *Tennessee v. Garner.*

Prior to the Garner case, and subsequent to the urban riots of the 1960s, many states replaced the fleeing felon rule with new state laws, internal rules of police departments, and court decisions. During the 1970s, many police departments developed an alternative to the fleeing felon doctrine, based in part on recommendations by the American Law Institute and the Police Foundation. This rule used the **"defense of life" standard,** which allowed police officers to use deadly force against people who were using deadly force against an officer or another person, as well as in certain violent felony situations. The replacement of the common-law fleeing felon rule by the defense of life standard changed the incidence of police shootings. O'Donnell found that police departments with effective deadly force rules showed sharp decreases not only in citizen deaths but also in officer deaths. In Kansas

YOU ARE THERE! »

Tennessee v. Garner

The Garner case finally ended the fleeing felon rule. On October 3, 1974, at about 10:45 P.M., two Memphis police officers, Elton Hymon and Leslie Wright, responded to a prowler run (a report of "prowler inside"). Upon reaching the location, they were met by a neighbor, who told them she had heard someone breaking into the house next to hers. Officer Wright radioed for assistance as Officer Hymon went to the rear of the house. As the officer approached the backyard, he heard a door slamming, and he observed someone running across the backyard. The fleeing person stopped at a 6-foot-high chain-link fence at the end of the yard. The officer shone his flashlight and saw what appeared to be a 17- or 18-year-old youth about 5 feet 7 inches tall. The officer yelled, "Police! Halt!" However, the youth began to climb the fence.

IF YOU WERE OFFICER HYMON, WHAT WOULD YOU DO?

The officer, thinking that the youth would escape, fired a shot at him, which struck him in the back of the head. The youth later died on the operating table. Ten dollars and a purse taken from the house were found on his body. The dead youth was later identified as Edward Garner, a 15-year-old eighth grader. At the trial, the officer admitted that he knew that Garner was unarmed and was trying to escape. The officer testified that he was acting under the provisions of Tennessee law that stated that an officer may use all the necessary means to effect an arrest if, after notice of the intention to arrest, the defendant either flees or forcibly resists.

The U.S. Supreme Court ruled 6 to 3 that the use of deadly force against apparently unarmed and nondangerous fleeing felons is an illegal seizure under the Fourth Amendment. The Court ended the common law fleeing felon rule by stating:

> The use of deadly force to prevent the escape of all felony suspects, whatever the circumstances, is constitutionally unreasonable. It is not better that all felony suspects die than they escape. Where the suspect poses no immediate threat to the officer and no threat to others, the harm resulting from failing to apprehend him does not justify the use of deadly force to do so. It is no doubt unfortunate when a suspect who is in sight escapes, but the fact that the police arrive a little late or are a little slower afoot does not always justify killing the suspect. A police officer may not seize an unarmed, nondangerous suspect by shooting him dead.

If you had been a member of the Court, would you have agreed with this ruling?

Source: Based on *Tennessee v. Garner,* 471 U.S. 1 (1985).

City, Missouri, for example, after the department adopted a rule that prohibited police from shooting juveniles except in self-defense, the number of youths under 18 shot by the police dropped dramatically.[41]

Fyfe found that the number of police shootings dropped sharply following the New York City Police Department's adoption of a strict deadly force rule (defense of life standard). He also found that the average number of shots fired by New York City police officers was reduced by 30 percent. The greatest reduction occurred in fleeing felon situations. Fyfe found, moreover, that the number of police officers shot also dropped. Hence, Fyfe concluded, stricter deadly force rules appear to reduce not only citizen but also police fatalities and woundings.[42] He observed that "reductions in police shooting frequency and changes in police shooting patterns have followed implementation of restrictive administrative policies on deadly force and weapon use."[43]

The Sherman and Cohn survey of police shooting trends in the 50 largest U.S. cities found that the total number of people shot and killed by the police per year was cut in half between 1970 and 1984.[44] In 1995, after tremendous negative publicity and after detailed investigations into the actions of federal agents at the deadly siege of the Branch Davidian compound in Waco, Texas, and at the home of antigovernment separatist Randy Weaver, in Ruby Ridge, Idaho, the federal government announced that it was refining the deadly force policy used by federal agents. The "imminent danger" standard, basically the same defense of life standard that law enforcement agencies have been following for years, restricts the use of deadly force to only those situations where the lives of agents or others are in imminent danger. The revised policy also permits deadly physical force against a prisoner attempting escape who was being held in or sentenced to a high-security prison. The new policy also forbids the firing

YOU ARE THERE! »

Alternatives to the Fleeing Felon Rule

In the 1970s, the American Law Institute proposed a Model Penal Code, which included new policies on the use of deadly force. Many states replaced their existing penal codes with this model code. Additionally, during the same time period, the Police Foundation proposed its own policies regarding the use of deadly force, which were adopted by many police departments.

MODEL PENAL CODE

The Model Penal Code, developed by the American Law Institute, permits the use of deadly force by police officers if an officer believes that (1) the felony for which the arrest is made involved the use, or the threatened use, of deadly force; or (2) there is a substantial risk that the suspect will cause death or serious bodily injury if not immediately apprehended; and (3) the force employed creates no substantial risk of injury to innocent people.

THE POLICE FOUNDATION STANDARD

After studying the deadly force policies of numerous police departments, including those of Birmingham, Detroit, Indianapolis, Kansas City (Missouri), Oakland, Portland (Oregon), and Washington, D.C., the Police Foundation recommended that police departments develop rules governing the use of deadly force after consultation with citizens and police line officers. It recommended that officers be allowed to shoot to defend themselves and others, as well as to apprehend

suspects in deadly or potentially deadly felonies. The Police Foundation also recommended several internal police policies that could lead to an improved use of deadly force by the police. These policies included carefully screening recruits to eliminate both unstable and violence-prone officers, dismissing probationary officers who demonstrate instability or propensity to violence, and providing more meaningful training in the rules of deadly force.

The Police Foundation proposed the following deadly force rules that departments might adopt: Officers might use deadly force to defend themselves or others from what the officers reasonably perceive as an immediate threat of death or serious injury, when there is no apparent alternative. Officers also might use deadly force to apprehend an armed and dangerous subject when alternative means of apprehension would involve a substantial risk of death or serious injury, and when the safety of innocent bystanders would not be additionally jeopardized by the officers' actions. Any of the following could make an armed subject dangerous enough to justify the use of deadly force: (1) the subject has recently shot, shot at, killed, or attempted to kill someone, or has done so more than once in the past; (2) the subject has recently committed a serious assault on a law enforcement officer acting in the line of duty; and (3) the subject has declared that he or she will kill, if necessary, to avoid arrest.

Source: Adapted from American Law Institute, *Model Penal Code,* section 307(2)(b); and Catherine H. Milton et al., *Police Use of Deadly Force* (Washington, DC: Police Foundation, 1977).

---

of warning shots and shooting at moving vehicles in an attempt to disable such vehicles.[45]

Realizing how important this issue is and the need for guidance for officers, most departments (93 percent) have a written policy on use of deadly force, including all departments serving a population over 25,000 people.[46]

Firearms Training

During the 1970s and 1980s, police departments came to the sad realization that officers needed more realistic firearms training and weapons at least equal to the criminals on the street.

A shootout in Miami in which four FBI agents were killed by heavily armed suspects indicated the need for police officers to carry automatic weapons, because most

criminals were armed with semiautomatics. Departments began to examine and research semiautomatic weapons in the '80s and began to convert to the more efficient sidearms. By 1990, 73 percent of all local departments had authorized the use of some type of semiautomatic weapon, and by 2000 that number had increased to 99 percent of all local departments.[47]

A 1970 gunfight in which four California Highway Patrol officers were killed shockingly indicated a need for better training. The four officers encountered two convicted felons and fired off fifteen rounds, including three shotgun rounds. All rounds were within seven yards, in darkness, and the officers inflicted only one superficial wound despite all the rounds fired.[48] This incident illustrated the need for improved training for officers in shooting situations.

In 1970, the NYPD began utilizing a "Firearms Discharge Report" to document all gunshots by NYPD officers.[49] By compiling this data, they were hoping to document where and when and under what conditions officers were firing their guns. Over the years, other departments followed suit in order to analyze shooting incidents and address training needs in an effort to keep officers safe. This included studies by Metro-Dade Miami and Los Angeles Sheriff's Departments. The old style of standing or kneeling at a range and firing at bull's-eye targets 25 or 50 yards downrange clearly wasn't preparing officers for the real-life conditions they encountered on the street.

In an article in *Law and Order* in August 2003, Thomas Aveni reviewed the information that departments have gathered. NYPD found 69 percent of shooting incidents occurred within zero to two yards, and 19 percent occurred within three to seven yards. Gunfight hit probability decreased significantly outside seven yards, yet most departments still qualify at 25 yards.[50] Sixty percent of police shootings occur in low-light situations, and the hit ratio diminished in these situations by 30 percent. These low-light situations also included over 75 percent of the mistake-of-fact shootings. A mistake-of-fact shooting was defined as a situation in which an officer shot an unarmed individual or an individual he or she thought was armed when the "weapon" was in fact another object. These shootings account for a small but significant and totally unnecessary percentage of police shootings—between 18 and 33 percent.[51]

Aveni also reports that shots fired in single officer incidents had a hit ratio of approximately 50 percent. The shots fired in "bunch" shootings (more than one officer) not only increased by 45 percent per officer, but the officer hit ratio declined by 82 percent. This phenomenon can be attributed to various emotional contagions and the dynamics of a chaotic complex crowd mentality. The officers face what they believe to be an imminent lethal threat and factors such as a misfire or someone falling can trigger the firing impulse.[52]

Most departments are attempting to incorporate real-life conditions such as low light, noise, sirens, flashing lights, and weather conditions into their training. They are also stressing the "shoot–don't shoot" aspect of shooting as much as accuracy. As much as agencies strive to make firearms training as realistic as possible, it will be difficult to simulate randomly moving targets and the emotional, life-threatening dynamics of the real thing; but the effort must continue.

Less-than-Lethal Force

Police agencies, states, and police organizations have felt it important to collect and analyze use-of-force information. In 1995, the Department of Justice proposed to develop and cofund a national use-of-force database by the International Association of Chiefs of Police. Initial activities and data collection began in 1996 and continues with the funding of the IACP.

These data indicate that police rarely use force. Fewer than 1 percent of people who had face-to-face contacts with police reported the officers used or threatened to use force. Research also found that excluding handcuffing, when police arrest individuals they used physical force in less than 20 percent of 7,512 arrests studied. In most of those cases they used weaponless tactics such as grabbing or holding. Police are trained to use force along a continuum, and most departments require that officers use the least amount of force necessary to obtain compliance. Most use of force by police occurs when officers are attempting to make an arrest and the subject is resisting; it is also more common when the officer is dealing with someone under the influence of drugs or alcohol or who is mentally ill. The most common type of force used by officers was hands and arms (77 percent) and if the subject claimed injury it was usually a bruise or abrasion (48 percent), followed by lacerations (24 percent) and gunshot injuries (4 percent).[53]

The Department of Justice also reports that, in 2000, 87 percent of all local departments had a policy regarding nonlethal force, and all departments serving a population of 1 million or more had one. Almost all departments authorized the use of one or more nonlethal weapons:

- 91 percent authorized use of chemical agents
- 88 percent authorized use of batons of some type
- 13 percent authorized the flash-bang grenade
- 7 percent authorized electronic devices of some type
- 7 percent authorized choke holds[54]

Departments have turned to some of these less-than-lethal weapons in an effort to give the officers options other than deadly force when faced with a combative subject. These devices have helped and have many supporters, but they are not without controversy. Various forms of chemical sprays have been in the police arsenal for years. Officers are required to get sprayed so that they know the effects and think about it before they use it on a citizen. Some people may be encountered for whom chemical

Forst's Law

The Public's Perception

It is difficult to know at the outset of a call how people are going to respond to your commands. We constantly need to adjust our perception of the situation and the amount of force that may be necessary to solve the problem. We also need to be aware that we are always being watched and that citizens may perceive things differently than we do.

I remember handling a call on a Friday evening during the height of tourist season in Boca. We received a call at a local restaurant/lounge advising of an elderly female threatening to "slash" the bartender with a knife. I was the first officer on the scene and contacted the bartender. He told me that the woman had left. He briefly described her and said that she did in fact show a kitchen knife and threaten to slash his face if he didn't serve her another drink. He felt she was unstable.

As I was talking to him, we got a similar call at the restaurant a few blocks away. This was a large chain-type bistro, and there was an elderly female in the restaurant yelling, acting irrationally, and stating she had a knife. I hopped in my car and drove to the restaurant. The restaurant was packed with families and tourists. I spoke with the manager who directed me to the woman in the back of the restaurant. By this time, two other officers had arrived. Two of us walked to the back and talked to the woman while the third officer waited by our cars. The

woman was agitated but agreed to come out front with us to discuss the situation. While we were talking she became increasingly irrational and started screaming that she was going to "slash" us. I patted her down and was attempting to take her knife from her when she went nuts and started fighting with us and screaming. This woman was only about 5' 4" and 65 to 70 years old and frail looking. We didn't want her to get hurt, and we didn't want one of us to get hurt; and we felt that by using three officers, we could handcuff her and minimize the chance of injuries by each officer taking an arm and another one doing the cuffing. She struggled and fought us but we got her cuffed without hurting her. We were standing by the back of one of the police cars right in front of the big plate glass window of the restaurant, and lots of people were watching. We used only as much force as we needed; even though she was old and frail, she was a danger to herself and others, but we knew it didn't look good—three officers in uniform handcuffing one elderly female. In fact, one individual leaving the restaurant made a comment to the effect that we were bullies. But we knew we had done the best we could under the circumstances and, despite outward appearances, were able to keep anyone from getting hurt. Officers are always going to be questioned about the amount of force they use in any given situation.

spray does not work; others may have an adverse reaction under certain conditions. Electronic devices have also given officers an alternative to deadly force, allowing a subject to be temporarily subdued without a gun. There have been several deaths in Taser or stun-gun situations, though none have been blamed on the taser itself. Most of the time, drugs were found to be the primary cause of death. Supporters of these weapons believe that the use of the Taser or stun-gun has saved many lives. The IACP has a model policy regarding the use of Tasers and other electronic devices and states their purpose is to save lives.[55]

Choke holds became a source of controversy after some deaths were associated with their use. Many departments have removed this option for officers from their policies. The use of K-9s is also considered by some to be less-than-lethal force, and there is a concern by some that they are utilized in a biased manner. Twenty-six percent of local departments used dogs for law enforcement purposes; the bigger the department, the more likely they are to use dogs, with 90 percent of departments serving over 100,000 using them. These departments will have policies in place governing when, where, and under what conditions dogs may be used.[56]

★ ★ ★

POLICE AUTOMOBILE PURSUITS

The police practice of using high-powered police vehicles to chase speeding motorists has resulted in numerous accidents, injuries, and deaths to innocent civilians, police officers, and the pursued drivers. The practice had not been studied until recently. Geoffrey P. Alpert and Lorie A. Fridell, however, in their 1992 book *Police Vehicles and Firearms: Instruments of Deadly Force,* report that in the past few years, a "great deal of progress has been made in the research, policy development and training associated with pursuit driving."[57]

Geoffrey Alpert and Patrick R. Anderson characterize the police high-speed automobile pursuit as the most deadly force available to the police.[58] They define high-speed pursuits as "an active attempt by a law enforcement officer operating an emergency vehicle to apprehend alleged criminals in a moving motor vehicle, when the driver of the vehicle, in an attempt to avoid apprehension, significantly increases his or her speed or takes other evasive action."[59] Alpert and Anderson point out several outcomes of such chases:

- The pursued driver stops the car and surrenders
- The chased vehicle crashes into a structure, and the driver and occupants are apprehended, escape, are injured, or are killed
- The chased vehicle crashes into another vehicle (with or without injuries to the driver and other occupants in the chased vehicle or another vehicle)
- The vehicle being chased strikes a pedestrian (with or without injuries or death)
- The police use some level of force to stop the pursued vehicle, including firearms, roadblocks, ramming, bumping, boxing, and so on
- The police car crashes (with or without injuries to officers or civilians)[60]

Clearly, not all of these possible outcomes are acceptable for the police or innocent civilians. A debate has begun that questions whether the police should pursue fleeing vehicles, especially when such a pursuit could risk injuries to the police or innocent civilians. Certainly, no one wants officers or civilians injured. According to the National Highway Traffic Safety Administration (NHTSA), about 520 people nationally who were not the subject of a chase died as a result of police pursuits from 1997 to 2001.[61] However, people on the other side in the debate say that if the police do not pursue fleeing drivers, they are sending a message to violators that they can get away with traffic violations by fleeing.

Studies Involving Police Pursuits

Studies have been conducted to determine what happens in a rapid pursuit. This information may help police administrators establish policies on rapid pursuits. A review by the California Highway Patrol of nearly 700 pursuits on its highways over a six-month period revealed the following about the typical pursuit:

- It starts as a traffic violation.
- It occurs at night.
- It covers only a mile or so.
- It takes approximately two minutes to resolve.
- It involves at least two police cars.
- It ends when the pursued driver stops his or her vehicle.
- It results in the apprehension of more than three-fourths of the pursued drivers.
- It ends without an accident 70 percent of the time.[62]

The California Highway Patrol Study also revealed that drivers failed to stop for the following reasons, based on the judgment of the pursuing officer:

- To avoid DWI or drug arrest (19 percent)
- To avoid a summons for a traffic infraction (14 percent)
- Because the driver was driving a stolen vehicle (12 percent)
- To avoid an arrest for a law violation (11 percent)
- Because of unknown or miscellaneous reasons, such as the driver's being afraid of the police, disliking the police, or enjoying the excitement of the chase (44 percent)[63]

The California Highway Patrol study concluded that although there are risks in high-speed pursuits, the pursuits are worth the risks:

> Attempted apprehension of motorists in violation of what appear to be minor traffic infractions is necessary for the preservation of order on the highways of California. . . . One can imagine what would happen if the police suddenly banned pursuits. Undoubtedly, innocent people may be injured or killed because an officer chooses to pursue a suspect, but this risk is necessary to avoid the even greater loss that would occur if law enforcement agencies were not allowed to aggressively pursue violators.[64]

A gunman hijacked this bus in Los Angeles after a shooting incident and then led police on a high-speed chase through downtown streets, killing one person and injuring seven. Many departments are instituting restrictive policies due to the extreme risks that pursuits pose and allowing them only in cases of violent offenses such as this one.

Geoffrey P. Alpert and Roger G. Dunham studied 952 pursuits in Dade County, Florida, by the area's two major police departments, the Metro-Dade Police Department and the City of Miami Police Department. The researchers found that 38 percent of the pursuits resulted in an accident, 17 percent in injury, and 0.7 percent in death. Of the 160 pursuits with injury, 30 involved injury to the police officer; 17, injury to an innocent bystander; and 113, injury to the fleeing driver, the passengers, or both. Alpert and Dunham also concluded that 54 percent of the pursuits were initiated for traffic offenses; 2 percent, for reckless driving or impaired driving; 33 percent, for serious

criminal activity; and 11 percent, for BOLO ("be on the lookout") alarms.[65]

Alpert and Fridell also studied high-speed pursuit data in Minnesota. The results indicated that 44 percent of pursuits resulted in accidents, and 24 percent resulted in injuries. The causes of the pursuits included traffic (76 percent), suspicion of DUI (6 percent), and suspicion of a felony (16 percent).[66] The National Highway Traffic Safety Administration has attributed 3,000 deaths to pursuits in the last decade, and they state that 40 percent of police chases end in crashes.[67]

In 2004, the University of Washington released a study conducted by two researchers at the Harborview Medical Center's Injury Prevention and Research Center. They examined all traffic fatalities in the nation from 1994 through 2002 and found 2,654 fatal crashes with 3,146 deaths resulting from police pursuits. Of those deaths, 1,048, or one-third, were of people not in fleeing vehicles. They were drivers or occupants of other vehicles, pedestrians, or bicyclists; 40 were police officers. The report did not determine how many police chases don't end in deaths or analyze the reasons for the pursuits. They did state that police chase fatalities make up 1 percent of all motor vehicle related deaths in the United States.[68]

Despite differences in the studies and confusion over the statistics, the fact remains that there is a high probability of a traffic accident when police involve themselves in rapid pursuits (30 percent in the California study and 38 percent in the Alpert and Dunham studies). Therefore, this area of police work requires much further study.

Establishment of Police Pursuit Policies

Alpert and Fridell state that "Policies on pursuit driving can be reduced to a simple concept: When the risk created by the driving outweighs the need for immediate apprehension of the suspect, such risky driving must be terminated. It is not only acceptable to terminate pursuits in which the potential benefit is minimal, but it is wise, safe and in good judgment to terminate pursuits which incorporate high risks!"[69]

The number of accidents and injuries resulting from police high-speed pursuits has led many U.S. police departments to establish formal **police pursuit policies** (policies regulating the circumstances and conditions under which the police should pursue or chase motorists driving at high speeds in a dangerous manner). Some departments are even telling their officers to discontinue a pursuit under certain circumstances.

Most departments have examined this issue closely over the last few years, and many have come to the conclusion that the dangers to officers, citizens, and even the individual being pursued often determine that pursuits are not an effective tactic and the dangers far outweigh the benefits. Policies give clear guidelines to officers and supervisors as to what their roles are. In 2000, 57 percent of local police agencies had a restrictive pursuit policy (restrictions based on speed, type of offense, and so on); 27 percent of departments had a judgmental pursuit policy leaving it to the officer's discretion; and 7 percent discouraged all vehicle pursuits.[69] Tire deflation spikes are used regularly by 26 percent of all departments as a tactic to end pursuits.[70] In 2003, major cities such as Los Angeles, Chicago, and Seattle joined the ranks of big-city departments using a restrictive policy. Seattle's policy dictates officers should chase drivers "only when the need for immediate capture outweighs the danger created by the pursuit itself." Officers are "allowed to chase drivers who have committed serious crimes, displayed weapons, or are creating a clear danger to others."[71] Additionally, sergeants complete special reports every time there is a pursuit, and the administration will analyze these reports on a yearly basis.

Most departments do not allow officers to shoot at moving vehicles unless they are returning fire to protect human life. Pursuit policies can also cause conflicts between neighboring towns or counties when their policies differ; one jurisdiction may initiate a pursuit that crosses a boundary into another jurisdiction where they won't pursue. The agencies need to sit down and communicate their policies and plan how they will handle the conflicts that may arise.

Considering the widely televised beatings of individuals after pursuits, a proposal by Geoffrey Alpert, a professor of criminology at the University of South Carolina, seems to make a great deal of sense. Alpert, in a 1996 study of police pursuit policies, recommended that suspects be apprehended by officers other than those who led the chase. Alpert found that officers chasing suspects experience an adrenaline high that can lead to the use of excessive force once they've caught up with the fleeing suspects.[72]

In 1997, in another study of police pursuits, Alpert concluded that police pursuit driving remains a controversial and dangerous activity. For generations the conventional police wisdom was that effective law enforcement demanded that officers apprehend suspects, even at great social costs. The tragic accidents that have resulted from pursuits testify to their danger.[73]

★ ★ ★

POLICE AND DOMESTIC VIOLENCE

Family violence is the most frequent type of violence that police encounter and though it is not necessarily considered the most dangerous police call (due to improved training and procedures) it is the most frequent type of violence in the United States.[74] Although it was once dismissed by police as a "civil matter," the latest statistics indicate the seriousness of this violence. According to the Commonwealth Fund 1998 survey of women's health, "One of 6 women experienced physical and/or sexual abuse during childhood. The equivalent of 3 million women nationwide reported experiencing domestic abuse in the past year. One in 5 said she's been raped or assaulted in her lifetime."[75] Female murder victims are far more likely than male murder victims to have been killed by an intimate. Three out of four women murder victims were attributed to intimate partner violence.[76]

Despite the sometimes hard criticism toward females reluctant to leave abusive partners, it is in fact a dangerous time. A woman is most at risk to be murdered when she tries to break off an abusive relationship.[77]

There is some dispute as to the prevalence of male battering, as some researchers believe it may be as prevalent as female battering, but due to reluctance to report or the reluctance traditionally of police to arrest females, it is not reflected in the statistics. Most experts accept the incidence rate to be approximately 15 percent of domestic violence.[78]

A 1997 University of Michigan study found that violence between intimate couples of opposite gender may start very early. In a survey of 635 suburban, middle-class high school students, about 36 percent of girls and 37 percent of boys said they had experienced physical abuse from a date. Half of the girls—and just 4 percent of the boys—had said their worst abusive experience "hurt a lot." Among the other key findings were that 44 percent of the girls stayed with boys after moderate violence, including slapping, and 36 percent stayed after severe abuse, including choking and punching.[79]

Traditional Police Response to Domestic Violence

A reviewer of two books on family violence writes that "domestic violence has a long history in all cultures, but it is only during the last 20 years or so, and only in some advanced industrial nations that this type of human conflict has gotten the attention and reactions of the criminal justice system."[80] The police, the courts, and society in general have traditionally adopted a hands-off policy toward domestic violence, treating it as a private affair that should be handled within the family. The police have generally not made arrests in domestic violence cases, even in those involving assaults with injuries that constitute a felony. Two assumptions prevailed: (1) that the arrest would make life worse for the victim, because the abuser might retaliate, and (2) that the victim would refuse to press charges.

Most police departments had no formal policies regarding domestic violence, and officers used many different techniques to deal with the problem when called to the scene. Among the techniques used were attempts to calm down both parties, mediating the conflict, and referring the participants to social service agencies for assistance in dealing with their problems. Often officers would escort abusive spouses out of the residence and advise them not to return until the next day or until things calmed down. Some officers would place abusive spouses in the police car and drive them to a location where it would take them an inordinate amount of time to find out where they were and to find their way home. Other officers just ignored domestic violence cases. Two important lawsuits—brought forward by women's groups in New York City (*Bruno* v. *Codd*, 1978) and Oakland, California (*Scott* v. *Hart,* 1979)—began to change the police response in domestic violence cases. The suits charged that the police departments had denied women equal protection of the law by failing to arrest people who had committed assaults against them. As a result of the lawsuits, both departments formulated official written policies mandating arrests in cases of felonious spousal assault.[81]

Minneapolis Domestic Violence Experiment

Subsequent to these lawsuits, the Police Foundation conducted the **Minneapolis Domestic Violence Experiment** (1981 to 1982). This experiment was designed to examine the deterrent effect of various methods of dealing with domestic violence, including mandatory arrest. During this experiment, officers called to incidents of domestic violence were required to select at random one of a group of instructions to tell them how to deal with the incidents. The officers' forced choice required them to do one of the following: (1) arrest the offender, (2) mediate the dispute, or (3) escort the offender from the home. Repeat violence over the next six months was measured through follow-up interviews with victims and police department records of calls to the same address.[82] The findings indicated that arrest prevented further domestic violence more effectively

than did separation or mediation. Repeat violence occurred in 10 percent of the arrest cases, compared with 19 percent of the mediation incidents and 24 percent of the separation incidents. The actual sanction imposed by arrest involved little more than an evening in jail; only 3 of the 136 people arrested were ever convicted and sentenced.[83] Lawrence Sherman and Richard Berk made three recommendations when concluding their Minneapolis Domestic Violence Experiment: First, the arrest would probably be the preferred response in domestic violence cases; second, that the experiment should be replicated to see if the results hold up; and third, that mandatory arrest should not be employed until more data were in, especially to avoid stifling future research into the topic.[84] Despite Sherman's concerns, mandatory arrest laws were adopted around the country, fueled by women's rights groups and battered women's advocates.

The Minneapolis experiment has been replicated in a number of other localities around the country to determine whether the results would be the same. These studies have had inconsistent results. In some areas, arrest provided no deterrence; in others, only certain types of offenders were deterred. Sherman and others have called for mandatory arrest laws to be repealed, and others feel a more holistic approach should be taken toward the issue of family violence, including close coordination with other criminal justice agencies and victim service providers.[85] A recent review of these replication studies indicates that mandatory arrest is still the preferred method of handling domestic violence and that it aids the individuals involved in getting into the system and getting help as well as educating the public that domestic violence is a crime.[86]

Police Response to Domestic Violence Today

Despite the lack of a clear consensus regarding the effectiveness of arrest in domestic violence cases, police departments nationwide have begun to establish new police guidelines for domestic violence cases. Currently, 91 percent of departments have special policies regarding arrest for domestic assault, 72 percent have mandatory arrest policies for domestic assault, and 16 percent have **proarrest policies** for domestic assault. Regarding violations of protection orders, 82 percent of departments had special polices, with 63 percent having mandatory arrest policies and 18 percent a proarrest policy. Bigger departments have higher percentages of such policies. Ninety-eight percent of departments serving a population of 25,000 or more have special policies regarding domestic assault and violation of protection orders.[87]

Mandatory arrests for domestic violence, however, are still controversial. Eve Buzawa argues that a mandatory arrest policy may deter female victims from calling the police in the first place; many victims simply want the police to help with the immediate crisis but do not necessarily want an arrest.[88] Also, some women feel that arresting an abusive spouse might make him angrier and cause him to commit further violence against her.

It has been found that oftentimes officers are making double arrests at scenes of domestic violence. They often cite the pressure to make arrests coupled with an inability to determine for sure which party is telling the truth. The feeling is that it is preferable to arrest both parties, get them in the system, and give them access to services as opposed to not making an arrest, with the individuals not receiving the services they need and the officers possibly facing departmental criticism. This alternative is frowned upon by victim's advocates, as victims are often afraid to call the police for fear of being arrested along with the partner, especially when they know the partner is particularly good at presenting his or her side of the story and perhaps "conning" others.

Many police departments throughout the country employ domestic violence specialists or coordinators to oversee the domestic violence cases the department handles. Depending on the size of the department and the size of the unit, they may or may not personally follow up on every domestic violence call. The specialist will ensure that all victims are aware of the services available and assist them in obtaining these services. The specialist will attempt to make sure that no cases slip through the cracks due to inaccurate reporting and provide assistance to the officers in handling these situations when requested.

The trend is to deal with domestic violence as part of the bigger picture involving family violence and provide a coordinated effort to all members of a family plagued by violence. It is no longer desirable or efficient for agencies to work independently, and there is increased communication and coordination, with use of liaisons and even task forces to deal with the issue of family violence. The impact of violence on our society, especially when witnessed or experienced at a young age, is becoming apparent, and service providers and criminal justice practitioners see the importance of intervening as early as possible.

The National Criminal Justice Reference Service (NCJRS) Web site describes family violence as a serious concern for criminal justice practitioners and society in general. They believe family violence, including child abuse, child neglect, elder abuse, and intimate partner violence are all interrelated and constitute a serious threat to the well-being of future generations. A study by the National Institute of Justice found that "being abused or neglected as a child increased the likelihood of arrest as a juvenile by 59%, as an adult by 28%, and for a violent crime by 30%."[89]

In 1996, the Domestic Violence Offender Gun Ban was passed by Congress. This law prohibits anyone with misdemeanor domestic violence convictions from possessing a firearm. (Persons with felony convictions are already prohibited from possessing a firearm.) Upon passage, the law began to rock law enforcement; it sparked lawsuits, forced police agencies to conduct background checks of officers to ensure compliance with the law, and, in some cases, cost officers their jobs. The law, police organizations say, threatens law enforcement careers by penalizing people convicted of spousal abuse without taking into account that they may have successfully dealt with their domestic problems.[90] The issue of domestic violence in police families is more fully discussed in Chapter 12.

★ ★ ★

POLICE AND RADICAL AND HATE GROUPS

Radical and hate groups have long presented a serious problem to the police. Throughout a major part of our history, the Ku Klux Klan terrorized and killed thousands of citizens. In the 1960s and 1970s, radical hate groups, such as the Black Panthers and the Black Liberation Army, raged urban warfare against the police, maiming and killing scores of police officers. Also, in that period of our history, militant student and antiwar groups caused tremendous problems for the police. Historically, in our nation, radical groups have been involved in assassinations, bombings, terrorism, and other crimes and acts of violence to protest the policies of the United States and to attempt to impose their distorted views on all members of our society.

Foreign terrorism has long threatened the lives and safety of U.S. citizens; however, in the 1990s, a new brand of home-grown terrorism has shocked America. These antigovernment groups are known by a myriad of names, including militias, Patriots, and white supremacists. The convicted bomber in the worst case of mass murder and domestic terrorism in U.S. history, Timothy McVeigh, who was executed in 2001 for the bombing of the Alfred P. Murrah Federal Building in Oklahoma City on April 19, 1995, was alleged to have had links to white supremacists and Patriot groups. The bombing killed 168 people.[91]

Domestic terrorism was also probably responsible for the bombing in Centennial Olympic Park at the Atlanta Olympics Games on July 27, 1996, in which one woman was killed and 111 other people were injured. It was reported in the media that the FBI originally suspected security guard Richard A. Jewell of complicity in the bombing, but later the FBI indicated that there was no evidence that he had any criminal part in it. On June 9, 1997, an FBI task force linked the Olympic bombing to the January 16, 1997, bombing at the Sandy Springs Professional Building (housing the Atlanta Northside Family Planning Services clinic—an abortion clinic) and the February 2, 1997, bombing at an Atlanta lesbian nightclub. The FBI claimed that letters mailed to the press by a militant religious cell known as the "Army of God" connected this group to the bombings.[92]

This mystery was finally cleared up in 2003. The FBI had earlier determined the primary suspect in the bombing at Centennial Olympic Park, as well as the gay bar and abortion clinics in Atlanta and Alabama, to be Eric Rudolph. He was arrested in 2003 after hiding in the mountains of North Carolina for five years. He had defeated all efforts to find him and was found not by an elite squad but by a rookie police officer in Murphy, North Carolina.[93] The concern of the government is that it is doubtful that Rudolph was able to survive and hide in the wilderness unaided for five years. It is believed that he had help, illustrating at the very least that sympathy and support for some of these domestic terrorist groups does exist.

One type of radical or hate group particularly worries the police. A 1997 report, *Two Years After: The Patriot Movement since Oklahoma City,* indicated that at least 858 so-called Patriot groups, including 380 armed militias, were active in the United States in 1996. This number represents a 6 percent increase over the number of such groups identified in 1994 and 1995 by the Klanwatch Project, an arm of the Montgomery, Alabama-based Southern Poverty Law Center, which monitors extremist groups around the nation.[94] The Klanwatch Project created its Militia Task Force in 1994, a year before the existence of the Patriot movement exploded into the national consciousness following the attack on the Oklahoma City Federal building. Six months before the blast on April 19, 1995, Klanwatch warned the U.S. Attorney General, "The mixture of armed groups and those who hate is a recipe for disaster."

In 1997, in response to fears regarding major terrorist threats to the nation, the federal government began a $42-million effort to conduct training exercises for police agencies to prepare them in responding to chemical or biological attacks.[95] FBI Special Agents James E. Duffy and Alan C. Brantley give us this profile of the typical militia member:

> Most militia organization members are white males who range in age from the early 20s to the mid-50s. The majority of militia members appear to be attracted to the movement because of gun control issues. . . . Militia members generally maintain strong Christian beliefs and justify their actions by claiming to be ardent defenders of the Constitution.[96]

Aggressive enforcement by federal and local law enforcement resulted in the following major cases against militia members around the nation in the last few years.

In West Virginia, four separate federal trials began against the Mountaineer Militia, accused of planning to bomb the FBI's new fingerprint facility in Clarksburg, West Virginia. The group's leader, Floyd Ray Looker, and one other man were indicted in 1996 on weapons, explosives, and terrorism charges. In Georgia, a government informant testified that two leaders of the Militia-at-Large for the Republic of Georgia had hoped to amass a stockpile of weapons at the Summer Olympics of 1996.

Militia leader John Pittner and seven others were arrested in Washington State on weapons and explosives charges. Informants testified in the trial that the militia members discussed blowing up radio towers and railroad tunnels.

Ten of twelve members of the Viper Militia in Arizona pled guilty to weapons and explosives charges. The group was accused of plotting to blow up government buildings in Arizona.[97]

Since September 11, 2001, concern for terrorism has been focused on enemies abroad but there are homegrown terrorists with which to be concerned. Some applauded the 9/11 attacks saying they were punishment from God as America had condoned things such as abortion, gay rights and women's rights.[98]

There are primarily two types of extremist groups, antigovernment groups and hate-oriented groups. In the last few years, the antigovernment groups have suffered due in part to the decline of the militia movement. The militias grew rapidly in the '90s but declined at the end of the decade due to some arrests, deaths, or illnesses of leaders; failures of their predictions (like the Y2K computer catastrophe); and infighting. They do still exist in many states and are advocates of violence. In October 2001, a Kentucky militia member followed through on his threats of violence against law enforcement by opening fire with an AK-47 on a deputy who pulled him over. Luckily, the deputy escaped injury.[99]

Some antigovernment movements have increased activities, including the Sovereign Citizen Movement, a tax-protest movement that stepped up activities after 1997 budget cuts weakened the IRS. They also advocate violence; in August 2002, a Sovereign Citizen killed a Massillon, Ohio, police officer during a traffic stop.

The white supremacist groups, however, have not suffered major declines in their ranks, though since 2002 they have experienced changes that have caused disruptions and instability. The major hate groups include the National Alliance (NA), which is the largest and most organized Neo-Nazi group with a recent faction breaking off called the White Revolution. The Aryan Nations is another Neo-Nazi group. Many of these "nations" have been competing against each other, with the Phineas Priests becoming self-appointed white supremacist vigilantes dedicated to targeting mixed-race couples, Jews, abortion providers, and homosexuals. The Illinois-based World Church of the Creator—now called the Creativity Movement—is another hate group at work. In January 2003, the leader was arrested for soliciting the murder of a judge who had ruled against the group.[100]

The criminal activities of the white supremacist groups have remained high. In 2002, there were numerous arrests for plotting to bomb public buildings and Jewish and African American landmarks, as well as to kill law enforcement officers. Local law enforcement is at the forefront of this fight.[101]

Many claim that the radical hate groups are motivated by what they consider to be oppressive federal government actions against groups like themselves. Two of these actions have received a great deal of criticism in the press and have caused the federal government to change many of their enforcement procedures.[102]

The most widely publicized of these actions—the 51-day siege of the Branch Davidian compound in Waco, Texas—ended on April 19, 1993, when 80 members of the Branch Davidian sect died after a fire and a shootout with police and federal agents. David Koresh, leader of the group, died of a gunshot wound to the head sometime during the blaze. Another controversial action occurred in 1992, when U.S. Marshals tried to arrest white separatist Randall C. Weaver on firearms charges. During the resulting siege in Ruby Ridge, Idaho, Weaver's unarmed wife, Vicki, and his son, Sammy, age 14 (as well as U.S. Marshal William Degan) were killed. In 1995, the U.S. government, without admitting guilt in the case, agreed to pay $3.1 million to Weaver and his three surviving children.[103] Regarding Ruby Ridge, one news source stated, "Like Waco, Ruby Ridge long ago entered the political mythology of the paranoid ultraright. Like Waco, it attests to the emergence of a reckless mentality that sullies the image of the FBI and plays straight into the hands of those who like to demagogue the federal government."[104]

There are also some environmental terrorist and animal-rights groups at work in the United States. They try to intervene and make a point regarding various environmental issues. They have released caged animals into the wild, targeted buildings where experimentation on animals has been conducted, and damaged vehicles they feel are not environmentally friendly. In August 2003, several car dealerships in Southern California were targeted by a radical group called Earth Liberation Front. They have claimed responsibility in the past for arsons against commercial entities they say damage the environment. On this evening, they burned dozens of SUVs as well as an auto dealership warehouse and also spray painted some vehicles with sayings such as "Fat, Lazy Americans." The vehicles they targeted were primarily Hummers.[105]

Anarchists have also been operating recently in the United States. They protest global and trade issues. Some of their members advocate violence and destruction of property and travel to trade meetings with the goal of disrupting the meetings and causing destruction in the streets, as happened in Seattle at the World Trade Organization talks.

★ ★ ★

BIAS-BASED POLICING

Racial profiling, the term commonly used for bias-based policing, is generally defined as any police-initiated activity that relies on a person's race or ethnic background rather than behavior as a basis for identifying that individual as being involved in criminal activity. Police may not use race or ethnicity to decide whom to stop or search, but they may use it to determine whether an individual matches a specific description of a suspect.[106]

The difficulty arises in the validity of stops when police are investigating a crime committed by a group of individuals who may share ethnic or racial characteristics. Some criminal enterprises are composed of persons with similar ethnic or racial or national origins, but under this definition using this characteristic as a determining factor could be interpreted as racial profiling.[107]

During the 1990s, racial profiling became a hot topic in the media. New terms were coined, such as "driving while black" (DWB). The media attention brought the topic up for discussion in communities. In December 1999, a

Gallup Poll revealed that only half of Americans believed that police engaged in racial profiling, and 81 percent disagreed with the practice.[108] This perception of the prevalence of the problem varied slightly by race, with 56 percent of whites and 77 percent of African Americans responding that racial profiling was widely used by police. Six percent of whites and 42 percent of African Americans felt they'd been stopped by the police due to their race, and a staggering 72 percent of African American males between 18 and 34 believed they'd been stopped because of their race. This perception of racial profiling correlates with animosity toward police in a community. According to the same Gallup poll, African American respondents had a lower opinion of police (58 percent had a favorable opinion of local police, and 64 percent favorably viewed state police versus 85 percent and 87 percent, respectively, by white residents). Fifty-three percent of African American males between 18 and 34 said they'd been treated unfairly by police.

Police officers have a lot of discretion in their jobs, and this is particularly evident in traffic stops. First, officers decide whether or not to stop a car; then, they decide how to handle the stop, i.e., remove occupants from the vehicle, call a drug dog, ask for a consent search, and so on. Questions have been raised by citizens as to how officers make these discretionary decisions, and some allege they are made based on race or ethnicity. Many members of minority groups feel they are being stopped for petty traffic violations such as failure to use a traffic signal or an equipment violation so that the officers can use the opportunity to question occupants or search vehicles.

The research that has recently been conducted on bias-based policing or racial profiling has been used in lawsuits. A study was done in Maryland by Dr. John Lamberth of Temple University. He did an analysis of police searches by Maryland State Police along I-95. He found that 74 percent of speeders were white, and 17.5 percent were African American, yet African Americans made up 79 percent of the drivers searched.[109] He was also asked to analyze New Jersey data when there were complaints that African American drivers were being stopped disproportionately by state troopers. He analyzed data from 1988 thru 1991 and found that African Americans comprised 13.5 percent of NJ Turnpike traffic and 15 percent of the drivers speeding, yet they represented 35 percent of those stopped and 73.2 percent of those arrested. He concluded African Americans were much more likely to be stopped and arrested than whites.[110] The Superior Court of New Jersey used these data when it suppressed evidence seized by troopers and agreed that troopers were relying on race in stopping and searching vehicles. In April of 1999, the Attorney General of New Jersey issued a report indicating New Jersey troopers had participated in racial profiling on the Jersey Turnpike; people of color were 40.6 percent of those stopped on the turnpike and 77.2 percent of the people searched. The report also found that 80 percent of consent searches involved minority motorists.[111]

The New York Attorney General analyzed New York City's stop-and-frisk practices and, in December 1999, released the results, which indicated that African Americans and Latinos were much more likely to be stopped and searched. This phenomenon has also been documented in Britain.[112]

These limited studies together with anecdotal evidence have helped criminal justice practitioners as well as community activists understand what is happening. To get a better handle on the situation and determine if there is a specific problem in various cities and states across the country, more data are needed. In response to the community outcry, most states have implemented some type of data collection system. In the year 2000, most states had taken some steps to address the problem, from California requiring cards with complaint numbers be given out to everyone stopped, to Arizona having over 100 police chiefs sign a declaration stating that racial profiling will not be tolerated, to Colorado collecting ethnicity data and providing antibias training to all certified officers. Though California failed to pass a measure mandating the collection of ethnicity data, over 60 percent of the departments in the state voluntarily track and analyze that data. Missouri has gone so far as to pass a law on racial profiling (which will be monitored by an 18-member task force), which requires police to keep data on motorists pulled over and allows the governor to withhold money from agencies failing to comply.[113]

Collecting these data will either help the community to see there is no problem with the activities of their police or help the police and community to understand the scope of the problems. This data collection will also send a message to all concerned that racial profiling is unacceptable. Analyzing the data together with an early warning system can also help to identify particular officers or squads who may be prone to inappropriate stops. There is a likelihood of initial resistance from officers asked to compile these data, but many have come to accept this collection process, especially when the data were used to examine trends and not target individual officers. Some departments have officers record information regarding ethnicity and other factors regarding their stops; others radio it in to dispatchers, who log the information for administrative review, as in "Operation Vanguard" in a couple of cities in Kansas.[114]

While some agencies may not be pleased with the analysis of their data, others will be reassured. The Washington State Patrol conducted a study of their stops and found that whites and African Americans were stopped more frequently than Native Americans or Asians. Whites make up 88.8 percent of the population and account for 92.2 percent of stops, African Americans are 3.4 percent of the population and 4 percent of the stops; Asian Americans are 5.9 percent of the population and 2.9 percent of the stops; and Native Americans are 1.9 percent of the population and .9 percent of the stops. They did discover, however, that Hispanic and African American drivers were arrested or ticketed more frequently than whites after being stopped.[115]

If analysis of these data reveals a problem, it can be addressed. New procedures, training, or counseling can be employed to make changes. Some departments are reassured when they find out there is not a bias-based policing problem, and in fact the data can help them counter allegations of unfair treatment. Having the data available is a starting point toward improvement, if there is a need for it, and documentation to defend the department's practices, if no problem is detected. Community support and relationships can be enhanced when the community has faith in the unbiased behavior of their police officers.

★ ★ ★

POLICE CIVIL AND CRIMINAL LIABILITY

Police officers may be held legally liable—that is arrested, sued, and prosecuted for their conduct. This concept of police legal liability comes in many different forms. **Police civil liability** means that a police officer may be sued in civil court for improper behavior, using such civil law concepts as negligence and torts. Civil liability is a relatively new approach to correcting improper actions by the police through lawsuits and the resultant monetary judgments. Officers may also be sued under the provisions of a state civil rights law for violation of a person's civil rights.

Rolando V. del Carmen has identified several major sources of police legal liability. Under state law, police are subject to (1) civil liabilities, including state tort laws and state civil rights laws; (2) criminal liabilities, including state penal code provisions applicable only to public officials and general state penal law provisions; and (3) administrative liabilities. Under federal law, police are subject to (1) civil liabilities, including three sections of Title 42 of the U.S. Code; (2) criminal liabilities, including three sections of Title 18 of the U.S. Code; and (3) administrative liabilities.[116]

State Liability

Police may be sued in state civil courts for torts. A tort is a private wrong, as opposed to a crime that is considered a public wrong. Torts can be classified as intentional torts or negligence torts. As for criminal liability, many states have provisions in their penal codes that make certain actions by police officers or other public servants a crime. Police officers, like everyone else, are also subject to being charged with violations of the state penal law, such as murder, assault, or larceny.

Police officers are also subject to administrative liability: They are liable for the rules and regulations established by their department to govern the conduct of its officers. Officers charged with violations of a department's internal rules and regulations may be subject to discipline in the form of fines, demotions, and even dismissal from the department.

Federal Liability

In recent years, an increasing number of lawsuits against police officers have been brought to federal courts on civil rights grounds. These federal suits are known as 1983 suits, because they are based on Section 1983 of Title 42 of the U.S. Code (Civil Action for Deprivation of Civil Rights):

> Every person who, under color of any statute, ordinance, regulation, custom, or usage, of any State or Territory, subjects or causes to be subjected, any citizen of the United States or other persons within the jurisdiction thereof to the deprivation of any rights, privileges or immunities secured by the Constitution and laws, shall be liable to the party injured in an action at law, suit in equity, or other proper proceeding for redress.

This law was passed in 1871 by Congress to ensure the civil rights of individuals. It requires due process of law before any person can be deprived of life, liberty, or property and provides redress for the denial of these constitutional rights by officials acting under color of state law (under the authority of their power as public officials).[117] Section 1983 of Title 42 of the U.S. Code was originally know as Section 1 of the Ku Klux Klan Act of April 20, 1871, enacted by Congress as a means of enforcing the Fourteenth Amendment guarantee of rights to the newly freed slaves. This law originally was given a narrow interpretation by the courts and was seldom used. Between 1871 and 1920, only 21 cases were decided under Section 1983.[118] Police officers who violate a person's civil rights by unlawfully searching or detaining a person can be sued under this law. It can also be used in abuse-of-force cases. Two other sections of Title 42 of the U.S. Code also apply to police officers. Section 1985 (Conspiracy to Interfere with Civil Rights) can be used against two or more officers who conspire to deprive a person of the equal protection of the law. Section 1981 (Equal Rights under the Law) can also be used against officers. In addition to being sued by a plaintiff civilly for violation of a person's civil rights, a police officer can face criminal charges by the government, using Title 18 of the U.S. Code, Section 242 (Criminal Liability for Deprivation of Civil Rights), and in conspiracy cases, Title 18 of the U.S. Code, Section 241 (Criminal Liability for Conspiracy to Deprive a Person of Rights). Title 18 of the U.S. Code, Section 245 (Federally Protected Activities), may be used against officers who interfere with certain activities such as voting, serving as a juror in a federal court, and other federally regulated activities.

Federal law enforcement officers are also subject to administrative liability—to the rules and regulations of their agencies—just as state officers are subject to the rules and regulations of their departments. The violation of these regulations may lead to such disciplinary action as fines, demotions, or dismissal.

Reasons for Suing Police Officers

Charles R. Swanson, Leonard Territo, and Robert W. Taylor report that the most common source of lawsuits against the police involve assault, battery, false imprisonment, and malicious prosecution.[119] Del Carmen found that a survey of police chiefs from the 20 largest U.S. cities and dozens of other municipalities with populations over 100,000 revealed that most of the chiefs, their officers, and their departments have been sued. The areas in which most suits were brought, in order of frequency, were as follows: (1) use of force; (2) auto pursuits; (3) arrests and searches; (4) employee drug tests; (5) hiring and promotion; (6) discrimination based on race, sex or age; (7) insurance or risk management; (8) record keeping and privacy; and (9) jail management.[120]

In *Civil Liabilities in American Policing: A Text for Law Enforcement Personnel,* del Carmen includes chapters on the following types of liabilities affecting law enforcement personnel: liability for nondeadly and deadly use of force; liability for false arrest and false imprisonment; liability for searches and seizures; liability for negligence, specific instances of negligence in police work; liability for jail management; liabilities of police supervisors for what their subordinates do; and liabilities of police supervisors for what they do to their subordinates.[121]

In his text *Critical Issues in Police Civil Liability,* Victor Kappeler addresses the issue of negligence and discusses areas of concern to law enforcement officers. These areas of potential liability include negligent operation of emergency vehicles, negligent failure to protect, negligent failure to arrest, negligent failure to render assistance, negligent selection, hiring and retention, negligent police supervision and direction, negligent entrustment and assignment, and negligent failure to discipline and investigate. Some of these issues are of more concern to law enforcement administrators, but many should be of concern to the street officer.[122]

Kappeler further discusses areas of concern to officers on the liability associated with excessive force, high-risk drug enforcement, abandoning citizens in dangerous places, failure to arrest intoxicated drivers, and negligence at accident scenes.

The following are some examples of civil lawsuits against the police. In *Biscoe* v. *Arlington,* Alvin Biscoe, an innocent bystander who was waiting to cross the street, was struck by a police car that had gone out of control while involved in a high-speed automobile pursuit. The accident caused Biscoe to lose both legs. Biscoe was awarded $5 million by the court.[123] *Kaplan* v. *Lloyd's Insurance Company* was another lawsuit involving an accident that resulted from a high-speed police chase. The officer driving the police car, who drove 75 miles per hour in a 40-mile-per-hour zone, was found to be negligent and was held liable for damages.[124]

The city of Boston agreed to pay $500,000 to the parents of a teenager who was shot to death by a police officer, even though the youth was in a stolen car involved in a high-speed chase with the police.[125] In *Prior* v. *Woods,* a Detroit police officer mistakenly shot and killed a man, David Prior, in front of his home, because the officer suspected Prior of being a burglar. A $5.7 million judgment was imposed against the Detroit Police Department.[126]

In 1996, Drewey and Mona Scarberry were awarded $950,000 by the city of Tacoma, Washington, as the result of a car crash that left Drewey Scarberry partially paralyzed. The couple's car was broadsided by a carload of gang members being pursued by the police.[127]

Effects of Lawsuits on Police Departments and Officers

The use of civil lawsuits against the police has been increasing at a rapid rate and is having a dramatic effect on the treasuries of some counties and cities. Advocates of police civil damage lawsuits see these lawsuits as a vehicle for stimulating police reform. They assume that the dollar cost of police misconduct will force other city officials to intervene and force improvements in the police department.

However, Edward J. Littlejohn's study of police misconduct litigation in Detroit suggested that this assumption is incorrect. Littlejohn found that even when damage awards increased substantially, there was no feedback from other agencies of city government. He found that one agency of government argued the case in court and another paid the bill when the case was lost. The damage awards did not create pressure for changes in police operations.[128]

This is changing, as lawsuits against police have exploded in recent years. Increased media attention, coupled with some high judgments and out-of-court settlements, have encouraged individuals and lawyers to go after the most visible arm of the criminal justice system—the police. There is also the perception by some of the government as having "deep pockets" and the ability to pay these judgments and settlements. Early estimates indicated that only 4 percent of the cases alleging police wrongdoing resulted in a verdict against the police, but more recently police have lost approximately 8 percent of cases reported. This number seems small, but departments feel a significant impact financially and in the area of morale.[129]

The cost to taxpayers for civil suits is extremely high when factoring in the cost of liability insurance, litigation, out-of-court settlements, and punitive damage awards. A recent study of police liability cases handed down by the federal district courst from 1978 to 1995 indicated the average reported award and attorney fees against police departments was $118,698, with judgments ranging from $1 to $1.6 million.[130] It's unfortunate, but due to the high costs, many governments pay minimal out-of-court settlements to get rid of the case and avoid the costs of litigation. This angers police officers, who feel they did nothing wrong and that the government should always defend them and stand up for what is right, rather than just looking at the least expensive way to resolve the situation. They also fear that settlements encourage frivolous lawsuits.

So many suits have been filed against the police that the U.S. Supreme Court, in *Canton v. Harris*, made it more difficult for victims to sue for damages. The Court ruled that to be liable, police departments must be deliberately indifferent to the needs of the people with whom police come in contact.[131] Joseph J. Senna and Larry J. Siegel said that despite this tightening of liability standards, "the threat of large civil penalties may prove to be the most effective deterrent yet to the police use of excessive force."[132]

There has been an increase in civil suits filed against the police since the 1960s; consequently, officers and administrators need to be aware of the issue of civil liability and the police. Unrealistic fears of civil liability have a number of negative effects, including morale problems as well as alienation from the public and sometimes misunderstandings. The increase in litigation does have a positive side in that it allows for proper redress of police wrongdoing and promotes better police training and more responsible police practices; it also sets the standard for police behavior.[133] Officers should seek to be as educated in this area as possible to have a realistic view and accurate understanding of the issue. Kappeler's text, *Critical Issues in Police Civil Liability,* is a good place to begin that education.

CHAPTER SUMMARY

Although police work can be dangerous, not many officers are murdered in the line of duty. Additionally, the number of murdered officers has decreased in recent years. Police shooting policies have changed significantly in recent years in response to changes in state laws, police philosophy, and court cases, including the landmark U.S. Supreme Court case of *Tennessee v. Garner.*

Additionally, police have begun to address the problem of rapid automobile pursuits, with many departments severely restricting them. Perhaps these changes will reduce the incidents of police civil liability, also discussed in this chapter.

The chapter also discussed the damage to U.S. society from domestic violence, along with efforts by the police to address this problem. Radical and hate groups and the threats that they pose to our police and our society were also covered, as was the issue of bias-based policing.

Finally, the chapter discussed how police officers can be held legally liable for their conduct. They can be arrested under their state's criminal law and sued under civil law.

Learning Check

1. Discuss how dangerous it is to be a police officer in the United States. Talk about whether this danger has changed at all during the past several years.

2. Explain the fleeing felon rule and why it existed.

3. Discuss some recent changes in police shooting policies and how they have affected officers' safety.

4. Explain why many police departments have started to introduce limited pursuit policies.

5. Discuss the seriousness of the domestic violence problem in our society.

Application Exercise

Last year you passed your local police department's entrance examination. During this year you have passed the department's physical agility, psychological, and medical examinations, as well as its background investigation. This morning you received a letter in the mail from the police department. It told you that you have been accepted for appointment and advised you to report to City Hall next Monday to be sworn in as a probationary police officer. You have never told your parents about your plans to become a police officer. You are sure they will object, because they consider police work to be extremely dangerous. Now you must tell your mother, an accountant, and your father, a high school English teacher, that you plan to become a police officer. You are sure they are going to be very upset about your decision and very concerned about your future safety. Plan what you will tell your parents about the degree of danger in police work.

Web Exercise

Research domestic violence sites on the Internet that target particular cultural groups (for example, Women's Justice Center, Asian Task Force against Domestic Violence, National Latino Alliance for the Elimination of Domestic Violence, Muslims against Family Violence, National Council of Jewish Women). What types of services and outreach do they provide?

Key Concepts

"Defense of life" standard
"Fleeing felon" doctrine
Minneapolis Domestic Violence Experiment
Police civil liability
Police pursuit policy
Proarrest policy
Radical and hate groups
Tennessee v. *Garner*

16 Policing and Homeland Defense

★ ★ ★

CHAPTER GOALS

- To introduce you to the concept of international and domestic terrorism and its disastrous results and the need for the government and the police to ensure homeland defense
- To explore the awful potential of weapons of mass destruction (WMD)
- To familiarize you with the rapid, unprecedented actions taken by the U.S. government and law enforcement to secure its homeland in reaction to the terrorist attacks of September 11, 2001
- To acquaint you with the many sophisticated efforts to prevent and deal with terrorism and ensure homeland defense by national, state, local, and private security agencies
- To show you the methods used to investigate acts of terrorism

The events of September 11, 2001, were an unprecedented challenge to the rescue personnel who responded. They tried to restore some order and calm, despite their own physical and emotional responses to viewing the tragedy and its effects up close.

On **September 11, 2001,** our world changed.

On September 11, 2001, a series of unthinkable and incomprehensible events led to ultimate disasters in New York City, Washington D.C., and a grassy field in Pennsylvania. Those events shocked the world and changed world history.

In the minutes before and after 8:00 A.M. on that date, four large commercial passenger jets lifted off at major airports in Boston, Newark, and just outside of Washington, D.C., en route to California. In several panicked calls from cell phones, passengers and airline crews told their families and loved ones about hijackers armed with knives attacking crew members and seizing control of the airliners.

At approximately 8:48 A.M., American Airlines Flight 11, a Boeing 767 scheduled to fly from Logan Airport in Boston to Los Angeles, with 92 people aboard, crashed into the 110-story north tower of the World Trade Center (WTC) in New York City's financial district (Building 1, 1 World Trade Center). The plane had departed Boston at 7:45. At approximately 9:03, United Airlines Flight 175, also a Boeing 767 and also headed for Los Angeles from Logan with 63 persons aboard, struck the south tower of the World Trade Center (Building 2, 2 World Trade Center). That flight had left Boston at 7:58.

Witnesses reported seeing the planes crash into the towers, with flames and smoke pouring out of the buildings, and bodies falling or jumping from the highest floors. Within an hour, the two towers, symbols of America's strength, giant structures that had dominated and symbolized the Manhattan skyline since they first opened in 1976, disappeared: imploding, crashing to the ground, reduced to ash and gigantic heaps of rubble. Smoke permeated the skies of the entire New York City metropolitan area; crushed vehicles, body parts, clothing, and building material were strewn about the streets. The thick gray ash spread throughout the area. Thousands of people ran screaming through the streets, crowded onto the bridges leading from Manhattan, and wandered the streets in a state of shock.

A massive emergency response, including the New York City Police Department, the New York City Fire Department, the police and rescue operations of the Port Authority of New York–New Jersey, and the city's emergency medical service, was immediate. These people entered the buildings in an attempt to rescue others. Many of them were lost forever,

A mail truck burns next to a police car after one of the twin towers of the World Trade Center collapses. What happened to the officers who had parked their car there to respond to the call? Many officers were inside the towers trying to help when they came crashing down.

YOU ARE THERE! »

New York City's Law Enforcement Heroes of 9/11

In memoriam to those who gave their lives on 9/11.

NEW YORK CITY POLICE DEPARTMENT

- Sergeant John Coughlin
- Sergeant Michael Curtin
- Sergeant Rodney Gillis
- Detective Claude Richards
- Detective Joseph Vigiano
- Officer John D'Allara
- Officer Vincent Danz
- Officer Jerome Dominguez
- Officer Stephen Driscoll
- Officer Mark Ellis
- Officer Robert Fazio
- Officer Ronald Kloepfer
- Officer Thomas Langone
- Officer James Leahy
- Officer Brian McDonnell
- Officer John Perry
- Officer Glenn Pettit
- Officer Tony Roy
- Officer Moria Smith
- Officer Ramon Suarez
- Officer Paul Talty
- Officer Santos Valentin
- Officer Walter Weaver

PORT AUTHORITY OF NEW YORK–NEW JERSEY POLICE DEPARTMENT

- Director Fred Marrone
- Chief James Romito
- Captain Kathy Mazza
- Lieutenant Robert Cirri
- Sergeant Robert Kaulfers
- Officer Christopher Amoroso
- Officer Maurice Barry
- Officer Liam Callahan
- Officer Clinton Davis
- Officer Donald Foreman
- Officer Gregg Froehner
- Officer Thomas Gorman
- Officer Uhuru Houston
- Officer George Howard
- Officer Steve Huczko
- Officer Anthony Infante
- Officer Paul Jurgens
- Officer Paul Laszcynksi
- Officer David Lemagne
- Officer John Lennon
- Officer John Levi
- Officer James Lynch
- Officer Donald McIntyre

- Officer Walter McNeil
- Officer Joseph Navas
- Officer James Nelson
- Officer Alfonse Niedermeyer
- Officer James Parham
- Officer Dominick Pezzulo
- Officer Bruce Reynolds
- Officer Antonio Rodrigues
- Officer Richard Rodriguez
- Officer James Romito
- Officer James Skala
- Officer Walwyn Stuart
- Officer Kenneth Tietjen
- Officer Nathaniel Webb
- Officer Michael Wholey

NEW YORK COURT ADMINISTRATION

- Captain William Thompson
- Court Officer Thomas Jurgens
- Court Officer Mitchell Wallace

including much of the high command of the fire and Port Authority departments. Medical and emergency response personnel from around the world responded. Triage centers went into operation, and ordinary residents passed out bottled water to the responding emergency personnel. By the evening of September 11, Buildings 5 and 7 of the World Trade Center had also collapsed, and many buildings began to tremble and show signs of imminent col-

lapse. The fires, smoke, and eerie ash continued blowing through the streets.

At approximately 9:39 A.M., American Airlines Flight 77, a Boeing 757 carrying 58 passengers and 6 crew members on a scheduled flight from Dulles International Airport in Virginia, just west of Washington, D.C., also bound for Los Angeles, slammed into one of the five-sided, five-story concrete-walled structures of the U.S. Pentagon

Dempsey's Law

"Professor—Where Were You on 9/11?"

Whenever we discuss the tragic terrorist attacks against the United States on September 11, 2001, and their impact on policing, a student will ask, "Professor Dempsey, where were you on 9/11? Were you there? What did you do? What were your reactions to it?"

Most people in my generation can still remember exactly where they were, whom they were with, and their initial reactions to the tragic assassination of President John F. Kennedy in Dallas, Texas, on November 22, 1963. The assassination of President Kennedy was a defining moment in the lives of most people of my generation. Now, sadly, we all have another defining moment in our lives, the September 11, 2001 attacks on the World Trade Center in New York City, on the Pentagon in northern Virginia, and the aborted attack on Washington, D.C., and the crash of a plane in a grassy field in Stony Creek Township, Pennsylvania.

On September 11, 2001, I was already retired as a captain with the New York City Police Department for 13 years after 24 years of service. I was in my office on Eastern Long Island, about 60 miles from the city, preparing for a 9:30 A.M. class when one of the other professors said to me, "Jack, a plane just crashed into the World Trade Center, and the radio says it may have been a terrorist attack." Of course, I was stunned and shocked and completely unprepared for this. My first thought was to get into my car and drive to the scene right away to help. That's what cops do, isn't it? They get to the scene as quickly as humanly possible to help. That's what I had done for 24 years, on-duty and off-duty.

Fortunately, as I got my wits about me, I realized that I had a responsibility right here, right now, to get to my classroom and help my students. That was my job now; I was no longer a cop; I was just a college professor. I went to my classroom right away to meet the students. When I got to the classroom, some of the students were already there, and some were just walking in. Many had heard dribs and drabs about the emergency as they were driving to school or walking on campus. They all appeared

nervous and extremely concerned; one young man was on his cell phone talking to his Mom because she had called him (his Dad worked in the World Trade Center). I started to talk to the students about the very little bit I knew about the situation, and not knowing what else to do, tried to reassure them that the very finest police, fire, and emergency medical personnel in the world were already at the scene or en route to it. I took the young man who was on the phone out into the hallway and stood with him as he talked to his Mom. Then I told him to get home to his Mom and family right away and to call me whenever he could.

At about 10 A.M., one of the administrative assistants who worked in the school walked into my classroom crying and in distress. Still, even after I had been retired for 13 years, most of the people on the campus perceived of me as the former city police captain instead of a professor and came to me whenever they needed assistance. She said to me, "Mr. Dempsey, the first tower just collapsed, and the second one is coming down." I went to comfort her immediately and made her sit down at one of the desks. I was still stunned, shocked, and unprepared for what she was saying. I couldn't even fathom the possibility of what she might be trying to tell me. Then I told the students that I was canceling class and asked them to go home immediately to help their parents, grandparents, younger brothers and sisters, and other loved ones to deal with this situation. I also asked them to pray.

I then went to the doorway of the classroom I was scheduled to teach in next and spoke to the students who were waiting in the hallway for the previous class to end. I briefed them about the little information we knew at this time and told them I was canceling class and gave them the same instructions I gave to the earlier class. One of my very best students, Nicole, a mom who had an 8-year-old daughter in a local school (Nicole is now an officer in the NYPD), came to me and asked me if I had any information about the local schools and whether the students there were affected. I just didn't know

Dempsey's Law

"Professor—Where Were You on 9/11?" (*continued*)

what to tell her. I felt hopeless. When I was a cop, everyone always came up to me with their problems, and I was able to help them the best I could. I told Nicole to drive over to her daughter's school and be ready to bring her home if school had been released.

Eventually, one of the professors came down the hall and said that all classes were cancelled. I brought the administrative assistant back to my office and then found out the full extent of what had happened that morning. As soon as I knew that she was being tended to, and my students were on their way home, I gathered my belongings to head to the parking lot to drive into the city. I noticed that there were many people, professors and students, crying and disoriented, in the hallways and classrooms, and I decided to deal with the closest emergency at hand, the immediate crisis that was right there. I attempted to comfort them. Later, I walked throughout the building and checked all the classrooms to make sure that they were empty and there was nobody else who needed help. Later, I called my family members at home and at work to make sure that they were all okay. We only live about 24 miles from lower Manhattan, and on a clear day we could see the towers from the bay down the block from the house.

Then, I went to my car and listened to the radio reports of the tragedy. Hearing about the chaos in Manhattan, and knowing that the roads would be blocked going into the city, I came back into the building and talked to the few remaining people who were there. I again walked through the building; after ensuring that no one needed help, I drove home. Later, I was glad I had not attempted to drive to the World Trade Center as the roads indeed were closed to all but emergency service vehicles. I also had to realize that the very finest emergency professionals in the world were at the scene, and that I was no longer a cop but just an old college professor now, and I probably would have gotten in the way.

Much later, reflecting back on the events of September 11, I kept recalling the first terrorist attack on the World Trade Center in 1993. At that time, I was already retired from the NYPD for five years and was visiting my daughter at the hospital where she was a patient. As the news broke that morning, both my daughter Anne Marie and I watched the dramatic rescues made by the NYPD that day. Anne Marie said to me, "Daddy, I'm so glad that you are retired, because you would have been down there." I said to Anne Marie, "I wish I had been there; look at all the people I could have helped." She smiled and said "Daddy, you'll never change— once a cop, always a cop. But, I am glad you are here helping me now."

I have since retired from my former school and now teach at SUNY–Empire State College. Many of my students are police officers in the NYPD attempting to finish up their four-year degrees as one of their requirements to rise to higher ranks. Among the study groups or seminars I teach now is a course called "Terrorism: Interdisciplinary Studies." The majority of my students in these groups had responded on September 11 to the World Trade Center or had spent a year working at the site (the pile; ground zero), or at the morgue with the family members, or at Fresh Kills (the location in Staten Island where the remains of the World Trade Center had been brought). Most of them had lost a brother- or sister-officer at the site. None of them will ever be the same as they were before the morning of September 11, 2001. I am very proud that I am associated with these students.

I know that my present students and all the members of the greatest emergency service professionals in the world did the very best that they could have that day. I think I did the best I could have done in my very small role as a professor where I was that day too. But I guess I'll always feel a little sad that I was not down there that day—as Anne Marie had said to me in 1993, "Once a cop . . ."

Forst's Law

Involvement in Major Incidents

I have always felt it was important for anyone in law enforcement to be aware of what was going on in their jurisdiction as well as nationally, to know about crime trends, unusual incidents, and investigations and court rulings.

I was no longer working for the police department when the attacks of 9/11 occurred. Like everyone, I was glued to the TV, and we discussed it quite a bit in class. When the anthrax threat occurred several weeks later and we didn't know whether there was a relationship or not, again I watched events unfold.

The anthrax incidents held particular interest as the American Media building is located in Boca Raton. When an employee died, another went to the hospital, and almost 1,000 lined up in the hot sun at the Health Department to obtain testing and precautionary antibiotics, I also looked at the situation as a former police administrator in that city.

The logistics and cost to the agency to serve in this highly unusual and unexpected situation created a challenge that they had to meet quickly. Securing the building 24 hours a day, documenting who came and went, interviewing employees, conferencing with other emergency response personnel and federal agencies, maintaining order among the anxious employees waiting for testing in the hot and humid conditions, collating information, and disseminating that information to a demanding press and a concerned public would tax their resources to the maximum. The city still required protection, but clearly all sworn personnel suspended their normal activities unless of an emergency nature. The calls for service were also increased with citizens bringing in "suspicious" packages and substances as well as calling in information regarding "suspicious" individuals who may be accomplices to the terrorists, some of whom had been living in the South Florida area.

These demands would require the administration to reassign personnel, change schedules, examine vehicle demands, devise procedures for handling the suspicious substances, define roles among the multiple investigatory agencies, establish procedures for handling the American Media scene, and clarify and disseminate information regarding the health risks to the public. These demands lasted quite a while and though they eventually de-escalated, the unusual level of activity continued. As the emergency nature of the situation slowly decreased, concern about paying for all these services did not.

It was exciting to watch the coverage and see friends and former coworkers being interviewed, giving press conferences, and walking around at the scene. It would have been an exciting and challenging time to be on the Boca Raton Police Department.

in northern Virginia—the headquarters and command center of the military forces of the United States of America. That plane had left Dulles at 8:10.

At approximately 10:10 A.M., United Airlines Flight 93, a Boeing 757, which had departed from Newark, New Jersey, bound for San Francisco, with 38 passengers, 2 pilots and 5 flight attendants on board, crashed into a grassy field in Stony Creek Township, Pennsylvania, about 80 miles southeast of Pittsburgh. The plane, which left Newark at 8:01, had nearly reached Cleveland when it made a sharp left turn and headed back toward Pennsylvania just before the crash. It was later revealed that the plane's target was Washington, D.C.

Immediately, all airports in the United States were shut down, and all air travel was terminated. U.S. military personnel from around the world were placed on Force Protection Condition Delta (DefCon Delta), the highest military alert possible. Aircraft carriers, warships, and jet fighters were dispatched into New York City harbor and other major harbors and areas across the nation. The U.S. borders were closed. High-rise buildings like the Sears Tower in Chicago, the Renaissance Center in Detroit, the Peachtree Center in Atlanta, the Gateway Arch in St. Louis, the Space Needle in Seattle, the Trans-America Pyramid in San Francisco, and the CNN Center in Atlanta, were evacuated and closed to the public. Walt Disney World and Sea

World in Orlando, as well as hundreds of shopping malls, including the huge Mall of America in Bloomington, Minnesota, were evacuated and closed. Government buildings and monuments were shut down. America's financial markets shut down as well.

The swiftness, scale, and sophistication of the coordinated operation, coupled with the extraordinary planning required, made most people realize that **terrorism** and mass murder had hit New York City, the United States, and indeed, the world. In the immediate aftermath of 9/11 it was reported that almost 5,000 people were missing and over 400 confirmed dead. Eventually it was determined that the missing persons included 23 New York City Police Officers, 38 New York–New Jersey Port Authority officers, 3 New York State court officers, and more than 300 New York City firefighters. These attacks shocked us, even though there had been similar events, although not as massive, before. Terrorism was not new to the United States.

For years most Americans had believed that terrorist attacks only occurred in foreign nations, but events in the past few years have changed American's perceptions:

- In 1993, the first terrorist attack on New York City's World Trade Center killed 6 and wounded 1,000.

- In 1995, the Alfred P. Murrah Federal Building in Oklahoma City was bombed, killing 168 persons and injuring 675 others.

- In 1996, a bombing at the Olympic Games in Atlanta, Georgia, killed 1 person and wounded 111 others.

During these years there were also terrorist acts committed against family planning clinics that provide abortions and against churches, and many other depraved, senseless incidents. These events awakened Americans to the fact that terrorism had actually come ashore. However, no other day in America's history had been quite like September 11, 2001.

The terrorist attacks of September 11, 2001, finally jolted Americans out of their sense of complacency, and perhaps lethargy, and made them realize that indeed they themselves were the targets of terrorism and that their lives and the lives of their loved ones were at extreme risk from brutal invaders and murderers. What really made the terrorism threat hit home to most Americans was that they were actually attacked in their homeland. The need for a strong homeland defense has been a primary interest of U.S. law enforcement since then.

This chapter will discuss terrorism directed against Americans and American interests abroad, including foreign terrorism and **domestic terrorism**, as well as cata-

strophic disasters and **weapons of mass destruction (WMD).** It will discuss the immediate aftermath of September 11, 2001 and the rapid, unprecedented efforts made by the U.S. government. It will describe federal, state, local, and private security efforts against terrorism and for homeland defense, and methods of investigating terrorism, including proactive and reactive methods and the federal–local Joint Terrorism Task Force concept.

★ ★ ★

TERRORISM

Terrorism has a long tradition in world history. Terrorist tactics have been used frequently by radical and criminal groups to influence public opinion and to attempt to force authorities to do their will. Terrorists have criminal, political, and other nefarious motives. Many may remember the terrorist activities that occurred during the 1972 Olympic Games in Munich, Germany, when terrorists attacked and took hostage the Israeli Olympic team and killed all of them; the 1988 explosion of Flight 103 in the air over Lockerbie, Scotland, killing all 270 persons aboard; the Oklahoma City Federal Building bombing; the first World Trade Center bombing in New York City; and the actions of the Unabomber. Of course, no one will ever forget the terrorist attacks against the United States of America on September 11, 2001. (See Exhibit 16.1.)

This section will discuss general concepts regarding terrorism, including international and domestic terrorism, catastrophic disasters, and weapons of mass destruction.

Many Americans and most major U.S. firms have been targeted by terrorists in some way. Political extremists and terrorists use the violence and suspense of terrorist acts such as bombing, kidnapping, and hostage situations to put pressure on those in authority to comply with their demands and cause the authorities and public to recognize their power. They use their activities to obtain money for

Exhibit 16.1	Some Types of Terrorism

- *Eco-terrorism:* Attempts to inflict economic damage to those who profit from the destruction of the natural environment.
- *Cyberterrorism:* Initiates, or threatens to initiate, the exploitation of or attack on information systems.
- *Narcoterrorism:* Hiring terrorists to protect the drug cartels as well as the sale and distribution of drugs by these cartels.
- *Bioterrorism:* Involves such weapons of mass destruction (WMD) as anthrax, botulism, and smallpox.

their causes, to alter business or government policies, or to change public opinion. Attacks against executives are common in Latin America, the Middle East, and Europe, and they have spread to the United States. Successful terrorist techniques employed in one country spread to others. Governments and corporations have had to develop extensive plans to deal with terrorism.

There are many definitions of terrorism. The FBI defines terrorism as "the unlawful use of force or violence against persons or property to intimidate or coerce a government, the civilian population, or a segment thereof, in furtherance of political or social objectives." The U.S. Defense Department defines it as "the unlawful use or threatened use of force or violence against individuals or property to coerce or intimidate governments or societies, often to achieve political, regligious, or ideological objectives."[1]

According to Louis J. Freeh, former director of the FBI:

> Terrorists are among the most ruthless of criminals, but their motivation rarely stems from personal need or a desire for material gain. Unlike the majority of violent criminals, terrorists do not know their victims; in fact, one of the hallmarks of terrorism is its indiscriminate victimization. Also, unlike most serious criminal activity, terrorism invites—and even depends upon—media attention to ensure a maximum yield of terror.[2]

Perhaps the most dramatic impression of terrorism these authors have read is the preface to Jonathan White's 2003 text, *Terrorism: An Introduction: 2002 Update*, in which he talks about a lecture on religious terrorism and the theology of violence he delivered at a training session on terrorism hosted by New York State Police Superintenant James McMahon a year before September 11, 2001:

> At the end of my two-hour lecture, a group of police officers stayed and asked questions. Their eagerness to learn reminded me of first semester graduate students, and they continued to take notes well into lunch. After a half-hour, my curiosity—and my hunger—were getting the best of me. I admitted the theology of violence fasinated me, but asked, "Why are you folks so interested?
>
> One of my new acquaintances smiled and said, "You're talking about the next attack. Religious terrorists are going to strike, and when it happens, it'll be in New York City." The young faces around him nodded in affirmation. The men and women who stayed were members of the New York City Police Department. Some of them charged into the burning trade towers to save lives on September 11. Not all of them returned.[3]

From 1968 to 2000, an average of 26 Americans per year have been killed as a result of terrorism. In 1998, the year of the Columbine tragedy, 28 students died in American schools. In 1999, of the 184 Americans abroad who were killed or injured by terrorists, 133 were businesspeople. U.S. interests remain the favored target of terrorists abroad.[4] It has been estimated that almost 3,000 people perished in the World Trade Center on September 11, 2001.

Another significant recent concern that falls into the terrorist camp is **cyberterrorism**, defined by the FBI as terrorism that initiates, or threatens to initiate, the exploitation of or attack on information systems.

The Terrorism Research Center, an independent institute dedicated to informing the public of the phenomena of terrorism, information warfare and security, critical infrastructure protection, homeland security, and other issues of low-intensity political violence and gray-area phenomena, offers an interesting Web site. It features essays and thought pieces on current issues as well as links to other terrorism documents, research, and resources.[5]

There have been several texts written on the subject of terrorism. The best text on terrorism the authors have used is Jonathan R. White's *Terrorism: An Introduction*. The latest edition of this text was published in 2003 as *Terrorism: An Introduction: 2002 Update*.[6] This text covers the phenomenon and history of terrorism in four parts. Part 1, "The Criminology of Terrorism," contains chapters on mutating forms of terrorism, individual and group behavior and terrorism, changing group structures and the metamorphosis of terrorism, and religion and terror. Part 2, "Essential Background," contains chapters on the origins of modern terrorism, the origins of the Irish troubles, the origins of Middle Eastern terrorism, and Latin American influences on terrorism. Part 3, "Modern Terrorism," includes chapters on international terrorism and the question of Palestine, religion and Middle Eastern terrorism, international terrorism (the rise and fall of the left and the right, nationalistic and ethnic terrorism), terrorism in the United States, and violent extremism in the United States. Part 4, "Issues in Modern Terrorism," contains chapters on technological terrorism and weapons of mass destruction; terrorism and the media; policy, liberty, security and the future; and responding to the tragedy of September 11. The

PATROLLING THE WEB

The Terrorism Research Center
   http://www.terrorism.com or
   http://www.homelandsecurity.com

text also includes an introductory dictionary of extremism and a selected bibliography; the book is fully indexed.

Also, for an excellent analysis on defending the homeland in the wake of 9/11, see Professor White's 2004 text *Defending The Homeland: Domestic Intelligence, Law Enforcement, and Security.*[7]

International Terrorism

According to John F. Lewis, Jr., retired assistant director of the FBI's National Security Division, the FBI divides the current international threat to the United States into three categories.[8]

First, there are threats from foreign sponsors of **international terrorism.** The U.S. Department of State has designated seven countries as state sponsors of terrorism: Iran, Iraq, Syria, Sudan, Libya, Cuba, and North Korea. These sponsors view terrorism as a tool of foreign policy. Their activities have changed over time. Past activities included direct terrorist support and operations by official state agents. Now these sponsors generally seek to conceal their support of terrorism by relying on surrogates to conduct operations. State sponsors remain involved in terrorist activities by funding, organizing, networking, and providing other support and instruction to formal terrorist groups and loosely affiliated extremists.

Second, there are threats from formalized terrorist groups, such as Al-Qaeda, the Lebanese Hizballah,

---

YOU ARE THERE! >>

A Profile of Osama bin Laden, the Murderer

The following is a brief profile of Osama bin Laden, the man responsible for numerous truly heinous terrorist incidents, including the September 11, 2001, terrorist attacks on U.S. soil and the destruction of the World Trade Center.

Osama bin Laden was born in 1955 or 1957 in the city of Riyadh, the capital of Saudi Arabia. He was raised in a wealthy family, one of more than 50 children born to a Yemeni father. The family made its fortune from Saudi Arabia's oil and construction riches. Osama bin Laden himself is believed to be worth $300 million. It is alleged that he uses his fortune to finance activities that involve anywhere from several hundred to several thousand terrorists.

In the 1980s, bin Laden became a leader in the Afghani insurgency against invading Soviet troops and earned a reputation as a fierce warrior on the battlefield. It has been said that during this 10-year struggle, bin Laden received money from the CIA, which covertly financed the Afghani insurgents.

In 1989, he returned home to Saudi Arabia; in 1990 he began a confrontation with the Saudi monarchy over its decision to invite U.S. troops into the country. This led to his arrest by Saudi officials for criticism of the monarchy. He has been involved in attempts to overthrow the secular regimes in Egypt, Jordan, Syria, and the Palestinian territories and replace them with Islamic states.

In 1992, bin Laden moved to the Sudan and began to form his Al-Qaeda (in Arabic this means "the base") terrorist organization, a worldwide network of radical Islamics. Investigators have uncovered a network of terrorist cells in Europe and Canada that mainly include Algerians, Tunisians, Libyans, and Moroccans affiliated with bin Laden. In 1996, Sudan, under intense pressure from the United States, forced bin Laden from that country. He resettled in Afghanistan with 180 followers and his three wives. There, sheltered by the ruling Taliban government, he trained terrorists at his training camps.

Bin Laden has been suspected of involvement in a number of major terrorist incidents:

- The February 26, 1993, bombing of the World Trade Center, which killed six and injured a thousand.

- The November 13, 1995, car bombing in Saudi Arabia that killed five American service people.

- The June 25, 1996, car bombing in Saudi Arabia that devastated an apartment complex housing U.S. service people. At least 19 were killed and 400 wounded.

- The August 7, 1998 bombings at the U.S. embassies in Kenya and Tanzania that killed 224 persons and injured thousands.

- The December 1999 plot to attack U.S. installations during the year 2000 millennium celebrations.

- The October 12, 2000, suicide bombing of the *U.S.S. Cole* off the coast of Yemen that killed 17 and injured 39 others.

- The September 11, 2001, attack on the World Trade Center in New York City that killed nearly 3,000 people.

- The September 11, 2001, attack on the United States Pentagon that killed approximately 200 people.

YOU ARE THERE! »

Details of Some Major International Terrorism Cases Affecting the United States

1993 WORLD TRADE CENTER ATTACK

Six persons were killed and more than 1,000 others were injured in the blast on February 26, 1993, in New York City. In 1994, four men were convicted of bombing the World Trade Center. Abdel Rahman, also known as Omar Ahmad Ali Abdel Rahman, a blind Egyptian religious leader, was charged with being one of the planners of the bombing conspiracy and leading a terrorist organization that sprang up in the United States in 1989. Investigators also say he participated in conversations involving the planned bombing of the United Nations building and the assassination of Egyptian President Hosni Mubarak. Rahman and 11 others were convicted in federal court on charges of trying to assassinate political leaders and bomb major New York City landmarks. In 1995 another man, Ramzi Ahmed Yousef, was arrested as the main plotter behind the World Trade Center bombing.

U.S. EMBASSY BOMBINGS

On August 7, 1998, simultaneous bombings occurred in the U.S. embassies in Dar es Salaam, Tanzania, and Nairobi, Kenya. These attacks killed over 200 persons, including 20 Americans. Osama bin Laden—who also uses the aliases of Usama bin Muhammad bin Ladin, Shaykh Usama bin Ladin, the Prince, the Emir, Abu Abdallah, Mujahid Shaykh, Hajj, and the Director—is still wanted by the FBI in connection with these bombings.

MILLENNIUM BOMB PLOT

On December 14, 1999, as the world was preparing to celebrate the year 2000 millennium, an Algerian terrorist at-

tempted to enter the United States from Canada with the intention of setting off a bomb at the Los Angeles International Airport during the celebrations. The would-be bomber, Ahmed Ressam, was arrested at the border near Seattle with a trunk full of explosives. The FBI started a sweeping search for other suspects and information about the plot. Investigators developed information that the plot was linked to a worldwide network of terrorists orchestrated by Osama bin Laden. Ressam was convicted and sentenced to prison in May 2000.

In July 2001, an Algerian-born shopkeeper, Mokhtar Haouari, age 32, who ran a gift shop in Montreal and as a sideline dealt in false identification documents, as well as check and credit card scams, was also convicted in the conspiracy. A third suspect, Abdel Ghani Meskini, offered testimony against the other plotters in exchange for a reduced sentence. The suspects said they were trained in guerilla camps in Afghanistan run by bin Laden.

BOMBING OF THE U.S.S. COLE

On October 12, 2000, two Arabic-speaking suicide bombers attacked the U.S. destroyer *Cole* in the waters off Aden, killing 17 American sailors. The FBI linked the bombing once again to Osama bin Laden, the fugitive Saudi, who had declared a worldwide "holy war" against the United States. Six men were arrested soon after the bombing. Bin Laden remains at large.

Egyptian Al-Gama's Al-Islamiyya, and Palestinian Hamas. These autonomous organizations have their own infrastructures, personnel, financial arrangements, and training facilities. They can plan and mount terrorist campaigns overseas as well as support terrorist operations inside the United States. Some groups use supporters in the United States to plan and coordinate acts of terrorism. In the past these formalized terrorist groups engaged in such criminal activities in the United States as illegally acquiring weapons, violating U.S. immigration laws, and providing safe havens to fugitives.

Third, there are threats from loosely affiliated international radical extremists, such as those who attacked the World Trade Center in 1993. These extremists do not represent a particular nation. Loosely affiliated extremists may pose the most urgent threat to the United States at this time because they remain relatively unknown to law enforcement. They can travel freely, obtain a variety of identities, and recruit like-minded sympathizers from various countries.

Many cases of international terrorism have involved this country primarily by targeting U.S. citizens and interests

---

Exhibit 16.2   Trends Indicating Probable Actions in International Terrorism

- The United States is the most frequently targeted nation.
- Terrorism is increasingly lethal.
- Incidents are declining, but results are more dramatic.
- Terrorism is increasingly based on religion.
- Terrorists make adaptations to changing technology.
- Terrorist structures are changing.
- Technological infrastructures will increasingly be targeted.
- International terrorists represent a new type of threat to law enforcement
- Political Islam will continue to grow, but this does not necessarily mean it will clash with the United States

Source: Jonathan R. White, *Defending the Homeland: Domestic Intelligence, Law Enforcement, and Security* (Belmont, CA: Wadsworth, 2004), p. 114.

---

abroad. Some memorable attacks in addition to the ones mentioned earlier in this chapter include the abduction of hostages in Lebanon in the mid-1980s; the 1996 detonation of an explosive device outside the Khobar Towers in Dhahran, Saudi Arabia, in which 10 U.S. military personnel were killed; the August 7, 1998, bombings of the U.S. embassies in Nairobi, Kenya, and Dar es Salaam, Tanzania, which resulted in the deaths of 12 Americans and 200 oth-

ers; the terrorist attack on the *U.S.S. Cole* in the waters of Aden, which killed 17 U.S. sailors; and the abduction and subsequent murder of *Wall Street Journal* journalist Daniel Pearl in February 2002. Prior to the September 11 attack, the most recent case of international terrorism occurring on our shores was on February 26, 1993, when foreign terrorists bombed the World Trade Center. (See Exhibit 16.2.)

Domestic Terrorism

According to John F. Lewis, Jr., domestic terrorism involves groups or individuals who operate without foreign direction entirely within the United States and target elements of the U.S. government or citizens.

He states that the 1995 federal building explosion in Oklahoma City and the pipe bomb explosion in Centennial Olympic Park during the 1996 Summer Olympic Games underscore the ever-present threat that exists from individuals determined to use violence to advance their agendas.

Lewis states that domestic terrorist groups today represent extreme right-wing, extreme left-wing, and special interest beliefs. The main themes espoused today by extremist right-wing groups are conspiracies having to do with the New World Order, gun control laws, and white supremacy. Many of these extremist groups also advocate antigovernment, antitaxation, or antiabortion sentiments and engage

---

YOU ARE THERE! ››

Details of Some Major Domestic Terrorism Cases

OKLAHOMA CITY FEDERAL BUILDING

At 9:05 A.M. on April 19, 1995, an explosion occurred at the Alfred P. Murrah Federal Building in Oklahoma City. The bombing destroyed the structure, killed 168 people, and injured 675. Later that day, an Oklahoma state trooper arrested Timothy McVeigh on Interstate 35 for driving without license plates. Several days later McVeigh was charged with the bombing. He was alleged to have links to white supremacist and patriot groups. McVeigh was convicted for his crimes in 1997 and executed in 2001.

ATLANTA OLYMPIC GAMES

On July 27, 1996, a bombing occurred in Centennial Olympic Park at the Atlanta Olympic Games; a women was killed and 111 other people were injured. In June 1997, the FBI linked

the Olympic bombing to the January 16, 1997, bombing at the Sandy Springs Professional Building, which housed the Atlanta Northside Family Planning Services clinic (a clinic that provided abortions) and the February 2, 1997, bombing of an Atlanta lesbian nightclub. The FBI claimed that letters mailed to the press by a militant religious cell known as the Army of God connected the group to the bombings.

After a five-year manhunt, Eric Robert Rudolph was arrested in the small town of Murphy, North Carolina, on May 31, 2003, by rookie police officer Jeff Postell. He was charged with these crimes, which killed and injured hundreds.

Sources: Kevin Sack, "Officials Link Atlanta Bombings and Ask for Help," *New York Times* (June 10, 1997), p. A1; Jo Thomas, "McVeigh Guilty on All Counts in the Oklahoma City Bombing," *New York Times* (June 3, 1997), p. A1; "FBI Ten Most Wanted Fugitives: Eric Robert Rudolph," retrieved from http://www.fbi.gov/mostwant/topten/fugitives/rudolph.htm.

YOU ARE THERE! »

A Domestic Terrorist: The Unabomber

Thomas J. Mosser, an executive with the Young & Rubicam advertising firm in Manhattan, was killed by a mail bomb on December 10, 1994. The parcel had been mailed to his home.

The explosion and Mosser's murder were attributed to the work of a serial bomber known as the Unabomber, who was believed to be responsible for 14 other bombings or attempted bombings beginning in 1978. The FBI reports that 2 people died and 23 others were injured in these explosions, which occurred over some 16 years, as this deranged man terrorized his fellow American citizens.

The sequence of events related to the Unabomber is

- A bomb exploded at Northwestern University in Illinois, May 25, 1978; a security guard was injured.

- A second person at Northwestern was injured on May 9, 1979, when a bomb exploded in the technical building.

- On American Airlines Flight 444 (Chicago to Boston), 12 persons suffered smoke inhalation injuries on November 15, 1979. This bomb was traced to a mailbag aboard the airliner.

- The president of United Airlines, Percy Wood, was injured by a bomb on June 10, 1980. Again, the bomb was in a package mailed to his home.

- A bomb in a business classroom at the University of Utah exploded on October 8, 1981.

- At Vanderbilt University in Nashville a secretary was injured on May 5, 1982, when a bomb mailed to the head of the computer science department exploded.

- Two people were injured, one seriously, at the University of California, Berkeley, as a result of bombings: an electrical engineering professor on July 2, 1982, and a student on May 15, 1985.

- Alert employees of the Boeing Company in Washington State had a bomb safely dismantled on May 18, 1985, when they realized a mailed package contained an explosive device.

- On November 15, 1985, the research assistant to a psychology professor at the University of Michigan at Ann Arbor was injured when a bomb received at the professor's home exploded.

- On December 11, 1985, Hugh Campbell, the owner of a computer rental store in Sacramento, California, was killed by a bomb left at his store.

- In Salt Lake City, another employee in the computer industry was maimed by a bomb placed in a bag in the company parking lot on February 20, 1987.

- A geneticist at the University of California at San Francisco sustained injuries when he opened a package received in the mail at his home on June 22, 1993.

- A computer scientist at Yale University opened a package mailed to his office and was injured by a bomb on June 24, 1993.

The FBI was certain that these bombings were related and attributable to one suspect, the Unabomber. The bombs were all built from similar materials and had a comparable, sophisticated design.

In 1996, based on a tip provided by his brother, Theodore Kaczynski was arrested and charged with all the Unabomber attacks. At trial he was found guilty and sentenced to life imprisonment.

Source: John S. Dempsey, *An Introduction to Public and Private Investigations*, (Minneapolis/St. Paul: West, 1996), pp. 16–17.

---

in survivalist training, with their goal to ensure the perpetuation of the United States as a white, Christian nation.

One particularly troubling element of right-wing extremism is the militia, or patriot, movement. Militia members want to remove federal involvement from various issues. They generally are law-abiding citizens who have become intolerant of what they perceive as violations of their constitutional rights. Membership in a militia organization is not entirely illegal in the United States, but certain states have legislated limits on militias, including on the

types of training (for example, paramilitary training) that they can offer. The FBI bases its interest in the militia movement on the risk of violence or the potential for violence and criminal activity.

Experts have traced the growth of the militia movement in part to the effective use of modern communication mediums. Videotapes and computer bulletin boards and networks, such as on the Internet, have been used with great effectiveness by militia sympathizers. Promilitia facsimile networks disseminate material from well-known hate group figures and conspiracy theorists. Organizers can promote their ideologies at militia meetings, patriot rallies, and gatherings of various other groups espousing antigovernment sentiments.

Left-wing extremist groups generally profess a revolutionary socialist doctrine and view themselves as protectors of the American people against capitalism and imperialism. They aim to change the nation through revolutionary means rather than by participating in the regular political and social process.

During the 1960s and 1970s, leftist-oriented extremist groups posed the predominant domestic terrorist threat in the United States. Beginning in the 1980s, however, the FBI dismantled many of these groups by arresting key members for their criminal activities. The transformation of the former Soviet Union also deprived many leftist groups of a coherent ideology or spiritual patron. As a result, membership and support for these groups has declined.

Special interest terrorist groups differ from both extreme left-wing and right-wing terrorist groups because their members seek to resolve specific interests rather than pursue widespread political change. Members of such groups include animal rights advocates, supporters of environmental issues, and antiabortion advocates. Although some consider the causes that these groups represent understandable or even noteworthy, they remain separated from traditional law-abiding special interest groups because of

their criminal activity. Through their violent actions, these terrorist groups attempt to force various segments of society, including the general public, to change their attitudes about issues they consider important.

See Chapter 15 of this text for further information on domestic terrorism and hate groups.

Catastrophic Disasters and Weapons of Mass Destuction (WMD)

According to an article by Joel Carlson, former FBI special agent and a member of the technical staff working on counterterrorism and the criminal use of nuclear materials at Sandia National Laboratories in New Mexico, catastrophic events, including terrorist attacks, that have plagued the United States for the past several years may become more frequent and deadly as criminals and terrorist groups exploit the availability of chemical substances, biological agents, and nuclear materials to construct weapons of mass destruction (WMD).[9]

Carlson writes that this material is available for several reasons, including the increased volume and types of substances produced, the failure of security systems to protect these materials, the transfer of prohibited weapons to irresponsible governments, and the proliferation of these materials in countries that previously did not perceive a need for sophisticated weaponry.

YOU ARE THERE! >>

Catching the Oklahoma City Bomber, Timothy McVeigh: Feds Took the Credit, But Charley Caught Him

Police Officer Charles J. Hanger of the Oklahoma Highway Patrol was on patrol on Interstate 35 in Oklahoma, 60 miles north of Oklahoma City, on April 19, 1995, when he observed a yellow 1977 Mercury Marquis in the opposite lane of traffic with no license plates. Hanger pursued the auto and stopped it, something he had done thousands of times in his police career.

When the driver reached for his license at the trooper's request, Hanger saw a bulge under his jacket. The bulge reminded Hanger of one of the dangers of his job: the armed felon. He ordered the driver out of the automobile and retrieved a loaded Glock semiautomatic pistol, two clips of ammunition, and a knife from under his jacket. The pistol had a live round in the chamber—a Black Talon bullet. The driver

was arrested for driving without license plates, having no insurance, and carrying a concealed weapon. The time of the arrest was approximately 90 minutes after the infamous bombing of the Alfred P. Murrah Federal Building, which killed and injured hundreds of people. Trooper Hanger testified at the driver's trial on April 29, 1997.

The driver, of course, was Timothy J. McVeigh.

We all know how the government cracked the case and charged McVeigh with the worst terrorist attack against the United States of America until that date. But would he have been apprehended if Hanger had not made that routine traffic stop on I-35?

Source: Peter Annin and Evan Thomas, "Judgement Day," *Newsweek* (March 24, 1997), p. 41.

PATROLLING THE WEB

Key Federal Agencies Concerning Catastrophic Disasters and WMD

Federal Bureau of Investigation (FBI)
   http://www.fbi.gov
Department of Homeland Security (DHS)
   http://www.dhs.gov
U.S. Department of State
   http://www.state.gov
U.S. Defense Department
   http://www.defenselink.mil
U.S. Department of Energy
   http://www.energy.gov

According to Carlson, the criminal use of chemical, biological, or nuclear materials could result in a disaster unparalleled in U.S. history and test the government's ability to avoid panic, disorientation, and loss of confidence in ensuring the public's safety. He writes that local and state public safety and emergency personnel may exhaust their experience, training, and capability attempting to protect the public from such potentially catastrophic and devastating consequences.

Because criminal misuse or the threat of misuse of chemical, biological, or nuclear materials on a domestic target poses the ultimate management challenge for public safety agencies and government leaders, the following federal responders will complement or supplement the resources of cities, counties, and states:

- The Federal Bureau of Investigation (FBI) serves as the lead federal agency for resolving a crisis perpetrated by a malevolent element in a WMD incident occurring inside the United States and its territories.

- The Federal Emergency Management Agency (FEMA) of the cabinet-level **Department of Homeland Security** (DHS) coordinates consequence management (evacuation planning or search-and-rescue efforts) of a WMD incident. FEMA also provides extensive training to local and state officials in preparation for mass disasters, including terrorist attacks. A mass disaster is defined as any catastrophic incident, criminal or otherwise, for which the local responsible government lacks the resources to fully investigate and restore order. FEMA provides assistance to local and state governments on request.

- The U.S. Department of State is the lead agency in coordinating U.S. resources in response to a WMD incident in a foreign country, should that government request such assistance.

- The U.S. Department of Defense provides specialized technical resources to assist in the mitigation of WMD devices or the consequences of their misuse, to supply logistical support to other federal responders, and to furnish additional assistance as defined by the situation and directed by the President.

- The U.S. Department of Energy provides technical and scientific assistance to locate hidden nuclear material; to diagnose a suspected, improvised nuclear device; to plan the disablement of a nuclear yield or radiological dispersal device; and to advise local authorities on the hazards and effects of this eventuality.

- The Public Health Service and the Centers for Disease Control and Prevention respond with technical and scientific personnel and equipment to assist in the mitigation of the health concerns that arise from various aspects of WMD misuse.

- Other federal agencies respond with personnel and resources if the threat or attack requires their unique resources or jurisdictional authority.

★ ★ ★

POST-9/11 RESPONSE TO TERRORISM AND HOMELAND DEFENSE

In the immediate aftermath of the terrorist attacks of September 11, 2001, strict security procedures were instituted at airports, government buildings, cultural centers and many other facilities. The FBI advised state and local law enforcement agencies to move to their highest level of alert and be prepared to respond to any further acts of terrorism. Armed National Guard troops supplemented airport security officers and local and state police in many jurisdictions. Military aircraft flew protective patrol over U.S. cities, and the Coast Guard patrolled coastlines and ports. Some other immediate responses included expanding the intelligence community's ability to intercept and translate messages in Arabic, Farsi, and other languages; fortification of cockpits to prevent access by hijackers; placing federal air marshals on commercial flights; and more intensive screening of luggage.

Approximately 4,000 FBI special agents and 3,000 support personnel were assigned to the September 11, 2001, attacks case nationwide; by early October, the FBI was handling more than a quarter-million potential leads and tips. It sent all law enforcement agencies a list of more than 190 witnesses, suspects, and others they wanted to interview and, in the two months following the attack, the Justice Department had arrested more than 1,000 people suspected of having links to terrorist groups.[10] The September 11, 2001, terrorist acts were attributed to the multinational terrorist group Al-Qaeda (the Base) operated by Osama bin Laden, a known terrorist residing in Afghanistan, sheltered by the ruling Taliban government.

On October 7, 2001, the United States launched a full-scale military assault—a war—against Afghanistan, the Taliban, and its allies, Al-Qaeda and Osama bin Laden. As a result of this military action the Taliban government has been replaced in Afghanistan and many members of Al-Qaeda were killed or arrested, but to the best of our current knowledge Osama bin Laden remains at large.

There has been much written about the failure of U.S. law enforcement, particularly federal law enforcement, to deal with terrorism. Some report that the failure to follow up leads and analyze information made the efforts of terrorists to commit terrorist attacks against America easier.[11] Others reported that a major flaw of counterterrorism measures was a lack of interagency cooperation and data sharing.

In order to address these concerns, on October 8, 2001, President Bush signed Executive Order 13228 establishing the Office of Homeland Security under the direction of former Pennsylvania Governor Tom Ridge.[12] The office's mission was to develop and coordinate the implementation of a comprehensive national strategy to secure the United States from threats and attacks. It coordinated the executive branch's efforts to detect, prepare for, prevent, and respond to terrorist attacks within this country. The President also established a Homeland Security Council that was responsible for advising and assisting him with all aspects of security. The council consisted of the President and Vice President, the Secretary of the Treasury, the Secretary of Defense, the Attorney General, the Secretary of Health and Human Services, the Secretary of Transportation, the director of the Federal Emergency Management Agency (FEMA), the director of the FBI, the director of the Central Intelligence Agency, and the assistant to the president for Homeland Security.[13]

PATROLLING THE WEB

White House Office of Homeland Security
http://www.whitehouse.gov/homeland

Additionally, on October 26, 2001, President Bush signed into law the USA **Patriot Act**—Uniting and Strengthening America by Providing Appropriate Tools Required to Intercept and Obstruct Terrorism, giving law enforcement new ability to search, seize, detain, or eavesdrop in their pursuit of possible terrorists. The law expanded the FBI's wiretapping and electronic surveillance authority and allowed nationwide jurisdiction for search warrants and electronic surveillance devices, including legal expansion of those devices to e-mail and the Internet. The Patriot Act also included money laundering provisions and set strong penalties for anyone harboring or financing terrorists. It also established new punishments for possession of biological weapons and made it a federal crime to commit an act of terrorism against a mass transit system. Additionally, the bill allowed law enforcement agents to detain terrorism suspects for up to seven days without filing charges against them.[14]

In November 2001, the President signed into law the Aviation and Transportation Security Act, which among other things established a new Transportation Security Administration (TSA), within the Department of Transportation, to protect the nation's transportation systems and ensure freedom of movement for people and commerce. This new agency assumed the duties formerly provided by the FAA. The newly established TSA recruited thousands of security personnel to perform screening duties at commercial airports and significantly expanded the federal air marshals program. It also created the positions of federal security directors to be directly responsible for security at airports, developed new passenger boarding procedures, trained pilots and flight crews in hijacking scenarios, and required all airport personnel to undergo background checks.[15]

Polls conducted immediately following the 9/11 attacks revealed that an overwhelming majority of Americans—approximately 75 percent—thought it necessary to give up some personal freedoms for the sake of security.[16]

Later, in June 2002, the President proposed creating a new cabinet-level agency, the U.S. Department of Homeland Security, to replace the Office of Homeland Security. With the new cabinet agency, duties formerly belonging to other government agencies would be merged, including border and transportation security, emergency preparedness and response, chemical, biological, radiological, and nuclear countermeasures, and information analysis and infrastructure protection.[17]

In the six months following September 11, a total of $10.6 billion was spent on creating new mechanisms for homeland security, responding to and investigating terrorist threats, and providing security for likely terrorist targets.[18]

★ ★ ★

FEDERAL EFFORTS
FOR HOMELAND SECURITY

Because **homeland defense** involves the participation
and coordination of myriad agencies of government and
the private sector, the federal government must play a
major role. The two major federal agencies charged with
homeland security are the U.S. Department of Homeland Security (DHS) and the Federal Bureau of Investigation (FBI). This section will discuss the role of these
two agencies, other federal agencies involved in homeland defense and federal budgetary support for homeland
defense.

The U.S. Department
of Homeland Security (DHS)

After much debate, study, and planning in the aftermath of
the terrorist attacks of September 11, 2001, the cabinet-
level U.S. Department of Homeland Security was established in March 2003.[19]

The new agency merged 22 previously disparate domestic agencies into one department to protect the nation
against threats to the homeland. The agency consists of
more than 170,000 employees. The creation of DHS was
the most significant transformation of the U.S. government
since 1947 when President Harry S. Truman merged the
various branches of the U.S. Armed Forces into the Department of Defense to better coordinate the nation's defense
against military threats. DHS represents a similar consolidation, both in style and substance. The DHS includes former

---

Exhibit 16.3   U.S. Department of Homeland Security (DHS) Organization

- Border and Transportation Security (BTS) directorate
  U.S. Citizenship and Immigration Services (USCIS)
  U.S. Immigration and Customs Enforcement (ICE)
  U.S. Customs and Border Protection (CBP)
  U.S. Coast Guard
  Transportation Security Administration
  Federal Law Enforcement Training Center
  Animal and Plant Health Inspection Service
  Federal Protective Service
  Office for Domestic Preparedness

- Emergency Preparedness and Response (EMR) directorate
  Federal Emergency Management Agency (FEMA)
  Strategic National Stockpile and the National Disaster
      Medical System
  Nuclear Incident Response Team
  Domestic Emergency Support Teams

- Science and Technology (S&T) directorate
  CBRN Countermeasures Programs
  Environmental Measurements Laboratory
  National BW Defense Analysis Center
  Plum Island Animal Disease Center

- Information Analysis and Infrastructure Protection (IAIP)
  directorate
  Critical Infrastructure Assurance Office
  Federal Computer Incident Response Center
  National Communications System
  National Infrastructure Protection Center
  Energy Security and Assurance Program

- Management directorate
  Office of State and Local Government Coordination
  Office of Private Sector Liaison
  Office of Inspector General

- U.S. Secret Service

Source: U.S. Department of Homeland Security. Retrieved on April 19, 2004,
from http://www.dhs.gov

PATROLLING THE WEB

U.S. Department of Homeland Security (DHS) and Some Major Subunits within DHS

U.S. Department of Homeland Security (DHS)
    http://www.dhs.gov
U.S. Bureau of Customs and Border Protection
    http://www.cbp.gov
U.S. Coast Guard
    http://www.uscg.mil
Secret Service
    http://www.secretservice.gov
Federal Emergency Management Agency (FEMA)
    http://www.fema.gov
Federal Law Enforcement Training Center (FLETC)
    http://www.fletc.gov
National Infrastructure Protection Center (NIPC)
    http://www.nipc.gov
U.S. Bureau of Citizenship and Immigration Services
    http://www.uscis.gov
Transportation Security Administration
    http://www.tsa.gov
Office of Energy Assurance
    http://www.doe.gov
National Communications System
    http://www.ncs.gov
U.S. Immigration and Customs Enforcement
    http://www.ice.gov

duties of many agencies, including the Coast Guard, U.S. Customs Service, the Secret Service, the Immigration and Naturalization Service, and the Transportation Security Administration, along with numerous other federal communications, science, and technology agencies. The DHS does not include the FBI, CIA, or National Security Agency, but these agencies are required to share their data with the department's new intelligence center.

The department's first priority is to protect the nation against further terrorist attacks. The department's agencies analyze threats and intelligence, guard our borders and airports, protect our critical infrastructure, and coordinate the responses of our nation for future emergencies.

The DHS has five major divisions or directorates, as well as several other critical subdivisions.

BORDER AND TRANSPORTATION SECURITY DIRECTORATE (BTS)   BTS is responsible for maintaining the security of our nation's borders. It assumed the former professional workforce, programs, and infrastructure of the Coast Guard, the Customs Service, the Immigration and Naturalization Service, including the Border Patrol, and the Transportation Security Administration. Through these agencies, the BTS protects our borders and enforces the nation's immigration laws. Its first priority is to prevent the entry of terrorists and the instruments of terrorism while simultaneously ensuring the efficient flow of lawful traffic and commerce into the nation. The BTS also directs the Animal and Plant Health Inspection Service, the Federal

YOU ARE THERE! »

Enormous Responsibilities for U.S. Border Protection

- The U.S. has 5,525 miles of border with Canada and 1,989 miles with Mexico.

- The U.S. maritime border includes 95,000 miles of shoreline and a 3.4 million mile exclusive economic zone with 350 official ports of entry.

- Each year, more than 500 million people cross the borders into the U.S., some 330 million of whom are noncitizens.

- Over 730 million people travel on commercial aircraft each year, and there are more than 700 million pieces of baggage screened for explosives each year.

- Approximately 11.2 million trucks and 2.2 million railcars cross into the U.S. each year.

- 7,500 foreign flagships make 51,000 calls in U.S. ports annually

Source: U.S. Department of Homeland Security.

YOU ARE THERE! »

Seeking a Job with the U.S. Department of Homeland Security (DHS)

Vacancies at DHS are listed on the federal government's Employment Information System, at http://www.USAJOBS.opm.gov. Anyone interested in a position with any of the DHS agencies should submit an application using the instructions provided in the vacancy announcement on the USAJOBS site. Anyone without access to the Internet can also access USAJOBS by calling (478) 757-3000 or TDD (478) 744-2299.

Source: U.S. Department of Homeland Security. Retrieved on March 28, 2003, from http://www.dhs.

Law Enforcement Training Center (FLETC), the Transportation Security Administration, the Federal Protective Service, and the Office for Domestic Preparedness.

EMERGENCY PREPAREDNESS AND RESPONSE DIRECTORATE (EPR)   EPR is responsible for ensuring that our nation is prepared to deal with and recover from terrorist attacks and natural disasters. It coordinates with first responders and oversees the federal government's national response and recovery strategy. A major component of EPR is the Federal Emergency Management Agency (FEMA), which protects our nation's institutions from all types of hazards through a comprehensive, risk-based emergency management program of preparedness, prevention, response, and recovery. The EPR has developed and managed a national training and evaluation system to design curriculums, set standards, evaluate, and reward performance in local, state, and federal training efforts. It also responds to any sort of biological or radiological attack and coordinates the involvement of other federal response teams, such as the National Guard, in the event of a major incident. In addition to FEMA, EPR also directs the Strategic National Stockpile, the National Disaster Medical

System, the Nuclear Incident Response Team, and the Domestic Emergency Support Teams.

SCIENCE AND TECHNOLOGY (S&T) DIRECTORATE

S&T is responsible for the coordination of the DHS's efforts in research and development, including preparing for and responding to the full range of terror threats involving weapons of mass destruction. S&T is the primary research and development arm of the DHS. It organizes the vast scientific and technological resources of the United States to prevent or mitigate the effects of catastrophic terrorism and unifies and coordinates the federal government's efforts to develop and implement scientific and technological countermeasures, including channeling the intellectual energy and extensive capacity of important scientific institutions, such as the national laboratories and academic institutions. It sponsors research, development, and testing to invent new vaccines, antidotes, diagnostics, and therapies against biological and chemical warfare agencies. S&T directs the CBRN Countermeasures Programs, the Environmental Measurements Laboratory, the National BW Defense Analysis Center, and the Plum Island Animal Disease Center.

INFORMATION ANALYSIS AND INFRASTRUCTURE PROTECTION DIRECTORATE (IAIP)

IAIP merges the governments' capability to identify and assess a broad range of intelligence information concerning threats to the homeland under one roof, to issue timely warnings, and to take appropriate preventive action. It analyzes intelligence and information from other agencies (including the CIA, FBI, DIA, and NSA) involving threats to homeland security and evaluates vulnerabilities in the nation's infrastructure. The primary mission of DHS is actionable intelligence—that is, information that can lead to stopping or apprehending terrorists. IAIP fuses and analyzes information from multiple sources pertaining to terrorist threats as a full partner and consumer of all the above-mentioned intelligence-generating agencies. It coordinates and consolidates the federal government's lines of communication with state and local public safety agencies and with the private sector, creating a coherent and efficient system for conveying actionable intelligence and other threat information. IAIP also administers the Homeland Security Advisory System.

IAIP takes the lead in coordinating the national effort to secure the nation's infrastructure through its National Infrastructure Protection Center (NIPC). Terrorists are capable of causing enormous damage to our county by attacking our critical infrastructure—food, water, agricul-

YOU ARE THERE! »

Operation Liberty Shield

At the outset of Operation Iraqi Freedom in March 2003, the U.S. Department of Homeland Security (DHS) put into effect Operation Liberty Shield to protect our borders and our critical infrastructure.

Operation Liberty Shield was a comprehensive national plan designed to increase protections for America's citizens and infrastructure while maintaining the free flow of goods and people across our border with minimal disruption to our economy and way of life.

It involved

- Increased security at borders

- Stronger transportation protections

- Ongoing measures to disrupt threats against our nation

- Greater protections for critical infrastructure and key assets

- Increased public health preparedness

- Federal response resources positioned and ready

Source: U.S. Department of Homeland Security. Retrieved on April 8, 2003, from http://www.dhs.gov/dhspublic/interapp/press_release_0115.xml.

ture, and health and emergency services; energy sources (electrical, nuclear, gas and oil, dams); transportation (air, road, rail, ports, waterways); information and telecommunications networks; banking and finance systems; postal and other assets and systems vital to our national security, public health and safety, economy, and way of life. The NIPC draws together personnel from federal law enforcement and intelligence agencies and state and local agencies, as well as experts from critical industries, to safeguard the interlocking computer, mass transport, and public utilities systems that power our society.

IAIP also administers the Cyber Security Protection Program. Our nation's information and telecommunications systems are directly connected to many other critical infrastructure sectors, including banking and finance, energy, and transportation. The consequences of an attack on our cyber infrastructure can cascade across many sectors, causing widespread disruption of essential services, damaging our economy, and imperiling public safety with speed, virulence, and maliciousness.

IAIP also provides our nation's Indications and Warning Advisories. In advance of real-time crisis or attack, IAIP provides

- Threat warnings and advisories against the homeland including physical (food, health, and weather warnings) and cyber events (computer viruses)

- National and sector-specific threat advisories through the **Homeland Security Advisory System** (color-coded alerts)

- Terrorist threat information for release to the public, private industry, and state and local governments

MANAGEMENT DIRECTORATE   The management directorate is responsible for budgetary, management, and personnel issues in the DHS.

UNITED STATES COAST GUARD   The U.S. Coast Guard is a military, multimission, maritime service and one of the nation's five armed services. Its mission is to protect the public, the environment, and U.S. economic interests—in the nation's ports and waterways, along the coast, on international waters, or in any maritime region as required to support national security. The commandant of the Coast Guard reports directly to the Secretary of Homeland Security.

UNITED STATES SECRET SERVICE   The primary mission of the Secret Service is the protection of the President and other government leaders, as well as security for designated national events. The Secret Service is also the primary agency responsible for protecting U.S. currency from counterfeiters and safeguarding Americans from credit card fraud. It provides security for designated national events and preserves the integrity of the nation's financial and critical infrastructures. It uses prevention-based training and methods to combat the cyber criminals and terrorists who attempt to use identity theft, telecommunications fraud, and other technology-based crimes to defraud and undermine American consumers and industry.

BUREAU OF CITIZENSHIP AND IMMIGRATION SERVICES (BCIS)   BCIS is responsible for providing efficient immigration services and easing the transition to American citizenship. It administers the nation's immigration laws and such services as immigrant and nonimmigrant sponsorship, adjustment of status, work authorization and other permits, naturalization of qualified applicants for U.S. citizenship, and asylum or refugee processing.

OFFICE OF STATE AND LOCAL GOVERNMENT CO-ORDINATION   This office ensures the close coordination between local, state, and federal governments, including first responders and emergency services.

OFFICE OF PRIVATE SECTOR LIAISON   This office provides America's business community a direct line of communication to the DHS. It works directly with individual businesses and through trade associations and other nongovernmental organizations to foster dialogue between the private sector and the DHS on the full range of issues

Members of the U.S. Coast Guard's Maritime Safety and Security Team (MSST) patrol the area near the Statue of Liberty during an antiterrorism response drill in September 2003. The team was created in response to the 9/11 terrorist attacks and is a specialized mobile unit capable of performing a broad spectrum of port safety and security operations. Members are trained to respond under threat of hostile chemical, biological, or radiological attacks; in explosives detection; and in antisabotage and commercial port protection.

YOU ARE THERE! »

Understanding the Homeland Security Advisory System—Threat Conditions

The world has changed since September 11, 2001. We remain a nation at risk to terrorist attacks and will remain at risk for the foreseeable future. At all threat conditions, we must remain vigilant, prepared, and ready to deter terrorist attacks. The following threat conditions each represent an increasing risk of terrorist attacks. Beneath each threat condition there are some suggested protective measures, recognizing that the heads of departments and agencies are responsible for developing and implementing appropriate agency-specific protective measures:

1. *Low condition (green):* This condition is declared when there is a low risk of terrorist attacks. Federal departments and agencies should consider the following general measures in addition to the agency-specific protective measures they develop and implement:
   ■ Refining and exercising, as appropriate, preplanned protective measures
   ■ Ensuring personnel receive proper training on the Homeland Security Advisory System and specific preplanned department or agency protective measures
   ■ Institutionalizing a process to assure that all facilities and regulated sectors are regularly assessed for vulnerabilities to terrorist attacks, and all reasonable measures are taken to mitigate these vulnerabilities

2. *Guarded condition (blue).* This condition is declared when there is a general threat of terrorist attacks. In addition to the protective measures taken in the previous threat condition, federal departments and agencies should consider the following general measures in addition to the agency-specific protective measures that they will develop and implement:
   ■ Checking communications with designated emergency response or command locations
   ■ Reviewing and updating emergency response procedures
   ■ Providing the public with any information that would strengthen its ability to respond appropriately

3. *Elevated condition (yellow):* An elevated condition is declared when there is a significant risk of terrorist attacks. In addition to the protective measures taken in the previous threat conditions, federal departments and agencies should consider the following general measures in addition to the protective measures that they will develop and implement:
   ■ Increasing surveillance of critical locations

■ Coordinating emergency plans as appropriate with nearby jurisdictions
■ Assessing whether the precise characteristics of the threat require the further refinement of preplanned protective measures
■ Implementing, as appropriate, contingency and emergency response plans

4. *High condition (orange):* A high condition is declared when there is a high risk of terrorist attacks. In addition to the protective measures taken in the previous threat conditions, federal departments and agencies should consider the following general measures in addition to the protective measures that they will direct and implement:
   ■ Coordinating necessary security efforts with federal, state, and local law enforcement agencies or any National Guard or other appropriate armed forces organizations
   ■ Taking additional precautions at public events and possibly considering alternative venues or even cancellation
   ■ Preparing to execute contingency procedures, such as moving to an alternative workplace or dispersing their workforce
   ■ Restricting threatened facility access to essential personnel only

5. *Severe condition (red):* A severe condition reflects a severe risk of terrorist attacks. Under most circumstances, the protective measures for a severe condition are not intended to be sustained for substantial periods of time. In addition to the protective measures taken in the previous threat conditions, federal departments and agencies should consider the following general measures in addition to the protective measures that they will develop and implement:
   ■ Increasing or redirecting personnel to address critical emergency needs
   ■ Assigning emergency response personnel and prepositioning and mobilizing specially trained teams or resources
   ■ Monitoring, redirecting, or constraining transportation systems
   ■ Closing public and government facilities

Source: U.S. Department of Homeland Security, "Homeland Advisory System." Retrieved on April 13, 2003, from http://www.dhs.gov/dhspublic/display?theme=29.

and challenges faced by America's business sector in the post-9/11 world.

OFFICE OF INSPECTOR GENERAL   This office serves as an independent and objective inspection, audit, and investigative body to promote effectiveness, efficiency, and economy in the DHS's programs and operations, and to prevent and detect fraud, abuse, mismanagement, and waste.[20]

The Federal Bureau of Investigation

The Federal Bureau of Investigation (FBI) has traditionally been the lead federal agency in the response to and investigation of terrorism. Realizing that both international and domestic terrorism were serious national concerns, the federal government took several law enforcement measures to deal with terrorism even before September 11.[21] From 1993 to 2001, the FBI's counterterrorism budget increased from $77 million to $376 million or 388 percent.

In May 2002, in the wake of massive criticism that the FBI had failed to properly handle information that could have led to the prevention of the September 11 attacks, FBI Director Robert S. Mueller issued a press release outlining its complete reorganization and creating a new strategic focus for the agency. The FBI's new focus placed the following as its three priorities: (1) protecting the United States from terrorist attack, (2) protecting the United States against foreign intelligence operations and espionage, and (3) protecting the Untied States against cyber-based attacks and high-technology crimes. The main organizational improvements Mueller implemented in a complete restructuring of the counterterrorism activities of the Bureau and a shift from a reactive to a proactive orientation were the development of special squads to coordinate national and international investigations; a reemphasis on the Joint Terrorism Task Forces; enhanced analytical capabilities with personnel and technological improvements; a permanent shift of additional resources to counterterrorism; the creation of a more mobile, agile, and flexible national terrorism response; and targeted recruitment to

PATROLLING THE WEB

Federal Bureau of Investigation
   http://www.fbi.gov

YOU ARE THERE! »

FBI Priorities Post-9/11

1. Protect the United States from terrorist attack
2. Protect the United States against foreign intelligence operations and espionage
3. Protect the United States against cyber-based attacks and high-technology crimes
4. Combat public corruption at all levels
5. Protect civil rights
6. Combat transnational and national criminal organizations and enterprises
7. Combat major white-collar crime
8. Combat significant violent crime
9. Support federal, state, local, and international partners
10. Upgrade technology to successfully perform the FBI's mission

Source: Federal Bureau of Investigation. Retrieved on April 8, 2003, from http://www.fbi.gov/priorities/priorities.htm.

acquire agents, analysts, translators, and others with specialized skills and backgrounds.[22]

Regarding their new role in counterterrorism, FBI Assistant Director Cassi Chandler stated in 2003 that

> The FBI, in conjunction with its law enforcement and intelligence community partners, is making a difference. Since September 11, 2001, more than 3,000 Al-Qa'ida leaders and foot soldiers have been taken into custody around the globe; nearly 200 suspected terrorist associates have been charged with crimes in the U.S.; and as many as a hundred terrorist attacks or plots have been broken up worldwide. The FBI is committed to preventing acts of terror and to protecting the security of the American people.[23]

The FBI has major **counterterrorism** and **counterintelligence** missions. Its counterterrorism mission is to prevent acts of terrorism before they occur or to react to them after they happen by bringing the offenders to justice. The major objectives of the FBI domestic and international terrorism programs are to identify and prevent terrorist acts and to pursue the arrest and prosecution of responsible individuals. As part of the prevention effort, the FBI collects foreign intelligence information on groups and individuals whose activities threaten the security of the United States. The FBI Counterterrorism Center combats terrorism three ways: It deals with international terrorism operations inside the United States and supports extraterritorial investigations; it deals with domestic terrorism operations; and it takes countermeasures relating to both international and domestic terrorism. Representatives from numerous federal agencies maintain a regular presence in the center and participate in its daily activities.

The FBI's mission makes it the lead counterintelligence agency in the United States. It is responsible for identifying and neutralizing ongoing national security threats. The FBI's Counterintelligence Division provides centralized management and oversight for all foreign counterintelligence investigations. It ensures that offensive operations and investigations are fully coordinated with the U.S. intelligence community and focused on those countries, foreign powers, or entities that pose the most significant threat to the United States. The Counterintelligence Division integrates law enforcement with intelligence efforts to investi-

gate violations of the espionage statutes under Title 18 of the U.S. Criminal Code. The investigative priorities of its Foreign Counterintelligence Program are to:

- Prevent or neutralize the foreign acquisition of weapons of mass destruction (WMD) technology or equipment
- Prevent the penetration of the U.S. intelligence community
- Prevent the penetration of U.S. government agencies or contractors
- Prevent the compromise of U.S. critical national assets

The FBI's primary terrorism investigative units are its Federal–Local **Joint Terrorism Task Forces (JTTFs).** The Federal–Local Joint Terrorism Task Forces operate in 16 communities across the nation to combine the resources of the FBI and other federal agencies with the street-level expertise of local and state law enforcement officers. These teams have been highly successful in numerous critical operations around the country. JTTFs are discussed more fully later in this chapter.

The FBI also maintains 40 legal attaché, or LEGAT, offices abroad who work with host governments to prevent crimes against U.S. interests and to investigate those that occur. Among the many benefits of establishing legal attachés are the close working relationships they form with the local law enforcement agencies, which have practical and operational familiarity with terrorist organizations that may pose a threat to Americans. These relationships enhance the FBI's ability to maintain a proactive, rather than reactive, posture in addressing threats. If a terrorist attack targeting U.S. citizens or interests does occur, the attachés can provide the FBI with an on-the-scene presence in the first critical hours of an investigation. Through this program, the U.S. government has successfully returned terrorists from other countries to stand trial for acts or planned acts of terrorism against U.S. citizens. Since the beginning of this program there have been approximately 350 extraterritorial jurisdiction cases.

The FBI also has implemented the Awareness of National Security Issues and Response Program (ANSIR) and the Strategic Information and Operations Center (SIOC).

ANSIR is designed to provide unclassified national security threat and warning information to as many as 40,000 U.S. corporate security directors and executives, law enforcement personnel, and other government agencies. ANSIR represents the first initiative by the U.S. government to provide this type of information to individual corporations that have critical technologies or sensitive economic information that could be targeted by foreign

YOU ARE THERE! >>

Then and Now: Changes at Airports and at Immigration

Changes at airports and Immigration between September 11, 2001, and April, 2003, include:

- *Airports:* After the September 11, 2001, attacks, no area of American life was subjected to more intense scrutiny than air travel. The federal government shouldered a far larger role, through the Transportation Security Administration, taking over airport security from a group of widely criticized contractors and imposing tougher rules for screening employees, passengers, and luggage. It has been an expensive undertaking. The powerful car-size X-ray machines being installed at airports to screen baggage cost about $1 million apiece. Two storage rooms at J.F.K. International Airport overflow with passengers' contraband, from chain saws to perfumes with names like "Time Bomb," whose bottles are shaped like explosives. Officials say the number of guns and knives seized at airport checkpoints nationwide has more than tripled since September 11, 2001.

  Before 9/11, fewer than 2 percent of checked bags were inspected; now all are either X-rayed, swabbed for explosive traces, or both. Before 9/11, there were 37 federal marshals assigned to riding airliners undercover; now there are thousands, according to airport officials.

- *Immigration:* Law enforcement and intelligence gathering have changed markedly since September 11th. Immigration agents, now part of the Department of

Homeland Security and the FBI, with the help of local law enforcement, are tracking and deporting more than 300,000 aliens who remained in the United States despite deportation orders. Schools are now being required to report all foreign students to the federal government. Visitors and immigrants from mostly Moslem nations are being subjected to far greater scrutiny than in the past. Male travelers from 26 nations are now fingerprinted and photographed upon arrival, and men from a long list of Muslim countries who are already in the United States are being required to register with the government—a process that immigration lawyers say means not only supplying an address and fingerprints, but also credit card numbers, video rental subscription numbers, family members' addresses, and e-mail addresses.

Domestic security officials reported in April, 2003, that they are beginning to use computer equipment that recognizes fingerprints and other features to verify the identities of foreign visitors as they enter and depart the U.S. They said the new security measures, which may also include the use of computerized facial-recognition technology, are intended to block the entry of terrorists and to verify that foreign visitors leave on schedule. This technology would be installed at some international airports, border crossings, and seaports. This biometric technology had been mandated by Congress as a result of the attacks of September 11, 2001.

---

governments or organizations. Each FBI ANSIR coordinator meets regularly with industry leaders and security directors for updates on current national security issues.

SIOC at the FBI headquarters operates as a round-the-clock operations facility that serves as a national command center during large-scale investigations or at times when risks to U.S. interests are heightened. This command center is staffed by personnel from several agencies depending on the nature of the incident or threat.

Other Federal Agencies

In addition to the BHS, the FBI, and the U.S. military, several other federal agencies are involved with crisis activities involving terrorism. One example is the Bureau of Alcohol, Tobacco, Firearms, and Explosives (ATFE), which has special responsibilities in cases of arson and explosives.

Some of its programs that have an impact on the U.S. efforts to prevent and investigate acts of terrorism are its accelerant and explosives detecting canines, arson and explosives training, arson task forces, criminal investigative analysis, explosives interdiction, explosives technology support, explosives tracing, forensic laboratory support, international response team, and national response team.[24]

PATROLLING THE WEB

Bureau of Alcohol, Tobacco, Firearms, and Explosives (ATFE)
   http://www.atf.gov

Federal Budgetary Support for Homeland Security

The federal effort to improve homeland security was given generous budgetary support under the federal 2004 fiscal budget. The Justice Department was allocated $600 million in additional funding for antiterror programs; the FBI received an additional $441 million to hire more agents and counterterrorism analysts and expand programs to combat cybercrime by terrorists. The Bureau also received $82 million to upgrade its technology. The new Department of Homeland Security was allocated a total of $36.2 billion: $18.1 billion for transportation and border security, including new inspection technology and training dogs to detect weapons of mass destruction and an entry-exit system to document visitors as they enter and leave the country; $6.7 billion to the Coast Guard for six new antiterrorist teams, new boats, and the upgrade of its cutters; $6 billion to the department's emergency preparedness and response unit for vaccines and medicines in case of bioterrorism. The budget also proposed a second installment of $3.5 billion for local homeland security investments by municipal law enforcement, emergency medical personnel, and firefighters.[25]

In April 2003, the U.S. Department of Homeland Security released a detailed breakdown of the $4 billion that it was provided under the $79 billion bill that Congress approved to pay for Operation Iraqi Freedom and related expenses. About $2.2 billion, the department said, was for state preparedness, money that state and local governments have long demanded from the federal government to help pay for counterterrorism efforts after September 11, 2001. Of that, $700 million was for high-threat urban areas, including New York, Washington, and other cities considered prime targets.[26]

The Transportation Security Administration, part of the department, received $665 million under the bill for such programs as improving security at commercial airports. The Coast Guard was provided $628 million, much of it to support war-related military activities. The Bureau of Customs and Border Protection received $333 million, with $90 million to produce detection and monitoring equipment to find radioactive material that terrorists might try to smuggle into the country. The department also distributed $2.4 billion to the airlines, which had sought the aid as reimbursement for their losses because of the war and continuing terrorist threats to the industry.[27]

★ ★ ★

STATE AND LOCAL EFFORTS FOR HOMELAND SECURITY

Although the previous section of this chapter emphasized the role of our national government in responding to and combating terrorism and homeland defense, we must remember that each act of terrorism is essentially a local problem that must be addressed by local authorities.

D. Douglas Bodrero, former commissioner of public safety for the state of Utah and a senior research associate with the Institute for Intergovernmental Research, writing in 1999, stated that "Every act of terrorism occurring within the United States remains local in nature."[28]

Bodrero, writing again in 2002, after the 2001 terrorist attacks upon the United States, reiterated his emphasis that terrorism is primarily a concern for local governments:

The planning or execution of terrorist acts on U.S. soil are the concern of every law enforcement agency, regardless of size or area of responsibility. Every terrorist event, every act of planning and preparation for that event occurs in some local law enforcement agency's jurisdiction. No agency is closer to the activities within its community than the law enforcement agency that has responsibility and jurisdiction for protecting that community.[29]

©Joe Raedle/Getty Images

A Citrus County sheriff's deputy stands guard at the entrance to the Florida Power Corporation's nuclear power plant in Crystal River, Florida. Nuclear power plants around the country have increased security measures since the September 11 terrorist attacks, placing an increased demand upon local law enforcement agencies around the country.

YOU ARE THERE! »

Training for the Unspeakable

Members of special weapons and tactics (SWAT) teams in the Tampa Bay, Florida, area participated in a five-day training program taught by Israelis to learn how to counter terrorism aimed at civilians using mass transportation.

Participants practiced response, entry, safety sweeps, searches for weapons and booby traps, protecting children and adults, and escorting civilians to safety. The training program covered operations such as mob control, hand-to-hand fighting, firearms and knives, behavior under stress, live fire drills and escalation, stealth fighting, live roadblock drills, terrorist booby traps, officer kidnapping situations, movement through crowds, car hijackings, and negotiations. The final focus of the training program was on bus intervention, including snipers, security, and penetration. In reenactments using a real school bus, participants learned techniques for approaching the bus, carrying out entry strikes, securing the bus perimeter, securing movement inside the bus, braking the bus in gear, and dealing with booby traps.

In one exercise, the complete response time from actual strike commencement to securing the terrorists and hostages was reduced to 7.5 minutes.

Source: Bruce Cameron, "School Bus Crisis: Preparing for the Unspeakable," *Law and Order* (May 2000), pp. 92–96.

Expressing similar concerns, in 2002, William B. Burger, chief of the North Miami Beach, Florida, police department and the president of the International Association of Chiefs of Police (IACP), stated

. . . state and local law enforcement agencies in the United States—and the 700,000 officers they employ—patrol the streets of our cities and towns daily and, as a result, have an intimate knowledge of those communities they serve. This unique relationship provides these agencies with a tremendous edge in effectively tracking down information related to terrorists.[30]

Even after the 1993 World Trade Center bombing, most state and local law enforcement administrators continued to view terrorism primarily as an international threat. Many administrators believed that metropolitan centers such as New York, Miami, and Chicago remained the most likely targets. A 1995 National Institute of Justice (NIJ) study confirmed that state and local law enforcement agencies viewed the threat of terrorism as real, but their response varied widely according to the size and resources of the agency and the nature of the threat in its community. Major cities developed prevention and preparation programs, often in cooperation with the FBI and its Joint Terrorism Task Forces (discussed later in this chapter); in contrast, smaller cities and counties usually operated on their own. Antiterrorism resources varied, based on the existing threat potential. Some smaller jurisdictions developed regional alliances to address specific extremist groups and organizations operating locally.[31]

But these perceptions changed after the 1995 Oklahoma City explosion. D. Douglas Bodrero wrote in a 1999 article in the *FBI Law Enforcement Bulletin* that most jurisdictions have more recently realized the threat presented by extremist individuals and groups and now assess the threat that such groups pose to their respective communities and to related operational planning and readiness issues.[32]

He reports that the key elements of the state and local response to the terrorism threat include planning, assessment, target identification, intelligence, and training. Many larger localities and agencies offer training for dealing with terrorist problems, but smaller ones offer little other than civil disturbance and special weapons and tactical training. The Federal Emergency Management Agency (FEMA) provides limited funding to state emergency management agencies. The FEMA training focuses mainly on the roles and duties of various responding agencies, stressing the need for emergency agencies to work together for a unified response.

Although the FBI maintains the lead federal role in the investigation and prevention of domestic terrorism, every terrorist act, as Bodrero and Burger wrote, is essentially local. Local law enforcement officers will respond first to a terrorist threat or incident and are the closest to sense the discontent among terrorist movements; they monitor the activity of extremist causes, respond to hate crimes, and serve as the foundation for an effective assessment of threatening activities in their own communities.

In the aftermath of the September 11, 2001, terrorist attacks, state and local agencies are being asked to play a bigger part as first responders to terrorist incidents and in gathering intelligence. Federal funding has been made available to state and local law enforcement for the development and enhancement of law enforcement information systems relating to terrorism, with an emphasis on information sharting.[33]

As an example of local efforts to address the problems of terrorism, in 2002 the New York City Police Department created two new deputy commissioner positions, a Deputy

YOU ARE THERE! »

They Stopped the Terrorists before They Could Attack: They Saved the City

The police officers who patrol New York City, the NYPD, are called New York's Finest—an accolade they deserve every day. The finest of the Finest has to be NYPD's elite Emergency Service Unit. These are the men and women who risk life and limb to climb to the tops of the city's myriad bridges and skyscrapers to rescue potential "jumpers" from themselves, enter blazing buildings, and breathe life back into cardiac victims and others who are near death. The NYPD's ESU is also the city's SWAT team. They are the Marine Corps of the city, called in daily with their automatic weapons to combat armed terrorists and maniacs. Their action on July 31, 1997, was just one of the heroic things cops in New York did that day, but it saved the city from certain disaster.

The events began unfolding with the frantic waving of a man along a darkened Brooklyn street. A Long Island Railroad police officer, on patrol in his radio car, observed the man acting irrationally at 10:45 P.M. on July 30, 1997. He was repeatedly screaming in Arabic, "Bomba" and cupping his hands and moving them apart to mimic an explosion. The officer took the man to the 88th Precinct station house in Fort Greene, Brooklyn, where an interpreter determined that bombs and plans to blow up New York City subways were at a house at 248 Fourth Avenue in the Park Slope neighborhood.

Just before dawn on July 31, the police closed off scores of blocks in Park Slope and called on the ESU to enter the building. The officers entered the cramped apartment, led by hero cops Joseph Dolan, age 34, and David Martinez, age 38, shouting, "Police! Don't move!" whereupon one man reached for one of the officers' weapons and another reached for one of

four toggle switches on a pipe bomb. Officers Dolan and Martinez shot both suspects before any actions against them could be taken. A 9-inch pipe packed with gunpowder and nails and a device in which four pipes had been wrapped together and equipped with toggle-switch detonators were among the explosives removed by the police. Further investigation revealed that the men were Middle Eastern terrorists who had planned to carry out a suicide bombing of the New York City subways on that very day.

The police action came a day after a suicide bombing in a Jerusalem market had killed and injured scores. The lives of over a million New York City commuters and residents were disrupted by the police action and investigation, but no injuries or deaths ensued. Says Officer Martinez, "I felt a little sick when I woke up the next day. I started to realize I almost wasn't here. I started to think of the magnitude of what these people were going to do. They would have killed hundreds of people, little children, mothers, people they don't even know. It's a great feeling to know in some way you helped alter the future."

Mayor Rudolph Giuliani said, "They prevented a major terrorist attack from taking place."

Sources: "They Saved the City: New York Would Be Counting Its Dead If These Hero Cops Had Not Acted," *New York Post* (Aug. 3, 1997), p. 1; Rocco Parascandola, "Hail Storm for City's Finest of Heroes," *New York Post* (Aug. 3, 1997), p. 1; "Heroes of Bomb Scare: Courageous Cops of Emergency Unit Honored," *Daily News* (Aug. 3, 1997), p. 3; William K. Rashbaum and Patrice O'Shaughnessy, "Raiders Knew Lethal Risk: With Seconds to Spare, Cops Nearly 'Naked' vs. Bomb," *Daily News* (Aug. 3, 1997), p. 2.

Commissioner for Intelligence and a Deputy Commissioner for Counterterrorism. They filled these positions with former high-ranking officials from the Central Intelligence Agency and the Marine Corps. The NYPD also created a Counter Terrorism Bureau consisting of 1,000 officers. The Bureau consists of the Counter Terrorism Division as its intelligence and research arm and the Federal–Local Joint Terrorism Task Force as its investigative arm. It has sent officers to Israel to learn more about suicide bombers and has officers working in concert with intelligence agencies throughout the world. New equipment, such as radiation-detection gear and biohazard suits, is now standard issue for all NYPD officers.

Police departments throughout the nation have participated in joint hazardous material response exercises with other emergency personnel. New joint antiterrorist task forces emerged from improved communications between the FBI and state and local departments. Statewide communication systems were enhanced; public terrorist tip lines were established; plans were developed by some local governments for evacuation and quarantine scenarios; and larger departments engaged in intelligence analysis training.[34]

The Florida Department of Law Enforcement (FDLE) entered into a partnership with DHS to train 35 municipal officers, sheriff's deputies, and FDLE agents, who would be assigned to regional antiterrorism task forces

YOU ARE THERE! >>

Policing the Waters of New York City: NYPD Harbor Patrol

At the outset of Operation Iraqi Freedom in March 2003, the members of the NYPD Harbor Patrol Unit worked 12-hour days with no days off, standing deck watch with machine guns and night-vision binoculars, scouring bridges, tunnels, power plants and hospitals. . . . The 27-boat harbor unit patrols the roughly 150 square miles of city waterways, and to spend a night on patrol with Squad 2 is to get an eerily calm view of a city on edge.

Each night, Squad 2 visits some 60 security-sensitive sites in its patrol area. Some are obvious (the Statue of Liberty, the huge support stanchions of the Brooklyn Bridge); others are less so (the large air vents for the Holland Tunnel, the hospitals on the Upper East Side). . . . The Harbor unit handles the city's waterfront. Sensitive areas include the United Nations, heliports and airports as well as Lower Manhattan, which from a boat seems to soar straight out of the water itself.

Source: Corey Kilgannon, "On the Water in Wartime, an Eerily Calm View," *New York Times* (March 21, 2003), p. B10.

and authorized to stop, question, and detain illegal aliens.[35]

Other local governments and local police agencies created new systems to protect their localities against terrorism. Some of these were

- The Pasadena, California, police department created its own threat matrix system to prioritize the continual stream of alerts from federal agencies, with the highest level reserved for those that specifically target Southern California.

- Des Moines, Iowa, police developed an intelligence-sharing system called Cop-Link, which has an artificial intelligence component allowing it to combine data so that municipal and county law enforcement do not have to call each other to find out what information the other might have.

- Portland, Oregon, is developing a $74 million National Center for Disaster Decision Making that will bring experts in law enforcement, politics, fire services, and other areas to the state for advanced simulation and classroom training.

- Stafford County, Virginia, developed a Homeland Security Neighborhood Watch to train participants living nearby railroads, airports, and other key areas for noting license plate numbers, directions of travel, and descriptions.[36]

The following description in the media gives a sense of the security changes in the New York City region at the onset of Operation Iraqi Freedom in 2003:

As the United States wages war on Iraq, New Yorkers and others across the region are witnessing an extraordinary state of heightened security. Police officers are armed like assault troops outside prominent buildings, police boats are combing the waterfronts and trucks are being inspected at bridges and tunnels. . . . No one can live or work in the region without having noticed the proliferation of armed security guards, surveillance cameras, handbag searches, metal detectors, electronic access cards and bomb-sniffing dogs, all of which have multiplied from Pennsylvania Station to the Metropolitan Museum of Art. Layered atop those are changes hidden from most eyes, like the detectives paying visits to chemical companies that terrorists might contact, the immigration agents demanding credit card numbers from foreign visitors, or the hospital emergency room stockpiles of nerve gas antidotes.[37]

Even in areas far from New York City, New York State Police troopers have been assigned to checkpoints along the Canadian border, a job that they did not perform before the September 11 attacks. At the onset of Operation Iraqi Freedom, troopers were covering all 12 international crossings where Customs and Border Patrol officers were already posted, and 120 troopers were assigned to patrol and periodically check the unmanned crossings. Other troopers have been shifted to the State Capitol in Albany for security reasons.[38]

In 2002, a four-day conference was held on the effect of community policing and homeland security. Conference speakers agreed that the community should be involved in countering any chronic crime problem facing the community. In the keynote address, U.S. Attorney General John Ashcroft noted that the agents of terror who committed the atrocities of September 11, 2001, lived in local communities for many months, moving unnoticed in neighborhoods and public places. He emphasized that citizens must become active stakeholders in securing their own safety by being trained by police agencies to become alert observers of dangerous signals, which can result in the supplying of valuable information to law enforcement agencies in their preventive efforts.[39]

Professor Melchor C. De Guzman of Indiana University South Bend, in a speech at a symposium on the changing role of criminal justice agencies in a time of terror, stated that the attacks of September 11, 2001,

YOU ARE THERE! »

Operations Atlas

In response to military actions in Iraq in March 2003, Operation Iraqi Freedom, the New York City Police Department implemented Operation Atlas, a comprehensive security package to protect New York City from possible reprisal attacks by terrorist groups and others.

Operation Atlas recently received high marks from the Secretary of Homeland Security, Tom Ridge:

Operation Atlas is a model for other communities to follow. There is no city in this country that does a better job of working across the board to prevent terrorism than the City of New York.

Core elements of Operation Atlas are

- Increased Personnel Deployment
- Transit System Security
- Patrol Operations/Increased Coverage
- Intelligence
- Airspace Security

INCREASED PERSONNEL DEPLOYMENT

- Increased deployments of harbor, aviation, and emergency service units
- COBRA (chemical, biological, or radiological actions) team deployments
- SAMPSON team deployments
- Harbor units to increase protection of commuter ferries
- Bomb-sniffing dogs assigned to the Staten Island Ferry
- ARCHANGEL teams, composed of Emergency Services Personnel, bomb experts, and investigators staged strategically in the city
- HAMMER teams, police, and fire department experts in hazardous materials deployed jointly
- Heavily armed HERCULES teams deployed randomly through the city
- Counter-assault teams in unmarked armored vehicles ("cat cars") with heavily armed officers
- Counterterrorism inspectors are coordinating mobilization drills

TRANSIT SYSTEM SECURITY

- Transportation Bureau working closely with the MTA and the Port Authority to ensure that war-related precautions are in place
- The National Guard assisting in patrolling the subway system
- Train Order Maintenance Sweeps, "TOMS," deployed to arrest fare evaders and others, whose initial low-level offenses are often precursors of more serious crimes in the subway system; TOMS may discourage or even intercept a terrorist attack
- Mobile arrest processing centers, MAPC BUSES, on standby
- Additional police officers patrolling high-density transit locations such as Times Square, Grand Central, and Penn Station
- Undercover teams riding the subways
- Radiation detection in the subways
- Conducting "surge responses," in which large numbers of officers saturate a given subway station
- Highway patrol officers on 12-hour tours
- Checkpoints in place along 96th Street and at all bridges and tunnels into the city, with locations subject to unannounced change
- Towing of vehicles parked in front of sensitive locations

PATROL OPERATIONS/INCREASED COVERAGE

- Counterterrorism inspectors working 12-hour shifts to guarantee round-the-clock coverage by executive staff
- Deployment of critical response vans to events, or simply to stop at certain locations, like hotels, restaurants, landmarks, or tourist attractions
- Intense 24-hour coverage of the financial district
- The Counterterrorism Bureau is supplying terrorist-related updates to APPLE, an association of New York City corporate and institutional security directors
- Stand-alone plans in place for each patrol borough commander to act as an autonomous police department should police headquarters command and control become disabled

(continued)

YOU ARE THERE! »

Operations Atlas (*continued*)

- Systematic citywide search for any radioactive material or devices

- Preparations to use up to 4,000 school safety officers in the event of an emergency to evacuate children, as well as adults, from the schools and to transport police resources throughout the city, as well as to staff emergency shelters

INTELLIGENCE

- Daily assessments to determine which synagogues and other houses of worship may merit additional protection

- Daily assessments to determine which hotels, museums, landmarks, and other attractions merit additional protection

- Greater surveillance at fuel depots in the greater metropolitan area

- Briefings by intelligence personnel for garage owners and attendants about suspect vehicles that might be left at parking lots in Manhattan

- In cooperation with New Jersey authorities, inspections of sites in New Jersey where radioactive material could be stored clandestinely in close proximity to New York City

- Daily assessment regarding which foreign missions merit additional protection and which dignitaries may need added security

- Review of the security at smaller airports in the metropolitan area to make sure general aviation is not used as a weapon against New York City

AIRSPACE SECURITY

- Restriction of air traffic over Manhattan by the FAA

- Combat aircraft assigned by the Department of Defense to protect New York City airspace

Source: New York City Police Department, "Operation Atlas." Retrieved on April 13, 2003, from http://www.nyc.gov/html/nypd/html/atlas.html.

clearly brought to the limelight not only the false sense of security of the United States but also its vulnerability to the violence of terrorism on its domestic soil. He said that our society must reexamine and revise our strategic thinking and paradigms about the way domestic security is maintained and that public policing has to make the necessary adjustments to contribute to the immediate security requirements of the nation. He concluded by stating:

> The roles and strategies of the police are shaped by the need of the times. In this time of terror, police are required to be more vigilant and perhaps more suspicious. They are required to be more proactive both in detecting and investigating acts of terrorism. The community policing roles that they have embraced for the last decade should be examined in the light of its opposing tenets to the demands of providing police service in time of terror. The police should lean toward a more legalistic style and begin to apply their innate talent for sensing danger. This is the philosophical shift that circumstances demand. This is probably the role that the American people demand from their law enforcement officers.[40]

The International Association of Chiefs of Police (IACP) offers numerous training programs to enable state and local law enforcement agencies to deal with the problems of terrorism. See Exhibit 16.4.

Exhibit 16.4	International Association of Chiefs of Police (IACP) Training Programs Regarding Terrorism and Homeland Defense

Critical Incident Management

Multi-Agency Incident Management for Law Enforcement and Fire Service

Terrorism Incidents Pre- and Post-Planning

Civil Disorder: Field Tactics

SWAT I: Basic Tactical Operations

SWAT II: Advanced Tactical and Hostage Rescue Operations

Organizing and Managing Small Agency and Area SWAT Teams

Source: International Association of Chiefs of Police, *Police Chief* (March 2003, April 2003).

A U.S. Capitol police officer stands outside the Capitol in Washington D.C. on October 17, 2001. Congressional leaders ordered an unprecedented shutdown of the House after more than two dozen people in Senator Tom Daschle's office tested positive for exposure to anthrax. The anthrax deaths and incidents in Florida and Washington, D.C., coming on the heels of the 9/11 tragedy, caused a panic among Americans as rumors ran rampant due to the lack of information about the anthrax incidents. Mail and U.S. governmental services were challenged as the need for security and safety was constantly weighed against the need for public access. Local departments were plagued with calls regarding suspicious substances that usually turned out to be harmless but nevertheless required a specialized response.

★ ★ ★

PRIVATE SECURITY EFFORTS FOR HOMELAND SECURITY

The private security industry in the United States has always attempted to address the issues of security in the workplace; however, the events of September 11, 2001, intensified the importance of security in the workplace. According to the Business Roundtable, an association of chief executive officers of leading American corporations, "Security is now a rising star in the corporate firmament. The people responsible for security have become much more visible to the top of the business and much more important to the business itself."[41] Also, market research on the security industry reported that the global security industry has moved from a peripheral activity to center stage.[42]

Members of corporate executive protection departments and others concerned with personal protection pay constant attention to terrorist possibilities and develop plans to deal with these eventualities in this country and abroad.[43] Most multinational corporations have detailed executive protection plans, crisis management teams, and threat assessment strategies. Sources of information about such security include the National Criminal Justice Reference Service of the National Institute of Justice; *Security Management*, the magazine of the American Society for Industrial Security (ASIS International); and the Office of Consular Affairs of the United States Department of State.[44]

Companies without security departments or those with smaller security departments often hire big contract security companies, such as the Wackenhut Corporation, Burns International, and Pinkerton Security and Investigation Services, to provide corporate and executive security services. These companies emphasize strategic prevention and conduct a threat assessment before establishing a prevention plan.

Often, executives without corporate security or executive protection specialists hire private investigators to advise them on matters of personal and corporate safety. These executives and celebrities also often hire their own personal bodyguards, sometimes referred to as chauffeurs, to accompany them through their travels and in their business and social activities. Private investigator licenses are generally not required for such employment. However, many of the people hired in these roles are former law enforcement officers because it is easier for them to obtain licenses to carry firearms in localities that require such licenses. Also, in localities that allow full-time police officers to "moonlight" (work in another capacity while off duty), many officers supplement their income this way.

As some examples of increased security:

■ The Empire State Building in New York City is more controlled now, and the building's managers say they have added $6 million a year worth of security measures.[45]

■ At Yankee Stadium, there are more police officers and private security guards during games. Bags and backpacks are forbidden, trash cans and parking have been eliminated along the perimeter wall, and there are more security cameras.

■ In New Jersey, state officals developed a list of the 110 privately owned sites they considered most likely to become targets, from office buildings to chemical plants, and even allocated $46 million to help pay for security.

Hospitals have made a big investment in security and emergency preparedness. Bellevue Hospital Center's former portable decontamination shower, hooked up to a hose, has been replaced by an enclosed, permanent, $500,000 structure with air filters, 56 high-speed water nozzles, and the ability to decontaminate as many as 500 people an hour. At St. Vincent's Manhattan Hospital, the pharmacy has a stockpile of 350 injection kits loaded with atropine, an antidote for some nerve gases, and more than 100 with a cyanide antidote. St. Vincent's ambulances have all been equipped with gas masks and body suits to protect the paramedics and with antidotes to chemical agents. Hospitals across New York State have spent more than $200 million on security and emergency reponse measures that were not contemplated before the Trade Center attack. They have built "negative air pressure" rooms that germs cannot escape, bought body suits and respirators, and installed backup computer systems. New York City's Health and Hospitals Corporation bought a radio system linking its 11 hospitals, in case the phones go dead.[46]

Immediately after the terrorist attacks of September 11, 2001, the ASIS International's Board of Directors realized that private security possesses such an incredible body of knowledge and is already involved in protecting so much of the nation's critical infrastructure that they needed to bring together representatives of security-related organizations to express the views of the security industry to the govern-

ment. In late 2002, ASIS International sponsored a security policy summit in Washington, D.C., involving representatives from the Office of Homeland Security and many attendees from security-related organizations. Panelists led discussions about the Homeland Security Act, privacy, and security officer standards. Frank Cilluffo, a director of policy for the Office of Homeland Security, stated, ". . . the private sector is on the front lines in this war [terrorism]."[47]

ASIS International also conducts professional development and training sessions for security management professionals relating to terrorism and homeland defense. See Exhibit 16.5 for a sample of their offerings.

METHODS OF INVESTIGATING TERRORISM

As with many types of investigations, there are two primary methods of investigating acts of terrorism: proactive and reactive. In addition, there is the Federal–Local Joint Terrorism Task Force concept. These three methods together can help prevent and detect acts of terrorism before they occur; and, when that is not possible, they can investigate their occurrences, determine who was involved in their commission, and bring the offenders to justice.

Proactive Methods

Much of this chapter has discussed proactive techniques that are in use constantly to prevent acts of terrorism before they occur. These methods include ongoing and coordinated planning, intelligence gathering, and investigating activity by various agencies.

Reactive Methods

Numerous reactive investigative methods can be used to investigate acts of terrorism after they occur, including response to the incident, crime scene processing and analysis, following up on leads and tips, use of informants, surveillance, and other normal investigative activities.

RESPONSE TO THE INCIDENT   The local law enforcement agency is usually the first responder to scenes of terrorist crimes—just as it is on any crime scene. These officers must follow the normal first-responder duties of rendering aid to the injured, arresting suspects, questioning witnesses, and other immediate response and investigatory issues. It is essential that they safeguard the scene and preserve the evidence for processing by laboratory per-

Exhibit 16.5	**ASIS International Professional Development and Training Conferences Relating to Terrorism and Homeland Security**

■ Disaster Management: The Incident Response Plan
■ Assets Protection Course: Concepts and Methods
■ Government Industry Conference on Global Terrorism and Political Instability
■ Bioterrorism Conference
■ Securing the Global Workplace
■ Security Force Management
■ Facility Security Design
■ Executive Protection
■ How to Conduct a Professional Investigation

Source: ASIS International, *ASIS Dynamics* (Jan./Feb., 2003), p. 18.

sonnel and arson and terrorist specialists. As with the crime of arson, much of the evidence is present in the debris that follows a terrorist explosion.

CRIME SCENE PROCESSING AND ANALYSIS   Crime scene specialists and trained personnel from the various federal, state, and local investigating units described earlier in the chapter use their special skills to seek the means used to commit the crime and any evidence that might connect the crime to the persons responsible for it. As an example of the importance of crime scene processing and analysis, two small pieces of evidence were the keys to determining the cause of the Pan Am explosion over Lockerbie, Scotland. Investigators had painstakingly searched a crime scene of over 845 square miles of debris to find this evidence.

How extensive are terrorist crime scenes? Consider the 2001 World Trade Center attack. When the jumbo jets crashed into the buildings, several things occurred. First, the explosive force of a plane entering the building destroyed much of the immediate internal structure and the victims within. The planes, just refueled for their flights, contained thousands of pounds of fuel. The ensuing fireball, reaching incredibly high temperatures, incinerated all in its path. The fuel then worked its way down to lower floors, continuing its destruction. Shortly after the initial explosion the weakened building, with some of its steel infrastructure actually melting in the intense heat, collapsed under the weight of the crumbling upper floors. The end result: millions of pounds of crime scene material and evidence.

The crime scene investigation was extensive. The first concern of this investigation was to account for and identify as many victims as possible. But before any identifications could be made, the remains had to be recovered. This required the detailed sifting of all the debris and material collected from the crime scene. Sifting was also conducted during the examination of the Oklahoma City bombing incident.

After suspected human remains were recovered from the debris, determinations needed to be made about their origin and identity. Efforts to identify recovered remains included such forensic disciplines as pathology, odontology, biology, and anthropology. For the most part, DNA was used to establish the identity of the deceased. Personal items found at the crime scene—such as jewelry and clothing—were also used for identification, but were considered presumptive in nature, because many of these items are not unique. Still, personal items provided investigators with information on the identity of the missing.

FOLLOWING UP ON LEADS AND TIPS   There must be canvasses and recanvasses, and interviews and reinterviews. (*Canvas* is an investigatory term for the search of an area for witnesses to an incident). Anyone with any information at all must be interviewed immediately. All leads must be followed through to their logical conclusions. Tip lines must be established, and all tips must be followed up.

USE OF INFORMANTS   Informants can be very important in the investigation of terrorist incidents. A good example of the value of an informant's information was the February 1995 arrest of Ramzi Ahmed Yousef, ranked at the time as number one on the FBI's Most Wanted List and believed to be the main plotter behind the 1993 World Trade Center bombing in New York City. Yousef was the target of an international manhunt spanning several countries and thousands of miles. He was located and arrested based on information provided by an unexpected informer who simply walked into the American Embassy in Islamabad, Pakistan. Authorities believed the informer was seeking to collect the $2 million reward that the U.S. State Department was offering for information resulting in Yousef's arrest. After receiving the informant's information, a team of Pakistani

Washington, D.C., Metropolitan Police stage near the site where a suspicious package was found in December 2003. The area was cordoned off as a major deployment of officers was set up and an investigation was conducted. Since the tragedy of 9/11, all police agencies are looking at these "suspicious" package/substance calls in a new way; consequently, the workload and demand on local agencies have increased.

©AP Photo/Pablo Martinez Monsivais

police and American law enforcement officials was assembled and sent to the hotel room where Yousef was believed to be; the team broke down the door and rushed into the room and found Yousef lying on his bed, a suitcase of explosives nearby.[48]

SURVEILLANCE   Surveillance is used in terrorist investigations to follow suspects identified as involved in the crime. (*Surveillance* is an investigatory term used for covertly following subjects in an investigation and recording their activities). Other methods of surveillance or information gathering techniques can also be used for intelligence purposes. Flight recorders in aircraft cockpits provide investigators with a multitude of details about a hijacking. Security cameras in public locations provide details on a terrorist's actions. Timothy McVeigh's truck was recorded on a security camera; terrorists involved in the September 11 attack were recorded on airport security systems. These types of surveillance systems are invaluable for the investigation of terrorist activities.

The Joint Terrorism Task Force (JTTF) Concept

Possibly the most important unit in investigating terrorism in the United States is the FBI–Local Joint Terrorist Task Force (JTTF). There are 16 such units across the United States. Before the establishment of these task forces, ad hoc task forces of local and federal authorities would be established to investigate each new terrorist case as it occurred and then disbanded after the investigation. The new concept ensures that the unit remains in place, becoming a close-knit, cohesive group capable of addressing the complex problems inherent in terrorism investigation. Because federal, state, and local law enforcement resources have been combined in these task forces, there is effective maximization of resources, provision of sophisticated investigative and technological resources, and linkage to all federal government resources in the United States and worldwide.[49]

The objectives of these task forces are twofold: to respond to and investigate terrorist incidents or terrorist-related criminal activity (reactive measures) and to investigate domestic and foreign terrorist groups and individuals targeting or operating in the area for the purpose of detecting, preventing, and prosecuting their criminal activity (proactive measures).

The key to the success of the JTTF task forces is the melding of personnel and talent from various law enforcement agencies in a single, focused unit. The local police members bring the insights that come from years of living and working with the people in their area. They have usually advanced through their careers from uniformed precinct patrol to various detective duties before being assigned to the task force. Each of the participating agencies similarly contributes its own resources and areas of expertise to the team. The integration of the many agencies, each bringing its own unique skills and investigative specialties to the task force, makes these units formidable in combating terrorism.

For example, the FBI–NYPD Joint Terrorism Task Force includes more than 140 members representing numerous federal and local agencies, such as the FBI, NYPD, U.S. Marshals Service, U.S. Department of State Diplomatic Security Service, the ATFE, the Immigration and Naturalization Service, the New York State Police, the New York–New Jersey Port Authority Police Department, and the U.S. Secret Service. In an excellent article in the *FBI Law Enforcement Bulletin*, Robert A. Martin, former deputy inspector for the NYPD and former member of the FBI-NYPD JTTF, describes the operation of the task force:

> The FBI special agents bring vast investigative experience from assignments all over the world. The FBI legal attachés, assigned to U.S. embassies throughout the world, provide initial law enforcement information on international terrorism cases. Since many terrorist events are committed by suspects from other countries, it is necessary to gain the cooperation of law enforcement agencies from the countries of origin. Interagency cooperation is essential when investigating crimes committed internationally. The FBI will work in tandem with other agencies to develop investigative leads.[50]

CHAPTER SUMMARY

Sergeant Rob Hill of the Oklahoma City Police Department was among the first officers to arrive at the scene of the explosion at the Alfred P. Murrah Federal Building on April 19, 1995. Sergeant Hill was trying to rescue survivors when firefighters warned of the possibility of another explosion. He was about to follow their advice and leave with other rescuers when he saw two women on the seventh floor. "Don't leave us!" they pleaded. Hill decided to return to try to rescue the women. He reached the seventh floor, crawled through a blown-out window, and came upon a 15-foot-wide pit. He could hear one of the two women trying to persuade her friend to jump from the window. Before either could jump, Hill yelled out that he was there. "I'll get you out!" he shouted. He pulled himself up onto a window frame, then moved carefully over two blown-out windows to get closer to the women. He hoisted one onto a window frame as Sergeant Robert Campbell, age 39, and Officer Jim Ramsey, age 27, both also of the Oklahoma City Police Department, threw a piece of metal over a narrow strip of floor to give the women an extra foothold. Using the metal plate to regain his own footing, Campbell grabbed one woman from the window frame and pulled her across as Hill and Ramsey returned to rescue the other.

Sergeant Hill and two of his colleagues were able to rescue the two women and bring them to safety. They were among the scores of heroes in Oklahoma City that morning. Imagine if you were one of the women trapped on the seventh floor. Imagine if you were Sergeant Hill or one of his colleagues faced with the responsibility to rescue these women despite the extreme danger to yourself. Such is the terror associated with terrorism.

There were thousands of heroes like Sergeant Hill and his colleagues at the disasters in New York City and at the Pentagon on September 11, 2001, but many of them went down in the rubble that those buildings became.

Now that you have read this chapter, we hope you are more aware of the tremendous threat that international and domestic terrorism poses to U.S. citizens at home and abroad and the need for homeland defense. We also hope that you realize how many professional, dedicated experts and investigators are on continual alert to prevent such terrorism, to investigate any occurrences and bring to justice those who commit them and to ensure homeland defense. Also, you should now realize that there are numerous investigating and specialized job opportunities for persons interested in the investigation of terrorism and ensuring homeland defense.

The lessons of September 11, 2001, have brought new techniques of investigation and new methods of protecting ourselves from the evils of terrorism. Terrorism is now a reality to all of us, and it is a reality that we will continue to fight to prevent.

This chapter discussed terrorism directed against Americans and American interests abroad, including foreign terrorism and domestic terrorism, as well as catastrophic disasters and weapons of mass destruction (WMD). It discussed the immediate aftermath of September 11, 2001, and the rapid, unprecedented efforts made by the U.S. government to ensure homeland defense. It described federal, state, local, and private security efforts for homeland defense and also methods of investigating terrorism, including proactive and reactive methods and the Federal–Local Joint Terrorism Task Force concept.

Learning Check

1. Define terrorism.
2. Describe some of the aspects of the immediate response of the U.S. government to the September 11, 2001, terrorist attacks.
3. List and describe three federal law enforcement programs to deal with the threat of international and domestic terrorism.
4. Discuss some aspects of state and local law enforcement efforts to deal with the threat of terrorism.
5. Name and discuss three methods used to investigate acts of terrorism.

Application Exercise

As part of an honors project, your professor has assigned the following final exercise for your class: List 10 significant changes in U.S. federal, state, and local law enforcement as a result of the September 11, 2001, terrorism attacks on U.S. soil and discuss them.

Web Exercise

Go to the Terrorism Research Center and prepare a list of five major terrorism groups, and under each group include:

- Group name
- Group status
- Other names (if any)
- Description
- Activities
- Other documented attacks (if any)
- Location/area of operation
- Strength
- External aid
- Key personalities
- Group narrative

Key Concepts

Counterintelligence
Counterterrorism
Cyberterrorism
Department of Homeland Security (DHS)
Domestic terrorism
Homeland defense

Homeland Security Advisory System
International terrorism
Joint Terrorism Task Force (JTTF) concept
Patriot Act (USA Patriot Act)
September 11, 2001
Terrorism
Weapons of mass destruction (WMD)

Epilogue

In the Line of Duty

DAVID H. SWIM

David H. Swim is a retired captain from the Stockton, California, Police Department, having spent 22 years with that agency. While with that department he worked the street as a police officer, sergeant, and lieutenant. He was also assigned to SWAT, serving 6 years as the SWAT unit's commander. He received his doctorate in public administration from the University of Southern California and is currently an associate professor of criminal justice administration and leadership, with California State University– Sacramento. He teaches upper-division courses in police administration, critical issues, and leadership, and two graduate courses in the history of criminal justice in America and collective bargaining.

In front of the Stockton Police Department stands a 10-foot high gray granite monument. It stands as a sentinel, to acknowledge those officers of our community who gave their all for law enforcement, in the line of duty. The 14 names etched into the granite will endure as long as the granite. They are enduring in the sense that the absence of these officers and their untimely deaths echo eternally; enduring in the sense that spouses, children, parents, and siblings will constantly feel their absence; enduring in the fact that each day, as officers arrive at work, they pass by this solemn sentinel, reminding them that they, too, could fall, in the line of duty.

The chiseled reality of loss is softened by a plaque occupying the top portion of the obelisk. The police officer holding a small child in his arms contrasts the kindness of the calling of police officer with the harshness of reality.

Death in the line of duty is not attended by some euphoric national pride or sense of mission. In fact, silently, over 100 officers are killed annually, simply doing their job. While we are not paid to die, it is a harsh reality of police work.

During my 22 years at the Stockton PD, seven of those names were added to that monument. Five were killed by gunfire, one was beaten to death, and one died during a foot pursuit. All were friends, some more so than others. Each had a family, most that I personally knew. Each death weathered my soul, extracted tears not cried, and demanded resolution of my shortcomings. Each death reminded me of my own mortality, but, most of all, my inadequacy to properly return to my maker.

One was killed during the exchange of gunfire at the end of a vehicle pursuit. Two were SWAT members whom I had trained to be the "best of the best"; the assailant's bullet pays no respect to training, skill, and finesse. One was ambushed from inside a residence with a rifle that no body armor could stop. One was shot in the face during an exchange of gunfire that also killed his assailant. At the hospital three of us stood around a gurney, silently weeping, knowing that, in the line of duty, real cops cry.

Two were narcotics officers killed on search warrants, by bullets that went over the top of or through the nonexistent side panel of body armor of the 1970s. One of these narcotics officers was the son of our chief of police, who responded to the hospital to find his pride and joy expired on the gurney. As we wept together, how does one console a father, let alone the chief of police? The other narcotics officer's father was working as a reserve the day of his death and expired of a heart attack when he heard of his son's death.

During a several-block foot pursuit of a fleeing suspect, a rare and undiagnosed heart malady stopped the heart of the pursuing officer, making him the sixth of those added to the list during my years with the department. Death was instantaneous, yet absolutely confusing to his attending officers, until the post mortem. A night time traffic stop of a parolee, bulked up by prison yard weight lifting, resulted in a beating with the seventh officer's own flashlight, so severe that the officer expired days later, never recovering from his comatose state.

Of the seven deaths, six were instant and finality came over us as immediately as the summer sun is eclipsed by clouds. The expiration of the beaten officer took days as the family and officers anticipated the eventuality of death. Each day was torture as we were literally or figuratively part of the death watch. Ironically, finality brought peace, commensurate with the immense pain.

Each of these deaths left widows and orphans. Each of these deaths tore the heart out of parents, whereas no parent should have a child precede him or her in death. Each left a community shocked, at least for the moment. Each created an atmosphere where spouses felt the visceral impact and fear for their loved one, in the line of duty. Each reminded us that we were mortal.

Seven viewings with the attendant honor guard in Class A uniforms at each end of the casket. Seven funerals with their respective masses or services. Seven funeral processions with hundreds of marching officers, with labor and management, for the moment, united in step and purpose. Miles of police vehicles with emergency lights beaconing heaven that another chosen servant is on his way. Seven postfuneral receptions where officers attempt to absorb some of the pain and loss of the family of the deceased and yet are confused as they sort out their own personal loss. I was asked by family to speak at two of those funerals. How does one comfort the family, his fellow officers, and express any justification at all for an officer's life being cut short, in the line of duty? Notwithstanding the nobility of the calling, the price is too high.

Policing is a noble calling. It is true, "and on the eighth day God created cops." The heroism of the many and the sacrifice of these few is tarnished by any who accept this calling and do not live up to the ethic required of this noble profession. We live in an era when our profession is under the greatest scrutiny and oftentimes disdain from an ambivalent public, due to the actions of those that disrespect their oath of office. Nonetheless, as with the centurions of old, the world is a better place, because the noble are willing to be in the line of duty.

Notes

Chapter 1

1. John Ayto, *Dictionary of Word Origins* (New York: Arcade, 1990), p. 402.

2. Excesses by the military in enforcing the law in the American West led to the Posse Comitatus Act of 1879. See the discussion of the frontier experience later in the chapter.

3. For a brief history of investigations, see Chapter 1 of John S. Dempsey, *Introduction to Investigations,* 2nd ed. (Belmont, CA.: Wadsworth, 2003).

4. This section on early policing is based on the following: William G. Bailey, ed., *The Encyclopedia of Police Science* (New York: Garland, 1989); John J. Fay, *The Police Dictionary and Encyclopedia* (Springfield, IL.: Charles C. Thomas, 1988); Sanford H. Kadish, *Encyclopedia of Crime and Justice* (New York: Free Press, 1983); George Thomas Kurian, *World Encyclopedia of Police Forces and Penal Systems* (New York: Facts on File, 1989); Jay Robert Nash, *Encyclopedia of World Crime* (Wilmette, IL.: Crime Books, 1990); Charles Reith, *The Blind Eye of History: A Study of the Origins of the Present Police Era* (London: Faber, 1912); and Philip J. Stead, *The Police of Paris* (London: Staples, 1957).

5. "The words [*vigilance* and *vigilante*] come from the Latin *vigilia,* which was derived from the adjective *vigil,* meaning 'awake, alert.' Another derivative of the Latin adjective was *vigilare,* meaning 'keep watch,' which lies behind the English *reveille, surveillance,* and *vigilant.*" Ayto, *Dictionary of Word Origins,* p. 559.

6. This section on the English roots of policing is based on the following: S. G. Chapman and T. E. St. Johnston, *The Police Heritage in England and America* (East Lansing: Michigan State University, 1962); Belton Cobb, *The First Detectives* (London: Faber & Faber, 1967), p. 51; T. A. Critchley, *A History of Police in England and Wales,* 2nd ed. (Montclair, NJ: Patterson Smith, 1972); Clive Emsley, *Policing and Its Context, 1750–1870* (New York: Schocken, 1984); A. C. Germann, Frank D. Day, and Robert R. J. Gallati, *Introduction to Law Enforcement and Criminal Justice* (Springfield, IL: Charles C. Thomas, 1969); W. E. Hunt, *History of England* (New York: Harper & Brothers, 1938); Luke Owen Pike, *A History of Crime in England* (London: Smith, Elder, 1873–1876); Patrick Pringle, *Highwaymen* (New York: Roy, 1963); Pringle, *Hue and Cry: The Story of Henry and John Fielding and Their Bow Street Runners* (New York: Morrow, 1965); Pringle, *The Thief Takers* (London: Museum Press, 1958); Reith, *A New Study of Police History* (London: Oliver & Boyd, 1956); Sir Leon Radiznowciz, *A History of English Criminal Law and Its Administration from 1750,* 4 vols. (London: Stevens & Sons, 1948–1968); Reith, *Blind Eye of History;* Thomas Reppetto, *The Blue Parade* (New York: Free Press, 1978); Albert Rieck, *Justice and Police in England* (London: Butterworth, 1936); Robert Sheehan and Gary W. Cordner, *Introduction to Police Administration,* 2nd ed. (Cincinnati: Anderson Publishing Co., 1989); and John J. H. Tobias, *Crime and Police in England, 1700–1900* (New York: St. Martin's Press, 1979).

7. Pringle, *Hue and Cry,* p. 81.

8. New Westminster Police Service, "Sir Robert Peel's Nine Principles of Policing," at http://www.newwestpolice.org/peel.html.

9. Reppetto, *The Blue Parade,* p. 19.

10. The sections on American colonial and 18th- and 19th-century policing are based on Bailey, *Encyclopedia of Police Science;* Carl Bridenbaugh, *Cities in Revolt: Urban Life in America, 1743–1776* (New York: Knopf,

1965); Bridenbaugh, *Cities in the Wilderness: Urban Life in America, 1625–1742* (New York: Capricorn, 1964); Emsley, *Policing and Its Context;* Robert M. Fogelson, *Big City Police* (Cambridge, MA: Harvard University Press, 1977); Roger Lane, *Policing the City, Boston 1822–1885* (Cambridge, MA: Harvard University Press, 1967); Eric Monkkonen, *Police in Urban America: 1860–1920* (Cambridge, MA: Harvard University Press, 1981); Reppetto, *Blue Parade;* James F. Richardson, *The New York Police: Colonial Times to 1901* (New York: Oxford University Press, 1976); Richardson, *Urban Police in the United States* (Port Washington, NY: Kennikat Press, 1974); Samuel Walker, *A Critical History of Police Reform: The Emergence of Professionalism* (Lexington, MA: Lexington Books, 1977); and Walker, *Popular Justice: History of American Criminal Justice* (New York: Oxford University Press, 1980).

11. Richardson, *New York Police,* p. 31.

12. *Commercial Advisor* (Aug. 20, 1840), as cited in Richardson, *New York Police,* p. 31.

13. Cited in Richardson, *New York Police,* p. 10.

14. Walker, *Popular Justice,* p. 61.

15. Luc Sante, *Low Life: Lures and Snares of Old New York* (New York: Farrar, Straus & Giroux, 1991), p. 236.

16. Walker, *Popular Justice,* p. 63.

17. Fogelson, *Big City Police,* p. 25.

18. Richard A. Staufenberger, *Progress in Policing: Essays on Change* (Cambridge, MA: Ballinger Publishing, 1980), pp. 8–9.

19. Walker, *Popular Justice,* p. 63.

20. Lincoln Steffens, *The Autobiography of Lincoln Steffens* (New York: Harcourt Brace Jovanovich, 1958; originally published in 1931), p. 207.

21. The section on the frontier experience is based on James D. Horan and Howard Swiggett, *The Pinkerton Story* (New York: Putnam, 1951); James D. Horan, *The Pinkertons: The Detective Dynasty That Made History* (New York: Crown, 1967); Edward Hungerford, *Wells Fargo: Advancing the American Frontier* (New York: Bonanza, 1949); David R. Johnson, *American Law Enforcement: A History* (St. Louis: Forum Press, 1981); Carolyn Lake, *Undercover for Wells Fargo* (Boston: Houghton Mifflin, 1969); Allan Pinkerton, *The Expressman and the Detective* (New York: Arno Press, 1976); Frank R. Prassel, *The Western Peace Officer: A Legacy of Law and Order* (Norman: University of Oklahoma Press, 1972); Charles A. Siringo, *A Cowboy Detective: A True Story of Twenty-Two Years with a World-Famous Detective Agency* (Lincoln: University of Nebraska Press, 1988); Bruce Smith, *Police Systems in the United States* (New York: Harper & Row, 1960); Smith, *Rural Crime Control* (New York: Columbia University Institute of Public Administration, 1933); and Walter Prescott Webb, *The Texas Rangers: A Century of Frontier Defense* (Boston: Houghton Mifflin, 1935).

22. This section on 20th-century policing is based on Jay Stuart Berman, *Police Administration and Progressive Reform: Theodore Roosevelt as Police Commissioner of New York* (New York: Greenwood Press, 1987); William J. Bopp and Donald D. Schultz, *A Short History of American Law Enforcement* (Springfield, IL: Charles C. Thomas, 1977); Fogelson, *Big City Police;* Richard Kluger, *Simple Justice* (New York: Vintage, 1977); Roger Lane, *Policing the City* (New York: Atheneum, 1975); Doug McAdam, *Freedom Summer* (New York: Oxford University Press, 1988); Wilbur R. Miller, *Cops and Bobbies: Police Authority in New York and London, 1830–1870*

(Chicago: University of Chicago Press, 1977); Monkkonen, *Police in Urban America;* Edward P. Morgan, *The 60's Experience: Hard Lessons about Modern America* (Philadelphia: Temple University Press, 1991); Albert J. Reiss, *The Police and the Public* (New Haven, CT: Yale University Press, 1971); Richardson, *Urban Police in the United States;* Jerome H., Skolnick, *Justice without Trial: Law Enforcement in a Democratic Society,* 2nd ed. (New York: Wiley, 1975); Jerome H. Skolnick and David H. Bayley, *The New Blue Line* (New York: Free Press, 1986); Milton Viorst, *Fire in the Streets: America in the 1960's* (New York: Simon & Schuster, 1970); Walker, *Popular Justice;* Walker, *Critical History of Police Reform;* Juan Williams, *Eyes on the Prize: America's Civil Rights Years, 1954–1965* (New York: Penguin, 1983); and James Q. Wilson, *Varieties of Police Behavior* (Cambridge, MA: Harvard University Press, 1968).

23. National Commission on Law Observance and Enforcement, *Lawlessness in Law Enforcement,* vol. 2 of the Wickersham Report (Washington, DC: U.S. Government Printing Office, 1931).

24. Johnson, *American Law Enforcement,* p. 121.

25. James Q. Wilson, *Thinking about Crime* (New York: Basic Books, 1983), p. 5.

26. *Mapp v. Ohio,* 367 U.S. 643 (1961).

27. *Escobedo v. Illinois,* 378 U.S. 478 (1964).

28. *Miranda v. Arizona,* 384 U.S. 436 (1966).

29. Cox Commission, *Crisis at Columbia: Report of the Fact-Finding Commission Appointed to Investigate the Disturbances at Columbia University in April and May 1968* (New York: Vintage, 1968), pp. 181–182.

30. National Advisory Commission on Civil Disorders, *Report of the National Advisory Commission on Civil Disorders* (New York: Bantam Books, 1967), p. 299.

31. Federal Bureau of Investigation, *Uniform Crime Reports: Crime in the United States* (Washington, DC: Federal Bureau of Investigation); Fox Butterfield, "Homicides Plunge 11 Percent in U.S., FBI Report Says 'A Stunningly Low' Rate," *New York Times* (June 2, 1997), pp. A1, B10; Michael Cooper, "As New York Homicides Fall, Rate of Solved Cases Goes Up," *New York Times* (June 2, 1997), pp. B1, B3; Michael Cooper, "Crime Reports Drop Sharply in New York: Murder and Car theft Leads Declines in 1997," *New York Times* (April 1, 1997), pp. B1, B9.

32. Peter C. Dodenhoff, "LEN Salutes Its 1996 People of the Year, the NYPD and Its Compstat Process: A Total Package of Re-engineering and Strategy-Making That Has Transformed the Nation's Largest Police Force—As It Will Law Enforcement in General," *Law Enforcement News* (December 31, 1996), pp. 1, 4; "There's No Going Back to Old Ways: Cities Vie to Board CompStat Bandwagon," *Law Enforcement News* (Dec. 31, 1996), p. 5; "What's on the Grill? In New York, It's Police Commanders," *Law Enforcement News* (Dec. 31, 1996), p. 5; Eli B. Silverman, "Mapping Change: How the New York City Police Department Re-engineered Itself to Drive Down Crime," *Law Enforcement News* (December 15, 1996), pp. 10–12.

33. Howard Safir, Police Commissioner, City of New York, *The Compstat Process* (New York: New York City Police Department, no date); William J. Bratton, Police Commissioner, City of New York, "Great Expectations: How Higher Expectation for Police Departments Can Lead to a Decrease in Crime," Paper presented at the National Institute of Justice Research Institute's "Measuring What Matters" Conference, Washington, DC (Nov. 28, 1995); Rudolf W. Giuliani, Randy M. Mastro, and Donna Lynne, *Mayor's Management Report: The City of New York* (New York: City of New York, 1997).

34. Peter C. Dodenhoff, "LEN Salutes Its 1996 People of the Year," p. 4.

35. "There's No Going Back to Old Ways," p.5.

36. Dan Barry, "A Clean Sweep for a Stained Station House: Heads of 70th Precinct Get New Assignment," *New York Times* (Aug. 15, 1997), pp. A1, 13; James Barron, "A Father Finds Charges Hard to Believe," *New York Times* (Aug. 15, 1997), p. A13; David Firestone, "A Police Case in the Context of Elector Politics: A Mayor Closely Tied to Police Successes Faces a Police Problem," *New York Times* (August 15, 1997), p. A13; Dan Barry, "2d Police Officer Charged in Attack on Arrested Man: Colleague Gave Details," *New York Times* (Aug. 16, 1997), pp. 1, 24.

37. Donald Johnston, "Report Criticizes Scientific Testing at FBI Lab: Serious Problems Cited," *New York Times* (April 16, 1997), pp. A1, D23; Mireya Navarro, "Doubts about FBI Lab Raise Hopes for Convict: On Death Row, but Seeking a New Trial," *New York Times* (April 22, 1997), p. A8.

38. "What's Wrong at the FBI?: The Fiasco at the Crime Lab," *Time* (April 28, 1997), pp. 28–35.

39. Seth Mydans, "23 Dead after 2d Day of Los Angeles Riot: Fires & Looting Persists Despite Curfew," *New York Times* (May 1, 1992), pp. A1, A20.

40. Seth Mydans, "Ex-Police Chief Blamed for Riot in Los Angeles: Gates Calls the Authors of the Report 'Liars,'" *New York Times* (Oct. 22, 1992), p. A12.

41. Richard Perez-Pena, "A Security Blanket, but With No Guarantees," *New York Times* (March 23, 2003), pp. A1, B14.

42. William K. Rashbaum, "Air Patrols and Officers at TV Stations as City Goes on Alert," *New York Times* (March 19, 2003), p. A21.

43. Jodi Wilgoren, "Higher Alert and Tighter Budgets," *New York Times* (March 19, 2003), pp. A1, A21.

44. Timothy Egan, "Pacific Northwest Keeps Watch on Many Vulnerable Points," *New York Times* (March 25, 2003), p. B-13.

45. Kate Zernike and Dean E. Murphy, "Across the Nation, Protesters Carry Out a Plan to 'Stop Business as Usual,'" *New York Times* (March 21, 2003), p. B4.

46. Zernike and Murphy, "Across the Nation, Protesters Carry Out a Plan."

47. Leslie Eaton, "Nationwide Peace Rallies Continue, Nonviolently," *New York Times* (March 22, 2003), p. B-9.

48. Leslie Eaton, "On New York's Streets and across the Nation, Protesters Speak Out," *New York Times* (March 23, 2003), p. B14.

Chapter 2

1. David H. Bayley, *Forces of Order: Police Behavior in Japan and the United States* (Berkeley: University of California Press, 1976).

2. Brian A. Reaves and Matthew J. Hickman, *Census of State and Local Law Enforcement Agencies, 2000* (Washington, DC: Bureau of Justice Statistics, 2002), p. 1; Brian A. Reaves and Matthew J. Hickman, *Local Police Departments, 2000,* p. v.

3. Reaves and Hickman, *Census of State and Local Law Enforcement Agencies, 2000;* Reaves and Hickman, *Local Police Departments, 2000* (Washington, D.C.: Bureau of Justice Statistics, 2003), p.v.

4. Sidra Lea Gifford, *Justice Expenditures and Employment in the United States, 1999* (Washington, DC: Bureau of Justice Statistics, 2002), p. 4.

5. Brian A. Reaves and Lynn M. Bauer, *Federal Law Enforcement Officers, 2002* (Washington, DC: Bureau of Justice Statistics, 2003), p. 1.

6. Reaves and Hickman, *Census of State and Local Law Enforcement Agencies, 2000*, p. 4.

7. William C. Cunningham, John J. Strauchs, and Clifford Van Meter, *The Hallcrest Report II: Private Security Trends: 1970 to 2000* (Boston: Butterworth-Heinemann, 1990).

8. U.S. Department of Labor, Bureau of Labor Statistics, *Occupational Outlook Handbook,* "Police and Detectives." Retrieved on May 15, 2003, from http://www.bls.gov/oco/ocos160.htm.

9. Reaves and Hickman, *Census of State and Local Law Enforcement Agencies,* 2000, pp. 5–7; also see Brian A. Reaves and Matthew J. Hickman, *Police Departments in Large Cities, 1990–2000* (Washington, DC: Bureau of Justice Statistics, 2002).

10. Reaves and Hickman, *Census of State and Local Law Enforcement Agencies, 2000,* pp. 12–14.

11. Lee P. Brown, "The Role of the Sheriff," in *The Future of Policing,* ed. Alvin Cohn (Beverly Hills, CA: Sage Publications, 1978), pp. 237–240.

12. Reaves and Hickman, *Census of State and Local Law Enforcement Agencies, 2000,* pp. 8–10; Matthew J. Hickman and Brian A. Reaves, Sheriff's Offices, 2000 (Washington, DC, 2003), p. 1.

13. John Hoffman, "Rural Policing," *Law and Order,* June 1992, pp. 20–24.

14. Hoffman, "Rural Policing."

15. Christopher S. Wren, "The Illegal Home Business: 'Speed' Manufacture," *New York Times* (July 8, 1997), p. A8.

16. Wren, "The Illegal Home Business."

17. Lee Colwell, "The National Center for Rural Law Enforcement: One Part of the Greater Whole," *Community Policing Exchange* (March/April 1997), p. 6.

18. Reeves and Hickman, *Census of State and Local Law Enforcement Agencies, 2000,* p. 11.

19. Reaves and Bauer, *Federal Law Enforcement Officers, 2002,* p. 1.

20. See, for example, Althan Theorharis and John Stuart Cox, *The Boss* (Philadelphia: Temple University Press, 1988). There are a myriad of books in college libraries and local public libraries regarding the history and operations of the FBI and the history of Director Hoover. An interesting class project or research paper may be to compare and contrast the treatment of the FBI and Hoover in the books published before his death in 1972 and after his death. Most authors needed the prior approval of Hoover and his officials prior to publication. The books published after his death generally paint a much different picture of Hoover and the FBI.

21. See, for example, Tony Proveda, *Lawlessness and Reform: The FBI in Transition* (Pacific Grove, CA: Brooks/Cole, 1990).

22. Federal Bureau of Investigation, www.fbi.gov/pressrel/speeches/speech052902.htm; http://www.fbi.gov/page2/52902.htm.

23. For a complete description of the DEA and many of its major programs, as well as a complete discussion of Controlled Substances and Drug Offenses see, John S. Dempsey, *Introduction to Investigations,* 2nd ed. (Belmont, CA: Wadsworth, 2003), Chapter 12.

24. See Rand Corporation, *Organizing for Homeland Security* (Santa Monica, CA: Rand Corporation, 2002); Randall A. Yim, *National Preparedness: Integration of Federal, State, Local and Private Sector Efforts Is Critical to an Effective National Strategy for Homeland Security* (Washington, DC: U.S. General Accounting Office, 2002); David M. Walker, *Homeland Security: Responsibility and Accountability for Achieving National Goals* (Washington, DC: U.S. General Accounting Office, 2002); Michael Barletta, *After 9/11: Preventing Mass-Destruction Terrorism and Weapons Proliferation* (Monterey, CA: Center for Nonproliferation Studies, 2002); and JayEtta Hecker, *Homeland Security: Intergovernmental Coordination and Partnership Will Be Critical to Success* (Washington, DC: U.S. General Accounting Office, 2002). All of these documents are available at NCJRS at http://www.ncjrs.gov.

25. U.S. Department of Homeland Security, DHS Organization. Retrieved on March 25, 2003, from http://www.dhs.gov/dhspublic/interapp/editorial/editorial_0086.xml.

26. Joel Brinkley, "Interior Department Struggles to Upgrade Its Police Forces," *New York Times* (Nov. 4, 2002), p. A11.

27. Reaves and Bauer, *Federal Law Enforcement Officers, 2002.*

28. William C. Cunningham and Todd H. Taylor, *The Hallcrest Report: Private Security and Police in America* (Portland, OR: Chancellor Press, 1985).

29. Cunningham, Strauchs, and Van Meter, *The Hallcrest Report II: Private Security Trends: 1970–2000* (Boston: Butterworth-Heinemann, 1990). This report was also published by the National Institute of Justice, in summary form, for the government as William C. Cunningham, John J. Strauchs, and Clifford W. Van Meter, *Private Security Patterns and Trends* (Washington, DC: U.S. Government Printing Office, 1991).

30. "ASIS Display Promotes Security Careers," *Security Management* (July 1997), pp. 137–138.

31. Security Industry Association. Retrieved on January 20, 2000, from http://www.siaonline.org/wp_size.html.

32. "Olympic Committee to Review Salt Lake Security in Wake of Terror Attacks," Associated Press (Sept. 17, 2001).

33. U.S. Department of Labor, Bureau of Labor Statistics, *Occupational Outlook Handbook,* "Security Guards and Gaming Surveillance Officers." Retrieved on May 15, 2003, from http://www.bls.gov/oco/ocos159.htm.

34. David H. Bayley and Clifford D. Shearing, *The New Structure of Policing: Description, Conceptualization and Research Agenda* (Washington, DC: National Institute of Justice, 2001).

35. "Welcome to the New World of Private Security," *Economist* (April 19, 1997).

36. Tucker Carlson, "Safety Inc.," *Policy Review* (Summer 1995), pp. 72–73.

37. See Law Commission of Canada, *In Search of Security: The Roles of Public Police and Private Agencies* (Ottawa, Ontario: Law Commission of Canada, 2002).

38. Cunningham, Strauchs, and Van Meter, *Private Security,* p. 2.

39. William C. Cunningham and Todd H. Taylor, *The Growth of Private Security* (Washington, DC: National Institute of Justice, 1984).

40. "George Smiley Joins the Firm," *Newsweek* (May 2,1988), pp. 46–47.

41. James F. Kakalik and Sorrel Wildhorn, *Private Police in the United States,* vol. 2 (Washington, DC: National Institute of Justice, 1971), p. 133.

42. Pamela A. Sexton-Alyea, "Police Versus Private Security: Whom Do We Trust?" in Deborah Mitchell Robinson, ed. *Policing and Crime Prevention* (Upper Saddle River, NJ: Prentice Hall Publishing, 2002), pp. 31–52.

43. Sherry L. Harowitz, "The New Centurions," *Security Management* (January 2003), pp. 51–58.

44. Joseph G. Deegan, "Mandated Training for Private Security," *FBI Law Enforcement Bulletin* (March 1987), pp. 6–8.

45. ASIS International, "About ASIS." Retrieved on June 24, 2003, from http://www.asisonline.org/about/index.xml.

46. Mary Alice Davidson, "It *Is* What You Know," *Security Management* (June 2003), p. 75.

47. "ASIS Display Promotes Security Careers," ASIS Online at http://www.asisonline.org.

48. Cunningham, Strauchs, and Van Meter, *Private Security,* p. 4.

49. Davidson, "It *Is* What You Know," p. 75.

50. Davidson, "It *Is* What You Know," p. 70.

51. Davidson, "It *Is* What You Know," p. 69.

52. Davidson, "It *Is* What You Know," p. 72.

53. "ASIS Display Promotes Security Careers."

54. U.S. Department of Labor, Bureau of Labor Statistics, *Occupational Outlook Handbook,* "Private Detectives and Investigators." Retrieved on May 15, 2003, from http://www.bls.gov/oco/ocos157.htm. For a complete description of the role and jobs performed by private investigators, see Chapter 15 of John S. Dempsey, *Introduction to Investigations,* 2nd ed. (Belmont: CA: Wadsworth, 2003).

55. Sandy Granville Sheehy, "The Adventures of Harold Smith, Art Supersleuth,"*Town and Country Monthly* (Oct. 1992), p. 118.

56. Dick Adler, "Brian Jenkin's Excellent Adventures," *Inc.* (Oct. 1991), p. 47.

57. Thomas Bancroft, "Growth Business," *Forbes* (Sept. 1992), p. 516.

58. Pamela Marin and Warren Kalbacker, "Love Dicks," *Playboy* (Jan. 1991), p. 102; Steven Edwards, "The Rush to Private Eyes: Wary Lovers Check Up on Partners," *Maclean's's* (March 1990), p. 49; and Bill Colligan, "Just Dial 1-900-CHEATER," *Newsweek* (July 29, 1991), p. 58.

59. Peter Wilkinson, "The Big Sleazy," *Gentlemen's Quarterly* (Jan. 1992), p. 112.

60. L. J. Davis, "International Gumshoe," *New York Times Magazine* (Aug. 30, 1992), p. 46.

61. "Checking Out Prospective Mates: Check-a-Mate, a Private Detective Service," *USA Today Magazine* (Dec. 1990), p. 4.

62. Tom Dunkel, "Holy sleuth frees innocent souls," *Insight* (Feb. 4, 1991), p. 52.

63. Scott Shuger, "Public Eye," *New York Times Magazine* (Sept. 13, 1992), p. 56.

64. Mark Ivey, "Philip Marlowe? No. Successful? Yes.," *Business Week* (Oct. 21, 1991), p. 60.

65. Amanda Gardner, "Corporate Eyes," *Inc.* (Nov. 1991), p. 61

66. "Doggone? Bloodhound Ron Dufault Runs around in Circles to Help Pet Owners Find Their Missing Pooches," *People Weekly* (Sept. 10, 1990), p. 151.

67. Ronnie Virgets, "Secret Services," *New Orleans Magazine* (March 1992), p. 36.

68. For a complete discussion of the role of private investigators in our society, see John S. Dempsey, *Introduction to Investigations,* 2nd ed., particularly Chapter 15.

69. Albert Reiss, *Private Employment of Public Police* (Washington, DC: National Institute of Justice, 1988).

70. Reiss, *Private Employment of Public Police.*

71. Reiss, *Private Employment of Public Police.*

72. Cunningham, Strauchs, and Van Meter, *Private Security,* p. 3. See the *New York Post* (Nov. 23, 1997), p.6, for a controversy involving a bill allowing New York City police officers to work in uniform for private employers.

73. For an excellent discussion of off-duty police officers working for private security concerns and the liability and constitutional issues involved, see David H. Peck, "When Police Walk the Security Beat," *Security Management* (Oct. 1999), pp. 39–45.

74. Catherine Whitaker, *Crime Prevention Measures* (Washington, DC: National Institute of Justice, 1986).

75. James Garofalo and Maureen McLeod, *Improving the Use and Effectiveness of Neighborhood Watch Programs* (Washington, DC: National Institutive of Justice, 1988).

Chapter 3

1. George W. Griesinger et al., *Civil Service Systems: Their Impact on Police Administration* (Washington, DC: U.S. Government Printing Office, 1979); Dorothy Guyot, "Blending Granite: Attempts to Change the Rank Structure of American Police Departments," *Journal of Police Science and Administration* 7 (1979), pp. 253–284.

2. *Criminal Procedure Law* of the State of New York, Article 140, Sections 140.10, 140.30.

3. National Institute of Law Enforcement and Criminal Justice, *Employing Civilians for Police Work* (Washington, DC: U.S. Government Printing Office, 1975), preface.

4. President's Commission on Law Enforcement and Administration of Justice, *Task Force Report: The Police* (Washington, DC: U.S. Government Printing Office, 1967), p.123.

5. International Association of Chiefs of Police, *Operational Issues in the Small Law Enforcement Agency* (Arlington, VA: International Association of Chiefs of Police, 1990).

6. L. I. Deitch and L. N. Thompson, "The Reserve Officer: One Alternative to the Need for Manpower," *Police Chief,* May 1985, pp. 59–61.

7. Randall Aragon, "Does Your Agency Need a Reserve Officer Program?" *Police Chief* (Nov. 1994), pp. 27–29.

8. Aragon, "Does Your Agency Need a Reserve Officer Program?"

9. Aragon, "Does Your Agency Need a Reserve Officer Program?"

10. President's Commission on Law Enforcement and Administration of Justice, *The Challenge of Crime in a Free Society* (Washington, DC: U.S. Government Printing Office, 1967), p. 112; and Geoffrey N. Calvert, *Portable Police Pensions Improving Inter-Agency Transfers* (Washington, DC: U.S. Government Printing Office, 1971).

11. Anthony V. Bouza, "Police Unions: How They Look from the Academic Side," in *Police Leadership in America,* ed. William A. Geller (New York: Praeger, 1985), p. 241.

12. Bouza, "Police Unions," p. 241.

13. Police Executive Research Forum, *Survey of Police Operational and Administrative Practice* (Washington, DC: Police Executive Research Forum, 1982), pp. 606–610.

14. Robert Sheehan and Gary W. Cordner, *Introduction to Police Administration,* 2nd ed. (Cincinnati, OH: Anderson Publishing, 1989), pp. 113–162.

Chapter 4

1. Troy Mineard, "Recruiting and Retaining Gen-X Officers," *Law and Order,* 51, 7(July 2003), pp. 94–95.

2. James J. Fyfe, "Police Personnel Practices, 1986," in *Municipal Yearbook 1987* (Washington, DC: International City Management Association, 1987), pp. 15–23.

3. Arthur Niederhoffer, *Behind the Shield: The Police in Urban Society* (Garden City, NY: Anchor Books, 1967), p. 1.

4. Robert Sheehan and Gary W. Cordner, *Introduction to Police Administration,* 2d ed. (Cincinnati: Anderson, 1989), p. 220.

5. Sheehan and Cordner, *Introduction to Police Administration,* p. 222.

6. U.S. Census Bureau Public Information Office. Retrieved on March 18, 2004, from www.census.gov/press-release.

7. Osborn, "Police Recruitment: Today's Standard—Tomorrow's Challenge," *FBI Law Enforcement Bulletin* (June 1992), p. 23.

8. Osborn, "Police Recruitment," p. 23.

9. Kathy Bushouse, "Creativity Tops off Police Recruitment." Retrieved on June 17, 2002, from www.sunsentinel.com.

10. Duane L. West, "Officer Looks Back at Recruitment Process—Things Have Changed," *Community Policing Exchange* (March/April 1997), p. 3. The author is a lieutenant with the Tallahassee, Florida, Police Department's Neighborhood Services Division.

11. *Guardians Association of NYC Police Department* v. *Civil Service Commission of New York,* 23 FEP 909 (1980).

12. D. Thompson and T. Thompson, "Court Standards for Job Analysis in Test Validation," *Personnel Psychology* (35): 865–874.

13. Matthew J. Hickman and Brian A. Reaves, *Law Enforcement Management & Administrative Statistics: Local Police Departments, 2000* (Washington, DC: Department of Justice, Bureau of Justices Statistics, 2002).

14. Timothy N. Oettmeier, "Perspectives on Selection Procedures," *Community Policing Exchange* (March/April 1997), p. 1. The author is a lieutenant in the Houston Police Department's police academy.

15. Allan Roe and Norma Roe, *Police Selection: A Technical Summary of Validity Studies* (Ogden, UT: Diagnostic Specialties, 1982).

16. Bernard Cohen and Jan Chaiken, *Investigators Who Perform Well* (Washington, DC: National Institute of Justice, 1987), pp. 16–20.

17. Cohen and Chaiken, *Investigators Who Perform Well,* p. 20.

18. Bernard Cohen and Jan M. Chaiken, *Police Background Characteristics and Performance* (Lexington, MA: Lexington Books, 1973), pp. 87, 90–91.

19. H. Saxenian, "To Select a Leader," *MIT Technology Review* 72 (1970): 55–61.

20. Hickman and Reaves, *Law Enforcement Management & Administrative Statistics: Local Police Departments, 2000.*

21. Charles R. Swanson, Leonard Territo, and Robert W. Taylor, *Police Administration,* 5th Ed. (Upper Saddle River, NJ: Prentice-Hall, 2001), p. 291.

22. Larry K. Gaines, John L. Worrall, Mittie T. Southerland, and John E. Angell, *Police Administration,* 2nd Ed. (New York: McGraw-Hill, 1991), p. 366.

23. Steven A. Lazer, "Common Sense, Can It Be Measured by Police Tests?" *Police Chief* (April 1997), pp. 157–158.

24. See James Kriebe, "Selection, Training, and Evaluation Ensure Success," *Police Chief,* 62(1994): 26–29. Also see T. Kenneth Moran, "Pathways toward a Nondiscriminatory Recruitment Policy," *Journal of Police Science and Administration* 16 (1988): 274–287.

25. G. E. Hargrave, "Using the MMPI and CPI to Screen Law Enforcement Applicants: A Study of Reliability and Validity of Clinician's Decisions," *Journal of Police Science and Administration* 13 (1985): 221–224.

26. Jack Aylward, "Psychological Testing and Police Selection," *Journal of Police Science and Administration,* 13(1985): 201–210.

27. George Pugh, "The California Psychological Inventory and Police Selection," *Journal of Police Science and Administration,* 3(1985): 172–177.

28. George Hargrave and Deidre Hiatt, "Law Enforcement Selection with the Interview, MMPI and CPI: A Study of Reliability and Validity," *Journal of Police Science and Administration,* 15(1987): 110–114.

29. Robert D. Meier and Richard E. Maxwell, "Psychological Screening of Police Candidates: Current Perspectives," *Journal of Police Science and Administration,* 15(1987): 210–215.

30. Alan Brenner, "Psychological Screening of Police Applicants," in *Critical Issues in Policing,* ed. Roger Dunham and Geoffrey Alper (Prospect Heights, IL: Waveland Press, 1989), pp. 72–87.

31. Elizabeth Burbeck and Adrian Furnham, "Police Officer Selection: A Critical Review of the Literature," *Journal of Police Science and Administration,* 13(1985): 58–69.

32. J. Douglas Grant and Joan Grant, "Officer Selection and the Prevention of Abuse of Force," in W. A. Geller and H. Toch, eds., *And Justice for All* (Washington, DC: PERF, 1995), pp. 161–162.

33. Wayne W. Bennett and Karen M. Hess, *Criminal Investigation,* 7th ed. (Belmont, CA: Wadsworth, 2004), p. 153.

34. F. Lee Bailey, Roger E. Zuckerman, and Kenneth R. Pierce, *The Employee Polygraph Protection Act: A Manual for Polygraph Examiners and Employers* (Severna Park, MD: American Polygraph Association, 1989). See also James J. Kouri, "Federal Polygraph Law: A Blow to Private Security," *The NarcOfficer* (May 1989), pp. 37–39; Hugh E. Jones, "The Employee Polygraph Protection Act: What Are the Consequences?" *The NarcOfficer,* May 1989, pp. 41–42; and Norman Ansley, "A Compendium on Polygraph Validity," *The NarcOfficer* (May 1989), pp. 43–48.

35. Gaines, Southerland, and Angell, *Police Administration,* p. 371.

36. Paula Rubin, *The Americans with Disabilities Act and Criminal Justice: Hiring New Employees* (Washington: DC: National Institute of Justice, 1994). Also see Michael Smith and Geoffrey Alpert, "The Police and the Americans with Disabilities Act—Who Is Being Discriminated Against?" *Criminal Law Bulletin,* 29 1993), pp. 516–528; T. Schneid and L. Gaines, "The Americans with Disabilities Act: Implications for Police Administrators," *American Journal of Police,* 10(1, 1991), pp. 47–58.

37. Thomas R. Collingwood, Robert Hoffman, and Jay Smith, "The Need for Physical Fitness," *Law and Order* (June 2003), pp. 44–50.

38. Thomas R. Collingwood, Robert Hoffman, and Jay Smith, "Underlying Physical Fitness Factors for Performing Police Officer Physical Tasks," *Police Chief* (March 2004), pp. 32–37.

39. John C. Klotter, Jaqueline R. Kanovitz, and Michael I. Kanovitz, *Constitutional Law,* 9th Ed. (Cincinnati, OH: Anderson, 2002).

40. Thomas H. Wright, "Preemployment Background Investigations," *FBI Law Enforcement Bulletin* (Nov. 1991), pp. 16–21.

41. President's Commission on Law Enforcement and Administration of Justice, *The Challenge of Crime in a Free Society* (Washington, DC: U.S. Government Printing Office, 1967).

42. Klotter, Kanovitz, and Kanovitz, *Constitutional Law,* p.489.

43. J. E. Sheedy et al., "Recommended Vision Standards for Police Officers," *Journal of the American Optometric Association* (Oct. 1983), pp. 925–928.

44. T. C. Cox et al., "A Theoretical Examination of Police Entry-Level Uncorrected Visual Acuity Standards," *American Journal of Criminal Justice* (Nov. 1987), pp. 199–208.

45. Gaines, Worrall, Southerland, and Angell, *Police Administration,* p. 271.

46. G. W. Good and A. R. Augsburger, "Uncorrected Visual Acuity Standards for Police Applicants," *Journal of Police Science and Administration* (Dec. 1987), pp. 18–23.

47. Mike Pearl, "'Age' Ruling Backs Cops in Battle of Blue & Grey," *New York Post* (May 31, 1997), p. 12; "Age before Duty? Police Brass Alter Ground Rules, Leaving Some Over-35 NYPD Rookies Standing at the Altar," *Law Enforcement News* (April 1997), p. 5.

48. James B. Jacobs and Samuel B. Magdovitz, "At LEEP's End: A Review of the Law Enforcement Education Program," *Journal of Police Science and Administration,* 5(1977), pp. 1–17. LEEP was also discussed in Chapter 1 of this text.

49. President's Commission on Law Enforcement and Administration of Justice, *Challenge of Crime,* p. 110.

50. B. E. Sanderson, "Police Officers: The Relationship of a College Education to Job Performance," *Police Chief,* 44(1977), p. 62.

51. Wayne Cascio, "Formal Education and Police Officer Performance," *Journal of Police Science and Administration,* 5(1977), pp. 57–60.

52. Lee Bowker, "A Theory of Educational Needs of Law Enforcement Officers," *Journal of Contemporary Criminal Justice,* 1(1980), pp. 17–24.

53. Mitchell Tyre and Susan Braunstein, "Higher Education and Ethical Policing," *FBI Law Enforcement Bulletin* (June 1992), pp. 6–10.

54. Lawrence Sherman et al., *The Quality of Police Education* (San Francisco: Jossey-Bass, 1978), pp. 185–188.

55. Sherman et al., *Quality of Police Education,* pp. 185–188.

56. T. Gest, *Crime and Politics: Big Government's Erratic Campaign for Law and Order* (New York: Oxford University Press, 2001).

57. J. T. Krimmel, "The Performance of College-Educated Police: A Study of Self-Rated Performance Measures," *American Journal of Policing,* 15(1996), pp. 85–96, and K. M. Lersch and L. Kunzman, "Misconduct Allegations and Higher Education in a Southern Sheriff's Department," *American Journal of Criminal Justice,* 25(2001), pp. 161–172.

58. Sheehan and Cordner, *Introduction to Police Administration,* p. 221.

59. "How Much Is Too Much? Prior Drug Use at Issue," *Law Enforcement News* (Feb. 2, 1997), p. 5. Also see "Md. Recruits Drug History Eyed," *Law Enforcement News* (April 15, 1997), p. 5.

60. Kevin Krause, "Police Agencies Mellow on Applicants' Drug Use." Retrieved on December 11, 2002, from www.sunsentinel.com.

61. Arthur Sharp, "Departmental Divergences on Marijuana use and New Recruits," *Law and Order* (Sept. 2003), pp. 80–81.

62. George W. Griesinger et al., *Civil Service Systems: Their Impact on Police Administration* (Washington, DC: National Institute of Justice, 1979), p. 102.

63. Gaines, Southerland, and Angell, *Police Administration,* p. 270.

64. Samuel Walker and Charles M. Katz, *Police in America,* 4th Ed. (New York: McGraw-Hill, 2002).

65. Harold Backer and Jack E. Whitehouse, *Police of America: A Personal View: Introduction and Commentary* (Springfield, IL: Charles C. Thomas, 1980), pp. 49–51.

66. Brian Reaves, *Local Law Enforcement* (Washington, DC: National Institute of Justice, 1996), p. 4.

67. Thomas Shaw, "The Evolution of Police Recruit Training: A Retrospective," *FBI Law Enforcement Bulletin* (Jan. 1992), pp. 2–6.

68. Thomas M. Frost and Magnus J. Seng, "The Administration of Police Training: A Thirty-Year Perspective," *Journal of Police Science and Administration* (March 1984), pp. 66–73.

69. President's Commission on Law Enforcement and Administration of Justice, pp. 112–113.

70. Hickman and Reaves, *Law Enforcement Management & Administrative Statistics: Local Police Departments, 2000.*

71. "Law Enforcement Training Week Resolution Awaits Passage in House," *CJ Update,* 21(1992), p. 10.

72. Michael S. Campbell, *Field Training for Police Officers: State of the Art* (Washington, DC: National Institute of Justice, 1986).

73. Jack B. Molden, "Training Officer Notes: Training as a Management Function," *Law and Order* (Sept. 1992), pp. 17–18.

74. James P. Morgan, Jr., "Police Firearms Training: The Missing Link," *FBI Law Enforcement Bulletin,* January 1992, pp. 14–15.

75. Hickman and Reeves, "Law Enforcement."

76. See, for example, "Kick-Start Training Strategies," *Community Policing Exchange* (March/April 1997), p. 4; Howard Lebowitz, "Academy Training Curriculum Emphasizes Moral Decision Making," *Community Policing Exchange* (March/April 1997), p. 2; John Gentile, "Recruit and In-Service Training: The Diversity Factor," *Community Policing Exchange* (March/April 1997), pp. 6–7; Clair Young, "Ohio Organizes Statewide Training," *Community Policing Exchange* (March/April 1997), p. 7; and Danny Shell, "State Makes Vision for Unity a Reality,"*Community Policing Exchange* (March/April 1997), p. 8.

77. "Free Community Policing Training Available to COPS Grantees," *Community Policing Exchange* (March/April 1997), p. 2. The Community Policing Consortium can be reached at 1726 M Street N.W., Suite 801, Washington, DC, 20036. 800-833-3085; Fax 202-833-9295. The consortium can also be clicked onto at its Web site at www.community-policing. org.

78. O. W. Wilson and Roy Clinton McLaren, *Police Administration,* 4th Ed. (New York: McGraw-Hill, 1977), p. 270.

Chapter 5

1. Herman Goldstein, *Policing a Free Society* (Cambridge, MA: Ballinger Press, 1977), p. 21.

2. George L. Kirkham and Laurin A. Wollan, Jr., *Introduction to Law Enforcement* (New York: Harper & Row, 1980), p. 336.

3. Federal Bureau of Investigations, *Uniform Crime Reports,* "Arrests 2002," p. 4. Retrieved on March 19, 2004, from http://www.fbi.gov.

4. Patrick A. Langan, Lawrence A. Greenfeld, Steven K. Smith, Matthew R. Durose, and David J. Levin, *Contacts Between Police and the Public: Findings from the 1999 National Survey* (Washington, DC: Bureau of Justice

Statistics, 2001); Lawrence A. Greenfeld, Patrick A. Langan, and Steven K. Smith, *Police Use of Force: Collection of National Data* (Washington, DC: Bureau of Justice Statistics, 1997).

5. John Webster, "Police Task and Time Study," *Journal of Criminal Law, Criminology, and Police Science,* 61(1970), pp. 94–100.

6. Robert Lilly, "What Are the Police Now Doing?" *Journal of Police Science and Administration,* 6(1978), pp. 51–53.

7. Eric J. Scott, *Calls for Service: Citizen Demand and Initial Police Response* (Washington, DC: National Institute of Justice, 1981), pp. 28–30.

8. Michael Brown, *Working the Street* (New York: Russell Sage Foundation, 1981); Norman Weiner, *The Role of Police in Urban Society: Conflict and Consequences* (Indianapolis: Bobbs-Merrill, 1976); and Albert J. Reiss, *The Police and the Public* (New Haven: CT: Yale University Press, 1971).

9. Stephen Meagher, "Police Patrol Styles: How Pervasive is Community Variation?" *Journal of Police Science and Administration,* 13(1985), pp. 36–45.

10. Alan Coffey, *Law Enforcement: A Human Relations Approach* (Englewood Cliffs, NJ: Prentice-Hall, 1990), p. 247. The author cites as an excellent example Bruce J. Terris, "The Role of the Police," *Annals of the American Academy of Political and Social Science*, November 1967.

11. George Pugh, "The Police Officer: Qualities, Roles and Concepts," *Journal of Police Science and Administration,* 14(1986), pp. 1–6.

12. Robert Sheehan and Gary W. Cordner, *Introduction to Police Administration*, 2d ed. (Cincinnati: Anderson, 1989), p. 62. In stating this core role, the authors cite the work of Egon Bittner, *The Functions of the Police in Modern Society*; Carl B. Klockars, ed., *Thinking about Police: Contemporary Readings* (New York: McGraw-Hill, 1983), pp. 227–231; and W. K. Muir, Jr., *Police: Streetcorner Politicians* (Chicago: University of Chicago Press, 1977).

13. Joseph J. Senna and Larry J. Siegel, *Introduction to Criminal Justice*, 5th ed. (St. Paul, MN: West, 1990).

14. Bittner, *Functions of the Police,* p. 8.

15. Sheehan and Cordner, *Introduction to Police Administration*, p. 16.

16. Senna and Siegel, *Introduction to Criminal Justice*, p. 217.

17. Sheehan and Cordner, *Introduction to Police Administration*, pp. 16–21.

18. John J. Broderick, *Police in a Time of Change*, 2nd ed. (Prospect Heights, IL: Waveland Press, 1987).

19. Broderick, *Police in a Time of Change*, pp. 21–46.

20. Broderick, *Police in a Time of Change*, pp. 47–74.

21. Broderick, *Police in a Time of Change*, pp. 75–95.

22. Broderick, *Police in a Time of Change*, p. 93.

23. Broderick, *Police in a Time of Change*, pp. 97–116.

24. The discussion of Wilson's police operational styles is based on James Q. Wilson, *Varieties of Police Behavior: The Management of Law and Order in Eight Communities* (Cambridge, MA: Harvard University Press, 1968).

25. Wilson, *Varieties of Police Behavior*, p. 187.

26. Michael R. Gottfredson and Don M. Gottfredson, *Decision Making in Criminal Justice: Toward the Rational Exercise of Discretion* (Cambridge, MA: Ballinger Press, 1980), p. 87.

27. Kenneth Culp Davis, *Police Discretion* (St. Paul, MN: West, 1975).

28. Donald Black, *The Manners and Customs of the Police* (New York: Academic Press, 1980), p. 90.

29. John A. Gardiner, *Traffic and the Police: Variations in Law Enforcement Policy* (Cambridge, MA: Harvard University Press, 1969).

30. Catherine H. Milton et al., *Police Use of Deadly Force* (Washington, DC: The Police Foundation, 1977).

31. Sheehan and Cordner, *Introduction to Police Administration,* pp. 52–53.

32. Herbert Jacob, *Urban Justice* (Boston: Little, Brown, 1973), p. 27.

33. Wilson, *Varieties of Police Behavior*, pp. 83–89.

34. Larry J. Siegel, Dennis Sullivan, and Jack R. Greene, "Decision Games Applied to Police Decision Making," *Journal of Criminal Justice* (Summer 1974), pp. 132–142.

35. Irving Pilavin and Scott Briar, "Police Encounters with Juveniles," *American Journal of Sociology,* 70(1964), pp. 206–214.

36. Dennis Powell, "Race, Rank, and Police Discretion," *Journal of Police Science and Administration,* 9(1981), pp. 383–389.

37. Dale Dannefer and Russel Schutt, "Race and Juvenile Justice Processing in Court and Police Agencies," *American Journal of Sociology,* 87(1982), pp. 113–132.

38. Douglas Smith, Christy Visher, and Laura Davidson, "Equity and Discretionary Justice: The Influence of Race on Police Arrest Decisions," *Journal of Criminal Law and Criminology,* 75(1984), pp. 234–249.

39. Cecil Willis and Richard Wells, "The Police and Child Abuse: An Analysis of Police Decisions to Report Illegal Behavior," *Criminology,* 26(1988), pp. 696–716.

40. Wilson, *Varieties of Police Behavior.*

41. William Willbanks, *The Myth of a Racist Criminal Justice System* (Monterey, CA: Brooks/Cole, 1987); Douglas Smith and Jody Klein, "Police Control of Interpersonal Disputes," pp. 468–481.

42. Smith and Klein, "Police Control of Interpersonal Disputes," pp. 468–481.

43. Douglas Smith and Christy Visher, "Street-Level Justice: Situational Determinants of Police Arrest Decisions," *Social Problems,* 29(1981), pp. 167–177.

44. Marvin Krohn, James Curry, and Shirley Nelson-Kilger, "Is Chivalry Dead? An Analysis of Changes in Police Dispositions of Males and Females," *Criminology,* 21(1983), pp. 417–437.

45. Christy Visher, "Arrest Decisions and Notions of Chivalry," *Criminology,* 21(1983), pp. 5–28.

46. For an interesting review of the literature on police discretion since 1980, see Eric Riksheim and Steven Cermak, "Causes of Police Behavior Revisited," *Journal of Criminal Justice,* 21(1993), pp. 353–382. For additional interesting and insightful studies see Larry Miller and Michael Braswell, "Police Perception of Ethical Decision Making: The Ideal vs. the Real," *American Journal of Police,* 11(1992), pp. 27–45; David Klinger, "Demeanor or Crime? Why 'Hostile' Citizens Are More Likely to Be Arrested," *Criminology,* 32(1994), pp. 475–493; Richard Lundman, "Demeanor or Crime? The Midwest City Police–Citizen Encounters Study," *Criminology,* 32(1994), pp. 631–653; Sandra Lee Browning et al., "Race and Getting Hassled by the Police: A Research Note," *Police Studies,* 17(1994), pp. 1–10; and Darlene Conley, "Adding Color to a Black and White Picture: Using Qualitative Data to Explain Racial Disproportionality in the Juvenile Justice System," *Journal of Research in Crime and Delinquency,* 31(1994), pp. 135–148.

47. See, for example, Davis, *Police Discretion.*

48. Davis. *Police Discretion*; and Herman Goldstein, "Police Discretion: The Ideal vs. the Real," *Public Administration Review,* 23(1963), pp. 148–156.

49. Goldstein, *Policing a Free Society*, p. 112.

50. Wilson, *Varieties of Police Behavior,* p. 33.

Chapter 6

1. Richard Lezin Jones, "New York Police Officers Face Counseling on September 11 Events," *New York Times* (Nov. 30, 2001), p. A1.

2. See, for example, Egon Bittner, *The Functions of Police in Modern Society* (Cambridge, MA.: Oelgeschlager, 1980); Michael K. Brown, *Working the Street* (New York: Russell Sage Foundation, 1981); and Malcolm Sparrow, Mark Moore, and David Kennedy, *Beyond 911: A New Era for Policing* (New York: Basic Books, 1990).

3. Brown, *Working the Street*, p. 82.

4. Brown, *Working the Street*, p. 82.

5. George L. Kirkham, "A Professor's Street Lessons," in *Order Under Law*, R. Culbertson and M. Tezak, eds. (Prospect Heights, IL: Waveland Press, 1981), p. 81.

6. Bittner, *Functions of Police*, p. 63.

7. See Richard Harris, *The Police Academy: An Inside View* (New York: Wiley, 1973); Jonathan Rubenstein, *City Police* (New York: Ballentine Books, 1973); and John Van Maanen, "Observations on the Making of a Policeman," in *Order Under Law*, R. Culbertson and M. Tezak, eds. (Prospect Heights, IL: Waveland Press, 1981), p. 81.

8. Bittner, *Functions of Police*, p. 63.

9. Robert Sheehan and Gary W. Cordner, *Introduction to Police Administration*, 2nd ed. (Cincinnati: Anderson, 1989), p. 286.

10. Sheehan and Cordner, *Introduction to Police Administration*, pp. 286–289.

11. William Westley, *Violence and the Police: A Sociological Study of Law, Custom, and Morality* (Cambridge, MA: MIT Press, 1970).

12. Richard Lundman, *Police and Policing* (New York: Holt, Rinehart & Winston, 1980); see also Jerome Skolnick, *Justice without Trial: Law Enforcement in a Democratic Society* (New York: Wiley, 1966).

13. Skolnick, *Justice without Trial*.

14. Skolnick, *Justice without Trial*.

15. Skolnick, *Justice without Trial*.

16. Elizabeth Burbeck and Adrian Furnham, "Police Officer Selection: A Critical Review of the Literature," *Journal of Police Science and Administration,* 13(1985), pp. 58–69.

17. Milton Rokeach, Martin Miller, and John Snyder, "The Value Gap between Police and Policed," *Journal of Social Issues,* 27(1971), pp. 155–171.

18. Bruce Carpenter and Susan Raza, "Personality Characteristics of Police Applicants: Comparisons across Subgroups and with Other Populations," *Journal of Police Science and Administration,* 15(1987), pp. 10–17; Richard Lawrence, "Police Stress and Personality Factors: A Conceptual Model," *Journal of Criminal Justice,* 12(1984), pp. 247–263; and James Teevan and Bernard Dolnick, "The Values of the Police: A Reconsideration and Interpretation," *Journal of Police Science and Administration,* 1(1973), pp. 366–369.

19. Richard Bennett and Theodore Greenstein, "The Police Personality: A Test of the Predispositional Model," *Journal of Police Science and Administration,* 3(1975), pp. 439–445.

20. Edward A. Thibault, Lawrence W. Lynch, and R. Bruce McBride, *Proactive Police Management* (Englewood Cliffs, NJ: Prentice-Hall, 1985).

21. Van Maanen, "Observations on the Making of a Policeman."

22. Van Maanen, "Observations on the Making of a Policeman."

23. Van Maanen, "Observations on the Making of a Policeman."

24. Lundman, *Police and Policing*, pp. 73, 82.

25. Larry A. Gould, "Longitudinal Approach to the Study of the Police Personality: Race/Gender Differences," *Journal of Police and Criminal Psychology,* 15:2(Fall 2000), pp. 41–51.

26. Larry Tifft, "The 'Cop Personality' Reconsidered," *Journal of Police Science and Administration,* 2(1974); David Bayley and Harold Mendelsohn, *Minorities and the Police* (New York: Free Press, 1969); and Robert Balch, "The Police Personality: Fact or Fiction?" *Journal of Criminal Law, Criminology, and Police Science,* 63(1972), p. 172.

27. Arthur Niederhoffer, *Behind the Shield: The Police in Urban Society* (Garden City, NY: Doubleday, 1967), pp. 41–42.

28. Niederhoffer, *Behind the Shield*.

29. Westley, *Violence and the Police*.

30. Niederhoffer, *Behind the Shield*, pp. 216–220.

31. Niederhoffer, *Behind the Shield*, p. 43.

32. Niederhoffer, *Behind the Shield*, p. 44.

33. Richard Anson, J. Dale Mann, and Dale Sherman, "Niederhoffer Cynicism Scale: Reliability and Beyond," *Journal of Criminal Justice,* 14(1986), pp. 295–307.

34. Carl B. Klockars, "The Dirty Harry Problem," *Annals* (Nov. 1980), pp. 33–47.

35. Klockars, "The Dirty Harry Problem," pp. 33–47.

36. Klockars, "The Dirty Harry Problem," pp. 33–47.

37. Edwin S. Geffner, ed., *The Internist's Compendium of Patient Information* (New York: McGraw-Hill, 1987), sec. 30.

38. Geffner, *Internist's Compendium*, sec. 30.

39. "Stress on the Job," *Newsweek* (April 25, 1988), p. 43.

40. Alison Mitchell, "A Night on Patrol: What's Behind Police Tensions and Discontent," *New York Times* (Oct. 19, 1992), pp. B1, B2.

41. W. Clinton Terry, "Police Stress: The Empirical Evidence," *Journal of Police Science and Administration,* 9(1981), pp. 67–70. This article has a substantial bibliography and discussion of the issue of police stress.

42. Clement Milanovich, "The Blue Pressure Cooker," *Police Chief,* 47(1980), p. 20.

43. Robert J. McGuire, "The Human Dimension in Urban Policing: Dealing with Stress in the 1980's," *Police Chief* (Nov. 1979), p. 27; and Joseph Victor, "Police Stress: Is Anybody Out There Listening?" *New York Law Enforcement Journal* (June 1986), pp. 19–20.

44. Gregory S. Anderson, Robin Litzenberger, Darryl Plecas, "Physical Evidence of Police Officer Stress," *Policing: An International Journal of Police Strategies and Management,* 25:2(2000), pp. 399–420.

45. Nancy Norvell, Dales Belles, and Holly Hills, "Perceived Stress Levels and Physical Symptoms in Supervisory Law Enforcement Personnel," *Journal of Police Science and Administration,* 6(1978), pp. 402–416.

46. Bryan Vila, "Tired Cops: Probable Connections between Fatigue and the Performance, Health, and Safety of Patrol Officers," *American Journal of Police,* 15:2(1996), pp. 51–92.

47. B. Healy, "The Aerobic Cop," *Police Chief* (Feb. 1981), pp. 67–70.

48. See J. Michael Rivard, Park Dietz, Daniel Martell, and Mel Widawski, "Acute Dissociative Responses in Law Enforcement Officers Involved in Critical Shooting Incidents: The Clinical and Forensic Implications," *Journal of Forensic Sciences*, 47:5(Sept. 2002), pp. 1093–1120, and Susan Taylor, "Post Shooting Emotional Meltdown?" *Police*, 25:9(Sept. 2001), pp. 40–43.

49. Sue Titus Reid, *Criminal Justice*, 3rd ed. (New York: Macmillan, 1993), p. 230.

50. Dorothy Bracey, "The Decline of the Vaccination Model: Criminal Justice Education for a Changing World," *CJ, The Americas* (April 1988), p. 1.

51. "On-the-Job Stress in Policing—Reducing It, Preventing It," *National Institute of Justice Journal* (Jan. 2000), pp. 18–24; also see Peter Finn and Julie Esselman Tomz, *Developing a Law Enforcement Stress Program for Officers and Their Families* (Washington, DC: National Institute of Justice, 1997).

52. John Blackmore, "Are Police Allowed to Have Problems of Their Own?" *Police*, 1(1978), pp. 47–55.

53. Charles Unkovic and William Brown, "The Drunken Cop," *Police Chief* (April 1978), p. 18.

54. James Hibberd, "Police Psychology," *On Patrol* (Fall 1996), p. 26.

55. "Dispatches," *On Patrol* (Summer 1996), p. 25.

56. *Justice Assistance News*, 4(1983), p. 5.

57. Ni He, Jihong Zhao, and Carol A. Archbold, "Gender and Police Stress: The Convergent and Divergent Impact of Work Environment, Work–Family Conflict, and Stress Coping Mechanisms of Female and Male Police Officers," *Policing: An International Journal of Police Strategies and Management*, 25:4(2002), pp. 687–708.

58. Jerry Dash and Martin Resier, "Suicide among Police in Urban Law Enforcement Agencies," *Journal of Police Science and Administration*, 6(1978), p. 18.

59. David Rafky, "My Husband the Cop," *Police Chief* (August 1984), p. 65.

60. Peter Maynard and Nancy Maynard, "Stress in Police Families: Some Policy Implications," *Journal of Police Science*, 10(1980), p. 309.

61. Ellen Scrivner, "Helping Families Cope with Stress," *Law Enforcement News*, 15 (June 1991), p. 6.

62. "On-the-Job Stress in Policing—Reducing It, Preventing It," *National Institute of Justice Journal* (Jan. 2000), pp. 18–24; also see Peter Finn and Julie Esselman Tomz, *Developing a Law Enforcement Stress Program for Officers and Their Families* (Washington, DC: National Institute of Justice, 1997) and R. Borum and C. Philpot, "Therapy with Law Enforcement Couples: Clinical Management of the 'High-Risk Lifestyle,'" *American Journal of Family Therapy*, 21(1993), pp. 122–135.

63. U.S. Commission on Civil Rights, *Who Is Guarding the Guardians? A Report on Police Practices* (Washington, DC: U.S. Government Printing Office, 1981).

64. *USA Today* (Sept. 15, 1986), p. 3.

65. National Criminal Justice Reference Service, *Program for the Reduction of Stress for New York City Police Officers and Their Families, Final Report* (Washington, DC: National Criminal Justice Reference Service, 1998).

66. *New York Times* (Sept. 15 1986), p. 14.

67. Nancy K. Bohl, "Hostage Negotiator Stress," *FBI Law Enforcement Bulletin* (August 1992), pp. 23–26.

68. James J. Ness and John Light, "Mandatory Physical Fitness Standards: Issues and Concerns," *Police Chief* (August 1992), pp. 23–26.

69. Ness and Light, "Mandatory Physical Fitness Standards," p. 77.

70. Ness and Light, "Mandatory Physical Fitness Standards," p. 75.

71. Robin N. Haarr and Merry Morash, "Gender, Race, and Strategies of Coping with Occupational Stress in Policing," *Justice Quarterly*, 16:2(June 1999), pp. 303–336.

72. Richard Lezin Jones, "New York Police Officers Face Counseling on September 11 Events," p. A1.

73. "Can We Talk? Officials Take Steps to Head Off 9/11 Post-Traumatic Stress," *Law Enforcement News* (Nov. 30, 2001), p. 1.

74. John M. Madonna, Jr., and Richard E. Kelly, *Treating Police Stress: The Work and the Words of Peer Counselors* (Springfield, IL: Charles C. Thomas, 2002).

75. Richard Kelly, "Critical Incident Debriefing," in John M. Madonna, Jr., and Richard E. Kelly, *Treating Police Stress: The Work and the Words of Peer Counselors*, pp. 139–149. Also see "Tactical Officers Get Help from Those Who've Been There," *Law Enforcement News* (April 15, 2002).

76. "On-the-Job Stress in Policing—Reducing It, Preventing It." Also see Peter Finn and Julie Esselman Tomz, *Developing a Law Enforcement Stress Program for Officers and Their Families*.

77. Robin E. Inwald and Elizabeth J. Shusman, "The IPA and MMPI as Predictors of Academy Performance for Police Recruits," *Journal of Police Science*, 12(1984), p. 1.

78. William Nagler and David Carlington, "Officer Fitness: The Officer at Risk Examination," *Law and Order* (Sept. 1992), p. 21.

79. Recently, significant attention is being addressed to police suicide and the stresses that can be attributed to it. See, for example, Thomas E. Baker and Jane P. Baker, "Preventing Police Suicide," *FBI Law Enforcement Bulletin* (Oct. 1996), pp. 24–27. See also John M. Violanti, "The Mystery Within: Understanding Police Suicide," *FBI Law Enforcement Bulletin* (Feb. 1995), pp. 19–23; Steven R. Standfest, "The Police Supervisor and Stress," *FBI Law Enforcement Bulletin* (May 1996), pp. 10–16; "What's Killing America's Cops? Mostly Themselves, According to New Study," *Law Enforcement News* (Nov. 1996), p. 1; and "The Greatest Threat to Cops' Lives—Themselves," *Law Enforcement News* (Dec. 31, 1997), p. 22. Also see Kevin Barrett, "More EAPs Needed in Police Departments to Quash Officers' Super-Human Self-Image," *EA Professional Report* (Jan. 1994), p. 3; and Barrett, "Police Suicide: Is Anyone Listening?" *Journal of Safe Management of Disruptive and Assaultive Behavior* (Spring 1997), pp. 6–9. Also see Violanti, "Police Suicide: Current Perspectives and Future Considerations," in Donald C. Sheehan and Janet I. Warren, eds. *Suicide and Law Enforcement* (Washington, DC: Federal Bureau of Investigation, 2001).

80. "Trooper in Suicide over Traffic-Stop Mistake," *Law Enforcement News* (Oct. 31, 2002), p. 5.

81. "The Greatest Threat to Cops' Lives—Themselves."

82. J. M. Violanti and J. E. Vena, "Epidemiology of Police Suicide," NIMH Grant MH47091-02.

83. "What's Killing America's Cops?"

84. Leonard Territo and Harold J. Vetter, "Stress and Police Personnel," *Journal of Police Science and Administration*, 9(1981), p. 200.

85. Violanti, "The Mystery Within: Understanding Police Suicide," p. 22.

86. Baker and Baker, "Preventing Police Suicide," p. 25.

87. "What's Killing America's Cops?"

88. Donald C. Sheehan and Janet I. Warren, eds., *Suicide and Law Enforcement*.

89. Denise Buffa, Linda Massarella, et al. "Suicide Teen Tricked Cops into Shooting Him: Dear Officer . . . Please Kill Me," *New York Post* (Nov. 17, 1997), p. 3.

90. John O'Mahony, "'Suicide by Cop' Not So Odd: Docs," *New York Post* (Nov. 17, 1997), p. 3.

91. Ronnie L. Paynter, "Suicide by Cop," *Law Enforcement Technology,* 27:6(June 2000), pp. 40–44.

92. J. Nick Marzella, "Psychological Effects of Suicide by Cop on Involved Officers," in Donald C. Sheehan and Janet I. Warren, eds., *Suicide and Law Enforcement* (Washington DC: U.S. Department of Justice, 2001).

Chapter 7

1. Robert Sheehan and Gary W. Cordner, *Introduction to Police Administration,* 2d ed. (Cincinnati: Anderson, 1989), p. 365.

2. Joan Petersilia, "The Influence of Research on Policing," in *Critical Issues in Policing: Contemporary Readings,* Roger G. Dunham and Geoffrey P. Albert, eds. (Prospect Heights, IL: Waveland Press, 1989), pp. 230–247.

3. George L. Kelling et al., *The Kansas City Preventive Patrol Experiment: A Summary Report* (Washington, DC: Police Foundation, 1974).

4. Kelling et al., *Kansas City Preventive Patrol Experiment,* p. 16.

5. James Q. Wilson, *Thinking about Crime* (New York: Vintage Books, 1975), p. 99.

6. Kelling et al., *Kansas City Preventive Patrol Experiment,* pp. v–vi.

7. Kelling et al., *Kansas City Preventive Patrol Experiment,* pp. 48–49.

8. Richard C. Larson, "What Happened to Patrol Operations in Kansas City? A Review of the Kansas City Preventive Patrol Experiment," *Journal of Criminal Justice,* 3(1975), pp. 267–297.

9. O. W. Wilson and Roy Clinton McLaren, *Police Administration,* 4th ed. (New York: McGraw-Hill, 1977), p. 4.

10. *Criminal Justice Newsletter* (August 27, 1979), p. 4.

11. Herbert Jacob and Michael J. Rich, "The Effects of the Police on Crime: A Second Look," *Law and Society Review,* 15(1980–1981), pp. 109–122.

12. Sheehan and Cordner, *Introduction to Police Administration,* pp. 367–368.

13. Samuel Walker, *The Police in America: An Introduction* (New York: McGraw-Hill, 1983), p. 118.

14. H. H. Isaacs, "A Study of Communications, Crimes, and Arrests in a Metropolitan Police Department," in President's Commission on Law Enforcement and Administration of Justice, *Task Force Report: Science and Technology* (Washington, DC: U.S. Government Printing Office, 1967).

15. U.S. National Advisory Commission on Criminal Justice Standards and Goals, *Police* (Washington, DC: U.S. Government Printing Office, 1973), p. 194.

16. Walker, *Police in America,* pp. 119–120.

17. Kansas City Police Department, *Response Time Analysis: Executive Summary* (Washington, DC: U.S. Government Printing Office, 1978); and William Spelman and D.K. Brown, *Calling the Police: Citizen Reporting of Serious Crime* (Washington, DC: Police Executive Research Forum, 1981).

18. Gary W. Cordner, Jack R. Greene, and T.S. Bynum, "The Sooner the Better: Some Effects of Police Response Time," in *Police at Work: Policy Issues and Analysis,* ed. R.R. Bennett (Beverly Hills: Sage Publications, 1983).

19. Peter W. Greenwood and Joan Petersilia, *The Criminal Investigation Process: Summary and Policy Implications* (Santa Monica, CA: Rand Corporation, 1975).

20. Greenwood and Petersilia, *Criminal Investigation Process,* p. vi.

21. Greenwood and Petersilia, *Criminal Investigation Process,* p. vii.

22. Spelman and Brown, *Calling the Police.*

23. Mark Willman and John Snortum, "Detective Work: The Criminal Investigation Process in a Medium-Size Police Department," *Criminal Justice Review,* 9(1984), pp. 33–39.

24. Anthony V. Bouza, *The Police Mystique: An Insider's Look at Cops, Crime, and the Criminal Justice System* (New York: Plenum Press, 1990), p. 27.

25. Walker, *Police in America,* p. 103.

26. American Bar Association, *Standards Relating to Urban Police Function* (New York: Institute of Judicial Administration, 1974), Standard 2.2.

27. W. Clinton Terry III, *Policing Society: An Occupational View* (New York: Wiley, 1985), pp. 259–260.

28. John Ayto, *Dictionary of Word Origins* (New York: Arcade, 1990), p. 386.

29. Samuel G. Chapman, *Police Patrol Readings,* 2d ed. (Springfield, IL: Charles C. Thomas, 1970), p. ix.

30. American Society for Industrial Security, "Innovations in Patrol," *The Educator* (Spring/Summer 1997), p.3.

31. Ralph Mroz, "Cops on Bikes," *Police* (Dec. 2001), pp. 41–45. For interesting and informative information on bicycle patrol see Tom Wood, "Starting a Bike Patrol: The Administrative Issues of Beginning and Running a Successful Bike Patrol," *Law and Order* (April 2002), pp. 78–80, 82–85; and David Olsen, "Patrolling by Bike in LA," *Law Enforcement Technology* (Feb. 2003), pp. 32, 34–37.

32. Charles E. Higginbotham, "Spotlight On: Specialized Patrol Vehicles, *Police Chief* (March 2003), pp. 53–54, 56, 59–60, 62–63.

33. O. W. Wilson, *Police Administration* (New York: McGraw-Hill, 1950). Later editions of this book, which was considered to be the "Bible of Policing" prior to the research revolution of the 1960s and 1970s, were published in 1963, 1972, and 1977. This book served as the college text for many of today's police chiefs and scholars, as well as for one of the authors of this text. A new edition was published in 1997 as *Police Administration,* 5th ed., by McGraw-Hill. The publishers selected three of the major researchers of policing in the 1980s, 1990s, and today to rewrite this classic text: James J. Fyfe, Jack R. Greene, and William F. Walsh.

34. Wilson and McLaren, *Police Administration,* pp. 320–321.

35. Wilson and McLaren, *Police Administration,* p. 320.

36. Alejandro del Carmen and Lori Guevara, "Police Officers on Two-Officer Units: A Study of Attitudinal Responses towards a Patrol Experiment," *Policing: An International Journal of Police Strategies & Management,* 26:1(2003), pp. 144–161.

37. Wilson and McLaren, *Police Administration.*

38. James J. Fyfe, Jack R. Greene, William F. Walsh, O. W. Wilson, and Roy Clinton McLaren, *Police Administration,* 5th ed. (New York: McGraw-Hill, 1997), p. xxiii. Fyfe is Deputy Commissioner of Training for the New York City Police Department, former Distinguished Professor at John Jay

College of Criminal Justice, former professor of criminal justice and Senior Public Policy Research Fellow at Temple University, Philadelphia, former professor of criminal justice at American University, and former NYPD lieutenant. Greene is professor of criminal justice at Temple University. Walsh is the director of the Southern Police Institute, associate professor in the Department of Justice Administration at the University of Louisville, and former NYPD lieutenant.

39. George L. Kelling and Mary A. Wycoff, *Evolving Strategy of Policing: Cases Studies of Strategic Change* (Cambridge, MA: Harvard University Press, 2001).

40. William G. Gay, Theodore H. Schell, and Steven Schack, *Routine Patrol: Improving Patrol Productivity, vol. 1* (Washington, DC: National Institute of Justice, 1977), p. 2.

41. Gay, Schell, and Schack, *Routine Patrol*, pp. 3–6.

42. James Q. Wilson, *Varieties of Police Behavior: The Management of Law and Order in Eight Communities* (Cambridge, MA: Harvard University Press, 1968).

43. Gary W. Cordner, "The Police on Patrol," in *Police and Policing: Contemporary Issues*, Dennis Jay Kenney, ed. (New York: Praeger, 1989), pp. 60–71.

44. Robert Lilly, "What Are the Police Now Doing?" *Journal of Police Science and Administration,* 6(1978), pp. 51–53.

45. George Antunes and Eric Scott, "Calling the Cops: Police Telephone Operations and Citizen Calls for Service," *Journal of Criminal Justice,* 9(1981), pp. 165–174.

46. Wilson, *Varieties of Police Behavior.*

47. Albert Reiss, *The Police and the Public* (New Haven, CT: Yale University Press, 1971).

48. Cordner, "Police on Patrol," p. 62.

49. T. Bercal, "Calls for Police Assistance," *American Behavioral Scientist,* 13(1970), pp. 267–277.

50. J. Tien, J. Simon, and R. Larson, *An Alternative Approach in Police Patrol: The Wilmington Split Force Experiment* (Washington,DC: National Institute of Justice, 1978).

51. Lawrence Sherman, *Repeat Calls to Police in Minneapolis* (Washington, DC: Crime Control Institute, 1987).

52. Cordner, "Police on Patrol," p. 63.

53. Reiss, *Police and the Public*, p. 19.

54. Egon Bittner, *The Functions of the Police in Modern Society* (Washington, DC: U.S. Government Printing Office, 1970), p. 127.

55. M. O'Neill and C. Bloom, "The Field Officer: Is He Really Fighting Crime?" *Police Chief* (Feb. 1972), pp. 30–32.

56. Kelling et al., *Kansas City Preventive Patrol Study.*

57. Cordner, "Police on Patrol," p. 65.

58. G. P. Whitaker, "What Is Patrol Work?" *Police Studies,* 4(1982), pp. 13–22.

59. Patrick A. Langan, Lawrence A. Greenfeld, Steven K. Smith, Matthew R. Durose, and David J. Levin, *Contacts Between Police and the Public: Findings from the 1999 National Survey* (Washington, D.C.: Bureau of Justice Statistics, 2001).

60. Jack R. Greene and Carl B. Klockars, "What Police Do," in *Thinking about Police: Contemporary Readings,* 2d ed., Carl B. Klockars and Stephen D. Mastrofski, eds. (New York: McGraw-Hill, 1991), pp. 273–284. This chapter for *Thinking about Police* was written for the book and is actually part of a larger resource allocation study published in Carl B. Klockars, Jack R. Greene, and S.Wissman, *An Evaluation of Resource Allocation in the Wilmington Police Department* (Wilmington, DE: Office of the Director of Public Safety, 1988).

61. Sheehan and Cordner, *Introduction to Police Administration*, pp. 57–58.

62. Wilson, *Thinking about Crime*, p. x.

63. Sheehan and Cordner, *Introduction to Police Administration*, pp. 57–58.

64. Bouza, *Police Mystique*, p. 84.

65. Bruce Smith, *Police Systems in the United States* (New York: Harper & Brothers, 1949), p. 14.

66. President's Commission on Law Enforcement and Administration of Justice, *Task Force Report: The Police* (Washington, DC: U.S. Government Printing Office, 1967), p. 55, Table 1.

67. President's Commission on Crime in the District of Columbia, *A Report on the President's Commission on Crime in the District of Columbia* (Washington, DC: U.S. Government Printing Office, 1966), p. 53.

68. Police Department of Kansas City, *1966 Survey of Municipal Police Departments* (Kansas City, MO: Police Department of Kansas City, 1966), p. 53.

69. International Association of Chiefs of Police, *A Survey of the Police Department of Youngstown, Ohio* (Washington, DC: International Association of Chiefs of Police, 1964), p. 89.

70. Walker, *Police in America*, p. 107.

71. William A. Westley, *Violence and the Police* (Cambridge, MA: MIT Press, 1970), p. 35.

72. Walker, *Police in America*, p. 107.

73. President's Commission on Law Enforcement and Administration of Justice, *Task Force Report: The Police*, p. 54.

74. John Heaphy, ed., *Police Practices: The General Administrative Survey* (Washington, DC: Police Foundation, 1978), p. 11.

75. Edward A. Thibault, Lawrence M. Lynch, and R. Bruce McBride, Proactive Police Management, 2d ed. (Englewood Cliffs, NJ: Prentice-Hall, 1990), p. 209.

76. Robert C. Trojanowicz and Dennis W. Banas, *Perceptions of Safety: A Comparison of Foot Patrol versus Motor Patrol Officers* (East Lansing, MI: National Neighborhood Foot Patrol Center, School of Criminal Justice, Michigan State University, 1985); and Trojanowicz and H. A. Harden, *The Status of Contemporary Community Policing Programs* (East Lansing, MI: National Neighborhood Foot Patrol Center, School of Criminal Justice, Michigan State University, 1984).

77. Kelling, *Foot Patrol* (Washington, DC: National Institute of Justice, 1987).

78. Police Foundation, *The Newark Foot Patrol Experiment* (Washington, DC: Police Foundation, 1981).

79. Trojanowicz and Banas, *Perceptions of Safety.*

80. Trojanowicz and Banas, *The Impact of Foot Patrol on Black and White Perceptions of Policing* (East Lansing: National Neighborhood Foot Patrol Center, School of Criminal Justice, Michigan State University, 1988).

81. G. Graves et al., *Developing a Street Patrol: A Guide for Neighborhood Crime Prevention Groups* (Boston: Neighborhood Crime Prevention Council, Justice Resource Institute, 1985).

82. George Napper, "Partnerships against Crime: Sharing Problems and Power," *Police Chief* (Feb. 1986), pp. 45–46.

83. S. Morrill, "Tampa Likes Sector Patrolling," *Law and Order,* 32(1984), pp. 37–40.

84. James Q. Wilson and George L. Kelling, "'Broken Windows': The Police and Neighborhood Safety," *Atlantic Monthly* (March 1982), pp. 29–38.

85. Ben Davis, "Foot Patrol," *Police Centurion* (June 1984), p. 41.

86. Wilson and Kelling, "Broken Windows," p. 30.

87. Herman Goldstein, *Policing a Free Society* (Cambridge, MA: Ballinger, 1977), pp. 55–56.

88. Greenwood and Petersilia, *Criminal Investigation Process,* p. vii.

89. Federal Bureau of Investigation, *Uniform Crime Reports,* issued annually.

90. Bureau of Justice Statistics, *Special Report: Reporting Crimes to the Police* (Washington, DC: U.S. Government Printing Office, 1985).

91. Reiss, *Police and the Public,* p. 104.

92. U.S. Department of Transportation, "USDOT Releases 2002 Highway Fatality Statistics." Retrieved on September 22, 2003, from http://www.nhtsa.dot.gov/nhtsa.

93. Thibault, Lynch, and McBride, *Proactive Police Management,* p. 174.

94. *Philadelphia Bulletin* (March 28, 1976), Sec. 3, p. 1.

95. "Paramilitary Police Units Are More Popular Than Ever," *Law Enforcement News* (May 15, 1997), p. 9.

96. Joseph Mancini, "NYPD's Hero Cops," *National Centurion* (August 1983), p. 22.

Chapter 8

1. Peter Johnson, "Crime Wave Sweeps Networks Newscasts," *USA Today* (August 13, 1997), p. 3D.

2. Retrieved on April 17, 2003 from www.cmpa.com.

3. J. W. Warren, M. L. Forst, and M. M. Estrella, "Directed Patrol: An Experiment That Worked," *Police Chief* (July 1979), pp. 48–49; Gary W. Cordner, "The Effects of Directed Patrol: A Natural Quasi-Experiment in Pontiac," in *Contemporary Issues in Law Enforcement,* James J. Fyfe, ed. (Beverly Hills, CA: Sage, 1981), pp. 242–261; George J. Sullivan, *Directed Patrol* (Kansas City, MO: Kansas City Police Department, Operations Resource Unit, 1976).

4. Lawrence Sherman, James Shaw, and Dennis Rogan, *The Kansas City Gun Experiment* (Washington, DC: National Institute of Justice, 1994).

5. Larry J. Siegel and Joseph J. Senna, *Essentials of Criminal Justice,* 4th ed. (Belmont, CA: Thompson-Wadsworth, 2004), p. 145.

6. James M. Tien, James W. Simon, and Richard C. Larson, *An Alternative Approach in Police Patrol: The Wilmington Split-Force Experiment* (Cambridge, MA: Public Systems Evaluation, 1977).

7. "Faced with a Crime Wave, Houston Cops 'Wave Back': Intensive Patrols Hit the Streets, but Union Blasts Directive Not to Field Calls for Service," *Law Enforcement News* (Dec. 15, 1991), p. 3.

8. "Houston Cops 'Wave Back,'" p. 3.

9. Michael T. Farmer, ed., *Differential Police Response Strategies* (Washington, DC: Police Executive Research Forum, 1981). Also see Robert Worden, "Toward Equity and Efficiency in Law Enforcement: Differential Police Response," *American Journal of Police, 12*(1993), pp. 1–24.

10. Robert Sheehan and Gary W. Cordner, *Introduction to Police Administration,* 2d ed. (Cincinnati, OH: Anderson, 1989), p. 554

11. Retrieved on May 24, 2004, from www.arlingtonpd.org.

12. R. E. Worden, "Toward Equity and Efficiency in Law Enforcement: Differential Police Response." In G. W. Cordner, L. K. Gaines, and V. E. Kappeler, eds., *Police Operations* (Cincinnati, OH: Anderson, 1996), pp. 131–156.

13. National Advisory Commission on Criminal Justice Standards and Goals, *Police* (Washington, DC: U.S. Government Printing Office, 1973).

14. Donald F. Cawley et al., *Managing Criminal Investigations: Manual* (Washington, DC: National Institute of Justice, 1977).

15. Ilene Greenberg and Robert Wasserman, *Managing Criminal Investigations* (Washington, DC: National Institute of Justice, 1975); and Cawley et al., *Managing Criminal Investigations.*

16. Greenberg and Wasserman, *Managing Criminal Investigations.*

17. Greenberg and Wasserman, *Managing Criminal Investigations.*

18. John E. Eck, *Managing Case Assignments: The Burglary Investigation Decision Model Replication* (Washington, DC: Police Executive Research Forum, 1979).

19. Federal Bureau of Investigation, *Uniformed Crime Reports: Crime in the United States* (Washington, DC: Federal Bureau of Investigation).

20. Christina Lewis, "Solving the cold case: Time, ingenuity and DNA can help." Retrieved on December 17, 2002, from www.cnn.com.

21. Retrieved on May 24, 2004, from http://unx1.shsu.edu/cjcenter/trcpi/7/Repeat_Offendor_Programs.

22. Retrieved on May 24, 2004, from http://www.maricopacountyattorney.org/SpecPros/gangrop.asp.

23. Susan E. Martin and Lawrence W. Sherman, "Selective Apprehension: A Police Strategy for Repeat Offenders,"*Criminology* (Feb. 1986), pp. 155–173.

24. Marcia Chaiken and Jan Chaiken, *Priority Prosecutors of High-Rate Dangerous Offenders* (Washington, DC: National Institute of Justice, 1991), as cited in Stephen Goldsmith, "Targeting High-Rate Offenders: Asking Some Tough Questions," *Law Enforcement News* (July/August 1991), p. 11.

25. Goldsmith, "Targeting High-Rate Offenders."

26. "Tough Chicago neighborhood to get extra attention from police, prosecutors," *Law Enforcement News* (March 15/31, 2003).

27. Stephen Schack, Theodore H. Schell, and William G. Gay, *Specialized Patrol: Improving Patrol Productivity,* vol. 2 (Washington, DC: National Institute of Justice, 1977), p. 1.

28. Charles Whited, *The Decoy Man* (New York: Playboy Press, 1973), p. 12.

29. Santa Barbara Police Department Web page. Retrieved on May 24, 2004, from www.sbpd.com.

30. J. E. Boydstun, *San Diego Field Interrogation: Final Report* (Washington, DC: Police Foundation, 1975).

31. James Q. Wilson and Barbara Boland, *The Effect of Police on Crime* (Washington, DC: National Institute of Justice, 1979).

32. H. Lawrence Ross, *Deterring the Drunk Driver: Legal Policy and Social Control* (Lexington, MA: D. C. Heath, 1982); and Samuel Walker, *Sense and Nonsense about Crime* (Monterey, CA: Brooks/Cole, 1985), pp. 82–85.

33. James Q. Wilson and Barbara Boland, "The Effect of Police on Crime," *Law and Society Review, 12*(1978), pp. 367–384.

34. Robert Sampson and Jacqueline Cohen, "Deterrent Effects of the Police on Crime: A Replication and Theoretical Extension," *Law and Society Review, 22*(1988), pp. 163–191.

35. Perry Shapiro and Harold Votey, "Deterrence and Subjective Probabilities of Arrest: Modeling Individual Decisions to Drink and Drive in Sweden," *Law and Society Review, 18*(1984), pp. 111–149.

36. Douglas Smith and Patrick Gartin, "Specifying Specific Deterrence: The Influence of Arrest on Future Criminal Activity," *American Sociological Review, 54*(1989), pp. 94–105.

37. Lawrence W. Sherman, "Police Crackdowns: Initial and Residual Deterrence," in *Crime and Justice: A Review of Research,* vol. 12, M. Tonry and N. Morris, eds. (Chicago: University of Chicago Press, 1990), pp. 1–48.

38. Jay S. Albanese and Robert D. Pursley, *Crime in America: Some Existing and Emerging Issues* (Englewood Cliffs, NJ: Regents/Prentice-Hall, 1993), p. 210.

39. Lawrence Sherman, Patrick Gartin, and Michael Buerger, "Hot Spots of Predatory Crime: Routine Activities and the Criminology of Place," *Criminology, 27*(1989), pp. 27–55. Also see Dennis Roncek and Pamela Maier, "Bars, Blocks, and Crimes Revisited: Linking the Theory of Routine Activities to the Empiricism of 'Hot Spots'," *Criminology, 29*(1991), pp. 725–753.

40. *Law Enforcement News* (October 31, 1995), p. 1. Also see John S. Dempsey, *Criminal Justice Update* (Minneapolis/St. Paul: West, 1996), p. 3.

41. Marie Simonetti Rosen, "Forget Events in the Spotlight—Local PD's Are Where the Action Is," *Law Enforcement News* (Dec. 31 1996), p. 1.

42. Rosen, "Forget Events in the Spotlight."

43. Lawrence Sherman, "Policing Communities: What Works," *Crime and Justice,* A. J. Reiss and Michael Tonry, eds. (Chicago: University of Chicago Press, 1986), pp. 366–379.

44. S. J. Press, *Some Effects of an Increase in Police Manpower in the 20th Precinct of New York* (New York: Rand Institute, 1971).

45. J. M. Chaiken, M. W. Lawless, and K. A. Stenson, *The Impact of Police Activity on Crime: Robberies in the New York City Subway System* (New York: Rand Institute, 1974).

46. J. P. Schnelle et al., "Social Evaluation Research: The Evaluation of Two Police Patrolling Strategies," *Journal of Applied Behavior Analysis, 8*(1975), pp. 232–240.

47. J. P. Schnelle et al., "Patrol Evaluation Research: A Multiple-Baseline Analysis of Saturation Police Patrolling during Day and Night Hours," *Journal of Applied Behavior Analysis, 10*(1977), pp. 33–40.

48. Lynn Zimmer, "Proactive Policing against Street-Level Drug Trafficking," *American Journal of Police, 9*(1990), pp. 43–65.

49. Larry K. Gaines and Victor E. Kappeler, *Policing in America,* 4th ed. (Cincinnati, OH: Anderson Publishing, 2003), p. 531.

50. ABT Associates, *New York City Anti-Crime Patrol: Exemplary Project Validation Report* (Washington, DC: National Institute of Justice, 1974); and Gary T. Marx, "The New Police Undercover Work," in *Thinking about Police: Contemporary Readings,* Carl B. Klockars, ed. (New York: McGraw-Hill, 1983), pp. 201–202.

51. "Miami Seeks to Aid Tourist-Crime Target," *Law Enforcement News* (Oct. 31, 1991), p. 4.

52. Andrew Halper and Richard Ku, *New York City Police Department Street Crime Unit* (Washington, DC: National Institute of Justice).

53. Patrick J. McGovern and Charles P. Connolly, "Decoys, Disguises, Danger—New York City's Nonuniform Street Patrol," *FBI Law Enforcement Bulletin* (Oct. 1976), pp. 16–26.

54. *New York Post* (Dec. 1995), p. 7. Also, see Dempsey, *Criminal Justice Update,* p. 2.

55. *Newsday* (Nov. 2, 1995), p. A7. Also see Dempsey, *Criminal Justice Update,* p. 2.

56. "Miami Seeks to Aid Tourist-Crime Targets," p. 4.

57. Bernard Edelman, "Blending," *Police* (Sept. 1979), pp. 53–58.

58. Anthony V. Bouza, *The Police Mystique: An Insider's Look at Cops, Crime, and the Criminal Justice System* (New York: Plenum Press, 1990), p. 93.

59. Bouza, *Police Mystique,* pp. 92–93.

60. Jeannie DeQuine, "High-Tech Drug Sting Zaps 93," *USA Today* (Dec. 7, 1988), p. 3.

61. "Car Ring Sting," *USA Today* (July 13, 1988), p. 3.

62. Carl B. Klockars, "The Modern Sting," in *Thinking about Police: Contemporary Readings,* Carl B. Klockars, ed.

63. Joseph M. Donisi, "Police Practices: Ft. Lauderdale's Code Enforcement Team," *FBI Law Enforcement Bulletin* (March 1992), pp. 24–25.

64. City of Fort Lauderdale Web site. Retrieved on May 24, 2004 from http://info.ci.ftlaud.fl.us.

65. Philip Arreola and Edward N. Kondracki, "Cutback Management, Cost Containment and Increased Productivity," *Police Chief* (Oct. 1992), p. 118.

66. "Expanding Zero Tolerance (the Crackdown, Not the Tolerance)," *Law Enforcement News* (April 30, 1997), pp. 1, 10.

67. John Sullivan, "Taking Back a Drug-Plagued Tenement, Step One: Get the Dealers Out," *New York Times* (Aug. 16, 1997), pp. 25–26.

68. "Slow Down, You're Movin' Too Fast: Highway Traffic Deaths Creep Upward," *Law Enforcement News* (Dec. 15, 1996), p. 5.

69. Mothers Against Drunk Driving Web site. Retrieved on June 24, 2003, from www.madd.org.

70. Jerome O. Campane, "The Constitutionality of Drunk Driver Roadblocks," *FBI Law Enforcement Bulletin* (July 1984), pp. 24–31.

71. City of Chicago Web site. Retrieved on May 24, 2004, from www.ci.chi.il.us.

72. "Alcohol and Highway Safety 2001: A Review of the State of Knowledge." (NHTSA, 2001).

73. National Highway Traffic Safety Administration Web site. Retrieved on June 24, 2003, from www.nhtsa.gov.

74. Washington State Patrol Web site. Retrieved on June 24, 2003, from www.wsp.wa.gov.

75. Washington State Patrol Web site. Retrieved on June 24, 2003, from www.wsp.wa.gov.

76. National Highway Traffic Safety Administration Web site. Retrieved on June 24, 2003, from www.nhtsa.gov.

77. Washington State Patrol Web site. Retrieved on June 24, 2003, from www.wsp.wa.gov.

78. Gary T. Marx, "The New Police Undercover Work," *Urban Life* (Jan. 1980), pp. 399–446.

79. Clifford Krauss, "Undercover Police Ride Wide Range of Emotion: Boredom and the Adrenaline Rush," *New York Times* (Aug. 29, 1994), p. B3.

80. Robert D. McFadden, "F.B.I. Sting: Hot Cars, Great Deals, 30 Suspects," *New York Times* (Sept. 9, 1994), p. B1.

81. Marx, "The New Police Undercover Work."

82. Wackenhut Investigations Division, *Integrity Testing and Other Shopping Services* (Coral Gables, FL: The Wackenhut Corporation, 1995).

83. Wackenhut Investigations Division, *Investigative Services* (Coral Gables, FL: The Wackenhut Corporation, 1995).

84. Pinkerton, *Pinkerton Reference Guide to Investigation Services,* 3rd ed. (Encino, CA: Pinkerton Security and Investigation Services, 1995), p. 10.

85. John McNamara, "Helping Merchants Mind the Store," *Police Chief* (Oct. 1993), pp. 90–92.

86. McNamara, "Helping Merchants Mind the Store."

87. George E. Rush, *The Dictionary of Criminal Justice,* 4th ed., (Guilford, CT: Dushkin Publishing Group, 1994), p. 124.

88. *Jacobson* v. *U.S.* 112 S.Ct. 1535 (1992); and Thomas V. Kukura, "Undercover Investigations and the Entrapment Defense: Recent Court Cases," *FBI Law Enforcement Bulletin* (April 1993), pp. 27–32.

89. Kukura, "Undercover Investigations and the Entrapment Defense."

Chapter 9

1. Lee P. Brown, "Police–Community Power Sharing," in *Police Leadership in America: Crisis and Opportunity,* ed. William A. Geller (New York: Praeger, 1985), p. 71. See also Lee P. Brown, "Violent Crime and Community Involvement," *FBI Law Enforcement Bulletin* (May 1992), pp. 2–5.

2. R. C. Davis, "Organizing the Community for Improved Policing," in *Police Leadership in America: Crisis and Opportunity,* William A. Geller, ed., pp. 84–85, p. 85.

3. Police Foundation, *Experiments in Police Improvement: A Progress Report* (Washington, DC: Police Foundation, 1972), p. 28.

4. Steven M. Cox and Jack D. Fitzgerald, *Police in Community Relations: Critical Issues,* 2nd ed. (Dubuque, IA: William C. Brown, 1992), p. 4.

5. Cox and Fitzgerald, *Police in Community Relations,* p. 7.

6. Cox and Fitzgerald, *Police in Community Relations,* p. 8.

7. President's Commission on Law Enforcement and Administration of Justice, *The Challenge of Crime in a Free Society* (Washington, DC: U.S. Government Printing Office, 1967), p. 100.

8. President's Commission on Law Enforcement and Administration of Justice, *Challenge of Crime.*

9. Louis A. Radelet, *The Police and the Community* (Encino, CA: Glencoe, 1980).

10. Egon Bittner, "Community Relations," in *Police Community Relations: Images, Roles, Realities,* Alvin W. Cohn and Emilio C. Viano, eds. (Philadelphia: Lippincott, 1976), pp. 77–82.

11. Cox and Fitzgerald, *Police in Community Relations,* p. 50.

12. George Gallup, Jr., and Alec Gallup, *The Gallup Poll Monthly* , no. 420 (Princeton, NJ: The Gallup Poll, 2000).

13. Timothy J. Flanagan and Kathleen Maguire, eds. *Sourcebook of Criminal Justice Statistics—1991* (Washington, DC: U.S. Department of Justice, Bureau of Justice Statistics, U.S. Government Printing Office, 1992), Table 2.15, p. 180.

14. Gallup Poll 2002. Retrieved on April 10, 2003, from http://www .gallup.com.

15. James Q. Wilson, *Thinking about Crime,* 2d ed. (New York: Basic Books, 1983), p. 91.

16. William A. Westley, *Violence and the Police* (Cambridge, MA: MIT Press, 1970), p. 93.

17. James Q. Wilson, *Varieties of Police Behavior* (New York: Atheneum, 1973), p. 28.

18. U.S. Census Bureau. Retrieved from http://www.census.gov /population/www/socdemo/foreign.html

19. Sherman Block, "Policing an Increasingly Diverse America," *FBI Law Enforcement Bulletin,* June 1994, pp. 24–26.

20. Block, "Policing an Increasingly Diverse America."

21. Brad R. Bennett, "Incorporating Diversity: Police Response to Multicultural Changes in Their Communities," *FBI Law Enforcement Bulletin,* December 1995, pp. 1–6.

22. International Association of Chiefs of Police, *1996 Training Catalog: IACP Educational Programs* (Alexandria, VA: International Association of Chiefs of Police, 1996), pp. 22–23. For more information on IACP training programs, contact the International Association of Chiefs of Police (IACP) at 515 N. Washington Street, Alexandria, Virginia, 22314-2357, call IACP at 1-800-THE-IACP, or fax 1-703-836-4543.

23. Bennett, "Incorporating Diversity."

24. Linda S. Miller, and Karen M. Hess, *The Police in the Community: Strategies for the 21st Century,* 3rd ed. (Belmont, CA: Wadsworth Publishing, 2002).

25. Miller and Hess, *The Police in the Community,* p. 63.

26. *Brown* v. *Board of Education of Topeka,* 347 U.S. 483 (1954).

27. National Advisory Commission on Civil Disorders, *Report of the National Advisory Commission on Civil Disorders* (Washington, DC: U.S. Government Printing Office, 1968); and Allen D. Grimshaw, *Racial Violence in the United States* (Chicago: Aldine, 1969), pp. 269–298.

28. Cox and Fitzgerald, *Police in Community Relations,* p. 130.

29. "Blacks and Criminal Justice—a Grim Picture," *Law Enforcement News* (Nov. 30, 1995), p. 11.

30. Miller and Hess, *The Police in the Community,* p. 177.

31. William P. McCamey, Gene L. Scaramella, and Steven M. Cox, *Contemporary Municipal Policing* (Boston, MA: Allyn & Bacon, 2003), p. 209.

32. *Sourcebook of Criminal Justice Statistics Online.* Retrieved from http://www.albany.edu/sourcebook/1995/tost_2.html#2-k.

33. *Sourcebook of Criminal Justice Statistics Online.* Retrieved from http://www.albany.edu/sourcebook/1995/tost_2.html#2-k.

34. Ronnie A. Carter, "Improving Minority Relations," *FBI Law Enforcement Bulletin* (Dec. 1995), pp. 14–17, p. 17.

35. Miller and Hess, *The Police in the Community,* p. 177.

36. U.S. Census Bureau. Retrieved from http://www.census.gov /population/www/socdemo/foreign.html

37. "LAPD Spices Things Up with a Little Mexican Flavor," *Law Enforcement News,* 30 April 1996, p. 1.

38. "Policing in Phoenix Gets a Little More Latin Flavor," *Law Enforcement News,* 30 June 1995, p. 5.

39. U.S. Census Bureau. Retrieved from http://www.census.gov/population/www/socdemo/foreign.html

40. Delbert Joe and Norman Robinson, "Chinatown's Immigrant Gangs: The New Warrior Class," *Criminology* 18 (1980), p. 337.

41. Bennett, "Incorporating Diversity," p. 2.

42. "Winning Strategies Offered for Working with Different Cultures." *Cultural Diversity* (Jan./Feb. 2000). Retrieved on April 27, 2003, from http://www.communitypolicing.org/publications/exchange/e30_00/e30wulff.htm.

43. "Winning Strategies Offered for Working with Different Cultures." *Cultural Diversity.*

44. U.S. Census Bureau. Retrieved on March 27, 2003, from http://www.census.gov/population/www/cen2000/tablist.html.

45. Alan Mentzer, "Policing in Indian Country: Understanding State Jurisdiction and Authority," *Law and Order* (June 1996), pp. 24–29. For further information on law enforcement and Indians, see B. T. Baker, *Law Enforcement within Indian Country: An Introduction* (Artesia, NM: Federal Law Enforcement Training Center, 1993); Bureau of Indian Affairs, Division of Law Enforcement, *Indian Law Enforcement History* (Washington, DC: U.S. Government Printing Office, 1975); *Indian Law Enforcement Reform Act of 1990, Public Law 101-379;* International Association of Chiefs of Police, Indian Country Law Enforcement Section, *A Report by the Indian Country Section of the International Association of Chiefs of Police* (Alexandria, VA: International Association of Chiefs of Police, 1994).

46. Jacob R. Clark, "Brutality, Abuse and Neglect: BIA Grapples with Chronic Problems," *Law Enforcement News* (May 15, 1996), p. 18.

47. "Culture, community and communication: An interview with Nancy Bill." *Building Bridges, 1*(2, Summer 1994). Retrieved April 3, 2003, from http://www.edc.org/buildingsafecommunities/buildbridges/bbl.2/nancy.html.

48. IACP, "Improving Safety in Indian Country: Recommendations from the IACP 2001 Summit," (2001). Retrieved on April 28, 2004, from http://www.theiacp.org/documents/index.cfm?fuseaction=document&document_id=108.

49. IACP, "Improving Safety in Indian Country: Recommendations from the IACP 2001 Summit."

50. Retrieved on March 27, 2003, from http://www.communitypolicing.org/publications/exchange/e30_00/e30telle.htm.

51. U.S. Department of Justice, Community Relations Service, *Twenty Plus Things Law Enforcement Agencies Can Do to Prevent or Respond to Hate Incidents against Arab-Americans, Muslims & Sikhs* (Washington, DC: Department of Justice). Retrieved on March 25, 2003, from www.usdoj.crs/twentyplus.htm.

52. "Examining Police Behavior under Nazi Rule Offers Contemporary Lessons on Moral Responsibility and Civil Liberties," Cultural Diversity (Jan/Feb 2000). Retrieved on March 27, 2003, from http://www.communitypolicing.org/publications/exchange/e30_00/e30milof.htm.

53. Neil Santaniello, "Jewish Agency, Boca Police to Teach Terror Response." Fort Lauderdale Sun-Sentinel (April 2, 2003). Retrieved on April 2, 2003, from www.sunsentinel.com.

54. Frank Schmallenger, *Criminal Justice Today: An Introductory Text for the Twenty-first Century* (Englewood Cliffs, NJ: Prentice-Hall, 1991), p. 213.

55. "The State of the Union: From Alabama to Wyoming, State-by-State Highlights of the Year in Policing," *Law Enforcement News* (Dec. 31, 1995/Jan. 15, 1996), p. 9.

56. Ruth Harlow, "Let's work to prevent, not just punish, hate crimes," *Lambda Legal* (Spring/summer 1999). Retrieved on April 19, 2003, from http://lambdalegal.org/cgi-bin/iowa/documents/record?record=453.

57. Marjorie Valbrun, "Haitians in New York," *APF Reporter, 20*(3, 2003). Retrieved on April 10, 2003, from http://www.aliciapatterson.org/APF2003/Valbrun/Valbrun.html.

58. Valbrun, "Haitians in New York."

59. New York City Police Department, *Annual Report—1985,* p. 50.

60. Betsy Cantrell, "Triad: Reducing Criminal Victimization of the Elderly," *FBI Law Enforcement Bulletin* (Feb. 1994), pp. 19–23.

61. Linda Forst, *The Aging of America: A handbook for police officers* (Springfield, IL: Charles C. Thomas Publishers, 2000), p. 7.

62. Forst, *The Aging of America,* p. 31.

63. Forst, *The Aging of America.*

64. William D. Miller, "The Graying of America: Implications towards Policing," *Law and Order* (Oct. 1991), pp. 96–97.

65. Cantrell, "Triad: Reducing Criminal Victimization of the Elderly."

66. Ordway P. Burden, "Adaptable, Low-Cost, Effective: That's Triad," *Law Enforcement News* (April 30, 1995), p. 17.

67. Burden, "Adaptable, Low-Cost, Effective."

68. Cantrell, "Triad: Reducing Criminal Victimization of the Elderly." See also Burden, "Adaptable, Low-Cost, Effective."

69. Lynne Bliss, "Assisting Senior Victims," *FBI Law Enforcement Bulletin* (Feb./March 1996), pp. 6–9.

70. Forst, *The Aging of America,* p. 133.

71. Forst, *The Aging of America,* p. 135.

72. Forst, *The Aging of America,* p. 136.

73. "Bulletin Reports: Crime and the Elderly," *FBI Law Enforcement Bulletin* (May 1994), p. 12. Note: Up to 50 copies of each brochure are available to law enforcement agencies, without charge, from AARP, ATTN: CJS B-5, 601 E Street, NW, Washington, D.C. 20049. Allow four to six weeks for delivery.

74. Federal Bureau of Investigation, *Uniform Crime Reports: Crime in the United States, 1993* (Washington, DC: U.S. Government Printing Office), 1994.

75. Barbara Allen Hagen and Melissa Sickmund, *Juveniles and Violence Fact Sheet* (Washington, DC: Office of Juvenile Justice and Delinquency, 1996).

76. "Ounces of Prevention: Chiefs Call for More Investment in Youth Programs," *Law Enforcement News* (Sept. 1996), p. 1.

77. "Ounces of Prevention," p. 10.

78. "Ounces of Prevention."

79. William DeJong, *Project DARE: Teaching Kids to Say "No" to Drugs and Alcohol* (Washington, DC: National Institute of Justice, March 1986), p. 4.

80. Joseph Santoro, *DARE works: A Police Chief's Perspective* (DARE America, 2002). Retrieved on April 3, 2003 from http://www.dare.com/newsroom/storypage.asp?N=NewsRoom&M=14&S=34&RecordID.

81. University of Akron, "Initial Results Positive for New DARE Program—Media Advisory" (Jan 10, 2002). Retrieved on April 3, 2003, from http://www.dare.com/new_site/positive_results.htm.

82. National Institute of Justice, *The D.A.R.E. Program: A Review of Prevalence, User Satisfaction, and Effectiveness* (Washington, DC: National Institute of Justice, 1994).

83. Joseph Santoro, *DARE works*.

84. Joseph Santoro, *DARE works*.

85. See Samuel Walker, *Sense and Nonsense about Crime and Drugs: A Policy Guide*, 4th ed. (Belmont, CA: Wadsworth/West, 1998), pp. 256–257.

86. Truth and DARE: Wash Cities Shelve Anti-Drug Curriculum," *Law Enforcement News* (Nov. 30, 1996), pp. 1, 15.

87. "Truth and DARE."

88. "Impact of a Drug Abuse Resistance Education (DARE) Program in Preventing the Initiation of Cigarette Smoking in Fifth and Sixth Grade Students" *Journal of National Medical Association*, 94(2002), pp 249–256.

89. Retrieved on April 3, 2003, from http://www.dare.com/new_site/curriculum/national_study.htm.

90. Youth Crime Watch of America. Retrieved on March 27, 2003, from www.ycwa.org.

91. Halley Smith-La Bombard, "Bullies Find No Refuge in Oak Harbor," *Community Policing Organization* (Sept. 2001). Retrieved on March 27, 2003, from www.communitypolicing.org/publications/comlinks/c116_labom.htm.

92. Retrieved on March 27, 2003, from http://www.usdoj.gov/crs/pubs/prevyouhatecrim.htm.

93. Retrieved on April 2, 2003, from http://www.cert-la.com/links/CERTinSchools.htm.

94. Cox and Fitzgerald, *Police in Community Relations*, p. 164.

95. "The Cops Are Rockin' with the Roll'rz Band," *Law and Order* (Dec. 1996), pp. 54–55.

96. R. John Schmidt, "Emergency Services Explorers, *Law and Order* (Dec. 1994), pp. 37–39.

97. Bernal F. Koehrsen, Jr., and Dennis L. Damon, "Police Practices: Collectible Cop Cards, *FBI Law Enforcement Bulletin* (Feb. 1993), pp. 4–5.

98. Lois Pilant, "Promoting Community Awareness," *Police Chief* (May 1995), pp. 36–42, p. 40.

99. Pilant, "Promoting Community Awareness," p. 41.

100. Michael K. Ahrens, "School Resource Officers: Community Outreach Benefits Everybody," *Law and Order* (July 1995), pp. 81–83. See also, "Keeping Kids in School," *FBI Law Enforcement Bulletin* (August 1992), pp. 10–11; Bill Zalud, "Back to School: Back to Security," *Security* (Sept. 1994), p. 7; and "T.A.S.R.O.: Texas Association of School Resource Officers," *Texas Police Journal* (August 1993), p. 7.

101. Ahrens, "School Resource Officers," pp. 81–83.

102. Betsy Showstack Young, "Project KidCare: Photo IDS and Safety Information Arm Parents against Child Abduction," *Law and Order* (Dec. 1995), pp. 22–24. For more information on Project KidCare, contact Polaroid at 1-800-662-8337, ext. 558.

103. "President Signs Protect Act." Retrieved on March 27, 2004, from www.Whitehouse.gov/news/releases2003/04/20030430-6.html.

104. National Association of Police Athletic Leagues (PAL). Retrieved on March 27, 2004, from www.nationalpal.org/Home.htm.

105. Kevin W. Dale, "College Internship Program: Prospective Recruits Get Hands-On Experience," *FBI Law Enforcement Bulletin* (Sept. 1996), pp. 21–24. See also "NCO Participants Learn Police Work," *Law and Order* (June 1995), p. 33.

106. Peter E. Finn and Monique Sullivan, *Police Response to Special Populations: Handling the Mentally Ill, Public Inebriate, and the Homeless* (Washington, DC: National Institute of Justice, January 1988), p. 1.

107. *Zinermon v. Burch*, 110 S.Ct. 975 (1990).

108. Alan R. Coffey, *Law Enforcement: A Human Relations Approach* (Englewood Cliffs, NJ: Prentice-Hall, 1990), pp. 136–137.

109. Jacob R. Clark, "Be It Ever So Humble . . . NY Transit Cops Reach Out to Those Who Would Make the Subways Their Home," *Law Enforcement News* (March 15, 1992), p. 11.

110. Peter Finn, *Street People: Crime File Study Guide* (Washington, DC: National Institute of Justice, 1988), p. 1.

111. Alison Hibbert, "Police Come to the Aid of the Homeless," *Police Chief* (May 2000). Retrieved on April 2, 2003, from http://ci.ftlaud.fl.us.police/homeless2.html.

112. Hibbert, "Police Come to the Aid of the Homeless."

113. Ronald W. Glensor and Ken Peak, "Policing the Homeless: A Problem-Oriented Response," *Police Chief* (Oct. 1994), pp. 101–103.

114. International Association of Chiefs of Police (IACP), "What do victims want? Effective strategies to achieve justice for victims of crime" (May 2000). Retrieved April 28, 2004, from http://www.theiacp.org/documents/index.cfm?fuseaction=document&document_id=150.

115. IACP.

116. National Center for Victims of Crime, *A police guide to first response: Domestic violence, residential burglary and automobile theft* (Washington DC: U.S. Department of Justice, 2000).

117. Denise Kindschi-Gosselin, Heavy hands: An introduction to the crimes of family violence, 2nd ed. (Upper Saddle River NJ: Prentice-Hall, 2003).

118. Susan G. Parker, "Establishing Victim Services within a Law Enforce-ment Agency: The Austin Experience," *OVC Bulletin* (March 2001), p. 2.

119. Kenneth R. Freeman and Terry Estrada-Mullaney, *Using Dolls to Interview Child Victims: Legal Concerns and Interview Procedures* (Washington, DC: National Institute of Justice, January/February 1988).

120. Peter Finn and Beverly N. W. Lee, *Establishing and Expanding Victim-Witness Assistance Programs* (Washington, DC: National Institute of Justice, August 1988).

121. Robert Snow, "Agencies Turned Advocate," *Law and Order* (Jan. 1992), pp. 285–287.

122. U.S. Census Bureau (2000). Retrieved on April 10, 2003, from http://www.census.gov/hhes/www/disable/disabcps.html.

123. Allan Lengel, "D.C. Police Learning to Hear the Deaf," Washington Post (Feb. 11, 2002), p. B1.

124. David J. Lee, "Officer Promotes Understanding between Police, Hearing Impaired," Odessa (Texas) American (Dec. 26, 2002). Retrieved from http://www.deaftoday.com/archives/000999.html.

125. "In Any language," *Law Enforcement News* (May 15, 1996), p. 4.

126. Lori M. B. Laffel and Cynthia Pasquarello, "Diabetes and Law Enforcement," *Police Chief* (Dec. 1996), p. 60.

127. George L. Kelling, "On the Accomplishments of the Police," in *Control of the Police Organization,* Maurice Punch, ed. (Cambridge, MA: MIT Press, 1983), p. 164.

128. Wesley G. Skogan, *Disorder and Decline: Crime and the Spiral of Decay in American Neighborhoods* (New York: Free Press, 1990), p. 125.

129. James Garofalo and Maureen McLeod, *Improving the Use and Effectiveness of Neighborhood Watch Programs* (Washington, DC: National Institute of Justice, 1988), p. 1.

130. Figgie International, *The Figgie Report, Part 4: Reducing Crime in America—Successful Community Efforts* (Willowby, OH: Figgie International, 1983).

131. Garofalo and McLeod, *Improving Neighborhood Watch Programs,* p. 1.

132. Garofalo and McLeod, *Improving Neighborhood Watch Programs.*

133. Skogan, *Disorder and Decline,* p. 130.

134. Dennis P. Rosenbaum, Arthur J. Lurigio, and Paul J. Lavrakas, *Crime Stoppers: A National Evaluation* (Washington, DC: National Institute of Justice, 1986).

135. Crime Stoppers U.S.A. Retrieved on March 27, 2004, from http://www.crimestopusa.com/stats.htm.

136. Virginia Beach Crime Solvers. Retrieved on March 27, 2004, from http://www.crimesolvers.com/stats.htm.

137. Dennis Jay Kenney, "The Guardian Angels: The Related Social Issues," in *Police and Policing: Contemporary Issues,* Dennis Jay Kenney, ed. (New York: Praeger, 1989), pp. 376–400.

138. Philip Messing, "Cops to Wing It with Angels in Park: Taking First Step Together—on Skates," *New York Post* (Dec. 1996), p. 6.

139. Susan Pennell et al., "Guardian Angels: A Unique Approach to Crime Prevention," *Crime and Delinquency* (July 1989), pp. 376–400.

140. The Guardian Angels. Retrieved on March 27, 2004, from www.guardianangels.org.

141. "Los Angeles Complex Calls in Muslim Guards," *New York Times* (Oct. 11, 1992), p. A38.

142. "Los Angeles Complex Calls in Muslim Guards."

143. Retrieved on April 10, 2003, from http://www.police.nashville.org/get_involved/default.htm.

144. Ordway P. Burden, "Volunteers: The Wave of the Future?" *Police Chief* (July 1988), pp. 25–26.

145. Retrieved on March 27, 2004, from http://police.nashville.org.

146. Retrieved on March 27, 2004, from http://police.ci.glendale.ca.us/.

147. Retrieved on March 27, 2004 from http://www.sanantonio.gov/sapd/vip/asp.

148. Houston Police Department, *Multiyear Report—1983–1987* (Houston: Houston Police Department, 1988), p. 25.

149. "Mobile Precincts: Police on Wheels," *FBI Law Enforcement Bulletin* (April 1992), p. 14.

150. Jeff Siegel, "The East Dallas Police Storefront," *Law and Order,* May 1995, pp. 53–55.

151. *Law Enforcement News* (May 15, 1995).

152. Alston A. Morgan, "Law Enforcement Community Benefits with State-Accredited Chaplain Academy," *Sheriff Times, 1*(10, Fall 1999), p. 1.

153. Alston A. Morgan, "Law Enforcement Community Benefits with State-Accredited Chaplain Academy," p. 2.

154. Bennett, "Incorporating Diversity."

155. Tracy Enns, "Citizens' Police Academies: The Farmington Experience," *Police Chief* (April 1995), pp. 133–135.

156. Robert J. Liddell, "Volunteers Help Shoulder the Load," *FBI Law Enforcement Bulletin* (August 1995), pp. 21–25.

157. Long Beach, California, Police Department. Retrieved on March 27, 2004, from www.longbeachpd.org.

158. "Law Enforcement around the Nation, 1995," p. 7.

159. "Law Enforcement around the Nation, 1995," p. 27.

160. "Law Enforcement around the Nation, 1995," p. 10.

161. Cheryl DuPree Kravetz, "Investing in Positive Community Relations: Newspaper's Police Trading Card Program Brings Cops and Kids Together," *Police* (Jan. 1997), pp. 18–19.

162. Pilant, "Promoting Community Awareness," p. 37.

163. Harvey Rachlin, "Something for Nothing: Making an Impact on the Community on a Zero Budget," *Law and Order* (Dec. 1996), pp. 24–28.

164. Harris Wofford, "AmeriCorps: An Important Resource for Police Executives," *Police Chief* (May 1996), pp. 59-62. Note: For information about applications or programs in your area, contact the AmeriCorps Office of Public Liaison at 1-202-606-5000, ext. 260, or contact your state commission.

165. Office of the Police Corps Web site. Retrieved on March 25, 2003, from http://www.ojp.usdoj.gov/opclee.

Chapter 10

1. George Kelling, *Police and Communities: The Quiet Revolution, Perspectives on Policing,* no. 1 (Washington, DC: National Institute of Justice, 1988).

2. Bureau of Justice Statistics. *Community Policing Impacts 86% of U.S. population Served by local police departments.* (Washington, DC: Department of Justice, 2001). Retrieved on April 23, 2003, from www.ojp.usdoj.gov/bjs/pub/press/cplp99pr.htm

3. The 12 monographs in the *Perspectives on Policing* series were published in 1988 and 1989 by the National Institute of Justice, Washington, D.C.

4. Mark H. Moore and Robert C. Trojanowicz, *Corporate Strategies for Policing, Perspectives on Policing,* no. 6 (Washington, DC: National Institute of Justice, 1988).

5. Albert J. Reiss, Jr., "Shaping and Serving the Community: The Role of the Police Chief Executive," in *Police Leadership in America: Crisis and Opportunity,* William A. Geller, ed. (New York: Praeger, 1985), p. 63.

6. James Q. Wilson and George Kelling, "'Broken Windows': The Police and Neighborhood Safety," *Atlantic Monthly* (March 1982), pp. 29–38.

7. Wilson and Kelling, "Broken Windows."

8. Wesley G. Skogan, *Disorder and Decline: Crime and the Spiral of Decay in American Neighborhoods* (New York: Free Press, 1990), pp. 21–50.

9. Robert C. Trojanowicz, "Building Support for Community Policing: An Effective Strategy," *FBI Law Enforcement Bulletin* (May 1992), pp. 7–12.

10. Jerome Skolnick and David Bayley, *Community Policing: Issues and Practices Around the World* (Washington, DC: National Institute of Justice, 1988).

11. Jeremy Travis, "What Difference Do the Police Make? Research Can Offer Some Answers," *Community Policing Exchange* (May/June 1997), p. 8.

12. Herman Goldstein, "Toward Community-Oriented Policing: Potential, Basic Requirements, and Threshold Questions,"*Crime and Delinquency, 33*(1987), pp. 6–30.

13. Malcolm K. Sparrow, Mark H. Moore, and David M. Kennedy, *Beyond 911: A New Era for Policing* (New York: Basic Books, 1990), p. 129.

14. James Ahern, *Police in Trouble* (New York: Hawthorn Books, 1992), pp. 83–85.

15. Mary Ann Wycoff et al., *Citizen Contact Patrol: Executive Summary* (Washington, DC: Police Foundation, 1985).

16. Michael J. Farrell, "The Development of the Community Patrol Officer Program: Community-Oriented Policing in the City of New York," in *Community Policing: Rhetoric or Reality?* Jack R. Greene and Stephen D. Mastrofski, eds. (New York: Praeger, 1988), pp. 73–88.

17. David L. Carter, *Community Policing and DARE: A Practitioner's Perspective* (Washington, DC: National Institute of Justice, 1995), p. 2.

18. Joseph E. Braun, "Progress through Partnerships," *Community Links* (Jan. 1997).

19. George L. Kelling, *"Broken Windows" and Police Discretion* (Washington, DC: U.S. Department of Justice, 1999).

20. Charles H. Wiegand, "Combining Tactical and Community Policing Considerations," *Law and Order* (May 1997), pp. 70–71.

21. Department of Justice, *Surveys in 12 Cities Show Widespread Community Support for Police* (Washington DC: Department of Justice, 1999).

22. Department of Justice, *Surveys in 12 Cities.*

23. Department of Justice, *Surveys in 12 Cities.*

24. Anthony V. Bouza, *The Police Mystique: An Insider's Look at Cops, Crime, and the Criminal Justice System* (New York: Plenum Press, 1990), pp. 236–237. Note: *Law Enforcement News* has an extensive interview with Professor Herman Goldstein in its Feb. 14, 1997, issue, "A LEN Interview with Professor Herman Goldstein, the 'Father' of Problem-Oriented Policing," pp. 8–11.

25. John E. Eck and William Spelman, "Who Ya Gonna Call? The Police as Problem Busters," *Crime and Delinquency, 33*(1987), p. 53.

26. Sparrow, Moore, and Kennedy, *Beyond 911,* pp. 16–17.

27. John E. Eck et al., *Problem Solving: Problem-Oriented Policing in Newport News* (Washington, DC: Police Executive Research Forum, 1987), pp. 100–101.

28. Sparrow, Moore, and Kennedy, *Beyond 911,* p. 129.

29. Herman Goldstein, *Problem-oriented Policing* (New York: McGraw-Hill, 1990).

30. Rachel Boba, "What is problem analysis?" *Problem Analysis in Policing: An Executive Summary, 5*(1, Winter 2003), p. 2.

31. Boba, "What is problem analysis?" p. 10.

32. Harvey Rachlin, "Creative Community Policing Programs," *Law and Order* (April 1997), pp. 24–34.

33. Charles A. Gruber, "Elgin Designs and Builds a Community Policing Facility," *Police Chief* (August 1996), pp. 16–24.

34. "A Place to Call Home: Resident Officer Programs Get a Federal Shot in the Arm," *Law Enforcement News* (July/August 1997), p. 17.

35. "A Place to Call Home."

36. Richard Glasser and Kevin P. Morison, "Examining Chicago's Alternative Policing Strategy," *Community Policing Exchange* (May/June 1997), pp. 1, 8.

37. Chicago's Alternative Policing Strategy Web site. Retrieved on May 25, 2003, from www.norhtwestern.edu/ipr/news/CAPS99release ,html.

38. Chris Krettler, "Small-Town Police Plan and Assess," *Community Policing Exchange,* (May/June 1997), p. 2.

39. Krettler, "Small-Town Police Plan and Assess."

40. Retrieved on May 25, 2003, from http://www.theiacp.org/awards.

41. Retrieved on May 25, 2003, from http://www.theiacp.org/awards.

42. Retrieved on May 25, 2003, from http://www.theiacp.org/awards.

43. Matthew Zolvinski, "Police Help Kids to Roam,"*Community Links* (March 2002), p. 6.

44. Sheila Schmitt, "ROPE: The Resident Officer Program of Elgin: If You Can't Beat 'Em, Join 'Em," *Law and Order* (May 1995), pp. 52, 56–57.

45. Schmitt, "ROPE: The Resident Officer Program of Elgin."

46. "A Place to Call Home." For more on Elgin's resident officer program, see "Resident Police Officers Go Beyond the Call of Duty," *Community Policing Exchange* (July/August 1997), p. 6.

47. "The State of the Union: From Alabama to Wyoming, State-by-State Highlights of the Year in Policing," *Law Enforcement News* (Dec. 31, 1995–Jan. 15, 1996), p. 13.

48. Walter Oleksy, "'Police Don't Live Here. They Don't Really Care?'": A New Idea in Community-Oriented Policing," *Law and Order* (August 1992), p. 45. See also Sheila Schmitt, "Columbia's Police Loan Program Houses Twice as Many Officers," *Law and Order* (May 1995), p. 59.

49. Schmitt, "Columbia's Police Loan Program Houses Twice as Many Officers."

50. Retrieved on May 25, 2004, from http://phoenix.gov /POLICE/pops1.html.

51. Tom Topousis, "Cops Get in on the Ground Floor: New Deal Gives Them Rent Break in Projects," *New York Post* (May 14, 1997), p. 20. See also "A Place to Call Home."

52. "A Place to Call Home."

53. Retrieved on May 25, 2004, from http://www.hud.gov/offices/hsg/sfh /reo/ond/ond.cfm.

54. "A Place to Call Home."

55. "The State of the Union," p. 10.

56. U.S.C. 3796dd-4, 3793.

57. Willard M. Oliver, "The COPS Office: The Office of Community Oriented Policing Services," *Law and Order,* April 1997, pp. 45–49.

58. Jeffrey A. Roth and Joseph F. Ryan, "The COPS Program after 4 Years: National Evaluation," *Research in Brief* (August 2000), p. 1.

59. Roth and Ryan, "The COPS Program after 4 Years," p. 1.

60. Roth and Ryan, "The COPS Program after 4 Years," p. 19.

61. Department of Justice, *On the beat, 19*(Fall 2002). Retrieved on April 2, 2004, from http://www.cops.usdoj.gov/mime/open.pdp?item=628.

62. Retrieved on May 25, 2004, from http://www.cops.usdoj.gov/default .asp?Item1062.

63. Tom McEwen and Stacy Milligan, *An Addendum to the Evaluation of the COPS Office Methamphetamine Initiative.* (Washington DC: U.S. Department of Justice, 2003).

64. McEwen and Milligan, *An Addendum to the Evaluation.*

65. National Institute of Justice, *Solicitation: Policing Research and Evaluation: Fiscal Year 1997* (Washington, DC: National Institute of Justice, 1997).

66. Department of Justice, *On the beat*.

67. Department of Justice, *On the beat*.

68. Department of Justice, *On the beat*.

69. "Is the COPS Office Fulfilling Its Mandate?" *Law Enforcement News, 26*(545, Dec. 2000). Retrieved on May 14, 2003, from http://www.lib .jjay.cuny.edu/len/2000/12.31/100cops.html

70. "Is the COPS Office Fulfilling Its Mandate?"

71. COMPASS. Retrieved on May 25, 2004, from http://www.ojp.usdoj .gov/commprograms/promising_programs.htm.

72. "Progress through Partnerships," *Community Links, 1*(1, Jan. 1997), p. 1. Those interested in contacting the Community Policing Consortium may do so at: The Community Policing Consortium, 1726 M St. N.W., Suite 801, Washington, D.C. 20036. Publications: 1-202-530-0639 or toll free: 1-800-833-3085; fax: 1-202-833-9295. You may get on their mailing list and receive future issues or may submit newsworthy articles or features for publication to them. The consortium may also be reached on the Internet at www.communitypolicing.org.

73. Brian Whitley, "Domestic Violence: Police Help Raise Awareness of Doctors and Interns." *Community Links* (Feb. 2003), p. 3. Retrieved on April 2, 2004, from http://www.communitypolicing.org/magazine.

74. "As Crime Rates Continue to Dip, Police Credit Community Efforts—and Their Own," *Law Enforcement News* (Sept. 15, 1996), pp. 1, 14.

75. "As Crime Rates Continue to Dip," p. 1.

76. "As Crime Rates Continue to Dip," p. 14.

77. "As Crime Rates Continue to Dip," p. 14.

78. "Going Down for the Third Time: UCR Shows Another Decrease in Part 1 Crime in '94," *Law Enforcement News* (June 15, 1995), pp. 1, 6.

79. "Going Down for the Third Time," p. 6.

80. Jacob R. Clark, "New Orleans Chief Touts Lofty Gains in Ambitious Plan to Reform Department," *Law Enforcement News* (Nov. 30, 1995), p. 1.

81. David Brown and Susan Iles, "Community Constable: A Study of a Policing Initiative," *NIJ International Summaries* (Washington, D.C.: National Institute of Justice, 1986).

82. Police Foundation, *The Newark Foot Patrol Experiment* (Washington, D.C.: Police Foundation, 1981).

83. Jack Greene and Steve Mastrofski, *Community Policing: Rhetoric or Reality?* (New York: Praeger, 1988).

84. Robert Sheehan and Gary W. Cordner, *Introduction to Police Administration* (Cincinnati: Anderson, 1989), p. 90.

85. Wesley Skogan and Mary Ann Wycoff, "Some Unexpected Effects of a Police Service for Victims," *Crime and Delinquency, 33*(1987), pp. 490–501.

86. "Audit Rips Houston's Policing Style as a Good Idea That Falls Short of the Mark," *Law Enforcement News* (Sept. 30 1991), p. 1.

87. Gary B. Schobel, Thomas A. Evans, and John L. Daly, "Community Policing: Does It Reduce Crime, or Just Displace It?," *Police Chief* (August 1997), pp. 64–71.

88. Lisa M. Riechers and Roy R. Roberg, "Community Policing: A Critical Review of Underlying Assumptions," *Journal of Police Science and Administration* (June 1990), p. 110.

89. "C-OP Lives on in Baltimore Co.: Police Brass Say They're Not Abandoning the Concept," *Law Enforcement News* (Dec. 15, 1996), p. 1.

90. "C-OP Lives on in Baltimore Co."

91. "C-OP Lives on in Baltimore Co."

92. Retrieved on May 25, 2004, from http://www.co.ba.md.us /Agencies/police/chief.html.

93. National Institute of Justice, "Policing Neighborhoods: A Report from St. Petersburg" *Research Preview* (July 1999).

94. National Institute of Justice, "Policing Neighborhoods."

95. Jacob R. Clark, "Time to Pay the Piper: COPS Funded Officers, Departments Near Day of Fiscal Reckoning," *Law Enforcement News* (Sept. 30, 1997), pp. 1, 14.

96. National Institute of Justice, "Policing Neighborhoods."

97. Clark, "Time to Pay the Piper," p. 1.

98. Clark, "Time to Pay the Piper," p. 14.

99. John L. Worrall, "Does 'Broken Windows' Law Enforcement Reduce Serious Crime?" California Institute for County Government Research Brief (2002), p. 9. Retrieved on April 2, 2004, from http://www .cicg.org/publications.

100. Retrieved on May 25, 2004, from http://www.chiefwalters.com /policing/Chapter5.html.

101. Retrieved on May 25, 2004, from http://www.policing.com/articl /cpanddv.html.

102. Retrieved on May 25, 2004, from http://www.cops.usdoj.gov/mime /open.pdf?item=1046.

103. Rob Chapman and Matthew C. Scheider, "Community Policing: Now More Than Ever." Retrieved on May 2, 2003, from http://www.cops.usdoj .gov/default.asp?item=716.

104. Malcolm K. Sparrow, *Implementing Community Policing: Perspectives on Policing,* (Washington, D.C.: National Institute of Justice, 1988).

105. Robert Wasserman and Mark H. Moore, *Values in Policing: Perspectives on Policing,* (Washington, D.C.: National Institute of Justice, 1988).

Chapter 11

1. Federal Bureau of Investigation, *Uniform Crime Reports, 2002.* Retrieved on April 1, 2004, from http://www.fbi.com.

2. *Weeks v. United States*, 232 U.S. 383 (1914).

3. *Brown v. Mississippi*, 297 U.S. 278 (1936).

4. *Mapp v. Ohio*, 367 U.S. 643 (1961); and *Miranda v. Arizona*, 384 U.S. 436 (1966).

5. *Weeks v. U.S.*

6. *Silverthorne Lumber Co. v. U.S.*, 251 U.S. 385 (1920).

7. *Wolf v. Colorado*, 338 U.S. 25 (1949).

8. *Rochin v. California*, 342 U.S. 165 (1952).

9. *Mapp v. Ohio*

10. National Institute of Justice, *The Effects of the Exclusionary Rule: A Study of California* (Washington, DC: National Institute of Justice, 1982), p. 12.

11. Peter Nardulli, "The Societal Cost of the Exclusionary Rule: An Empirical Assessment," *ABF Research Journal* (1983), pp. 585–609.

12. *Atwater v. City of Lago Vista*, 121 S.Ct. 1536 (2001).

13. *Payton v. New York*, 445 U.S. 573 (1980).

14. *Henry v. United States*, 361 U.S. 98 (1959).

15. *Brinegar v. United States*, 338 U.S. 160 (1949).

16. *Draper v. United States*, 358 U.S. 307 (1959).

17. *County of Riverside v. McLoughlin*, 111 S.Ct. 1661 (1991).

18. *Delaware v. Prouse*, 440 U.S. 648 (1979).

19. *Mimms v. Pennsylvania*, 434 U.S. 106 (1977). For a thorough discussion of *Mimms* and *Wilson*, see Lisa A. Regini, "Extending the Mimms Rule to Include Passengers," *FBI Law Enforcement Bulletin* (June 1997), pp. 27–32.

20. *Maryland v. Wilson*, 117 S.Ct. 882 (1997).

21. *Maryland v. Wilson*, citing Federal Bureau of Investigation, *Uniform Crime Reports: Law Enforcement Officers Killed and Assaulted* (Washington, DC: Federal Bureau of Investigation, 1994).

22. *Michigan Department of State Police v. Sitz*, 496 U.S. 444 (1990).

23. *City of Indianapolis v. Edmond*, 121 S.Ct. 447 (2000).

24. *Whren v. United States*, 116 S.Ct. 1769 (1996).

25. *Payton v. New York*

26. *Minnesota v. Olson* 495 U.S. 91 (1990).

27. *Minnesota v. Carter* 119 S.Ct. 469 (1998).

28. *Kirk v. Louisiana*, U.S. Supreme Court, No.01-8419 (2002).

29. Sophia Y. Kil, "Supreme Court Cases: 1999–2000 Term," *FBI Law Enforcement Bulletin* (Nov. 2000), pp. 28–29.

30. *Katz v. United States*, 389 U.S. 347 (1967).

31. *Wilson v. Arkansas*, 115 S.Ct. 1914 (1995). For a complete discussion of Fourth Amendment standards on search warrants, see Michael J. Bulzomi, "Knock and Announce: A Fourth Amendment Standard," *FBI Law Enforcement Bulletin* (May 1997), pp. 27–32.

32. *Aguilar v. Texas*, 378 U.S. 108 (1964); and *Spinelli v. United States*, 393 U.S. 410 (1969).

33. *Illinois v. Gates*, 462 U.S. 213 (1983).

34. For an excellent article on *Illinois v. Gates* and other cases involving probable cause and search warrants, see Edward Hendrie, "Inferring Probable Cause: Obtaining a Search Warrant for a Suspect's Home Without Direct Information that Evidence Is Inside," *FBI Law Enforcement Bulletin* (Feb. 2002), pp. 23–32.

35. *Chimel v. California*, 395 U.S. 213 (1969).

36. *United States v. Robinson*, 414 U.S.218 (1973).

37. *Maryland v. Buie*, 110 S.Ct. 1093 (1990).

38. *Illinois v. McArthur*, 121 S.Ct. 946 (2001).

39. *Knowles v. Iowa*, 119 S.Ct. 484 (1998). For an excellent article on the history of searches incident to arrest, see Thomas D. Colbridge, "Search Incident to Arrest: Another Look," *FBI Law Enforcement Bulletin* (May 1999), pp. 27–32.

40. *Terry v. Ohio*, 392 U.S. 1 (1968).

41. *Terry v. Ohio*.

42. *Minnesota v. Dickerson*, 113 S.Ct. 2130 (1993).

43. *Illinois v. Wardlow*, 120 S.Ct. 673 (2000).

44. *Illinois v. Wardlow,* citing *Terry*, 392 U.S. at 30.

45. Sophia Y. Kil, "Supreme Court Cases: 1999–2000 Term," pp. 28–32. For an excellent discussion of the Wardlow decision and flight as justification for seizure see Michel E. Brooks, "Flight as Justification for Seizure: Supreme Court Rulings, *FBI Law Enforcement Bulletin* (June 2000), pp. 28–32.

46. *Florida v. J.L.*, 120 S.Ct. 1375 (2000). For an interesting, informative article on *Terry* stops in response to anonymous tips, see Michael J. Bulzomi, "Anonymous Tips and Frisks: Determining Reasonable Suspicion," *FBI Law Enforcement Bulletin* (August 2000), pp. 28–30.

47. *Payton v. New York*.

48. *Arkansas v. Sanders*, 442 U.S. 753 (1979).

49. Michael L. Ciminelli, "Police Response to Anonymous Emergency Calls," *FBI Law Enforcement Bulletin* (May 2003), pp. 23–32.

50. *Warden v. Hayden*, 387 U.S. 294 (1967).

51. *Mincey v. Arizona*, 437 U.S/ 385 (1978).

52. *Maryland v. Buie*, 110 S.Ct. 1093 (1990).

53. *Wilson v. Arkansas*, 115 S.Ct. 1914 (1995).

54. *Illinois v. McArthur*, 531 U.S. 326 (2001).

55. *United States v. Holloway*, 290 F.3d 1331 (11th Cir., 2002); see also *State v. Applegate* 626 N.E.2d 942 (Ohio 1994), and *United States v. Richardson*, 208 F.3d 626 (7th Cir.), cert. denied, 531 U.S. 910 (2000).

56. Michael L. Ciminelli, "Police Response to Anonymous Emergency Calls," *FBI Law Enforcement Bulletin* (May 2003), pp. 23–31.

57. Jayme Walker Holcomb, "Consent Searches: Factors Courts Consider in Determining Voluntariness," *FBI Law Enforcement Bulletin* (May 2002), pp. 25–31; also see Holcomb, "Obtaining Written Consent to Search," *FBI Law Enforcement Bulletin* (March 2003), pp. 26–32.

58. *Schneckloth v. Bustamonte*, 412 U.S. 218 (1973).

59. *United States v. Matlock*, 415 U.S. 164 (1974).

60. *Bumper v. North Carolina*, 391 U.S. 543 (1968).

61. *Illinois v. Rodriguez*, 110 S.Ct. 2793 (1990).

62. *Florida v. Bostick*, 111 S.Ct. 2382 (1991).

63. Edward M. Hendrie, "Consent Once Removed," *FBI Law Enforcement Bulletin* (Feb. 2003), pp. 24–32.

64. *United States v. Pollard*, 215 F.3d 643 (6th Cir. 2000).

65. *Harris v. United States*, 390 U.S. 234 (1968). See also *Horton v. California* 110 S.Ct. 2301 (1990).

66. *Arizona v. Hicks*, 107 S.Ct. 1149 (1987).

67. *Mincey v. Arizona*.

68. Kimberly A. Crawford, "Crime Scene Searches: The Need for Fourth Amendment Compliance," *FBI Law Enforcement Bulletin* (Jan. 1999), pp. 26–31. For a complete discussion of crime scenes and crime scene procedures see John S. Dempsey, *An Introduction to Investigations*, 2nd ed. (Belmont, CA: Wadsworth, 2001), Chapter 3.

69. *Illinois v. Rodriguez*.

70. Kimberly A. Crawford, "Crime Scene Searches: The Need for Fourth Amendment Compliance."

71. *Abel v. United States*, 362 U.S. 217 (1960).

72. *California v. Greenwood*, 486 U.S. 35 (1988).

73. *California v. Hodari, D.*, 111 S.Ct. 1547 (1991).

74. *Colorado v. Bertine*, 479 U.S. 367 (1987).

75. *Hester v. United States*, 265 U.S. 57 (1924).

76. *Oliver v. United States*, 466 U.S. 170 (1984).

77. *California v. Ciraola*, 476 U.S. 207 (1986).

78. *Florida v. Riley*, 488 U.S. 445 (1989).

79. *Carroll v. United States*, 267 U.S. 132 (1925).

80. *New York v. Belton*, 453 U.S. 454 (1981).

81. *United States v. Ross*, 456 U.S. 454 (1981).

82. *United States v. Villamonte-Marquez*, 462 U.S. 579 (1983) and *California v. Carney*, 471 U.S. 386 (1985).

83. *California v. Acevedo*, 111 S.Ct. 1982 (1991); and *Florida v. Jimeno*, 111 S.Ct. 1801 (1991).

84. *Pennsylvania v. Labron*, 518 U.S. 938 (1996).

85. *Maryland v. Dyson*, 119 S.Ct. 2013 (1999).

86. *Wyoming v. Houghton*, 119 S.Ct. 1297 (1999). For an excellent article on the auto exception to the search warrant, see "The Motor Vehicle Exception: When and Where to Search," *FBI Law Enforcement Bulletin* (July 1999).

87. *United States v. Martinez-Fuerte*, 428 U.S. 543 (1976).

88. *United States v. Leon*, 468 U.S. 897 (1984).

89. *Massachusetts v. Sheppard*, 104 S.Ct.3424; *Illinois v. Krull*, 107 S.Ct. 1160 (1987); and *Maryland v. Garrison*, 107 S.Ct. 1013 (1987).

90. *Arizona v. Isaac Evans*, 514 U.S. 1 (1995).

91. *Burdeau v. McDowell*, 256 U.S. 465 (1921).

92. *United States v. Place*, 462 U.S. 696 (1983).

93. See Michael J. Bulzomi, "Drug Detection Dogs: Legal Considerations," *FBI Law Enforcement Bulletin* (Jan. 2000), pp. 27–31.

94. Michael J. Bulzomi, "Drug Detection Dogs: Legal Considerations," pp. 30–31.

95. Jayme S. Walker, "Using Drug Detection Dogs: An Update," *FBI Law Enforcement Bulletin* (April 2001), pp. 25 to 32

96. *Miranda v. Arizona*.

97. Kimberly A. Crawford, "Constitutional Rights to Counsel During Interrogation: Comparing Rights Under the Fifth and Sixth Amendments," *FBI Law Enforcement Bulletin* (Sept. 2002), pp. 28–32.

98. James W. Osterburg and Richard H. Ward, *Criminal Investigation: A Method for Reconstructing the Past* (Cincinnati, OH: Anderson Publishing, 1992), p. 377.

99. Louis DiPietro, "Lies, Promises, or Threats: The Voluntariness of Confessions," *FBI Law Enforcement Bulletin* (July 1993), pp. 27–32, p. 27.

100. *Brown v. Mississippi*.

101. *McNabb v. United States*, 318 U.S. 332 (1943); *Mallory v. United States*, 354 U.S. 449 (1957).

102. *Escobedo v. Illinois*, 378 U.S. 478 (1964).

103. *Miranda v. Arizona*.

104. Based on *Miranda v. Arizona*.

105. Lisa A. Judge, "Miranda Revisited," *Police Chief* (August 2003), pp. 13–15.

106. *Oregon v. Mathiason*, 429 U.S. 492 (1977).

107. *Berkemer v. McCarty*, 468 U.S. 420 (1984); *Beckwith v. United States*, 425 U.S. 341 (1976).

108. *Moran v. Burbine*, 475 U.S. 412 (1986); *Michigan v. Mosley*, 423 U.S. 96 (1975); *Edwards v. Arizona*, 451 U.S. 477 (1981); *Arizona v. Roberson*, 486 U.S. 675 (1988); and *Minnick v. Mississippi*, 495 U.S. 903 (1990).

109. *Colorado v. Connelly*, 107 S. Ct. 515 (1986).

110. *Arizona v. Roberson*.

111. Alan M. Dershowitz, *Taking Liberties: A Decade of Hard Cases, Bad Laws and Bum Raps* (Chicago: Contemporary Books, 1988), p. 10.

112. Dershowitz, *Taking Liberties: A Decade of Hard Cases, Bad Laws and Bum Raps*, p. 12.

113. *Harris v. New York*, 401 U.S. 222 (1971).

114. *Michigan v. Mosley*, 423 U.S. 96 (1975).

115. *Brewer v. Williams*, 430 U.S. 387 (1977).

116. *Nix v. Williams*, 467 U.S. 431 (1984).

117. *Rhode Island v. Innis*, 446 U.S. 291 (1980).

118. *New York v. Quarles*, 104 S.Ct. 2626 (1984).

119. *Moran v. Burbine*, 475 U.S. 412 (1986).

120. *Illinois v. Perkins*, 110 S.Ct. 2394 (1990).

121. *Pennsylvania v. Muniz*, 496 U.S. 582 (1990).

122. *Arizona v. Fulminante*, 111 S.Ct. 1246 (1991).

123. *Minnick v. Mississippi*, 111 S.Ct. 486 (1991).

124. *McNeil v. Wisconsin*, 111 S.Ct. 2204 (1991).

125. *Withrow v. Williams*, 112 S.Ct. 1745 (1993).

126. *Davis v. United States*, 114 S.Ct. 2350 (1994).

127. *Stansbury v. California*, 114 S.Ct. 1526 (1994).

128. *Dickerson v. United States* 20 S.Ct. 2326 (2000). See Thomas D. Petrowski, "*Miranda* Revisited: *Dickerson v. United States*," *FBI Law Enforcement Bulletin* (August 2001), pp. 25–32.

129. *Dickerson v. United States*; Sophia Y. Kil, "Supreme Court Cases: 1999–2000 Term," pp. 28–32.

130. Samuel C. Rickless, "*Miranda, Dickerson,* and the Problem of Actual Innocence," *Criminal Justice Ethics, 19*(2, Summer/Fall 2000), pp. 2–55.

131. *Texas v. Cobb*, 121 S.Ct. 1335 (2001); also see Kimberly A. Crawford, "The Sixth Amendment Right to Counsel: Application and Limitations," *FBI Law Enforcement Bulletin* (July 2001), pp. 27–32.

132. Kimberly A. Crawford, "Surreptitious Recording of Suspects' Conversations," *FBI Law Enforcement Bulletin* (Sept. 1993), pp. 26–32; also see Richard G. Schott, "Warrantless Interception of Communications: When, Where, and Why It Can Be Done," *FBI Law Enforcement Bulletin* (Jan. 2003), pp. 25–31.

133. *Stanley v. Wainwright*, 604 F.2d 379 (5th Cir. 1979).

134. *United States v. McKinnon*, 985 F.2d 1425 (11th Cir.), cert. denied, 510 U.S. 843 (1993).

135. *Kuhlmann v. Wilson*, 106 S.Ct. 2616 (1986).

136. *Ahmad A. v. Superior Court,* 263 Cal.Rptr. 747 (Cal.App. 2 Dist. 1989), cert. denied, 498 U.S. 834 (1990).

137. *Belmar v.. Commonwealth,* 553 S.E.2d 123 (Va App. Ct. 2001).

138. Crawford, "Surreptitious Recording of Suspects' Conversations," pp. 29–31.

139. *United States v. Wade,* 388 U.S. 218 (1967).

140. *Kirby v.. Illinois,* 406 U.S. 682 (1972).

141. *Stoval v. Denno,* 388 U.S. 293 (1967).

142. *United States v. O'Connor,* 282 F.Supp. 963 (D.D.C. 1968).

143. *United States v. Ash,* 413 U.S. 300 (1973).

144. *Schmerber v. California,* 384 U.S. 757 (1966).

145. *Winston v. Lee,* 470 U.S. 753 (1985).

146. *Schmerber v. California.*

147. *Winston v. Lee.*

148. *United States v. Dionisio,* 410 U.S. 1 (1973).

149. *United States v. Mara,* 410 U.S. 19 (1973).

150. "Eyewitness Evidence," *FBI Law Enforcement Bulletin* (July 2001), p. 15.

Chapter 12

1. James N. Gilbert, "Investigative Ethics," in Michael J. Palmiotto, ed., *Critical Issues in Criminal Investigations,* 2nd ed. (Cincinnati, OH: Anderson, 1988), pp. 7–14. This article is also contained in its entirety in John S. Dempsey, *An Introduction to Public and Private Investigations,* 2nd ed.(Minneapolis/ St. Paul:West, 1996), pp. 376–380.

2. Gilbert, "Investigative Ethics," p. 14.

3. See Joycelyn M. Pollock, *Ethics in Crime and Justice: Dilemmas and Decisions,* 4th ed. (Belmont, CA: Thomson/Wadsworth, 2004); Victor Kappeler, Richard Sluder, and Geoffrey Alpert, *Forces of Deviance, Understanding the Dark Side of Policing* (Prospect Heights, IL: Waveland Press, 1994); Jerome H. Skolnick and James J. Fyfe, *Above the Law: Police and the Excessive Use of Force* (New York: Free Press, 1993); Thomas Barker and David L. Carter, *Police Deviance* (Cincinnati, OH: Anderson, 1986); S. Bok, *Lying: Moral Choice in Public and Private Life* (New York: Pantheon, 1978); Frederick A. Elliston and Michael Feldberg, eds., *Moral Issues in Police Work* (Totowa, NJ: Rowman and Allanheld, 1985); W. Heffernan and T. Stroup, eds., *Police Ethics: Hard Choices in Law Enforcement* (New York: John Jay Press, 1985); and Carl B. Klockars, "The Dirty Harry Problem," *Annals of the American Association of Political and Social Science, 452*(November 1980), pp.33–37.

4. Michelle A. Mortensen and Michael Cortrite, "Ethics Training: A Passing Fad or Sustaining Component?" *Community Policing Exchange* (March/April1998). Retrieved on May 2, 2003, from www .communitypolicingt.org/

5. Aristotle, *Nicomachean Ethics, 1094*(a): 1–22.

6. Pollock, *Ethics in Crime and Justice,* pp. 140–141.

7. Pollock, *Ethics in Crime and Justice,* p. 149.

8. Albert Cantara, "Ramblings about Ethics: A Shrink Speaks," *Community Policing Exchange* (March/April1998). Retrieved on May 2, 2003, from www.communitypolicing.org/.

9. Found in Table 2.21, "Ratings of the Honesty and Ethical Standards of Various Occupations," in *Sourcebook of Criminal Justice Statistics, 2001.* Retrieved on January 4, 2002, from http:www.gallup.com/poll/topics /hnsty_ethics.asp.

10. Catherine Gallagher, Edward Maguire, Stephen D. Mastrofski, and Michael D. Reisig, "The Public Image of Police" (2001). Retrieved on March 27, 2003, from www.theiacp.org/.

11. Jerome Skolnick, *Justice without Trial: Law Enforcement in a Democratic Society,* 2d ed. (New York: Wiley, 1975).

12. Howard Abadinski, *Crime and Justice: An Introduction* (Chicago: Nelson Hall, 1987), p. 169.

13. Elmer Johnson, "Police: An Analysis of Role Conflict," (Paper presented at a symposium on criminology, Indiana State University at Terre Haute, 24 July 1969), as cited in Abadinsky, *Crime and Justice,* p. 169.

14. National Commission on Law Observance and Enforcement, *Report on Police* (Washington, DC: U.S. Government Printing Office, 1931); President's Commission on Law Enforcement and Administration of Justice, *The Challenge of Crime in a Free Society* (Washington, DC: U.S. Government Printing Office, 1968); National Advisory Commission on Criminal Justice Standards and Goals, *Police* (Washington, DC: U.S. Government Printing Office, 1973); and *Standards for Law Enforcement Agencies,* 2d ed. (Fairfax, VA: Commission on Accreditation for Law Enforcement Agencies, 1987).

15. Knapp Commission, *Report on Police Corruption* (New York: Braziller, 1973).

16. Vincent J. Palmiotto, "Legal Authority of Police," in *Police Misconduct* by Michael Palmiotto. (Upper Saddle River, NJ: Prentice-Hall, 2001).

17. Herman Goldstein, *Police Corruption: A Perspective on Its Nature and Control* (Washington, DC: The Police Foundation, 1975), p. 3.

18. Elliston and Feldberg, eds., *Moral Issues in Police Work.*

19. Richard J. Lundman, "Police Misconduct," in *The Ambivalent Force: Perspectives on the Police,* 3d ed., Abraham S. Blumberg and Elaine Niederhoffer, eds. (New York: Holt, Rinehart & Winston, 1985), p. 158.

20. Michael Feldberg, "Gratuities, Corruption and the Democratic Ethos of Policing: The Case of the Free Cup of Coffee," in *Moral Issues in Police Work,* ed. Elliston and Feldberg, p. 21.

21. Goldstein, *Police Corruption,* p. 29.

22. Peter Maas, *Serpico* (New York: Bantam Books, 1974).

23. Robert Daley, *Prince of the City: The Story of a Cop Who Knew Too Much* (Boston: Houghton Mifflin, 1978).

24. Mike McAlary, *Buddy Boys: When Good Cops Turn Bad* (New York: Putnam, 1987).

25. John Dorschner, "The Dark Side of Force," in *Critical Issues in Policing: Contemporary Readings,* Roger G. Dunham and Geoffrey P. Alpert, eds. (Prospect Heights, IL: Waveland Press, 1989), pp. 250–270.

26. Selwyn Raab, "Ex-Rogue Officer Tells Panel of Police Graft in New York," *New York Times* (Sept. 28, 1993), pp. A1, B3.

27. "On the Side of the Law? Not Necessarily," *Law Enforcement News* (Dec. 31, 1996), p. 19.

28. "On the Side of the Law?"

29. "Sentencing in City of Miami Cops Case,"press release from U.S. Department of Justice, U.S. Attorney for Southern District of Florida (Oct. 29, 2003). Retrieved on April 9, 2004, from www.usdoj.gov/isap/fls.

30. "Hart Broken in Detroit: Embezzlement Conviction Topples Veteran Chief," *Law Enforcement News* (May 15, 1992), p. 6.

31. "On the Side of the Law?"

32. Associated Press, "Former Miami City Manager Warshaw Loses Pension-Again." Retrieved on August 6, 2003, from www .sun-sentinel.com.

33. Peter Pochna, (2003, April 29). "Ex-Cop Admits Stealing $180,000." Retrieved on April 29, 2003, from www.northjersey.com.

34. "FBI Agent Who Spied Is Sentenced to 27 Years," *New York Times* (June 24, 1997), p. A14; Evan Thomas, "Inside the Mind of a Spy," *Newsweek* (July 7, 1997), p. 35.

35. "FBI Leader in Gambino Case Is Indicted," *New York Times* (June 27, 1997), p. B3. Also see Selwyn Raab, "Arrest of an Agent Threatens to Taint a Major Mob Case," *New York Times* (June 14, 1997), pp. A1, 26.

36. Andy Friedberg, and Jon Burstein, (2003, April 14). "Farrall Settles Suit in Deadly Collision." Retrieved on April 14, 2003, www .sun-sentinel.com.

37. Kappeler, Sluder, and Alpert, *Forces of Deviance, Understanding the Dark Side of Policing,* and Skolnick and Fyfe, *Above the Law;* and Palmietto, *Police Misconduct.*

38. Lawrence W. Sherman, ed., *Police Corruption: A Sociological Perspective* (Garden City, NY: Doubleday, 1974), p. 1.

39. Herman Goldstein, *Policing a Free Society* (Cambridge, MA: Ballinger Publishing, 1977), p. 218.

40. Frank Schmalleger, *Criminal Justice Today: An Introductory Text for the Twenty-first Century* (Englewood Cliffs, N.J.: Prentice-Hall, 1991), p. 191.

41. Samuel Walker, *The Police in America: An Introduction,* 2d ed. (New York: McGraw-Hill, 1992), pp. 175–177.

42. Thomas Barker and Julian Roebuck, *An Empirical Typology of Police Corruption: A Study in Organizational Deviance* (Springfield, IL: Charles C. Thomas, 1973), pp. 26–27.

43. Sherman, *Police Corruption,* p. 7.

44. Patrick V. Murphy and Thomas Plate, *Commissioner: A View from the Top of American Law Enforcement* (New York: Simon and Schuster, 1977).

45. Sherman, *Police Corruption.*

46. Lawrence W. Sherman, "Becoming Bent: Moral Careers of Corrupt Policemen," in *Police Corruption,* ed. Lawrence W. Sherman, pp. 191–208.

47. Douglas W. Perez, and J. Alan Moore, *Police Ethics: A Matter of Character.* (Cincinatti, OH: Atomic Dog Publishing, 2002), p. 134.

48. E. Delattre, *Character and cops,* 3rd ed. (Washington DC: AEI Press, 1996).

49. President's Commission on Law Enforcement and Administration of Justice, *Task Force Report: The Police* (Washington, DC: U.S. Government Printing Office, 1967), p. 208.

50. David Burnham, "How Police Corruption Is Built into the System— And a Few Ideas forWhat to Do about It," in *Police Corruption,* Lawrence W. Sherman, ed., pp. 310–311.

51. Edwin H. Sutherland and Donald Cressey, *Principles of Criminology,* 8th ed. (Philadelphia: Lippincott, 1970).

52. Schmalleger, *Criminal Justice Today,* p. 193.

53. National Commission on Law Observance and Enforcement, *Report on Police.*

54. James Q. Wilson, *Varieties of Police Behavior: The Management of Law and Order in Eight Communities* (Cambridge, MA: Harvard University Press, 1968).

55. Goldstein, *Police Corruption,* pp. 6–8.

56. "Police Officer Accused of Stealing $6,000," *New York Times* (June 28, 1997), p. 24; Rocco Parascandola, "Wash. Hts. Sting Bags 'Rogue Cop'", *New York Post* (June 28, 1997), p. 9.

57. David M. Herszenhorn, "Police in West New York Arrested in Bribery Inquiry; 9 Current and Former Officers are Charged," *New York Times* (Jan. 14, 1998), p. B5.

58. Marlon A. Defillo, "Police integrity-New Orleans Style," *Community Policing Exchange* (Mar/April1998). Retrieved on May 2, 2003, from www.communitypolicing.org.

59. Diana Marrero, "Miami Chief Reaches Out to Rank and File after Verdicts." Retrieved on April 11, 2003, from www.sun-sentinel.com.

60. "San Francisco Police Chief retires after brawl cover-up incident," *Associated Press.* Retrieved on August 11, 2003, from www. newsobserver.com.

61. Jeffrey Higginbotham, "Urinalysis Drug Testing Programs for Law Enforcement," *FBI Law Enforcement Bulletin* (Oct. 1986).

62. *National Treasury Employees Union* v. *Von Raab,* 489 U.S. 656 (1989).

63. Ordway Burden, "Police and Drug Abuse: What's All the Hullabaloo?" *Crime Control Digest* (June 15, 1987).

64. *Employee Drug Testing Policies in Police Departments* (Washington, DC: National Institute of Justice, 1986).

65. *Employee Drug Testing Policies.*

66. Nancy L. Othon, "Veteran Officer Held on Cocaine Charges." Retrieved on February 24, 2002, from www.sun-sentinel.com.

67. U.S. General Accounting Office, *Information on drug-related police corruption.* (Washington DC: #GAO/GGD-98-111, 1998).

68. U.S. General Accounting Office (1998).

69. U.S. Department of Justice, Southern District of Florida. Press release (Sept. 12, 2002). Retrieved from www.justice.gov/usao/fls.

70. Skolnick, *Justice without Trial,* pp. 42–49.

71. Danielle Hitz, "Drunken Sailors and Others: Drinking Problems in Specific Occupations," *Quarterly Journal of Studies on Alcohol,* 34(1973), pp. 496–505.

72. W. Kroes, *Society's Victim, The Policeman: An Analysis of Job Stress in Policing* (Springfield, IL: Charles C. Thomas, 1976); and R. C. Van Raalte, "Alcohol as a Problem among Officers," *Police Chief,* 44, pp. 38–40.

73. Gene Radano, *Walking the Beat: A New York Policeman Tells What It's Like on His Side of the Law* (Cleveland, OH: World Publishing, 1968), p. 13.

74. Joseph Wambaugh, *The Blue Knight* (Boston: Little, Brown, 1973).

75. Jerome H. Skolnick, "Deception by Police," in *Moral Issues in Police Work,* Elliston and Feldberg, eds., pp. 76–77.

76. *Mapp* v. *Ohio,* 367 U.S. 643 (1961).

77. Skolnick, "Deception by Police," pp. 76–77.

78. Tony G. Poveda, *Lawlessness and Reform: The FBI in Transition* (Pacific Grove, CA: Brooks/Cole, 1990), especially Chapters 4 and 5; see also Tony G. Poveda, "The Effects of Scandal on Organizational Deviance: The Case of the FBI," *Justice Quarterly,* 2(1985), pp. 237–258. Note: There are a myriad of books regarding the history of the FBI, some reflecting views differing from Poveda's.

79. "Officer Sentenced for Felony." Retrieved on May 2, 2003, from www.wtol.com.

80. Crystal Carreon, "San Jose Officer's deceit Raises Racial Tensions," *San Jose Mercury News.* Retrieved on May 25, 2003, from www.bayarea.com

81. Barker and Carter, *Police Deviance.*

82. Alan N. Kornblum, *The Moral Hazards* (Lexington, MA: Lexington Books, 1976), p. 6.

83. Robert D. Pursley, *Introduction to Criminal Justice,* 5th ed. (New York: Macmillan, 1991), p. 236.

84. P. B. Kraska and V. E. Kappeler, "To Serve and Pursue: Exploring Police Sexual Violence against Women, *Justice Quarterly*, 12(1), pp. 85–111.

85. Daniel Borunda, "Ex-Deputy Sentenced." Retrieved on June 18, 2003, from www.elpasotimes.com.

86. Jeremy Milarsky, "Ex-Margate Cop Gets 20 Months in Jail for Having Sex in Back Seat of Cruiser." Retrieved on March 4, 2002, from www.sun-sentinel.com.

87. Scott Hiaaasen, "Lakewood Officer Pleads to Charges, Admits Having Sex in Back of Cruiser." Retrieved on May 14, 2003, from www.cleveland.com.

88. Associated Press, "Ex-LA Police Officer Sentenced to Prison for On-Duty Rape." Retrieved on April 24, 2003, from www.bayarea.com/mid/mercurynews.

89. National Center for Women and Policing, Police Family Violence Fact Sheet. Retrieved on April 23, 2003, from www.womenandpolicing.org.

90. National Center for Women and Policing.

91. Michael Ko, "Brame Inquiry: Poor Judgment but No Charges" (Nov. 18, 2003). Retrieved on November 20, 2003, from http://seattletimes.nwsource.com.

92. Gerald D. Robin and Richard H. Anson, *Introduction to the Criminal Justice System,* 4th ed. (New York: Harper & Row, 1988), p. 86.

93. David Weisburd, Rosann Greenspan, Edwin H. Hamilton, Hubert Williams, and Kellie A. Bryant, *Police attitudes toward abuses of authority: Findings from a national study.* (Washington DC: U.S. Department of Justice, National Institute of Justice, 2002).

94. Albert J. Reiss, Jr., "Police Brutality," *Transaction Magazine,* 5(1968), reprinted in Richard J. Lundman, ed., *Police Behavior: A Sociological Perspective* (New York: Oxford University Press, 1980), pp. 274–275.

95. Luc Sante, *Low Life: Lures and Snares of Old New York* (New York: Farrar, Straus & Giroux, 1991), p. 247.

96. Sante, *Low Life,* p. 243.

97. Joseph P. Senna and Larry J. Siegel, *Introduction to Criminal Justice,* 5th ed. (St. Paul, MN: West, 1990), p. 265. For a complete discussion of the police and the third degree, see Dempsey, *Introduction to Public and Private Investigations* and Skolnick and Fyfe, *Above the Law.*

98. *Brown v. Mississippi,* 297 U.S. 278 (1936).

99. Samuel Walker, *Popular Justice* (New York: Oxford University Press, 1980), p. 197.

100. For an excellent analysis of the Rodney King incident and the history and tradition of police brutality, see Skolnick and Fyfe, *Above the Law.*

101. George Hackett et al., "All of Us Are in Trouble," *Newsweek* (Jan. 30, 1989), pp. 36–37.

102. *U.S. News and World Report* (Aug. 27, 1979), p. 27.

103. *U.S. News and World Report,* p. 27.

104. *Time* (Aug. 27, 1979), p. 27.

105. "Man Who Taped Beating to Be Extradited." Retrieved on July 13, 2002, from http://cnn.usnews.

106. Matt Lait, and Scott Glover, "Inglewood Officers Face More Abuse Allegations," *Los Angeles Times in Everett Herald* (July 15, 2002), p. A6.

107. Bill Girdner, "Charges of Racism by Calif. Police Is Latest in Long Line," *Boston Globe* (Jan. 19, 1989), p. 3.

108. President's Commission on Law Enforcement and Administration of Justice, *Task Force Report: The Police,* pp. 181–182.

109. Albert J. Reiss, Jr., *The Police and the Public* (New Haven, CT: Yale University Press, 1972).

110. Paul Chevigny, *Police Power: Police Abuses in New York City* (New York: Pantheon, 1969).

111. Peter Scharf and Arnold Binder, *The Badge and the Bullet: Police Use of Deadly Force* (New York: Praeger, 1983), p. 135.

112. David Bayley and James Garofalo, "The Management of Violence by Police Patrol Officers," Criminology, 27(1989), pp. 1–27.

113. Robin and Anson, *Introduction to the Criminal Justice System,* p. 86.

114. "Police Abuse Rare, Study Says," *New York Times* (Nov. 23, 1997), p. 29.

115. Carl B. Klockars, "The Only Way to Make Any Real Progress in Controlling Excessive Force by Police," *Law Enforcement News,* 15(May 1992), p. 12.

116. Samuel Walker, "The Rule Revolution: Reflections on the Transformation of American Criminal Justice, 1950–1988" (Working Papers, series 3, Institute for Legal Studies, University of Wisconsin Law School, Madison, December 1988), reprinted in Senna and Siegel, *Introduction to Criminal Justice,* p. 267.

117. National Minority Advisory Council on Criminal Justice, *The Inequality of Justice: A Report on Crime and the Administration of Justice in the Minority Community* (Washington, DC: U.S. Government Printing Office, 1980), pp. 15–16.

118. Gerald W. Lynch and Edward Diamond, "Police Misconduct," in *Encyclopedia of Crime and Justice,* vol. 3, Sanford H. Kadish, ed. (New York: Free Press, 1983), p. 1160.

119. Wayne Kerstetter, "Who Disciplines the Police? Who Should?" in *Police Leadership in America: Crisis and Opportunity,* William A. Geller, ed. (New York: Praeger, 1985), pp. 160–161.

120. U.S. Commission on Civil Rights, *Who Is Guarding the Guardians: A Report on Police Practices* (Washington, DC: U.S. Government Printing Office, 1981), p. 163.

121. "The Voters Speak: Miami Police Review Board Will Have to Make Do without Subpoena Powers," *Law Enforcement News* (Dec.15, 1991), p. 1.

122. Terry Hensley, "Civilian Reviews Boards: A Means to Police Accountability," *Police Chief,* (Sept. 1988), pp. 45–47.

123. Hensley, "Civilian Review Boards."

124. Albert J. Reiss, Jr., "Shaping and Servicing the Community: The Role of the Police Chief Executive," in *Police Leadership in America,* William A. Geller, ed., p. 61.

125. "Systems Failures: Albuquerque Police Oversight Mechanisms Blasted in Report," *Law Enforcement News* (May 31, 1997), pp. 1, 11.

126. "New Faces Look over Cops' Shoulders: Review Board, Auditor to Monitor Handling of Complaints against Tucson Cops," *Law Enforcement News* (April 30, 1997), p. 6.

127. Joe Farrow and Trac Pham, "Citizen Oversight of Law Enforcement: Challenge and Opportunity," *Police Chief Magazine,* 70(10, Oct. 2003), pp. 22–29.

128. U.S. Department of Justice, *Principles for promoting police integrity* (Washington DC: Department of Justice, 2001).

129. *Principles for promoting police integrity.*

130. *Principles for promoting police integrity.*

Chapter 13

1. Jack Kuykendall and David E. Burns, "The Black Police Officer: An Historical Perspective," *Journal of Contemporary Criminal Justice,* 1(1980), pp. 4–13.

2. Samuel Walker, "Employment of Black and Hispanic Police Officers," *Academy of Criminal Justice Sciences Today,* 10(1983), pp. 1–5.

3. Samuel Walker, *A Critical History of Police Reform: The Emergence of Professionalism* (Lexington, MA: Lexington Books, 1977), pp. 84–94.

4. U.S. Department of Justice, *Civil Service System: Affirmative Action and Equal Employment: A Guidebook for Employers,* vol. 1 (Washington, DC: U.S. Department of Justice, 1974).

5. Gerald Carden, *Police Revitalization* (Lexington, MA: Lexington Books, 1977).

6. Chloe Owings, *Women Police* (Montclair, NJ: Patterson Smith, 1969; originally published in 1925).

7. Catherine H. Milton, *Women in Policing* (Washington, DC: Police Foundation, 1972).

8. Samuel Walker, *The Police in America: An Introduction* (New York: McGraw-Hill, 1983), p. 24.

9. Timothy Egan, "New Faces, and New Roles, for the Police," in *Annual Editions: Criminal Justice 92/93,* John J. Sullivan, ed. (Guilford, CT: Dushkin Publishing, 1992), p. 96; reprinted from *The New York Times* (April 25, 1991), pp. A1, B10.

10. For an excellent look at the evolution of women as patrol officers, see educator and scholar Dorothy Moses Schulz's *From Social Worker to Crimefighter: Women in United States Municipal Policing* (New York: Praeger, 1995). Ms. Schulz is a former patrol captain with New York's Metro North Railroad Police and a professor at John Jay College of Criminal Justice in New York City. See the book review in Law Enforcement News (Sept. 15 1996), p. 13.

11. Kuykendall and Burns, "Black Police Officer."

12. Kuykendall and Burns, "Black Police Officer."

13. Nicholas Alex, *Black in Blue: A Study of the Negro Policeman* (New York: Appleton-Century-Crofts, 1969), pp. 87, 111.

14. Alex, *Black in Blue,* p. 87.

15. Nicholas Alex, *New York Cops Talk Back* (New York: Wiley, 1976).

16. Steven Leinen, *Black Police, White Society* (New York: New York University Press, 1984).

17. Leinen, *Black Police, White Society,* pp. 255–256.

18. National Advisory Commission on Civil Disorders, *Report* (Washington, DC: U.S. Government Printing Office, 1968), Chap. 11.

19. National Advisory Commission on Civil Disorders, *Report,* p. 322.

20. National Advisory Commission on Criminal Justice Standards and Goals, *Police* (Washington, DC: U.S. Government Printing Office, 1973), p. 343.

21. National Advisory Commission on Criminal Justice Standards and Goals, *Police,* p. 329.

22. *Law Enforcement News* (Oct. 1990), p. 1.

23. Charles R. Swanson, Leonard Territo, and Robert W. Taylor, *Police Administration: Structures, Processes, and Behavior,* 2d ed. (New York: Macmillan, 1988), p. 224.

24. Karla D. Shores, "Manors Should Hire an Openly Gay Officer, Mayor Says." Retrieved on January 22, 2002, from www.sunsentinel.com.

25. Shores, "Manors Should Hire."

26. Shores, "Manors Should Hire."

27. 42 U.S.C.S. 2000 et seq.

28. Public Law No. 92–261.

29. *Griggs* v. *Duke Power Company,* 401 U.S. 424 (1971).

30. U.S. Equal Employment Opportunity Commission, *Affirmative Action and Equal Employment,* vol. 2 (Washington, DC: U.S. Government Printing Office, 1974), p. D-2.

31. *Mieth v. Dollard,* 418 F. Supp. 1169 (1976).

32. *Vanguard Justice Society v. Hughes,* 471 F. Supp. 670 (1979).

33. E. Hernandez, "Problems and Implications in Validating Physical Ability Test Criteria in Law Enforcement" (Paper presented at the annual meeting of the American Society of Criminology), as cited in Larry K. Gaines, Mittie D. Southerland, and John E. Angell, *Police Administration* (New York: McGraw-Hill, 1991), p. 274.

34. P. Maher, "Police Physical Ability Tests: Can They Ever Be Valid?" *Public Personnel Management Journal,* 13, pp. 73–183.

35. D. Thompson and T. Thompson, "Court Standards for Job Analysis in Test Validation," *Personnel Psychology,* 35, pp. 865–874.

36. *Vulcan Society v. Civil Service Commission,* 5 FEP 1229 (1973).

37. United States v. State of New York, 21 FEP 1986 (1979).

38. *Guardians Association of New York City Police Department* v. *Civil Service Commission of New York,* 23 FEP 909 (1980).

39. U.S. Equal Employment Opportunity Commission, *Affirmative Action and Equal Employment,* vol. 2, pp. D15–D25.

40. Lawrence W. Sherman, "Enforcement Workshop: Minority Quotas for Promotions," *Criminal Law Bulletin* 15 (January/February 1979): 79–84.

41. Robert Sheehan and Gary W. Cordner, *Introduction to Police Administration,* 2d ed. (Cincinnati: Anderson, 1989), p. 135.

42. Charles R., Swanson, Leonard Territo, and Robert W. Taylor, *Police Administration,* 5th ed. (Upper Saddle River, NJ: Prentice-Hall, 2001).

43. James Jacobs and Jay Cohen, "The Impact of Racial Integration on the Police," *Journal of Police Science and Administration,* 6(1978), p. 182.

44. *Afro-American Patrolmen's League v. Duck,* 538 F.2d 328 (1976).

45. *Detroit Police Officers Association v. Young,* 46 U.S. Law Week 2463 (E.D. Mich. 1978). See also Sherman, "Enforcement Workshop," pp. 79–84.

46. "The State of the Union," *Law Enforcement News* (Jan. 15, 1996), p. 10.

47. The State of the Union," p. 18.

48. "Affirmative-Action Programs Looking a Little Black & Blue," *Law Enforcement News* (April 30, 1995), pp. 1, 7.

49. Peter B. Bloch and Deborah Anderson, *Policewomen on Patrol: Final Report* (Washington, DC: Police Foundation, 1974); and Joyce Sichel et al., Women on Patrol: A Pilot Study of Police Performance in New York City (Washington, DC: Department of Justice, 1978).

50. Sichel et al., *Women on Patrol,* foreword.

51. Sichel et al., *Women on Patrol,* foreword.

52. Anthony V. Bouza, "Women in Policing," *FBI Law Enforcement Bulletin* (Sept. 1975), pp. 4–7.

53. James David, "Perspectives of Policewomen in Texas and Oklahoma," *Journal of Police Science and Administration,* 12(1984), pp. 395–403.

54. Robert Homant and Daniel Kennedy, "Police Perceptions of Spouse Abuse: A Comparison of Male and Female Officers," *Journal of Criminal Justice,* 13(1985), pp. 49–64.

55. Loretta J. Stalans and Mary A. Finn, "Gender Differences in Officers' Perceptions and decisions about Domestic Violence Cases." *Women and Criminal Justice,* 11(3, 2000), pp. 1–24g.

56. Merry Morash and Jack Greene, "Evaluating Women on Patrol: A Critique of Contemporary Wisdom," *Evaluation Review* 10 (1986): 230–255.

57. Sean Grennan, "Findings of the Role of Officer Gender in Violent Encounters with Citizens," *Journal of Police Science and Administration* 15 (1988): 75–78.

58. Report of the Independent Commission on the Los Angeles Police Department (Los Angeles, CA: Independent Commission on the Los Angeles Police Department, 1991).

59. Zev Yarolslavsky, "Gender Balance in the Los Angeles Police Department," *WomenPolice* 26(3, Winter 1992), pp. 14–15.

60. Jeanne McDowell, "Are Women Better Cops?" *Time* (Feb. 17, 1992), pp. 70–72.

61. Kim Michelle Lersch, "Exploring Gender Differences in Citizen Allegations of Misconduct: An Analysis of a Municipal Police Department," *Women and Criminal Justice,* 9(4, 1998), pp. 69–79.

62. Richard M. Seklecki, "A Quantitative Analysis of Atttitude and Behavior Differences between Male and Female Police Officers toward Citizens in a Highly Conflictive and Densely Populated Urban Area." Paper presented at the Academy of Criminal Justice Sciences Annual Meeting in Washington, DC, April 2001.

63. Kristen Leger, "Public Perceptions of Female Police Officers on Patrol," *American Journal of Criminal Justice,* 21(2, 1997), pp. 231–249.

64. Diana R. Grant, "Perceived Gender Difference in Policing: The Impact of Gendered Perceptions of Officer-Situation Fit," *Women and Criminal Justice,* 12(1, 2000), pp. 53–74.

65. Michael Charles, "Women in Policing: The Physical Aspects," *Journal of Police Science and Administration,* 10(1982), pp. 194–205.

66. International Association of Chiefs of Police, "The Future of Women in Policing: Mandates for Action" (November, 1998). Retrieved on April 12, 2004, from www.theiacp.org/documents/index

67. Kimberly Lonsway, "The Role of Women in Community Policing: Dismantling the Warrior Image" (2001, September). Retrieved on April 12, 2004, from www.communitypolicing.org/publications/comlinks/.

68. National Center for Women and Policing, "Men, Women and Police Excessive Force: A Tale of Two Genders. A Content Analysis of Civil Liability Cases, Sustained Allegations and Citizen Complaints" (2002). Retrieved on April 12, 2004, from www.womenandpolicing.org.

69. Bruce Berg, Edmond True, and Marc Gertz, "Police, Riots, and Alienation," *Journal of Police Science and Administration,* 12(1984), pp. 186–190.

70. "Diversity Rules for Sheriff's Office: Minorities Are a Majority for San Francisco Agency," *Law Enforcement News* (Oct. 15, 1996), p. 7.

71. "For She's a Jolly Good Fellow. Watson Leaves Austin PD for COPS Office Visiting Fellowship," *Law Enforcement News* (Feb. 14,1997), p. 4.

72. "Meara Image," *Law Enforcement News* (Dec. 31, 1997), p. 16.

73. "First, Again," *Law Enforcement News* (Feb. 28, 1997), p. 4.

74. "Straight to the Top," *Law Enforcement News* (April 30, 1995), p. 4.

75. IACP, The Future of Women in Policing.

76. Matthew J Hickman and Brian A. Reaves, *Local Police Departments, 2000* (Washington DC: U.S. Department of Justice, Bureau of Justice Statistics, NCJ # 196002, 2003).

77. Dean J. Champion, *Criminal Justice in the United States* (Columbus, OH: Merrill, 1989), pp. 150–151.

78. Gaines, Southerland, and Angel, *Police Administration,* p. 455.

79. National Center for Women and Policing, The Effect of Consent Decrees on the Representation of Women in Sworn Law Enforcement (Spring 2003). Retrieved on April 12, 2004, from http://www .womenandpolicing.org/.

80. National Center for Women and Policing, The Status of Women in Policing: 2001 (April 2002). Retrieved on April 12, 2004, from http://www.womenand policing.org/.

81. "Father Figure," *Law Enforcement News* (Feb. 28, 1997).

82. "New Tune for Indiana SP: Superintendent Hopes to Have Agency Humming Along," *Law Enforcement News,* 15 April 1997.

83. Peggy Sullivan, "Minorities in Policing," in *Critical Issues in Policing,* Roger G. Dunham and Geoffrey P. Alpert, eds. (Prospect Heights, IL: Waveland Press, 1988), pp.331–345.

84. "He Accepts," *Law Enforcement News* (Dec. 31, 1996), p. 14.

85. Hickman and Reaves, *Local Police Departments, 2000.*

86. Adapted from "How State Patrol Stacks Up," *Everett Herald* (Sept. 13, 2002), p. 1B; and telephone interview with WSP Diversity Coordinator (April 12, 2004).

87. For an interesting and entertaining book on women and their history and experiences in law enforcement, see Connie Fletcher, *Breaking and Entering: Women Cops Break the Code of Silence to Tell Their Stories from the Inside* (New York: Simon & Schuster, 1995). Fletcher is also the author of two other books on law enforcement, *What Cops Know* and *Pure Cop.*

88. Gaines, Southerland, and Angel, *Police Administration,* p. 233.

89. Thomas Austin and Don Hummer, "What Do College Students Think of Policewomen? An Attitudinal Assessment of Future Law Enforcement Personnel," *Women and Criminal Justice,* 10(4, 1999), pp. 1–24.

90. William L. Pelkey and Michelle L. DeGrange, "Gender Bias in Field Training Evaluation Programs: An Exploratory Analysis," *Women and Criminal Justice,* 8(2, 1996), pp. 79–90.

91. Jennifer Lynn Gossett and Joyce E. Williams, "Perceived Discrimination among Women in Law Enforcement," *Women and Criminal Justice,* 10(1, 1998), pp. 53–73.

92. Lance D. Jones, "Matrons to Chiefs in One Short Century: The Transition of Women in U.S. Law Enforcement," *Women Police* (2003, Summer), pp. 6–9.

93. Carole Moore, "Pregnant Officer Policies," *Law and Order,* 51(9, Sept. 2003), pp. 73–78, p. 75.

94. Moore, "Pregnant Officer Policies," p. 76.

95. Donna Stuccio, "Blue Moon" *Women and Criminal Justice,* 14(1, 2002).

96. "The State of the Union," p. 9.

97. "The High Cost of Discrimination," *Law Enforcement News* (Dec. 31, 1996), p. 19.

98. Robert D. McFadden, "Darkness and Disorder in Subway: Questions Swirl in Police Shooting," *New York Times* (Nov. 20, 1992), pp. A1, B2.

99. Craig Wolff, "Alone, Undercover, and Black: Hazards of Mistaken Identity," *New York Times* (Nov. 22, 1992), pp. A1, A48.

100. Wolff, "Alone, Undercover, and Black," p. A48.

101. Clifford Krauss, "Undercover Police Ride Wide Range of Emotion: Boredom and the Adrenaline Rush," *New York Times* (August 1994), p. B3.

Chapter 14

1. John Ashcroft, *A Resource Guide to Law Enforcement, Corrections and Forensic Technologies,* (Washington, DC: U.S. Department of Justice, 2001), p. iii.

2. Matthew Hickman and Brian Reaves, *Local Police Departments 1999* (Washington, DC: Bureau of Justice Statistics, 2001); Mark Birchlet, "Computers in a Small Police Agency," *FBI Law Enforcement Bulletin* (1989), pp. 7–9.

3. Charles R. Swanson, Leonard Territo, and Robert W. Taylor, *Police Administration: Structures, Processes and Behavior* (New York: Macmillan, 1988), p. 367.

4. Bruce Williams, "Small Agencies Can Afford to Computerize," *Law and Order* (Dec. 1989), p. 45.

5. Christa Miller, "Mobile Computing Options for 21st Century Law Enforcement," *Law Enforcement Technology* (July 2002), pp. 34, 36–39, 40.

6. National Institute of Justice, *Local Police Departments,* 1993 (Washington, DC: National Institute of Justice, 1996), p. 18; and National Institute of Justice, *Sheriffs' Departments,* 1993 (Washington, DC: National Institute of Justice, 1996), p. 20. For two recent articles on CAD, see Donna Rogers, "CAD Selection 101: The Nuts and Bolts of Finding a CAD System That Works for You," *Law Enforcement Technology* (Oct. 2001), pp. 120–124, 126–127, and Charles E. Higginbotham, "High-Tech Solutions to Police Problems," *Police Chief* (Feb. 2003, pp. 32, 34–35, 36.

7. Swanson, Territo, and Taylor, *Police Administration,* pp. 381–383.

8. Jerome H. Skolnick and David H. Bayley, *The New Blue Line: Police Innovation in Six American Cities* (New York: Free Press, 1986), pp. 100–101.

9. Nassau County Police Department, *1990 Annual Report* (Mineola, NY: Nassau County Police Department, 1991).

10. Andrew K. Ruotolo Jr., "MDTs Aid Auto Theft Task Force," *Police Chief* (Sept. 1992), pp. 29–24.

11. Elizabeth Daigneau, "Calling All Citizens: A Growing Number of Municipalities are Using 'Reverse 911' to Alert Residents in the Event of an Emergency," *Governance* (July 2002), pp. 44–45.

12. "Cellular Digital Packet Data (CDPD) Technology Assists Plainclothes Officers," *Police Chief* (March 1997), pp. 14–15.

13. Federal Bureau of Investigation, *NCIC: National Crime Information Center.* Retrieved on August 17, 2002, from http://www.fbi.gov/hq/cjisd/ncic.htm; also see Stephanie L. Hitt, "NCIC 2000," *FBI Law Enforcement Bulletin* (July 2000), pp. 12–15; and Christopher Swope, "Sherlock Online," *Governing* (Sept. 2000), pp. 80–84.

14. Federal Bureau of Investigation, *NICS: National Instant Criminal Background Check System.* Retrieved on July 17, 2001, from http://www.fbi.gov/hq/cjisd/nics.htm.

15. For the latest on ViCAP see Eric W. Witzig, "The New ViCAP: More User-Friendly and Used by More Agencies," *FBI Law Enforcement Bulletin* (June 2003), pp. 1–7. For a further description of ViCAP and sample ViCAP Alerts see John S. Dempsey, *Introduction to Investigations,* 2nd ed. (Belmont, CA: Wadsworth, 2003), Chapter 10.

16. Preston Gralla, "Hollywood Confidential: PC Crime Fighters," *PC Computing* (Jan. 1989), p. 188.

17. Bill Clede, "Storing Massive Records," *Law and Order* (Jan. 1994), p. 45.

18. See Vincent E. Henry, *The Compstat Paradigm: Management Accountability in Policing, Business and the Public Sector* (New York: Looseleaf Law Publications, 2002); Howard Safir, *The Compstat Process* (New York: New York City Police Department, nd); William J. Bratton, "Great Expectations: How Higher Expectations for Police Departments Can Lead to a Decrease in Crime," Paper presented at the National Institute of Justice's Research Institute's "Measuring What Matters" Conference, Washington, DC, November 28, 1995; Rudolph W. Giuliani, Randy M. Mastro, and Donna Lynne, *Mayor's Management Report: The City of New York* (New York: City of New York, 1997); William W. Bratton and Peter Knobler, *Turnaround: How America's Top Cop Reversed the Crime Epidemic* (New York: Random House, 1998); Jeremy Travis, "Computerized Crime Mapping," *NIJ News* (Washington, DC: National Institute of Justice, 1999).

19. Travis, "Computerized Crime Mapping."

20. Gralla, "Hollywood Confidential: PC Crime Fighters," p. 188.

21. Sharon Hollis Sutter, "Holmes . . . Still Aiding Complex Investigations," *Law and Order* (Nov. 1991), pp. 50–52.

22. Sutter, "Holmes . . . Still Aiding Complex Investigations," p. 52.

23. Terry Morgan, "HITS/SMART: Washington State's Crime-Fighting Tool," *FBI Law Enforcement Bulletin* (Feb.2002), pp. 1–10; and Robert D. Keppel and Joseph G. Weis, "HITS: Catching Criminals in the Northwest," *FBI Law Enforcement Bulletin* (April 1993), pp. 14–19.

24. Lois Pilant, "Equipping a Forensics Lab," *Police Chief* (Sept. 1992), pp. 37–47.

25. "International News: Crime Analysis Program," *Law and Order* (July 1992), p. 6.

26. Lois Pilant, "Spotlight on . . . Computerized Criminal Investigations," Police Chief (Jan. 1993), pp. 39–41.

27. Robert Sheehan and Gary W. Cordner, *Introduction to Police Administration,* 2d ed. (Cincinnati, OH: Anderson, 1989), p. 419.

28. Sheehan and Cordner, *Introduction to Police Administration,* p. 422.

29. "PG County Police Opt for Computer-Aided System to Red-Flag Stressed-Out Officers," *Law Enforcement News* (June 30, 1997), p. 5.

30. Swanson, Territo, and Taylor, *Police Administration,* pp. 380–381.

31. Sheehan and Cordner, *Introduction to Police Administration,* p. 428.

32. Julie Wartell, "Putting Crime on the Map," *Police* (June 2000), pp. 52–55.

33. For a brief but interesting history of the use of fingerprints as identification see John S. Dempsey, *Introduction to Investigations,* 2nd ed. (Belmont, CA: Wadsworth, 2003), Chapter 6.

34. Federal Bureau of Investigation, "Fingerprint Identification: An Overview." Retrieved on June 12, 2001, from http://www.fbi.gov/hq/cjisd/ident.htm.

35. Curtis C. Frame, "Lifting Latent Prints in Dust," *Law and Order* (June 2000), p. 75; also see Frame, "Picking Up Latent Prints in Dust," *Police Chief* (April 2000), p. 180.

36. "High-Tech Crime Hunters," *Popular Mechanics* (Dec. 1991), p. 30.

37. T. F. Wilson and P. L. Woodard, *Automated Fingerprint Identification Systems—Technology and Policy Issues* (Washington, DC: U.S. Department of Justice, 1987), p. 5.

38. Harold J. Grasman, "New Fingerprint Technology Boosts Odds in Fight against Terrorism," *Police Chief* (Jan. 1997), pp. 23–28.

39. U.S. Congress, Office of Technology Assessment, *Criminal Justice: New Technologies and the Constitution: A Special Report* (Washington DC: U.S. Government Printing Office, 1988), p. 18.

40. William Folsom, "Automated Fingerprint Identification Systems," *Law and Order* (July 1986), pp. 27–28.

41. Los Angeles Police Department, *Annual Report, 1985* (Los Angeles: Los Angeles Police Department, 1986), p. 26.

42. William Stover, "Automated Fingerprint Identification—Regional Application of Technology," *FBI Law Enforcement Bulletin* 53 (1984), pp. 1–4.

43. Judith Blair Schmitt, "Computerized ID Systems," *Police Chief* (Feb. 1992), p. 35.

44. Schmitt, "Computerized ID Systems."

45. Schmitt, "Computerized ID Systems."

46. John Ryan, "AFIS Pays Big Dividends For a Small City," *Law and Order* (June 2000), p. 70–72.

47. "Something for Everyone in High-tech," *Law Enforcement News* (Dec. 15/31, 1998), p. 17.

48. "Mobile Identification Technology," *Law and Order* (June 2000), pp. 76–78; Stephen Coleman, "Biometrics: Solving Cases of Mistaken Identity and More," *FBI Law Enforcement Bulletin* (June 2000), pp. 9–16.

49. Tony Lesce, "Verafind AFIS System: Flexible and Software Based," *Law and Order* (Dec. 1994), pp. 53–54.

50. Rebecca Kanable, "Live-Scan Is Making Its Print," *Law Enforcement Technology* (April 1999), pp. 77–81.

51. FBI, "Integrated Automated Fingerprint Identification system (IAFIS)." Retrieved on June 12, 2001, from http://www.fbi.gov/hq/lab/org/systems.htm.

52. FBI, "Latent Print Unit." Retrieved on June 2, 2001, from http://www.fbi.gov/hq/lab/org/lpu.htm.

53. "INS, FBI Plan a $200M Wedding—Of Their Fingerprint Databases," *Law Enforcement News* (March 31, 2000), p. 7.

54. Rebecca Kanable, "Fingerprints Making the Case: AFIS and IAFIS Are Helping Find Matching Prints, But There Are More To Be Found," *Law Enforcement Technology* (March 2003), pp. 48, 50–53.

55. Rebecca Kanable, "Grip on Identification Information," *Law Enforcement Technology* (June 2000), pp. 122–126.

56. Dominic Andrae, "New Zealand Fingerprint Technology," *Law and Order* (Nov. 1993), pp. 37–38.

57. "NAFIS Launched in South Wales," *Law and Order* (June 2000), p. 74.

58. Tony Doonan, "Palmprint Technology Comes of Age,"*Law and Order* (Nov. 2000), pp. 63–65.

59. See Ronnie Paynter, "Less-Lethal Weaponry, Law Enforcement Technology, (Oct. 1999), pp. 78–84; and Lois Pilant, *Less-Than-Lethal Weapons: New Solutions for Law Enforcement* (Alexandria, VA: International Association of Chiefs of Police, 2000).

60. Christopher Reilly, "The Science of Pepper Spray," *Law and Order* (July 2003), pp. 124–130; and Bill Clede, "A Banquet of Aerosol Sprays," *Law and Order* (Sept. 1992), pp. 57–59.

61. Michael Cooper, "Hoping for Less Lethal Force, Police to Switch to Stronger Pepper Spray," *New York Times* (March 27, 1997), p. B3. See also "NYPD Wants More Potent Pepper," *Law Enforcement News* (April 30, 1997), p. 7.

62. Cooper, "Hoping for Less Lethal Force."

63. "OC Is OK: Pepper Spray Gets a Qualified Thumbs-Up," *Law Enforcement News* (April 30, 1997), p. 7. See also Cooper, "Hoping for Less Lethal Force."

64. "Pepper Sprays Get Yet Another Shake," *Security Management* (Aug. 2003), p. 18.

65. For a recent report on the Taser, see George T. Williams and Richard V. Simon, "Tasertron's 95HP: The Law Enforcement Taser," *Law and Order* (Nov. 2001), pp. 80–83.

66. Grey Meyer, "Nonlethal Weapons vs. Conventional Police Tactics: Assessing Injuries and Liabilities," *Police Chief* (Aug. 1992), p. 13. See also Sherri Sweetman, *Report on the Attorney General's Conference on Less-Than-Lethal Weapons* (Washington, DC: U.S. Government Printing Office, 1987).

67. John Graham, "Officers Armed with Beanbags," *Law and Order* (June 1997), pp. 67–68.

68. Joan A. Hopper, "Less-Lethal Litigation: Departments and the Courts React to Less-Lethal Standards," *Law and Order* (Nov. 2001), pp. 87–91.

69. J. P. Morgan, "Oleoresin Capsicum Policy," *Police Chief* (Aug. 1992), p. 26.

70. Meyer, "Nonlethal Weapons vs. Conventional Police Tactics," pp. 15–16.

71. Meyer, "Nonlethal Weapons vs. Conventional Police Tactics," p. 18.

72. *Michenfelder v. Sumner,* 860 F.2d 328 (9th Cir. 1988).

73. Peter D. Button, *Less-Lethal Force Technology,* (Toronto: Toronto Metropolitan Police Commission, 2001).

74. T. Donnelly, *Less Lethal Technologies: Initial Prioritisation and Evaluation* (London: Great Britain Home Office, Policing and Reducing Crime Unit, 2001).

75. Dale Yeager, "Less Lethal: A New Look at the State of Tactical Training, *Law Enforcement Technology* (Oct. 2002), pp. 52, 54–56.

76. For a comprehensive article on advanced surveillance devices, see Lois Pilant, "Spotlight on . . . Achieving State-of-the-Art Surveillance," *Police Chief* (June 1993), pp. 25–34.

77. Albert E. Brandenstein, "Advanced Technologies Bolster Law Enforcement's Counterdrug Efforts," *Police Chief* (Jan. 1997), pp. 32–34.

78. Tom Yates, "Surveillance Vans," *Law and Order* (Dec. 1991), pp. 52, 56.

79. Yates, "Surveillance Vans," p. 53.

80. Bill Siuru, "Seeing in the Dark and Much More: Thermal Imaging," *Law and Order* (Nov. 1993), pp. 18–20.

81. Siuru, "Seeing in the Dark and Much More: Thermal Imaging," pp. 18–20."

82. Yates, "'Eyes' in the Night," *Law and Order* (Nov.1993), pp. 19–24.

83. Donna Rogers, "Contraband Cops: U.S. Customs and Border Patrol Agents Stem the Tide of Smuggling with High-Tech Tools," *Law Enforcement Technology* (April 2000), pp. 68–72.

84. R. Paynter, "Images in the Night: Law Enforcement Sheds Light on Applications for Night Vision Technologies," *Law Enforcement Technology* (May 1999), pp. 22–26.

85. Donna Rogers, "GPS: Getting the Proper Positioning," *Law Enforcement Technology* (Sept. 2000), pp. 44–50; See also, National Institute of Justice, *GPS Applications in Law Enforcement: The SkyTracker Surveillance System, Final Report* (Washington, DC: National Institute of Justice, 1998).

86. Keith Harries, *Mapping Crime: Principle and Practice* (Washington, DC: National Institute of Justice, 1999); Ron Mercer, Murray Brooks, and Paula T. Bryant, "Global Positioning Satellite System: Tracking Offenders in Real Time," *Corrections Today* (July 2000), pp. 76–80; Bill Siuru, "Tracking 'Down': Space-Age GPS Technology Is Here," *Corrections Technology and Management* (Sept.–Oct. 1999), pp. 1–14.

87. National Sheriffs' Association, "Law Enforcement Aircraft: A Vital Force Multiplier," (Jan.–Feb. 2000), pp. 32–60.

88. John J. Pavlis, "Mug-shot Imaging Systems," *FBI Law Enforcement Bulletin* (Aug. 1992), pp. 20–22.

89. "Pavlis, "Mug-shot Imaging Systems," p. 22.

90. "Darrel L. Sanders, "The Critical Role of Technology," *Police Chief* (July 1997), p. 6.

91. "Picture This: Digital Photos Beam from Texas to Virginia via High-Tech Patrol Cars," *Law Enforcement News* (June 15, 1997), p. 1.

92. Stephen Coleman, "Biometrics: Solving Cases of Mistaken Identity and More," *FBI Law Enforcement Bulletin* (June 2000), p. 13.

93. "High-Tech Crime Hunters," p. 31.

94. "High-Tech Crime Hunters," p. 31. See also Gene O'Donnell, "Forensic Imaging Comes of Age," *FBI Law Enforcement Bulletin* (Jan. 1994), pp. 5–10.

95. "High-Tech Crime Hunters," p. 31. See also O'Donnell, "Forensic Imaging Comes of Age."

96. "No More Pencils, No More Books?" *Law Enforcement News* (Jan. 31, 1998), p. 5.

97. "The Face is Familiar—and Computer-Generated," *Law Enforcement News* (Oct. 31, 1999), p. 7.

98. Donna Rogers, "Drawing the Line," *Law Enforcement Technology* (May 2003), pp. 44, 46–50.

99. Marc H. Caplan and Joe Holt Anderson, *Forensic: When Science Bears Witness* (Washington, DC: National Institute of Justice, 1984), p. 2.

100. Peter R. DeForest, N. Petraco, and L. Koblinsky, "Chemistry and the Challenge of Crime," in S. Gerber, ed. *Chemistry and Crime* (Washington, DC: American Chemical Society, 1983), p. 45.

101. David Johnston, "Report Criticizes Scientific Testing at FBI Lab: Serious Problems Cited," *New York Times* (April 16, 1997), pp. A1, D23; Mireya Navarro, "Doubts about FBI Lab Raise Hopes for Convict: On Death Row, but Seeking a New Trial," *New York Times* (April 1997), p. A8.

102. "What's Wrong at the FBI?: The Fiasco at the Crime Lab," *Time* (April 28, 1997), pp. 28–35.

103. Belinda Luscombe, "When the Evidence Lies: Joyce Gilchrist Helped Send Dozens to Death Row. The Forensic Scientist's Errors Are Putting Capital Punishment under the Microscope," *Time* (May 21, 2001), pp. 37–40.

104. "Indiana: DNA Evidence Under Review," *New York Times* (July 19, 2003), p. A10.

105. Joseph L. Peterson, *Use of Forensic Evidence by the Police and Courts* (Washington, DC: National Institute of Justice, 1987).

106. "Hey Buddy, Got a Match? New System Does for Bullets What AFIS Did for Prints," *Law Enforcement News* (April 30, 1994), p. 1.

107. Terry L. Knowles, "Meeting the Challenges of the 21st Century," *Police Chief* (June 1997), pp. 39–43.

108. "ATF Tightens Screws on Illicit Gun Sales with Gun- & Bullet-Tracing Databases," *Law Enforcement News* (Feb. 14, 2000), pp. 1, 6.

109. Carl E. King, "Make Drug Testing a Positive Experience," *Security Management* (Nov. 1993), pp. 22–26, p. 25.

110. Robert D. McCrie, ed., *Security Letter Source Book* (New York: Security Letter, Inc., 1992), p. 62.

111. Richard A. Dusak, "Automated Handwriting Technology a Boon to Police," *Police Chief* (Jan. 1997), pp. 39–41

112. American Society of Crime Laboratory Directors. Retrieved on May 31, 2001, from http://www.ascld.org.

113. Pilant, "Crime Laboratory Developments," *Police Chief* (June 1997), p. 31.

114. Saferstein, *Criminalistics: An Introduction to Forensic Science,* 7th ed., pp. 353–394.

115. Judith Martin, "The Power of DNA," *Law and Order* (May 2001), pp. 31–35.

116. Peter J. Neufeld and Neville Colman, "When Science Takes the Witness Stand," *Scientific American* (May 1990), p. 46.

117. Warren E. Leary, "Genetic Record to be Kept on Members of Military," *New York Times* (Jan. 12, 1992), p. A15.

118. C. Thomas Caskey and Holly A. Hammond, *Automated DNA Typing: Method of the Future?* (Washington, DC: National Institute of Justice, 1997), p. 1.

119. Federal Bureau of Investigation, *DNA Analysis.* Retrieved on June 2, 2001, from http://www.fbi.gov/hq/lab/org/dnau.htm.

120. Knowles, "Meeting the Challenges of the 21st Century," pp. 39–43.

121. Federal Bureau of Investigation, *Combined DNA Index System (CODIS).* Retrieved on June 2, 2001, from http:www.fbi.gov/hq/lab/org/systems.htm.

122. National Commission on the Future of DNA Testing, *The Future of Forensic DNA Testing: Predictions of the Research and Development Working Group* (Washington, DC: National Institute of Justice, 2000), pp. 19–20. For the latest information on DNA, see the following reports: National Institute of Justice, *Using DNA to Solve Cold Cases* (Washington, DC: National Institute of Justice, 2002); Executive Office of the President of the United States, *Advancing Justice through DNA Technology* (Washington, DC: National Institute of Justice, 2003); National Institute of Justice, *Report to the Attorney General on Delays in Forensic DNA Analysis* (Washington, DC: National Institute of Justice, 2003); Nicholas P. Lovich, Travis C. Pratt, Michael J. Gaffney, and Charles J. Johnson, *National Forensic DNA Study Report* (Washington, DC: National Institute of Justice, 2004).

123. Martin, "The Power of DNA," pp. 30–35.

124. Jeff Wise and Richard Li, "The Future of DNA Evidence," *Crime and Justice International,* 19(70, Feb. 2003), pp. 31–32.

125. Janet C. Hoeffel, "The Dark Side of DNA Profiling: Unreliable Scientific Evidence Meets the Criminal Defendant," *Stanford Law Review,* 42(1990), pp. 465–538.

126. *Frye v.. United States, 293 F. 1013 (D.C. Cir.) 1923.*

127. "DNA Fingerprinting ID Method May Streamline Investigations," *Current Reports: BNA Criminal Practice Manual,* 1(19, 1987), p. 1.

128. Ronald Sullivan, "Appeals Court Eases Rules on Genetic Evidence," *New York Times* (Jan.11, 1992), p. 8.

129. "Supreme Court Clarifies Ruling on Admitting Scientific Evidence," *Criminal Justice Newsletter* (Dec. 1, 1997), p. 1.

130. "DNA Typing Endorsed by National Academy of Sciences," *CJ Update* (Fall 1992), p. 1.

131. National Commission on the Future of DNA Evidence, *The Future of Forensic DNA Testing . . .* , p. v.

132. National Commission on the Future of DNA Evidence, *The Future of Forensic DNA Testing . . .* , p. 1.

133. National Commission on the Future of DNA Evidence, *The Future of Forensic DNA Testing . . .* , pp. 3–6.

134. "The Truth Is in Your Genes," *Law Enforcement News* (Dec. 15/31, 2000), p. 7.

135. Rebecca S. Peterson, "DNA Databases: When Fear Goes Too Far," *American Criminal Law Review,* 37(3, Summer 2000), pp. 1219–1237.

136. Executive Office of the President of the United States, *Advancing Justice Through DNA Technology.*

137. Nicholas Lovrich, Travis C. Pratt, Michael J. Gaffney, and Charles J. Johnson, *National Forensic DNA Study Report* (Washington, DC: National Institute of Justice, 2004.)

138. Josee Charron, "Canada's DNA Data Bank: A Valuable Resource for Criminal Investigators," *Canadian Police Chief Magazine* (Winter 2003), pp. 19–21; and W.R. Kuperus et al., "Crime Scene Links through DNA Evidence: The Practical Experience From Saskatchewan Casework," *Journal of the Canadian Society of Forensic Science,* 36(1, March 2003), pp. 19–28.

139. Jenny Mouzos, *Investigating Homicide: New Responses for an Old Crime* (Canberra ACT: Australia, Australian Institute of Criminology, 2001).

140. National Commission on the Future of DNA Evidence, *What Every Law Enforcement Officer Should Know about DNA Evidence* (Washington, DC: National Institute of Justice, 2000).

141. National Institute of Justice, *Understanding DNA Evidence: A Guide for Victim Service Providers* (Washington, DC: National Institute of Justice, 2001).

142. Tod W. Burke and Jason M. Rexrode, "DNA Warrants," *Law and Order* (July 2000), pp. 121–124.

143. William K. Rashbaum, "New York Pursues Old Cases of Rape Based Just on DNA: Indicting with No Name: May Allow Hundreds of Crimes to Be Prosecuted Despite Statute of Limitations," *New York Times* (Aug. 5, 2003), pp. A1, B6.

144. Coleman, "Biometrics: Solving Cases of Mistaken Identity and More."

145. J. A. West, *Facial Identification Technology and Law Enforcement* (Sacramento, CA: California Commission on Peace Officer Standards and Training, 1996).

146. Visionics Corporation, *Adaptive Surveillance: A Novel Approach to Facial Surveillance for CCTV Systems, Final Progress Report* (Jersey City, NJ: Visionics Corporation, 2001).

147. Stephen Coleman, "Biometrics: Solving Cases of Mistaken Identity and More," *FBI Law Enforcement Bulletin* (June 2000), p.13.

148. Associated Press, "High-Tech Security on Tampa Streets." Retrieved on July 3, 2001, from http://www.washingtonpost.com; Dana Canedy, "Tampa Scans the Faces in Its Crowds for Criminals," *New York Times* (July 4, 2001), pp. A1, A11.

149. Michael Giacoppo, "The Expanding Role of Videotape in Court," *FBI Law Enforcement Bulletin* (Nov. 1991), p. 3.

150. Dale Stockton, "Police Video: Up Close and Personal," *Law and Order* (Aug. 1999), pp. 78–82; Ronnie L. Paynter, "Patrol Car Video," *Law Enforcement Technology* (June 1999), pp. 34–37; Giacoppo, "The Expanding Role of Videotape."

151. Joseph G. Estey, "2,000 Survivors' Club Hits: In the Past 10 Years, 2,000 Officers Have 'Dressed For Survival'," *Police Chief* (May 1997), p. 19.

152. Douglas Page, "Small Fry Robots Becoming Big Law Enforcement Deal," *Law Enforcement Technology* (May 2002), pp. 34–37; Douglas Page, "Get Smart: A Bomb 'Bot with Know-How," *Law Enforcement Technology* (July 2002), pp. 136, 138–140, 142; Lois Pilant, "Spotlight on . . . Equipping a Bomb Unit," *Police Chief* (Oct. 1992), pp. 58–67.

153. U.S. Congress, Office of Technology Assessment, Criminal Justice.

154. "High-Tech Crime Hunters," p. 31.

155. *California v. Ciraolo, 476 U.S. 207 (1986).*

156. Alan M. Dershowitz, *Taking Liberties: A Decade of Hard Cases, Bad Laws, and Bum Raps* (Chicago: Contemporary Books, 1988), p. 209.

Chapter 15

1. BJS, "Law Enforcement Officers Most at Risk for Workplace Violence." Retrieved on April 16, 2004, from www.ojp.usdoj.gov/bjs/abstract/vw99.htm.

2. Barbara Raffel Price, as quoted in Karen Polk, "New York Police: Caught in the Middle and Losing Faith," *Boston Globe* (Dec. 28, 1988), p. 3.

3. BJS, *Policing and Homicide, 1976–1998: Justifiable Homicide by Police, Police Officers Murdered by Felons.* (Washington DC: Department of Justice, NCJ# 180987, 2001).

4. BJS, *Policing and Homicide, 1976–1998.*

5. BJS, *Local Police Departments.* (Washington, DC: Department of Justice, 2003).

6. BJS, *Policing and Homicide, 1976–1998.*

7. U.S. Department of Justice, "Uniform Crime Reporting Program Releases LEOKA Statistics for 2002" (Nov. 17, 2003). Retrieved on April 16, 2004, from http://www.fbi.gov/pressrel/pressrel103/leoka02press.htm.

8. U.S. Department of Justice, "Law Enforcement Officers Killed and Assaulted, 2001" (Dec. 2, 2002). Retrieved September 4, 2003, from http://www.fbi.gov/pressrel/pressrel102/leoka120202.htm.

9. Maguire and Pastore, *Sourcebook-1996,* Table 3.16, p. 356. Table 15.3 lists reasons for the accidental deaths of police officers from 1980 to 1995.

10. U.S. Department of Justice, "Law Enforcement Officers Killed and Assaulted, 2001."

11. William Geller and Michael S. Scott, *Deadly Force: What We Know* (Washington, DC : Police Executive Research Forum, 1992), pp. 549–550.

12. David Lester, "The Murder of Police Officers in American Cities," *Criminal Justice and Behavior* (Jan. 1984), pp. 101–113.

13. William Geller, "Deadly Force: What We Know," *Journal of Police Science and Administration, 10*(1982), pp. 151–177.

14. Frances T. Cullen et al., "Paradox in Policing: A Note on Perceptions of Danger," *Journal of Police Science and Administration, 11*(1983), pp. 457–462.

15. National Law Enforcement Officers Memorial Fund, "Police Facts" (June 11, 2003). Retrieved on August 26, 2003, from http://www.nleomf.com/factsfigures/polfacts.html

16. Concerns of Police Survivors, Inc. Retrieved on May 30, 2004, from http://www.national cops.org.

17. U.S. Department of Justice, "Law Enforcement Officers Killed and Assaulted, 2001."

18. U.S. Department of Justice, "Uniform Crime Reporting Program Releases LEOKA Statistics for 2002."

19. Centers for Disease Control and Prevention, "Basic Statistics" (Dec. 2003). Retrieved on April 16, 2004, from http://www.cdc.gov/hiv/stats.htm.

20. IACP, "HIV/AIDS Prevention: Concepts and Issues Paper" (May 1,2000).

21. Theodore M. Hammett and Walter Bond, *Risks of Infection with the AIDS Virus through Exposures to Blood* (Washington, DC: National Institute of Justice, 1987).

22. IACP, "HIV/AIDS Prevention."

23. Federal Bureau of Investigation, "Collecting and Handling Evidence Infected with Human Disease-causing Organisms," *FBI Law Enforcement Bulletin,* July 1987.

24. Theodore M. Hammett, *Precautionary Measures and Protective Equipment: Developing a Reasonable Response* (Washington, DC: National Institute of Justice, 1988).

25. Theodore M. Hammett, *AIDS and the Law Enforcement Officer: Concerns and Policy Responses* (Washington, DC: National Institute of Justice, 1987).

26. IACP, "HIV/AIDS Prevention."

27. James Q. Wilson, "Police Use of Deadly Force," *FBI Law Enforcement Bulletin* (August 1980), p. 16.

28. James J. Fyfe, "Police Use of Deadly Force: Research and Reform," *Justice Quarterly, 5*(1988), pp. 164–205.

29. BJS, *Policing and Homicide, 1976–1998.*

30. BJS, *Policing and Homicide, 1976–1998.*

31. BJS, *Policing and Homicide, 1976–1998.*

32. BJS, *Policing and Homicide, 1976–1998.*

33. BJS, *Policing and Homicide, 1976–1998.*

34. Gerald Robin, "Justifiable Homicide by Police," *Journal of Criminal Law, Criminology, and Police Science* (May/June 1963), pp. 225–231.

35. James J. Fyfe, "Reducing the Use of Deadly Force: The New York Experience," in *Police Use of Deadly Force* (Washington, DC: National Institute of Justice, 1978), p. 29.

36. William A. Geller and Kevin J. Karales, *Split-Second Decisions* (Chicago: Chicago Law Enforcement Study Group, 1981), p. 119.

37. James Fyfe, "Shots Fired" (Ph.D. dissertation, State University of New York, Albany, 1978).

38. David Lester, "Predicting the Rate of Justifiable Homicide by Police Officers," *Police Studies,* 16(1993), p. 43; see also Kania and Mackey, "Police Violence."

39. Michael D. White, "Identifying Situational Predictors of Police Shootings Using Multivariate Analysis," *Policing, 25*(4, 2002), pp. 726–752.

40. Florangela Davila, "Study: People more likely to see blacks as a threat," *Seattle Times* (July 9, 2003), pp. B1–B2.

41. Lawrence O'Donnell, *Deadly Force* (New York: William Morrow, 1983), p. 14. See also Abraham Tennenbaum, "The Influence of the Garner Decision on Police. Use of Deadly Force," *Journal of Law and Criminology,* 85(1994).

42. James J. Fyfe, "Administrative Interventions on Police Shooting Discretion: An Empirical Analysis," *Journal of Criminal Justice,* 7(1979), pp. 309–323; and James J. Fyfe, cited in O'Donnell, *Deadly Force.*

43. Fyfe, "Police Use of Deadly Force," p. 181.

44. Lawrence W. Sherman and Ellen G. Cohn, *Citizens Killed by Big-City Police, 1970–1984* (Washington, DC: Crime Control Institute, 1986).

45. *Law Enforcement News* (Nov. 15, 1995), p. 1. See also John S. Dempsey, *West Home Page,* April 1996.

46. BJS, *Local Police Departments.*

47. BJS, *Local Police Departments.*

48. Thomas Aveni, "Special Report: Firearms Following Standard Procedure-A Long Term Analysis of Gunfights and Their Effects on Policy and Training," *Law and Order,* 51(8, Aug. 2003), pp. 78–87.

49. Aveni, "Special Report."

50. Aveni, "Special Report."

51. Aveni, "Special Report."

52. Aveni, "Special Report."

53. BJS, *Use of Force by Police* (Washington DC: Department of Justice, 1999).

54. BJS, *Local Police Departments.*

55. Karen Krause, "Boca Police Find Taser Guns Help Subdue Suspect, but Some Questions Remain." Retrieved on April 26, 2002, from www .sun-sentinel.com.

56. BJS, *Local Police Departments.*

57. Geoffrey P. Alpert and Lorie A. Fridell, *Police Vehicles and Firearms: Instruments of Deadly Force* (Prospect Heights, IL: Waveland Press, 1992), pp. 105–106.

58. Geoffrey Alpert and Patrick R. Anderson, "The Most Deadly Force: Police Pursuits," *Justice Quarterly,* 3(1986), pp. 1–14.

59. Alpert and Anderson, "Most Deadly Force," p. 5.

60. Alpert and Anderson, "Most Deadly Force," p. 3.

61. Amy C. Rippel, "Orange Settles over Fatal Cop Chase." Retrieved on April 15, 2003, from www.sun-sentinel.com.

62. California Highway Patrol, *Pursuit Study* (Sacramento, CA: California Highway Patrol, 1993).

63. California Highway Patrol, *Pursuit Study,* p. 72.

64. California Highway Patrol, *Pursuit Study,* p. 21.

65. Geoffrey P. Alpert and Roger G. Dunham, *Police Pursuit Driving: Controlled Responses to Emergency Situations* (Westport, CT: Greenwood Press, 1990); Geoffrey P. Alpert, "Questioning Police Pursuit in Urban Areas," *Journal of Police Science and Administration* (1987), pp. 298–306; and Geoffrey P. Alpert and Roger G. Dunham, "Research on Police Pursuits: Applications for Law Enforcement," *American Journal of Police,* 7(1988), pp. 123–131. For a discussion of these three studies, see Alpert and Fridell, *Police Vehicles and Firearms,* pp. 105–106.

66. Alpert and Fridell, *Police Vehicles and Firearms.*

67. Ian Ith, "Seattle Police Told to Avoid High-Speed Car Chases," *Seattle Times* (Aug. 15, 2003), pp. B1, B4.

68. Michael Ko, "Harborview Researchers Tally Police Chase Toll," *Seattle Times*. Retrieved on April 8, 2004, from http://www.seattletimes.nwsource.com.

69. Alpert and Fridell, *Police Vehicles and Firearms*, p. 115.

70. BJS, *Local Police Departments.*

71. Ith, "Seattle Police Told to Avoid High-Speed Car Chases."

72. "Life, Liberty and Pursuits," *Law Enforcement News* (Dec. 31, 1996), p. 26.

73. Geoffrey P. Alpert, *Police Pursuit: Policies and Training* (Washington, DC: National Institute of Justice, 1997).

74. Denise Kindschi Gosselin, *Heavy Hands: An introduction to the Crimes of Family Violence,* 2nd ed. (Upper Saddle River, NJ: Prentice Hall, 2003).http://www.sun-sentinel.com

75. Karen S. Collins, Cathy Schoen, Susan Joseph, Lisa Duchon, Elisabeth Simantov, and Michele Yellowitz, "Health Concerns across a woman's lifespan" (1999). Retrieved on April 15, 2004, from http://www.cmwf.org/programs/women/ksc_whsurvey99_332.asp.2002.

76. Callie Marie Rennison and Sarah Welchans, *Intimate Partner Violence* (NIJ 178247) (Washington DC: U.S. Department of Justice, 2000).

77. Daniel J. Sonkin and Michael Durphy, *Learning to live without violence: A handbook for men,* 5th ed. (Volcano, CA: Volcano Press., 1997).

78. Gosselin, *Heavy Hands.*

79. "Where New York's Anti-crime Miracle Ends: Crime-Reduction Strategies Aren't Having as Much Impact on Domestic Homicide," *Law Enforcement News* (April 30, 1997), p. 7.

80. T. S. Duncan, "Changing Perception of Domestic Violence," *Law Enforcement News* (Oct. 31, 1991), p. 13. The two books reviewed are Michael Steinman, ed., *Woman Battering: Policy Responses* (Cincinnati: Anderson, 1991); and Douglas J. Besharov, ed., *Family Violence: Research and Public Policy Issues* (Washington, DC: University Press of America, 1990).

81. Nancy Loving, *Responding to Spouse Abuse and Wife Beating: A Guide for Police* (Washington, DC: Police Executive Research Forum, 1980).

82. Lawrence W. Sherman and Richard A. Berk, *The Minneapolis Domestic Violence Experiment* (Washington, DC: Police Foundation, 1984).

83. Sherman and Berk, *Minneapolis Domestic Violence Experiment.*

84. Lawrence Sherman and Dennis Rogan, *Policing Domestic Violence: Experiments and Dilemmas* (New York: Free Press, 1992), p. 46.

85. Gosselin, *Heavy Hands.*

86. Gosselin, *Heavy Hands.*

87. Bureau of Justice Statistics, *Local Police Departments, 2000* (Washington, DC: Department of Justice, 2003), p. 27.

88. Eve Buzawa, "Police Officer Response to Domestic Violence Legislation in Michigan," *Journal of Police Science and Administration*, 10(1982), pp. 415–424.

89. National Criminal Justice Reference Service, "An Update on the Cycle of Violence, 2001." Retrieved on September 4, 2003, from http://www.ncjrs.org/family-violence/summary.html.

90. Jacob R. Clark, "Police Careers May Take a Beating from Fed Domestic-Violence Law," *Law Enforcement News* (Feb. 14, 1997), pp. 1, 14.

See also "Battle Lines Form on Law Disarming Some Cops," *Law Enforcement News* (March 15, 1997), p. 7.

91. Jo Thomas, "Army Buddy Says McVeigh Saw Victims as Part of 'Evil Empire,'" *New York Times* (May 13, 1997), pp. A1, 14; Michael Fleeman, "Prosecutor Says McVeigh Wanted Blood," *Tampa Tribune* (April 25, 1997), pp. 1, 9; "Families Break into Tears as Victims' Names Recited,"*Tampa Tribune* (April 25, 1997), p. 9; Jo Thomas, "McVeigh Guilty on All Counts in the Oklahoma City Bombing," *New York Times* (June 3, 1997), pp. A1, 18; Rick Bragg, "Survivors Respond: Still Haunted, Families See Justice in Shape of a Killer's Grave, *New York Times* (June 3, 1997), pp. A1, 19; James Collins, "The Weight of Evidence," *Time* (April 28, 1997), pp. 37–43.

92. Kevin Sack, "U.S. Says FBI Erred in Using Deception in Olympic Bomb Inquiry," *New York Times* (April 9, 1997), p. A47; Sack, "Officials Link Atlanta Bombings and Ask for Help," *New York Times* (June 10, 1997), pp. A1, D24.

93. Mark Pitcavage, "Domestic Extremism: Still a Potent Threat" *Police Chief* (Aug. 2003), pp. 32–35.

94. "In Okla. City Bombing's Wake, Militias Still Seen Posing Public-Safety Threat," *Law Enforcement News* (April 15, 1997), p. 5.

95. "Coming to Your Town: Bio-Chem Terror Training," *Law Enforcement News* (May 15, 1997), p. 8.

96. James E. Duffy and Alan C. Brantley, "Militias: Initiating Contact," *FBI Law Enforcement Bulletin* (July 1997), pp. 22–26, p. 23.

97. "Policing Keeps an Eye on the Radical Right," *Law Enforcement News* (Dec. 31, 1996), p. 8; "FBI Turns up the Heat on Domestic Terror," *Law Enforcement News* (April 30,1997), p. 9; "Agents Tell of Militia Life from Within," *New York Times* (June 6, 1997), p. A22.

98. Pitcavage, "Domestic Extremism: Still a Potent Threat."

99. Pitcavage, "Domestic Extremism: Still a Potent Threat."

100. Pitcavage, "Domestic Extremism: Still a Potent Threat."

101. Pitcavage, "Domestic Extremism: Still a Potent Threat."

102. Duffy and Brantley, "Militias: Initiating Contact."

103. "Ruby Ridge," *Newsweek*, 28 August 1995, pp. 25–33.

104. "Ruby Ridge," p. 25.

105. Associated Press, "$1 Million in Luxury SUVs Destroyed in California Arson," *Everett Herald* (Aug. 23, 2003), p. A4.

106. *A resource guide on racial profiling data collection systems: Promising practices and lessons learned* (NCJ# 184768). (Washington DC: Department of Justice, 2000).

107. *A resource guide on racial profiling data collection systems.*

108. *A resource guide on racial profiling data collection systems.*

109. BJS, *Policing and Homicide, 1976–1998.*

110. BJS, *Policing and Homicide, 1976–1998.*

111. *A resource guide on racial profiling data collection systems.*

112. *A resource guide on racial profiling data collection systems.*

113. "Facing up to an unflattering profile," *Law Enforcement News* (Dec. 2000).

114. "Facing up to an unflattering profile."

115. "Facing up to an unflattering profile."

116. Rolando V. del Carmen, *Civil Liabilities in American Policing: A Text for Law Enforcement Personnel* (Englewood Cliffs, NJ: Prentice-Hall, 1991), pp. 7-14.

117. Frank Schmallenger, *Criminal Justice Today: An Introductory Text for the Twenty-first Century* (Englewood Cliffs, NJ: Prentice-Hall, 1991), p. 205.

118. del Carmen, *Civil Liabilities in American Policing,* p. 29.

119. Charles R. Swanson, Leonard Territo, and Robert W. Taylor, *Police Administration: Structures, Processes, and Behavior,* 2d ed. (New York: Macmillan, 1988).

120. del Carmen, *Civil Liabilities in American Policing,* pp. 2–3.

121. del Carmen, *Civil Liabilities in American Policing.*

122. Victor Kappeler, *Critical Issues in Police Civil Liability,* 3rd ed. (Prospect Heights, IL: Waveland Press, 2001), p. 26.

123. *Biscoe* v. *Arlington* (1984) 80–0766, *National Law Journal* (May 13, 1985).

124. *Kaplan* v. *Lloyd's Insurance Co.,* 479 So.2d 961 (La.App. 1985).

125. Sean Murphy, "City Made $500,000 Settlement in Shooting," *Boston Globe* (Dec. 6, 1988), p. 1.

126. *Prior* v. *Woods* (1981), *National Law Journal* (Nov. 2, 1981).

127. "Life, Liberty and Pursuits."

128. Edward J. Littlejohn, "Civil Liability and the Police Officer: The Need for New Deterrents to Police Misconduct,"*University of Detroit Journal of Urban Law, 58*(1981), pp. 365–431.

129. Kappeler, *Critical Issues in Police Civil Liability.*

130. Kappeler, *Critical Issues in Police Civil Liability.*

131. *Canton* v. *Harris,* 86–1088, 44 Crl. 3157 (1989).

132. Joseph J. Senna and Larry J. Siegel, *Introduction to Criminal Justice,* 5th ed. (St. Paul, MN:West, 1990), p. 273.

133. Kappeler, *Critical Issues in Police Civil Liability.*

Chapter 16

1. See Jonathan R. White, *Terrorism: An Introduction: 2002 Update,* 4th ed. (Belmont, CA: Wadsworth, 2003), pp. 7–10.

2. Louis J. Freeh, "Responding to Terrorism," *FBI Law Enforcement Bulletin* (March 1999), pp. 1–2.

3. White, *Terrorism: An Introduction*, p. xv.

4. "Terrorism," *Security Management* (July 2001), pp. 20–21.

5. The Terrorism Research Center, http://www.terrorism.com.

6. White, *Terrorism: An Introduction: 2002 Update*.

7. Jonathan R. White, *Defending The Homeland: Domestic Intelligence, Law Enforcement, and Security* (Belmont, CA: Wadsworth, 2004).

8. John F. Lewis, Jr. "Fighting Terrorism in the 21st Century," *FBI Law Enforcement Bulletin* (March 1999), pp. 3–10.

9. Joel Carlson, "Critical Incident Management in the Ultimate Crisis," *FBI Law Enforcement Bulletin* (March 1999), pp. 19–22.

10. "Ashcroft Announces Plan for DOJ 'Wartime Reorganization,'" *Criminal Justice Newsletter* (Nov. 14, 2001), pp. 1–2.

11. For example, see: Evan Thomas, et al., "The Road to September 11th," *Newsweek* (Oct. 1, 2001), pp. 38–49; John Miller and Michael Stone with Chris Mitchell, *The Cell: Inside the 9/11 Plot, Why the FBI and CIA Failed to Stop It* (New York: Hyperion, 2002).

12. "President Signs Homeland Security EO and Ridge Sworn In as Its Director," *NCIA Justice Bulletin* (Oct. 2001), pp. 8–10.

13. Office of Homeland Security, http://www.whitehouse,gov/response /faq–homeland.html; http://www.whitehouse.gov/news/releases /2001/10/200111008.html.

14. Public Law No. 107–56, USA Patriot Act of 2001.

15. Transportation Security Administration, http://www.tsa.gov/Agency/ mission.htm; Office of Homeland Security, http://www.whitehouse. gov/homeland/six_month_update.html.

16. "Polls: Trade Some Freedom for Security," *Law Enforcement News* (Sept. 15, 2001), p. 1.

17. Office of Homeland Security, http://www.whitehouse.gov /deptofhomeland/.

18. Office of Homeland Security, http://www.whitehouse.gov/homeland /six_month_update.html.

19. See Rand Corporation, *Organizing for Homeland Security* (Santa Monica: CA: Rand Corporation, 2002); Randall A. Yim, *National Preparedness: Integration of Federal, State, Local and Private Sector Efforts Is Critical to an Effective National Strategy for Homeland Security* (Washington, DC: U.S. General Accounting Office, 2002); David M. Walker, *Homeland Security: Responsibility and Accountability for Achieving National Goals* (Washington, DC: U.S. General Accounting Office, 2002); Michael Barletta, *After 9/11: Preventing Mass-Destruction Terrorism and Weapons Proliferation* (Monterey, CA: Center for Nonproliferation Studies, 2002); JayEtta Hecker, *Homeland Security: Intergovernmental Coordination and Partnership Will Be Critical to Success* (Washington, DC: U.S. General Accounting Office, 2002). All of these documents are available at NCJRS at http://www.ncjrs.gov.

20. U.S. Department of Homeland Security, DHS Organization. Retrieved on March 25, 2003, from http://www.dhs.gov/dhspublic/interapp /editorial/editorial_0086.xml.

21. Lewis, "Fighting Terrorism"; Freeh, "Responding to Terrorism."

22. Federal Bureau of Investigation, www.fbi.gov/pressrel/speeches/ speech052902.htm; http://www.fbi.gov/page2/52902.htm.

23. Cassi Chandler, "FBI Counterterrorism." Retrieved on April 8, 2003, from www.fbi.gov/terrorinfo/counterrorism/waronterrorhome.htm.

24. Bureau of Alcohol, Tobacco, Firearms, and Explosives, *ATF Online: Arson and Explosives: Programs,* http://www.atf.treas.gov/explarson /index.htm.

25. "FY 2004 Budget Seen as Mixed Bag," *Law Enforcement News* (Feb. 28, 2003), p. 6.

26. Philip Shenon, "Administration Reduces Level of Terrorism Alert to Yellow, Citing the Fall of Hussein," *New York Times* (April 17, 2003), p. B7.

27. Shenon, "Administration Reduces Level of Terrorism Alert to Yellow, Citing the Fall of Hussein."

28. D. Douglas Bodrero, "Confronting Terrorism on the State and Local Level," *FBI Law Enforcement Bulletin* (March 1999), pp. 11–18.

29. D. Douglas Bodrero, "Law Enforcement's New Challenge to Investigate, Interdict and Prevent Terrorism," *Police Chief* (Feb. 2002), pp. 41–48.

30. Gene Voegtlin, "IACP Testifies on Local Law Enforcement Role in Homeland Defense," *Police Chief* (Feb. 2002), p. 8.

31. Kevin Riley and Bruce Hoffman, *Domestic Terrorism: A National Assessment of State and Local Law Enforcement Preparedness* (Santa Monica, CA: Rand Corporation, National Institute of Justice, 1995).

32. Bodrero, "Confronting Terrorism on the State and Local Level."

33. Mathew J. Hickman and Brian A. Reaves, "Local Police and Homeland Security: Some Baseline Data," *Police Chief* (Oct. 2002), pp. 83–88.

34. Marie Simonetti Rosen, "2002: A Year in Retrospect: What a Difference 12 Months Can Make for Law Enforcement," *Law Enforcement News* (Dec. 15/31, 2002), pp. 1, 4.

35. Rosen, "2002: A Year in Retrospect."

36. "Domestic Security Demands More of Local PDs," *Law Enforcement News* (Dec. 15/31, 2002), p. 9.

37. Richard Perez-Pena, "A security blanket, but with no guarantees," *New York Times* (March 23, 2003), pp. 1, B14, B15, p.1.

38. Perez-Pena, "A Security Blanket, but with No Guarantees."

39. Mike Terault, "Community Policing: Essential to Homeland Security," *Sheriff* (Sept./Oct. 2002), pp. 36–37.

40. Melchor C. De Guzman, "The Changing Roles and Strategies of the Police in Time of Terror," *Academy of Criminal Justice Sciences Today* (Sept./Oct. 2002), pp. 8–13.

41. Sherry L. Harowitz, "The New Centurions," *Security Management* (Jan. 2003), pp. 51–58, p. 52. Also see Teresa Anderson, "A Year of Reassessment," *Security Management* (Jan. 2003), pp. 61–65.

42. Harowitz, "The New Centurions," p. 52.

43. E. Meyr, "Tactical Response to Terrorism: The Concept and Its Application," *Law and Order* (March 1999), pp. 44–47.

44. C. Roda, *Executive Safety* (Washington, DC: National Criminal Justice Reference Service, 1997).

45. Perez-Pena, "A Security Blanket, but with No Guarantees."

46. Perez-Pena, "A Security Blanket, but with No Guarantees."

47. "Summit Focuses on Homeland Security," *ASIS Dynamics* (Jan./Feb. 2003), pp. 1, 12.

48. Richard Bernstein, "Behind Arrest of Bomb Fugitive, Informer's Tip, Then Fast Action," *New York Times* (Feb. 10, 1995), p. 1.

49. Robert A. Martin, "The Joint Terrorism Task Force: A Concept That Works," *FBI Law Enforcement Bulletin* (March 1999), pp. 23–27.

50. Martin, "The Joint Terrorism Task Force," p. 27.

Glossary

Adverse impact   A form of defacto discrimination resulting from a testing element that discriminates against a particular group, essentially keeping them out of the applicant pool.

Affirmative action regulations   Rules designed to achieve a ratio of minority group employees in approximate proportion to their makeup in the population of a locality, as well as to remedy past discriminatory employment and promotional practices.

Age-progression photos   Photo systems that show changes that will naturally occur to the face with age; also called age-enhanced photos.

Aggressive driving   Overly assertive maneuvers in traffic, including violations such as following too closely, changing lanes abruptly, and sudden stopping; these are often the cause as well as the result of road rage.

Ambiguous   The concept that the police role is very diverse and dynamic.

Anatomically correct doll   Doll made to resemble an actual person, including genitalia and other appropriate body parts.

ASIS International   Professional organization of private security professionals.

Assessment Center   Promotional process in which participants perform tasks related to the anticipated position in a simulated exercise.

Automated crime analysis (crime mapping)   Computerized analysis of crime statistics, patterns, and trends.

Automated fingerprint identification system (AFIS)   Fingerprinting innovation begun in the 1980s in which a print technician can enter unidentified latent fingerprints into a computer. The computer then automatically searches its files and presents a list of likely matches.

Automated palmprint technology   Allows fingerprint technicians to match palmprints from crime scenes to those stored in a computer.

Ballistics   Scientific analysis of guns and bullets.

Beat   The smallest geographical area an individual officer can patrol.

Beat system   System of policing created by Sir Robert Peel for the London Metropolitan Police in 1829, in which officers were assigned to relatively small permanent posts.

Bias-based policing   *See* racial profiling.

Biometric identification   Automated identification systems that use particular physical characteristics to distinguish one person from another; can identify criminals or provide authentication.

Blending   Plainclothes officers' effort to blend into an area and attempt to catch a criminal.

Blue curtain   A concept developed by William Westley that claims that police officers trust only other police officers and do not aid in the investigation of wrongdoing by other officers.

Blue flu   Informal job action by officers in which they call in sick as a way of refusing to perform certain job functions in an attempt to win labor concessions from their employers.

Blue wall of silence   A figurative protective barrier erected by the police by which officers protect one another from outsiders, often even refusing to aid police superiors or other law enforcement officials in investigating wrongdoing of other officers.

Bona fide occupational qualification (BFOQ)   A qualification reasonably necessary to perform a job; the essential functions of a job.

"Broken windows" model   Theory that unrepaired broken windows indicate to others that members of the community do not care about the quality of life in the neighborhood and are unlikely to get involved; consequently, disorder and crime will thrive.

Carroll doctrine   The legal doctrine that automobiles have less Fourth Amendment protection than other places. Arose from the landmark 1925 U.S. Supreme Court case *Carroll* v. *United States.*

Centralized model of state law enforcement   Combines the duties of major criminal investigations with the patrol of state highways.

Chain of command   Managerial concept stating that each individual in an organization is supervised by and reports to only one immediate supervisor.

Citizen oversight   Process by which citizens appointed by government executives review allegations of brutality or abuse by police officers. Generally, they have no power to discipline but can make recommendations to police officials.

Citizen patrols   Citizen volunteers who patrol their community and report any suspicious activity to the police.

Citizen police academies   Educational programs put on by police officers for residents to learn about police roles and responsibilities and gain familiarity with their police department.

Civil forfeiture   Situation in which property is confiscated from an owner by the government.

Civil Rights Act of 1964 (Title VII)   Law that prohibits discrimination based on race, color, religion, sex, or national origin for employers with more than 15 employees, as well as unions and governmental agencies.

Civil service system   A method of hiring and managing government employees designed to eliminate political influence, favoritism, nepotism, and bias.

Civilianization   The process of removing sworn officers from noncritical or nonenforcement tasks and replacing them with civilians or nonsworn employees.

Cold case squads   Investigative units who open old, unsolved cases and determine the feasibility of reinvestigating them.

Combined DNA Index System (CODIS)   Database that contains DNA profiles obtained from subjects convicted of homicide, sexual assault, and other serious felonies.

Community policing   Philosophy of empowering citizens and developing a partnership between the police and the community to work together to solve problems.

Community Policing Consortium   An organization reporting on and encouraging the latest community policing activities. It is made up of the International Association of Chiefs of Police (IACP), the National Organization of Black Law Enforcement Executives (NOBLE), the National Sheriffs Association (NSA), the Police Executive Research Forum (PERF), and the Police Foundation.

Community service officers (CSOs)   An entry-level police employee without general law enforcement powers suggested by the President's Commission on Law Enforcement and Administration of Justice.

Composite sketches   Sketches prepared by forensic artists or automated means of people wanted by the police for a crime.

Compstat   Weekly crime strategy meetings, featuring the latest computerized crime statistics and high-stress brain storming; developed by the New York City Police Department in the mid-1990s.

Computer-aided dispatch (CAD)   System that allows almost immediate communication between the police dispatcher and police units in the field.

Computer-aided investigations (computer-aided case management)   The use of computers to perform case management and other functions in investigations.

Constable   An official assigned to keep the peace in the Mutual Pledge system in England.

Contract security   Private security services offered by industrial security firms and guard agencies to private employers or individuals on a contract basis.

Control group   One of the groups studied in a controlled experiment; no changes are made to this group.

Controlled experiment   A scientific experiment in which changes are made to an experimental group to see the effects of a newly introduced variable; the experimental group is then compared to the control group to attempt to observe the effect of the variable, if any.

Cooping   Sleeping, resting, or avoiding work while on duty.

Counterintelligence   Intelligence efforts directed against terrorist organizations.

Counterterrorism   Enforcement efforts made against terrorist organizations.

Crime analysis   The use of analytical methods to obtain pertinent information on crime patterns and trends that can then be disseminated to officers on the street.

The Crime Bill of 1994   The Violent Crime Control and Law Enforcement Act, signed by President Clinton in 1994.

Crime-fighting role   A major view of the role of the police that emphasizes crime fighting or law enforcement.

Crime scene   The geographic location where a crime has been committed.

Crime Stoppers   Program in which unsolved crimes are publicized and cash rewards offered to citizens for information leading to the capture of the person responsible.

Criminalistics   The branch of forensic science that deals with the study of physical evidence related to crime.

Custodial interrogation   The questioning of a person in police custody regarding his or her participation in a crime.

Cyberterrorism   Terrorism that initiates, or threatens to initiate, the exploitation of or attack on information systems.

Deadly force   Force that can cause death.

Decentralized model of state law enforcement   A clear distinction between traffic enforcement on state highways and other state-level law enforcement functions.

Decoy operations   Operations in which officers dress as and play the role of potential victims in the hope of attracting and catching a criminal.

De facto discrimination   Discrimination that is the indirect result of policies or practices that are not intended to discriminate but do, in fact, discriminate.

Defense of life standard   Doctrine allowing police officers to use deadly force against individuals using deadly force against an officer or others.

Deoxyribonucleic acid (DNA)   The basic building code for all of the human body's chromosomes.

Department of Homeland Security   Federal cabinet department established in the aftermath of the terrorist attacks of September 11, 2001.

Detective mystique   The idea that detective work is glamorous, exciting, and dangerous, as it is depicted in the movies and on television.

Differential response to calls for service   Varying the rapidity of responses to calls for service, based on the type of incident.

Directed patrol   The use of officers' available discretionary time to focus on specific crime problems.

Dirty Harry problem   A moral dilemma faced by police officers in which they may feel forced to take certain illegal actions to achieve a greater good.

Discretion   Freedom to act or decide a matter on one's own.

Discrimination   Treating an individual or group differently based on membership in a particular group.

DNA profiling (genetic fingerprinting, or DNA typing) The examination of DNA samples from a body fluid to determine whether they came from a particular subject.

Domestic terrorism Terrorism committed by citizens of the United States in the United States.

Double marginality The social burden carried by African American police officers of being members of a minority group as well as law enforcement officers.

Drug Abuse Resistance Education (DARE) A school program taught by police officers aimed at teaching older elementary students to resist drugs.

Eighteenth Amendment *See* Volstead Act.

Enhanced CAD (enhanced 911, or E-911) Sophisticated CAD system utilizing mobile digital terminals in each patrol unit; replaces voice communication.

Entrapment A legal defense that holds that police originated the criminal idea or initiated the criminal action.

Equal Employment Opportunity Act of 1972 (EEOA) This act extended the 1964 Civil Rights Act and made its provisions, including Title VII, applicable to state and local governments.

Equal opportunity employment regulations Rules designed to ensure that members of minority groups are treated equally with members of dominant groups and that race, gender, ethnicity, and religion will not affect a person's chances of being hired or promoted.

Ethics Standards of fair and honest conduct; conduct examined in terms of morality.

Exclusionary rule An interpretation of the U.S. Constitution by the U.S. Supreme Court that holds that evidence seized in violation of the U.S. Constitution cannot be used in court against a defendant.

Exigent circumstances Emergency situation that allows the police to enter a premise and search without a warrant.

Experimental group One of the groups studied in a controlled experiment; changes are made to this group.

Field training Training program on the job and under the direction of an FTO.

Field training officer (FTO) Experienced officer who mentors and trains a new police officer.

Fingerprints The impressions made from the series of friction ridge outlines on the fleshy side of the end joint of each finger.

Fleeing felon doctrine Doctrine widely followed prior to the 1960s that allowed police officers to use deadly force to apprehend a fleeing felon.

Flight-or-fight response The body's reaction to highly stressful situations in which it is getting prepared for extraordinary physical exertion.

Foot patrol A method of deploying police officers that gives them responsibility for all policing activity by requiring them to walk around a defined geographical area.

Forensic science The branch of science that answers legal questions.

Fourteenth Amendment Amendment to the U.S. Constitution that guarantees "equal protection under the law" to all citizens of the United States.

Frye test Standard for admitting new scientific evidence into U.S. Courts; based on the U.S. Supreme Court case *Frye* v. *United States* (1923).

Global positioning system (GPS) A satellite system used to locate a position on the map.

Griggs* v. *Duke Power Company Landmark U.S. Supreme Court case that ruled that a company's job requirements are discriminatory if they cannot be shown to measure the abilities needed to perform a certain job.

Guardians Association of New York City Police Department* v. *Civil Service Commission of New York A landmark appellate court decision on the issue of job analysis.

Hallcrest Reports Two comprehensive reports commissioned by the National Institute of Justice on the private security industry in the United States.

Hate crime Crime committed against persons or property that is at least partially motivated by the offender's hatred or bias toward the victim's race, religion, ethnicity, gender, age, disability, or sexual orientation.

Hogan's Alley A shooting course in which simulated "good guys" and "bad guys" pop up, requiring police officers to make split-second decisions.

Homeland defense Efforts made since the terrorist acts of September 11, 2001, to protect the United States against terrorist acts.

Homeland security advisory system Series of color-coded alerts issued by the Department of Homeland Security to advise the nation of the level of the current terrorism threat.

Hot spots Locations where many crimes occur, usually by different offenders.

Hue and cry A method developed in early England for citizens to summon assistance from fellow members of the community.

Index crimes The major crimes studied in the Uniform Crime Reports, including murder and nonnegligent manslaughter, forcible rape, robbery, aggravated assault, burglary, larceny/theft, arson, and motor vehicle theft.

Inked prints (ten-prints) Fingerprints made by rolling each finger onto a ten-print card.

In-service training In-house training.

Integrated automated fingerprint identification system (IAFIS) A system for searching an individual's fingerprints against a computerized database of all fingerprints.

Integrity test Testing the integrity of employees through the presentation of corruption opportunities.

Internal Affairs Division (IA, IAD)   Also sometimes called the Professional Standards Unit; investigates allegations of police misconduct.

International terrorism   Terrorism on an international level.

Job analysis   Identifies the important skills that must be performed by police officers, and then identifies the knowledge, skills, and abilities necessary to perform those tasks.

Job description   Formal summary of duties and responsibilities for a position.

Job relatedness   Concept that job requirements must be necessary for the performance of the job a person is applying for.

Joint Federal/Local Task Force   Use of federal, state, and local law enforcement agents in a focused task force to address particular crime problems.

Joint Terrorism Task Force (JTTF) concept   Use of single-focused investigative units that meld personnel and talent from various law enforcement agencies to conduct reactive and proactive investigations of terrorist-related activities.

Judicial review   Process by which actions of the police in areas such as arrests, search and seizure, and interrogations are reviewed by the U.S. court system at various levels to ensure the constitutionality of these actions.

Kansas City Study   A controlled experiment conducted during 1972 and 1973 to determine whether increasing or decreasing random routine patrol had an effect on crime rates and other indicators of police service.

Knapp Commission   A public body that conducted an investigation into police corruption in New York City in the early 1970s and discovered a widespread network of payoffs and bribes.

Knowledge, skills, and abilities (KSAs)   Talents or attributes necessary to do a particular job.

Latent prints   Fingerprint impressions left at a crime scene.

Lateral transfers   The ability and opportunity to transfer from one police department to another.

Law Enforcement Assistance Administration (LEAA)   Agency funded by the Federal Safe Streets Act that provided for technical assistance and millions of dollars in aid to local and state justice agencies between 1969 and 1982.

Law Enforcement Employee Average   Number of law enforcement employees for each 1,000 residents.

Law Enforcement Management and Administrative Statistics (LEMAS)   Statistical reports on law enforcement personnel data issued by the National Institute of Justice under its Law Enforcement Management and Administrative Statistics program.

Law Enforcement Officers Memorial Fund   A memorial in Washington, D.C., established to recognize the ultimate sacrifice of police officers killed in the line of duty.

Less-than-lethal weapons   Innovative alternatives to traditional firearms, such as batons, flashlights, bodily force techniques, chemical irritant sprays, and TASERS.

Lineup   Police identification procedure involving the placing of a suspect with a group of other people of similar physical characteristics so that a witness or victim of a crime can have the opportunity to identify the perpetrator of the crime.

Live-Scan   The electronic taking and transmission of fingerprints as opposed to traditional ink methods.

Local control   The formal and informal use of local or neighborhood forms of government and measures to deter abhorrent behaviors.

Managing Criminal Investigations (MCI)   Proposal recommended by the Rand Study regarding a more effective way of investigating crimes, including allowing patrol officers to follow up cases and the use of solvability factors in determining which cases to follow up.

Metropolitan Police   Police department created in 1829 for London, England.

Minneapolis Domestic Violence Experiment   An experiment conducted in 1981 and 1982 to examine the deterrent effect of various methods of handling domestic violence calls.

***Miranda* rules (*Miranda* warnings)**   Rules established by the U.S. Supreme Court in the landmark case *Miranda* v. *Arizona* (1966) that require the police to advise suspects confronting custodial interrogation of their constitutional rights.

Mitochondrial DNA (MtDNA)   DNA analysis applied to evidence containing very small or degraded quantities from hair, bones, teeth, and body fluids.

Mobile digital terminal (MDT)   A device put into a police vehicle that allows the electronic transmission of messages between the police dispatcher and the officer in the field.

Moonlighting   Term for police officers working in private security jobs during their off-duty hours.

Mug shot imaging   A system of digitizing a mug shot picture and storing its image on a computer so that it can be retrieved at a later time.

Mutual pledge   A form of community self-protection developed by England's King Alfred the Great in the later part of the ninth century.

National Advisory Commission on Civil Disorders (Kerner Commission)   Commission created in 1968 to address the reasons for the riots of the 1960s.

National Crime Information Center (NCIC, NCIC 2000)   Computerized database of criminal information maintained by the FBI.

National Crime Victimization Survey (NCVS)   National Institute of Justice survey of a random sample of U.S. households, asking them if a crime was committed against anyone in the household during the prior six months.

National Criminal Justice Reference Service (NCJRS)   A national clearinghouse of criminal justice information maintained by the National Institute of Justice.

National DNA Index System (NDIS)   Databank consisting of DNA profiles. Includes two sections: a Convicted Offender Index and a Forensic Index.

National Institute of Justice (NIJ)   The research arm of the U.S. Justice Department.

National Treasury Employees Union v. Von Raab   1989 case in which the U.S. Supreme Court ruled that random drug testing was constitutional for U.S. Customs personnel involved in drug interdiction and/or carrying firearms.

Neighborhood watch programs   Crime-prevention programs in which community members watch over activities in their neighborhood.

Newark Foot patrol studies   Studies made in the 1980s to observe the effect of foot patrol in Newark, New Jersey.

Night vision devices   Photographic and viewing devices that allow visibility in darkness.

Noble cause corruption   The idea that police officers may lie or commit unethical acts for a good end, such as putting a criminal behind bars.

Nonlethal force   Force that is not likely to result in death.

Nonsworn (civilian) members   Police employees without traditional police powers generally assigned to noncritical or nonenforcement tasks.

Office of Community Oriented Policing Services (COPS)   Established to administer the grant money provided by the 1994 Crime Bill and to promote community policing.

Omnipresence   A concept that suggests that the police are always present or always seem to be present.

Operation identification   A program in which owners mark property with identifying marks and post signs advertising that fact in an effort to deter theft.

Order maintenance   A major view of the role of the police that emphasizes keeping the peace and providing social services.

PAL (Police Athletic League)   Program developed to provide opportunities for youth to interact with police officers in gyms or on playing fields rather than in adversarial situations.

Palmprints   The impressions made from the series of friction ridge outlines on the palm of each hand.

Patriot Act (USA Patriot Act)   Public Law No. 107-56, passed in 2001, giving law enforcement new ability to search, seize, detain, or evesdrop in their pursuit of possible terrorists; the full title of the law is U.S.A. Patriot Act—Uniting and Strengthening America by Providing Appropriate Tools Required to Intercept and Obstruct Terrorism.

PCR-STR (polymerase chain reaction-short tandem repeat)   One of the latest DNA technology systems. Requires only pin-size samples rather than dime-size samples needed for RFLP.

Peel's Nine Principles   Basic guidelines created by Sir Robert Peel for the London Metropolitan Police in 1829.

Pendleton Act   A federal law passed in 1883 to establish a civil service system that tested, appointed, and promoted officers on a merit system.

Photo array   Police identification procedure similar to a lineup, except that photos of the suspect (who is not in custody) and others are shown to a witness or victim of a crime.

Plain view evidence   Evidence seized without a warrant by police who have the right to be in a position to observe it.

Platoon   All of the people working on a particular tour or shift.

Police brutality   Actions including using abusive language, making threats, or using force or coercion unnecessarily.

Police civil liability   Concept that a police officer can be sued in civil court for improper behavior using such civil law vehicles as negligence and torts.

Police–community relations   Efforts to interact and communicate with the public.

Police community relations (PCR) movement   A movement that began in the 50s with the assignment of specific officers to specialized community relations duties.

Police corruption   Misuse of police authority, resulting in a benefit to the officer or others.

Police culture or police subculture   A combination of shared norms, values, goals, career patterns, lifestyles, and occupational structures that is substantially different from that held by the rest of society.

Police cynicism   An attitude that there is no hope for the world and a view of humanity at its worst.

Police deception   Deceptive behavior, including perjury and attempts to circumvent the rules regarding search and seizure of evidence.

Police human relations   Efforts to understand and relate to individuals and groups by police agencies.

Police operational styles   Styles adopted by police officers as a way of thinking about the role of the police and law in society.

Police personality   Traits common to most police officers, thought to include authoritarianism, suspicion, racism, hostility, insecurity, conservatism, and cynicism.

Police–Public Contact Survey (PPCS)   A 2001 National Institute of Justice survey of contacts between the police and citizens.

Police–public relations   Activities sponsored by a police agency with the intent of creating a favorable image of the police.

Police pursuit policy   Police department policy that regulates the circumstances and conditions under which police can pursue a motor vehicle.

Police role   The concept of "what the police do."

Police selection process   A series of examinations, interviews, and investigative steps designed to select the best candidates from the many who apply for positions in a police department.

Police storefront station or ministation   Satellite offices where small numbers of officers work, allowing for increased accessibility by the community.

Police suicide   The intentional taking of his or her own life by a police officer.

Posse comitatus   A common-law descendent of the old hue and cry found on the American frontier. If a crime spree occurred or a dangerous criminal was in the area, the U.S. frontier sheriff would call upon the posse comitatus. In Latin, it means "the power of the county."

Praetorian Guard   Select group of highly qualified members of the military established by Roman emperor Augustus to protect him and his palace.

Precinct   The entire collection of beats in a given geographic area; the organizational headquarters of a police department.

Preliminary investigation   The investigation conducted at a crime scene upon arrival, including interviews of victims and witnesses and crime scene searches.

President's Commission on Law Enforcement and Administration of Justice   Commission that issued a report in 1967 entitled *The Challenge of Crime in a Free Society*. The commission was created in the wake of the problems of the 1960s, particularly the problems between police and citizens.

Pretext stop   A traffic stop conducted by a police officer based ostensibly on a traffic violation but actually made in order to conduct an investigation.

Private security industry   The industry that provides private and corporate security programs in the United States.

Privatization   Contracting out various services to private agencies to help a police department fulfill its mission.

Proarrest policy   Policy that the abusive spouse must be arrested regardless of the wishes of the victim.

Proactive investigation   Anticipating problems and working to solve them rather than responding after the fact.

Probable cause   Evidence that may lead a reasonable person to believe that a crime has been committed and that a certain person committed it.

Probationary period   The period of time that a department has to evaluate a new officer's ability to perform his or her job effectively—generally a year or more.

Problem-solving policing   Proactive approach to policing that focuses on solving problems rather than responding to calls for service after the fact.

Proprietary security   Security services provided by the organization or company itself.

Pursuits   Attempts by police officers in patrol vehicles to stop a motor vehicle when the driver is aware and resists by increasing speed or ignoring the officer's directions to stop.

Quasi-military organization   An organization similar to the military along structures of strict authority and reporting relations.

Racial profiling   Inconsistent and discriminatory enforcement of the law; officers' use of a person's race or ethnicity to assess the likelihood of criminal conduct or wrongdoing.

Radical and hate groups   Groups that use violence and terrorism against certain other groups of people to further their political or social objectives

Rand Study of the Criminal Investigation Process   Studies made of the criminal investigation process by the Rand Corporation "think tank."

Random routine patrol   An officer driving or walking around a designated geographic area.

Rapid response to citizens' calls to 911   Responding to calls made by citizens to 911 and performing whatever police work is required.

Reasonable force   The amount of force an officer can use when making an arrest.

Reasonable suspicion   The standard of proof that is necessary for police officers to conduct a stop and frisk.

Repeat offender programs (ROPS)   Enforcement efforts directed at known repeat offenders through surveillance or case enhancement.

Reserve officer   Either part-time compensated or noncompensated police employees who serve when needed.

Resident officer programs   Programs through which officers live in particular communities to strengthen relations between the police and that community.

Restricted fragment length polymorphism (RFLP)   Traditional method of DNA technology analysis.

Retroactive investigation of past crimes by detectives   Follow-up investigation of past crimes.

Reverse discrimination   Giving preferential treatment to women and minorities to the detriment of white males in hiring and promotions.

Reverse 911 (R-911)   An automated telephonic method by which the police can immediately contact the public or selected members of the public.

Rodney King incident   The 1991 videotaped beating of an African American citizen by members of the Los Angeles police department.

Saturation patrol   A type of uniformed tactical operation in which a larger-than-usual number of uniformed officers are assigned to a particular area to deal with a particular crime problem.

Search and seizure   Legal concept relating to the searching for and confiscation of evidence by the police.

Search warrant   A written order, based on probable cause and signed by a judge, authorizing police to search a specific person, place, or property to obtain evidence.

Section 1983 of the Civil Rights Act   Law allowing anyone acting under the authority of law who violates another person's constitutional rights to be sued; the legal authority for most lawsuits against law enforcement officers and agencies.

Selection process   The steps/tests an individual must progress through in order to be hired as a police officer.

Selective enforcement   Police discretion used to concentrate efforts on certain crimes and not others.

September 11, 2001   The date of a series of terrorist attacks against the United States of American by members of al Qaeda.

Serology   Scientific analysis of blood, semen, and other body fluids.

Shift   Time span to which personnel are assigned; can be 8, 10, or 12 hours. Also called a *tour.*

Shire-reeve   Early English official placed in charge of shires as part of the system of mutual pledge; evolved into the modern concept of the sheriff.

Showup   Police identification process involving bringing a suspect back to the scene of the crime or another place (for example, a hospital where an injured victim is) where the suspect can be seen and possibly identified by a victim or witness of a crime.

Silver platter doctrine   Legal tactic that allowed federal prosecutors to use evidence obtained by state police officers seized through unreasonable searches and seizures.

Solvability factors   Factors considered in determining whether or not a case should be assigned for a follow-up investigation.

Span of control   The number of officers or subordinates that a superior can supervise effectively.

Split force patrol   The designation of half of the patrol force to handle calls for service, allowing the other half to devote their time to directed patrol.

Squad   A group of officers who generally work together all the time under the supervision of a particular sergeant.

Sting operation   Undercover police operations in which police pose as criminals to arrest law violators.

Stop and frisk   The detaining of a person by law enforcement officers for the purpose of investigation, accompanied by a superficial examination of the person's body surface or clothing to discover weapons, contraband, or other objects relating to criminal activity.

Suicide by cop   The phenomenon in which a person wishing to die deliberately places an officer in a life-threatening situation, causing the officer to use deadly force against that person.

Sworn Law Enforcement Employee Average   Number of sworn law enforcement employees for each 1,000 residents.

Sworn members   Police employees given traditional police powers by state and local laws, including penal or criminal laws and criminal procedure laws.

Target hardening   The process of making a home or business as crime-proof as possible by installing locks, bars, alarms, and other protective devices.

Tennessee v. Garner   A U.S. Supreme Court case that ended the use of the fleeing felon rule.

Terrorism   The use of terrorist actions; one of the hallmarks of terrorism is indscriminate victimization.

Terrorist attacks against the United States of America on September 11, 2001   The terrorist attacks committed by al Qaeda.

Thief-takers   Private English citizens with no official status who were paid by the king for every criminal they arrested. They were similar to the bounty hunters of the American West.

Time-in-rank system   Promotional system in which police officers can advance in rank only after a specified time spent in the preceding rank.

Title IV   See Civil Rights Act of 1964

Undercover investigations   Covert investigations involving plainclothes officers.

Uniform Crime Reports (UCR)   Yearly collection of aggregate crime statistics prepared by the FBI based upon citizens' reports of crimes to the police.

Unity of command   A managerial concept that specifies that each individual in an organization is directly accountable to only one supervisor.

Vehicle tracking systems   Transmitters that enable investigators to track a vehicle during a surveillance. Also called transponders, bumper beepers, or homing devices.

Vigiles   Early Roman firefighters who also patrolled the streets to protect citizens.

Volstead Act (National Prohibition)   The Eighteenth Amendment to the U.S. Constitution, which became law in 1920 and forbade the sale and manufacture of alcohol.

Watch and ward   A rudimentary form of policing, designed to protect against crime, disturbances, and fire. All men were required to serve on it.

Weapons of mass destruction (WMD)   Chemical substances, biological agents, and nuclear materials that can be used for unparalleled destruction.

Wickersham Commission   The first national study of the U.S. criminal justice system, published in 1931.

Bibliography

Books

Abadinski, Howard. *Crime and Justice: An Introduction.* Chicago: Nelson-Hall, 1987.

Ahern, James. *Police in Trouble.* New York: Hawthorn Books, 1972.

Albanese, Jay S., and Robert D. Pursley. *Crime in America: Some Existing and Emerging Issues.* Englewood Cliffs, NJ: Regents/Prentice-Hall, 1993.

Alex, Nicholas. *Black in Blue: A Study of the Negro Policeman.* New York: Appleton- Century-Crofts, 1969.

Alex, Nicholas. *New York Cops Talk Back.* New York: Wiley, 1976.

Alpert, Geoffrey P., and Roger G. Dunham. *Police Pursuit Driving: Controlling Responses to Emergency Situations.* Westport, CT: Greenwood Press, 1990.

Alpert, Geoffrey P., and Roger G. Dunham. *Policing Urban America,* 2nd ed. Prospect Heights, IL: Waveland Press, 1992.

Alpert, Geoffrey P., and Lorie A. Fridell. *Police Vehicles and Firearms: Instruments of Deadly Force.* Prospect Heights, IL: Waveland Press, 1992.

American Bar Association. *Standards Relating to Urban Police Function.* New York: Institute of Judicial Administration, 1974.

Aristotle. *Nicomachean Ethics.*

Asbury, Herbert. *The Gangs of New York.* New York: Capricorn, 1970. Original edition, 1927.

Ayres, Richard M., and George S. Flanagan. *Preventing Law Enforcement Stress: The Organization's Role.* Washington, DC: National Sheriff's Association, 1990.

Ayto, John. *Dictionary of Word Origins.* New York: Arcade, 1990.

Bailey, F. Lee, Roger E. Zuckerman, and Kenneth R. Pierce. *The Employee Polygraph Protection Act: A Manual for Polygraph Examiners and Employers.* Severna Park, MD: American Polygraph Association, 1989.

Bailey, William G., ed. *The Encyclopedia of Police Science.* New York: Garland, 1989.

Baker, Mark. *Cops: Their Lives in Their Own Words.* New York: Simon & Schuster, 1985.

Barker, Thomas, and David L. Carter. *Police Deviance.* Cincinnati, OH: Anderson, 1986.

Barker, Thomas, and Julian Roebuck. *An Empirical Typology of Police Corruption: A Study in Organizational Deviance.* Springfield, IL: Charles C. Thomas, 1973.

Barletta, Michael. *After 9/11: Preventing Mass-Destruction Terrorism and Weapons Proliferation.* Monterey, CA: Center for Nonproliferation Studies, 2002.

Bayley, David, and Harold Mendelsohn. *Minorities and the Police.* New York: Free Press, 1969.

Bayley, David H. *Forces of Order: Police Behavior in Japan and the United States.* Berkeley: University of California Press, 1976.

Bayley, David H. *Patterns of Policing: A Comparative International Analysis,* New Brunswick, NJ: Rutgers University Press, 1985.

Becker, Harold K., and Jack E. Whitehouse. *Police of America: A Personal View: Introduction and Commentary.* Springfield, IL: Charles C. Thomas, 1980.

Bennett, R., ed. *Police at Work: Policy Issues and Analysis.* Beverly Hills, CA: Sage Publications, 1983.

Bennett, Wayne W., and Karen M. Hess. *Criminal Investigation.* St. Paul, MN: West, 1991, 1994.

Benyon, J., L. Turnbull, A. Willis, R. Woodward, and A. Beck. *Police Co-operation in Europe: An Investigation.* Leicester, U.K.: Centre for the Study of Public Orders, University of Leicester, 1993, reprinted 1995.

Berman, Jay Stuart. *Police Administration and Progressive Reform: Theodore Roosevelt as Police Commissioner of New York.* New York: Greenwood Press, 1987.

Besharov, Douglas J., ed. *Family Violence: Research and Public Policy Issues.* Washington, DC: University Press of America, 1990.

Bittner, Egon. *The Function of Police in Modern Society.* Cambridge, MA: Oelgeschlager, 1980.

Black, Donald. *The Manners and Customs of the Police.* New York: Academic Press, 1980.

Bloch, Peter B., and Deborah Anderson, *Policewomen on Patrol: Final Report.* Washington, DC: Police Foundation, 1974.

Blumberg, Abraham S., and Elaine Niederhoffer, eds. *The Ambivalent Force: Perspectives on the Police.* New York: Holt, Rinehart & Winston, 1985.

Boba, Rachel. *What is Problem Analysis? Problem Analysis in Policing: An Executive Summary.* Washington, DC: Police Foundation, 2003.

Bok, S. *Lying: Moral Choice in Public and Private Life.* New York: Pantheon, 1978.

Bopp, William J., and Donald O. Schultz. *A Short History of American Law Enforcement.* Springfield, IL: Charles C. Thomas, 1977.

Bouza, Anthony V. *The Police Mystique: An Insider's Look at Cops, Crime, and the Criminal Justice System.* New York: Plenum Press, 1990.

Boydstun, J. E. *San Diego Field Interrogation: Final Report.* Washington, DC: Police Foundation, 1975.

Bratton, William W., and Peter Knobler. *Turnaround: How America's Top Cop Reversed the Crime Epidemic.* New York: Random House, 1998.

Bridenbaugh, Carl. *Cities in Revolt: Urban Life in America, 1743–1776.* New York: Knopf, 1965.

Bridenbaugh, Carl. *Cities in the Wilderness: Urban Life in America, 1625–1742.* New York: Capricorn, 1964.

Broderick, John J. *Police in a Time of Change,* 2d ed. Prospect Heights, IL: Waveland Press, 1987.

Brown, Michael. *Working the Street.* New York: Russell Sage Foundation, 1981.

Brown, Sam, and Gini Graham Scott. *Private Eyes: The Role of the Private Investigator in American Marriage, Business, and Industry.* New York: Citadel Press, 1991.

Burgess, Ann Wolbert. *Sexual Assault of Children and Adolescents.* Lexington, MA: D. C. Heath, 1978.

Cahn, Michael F., and James M. Tien. *An Alternative Approach in Police Response: The Wilmington Management of Demand Program.* Cambridge, MA: Public Systems Evaluation, 1981.

Carden, Gerald. *Police Revitalization.* Lexington, MA: Lexington Books, 1977.

Carter, David L., Allen D. Sapp, and Darrel W. Stephens. *The State of Police Education: Policy Direction for the 21st Century.* Washington, DC: Police Executive Research Forum, 1989.

Chaiken, J. M., M. W. Lawless, and K. A. Stenson. *The Impact of Police Activity on Crime: Robberies in the New York City Subway System.* New York: Rand Institute, 1974.

Champion, Dean J. *Criminal Justice in the United States.* Columbus, OH: Merrill, 1989.

Chapman, Samuel G. *Police Patrol Readings,* 2d ed. Springfield, IL: Charles C. Thomas, 1970.

Chapman, S. G., and T. E. St. Johnston. *The Police Heritage in England and America.* East Lansing: Michigan State University, 1962.

Chevigny, Paul. *Police Power: Police Abuses in New York City.* New York: Pantheon, 1969.

Coffey, Alan. *Law Enforcement: A Human Relations Approach.* Englewood Cliffs, NJ: Prentice-Hall, 1990.

Cohen, Bernard, and Jan M. Chaiken. *Police Background Characteristics and Performance.* Lexington, MA: Lexington Books, 1973.

Cohn, Alvin, ed. *The Future of Policing.* Beverly Hills, CA: Sage Publications, 1978.

Cohn, Alvin W., and Emilio C. Viano. *Police Community Relations: Images, Roles, Realities.* Philadelphia: Lippincott, 1976.

Cohn, Ellen G., and Lawrence W. Sherman. *Police Policy on Domestic Violence, 1986: A National Survey.* Washington, DC: Crime Control Institute, 1987.

Cole, George F. *The American System of Criminal Justice,* 6th ed. Pacific Grove, CA: Brooks/Cole, 1992.

Cunliffe, F., and P. B. Piazza. *Criminalistics and Scientific Investigation.* Englewood Cliffs, NJ: Prentice-Hall, 1980.

Cox, Steven M., and Jack D. Fitzgerald. *Police in Community Relations: Critical Issues,* 2d ed. Dubuque, IA: William C. Brown, 1992.

Cox Commission. *Crisis at Columbia: Report of the Fact-Finding Commission Appointed to Investigate the Disturbances at Columbia University in April and May 1968.* New York: Vintage, 1968.

Critchley, T. A. *A History of Police in England and Wales,* 2d ed. Montclair, NJ: Patterson Smith, 1972.

Culbertson, R., and M. Tezak, eds. *Order under Law.* Prospect Heights, IL: Waveland Press, 1981.

Cunningham, William C., John J. Strauchs, and Clifford W. Van Meter. *The Hallcrest Report: Private Security and Police in America.* Portland, OR: Chancellor Press, 1985.

Cunningham, William C., John J. Strauchs, and Clifford W. Van Meter. *The Hallcrest Report II: Private Security Trends, 1970–2000.* Boston: Butterworth-Heinemann, 1990.

Daley, Robert. *Prince of the City: The Story of a Cop Who Knew Too Much.* Boston: Houghton Mifflin, 1978.

Davis, Kenneth Culp. *Police Discretion.* St. Paul, MN: West, 1975.

DeForest, Peter. *Forensic Science: An Introduction to Criminalistics.* New York: McGraw-Hill, 1983.

Delattre, E. *Character and Cops,* 3rd ed. Washington, DC: AEI Press, 1996.

del Carmen, Rolando V. *Civil Liabilities in American Policing: A Text for Law Enforcement Personnel.* Englewood Cliffs, NJ: Prentice-Hall, 1991.

Dempsey, John S. *Criminal Justice Update.* Minneapolis/St. Paul, MN: West, 1996.

Dempsey, John S. *Introduction to Investigations,* Belmont, CA: Wadsworth, 2003.

Dempsey, John S. *Policing: An Introduction to Law Enforcement.* Minneapolis/St. Paul, MN: West, 1994.

Dempsey, John S. *An Introduction to Policing.* Belmont, CA: Wadsworth/West, 1999.

Dempsey, John S. *An Introduction to Public and Private Investigations.* Minneapolis/St. Paul, MN: West, 1996.

Dershowitz, Alan M. *Taking Liberties: A Decade of Hard Cases, Bad Laws, and Bum Raps.* Chicago: Contemporary Books, 1988.

Dunham, Roger G., and Geoffrey P. Alpert. *Critical Issues in Policing,* 3rd ed. Prospect Heights, IL: Waveland Press, 1997.

Eck, John E. *Managing Case Assignments: The Burglary Investigation Decision Model Replication.* Washington, DC: Police Executive Research Forum, 1979.

Eck, John E., et al. *Problem Solving: Problem-Oriented Policing in Newport News.* Washington, DC: Police Executive Research Forum, 1987.

Eisenberg, Terry, et al. *Police Personnel Practices in State and Local Governments.* Washington, DC: Police Foundation, 1973.

Elliston, Frederick A., and Michael Feldberg, eds. *Moral Issues in Police Work.* Totowa, NJ: Rowman and Allanheld, 1985.

Emsley, Clive. *Policing and Its Context, 1750–1870.* New York: Schocken, 1984.

Faller, Kathleen Couborn. *Child Sexual Abuse: An Interdisciplinary Manual for the Diagnosis, Case Management and Treatment.* New York: Columbia University Press, 1988.

Farmer, Michael T., ed. *Differential Police Response Strategies.* Washington, DC: Police Executive Research Forum, 1981.

Fay, John J. *The Police Dictionary and Encyclopedia.* Springfield, IL: Charles C. Thomas, 1988.

Figgie International. *The Figgie Report, Part 4: Reducing Crime in America—Successful Community Efforts.* Willowby, OH: Figgie International, 1983.

Fletcher, Connie. *Breaking and Entering: Women Cops Break the Code of Silence to Tell Their Stories from the Inside.* New York: Simon & Schuster, 1995.

Fogelson, Robert M. *Big City Police.* Cambridge, MA: Harvard University Press, 1977.

Forst, Linda. *The Aging of America: A Handbook for Police Officers.* Springfield, IL: Charles C. Thomas, 2000.

Friendly, Fred W., and Martha J. H. Elliot. *The Constitution: That Delicate Balance: Landmark Cases That Shaped the Constitution.* New York: McGraw-Hill, 1984.

Fyfe, James J. *Contemporary Issues in Law Enforcement.* Beverly Hills, CA: Sage, 1981.

Fyfe, James J. "Shots Fired." Ph.D. diss., State University of New York–Albany, 1978.

Fyfe, James J., Jack R. Greene, William F. Walsh, O. W. Wilson, and Roy Clinton McLaren. *Police Administration,* 5th ed. New York: McGraw-Hill, 1997.

Gaines, Larry K., and Roger Miller. *Criminal Justice in Action.* Belmont, CA: Wadsworth/Thomson Learning, 2003.

Gaines, Larry K., Mittie T. Southerland, and John E. Angell. *Police Administration.* New York: McGraw-Hill, 1991.

Gallati, Robert J. *Introduction to Law Enforcement and Criminal Justice.* Springfield, IL: Charles E. Thomas, 1969.

Gallup, George Jr., and Alex Gallup. *The Gallup Poll Monthly Number 420.* Princeton, NJ: The Gallup Poll, 2000.

Gardiner, John A. *Traffic and the Police: Variations in Law Enforcement Policy.* Cambridge, MA: Harvard University Press, 1969.

Geffner, Edwin S. *The Internist's Compendium of Patient Information.* New York: McGraw-Hill, 1987.

Geller, William A., ed. *Police Leadership in America.* New York: Praeger, 1985.

Geller, William A., and Kevin J. Karales. *Split-Second Decisions.* Chicago: Chicago Law Enforcement Study Group, 1981.

Geller, William, and Michael S. Scott. *Deadly Force: What We Know.* Washington, DC: Police Executive Research Forum, 1992.

Gellerman, S. W. *Motivation and Productivity.* New York: American Management Association, 1963.

Gerber, S., ed. *Chemistry and Crime.* Washington, DC: American Chemical Society, 1983.

Germann, A. C., Frank D. Day, and Robert R. J. Gallati. *Introduction to Law Enforcement and Criminal Justice.* Springfield, IL: Charles C. Thomas, 1969.

Gold, Marion E. *Top Cops: Profiles of Women in Command.* Chicago: Brittany Publications Ltd., 1999

Goldstein, Herman. *Police Corruption: A Perspective on Its Nature and Control.* Washington, DC: Police Foundation, 1975.

Goldstein, Herman. *Policing a Free Society.* Cambridge, MA: Ballinger Press, 1977.

Goldstein, Herman. *Problem-Oriented Policing*. New York: McGraw-Hill, 1990.

Gottfredson, Michael R., and Don M. Gottfredson. *Decision Making in Criminal Justice: Toward the Rational Exercise of Discretion*. Cambridge, MA: Ballinger Press, 1980.

Graves, G., et al. *Developing a Street Patrol: A Guide for Neighborhood Crime Prevention Groups*. Boston: Neighborhood Crime Prevention Council, Justice Resource Institute, 1985.

Greene, Jack, and S. Mastrofski. *Community Policing: Rhetoric or Reality?* New York: Praeger, 1988.

Greenwood, Peter W., and Joan Petersilia. *The Criminal Investigation Process: Summary and Policy Implications*. Santa Monica, CA: Rand Corporation, 1975.

Grimshaw, Allen D. *Racial Violence in the United States*. Chicago: Aldine, 1969.

Harris, Richard. *The Police Academy: An Inside View*. New York: Wiley, 1973.

Heaphy, John, ed. *Police Practices: The General Administrative Survey*. Washington, DC: Police Foundation, 1978.

Heffernan, W., and T. Stroup, eds. *Police Ethics: Hard Choices in Law Enforcement*. New York: John Jay Press, 1985.

Henry, Vincent E. *The Compstat Paradigm: Management Accountability in Policing, Business and the Public Sector*. New York: Looseleaf Law Publications, 2002.

Horan, James D., and Howard Swiggett. *The Detective Dynasty That Made History*. New York: Crown, 1967.

Horan, James D., and Howard Swiggett. *The Pinkerton Story*. New York: Putnam, 1951.

Hungerford, Edward. *Wells Fargo: Advancing the American Frontier*. New York: Bonanza, 1949.

Hunt, W. E. *History of England*. New York: Harper & Brothers, 1938.

Inciardi, James A. *Criminal Justice*, 3rd ed. Orlando, FL: Harcourt Brace Jovanovich, 1990.

International Association of Chiefs of Police. *The Future of Women in Policing*, at www.theiacp.,org, 1998.

International Association of Chiefs of Police. *Improving Safety in Indian Country: Recommendations from the IACP 2001 Summit*. Alexandria, VA: International Association of Chiefs of Police, 2001.

International Association of Chiefs of Police. *Operational Issues in the Small Law Enforcement Agency*. Arlington, VA: International Association of Chiefs of Police, 1990.

International Association of Chiefs of Police. *A Report by the Indian Country Section of the International Association of Chiefs of Police*. Alexandria, VA: International Association of Chiefs of Police, 1994.

International Association of Chiefs of Police. *A Survey of the Police Department of Youngstown, Ohio*. Washington, DC: International Association of Chiefs of Police, 1964.

International Association of Chiefs of Police. *Training Catalog: IACP Educational Programs*. Alexandria, VA: International Association of Chiefs of Police, published yearly.

International Association of Chiefs of Police. *What Do Victims Want? Effective Strategies to Achieve Justice for Victims of Crime*. Alexandria, VA: International Association of Chiefs of Police, 2002.

Jacob, Herbert. *Urban Justice*. Boston: Little, Brown, 1973.

Johnson, David R. *American Law Enforcement: A History*. St. Louis, MO: Forum Press, 1981.

Kadish, Sanford H. *Encyclopedia of Crime and Justice*. New York: Free Press, 1983.

Kappeler, Victor, Richard Sluder, and Geoffrey Alpert. *Forces of Deviance, Understanding the Dark Side of Policing*. Prospect Heights, IL: Waveland Press, 1994.

Kelling, George L. *The Kansas City Preventive Patrol Experiment: A Summary Report*. Washington, DC: Police Foundation, 1974.

Kenney, Dennis Jay, ed. *Police and Policing: Contemporary Issues*. New York: Praeger, 1989.

Kindschi-Gosselin, Denise. *Heavy Hands: An Introduction to the Crimes of Family Violence*, 2nd ed. Upper Saddle River, NJ: Prentice Hall, 2003.

Kirkham, George L., and Laurin A. Wollan, Jr. *Introduction to Law Enforcement*. New York: Harper & Row, 1980.

Klein, Irving J. *Constitutional Law for Criminal Justice Professionals*. Miami, FL: Coral Gables, 1986, 1993.

Klockars, Carl B., ed. *Thinking about Police: Contemporary Readings*. New York: McGraw-Hill, 1983.

Klockars, Carl B., and Stephen D. Mastrofski, eds. *Thinking about Police: Contemporary Readings*, 2d ed. New York: McGraw-Hill, 1991.

Kluger, Richard. *Simple Justice*. New York: Vintage, 1977.

Knapp Commission. *Report on Police Corruption*. New York: Braziller, 1973.

Kornblum, Alan N. *The Moral Hazards*. Lexington, MA: Lexington Books, 1976.

Kroes, W. *Society's Victim, The Policeman: An Analysis of Job Stress in Policing*. Springfield, IL: Charles C. Thomas, 1976.

Kurian, George Thomas. *World Encyclopedia of Police Forces and Penal Systems*. New York: Facts on File, 1989.

Kurland, Daniel J., and Christina Polsenberg. *Internet Guide for Criminal Justice*. Belmont, CA: Wadsworth, 1997.

Lake, Carolyn. *Undercover for Wells Fargo*. Boston: Houghton Mifflin, 1969.

Lane, Roger. *Policing the City*. New York: Atheneum, 1975.

Lane, Roger. *Policing the City: Boston 1822–1885*. Cambridge, MA: Harvard University Press, 1967.

Leinen, Steven. *Black Police, White Society*. New York: New York University Press, 1984.

Lonsway, Kimberly. *Hiring and Retaining More Women: The Advantages to Law Enforcement Agencies*, 2000. Available at www.womenandpolicing.org.

Lonsway, Kimberly. *The Role of Women in Community Policing: Dismantling the Warrior Image*, 2001. Available at www.communitypolicing.org.

Loving, Nancy. *Responding to Spouse Abuse and Wife Beating: A Guide for Police*. Washington, DC: Police Executive Research Forum, 1980.

Lundman, Richard. *Police and Policing*. New York: Holt, Rinehart & Winston, 1980.

Lundman, Richard. *Police Behavior: A Sociological Perspective*. New York: Oxford University Press, 1980.

Madonna, John M., and Richard E. Kelly, *Treating Police Stress: The Work and the Words of Peer Counselors*. Springfield, IL: Charles C. Thomas, 2002.

Martin, Susan E. *Women on the Move? A Report on the Status of Women in Policing*. Washington, DC: Police Foundation, 1989.

Mass, Peter. *Serpico*. New York: Bantam Books, 1974.

Matulia, Kenneth J. *A Balance of Forces*, 2d ed. Gaithersburg, MD: International Association of Chiefs of Police, 1985.

McAdam, Doug. *Freedom Summer*. New York: Oxford University Press, 1988.

McAlary, Mike. *Buddy Boys: When Good Cops Turn Bad*. New York: Putnam, 1987.

McCamey, William P., Gene L. Caramella, and Steven M. Cox, *Contemporary Municipal Policing*. Boston: Allyn & Bacon, 2003.

McCrie, Robert D., ed. *Security Letter Source Book*. New York: Security Letter, published annually.

Miller, John, and Michael Stone with Chris Mitchell. *The Cell: Inside the 9/11 Plot, Why the FBI and CIA Failed to Stop It.* New York: Hyperion, 2002.

Miller, Linda S., and Karen M. Hess. *The Police in the Community: Strategies for the 21stt Century*, 3rd ed. Belmont, CA: Wadsworth, 2002.

Miller, Wilbur R. *Cops and Bobbies: Police Authority in New York and London, 1830–1870.* Chicago: University of Chicago Press, 1977.

Milton, Catherine H. *Women in Policing.* Washington, DC: Police Foundation, 1972.

Milton, Catherine H., et al. *Police Use of Deadly Force.* Washington, DC: Police Foundation, 1977.

Monkkonen, Eric. *Police in Urban America: 1860–1920.* Cambridge, MA: Harvard University Press, 1981.

Morgan, Edward P. *The 60's Experience: Hard Lessons about Modern America.* Philadelphia: Temple University Press, 1991.

Mouzos, Jenny. *Investigating Homicide: New Responses for an Old Crime.* Canberra ACT, Australia, Australian Institute of Criminology, 2001.

Muir, W. K., Jr. *Police: Streetcorner Politicians.* Chicago: University of Chicago Press, 1977.

Murphy, Patrick V., and Thomas Plate. *Commissioner: A View from the Top of American Law Enforcement.* New York: Simon & Schuster, 1977.

Nash, Jay Robert. *Encyclopedia of World Crime.* Wilmette, IL: Crime Books, 1990.

National Center for Women and Policing. *Men, Women and Police Excessive Force: A Tale of Two Genders: A Content Analysis of Civil Liability Cases, Sustained Allegations and Citizen Complaints*, 2002. Available at www.womenandpolicing.org.

National Police Chiefs and Sheriffs Information Bureau. *National Directory of Law Enforcement Administrators.* Stevens Point, WI: National Police Chiefs and Sheriffs Information Bureau, published yearly.

Niederhoffer, Arthur. *Behind the Shield: The Police in Urban Society.* Garden City, NY: Anchor Books, 1967.

O'Donnell, Kenneth. *Deadly Force.* New York: William Morrow, 1983.

Osterburg, James W., and Richard H. Ward, *Criminal Investigation: A Method for Reconstructing the Past.* Cincinnati, OH: Anderson Publishing, 1992.

Owings, Chloe. *Women Police.* Montclair, NJ: Patterson Smith, 1969. (Original edition, 1925.)

Palmiotto, Michael J., ed. *Critical Issues in Criminal Justice.* Cincinnati, OH: Anderson, 1988.

Palmiotto, Michael J., ed. *Police Misconduct.* Upper Saddle River, NJ: Prentice Hall, 2001.

Pike, Owen. *A History of Crime in England.* London, U.K.: Smith, Elder, 1873–1876.

Perez, Douglas W. and J. Alan Moore. *Police Ethics: A Matter of Character.* Cincinnati, OH: Atomic Dog Publishing, 2002.

Pilant, Lois. *Less-Than-Lethal-Weapons: New Solutions for Law Enforcement.* Alexandria, VA: International Association of Chiefs of Police, 2000.

Pinkerton, Allan. *The Expressman and the Detective.* New York: Arno Press, 1976.

Pinkerton Investigation Division. *Investigations Department Training Manual.* Encino, CA: Pinkerton's Security and Investigations Services, 1990.

Pinkerton Investigation Division. *Pinkerton Reference Guide to Investigation Services.* Encino, CA: Pinkerton Security and Investigation Services, 1995.

Police Executive Research Forum. *Survey of Police Operational and Administrative Practice, 1981.* Washington, DC: Police Executive Research Forum, 1982.

Police Foundation. *Domestic Violence and the Police: Studies in Detroit and Kansas City.* Washington, DC: Police Foundation, 1977.

Police Foundation. *Experiments in Police Improvement: A Progress Report.* Washington, DC: Police Foundation, 1972.

Police Foundation. *The Newark Foot Patrol Experiment.* Washington: DC: Police Foundation, 1991.

Pollock, Joycelyn M. *Ethics in Crime and Justice: Dilemmas and Decisions,* 3rd ed. Belmont, CA: West/Wadsworth, 1998.

Poveda, Tony. *Lawlessness and Reform: The FBI in Transition.* Pacific Grove, CA: Brooks/Cole, 1990.

Prassel, Frank R. *The Western Peace Officer: A Legacy of Law and Order.* Norman: University of Oklahoma Press, 1972.

Press, S. J. *Some Effects of an Increase in Police Manpower in the 20th Precinct of New York.* New York: Rand Institute, 1971.

Pringle, Patrick. *Highwaymen.* New York: Roy, 1963.

Pringle, Patrick. *Hue and Cry: The Story of Henry and John Fielding and Their Bow Street Runners.* New York: Morrow, 1965.

Pringle, Patrick. *The Thief Takers.* London, U.K.: Museum Press, 1958.

Punch, Maurice. *Control of the Police Organization.* Cambridge, MA: MIT Press, 1983.

Pursley, Robert D. *Introduction to Criminal Justice,* 5th ed. New York: Macmillan, 1991.

Radano, Gene. *Walking the Beat: A New York Policeman Tells What It's Like on His Side of the Law.* Cleveland, OH: World Publishing, 1968.

Rand Corporation. *Organizing for Homeland Security.* Santa Monica: CA: Rand Corporation, 2002.

Radelet, Louis A. *The Police and the Community.* Encino, CA: Glencoe, 1980.

Reid, Sue Titus. *Criminal Justice.* New York: Macmillan, 1993.

Reiss, Albert J. *The Police and the Public.* New Haven, CT: Yale University Press, 1971.

Reiss, Albert J., and Michael Tonry, eds. *Crime and Justice.* Chicago: University of Chicago Press, 1986.

Reith, Charles. *The Blind Eye of History: A Study of the Origins of the Present Police Era.* London, U.K.: Faber, 1912.

Reppetto, Thomas. *The Blue Parade.* New York: Free Press, 1978.

Reuter, Peter, et al. *Drug Use and Drug Programs in the Washington Metropolitan Area.* Santa Monica, CA: Rand Corporation, 1988.

Richardson, James F. *The New York Police: Colonial Times to 1901.* New York: Oxford University Press, 1976.

Richardson, James F. *Urban Police in the United States.* Port Washington, NY: Kennikat Press, 1974.

Rieck, Albert. *Justice and Police in England.* London, U.K.: Butterworth, 1936.

Robin, Gerald D., and Richard H. Anson. *Introduction to the American Criminal Justice System,* 4th ed. New York: Harper & Row, 1988.

Robinson, Deborah Mitchell, ed. *Policing and Crime Prevention.* Upper Saddle River, NJ: Prentice Hall, 2002.

Roe, Allan, and Norma Roe. *Police Selection: A Technical Summary of Validity Studies.* Ogden, UT: Diagnostic Specialists, 1982.

Ross, H. Lawrence. *Deterring the Drunk Driver: Legal Policy and Social Control.* Lexington, MA: D. C. Heath, 1982.

Rubenstein, Jonathan. *City Police.* New York: Ballentine Books, 1978.

Ruchelman, Leonard. *Who Rules the Police?* New York: New York University Press, 1973.

Rush, George E. *The Dictionary of Criminal Justice.* Guilford, CT: Dushkin Publishing, 1994.

Saferstein, R. *Criminalistics: An Introduction to Forensic Science.* Englewood Cliffs, NJ: Prentice-Hall, 1987.

Saferstein, R. *Forensic Science Handbook.* Englewood Cliffs, NJ: Prentice-Hall, 1988.

Sante, Luc. *Low Life: Lures and Snares of Old New York.* New York: Farrar, Straus & Giroux, 1991.

Scharf, Peter, and Arnold Binder. *The Badge and the Bullet: Police Use of Deadly Force*. New York: Praeger, 1983.

Schmalleger, Frank. *Criminal Justice Today: An Introductory Text for the Twenty-First Century*. Englewood Cliffs, NJ: Prentice-Hall, 1991, 1994, 1997.

Senna, Joseph J., and Larry J. Siegel. *Introduction to Criminal Justice*. St. Paul, MN: West, 1993, 1996.

Shaffer, Ron, Kevin Klose, and Alfred E. Lewis. *Surprise! Surprise!* New York: Viking, 1979.

Sheehan, Robert, and Gary W. Cordner. *Introduction to Police Administration*. Cincinnati, OH: Anderson, 1989, 1995.

Sherman, Lawrence W., ed. *Police Corruption: A Sociological Perspective*. Garden City, NY: Doubleday, 1974.

Sherman, Lawrence W. *Repeat Calls to Police in Minneapolis*. Washington, DC: Crime Control Institute, 1987.

Sherman, Lawrence W. *Scandal and Reform: Controlling Police Corruption*. Berkeley: University of California Press, 1978.

Sherman, Lawrence W., and Richard A. Berk. *The Minneapolis Domestic Violence Experiment*. Washington, DC: Police Foundation, 1984.

Sherman, Lawrence W., and Ellen G. Cohn. *Citizens Killed by Big-City Police, 1970–1984*. Washington, DC: Crime Control Institute, 1986.

Sherman, Lawrence W., et al. *The Quality of Police Education*. San Francisco: Jossey-Bass, 1978.

Sherman, Lawrence W. and Dennis Rogan. *Policing Domestic Violence: Experimentsand Dilemmas*. New York: Free Press, 1992.

Schulz, Dorothy Moses. *From Social Worker to Crimefighter: Women in United States Municipal Policing*. New York: Praeger, 1995.

Shusta, Robert M., Deena R. Levine, Philip P. Harris, and Herbert Z. Wong. *Multicultural Law Enforcement: Strategies for Peacekeeping in a Diverse Society*. Englewoods Cliffs, NJ: Prentice-Hall, 1995.

Silberman, Charles. *Criminal Violence, Criminal Justice*. New York: Vintage Books, 1978.

Siegel, Larry J. and Joseph J. Senna. *Essentials of Criminal Justice*. Belmont, CA: Wadsworth/Thomson Learning, 2004.

Siringo, Charles A. *A Cowboy Detective: A True Story of Twenty-Two Years with a World-Famous Detective Agency*. Lincoln: University of Nebraska Press, 1988.

Skogan, Wesley G. *Disorder and Decline: Crime and the Spiral of Decay in American Neighborhoods*. New York: Free Press, 1990.

Skolnick, Jerome H. *Justice without Trial: Law Enforcement in a Democratic Society*. New York: Wiley, 1975, 1995.

Skolnick, Jerome H., and David H. Bayley. *The New Blue Line: Police Innovation in Six American Cities*. New York: Free Press, 1986.

Skolnick, Jerome H., and James J. Fyfe. *Above the Law: Police and the Excessive Use of Force*. New York: Free Press, 1993.

Smith, Bruce. *Police Systems in the United States*. New York: Harper & Row, 1950.

Smith, Bruce. *Rural Crime Control*. New York: Columbia University Institute of Public Administration, 1933.

Sonkin, Daniel J. and Michael Durphy. *Learning to Live Without Violence: A Handbook for Men*, 5th ed. Volcano, CA: Volcano Press, 1997.

Sparrow, Malcolm, Mark Moore, and David Kennedy. *Beyond 911: A New Era for Policing*. New York: Basic Books, 1990.

Spelman,W., and D. K. Brown. *Calling the Police: Citizen Reporting of Serious Crime*. Washington, DC: Police Executive Research Forum, 1981.

Staufenberger, Richard A. *Progress in Policing: Essays on Change*. Cambridge, MA: Ballinger Press, 1980.

Steffens, Lincoln. *The Autobiography of Lincoln Steffens*. New York: Harcourt Brace Jovanovich, 1958. (Original edition, 1931.)

Steffens, Lincoln. *The Shame of the Cities*. New York: Hill and Wang, 1957. (Original edition, 1902.)

Steinman, Michael, ed. *Woman Battering: Policy Responses*. Cincinnati, OH: Anderson, 1991.

Straus, Murray A., Richard J. Gelles, and Suzanne Steinmetz. *Behind Closed Doors: Violence in the American Family*. Garden City, NY: Anchor Press, 1980.

Sutherland, Edwin H., and Donald Cressey. *Principles of Criminology*. 8th ed. Philadelphia: Lippincott, 1970.

Swank, C., and J. Conser, eds. *The Police Personnel System*. New York: Wiley, 1983.

Swanson, Charles R., Leonard Territo, and Robert W. Taylor. *Police Administration: Structures, Processes, and Behavior*, 2nd ed. New York: Macmillan, 1988.

Swanson, Charles R., Leonard Territo, and Robert W. Taylor. *Police Administration*, 5th ed. Upper Saddle River, NJ: Prentice-Hall, 2001.

Territo, Leonard, Charles R. Swanson, and N. C. Chamelin. *The Police Personnel Selection Process*. Indianapolis: Bobbs-Merrill, 1977.

Terry, W. Clinton. *Policing Society: An Occupational View*. New York: Wiley, 1985.

Theoharis, Althan, and John Stuart Cox. *The Boss*. Philadelphia: Temple University Press, 1988.

Thibault, Edward A., Lawrence M. Lynch, and R. Bruce McBride. *Proactive Police Management*. Englewood Cliffs, NJ: Prentice-Hall, 1985, 1991, 2004.

Tien, James M., James W. Simon, and Richard C. Larson, *An Alternative Approach in Police Patrol: The Wilmington Split-Force Experiment*. Cambridge, MA: Public Systems Evaluation, 1977.

Tobias, John J. *Crime and Police in England, 1700–1900*. New York: St. Martin's Press, 1979.

Tonry, Michael, and Morris, N. *Crime and Justice: A Review of Research*. Chicago: University of Chicago Press, 1990.

Trojanowicz, Robert C., and Dennis W. Banas. *The Impact of Foot Patrol on Black and White Perceptions of Policing*. East Lansing: National Neighborhood Foot Patrol Center, School of Criminal Justice, Michigan State University, 1988.

Trojanowicz, Robert C., and Dennis W. Banas. *Perceptions of Safety: A Comparison of Foot Patrol versus Motor Patrol Officers*. East Lansing: National Neighborhood Foot Patrol Center, School of Criminal Justice, Michigan State University, 1985.

Trojanowicz, Robert C., and Bonnie Bucqueroux. *Community Policing: A Contemporary Perspective*. Cincinnati, OH: Anderson, 1990.

Trojanowicz, Robert C., and H. A. Harden. *The Status of Contemporary Community Policing Programs*. East Lansing: National Neighborhood Foot Patrol Center, School of Criminal Justice, Michigan State University, 1984.

Viorst, Milton. *Fire in the Streets: America in the 1960's*. New York: Simon & Schuster, 1970.

Visionics Corporation. *Adaptive Surveillance: A Novel Approach to Facial Surveillance for CCTV Systems, Final Progress Report*. Jersey City, NJ: Visionics Corporation, 2001.

Wackenhut Investigations Division. *Integrity Testing and Other Shopping Services*. Coral Gables, FL: The Wackenhut Corporation, 1995.

Wackenhut Investigations Division. *Investigative Services*. Coral Gables: FL: The Wackenhut Corporation, 1995.

Waldron, Ronald J. *The Criminal Justice System: An Introduction*, 4th ed. New York: Harper & Row, 1989.

Walker, Samuel. *A Critical History of Police Reform: The Emergence of Professionalism*. Lexington, MA: Lexington Books, 1977.

Walker, Samuel. *The Police in America: An Introduction*. New York: McGraw-Hill, 1992, 1995.

Walker, Samuel. *Popular Justice: History of American Criminal Justice*. New York: Oxford University Press, 1980.

Walker, Samuel. *Sense and Nonsense about Crime*. Monterey, CA: Brooks/Cole, 1985.

Walker, Samuel, and Vic Bumphus. *A National Survey of Civilian Oversight of the Police*. Omaha: University of Nebraska at Omaha, 1991.

Walker, Samuel, and Charles M. Katz. *Police in America* 4th ed. New York: McGraw-Hill, 2002.

Wambaugh, Joseph. *The Blue Knight*. Boston: Little, Brown, 1973.

Webb, Walter Prescott. *The Texas Rangers: A Century of Frontier Defense*. Boston: Houghton Mifflin, 1935.

Weiner, Norman. *The Role of Police in Urban Society: Conflict and Consequences*. Indianapolis: Bobbs-Merrill, 1976.

West, J. A. *Facial Identification Technology and Law Enforcement*. Sacramento, CA: California Commission on Peace Officer Standards and Training, 1996.

Westley, William. *Violence and the Police: A Sociological Study of Law, Custom, and Morality*. Cambridge, MA: MIT Press, 1970.

White, Jonathan R. *Defending the Homeland: Domestic Intelligence, Law Enforcement, and Security*. Belmont, CA: Wadsworth, 2004.

White, Jonathan R. *Terrorism: An Introduction*, 3rd ed. Belmont, CA: Wadsworth, 2001.

White, Jonathan R. *Terrorism: An Introduction: 2002 Update*, 4th ed. Belmont, CA: Wadsworth, 2003.

Whited, Charles. *The Decoy Man*. New York: Playboy Press, 1973.

Wilber, Charles C. *Ballistic Science for the Law Enforcement Officer*. Springfield, IL: Charles C. Thomas, 1977.

Willbanks, William. *The Myth of a Racist Criminal Justice System*. Monterey, CA: Brooks/Cole, 1987.

Williams, Juan. *Eyes on the Prize: America's Civil Rights Years, 1954–1965*. New York: Penguin, 1983.

Wilson, James Q. *Thinking about Crime*. New York: Basic Books, 1983.

Wilson, James Q. *Varieties of Police Behavior: The Management of Law and Order in Eight Communities*. Cambridge, MA: Harvard University Press, 1968.

Wilson, O. W. *Police Administration*. New York: McGraw-Hill, 1950.

Wilson, O. W., and Roy Clinton McLaren. *Police Administration*, 4th ed. New York: McGraw-Hill, 1977.

Wycoff, Mary Ann, et al. *Citizen Contact Patrol: Executive Summary*. Washington, DC: Police Foundation, 1985.

Yuille, John C., ed. *Police Selection and Training: The Role of Psychology*. Dordrecht, The Netherlands: Martinus Nijhoff Publishers, 1986.

Government Reports

ABT Associates. *New York City Anti-Crime Patrol: Exemplary Project Validation Report*. Washington, DC: U.S. Government Printing Office, 1974.

Ashcroft, John. *A Resource Guide to Law Enforcement, Corrections and Forensic Technologies*. Washington, DC: U.S. Department of Justice, 2001.

Baker, B. T. *Law Enforcement within Indian Country: An Introduction*. Artesia, NM: Federal Law Enforcement Training Center, 1993.

Bayley, David H. and Clifford D. Shearing. *The New Structure of Policing: Description, Conceptualization and Research Agenda*. Washington, DC: National Institute of Justice, 2001.

Bittner, Egon. *The Functions of the Police in Modern Society*. Washington, DC: U.S. Government Printing Office, 1970.

Brown, Lee P. *Community Policing: A Practical Guide for Police Officials. Perspectives on Policing, no. 12*. Washington, DC: U.S. Government Printing Office, 1989.

Bureau of Indian Affairs, Division of Law Enforcement. *Indian Law Enforcement History*. Washington, DC: U.S. Government Printing Office, 1975.

Button, Peter D. *Less-Lethal Force Technology*. Toronto: Toronto Metropolitan Police Commission, 2001.

California Highway Patrol. *Pursuit Study*. Sacramento: California Highway Patrol, 1983.

Calvert, Geoffrey N. *Portable Police Pensions—Improving Inter-Agency Transfers*. Washington, DC: U.S. Government Printing Office, 1971.

Caplan, Marc H., and Joe Holt Anderson. *Forensic: When Science Bears Witness*. Washington, DC: National Institute of Justice, 1984.

Campbell, Michael S. *Field Training for Police Officers: State of the Art*. Washington, DC: U.S. Government Printing Office, 1986.

Caskey, C. Thomas, and Holly A. Hammond. *Automated DNA Typing: Method of the Future?* Washington, DC: National Institute of Justice, 1997.

Cawley, Donald F., et al. *Managing Criminal Investigations: Manual*. Washington, DC: U.S. Government Printing Office, 1977.

Chaiken, M., ed. *Street Level Drug Enforcement: Examining the Issues*. Washington, DC: National Institute of Justice, 1988.

Chaiken, Marcia, and Jan Chaiken. *Priority Prosecutors of High Rate Dangerous Offenders*. Washington, DC: National Institute of Justice, 1991.

Cohen, Bernard, and Jan Chaiken. *Investigators Who Perform Well*. Washington, DC: National Institute of Justice, 1987.

Commission on Accreditation for Law Enforcement Agencies. *Standards for Law Enforcement Agencies*. Fairfax, VA: Commission on Accreditation for Law Enforcement Agencies, 1987.

Connors, Edward. *Convicted by Juries, Exonerated by Science: Case Studies in the Use of DNA Evidence to Establish Innocence After Trial*. Washington, DC: National Institute of Justice, 1996.

Cox Commission. *Crisis at Columbia: Report of the Fact-Finding Commission Appointed to Investigate the Disturbances at Columbia University in April and May 1968*. New York: Vintage, 1968.

Cunningham, William C., John J. Strauchs, and Clifford W. Van Meter. *Private Security: Patterns and Trends*. Washington, DC: U.S. Government Printing Office, 1991.

Cunningham, William C., and Todd H. Taylor. *The Growth of Private Security*. Washington, DC: U.S. Government Printing Office, 1984.

DeJong, William. *Project DARE: Teaching Kids to Say "No" to Drugs and Alcohol*. Washington, DC: National Institute of Justice, 1986.

Donnelly, T. *Less Lethal Technologies: Initial Prioritisation and Evaluation*. London, U.K.: Great Britain Home Office, Policing and Reducing Crime Unit, 2001.

Executive Office of the President of the United States. *Advancing Justice Through DNA Technology*. Washington, DC: National Institute of Justice, 2003.

Federal Bureau of Investigation. *FBI Law Enforcement Bulletin*. Washington, DC: Federal Bureau of Investigation, published monthly.

Federal Bureau of Investigation. *Law Enforcement Officers Killed and Assaulted*. Washington, DC: U.S. Government Printing Office, published annually.

Federal Bureau of Investigation. *Uniform Crime Reports: Crime in the United States*. Washington, DC: U.S. Government Printing Office, published annually.

Finn, Peter E. *Block Watches Help Crime Victims in Philadelphia*. Washington, DC: National Institute of Justice, 1986.

Finn, Peter E., and Beverly N. W. Lee. *Establishing and Expanding Victim–Witness Assistance Programs*. Washington, DC: U.S. Government Printing Office, 1988.

Finn, Peter E., and Monique Sullivan. *Police Response to Special Populations: Handling the Mentally Ill, Public Inebriate, and the Homeless*. Washington, DC: National Institute of Justice, 1988.

Finn, Peter E. and Julie Esselman Tomz. *Developing a Law Enforcement Stress Program for Officers and Their Families*. Washington, DC: National Institute of Justice, 1997.

Foti, Charles C., Jr. *The Effect of Drug Testing in New Orleans*. Washington, DC: National Institute of Justice, 1993.

Freedman, Kenneth R., and Terry Estrada-Mullaney. *Using Dolls to Interview Child Victims: Legal Concerns and Interview Procedures*. Washington, DC: National Institute of Justice, 1988.

Garofalo, James, and Maureen McLeod. *Improving the Use and Effectiveness of Neighborhood Watch Programs*. Washington, DC: National Institute of Justice, 1988.

Geller, William. *Crime File: Deadly Force*. Washington, DC: National Institute of Justice, 1985.

Gifford, Sidra Lea. *Justice Expenditures and Employment in the United States, 1999*. Washington, DC: Bureau of Justice Statistics, 2002.

Greenberg, Ilene, and Robert Wasserman. *Managing Criminal Investigations*. Washington, DC: U.S. Government Printing Office, 1979.

Griesinger, George W., et al. *Civil Service Systems: Their Impact on Police Administration*. Washington, DC: U.S. Government Printing Office, 1979.

Guiliani, Rudolph W., Randy M. Mastro, and Donna Lynn. *Mayor's Management Report: The City of New York*. New York: City of New York, 1997.

Halper, Andrew, and Richard Ku. *New York City Police Department Street Crime Unit*. Washington, DC: U.S. Government Printing Office, nd.

Hammett., Theodore M. *AIDS and the Law Enforcement Officer: Concerns and Policy Responses*. Washington, DC: U.S. Government Printing Office, 1987.

Hammett., Theodore M. *Precautionary Measures and Protective Equipment: Developing a Reasonable Response: National Institute of Justice AIDS Bulletin*. Washington, DC: National Institute of Justice, 1988.

Hammett, Theodore M., and Walter Bond. *Risks of Infection with the AIDS Virus through Exposures to Blood: National Institute of Justice AIDS Bulletin*. Washington, DC: National Institute of Justice, 1987.

Hammett, Theodore M., Harold W. Jaffe, and Bruce A. Johnson. *The Cause, Transmission and Incidence of AIDS: National Institute of Justice AIDS Bulletin*. Washington, DC: National Institute of Justice, 1987.

Harries, Keith. *Mapping Crime: Principle and Practice*. Washington, DC: National Institute of Justice, 1999.

Hartman, Francis X., ed. *Debating the Evolution of American Policing. Perspectives on Policing, no. 5*. Washington, DC: U.S. Government Printing Office, 1988.

Hayeslip, David W. *Local-Level Drug Enforcement: New Strategies*. Washington, DC: National Institute of Justice, 1989.

Hecker, JayEtta. *Homeland Security: Intergovernmental Coordination and Partnership Will Be Critical to Success*. Washington, DC: General Accounting Office, 2002.

Hickman, Matthew J., and Brian Reaves. *Local Police Departments 1999*. Washington, DC: Bureau of Justice Statistics, 2001.

Hickman, Matthew J., and Brian Reaves. *Local Police Departments, 2000*. Washington, DC: Bureau of Justice Statistics, 2003.

Houston Police Department. *Annual Report*. Houston: Houston Police Department, published annually.

International City Management Association. *Municipal Yearbook*. Washington, DC: International City Management Association, published annually.

Kakalik, James F., and Sorrel Wildhorn. *Private Police in the United States*. Washington, DC: National Institute of Justice, 1971.

Kansas City Police Department. *Response Time Analysis: Executive Summary*. Washington, DC: U.S. Government Printing Office, 1978.

Kelling, George L. *"Broken Windows" and Police Discretion*. Washington, DC: National Institute of Justice, 1999.

Kelling, George L. *Foot Patrol*. Washington, DC: National Institute of Justice, 1987.

Kelling, George L. *Police and Communities: The Quiet Revolution. Perspectives on Policing, no. 1*. Washington, DC: U.S. Government Printing Office, 1988.

Kelling, George L. *What Works? Research and the Police*. Washington, DC: National Institute of Justice, nd.

Kelling, George L., and Mark H. Moore. *The Evolving Strategy of Policing. Perspectives on Policing, no. 4*. Washington, DC: U.S. Government Printing Office, 1988.

Kelling, George L., and James K. Stewart. *Neighborhoods and Police: The Maintenance of Civil Authority. Perspectives on Policing, no. 10*. Washington, DC: U.S. Government Printing Office, 1989.

Kelling, George L., Robert Wasserman, and Hubert Williams. *Police Accountability and Community Policing. Perspectives on Policing, no. 7*.Washington, DC: U.S. Government Printing Office, 1988.

Klockars, Carl B., Jack R. Greene, and S. Wissmann. *An Evaluation of Resource Allocation in the Wilmington Police Department*. Wilmington, DE: Office of the Director of Public Safety, 1988.

Levine, Margaret J., and J. Thomas McEwen. *Patrol Deployment*. Washington, DC: National Institute of Justice, 1985.

Los Angeles Police Department. *Annual Report*. Los Angeles: Los Angeles Police Department, published annually.

Maguire, Kathleen, and Ann L. Pastore, eds. *Sourcebook of Criminal Justice Statistics*. Washington, DC: U.S. Department of Justice, Bureau of Justice Statistics, U.S. Government Printing Office, published annually.

Manili, Barbara, and Edward Connors. *Police Chiefs and Sheriffs Rank Their Criminal Justice Needs*. Washington, DC: National Institute of Justice, 1988.

McEwen, J. Thomas, Edward F. Connors III, and Marcia J. Cohen. *Evaluation of the Differential Police Responses Field Test*. Washington, DC: U.S. Government Printing Office, 1986.

McEwen, J. Thomas, Barbara Manili, and Edward Connors. *Employee Drug Testing Policies in Police Departments*. Washington, DC: National Institute of Justice, 1986.

Moore, Mark H., and Mark A. R. Kleiman. *The Police and Drugs. Perspectives on Policing, no. 11*. Washington, DC: U.S. Government Printing Office, 1989.

Moore, Mark H., and Robert C. Trojanowitz. *Corporate Strategies for Policing. Perspectives on Policing, no. 6*. Washington, DC: U.S. Government Printing Office, 1988.

Moore, Mark H., and Robert C. Trojanowitz. *Policing and the Fear of Crime. Perspectives on Policing, no. 3*. Washington, DC: U.S. Government Printing Office, 1988.

Moore, Mark H., Robert C. Trojanowicz, and George L. Kelling. *Crime and Policing. Perspectives on Policing, no. 2*. Washington, DC: U.S. Government Printing Office, 1988.

Nassau County Police Department. *Annual Report*. New York: Nassau County Police Department, published annually.

National Advisory Commission on Civil Disorders. *Report*. Washington, DC: U.S. Government Printing Office, 1968.

National Advisory Commission on Criminal Justice Standards and Goals. *Police*. Washington, DC: U.S. Government Printing Office, 1973.

National Center for Victims of Crime. *A Police Guide to First Response: Domestic Violence, Residential Burglary and Automobile Theft*. Washington, DC: U.S. Department of Justice, 2002.

National Commission on the Future of DNA Testing. *The Future of Forensic DNA Testing: Predictions of the Research and Development Working Group* Washington, DC: National Institute of Justice, 2000.

National Commission on the Future of DNA Testing. *Understanding DNA Evidence: A Guide for Victim Service Providers*. Washington, DC: National Institute of Justice, 2001.

National Commission on the Future of DNA Testing. *Understanding DNA Evidence, What Every Law Enforcement Officer Should Know about DNA Evidence*. Washington, DC: National Institute of Justice, 2000.

National Commission on Law Observance and Enforcement. *Lawlessness in Law Enforcement*. Washington, DC: U.S. Government Printing Office, 1931.

National Commission on Law Observance and Enforcement. *Report on Police*. Washington, DC: U.S. Government Printing Office, 1931.

National Criminal Justice Reference Service. *Program for the Reduction of Stress for New York City Police Officers and Their Families, Final Report*. Washington, DC: National Criminal Justice Reference Service, 1998.

National Institute of Justice. *Community Policing Impacts 86% of U.S. Population Served by Local Police Departments*. Washington, DC: National Institute of Justice, 2001.

National Institute of Justice. *Community Policing in Seattle: A Modal Partnership between Citizens and Police*. Washington, DC: National Institute of Justice, 1992.

National Institute of Justice. *Confronting Domestic Violence: A Guide for Criminal Justice Agencies*. Washington, DC: National Institute of Justice, 1986.

National Institute of Justice. *The DARE Program: A Review of Prevalence, User Satisfaction, and Effectiveness*. Washington, DC: National Institute of Justice, 1994.

National Institute of Justice. *The Effects of the Exclusionary Rule: A Study of California*. Washington, DC: National Institute of Justice, 1982.

National Institute of Justice. *Employee Drug Testing Policies in Police Departments: Research in Brief*. Washington, DC: National Institute of Justice, 1986.

National Institute of Justice. *GPS Applications in Law Enforcement: The SkyTracker Surveillance System, Final Report*. Washington, DC: National Institute of Justice, 1998.

National Institute of Justice. *Local Police Departments, 1993*. Washington, DC: National Institute of Justice, 1996.

National Institute of Justice. *Policing and Homicide, 1976–1998: Justifiable Homicide by Police, Police Officers Murdered by Felons*. Washington, DC: National Institute of Justice, 2001.

National Institute of Justice. *Policing Neighborhoods: A Report from St. Petersburg*. Washington, DC: National Institute of Justice, 1999.

National Institute of Justice. *Principles for Promoting Police Integrity*. Washington, DC: National Institute of Justice, 2001.

National Institute of Justice. *Research Plan*. Washington, DC: National Institute of Justice, issued yearly.

National Institute of Justice. *A Resource Guide on Racial Profiling Data Collection Systems: Promising Practices and Lessons Learned*. Washington, DC: National Institute of Justice, 2000.

National Institute of Justice. *Sheriffs' Departments 1993*. Washington, DC: National Institute of Justice, 1996.

National Institute of Justice. *Surveys in 12 Cities Show Widespread Community Support for Police*. Washington, DC: National Institute of Justice, 1999.

National Institute of Justice. *Toward the Paperless Police Department: The Use of Laptop Computers*. Washington, DC: National Institute of Justice, 1993.

National Institute of Justice. *Use of Force by Police*. Washington, DC: National Institute of Justice, 1999.

National Institute of Law Enforcement and Criminal Justice. *Controlling Police Corruption: The Effects of Reform Policies, Summary Report*. Washington, DC: U.S. Department of Justice, 1978.

National Institute of Law Enforcement and Criminal Justice. *Employing Civilians for Police Work*. Washington, DC: U.S. Government Printing Office, 1975.

National Minority Advisory Council on Criminal Justice. *The Inequality of Justice: A Report on Crime and the Administration of Justice in the Minority Community*. Washington, DC: U.S. Government Printing Office, 1980.

New York City Police Department. *AIDS and Our Workplace*. New York: New York City Police Department, 1987.

New York City Police Department. *Annual Report*. New York: New York City Police Department, published annually.

New York City Police Department. *Problem-Solving Strategies for Community Policing: A Practical Guide*. New York: New York City Police Department.

Peterson, Joseph L. *Use of Forensic Evidence by the Police and Courts*. Washington, DC: National Institute of Justice, 1987.

Police Department of Kansas City. *1966 Survey of Municipal Police Departments*. Kansas City, MO: Police Department of Kansas City, 1966.

President's Commission on Crime in the District of Columbia. *A Report on the President's Commission on Crime in the District of Columbia*. Washington, DC: U.S. Government Printing Office, 1966.

President's Commission on Law Enforcement and Administration of Justice. *The Challenge of Crime in a Free Society*. Washington, DC: U.S. Government Printing Office, 1967.

President's Commission on Law Enforcement and Administration of Justice. *Task Force Report: The Police*. Washington, DC: U.S. Government Printing Office, 1967.

President's Commission on Law Enforcement and Administration of Justice. *Task Force Report: Science and Technology*. Washington, DC: U.S. Government Printing Office, 1967.

Reaves, Brian. *Local Police Departments—1993*. Washington, DC: National Institute of Justice, 1996.

Reaves, Brian. *Profile of State and Local Law Enforcement Agencies, 1992*. Washington, DC: National Institute of Justice, 1993.

Reaves, Brian. *Sheriffs' Departments: 1990*. Washington, DC: National Institute of Justice, 1992.

Reaves, Brian. *Sheriffs' Departments: 1993*. Washington, D.C.: National Institute of Justice, 1996.

Reaves, Brian A., and Timothy C. Hart, *Federal Law Enforcement Officers, 2000*. Washington, DC: Bureau of Justice Statistics, 2001.

Reaves, Brian A., and Mathew Hickman. *Census of State and Local Law Enforcement Agencies, 2000*. Washington, DC: Bureau of Justice Statistics, 2002.

Rennison, Callie Marie, and Sarah Welchans. *Intimate Partner Violence*. Washington, DC: National Institute of Justice, 2000.

Riley, Kevin, and Bruce Hoffman, *Domestic Terrorism: A National Assessment of State and Local Law Enforcement Preparedness*. Santa Monica, CA: Rand Corporation, National Institute of Justice, 1995.

Reiss, Albert. *Private Employment of Public Police*. Washington, DC: National Institute of Justice, 1988.

Roda, C. *Executive Safety*. Washington, DC: National Criminal Justice Reference Service, 1997.

Rosenbaum, Dennis P., Arthur J. Lurigio, and Paul J. Lavrakas. *Crime Stoppers: A National Evaluation*. Washington, DC: National Institute of Justice, 1986.

Roth, Jeffrey A., and Joseph F. Ryan. *The COPS Program After 4 Years: National Evaluation, Research in Brief*. Washington, D.C.: National Institute of Justice, 2000.

Rubin, Paula. *The Americans with Disabilities Act and Criminal Justice: Hiring New Employees*. Washington, DC: National Institute of Justice, 1994.

Safir, Howard. *The Compstat Process*. New York: New York City Police Department, nd.

Schack, Stephen, Theodore H. Schell, and William G. Gay. *Specialized Patrol: Improving Patrol Productivity*. Washington, DC: U.S. Government Printing Office, 1977.

Scott, Eric J. *Calls for Service: Citizen Demand and Initial Police Response*. Washington, DC: U.S. Government Printing Office, 1981.

Sheehan, Donald C., and Janet I. Warren, eds. *Suicide and Law Enforcement*. Washington, DC: Federal Bureau of Investigation, 2001.

Sherman, Lawrence, James Shaw, and Dennis Rogan. *The Kansas City Gun Experiment*. Washington, DC: National Institute of Justice, 1994.

Shubin, Lester D. *Research, Testing Upgrade Criminal Justice Technology*. Washington, DC: National Institute of Justice, 1988.

Sichel, Joyce, et al. *Women on Patrol: A Pilot Study of Police Performance in New York City*. Washington, DC: Department of Justice, 1978.

Skolnick, Jerome, and D. Bayley. *Community Policing: Issues and Practices around the World*. Washington, DC: National Institute of Justice, 1988.

Sparrow, Malcolm K. *Implementing Community Policing. Perspectives on Policing, no. 9*. Washington, DC: U.S. Government Printing Office, 1988.

Sparrow, Malcolm K. *Information Systems and the Development of Policing. Perspectives on Policing, no. 16*, Washington, DC: U.S. Government Printing Office, 1993.

Spelman, William, and John E. Eck. *Newport News Tests Problem-Oriented Policing*. Washington, DC: National Institute of Justice, 1987.

Stillman, Frances A. *Line of Duty Deaths: Survivor and Departmental Responses*. Washington, DC: National Institute of Justice, 1987.

Sullivan, George J. *Directed Patrol*. Kansas City, MO: Kansas City Police Department, Operations Resource Unit, 1976.

Sweetman, Sherri. *Report on the Attorney General's Conference on Less-than-Lethal Weapons*. Washington, DC: National Institute of Justice, 1987.

Tien, J., J. Simon, and R. Larson. *An Alternative Approach in Police Patrol: The Wilmington Split Force Experiment*. Washington, DC: U.S. Government Printing Office, 1978.

Uchida, Craig D., Brian Forst, and Sampson O. Annan. *Controlling Street-Level Drug Trafficking: Evidence from Oakland and Birmingham*. Washington, DC: National Institute of Justice, 1992.

U.S. Bureau of Census. *1990 Census of Population*. Washington, DC: U.S. Bureau of Census, 1991.

U.S. Commission on Civil Rights. *Who Is Guarding the Guardians? A Report on Police Practices*. Washington, DC: U.S. Government Printing Office, 1981.

U.S. Congress, Office of Technology Assessment. *Criminal Justice: New Technologies and the Constitution: A Special Report*. Washington, DC: U.S. Government Printing Office, 1988.

U.S. Department of Justice. *Civil Service Systems: Affirmative Action and Equal Employment: A Guidebook for Employers*. Washington, DC: U.S. Government Printing Office, 1974.

U.S. Department of Justice. *Justice Expenditure and Employment*. Washington, DC: U.S. Government Printing Office, published annually.

U.S. Department of Justice. *Police Departments in Large Cities, 1987*. Washington, DC: U.S. Government Printing Office, 1989.

U.S. Department of Justice. *Police Use of Deadly Force*. Washington, DC: U.S. Government Printing Office, 1978.

U.S. Department of Justice, Bureau of Justice Statistics. *Crime and the Nation's Households*. Washington, DC: U.S. Government Printing Office, published annually.

U.S. Department of Justice, Bureau of Justice Statistics. *Criminal Victimization in the Untied States*. Washington, DC: National Institute of Justice, published annually.

U.S. Department of Justice, Bureau of Justice Statistics. *Report to the Nation on Crime and Justice,* 2nd ed. Washington, DC: U.S. Government Printing Office, 1991.

U.S. Department of Justice, Bureau of Justice Statistics. *Sourcebook of Criminal Justice Statistics*. Washington, DC: U.S. Government Printing Office, published annually.

U.S. Department of Justice, Bureau of Justice Statistics. *Special Report: Reporting Crimes to the Police*. Washington, DC: U.S. Government Printing Office, 1985.

U.S. Department of Labor, Bureau of Labor Statistics, *Occupational Outlook Handbook*, Washington DC: U.S. Department of Labor, published annually.

Walker, David M. *Homeland Security: Responsibility and Accountability for Achieving National Goals*. Washington, DC: U.S. General Accounting Office, 2002.

Wasserman, Robert, and Mark H. Moore. *Values in Policing. Perspectives on Policing, no. 8*. Washington, DC: U.S. Government Printing Office, 1988.

Weisburd, David, Roseann Greenspan, Edwin H. Hamilton, Hubert Williams, and Kellie A. Bryant, *Police Attitudes toward Abuses of Authority: Findings from a National Study*. Washington, DC: National Institute of Justice, 2000.

Whitaker, Catherine. *Crime Prevention Measures*. Washington, DC: Bureau of Justice Statistics, 1986.

Wilson, James Q., and Barbara Boland. *The Effect of Police on Crime*. Washington, DC: U.S. Government Printing Office, 1979.

Wilson, T. F., and P. L. Woodard. *Automated Fingerprint Identification Systems—Technology and Policy Issues*. Washington, DC: U.S. Department of Justice, 1987.

Yim, Randall A. *National Preparedness: Integration of Federal, State, Local and Private Sector Efforts Is Critical to an Effective National Strategy for Homeland Security*. Washington, DC: U.S. General Accounting Office, 2002.

Academic and Professional Journals

ABF Research Journal
Academy of Criminal Justice Sciences Today
American Behavioral Scientist
American Criminal Law Review
American Demographics
American Journal of Family Therapy
American Journal of Police
American Journal of Sociology
American Sociological Review

Annals of the American Association of Political and Social Science
Building Bridges
CJ, The Americas
Community Policing Exchange
Cultural Diversity
Crime and Justice International
Crime and Social Justice
Crime Control Digest
Criminal Justice and Behavior
Criminal Justice Journal
Criminal Justice Newsletter
Criminal Law Bulletin
Criminology
Detroit Journal of Urban Law
EA Professional Report
Economist
Educator
Evaluation Review
FBI Law Enforcement Bulletin
Futurist
Governance
Journal of the American Optometric Association
Journal of Applied Behavior Analysis
Journal of California Law Enforcement
Journal of the Canadian Society of Forensic Science
Journal of Contemporary Criminal Justice
Journal of Criminal Law, Criminology, and Police Science
Journal of Forensic Sciences
Journal of Law and Criminology
Journal of National Medical Association
Journal of Police and Criminal Psychology
Journal of Police Science and Administration
Journal of Research in Crime and Delinquency
Journal of Safe Management of Disruptive and Assaultive Behavior
Journal of Social Issues
Justice Assistance News
Justice Quarterly
Law and Society Review
National Institute of Justice Journal
National Law Journal
NCIA Justice Bulletin
New York Law Enforcement Journal
Northwestern Law Journal
Police Journal
Police Studies
Policing: An International Journal of Police Strategies and Management
Public Administration Review
Public Personnel Management Journal
Quarterly Journal of Studies on Alcohol
Security Journal
Social Problems
Stanford Law Review
Texas Police Journal
University of Chicago Law Journal
Urban Life
Women in Criminal Justice
Women Police
Yale Law Journal

Newspapers and National Magazines

Boston Globe
Business Week
Commercial Advisor
Forbes
Fort Lauderdale Sun-Sentinel
Gentlemen's Quarterly
Inc.
Insight
Law Enforcement News
MacLean's
New Orleans Magazine
Newsday
Newsweek
New York Post
New York Times
New York Times Magazine
Odessa American
People Weekly
Philadelphia Bulletin
Sun Sentinel
Tampa Tribune
Time
Town and Country Monthly
USA Today
USA Today Magazine
U.S. News and World Report
Wall Street Journal
Washington Post

Trade Magazines

APF Reporter
ASIS Dynamics
Canadian Police Chief Magazine
Corrections Technology and Management
Corrections Today
Crime Prevention Technology
Lambda Legal
Law and Order
Law Enforcement Technology
National Centurion
PC Computing
Police
Police Centurion
Police Chief
Popular Mechanics
Scientific America
Security
Security Management
The NarcOfficer

Photo Credits

Chapter 1 p. 9, Corbis/Bettmann; p. 17, © Underwood & Underwood/Corbis; p. 29, © Richard B. Levine.

Chapter 2 p. 34, © Tony Savino/The Image Works; p. 38, © Ramin Talaie/Corbis; p. 40, © Ilkka Uimonen/ Magnum Photos Inc.; p. 48, © Reuters/Corbis.

Chapter 3 p. 62, Organizational Chart provided Courtesy of the City of Madison Police Department, Madison, Wisconsin; p. 66, © Daemmrich Photography; p. 68, © Spencer Grant/ Photoedit; p. 74, © Joel Gordon.

Chapter 4 p. 87, © Michael Newman/PhotoEdit; p. 89, © AP Photo/Marta Lavandier; p. 95, © Journal-Courier/ Tiffany M. Hermon/The Image Works; p. 105, © Stephen D. Cannerelli/Syracuse Newspapers/The Image Works.

Chapter 5 p. 111, © Dorothy Littell Greco/The Image Works; p. 117, © Richard Lord/PhotoEdit; p. 123, © William Thomas Cain/Getty Images.

Chapter 6 p. 126, Courtesy of Linda Forst; p. 128, © Frederic Larson/San Francisco Chronicle/Corbis SABA; p. 133, © Joel Gordon; p. 136, © Mark Peterson/Corbis.

Chapter 7 p. 151, © Lester Lefkowitz/Corbis; p. 161 (top), © Tony Freeman/PhotoEdit; p. 161 (bottom), © Larry Mulvehill/The Image Works; p. 165, © AP Photo/ Mary Altaffer.

Chapter 8 p. 173, © Bob Daemmrich/The Image Works; p. 177, © Frances M. Roberts/Levine-Roberts Photography; p. 181, © Nancy Pierce/The New York Times; p. 186, © A. Ramey/PhotoEdit.

Chapter 9 p. 192, © Spencer Grant/PhotEdit; p. 198, © Joel Gordon; p. 205, Courtesy of Boca Raton Police Department; p. 211, © Frances M. Roberts/Levine-Roberts Photography; p. 213, © AP Photo/Richard Sheinwald.

Chapter 10 p. 230, Courtesy of Boca Raton Police Department; p. 238, © Robert Holmes/Corbis; p. 230, Courtesy of Boca Raton Police Department; p. 240, © AP Photo/Alan Diaz; p. 241, © Reuters/Mike Thieler/ Archive Photos.

Chapter 11 p. 264, © Bob Daemmrich/PhotoEdit; p. 269, © AP Photo/The Progress-Index, Jeff Mankeie; p. 279, © UPI/Corbis-Bettmann; p. 279, © UPI/Corbis-Bettmann.

Chapter 12 p. 294, © UPI/Corbis-Bettmann; p. 305, © photo by Joe Raedle/Getty Images; p. 328, © Hal Rubin.

Chapter 13 p. 333, (top) © AP Photo/Victoria Arocho; p. 333, (bottom) © AP Photo/Ben Margo; p. 339, © Frances M. Roberts/Levine-Roberts Photography.

Chapter 14 p. 344, © AP Photo/E. B. McGovern; p. 360, © AP Photo/Wilfredo Lee; p. 381, © AP Photo/ Visionics.

Chapter 15 p. 388, © Richard Cohen/Corbis; p. 391, © AP Photo/Michael S. Green; p. 399, © David McNew/Newsmakers/ Getty Images.

Chapter 16 p. 411, (top) © Robert Brenner/PhotoEdit; p. 411(bottom), © Reuters/Robby Berman/Corbis; p. 425, © AP Photo/Kathy Willens; p. 433, © Joe Raedle/Getty Images; p. 439, © AP Photo/Rick Bowmer; p. 441, © AP Photo/Pablo Martinez Monsivias.

Index

Note: *e* = exhibit; *f* = figure; *t* = table